Ninth Edition

THE ORGANIZATIONAL BEHAVIOR READER

Edited by:

Joyce S. Osland
San Jose State University

Marlene E. Turner
San Jose State University

Prentice Hall

Boston Columbus Indianapolis New York San Francisco Upper Saddle River
Amsterdam Cape Town Dubai London Madrid Milan Munich Paris Montreal Toronto
Delhi Mexico City Sao Paulo Sydney Hong Kong Seoul Singapore Taipei Tokyo

Editorial Director: Sally Yagan
Editor in Chief: Eric Svendsen
Director of Editorial Services: Ashley Santora
Editorial Project Manager: Meg O'Rourke
Editorial Assistant: Carter Anderson
Director of Marketing: Patrice Lamumba Jones
Senior Marketing Manager: Nikki Jones
Marketing Assistant: Ian Gold
Senior Managing Editor: Judy Leale
Production Editor: Debbie Ryan
Operations Specialist: Clara Bartunek
Creative Art Director: Jayne Conte
Cover Designer: Bruce Kenselaar
Manager, Visual Research: Beth Brenzel
Manager, Rights and Permissions: Shannon Barbe
Manager, Cover Visual Research & Permissions: Karen Sanatar
Cover Art: Fotolia
Full-Service Project Management:
Printer/Binder: STP Courier w/Cover, Stoughton
Text Font: 10/12, Times Roman

Credits and acknowledgments borrowed from other sources and reproduced, with permission, in this textbook appear on appropriate page within text.

Library of Congress Cataloging-in-Publication Data
The organizational behavior reader / edited by Joyce S. Osland, Marlene Turner.—9th ed.
    p. cm.
    Includes bibliographical references and index.
    ISBN-13: 978-0-13-612551-8 (alk. paper)
    ISBN-10: 0-13-612551-4 (alk. paper)
    1. Psychology, Industrial.   2. Organizational behavior.   I. Osland, Joyce.   II. Turner, Marlene E.
HF5548.8.K552 2011
158.7—dc22

2010022922

10 9 8 7 6 5 4 3 2 1

Prentice Hall
is an imprint of

www.pearsonhighered.com

ISBN 10:   0-13-612552-2
ISBN 13: 978-0-13-612552-5

CONTENTS

PREFACE

NEW TO THIS EDITION

Compared to previous editions, the ninth edition contains:

- Seventeen new articles by well-known experts, some of which were written or revised specifically for the *Reader*
- Expanded content on intercultural competence in response to the global nature of many jobs
- Best practices for engaging workers in a period of downsizing and building civilized, high-performing workplaces
- Even greater emphasis on ethics and understanding the system that caused the economic crisis
- New research on motivation, stereotypes, virtual teams, international negotiations, leadership, female leaders, coaching, and global change
- Practical advice for cross-sector collaboration on the sustainability challenge

This book is a primer on human behavior in organizations for students of management at three different levels—undergraduate, graduate, and executive education. Our goal in this volume is to prepare employees and managers to diagnose and understand organizational issues so they can be more effective. We address essential topics that fall into four key areas of organizational behavior: "Understanding Yourself and Other People at Work," "Creating Effective Work Groups," "Leadership and Management," and "Managing Effective Organizations." The *Reader* contains basic ideas and concepts, new research findings and practical applications, as well as emerging perspectives that suggest the future shape of the field.

Our aim was to compile an exciting collection of significant theoretical, and practical work that is both reader friendly and topical. We have read hundreds of articles to find "just the right ones," which can be classified in one or more of the following categories:

1. Classic, groundbreaking articles that, although written years ago, still provide the definitive treatment of a subject and deserve to be read in the scholar's original words.
2. Lucid overviews of research findings and theories on an important topic.
3. Descriptions of cutting-edge research.
4. Practical guides for managers based on research findings.

Each chapter has a brief introduction to give readers some contextual background and provide a glimpse of what they can expect.

The *Reader* can be used on its own or with its companion volume , *Organizational Behavior: An Experiential Approach, Ninth Edition* (forthcoming), by Osland and Turner. The articles contained herein form a complete package with the exercises and theory presented in the companion volume, allowing the student to go through all the phases of the experiential learning process. The *Reader* is useful to teachers, managers, and consultants for the breadth of viewpoints and the wealth of data that it provides about the field of organizational behavior and industrial and organizational psychology.

This is the first edition of the *Reader* that does not carry the names of the original *Reader* authors, David Kolb and Irwin Rubin, who are focusing now on other interests and passions. In 1971, their vision of advancing knowledge in a young field of study became a reality in the *Reader's* first edition. We want to acknowledge their invaluable contribution to management education over the years. It has been an honor to work with them, and we will do our best to carry on their vision.

To acknowledge other contributions to this edition, we would like to first thank Jessica Navarro, Emalynn Robinson, and Anu Sairaj, research assistants extraordinaire, our meticulous proofreaders, Carol Henson and Stacy Wheeler. We owe a special debt of gratitude to the authors who responded to our pleas for tailor-made pieces for the book: Janet Bennett, Cristina Gibson, Roy Lubit, and Richard Neilsen. At our organizational home, San Jose State University, we are deeply grateful to Prabha Chandrasekar, Barbara Somers, Erica Rivera, Kathryn Hetzner, and Megan Phillips for their cheerful, unwavering support and to our own exemplary managers, Dean David Steele and William Jiang (chair). The reviewers of the previous edition were extremely helpful and thorough: David Bright, Wright State University; Suzanne Crampton, Grand Valley State University; Evelyn Daniel, University of North Carolina–Chapel Hill; Nancy Meyer-Emerick, Cleveland State University; Stephen Miller, California State University–East Bay; and Chris Roberts, University of Massachusetts–Amherst. It was a pleasure, as always, to work with the Prentice Hall crew—Ashley Santora, Meg O'Rourke, and Clara Bartunek—and with George Jacob at Integra.

An effort like this is never completed without numerous family sacrifices and favors for which no words of gratitude are ever adequate—our heartfelt thanks to our spouses, Asbjorn and Anthony, our children, grandchildren, and parents.

Joyce S. Osland
Marlene E. Turner

SECTION ONE

Understanding Yourself and Other People at Work

The goal of the first section is to help you become aware of your mental maps or models, as well as those of people with whom you work. Although the concept has existed since ancient times, the term *mental models* was coined by Kenneth Craik, a Scottish psychologist, in the 1940s. It refers to "the images, assumptions, and stories that we carry in our minds of ourselves, other people, institutions, and every aspect of the world. Like a pane of glass framing and subtly distorting our vision, mental models determine what we see and then how we act."* One way to understand our behavior is to make these usually tacit maps visible. In this section, you will have an opportunity to examine mental maps about cultural differences, psychological contracts, theories of management, learning styles, human behavior, ethics, and values. We hope you will finish the section with more self-knowledge and a greater appreciation for the differences you discover in other people.

---

*P. Senge, A. Kleiner, C. Roberts, R. Ross, and B. Smith, *The Fifth Discipline Fieldbook: Strategies and Tools for Building a Learning Organization* (New York: Currency, 1993): 235.

1

Setting the Global Stage

BROADENING THE DEBATE: THE PROS AND CONS OF GLOBALIZATION
Joyce S. Osland

THE NEW GLOBAL MANAGER: LEARNING CULTURES ON THE FLY
Luciara Nardon
Richard M. Steers

DEVELOPING INTERCULTURAL COMPETENCE: THE INTERCULTURAL POSITIONING SYSTEM
Janet M. Bennett

Although some companies are slower than others to develop a global mindset and adopt a global business strategy, we all operate, either passively or proactively, in a global economy. This necessitates a broader understanding of the world—in terms of macro issues like global trade, economics, and international politics and in terms of micro issues such as the cultural differences we observe in an increasingly multicultural workplace. The selections in this chapter reflect both a macro and micro approach to understanding the global stage. As such, they lay the groundwork for managing in a global context.

A macro view of globalization equips managers and employees with a global perspective on a complex, controversial topic. Joyce Osland, a global leadership professor, wrote "Broadening the Debate: The Pros and Cons of Globalization," the first systemic view outlining the benefits and disadvantages of globalization. After reviewing the empirical research on globalization, she concluded that where people stood on the globalization issue was often determined by how narrowly or broadly they defined globalization. To help readers understand these different views, Osland identifies the major "bones of contention" surrounding globalization and the pros and cons identified by research. The economic crisis beginning in 2008 has been a sobering lesson on the interdependencies of a global economy. The crisis and the resulting recession in some countries have caused an even larger gap between rich and poor than when this article was written.

One of the major challenges in global business is finding the time to educate oneself about the cultural behavior and background of work colleagues from numerous countries. In the past, expatriate assignments that provided an opportunity to master another culture in depth were a common path to international work. Today, people can be catapulted into a virtual, multicultural workplace without any personal experience of living abroad. Luciara Nardon, a Brazilian who studied in Argentina and the United States and now a professor in Belgium, and Richard Steers, a professor emeritus who specialized in international management and continues to teach in Europe and Asia, combined their collective international experience and knowledge in "The New Global Manager: Learning Cultures on the Fly." They created an intercultural interaction learning model in which both parties learn about the other culture and negotiate effective ways of relating.

How much we learn about another culture is determined in large part by the number and type of cultural differences that we have on our "radar screen"—the mental map we hold about culture. In "Developing Intercultural Competence: The Intercultural Positioning System," Janet Bennett, executive director and co-founder of the Intercultural Communication Institute and a leading scholar in that field, describes several cultural maps, such as cognitive styles, that can be used to determine one's own cultural views and practices relative to others. Bennett provides helpful guidelines for developing intercultural competence.

BROADENING THE DEBATE: THE PROS AND CONS OF GLOBALIZATION*

Joyce S. Osland

The roots of globalization began to take hold in the 15th century with voyages by intrepid explorers who were funded by European monarchs seeking new trade routes. It continued throughout the years of the imperial expansion of Europe and the colonization of other lands primarily for the purpose of trade. In the mercantilist era, trading companies (such as the Hudson Bay Company and the East India Tea Company) served as surrogate colonial governments, merging trade and government. Later, trading companies were privatized, and intercontinental railways and transoceanic steamships made it possible to open previously protected markets. The global markets present in the early 20th century were disrupted by both world wars. After World War II, the World Bank and the International Monetary Fund (IMF) were founded to aid development in war-ravaged countries and lesser developed countries (LDCs). The English term *globalization* first made its appearance around 1960 (Waters, 1995). In 1995, the World Trade Organization (WTO) was created as a successor to the General Agreement on Tariffs and Trade (GATT) "to help trade flow smoothly, freely, fairly and predictably" (World, 2003, p. 3).[1] In recent years, many nations have liberalized their trade policies—removing trade barriers and focusing on exports—which further stimulated globalization.

The level of global trade increased 14-fold in the period from 1950 to 1997 (World, 2003, p. 2). In addition to increased volume, beginning in the 1970s and 1980s, a shift to foreign direct investment and technology characterized globalization. Recent growth in globalization has been facilitated and driven by rapid improvements in international transportation, technology, and telecommunications (Wood, 1995). The Internet opened up service markets that were previously protected by geographical distance (Valaskakis, 1998). Today, cross-border capital flows are more important than trade flows, and some multinational enterprises (MNEs) now have budgets larger than the economies of many countries. Kobrin (1997), however, argued that foreign trade and investment are less important drivers of globalization than are increasing technological scale, interfirm alliances, and information flows.

Many businesspeople and, judging by the international business literature, many business scholars accept globalization as a fait accompli whose presence and benefits are largely unquestioned. In other circles, however, globalization has become

*Reprinted with permission from *Journal of Management Inquiry* 12(2) (June 2003): 137–54. Reprinted by permission of Sage Publications.

a controversial topic, as first evidenced by labor protests in Korea and France, student riots in Indonesia, and the anti-World Trade Organization demonstrations in Seattle. A small but growing number of respected economists, sociologists, and political scientists criticize globalization and warn that protesters must be taken seriously to avoid dire consequences (Press, 2002, p. 12). Antiglobalization protests have become a familiar part of the social landscape, and there is little reason to suppose they will simply disappear. Furthermore, the issue is still fairly polarized with fervent free traders on one end of the continuum and radical protesters on the other. Polarization that prohibits room for dialogue seldom leads to lasting solutions, particularly in the case of complex issues. Therefore, this article is an attempt to help business practitioners, scholars, and students better understand the complexity of the issue and to challenge readers to think about win-win solutions benefiting more stakeholders.

The globalization debate continuum is anchored by these views: Proponents generally view globalization as an opportunity for economic growth and prosperity, whereas opponents perceive it as a threat to prosperity, political sovereignty, cultural integrity, and the environment. In developed countries, the primary concerns are the potential job loss for workers and the risk to contracting industries; developing countries worry about political sovereignty and losing control of their economies (Champlin and Olson, 1999). The burgeoning literature on globalization includes so many impassioned ideological arguments for or against it that a reader's first concern is to ascertain the potential bias of the author.[2] Many of these arguments lack empirical support. To complicate matters further, some of the existing economic research findings are highly contradictory. Much of the academic literature seems to fall primarily into pro and con categories. A recent review of the social science literature on globalization categorized it in terms of Hirschman's (1982) metaphor as either civilizing (positive), destructive (negative), or feeble (having no significant impact) and concluded that the feeble category was the least compelling (Guillén, 2001).

Disagreement over the definition of globalization impedes the debate. As Champlin and Olson (1999) noted, the debate cannot be resolved, not because we lack the definitive econometric analysis but because the debate is defined or framed in different ways. Is it simply an argument about the virtues of free markets and supply and demand, or does it include the broader sociocultural and environmental impact? Robert Reich described globalization as one of those concepts "that has passed from obscurity to meaninglessness without ever having an intervening period of coherence" (Duin, 2000, p. B-1). This meaninglessness can be traced to its usage as an "all-purpose catchword in public and scholarly debate" (Lechner and Boli, 2000, p. 1) with different connotations for different parties who support or oppose globalization.

Some definitions of globalization focus solely on cross-border trade—for example, globalization as the absence of borders and barriers to trade between nations (Ohmae, 1995). The International Monetary Fund describes globalization as "the growing economic interdependence of countries worldwide through the increasing volume and variety of cross-border transactions in goods and services and of international capital flows, and also through the more rapid and widespread diffusion of technology" (International, 1999, p. 45). Although these definitions convey a sense of dynamic change and boundarylessness, they portray the outcomes of globalization too narrowly. Brown (1992) and Renesch (1992) defined globalization as the interconnections between the overlapping interests of business and society, a definition that acknowledges the broader context in which globalization takes place. To ensure a systems view, globalization is defined here as a process leading to greater economic interdependence and networks and the economic, political, social, cultural, and environmental results of that process. There is plentiful, if sometimes contradictory, research on the financial and economic aspects of globalization; the broader impact of these phenomena, however, has received less attention by business scholars.

This article intends to make three contributions to the existing debate and literature: (a) expand the boundaries of the debate by examining the impact of globalization on other areas in the broader system; (b) provide a balanced, objective analysis of the benefits and liabilities of globalization based on scientific research rather than on rhetoric; and (c) offer a description of the more common stakeholder perspectives in the debate. The empirical data on the impact of globalization indicate that it is an uneven process yielding mixed results. Therefore, most of the findings in this article are presented in terms of trade-offs, highlighting both the positive and negative effects of globalization in the areas most affected: equality, labor, government, culture and community, and the environment.

The Impact of Globalization on Equality

On the positive side of the ledger, globalization has resulted in increased access to more goods for consumers in many countries (Evenett, 1999), reduced prices due to competition with local monopolies, and increased food supply due to industrial agriculture in some countries (Mander and Goldsmith, 1996). Poor people in some countries have been able to buy cheaper imported goods rather than shoddy goods produced by local monopolies (Graham and Krugman, 1991). A recent study by the London-based Center for Economic Policy Research reports that globalization increased economic growth and improved the incomes of both rich and poor people. The researchers claim that the number of people living in poverty today would be even greater without globalization (Gaunt, 2002).

A look at the statistics on equality indicates that globalization has resulted in both winners and losers, which is supported by Lee's (1996) economic analysis of income levels. According to one expert estimate,[3] 30–40% of the world population has benefited from globalization, whereas the rest has not (Valaskakis, 1998). Globalization is blamed for increasing the chasm between new groups of haves and have-nots—between the well educated and the poorly educated, between the technologically skilled and the unskilled, and between those living in countries that compete successfully in the global economy and those who do not (Frank and Cook, 1995; Pritchett, 1997; United Nations Development, 1999). Globalization has resulted in more jobs in developing countries, creating another group of winners depending on the level of wages they receive. There have been examples of spectacular development, like the Asian Tigers (Singapore, Taiwan, Hong Kong, and South Korea), as well as examples of countries that are marginalized from the global economy, such as sub-Saharan Africa. Some developing countries have suffered job losses in local industries that could not compete with foreign multinationals once formerly protected markets were opened (Lee, 1996). Some critics believe that the structure of the global economy favors developed countries over lesser developed countries.

Amidst the occasionally contradictory economic findings, one piece of incontrovertible evidence stands out. There is more inequality among and within countries today than in the past. Between 1870 and 1990, the gap in per capita income between rich and developing countries has grown fivefold (Temple, 1999). The gap between the richest and poorest 20% of the world population has widened significantly since 1960, when the income ratio of the richest to the poorest was 30:1, to 82:1 in 1995 (United Nations Development, 1996). There are 1.2 billion people living on less than $1 a day (United Nations Development, 2001), a figure that is increasing rather than diminishing. The richest 20% of the world's population receives 86% of the world's GDP, 82% of the export trade, and 68% of foreign direct investment; the lowest 20%

receives only 1% of each (United Nations Development, 1999). A total of 358 people own as much wealth as 2.5 billion people own together—nearly half the world's population (United Nations Development, 1996). The global income of the poorest 20% of the world dropped from 2.3% to 1.4% of world GDP between 1989 and 1998 (Giddens, 2000). In virtually all developed countries, the gaps between skilled and unskilled workers in wages and/or unemployment rates have widened (Gottschalk and Smeeding, 1997; Murphy and Topel, 1997; Organization, 1997).

The notable exceptions—countries or commonwealths that have significantly reduced the gap since 1960—include South Korea, Taiwan, Singapore, Ireland, and Puerto Rico. In the East Asian economies, trade liberalization contributed to reduced wage inequality accompanied by rapid economic growth (Lee, 1996). In Latin America, however, wage inequality increased following liberalization, meaning that skilled workers benefited disproportionately (Berry, 1996; Robbins, 1995; see also United Nations Conference, 1997; Wood, 1997).

Given its egalitarian roots and the historic propensity of most U.S. citizens to consider themselves middle class, it is surprising to discover that nowhere is the inequality between the rich and the poor as great as in the United States (Longworth, 1999). The worth of the average hourly wage is 12% lower than it was in 1973 (Longworth, 1999), whereas the average pay for a U.S. CEO is 200 times higher, $7.4 million in 2002 (almost half the 2000 average) (Lavelle, Jespersen, Ante, and Kerstetter, 2003). The after-tax income of the richest 1% of U.S. households increased 72% from 1977 to 1994, whereas that of the poorest 20% of U.S. households decreased by 16% (Scott, Lee, and Schmidt, 1997). As in other countries, some parts of the United States have prospered from globalization, whereas other regions struggle to keep up.

The Silicon Valley, for example, benefited from globalization until the recent economic downturn; since 2001, employment has decreased 20% (Joint Venture, 2003). Previously, developed countries were concerned about losing blue-collar jobs, but the next wave of globalization is shifting white-collar jobs—highly trained knowledge workers and service jobs—off-shore to less expensive labor markets in Asia, Latin America, and Eastern Europe (Engardio, Bernstein, and Kripalani, 2003).

Researchers agree that the gap between rich and poor has widened; they disagree, however, on whether globalization has caused the gap by influencing wages. Although U.S. wages rose only 5.5% between 1979 and 1993, some economists claim that this is not the fault of globalization because international trade and investment have had little impact (Lawrence, 1995; Sachs and Schatz, 1994). Estimated shifts in product market demand, including the impact of imports, account for less than 10% of the increase in wage differential (Slaughter and Swagel, 2000). Other economists attribute labor inequalities to technological changes (Lawrence and Slaughter, 1993; Organization, 1997) rather than to globalization. Another contingent of scholars, however, points to globalization as the cause of inequality (Learner, 1998; Rodrik, 1997; Wood, 1994). More recent research by Wood (1998) indicated a causal relationship between globalization and the increased demand for skilled rather than unskilled workers in developed countries. Furthermore, Zhao's research (1998) found that foreign direct investments adversely affect union wages and employment. Baldwin and Martin (1999) summarized the empirical literature, writing that virtually all studies found some effect of trade on the labor market in both the United States and Europe; the findings ranged, however, from almost 0% to 100% with a consensus range of perhaps 10–20% (p. 21).

Although globalization may not be the only factor involved in growing social inequality, it does seem safe to conclude that it has produced winners and losers on both the individual and country levels. The increasing gap between the haves and the have-nots raises the question of fairness. Intense debates over the fairness of the competitive advantages held by various countries are fought out at World Trade

Table 1   The Impact of Globalization on Equality

Positive Effects	Negative Effects
Income increased globally for both rich and poor, decreasing poverty	Greater chasm between haves and have-nots on individual and country levels
Increased wages for the well educated	Some downward pressure on wages for the poorly educated
Increased wages for technologically skilled	Some downward pressure on wages for technologically unskilled
Improved economic conditions in countries and regions that successfully compete in the global economy	Worsened economic conditions in countries marginalized from the global economy and in certain regions of developed countries
Rich have become richer	Poor have become poorer
Increased access to more goods	
Reduced prices due to competition with local monopolies	
Increased food supply in some countries	

Organization meetings and trade negotiations. Increasingly, there are expressions of concern about the threat to political stability, because historically large, apparently insurmountable gaps between rich and poor have been a factor in revolutions (Marquand, 1998). In the opinion of Anthony Giddens (2000), sociologist and director of the London School of Economics, "Along with ecological risk, expanding inequality is the most serious problem facing world society" (p. 34).

The positive and negative effects that globalization has on equality and wages appear in Table 1.

The Impact of Globalization on Labor Conditions

Closely related to equality and wages, labor conditions is another area influenced by globalization. On the positive side, some workers in lesser developed countries have received more education and training from multinational companies due to globalization. Furthermore, there is some evidence that increased competition has resulted in upgrading educational systems to produce a more highly qualified workforce (Mander and Goldsmith, 1996; Schmidheiny, 1992).

The threat of job displacement is one of the most tangible concerns that critics have regarding globalization. Workers have more employment opportunities in some countries, but they have less in others where certain industries and firms (e.g., the import sector and small farmers) have been put out of business by global competition (Mander and Goldsmith, 1996). Daly (1996) noted that some people have less choice about how they make their living as a result of globalization. Increasing imports from low-wage countries are perceived by some as a threat to manufacturing jobs in industrialized countries, particularly in labor-intensive sectors (Wood, 1994).

The labor movement and human rights advocates argue that globalization has had a negative effect on labor standards and that it threatens hard-won improvements in labor conditions. They warn about the *race to the bottom*, which assumes that competition will drive labor standards (and also environmental standards) to the lowest common denominator. Rodrik (1997) found evidence of negative impact on labor conditions, but Drezner (2000) insisted that the race to the bottom is merely a myth used as a scare tactic by both multinational enterprises and activists. For example, Drezner (2000) cited a 1996 Organization for Economic Cooperation and Development

(OECD) study that found a positive correlation between "successfully sustained trade reforms" and improved core labor standards because multinationals tend to pay higher than average wages to attract better workers in developing countries (p. 65). Furthermore, the majority of global foreign direct investment (FDI) went to developed countries, which generally boast higher labor standards, during the 1990s (68.9% in 1992, 63.4% in 1995, and 71.5% in 1998), according to the United Nations Conference on Trade and Development (UNCTAD) (1992, 1995, 1998). There is no evidence that multinational enterprises choose to locate in countries where labor and environmental standards are absent or less stringent; other factors like stability, infrastructure, and the size of potential markets play stronger roles in strategic decisions.

Globalization critics, however, worry about the dynamics that occur when firms in developed nations with high wages transfer their manufacturing or processing operations to low-cost, lesser developed countries. Such transfers can be advantageous for the lesser developed countries, the recipients of new jobs, and the firms. When LDCs compete against one another to attract foreign employers to free trade zones or export processing zones (EPZs), however, critics fear this will degrade labor conditions.[4] Multinational enterprises are wooed with the lure of tax-free status for a set number of years, with facilities and infrastructure, and, in some countries, with exemptions from adhering to the national labor code. Five of the 11 nations examined in a U.S. Department of Labor study restricted their citizens' labor rights in export processing zones by allowing foreign firms to ignore national labor laws that were enforced elsewhere in the country (Charnovitz, 1992), which supports the race to the bottom argument. According to some sources, export processing zone workers are often temporary workers who are fired and rehired as needed to avoid having to provide them with benefits or career paths. When zone workers complain about working conditions, they may be fired (Klein, 2000).

The exploitative practices most commonly cited in export processing zones and outsourced factories are child labor, hazardous and unhealthy working conditions, absence of collective bargaining, repression of labor unions (Lawrence, Rodrik, and Whalley, 1996), and forced overtime (Klein, 2000). Labor union advocates and others fear that "exploitative practices in low-wage exporting countries artificially depress labor costs, leading to unfair competitive advantage in world markets and a downward pressure on labor standards in rich countries" (Lawrence et al., 1996, p. 12). There is some evidence that globalization has caused downward pressure on wages (Lawrence, 1995) as well as on pensions and benefits (Krishnan, 1996; Sutherland, 1998) and has diminished the power of unions (Levi, 2000). Other economists argue that globalization has had very little negative impact on labor conditions and wages (Krugman, 1994).

The form of ownership and the transitory nature of many overseas factories have resulted in a different form of social contract between employer and employee. The reliance of some multinational enterprises on local subcontractors who run their factories means that workers do not "belong" to the company. This arm's-length relationship facilitates the closure of factories when labor costs rise prohibitively and another country becomes more attractive. In these cases, the social contract between employer and employee is limited to the simplest, most expedient transaction—pay for work, which is a stripped-down version of the social contract that exists in most developed countries (albeit with the exception of temporary workers). There have been instances of unscrupulous foreign factory operators in export processing zones who have closed down and fled the country without any warning or termination pay to employees.

Moving jobs offshore also affects the social contract that firms have with domestic employees. Boeing's engineers' union threatened to strike in December 2002 if the company didn't decrease the number of engineers working in the firm's Russian facility. The union's concerns were job loss and the potential danger of sharing technology; management's interests were significantly lower wages for engineers ($5,400 yearly) and entry into the Russian market (Holmes and Ostrovsky, 2003). Such disparate goals do not fit the preexisting social contract.

The onset of globalization served as a trigger event in some companies—a wake-up call that people must work more efficiently and more intelligently, which resulted in increased productivity (Evenett, 1999). The threat of globalization has, however, also been held over workers' heads. According to Longworth (1999),

> The rhetoric is probably a more potent force than globalization itself. An employer doesn't have to move jobs to Asia to persuade those left behind to take pay cuts. The mere possibility that, in this global age, he can do it is enough. (p. 10)

Interestingly, other aspects of globalization—worldwide telecommunications and the Internet—have contributed to calls for basic labor standards. The increased publicity and communications about poor working conditions in other countries, which is known as the *CNN effect*, has resulted in greater pressure from human rights groups and labor unions (Lawrence et al., 1996). The threat of Internet-driven international boycotts of goods made by offending multinationals exerts a counterbalancing force for better labor practices in some cases. Companies that engage in exploitative practices are subject to boycotts, negative publicity, and loss of both goodwill and revenue (Dohrs and Garfunkel, 1999). Widespread criticism from consumers and protesters induced some MNEs like Nike to demand that their subcontractors provide better working conditions in overseas factories. To avoid bad publicity, firms like Nike, Mattel, and Levi Strauss have established guidelines and invited monitors to inspect their operations.

In sum, there is both positive and negative evidence concerning the impact of globalization on labor conditions, as shown in Table 2.

Table 2 The Impact of Globalization on Labor Conditions	
Positive Effects	**Negative Effects**
Increased job opportunities in some countries	Certain industries and companies were forced out of business
Upgraded educational system and more training in some countries	Job displacement affected some individuals
Increased labor standards or no change due to globalization*	Decreased labor standards*
Increased labor productivity	Caused downward pressure on benefits and pensions
CNN effect pressures firms to correct labor abuses	Decreased power of unions
Some firms taking proactive steps to avoid labor abuses	Child labor, unhealthy work conditions, and forced overtime in export processing zones (EPZs)
	Diminished social contract between employer and employee

*Contradictory findings.

The Impact of Globalization on Governments

The key question regarding globalization and governments is whether or not globalization threatens national sovereignty. Historically, governments played a major role in promoting their country's economic development and managing its economy, albeit in quite varied forms. Today, however, some critics argue that government matters less and less in a global economy. Nation-states are simply other actors on the global stage rather than its directors. Aggressive global production systems and capital markets now occupy the "commanding heights" of global development, forcing governments on the defensive and pressuring them to deregulate, downsize, and privatize many of the social management functions they assumed during the past century (Yergin and Stanislaw, 2000). The political boundaries that define nation-states place them at a disadvantage when confronting the unique pressures of a boundaryless global economy. There is a "jurisdictional asymmetry" between an economic system composed of centrally controlled, transnational MNEs on one hand and a political system structured into geographically defined sovereign states on the other (Kobrin, 2001b). Yergin and Stanislaw (2000) argued:

> Information technology—through computers—is creating a "woven world" by promoting communication, coordination, integration, and contact at a pace and scale of change that far outrun the ability of any government to manage. The accelerating connections make national borders increasingly porous—and, in terms of some forms of control, increasingly irrelevant. (p. 215)

The growing power of globalized financial markets limits the scope of national policy (Lee, 1996). Because the world has become so interdependent and networked, nation-states are criticized if the "playing field" for business is not level, which limits the degree of freedom in their decision making. This brings us to the key question: "Who governs MNEs and a global economy?" "The market" is not a satisfactory answer for globalization critics and some governments, and the sense that globalization is out of control creates a feeling of powerlessness and resentment in protesters. Nation-states are not designed to govern MNEs, but the idea of yielding their power to international governing bodies is perceived by some countries as yet another threat to national sovereignty (Longworth, 1999).

On the positive side of the ledger, for some governments, globalization has resulted in expanded infrastructure, more jobs, and more economic development for their citizenry. Certain countries have benefited from the transfer of modern, more effective management techniques to their business sector. Furthermore, some observers believe that the increased interdependence of trading and investment partners will draw countries closer together and serve as a deterrent against war (Harris and Goodwin, 1995; Tyson, 1999).

On the negative side, MNEs have exerted pressure on governments in several ways. International competitiveness has influenced public policy in some countries by encouraging government officials to lower labor standards (Lee, 1997). Because governments may view themselves in competition with others in a race to the bottom to attract MNEs to their country, foreign firms can have the upper hand in negotiations unless governments have something unique to offer (such as rare natural resources, highly trained people, and a large consumer market). Singapore, for example, invested heavily in education, attracting high-tech and professional industry rather than limiting its population to employment in low-wage factories.

George Soros (2002) criticized globalization for making the provision of private goods more important than public goods such as peace, the eradication of poverty, the protection of human and labor rights, and the environment. Governments of developed countries with extensive entitlement programs—social security systems, health-care programs, and unemployment pay or welfare systems—are experiencing greater pressure to decrease such expenditures because they raise the rate of corporate taxation (Longworth, 1999). Nevertheless, Lee (1996) concluded that in spite of increasing globalization, national policies still determine levels of employment and labor standards. He warned, however, that there is a worldwide trend toward smaller government, which is evident in public expenditure reductions, lower taxes, less support for redistributive measures, and greater deregulation of markets, including the labor market. Thus, governments are less likely to compensate the losers from globalization at a time when globalization increases the demand for social insurance (Sutherland, 1998). A global economy allows companies (and the wealthiest citizens) to spread their tax liability to countries with the lowest rates and thereby decrease the taxes that national governments receive from formerly "local" companies. Capital mobility weakens the tax base, which means that there are less funds available for social insurance (Sutherland, 1998) in countries that previously received tax payments.

The blueprint for economic development promoted by the International Monetary Fund and World Bank decreased the role of government with calls for privatization, deregulation, and the reduction of corporate, trade, and capital gains taxes (United Nations Conference, 1999; United Nations Development, 1999). Not only did this make some government functions irrelevant, but it also left governments with less money in their coffers. Grunberg (1998) reported that governments have fewer funds available as a result of globalization. The proportion of corporate taxes has decreased as a percentage of the total revenues in the United States, and it has also decreased relative to the share of corporate profits in all of the Organization for Economic Cooperation and Development countries (Kobrin, 2001a).[5] Hines (1999) found complex reasons for this phenomenon but also found evidence of aggressive tax avoidance behavior by MNEs and a race to the bottom by governments who reduced corporate tax rates to attract investment. Many EPZs grant tax-free status for the first years, but some MNEs shut down operations and leave as soon as the period is over, because they can take advantage of the same tax-free status elsewhere (Klein, 2000). Furthermore, MNEs sometimes influence local government policy and threaten to leave if their demands are not met. In this way, corporations externalize their costs to others.

Globalization makes it more difficult for governments to exercise their regulatory powers (Cox, 1996) and maintain their autonomy and independent decision making (Kobrin, 1997). In a literature review that examined whether globalization undermines the authority of nation-states, Guillén (2001) found mixed results. Some research concludes that MNEs have the upper hand with governments that now have less autonomy, whereas political scientists contend that the role of government has simply changed to include dealing with the problems of globalization. Kobrin (2001b) concluded that governments are not irrelevant, but they have been weakened as a result of globalization; they will continue to play a major role, but instead of exercising supreme authority, a nation may find that its sovereignty comes to mean simply being one of several prominent parties involved in international negotiations.

There is widespread agreement that governments are not designed or structured to deal with the problems of global business (Giddens, 2000), particularly problems like global warming and environmental degradation, that have accompanied economic development (Lechner and Boli, 2000). Partially to fill this gap, a growing number of nongovernmental organizations (NGOs) are trying to counterbalance the power of MNEs (Dohrs and Garfunkel, 1999). Nongovernmental organizations that focus on topics like human rights and environmental issues have organized themselves to exert pressure on MNEs, governments, and international organizations to ensure their agenda is heard. If one looks at globalization solely in terms of power, it has shifted from governments and organized labor to MNEs, markets, and international organizations (Kobrin, 2001a). This shift took place without a democratic vote—a silent coup that rankles protesters (Clarke, 2001). International organizations like the International Monetary Fund, World Bank, and World Trade Organization are not trusted by some factions of the antiglobalization protest movement because of the partiality these organizations show toward corporate interests and powerful governments. Stiglitz (2002), a former senior vice president and chief economist at the World Bank, claims that some of the protesters' complaints about the International Monetary Fund are based in fact—namely, that free-trade agreements primarily benefit the rich, that privatization has not proved successful in many countries, and that the IMF's vaunted structural adjustment programs have resulted in hardship for many.

UN Secretary-General Kofi Annan (1999) gave this warning at Davos:

> The spread of markets outpaces the ability of societies and their political systems to adjust to them, let alone to guide the course they take. History teaches us that such an imbalance between the economic, social; and political worlds can never be sustained for very long.

Table 3 summarizes the positive and negative impacts of globalization on governments.

Table 3 The Impact of Globalization on Government	
Positive Effects	**Negative Effects**
Increased economic development benefits some governments	Power of multinational enterprises (MNEs) increased at the expense of government power, sovereignty, and ability to regulate business
Increased jobs and expanded infrastructure benefit some countries	MNEs externalize some of their costs to countries
Transfer of modern management techniques into business sector	Competition for factories and foreign direct investment (FDI) result in too many concessions to MNEs by some governments
Greater interdependence among trading and investment partners may deter war	Some MNEs influence local government policy and threaten to leave if their demands are not met
Proliferation of non-governmental organizations (NGOs) to counter-balance decreased governmental power	MNEs pay fewer taxes to governments and incorporate where the tax rate is lowest, depriving their own country of revenue
	Governments are pressured to reduce tax rates and decrease social benefits that may affect stability

The Impact of Globalization on Culture and Community

Globalization may be a positive force for greater cross-cultural understanding via more cross-cultural exposure and closer cross-border ties. As Tomlinson (1999) stated,

> A world of complex connectivity (a global market place, international fashion codes, an international division of labor, a shared ecosystem) thus links the myriad small everyday actions of millions with the fates of distant, unknown others and even with the possible fate of the planet. (p. 25)

Tomlinson (1999) referred to the increased connectivity of the world as a double-edged sword that provides new and wider understanding at the same time that it takes away the securities of one's local world.

Critics claim that globalization is creating a monoculture that is rapidly spreading around the world. MTV culture, for instance, offends social conservatives in many countries. By this view, weakened cultural traditions combined with the importation of foreign media, stores, and goods encourage cultural homogenization. Multinational news outlets, like CNN and Rupert Murdoch's News Corporation, provoked the complaint that the "flow of information" (a term that includes both ideas and attitudes) is dominated by multinational entities based in the most powerful nations (MacBride and Roach, 2000, p. 286). Chains like Wal-Mart, with lower prices and extensive, standardized inventory, force uniquely local small stores out of business because consumers prefer the service and prices at Wal-Mart. Monbiot (1995) claimed that the use of English as the language of business and in the media drives out and threatens minority languages. As transnational corporations grow and become more powerful, there is a concern that the culture of capitalism, which is heavily influenced by Western or U.S. culture and commoditization, will develop into a world monoculture. *Commoditization* is the process by which market capitalism transforms things that were previously not viewed as economic goods (such as human genes) into something with a price. In fact, many aspects of culture have been *commodified* as evidenced in the shopping opportunities incorporated into experiences in which they previously did not exist (Tomlinson, 1999) such as visits to natural wonders or religious ceremonies. Cultures have always influenced one another, often enriching each other in the process, but some observers conclude that cultural synchronization has been occurring at an unprecedented rate and that "never before has one particular cultural pattern been of such global dimensions and so comprehensive" (Hamelink, 1988).

Not all communication experts, however, share this opinion. Some maintain that the media have been decentralizing with the development of regional centers (e.g., Mexico for Spanish television, India for film, and Hong Kong for East Asian film and television) and indigenized programming. Thus, they argue that the homogenizing forces of the media, like satellite television, exist in tension with *heterogenization* (Sinclair, Jacka, and Cunningham, 1996). Tomlinson (1999) agreed with Hamelink that cultural synchronization is an unprecedented feature of global modernity but argued, "Movement between cultural/geographical areas always involves interpretation, translation, mutation, adaptation, and 'indigenisation' as the receiving culture brings its own cultural resources to bear, in dialectical fashion, upon 'cultural imports'" (p. 84). And as Howes (1996) noted,

> No imported object, Coca-Cola included, is completely immune from creolization. Indeed, one finds that Coke is often attributed with meanings

and uses within particular cultures that are different from those imagined by the manufacturer. These include that it can smooth wrinkles (Russia), that it can revive a person from the dead (Haiti), indigenised through being mixed with other drinks, such as rum in the Caribbean to make Cuba Libre or aguardiente in Bolivia to produce Ponche Negro. Finally, it seems that Coke is perceived as a "native product" in many different places—that you will often find people who believe the drink originated in their country not in the United States. (p. 6)

Pressures for a global monoculture are counterbalanced by greater attention and efforts to maintain ethnic identity. Karliner (2000) argued that globalization may be responsible for the increasing popularity of indigenous movements to maintain ethnic identity. Although globalization was not the only cause of the Islamic revolution in Iran, it provided a target for rebellion and also forced the Muslims to "identify" themselves and determine how they wanted to live in a global society (Lechner and Boli, 2000). Anthropologist Clifford Geertz (1998) wrote that the world is "growing both more global and more divided, more thoroughly interconnected and more intricately partitioned at the same time" (p. 107). Although few social scientists support the creation of a monoculture (Guillén, 2001), this is a common fear among protesters.

Critics claim that globalization has irrevocably changed the social landscape of communities and constitutes a threat to national culture in various ways. For example, transnational agribusiness has replaced family farms in some areas, and cutting down forests inhabited by indigenous people makes it difficult if not impossible for them to maintain their traditional way of life (Brown, Renner, and Flavin, 1998; Keck and Sikkink, 2000). The spread of newer cultures and technologies may result in the loss of knowledge about traditional practices and arts more compatible with natural systems. EPZs draw people from rural areas, moving them out of reach of their traditional safety nets. It is difficult to pinpoint how much of this migration from their traditional communities and ways of life can be attributed directly to globalization versus traditional economic development and a desire to better one's life. People, particularly men, have been forced to migrate to find work throughout history. In the case of the Mexican maquiladoras (a type of EPZ) along the U.S. border, however, the primary employees are young women, which has had a marked impact on the social structure.

Table 4 summarizes the positive and negative impacts of globalization on culture and community.

Table 4 The Impact of Globalization on Culture and Community	
Positive Effects	**Negative Effects**
Increased cultural exposure, understanding, and cross-border ties	More mobility and disruption of rural life away from traditional safety nets
Encouraged proliferation of indigenous organizations and movements to preserve ethnic identity	Increased exposure to cultural homogenization
	Disintegration of some local communities

The Impact of Globalization on Environmental Sustainability

Sustainability is defined as meeting the needs of present generations without compromising the ability of future generations to meet their own needs. The moral basis for sustainability is the ethical position that destroying Earth's future capacity to support life is wrong. Global environmental issues such as global warming, deforestation, ozone depletion, reduction of biodiversity, degradation of ocean habitats (Lawrence et al., 1996), and pollution are the key areas affected by globalization.[6] Most of the empirical studies found in a literature review on globalization's impact on the environment, which are summarized below, focused on small pieces of the puzzle—they are "local" in nature due to the difficulty of studying the environment as a whole (Osland, Dhanda, and Yuthas, 2002).

On the positive side of the ledger, globalization has caused some countries to make a narrower range of products more efficiently; in other words, it has given them a comparative advantage. It has been responsible for creating and exporting technologies that use fewer natural resources and result in less waste and pollution.[7] Globalization has facilitated the dissemination of practices like improved energy efficiency, lowered carbon combustion, dematerialization (reducing overall use of materials), substitution of resources with reduced environmental impact, and metal recovery technologies (Allenby and Richards, 1994; Graedel and Allenby, 1995; Socolow, Andrews, Berkhout, and Thomas, 1994). The industrial ecology movement has sought to improve environmental responsiveness at the same time that it reduces the global cost of production for corporations.

On the negative side, because of globalization, harmful technologies and activities have also been exported. Although better technology is available, companies do not always use it because it can be highly capital intensive (Socolow et al., 1994).

Globalization is blamed as a source of pollution. For instance, industrial toxic effluents and pesticide runoffs from agribusiness have destroyed river fish (Khor, 1996). A recent study overseen by the UN Environment Program warns of the danger of the *Asian cloud*, which may be causing premature death, flooding, and drought. Not all of the two-mile-thick cloud is a direct result of increased industrialization and globalization; traditional practices and forest clearing are also responsible in addition to auto emission, factories, and waste incineration.[8] Since prevailing winds can carry pollution clouds around the world in a short period, they are becoming a global environmental problem (United Nations Environment, 2002).

The spread of factories around the world has made more infrastructure necessary, which requires extracted substances from the earth. Globalization promotes the transportation of raw materials and goods using nonrenewable resources. Increased travel by workers seeking jobs (Brown, Renner, and Flavin, 1998) and by MNE employees uses fossil fuel and contributes to global warming. Additionally, because MNEs have moved their operations to countries where environmental laws are absent or not enforced, greater environmental degradation has occurred. Some MNEs have taken advantage of lowered environmental protection to sell harmful products abroad that are banned in more developed countries.

Critics claim that countries are more likely to export more commodities that increase the exploitation of natural resources as a result of globalization (French, 1993). There are numerous examples of environmental degradation such as deforestation, threats to biodiversity, and depletion of fish stocks (French, 1993; Goldsmith, 1997; Wilkes, 1995). Some of these problems stem from inappropriate use or overuse, whereas others involve inappropriate modern technologies such as modern trawl fishing that scrapes the bottom of the seabed and disturbs breeding grounds (Khor, 1996). Deforestation and technological innovations in agriculture have also resulted in habitat damage and extinction of species (Rackham, 1986).

Wackernagel and Rees (1996) popularized the concept of the *environmental footprint*. They demonstrated that developed countries require greater per capita material and energy flows, and therefore greater land surface, than do developing countries. The per capita effect on the earth's crust is greatest in the wealthiest countries that extract resources at a far greater rate than they can be replaced. The globalization of materially affluent lifestyles promulgated by the media and increased travel intensifies the demand for extracted materials (Duchin, 1996).

A conflict has arisen over the view of many developing countries that it is their turn to develop, as the more advanced developed countries did, without the constraints of environmental regulations. This dilemma pits the principle of equal capacity for economic development against the competing value of environmental sustainability.

The 1992 GATT annual report laid out the argument that increased trade will produce increased incomes, which will then result in more concern about the environment (Lawrence et al., 1996). Environmentalists, however, worry that globalization will encourage greater consumption as more goods are marketed to more people, creating artificial needs and using more natural resources (Mander and Goldsmith, 1996). Although globalization theoretically should result in greater efficiency in production, it has caused more surplus and scarcity (Brown, Renner, and Flavin, 1998), which points to a less than perfect use of resources.

It would be impossible to calculate the total impact of globalization on the environment, but there is a growing body of evidence documenting its harmful effects (Osland et al., 2002). Table 5 summarizes the positive and negative impacts of globalization on environmental sustainability.

Table 5 The Impact of Globalization on Environmental Sustainability	
Positive Effects	**Negative Effects**
Countries make a narrower range of products more efficiently	Causes surplus and scarcity
Relative efficiency of energy use is improving	Development and increased affluence lead to larger demands for materials and energy as well as increased waste and energy-related pollution
More systematic dematerialization through manufacturing changes	Export of damaging extraction technologies continues despite existence of alternative technologies
Substitution of harmful materials by resources with reduced environmental impact	Spread of factories requires increased infrastructure that uses more extracted materials
Some firms do environmental impact studies of product's entire lifecycle	Increased travel of workers and multinational enterprise employees uses fossil fuel and contributes to global warming
Transfer of efficient technologies to assist developing countries to increase production	Some developing nations are exposed to toxic or dangerous products and technologies
Creation and transfer of more efficient technologies to some countries	Increased consumption uses more natural resources
Use of alternative energy sources decreases carbon combustion	Increased advertising creates artificial needs

(Continued)

Positive Effects	Negative Effects
Increased income may lead to concern for environmental protection	Increasing fossil fuel combustion emits gases and particles into the atmosphere
	Increased transportation of raw materials uses non-renewable resources
	Increased environmental degradation from factories in countries without enforced environmental protection laws
Modern trawl fishing maximizes the catch for maximum immediate revenue	Degradation due to agribusiness, logging, commercial fishing, and industrial waste
	Deforestation threatens species survival

Conclusions

The current debate raging on globalization and the explosion of publications on this topic reflect the importance this phenomenon has gained in recent years. When we expand the boundaries of the debate beyond the merits of free trade, a picture emerges of globalization as an uneven process that has resulted in both positive and negative consequences, both winners and losers. Thus, the quick answer to the question "What is the impact of globalization?" is "It's mixed." Globalization is neither a panacea nor an unmitigated plague. Given the complexity and scope of the topic, it is difficult to determine with precision whether some of the problems linked to globalization would exist independently and to what degree. We can conclude, however, that globalization in its current state often involves serious trade-offs such as economic development and jobs at the cost of environmental degradation and weakened labor protection. One important lesson is to include these trade-offs in the debate and in calculating the total cost of global business.

Where people stand with regard to these trade-offs often depends on their values and mindsets—in particular their beliefs regarding free markets, government intervention, the importance of local versus global concerns, and individualist versus communitarian views about the common good (Gladwin, 2002). Understanding these differences in basic assumptions is the first step in creating a civil discourse on the topic. Although businesspeople may disagree with antiglobalization protesters' rhetoric or tactics, another key lesson is that some of their criticisms are valid and should be taken into consideration. In Kobrin's (2001a) description of the antiglobalization protest movement, he concluded that their protests may be "the canary in the mine"—the warning signal about globalization and the role of MNEs.

A third lesson is that businesspeople (and academics) should take a systems approach to globalization to avoid problems. Customers and protesters often see more linkages than some firms seem to consider, and many consumers do care about where their purchases come from. For example, the employees of a major company warned top executives about problems in overseas factories that could result in bad publicity. The person in charge ignored the warning, insisting, "These are just contract workers—they aren't really a part of our company." Years later, the company is still dealing with the PR fallout and targeting by protest groups. To the public, the distinction about whose employees they were was both legalistic and irrelevant. To avoid such problems, some MNEs are now entering into dialogue with all their various stakeholders, including non-governmental organizations.

The accounting systems used by governments and businesses discourage a systems perspective. As long as accounting systems fail to take into consideration the environmental and social costs of doing business, firms can "look good" while doing a fair amount of harm to the larger society. Social accounting is admittedly difficult, but its advantages may now outweigh its disadvantages (Sherman, Steingard, and Fitzgibbons, 2002).

As teachers, we need to make sure our students learn about the whole picture of globalization, including its unintended consequences. Yet my examination of international business textbooks yielded virtually no mention of the impact of globalization on the environment. Globalization is one of the most challenging and complex issues humans have ever faced. The way we teach it should reflect its requisite variety— a multidisciplinary focus including all stakeholders, understanding both the abstract as well as the human and environmental impact, teaching a thorough understanding of the pros and cons, and examining the solutions offered to counteract its problems.

Globalization is driven in large part by a mindset—the belief in the sanctity of markets, which Soros (1998) called "market fundamentalism." Some obvious caveats come to mind, however. First, some economists question whether markets are really "free" (see Stiglitz, 2002, for an alternative view).

Second, once we broaden the globalization debate to include more than economic arguments, it seems obvious that free trade without any regulations or constraints has not been wholly successful (Giddens, 2000). The nations that have prospered under free trade have done so in part because they have laws and institutions that serve as checks and balances. In Giddens's (2000) view,

> Trade always needs a framework of institutions, as do other forms of economic development. Markets cannot be created by purely economic means, and how far a given economy should be exposed to the world marketplace must depend upon a range of criteria . . . Opening up a country or regions within it to free trade can undermine a local subsistence economy. An area that becomes dependent upon a few products sold on world markets is very vulnerable to shifts in prices as well as to technological change. (p. 35)

Business scholars could help identify the criteria that Giddens mentioned and conceptualize globalization as occurring with a broader systemic context. Cookie-cutter approaches to economic development seldom work. Strategies have to fit the local context of each country with its unique institutions and historical, political, and social context.

Third, in addition to a framework of institutions, trade has to be embedded in a broader framework of shared social values that include at least some degree of concern for social justice and the common good.[9] Privatization has been successful in some countries but not where government officials or their cronies bought undervalued state assets and established monopolies. Either the rule of law or shared values is needed to prevent a winner-takes-all mentality. In their absence, perhaps MNEs have to accept that they too have social responsibilities and a broader role to play in society than maximizing shareholder wealth.[10] Concentration solely on economic growth no doubt made sense in an earlier time, but given what is known today about globalization and its impact, our focus should broaden to include a more balanced, integrated approach to economic development (United Nations Development, 2002).

If we needed further convincing that globalization demands a systems view, we might be persuaded by the backlash and counterbalancing forces it has provoked. The protest movements,[11] the growth of nongovernmental organizations, and the movements affirming ethnic identity are all reactions in part to globalization or perhaps an inherent part of globalization. It is more difficult to forecast how the nature of globalization might change in response to these forces. Some observers assume that the current state of globalization is akin to the robber baron era in the United States—a period of excess and abuse that eventually sparked a backlash resulting in policies and laws. Kell and Levin (2002) described globalization as an incomplete experiment in human history with systemic deficiencies that cause instability and social injustice. A consensus of sorts seems to be building around the need to somehow "tame" globalization, but there is no clarity yet about how this will occur, what form it will take, and who has the requisite authority to pull it off.[12]

One interesting response to globalization is the United Nations' Global Compact. This initiative, led by Secretary-General Kofi Annan, consists of a global network of companies, non-governmental organizations, major international labor federations, and several UN agencies. Its objective is to "create a more stable, equitable and inclusive global market by making its nine principles an integral part of business activities everywhere" (United Nations, 2002). These principles, which involve human rights, labor standards, and environmental practices, are an attempt to establish a universal standard.

Principle 1: Support and respect the protection of international human rights within their sphere of influence.

Principle 2: Make sure their own corporations are not complicit in human rights abuses.

Principle 3: Uphold freedom of association and the effective recognition of the right to collective bargaining.

Principle 4: Uphold the elimination of all forms of forced and compulsory labor.

Principle 5: Uphold the effective abolition of child labor.

Principle 6: Uphold the elimination of discrimination in respect of employment and occupation.

Principle 7: Support a precautionary approach to environmental challenges.

Principle 8: Undertake initiatives to promote greater environmental responsibility.

Principle 9: Encourage the development and diffusion of environmentally friendly technologies (United Nations, 2002).

The Global Compact is attempting to build shared values and create a forum for dialogue and institutional learning that will result in social change. In addition to recruiting companies who agree to integrate the nine principles into their business operations, the program's goals are to establish a learning bank that shares lessons on applying the principles, conducts issues dialogues, and generates partnership projects among the different stakeholders. Such partnerships could theoretically decrease the polarization among various groups. The architects of the Global Compact hope that it will be part of the solution to globalization's problems but do not view it as the definitive solution. To date, 700 companies have voluntarily joined the compact.

As stated in the introduction, much of the globalization literature has an ideological bent, which means there is a need for objective research on globalization's impact and for more questioning about the basic assumption of globalization itself. The U.S. acceptance of globalization as the status quo may reflect cultural and historical influences. In his Pulitzer Prize-winning book, *The Global Squeeze*, journalist Richard Longworth (1999) concluded:

The global economy is not an act of God, like a virus or a volcano, but the result of economic actions taken by human beings and thus responsive to human control. There is no need to say, as many American economists and businesspeople do, that the market knows best and must be obeyed. This cultural capitalism is confined mostly to the United States and the other English-speaking nations. Other nations, in Europe and in Asia, see the market as the source of both bountiful benefits and lethal damage and are determined to temper this force to their own priorities. (pp. 4–5)

Given the ever-evolving history of economic development, trade, and international relations, there is little reason for scholars to assume that globalization as we know it today is the final version. Such an assumption is dangerous if it prevents us from seeing other possibilities and the systemic consequences of the current system. Business scholars have made good progress in describing this system and documenting what it takes to be profitable. Now it's time for us to consider what else we can contribute to the debate on globalization and whether we can take a stronger leadership role in influencing the way people think about and practice global business in the future.

Notes

1. The World Trade Organization's major functions are to administer trade agreements, serve as a forum for trade negotiations, settle trade disputes, review national trade policies, and assist developing nations in trade policy issues.

2. Having warned you about the potential biases of globalization writers, it's only fair to explain my own stance and my impetus for writing this article. At the behest of the Northwest Earth Institute, I joined a discussion group on the impact of globalization on the environment and commenced reading. I began with few preconceived notions and with no strong inclination either for or against globalization. If anything, I was positively disposed to creating jobs in lesser developed countries, since I had learned during a previous career in international development that providing employment goes a long way toward solving a variety of social ills for poor people. In the conclusion, I will explain my current position.

3. Simon Valaskakis is Canada's ambassador to the Organization for Economic Cooperation and Development (OECD) in Paris and a professor of economics at the University of Montreal.

4. As of 2002, there were more than 850 export processing zones in the world employing 27 million workers (Drezner, 2000). See International Labour Organization, *Labour and Social Issues Relating to Export Processing Zones* (1998), for information on conditions.

5. The Organization for Economic Cooperation and Development is an international organization that consists of 30 industrialized, market-economy countries. Their representatives meet "to exchange information and harmonize policy with a view to maximizing economic growth within Member countries and assisting non-Member countries develop more rapidly" (Organization, 2003). For more

information, see http://www.oecdwash.org/ ABOUT/aboutmain.htm.

6. Bioengineering is another controversial topic. Genetic engineering can preserve existing species and create new varieties, but the impact of the latter on biological systems is still unknown. There are also ethical concerns about the ability to patent genetically engineered species and human tissues, cells, and organs.

7. See the United Nations Conference on Environment and Development (1992) for information on the successful transfer of technological innovations. For a more complete analysis of the environmental impact of globalization, see J. Osland, K. Dhanda, and K. Yuthas (2002).

8. The Asian cloud is the result of traditional practices such as wood- and dung-burning stoves, cooking fires, and forest clearing as well as auto emissions, factories, and waste incineration.

9. See John Ruggie's (1982) description of embedded liberalism, which was originally conceptualized as a compromise of multilateral trade and domestic stability.

10. *BusinessWeek* devoted its cover story to "Global Capitalism: Can It Be Made to Work Better?" in its November 6, 2000 issue (Engardio and Belton, 2000). Its conclusions are similar to those found here and acknowledge the need for more social responsibility on the part of multinationals and a more realistic view of the economic policy that has driven globalization.

11. For an interesting account of this movement, see Kobrin (2001a).

12. Articulating the suggested solutions lies outside the scope of this article, but one starting point is to look at the lessons learned from 50 years of tackling various global problems in Simmons and Oudraat (2001).

References

Allenby, B. R., & Richards, D. (1994). *Greening of industrial ecosystems.* Washington, DC: National Academy Press.

Annan, K. (1999, January 31). *Address to Davos World Economic Forum*, Davos, Switzerland.

Baldwin, R. E., & Martin, P. (1999). *Two waves of globalization: Superficial similarities, fundamental differences* (NBER Working Paper Series 6904). Cambridge, MA: National Bureau of Economic Research.

Berry, A. (1996, January). *Distributional impact of market-oriented reforms*, Paper prepared at the Association for Comparative Economic Studies, San Francisco.

Brown, C. R., Renner, M., & Flavin, C. (1998). *Vital Signs.* New York: Norton.

Brown, J. (1992). Corporation as community: A new image for a new era. In J. Renesch (Ed.). *New traditions in business* (123–139). San Francisco: Barrett-Kohler.

Champlin, D., & Olson, P. (1999). The impact of globalization on U.S. labor markets: Redefining the debate. *Journal of Economic Issues, 33*(2), 443–451.

Charnovitz, S. (1992, May). Environmental and labour standards in trade. *The World Economy, 15*(8): 343.

Clarke, T. (2001). *Silent coup: Confronting the big business takeover of Canada.* Retrieved January 12, 2001, from www3.simpatico.ca/ tryegrowth/MAI_can.htm

Cox, R. W. (1996). A perspective on globalization. In J. H. Mittelman (Ed.), *Globalization: Critical reflections* (21–30). Boulder, CO: Lynne Rienner.

Daly, H. (1996). *Beyond growth.* Boston: Beacon.

Dohrs, L., & Garfunkel, J. (1999, February). *Time to talk about trade and human rights? Trade and human rights: A Pacific Rim perspective, a source handbook.* Seattle, WA: Global Source Education.

Drezner, D. W. (2000, November/December). Bottom feeders. *Foreign Policy*, 64–70.

Duchin, F. (1996). Population change, lifestyles, and technology: How much difference can they make? *Population and Development Review, 22*(2), 321–330.

Duin, S. (2000, December 3). Reich displays designer hips and a deft mind. *The Oregonian*, B-1.

Engardio, P., & Belton, C. (2000, November 6). Global capitalism: Can it be made to work better? *BusinessWeek*, 72–76.

Engardio, P., Bernstein, A., & Kripalani, M. (2003, February 3). Is your job next? *BusinessWeek*, 50–60.

Evenett, S. J. (1999). The world trading system: The road ahead. *Finance and Development, 36*(4), 22.

Frank, R. H., & Cook, P. J. (1995). *The winner-takes-all society.* New York: Free Press.

French, H. (1993). *Costly tradeoffs: Reconciling trade and the environment.* Washington, DC: World Watch Institute.

Gaunt, J. (2002, July 7). Globalization has helped the poor, study says. Reuters.

Geertz, C. (1998). The world in pieces: Culture and politics at the end of the century. *Focaal: Tigdschrift voor Antropologie, 32*, 91–117.

Giddens, A. (2000). *Runaway world: How globalization is reshaping our lives.* New York: Routledge.

Gladwin, T. (2002, March). *Keynote address presented at the Western Academy of Management*, Santa Fe, New Mexico.

Goldsmith, E. (1997). Can the environment survive the global economy? *The Ecologist, 27*(6), 242–249.

Gottschalk, P., & Smeeding, T. (1997). Cross national comparisons of earnings and income inequality. *Journal of Economic Literature, 35*(2), 633–687.

Graedel, T. E., & Allenby, B. R. (1995). *Industrial ecology.* New York: Prentice Hall.

Graham, E. M., & Krugman, P. R. (1991). *Foreign direct investment in the United States* (2nd ed.). Washington, DC: Institute for International Economics.

Grunberg, I. (1998). Double Jeopardy: Globalization, liberalization and the fiscal squeeze. *World Development, 26*(4), 591–605.

Guillén, M. F. (2001). Is globalization civilizing, destructive or feeble? A critique of six key debates in the social science literature. *Annual Review of Sociology, 27*, 235–260.

Hamelink, C. J. (1998). *Cultural autonomy in global communications.* New York: Longman.

Harris, J. M., & Goodwin, N. R. (1995). *A survey of ecological economics.* Washington, DC: Island Press.

Hirschman, A. O. (1982, December). Rival interpretations of market society: Civilizing, destructive, or feeble? *Journal of Economic Literature, 20*, 1463–1484.

Holmes, S., & Ostrovsky, S. (2003, February 3). The new cold war at Boeing. *Business Week*: 58–59.

Howes, D. (Ed.). (1996). *Cross-cultural consumption: Global markets, local realities.* London: Routledge.

International Labour Organization. (1998). *Labour and social issues relating to export processing zones.* Geneva: Author.

International Monetary Fund. (1999, May). *World economic outlook: A survey by the staff of the International Monetary Fund.* Washington, DC: Author.

Joint Venture. (2003). *Joint Venture's 2003 index of Silicon Valley.* San Jose, CA: Author.

Karliner, J. (2000). Grassroots globalization: Reclaiming the blue planet. In F. J. Lechner & J. Boli (Eds.), *The globalization reader* (pp. 34–38). Oxford: Blackwell.

Keck, M. E., & Sikkink, K. (2000). Environmental advocacy networks. In F. J. Lechner & J. Boli (Eds.), *The globalization reader* (pp. 392–399). Oxford: Blackwell.

Kell, G., & Levin, D. (2002, August). *The evolution of the global compact network: An historic experiment in learning and action.* Paper presented at the Academy of Management meeting, Denver, Colorado.

Khor, M. (1996). Global economy and the third world. In J. Mander and J. Goldsmith (Eds.), *The case against the global economy and for a turn toward the local* (47–59). San Francisco: Sierra Club.

Klein, N. (2000). *No Logo.* New York: Picador.

Kobrin, S. J. (1997). The architecture of globalization: State sovereignty in a networked global economy. In J. H. Dunning (Ed.), *Governments, globalization, and international business* (pp. 146–171). New York: Oxford University Press.

Kobrin, S. J. (2001a, February). *Our resistance is as global as your oppression: Multinational corporations, the protest movement and the future of global governance.* Paper presented at the meeting of the International Studies Association, Chicago.

Kobrin, S. J. (2001b). Sovereignty @ bay: Globalization, multinational enterprise, and the international political system. In A. Rugman & T. Brewer (Eds.), *The Oxford handbook of international business* (pp. 181–205). New York: Oxford University Press.

Krishnan, R. (1996). December 1995: The first revolt against globalization. *Monthly Review, 48*(1): 1–23.

Krugman, P. (1994). Does third world growth hurt first world prosperity? *Harvard Business Review, 72*(4), 113–121.

Lavelle, L., Jespersen, F., Ante, S., & Kerstetter, J. (2003, April 21). Executive pay. *Business Week,* 86–90.

Lawrence, R. A. (1995, January). U.S. wage trends in the 1980s: The role of international factors. *Federal Reserve Bank of New York Economic Policy Review, 2*(1), 18–25.

Lawrence, R. Z., Rodrik, D., & Whalley, J. (1996). *Emerging agenda for global trade: High stakes for developing countries.* Washington, DC: Overseas Development Council.

Lawrence, R. Z., & Slaughter, M. (1993). Trade and U.S. wages in the 1980s: Giant sucking sound or small hiccup? *Brookings Papers on Economic Activity: Microeconomics, 2,* 161–210.

Learner, E. (1998). In search of Stopler-Samuelson linkages between international trade and lower wages. In S. Collins (Ed.), *Imports, exports, and the American worker* (141–214). Washington, DC: Brookings Institution Press.

Lechner, F. J., & Boli, J. (Eds.). (2000). *The globalization reader.* Oxford: Blackwell.

Lee, E. (1996). Globalization and employment: Is anxiety justified? *International Labour Review, 135*(5), 486–497.

Lee, E. (1997). Globalization and labour standards: A review of issues. *International Labour Review, 136*(2), 173–189.

Levi, M. (2000, February). *Labor unions and the WTO.* Speech given at the University of Washington, Seattle.

Longworth, R. C. (1999). *The global squeeze.* Chicago: Contemporary Books.

MacBride, S., & Roach, C. (2000). The new international information order. In F. J. Lechner and J. Boli (Eds.), *The globalization reader* (pp. 286–292). Oxford: Blackwell.

Mander, J., & Goldsmith, E. (Eds.). (1996). *The case against the global economy and for a turn toward the local.* San Francisco: Sierra Club.

Marquand, D. (1998). *The new reckoning.* Cambridge: Polity.

Monbiot, G. (1995, August 13). Global villagers speak with forked tongues. *Guardian,* 24.

Murphy, K., & Topel, R. (1997). Unemployment and nonemployment. *American Economic Review, 87*(2), 295–300.

Ohmae, K. (1995). *The end of the nation state.* New York: Free Press.

Organization for Economic Cooperation and Development (OECD) (1996). *Trade, employment, and labour standards: A study of core workers' rights and international trade.* Paris: Author.

Organization for Economic Cooperation and Development (OECD). (1997). Trade, Earnings and employment: Assessing the impact of trade with emerging economies on OECD labour markets. *OECD Employment Outlook,* 93–128.

Organization for Economic Cooperation and Development (OECD). (2003). *About the OECD.* Retrieved on March 27, 2003, from http://www.oecdwash.org/ABOUT/aboutmain.htm

Osland, J. S., Dhanda, K., & Yuthas, K. (2002). Globalization and environmental sustainability: An analysis of the impact of globalization using the Natural Step framework. In S. Sharma & M. Starik (Eds.), *Research in corporate sustainability: The evolving theory and practice of organizations in the natural environment* (pp. 31–60). Cheltenham, UK: Edward Elgar.

Press, E. (2002, June 10). Rebel with a cause: The re-education of Joseph Stiglitz. *The Nation,* 11–16.

Pritchett, I., (1997, 3rd trimester). La distribution passee et future du revenu mondial. [The once (and future) distribution of world income.] *Economie Internationale, 0*(71), 19–42.

Rackham, O. (1986). *The history of the countryside.* London: J. M. Dent & Sons.

Renesch, J. (Ed.). (1992). *New traditions in business.* San Francisco: Barrett-Kohler.

Robbins, D. J. (1995). *Trade, trade liberalization and inequality in Latin America and East Asia: Synthesis of seven country studies.* Unpublished manuscript, Harvard University.

Rodrik, D. (1997). *Has globalization gone too far?* Washington, DC: Institute for International Economics.

Ruggie, J. (1982). International regimes, transactions and change: Embedded liberalism in the postwar economic order. *International Organization, 36*(2), 379–415.

Sachs, J., & Schatz, H. (1994). *Trade and jobs in US manufacturing* (Brookings Papers on Economic Activity, 1, pp. 1–84). Washington, DC: Brookings Institution.

Schmidheiny, S. (1992). *Changing course.* Cambridge, MA: MIT Press.

Scott, R. E., Lee, T., & Schmitt, J. (1997). *Trading away good jobs: An examination of employment and wages in the US 1979–94.* Washington, DC: Economic Policy Institute.

Sherman, R. W., Steingard, D. S., & Fitzgibbons, D. E. (2002). Sustainable stakeholder accounting: Beyond complementarity and towards integration in environmental accounting. In S. Sharma & M. Starik (Eds.), *Research in corporate sustainability: The evolving theory and practice of organizations in the natural environment* (257–294). Cheltenham, UK: Edward Elgar.

Simmons, P. J., & de Jonge Oudraat, C. (Eds.). (2001). *Managing global issues: Lessons learned.* Washington, DC: Carnegie Endowment.

Sinclair, J., Jacka, E., & Cunningham, S. (1996). *New patterns in global television: Peripheral vision.* Oxford: Oxford University Press.

Slaughter, M. J., & Swagel, P. (2000). Does globalization lower wages and export jobs? In F. J. Lechner & J. Boli (Eds.), *The globalization reader* (pp. 177–180). Oxford: Blackwell.

Socolow, R., Andrews, C., Berkhout, F., & Thomas, V. (1994). *Industrial ecology and global change.* New York: Cambridge University Press.

Soros, G. (1998). *The crisis of global capitalism.* New York: Public Affairs.

Soros, G. (2002). *George Soros on globalization.* New York: Public Affairs.

Stiglitz, J. (2002). *Globalization and its discontent.* New York: Norton.

Sutherland, P. D. (1998, November 1). Sharing the bounty. *Banker, 148*(873).

Takashi, I. (1997). Changing Japanese labor and employment system. *Journal of Japanese Trade & Industry, 16*(4), 20–24.

Temple, J. (1999). The new growth evidence. *Journal of Economic Literature, 37,* 112–156.

Tisdell, C. (1997). Local communities, conservation and sustainability: Institutional change, altered governance and Kant's social philosophy. *International Journal of Social Economics, 24*(12), 1361–1320.

Tomlinson, J. (1999). *Globalization and culture.* Chicago: University of Chicago Press.

Tyson, D. L. (1999, May 31). Why the US should welcome China to the WTO. *BusinessWeek,* 30.

United Nations. (2002). *Global Compact.* Retrieved on August 29, 2002, from http://65.214.34.30/un/gc/unweb.nsf/webprintview/thenine.htm

United Nations Conference on Trade and Development (UNCTAD) (1992). *World investment report.* Geneva: Author.

United Nations Conference on Trade and Development (UNCTAD) (1995). *World investment report.* Geneva: Author

United Nations Conference on Trade and Development (UNCTAD) (1997). *Trade and development report.* Geneva: Author.

United Nations Conference on Trade and Development (UNCTAD) (1998). *World investment report.* Geneva: Author.

United Nations Conference on Trade and Development (UNCTAD) (1999). *North-South trade, employment and inequality: The social responsibility of transactional corporations.* Geneva: Author.

United Nations Development Programme (UNDP). (1996). *Human development report 1996.* New York: Oxford University Press.

United Nations Development Programme (UNDP). (1999). *Human development report 1999.* New York: Oxford University Press.

United Nations Development Programme (UNDP). (2001). *Human development report 2001.* New York: Oxford University Press.

United Nations Development Programme (UNDP). (2002). *Human development reports—fast facts.* Retrieved on September 9, 2002, from http://www/undp.org/ dpa/publications

Valaskakis, K. (1998, Summer). The challenge of strategic governance: Can globalization be managed? *Optimum, 28*(2), 26–40.

Wackernagel, M., & Rees, W. (1996). *Our ecological footprint.* Gabriola Island, BC: New Society Publishers.

Waters, M. (1995). *Globalization.* New York: Routledge.

Wilkes, A. (1995). Prawns, profits and protein: Aquaculture and food production. *Ecologist, 25,* 2–3.

Wood, A. (1994). *North-south trade, employment and inequality: Changing fortunes in a skill-driven world.* Oxford: Clarendon.

Wood, A. (1995, Summer). How trade hurt unskilled workers. *Journal of Economic Perspectives, 9*(3), 57–81.

Wood, A. (1997). Openness and wage inequality in developing countries: The Latin American challenge to East Asian conventional wisdom. *World Bank Economic Review, 11*(1), 33–57.

Wood, A. (1998, September). Globalization and the rise in labour market inequalities. *Economic Journal, 198*(450), 1463–1483.

World Trade Organization (2003). Retrieved March 28, 2003, from http://www.wto.org

Yergin, D., & Stanislaw, J. (2000). The commanding heights: The battle between government and the marketplace that is remaking the modern world. In F. J. Lechner & J. Boli (Eds.), *The globalization reader* (pp. 212–220). Oxford: Blackwell.

Zhao, L. (1998, April). The impact of foreign direct investment on wages and employment. *Oxford Economic Papers, 50*(2), 284–302.

THE NEW GLOBAL MANAGER: LEARNING CULTURES ON THE FLY*

Luciara Nardon

Richard M. Steers

Many years ago, a popular film making the rounds of the local movie theatres was *If It's Tuesday, It Must Be Belgium.* The film used humor to highlight the plight of a typical American tourist who was overcome by the cultural differences across the countries included in her whirlwind tour of Europe. The film's underlying

*Reprinted from *Organizational Dynamics*, 37(1), Luciara Nardon and Richard M. Steers, "The New Global Manager: Learning Cultures on the Fly," pp. 47–59, © 2008, with permission from Elsevier.

message was that tourists—at least American tourists—seldom allow sufficient time in their travels to learn about cultural differences, preferring instead to race from one popular tourist site to another in search of good food, unique experiences, and photographs to show to their friends and family back home. The issue is one of having *been* there, not having *learned* anything. Today, despite a widespread recognition that we live and work in an increasingly interconnected global economy, it is curious that the dilemma posed in this old film is still salient for many contemporary managers and entrepreneurs alike. How serious are we about learning about other cultures? And if we are serious, how do we accomplish this in meaningful ways as part of our busy work schedules?

Working with Global Partners

Today, a major challenge facing managers and entrepreneurs is how to deal with both partners and competitors abroad whom we simply don't understand. More often than not, the problem is not just language differences; it is *cultural* differences. Consider: How can we trust or do business with prospective foreign business partners who won't:

- "put their cards on the table" and say what they actually mean?
- work "24/7" and "stay on target" until the job is completed?
- "step up to the plate," make concrete commitments, and accept responsibility for their side of the partnership?
- "let their hair down" and open up to us, so we can get to know each other?

In other words, how can we trust or do business with prospective foreign business partners when we know so little about them, their backgrounds, their approaches to business, or their future intents? The obvious question here is what to do. Unfortunately, the answer to this question is not as simple as perhaps it once was. Gone are the days when prospective managers could learn French or German or Spanish in college to prepare themselves for their careers. Learning a foreign language and foreign culture is obviously helpful, but it is often impractical in view of the rapidity with which business opportunities appear and disappear around the world.

This challenge of understanding people from other cultures is made more difficult by the increasing speed with which business often occurs. A key factor here is the way in which recent technological advancements have pushed both the pace and complexity of globalization to new heights. Communication and information technology makes it possible to collaborate—or compete—globally from anywhere in the world, regardless of one's country of origin or cultural background. As a growing number of organizations have established increased operations around the world, managers' exposure to both partners and competitors from significantly different cultural backgrounds has increased at a rate that has surprised both economists and social scientists. The implication for managers of all types is clear: Managers with a capability to think and understand business relationships from a *global* perspective will more often than not succeed over those with more limited nation-based mindsets.

In this regard, consider a day in the life of Adhira Iyengar, an entrepreneur from Bangalore, India. Adhira woke up early one recent morning, prepared a cup of tea, and logged onto her computer. As expected, Debra Brown, her business partner in California, was already logged on. "Good morning! I have a few questions about your last report and would like to discuss them with you before I leave for the day." As they finished their online meeting, Adhira stared at her calendar and realized that, again, it was going to be a long day. At 10:00 that morning she had a conference call with Mr. Wu, a client from Hong Kong, about some changes in their service contract. At 1:30 p.m. she had a face-to-face meeting with a group of prospective Australian clients in her office in Bangalore. Before the end of the day, she had to complete a report and e-mail it to Mrs. Sanchez, a partner in Mexico City, and she still needed to prepare for her trip to Berlin coming up in the following week.

Developing successful relationships with people from different cultures, as Adhira has done, is challenging by definition. Several reasons account for this, including people's tendencies to have preconceived notions about how the world works (or should work), how individuals behave (or should behave), and which behaviors are acceptable (or unacceptable). These ideas are largely influenced by our personal experiences and the cultures in which we grew up. We tend to approach intercultural interactions based on our own perceptions, beliefs, values, biases, and misconceptions about what is likely to happen. As a result, when we engage in exchanges with people from different cultures, we frequently discover that the consequences of our actions are quite different than the ones we anticipated. The results can range from embarrassment to insult to lost business opportunities. Such consequences can also be career-limiting, to say the least.

Preparing for Global Assignments

How can people like Adhira prepare to succeed in today's highly competitive global economy? More to the point, what can relatively inexperienced managers from any country do when they are assigned to go abroad—for short or long periods—to represent their company's critical business interests? And what can they do when they are required to work with people from other countries before they even have a chance to see what it is like to live abroad? At least three strategies can be identified to help such inexperienced managers: cultural fluency, developing a global mindset, and learning cultures on the fly.

Cultural Fluency

Traditionally, managers have been advised to prepare themselves for an international assignment through *cultural fluency*—that is, by mastering the culture and language of the country to which they were being assigned. Management training programs, both in the home country and host country, have long been used to achieve such goals. Through such programs, managers develop capabilities to interact more effectively with people from another country through learning the local language and culture in depth and behaving in ways that are appropriate to that culture. Thus, a manager who is assigned to work in France for several years may be advised to study French language and culture, make local friends upon arrival in the new location, and be tolerant of experiences that are new or unique.

A key part of such programs is to develop a clear recognition in the minds of the managers that new expatriates frequently experience stress and anxiety as a result of being immersed in an unfamiliar culture—generally referred to as culture shock. Over time, such managers typically learn new ways of coping and eventually become more comfortable living in the culture of the host country. This learning strategy has considerable merit when a manager is being assigned to a specific country for a long period of time. It works less well, however, when the manager in question will be spending the coming years doing business across multiple cultures.

Developing a Global Mindset

With this new multicultural reality, managers are being increasingly advised to develop what has been called a *global mindset.* That is, managers are told to expand their knowledge and understanding of multiple cultures in ways that will help them successfully interact with people from highly diverse backgrounds. Reaching a critical mass of understanding here enables the informed traveler to venture forth and conduct business in multiple locations with competence. As noted by Mansour Javidan and his colleagues, "It is insufficient for a manager who is likely to assume, mistakenly, that being open minded in Atlanta, Helsinki, and Beijing will be perceived identically, or that walking in someone else's shoes will feel the same in Houston, Jakarta, or Madrid. Because of the lack of scientifically compiled information, businesspeople have not had sufficient detailed and context-specific suggestions about how to handle these cross-cultural challenges." Developing a global mindset is advocated as one way to resolve this deficiency.

While some variations exist, most definitions of global mindset suggest that it is an ability to develop and interpret criteria for personal and business performance that are independent of the assumptions of a single country, culture, or context, and to implement those criteria appropriately in different countries, cultures, and contexts. In other words, a global mindset is a cognitive structure or knowledge structure that contains information about several cultures and realities. This knowledge allows managers to interpret situations using multiple cultural frameworks and then select the most appropriate action for each particular situation.

Learning Cultures on the Fly

While both of these approaches—cultural fluency and developing a global mindset—can be very useful, we suggest that the increasing intensity, time sensitivity, and diversity that characterizes today's global business environment may require a third approach. Developing broad-based knowledge about one or several cultures, and using such knowledge in appropriate ways, is ideal. In reality, however, achieving this level of understanding is difficult, if not impossible, for at least two reasons. First, learning about another culture from a distance is difficult at best. Second, most managers do not have the time to learn about other cultures and develop a global mindset well before they are asked to be effective in the field. In such cases, we offer an alternative—not a better alternative, but perhaps a more practical one when time is of the essence. We call it *learning cultures on the fly.*

Learning Cultures on the Fly: From Individual to Interdependent Learning

As the international business environment has shifted from a collection of principally bi-cultural business relationships to a more genuinely integrated intercultural one, managers are faced with three principal challenges in attempting to adapt quickly to the new realities on the ground:

1. *Many intercultural encounters happen on short notice, leaving little time to learn about the other culture.* Imagine that you just returned from a week's stay in India where you were negotiating an outsourcing agreement. As you arrive in your home office you learn that an incredible acquisition opportunity just turned up in South Africa and that you are supposed to leave in a week to explore the matter further. You have never been to South Africa, nor do you know anybody from there. What do you do? While there are many books covering the "do's and don'ts" of cultures, they are typically

helpful guides on how to eat or behave politely and say little about how local managers behave.

2. *It is often unclear to which culture we should adapt.* Suppose your company has asked you to join a global project team to work in a six-month research and development (R&D) project. The team includes people from Mexico, Germany, China, and Russia. Every member of the team has a permanent appointment in his or her home country, but is temporarily assigned to work on this project at company headquarters in Switzerland. Which culture should team members adapt to? In this case, there is no dominant cultural group to dictate the rules. Considering the multiple cultures involved, and the little exposure each manager has likely had with the other cultures, the traditional approach of adaptation is unlikely to be successful. Nevertheless, the group must be able to work together quickly and effectively to produce results—and protect their careers—despite their differences. What would you do?

3. *Intercultural meetings increasingly occur virtually, not face-to-face.* Suppose you were asked to build a partnership with a Korean partner whom you have never met, and that you know little about Korean culture. Suppose further that this task is to be completed online, without any face-to-face communication or interactions. Your boss is in a hurry for results. What would you do?

Taken together, these three challenges demonstrate how difficult it can be to work across cultures in today's rapidly changing technology-based business environment. The old ways of communicating and doing business are simply less effective than in the past. The question before us, then, is how to facilitate management success in such situations. To accomplish this, we suggest that managers need to *learn how to learn* to deal with other cultures and make sense of varied environments. To this end, consider how individuals learn from experience and how models of learning can be applied to help managers succeed in intercultural contexts.

Individual Learning: Experiential Learning Theory

Following experiential learning theory, developed by David Kolb, individual learning occurs through a combination of grasping and transforming experiences. The learning process is composed of four stages that include the two modes of constructing knowledge: knowledge is grasped through *concrete experience* and *abstract conceptualization* and then transformed through *reflective observation* and *active experimentation*. While it may begin in any of the four stages, learning is a process of experience, observation, and reflection, abstract conceptualization, and active experimentation, as illustrated in Figure 1.

Concrete Experience

To understand how experiential learning theory works in practice, imagine that you come from a culture that values direct, straightforward communication. As you engage in a conversation with another individual, you are likely to think that direct questioning is appropriate and will result in a straightforward answer. Now imagine that the individual with whom you are communicating comes from a culture that values indirect communication and the avoidance of public embarrassment. For this person direct questions are inappropriate, and information is exchanged indirectly through subtle suggestions and hints. Now, consider that

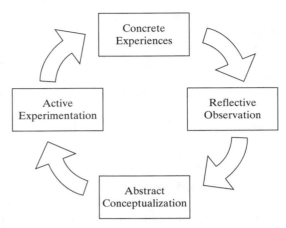

FIGURE 1 The Experiential Learning Process

neither of you is sufficiently knowledgeable to adapt your communication style to suit the other's culture. The most likely result of this scenario is that you will ask a direct question and will get what you perceive as an unsatisfactory response. At this point, you are likely to experience an emotional reaction—discomfort, perplexity, offense, or surprise. The feelings you experience as a result of your actions are referred to as *concrete experience*. In other words, it is your emotional reaction to the results of your actions.

Observation and Reflection

Your experience or feelings may then prompt you to try to understand what is happening. You may engage in *observation and reflection.* That is, once you realize that there is a disconnect between what is happening and what you thought would happen, you observe the other person and try to guess why he or she responded as they did. You may mentally run thorough a list of possible problems: maybe she did not hear you, maybe she did not understand the question, maybe she does not speak English very well, maybe she is shy, maybe she is not comfortable with the question, and so forth. You then search for other clues to her behavior in the context of the situation that can help understand her behavior. Simply put, you look for additional information that will help you make sense of the situation.

Abstract Concepts and Generalizations

This observation and reflection forms the basis of *abstract concepts and generalizations.* As you think about it, you develop a theory of what is happening. You identify a plausible explanation for her behavior and begin searching for alternative solutions to your problem. Let's suppose that you concluded that your partner is uncomfortable with your question. Her body language suggests that she feels embarrassed to answer. Therefore, you theorize that you should pose the question in a different way.

Testing Implications of Concepts

Your newly developed theory will guide any future actions you take to deal with this individual and others from the same culture. As you practice these new actions, you are *testing implications of concepts.* You decide, for example, to formulate your question in a different way, you observe the results, and start a new learning cycle. The cycle continues until you are able to identify successful behaviors. Learning through experience is a process of trial and error in which we perceive a mismatch, reflect on it, identify solutions, and initiate new behaviors. When we identify successful behaviors, we incorporate them into our theories of how to behave. The next time we engage in a similar situation, we draw upon our latest theory for guidance.

We may initiate our learning process at different points of the circular cycle, depending on the situation and our learning preferences. For instance, some people have a preference for abstract concepts and generalizations, preferring to go to the library and read about the other culture prior to engaging with its members. These individuals will strive to develop a theory beforehand and will improve their theory in the course of the interaction. Others have a preference for observation and may choose to watch foreigners interacting prior to engaging with them. In other words, they will fine-tune their theories based on their observations. Still others may prefer to jump to the situation without prior exposure and draw on their feelings to decide how to behave. As the circular model suggests, individuals that are able to utilize all four types of abilities are better equipped to learn in the complex environment of intercultural interactions.

Interdependent Learning: The Intercultural Interaction Learning Model

While experiential learning theory has remained one of the most influential theories of management development, it has been criticized for its failure to account for the *social* aspects of learning; that is, it ignores the role of learning from and with others. In an effort to fill this void, the *intercultural interaction learning model* focuses on two or more individuals who are simultaneously experiencing problems, reflecting on them, theorizing about them, and engaging in new corrective actions. In other words, the learning process is seen as interdependent and interactive, not independent or linear. The learning of one party to an intercultural exchange leads to learning by the other party and so forth.

In principle, as people's learning processes interact, new and hopefully better ways of communicating emerge. However, if learning is short-circuited, the relationship suffers, and the interaction fails. For instance, if after asking a question and receiving an unsatisfactory answer the person does not stop to observe the other party and reflect on her behavior, he or she may engage in actions that are detrimental to the relationship. In sum, an effective intercultural interaction is the result of a successful interdependent learning process, in which all parties to an exchange learn to work together more effectively.

In our view, an *intercultural interaction* is an opportunity for interdependent learning in which individuals *both* learn about the other's culture *and* negotiate effective ways of relating to one another. Building on previous communications research, we suggest four main areas that need to be negotiated in intercultural exchanges: identities, meaning, rules, and behaviors. Each of these negotiating activities is based on a specific learning ability: 1) the ability to *negotiate identity* draws on the ability to engage in concrete experiences: 2) the ability to *negotiate meaning* builds on the ability to reflect and observe; and 3) the ability to *negotiate new rules* is based on the ability to develop new theories; and 4) the ability to *negotiate new behaviors* is based on the ability to take actions.

Step #1: Negotiating Identity

An individual's self-identity consists of those attributes that are central, enduring, and distinctive about the individual. In other words, identity is the answer to the question,

"Who am I?" Identity is constructed through social interactions, whereby individuals create categories and define themselves in relation to others. This process of categorization influences not only how individuals position themselves in relation to others, but also how people act and feel about the interaction. Our own identity or self-image is closely linked to our interpretations of reality. In other words, we make sense of the world based on how we see ourselves. Or as noted in the *Talmud,* "We do not see things as they are, we see them as we are." Social identification theory suggests that one's actions will be congruent with one's self-identity. Individuals tend to engage in activities that are harmonious with their self-concept and to support institutions that embody their identities.

It is for this reason that intercultural interactions are potentially challenging. When we engage with others from a different cultural background, our assumptions, values, and beliefs are often questioned. Our perceptions about who we are, our competence, status, and self-worth may be challenged. An inter-cultural interaction is likely to produce strong feelings associated with our own identity and how we expect to be treated. For these feelings to be positive, individuals must engage in a process of managing or *negotiating identity.*

Intercultural relations scholars have recognized the importance of negotiating identity in cross-cultural conflicts. According to them, conflicts of interests among different groups or individuals are projected on the basis of identity, and differences in international conflicts must involve a resolution of the parties' identities. Dealing with international conflicts requires first dealing with oneself through reflexive dialogue. In other words, it requires addressing how the issue is reflected 'inside' one's mind and how one's identity is challenged or threatened by it.

Negotiating identity is particularly important in situations in which one culture is perceived to be in a more powerful position than the other. For instance, in global business acquisitions, managers from an acquiring company are generally more powerful, have greater status, and may try to impose the "right" way of doing things on the people from the acquired company. Individuals from the less powerful group may find that their cultural-based assumptions and values are criticized, considered inappropriate, and may feel that their own sense of self is being challenged. In other words, their position in the social environment is decreased.

For instance, a Spanish manager may consider that arriving 30 minutes late to a meeting is normal and acceptable. However, the manager of the recently acquired Polish company may see this as a sign of disrespect, and a sign that she is no longer important to the organization. Having one's identity threatened may close off communication, impede learning, and eventually compromise the success of the interaction. Unless both parties can negotiate an acceptable identity for themselves, the interaction is likely to fail.

The process of identity negotiation involves two identities—our own and the other's identity. For an intercultural interaction to be successful, we need to be able to preserve a satisfactory identity for ourselves, while at the same time respecting and preserving the other's identity.

- To preserve our own identity, we need to develop self-awareness. Self-awareness refers to understanding who we are, what our values are, and what our place in the social interaction is. In other words, we need to understand that we are complex cultural beings and that our values, beliefs, and assumptions are a product of our cultural heritage. When we understand that who we are is heavily influenced by our own cultural experiences, we are better equipped to separate our sense of worth from the situation. For example, the Polish manager above may think "As a Polish manager, I do not like to wait," rather than "only people who are not important are kept waiting." The first statement preserves her identity, the second challenges it.

• To preserve the other's identity, it is important to develop empathy towards the other. Empathy refers to the ability to identify and understand the other's feelings and motives. In other words, empathy suggests an understanding that the other is also a complex cultural being and that their actions—like ours—are a product of deep-seated cultural values and beliefs. In other words, when there is a misunderstanding, successful global managers tend to search for a cultural explanation for the other's behavior, before judging the other party's behavior.

For example, suppose you had asked your Egyptian counterpart if an important report would be ready today, and he had answered "yes," but did not deliver it. Instead of judging him based on your own culture (perhaps suggesting that he is not dependable, trustworthy, or competent), you empathize with him on the grounds that his behavior is also a product of culture. Maybe he indirectly told you that he could not finish the report, but you did not understand. Maybe your request was not appropriate or time expectations were not clear. Therefore, you assume that he is acting consistently with his own cultural rules even though you do not understand it. You then proceed to understand what happened, trying to identify a possible miscommunication.

Managers that are open-minded and willing to suspend judgment are more likely to be successful. Skilled managers empathize with others not based on shared values and assumptions, but based on the common fact that we are complex cultural beings and behave in accordance to a complex web of cultural values and beliefs.

In other words, in order to negotiate identities effectively we need to understand that we are cultural beings. We need to know our own values and assumptions, and their relationship with our own culture. We also need to empathize with the other, knowing that he or she is also influenced by culture, even if we do not know what it means. With this in mind, we can negotiate acceptable identities in which our own and the other's sense of self are preserved. When our sense of self is preserved, our feelings in the interaction are more likely to be positive and it becomes easier to continue with the learning experience.

Step #2: Negotiating Meaning

Meaning refers to the interpretation we give to things. For example, what does signing a contract really mean? For some cultures a contract means the end of a negotiation, for others it means the beginning of a relationship. New assignments of meaning are based on current and past experience. Jointly understood meaning is constructed through interaction, as individuals exchange information. Therefore, when two individuals from different cultures interact, they are likely to start with different understandings about the meaning of the concrete topic that they are discussing (for example a contract). However, to be effective, they will need to arrive at a common understanding of the issue; that is, they need to *negotiate meaning.*

In interpersonal interactions, the meanings of messages cannot be transmitted from one person to another, only the message itself can be. When we send a message to another we attach certain meaning to it, based on our interpretation of the issue, ourselves, and the other. When others receive our message, they attach meaning to it based on their interpretation of the issue, the message, themselves, and us.

For example, when you say, "I am glad we were able to sign a contract," you may mean "I am glad the negotiations are over and I can go back to business." However, your Asian counterpart may hear "I am glad we agreed to start a relationship and will continue the negotiations for a long time to come." A common meaning must be constructed for this interaction to be effective.

Most frequently, meaning is constructed through interaction as individuals exchange information. Negotiating meaning involves uncovering hidden cultural assumptions, becoming aware of how culture is shaping perceptions, expectations, and behaviors for all parties involved. To negotiate meaning effectively, individuals must engage in two behaviors: inquiry and advocacy.

- *Inquiry* refers to exploring and questioning one's own reasoning and the reasoning of others. In other words, individuals strive to create and accept a new, common meaning, by asking the following questions: How do I/you perceive the situation? What do I/you wish to achieve in this situation? Which actions am I/are you taking to achieve this goal? Inquiry requires suspending judgment, letting go of a previous understanding, and tolerating uncertainty until a new understanding may be created.
- *Advocacy* refers to expressing and standing for what one thinks and desires. Advocacy suggests stating clearly what you think and want, and explaining the reasoning behind your view. When individuals combine inquiry with advocacy they share information about their cultural assumptions, the meanings they associate with the issue, and the reasoning for their thinking. This sharing of assumptions and interpretations creates the basis for a new, mutually acceptable meaning to emerge.

Engaging in inquiry and advocacy is challenging because it requires uncovering our own perceptions, exposing ourselves, being open to listen to the other's perception, and being willing to give up the safety of our own previous interpretations in order for a new culture-free interpretation to emerge. To make matters worse, cultural-based preferences can also influence how individuals may go about doing this.

For example, in some cultures, individuals prefer to express themselves using open and direct communication, whereas in other cultures individuals are likely to share their assumptions indirectly, making it difficult for direct communicators to fully understand. Some indirect communicators may even feel uncomfortable with direct questioning of their assumptions, which could potentially close communication even further.

Additionally, cultural-based preferences may suggest circumstances in which inquiry and advocacy are more likely to be successful. For instance, in some cultures it may be during formal meetings, in other cultures it may be late at night over drinks, and in still others it may be through informal one-on-one conversations.

As a result, in order to negotiate meaning, individuals must gather information in several different ways, relying on the context, body language, subtle cues, and messages. These abilities typically rely heavily on learning skills associated with observation and reflection: information gathering and analysis.

- *Information gathering* refers to the ability to collect information through various means in order to understand the point of view of others. Competent managers gather information by observing context, body language, face expression, and other behavioral cues, listening to what is being communicated, and asking questions when appropriate, and in a way that is appropriate.

- *Information analysis* refers to the ability to interpret this information in light of what is being discussed, the people involved, and the context in which the interaction is happening.

Step #3: Negotiating New Rules

In a typical intercultural interaction, once the parties agree on acceptable identities and meanings, they turn their attention on developing or *negotiating new rules* that will inform and guide their relationship in the future. These rules are akin to theories of action and over time will ideally create a common context for behavior and interaction.

For example, parties to an interaction need to establish rules about acceptable behaviors regarding time. How late is too late? Managers may agree that, for instance, fifteen minutes is not considered late, but that further delays should be avoided—or at a minimum deserve an apology. Alternatively, they may agree on a more clear specification of time when making appointments: 8:00 Mexican time typically means that delays are expected, while 8:00 American time typically means that punctuality is expected. These rules should cover the most important cultural obstacles to the success of the relationship, whether they are about time, use of titles, style of communication, or any other thing.

In time, these rules will evolve into a new shared culture for the individuals involved. This culture may be a combination of the several cultures involved, or it may be a culture that is unlike any other but is acceptable to all. Sometimes one of the parties will embrace the other's cultural rules in their entirety and adopt them as their own. This last scenario is more common when one of the parties has been exposed to the other's culture for a long time and can adapt. In any case, to develop new rules managers must develop the learning skills associated with integration and transformation of information.

- *Integration of information* refers to the ability to assimilate all the information gathered in the negotiating meaning stage into a coherent theory of action. For example, you noticed that your counterpart looked annoyed when you answered the phone during a meeting, you noticed that he turned his cell phone off, and you noticed that he signaled to the secretary that he should not be interrupted. You integrate all these disparate pieces of information into one theory: your counterpart does not appreciate interruptions.
- *Transformation of information* refers to creating a theory of action based on the information you have. Continuing with the interruption example, you may transform your theory about the other into a theory about what you should do: you should avoid interruptions if at all possible. As these behaviors take place, rules are adjusted and fine-tuned.

Step #4: Negotiating New Behaviors

To complete the cycle after individuals develop new theories of action and agree on a common set of cultural rules to guide the interaction, they will likely move to complete the learning loop by *negotiating new behaviors*.

For example, if the negotiated rule is that delays of more than fifteen minutes should be avoided, you must learn to engage in a new set of behaviors that will allow you to control time, prioritize things differently, and arrive on time.

Or, perhaps the new rule suggests that direct communication should be avoided, in which case you will need to learn to engage in a communication style that is more indirect, subtle, and diplomatic.

Clearly, engaging in new behaviors requires high levels of behavioral flexibility, including an ability to engage in different behaviors—being able to switch styles and accomplish things in more than one way. For some individuals it is easy to engage in some behaviors but not others. Successful managers are able to recognize which behaviors are challenging for them, and compensate with other behaviors. For instance, for some individuals it is very difficult to communicate indirectly. They recognize this limitation, and to compensate for it search for opportunities to discuss issues privately so any public embarrassments can be avoided.

Finally, managers need to be mindful of themselves, the other, and the interaction between the two. That is, they must constantly pay attention to what they are feeling and doing, what the other is doing, and how the other reacts to what they say and do. In the process of learning about the other and testing ways to interact, individuals are aware of their own behavior and the effects of their behavior on others involved.

Conclusion

As most successful managers realize, working with foreign partners and competitors is increasingly unavoidable. As the examples throughout this paper suggest, the realities of today's global environment imply that managers often need to do business in several countries and deal with several cultures simultaneously or, at the very least, sequentially. While the examples provided here may suggest easy solutions—for example, when dealing with Spaniards, know they will be late—the reality of intercultural encounters is considerably more complex for several reasons:

- Individuals are often influenced by multiple cultures—national, regional, organizational, functional, and professional.
- In no country are people monolithic in their beliefs, values, and behaviors. People are different, despite having the same country of origin.
- Our business counterparts are also learning how to deal with foreigners and may deal with us in ways that are not typical of their own culture.
- Culture itself is very complex and may seem paradoxical to an outsider. For this reason, simplistic categorizations of cultures may be helpful explanations of behavior, or good first guesses, but they are not good predictors.

In order to succeed in this business environment, managers are encouraged to develop skills that will allow them to learn how to succeed in each interaction by uncovering cultural assumptions and learning how to deal with them. The Indian manager in our earlier example has to deal with four or five different cultures in one day. It would be difficult for her to acquire fluency in these cultures, while sitting in her office in Bangalore. Instead, she needs to develop learning skills that will compensate for cultural knowledge gaps, helping her to negotiate her interactions as they evolve.

In summary, we have suggested that intercultural interactions involve four types of negotiation relating to identities, meaning, rules, and behaviors.

- The negotiation of identities relies on strong self-awareness and empathy, so the emotional experience is managed and the learning experience can proceed.
- The negotiation of meaning relies on information gathering and analysis, which uncovers a new basis of information from which new meanings can be created.

- The negotiation of rules relies on the individual's ability to integrate and transform information into new theories of action.
- Finally, the negotiation of behaviors relies on behavioral flexibility and mindfulness, where managers are able to engage in alternative behaviors accordingly as each situation demands.

The prospects of dealing with people from different cultural backgrounds can be very challenging, but at the same time very rewarding. Interacting with others brings the possibility of learning more about ourselves, discovering new ways of doing things, and finding creative solutions to both new problems and old. It also contributes in no small way to business success. In this endeavor, intercultural learning processes play a significant—and often underappreciated—role.

Selected Bibliography

For learning and intercultural learning, we recommend A. Y. Kolb and D. A. Kolb, "Learning Styles and Learning Spaces: Enhancing Experiential Learning in Higher Education," *Academy of Management Learning and Education,* 2005, 4, 193–212; M. J. Bennet (Ed.), *Basic Concepts of Intercultural Communication: Selected Readings* (Yarmouth, ME: Intercultural Press, 1998) 31–51; D. C. Kayes, "Experiential Learning and its Critics: Preserving the Role of Experience in Management Learning and Education," *Academy of Management Learning and Education,* 2002, 1(2), 137–149; Y. Yamazaki and D. C. Kayes, "An Experiential Approach to Cross-Cultural Learning: A Review and Integration of Competencies for Successful Expatriate Adaptation," *Academy of Management Learning and Education,* 2004, 3(4), 362–379; T. Imahori and W. R. Cupach, "Identity Management Theory: Facework in Intercultural Relationships." in William Gudykunst (Ed.), *Theorizing about Intercultural Communication* (Thousand Oaks, CA: Sage Publications, 2005), 195–210.

For cultural intelligence, see D. C. Thomas and K. Inkson, *Cultural Intelligence: People Skills for Global Business* (San Francisco: Berret-Koehler, 2004); P. C. Earley and S. Ang, *Cultural Intelligence: An Analysis of Individual Interactions Across Cultures* (Palo Alto, CA: Stanford University Press); and P. C. Earley and E. Mosakowski, "Cultural Intelligence," *Harvard Business Review,* 2004, 82(10), 139–146.

For recent research on global mindset, readers are referred to Mansour Javidan, Peter Dorfman, Marie S. de Luque, and Robert J. House, "In the Eye of the Beholder: Cross-Cultural Lessons in Leadership from GLOBE Project," *Academy of Management Perspectives,* 2006, 67–90; and Luciara Nardon and Richard M. Steers, "Learning Cultures on the Fly," in Mansour Javidan, Richard M. Steers, and Michael Hitt (Eds.), *Advances in International Management: The Global Mindset* (Amsterdam: Elsevier, 2007), 179–198.

Finally, for more on negotiation of meaning within a cross-cultural setting, we recommend V. J. Friedman and A. Berthoin Antal, "Negotiating Reality: A Theory of Action Approach to Intercultural Competence," *Management Learning,* 2005, 36, 69–86; and Allan Bird and Joyce S. Osland, "Teaching Cultural Sense-Making," in N. Boyacigiller, R. A. Goodman, and M. E. Phillips (Eds.), *Crossing Cultures: Insights from Master Teachers* (London: Routledge, 2003), 89–100.

CULTIVATING INTERCULTURAL COMPETENCE: THE INTERCULTURAL POSITIONING SYSTEM*

By *Janet M. Bennett*

"And how was your flight today?"

The taxi driver in Montgomery, Alabama, greeted my colleague. Indeed, she had experienced one of those days of flying that many of us know all too well: a two-hour delay of her first flight, a mad dash to barely make the connection to her second flight, an hour and a half sitting on the tarmac while thunderstorms passed, and, of

*Reprinted with permission from D. Deardorff (Ed.), *The SAGE Handbook of Intercultural Competence,* 2009. Reprinted by permission of Sage Publications.

course, at the end of the day, lost luggage. She started to release her pent-up frustrations, when she took a breath and scanned her context. A driver identity card on the visor revealed a Moslem name, while prayer beads dangled from the mirror. His accent suggested Africa to her and instead of sharing her litany of travel travails, she said it had been a fine day, and by the way, where was he from?

"I am from Africa," he responded.

"Northern Africa?" she asked.

"Why, yes," he said.

"From Sudan?" she asked.

And soon they were discussing the tragic events in Darfur that had led him to seek refuge in the United States. It occurred to her that she had nearly whined about lost luggage to a man whose family had been murdered before his eyes only months earlier.

A small moment in time, no doubt. But a moment that reflects the value of cultural competence during even the most transitory interactions.

Her experience illustrates an important truth: if we are to thrive in "a world lived in common with others" (Green, 1988), we must step outside of our own frame of reference and interact meaningfully with different cultural realities. That means engaging profound cultural differences with deep cultural humility; our way is only one way of viewing the world, and perhaps we haven't a clue about what is really going on! (Guskin, 1991).

Learning to identify our own cultural patterns, to acknowledge the patterns of others, and, eventually, to adapt to other cultures, is a developmental process for each of us, regardless of our place in the world (J. Bennett & M. Bennett, 2004). The call to develop the skills and abilities to live and work with culturally different others is no longer specific to a few particular disciplines and professions, but is a call to cultural consciousness for everyone.

This reading provides a definition of intercultural competence and explores how it can be cultivated using the intercultural positioning system.

Definition of Intercultural Competence

Whether described as a "global mindset " (Bird & Osland, 2004); "global competence" (Hunter, White & Godbey, 2006); "global learning" (Hovland, 2006; Musil, 2006); "culture learning" (Paige, Cohen, Kappler, Chi & Lassegard, 2002); "intercultural effectiveness," (Vulpe, Kealey, Protheroe & MacDonald, 2001); "cultural intelligence" (Peterson, 2004; Thomas & Inkson, 2004; Earley & Ang, 2003); "global leadership competence" (Osland, 2008; Jokinen, 2005); "intercultural communication competence" (Dinges & Baldwin, 1996; Kim, 1991; Collier, 1989; Hammer, 1989; Spitzberg, 1989, 1994; Dinges, 1983); or, of course, intercultural competence (Deardorff, 2005, 2006, 2009; Graf, 2004), many of the disciplinary roads lead to a similar place. There is clearly an "emerging consensus around what constitutes intercultural competence, which is most often viewed as a set of cognitive, affective, and behavioral skills and characteristics that support effective and appropriate interaction in a variety of cultural contexts" (J. Bennett, 2008, p. 97).

There are lengthy lists that describe precisely which knowledge, skills, and attitudes constitute intercultural competence (Jokinen, 2005; Bird & Osland, 2004; Mendenhall, 2001; Spitzberg & Changnon, 2009; Yershova, DeJaeghere & Mestenhauser, 2000). Such lists provide an excellent starting point for assessing the appropriate characteristics for the specific situation, but, of course, no list fits all cultures, all contexts, all conditions.

One consistent concern is that such lists do not address the application of knowledge and skills to complex interactions with culturally different others with whom we must negotiate shared meaning (King & Baxter Magolda, 2005; Deardorff, 2006, 2009). Cultural knowledge does not equal intercultural competence, since a person can be an expert on a particular aspect of Chinese culture, and yet be unable to negotiate well with his Chinese counterparts. This gap between knowledge and competence may be due in part to being unaware of one's own culture, and therefore not fully capable of assessing the cultural position of others. Or it may reflect an over reliance on the cognitive domain, with less development of affective and behavioral capacities. This reading will suggest approaches for putting knowledge into practice, underscoring the importance of the process inherent in intercultural competence development.

In the past 20 years, there has been a growing acknowledgement that intercultural competence contributes to effectiveness in both global and domestic interaction. In fact, such competence may be a prerequisite for capably addressing issues of race, class, and gender (J. Bennett & M. Bennett, 2004). Organizations now frequently incorporate both global and domestic diversity under the umbrella of intercultural competence initiatives, where differences are recognized as contributions to the productivity of the organization, not barriers to overcome (Gundling & Zanchettin, 2006; J. Bennett & M. Bennett, 2004; Gardenswartz, Rowe, Digh, & M. Bennett, 2003; Wentling & Palma-Rivas, 2000; Cornwell & Stoddard, 1999).

Referring to the work of Gurin, Dey, Hurtado, and Gurin (2002), King and Baxter Magolda (2005) observed, "In times of increased global interdependence, producing interculturally competent citizens who can engage in informed, ethical decision-making when confronted with problems that involve a diversity of perspectives is becoming an urgent educational priority" (p. 571). The *Workforce 2020* report sums up this new reality, noting "the rest of the world matters" (Judy & D'Amico, 1997, p. 3).

Literally tens of thousands of educators and trainers in the United States have been working intensively since the 1980s to ensure that most students and professionals have at least been exposed to the idea that culture matters. In business education, one of the most significant ways that culture matters is in its influence on the way management theories are built. For instance, one of Hofstede's (1980) greatest contributions was to ask whether these theories are culturally biased. He warned that three unique elements in American management theories—the emphasis on market forces, the individual, and managers rather than workers—reflect U.S. values, which might limit their applicability to other cultures. Hofstede (1980) also noted that the term 'management' has varied meanings as do managerial roles and status in different countries. As a result, we have become more sensitive to potential cultural constraints in our theories.

This reading offers a tool for developing intercultural competence through the metaphor of an intercultural positioning system. Modeled on the metaphor of a global positioning system, the intercultural positioning system involves the following four steps, which will be described in detail further on in this reading:

1. Fostering attitudes that motivate us
2. Discovering knowledge that informs us of our own and others' cultural position
3. Assessing the challenge and support factors that impact our adaptation
4. Developing skills that enable us to interact effectively and appropriately

Intercultural Competence: Positioning Systems

As we think about the process of building intercultural competence, let us first consider the metaphor of a global positioning system (GPS). We routinely rely on this helpful technology not only to discover where we are, but also where we are going.

The GPS is a global navigation system developed by the U.S. Department of Defense that uses more than 25 satellites to precisely determine our location, speed, direction, and time. The locating capacity of a single satellite is insufficient for precision, but through the use of multiple satellite messages, we can accurately assess where we are, bringing in additional satellite signals to enhance the clarity of our position.

For example, by gathering data from at least three, often four, satellites, we know exactly where we are. If someone tells us that we are 116 miles from Los Angeles, we now have a radius from which to make guesses about our location. When we add the information that we are 15 miles from Tijuana, that begins to narrow the range of where we might be. But once we add a third distance, say, we are 299 miles from Phoenix, we have triangulated our position and can conclude confidently that we are in San Diego! In fact, if we figure out a fourth dimension, knowing that Las Vegas is 331 miles away, it assures even more precise information about our location in San Diego.

An Intercultural Positioning System

If we view developing intercultural competence as a process similar to triangulation, using the contemporary metaphor of a global positioning system, Stoddard and Cornwell (2003) suggest that this can be "A model for the way one needs to collect perspectives from differently situated knowers and citizens around the world in order to be able to make informed judgments, to have a sufficient basis for knowledge" (p. 5).

In order to identify our own *cultural* position in the context of others, we need to parallel the process of the global positioning system, using multiple culture maps as a tool to assess our own cultural views relative to others in what we call an intercultural positioning system.

The distinction here between *cultural* and *intercultural* is an important one. When we describe cultural generalizations about the attributes of one person with whom we are interacting, or one culture group about which we are conducting research, we are often using anthropological, linguistic, or psychological frameworks as our culture maps. When we use the intercultural positioning tool, we are looking at the *interface* between two or more individuals with differing culture maps and attempting to develop a strategy for integrating their values, beliefs, and behaviors in order to enhance the effectiveness of their interaction.

Culture maps are simply frameworks that provide a *culture-general* (etic) perspective for comparing and contrasting cultures. Originally from linguistics, *etic* is derived from phonetics, referring "to sounds that are found across all languages" in contrast to *emic*, derived from phonemics, referring to "sounds used in a particular language" (Pike, 1967, as cited in Gelfand, Erez, & Aycan, 2007, p. 482). Based on abstract categories, such frameworks do not refer to any *specific* culture but rather provide general categories that allow us to explore cultural variables in *any* culture.

Culture maps are readily available for examining the following topics, which are accompanied by a few examples:

1. Nonverbal behavior such as the use of space and time, touching, gestures, facial expressions, voice pitch, eye contact (Knapp & Hall, 2005; Ting-Toomey, 1999)
2. Communication styles such as high- versus low-context, emotionally restrained versus emotionally expressive, linear versus circular (contextual) (Saphiere, Mikk, & Devries, 2005; Wurzel, 2005; Kim, 1998; Gudykunst & Ting-Toomey, 1988)
3. Value orientations such as status, collectivism versus individualism, universalistic versus particularistic (Chhokar, Brodbeck, & House, 2007; Saphiere, 2007; House, Hanges, Javidan, Dorfman, & Gupta, 2004; Hofstede, 2001; Lane, DiStefano, & Maznevski, 2000; Trompenaars & Hampden-Turner, 1997; Brake & Walker, 1995)

4. Interaction rituals such as greetings, farewells, and turn-taking in conversation (Tannen, 1994; Ting-Toomey, 1999)
5. Conflict styles such as controlling, direct, collaborative, avoiding (Ting-Toomey & Oetzel, 2001; Hammer, 2003)
6. Cognitive and learning styles such as attention, use of logic, holistic versus analytical, divergent versus convergent, abstract versus concrete (Edmundson, 2007; King & Baxter Magolda, 2005; Riding & Rayner, 2000; Yershova et al., 2000; Nisbett, 2003; Belenky, Clinchy, Goldberger, & Tarule, 1996; Dunn & Griggs, 1988, 1990; Kolb, 1984; Elbow, 1973)
7. Identity development, which includes the ways that people adapt to other cultures, such as assimilation, biculturalism, marginality (Sue, 2007; Schaetti, 2000; Evans, Forney, & Guido-DiBrito, 1998; Phinney, 1991; Sabnani, Ponterotto, & Borodovsky, 1991; Parham, 1989; Helms, 1984; Cross, 1978)

For instance, the cultural map on nonverbal behavior allows us to compare and contrast our turn-taking conversational rituals with those of other cultures. In fact, it brings into awareness that we actually *have* a turn-taking ritual, an idea that may never have occurred to us!

Once we have successfully navigated several culture-general maps, then we can begin to employ *culture-specific* categories (emic) based on specific ethnographic information for a particular culture that we want to understand. Here we may ask, "What are the turn-taking rituals in Ghana?"

Through exploration of our own position on cultural variables, we can identify similarities and differences with others and thus begin the process of building intercultural competence. Careful analysis of our position relative to the cultural position of others suggests a way of calibrating the degree of adaptation we may wish to make in our interactions. We may note that if our turn taking requires direct eye contact and rapid insertion of our opinion in the dialogue, we may have to make a substantive adaptation to a culture that relies on silence for an opening to speak, while averting eye contact.

However, the first use of an intercultural positioning system is to locate *ourselves*, to develop our own cultural self-awareness through understanding our cultural patterns. Only then can we begin exploring the gap between our values, beliefs, and behaviors and those of others. Some cultural distances will be short and readily adjusted; others, of course, may defy negotiation. For instance, while we may easily replace a handshake with a bow, it is often more difficult to replace directness with subtlety. Our own cultural patterns are deep and resist adjustment. And, finally, it is a joint venture to build a third culture bridge between our intercultural positions, requiring two parties willing to tolerate the ambiguity this involves. If I really attempt to resolve conflict in an indirect way through a third person intermediary, it means suspending my sense that face-to-face discussion always yields a superior result.

Frequently, the prospect of adapting to other cultures brings up the question of whether to adapt, how much to adapt, or, perhaps of most importance, do we have to give up ourselves if we adapt to this other person? In fact, this perspective suggests a rather reified self, as if compromising with others somehow subtracts from our personhood, and feels inauthentic. People with intercultural experience tend to see it more as an additive process; not only do we remain intact, but we have added more skills to our repertoire. We adapt when we hope to achieve shared meaning, complete an effective business transaction, teach across cultures, or accomplish anything well that involves culturally different others. We may choose not to adapt when deep culture values are substantially violated, when our safety is involved, or when the risk is higher than our tolerance.

Fostering Attitudes That Motivate Us

Perhaps the place to begin developing intercultural competence is with motivation: what inspires us to want to learn about others? Mendenhall (2001) suggests that inquisitiveness is the critical factor, perhaps the keystone in developing intercultural effectiveness, a position also supported by Deardorff's recent study that examined intercultural competence and internationalization (2006).

Gregersen, Morrison, and Black (1998) define curiosity as "unbridled inquisitiveness," noting that global leaders "stated repeatedly that inquisitiveness is the fuel for increasing their global savvy, enhancing their ability to understand people and maintain integrity, and augmenting their capacity for dealing with uncertainty and managing tension" (p. 23). In defining curiosity, Opdal (2001) describes it as a sense of wonder:

> Wonder . . . always points to something beyond the accepted rules. Because of this, the feeling of being overwhelmed, or the experience of humbleness and even awe could accompany it. Wonder is the state of mind that signals we have reached the limits of our present understanding, and that things may be different from how they look (p. 33).

When we are interacting across cultures, things are often different from how they look. We frequently encounter these teachable moments or trigger events (Osland, Bird, & Gundersen, 2007) for which we have no map—which have not yet been registered in our intercultural positioning systems, events that have no precedent in our past—that may yet inspire us to see the world in different ways. Whether we are shocked at our own negative response to a busy market in India, puzzled by an African American colleague's response to a political event, perplexed by a European American's reluctance to apologize, or confounded by the argument style of someone of the opposite gender—it can be a teachable moment. While this can inspire a flight response, there are attitudes and approaches that can turn flight into filtering ideas and flexing positions in the new context (Sergeant, 1973).

For curiosity to thrive, the first action is suspending assumptions and judgments, leaving our minds open to multiple perspectives. This requires cognitive flexibility, the capacity to shift frames of reference. By asking, "What do I see here? What might it mean? What else might it mean? And yet again, what might *others* think it means?," we enhance our own perceptions and practice cultural humility (Guskin, 1991). Our way is not the only way and may not necessarily be the best way.

The second action is to increase our tolerance of ambiguity, an essential characteristic for working effectively across cultures. Hofstede's work (2001) examined the value map of "uncertainty avoidance," suggesting that cultures have a different tolerance of the extent to which they handle ambiguity and what it takes to "allow us to sleep peacefully" (p. 146). For example, in a training context, Americans will often (not always) exhibit a relatively high tolerance for uncertainty in adjusting to vague directions or generalized case studies with few details. People from cultures with greater uncertainty avoidance may seek every detail of the instructor's expectations and the case study context before agreeing to proceed.

Curiosity, suspension of judgment, cognitive flexibility, cultural humility, and tolerance of ambiguity are critical core components of intercultural competence. For instance, in a common business dilemma, our global colleagues may have overlooked the promised deadline for delivering the product. We can have a judgmental response, suggesting the supplier may be devious, or even lying. ("But he agreed to this due date!") We might make this judgment from our own point of view, presuming our culture has the best perspective on meeting deadlines. ("What don't you understand about September 15th?") However, curiosity would lead us to ask a few questions about how that deadline was originally established and how the timing of this deadline ignored a cultural issue that we were not aware of. ("Oh, we imposed the deadline during the week of your most significant national holiday?")

Discovering Knowledge That Informs Us

After building on the motivation to respond appropriately to the unfamiliar cultural event, seeking knowledge is often the next step. The intercultural positioning system, with its series of culture maps, provides a tool that can move through the necessary cultural self-awareness to analysis of the other cultures with whom we are interacting. While there are many culture maps we might choose to use for illustration, let us consider the culture map of thinking styles. While the nonverbal map may be more playful, and the communication styles map more readily defined, thinking styles are often a subtle barrier in our classrooms and workplaces and therefore provide an intriguing map. To use the intercultural positioning system, we might ask, "Where do I fit in the framework of thinking styles? And where does my colleague fit?"

There are no agreed-upon definitions of thinking and learning styles, and many researchers use the terms interchangeably. However, the term *cognitive styles* is used most frequently to refer to an individual's preferred patterns of interacting with the environment, through perception, gathering information, constructing meaning, and organizing and applying knowledge (Jonassen & Grabowski, 1993; Irvine & York, 1995; Oxford & Anderson, 1995). What this means in practice is that colleagues working on our intercultural team may be approaching our joint project through a completely different constructed meaning and have an entirely different sense of the application. While I was conducting a seminar on change agentry in Japan, I queried my participants on their response to change. One senior member of the group quietly offered, "The Buddha teaches us that we are all on a path that winds through life until we inevitably perish." Another responded, "Change has nothing to do with us. It can't be helped." My Western sense that we have agency, that as individuals we can make a difference, that we can apply models and anticipate outcomes felt irrelevant, as I responded to the reality that perhaps my seminar design needed some rapid rethinking.

When using a culture map of thinking styles, it is essential to underscore that all members of each culture may apply a number of styles in their interactions, depending on the situation. However, we can benefit from mapping styles as a way to assess useful adaptations for interacting with others. We develop culture maps by consulting theory, research, and practice about the topic at hand. We then synthesize a series of dimensions that will help us to explore our own culture and that of others. While based on credible literature, we still hold our generalizations lightly (J. Bennett & M. Bennett, 2004), acknowledging that no individual can ever be expected to conform to research or precise culture maps, no matter how well developed.

We begin the thinking styles map construction with psychologist Richard Nisbett (2003), who interprets the chasm between Western and Eastern patterns of thinking, based on contrasting Greek and Confucian philosophy in his lively text *The Geography of Thought*. Nisbett was engaged one day in his own teachable moment when one of his Chinese students mentioned that he thought on a circle, while his professor thought on a line. Based on his subsequent research connecting social values with thought processes, Nisbett describes a series of dimensions for a culture map suggesting that "We might expect to find differences in: patterns of attention and perception . . . preferred patterns of explanation for events . . . habits of organizing the world . . . use of formal logic rules . . . application of dialectical approaches" (pp. 44-45). Contrasting U.S. American with Eastern ways of thinking, he observes:

> The rhetoric of scientific papers consists of an overview of the ideas to be considered, a description of the relevant basic theories, a specific hypothesis, a statement of the methods and justification of them, a presentation of the evidence produced by the methods, an argument as to why the evidence supports the hypothesis, a refutation of possible counter-arguments, a reference back to the basic theory and a comment on the larger territory of which the article is a part. For Americans, this rhetoric is constructed bit by bit from nursery school through college (p. 74).

Compare this way of thinking to a recent presentation I attended by a researcher (Yamashita, 2007) investigating why the U.S. American classroom constitutes a chilly climate for Asians. She produced a Japanese writing pattern, called *ki-sho-ten-ketsu*, undoubtedly a rhetoric constructed bit by bit from nursery school through college. The method suggests starting with the topic (ki), expanding it (sho), giving it a 180-degree turn (ten), and stating the conclusion (ketsu). She illustrated her very Western PowerPoint presentation with the following example commonly taught to young writers in Japan to help them present their thoughts:

KI:	Mr. Itoya has two daughters.
SHO:	His daughters are age fourteen and sixteen.
TEN:	Feudal lords kill with their bows and arrows.
KETSU:	Mr. Itoya's daughters kill with their eyes.

After she repeated it twice to her rapt Western audience, we learned that the gap between our way of thinking and hers was more intriguing than we had ever imagined. We had reached the limits of our understanding, and we were curious.

In building the thinking styles map, the traditional constructs of field independence and field dependence (now frequently called field sensitive) styles also prove useful. Field independence refers to a style that often reflects a task orientation; abstract, analytical, digital, objective thinking; a focus on details and precision; inner-direction; and autonomy. Field sensitivity refers to a style that often reflects relationship orientation; concrete, global, analogic, metaphorical thinking; a focus on people rather than things; and group consciousness (Hayashi & Jolley, 2002; Irvine & York, 1995; Oxford & Anderson, 1995). On the same theme, discussing women's ways of knowing, Belenky and her colleagues (1996) distinguished separate ways of knowing (objective, analytical, rational, concerned with validity, detached) from connected ways of knowing (subjective, metaphorical, empathic, concerned with meaning, engaged).

Finally, educator Peter Elbow (1973) contributes to our discussion with his contrast between the Doubting Game and the Believing Game, in which he suggests (similar to Belenky et al.) that one approach to grasping ideas is to doubt the author, critique the ideas, and prove or disprove their validity. In contrast, the Believing Game suggests engaging the ideas, understanding them deeply, and exploring and sharing a synthesis.

While at least 20 dimensions of cognitive styles have been widely researched (Yershova et al., 2000; Oxford & Anderson, 1995), for purposes of an introductory thinking styles map, we can now synthesize a few of the questions to explore as we examine our intercultural positions:

1. To what extent is the thinking pattern based on analytical logic in contrast to holistic/global thinking? (Nisbett, 2003; Oxford & Anderson, 1995)
2. To what extent are thinking patterns verbalized abstractly in contrast to metaphorically? (Belenky et al., 1996)
3. To what extent is the thinking pattern based on objective in contrast to subjective ways of knowing? (Hayashi & Jolley, 2002; Belenky et al., 1996; Elbow, 1973)
4. To what extent is the thinking pattern dialectic in contrast to integrative? (Nisbett, 2003; Belenky et al., 1996; Elbow, 1973)
5. To what extent is the thinking pattern based on the Doubting Game in contrast to the Believing Game? (Elbow, 1973)

Intercultural positioning would allow us to compare our own perspective on these questions with the perspective of those with whom we are interacting to determine the distance from our pattern of thinking and theirs, the map gap. For instance, if a European American man was acculturated, educated, and employed in North America, he might have thinking patterns closer to the first of the two elements in each of the above questions. If he were interacting with another similar man, his adaptation distance might be negligible. However, if he were assigned to go to Vietnam to negotiate with a man who was acculturated, educated, and employed in Vietnam, he might have quite a distance between his pattern of thinking and his counterpart's, which might be more similar to the second element in each of the above questions. In that case, he would need to examine how challenging he finds this degree of compromise, adaptation, and adjustment.

While this thinking styles culture map gives us only one dimension of where we are in relationship to culturally different others, the use of multiple culture maps increases the potential for more significant knowledge about our intercultural bearings. As we gather a more precise definition of our cultural whereabouts, it is important to assess the level of challenge we face in our interactions.

Assessing the Challenge and Support Factors

Nevitt Sanford (1966) noted the essential balance required between the challenges any individual faces in a new situation and the level of support required for that person to learn about the new context. These challenges are powerfully described by Paige (1993) who has constructed a list of the primary intensity factors that influence the challenge of intercultural experience, including factors in the person as well as those in the environment. For instance, the degree to which a person is ethnocentric, culturally different, and immersed in a new cultural context impacts the challenge of the experience. The business professional who is confident of her European culture's perspective and broadly inflexible, and finds herself immersed in an Indian corporation in Bangalore with completely different cultural values is more likely to perceive this as a very intense, highly challenging context. The gap between her cultural position and that of her Indian counterparts may, in fact, be excessively challenging. Somehow, her organization or she herself needs to increase the support for her adaptation, perhaps with coaching, training, cultural mediators, etc. Paige's intensity factors provide a barometer to assess the degree of challenge, in order to balance that intensity with adequate support.

For each of us, it is important to recognize what aspects of the intercultural context can provide support for our learning and adaptation, as well as what aspects present challenges. Depending on our own culture and developmental worldview, some of us may find certain culture distances very challenging while we find others affirming. If we are overly supported, adaptation or development is less likely. For instance, if we avoid interaction in the host culture, buffering ourselves against excess challenge, we will be less effective in our jobs. On the other hand, if we are overly challenged, we may want to flee the intercultural context, whether psychologically, physically, or both. Early returns of transferees speak eloquently to this issue. Each of us needs to balance challenge and support to maximize adaptation across cultures.

Developing Skills That Enable Us

Having increased our cultural self-awareness, examined the distance from our position to that of others, and assessed the level of challenge and support required, the next step in the intercultural positioning system process is to continue the lifetime task of developing the requisite skills for adaptation.

The intercultural skillset typically includes such characteristics and competencies as the ability to empathize, gather appropriate information, listen, adapt, resolve conflict, and manage social interactions and anxiety.

In the past, many professionals assumed that *any* contact across cultures was useful contact and would reduce stereotypes and prejudice, allowing intercultural competence to "naturally" evolve. Well-intentioned but uncoordinated efforts to bring differences into the workplace often generated more heat than light.

However, recent research suggests that contact *does* reduce prejudice among many culture groups, under many conditions. Pettigrew and Tropp's (2000) meta-analysis of 516 studies completed over 50 years on the contact hypothesis reports that 95% of these studies reflect a negative relationship between contact and prejudice of many types. They note that maintaining certain conditions, such as shared goals and equal status, can enhance the impact of contact.

But intercultural competence is more than the diminishment of prejudice; it does *not* naturally evolve in the presence of difference. Pettigrew notes that two of the core intercultural competencies—empathy and anxiety management—contribute importantly to enhancing the impact of intercultural contact, even more than the acquisition of knowledge about other cultures, whom he describes as the "outgroup," referring to nondominant cultures. Pettigrew's most recent research (2008) examines three variables relevant to our discussion of skill building: exploring how new knowledge about others affects attitudes, how anxiety reduction facilitates interactions, and how empathy with the others impacts our understanding. He concludes:

> Early theorists thought that intergroup contact led to learning about the outgroup, and this new knowledge in turn reduced prejudice. Recent work, however, reveals that this knowledge mediation does exist but is of minor importance. Empathy and perspective taking are far more important. (p. 190)

He also notes that friendship fosters empathy with others and often requires frame shifting that is effective in reducing prejudice, which is correlated with authoritarianism and social dominance. Finally, he underlines the importance of reducing anxiety, the "threat and uncertainty that people experience in intergroup contexts" (p. 190).

In addition to recognizing that empathy and reduced anxiety enhance prejudice reduction, we also know that positive contact requires more than being in the presence of cultural difference. It must also foster engagement with that difference (Williams, Berger, & McClendon, 2005). Facilitated contact—through mentoring, coaching, training, transformative learning, or reflection—often develops more intercultural competence than autonomous, unguided contact (Paige, 2008; Vande Berg, 2007, 2009).

Training is one effective approach, although not the only one, for developing intercultural skills. Anthropologists, such as Spradley (1979, 1980), also support skill building, since they offer their well-honed disciplinary perspective on interviewing across cultures and participant observation. To satisfy curiosity, some individuals may ask questions directly, while some cultures clearly prefer the more indirect learning acquired through participant observation. Although gathering information across cultures is an essential component of intercultural competence, asking questions is not. Therefore, using credible cultural mentors can also facilitate skill building (Osland & Bird, 2000). Such bicultural, bilingual individuals may graciously offer to decode their culture for outsiders, expecting only in return that the newcomers move with equal graciousness through their communities.

Strategies for developing skills of empathy (M. Bennett, 1998) and resolving conflict (Hammer, 2003) are readily available in the intercultural communication and psychology literature. Each requires cognitive flexibility, as discussed earlier. A quick three-step analysis from multiple perspectives can be used to bridge cultural differences empathically by assessing the mutual negative evaluation of any particular pattern, the benefits of using that pattern, and adaptive strategies for working effectively with it. This analysis offers skills practice in cognitive flexibility, empathy, listening, and, potentially, managing interactions.

Step One: Using the thinking styles map discussed earlier in this chapter as an example, we can empathize with the perspective of others and reflect on how someone from a different culture might feel about the style of being analytically logical, abstract, objective, dialectic, and doubting. Someone not accustomed to that style might find it cold, argumentative, simplistic, critical, and downright unpleasant. In turn, the logical partner in the interaction might find the style of being holistic, metaphorical, subjective, integrative, and believing to be naïve, uncritical, incoherent, illogical, and downright confusing.

Step Two: The second step involves describing the strengths of each style. We might note that one style is particularly good for creating policies, procedures, and legal contexts, while the other may be more successful with human resources management and leadership.

Step Three: The third step—perhaps the most difficult—designs adaptive processes, overtly building on the strengths of each style. For instance, this might include designing the style of meetings to take into account multiple voices, or deliberately reviewing reports for diverse perspectives and, of course, eventually being able to generate those multiple perspectives individually.

If being interculturally competent is a lifetime developmental opportunity, then using the intercultural positioning system is but one of many ways we can enhance our competence. If our efforts are consistently intentional, developmental, and inclusive, we will begin to acquire the necessary knowledge, attitudes, and skills to make a small claim on intercultural competence, with a great deal of cultural humility.

Conclusion

If intercultural competence is to achieve its potential, intercultural positioning systems must become part of our daily lives. With this perspective, such a calibration holds the possibility that we can "cultivate the factual and imaginative prerequisites for recognizing humanity in the stranger and the other. . . . Ignorance and distance cramp the consciousness" (Nussbaum, 2002, p. 133). We know that contact is useful, but perhaps not useful enough if we are not transformed in important ways by our experience. And we know that to achieve that transformation, we have to intentionally and proactively seek opportunities to use our intercultural positioning system and to expose ourselves to other cultures and people who are different. Edwin O. Reischauer (1986), highly respected former U.S. ambassador to Japan, offers us a powerful goal for doing so:

> We had acquired the habit of looking at things two different ways—from the Japanese angle of vision as well as from our own national viewpoint. This proved to be the key to my career and, extended worldwide, is the only hope I can see for world peace and human survival. (pp. xi–xii)

References

Belenky, M. F., Clinchy, B. M., Goldberger, N. R., & Tarule, J. M. (1996). *Woman's ways of knowing: The development of self, voice, and mind* (10th ed.). New York: Basic Books (Harper Collins).

Bennett, J. M. (2008). Transformative training: Designing programs for culture learning. In M. A. Moodian (Ed.), *Contemporary leadership and intercultural competence: Understanding and utilizing cultural diversity to build successful organizations* (pp. 95–110). Thousand Oaks, CA: Sage.

Bennett, J. M., & Bennett, M. J. (2004). Developing intercultural sensitivity: An integrative approach to global and domestic diversity. In D. Landis, J. M. Bennett, & M. J. Bennett (Eds.), *Handbook of intercultural training* (3rd ed., pp. 147–165). Thousand Oaks, CA: Sage.

Bennett, M. J. (1998). Overcoming the golden rule: Sympathy and empathy. In M. J. Bennett (Ed.), *Basic concepts of intercultural communication: A reader* (pp. 191–214). Yarmouth, ME: Intercultural Press, Inc.

Bird, A., & Osland, J. S. (2004). Global competencies: An introduction. In H. W. Lane, M. L. Maznevski, M. E. Mendenhall, & J. McNett (Eds.), *The Blackwell handbook of global management: A guide to managing complexity* (pp. 57–80). Malden, MA: Blackwell.

Brake, T., & Walker, D. (1995). *Doing business internationally: The workbook for cross-cultural success.* Princeton, NJ: Princeton Training Press.

Chhokar, J. S., Brodbeck, F. C., & House, R. J. (Eds.). (2007). *Culture and leadership across the world: The GLOBE book of in-depth studies of 25 societies.* Mahwah, NJ: Lawrence Erlbaum.

Collier, M. J. (1989). Cultural and intercultural communication competence: Current approaches and directions for future research. *International Journal of Intercultural Relations, 13,* 287–302.

Cornwell, G. H., & Stoddard, E. W. (1999). *Globalizing knowledge: Connecting international and intercultural studies.* Washington, DC: Association of American Colleges and Universities.

Cross, W. E., Jr. (1978). The Thomas and Cross models of psychological nigrescence: A review. *Journal of Black Psychology 5*(1), 13–31.

Deardorff, D. K. (2005). A matter of logic? *International Educator, XIV(3),* 26–31. *Description, interpretation, and evaluation.* (n.d.). Retrieved August 24, 2007, from http://www.intercultural.org/documents/resources/die.doc/

Deardorff, D. K. (2006, Fall). Identification and assessment of intercultural competence as a student outcome of internationalization. *Journal of Studies in International Education, 10*(3), 241–266.

Deardorff, D. K. (2009). *The SAGE handbook of intercultural competence.* Los Angeles, CA: Sage.

Dinges, N. (1983). Intercultural competence. In D. Landis & R. Brislin (Eds.), *Handbook of intercultural relations: Vol. 1. Theory and practice* (pp. 176–202). Elmsford, NY: Pergamon.

Dinges, N. G., & Baldwin, K. D. (1996). Intercultural competence: A research perspective. In D. Landis & R. S. Bhagat (Eds.), *Handbook of intercultural training* (2nd ed., pp. 106–123). Thousand Oaks, CA: Sage.

Dunn, R., & Griggs, S. (1988). *Learning styles: Quiet revolution in American secondary schools.* Reston, VA: National Association of Secondary School Principals.

Dunn, R., & Griggs, S. (1990). Research on the learning style characteristics of selected racial and ethnic groups. *Reading, Writing, and Learning Disabilities, 6,* 261–80.

Earley, P. C., & Ang, S. (2003). *Cultural intelligence: Individual interactions across cultures.* Stanford, CA: Stanford University Press.

Edmundson, A. (2007). *Globalized e-learning cultural challenges.* Hershey, PA: Information Science Publishing (an imprint of Idea Group Inc.).

Elbow, P. (1973). *Writing without teachers.* New York: Oxford Press.

Evans, N. J., Forney, D. S., & Guido-DiBrito, F. (1998). Gay, lesbian, and bisexual identity development. *Student development in college: Theory, research, and practice* (pp. 89–106). San Francisco: Jossey-Bass.

Gardenswartz, L., Rowe, A., Digh, P., & Bennett, M. (2003). *The global diversity desk reference: Managing an international workforce.* San Francisco: Jossey-Bass.

Gelfand, M. J., Erez, M., & Aycan, Z. (2007, January). Cross-cultural organizational behavior. *Annual Review of Psychology, 58,* 479–514.

Graf, A. (2004, September). Screening and training inter-cultural competencies: Evaluating the impact of national culture on inter-cultural competencies. *The International Journal of Human Resource Management, 15*(6), 1124–1148.

Green, M. (1988). *The dialectic of freedom.* New York: Teachers College Press.

Gregersen, J. B., Morrison, A., & Black, J. S. (1998). Developing leaders for the global frontier. *Sloan Management Review, 40*(1), 21–33.

Gudykunst, W. B., & Ting-Toomey, S. (1988). *Culture and interpersonal communication.* Newbury Park, CA: Sage.

Gundling, E., & Zanchettin, A. (2006). *Global diversity: Winning customers and engaging employees in world markets.* Boston: Nicholas Brealey.

Gurin, P., Dey, E. L., Hurtado, S., & Gurin, G. (2002). Diversity and higher education: Theory and impact on educational outcomes. *Harvard Educational Review, 72*(3), 330–366.

Guskin, A. (1991). Cultural humility: A way of being in the world. *Antioch Notes, 59*(1). Yellow Springs, OH: Antioch Publications Office.

Hammer, M. R. (1989). Intercultural communication competence. In M. K. Asante & W. B. Gudykunst (Eds.), *Handbook of international and intercultural communication* (pp. 247–260). Newbury Park, CA: Sage.

Hammer, M. R. (2003). *ICS interpretive guide.* Ocean Pines, MD: Hammer Consulting.

Hayashi, K., & Jolley, G. (2002, October). Two thoughts on analog and digital language. *Aoyama Journal of International Politics, Economics and Business, 58,* 179–196.

Helms, J. E. (1984). Toward a theoretical explanation of the effects of race on counseling: A black and white model. *Counseling Psychologist, 12,* 153–165.

Hofstede, G. (1980). *Culture's consequences: International differences in work-related values.* Beverly Hills, CA: Sage.

Hofstede, G. (2001). *Culture's consequences: Comparing values, behaviors, institutions, and organizations across nations* (2nd ed.). Thousand Oaks, CA: Sage.

House, R. J., Hanges, P. J., Javidan M., Dorfman, P. W., & Gupta, V. (Eds.). (2004). *Culture, leadership, and organizations: The GLOBE study of 62 societies.* Thousand Oaks, CA: Sage.

Hovland, K. (2006). *Shared futures: Global learning and liberal education.* Washington, DC: Association of American Colleges and Universities.

Hunter, B., White, G. P., & Godbey, G. C. (2006). What does it mean to be globally competent? *Journal of Studies in International Education, 10*(3), 267–285.

Irvine, J. J., & York, D. E. (1995). Learning styles and culturally diverse students: A literature review. In J. A. Banks & C. A. M. Banks (Eds.), *Handbook of research on multicultural education* (pp. 484–497). New York: Macmillan.

Jokinen, T. (2005). Global leadership competencies: A review and discussion. *Journal of European Industrial Training, 29*(3), 199–216.

Jonassen, D. H., & Grabowski, B. L. (1993). *Handbook of individual differences, learning, and instruction.* Hillsdale, NJ: Lawrence Erlbaum.

Judy, R. W., & D'Amico, C. (1997). *Workforce 2020: Work and workers in the 21st century.* Indianapolis, IN: Hudson Institute.

Kim, M. (1998). Conversational constraints as a tool for understanding communication styles. In T. M. Singelis (Ed.), *Teaching about culture, ethnicity, and diversity* (pp. 101–109). Thousand Oaks, CA: Sage.

Kim, Y. Y. (1991). Intercultural communication competence: A systems-theoretic view. In S. Ting-Toomey & F. Korzenny (Eds.), *International and intercultural communication annual (Vol. 15): Cross-cultural interpersonal communication* (pp. 230–275). Newbury Park, CA: Sage.

King, P. M., & Baxter Magolda, M. B. (2005, November/December). A developmental model of intercultural maturity. *Journal of College Student Development, 46*(6), 571–592.

Knapp, M. L., & Hall, J. A. (2005). *Nonverbal communication in human interaction* (6th ed.). Belmont, CA: Wadsworth.

Kolb, D. A. (1984). *Experiential learning: Experience as the source of learning and development.* Englewood Cliffs, NJ: Prentice Hall.

Lane, H. W., DiStefano, J. J., & Maznevski, M. L. (2000). *International management behavior: Text, readings and cases* (4th ed.). Malden, MA: Blackwell Business.

Mendenhall, M. E. (2001). Introduction: New perspectives on expatriate adjustment and its relationship to global leadership development. In M. E. Mendenhall, T. M. Kühlmann, & G. K. Stahl (Eds.), *Developing global business leaders: Policies, processes, and innovations* (pp. 1–18). Westport, CT: Greenwood.

Musil, C. M. (2006). *Assessing global learning: Matching good intentions with good practice.* Washington, DC: Association of American Colleges and Universities.

Nisbett, R. E. (2003). The geography of thought: How Asians and westerners think differently . . . and why. New York: Free Press.

Nussbaum, M. C. (2002). *For love of country? Debating the limits of patriotism.* Boston: Beacon Press.

Opdal, P. M. (2001). Curiosity, wonder and education seen as perspective. *Studies in Philosophy and Education,* 20, 331–344.

Osland, J. (2008). An overview of the global leadership literature. In M. Mendenhall, J. Osland, A. Bird, G. Oddou & M. Maznevski (Eds.), *Global leadership: Research, practice and development* (pp. 34–63). London: Routledge.

Osland, J. & Bird, A. (2000). *Beyond sophisticated stereotyping: Cultural sensemaking in context. Academy of Management Executive,* 14, 65–79.

Osland, J. S., Bird, A., & Gundersen, A. (2007, August). *Trigger events in intercultural sensemaking.* Paper presented at the Academy of Management Meeting: Philadelphia, PA.

Oxford, R. L., & Anderson, N. J. (1995). A crosscultural view of learning styles. *Language Teaching,* 28, 201–215.

Paige, R. M. (Ed.). (1993). *Education for the intercultural experience.* (2nd ed., pp. 109–135). Yarmouth, ME: Intercultural Press, Inc.

Paige, R. M. (2008, October 3–4). *Using the IDI to guide personal and organizational development: Challenges and opportunities* (PowerPoint). Presented at the first annual Intercultural Development Inventory Conference, Minneapolis, MN.

Paige, R. M., Cohen, A. D., Kappler, B., Chi, J. C., & Lassegard, J. P. (2002). *Maximizing study abroad: A students' guide to strategies for language and culture learning and use.* Minneapolis, MN: University of Minnesota.

Parham, T. A. (1989). Cycles of psychological nigrescence. *Counseling Psychologist, 17*(2), 187–226.

Peterson, B. (2004). *Cultural intelligence: A guide to working with people from other cultures.* Yarmouth, ME: Intercultural Press, Inc.

Pettigrew, T. F. (2008, May). Future directions for intergroup contact theory and research. *International Journal 2 of Intercultural Relations, 32*(3), 182–199.

Pettigrew, T. F., & Tropp, L. R. (2000). Does intergroup contact reduce prejudice? Recent meta-analytic findings. In S. Oskamp (Ed.), *Reducing prejudice and discrimination* (pp. 93–114). Mahwah, NJ: Lawrence Erlbaum.

Phinney, J. S. (1991). Ethnic identity and self-esteem: A review and integration. *Hispanic Journal of Behavioral Sciences, 13*(2), 193–208.

Reischauer, E. O. (1986). *My life between Japan and America.* New York: Harper & Row.

Riding, R., & Rayner, S. (Eds.). (2000). *Cognitive styles and learning strategies: Understanding style differences in learning and behavior.* London: David Fulton Publishers.

Sabnani, H. B., Ponterotto, J. G., & Borodovsky, L. G. (1991). White racial identity development and cross-cultural counselor training: A stage model. *The Counseling Psychologist, 19*(1), 76–102.

Sanford, N. (1966). *Self and society: Social change and individual development.* New York: Atherton Press.

Saphiere, D. H. (2007). The Cultural Detective®. http://www.culturaldetective.com

Saphiere, D. H., Mikk, B. K., & Devries, B. I. (2005). *Communication highwire: Leveraging the power of diverse communication styles.* Yarmouth, ME: Intercultural Press, Inc.

Schaetti, B. F. (2000, November). Global nomad identity: Hypothesizing a developmental model (Doctoral dissertation, The Union Institute, 2000). *Dissertation Abstracts, 6110*(A), Catalogue number 9992721.

Sergeant, C. (1973). *U.S. Navy overseas diplomacy guidelines for I. C. R. specialists* (pp. 42–45). Washington, DC: Bureau of Naval Personnel.

Spitzberg, B. H. (1989). Theoretical issues: Issues in the development of a theory of interpersonal competence in the intercultural context. *International Journal of Intercultural Relations, 13*, 241–268.

Spitzberg, B. H. (1994). A model of intercultural communication competence. In L. A. Samovar & R. E. Porter (Eds.), *Intercultural communication: A reader* (7th ed., pp. 347–359). Belmont, CA: Wadsworth.

Spitzberg, B. H. & Changnon, G. (2009). Conceptualizing intercultural competence. In D. K. Deardorff (Ed.), *The SAGE handbook of intercultural competence.* Los Angeles, CA: Sage.

Spradley, J. P. (1979). *Ethnographic interview.* New York: Holt, Rinehart & Winston.

Spradley, J. P. (1980). *Participation observation.* New York: Holt, Rinehart & Winston.

Stoddard, E. W., & Cornwell, G. H. (2003). Peripheral visions: Toward a geoethics of citizenship. *Liberal Education.* Retrieved January 29, 2008, from http://www.aacu.org/liberaleducation/le-su03/le-su3fperspective.cfm.

Sue, D. W. (2007). *Counseling the culturally diverse: Theory and practice* (5th ed.). Hoboken, NJ: Wiley.

Tannen, D. (1994). *Talking from 9 to 5: How women's and men's conversational styles affect who gets heard, who gets credit, and what gets done at work.* New York: William Morrow.

Thomas, D. C., & Inkson, K. (2004). *Cultural intelligence: People skills for global business.* San Francisco: Berrett-Koehler.

Ting-Toomey, S. (1999). *Communicating across cultures.* New York: Guilford.

Ting-Toomey, S., & Oetzel, J. G. (2001). *Managing intercultural conflict effectively.* Thousand Oaks, CA: Sage.

Trompenaars, F., & Hampden-Turner, C. (1997). *Riding the waves of culture: Understanding cultural diversity in business* (2nd ed.). Naperville, IL: Intercultural Management Publishers NV/Nicholas Brealey.

Vande Berg, M. (2007, February). *It's not all about the numbers: Maximizing student learning abroad.* Paper presented at the meeting of the Association of International Education Administrators, Washington, DC.

Vande Berg, M. (2009). Intervening in student learning abroad: A research-based inquiry. Intercultural Education, 20(1–2), 15–27.

Vulpe, T., Kealey, D., Protheroe, D., & MacDonald, D. (2001). *A profile of the interculturally effective person* (2nd ed.). Quebec, Canada: Canadian Department of Foreign Affairs and International Trade, Centre for Intercultural Learning.

Wentling, R. M., & Palma-Rivas, N. (2000, Spring). Current status of diversity initiatives in selected multinational corporations. *Human Resource Development Quarterly, 11*(1), 35–60.

Wurzel, J. S. (2005). *Building community in the classroom: An intercultural approach.* Newton, MA: Intercultural Resource Corporation.

Yamashita, M. (2007). *Integrating East Asian International Students into U.S. Classrooms: An Investigation of Challenges and Opportunities.* Presentation at doctoral dissertation meeting, School of Education, Portland State University, Portland, OR.

Yershova, Y., DeJaeghere, J., & Mestenhauser, J. (2000, Spring). Thinking not as usual: Adding the intercultural perspective. *Journal of Studies in International Education, 4*(1), 39–78.

2

The Psychological Contract and Commitment

THE PSYCHOLOGICAL CONTRACT: VIOLATIONS AND MODIFICATIONS
Denise M. Rousseau
EMPLOYEE ENGAGEMENT: BEYOND THE FAD AND INTO THE EXECUTIVE SUITE
Theresa M. Welbourne

The second mental map we are going to examine concerns the psychological contract, an individual's beliefs, shaped by the organization, regarding the terms and conditions of a reciprocal exchange agreement between individuals and their organization. People frame events at work, such as promises, expectations, and future payoffs for their contributions, according to their own mental model and past history. There are negative consequences when psychological contracts are violated; understanding this concept can prevent managers from making mistakes and harming their relationship with employees.

Denise Rousseau, an expert on psychological contracts and professor at Carnegie Mellon, describes what happens when people fail to comply with the terms of a contract in "The Psychological Contracts: Violations and Modifications." Rousseau identifies common sources of contract violation and typical responses. In a rapidly changing environment, it is sometimes impossible to avoid modifying psychological contracts. Rousseau explains how to change psychological contracts with the least possible disruption.

Psychological contracts are the link between the individual and the organization. In successful firms, that link is based on mutual expectations about what employees are capable of performing and how employees should be treated. In "Employee Engagement: Beyond the Fad and into the Executive Suite," Theresa Welbourne, a researcher at the University of Southern California's Center for Effective Organizations, argues that a systematic approach to building employee engagement fully supported by senior management is key to ensuring organizational and employee success. Advocating a role-based performance approach, she identifies critical practices that contribute toward developing an environment in which employees and indeed leaders are fully engaged and contribute to firm success.

The Psychological Contract: Violations and Modifications*

Denise M. Rousseau

> "They promised me a job in marketing and here I am doing telephone sales."
>
> "The company promised that no one would be fired out of the training program—that all of us were 'safe' until placement. In return for this security, we accepted lower pay. The company subsequently fired four people from the training program."
>
> "Original representations of the company's financial and market strength (were) clearly fraudulent."

The common thread found in these quotations from recently hired employees is a violation of the psychological contract, which is defined as individual beliefs, shaped by the organization, regarding terms of an exchange agreement between individuals and their organizations. A contract is a mental model that people use to frame events such as promises, acceptance, and reliance. The promises that make up contracts have no objective meaning. Promises ultimately are perceptions of what was sent and what was meant. Perceptions, however, are not simply passive interpretations of reality; people create their own meaning for many events. The close supervision one person sees as controlling may seem supportive and helpful to her co-worker. Yet reality is not constructed wholly in the minds of individuals. Groups sometimes do agree on events and their meaning. Investment bankers, for example, may share a belief that their firm rewards those who make profitable deals.

Contract violation erodes trust. It undermines the employment relationship, yielding both lower employee contributions (e.g., performance and attendance) and lower employer investments (e.g., retention and promotion) in employees. Therefore, it's important for managers to understand how to avoid violating psychological contracts unnecessarily and how to modify them without eroding trust when change is essential.

Psychological contract violation can run the gamut from subtle misperceptions to stark breaches of good faith. In organizations, violated contracts are at the heart of many lawsuits brought by customers and employees. Although potentially damaging to reputations, careers, and relationships, violations also appear to be both frequent and survivable.

The basic facts of contract violation are these:

- Contract violation is commonplace.
- Violated contracts lead to adverse reactions by the injured party.
- Failure to fulfill a contract need not be fatal to the relationship.

What is Contract Violation?

In the strictest sense, violation is a failure to comply with the terms of a contract. But, given the subjective nature of psychological contracts, how people interpret the circumstances of this failure determines whether they experience a violation. Violation takes three forms (Table 1). *Inadvertent violation* occurs when both parties are able and willing to keep their bargain, but divergent interpretations lead one party

---

*Excerpted and reprinted with permission from D. M. Rousseau, *Psychological Contracts in Organizations*, Sage Publications, 1995.

Table 1 Sources of Experienced Violation	
Inadvertent	Able and willing (divergent interpretations made in good faith)
Disruption	Willing but unable (inability to fulfill a contract)
Breach of contract	Able but unwilling (reneging)

to act in a manner at odds with the understanding and interests of the other. Two people who misunderstand the time of a meeting will inadvertently fail to honor their mutual commitment to attend. *Disruption* to the contract occurs when circumstances make it impossible for one or both parties to fulfill their end of the contract, despite the fact that they are willing to do so. A plant closing forced by a hurricane can prevent an employer from providing work. Similarly, a car accident can keep an employee from showing up to work on time. Reneging or *breach of contract* occurs when one side, otherwise capable of performing the contract, refuses to do so. A bank manager who wants to spend more time with his family leaves a high demand/high pay job with one bank for another with a smaller financial institution. The major attraction of the new bank for the manager is its low pressure environment, which is played up by the officers who recruit him. Within two weeks of taking the job, the manager learns that the smaller firm is starting an aggressive marketing campaign he is expected to head, which will keep him away from his family for even longer hours than before. Damages include increased stress and family conflict along with loss of reputation if he tries to change jobs again soon. The sense of betrayal and entrapment this manager feels exacerbates his personal costs from the organization's actions. Whether the victim understands the source of violation to be unwillingness or inability to comply has a tremendous impact on how violation is experienced and what victims do in response (Bies and Moag, 1986).

Although contracts can be violated in innumerable ways, there are a number of common forms (Table 2). Recruiters may overpromise a job's opportunity for challenge, growth, or development, while at the same time, eager job seekers may read into a promise what they want to hear. Managers, co-workers, or executives who say one thing and do another all can engender violation. A common cause of violation for many employees involves a change in superiors. When one's boss or mentor is promoted, terminated, or retired, old deals may be abrogated. Similarly, changes in human resource practices, even with constructive intent (e.g., to align with a new business strategy) can appear to break old commitments (e.g., introducing new results-based performance criteria among veteran employees used to a seniority system). Then there is the phenomenon of mixed messages, where different contract makers express divergent intentions. A mission statement can convey that the organization rewards based upon merit ("commitment to excellence") while the compensation system is based on seniority. Different contract sources may each convey mutually exclusive promises.

When is Violation Most Likely?

- When there is a history of conflict and low trust in the relationship.
- When social distance exists between the parties such that one does not understand the perspective of the other.
- When an external pattern of violations exists (e.g., an era of business retrenchment).
- When incentives to breach contracts are very high or when perpetrators perceive themselves to have no alternatives (e.g., organizational crises).
- When one party places little value in the relationship (e.g., alternative parties are relatively available and there are few sunk costs).

Table 2	Sources of Violation by Contract Makers and Systems
Sources	**Violations**
Contract Makers:	
recruiters	• unfamiliar with actual job
	• overpromise
managers	• say one thing, do another
co-workers	• failure to provide support
mentors	• little follow-through
	• few interactions
top management	• mixed messages
Systems:	
compensation	• changing criteria
	• reward seniority, low job security
benefits	• changing coverage
career paths	• dependent on one's manager
	• inconsistent application
performance review	• not done on time
	• little feedback
training	• skills learned not tied to job
documentation	• stated procedures at odds with actual practice

When a Contract is Violated

Responses to violation take many forms. Violated contracts promote mistrust, anger, and attrition and change the way people behave in subsequent interactions. The aftermath of contract violation can be seen in declining corporate loyalty and increased litigation. Managers decry the decline of employee loyalty, while at the same time, the workforce has been counseled to eschew reliance on job security and employee commitments, and to "pack its own parachute" instead. In both instances there is the suggestion of contract violation, and the implication that at least one party has failed to keep its side of the bargain.

Types of Responses

Whether organizations and individuals choose to end their relationship, resolve their dispute, sue, or suffer in silence is a function of both situational factors and the predispositions of the parties. Previous research on responses to the more general phenomenon of dissatisfaction has largely focused on four courses of action: exit, voice, loyalty, and destruction. Although studied in various combinations (e.g., Hirschman, 1970s, *Exit, Voice, and Loyalty*) and labels (e.g., Farrell's, 1983, *Exit, Voice, Loyalty, and Neglect*), these courses of action reflect two essential dimensions: active-passive and constructive-destructive.

Personal characteristics predisposing the victim to believe that the relationship is valuable or can be saved should promote either relationship-building behaviors of voice or loyalty. Without this belief, behaviors that undermine the relationship, exit or destruction, are more likely. Research on individual reactions to inequitable situations suggests that people differ in terms of their willingness to tolerate unfair or inequitable exchanges (Berscheid and Walster, 1973). "Equity-sensitives" are people who tend to monitor their exchanges with others very carefully. "Beneficient" individuals are those who tend to be other-oriented, or comfortable when exchanges benefit others more than themselves. There is some evidence that men are more likely to be equity-sensitive and women more beneficent, although personality and other factors also enter in.

Situational factors promoting certain behaviors and inhibiting others also affect responses to violation. Social learning and the presence of behavioral role models tend to induce certain types of behaviors. Thus, employees in organizations where other victims have left might be inclined to leave themselves. Similarly, individuals who have observed others successfully complain about their treatment might themselves be inclined to complain (Robinson, 1992). It is likely that the culture of the organization shapes the type of violation responses people make. A very bureaucratic organization that stifles communication and deviant behavior probably engenders little voice and more neglect and disloyalty. An open, communal organization might foster more overt complaints, as well as attempting to repair the contract by communicating with superiors.

Exit is voluntary termination of the relationship. Employers can terminate workers whose performance does not meet standards (e.g., too frequently tardy, absent, or careless), while workers can quit an untrustworthy or unreliable employer (e.g., who fails to deliver promised training or promotions). Exit is most likely in employment with transactional terms, where its costs are relatively low. Transactional terms are exemplified by *a fair day's work for a fair day's pay*—focusing on short-term and monetizable exchanges. Employment agencies such as Manpower, Kelly, Nursetemps, and other temporary employment services offer organizations the opportunity to create purely transactional agreements with workers. Transactional contract terms include: specific economic conditions (e.g., wage rate) as the primary incentive, limited personal involvement in the job, closed-ended time frame (e.g., seasonal employment), commitments limited to well-specified conditions (e.g., union contract), unambiguous terms readily understood by outsiders, and the use of existing skills (no development).

Both active and destructive, exit terminates the relationship. The vast majority of people quitting jobs within the first two years of employment report that their employer had violated commitments it had made (Robinson and Rousseau, 1994).

Exit is most likely following violation when:

1. the contract is transactional;
2. many other potential jobs or potential employees are available;
3. the relationship is relatively brief;
4. other people are also exiting; and
5. attempts to remedy a violated contract have failed.

However, it should be pointed out that violations don't always lead to exit. Robinson and Rousseau (1994) found that although 79 percent of leavers reported violated contracts, so too did 52 percent of stayers. While enduring violation, stayers can manifest three forms of response: voice, loyalty, or neglect.

Voice refers to the actions victims take to remedy the violation. Any attempt to change the objectionable features in the situation, such as complaints to one's boss or to human resources, or the filing of a grievance, are efforts made to remedy or compensate for the violation while remaining in the relationship. As a means of expressing general dissatisfaction, voice has received wide study in terms of grievance filing (Allen and Keaveny, 1981), willingness to vote for unions (Getman, Goldberg, and Herman, 1976), and whistle-blowing (Near and Miceli, 1986). However, as a means of remediating a contract violation, voice has distinct features from reparations for dissatisfaction. Voice in contract violation focuses on (1) reducing losses and (2) restoring trust.

As a response to dissatisfaction, voice often has been associated with relationship-threatening alternatives, where members in effect burn their bridges (e.g., whistle-blowing). Voice in response to contract violation is an active, constructive effort and is manifest in a number of ways. In a study of MBA alumni, there were three major types of employee voice behaviors: talking with superiors, threats, and changes in behavior (Rousseau, Robinson, and Kraatz, 1992).

Talking with superiors was the most frequent type of voice:

> *I discussed my disappointment with my boss and also with my mentor. I was assured that, although I did not receive a bonus, my performance was above average. I was promoted and received a salary increase six months later*

Some complaints obtain some sort of substitution:

> They said the situation was out of their hands and gave me a substantial salary increase.

Some complaints elicit no response:

> My boss paid lip service to making changes, but nothing actually occurred.

Voice can take the form of a threat in a smaller number of cases:

> I threatened to leave based on my work assignment, training, and development opportunities. I was given new assignments, more training, and was allowed to stretch for development . . . however, I believe that happened primarily because of my director; another director probably would have let me leave.

In a few instances, a change in the victim's behavior generates a response:

> I was unhappy with the situation and my performance reflected it. The decision was made by (my) managers to reverse the situation. I now report to the marketing manager with a dotted line reporting relationship with the financial manager (a reversal of the previous situation).

Exit was the final resort for some:

> First there was a confrontation on my part to bring the problem forth, then following further unkept promises, I left the company (giving over a month's notice).

Voice is most likely when:

1. A positive relationship and trust exist.
2. Voice channels exist.
3. Other people are using voice.
4. People believe that they can influence the other contract party.

Silence is a form of non-response. Manifest as loyalty or as avoidance, silence reflects a willingness to endure or accept unfavorable circumstances. Silence can imply pessimism, in terms of believing that one has no available alternatives. Or, silence can reflect loyalty—optimistically waiting for conditions to improve (Rusbult, Farrell, Rogers, and Mainous, 1988). As a passive, constructive response, silence serves to perpetuate the existing relationship:

> I started spending more time with my family and worrying less about what was happening at work.

Silence is likely when:

1. there are no voice channels, or established ways of complaining or communicating violations, and
2. no available alternative opportunities exist elsewhere.

Neglect, which entails passive negligence or active destruction, is a complex form of response. It can involve neglect of one's duties to the detriment of the interests of the other party. Passive-aggressive employee behavior, as in work slowdowns or providing customers with poor service, is a form of neglect, as is an organization's failure to invest in certain employees while developing others. Even when passive, neglect reflects erosion of the relationship between the parties. Destruction involves more active examples of counterproductive behaviors, including vandalism, theft, and interpersonal aggression (e.g., violence at work).

Violation Isn't the End of the Contract

Exit is only one of many results of contract violation. The fact that so many people with violated contracts remain with their employer suggests although violation may be based on a discrete event (e.g., a willful breach of contract terms), a contract's fulfillment is more a matter of degree. When Robinson and Rousseau (1994) asked employees to indicate whether their contract had been violated using a yes/no format, a total of 59 percent indicated *Yes*. However, when respondents were asked if their contract had been ultimately fulfilled by their employer, a large proportion (73 percent) indicated that their employer had honored its commitments at least moderately well. Among those employees reporting a violation at some point in the first two years of employment, 48 percent indicated that their contract had been honored at least somewhat by their employer. The major difference was that for victims of violation, the model rating of fulfillment was 3 on a 5 point scale (mean = 2.65) while for non-victims it was 4 (mean = 3.93). Extent of contract keeping was affected by what benefits the employee received (e.g., if not the promotion as scheduled, then a later promotion) as well as whether the violation was an isolated incident or part of a larger pattern. These findings suggest that although violation is a discrete event, contract fulfillment is not. Rather, fulfillment is a continuum shaped by both the quality of the relationship and post-violation behavior of both the victim and perpetrator.

How people respond to violation is largely a function of attributions made regarding the violators' motives, the behavior of the violator, and the scope of losses incurred. To understand how events are experienced as violations, it is necessary to take into account the perspective of the victim and the behavior of the perpetrator. For the prospective victim, the experience of violation is heightened when:

• Losses seem greater; experienced violation is a matter of degree rather than a discrete event (all or nothing).
• The event occurs in a context where it poses a threat to the relationship between the parties (e.g., a history of previous breach or conflict).

- The violation event appears to be voluntary, as opposed to inadvertent, accidental, or due to forces beyond the violator's control.
- No evidence of good faith efforts to avoid violation (the appearance of irresponsibility or neglect) is perceived by the victim.

The strength and quality of the relationship affects not only the extent to which violation is tolerated or leads to dissolution of the contract, but also affects the ability of the parties to repair the relationship. How people are treated following violation can repair the relationship or exacerbate its problems.

The dynamics of psychological contract violation offer some lessons for both managers and workers. Perceptions are facts to the person who shares them and must be taken into account in a successful worker-manager relationship. When changes are introduced it is quite possible that workers will believe that new practices will violate old promises. Rather than merely accepting the inevitability of violation, a number of steps spell the difference between a well managed employment relationship and violation, anger, and mistrust.

Actively seek to understand what the people we work with interpret to be our and the organization's commitments to them. This understanding makes it easier to both honor existing commitments as well as to know how to effectively change a deal or create a new one.

Recognize that any departure from the status quo can involve losses, painful consequences for the people who have enjoyed its benefits. Managing these losses, first by recognizing what forms they might take, and then taking steps to offset or accommodate them, can spell the difference between successful management and a breach of trust.

Even when complaints and anger indicate a violation has been experienced, a sense of good faith can be restored when the issues are directly addressed through a joint problem-solving process. Such actions can make a so-so relationship far stronger by showing commitment to joint agreement and respect for the people involved.

References

R. Allen & T. Keaveny, Correlates of faculty interests in unionization: A replication and extension. *Journal of applied psychology 66* (1981), 582–588.

R. Bies & J. Moag, Interactional justice communication criteria of fairness. M. Bazerman, R. Lewicki, and B. Shepard (Eds.) *Research on negotiations in organizations 1* (Greenwich, CT: JAI Press, 1986), 43–45.

D. Farrell. Exit, Voice, Loyalty, and neglect as responses to job dissatisfaction: A multidimensional scaling study. *Academy of Management Journal 26* (1983), 596–607.

J. Getman, S. Goldberg, & J. Herman, *Union representation elections: Law and reality* (New York: Russell Sage, 1976).

A. O. Hirschman, *Exit, Voice, and Loyalty* (Cambridge, MA: Harvard University Press, 1970).

J. Near & M. Miceli, Retaliation against whistleblowers: Predictors and effects. *Journal of applied psychology 71* (1986), 137–145.

S. L. Robinson, *Responses to dissatisfaction.* Unpublished dissertation, Northwestern University, Kellogg graduate school of management, 1992.

S. L. Robinson & D. M. Rousseau, Violating the Psychological Contract: Not the Exception but the Norm," *Journal of Organizational Behavior 15* (1994), 245–259.

D. M. Rousseau, S. L. Robinson, & M. S. Kraatz, Renegotiating the psychological contract. Paper presented at the society for industrial organizational psychology meetings, Montreal, May 1992.

C. Rusbult, D. Farrell, G. Rogers, & A. Mainous, Impact of exchange variables on exit, voice, loyalty, and neglect: An integrative model of response to declining job satisfaction. *Academy of management journal 31* (1988), 599–627.

E. Walster, E. Bercheid, & G. Walster, New directions in equity research. *Journal of personality and social psychology 25* (1973), 151–176.

EMPLOYEE ENGAGEMENT: BEYOND THE FAD AND INTO THE EXECUTIVE SUITE*

Theresa M. Welbourne

When you hear the word *engagement*, you might think of long-term commitment, marriage, diamonds, family, and celebration; however, today the word is associated with one of the hottest topics in management. Everyone seems to be on the path to getting their employees engaged. The claim has been made that engagement is needed for higher levels of firm performance, and consultant studies estimate that only 14 percent to 30 percent of employees are engaged at work.

But to date, despite a surge in interest in improving engagement, people still disagree about what employee engagement is, how to go about getting it, and what it looks like when it is achieved. Additionally, with all the attention given to reported levels of low employee engagement, there are few if any statistics on what a realistic level of engagement should be for employees overall and for various subgroups of workers. In particular, very little attention has been given to the engagement levels of the people running organizations—the leadership and management teams. Regardless of what definition of engagement is used, if it is something organizations are trying to do to employees rather than a quality that leaders are demonstrating through example, the interventions associated with engagement will fail.

In this article, I focus on the context and behaviors of employee engagement. I do this to understand what may be causing the reported low levels of engagement and to spell out the critical role that leaders play in improving performance through employee engagement. To study the framework for engagement, I introduce the role-based model of performance. This model spells out five specific roles that employees occupy at work—and the links between these roles and improved firm performance tell the story of what happens when employees become engaged at work.

Knowing the relationship between employee behavior and firm performance, while simultaneously understanding the context in which leaders are running their organizations, it becomes clear that engagement is not going to be a quick fix. Leaders face challenges of being engaged themselves, getting structural barriers out of the way of engagement, and dealing with an employee contract that does not support engagement at work.

Origins of Employee Engagement

Employee engagement has appeared on the management scene in a big way fairly recently. A review of recent history helps to clarify why it is so popular today. Prior to the 1980s, employers expected loyalty to the organization, and in exchange for that commitment, they offered lifetime employment. Then in the 1980s organizations started to change that contract.

With increased global competition, employers needed to be more flexible in their deployment of employees. Plants were closed and then reopened in countries where wages were lower, and as business became global, leaders needed more control over wage and benefit costs to compete effectively. Employees learned the hard way (through layoffs) that loyalty was no longer rewarded. College seniors were told they could no longer expect long-term employment, and career progress became viewed as a spiral instead of a ladder. The rules of the game changed, and leaders in business initiated the evolution.

---

*Reprinted with permission from *Leader to Leader* (Spring 2007): 45–51.

The workforce has changed. Employers wanted it to change; however, in many cases, they did not quite want *everyone* to change. The new employment contract backfired. High-quality talent left organizations, and productivity suffered. Skilled employees were not willing to put in overtime and extra effort, and employers started to see increases in productivity slow down. This situation created the need for something new, and at least one of the initiatives was employee engagement.

The driving need today is for business to continue to improve productivity in a global environment where continuous change is making it difficult to compete. This desire to do more is combined with the mandate to do so with less, and one of the only outlets left for making this happen *is* employees. However, given the employee contract as it has been redefined, it is not easy for employers to snap their fingers and simply get employees to do more. Thus, the employee engagement movement arrived as a way to solve this problem. The experts claim that engaged employees do more; therefore, to get more out of less, the logic would be that managers simply need to engage their people.

Behavior, not Attitudes

Many case studies detail how efforts to improve employee engagement can improve firm performance outcomes (such as sales and profitability) and other outcomes such as absenteeism, customer service scores, and more. However, these data are primarily focused on employee attitudes (that is, the degree to which employees describe themselves as motivated, inspired, feeling liked by coworkers, having opportunities to excel, and so on), and they do not spell out the process by which these employee attitudes lead to changed behaviors or what specific actions drive performance. In today's environment, where the employee contract has evolved considerably, the process by which we expect engagement to happen needs to be fully understood so that managers can change contract terms or other context issues to enable full employee engagement. The only way to improve employee engagement across multiple organizations is to know what it looks like; the behaviors (not just attitudes) must be specified. Behaviors, to date, are the missing link in employee engagement. Thus, to fill that void, I suggest a role-based performance model as an option for providing a definition of the behaviors of employee engagement.

Role-Based Performance

The role-based performance model helps explain employee engagement by starting with the end goal in mind. The objective of all employee engagement initiatives is improved firm performance. The role-based performance model helps identify the types of behaviors needed from employees to drive performance. The model defines five key roles that employees occupy at work:

- Core job-holder role (what's in the job description)
- Entrepreneur or innovator role (improving process, coming up with new ideas, participating in others' innovations)
- Team member role (participating in teams, working with others in different jobs)
- Career role (learning, engaging in activities to improve personal skills and knowledge)
- Organizational member role (citizenship role or doing things that are good for the company)

I developed the role-based model for a large research project I conducted that focused on the determinants of long-term firm performance. The study was based on theories and prior work on what employers need from employees and what they reward. The model was validated with results obtained from numerous within-firm studies. The core ideas behind use of the model are that firms win in the market when they develop human resources in a way that is not easily replicated by their competition.

The roles that are not easily copied are the non-core job roles. When employees put in enough time within an organization to understand how to innovate (not just new products, but processes), they add value that an employee newly off the street cannot contribute. When employees are part of a team and all team members develop company-specific knowledge, that asset is something that cannot be easily copied by a competitor. As employees move from job to job within the organization and they build their own company-specific career knowledge, or as they teach others within the firm, the advantages of this firm-specific, career-based action cannot be easily imitated by another organization. When employees understand the inner workings of the organization, and they begin to engage in behaviors that support the company overall (instead of just their own job), this type of activity is not easily replicated by another organization, and these behaviors bring high value.

However, on the opposite side of the spectrum, if a company values only the core job role, and employees engage in behaviors exclusively associated with the core job, these jobs are very easy for competitors to copy. It *is* a simple matter to replicate this type of company, hire employees in another region or country who can be paid less money, and then compete with the original employer.

The net is that the core job role is important, but it alone will not result in long-term competitive advantage. This notion is *consistent* with what we are hearing in the employee engagement articles and books. Writers and experts talk about "above and beyond" behaviors, and they discuss discretionary effort, but these outcomes are rarely specifically defined or measured. Using the role-based model, one can describe what it looks like to be engaged at work.

> *Employee engagement improves when employees are successful working in both the core job and the non-core job roles.*

The result of employees' engaging in the non-core job roles will be new ideas, improved process, enhanced product lines, more skilled employees, higher service levels, career movement within the organization, employees' going above and beyond to help the company even when a project is not officially part of the immediate job, employees' working on teams to create new synergy that was not there in the past, employees' caring about the outcomes of projects because they know that the organization values their going beyond their core job, and more. The result of spending time and doing the non-core job roles well is company-specific assets that cannot be easily copied. These assets, then, drive long-term competitive advantage and firm performance.

Leader Energy and Engagement

To provide the environment where employees can be successful in both the core job and the non-core job roles, a few things are necessary:

- Leaders themselves have to be engaged; they need to work and succeed in both their core job and non-core job roles.
- Leaders need to clearly articulate how each role helps support the business strategy and plan.
- Leaders have to create an environment where the non-core job roles are valued, and they must remove barriers to employees' working in the non-core job roles.

These three conditions for engagement are not easy for leaders to meet. The work environment in most organizations is becoming more stressful, with employees not being able to do their core jobs in 60-hour work weeks, and leaders themselves are becoming burned out, confused, and disengaged. This is not a ripe environment for engaging employees or leaders.

Data on the context of engagement come from a study that I have been conducting over the last three years. The research is designed to examine leadership through an ongoing dialogue and data-collection process with leaders from multiple organizations. The study involves short pulse surveys sent every two months to more than 4,000 executives.

A subset of these data-collection efforts includes a measure of personal energy (or sense of urgency) at work, and the measurement process includes an open-ended comment question that asks respondents to explain the factors affecting their energy. The study focuses on energy because my prior research found it to be an important determinant of both individual and firm performance in several large-scale studies involving thousands of organizations and then in multiple case studies conducted since 1996.

The leadership pulse results show that, overall, leaders are reporting personal energy levels at work to be lower than where they say they are most productive. To understand this data, I asked respondents to explain their energy scores and why they are suboptimal. Below are some sample quotes from the data:

"Unclear and conflicting signals,"

"Lack of information."

"Personnel problems."

"Non-recognition of extra effort—nobody appreciates."

"Stress, overwork, constantly changing priorities."

"Continuous crisis management and cost cutting moved energy level to both extremes."

"Too many projects; lack of completion."

"The feeling of overloading in the workplace."

"Today's pace is too fast, at home and at work, and it is difficult to stay ahead of the game."

In this study I obtained more than 250 single-spaced pages of comments that indicate that many senior executives are tired, struggling to keep pace with their workloads, unclear about their own priorities, not confident in their own business strategies, and overall not doing well. This leadership research is only the tip of the iceberg. When leaders and managers are feeling confused, distracted, and overworked, their employees are doing much worse. I have been collecting energy data from employees throughout the world since 1996. The research shows that a decline in leader energy predicts reduced employee energy scores.

For example, here are sample quotes from a group of employees reporting to a manager whose own energy levels are suboptimal, low, and declining:

"Workload is not evenly distributed."

"Too much work and not enough time to get it done."

"The pace of my work is too much."

"I don't know how to spend my time; I have too much to do."

"I need help."

"There are not enough resources to get the job done."

"Many of us are just burned out."

"We have no idea what the strategy is or where we are going."

"There are not enough communications."

The Leader and Employee Engagement Challenge

This research suggests that many leaders are creating or are in an environment where employee engagement will be very difficult to achieve. When leaders are working at an energy level that is suboptimal, and when they have a difficult time merely getting their own jobs done, they will not value nor be interested in anyone engaging in the non-core job roles.

The type of environment leaders are discussing in the leadership pulse project is not conducive to high levels of employee or leader engagement. This is why having a concrete definition of what engagement looks like is so important for leaders. The organization must provide a context where people who move to the engaged state are rewarded or at least not punished for what they are doing. In a company where everyone is reporting being overworked, employees and managers will not tolerate time spent in the non-core job role even if a logical argument can be made for how that effort will benefit the organization in the long run.

In sum, the leadership pulse data reports a large proportion of leaders are not optimally energized at work, and the cause seems to be related to workload and a heavy focus on the core job role. At the same time, employees do not expect their employers to be loyal to them; they do not anticipate nor want jobs for life, and they are willing to leave their company when a new opportunity arises. In this highly complex environment, we need to ask some hard questions:

- Should anyone be surprised that only a small majority of employees are reporting being "engaged"? The employee contract was changed in ways that mean employers should have anticipated disengagement.
- Can anyone realistically expect to raise "engagement" when there are no associated rewards?
- Should we expect to improve engagement (if we define it as doing the non-core job roles) if employees are working for leaders who are having problems energizing themselves at work?
- Can employees or leaders afford to take time away from the job role when there are so many pressures on merely getting the job done?
- If the leadership team has no time to engage in anything other than the core job role, why would they value non-core job role-based behavior from their own employees?

Putting the pieces together, one could speculate that the millions of dollars being spent on employee engagement programs may be wasted money when the context for engagement does not exist. To change firm performance through people, a significant effort must begin with the leadership team. The leadership team must be engaged themselves; they need to know what it looks like to engage people at work, and they must be role models for this behavior with their direct reports—who then do the same for their employees.

Suggestions for Success

Improving conditions for employees and leaders at work so that they can engage in both core job and non-core job roles is an important goal for firms that want to gain competitive advantage. The role-based model is a way to start systematically addressing the problem of performance and the proposed solution of engagement.

If we define "engaged" employees as those who work and succeed in the non-core job roles, then a systematic approach to employee engagement would not start with an all-employee attitude survey (as has been done in many engagement programs). Instead, it would begin with the leadership team. Here are some suggested actions leaders can take to ensure that the people in charge of engagement are engaged themselves and that their organization has an environment that can support employees' contributing to productivity in a way that is defined by the role-based model:

- Conduct a business analysis to determine what roles are really valued in their organization and what roles are needed to achieve business plan objectives. This analysis should lead to identification of any gap in shared understanding of how employees should be allocating time and effort and what is rewarded in the organization.
- If the non-core job roles are not valued (by the managers who interact with employees daily), analyze the types of structural and strategic changes required to align the organization so it can compete effectively.
- Determine what leadership education is necessary to create a culture where both core job and non-core job roles are valued and rewarded.
- Examine in detail what structural impediments may exist to spending time in the non-core roles. These can be formal processes such as performance management systems that only focus on the job, or they can be informal norms.
- Assess the ways in which the various roles need to be enacted throughout the year. The importance of roles may change based on seasonality of the industry or work demands; they also may be different for various occupations. This type of detailed understanding is needed to assure continuous alignment.
- Engage employees in the right roles at the right time. Conduct assessments to understand the determinants of engagement in the various roles as opposed to engagement overall. Using this data, you can develop interventions to help retain employees who are interested in engaging in both the core job and non-core job roles.

Organizations need more engagement at work. They need leaders, managers, supervisors, and employees who will take time to go above their core job roles if the business is to remain competitive in the global economy. However, employers cannot expect a magic formula to make engagement happen. It will be a long journey that starts at the top of the organization and moves its way throughout the business.

CHAPTER

3

Theories of Managing People

THE MANAGER'S JOB
Henry Mintzberg

MASTERING COMPETING VALUES: AN INTEGRATED APPROACH
TO MANAGEMENT
Robert E. Quinn

The third mental map we will examine concerns theories of management. We all carry around implicit models of how managers should best carry out their job and manage people. Sometimes these models are not made explicit or put into words until we bump into managers who fail to act as we think they should. Although discrepant ideas and mental models of management can be a source of conflict in the workplace, they can also be a potential trigger for personal development if we are willing to learn from others who think about and enact the managerial role in different ways.

Business theorists also have conflicting views on the best way to manage. To provide a definitive answer on what managers actually do, Henry Mintzberg, renowned Canadian management scholar at McGill University, carried out an observational study of five chief executives at work. He noted and timed everything they did with their time and produced a classic description of managerial work. In "The Manager's Job," a later version of his original conclusions, Mintzberg distinguishes between the folklore and the fact surrounding managerial work and characterizes the job as managing action, people, and information. You will notice that Mintzberg describes how managers handle mail rather than contemporary forms of communication. While the modes of communication and some processes have changed, the basic challenges for managers remain the same.

Successful management involves a careful balancing act and the ability to manage paradox. Robert Quinn captures both in "Mastering Competing Values: An Integrated Approach to Management." A consultant and University of Michigan professor, Quinn developed a framework that juxtaposes four classic theories of management and explains how master managers analyze situations and choose the most effective action. This is a very useful, practical model that brings to life the challenges that managers face in complex organizations.

THE MANAGER'S JOB*

Henry Mintzberg

Some Folklore and Facts about Managerial Work

There are four myths about the manager's job that do not bear up under careful scrutiny of the facts.

Folklore: The manager is a reflective, systematic planner.

The evidence on this issue is overwhelming, but not a shred of it supports this statement.

Fact: Study after study has shown that managers work at an unrelenting pace, that their activities are characterized by brevity, variety, and discontinuity, and that they are strongly oriented to action and dislike reflective activities.

Consider this evidence:

• Half the activities engaged in by the five [American] chief executives [that I studied in my own research (Mintzberg, 1973a)] lasted less than nine minutes, and only 10 percent exceeded one hour. A study of 56 U.S. foremen found that they averaged 583 activities per eight-hour shift, an average of 1 every 48 seconds (Guest, 1956, p.478). The work pace for both chief executives and foremen was unrelenting. The chief executives met a steady stream of callers and mail from the moment they arrived in the morning until they left in the evening. Coffee breaks and lunches were inevitably work related, and ever-present subordinates seemed to usurp any free moment.

• A diary study of 160 British middle and top managers found that they worked for a half hour or more without interruption only about once every two days (Stewart, 1967).

• Of the verbal contacts of the chief executives in my study, 93 percent were arranged on an ad hoc basis. Only 1 percent of the executives' time was spent in open-ended observational tours. Only 1 out of 368 verbal contacts was unrelated to a specific issue and could be called general planning.

• No study has found important patterns in the way managers schedule their time. They seem to jump from issue to issue, continually responding to the needs of the moment.

Is this the planner that the classical view describes? Hardly. The manager is simply responding to the pressures of the job. Clearly, these managers wanted to encourage the flow of current information. But more significantly, they seemed to be conditioned by their own work loads. They appreciated the opportunity cost of their own time, and they were continually aware of their ever-present obligations—mail to

---

*Adapted and reprinted with permission from *The Strategy Process: Concepts, Contexts, Cases* (Upper Saddle River, NJ: Prentice Hall, 1996): 19–34.

be answered, callers to attend to, and so on. It seems that no matter what he or she is doing, the manager is plagued by the possibilities of what he or she might do and must do.

When the manager must plan, he or she seems to do so implicitly in the context of daily actions, not in some abstract process reserved for two weeks in the organization's mountain retreat. The plans of the chief executives I studied seemed to exist only in their heads—as flexible, but often specific, intentions. The traditional literature notwithstanding, the job of managing does not breed reflective planners; the manager is a real-time responder to stimuli, an individual who is conditioned by his or her job to prefer live to delayed action.

Folklore: The effective manager has no regular duties to perform.

Managers are constantly being told to spend more time planning and delegating, and less time on operating details. These are not, after all, the true tasks of the manager. To use the popular analogy, the good manager, like the good conductor, carefully orchestrates everything in advance, then sits back to enjoy the fruits of his or her labor, responding occasionally to an unforeseeable exception.

Fact: In addition to handling exceptions, managerial work involves performing a number of regular duties, including ritual and ceremony, negotiations, and processing of soft information that links the organization with its environment.

Consider some evidence from the early research studies:

- A study of the work of the presidents of small companies found that they engaged in routine activities because their companies could not afford staff specialists and were so thin on operating personnel that a single absence often required the president to substitute (Choran in Mintzberg, 1973a).
- One study of field sales managers and another of chief executives suggest that it is a natural part of both jobs to see important customers, assuming the managers wish to keep those customers (Davis, 1957; Copeman, 1963).
- Someone, only half in jest, once described the manager as that person who sees visitors so that everyone else can get his or her work done. In my study, I found that certain ceremonial duties—meeting visiting dignitaries, giving out gold watches, presiding at Christmas dinners—were an intrinsic part of the chief executive's job.
- Studies of managers' information flow suggest that managers play a key role in securing "soft" external information (much of it available only to them because of their status) and in passing it along to their subordinates.

Folklore: The senior manager needs aggregated information, which a formal management information system best provides.

But this never proved true at all. A look at how managers actually process information makes the reason quite clear. Managers have five media at their command—documents, telephone calls, scheduled and unscheduled meetings, and observational tours.

Fact: Managers strongly favor the verbal media—namely, telephone calls and meetings.

The evidence comes from every one of the early studies of managerial work. Consider the following:

- In two British studies, managers spent an average of 66 percent and 80 percent of their time in verbal (oral) communication (Stewart, 1967; Burns, 1954). In my study of five American chief executives, the figure was 78 percent.
- These five chief executives treated mail processing as a burden to be dispensed with. One came in Saturday morning to process 142 pieces of mail in just over three hours, to "get rid of all the stuff." This same manager looked at the first piece of "hard" mail he had received all week, a standard cost report, and put it aside with the comment, "I never look at this."
- These same five chief executives responded immediately to 2 of the 40 routine reports they received during the five weeks of my study and to four items in the 104 periodicals. In all, these chief executives of good-sized organizations initiated on their own—that is, not in response to something else—a grand total of 25 pieces of mail during the 25 days I observed them.

Consider another interesting finding. Managers seem to cherish "soft" information, especially gossip, hearsay, and speculation. Why? The reason is its timeliness; today's gossip may be tomorrow's fact. The manager who is not accessible for the telephone call informing him or her that the firm's biggest customer was seen golfing with its main competitor may read about a dramatic drop in sales in the next quarterly report. But then it's too late.

The manager's emphasis on the verbal media raises two important points:

First, verbal information is stored in the brains of people. Only when people write this information down can it be stored in the files of the organization—whether in metal cabinets or computer memory—and managers apparently do not write down much of what they hear. Thus the strategic data bank of the organization is not in the memory of its computers but in the minds of its managers.

Second, the managers' extensive use of verbal media helps to explain why they are reluctant to delegate tasks. When we note that most of the managers' important information comes in verbal form and is stored in their heads, we can well appreciate their reluctance. It is not as if they can hand a dossier over to someone; they must take the time to "dump memory"—to tell that someone all they know about the subject. But this could take so long that the managers find it easier to do the task themselves. Thus the managers are damned by their own information systems to a "dilemma of delegation"—to do too much themselves or to delegate to their subordinates with inadequate briefing.

Folklore: Management is, or at least is quickly becoming, a science and a profession.

By almost any definitions of science and profession, this statement is false. Brief observation of any manager will quickly lay to rest the notion that managers practice a science. A science involves the enaction of systematic, analytically determined procedures or programs. If we do not even know what procedures managers use, how can we prescribe them by scientific analysis? And how can we call management a profession if we cannot specify what managers are to learn?

Fact: The managers' programs—to schedule time, process information, make decisions, and so on—remain locked deep inside their brains.

I was struck during my study by the fact that the executives I was observing—all very competent by any standard—are fundamentally indistinguishable from their counterparts of a hundred years ago (or a thousand years ago, for that matter). The information they need differs, but they seek it in the same way—by word of mouth. Their decisions concern modern technology, but the procedures they use to make them are the same as the procedures of the nineteenth-century manager.

Toward a Basic Description of Managerial Work

Now let us try to put some of the pieces of this puzzle together. The manager can be defined as that person in charge of an organization or one of its units. Besides chief executive officers, this definition would include vice presidents, head nurses, hockey coaches, and prime ministers. Our description takes the form of a model, building the image of the manager's job from the inside out, beginning at the center with the person and his or her frame and working out from there, layer by layer.

The Person in the Job

We begin at the center, with the person who comes to the job. Figure 1 shows that an individual comes to a managerial job with a set of *values*, by this stage in life probably rather firmly set, also a body of experience that, on the one hand, has forged a set of skills or *competencies*, perhaps honed by training, and, on the other, has provided a base of *knowledge*. That knowledge is, of course, used directly, but it is also converted into a set of *mental models*, key means by which managers interpret the world around them—for example, how the head nurse on a hospital ward perceives the behavior of the surgeons with whom she must work. Together, all these characteristics greatly determine how any manager approaches a given job—his or her *style* of managing. Style will come to life as we begin to see *how* a manager carries out *what* his or her job requires.

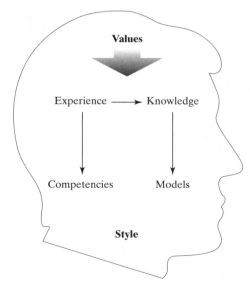

FIGURE 1 The Person in the Job

The Frame of the Job

Embed the person depicted in a given managerial job and you get managerial work. At the core of it is some kind of *frame* for the job, the mental set the incumbent assumes to carry it out. Frame is strategy, to be sure, possibly even vision, but it is more than that. It is purpose, whether to create something in the first place, maintain something that has already been created or adapt it to changes, or else recreate something. Frame is also *perspective*—the broad view of the organization and its mission—and *positions*—concerning specific products, services, and markets.

The Agenda of the Work

Given a person in a particular managerial job with a particular frame, the question arises of how this is manifested in the form of specific activities. That happens through the *agenda* to carry out the work, and the associated role of **scheduling**, which has received considerable mention in the literature of management. Agenda is considered in two respects here. First, the frame gets manifested as a set of current issues, in effect, whatever is of concern to the manager, broken down into manageable units—what Tom Peters likes to call "chunks." Ask any manager about his or her work, and the almost inevitable first reply will be about the "issues" of central concern, those things "on the plate," as the saying goes.

Second, the frame and the issues get manifested in the more tangible *schedule*, the specific allocations of managerial time on a day-to-day basis. Also included here, however implicitly, is the setting of priorities among the issues.

The Core in Context

If we label the person in the job with a frame manifested by an agenda, the central core of the manager's job (shown by the concentric circles in Figure 2), then we turn next to the context in which this core is embedded, the milieu in which the work is practiced.

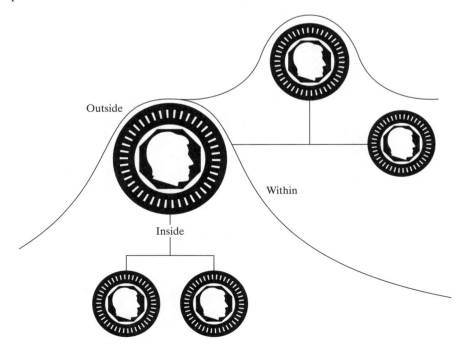

FIGURE 2   **The Core in Context**

The context of the job is depicted in Figure 2 by the lines that surround the core. Context can be split into three areas, labeled Inside, Within, and Outside in Figure 2.

Inside refers to the unit being managed, shown below the manager to represent his or her formal authority over its people and activities—the hospital ward in the case of the head nurse, for example. *Within*, shown to the right, refers to the rest of the organization—other members and other units with which the manager must work but over which he or she has no formal authority, for example, the doctors, the kitchen, the physiotherapists in the rest of the hospital, to continue with the same example. And *outside* refers to the rest of the context not formally part of the organization with which the manager must work—in this example, patients' relatives, long-term care institutions to which some of the unit's patients are discharged, nursing associations, and so on. The importance of this distinction (for convenience, we shall mostly refer to inside versus outside) is that much of managerial work is clearly directed either to the unit itself, for which the manager has official responsibility, or at its various boundary contexts, through which the manager must act without that responsibility.

Managing on Three Levels

We are now ready to address the actual behaviors that managers engage in to do their jobs. The essence of the model, designed to enable us to "see" managerial work comprehensively, in one figure, is that these roles are carried out on three successive levels, each inside and outside the unit. This is depicted by concentric circles of increasing specificity, shown in Figure 3.

From the outside (or most tangible level) in, managers can manage *action* directly, they can manage *people* to encourage them to take the necessary actions, and

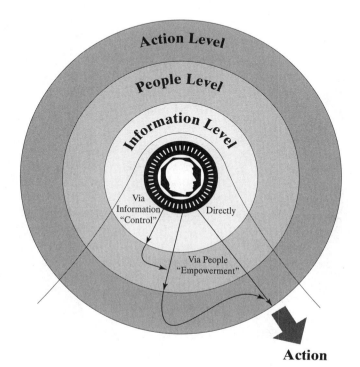

FIGURE 3 **Three Levels of Evoking Action**

they can manage *information* to influence the people in turn to take their necessary actions. In other words, the ultimate objective of managerial work, and of the functioning of any organizational unit, the taking of action, can be managed directly, indirectly through people, or even more indirectly by information through people. The manager can thus choose to intervene at any of the three levels, but once done, he or she must work through the remaining ones. Later we shall see that the level a given manager favors becomes an important determinant of his or her managerial style, especially distinguishing so-called "doers" who prefer direct action, "leaders" who prefer working through people, and "administrators" who prefer to work by information.

Managing by Information

To manage by information is to sit two steps removed from the purpose of managerial work. The manager processes information to drive other people who, in turn, are supposed to ensure that necessary actions are taken. In other words, here the managers' own activities focus neither on people nor on actions per se, but rather on information as an indirect way to make things happen.

The manager's various informational behaviors may be grouped into two broad roles, here labeled communicating and controlling, shown in Figure 4. **Communicating** refers to the collection and dissemination of information. In Figure 4, communicating is shown by double arrows to indicate that managers devote a great deal of effort to the two-way flow of information with the people all around them—employees inside their own units, others in the rest of the organization, and especially, as the empirical evidence makes abundantly clear, a great number of outsiders with whom they maintain regular contact. Thus the head of one regional division of the national police force spent a good part of the day I observed him passing information back and forth between the central headquarters and the people on his staff.

Managers "scan" their environments, they monitor their own units, and they share with and disseminate to others considerable amounts of the information they

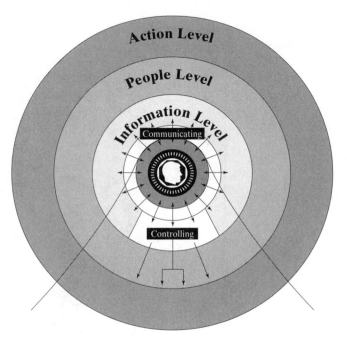

FIGURE 4 **The Information Roles**

pick up. Managers can be described as "nerve centers" of their units, who use their status of office to gain access to a wide variety of informational sources. Inside the unit, everyone else is a specialist who generally knows more about his or her specialty than the manager. But, because the manager is connected to all those specialists, he or she should have the broadest base of knowledge about the unit in general. This should apply to the head of a huge health care system, with regard to broad policy issues, no less than to the clinical director of one of its hospital units, with regard to the service rendered there. And externally, by virtue of their status, managers have access to other managers who are themselves nerve centers of their own units. And so they tend to be exposed to powerful sources of external information and thus emerge as external nerve centers as well.

The result of all this is that a considerable amount of the manager's information turns out to be privileged, especially when we consider how much of it is oral and nonverbal. Accordingly, to function effectively with the people around them, managers have to spend considerable time sharing their information, both with outsiders (in a kind of spokesperson role) and with insiders (in a kind of disseminator role).

I found in my initial study of chief executives that perhaps 40 percent of their time was devoted almost exclusively to the communicating role—just to gaining and sharing information—leaving aside the information processing aspects of all the other roles. In other words, the job of managing is fundamentally one of processing information, notably by talking and especially listening. Thus Figure 4 shows the inner core (the person in the job, conceiving and scheduling) connected to the outer rings (the more tangible roles of managing people and action) through what can be called the membrane of information processing all around the job.

What can be called the **controlling** role describes the managers' efforts, not just to gain and share information, but to use it in a directive way inside their units: to evoke or provoke general action by the people who report to them. They do this in three broad ways: they develop systems, they design structures, and they impose directives. Each of these seeks to control how other people work, especially with regard to the allocation of resources, and to what actions they are inclined to take.

First, developing systems is the most general of these three, and the closest to conceiving. It uses information to control peoples' behaviors. Managers often take charge of establishing and even running such systems in their units, including those of planning and performance control (such as budgeting).

Second, managers exercise control through designing the structures of their units. By establishing responsibilities and defining hierarchical authority, they again exercise control rather passively, through the processing of information. People are informed of their duties, which in turn is expected to drive them to carry out the appropriate actions.

Third is imposing directives, which is the most direct of the three, closest to the people and action, although still informational in nature. Managers pronounce: They make specific choices and give specific orders, usually in the process of "delegating" particular responsibilities and "authorizing" particular requests. In effect, managers manage by transmitting information to people so that they can act.

Managing Through People

To manage through people, instead of by information, is to move one step closer to action, but still to remain removed from it. That is because here the focus of managerial attention becomes affect instead of effect. Other people become the means to get things done, not the manager him or herself, or even the substance of the manager's thoughts.

Not until serious research on managerial work began did it become evident how important to managers were contacts with individuals outside their units.

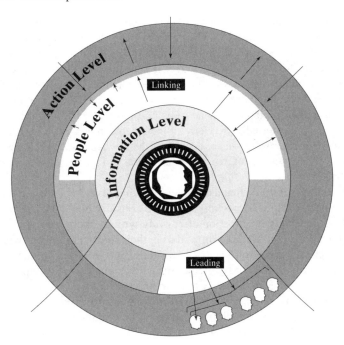

FIGURE 5   **The People Roles**

Virtually every single study of how all kinds of managers spent their time has indicated that outsiders, of an enormously wide variety, generally take as much of the managers' attention as so-called "subordinates." We shall thus describe two people roles here, shown in Figure 5, one internal, called *leading*, and one external, called *linking*.

The **leading** role has probably received more attention in the literature of management than all the other roles combined. And so we need not dwell on it here. But neither can we ignore it: managers certainly do much more than lead the people in their own units, and leading certainly infuses much else of what managers do (as, in fact, do all the roles, as we have already noted about communicating). But their work just as certainly cannot be understood without this dimension. We can describe the role of leading on three levels, as indicated in Figure 5-"The People Roles".

First, managers lead on the *individual* level, "one on one," as the expression goes. They encourage and drive the people of their units—motivate them, inspire them, coach them, nurture them, push them, mentor them, and so on. All the managers I observed, from the chief executive of a major police force to the front-country manager in a mountain park, stopped to chat with their people informally during the day to encourage them in their work. Second, managers lead on the *group* level, especially by building and managing teams, an effort that has received considerable attention in recent years. And third, they lead on the *unit* level, especially with regard to the creation and maintenance of culture, another subject of increasing attention in recent years (thanks especially to the Japanese). Managers, for example, engage in many acts of symbolic nature ("figurehead" duties) to sustain culture, as when the head of the national police force visited its officer training institute (as he did frequently) to imbue the force's norms and attitudes in its graduating class.

The excess attention to the role of leading has probably been matched by the inadequate attention to the role of **linking**. For, in their sheer allocation of time, managers have been shown to be external linkers as much as they are internal leaders, in study after study. Indeed, now more than ever, it must be understood, given the great growth of joint ventures and other collaborating and networking relationships between organizations, as well as the gradual reconception of the "captive" employee as an autonomous "agent" who supplies labor.

Figure 5 suggests a small model of the linking role. The arrows go in and out to indicate that the manager is both an advocate of its influence outside the unit and, in turn, a recipient of much of the influence exerted on it from the outside. In the middle are two parallel lines to represent the buffering aspect of this role—that managers must regulate the receipt of external influence to protect their units. To use a popular term, they are the *gate-keepers* of influence. Or, to add a metaphor, the manager acts as a kind of valve between the unit and its environment. Nowhere was this clearer than in my observation of three levels of management in a national park system—a regional director, the head of one mountain park, and the front-country manager of that park. They sit in an immensely complex array of forces—developers who want to enhance their business opportunities, environmentalists who want to preserve the natural habitat, tourists who want to enjoy the beauty, truckers who want to drive through the park unimpeded, politicians who want to avoid negative publicity, etc.

All managers appear to spend a great deal of time "networking"—building vast arrays of contacts and intricate coalitions of supporters beyond their own units, whether within the rest of the organization or outside, in the world at large. To all these contacts, the manager represents the unit externally, promotes its needs, and lobbies for its causes. In response, these people are expected to provide a steady inflow of information to the unit as well as various means of support and specific favors for it.

In turn, people intent on influencing the behavior of an organization or one of its sub-units will often exercise pressure directly on its manager, expecting that person to transmit the influence inside, as was most pointedly clear in the work of the parks manager. Here, then, the managerial job becomes one of delicate balance, a tricky act of mediation. Those managers who let external influence pass inside too freely—who act like sieves—are apt to drive their people crazy. (Of course, those who act like sponges and absorb all the influence personally are apt to drive themselves crazy!) And those who block out all influence—who act like lead to X-rays—are apt to detach their units from reality (and so dry up the sources of external support). Thus, what influence to pass on and how, bearing in mind the quid pro quo that influence exerted out is likely to be mirrored by influence coming back in, becomes another key aspect of managerial style, worthy of greatly increased attention in both the study of the job and the training of its occupants.

Managing Action

If managers manage passively by information and affectively through people, then they also manage actively and instrumentally by their own direct involvement in action. Indeed, this has been a long-established view of managerial work, although the excess attention in this century, first to controlling and then to leading and more recently to conceiving (of planned strategy), has obscured its importance.

I shall refer to this involvement as the **doing role**. But, in using this label, it is necessary to point out that managers, in fact, hardly ever "do" anything. Many barely even dial their own telephones! Watch a manager and you will see someone whose work consists almost exclusively of talking and listening, alongside, of course, watching and "feeling." (That, incidentally, is why I show the manager at the core of the model as a head and not a full body!)

What "doing" presumably means, therefore, is getting closer to the action, ultimately being just one step removed from it. Managers as doers manage the carrying out of action directly, instead of indirectly through managing people or by processing information. In the terms of decision making introduced earlier, here

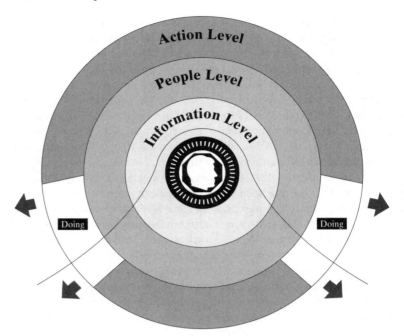

FIGURE 6 The Action Roles

the manager diagnoses and designs as well as decides: he or she gets deeply and fully involved in the management of particular activities. Thus, in the day I spent with the head of the small retail chain, I saw a steady stream of all sorts of people coming and going, most involved with some aspect of store development or store operations, and there to get specific instructions on how to proceed next. He was not delegating or authorizing, but very clearly managing specific development projects step by step.

Just as they communicate all around the circle, so too do managers "do" all around it, as shown in Figure 6. *Doing inside* involves projects and problems. In other words, much "doing" has to do with changing the unit itself, both proactively and reactively. Managers champion change to exploit opportunities for their units, and they handle its problems and resolve its crises, often with "hands on" involvement. And the evidence, in fact, is that managers at all levels typically juggle many such projects concurrently, perhaps several dozen in the case of chief executives.

Some managers continue to do regular work after they have become managers as well. For example, a head nurse might see a patient, just as the Pope leads prayers, or a dean might teach a class. Done for its own sake, this might be considered separate from managerial work. But such things are often done for very managerial reasons as well. This may be an effective way of "keeping in touch" with the unit's work and finding out about its problems, in which case it falls under the role of communicating. Or it may be done to demonstrate involvement and commitment with others in the unit, in which case it falls under the role of culture building in the role of leading.

Doing outside takes place in terms of deals and negotiations. Again, there is no shortage of evidence on the importance of negotiating as well as dealing in managerial work. Most evident in my observations was the managing director of the film company, who was working on one intricate deal after another. This was a small company, and making deals was a key part of her job. But even in larger organizations, senior managers have to spend considerable time on negotiations themselves, especially when critical moments arise. After all, they are the ones who have the authority to commit the resources of their unit, and it is they who are the nerve centers of its information as well as the energy centers of its activity, not to mention the conceptual centers of its strategy. All around the circles, therefore, action connects to people who connect to information, which connects to the frame.

The Well-Rounded Job of Managing

A final aspect of managerial style has to do with the interrelationships among the various components of managerial work. For example, an important distinction can be made between *deductive* and *inductive* approaches to managerial work. The former proceeds from the core out, as the conceived frame is implemented through scheduling that uses information to drive people to get action done. We can call this a *cerebral* style of managing—highly deliberate. But there is an alternate, emergent view of the management process as well, which proceeds inductively, from the outer surface to the inner core. We might label it an *insightful* style. As Karl Weick puts it, managers act in order to think. They try things to gain experience, retain what works, and then, by interpreting the results, gradually evolve their frames (Weick, 1979).

Clearly, there is an infinity of possible contexts within which management can be practiced. But just as clearly, perhaps, a model such as the one presented here can help to order them and so come to grips with the difficult requirements of designing managerial jobs, selecting the right people to fill them, and training people accordingly.

MASTERING COMPETING VALUES: AN INTEGRATED APPROACH TO MANAGEMENT*

Robert E. Quinn

It was awful. Everything was always changing and nothing ever seemed to happen. The people above me would sit around forever and talk about things. The technically right answer didn't matter. They were always making what I thought were wrong decisions, and when I insisted on doing what was right, they got pissed off and would ignore what I was saying. Everything was suddenly political. They would worry about what everyone was going to think about every issue. How you looked, attending cocktail parties—that stuff to me was unreal and unimportant.

I went through five and a half terrible years. I occasionally thought I had reached my level of incompetence, but I refused to give up. In the end, the frustration and pain turned out to be a positive thing because it forced me to consider some alternative perspectives. I eventually learned that there were other realities besides the technical reality.

I discovered perception and long time lines. At higher levels what matters is how people see the world, and everyone sees it a little differently.

---

*Adapted with permission from *Beyond Rational Management* (San Francisco: Jossey-Bass, 1988).

Technical facts are not as available or as important. Things are changing more rapidly at higher levels, you are no longer buffered from the outside world. Things are more complex, and it takes longer to get people on board. I decided I had to be a lot more receptive and a lot more patient. It was an enormous adjustment, but then things started to change. I think I became a heck of a lot better manager.

The Concept of Mastery

If there is such a thing as a master of management, what is it that differentiates the master from others? The answer has to do with how the master of management sees the world.

Most of us learn to think of the concept of organization in a very static way. Particularly at the lower levels, organizations seem to be characterized by relatively stable, predictable patterns of action. They appear to be, or at least we expect them to be, the product of rational-deductive thinking. We think of them as static mechanisms designed to accomplish some single purpose.

One of the most difficult things for most of us to understand is that organizations are dynamic. Particularly as one moves up the organizational ladder, matters become less tangible and less predictable. A primary characteristic of managing, particularly at higher levels, is the confrontation of change, ambiguity, and contradiction. Managers spend much of their time living in fields of perceived tensions. They are constantly forced to make tradeoffs, and they often find that there are no right answers. The higher one goes in an organization, the more exaggerated this phenomenon becomes. One-dimensional bromides (care for people, work harder, get control, be innovative) are simply half-truths representing single domains of action. What exists in reality are contradictory pressures, emanating from a variety of domains. This fact is important because much of the time the choice is not between good and bad, but between one good and another or between two unpleasant alternatives. In such cases the need is for complex, intuitive decisions, and many people fail to cope successfully with the resulting tension, stress, and uncertainty. This is well illustrated by the initial failure and frustration of the engineer who was quoted earlier.

The people who come to be masters of management do not see their work environment only in structured, analytic ways. Instead, they also have the capacity to see it as a complex, dynamic system that is constantly evolving. In order to interact effectively with it, they employ a variety of different perspectives or frames. As one set of conditions arises, they focus on certain cues that lead them to apply a very analytic and structured approach. As these cues fade, they focus on new cues of emerging importance and apply another frame, perhaps this time an intuitive and flexible one. At another time they may emphasize the overall task, and at still another they may focus on the welfare of a single individual.

Because of these shifts, masters of management may appear to act in paradoxical ways. They engage the contradictions of organizational life by using paradoxical frames. Viewed from a single point in time, their behaviors may seem illogical and contradictory. Yet these seeming contradictions come together in a fluid whole. Things work out well for these people.

The ability to see the world in a dynamic fashion does not come naturally. It requires a dramatic change in outlook, a redefinition of one's world view. It means transcending the rules of mechanistic logic used for solving well-defined problems and adopting a more comprehensive and flexible kind of logic. It is a logic that comes from experience rather than from textbooks. It requires a change not unlike a religious conversion.

The Evolution of Mastery

Dreyfus, Dreyfus, and Athanasion (1986) provide a five-stage model that describes the evolution from novice to expert.

In the novice stage people learn facts and rules. The rules are learned as absolutes that are never to be violated. For example, in playing chess people learn the names of the pieces, how they are moved, and their value. They are told to exchange pieces of lower value for pieces of higher value. In management, this might be the equivalent of the classroom education of an M.B.A.

In the advanced beginner stage, experience becomes critical. Performance improves somewhat as real situations are encountered. Understanding begins to exceed the stated facts and rules. Observation of certain basic patterns leads to the recognition of factors that were not set forth in the rules. A chess player, for example, begins to recognize certain basic board positions that should be pursued. The M.B.A. discovers the basic norms, values, and culture of the workplace on the first job.

The third stage is competence. Here the individual has begun to appreciate the complexity of the task and now recognizes a much larger set of cues. The person develops the ability to select and concentrate on the most important cues. With this ability competence grows. Here the reliance on absolute rules begins to disappear. People take calculated risks and engage in complex trade-offs. A chess player may, for example, weaken board position in order to attack the opposing king. This plan may or may not follow any rules that the person was ever taught. The M.B.A. may go beyond the technical analysis taught in graduate school as he or she experiments with an innovation of some sort. Flow or excellence may even be experienced in certain specific domains or subareas of management, as in the case of the engineer at the beginning of the article who displayed technical brilliance.

In the proficiency stage, calculation and rational analysis seem to disappear and unconscious, fluid, and effortless performance begins to emerge. Here no one plan is held sacred. The person learns to unconsciously "read" the evolving situation. Cues are noticed and responded to, and attention shifts to new cues as the importance of the old ones recedes. New plans are triggered as emerging patterns call to mind plans that worked previously. Here there is a holistic and intuitive grasp of the situation. Here we are talking, for example, about the top 1 percent of all chess players, the people with the ability to intuitively recognize and respond to change in board positions. Here the M.B.A. has become an effective, upper-level manager, capable of meeting a wide variety of demands and contradictions.

Experts, those at the fifth stage, do what comes naturally. They do not apply rules but use holistic recognition in a way that allows them to deeply understand the situation. They have maps of the territory programmed into their heads that the rest of us are not aware of. They see and know things intuitively that the rest of us do not know or see (many dimensions). They frame and reframe strategies as they read changing cues (action inquiry). Here the manager has fully transcended personal style. The master manager seems to meet the contradictions of organizational life effortlessly.

The Need for More Complex Theory

In their popular book, *In Search of Excellence* (1982), Peters and Waterman seek to discover what differentiates excellent companies from ordinary ones. Embedded in their work is an observation that is quite consistent with our observations. They conclude that managers in excellent companies have an unusual ability to resolve paradox, to translate conflicts and tensions into excitement, high commitment, and superior performance. In reviewing the book, Van de Ven (1983) applauds this insight and notes a grave inadequacy in the theories generated by administrative researchers. He argues that while the managers of excellent companies seem to have a capacity for dealing with paradox, administrative theories are not designed to take this phenomenon into account. In order to be internally consistent, theorists tend to eliminate contradiction. Hence, there is a need for a dynamic theory that can handle both stability and change, that can consider the tensions and conflicts inherent in human systems. Among other things, the theory would view people as complex actors in tension-filled social systems, constantly interacting with a "fast-paced, ever-changing array of forces" (Van de Ven, 1983, p. 624). The theory would center on transforming leadership that focuses on "the ethics and value judgments that are implied when leaders and followers raise one another to higher levels of motivation and morality" (Van de Ven, p. 624).

For most of us, discovering the contradictory nature of organizing is not easy. We have biases in how we process information, and we prefer to live in certain kinds of settings. Our biases are further influenced by our organizational experience at both the functional and cultural levels. At the functional level, for example, accountants and marketing people tend to develop very different assumptions about what is "good." At the cultural level, there is often a set of values that conveys "how we do things around here." Because these values tend to be so powerful, it is very difficult to see past them. It is difficult to recognize that there are weaknesses in our own perspective and advantages in opposing perspectives. It is particularly difficult to realize that these various perspectives must be understood, juxtaposed, and blended in a delicate, complex, and dynamic way. It is much more natural to see them as either/or positions in which one must triumph over the other.

A Competing Values Model

In the late seventies and early eighties, many of my colleagues and I became interested in the issue of organizational effectiveness. We were asking the question, What are the characteristics of effective organizations? Many studies were done in which people set out to measure the characteristics of organizations. These measures were then submitted to a technique called factor analysis. It produced lists of variables that characterized effective organizations. The problem was that these variables differed from one study to another. It seemed that the more we learned, the less we knew.

My colleague, John Rohrbaugh, and I therefore tried to reframe the question. Instead of asking what effective organizations looked like, we decided to ask how experts think about effective organizations. This would allow us to get to the assumptions behind the studies and perhaps make sense of what was causing the confusion. In a series of studies (Quinn and Rohrbaugh, 1983), we had organizational theorists and researchers make judgments regarding the similarity or dissimilarity between pairs of effectiveness criteria. The data were analyzed using a technique called multidimensional scaling. Results of the analyses suggested that organizational theorists and researchers share an implicit theoretical framework, or cognitive map (Figure 1).

Note that the two axes in the figure create four quadrants. The vertical axis ranges from flexibility to control, the horizontal axis ranges from an internal to an external focus. Each quadrant of the framework represents one of the four major models in organizational theory. The human relations model, for example, stresses criteria such as those in the upper-left quadrant: cohesion and morale, along with human resource development. The open systems model stresses criteria such as those in the upper-right quadrant. These include flexibility and readiness as well as growth, resource acquisition, and external support. The rational goal model stresses the kind of criteria found in the lower-right quadrant, including planning and goal setting and productivity and efficiency.

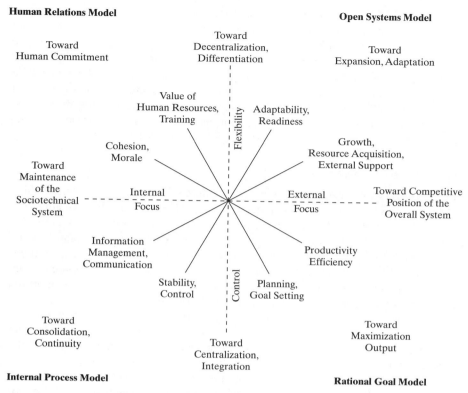

FIGURE 1 Competing Values Framework: Effectiveness

The internal process model is represented in the lower-left quadrant. It stresses information management and communication, along with stability and control.

Each model has a polar opposite. The human relations model, which emphasizes flexibility and internal focus, stands in stark contrast to the rational goal model, which stresses control and external focus. The open systems model, which is characterized by flexibility and external focus, runs counter to the internal process model, which emphasizes control and internal focus. Parallels among the models are also important. The human relations and open systems models share an emphasis on flexibility. The open systems and rational goal models have an external focus (responding to outside change and producing in a competitive market). The rational goal and internal process models are rooted in the value of control. Finally, the internal process and human relations models share an internal focus (concern for the human and technical systems inside the organization).

Each model suggests a mode or type of organizing. The two sets of criteria in each quadrant also suggest an implicit means-ends theory that is associated with each mode. Thus, the rational goal model suggests that an organization is a rational economic firm. Here planning and goal setting are viewed as a means of achieving productivity and efficiency. In the open systems model we find the adhocracy, where adaptability and readiness are viewed as a means to growth, resource acquisition, and external support. In the internal process model is the hierarchy, where information management and communication are viewed as a means of arriving at stability and control. In the human relations quadrant we find the team. Here cohesion and morale are viewed as a means of increasing the value of human resources.

This scheme is called the competing values framework because the criteria seem to initially carry a conflictual message. We want our organizations to be adaptable and flexible, but we also want them to be stable and controlled. We want growth, resource acquisition, and external support, but we also want tight information management and formal communication. We want an emphasis on the value of human resources, but we also want an emphasis on planning and goal setting. The model does not suggest that these oppositions cannot mutually exist in a real system. It suggests, rather, that these criteria, values, and assumptions are oppositions in our minds. We tend to think that they are very different from one another, and we sometimes assume them to be mutually exclusive. In order to illustrate this point we will consider how values manifest themselves and, in so doing, consider some applied examples.

How Values Manifest Themselves

In recent years much has been written about culture in organizations. When we think of the manifestation of values in organizations, it is their cultures that we are thinking of. Simply put, culture is the set of values and assumptions that underlie the statement "This is how we do things around here." Culture at the organizational level, like information processing at the individual level, tends to take on moral overtones. While cultures tend to vary dramatically, they share the common characteristic of providing integration of effort in one direction while often sealing off the possibility of moving in another direction. An illustration may be helpful.

In October 1980 *Business Week* ran an article contrasting the cultures at JCPenney and PepsiCo. At Penney the culture focuses on the values of fairness and long-term loyalty. Indeed, a manager was once chewed out by the president of the company for making too much money! To do so was unfair to the customers, and at Penney one must never take advantage of the customer. Customers are free to return merchandise with which they are not satisfied. Suppliers know that they can establish stable, long-term relationships with Penney. Employees know that if their ability to perform a given job begins to deteriorate, they will not find themselves out on the street; rather, an appropriate alternative position will be found for them.

The core of the company's culture is captured in "The Penney Idea." Although it was adopted in 1913, it is a very modern-sounding statement, consisting of seven points:

> To serve the public, as nearly as we can, to its complete satisfaction; to expect for the service we render a fair remuneration and not all the profit the traffic will bear; to do all in our power to pack the customer's dollar full of value, quality, and satisfaction; to continue to train ourselves and our associates so that the service we give will be more and more intelligently performed; to improve constantly the human factor in our business; to reward men and women in our organization through participation in what the business produces; to test our every policy, method, and act in this wise: "Does it square with what is right and just?"

The culture at PepsiCo is in stark contrast to that at Penney's. After years as a sleepy company that took the back seat to Coca-Cola, PepsiCo underwent a major change by adopting a much more competitive culture. This new culture was manifest both externally and internally. On the outside PepsiCo directly confronted Coca-Cola. In bold ads customers were asked to taste and compare the products of the two companies. Internally, managers knew that their jobs were on the line and that they had to produce results. There was continuous pressure to show improvement in market share, product volume, and profits. Jobs were won or lost over a "tenth of a point" difference in these areas.

Staffs were kept small. Managers were constantly moved from job to job and expected to work long hours. The pressure never let up. During a blizzard, for example, the chief executive officer found a snowmobile and drove it to work. (This story is told regularly at PepsiCo.) Competitive team and individual sports are emphasized, and people are expected to stay in shape. The overall climate is reflected in the often repeated phrase, "We are the marines, not the army."

The differences between these two companies could hardly be greater. Reading this account, you have probably concluded that one culture is more attractive than the other, and you would expect others to agree with your choice. But it is very likely that if you visited PepsiCo and spoke of "The Penney Idea," you would be laughed at. If you tried to press it upon PepsiCo employees, they would probably become incensed. Likewise, if you visited Penney's and described or tried to press upon them the values of PepsiCo, they would have the same reaction. You would be violating sacred assumptions.

Interestingly, the major problem at PepsiCo was seen as the absence of loyalty. Coca-Cola's response to the PepsiCo attack, for example, was to hire away some of PepsiCo's best "Tigers" and they were, because of the constant pressure, willing to go. (PepsiCo's rate of tenure is less than one-third of the rate at Penney.) And what, according to *Business Week*, was the major problem at Penney? Lack of competitiveness. Despite a reputation as one of the best places to work, and despite intense employee and customer loyalty, J. C. Penney had been rapidly losing market share to K-Mart. Some critics expressed doubt that Penney could respond to the challenge.

What is happening here? The surface conclusion is that two opposite cultures exist. Penney's reflects the human relations model in that the company seems to resemble a team, clan, or family. PepsiCo reflects the rational goal model in that it appears to be an instrumental firm. The strength of one is the weakness of the other. While this conclusion is true, there is a deeper insight to be gained. I will later return to this interesting contrast after considering the transformation of values.

Ineffectiveness

The competing values framework consists of juxtaposed sets of organizational effectiveness criteria. Each of these "good" criteria can become overvalued by an individual and pursued in an unidimensional fashion. When this zealous pursuit of a single set of criteria takes place, a strange inversion can result. Good things can mysteriously become bad things. In Figure 2, I show how criteria of effectiveness, when pursued blindly, become criteria of ineffectiveness. These latter criteria are depicted in the negative zone on the outside of the diagram.

The structure of this model parallels the competing values framework of effectiveness. The axes, however, are negatively, rather than positively, labeled. Thus, the vertical dimension ranges from chaos (too much flexibility and spontaneity) to rigidity (too much order and predictability). The horizontal dimension ranges from belligerence and hostility (too much external focus and too much emphasis on competition and engagement) to apathy and indifference (too much internal focus and too much emphasis on maintenance and coordination within the system). Each quadrant represents a negative culture with negative effectiveness criteria. Embedded within these quadrants are eight criteria of ineffectiveness.

In the upper-left quadrant is the irresponsible country club. In this quadrant, human relations criteria are emphasized to the point of encouraging laxity and negligence. Discussion and participation, good in themselves, are carried to inappropriate lengths. Commitment, morale, and human development turn into extreme permissiveness and uncontrolled individualism. Here, administrators are concerned only with employees, to the exclusion of the task.

In the upper-right quadrant is the tumultuous anarchy. In this quadrant, there is so much emphasis on the open systems criteria of effectiveness that disruption and

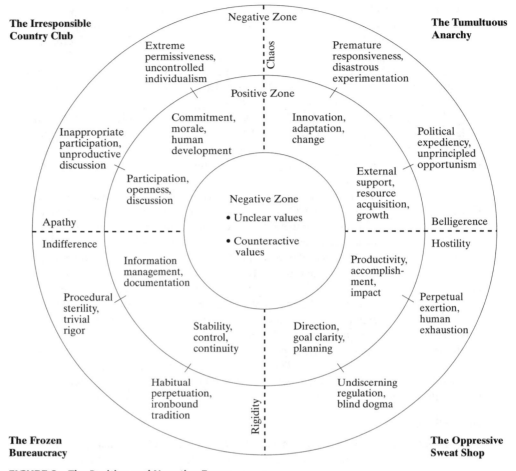

FIGURE 2   The Positive and Negative Zones

discontinuity result. Emphasis on insight, innovation, and change turns into premature responsiveness and disastrous experimentation. Concern for external support, resource acquisition, and growth turns into political expediency and unprincipled opportunism. Here, administrators are concerned only with having a competitive advantage and show no interest in continuity and control of the work flow.

In the lower-right quadrant is the oppressive sweatshop. In this quadrant, there is too much emphasis on the criteria of effectiveness associated with the rational goal model. Effort, productivity, and emphasis on profit or impact of service turn into perpetual exertion and human exhaustion. Here, we see symptoms of burnout. Concern for goal clarification, authority, and decisiveness turns into an emphasis on strict regulation and blind dogma. There is no room for individual differences; the boss has the final say.

Finally, in the lower-left quadrant is the frozen bureaucracy. Here, there is too much concern with internal processes. The organization becomes atrophied as a result of excessive measurement and documentation; it becomes a system of red tape. Control measures, documentation, and computation turn into procedural sterility and trivial rigor. Everything is "by the book." The emphasis on stability, control, and continuity leads to the blind perpetuation of habits and traditions. Procedures are followed because "we've always done it this way"; there is no room for trying something new.

Strength Becoming Weakness

Let us return to PepsiCo and JCPenney. Earlier I said that introducing the culture of one company into the other would be highly conflictual. Further, I pointed out that each culture had weaknesses. Now we can see that their very strengths put them at risk.

Because of the inability of the PepsiCo culture to tolerate the values in the human relations quadrant, the company is in danger of moving into the negative zone on the right side of Figure 2. Because of the inability of the JCPenney culture to more fully absorb the values on the right side of the figure, the company is in danger of moving into the negative zone on the left side of the figure. The more fully that each company pushes a particular set of positive values, without tending to the opposite positive values, the greater the danger to it.

The major point here is that everything in the two outer circles is related. The more that success is pursued around one set of positive values, the greater will be the pressure to take into account the opposite positive values. If these other values are ignored long enough, crisis and catastrophe will result.

Staying in the Positive Zone: Mastering Paradox

Staying in the positive zone requires high levels of complex thought. Consider, for example, the stereotypical entrepreneur, like Steve Jobs of Apple Computer. Entrepreneurs are typically very creative and action oriented. They are usually not very sympathetic to the values in the hierarchy quadrant. When they build a new organization they often try to avoid hierarchy. Unfortunately, if their initial vision is successful, and their new company expands rapidly, the growth (an indicator of success) stimulates a need for hierarchical coordinating mechanisms (often seen as an indication of failure). This phenomenon is often called the formalization crisis. Many successful entrepreneurs are forced, like Steve Jobs at one point, to leave their company because they cannot comprehend the paradox or manage the competing values. For this reason, it is instructive to consider Bill Gates of Microsoft.

Microsoft is one of the largest software companies in the world. Run by Bill Gates, Microsoft had been best known for its widely used MS DOS system. But in 1987 Gates was successful in convincing IBM to adopt its newest product, called Windows, for use in IBM's new line of personal computers. Upon completion of the agreement, analysts began to predict that within 12 months Microsoft would become the largest software company in the world.

In many ways, Gates is the stereotypical entrepreneur. He is a technical genius with a burning mission. He feels a drive to bring the power of computing to the masses. His company is marked by considerable flexibility and excitement. The median age of the workforce is 31. People work long days, with Gates himself setting the example with an early morning to midnight routine. There are frequent picnics, programmers set their own hours, dress is casual, and the turnover rate is less than 10 percent.

The company has grown rapidly. From 1980 to 1981, Gates watched his company go from 80 to 125 employees and saw profits double to $16 million. Given our earlier cases, all these indicators would lead us to worry about Gates and his ability to meet the demands for formalization.

In fact, however, Gates has already faced the formalization crisis and has come off well. What were the keys to this success? First, he made a very significant decision to bring in professional managers and to focus his own energies on technology. He seemed to grasp an important paradox that eludes most entrepreneurs: To have power means one must give up power. Maintaining a primary focus on technology, however, does not mean that he has abandoned the tasks of leadership. Instead, he has taken the time to learn the principles of law, marketing, distribution, and accounting and apply them to his work. He also has the paradoxical capacity of simultaneously caring and being tough. For example, dissatisfied with the performance of Microsoft's president, Gates removed him from office after only one year. But not long after, Gates was invited to be the best man at the wedding of the former president.

Perhaps the best summary of Gates and his abilities comes from one of his colleagues: "Bill Gates is very good at evaluating situations as they change." This, of course, is a key characteristic for staying in the positive zone.

Figure 2 has some important implications for management. It suggests that managers need to stay in the positive zone; that is, they need to pursue the seemingly "competing" positive values in the middle circle while also being careful to stay out of the external negative zone. They must maintain a dynamic, creative tension. Over time they must, like Bill Gates, be able to frame and reframe; that is, to move from one set of competing values to another.

Some Implications for Management

The notions of mastery and competing values suggest a more complex and dynamic approach to management. The novice-like "rules" taught in the textbooks are misleading in that they usually represent only one of the competing perspectives or polarities embedded in organizational life. Theory X is not inherently better than theory Y. Change is not inherently better than the status quo. Productivity is not inherently better than cohesion and morale.

The challenge for experienced managers is threefold: the first is far more difficult than it sounds, to recognize and appreciate the positive (and the negative) aspects of all areas of the competing values framework; second, to assess and work on the roles and skills associated with each area; third, to analyze the present organizational moment, with all its dilemmas, and trust one's ability to integrate and employ the skills appropriate to that moment. Together these three steps are key points in the process of mastering management.

References

H. Dreyfus, S. Dreyfus, and T. Athanasion, *Mind Over Machine: The Power of Human Intuition and Expertise in the Era of the Computer* (New York: Free Press, 1986).

R. Quinn and J. Rohrbaugh, "A Spatial Model of Effectiveness Criteria: Towards a Competing Values Approach to Organizational Analysis," *Management Science 39*, no. 3 (1983): 363–377.

T. Peters and R. Waterman Jr., *In Search of Excellence* (New York: Harper & Row, 1982).

A. Van de Ven, "In Search of Excellence: Lessons from America's Best Run Companies," *Administrative Science Quarterly 28*, no. 4 (1993): 621–624.

4

Individual and Organizational Learning

DEEP SMARTS
Dorothy Leonard
Walter Swap

THE LEADER'S NEW WORK: BUILDING LEARNING ORGANIZATIONS
Peter M. Senge

The ability to learn and to transfer that knowledge has become a key factor in organizational survival. Intellectual capital is a firm's most important asset in a knowledge economy and one that requires careful management. Individuals may have different learning styles and take different approaches to learning, but effective learning, mastery, and years of experience have the same end result—expert knowledge and cognition. Firms can help employees become experts by investing in their training and development, by hiring people who already possess expert knowledge, or by paying consultants for their knowledge. Regardless of the approach they use, many successful firms wisely pay close attention to the learning needs of their employees and of the organization as a whole.

Dorothy Leonard, a Harvard professor and innovation and creativity consultant, and Walter Swap, former psychology professor and dean at Tufts, examine the development of "Deep Smarts"—the explicit and tacit knowledge that extraordinarily competent people possess. Deep smarts allows them to both see the big picture and dive deep into the details of problems and decisions. Since it resides in the heads of individual employees, this expert knowledge can be a difficult asset to manage if they retire or leave the organization. Leonard and Swap discuss how to cultivate deep smarts in individual employees and in the organization as a whole.

The ability to learn from experience and adapt rapidly, both on the individual and the organizational levels, is a critical skill in a quickly changing business environment. In the classic article "The Leader's New Work: Building Learning Organizations," Peter Senge, a former engineer and the director of the Society for Organizational Learning at MIT, argues that companies have to surface and examine their mental maps—the assumptions on which decisions are based—in order to learn and survive. Senge describes what leaders must do to build learning organizations and provides many practical suggestions about the skills and tools they need to develop in themselves and others.

DEEP SMARTS*

Dorothy Leonard

Walter Swap

When a person sizes up a complex situation and comes to a rapid decision that proves to be not just good but brilliant, you think, "That was smart." After you've watched him do this a few times, you realize you're in the presence of something special. It's not raw brainpower, though that helps. It's not emotional intelligence, either, though that, too, is often involved. It's deep smarts, the stuff that produces that mysterious quality, good judgment. Those who have deep smarts can see the whole picture and yet zoom in on a specific problem others haven't been able to diagnose. Almost intuitively, they can make the right decision, at the right level, with the right people. The manager who understands when and how to move into a new international market, the executive who knows just what kind of talk to give when her organization is in crisis, the technician who can track a product failure back to an interaction between independently produced elements—these are people whose knowledge would be hard to purchase on the open market. Their insight is based more on know-how than on facts; it comprises a system view as well as expertise in individual areas. Deep smarts are not philosophical—they're not "wisdom" in that sense—but they're as close to wisdom as business gets.

Throughout your organization, there are people with deep smarts. Their judgment and knowledge—both explicit and tacit—are stored in their heads and hands. Their knowledge is essential. The organization cannot progress without it. You will be a more effective manager if you understand what deep smarts are, how they are cultivated, and how they can be transferred from one person to another.

Very few organizations manage this asset well, perhaps because it's difficult to pin down and measure. Such neglect is risky. Individuals develop practical, often organization-specific expertise over the course of many years but can walk out the door in only a minute, taking their smarts with them. As the baby-boom-retirement tsunami approaches, lots of valuable employees and leaders will do precisely that. By 2006, for example, half of NASA's workforce will be eligible for retirement. It's not easy to harvest future retirees' knowledge, since much of it depends on context. Those with deep smarts know your business, your customers, and your product lines, both overall and in depth. And much of their insight is neither documented nor even articulated. You may not know you have lost it until you feel the cold breezes of ignorance blowing through the cracks in your product or service architecture.

Smaller-scale losses occur when employees with deep smarts are transferred to new locations, functions, or roles. A marketing director we know was promoted to a general management position, which encompassed new functions and required new skills. Her predecessor was scheduled to be on a plane to take a new position in Thailand within two days of the promotion, so she needed to learn about engineering, manufacturing, finance, and sales—fast. She couldn't possibly pick up the necessary skills in such a short time, but her superiors didn't even consider the costs of forcing her to muddle through on her own. Much of her predecessor's knowledge was lost.

When veterans leave, it is painful to lose strategic capabilities partly because growing them in the first place is extraordinarily challenging. Deep smarts are experience based. They can't be produced overnight or imported readily, as many companies pursuing a new strategy have discovered to their dismay. But with the right techniques, this sort of knowledge can be taught—if a company is willing to invest. Brad Anderson, the CEO of Best Buy, recently decided that the future success of his company depended on building an internal capability to innovate continuously. His employees were bright, hardworking, and terrific at delivering on set goals, but innovation had never been part of their job. Exhortation alone would not change the DNA of the organization. Anderson needed to have some deep smarts about the innovation process transferred into the company. He hired the consulting firm Strategos to coach a cohort of employees through a six-month innovation journey. He hoped participants would gain enough experience to start embedding innovative practices throughout the organization.

Best Buy's deliberate decision to build companywide expertise is unusual. In most organizations, deep smarts develop more by chance than by intent—and often in spite of management practices rather than because of them. Leaders toss people willy-nilly into new situations, incurring the costs of trial-and-error learning instead of those associated with more carefully planned transitions. But it is neither effective nor efficient to cultivate experience-based know-how in such an ad hoc fashion or to rely on a company's existing processes for transferring knowledge. Most organizational practices are not grounded in a fundamental understanding of how people learn. Furthermore, most companies' training and development programs are designed to transfer explicit technical or managerial knowledge—but not deep smarts.

We learned to appreciate the importance of deep smarts when we studied how novices acquire complex managerial skills. Over two years, we conducted research at 35 start-up companies in the United States and Asia, looking most closely at how experienced coaches helped novice entrepreneurs. We also examined a number of mature organizations, including Jet Propulsion Laboratory in Pasadena, California, and Best Buy, in which managers were struggling with how to cultivate business wisdom. We interviewed more than 200 people (including each of the novice entrepreneurs and their coaches) twice, a year apart; sat in on dozens of meetings; shadowed one experienced leader as he made rounds to various protégés in India; and reviewed scores of videotapes made by people undergoing the intensive knowledge transfer effort at Best Buy. In the following pages, we draw on this field research to illustrate how organizations can develop and sustain profound institutional knowledge among their employees.

How Did He *Do* That?

Let's look in particular at two examples of deep smarts—one technical and the other managerial.

In the 1980s, two companies were competing for a multibillion-dollar, decades-long government contract for tactical missiles. Neither had a performance advantage. The stalemate was broken by a scientist in one of the companies who was not a member of the project team. His reputation as a technical wizard (based on more than 20 years of experience developing missiles) was such that when he called a meeting of the primary project participants, they all came. For several hours, he enthralled them with a detailed proposal for design changes that he had worked out over a single week of dedicated effort. Without notes, he walked them through the redesign of an entire weapon. To put the extensive software, wiring, and hardware changes he suggested into production, as many as 400 people would have to work full time for up to a year and a half—but the expert's audience saw immediately that the modifications would create tremendous competitive advantage. His proposal precipitated a frenzy of activity, and his company won the contract. More than 20 years later, it is still reaping the harvest sown by this man with deep smarts.

Deep smarts are most easily recognized when, as in the previous example, they are based on technical knowledge. Managerial deep smarts are harder to identify, but we know that people who have them are compelling leaders. Take the case of a CEO who, in an unusual reversal of roles, had to talk his board of directors out of allowing the company to miss its earnings commitment. In early 1997, Intuit had just sold off its bill-paying operations. The board met to consider a new strategic direction. Because revenues were down, the sentiment around the boardroom table was that the company would have to miss its earnings commitments not only for that quarter but for the foreseeable future. Board members were further resigned to a drop in stock price when the earnings were announced.

CEO Bill Campbell argued passionately against this fatalistic viewpoint. Wall Street analysts, he said, had already discounted the slower growth and the resulting decline in the top line. Lower revenues would not hurt the stock price. But deliberately deciding midway through the quarter to miss earnings was contrary to good management practices. Perhaps even more important, Campbell pointed out, if the stock dropped, employee options would be worthless—and some critical individuals might well leave the company. Such defections could hurt Intuit even more than the financial blow per se. It was pure baloney that they could not make the bottom line! He knew how to cut costs—and where to start.

The board members were persuaded by Campbell, and the next few months proved him right. Managers cut expenses and hit their quarterly financial targets, and the stock stayed steady. The course set out in the board meeting was successful for Intuit, and Campbell's promise to employees that the stock would double within a year was fulfilled. What smarts did Campbell have that allowed him to make the right decision—and to sway his board? He knew, of course, the details of his company's operations well enough to pinpoint areas for potential cost cutting. But he also understood the big picture, the financial environment within which he operated; he knew how resilient Intuit could be and how to release the company's untapped energies. He could foresee both Wall Street's reactions and those of his employees. And finally, he understood group dynamics and the personalities of his board members well enough to offer persuasive arguments.

Both the missile expert and Bill Campbell demonstrated an ability to do systems thinking *and* to dive into the details. The former, who redesigned a whole weapon by himself, knew a lot about each piece of software and hardware—but also about how they had to interact and which parts might need to be suboptimized in order to make the whole system perform better. Campbell could pull operational details about his company out of his head, but he also was emotionally intelligent about his organization as a collection of people and understood the larger financial milieu in which Intuit functioned.

The Science Behind Deep Smarts

Experience is the obvious reason that such deeply knowledgeable individuals make swift, smart decisions. We would all rather fly with a pilot who has taken off, flown, and (especially) landed in all kinds of extreme weather than with one who has always enjoyed smooth conditions. Similarly, if we're about to go under anesthesia, we don't want to hear the surgeon exclaim, "Wow—never seen one of *these* before!" And when launching a new product, we would prefer a boss who understands design, marketing, and manufacturing over one who sees the world through only one lens. But what is it about experience that separates novices from experts?

Think about something you are really, really good at—chess or cooking or interviewing job candidates. Chances are, if you are not just competent, but truly expert, it took ten years or more to develop that expertise—in which time you've come across countless different situations. With so many of them under your belt, you have likely found some common ground and discovered a few rules of thumb that usually work: "Control the center of the board" in chess, for instance, or "Err on the side of letting people go early rather than late" in management. However, as an expert, you have the perspective to go beyond generalizations and respond to unusual situations. You know when facile rules don't apply, because you've seen so many exceptions. When confronted with a setback or a surprise, you can modify your course of action by combining elements from your menu of familiar options. In short, you can exploit an extensive *experience repertoire.*

Experts who encounter a wide variety of situations over many years accumulate a storehouse of knowledge and, with it, the ability to reason swiftly and without a lot of conscious effort. Those with keen managerial or technical intuition can rapidly determine whether current cases fit any patterns that have emerged in the past; they're also adept at coherently (though not always consciously) assembling disparate elements into a whole that makes sense. They can identify both trends and anomalies that would escape the notice of less-experienced individuals. When you ask your financial wizard how she decided so quickly that there was something wrong with the numbers on a page, she may not be able to tell you exactly how she homed in on the odd figure. In fact, when asked to explain a decision, experts often cannot re-create all the pathways their brains checked out and so cannot give a carefully reasoned answer. They chalk up to gut *feel* what is really a form of gut *knowledge.*

Of course, the experts aren't always right. Their confidence can lead to myopia or arrogance, blinding them to truly novel solutions or causing them to reject contributions from others. They can underestimate the extent to which knowledge is actually a set of beliefs and assumptions. When a physician confidently prescribes an acid suppressant for a woman who is in fact having a heart attack, not indigestion, he may be fitting her symptoms into a schema built on research about men. No chest pains—ergo, no heart attack. Only as research reveals that women's heart attack symptoms differ from men's, and as medicine builds enough knowledge to characterize these differences, will the physician be prepared to recognize the danger of his snap judgment.

Making Sure the Catcher is Ready Before You Pitch

Many times in our lives, we need either to transfer our knowledge to someone else (a child, a junior colleague, a peer) or to access bits of wisdom accumulated in someone else's cranium. But before we can even begin to plan such a transfer, we must understand how our brains process incoming information.

What we already have in our heads determines how we assimilate new experiences. Without receptors—hooks on which to hang new information—we may not even perceive and process the information. It's like being sent boxes of documents but having no idea how they could or should be organized. Scientists who study specialized functions of the brain note that specific areas link our perceptions to long-term memory. For someone to capture complex, experience-based knowledge, his brain has to contain some frameworks, domain knowledge, or prior experiences

PASSIVE RECEPTION							ACTIVE LEARNING
Directives, Presentations, Lectures	Rules of Thumb	Stories with a Moral	Socratic Questioning	Guided Practice	Guided Observation	Guided Problem Solving	Guided Experimentation

FIGURE 1   **Moving Toward Deep Smarts**

to which current inputs can connect. Otherwise, the messages and information sent remain relatively meaningless suggestions. To a person who is unfamiliar with finance, the following advice is merely a string of words: "If you borrow money to buy back a lot of stock, you increase return on equity, but not in a way that those hawks at Moody's would approve of." Take a non-business example: "What three-dimensional avatar would you like to be in the next MUD you enter?" To many people, that question is almost unintelligible—but not to an online gamer who has represented herself in cyberspace as a three-dimensional object (an avatar) while playing in a multiuser domain (MUD). Even when the terms are explained, however, a non-gamer will not know what criteria to use in selecting an avatar. Someone who has not played such games lacks the receptors to process the query intelligently.

This cognitive limitation exists at an organizational level as well. When GE Healthcare sets up or transfers operations from one location to another, for instance, it appoints an experienced manager and team to be the "pitcher" and a team in the receiving plant to be the "catcher." These two teams work together, often over a period of years, first at the pitcher's location and then at the catcher's. To ensure a smooth transition, the pitcher team needs to be sensitive to the catcher team's level of experience and familiarity with GE Healthcare procedures. When a veteran operations manager arrived at a growing GE Healthcare plant in China, the local team was getting ready to move raw materials from the manufacturing facility into a warehouse. The operations manager could see numerous potential problems with the chosen site, but he knew that simply vetoing it would have transferred little knowledge. So he helped the team develop a list of critical-to-quality (CTQ) factors against which to evaluate potential sites. (Although this analytic process is standard operating procedure at GE, the Chinese plant hadn't adopted it yet.) The list included such factors as proximity to the manufacturing plant, easy access for large trucks, road conditions between facilities, and basic amenities for employees. List in hand, the catchers visited the selected site and could see that it met few of their criteria. They then understood the reasons for using the CTQ model for even apparently simple choices; they had a framework and some basic experience on which to build future decisions.

In many situations requiring the transfer of deep smarts, new people are thrown in to sink or swim. Sometimes they make it. They're often quick studies and have other adaptive skills. If they come into the job with few preconceptions about what does and doesn't work, they may suggest smart changes. So a deliberate decision *not* to transfer knowledge to the newcomer can have advantages. But usually, the sink-or-swim strategy is inefficient and—more important—ineffective. It is far better to deliberately create receptors by providing frameworks and tools or other types of mental structures to which experience can be tied.

Transfer Techniques

Receptors, of course, are not enough. The most valuable part of deep smarts is the tacit know-how (and often, know-who) that a person has built up over years of experience. This knowledge cannot be easily documented and handed over in a filing cabinet or on a CD. Managers are sophisticated; they recognize that documentation and software are inadequate to capture deep knowledge. Why, then, do they persist in relying on a thick deck of PowerPoint slides, a Web site of best practices, a repository of project reports, online training, or even in-person lectures for the transfer? Even the smartest people have difficulty gaining insight from such materials, because so much of the knowledge they need is tied to specific contexts and has tacit dimensions.

The central paradox in transferring deep smarts is that constantly reinventing the wheel is inefficient, but people learn only by doing. So what's the best way to get

Table 1	Guided Experience versus Other Types of Learning

Guided experience—learning by doing with feedback from a knowledge coach—creates deep understanding. It is especially valuable when:

Situations	Examples
The skills to be learned involve interpersonal relations, so there is no set of absolute steps but rather an array of possible responses to the actions and emotions of others.	• working with a board of directors • negotiating a merger or acquisition • handling a talented prima donna
There are many tacit dimensions to the skills, so even an expert may not be able to make them all explicit.	• closing a sale • dissipating tension in a meeting • creating a new perfume or best-selling wine
The knowledge is context specific so it's appropriate to be adaptive rather than apply formulas.	• managing in a foreign culture • manufacturing with proprietary, plant-specific equipment • handling sexual harassment cases
The situation is new, so there is great uncertainty.	• launching a new service product in a new market using a new mode of manufacturing

Rules create a mental scaffold on which to hang experience. They help people make sense of their experience but do not serve as a substitute for it. People with deep smarts will know exceptions to the rules in their domain and will feel comfortable augmenting them. But guidelines can be appropriate and helpful as a starting point especially when:

Situations	Examples
The skills to be learned are largely cognitive, generate little emotion, and are relatively independent of individual differences.	• accounting practices • statistical analysis of market segments
There are explicit, communicable ideas and models.	• strategic analysis using Michael Porter's "five forces" model • financial analysis of a business plan
The processes are unvarying and relatively independent of context.	• Six Sigma applications • the running of democratic meetings
The domain is well understood and expired, and there is little uncertainty about what works.	• high-volume assembly line manufacturing • product positioning on shelves

them up to speed? In our research, we identified a number of techniques used by what we call knowledge coaches—experts who were motivated to share some of their deep smarts with protégés. While some played the traditional mentor role of helping their protégés navigate organizations or providing personal advice, the coaches primarily served as teachers transmitting experience-based expertise.

As the exhibit "Moving Toward Deep Smarts" suggests, approaches vary considerably—and predictably—in how effectively they address the deep smarts paradox. Most of these modes are well understood. A number of books have been written about storytelling, for example, as a potent way to convey nuanced information. And Socratic questioning is pretty common. Queries such as "How do you know?" and "What would happen if . . . ?" stimulate reflection and active learning. However, the learning-by-doing methods are not as familiar to many readers. They require active engagement from both the teacher and the student, they take time, and they usually happen one-on-one.

Recall that deep smarts are based on an extensive experience repertoire. While it's true that merely describing experiences to people (or telling them what to do or giving them rules) may create some mental receptors upon which to hang experience, the tacit dimensions of an expert's deep smarts have to be *re-created* to take hold. That is, the novice needs to discover the expert's know-how through practice, observation, problem solving, and experimentation—all under the direction of a knowledge coach. In the process, the smarts of both the expert and the novice are deepened.

GUIDED PRACTICE The old adage is right: Practice *does* make perfect—or at least better. But mindless repetition can hone the wrong skills. Better is mindful, reflective practice, in which outcomes are assessed and the method adjusted appropriately. But

Table 2   Characteristics and Limitations of Deep Smarts

Sometimes an expert is the key actor in a managerial setting. Sometimes a novice is. Give them both a managerial task, and they'll approach it in characteristically different ways. And the experts aren't always right—they run risks, too.

Tasks	Novice	Expert	Expert's Limitations
Making decisions	Needs to review all facts and choose deliberately among alternatives	Makes decisions swiftly, efficiently without reviewing basic facts	Overconfidence; expert may ignore relevant data
Considering context	Relies on rules of thumb that minimize context	Takes context into account when solving problems	Difficulty transferring expert knowledge, because it is highly contextualized
Extrapolating information	Lacks receptors and thus has limited basis for extrapolation	Can extrapolate from a novel situation to find a solution	May base solution on inappropriate pattern
Exercising discrimination	Uses rules of thumb to obscure fine distinctions	Can make fine distinctions	May not communicate well to a novice who lacks receptors to understand distinctions
Being aware of knowledge gaps	Doesn't know what he doesn't know	Knows when rules don't apply	May assume expertise where none exists
Recognizing patterns	Has limited experience from which to draw patterns	Has large inventory of patterns drawn from experience	May be no better than novice when no patterns exist
Using tacit knowledge	Relies largely on explicit knowledge	Uses extensive tacit knowledge to drive decision making	May have a hard time articulating and thus transferring tacit knowledge

best of all is practice under the tutelage of someone who can guide the reflection and provide performance feedback. This is where an experienced coach comes in.

At SAIC, a consulting firm in San Diego that works primarily with the U.S. government, consultants learn their trade from a seasoned pro first by watching the expert help a client pick up a particular knowledge management process, next by leading a client session and receiving feedback from the coach, and then by teaching another consultant how to work with a client. This "see one, lead one, teach one" approach is one of SAIC's most useful knowledge transfer tools.

GUIDED OBSERVATION Another powerful technique, guided observation, can be used for two very different purposes: to re-create deep smarts and to challenge ossified assumptions that may be based on outdated experience.

If your goal is to re-create deep smarts, you can have a "catcher" shadow an experienced, skilled colleague and arrange for the two to meet afterward to discuss what the catcher observed. A top consultant was once asked where and how he learned his skills in closing deals with clients. He explained that when he joined the company, an elder statesman in the firm asked him to sit in on client meetings. "You don't have to say a word," the older consultant told him. "Just listen and learn." The junior consultant rightly took that invitation as more than a suggestion and sat at the back of the room. After the meetings, he and the older consultant discussed what had occurred. "I learned more from those debriefs," he said, "than in four years at my prior company and two years of business school."

The combination of shadowing and feedback sessions works because, as we have said, deep smarts are based largely on pattern recognition and are highly contextual. Because there are so many tacit dimensions to this sort of insight, the individual possessing it will not always realize what she knows until a particular challenge calls her knowledge forth. This makes it difficult for her to give her protégé absolute, detailed directives to follow in general. She might not be able to tell a novice what the response should be to a particular situation, but she can show him.

What if the issue is not so much teaching new skills but convincing individuals to unlearn what they take for granted? We can't deepen our smarts without challenging our beliefs about our clients, our organizations, our services. Field trips—playing anthropologist for a few days to observe behaviors at other sites or companies—can help. Exposed to foreign ways of thinking and behaving, people not only extend their experience repertoire but are often shocked into questioning their own complacent understanding of the world.

When consultants from Strategos guided teams from Best Buy through the intricate steps of identifying, exploring, and prototyping new business opportunities, they first challenged the team members' assumptions about the company's uses of technology to attract typical Best Buy customers—young males who purchase powerful, feature-rich electronics. The consultants then sent team members on the road. Best Buy's Toby Nord took a trip with some colleagues to American Girl Place in Chicago that proved invaluable, though initially unsettling. American Girl specializes in a line of dolls representing historical eras. More of a destination than a retail outlet, the store features doll-centric activities: You can get a new hairdo for your doll, for example, or have tea and scones at the American Girl Cafe, where dolls sit at the table. Nord and his male colleagues were pushed out of their comfort zone. But Nord realized that the dolls at American Girl Place were a kind of platform for intergenerational socializing among grandmothers, mothers, and daughters. The store was entertaining, and its business focused tightly on a community built for a given demographic: women and girls.

The Best Buy team combined observations from this trip to Chicago and others to Mexico City, the Amish countryside in Indiana, and Seoul, South Korea, and began to see behavior patterns. All these visits stimulated thinking about social, communal behavior focused on a platform, product, or technology. The team began to generate ideas for products and services that would offer an experience or a social happening. Inspired by the groups of teens they saw in Seoul gathering to play video games, the Best Buy folks came up with a youth-centered entertainment concept: a "PCBang," where teenagers and people in their early twenties (a demographic group younger than Best Buy's typical consumers) will be able to play computer games together and socialize.

GUIDED PROBLEM SOLVING Guided problem solving serves different purposes and requires more active engagement from the protégé than does guided observation. A knowledge coach may or may not already know the answer to a problem. But either way, if he works on it with his protégé, the novice can learn how to approach the problem. That is, the knowledge coach transfers know-how more than know-what. During their residencies, newly minted physicians convert their book smarts into deeper, experience-based smarts as they work beside veteran doctors over a period of years.

Apprenticeships in business are less formalized—but they do occur in companies where managers are alert to the need for re-creating tacit knowledge. In an engineering company, a highly experienced design engineer was asked to train a younger colleague in the kind of systems thinking for which the older man was renowned. One of the senior engineer's most valued skills was the ability to bring multiple perspectives to any design—not just engineering knowledge about every component (software and hardware) in the complex systems the company manufactured, but also an understanding of how the systems were to be produced. He was famous for detecting and avoiding potential assembly problems and performance shortfalls. To transfer his understanding of the overall product architecture and his respect for manufacturing constraints, he had his protégé go down to the assembly line and work on problems with a test engineer for several months. The senior engineer joined many of these problem-solving sessions, adding information that the test technician lacked, such as historic customer biases and preferences. While the protégé gained specific knowledge about component parts, the more important know-how transferred was the ability to look at the whole system, see how the interfaces worked, and understand how different functional priorities led to specific design flaws. The protégé also got to know and respect the knowledge of people working on the assembly line. This experience enhanced his organizational know-who, altered his belief systems, and contributed to his technical expertise.

Guided problem solving combines many of the best features of the transfer techniques mentioned previously: focusing attention, sharpening process skills, giving feedback, providing an opportunity to mimic an expert, engaging the learner actively in developing her own deep smarts, and building an experience repertoire.

GUIDED EXPERIMENTATION In the first few years of their lives, children learn at a fantastic rate, partly because they are constantly experimenting. (Of course, that's what makes parents of toddlers so nervous.) Too often in organizations, we assume that experimentation is both a risky and an expensive way of learning. It doesn't have to be. The best entrepreneurial coaches in our study of 35 start-ups encouraged their charges to set up deliberate but modest experiments. This was the case with ActivePhoto, a company based on a software system that instantly downloads and catalogs digital photographs for use in a business process. In search of its best market, ActivePhoto initially considered three promising customer bases: public emergency services, insurance claims processing, and online auctioning. The tiny seven-person firm would ultimately have to choose one or two markets, but in its first few months of life it experimented with all three. Pilot studies, along with discussions with knowledge coaches, allowed the ActivePhoto people to evaluate the results of each experiment and quickly eliminate the first market.

Most retail companies use pilot markets to test new products—rolling them out in one area of the country before going national. When Whirlpool was considering custom-built appliances, the company was advised to find out whether customers were interested and whether customization would generate more market share or more profit. In a fairly simple and inexpensive experiment, Whirlpool selected two retail outlets in each of two cities (Dallas and Philadelphia) in which to set up tests for custom appliances. To draw crowds, the stores funded local advertising campaigns ("Come build your own Whirlpool refrigerator down at XYZ Appliances"). Computer kiosks in the stores allowed customers to choose from a variety of appliance features, and workers in the back busily assembled what people ordered. What did Whirlpool learn? As expected, customizing helped in the share game, at least for these four outlets. But the experiment also produced an unanticipated outcome: Customers ordered more features—approximately $70 more per refrigerator.

Coaches can offer good advice about where and how much to experiment— and more important, they can improve a team's attitude toward adding to deep smarts through experimentation. The Toyota Production System is admired for its efficient manufacturing and has attracted imitators worldwide. But researchers who have investigated the deep smarts underlying TPS have discovered that the explicit techniques so widely copied (kanban cards, andon cords, just-in-time inventory delivery) do not account for the true advantage that Toyota has. The real secret to Toyota's success is the mind-set of its employees: to constantly hypothesize about possible improvements and test those hypotheses in experiments. (See "Decoding the DNA of the Toyota Production System," by Steven Spear and H. Kent Bowen, in the September–October 1999 issue of *HBR*.) This sort of mind-set is possible in any industry, including service. At any given time, Bank of America's innovation and development teams are conducting more than two dozen experiments in operating branches, such as "virtual tellers," video monitors displaying financial and investment news, computer stations where customers can upload images of their canceled checks, and kiosks staffed by associates ready to open accounts or process loan applications.

But Does It Cost Too Much?

In our world of fast brain food, one might think that guided experience is passé at best—or at least too costly. We have heard an executive from a well-run *Fortune* 100 company say, "The days of apprenticeship are over. We don't have enough people to mentor newcomers." Many who share this view will nonetheless willingly spend millions of dollars and years of effort on data repositories and formal training. We certainly do not wish to suggest that all such investments are wasteful. But we're convinced that guided experience is the only way to cultivate deep smarts—and that managers need to be realistic about how much tacit, context-specific knowledge can be created or transferred through other means.

Fortunately, guided experience can deliver two benefits simultaneously and thus is not as costly as it might seem: first, a lasting asset in the form of transferred know-how, and second, delivery of a new business process, product idea, or capability. The learning happens on the job, so the business situations are real and relevant to today's problems. SAIC's training of U.S. Army personnel in the "peer assist" technique, for example, not only transfers process knowledge but does so in the context of a real problem—how to improve the performance of contract officers. Similarly, Strategos consultants were not only training Whirlpool and Best Buy employees to develop innovation processes; they were also showing these clients how to identify new business opportunities.

Guided experience increases value exponentially—it promotes dual-purpose learning and builds on all that we know about how people accumulate and retain knowledge. How can companies afford *not* to invest in it?

THE LEADER'S NEW WORK: BUILDING LEARNING ORGANIZATIONS*

Peter M. Senge

Human beings are designed for learning. No one has to teach an infant to walk, or talk, or master the spatial relationships needed to stack eight building blocks that don't topple. Children come fully equipped with an insatiable drive to explore and experiment. Unfortunately the primary institutions of our society are oriented predominately toward controlling rather than learning, rewarding individuals for performing for others rather than for cultivating their natural curiosity and impulse to learn. The young child entering school discovers quickly that the name of the game is getting the right answer and avoiding mistakes—a mandate no less compelling to the aspiring manager.

"Our prevailing system of management has destroyed our people," writes W. Edwards Deming, leader in the quality movement.[1] "People are born with intrinsic motivation, self-esteem, dignity, curiosity to learn, joy in learning. The forces of destruction begin with toddlers—a prize for the best Halloween costume, grades in school, gold stars, and up on through the university. On the job, people, teams, divisions are ranked—reward for the one at the top, punishment at the bottom. MBO, quotas, incentive pay, business plans, put together separately, division by division, cause further loss, unknown and unknowable."

Ironically, by focusing on performing for someone else's approval, corporations create the very conditions that predestine them to mediocre performance. Over the long run, superior performance depends on superior learning. A Shell study showed that, according to former planning director Arie de Geus, "a full one-third of the *Fortune* 500 industrials listed in 1970 have vanished by 1983."[2] Today, the average lifetime of the largest industrial enterprises is probably less than *half* the average life-time of a person in an industrial society. On the other hand, de Geus and his colleagues at Shell also found a small number of companies that survived for seventy-five years or longer. Interestingly, the key to their survival was the ability to run "experiments in the margin," to continually explore new businesses and organizational opportunities that create potential new sources of growth.

If anything, the need for understanding how organizations learn and accelerating that learning is greater today than ever before. The old days when a Henry Ford, Alfred Sloan, or Tom Watson *learned for the organization* are gone. In an increasingly dynamic, interdependent, and unpredictable world, it is simply no longer possible for anyone to "figure it all out at the top." The old model, "the top thinks and the local acts,"

*Reprinted with permission from *MIT Sloan Management Review* 48(2) (winter 2007): 65–71.

must now give way to integrating thinking and acting at all levels. While the challenge is great, so is the potential payoff. "The person who figures out how to harness the collective genius of the people in his or her organization," according to former Citibank CEO Walter Wriston, "is going to blow the competition away."

Adaptive Learning and Generative Learning

The prevailing view of learning organizations emphasizes increased adaptability. Given the accelerating pace of change, or so the standard view goes, "the most successful corporation of the 1990s," according to *Fortune,* "will be something called a learning organization, a consummately adaptive enterprise."[3] As the Shell study shows, examples of traditional authoritarian bureaucracies that responded too slowly to survive in changing business environments are legion.

But increasing adaptiveness is only the first stage in moving toward learning organizations. The impulse to learn in children goes deeper than desire to respond and adapt more effectively to environmental change. The impulse to learn, at its heart, is an impulse to be generative, to expand our capability. This is why leading corporations are focusing on *generative* learning, which is about creating, as well as *adaptive* learning, which is about coping.[4]

The total quality movement in Japan illustrates the evolution from adaptive to generative learning. With its emphasis on continuous experimentation and feedback, the total quality movement has been the first wave in building learning organizations. But Japanese firms' view of serving the customer has evolved. In the early years of total quality, the focus was on "fitness to standard," making a product reliably so that it would do what its designers intended it to do and what the firm told its customers it would do. Then came a focus on "fitness to need," understanding better what the customer wanted and then providing products that reliably *met* those needs. Today, leading edge firms seek to understand and meet the "latent need" of customers— what customers might truly value but have never experienced or would never think to ask for. As one Detroit executive commented recently, "You could never produce the Mazda Miata solely from market research. It required a leap of imagination to see what the customer *might* want."[5]

Generative learning, unlike adaptive learning, requires new ways of looking at the world, whether in understanding customers or in understanding how to better manage a business. For years, U.S. manufacturers sought competitive advantage in aggressive controls on inventories, incentive against overproduction, and rigid adherence to production forecasts. Despite these incentives, their performance was eventually eclipsed by Japanese firms who saw the challenges of manufacturing differently. They realized that eliminating delays in the production process was the key to reducing instability and improving cost, productivity, and service. They worked to build networks of relationships with trusted suppliers and to redesign physical production processes so as to reduce delays in materials procurement, production setup, and in-process inventory—a much higher-leverage approach to improving both cost and customer loyalty.

As Boston Consulting Group's George Stalk has observed, the Japanese saw the significance of delays because they see the process of order entry, production scheduling, materials procurement, production, and distribution *as an integrated system.* "What distorts the system so badly is time," observed Stalk—the multiple delays between events and responses. "These distortions reverberate throughout the system, producing disruptions, waste, and inefficiency."[6] Generative learning requires seeing the systems that control events. When we fail to grasp the systematic source of problems, we are left to "push on" symptoms rather than eliminate underlying causes. The best we can ever do is adaptive learning.

The Leaders' New Work

"I talk with people all over the country about learning organizations, and the response is always very positive," says William O'Brien, CEO of the Hanover Insurance companies. "If this type of organization is so widely preferred, why don't people create such organizations? I think the answer is leadership. People have no real comprehension of the type of commitment it requires to build such an organization."[7]

Our traditional view of leaders—as special people who set the direction, make the key decisions, and energize the troops—is deeply rooted in an individualistic and nonsystemic worldview, especially in the West, leaders are *heroes*—great men (and occasionally women) who rise to the fore in times of crisis. So long as such myths prevail, they reinforce a focus on short-term events and charismatic heroes rather than on systematic forces and collective learning.

Leadership in learning organizations centers on subtler and ultimately more important work. In a learning organization, leaders' roles differ dramatically from that of the charismatic decision maker. Leaders are designers, teachers, stewards. These roles require new skills: the ability to build shared vision, to bring to the surface and challenge prevailing mental models, and to foster more systematic patterns of thinking. In short, leaders in learning organizations are responsible for *building organizations* where people are continually expanding their capabilities to shape their future—that is, leaders are responsible for learning.

Creative Tension: the Integrating Principle

Leadership in a learning organization starts with the principle of creative tension.[8] Creative tension comes from seeing clearly where we want to be, our "vision," and telling the truth about where we are, our "current reality." The gap between the two generates a natural tension. (See Figure 1.)

Creative tension can be resolved in two basic ways: by raising current reality toward the vision, or by lowering the vision toward current reality. Individuals, groups, and organizations who learn how to work with creative tension learn how to use the energy it generates to move reality more reliably toward their visions.

The principle of creative tension has long been recognized by leaders. Martin Luther King, Jr. once said, "Just as Socrates felt that it was necessary to create a

Vision

Current reality

FIGURE 1 The Principle of Creative Tension

tension in the mind, so that individuals could rise from the bondage of myths and half truths . . . so must we . . . create the kind of tension in society that will help men rise from the dark depths of prejudice and racism."[9]

Without vision there is no creative tension. Creative tension cannot be generated from current reality alone. All the analysis in the world will never generate a vision. Many who are otherwise qualified to lead fail to do so because they try to substitute analysis for vision. They believe that, if only people understood current reality, they would surely feel the motivation to change. They are then disappointed to discover that people "resist" the personal and organizational changes that must be made to alter reality. What they never grasp is that the natural energy for changing reality comes from holding a picture of what might be that is more important to people than what is.

But creative tension cannot be generated from vision alone; it demands an accurate picture of current reality as well. Just as King had a dream, so too did he continually strive to "dramatize the shameful conditions" of racism and prejudice so that they could no longer be ignored. Vision without an understanding of current reality will more likely foster cynicism than creativity. The principle of creative tension teaches that *an accurate picture of current reality is just as important as a compelling picture of a desired future.*

Leading through creative tension is different than solving problems. In problem solving, the energy for change comes from attempting to get away from an aspect of current reality that is undesirable. With creative tension the energy for change comes from the vision, from what we want to create, juxtaposed with current reality. While the distinction may seem small, the consequences are not. Many people and organizations find themselves motivated to change only when their problems are bad enough to cause them to change. This works for a while, but the change process runs out of steam as soon as the problems driving the change become less pressing. With problem solving, the motivation for change is extrinsic. With creative tension, the motivation is intrinsic. This distinction mirrors the distinction between adaptive and generative learning.

New Roles

The traditional authoritarian image of the leader as "the boss calling the shots" has been recognized as oversimplified and inadequate for some time. According to Edgar Schein, "Leadership is intertwined with culture formation." Building an organization's culture and shaping its evolution is the "unique and essential function" of leadership.[10] In a learning organization, the critical roles of leadership—designer, teacher, and steward have antecedents in the ways leaders have contributed to building organizations in the past. But each role takes on a new meaning in the learning organizations and, as will be seen in the following sections, demands new skills and tools.

Leader as Designer

Imagine that your organization is an ocean liner and that you are "the leader." What is your role?

I have asked this question of groups of managers many times. The most common answer, not surprisingly, is "the captain." Others say, "The navigator, setting the direction." Still others say, "The helmsman, actually controlling the direction," or, "The engineer down there stroking the fire, providing energy," or, "The social director, making sure everybody's enrolled, involved, and communicating." While these are legitimate leadership roles, there is another which, in many ways, eclipses them all in importance. Yet rarely does anyone mention it.

The neglected leadership role is the *designer* of the ship. No one has a more sweeping influence than the designer. What good does it do for the captain to say,

"Turn starboard 30 degrees," when the designer has built a rudder that will only turn to port, or which takes six hours to turn to starboard? It's fruitless to be the leader in an organization that is poorly designed.

The functions of design, or what some have called "social architecture," are rarely visible; they take place behind the scenes. The consequences that appear today are the result of work done long in the past, and work today will show its benefits far in the future. Those who aspire to lead out of a desire to control, or gain fame, or simply to be at the center of the action, will find little to attract them to the quiet design work of leadership.

But what, specifically, is involved in organizational design? "Organizational design is widely misconstrued as moving around boxes and lines," says Hanover's O'Brien. "The first task of organization design concerns designing the governing ideas of purpose, vision, and core values by which people will live." Few acts of leadership have a more enduring impact on an organization than building a foundation of purpose and core values.

In 1982, Johnson & Johnson found itself facing a corporate nightmare when bottles of its bestselling Tylenol were tampered with, resulting in several deaths. The corporation's immediate response was to pull all Tylenol off the shelves of retail outlets. Thirty-one million capsules were destroyed, even though they were tested and found safe. Although the immediate cost was significant, no other action was possible given the firm's credo. Authored almost 40 years earlier by president Robert Wood Johnson, Johnson & Johnson's credo states that permanent success is possible only when modern industry realizes that:

- service to its customers comes first;
- service to its employees and management comes second;
- service to the community comes third; and
- service to its stockholders, last.

Such statements might seem like motherhood and apple pie to those who have not seen the way a clear sense of purpose and values can affect key business decisions. Johnson & Johnson's crisis management in this case was based on that credo. It was simple, it was right, and it worked.

If governing ideas constitute the first design task of leadership, the second design task involves the policies, strategies, and structures that translate guiding ideas into business decisions. Leadership theorist Philip Selznick calls policy and structure the "institutional embodiment of purpose."[11] "Policy making (the rules that guide decisions) ought to be separated from decision making," says Jay Forrester.[12] "Otherwise, short-term pressures will usurp time from policy creation."

Traditionally, writers like Selznick and Forrester have tended to see policy making and implementation as the work of a small number of senior managers. But that view is changing. Both the dynamic business environment and the mandate of the learning organization to engage people at all levels now make it clear that this second design task is more subtle. Henry Mintzberg has argued that strategy is less a rational plan arrived at in the abstract and implemented throughout the organization than an "emergent phenomenon." Successful organizations "craft strategy" according to Mintzberg, as they continually learn about shifting business conditions and balance what is desired and what is possible.[13] The key is not getting the right strategy but fostering strategic thinking. "The choice of individual action is only part of the policymaker's need," according to Mason and Mitroff.[14] "More important is the need to achieve insight into the nature of the complexity and to formulate concepts and world views for coping with it."

Behind appropriate policies, strategies, and structures are effective learning processes; their creation is the third key design responsibility in learning organizations. This does not absolve senior managers of their strategic responsibilities. Now, they are not only responsible for ensuring that an organization have well-developed strategies and policies, but also for ensuring that processes exist whereby these are continually improved.

In the early 1970s, Shell was the weakest of the big seven oil companies. Today, Shell and Exxon are arguably the strongest, both in size and financial health. Shell's ascendance began with frustration. Around 1971 members of Shell's "Group Planning" in London began to foresee dramatic change and unpredictability in world oil markets. However, it proved impossible to persuade managers that the stable world of steady growth in oil demand and supply they had known for 20 years was about to change. Despite brilliant analysis and artful presentation, Shell's planners realized, in the words of Pierre Wack, that they "had failed to change behavior in much of the Shell organization."[15] Progress would probably have ended there, had the frustration not given way to a radically new view of corporate planning.

As they pondered this failure, the planner's view of their basic task shifted: "We no longer saw our task as producing a documented view of the future business environment 5 or 10 years ahead. Our real target was the microcosm (the 'mental model') of our decision makers." Only when the planners reconceptualized their basic task as fostering learning rather than devising plans did their insights begin to have an impact. The initial tool used was "scenario analysis," through which planners encouraged operating managers to think through how they would manage in the future under different possible scenarios. It mattered not that the managers believed the planners' scenarios absolutely, only that they became engaged in ferreting out the implications. In this way, Shell's planners conditioned managers to be mentally prepared for a shift from low prices to high prices and from stability to instability. The results were significant. When OPEC became a reality, Shell quickly responded by increasing local operating company control (to enhance maneuverability in the new political environment), building buffer stocks, and accelerating development of non-OPEC sources—actions that its competitors took much more slowly or not at all.

Somewhat inadvertently, Shell planners had discovered the leverage of designing institutional learning processes, whereby, in the words of former planning director de Geus, "Management teams change their shared mental models of their company, their markets, and their competitors."[16] Since then, "planning as learning" has become a byword at Shell, and Group Planning has continually sought out new learning tools that can be integrated into the planning process. Some of these are described later.

Leader as Teacher

"The first responsibility of a leader," writes retired Herman Miller CEO Max de Pree, "is to define reality."[17] Much of the leverage leaders can actually exert lies in helping people achieve more accurate, more insightful, and more *empowering* views of reality.

Leader as teacher does *not* mean leader as authoritarian expert whose job it is to teach people the "correct" view of reality. Rather, it is about helping everyone in the organization, oneself included, to gain more insightful views of current reality. This is in line with a popular emerging view of leaders as coaches, guides, or facilitators.[18] In learning organizations, this teaching role is developed further by virtue of explicit attention to people's mental models and by the influence of the system's perspective.

The role of leader as teacher starts with bringing to the surface people's mental models of important issues. No one carries an organization, a market, or a state of technology in his or her head. What we carry in our heads are assumptions. These mental pictures of how the world works have a significant influence on how we perceive problems and opportunities, identify courses of action, and make choices.

One reason that mental models are so deeply entrenched is that they are largely tacit. Ian Mitroff, in his study of General Motors, argues that an assumption that prevailed for years was that, in the United States, "Cars are status symbols. Styling is therefore more important than quality."[19] The Detroit automakers didn't say, "We have a mental model that all people care about is styling." Few actual managers would even say publicly that all people care about is styling. So long as the view remained unexpressed, there was little possibility of challenging its validity or forming more accurate assumptions.

But working with mental models goes beyond revealing hidden assumptions. "Reality," as perceived by most people in most organizations, means pressures that must be borne, crises that must be reacted to, and limitations that must be accepted. Leaders as teachers help people restructure their views of reality to see beyond the superficial conditions and events into the underlying causes of problems—and therefore to see new possibilities for shaping the future.

Specifically, leaders can influence people to view reality at three distinct levels: events, patterns of behavior, and systemic structure.

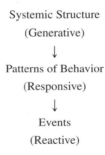

Systemic Structure

(Generative)

↓

Patterns of Behavior

(Responsive)

↓

Events

(Reactive)

The key question becomes *where do leaders predominantly focus their own and their organization's attention*?

Contemporary society focuses predominantly on events. The media reinforces this perspective, with almost exclusive attention to short-term, dramatic events. This focus leads naturally to explaining what happens in terms of those events: "The Dow Jones average went up 16 points because high fourth-quarter profits were announced yesterday."

Pattern-of-behavior explanations are rarer, in contemporary culture, than event explanations, but they do occur. "Trend analysis" is an example of seeing patterns of behavior. A good editorial that interprets a set of current events in the context of long-term historical changes is another example. Systemic, structural explanations go even further by addressing the questions, "What causes the patterns of behavior?"

In some sense, all three levels of explanation are equally true. But their usefulness is quite different. Event explanations—who did what to whom—doom their holders to a reactive stance toward change. Pattern-of-behavior explanations focus on identifying long-term trends and assessing their implications. They at least suggest how, over time, we can respond to shifting conditions. Structural explanations are the most powerful. Only they address the underlying causes of behavior at a level such that patterns of behavior can be changed.

By and large, leaders of our current institutions focus their attention on events and patterns of behavior, and, under their influence, their organizations do likewise. That is why contemporary organizations are predominantly reactive, or at best responsive—rarely generative. On the other hand, leaders in learning organizations pay attention to all three levels, but focus especially on systemic structure; largely by example, they teach people throughout the organization to do likewise.

Leader as Steward

This is the subtlest role of leadership. Unlike the roles of designer and teacher, it is almost solely a matter of attitude. It is an attitude critical to learning organizations.

While stewardship has long been recognized as an aspect of leadership, its source is still not widely understood. I believe Robert Greenleaf came closest to explaining real stewardship, in his seminal book *Servant Leadership.*[20] There, Greenleaf argues that "the servant leader is servant *first.* . . . It begins with the natural feeling that one wants to serve, to serve *first.* This conscious choice brings one to aspire to lead. That person is sharply different from one who is leader *first,* perhaps because of the need to assuage an unusual power drive or to acquire material possessions."

Leaders' sense of stewardship operates on two levels: stewardship for the people they lead and stewardship for the larger purpose or mission that underlies the enterprise. The first type arises from a keen appreciation of the impact one's leadership can have on others. People can suffer economically, emotionally, and spiritually under inept leadership. If anything, people in a learning organization are more vulnerable because of their commitment and sense of shared ownership. Appreciating this naturally instills a sense of responsibility in leaders. The second type of stewardship arises from a leader's sense of personal purpose and commitment to the organization's larger mission. People's natural impulse to learn is unleashed when they are engaged in an endeavor they consider worthy of their fullest commitment. Or, as Lawrence Miller puts it, "Achieving return on equity does not, as a goal, mobilize the most noble forces of our soul."[21]

Leaders engaged in building learning organizations naturally feel part of a larger purpose that goes beyond their organization. They are part of changing the way businesses operate, not from a vague philanthropic urge, but from a conviction that their efforts will produce more productive organizations, capable of achieving higher levels of organizational success and personal satisfaction than more traditional organizations. Their sense of stewardship was succinctly captured by George Bernard Shaw when he said,

> This is the true joy in life, the being used for a purpose you consider a mighty one, the being a force of nature rather than a feverish, selfish clod of ailments and grievances complaining that the world will not devote itself to making you happy.

New Skills

New leadership roles require new leadership skills. These skills can only be developed, in my judgment, through a lifetime commitment. It is not enough for one or two individuals to develop these skills. They must be distributed widely throughout the organization. This is one reason that understanding the disciplines of a learning organization is so important. These disciplines embody the principles and practices that can widely foster leadership development.

Three critical areas of skills (disciplines) are building shared vision, surfacing and challenging mental models, and engaging in systems thinking.[22]

Building Shared Vision

How do individual visions come together to create shared visions? A useful metaphor is the hologram, the three-dimensional image created by interacting light sources.

If you cut a photograph in half, each half shows only part of the whole image. But if you divide a hologram, each part, no matter how small, shows the whole image intact. Likewise, when a group of people come to share a vision for an organization, each person sees an individual picture of the organization at its best. Each shares responsibility for the whole, not just for one piece. But the component pieces of the hologram are not identical. Each represents the whole image from a different point of view. It's something like poking holes in a window shade; each hole offers a unique angle for viewing the whole image. So, too, is each individual's vision unique.

When you add up the pieces of a hologram, something interesting happens. The image becomes more intense, more lifelike. When more people come to share a vision, the vision becomes more real in the sense of a mental reality that people can truly imagine achieving. They now have partners, co-creators; the vision no longer rests on their shoulders alone. Early on, when they are nurturing an individual vision, people may say it is "my vision." But, as the shared vision develops, it becomes both "my vision" and "our vision."

The skills involved in building shared vision include the following:

- *Encouraging Personal Vision.* Shared visions emerge from personal visions. It is not that people only care about their own self-interest—in fact, people's values usually include dimensions that concern family, organization, community, and even the world. Rather, it is that people's capacity for caring is personal.
- *Communicating and Asking for Support.* Leaders must be willing to continually share their own vision, rather than being the official representative of the corporate vision. They also must be prepared to ask, "Is this the vision worthy of your commitment?" This can be difficult for a person used to setting goals and presuming compliance.
- *Visioning as an Ongoing Process.* Building shared vision is a never-ending process. At any one point there will be a particular image of the future that is predominant, but that image will evolve. Today, too many managers want to dispense with the "vision business" by going off and writing the Official Vision Statement. Such statements almost always lack the vitality, freshness, and excitement of a genuine vision that comes from people asking, "What do we really want to achieve?"
- *Blending Extrinsic and Intrinsic Visions.* Many energizing visions are extrinsic—that is, they focus on achieving something relative to an outsider, such as a competitor. But a goal that is limited to defeating an opponent can, once the vision is achieved, easily become a defensive posture. In contrast, intrinsic goals like creating a new type of product, taking an established product to a new level, or setting a new standard for customer satisfaction can call forth a new level of creativity and innovation. Intrinsic and extrinsic visions need to coexist; a vision solely predicated on defeating an adversary will eventually weaken an organization.
- *Distinguishing Positive from Negative Visions.* Many organizations only truly pull together when their survival is threatened. Similarly, most social movements aim at eliminating what people don't want: for example, anti-drugs, anti-smoking, or anti-nuclear arms movements. Negative visions carry a subtle message of powerlessness: People will only pull together when there is sufficient threat. Negative visions also tend to be short term. Two fundamental sources of energy can motivate organizations: fear and aspiration. Fear, the energy source behind negative visions, can produce extraordinary changes in short periods, but aspiration endures as a continuing source of learning and growth.

Surfacing and Testing Mental Models

Many of the best ideas in organizations never get put into practice. One reason is that new insights and initiatives often conflict with established mental models. The leadership task of challenging assumptions without invoking defensiveness requires reflection and inquiry skills possessed by a few leaders in traditional controlling organizations.[23]

- *Seeing Leaps of Abstraction.* Our minds literally move at lightning speed. Ironically, this often slows our learning, because we leap to generalizations so quickly that we never think to test them. We then confuse our generalizations with the observable data upon which they are based, treating the generalizations as if they were data. The frustrated sales rep reports to the home office that "customers don't really care about quality, price is what matters," when what actually happened was that three consecutive large customers refused to place an order unless a larger discount was offered. The sales rep treats her generalization, "customers care only about price," as if it were absolute fact rather than an assumption (very likely an assumption reflecting her own views of customers and the market). This thwarts future learning because she starts to focus on how to offer attractive discounts rather than probing behind the customers' statements. For example, the customers may have been so disgruntled with the firm's delivery or customer service that they are unwilling to purchase again without larger discounts.

- *Balancing Inquiry and Advocacy.* Most managers are skilled at articulating their views and presenting them persuasively. While important, advocacy skills can become counterproductive as managers rise in responsibility and confront increasingly complex issues that require collaborative learning among different, equally knowledgeable people. Leaders in learning organizations need to have both inquiry and advocacy skills.[24]

    Specifically, when advocating a view, they need to be able to:
    - explain the reasoning and data that led to their view;
    - encourage others to test their view (e.g., Do you see gaps in my reasoning? Do you disagree with the data upon which my view is based?); and
    - encourage others to provide different views (e.g., Do you have either different data, different conclusions, or both?).

    When inquiring into another's views, they need to:
    - actively seek to understand the other's view, rather than simply restating their own view and how it differs from the other's view; and
    - make their attributions about the other's view explicit (e.g., Based on your statement that . . . ; I am assuming that you believe . . . ; Am I representing your views fairly?).

    If they reach an impasse (others no longer appear open to inquiry), they need to:
    - ask what data or logic might unfreeze the impasse, or if an experiment (or some other inquiry) might be designed to provide new information.

- *Distinguishing Espoused Theory from Theory in Use.* We all like to think that we hold certain views, but often our actions reveal deeper views. For example, I may proclaim that people are trustworthy, but never lend friends money and jealously guard my possessions. Obviously, my deeper mental model (my theory in use) differs from my espoused theory. Recognizing gaps between espoused views and theories in use (which often requires the help of others) can be pivotal to deeper learning.

- *Recognizing and Defusing Defensive Routines.* As one CEO in our research program puts it, "Nobody ever talks about an issue at the 8:00 business meeting exactly the same way they talk about it at home that evening or over drinks at the end of the day." The reason is what Chris Argyris calls "defensive routines," entrenched habits used to protect ourselves from the embarrassment and threat that come with exposing our thinking. For most of us, such defenses began to build early in life in response to pressures to have the right answers in school or at home. Organizations add new levels of performance anxiety and thereby amplify and exacerbate this defensiveness. Ironically, this makes it even more difficult to expose hidden mental models, and thereby lessens learning.

The first challenge is to recognize defensive routines, then to inquire into their operation. Those who are best at revealing and defusing defensive routines operate with a high degree of self-disclosure regarding their own defensiveness (e.g., I notice that I am feeling uneasy about how this conversation is going. Perhaps I don't understand it or it is threatening to me in ways I don't yet see. Can you help me see this better?).

Systems Thinking

We all know that leaders should help people see the big picture. But the actual skills whereby leaders are supposed to achieve this are not well understood. In my experience, successful leaders often are "systems thinkers" to a considerable extent. They focus less on day-to-day events and more on underlying trends and forces of change. But they do this almost completely intuitively. The consequence is that they are often unable to explain their intuitions to others and feel frustrated that others cannot see the world the way they do.

One of the most significant developments in management science today is the gradual coalescence of managerial systems thinking as a field of study and practice. This field suggests some key skills for future leaders:

- *Seeing Interrelationships, Not Things, and Processes, Not Snapshots.* Most of us have been conditioned throughout our lives to focus on things and to see the world in static images. This leads us to linear explanations of systemic phenomenon. For instance, in an arms race each party is convinced that the other is the cause of problems. They react to each new move as an isolated event, not as part of a process. So long as they fail to see the interrelationships of these actions, they are trapped.
- *Moving Beyond Blame.* We tend to blame each other or outside circumstances for our problems. But it is poorly designed systems, not incompetent or unmotivated individuals, that cause most organizational problems. System thinking shows us that there is no outside—that you and the cause of your problems are part of a single system.
- *Distinguishing Detail Complexity from Dynamic Complexity.* Some types of complexity are more important strategically than others. Detail complexity arises when there are many variables. Dynamic complexity arises when cause and effect are distant in time and space, and when the consequences over time of interventions are subtle and not obvious to many participants in the system. The leverage in most management situations lies in understanding dynamic complexity, not detail complexity.
- *Focusing on Areas of Higher Leverage.* Some have called systems thinking the "new dismal science" because it teaches that most obvious solutions don't

work—at best, they improve matters in the short run, only to make things worse in the long run. But there is another side to the story. Systems thinking also shows that small, well-focused actions can produce significant, enduring improvements, if they are in the right place. Systems thinkers refer to this idea as the principle of "leverage." Tackling a difficult problem is often a matter of seeing where the high leverage lies, where a change—with a minimum of effort—would lead to lasting, significant improvement.

- *Avoiding Symptomatic Solutions.* The pressures to intervene in management systems that are going awry can be overwhelming. Unfortunately, given the linear thinking that predominates in most organizations, interventions usually focus on symptomatic fixes, not underlying causes. This results in only temporary relief, and it tends to create still more pressures later and for further, low leverage intervention. If leaders acquiesce to these pressures, they can be sucked into an endless spiral of increasing intervention. Sometimes the most difficult leadership acts are to refrain from intervening through popular quick fixes and to keep the pressure on everyone to identify more enduring solutions.

While leaders who can articulate systemic explanations are rare, those who can will leave their stamps on an organization. One person who had this gift was Bill Gore, the founder and longtime CEO of W.L. Gore and Associates (makers of Gore Tex and other synthetic fiber products). Bill Gore was adept at telling stories that showed how the organization's core values of freedom and individual responsibility required particular operating policies. He was proud of his egalitarian organization, in which there were (and still are) no "employees," only "associates," all of whom own shares in the company and participate in its management. At one talk, he explained the company's policy of controlled growth: "Our limitation is not financial resources. Our limitation is the rate at which we can bring in new associates. Our experience has been that if we try to bring in more than a 25 percent per year increase, we begin to bog down. Twenty-five percent per year growth is a real limitation; you can do much better than that with an authoritarian organization." As Gore tells the story, one of the associates, Esther Baum, went home after this talk and reported the limitation to her husband. As it happened, he was an astronomer and mathematician at Lowell Observatory. He said, "That's a very interesting figure." He took out his pencil and paper and calculated and said, "Do you realize that in only fifty-seven and a half years, everyone in the world will be working for Gore?"

Through the story, Gore explains the systemic rationale behind a key policy, limited growth rate—a policy that undoubtedly caused a lot of stress in the organization. He suggests that, at larger rates of growth, the adverse effects of attempting to integrate too many new people too rapidly would begin to dominate. (This is the "limits to growth" systems archetype explained later.) The story also reaffirms the organization's commitment to creating a unique environment for its associates and illustrates the types of sacrifices that the firm is prepared to make in order to remain true to its vision. The last part of the story shows that, despite the self-imposed limit, the company is still very much a growth company.

The consequences of leaders who lack systems thinking skills can be devastating. Many charismatic leaders manage almost exclusively at the level of events. They deal in visions and in crises, and little in between. Under the leadership, an organization hurtles from crisis to crisis. Eventually, the worldview of people in the organization becomes dominated by events and reactiveness. Many, especially those who are deeply committed, become burned out. Eventually, cynicism comes to pervade the organization. People have no control over their time, let alone their destiny.

Similar problems arise with the "visionary strategist," the leader with vision who sees both patterns of change and events. This leader is better prepared to manage change. She or he can explain strategies in terms of emerging trends, and thereby foster a climate that is less reactive. But such leaders still impart a responsive orientation rather than a generative one.

Many talented leaders have rich, highly systemic intuitions but cannot explain those intuitions to others. Ironically, they often end up being authoritarian leaders, even if they don't want to, because only they see the decisions that need to be made. They are unable to conceptualize their strategic insights so that these can become public knowledge, open to challenge and further improvement.

New Tools

Developing the skills described previously requires new tools—tools that will enhance leaders' conceptual abilities and foster communication and collaborative inquiry. What follows is a sampling of tools starting to find use in learning organizations.

Systems Archetypes

One of the insights of the budding, managerial systems-thinking field is that certain types of systemic structures recur again and again. Countless systems grow for a period, then encounter problems and cease to grow (or even collapse) well before they have reached intrinsic limits to growth. Many other systems get locked in runaway vicious spirals where every actor has to run faster and faster to stay in the same place. Still others lure individual actors into doing what seems right locally, yet which eventually causes suffering for all.[25]

Some of the system archetypes that have the broadest relevance include:

- *Balancing Process with Delay.* In this archetype, decision makers fail to appreciate the time delays involved as they move toward a goal. As a result, they overshoot the goal and may even produce recurring cycles. Classic example: Real estate developers who keep starting new projects until the market has gone soft, by which time an eventual glut is guaranteed by the properties still under construction.
- *Limits to Growth.* A reinforcing cycle of growth grinds to a halt, and may even reverse itself, as limits are approached. The limits can be resource constraints, or external or internal responses to growth. Classic examples: Product life cycles that peak prematurely due to poor quality or service, the growth and decline of communication in a management team, and the spread of a new movement.
- *Shifting the Burden.* A short-term "solution" is used to correct a problem, with seemingly happy immediate results. As this correction is used more and more, fundamental long-term corrective measures are used less. Over time, the mechanisms of the fundamental solution may atrophy or become disabled, leading to an even greater reliance on the symptomatic solution. Classic example: Using corporate human resource staff to solve local personnel problems, thereby keeping managers from developing their own interpersonal skills.
- *Eroding Goals.* When all else fails, lower your standards. This is like "shifting the burden," except that the short-term solution involves letting a fundamental goal, such as quality standards or employee morale standards, atrophy. Classic

example: A company that responds to delivery problems by continually upping its quoted delivery times.

- *Escalation.* Two people or two organizations, who each see their welfare as depending on a relative advantage over the other, continually react to the other's advances. Whenever one side gets ahead, the other is threatened, leading it to act more aggressively to reestablish its advantage, which threatens the first, and so on. Classic examples: Arms race, gang warfare, price wars.

- *Tragedy of the Commons.*[26] Individuals keep intensifying their use of a commonly available but limited resource until all individuals start to experience severely diminishing returns. Classic examples: Sheepherders who keep increasing their flocks until they overgraze the common pasture; divisions in a firm that share a common sales force and compete for the use of sales reps by upping their sales targets, until the sales force burns out from overextension.

- *Growth and Underinvestment.* Rapid growth approaches a limit that could be eliminated or pushed into the future, but only by aggressive investment in physical and human capacity. Eroding goals or standards cause investment that is too weak, or too slow, and customers get increasingly unhappy, slowing demand growth and thereby making the needed investment (apparently) unnecessary or impossible. Classic example: Countless once-successful growth firms that allowed product or service quality to erode, and were unable to generate enough revenues to invest in remedies.

The Archetype Template is a specific tool that is helping managers identify archetypes operating in their own strategic areas (see Figure 2).[27] The template shows the basic structural form of the archetype but lets managers fill in the variables of their own situation. For example, the shifting the burden template involves two balancing processes ("B") that compete for control of a problem

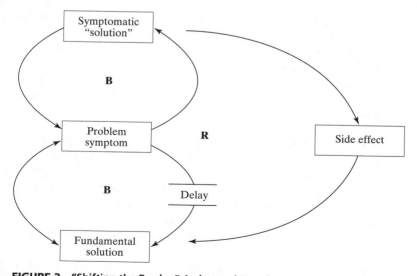

FIGURE 2   "Shifting the Burden" Archetypal Template.
In the "shifting the burden" template, two balancing processes (B) compete for control of a problem symptom. Both solutions affect the symptom, but only the fundamental solution treats the cause. The symptomatic "solution" creates the additional side effect (R) of deferring the fundamental solution, making it harder and harder to achieve.

symptom. The upper, symptomatic solution provides a short-term fix that will make the problem symptom go away for a while. The lower, fundamental solution provides a more enduring solution. The side-effect feedback ("R") around the outside of the diagram identifies unintended exacerbating effects of the symptomatic solution, which, over time, make it more and more difficult to invoke the fundamental solution.

Several years ago, a team of managers from a leading consumer goods producer used the shifting the burden archetype in a revealing way. The problem they focused on was financial stress, which could be dealt with in two different ways: by running marketing promotions (the symptomatic solution) or by product innovation (the fundamental solution). Marketing promotions were fast. The company was expert in their design and implementation. The results were highly predictable. Product innovation was slow and much less predictable, and the company had a history over the past ten years of product-innovation mismanagement. Yet only through innovation could they retain a leadership position in their industry, which had slid over the past ten to twenty years. What the managers saw clearly was that the more skillful they became at promotions, the more they shifted the burden away from product innovation. But what really struck home was when one member identified the unintended side effect: The last three CEOs had all come from advertising, which had become the politically dominant function in the corporation, thereby institutionalizing the symptomatic solution. Unless the political values shifted back toward product and process innovation, the managers realized, the firm's decline would accelerate—which is just the shift that had happened over the past several years.

Charting Strategic Dilemmas

Management teams typically come unglued when confronted with core dilemmas. A classic example was the way U.S. manufacturers faced the low cost–high quality choice. For years, most assumed that it was necessary to choose between the two. Not surprisingly, given the short-term pressures perceived by most managements, the prevailing choice was low cost. Firms that chose high quality usually perceived themselves as aiming exclusively for high quality, high price market niche. The consequences of this perceived either–or choice have been disastrous, even fatal, as U.S. manufacturers have encountered increasing international competition from firms that have chosen to consistently improve quality and cost.

In a recent book, Charles Hampden-Turner presented a variety of tools for helping management teams confront strategic dilemmas creatively.[28] He summarizes the process in seven steps:

- *Eliciting the Dilemmas.* Identifying the opposed values that form the "horns" of the dilemma, for example, cost as opposed to quality, or local initiative as opposed to central coordination and control. Hampden-Turner suggests that humor can be a distinct asset in this process since "the admission that dilemmas even exist tends to be difficult for some companies."
- *Mapping.* Locating the opposing values as two axes and helping managers identify where they see themselves, or their organization, along the axes.
- *Processing.* Getting rid of nouns to describe the axes of the dilemma. Present participles formed by adding "ing" convert rigid nouns into processes that imply movement. For example, central control versus local control becomes "strengthening national office" and "growing local initiatives." This loosens the bond of implied opposition between the two values. For example, it becomes possible to think of "strengthening national services" from which local branches can benefit.

- *Framing/Contextualizing.* Further softening the adversarial structure among different values by letting "each side in turn be the frame or context for the other." This shifting of the "figure–ground" relationship undermines any implicit attempts to hold one value as intrinsically superior to the other, and thereby to become mentally closed to creative strategies for continuous improvement of both.
- *Sequencing.* Breaking the hold of static thinking. Very often, values like low cost and high quality appear to be in opposition because we think in terms of a point in time, not in terms of an ongoing process. For example, a strategy of investing in a new process technology and developing a new production-floor culture of worker responsibility may take time and money in the near term, yet reap significant long-term financial rewards.
- *Waving/Cycling.* Sometimes the strategic path toward improving both values involves cycles where both values will get "worse" for a time. Yet, at a deeper level, learning is occurring that will cause the next cycle to be at a higher plateau for both values.
- *Synergizing.* Achieving synergy where significant improvement is occurring along all axes of all relevant dilemmas. (This is the ultimate goal, of course.) Synergy, as Hampden-Turner points out, is a uniquely systemic notion, coming from the Greek *Syn-ergo* or "work together."

"The Left-Hand Column": Surfacing Mental Models

The idea that the mental models can dominate business decisions and that these models are often tacit and even contradictory to what people espouse can be very threatening to managers who pride themselves on rationality and judicious decision making. It is important to have tools to help managers discover for themselves how their mental models operate to undermine their own intentions.

One tool that has worked consistently to help managers see their own mental models in action is the "left-hand column" exercise developed by Chris Argyris and his colleagues. This tool is especially helpful in showing how we leap from data to generalization without testing the validity of our generalizations.

When working with managers, I start this exercise by selecting a specific situation in which I am interacting with other people in a way that is not working, that is not producing the learning that is needed. I write out a sample of the exchange, with the script on the right-hand side of the page. On the left-hand side, I write what I am thinking but not saying at each stage in the exchange (see sidebar).

The left-hand column exercise not only brings hidden assumptions to the surface, it shows how they influence behavior. In the example, I make two key assumptions about Bill: he lacks confidence and he lacks initiative. Neither may be literally true, but both are evident in my internal dialogue, and both influence the way I handle the situation. Believing that he lacks confidence, I skirt the fact that I've heard the presentation was a bomb. I'm afraid that if I say it directly, he will lose what little confidence he has, or he will see me as unsupportive. So I bring up the subject of the presentation obliquely. When I ask Bill what we should do next, he gives no specific course of action. Believing he lacks initiative, I take this as evidence of his laziness; he is content to do nothing when action is definitely required. I conclude that I will have to manufacture some form of pressure to motivate him, or else I will simply have to take matters into my own hands.

The exercise reveals the elaborate webs of assumptions we weave, within which we become our own victims. Rather than dealing directly with my assumptions about Bill and the situation, we talk around the subject. The reasons for my avoidance are

---

The Left-Hand Column: An Exercise

Imagine my exchange with a colleague, Bill, after he made a big presentation to our boss on a project we are doing together. I had to miss the presentation, but I've heard that it was poorly received.

ME: How did the presentation go?
BILL: Well, I don't know. It's really too early to say. Besides, we're breaking new ground here.
ME: Well, what do you think we should do? I believe that the issues you were raising were important.
BILL: I'm not so sure. Let's just wait and see what happens.
ME: You may be right, but I think we may need to do more than just wait.

Now, here is what the exchange looks like with my "left-hand column"

WHAT I'M THINKING	WHAT IS SAID
Everyone says the presentation was a bomb.	ME: How did the presentation go?
Does he really not know how bad it was? Or is he not willing to face up to it?	BILL: Well, I don't know. It's too early to say. Besides, we're breaking new ground here.
He really is afraid to see the truth. If he only had more confidence, he could probably learn from a situation like this.	ME: Well, what do you think we should do? I believe that the issues you were raising are important.
I can't believe he doesn't realize how disastrous that presentation was to our moving ahead.	BILL: I'm not so sure. Let's just wait and see what happens.
I've got to find some way to light a fire under the guy.	ME: You may be right, but I think we may need to do more than just wait.

---

self-evident: I assume that if I raised my doubts, I would provoke a defensive reaction that would only make matters worse. But the price of avoiding the issue is high. Instead of determining how to move forward to resolve problems, we end our exchange with no clear course of action. My assumptions about Bill's limitations have been reinforced. I resort to a manipulative strategy to move things forward.

The exercise not only reveals the need for skills in surfacing assumptions, but that we are the ones most in need of help. There is no one right way to handle difficult situations like my exchange with Bill, but any productive strategy revolves around a high level of self-disclosure and willingness to have my views challenged. I need to recognize my own leaps of abstraction regarding Bill, share the events and reasoning that are leading to my concern over the project, and be open to Bill's views on both. The skills to carry on such conversations without invoking defensiveness take time to develop. But if both parties in a learning impasse start by doing their own left-hand column exercise and sharing them with each other, it is remarkable how quickly everyone recognizes their contribution to the impasse and progress starts to be made.

Learning Laboratories: Practice Fields for Management Teams

One of the most promising new tools is the learning laboratory or "microworld": constructed microcosms of real-life settings in which management teams can learn how to learn together.

The rationale behind learning laboratories can be best explained by analogy. Although most management teams have great difficulty learning (enhancing their collective intelligence and capacity to create), in other domains team learning is the norm rather than the exception—team sports and the performing arts, for example. Great basketball teams do not start off great. They learn. But the process by which these teams learn is, by and large, absent from modern organizations. The process is a continual movement between practice and performance.

The vision guiding current research in management learning laboratories is to design and construct effective practice fields for management teams. Much remains to be done, but the broad outlines are emerging.

First, since team learning in organizations is an individual-to-individual and individual-to-system phenomenon, learning laboratories must combine meaningful business issues with meaningful interpersonal dynamics. Either alone is incomplete.

Second, the factors that thwart learning about complex business issues must be eliminated in the learning lab. Chief among these is the inability to experience the long-term, systemic consequences of key strategic decisions. We all learn best from experience, but we are unable to experience the consequences of many important organizational decisions. Learning laboratories remove this constraint through system dynamics simulation games that compress time and space.

Third, new learning skills must be developed. One constraint on learning is the inability of managers to reflect insightfully on their assumptions, and to inquire effectively into each other's assumptions. Both skills can be enhanced in a learning laboratory, where people can practice surfacing assumptions in a low-risk setting. A note of caution: It is far easier to design an entertaining learning laboratory than it is to have an impact on real management practices and firm traditions outside the learning lab. Research on management simulations has shown that they often have greater entertainment value than the educational value. One of the reasons appears to be that many simulations do not offer deep insights into systemic structures causing business problems. Another reason is that they do not foster new learning skills. Also, there is no connection between experiments in the learning lab and real-life experiments. These are significant problems that research on laboratory design is now addressing.

Learning at Hanover Insurance

Hanover Insurance has gone from the bottom of the property and liability industry to a position among the top 25 percent of U.S. insurance companies over the past 20 years, largely through the efforts of CEO William O'Brien and his predecessor, Jack Adam. The following comments are excerpted from series of interviews Senge conducted with O'Brien as background for his book.

SENGE: Why do you think there is so much change occurring in management and organizations today? Is it primarily because of increased competitive pressures?

O'BRIEN: That's a factor, but not the most significant factor. The ferment in management will continue until we find models that are more congruent with human nature.

One of the great insights of modern psychology is the hierarchy of human needs. As Maslow expressed this idea, the most basic needs are food and shelter. Then comes belonging. Once these three basic needs are satisfied, people begin to aspire toward self-respect and esteem, and toward self-actualization—the fourth- and fifth-order needs.

Our traditional hierarchical organizations are designed to provide for the first three levels, but not the fourth and fifth. These first three levels are now widely available to members of industrial society, but our organizations do not offer people sufficient opportunities for growth.

SENGE: How would you assess Hanover's progress to date?

O'BRIEN: We have been on a long journey away from traditional hierarchical culture. The journey began with everyone understanding some guiding ideas about purpose, vision, and values as a basis for participative management. This is a better way to begin building a participative culture than by simply "letting people in on decision making." Before there can be meaningful participation, people must share certain values and pictures about where we are trying to go. We discovered that people have real need to feel that they're part of an ennobling mission. But developing shared visions and values is not the end, only the beginning.

(continued)

(continued)

Next we had to get beyond mechanical, linear thinking. The essence of our jobs as managers is to deal with "divergent" problems—problems that have no simple answer.

"Convergent" problems—problems that have a "right" answer—should be solved locally. Yet we are deeply conditioned to see the world in terms of convergent problems. Most managers try to force-fit simplistic solutions and undermine the potential for learning when divergent problems arise. Since everyone handles the linear issues fairly well, companies that learn how to handle divergent issues will have a great advantage.

The next basic stage in our progression was coming to understand inquiry and advocacy. We learned that real openness is rooted in people's ability to continually inquire into their own thinking. This requires exposing yourself to being wrong—not something that most managers are rewarded for. But learning is very difficult if you cannot look for errors or incompleteness in your own ideas.

What all this builds to is the capability throughout an organization to manage mental models. In a locally controlled organization, you have the fundamental challenge of learning how to help people make good decisions without coercing them into making particular decisions. By managing mental models, we create "self-concluding" decisions—decisions that people come to themselves—which will result in deeper conviction, better implementation, and the ability to make better adjustments when the situation changes.

SENGE: What concrete steps can top managers take to begin moving toward learning organizations?

O'BRIEN: Look at the signals you send through the organization. For example, one critical signal is how you spend your time. It's hard to build a learning organization if people are unable to take the time to think through important matters. I rarely set up an appointment for less than one hour. If the subject is not worth an hour, it shouldn't be on my calendar.

SENGE: Why is this so hard for so many managers?

O'BRIEN: It comes back to what you believe about the nature of your work. The authoritarian manager has a "chain gang" mental model: "The speed of the boss is the speed of the gang. I've got to keep things moving fast, because I've got to keep people working." In a learning organization, the manager shoulders an almost sacred responsibility: to create conditions that enable people to have happy and productive lives. If you understand the effects the ideas we are discussing can have on the lives of people in your organization, you will take the time.

Developing Leaders and Learning Organizations

In a recently published retrospective on organization development in the 1980s, Marshall Sashkin and N. Warner Burke observe the return of an emphasis on developing leaders who can develop organizations.[29] They also note Schein's critique that most top executives are not qualified for the task of developing culture.[30] Learning organizations represent a potentially significant evolution of organizational culture. So it should come as no surprise that such organization will remain a distant vision until the leadership capabilities they demand are developed. "The 1990s may be the period," suggest Sashkin and Burke, "during which organization development and (a new sort) of management development are reconnected."

I believe that this new sort of management development will focus on the roles, skills, and tools for leadership in learning organizations. Undoubtedly, the ideas offered in this article are only a rough approximation of this new territory. The sooner we begin seriously exploring the territory, the sooner the initial map can be improved—and the sooner we will realize an age-old vision of leadership.

> *The wicked leader is he who the people despise.*
> *The good leader is he who the people revere.*
> *The great leader is he who the people say, "We did it ourselves."*
>
> *—Lao Tsu*

References

1. P. Senge, *The Fifth Discipline: The Art and Practice of the Learning Organization* (New York: Doubleday/Currency, 1990).
2. A. P. de Geus, "Planning as Learning," *Harvard Business Review* (March–April 1988): 70–74.
3. B. Domain, *Fortune,* July 3, 1989, 48–62.
4. The distinction between adaptive and generative learning has its roots in the distinction between what Argyris and Schon have called their "single-loop" learning, in which individuals or groups adjust their behavior relative to fixed goals, norms, and assumptions, and "double-loop" learning, in which goals, norms, and assumptions, as well as behavior, are open to change (e.g., see C. Argyris and D. Schon, *Organizational Learning: A Theory-in-Action Perspective* [Reading, MA: Addison-Wesley, 1978]).
5. All unattributed quotes are from personal communications with the author.
6. G. Stalk, Jr., "Time: The Next Source of Competitive Advantage," *Harvard Business Review* (July–August 1988): 41–51.
7. Senge (1990).
8. The principle of creative tension comes from Robert Fritz's work on creativity. See R. Fritz, *The Path of Least Resistance* (New York: Ballantine, 1989) and *Creating* (New York: Ballantine, 1990).
9. M. L. King, Jr., "Letter from Birmingham Jail," *American Visions* (January–February 1986): 52–59.
10. E. Schein, *Organizational Culture and Leadership* (San Francisco: Jossey-Bass, 1985). Similar views have been expressed by many leadership theorists. For example, see: P. Selznick, *Leadership in Administration* (New York: Harper & Row, 1957); W. Bennis and B. Nanus, *Leaders* (New York: Harper & Row, 1985); and N. M. Tichy and M. A. Devanna, *The Transformational Leader* (New York: John Wiley & Sons, 1986).
11. Selznick (1957).
12. J. W. Forrester, "A New Corporate Design," *Sloan Management Review* (formerly *Industrial Management Review*) (Fall 1965): 5–17.
13. See, for example, H. Mintzberg, "Crafting Strategy," *Harvard Business Review* (July–August 1987): 66–75.
14. R. Mason and I. Mitroff, *Challenging Strategic Planning Assumptions* (New York: John Wiley & Sons, 1981): 16.
15. P. Wack, "Scenarios: Uncharted Waters Ahead," *Harvard Business Review* (September–October 1985): 73–89.
16. de Geus (1988).
17. M. de Pree, *Leadership Is an Art* (New York: Doubleday, 1989): 9.
18. For example, see T. Peters and N. Austin, *A Passion for Excellence* (New York: Random House, 1985); and J. M. Kouzes and B. Z. Posner, *The Leadership Challenge* (San Francisco: Jossey-Bass, 1987).
19. I. Mitroff, *Break-Away Thinking* (New York: John Wiley & Sons, 1988): 66–67.
20. R. K. Greenleaf, *Servant Leadership: A Journey into the Nature of Legitimate Power and Greatness* (New York: Paulist Press, 1977).
21. L. Miller, *American Spirit: Visions of a New Corporate Culture* (New York: William Morrow, 1984): 15.
22. These points are condensed from the practices of the five disciplines examined in Senge (1990).
23. The ideas below are based to a considerable extent on the work of Chris Argyris, Donald Schon, and their Action Science colleagues: C. Argyris and D. Schon, *Organizational Learning: A Theory-in-Action Perspective* (Reading, MA: Addison-Wesley, 1978); C. Argyris, R. Putnam, and D. Smith, *Action Science* (San Francisco: Jossey-Bass, 1985); C. Argyris, *Strategy Change and Defensive Routines* (Boston: Pitman, 1985); and C. Argyris, *Overcoming Organizational Defenses* (Upper Saddle River, NJ: Prentice Hall, 1990).
24. I am indebted to Diana Smith for the summary points that follow.
25. The system archetypes are one of several systems diagramming and communication tools. See D. H. Kim, "Toward Learning Organizations: Integrating Total Quality Control and Systems Thinking" (Cambridge, MA: MIT Sloan School of Management, Working Paper No. 3037-89-BPS, June 1989).
26. This archetype is closely associated with the work of ecologist Garrett Hardin, who coined its label: G. Hardin, "The Tragedy of the Commons," *Science,* December 13, 1968.
27. These templates were originally developed by Jennifer Kemeny, Charles Kiefer, and Michael Goodman of Innovation Associates, Inc., Framingham, Massachusetts.
28. C. Hampden-Turner, *Charting the Corporate Mind* (New York: The Free Press, 1990).
29. M. Sashkin and W. W. Burke, "Organization Development in the 1980s" and "An End-of-the-Eighties Retrospective," *Advances in Organization Development,* ed. F. Masarik (Norwood, NJ: Ablex, 1990).
30. E. Schein (1985).

CHAPTER

5

Decoding Human Behavior

THE TYRANNY OF TOXIC MANAGERS: APPLYING EMOTIONAL INTELLIGENCE
TO DEAL WITH DIFFICULT PERSONALITIES
Roy Lubit

THE ROLE OF PSYCHOLOGICAL WELL-BEING IN JOB PERFORMANCE:
A FRESH LOOK AT AN AGE-OLD QUEST
Thomas A. Wright
Russell Cropanzano

BUILDING THE CIVILIZED WORKPLACE
Robert I. Sutton

One of the major challenges people face lies in understanding why others, in particular those who are very different from oneself, behave the way they do. There are many reasons that explain behavior, such as personality, individual background and attitudes, group norms, and culture. The articles in this chapter were chosen to help you decode behavior and understand why people act as they do.

The first article, "The Tyranny of Toxic Managers," was written by Roy Lubit, a New York psychiatrist who does executive coaching to develop emotional intelligence in people with difficult personalities. Lubit's article provides a framework for understanding toxic behavior in the workplace and provides advice on how to deal with each personality type. The article emphasizes the importance of developing emotional intelligence and explains how it can be increased. He also identifies the major behavioral differences that people struggle to accept in others in the workplace. Understanding how we are different from others is often the first step in appreciating, tolerating, and leveraging the strengths of their behavior (and our own).

A new movement in research, Positive Psychology and Positive Organizational Behavior, focuses on the positive aspects of work and life, rather than the traditional concern with negative aspects. For example, Fred Luthans and his colleagues argue that personal characteristics like confidence, hope, optimism, and resilience constitute an organization's positive psychological capital. These qualities, as well as happiness, the subject of the second article in this chapter, seldom made their way into research or textbooks in the past. Thomas Wright, director of the Center for Character-Based Leadership at Kansas State, and Russell Cropanzano, an industrial and organizational psychologist at the University of Arizona, shed new light for both scholars and practitioners in "The Role of Psychological Well-Being in Job Performance: A Fresh Look at an Age-Old Quest."

Moving back to negative forces in the workplace, we consider the challenge of understanding and dealing with jerks in the workplace. In "Building the Civilized Workplace," Stanford University professor Robert Sutton describes the damage done by jerks, defined as employees who are nasty, demeaning, and extremely hard to get along with. They can decrease creativity, harm performance, impair collaboration, damage reputations, and make client and even investor relations precarious. Sutton details 12 common tactics used by jerks to wreak organizational havoc. To build a civilized workplace, he recommends a set of five integrated practices including a zero-tolerance policy as well as hiring and firing procedures that reinforce that policy.

THE TYRANNY OF TOXIC MANAGERS: APPLYING EMOTIONAL INTELLIGENCE TO DEAL WITH DIFFICULT PERSONALITIES*

Roy Lubit

Toxic managers are a fact of life. Some managers are toxic most of the time; most managers are toxic some of the time. Knowing how to deal with people who are rigid, aggressive, or self-centered, or who exhibit other types of dysfunctional behavior can improve your own health and that of others in the workplace. This author describes the mechanisms for coping.

Toxic managers dot the landscape in most organizations, making them seem, at times, like war zones. These managers can complicate your work, drain your energy, compromise your sanity, derail your projects, and destroy your career. Your ability to deal with these corporate land mines will have a significant impact on your career. Those who are able to recognize toxic managers quickly and understand what makes them tick will be in the best position to protect themselves. Difficult managers are a fact of life and how they affect your life depends upon the skills you develop to deal with them.

The issue is not simply a matter of individual survival. Toxic managers divert people's energy from the real work of the organization, destroy morale, impair retention, and interfere with cooperation and information sharing. Their behavior, like a rock thrown into a pond, can cause ripples distorting the organization's culture and affecting people far beyond the point of impact. Senior management and HR can significantly improve an organization's culture and functioning by taking steps to find and contain those who are most destructive. Leadership can spare an organization serious damage by learning how to recognize problematic personality traits quickly, placing difficult managers in positions in which their behavior will do the least harm, arranging for coaching for those who are able to grow, and knowing which managers are time bombs that need to be let go.

This article will help you learn how to avoid becoming a scapegoat, to survive aggressive managers' assaults, and to give narcissistic and rigid managers the things they need to be satisfied with you. It will also help senior management and HR to recognize toxic managers before they do serious damage. *The basic theme of the article is that to deal effectively with toxic behavior you need to understand what lies*

---

*Written for *The Organizational Behavior Reader*, based on The Tyranny of Toxic Managers: Applying Emotional Intelligence to Deal with Difficult Personalities, *Ivey Business Journal Online*, March–April 2004, 68(4).

underneath it, design an intervention to target those underlying factors, and have sufficient control of your own feelings and behavior so that you can do what is most effective, rather than let your own anger or anxiety get the best of you. To do this, you need to develop your emotional intelligence (including your self-control) along with your understanding of how difficult people view the world and what motivates them.

Types of Difficult Co-Workers

Toxic managers can be divided into four categories: narcissistic, aggressive, rigid, and impaired. Underneath these difficult behaviors are either problematic personality traits, mood disorders, or impulsivity. By personality traits, we mean enduring patterns of perceiving, interpreting, and relating to the world and oneself. Problems of mood and concentration can often mimic personality problems. When people are stressed by anxiety, depression, trauma, Attention Deficit Hyperactivity Disorder, alcohol, drugs, or a difficult environment, any tendency they have for aggressive, rigid, or narcissistic behavior intensifies. Having a professional assess whether the problem is due primarily to personality problems or to a problem of mood and concentration is crucial, since problems of mood and concentration can often be ameliorated fairly quickly with appropriate treatment.

The four types of toxic managers are described below as are ways for coping with, and even changing, their behavior.

Narcissistic Managers

Preoccupied with their own importance, narcissistic managers are grandiose and arrogant. They devalue others, lack empathy for others, and have little, if any, conscience. Feeling exempt from the normal rules of society, they exploit people without remorse. Narcissistic individuals are also very sensitive to anything that threatens their self-esteem. Challenges to their grandiose self-image can lead to narcissistic rage that sees them lose all judgment and attack in ways that are destructive to themselves and their victims.

Arrogant with peers and subordinates, they may suddenly become submissive in the presence of a superior. Once the superior has left, they may well disparage her. They generally deprecate and exploit others, including former idols. They may, however, idealize powerful individuals who support them, though only for a short time.

Under the surface, narcissistic managers struggle with fragile self-esteem. They also have a sense of emptiness arising from their lack of true self-love and inability to care about other people or about abstract values such as honesty and integrity. Their grandiose fantasies are attempts to fill the emptiness and reinforce their fragile self-esteem.

The classic narcissistic manager is grandiose. Grandiose managers are legends in their own minds. Preoccupied with their exaggerated accomplishments and grandiose expectations for the future, they expect others to hold them in awe. Constantly boasting, they resemble peacocks strutting around with their tail feathers unfurled.

Some narcissistic managers are not effusive about their abilities and accomplishments. What stands out about them is a willingness to exploit others, a willingness to break the law, or a desire to control and dominate others.

Narcissistic managers are less likely to make major changes in their behavior than are managers with other issues. They are also particularly likely to become outraged and vindictive if someone challenges their behavior. Therefore, when you are dealing with managers who are rigid or aggressive, it is important to know whether narcissism or other disorders lie underneath their destructive behavior.

A milder variant of narcissistic managers are those with learned narcissism. They are not desperately trying to hide and shield fragile self-esteem arising from a troubled childhood. Rather, their success in some area has brought sufficient fame and fortune that they have been shielded from the normal consequences of behaving arrogantly and treating others poorly. Moreover, as people incessantly flatter them, they come to believe the glorifying compliments. Although somewhat grandiose and inconsiderate of others, these people have a conscience and can feel empathy for others; they simply do not realize the full impact of their behavior on others. People with learned narcissism are far more amenable to change than are those with narcissism resulting from problems early on in emotional development. Another variety of narcissist focuses on power more than adulation and becomes control freaks. Their micromanagement comes from both a desire to be in control in order to prove that they are superior, and from devaluation of others and the need to control things lest they fall apart.

The most prominent trait for the antisocial variety is the devaluation of others and the willingness to violate their rights. They take whatever they wish, whether it is credit for work done or more than their share. They play by a different set of rules: All is fair in love, war, and business.

Coping with narcissistic managers is very difficult for most people. You can't make it a fun experience, but there are things you can do to make yourself less vulnerable to them, as shown in Table 1.

Table 1   Types of Narcissistic Managers

Varieties	Primary Traits	Objective	Subordinate Survival Tactics	Superior's Actions For All Varieties
Grandiose: Psychodynamic	Outward grandiose self-image; exploits others; devalues others; enraged if self-esteem threatened; limited conscience and capacity for empathy; desperately protects underlying fragile self-esteem	Be admired	General tactics: Avoid criticizing them; show admiration; outshine them; don't play down your accomplishments and ambition; document your work; build relationships with a mentor; keep your eyes open for other positions; do not take their behavior personally; consult with mentor or executive coach	Maintain close oversight to continually assess their treatment of others; do not automatically believe superiors over their subordinates; get 360° feedback on them; get coaching for them; place them where they cannot do serious harm; consider getting rid of them; don't ignore signs of trouble; consider possible presence of depression, anxiety, alcohol abuse
Grandiose: Learned	Grandiose self-image; exploits others out of carelessness; is inconsiderate in treatment of others due to not receiving negative feedback for behavior	Be admired	See general tactics above	

(continued)

Table 1 Continued

Varieties	Primary Traits	Objective	Subordinate Survival Tactics	Superior's Actions For All Varieties
Control Freak	Micromanages; seeks absolute control of everything; inflated self-image and devaluation of others' abilities; fear of chaos	Control others	See general tactics plus: Avoid direct suggestions; let them think new ideas are their own	
Antisocial	Takes what he wants, lies to get ahead, hurts others if they are in his way; lacks both a conscience and capacity for empathy	Excitement of violating rules and abusing others	Avoid provoking them; transfer out before they destroy you; do not get dragged into their unethical/illegal activities; seek allies in co-workers and mentors; seek executive coach to help you cope	

Aggressive Managers

There are a variety of factors that can lead to aggressive behavior. Frantic and irritable managers have enduring problems modulating the intensity of their feelings. They are often flooded by them, and then ignore the feelings and rights of others in desperate attempts to deal with their distress. They are often clueless about the impact of their behavior on others. Some aggressive individuals chronically view themselves as victims; what others view as aggression they see as self-defense or compensation for wrongs done to them in the past. The most problematic aggressive managers have underlying narcissistic personality traits. For example, ruthless managers lack empathy and concern for the well-being of others. Moreover, they perceive the world as a dog-eat-dog competition in which people are out to get you. In their eyes, if you are not a predator, you will become someone's prey. Bullies derive a perverse pleasure from intimidating others.

Rigid Managers

Rigid managers insist on doing things their way. Underneath this insistence can be a variety of factors. Compulsive managers fear being wrong. They live in a world of "should" and "should have." Avoiding making mistakes dominates their decision making. Authoritarian managers believe that rigid hierarchies are the best way to run organizations. Oppositional and passive-aggressive individuals perpetually feel that their autonomy is constantly being threatened, and they must push back in order to defend themselves. They fail to see that in doing so they are stepping on the rights of others. Narcissistic managers who are rigid feel that their way is best and that there is no reason to listen to others' ideas.

Impaired Managers

Many managers, at one time or another, suffer from depression, an anxiety disorder, burnout, or alcohol abuse. Many have attention deficit disorder that has never been diagnosed. Each of these can significantly impair someone's performance and ability to work effectively with others. Failure to recognize and treat these common problems costs businesses billions of dollars a year in lost productivity.

Table 2	Types of Aggressive Managers		
Varieties	**Primary Traits**	**Objective**	**Surviving Them**
Frantic	Always hyper and pressured	Avoid being in trouble; accomplishing a lot	Help them with their objectives; help them see that a frantic pace may be inefficient; evaluate for anxiety and depression
Irritable	Difficulty modulating their stress level; highly reactive to certain things	Varies	Find out what upsets them and avoid pushing their buttons; provide support; evaluate for depression and anxiety problems; gently let them know their behavior is destructive
Narcissistic	Underlying fragile self-esteem leads to eruptions of anger if the self-esteem is challenged	Maintain their self-esteem	Show deference; play down your accomplishments, avoid outshining them, never criticize them
Ruthless	Calmly goes after what he or she wants	Get what he wants	Watch your back
Bully	Seeks to intimidate for the pure excitement of it	Dominate and intimidate	Stay out of their way; don't let them see you are intimidated

Unfortunately, most of the time, the nature of the problem is not recognized. In addition to damaging productivity, these problems can markedly exacerbate, or even mimic, the various personality disorders discussed above. Most of these can be treated relatively quickly and yield a marked improvement in performance.

Table 3	Types of Rigid Managers		
Type	**Belief System**	**Underlying Dynamics**	**How to Deal With Them**
Compulsive	His way is the only way, since trying a new way would be very hard	Fears being wrong	Show them that many, many respected people do it a different way and that this way will work out in this particular situation; avoid arguing about what way is best
Authoritarian	The bosses' way is the way it should be done	Fears the world being out of control unless someone is rigidly in charge	Show them that an authority they respect does things differently
Oppositional	People are trying to dominate him and he must speak up	Feels that they are always being dominated and need to push back	Let them feel a part of the decision
Passive-Aggressive	People are trying to dominate him, and he can't speak up	Feels pushed around	Encourage their participation
Narcissistic	Feels he is remarkably skilled and knows better than anyone	Covering over fragile self-esteem by a rigid grandiose self-image	Feed their ego; don't criticize them; explain how your ideas fit into their plans

Table 4	Types of Impaired Managers	
	Main Symptoms	**Dealing with Them**
ADHD	Easily distracted, disorganized, talks incessantly, interrupts others	Get them treatment
Anxiety	Fearful—generally or with a focus	Get them treatment
PTSD	Preoccupied, emotionally numb, withdrawn, jumpy, fearful, irritable	Get them treatment
Depression	Loss of interest and energy, pessimistic, tends to worry, sleep and appetite changes	Get them treatment
Burnout	Feels overwhelmed, loss of motivation and interest	Get them treatment
Alcohol Abuse	Declining performance, often late or absent	Get them treatment

Designing Effective Interventions

Effective interventions take into consideration what is driving difficult behavior, and not simply what appears on the surface. Interventions that would lead to a positive change in a manager with one underlying personality type could intensify the problematic behavior of someone with another personality type. For example, aggressive and rigid behavior can be driven by fear and insecurity, by cluelessness, or by a ruthless desire to dominate and control people. Managers whose aggression

Case Study

Dealing with a Narcissistic VP

Bill was the vice president of a mid-sized company. His unit had grown rapidly and was profitable. He had special knowledge and skills that made him very valuable to the company. At the same time, the company's president was increasingly aware that the morale in Bill's unit was poor and that turnover was high. The president instructed Bill to obtain some coaching. He balked and the CEO relented. In time, however, things went from bad to worse. The CEO considered firing Bill. The cost of finding a replacement, and the inefficiencies suffered while the new person came up to speed, would be high. Nevertheless, he couldn't let the unit continue to bleed people. Faced with the possibility of being fired, Bill agreed to executive coaching.

Bill balked at 360° feedback but he agreed to let the coach speak with people and observe his ways of interacting. What people reported, and what the coach saw, was a driven person who lacked concern for others, focused on his own needs, was constantly snapping at people, rarely gave a pat on the back, and sometimes stole credit for others' work. He certainly fit the description of the narcissistic manager.

There was, however, another part of him. At times, he really seemed concerned about others. In individual discussions with the coach, Bill's insecurity and depression stood out more than his grandiosity. The coach determined that rather than having the core personality structure of a narcissistic individual, Bill had been so successful that he had been able to get away with stepping on people and was relatively clueless about how others felt and how his behavior affected their performance.

A major factor in Bill's behavior was a mild chronic depression. He did not enjoy things that much and rarely smiled. A great deal of his irritability came from the mild depression. The coach convinced him to try an antidepressant. Bill's snapping at people declined in a few days. In a month he seemed like a different person. With his depression gone he not only felt much less irritable, but had the emotional energy to think about others' feelings and to begin to look at his own behavior more than he had before. He had many bad habits in how he related to people, but he was now able to begin to look at them and gradually make changes.

or rigidity arises from fear and insecurity are likely to improve if treated with tolerance and reassurance. Tolerance of toxic behavior arising from ruthlessness, however, is likely to exacerbate the situation. Similarly, while a strong negative response to aggressive or rigid behavior may deter someone who is ruthless, it could increase the anxiety and tension of someone who is driven by fear, and thereby worsen the problem. *The better you understand how other people view the world and what motivates them, the better you will be able to influence their behavior.*

Senior management and human resources professionals also need to understand why someone is doing poorly in order to know whether to work with the person to improve the troubling behavior or to let him or her go. You do not want to give too many chances to someone who rains chaos and problems on others. At the same time, you do not want to get rid of a potentially fine manager who is suffering from readily treatable anxiety, depression, or stress, or who could learn better social skills in a reasonable period of time.

Developing Your Emotional Intelligence

It is puzzling that we seek expert advice on improving our golf game but avoid professional advice on how we can deal with other people. We pay personal trainers remarkable fees one or more times a week to encourage us to exercise harder. We avoid, however, engaging an expert to help us learn more about ourselves and others—someone who could help us learn to deal with different types of difficult people. Somehow, we are supposed to be experts on dealing with other people and with our own emotions even though these issues were never formally addressed in our education and training.

You are unlikely to bring about wholesale personality change in someone, but you do not need to. Rounding off rough spots and bringing greater flexibility and responsiveness to situations is all that is needed to make a significant improvement in the quality of the work environment and work output. This is very doable if handled with skill and understanding of what is needed for change.

Enhancing your emotional intelligence is preventative medicine, a vaccine against the development of toxic relationships as well as a suit of armor limiting the damage that toxic managers can do. Emotional intelligence is the key to understanding others' perspectives and needs, resolving conflicts, and wielding influence. It also helps you to know who is dangerous before problems begin, enabling you to take steps to decrease your vulnerability. Emotional intelligence helps you deal with the rigid, aggressive, and grandiose behavior you may be subjected to. Emotional intelligence also enables leaders to spot, and then either coach or remove, managers who behave in ways that are toxic to others.

There are two major components of emotional intelligence, personal competence and social competence. Personal competence refers to the ability to understand your own feelings, strengths, and weaknesses (self-awareness), and the ability to manage those feelings effectively (self-management). For example, being able to contain your anger and anxiety and thereby think clearly in upsetting situations is crucial to making good decisions and influencing others.

Social competence refers to the ability to understand what others are feeling (social awareness) and having the skills to work effectively with others (relationship management). The ability to understand what people think and feel, and then to know how to persuade, motivate, and resolve conflicts with specific individuals is among the most important skills of successful leaders and managers.

Components of Emotional Intelligence

PERSONAL COMPETENCE

Self-Awareness

- Aware of your emotions and their impact
- Aware of your strengths and weaknesses

Self-Management

- Emotional self-control
- Adaptability: flexibility in adapting to changing situations and obstacles
- Integrity, honesty, trustworthiness
- Drive to grow and achieve
  - Achievement oriented
  - Continuous learner
  - Willing to take initiative
  - Optimistic

SOCIAL COMPETENCE

Social Awareness

- Empathy and insight
  - Understanding others' perspectives and feelings
  - Appreciation of others' strengths and weaknesses
- Political awareness

Relationship Management

- Respect for others
- Conflict management skills
- Collaborative approach
- Sense of humor
- Persuasive: visionary, diplomatic
- Able to leverage diversity

People are born with varying levels of talent for understanding their own feelings and the feelings of others. Nevertheless, with conscious effort most people can make significant strides in improving their emotional intelligence.

The keys to developing your personal competence (self-awareness and self-management) are (1) paying attention to your emotional reactions to situations, (2) enhancing your understanding of why you react as you do, (3) thinking of alternate ways to interpret upsetting situations, and (4) finding constructive ways to deal with whatever emotional stress remains. The more time you invest in introspection and talking with confidants about how to understand your emotional reactions and behavior, the more your personal competence will grow.

Certain psychological issues can present an enormous barrier to developing emotional intelligence. Obstacles include a tendency to interpret situations in ways that lead to self-fulfilling prophecies, black-and-white thinking, having interpretations controlled by past painful memories, and holding attitudes that color your interpretation of experiences. These blinders can block learning. Executive coaching with someone trained as a therapist can remove the obstacles and enable you to learn.

Social competence involves understanding why people behave as they do and being able to select a course of action that will be most effective in dealing with them. The first part of this paper discussed why people may engage in various types of toxic behavior. If you understand the concepts presented and are now better able to assess why someone is engaging in toxic behavior, your social competence has grown.

In general, social competence grows through a process of (1) paying attention to the emotions and behavior of others, (2) seeking to understand others' behavior through reflection and discussions with third parties, (3) thinking of various ways to deal with situations, and (4) observing the effects of your actions. You do not have to be directly involved in situations to learn from them. You can enhance your social competence by observing others, thinking about why people are behaving and reacting as they do, and seeing what behavior seems helpful in which situations.

Whether or not they engage in toxic behavior, it is valuable to understand the personality types and work styles of people you work with. Any relationship can become toxic if the people do not understand each other and become locked in a disagreement. Having the tools to understand people is preventative medicine. The key to being a good manager lies in recognizing people's strengths and weaknesses, being able to place them in positions where their strengths will be utilized and their weaknesses will not interfere with the work, and knowing how to communicate with and work with people whose style differs from your own.

Decoding Work Styles

Everyone's style is unique and made up of innumerable factors. Nevertheless, there are certain key factors to look at when deciding on whether someone would be a good fit for a position. Familiarity with one or more models can help you to understand the people you work with by providing structure to your thoughts about them. Several typologies of personality styles have been developed including the "Five-Factor Model," Myers-Briggs Type Indicator, and Bolton's "People Styles at Work." I have created a "Work Styles Model" by integrating the insights from these three models [See *The Five-Factor Model of Personality* edited by J. S. Wiggins (Guilford Press, 1996); *Introduction to Type in Organizations* by Sandra K. Hirsh and Jean M. Kummerow (CPP, 1998); *Work It Out: Clues for Solving People Problems at Work* by Sandra Krebs Hirsh and Jane A. G. Kise (Davies-Black, 1996); *WorkTypes: Understanding Your Work Personality—How It Helps You and Holds You Back, and What You Can Do to Understand It* by Jean M. Kummerow, Nancy J. Barger, and Linda Kirby (Warner Books, 1997); *People Styles at Work: Making Bad Relationships Good and Good Relationships Better* by Robert Bolton and Dorothy Grover Bolton (Touchstone, 1986)].

Work Styles Model	
Introverts	Extroverts
Detail-Oriented	Big Picture
Task-Oriented	People-Oriented
Emotional Intelligence	Limited Social Skills
Planners	Spontaneous
Self-Centered	Group-Oriented
Conservative	Imaginative
Initiative	Followers
Conscientious	Unreliable
Strong Conscience and Moral Values	Machiavellian Attitude

INTROVERTS VS. EXTROVERTS "Extroverts" are energized by external factors (being with people) while "introverts" rejuvenate themselves by spending time alone. Extroverts are outgoing and enjoy being with groups of people whenever possible. Introverts avoid loud parties preferring one-on-one interactions or doing something on their own. Introverts find their ideas and energy inside. Interacting with others, even if fun, absorbs energy rather than creates it.

Extroverts tend to speak before they have thought a matter through, while introverts tend to gather their thoughts before thinking. Because of their tendency to talk a lot, extreme extroverts often make it hard for others to be heard, particularly introverts. On the other hand, when people are unsure of what to do, extroverts can be very helpful in getting the discussion going.

Teams benefit from having a mix of introverts and extroverts. A team consisting only of introverts could sit and say little to each other and have a hard time getting a conversation going and getting the work done. A group of extroverts could slowly and progressively increase in tension since most of the people are used to speaking 30 to 50% of the time in groups and can't when they are facing other extroverts rather than introverts.

The key to dealing with these differences is first to understand them, second to respect the strengths and limitations of each, and then to have each do what he or she are good at. Introverts should not be assigned to positions in which rapid networking is crucial. Extroverts are likely to run into trouble when someone is needed who will listen more than speak.

DETAIL PEOPLE VS. BIG-PICTURE PEOPLE Detail people are invaluable when being meticulous is important, such as in planning and implementation. At the same time, they can miss the big picture. Overly focused on getting every detail correct, they may needlessly drive up costs and run behind schedule.

Big-picture people are the ones to create visions and to make sure that a team is going in the right direction. They generally have good intuition and can synthesize large amounts of material and come up with a plan and direction. Implementing is usually not their forte, however, and they can miss important details unless a detail person is backing them up.

TASK-ORIENTED VS. PEOPLE-ORIENTED Some people are overwhelmingly focused on the tasks they have been assigned, ignoring the cost to people of accomplishing the task. They try to be unemotional and avoid letting feelings or the well-being of individuals get in the way of careful analyses of problems. They are all business at work and interact with people primarily when it is necessary to get the work done.

People-oriented individuals are much more concerned about their relationships. They want to have friends at work. They care as much about whom they work with as what they are doing. They spend time and energy talking around the water cooler because it is fun, and not simply because they need to exchange information.

While task-oriented individuals provide the direction and drive for action to overcome obstacles (including the needs and desires of some people), people-oriented individuals provide the glue that holds the office together and the support to keep people engaged and motivated. Both are needed.

EMOTIONAL INTELLIGENCE VS. LIMITED SOCIAL SKILLS Being interested in people is not the same as having social skills. Some people like to talk and to have an audience more than they like to get to know other people and listen to other people. They don't really converse with people, they talk at them. They are so preoccupied with expressing what they are feeling and thinking that they have no energy to find out what you are thinking and feeling and wish. Some people fail to pick up on messages that someone has heard enough about a topic or that he or she is busy and does not want to be interrupted. Some people do not know how to make small talk and develop a relationship and trust before jumping into business. Having limited social skills will almost always interfere with someone's success. Whether it is a minor obstacle or a disaster waiting to happen depends upon the position and the situation. It is important that people with limited social skills be placed where their limitations will not severely undermine their success, and that they obtain some coaching to improve their skills.

PLANNERS VS. SPONTANEOUS Planners like order and predictability. They like to plan carefully and then follow through. They want to know in advance that everything is set, and they seek to avoid surprises. Once decisions are made they don't want to revisit them.

Spontaneous people like spontaneity; they like to keep options open and don't want to be locked into old decisions. They will keep their eyes open to new opportunities, be flexible about timetables, and head off in new directions that seem promising.

Teams generally benefit from having a combination of planners and spontaneous people. You both want your team to get the job done and want someone to keep their eyes open to new opportunities.

SELF-CENTERED VS. GROUP-ORIENTED Some people have difficulty seeing beyond their own perspectives and wishes to such an extent that they label anyone who disagrees with them as unfair, unreasonable, or stupid. Other people are very concerned with the views and wishes of others and readily give up some of what they want in order to respect the wishes and needs of others. Group-oriented people are better team players and more trustworthy. Self-centered individuals, however, may be easier to motivate and convince to put in enormous hours in the pursuit of building their career and power.

CONSERVATIVE VS. IMAGINATIVE Some individuals strongly prefer to stay with standard ways of doing things while others want to try something new. A conservative style can come from being risk prone averse, from having difficulty learning new ways, or from difficulty imagining new ways of doing things. Imaginative individuals are able to think of new options, willing to consider taking risks, and able to learn new things. You want people with both traits on most teams, unless the task is very mundane, has been well assessed for potential new ways of doing things and no amount of imagination could improve current practices.

INITIATIVE VS. FOLLOWERS Some individuals are self-starters. If given an opportunity they will find useful things to do and will deliver. Others are good at following directions, but they are likely to sit and do little if not given explicit directions. A follower does not necessarily need close supervision, but a follower needs clear directions.

CONSCIENTIOUS AND RELIABLE VS. UNRELIABLE There are "can do" people you can go to with a very difficult task and feel confident that they will get it done somehow. Other people have marked difficulty with organizing themselves or figuring out how to do things if any glitches arise. It is important to know the reliability and resourcefulness of an individual when you select someone for a task that you will not be able to carefully supervise and support.

STRONG CONSCIENCE AND MORALS VS. MACHIAVELLIAN Some people have a strong sense of right and wrong, while others are more Machiavellian and believe that the ends justify the means. Some believe that anything that serves their personal goals is acceptable. The latter leaves the gate open to unethical behavior. Positions that present opportunities for personal gain through unethical behavior should not be filled with Machiavellian individuals unless they are well monitored. This is particularly the case if such behavior could do the company great harm.

Conclusion

Toxic managers and subordinates are a fact of life in organizations. Some are toxic most of the time; most are toxic some of the time. Knowing how to deal with people when they are being rigid, aggressive, self-centered, or performing poorly separates the good from the great managers. Using your emotional intelligence and analytic skills to understand what motivates toxic behavior enables you to find an appropriate intervention to ameliorate the impact on the work environment, including making the right decision about retaining them or letting them go.

Even when individuals are not toxic, your interactions with them can become inefficient if you do not understand their styles and cannot adjust your style to effectively work with them. Moreover, you need to understand the skills and weaknesses of people to know what jobs to assign subordinates, how to combine people to make effective teams, and how to work effectively with your boss.

THE ROLE OF PSYCHOLOGICAL WELL-BEING IN JOB PERFORMANCE: A FRESH LOOK AT AN AGE-OLD QUEST*

Thomas A. Wright

Russell Cropanzano

The thirst after happiness is never extinguished in the heart of man.

—Jean Jacques Rousseau,
Les Confessions [1781–1788], IX

Like social philosophers such as Rousseau, both business executives and organizational researchers have long been fascinated with the happy/productive worker thesis. There is a very strong practical basis for this interest. Most readers are familiar with the famous Hawthorne experiments undertaken during the 1920s and 1930s at the Western Electric Company in Cicero, Illinois. Initially undertaken to examine the role of such physical job factors as level of illumination on productivity, the studies evolved into much more, eventually securing a prominent spot in the folklore of modern management thought. In particular was the belief widely held by a number of Hawthorne researchers, including Elton Mayo and G.A. Pennock, suggesting that happiness (broadly defined) *should* produce better job performance. In addition, happiness provides a number of positive benefits for not only the happy individuals themselves, but also for those with whom they come in contact. Seen in this light, happiness is almost a responsibility to ourselves, to be sure, but also to our co-workers, who often rely on us to be steadfast and supportive in difficult times.

Prior research efforts to test the thesis have, unfortunately, often not matched this strong practical appeal. Simply stated, the results to date have been rather disappointing and, similar to the conclusions reached by Barry M. Staw and his colleagues in the mid-1980s, still remain a source of much controversy and confusion. Extending the seminal

*Reprinted from *Organizational Dynamics,* 33(4), Thomas A. Wright and Robert Cropanzane, "The Role of Psychological Well-Being in Job Performance: A Fresh Look at an Age-Old Quest," pp. 338–351, © 2004, with permission from Elsevier.

work of Staw, we suggest that the primary reason for these disappointing findings lies in how happiness has been operationalized. Traditionally, happiness has been considered as employee job satisfaction, with literally thousands of job satisfaction studies already published and hundreds more published every year. In the pages that follow, we will explore our ideas in greater detail. As we shall see, our central theme is that it is both reasonable and highly practical for both business executives and management scholars to understand that happiness is a valuable tool for maximizing both personal betterment and employee job performance.

But first, as proof positive of this trend toward the positive, consider the uplifting results from a study on the handwritten autobiographies of 180 Catholic nuns. The autobiographies, composed before the nuns took their final vows at a mean age of 22 years, were coded for both positive and emotional content. An example of positive emotional content is taken from one nun's autobiography: " . . . The past year which I have spent as a candidate studying at Notre Dame College has been a very happy one. Now I look forward with eager joy to receiving the Holy Habit of Our Lady and to a life of union with Love Divine." Providing solid testimony to the value of "thinking positively," positive emotional content was strongly associated with longevity six decades later. Happier, more productive nuns lived significantly longer (and healthier). Nuns in the highest quartile of reported positive emotion sentences taken from their autobiographies lived healthier and an average of 6.9 years longer, compared with those in the lowest quartile. The moral of the story: Being happy and positive in one's outlook on work and life has a number of tangible benefits, including living longer and healthier. As much as this may make intuitive sense to many of us, an emphasis on the positive has been a surprisingly neglected topic in organizational research.

Accentuate the Negative!

Historically, the organizational sciences have been preoccupied with negative aspects of work and life. This focus on the negative can be traced back over 100 years to the very beginnings of applied research in the latter part of the 19th/early part of the 20th centuries. The prevailing belief of early organizational research was that the most profitable business techniques were those that focused on the negative, as opposed to positive, aspects of human motivation. As a case in point, the following example, taken from a series of studies conducted in the 1920s and published in the *Journal of Applied Psychology*, clearly emphasizes this early, applied focus on the negative. In particular, and strongly influencing this accentuation on the negative, the first systematic applications of applied psychology to business problems involved how to generate increased sales dollars through "better" advertising. Essentially, increased sales were thought to result from advertisements all too often designed to frighten and scare potential customers into buying the product!

The research involved an ad test campaign for a proprietary medicine. Five advertisements were created and circulated in 15 eastern American cities of roughly equal size. The advertising appeals ranged from a highly positive one promoting the attainment of good health and its preservation, to a strongly negative one warning against the dire and costly consequences of ill health. The results speak volumes: Positive appeals to good health met with so little success (sales actually went down 10%) that they were, for the most part, discarded. Alternatively, negative appeals to the potential consequences of ill health from not purchasing the medicine met with tremendous success, with sales increasing 171%! Drawing on recent, fascinating work on human emotions, we provide a brief explanation for *why* this widespread focus on the negative, to the apparent neglect of the positive.

A key assertion made by many traditional models of emotion is that human emotions are associated with specific action tendencies. A leading positive psychologist, Barbara Fredrickson, defines a specific action tendency as "the outcome of a psychological process that narrows a person's momentary thought-action repertoire by calling to mind an urge to act in a particular way." In other words, a specific action tendency is what helps to get our attention. For example, anger leads to attacking behavior and fear leads to escape behavior. In a distinction that will become more relevant as our discussion unfolds, a number of prominent researchers on human emotions suggest that specific action tendencies better describe both the form and function of negative, as opposed to positive, emotions.

To further illustrate this critical distinction, consider the primary role of negative emotion in our most basic decision to "fight or flee" in a given situation. In the fight or flight (flee) scenario, the negative emotion of fear is best viewed as an evolved adaptation that was highly instrumental in assisting our prehistoric ancestors to survive various life-threatening situations. For instance, one of the authors currently lives at the base of the Sierra Nevada Mountains on the Nevada/California border. The mountain area is highly populated with such wild animals as mountain lions and bears. If, on one of his hikes in the mountains, the author happened upon a huge, ferocious bear, his initial response would most likely be to become frightened and then attempt to escape from this dangerous situation. In other words, the negative emotion of fear initiates the specific action tendency to flee from the fear-evoking stimulus of the man-eating bear. As our thoughts about various actions narrow to, and then focus on, these specific urges, the body's role becomes one of mobilizing optimal physiological resources to meet the life-threatening challenge. Our prehistoric survival instincts take over. This constricted or narrowed thought–action sequence can be highly adaptive in nature and helps foster quick, decisive, and potentially life-saving action.

While potentially adaptive in nature, the focus on negative, to the neglect of positive emotions, can be [and has been] very problematic if overindulged in the business environment. An excellent example of this negative focus is the typical yearly performance evaluation procedure. Why so? The answer rests on the apparent need of many evaluators to primarily focus on various negative aspects of employee behavior. Your employee neglected to do this, or your employee failed to do that. This overemphasis on the negative by many evaluators has repeatedly been shown to have a detrimental effect on subsequent employee goal achievement. Is it any wonder that managers and employees alike widely report that the most stressful job-related task is to give/get performance evaluations?

How "successful" or widespread has this buy-in to the negative been in social science research? Well, a recent computer search of contemporary literature in psychology found approximately 375,000 articles on "negative" concepts (i.e., mental illness, depression, burnout, anxiety, fear, and anger) and only about 1,000 articles on various positive concepts and capabilities of people. This constitutes a negative/positive ratio of approximately 375/1.

Once again, consider our advertising example. The primary purpose of the negative warnings against the dire and costly effects of ill health was to narrow the potential product buyer's thought–action response repertoire to focus on the detrimental consequences of not purchasing the product. The negative message was one intentionally framed to be perceived by the potential customer as distressing, fearful, or anxiety inducing. The intended message was that a failure to take this medicine would result in grave consequences. Similar to the bear scenario, in our advertising example, the effect is immediate and significant. Over the years, these and many similar results, covering a wide gamut of organizational topics, got the full attention of a business audience highly interested in maximizing short-term revenue.

This prevailing emphasis on the negative is especially ironic when one considers the increasing prominence of the Positive Psychology and Positive Organizational Behavior/Scholarship movements. We say ironic because Abraham Maslow first introduced the term "positive psychology" to us 50 years ago in his ground-breaking book, *Motivation and Personality*. In his last chapter titled "Toward a Positive Psychology," Maslow laid out a research agenda proposing investigation of such "new" and "central" concepts as growth, self-sacrifice, love, optimism, spontaneity, courage, acceptance, contentment, humility, kindness, and actualization of potential. Do these concepts sound familiar today? Given Maslow's earlier work, they should! However, Maslow was unsuccessful in bucking the prevailing viewpoint and, unfortunately, as a result, organizational research continues to focus on the negative. Adopting a "repair shop" perspective, and extending our advertising example, applied research has tended to unduly concentrate on identification of the pecuniary costs to the organization of distressed, dissatisfied, and unhappy employees. In addition, the cause of this employee dissatisfaction and unhappiness is typically seen from this negative-based or "repair shop" perspective as being deeply embedded in the emotional maladjustment of the employee, as opposed to aspects of the job itself. As a result, the "cure" for this malady usually involves some type of prevention-based employee therapy. Among others, the authors have previously referred to this approach as the disease model and suggest that while important, the disease approach is incomplete in scope. However, as we now demonstrate, the potential benefits of a positive, what we call a health approach, can also be very evident, especially over time, when considering the role of employee psychological well-being (PWB) in the happy/productive worker thesis.

Back to the Future: Psychological Well-Being and Happiness

"Happiness" is a lay construct, replete with personal meaning for each of us. In order to study the idea scientifically, we need a more precise definition that lends itself to systematic measurement. In this regard, scholars have tended to treat "happiness" as PWB, also referred to as emotional well-being or subjective well-being.

PWB is usually thought of in terms of the overall effectiveness of an employee's psychological functioning. Definitions of happiness/PWB have at least three characteristics. First, happiness is a subjective experience. People are happy to the extent that they believe themselves to be happy. Second, happiness includes both the relative presence of positive emotion and the relative absence of negative emotions. Third, happiness is a global judgment. It refers to one's life as a whole. PWB is not tied to any particular situation. Additionally, PWB has been shown to exhibit consistency over time. How one feels today influences how one feels tomorrow, next week, next month, next year, even years in the future. Fortunately, this does not mean that PWB is immutable to change. PWB has been shown to be strongly influenced by any number of environmental events and is considered to be responsive to therapeutic interventions. In sum, it is generally accepted that happiness refers to a subjective and global judgment that one is experiencing a good deal of positive emotion and relatively little negative emotion. As we shall see, recent research has consistently demonstrated that high levels of PWB can boost performance on the job, while simultaneously increasing each individual's capacity to appreciate new opportunities and experiences.

Job Performance: The Organizational Consequences of Happiness

In support of the happy/productive worker thesis, a growing body of empirical research has found significant links between various measures of employee PWB and measures of job-related performance. In one study involving M.B.A. students, participants high on well-being were shown to be superior decision makers, demonstrated better interpersonal behaviors, and received higher overall performance ratings. These results are important for two reasons. First, the study design used objective, quantifiable indices of performance (e.g., an "in-basket" measure). This argues against the possibility that correlations between well-being and job performance are simply misperceptions. Second, the experimental design of this research suggests a causal relation: that performance increases when PWB is high. In another study, employees high in well-being had superior performance evaluations and higher pay 18 months later. Considered together, these PWB studies clearly demonstrate that PWB is predictive of both a subjective measure of performance, supervisory performance evaluations, and a more objective indicator of performance, actual pay. In addition, the consistency of PWB over time is especially relevant for practitioners concerned with issues involving employee selection, training and development, and placement. Using a sample of experienced management personnel, our next example clearly demonstrates the magnitude of this stability.

Incorporating multiple measures of both PWB and performance, one of the present authors recently found that PWB significantly predicted not only contemporaneous employee performance, but also subsequent supervisory performance ratings several *years* in the future. In addition, PWB predicted subsequent employee performance even after controlling for their prior performance. In a series of studies involving well-paid management personnel from a variety of different organizations and occupations, the current authors have found that PWB remained significantly related to performance even after controlling for employee age, gender, ethnicity, job tenure, and educational attainment level.

These findings are important for at least three reasons. First, the use of longitudinal research designs supports the possibility that PWB is not only correlated with performance, but could also be a cause of job performance. Incorporating multiple measures of both performance and PWB, these research designs provide a measure of rigor not typically found in research conducted in actual organizational settings. Second, the fact that both subjective *and* objective quantifiable indices of performance have consistently been found to be related to PWB strongly argues against the possibility that the significant findings are the result of supervisory misperceptions, a consequence of what is typically referred to as the "halo" error.

Halo error is a potentially serious problem in performance evaluation. Halo error is defined as the tendency to evaluate an employee's overall job performance primarily based upon how well they perform, or are perceived to perform, on one salient performance dimension. In the present case, this salient performance dimension might be the employee's level of PWB and the possibility of halo error can be explained in the following manner. Employees who are more psychologically well may be seen by their supervisors as more likeable and fun to be around. Because people in general, and supervisors in particular, tend to be more tolerant of those they like, they may provide more positive performance evaluations for those subordinates considered to be more psychologically well. As a result, rather than being directly related to changes in performance, PWB could serve as a systematic source of halo in performance evaluations. If true, halo error could bias our ability to interpret these findings of a relationship between PWB and job performance.

Though one cannot totally rule out the halo alternative, drawing on previous research in the area, we offer three basic arguments minimizing the possibility of halo error. First, a number of the studies reported here have used longitudinal designs, affording the opportunity to measure the influence of PWB on incremental changes in job performance evaluations over time. A major strength of having multiple measures of performance over time is the ability to capture any halo contained in the prior measure(s) of job performance. Second, PWB has been related to job performance in a number of studies which have also examined a number of possible third variable explanations, including job satisfaction, positive employee affect, negative employee affect, and employee burnout. If halo bias was accounting for the obtained relationship between PWB and job performance, then we can also expect significant relations between these other measures of employee affect/emotion and job performance. The results have consistently demonstrated that this is not the case. In fact, the available data point to a common conclusion: When employee happiness is operationalized as PWB, it is positively related to various measures of employee job performance.

Third, this line of research is important because significant correlations between PWB and job performance have typically been found in the .30–.50 range. Not only are these findings *statistically* significant, they are *practically* relevant. As a case in point, taking a correlation of .30 between PWB and job performance indicates that roughly 10% of the variance in job performance is associated with differences in PWB, while taking a correlation of .50 points to a substantial 25% of the variance in job performance being associated with differences in PWB.

The available data consistently point to a common, highly practical conclusion. Whether measured with subjective ratings or objective indices, whether examined in quasi-experimental, cross-sectional, or longitudinal designs, even after controlling for the effects of a number of possible confounding variables, when happiness is measured as PWB, it is consistently and positively related to various measures of job performance. In the following sections, using current research and theory emanating from the Positive Psychology/Positive Organizational Behavior movements, we propose an expanded role of PWB for those interested in enhancing worker performance.

Broaden-and-Build: The Human Consequences of Happiness

All things being equal, not many individuals would prefer to be unhappy when they could be happy. At least since the time of the famous utilitarian philosopher Jeremy Bentham (circa 1748–1832), many would agree that seeking pleasure and avoiding pain is fundamental to human motivation. Certainly many organizational reward systems are predicated on this assumption. Consistent with this hedonistic approach, positive emotions can be seen as providing the distinct value-added of making us feel good. In fact, the balance between positive and negative emotions contributes to how we view our life.

Of noteworthy relevance is Barbara Fredrickson's broaden-and-build model of positive emotions. According to the broaden-and-build model, a number of positive emotions, including the experience of employee PWB, all share the capacity to "broaden" an individual's momentary thought–action repertoires through expanding the selection of potential thoughts and actions that come to mind. For example, the positive emotion, interest, fosters the desire to explore, assimilate new experiences, encounter new information, and grow. Likewise, the positive emotion, joy, creates the urge to play, to think outside the box and be creative. Positive emotions have the beneficial effect of potentially widening one's available arsenal of thoughts and actions by "enlarging" the available cognitive context. Properly implemented in the workplace environment, the manifestation of such positive employee emotions as joy and interest fosters employee perceptions of enhanced meaning from their work. As a result, those employees who see positive meaning in their work often come to view it as a Calling, not just as a Job or Career. Those with a Calling orientation work not only for the positive financial rewards (Job orientation) or personal achievement (Career orientation), but also for the personal fulfillment that doing one's job can bring. One practical consequence is that those who view their work as a Calling may well be more productive.

Executive Illustration

"Today's workers are not committed anymore" is a lament we hear expressed by an ever-increasing number of corporate executives. If accurate, and using the Job, Career, and Calling categories as our framework, more and more of today's employees view their work as merely a Job. When work is considered as a Job, the employee focuses on the material benefits derived from working. Work is simply the necessary means to a financial end. The fulfillment of personal happiness and contentment are sought during one's time off the job. On the other hand, those with a Career orientation work for the rewards that accompany their advancement, either organizational or professional in nature. Employees with a Career orientation are driven by the strong desire to obtain power and prestige through the increased pay and promotional opportunities that Career advancement brings. Alternatively, employees with a Calling orientation do not work primarily for either financial or promotional advancement opportunities. Instead, they work for the fulfillment that doing their work affords. Doing their work well is considered an end in and of itself. Considered together, employees with a Calling orientation report a much more rewarding relation with the work itself, spend more time on work-related activities, and appear to gain more enjoyment, fulfillment, and satisfaction from it. Those who are optimistic and conscientious appear to be more likely to report themselves as having a Calling orientation. Interestingly, and highly relevant when one considers possible intervention strategies, recent research indicates that many employees have the ability to accurately differentiate their work orientation among the Job, Career, and Calling categories.

Fascinating research has further confirmed that the enlarging effect of positive emotion has a physiological base and is linked to increases in brain dopamine levels. In addition, while negative emotions have been shown to adversely increase both heart rate and blood pressure, positive emotions can suppress or "undo" these lingering maladaptive effects! More specifically, compared to such negative emotions as anger and sadness, positive emotions have been shown to produce more rapid returns to the individuals's normal cardiovascular baseline levels. In other words, following the initial, evolutionary surge in heart and blood pressure rates which typically accompany our response to stressful situations, positive emotions help speed the body's recovery to its normal, pre-stress levels.

Based on Fredrickson's work, we also propose that these positive emotions assist in "building" the individual's enduring personal resources, ranging from physical, psychological, intellectual, and social in nature. This capacity to experience the positive seems to be crucial to one's capacity to thrive, mentally flourish, and psychologically grow. This sense of flourishing appears to make psychologically well or happy people more proactive, resilient to adverse situations, and less prone to stress symptoms. As a result, a continued focus on these positive feelings expands (broadens) and builds on these positive urges, creating a potentially moderating "upward spiral" effect, which can further enhance employee character development. This capacity to experience positive feelings is considered to be a fundamental human strength.

Good Morning America Case

Positive emotions help people to not only survive, but also to thrive when confronted with adverse situations. This capacity to overcome potential adversity was vividly demonstrated on a segment of the *Good Morning America* program. C. R. Snyder, one of the founding fathers of positive psychology and a psychology professor at the University of Kansas, gave a test of positive emotion to the *Good Morning America* regular cast.

Not surprisingly for many regular viewers of the popular show, host Charles Gibson outscored everyone else by a wide margin. Then, testing the hypothesis that positive or happy people have developed the necessary psychological and physical resources for coping with adversity, Snyder had the members of the crew hold their hand in a bucket of ice before the live cameras and studio audience. Consistent with Snyder's prediction, everyone in the cast removed his or her hand before 90 seconds had elapsed—everyone, that is, except Charles Gibson! In fact, Gibson still had his hand in the ice bucket [while continuing to smile, not grimace] right up until the commercial break, well beyond the time endured by the rest of the program crew. Gibson's resilience to the pain and ability to cope with adversity was clearly attributable to his positive, optimistic personality.

Consider the positive emotion *interest*. Interest has both individual and organizational benefits. At the individual level, interest creates the urge to explore, take in new information and experiences, and expand oneself in the process. At the organizational level, interest, considered collectively, can facilitate meaningful interpersonal encounters. These meaningful interpersonal encounters result in enhanced social connections and team-building behavior. A beneficial organizational consequence is the creation of a better work climate and increased productivity.

This upward spiraling effect is in marked contrast to the effects of a number of negative emotions. Consider the case of depression. Distressingly, depression has reached epidemic proportions in the United States. Recent figures indicate that literally tens of millions of Americans have taken (or are currently taking) various forms of antidepression medications. Unlike the uplifting effect of positive emotion, negative feelings of depression or anger or fear tend to lead to narrowed, pessimistic thinking, which can produce a further downward spiral, leading to ever-worsening moods and feelings.

How Happiness Helps Us to Grow: A Demonstration of the Broaden-and-Build Approach to Management

We have already seen that happiness, when defined as PWB, promotes higher levels of job performance. We have also learned that those high in PWB are in a better position to benefit from positive work experiences than are their counterparts who are lower in PWB. Through the impetus provided by high levels of PWB, happier or more psychologically well employees are more easily able to "broaden-and-build" themselves and become more creative, resilient, socially connected, physically and mentally healthy, and more productively effective. In addition, and of further benefit, these effects are seen as persisting over time and across situations.

As an illustration of this idea, consider a recent study by the present authors. In this study we found strong empirical support for the idea that those high in PWB can benefit more from a satisfying job than do those low in PWB. In other words, employee PWB moderated or influenced the job satisfaction to job performance relation. Specifically, the more positive the PWB of the employee, the stronger [more statistically robust] was the observed relation between job satisfaction and job performance. Considered together, PWB, job satisfaction and the PWB by job satisfaction interaction (the moderator effect) accounted for approximately 25% of the variance in employee job performance ratings. This finding strongly supports our premise of a distinct competitive advantage for those organizations able and willing to foster a psychologically well workforce and work environment.

To emphasize the potential pecuniary benefits of these findings, consider the following example. Suppose you manage 10 electrical engineers. Furthermore, each engineer is paid $1,250 per week, or $65,000 a year in salary. You know that, for a number of reasons—including their PWB—each engineer's productivity varies by as much as $500 a week, or roughly $25,000 a year. (This is consistent with national averages across occupations, which indicate your engineers are typically productive for only 4.8 hours for every 8 hours that you pay them!) Let us put this in the context of our reported results. PWB and job satisfaction account for roughly 25% of this $500 a week in performance variance for our engineers. This translates into $125 per week/per person in lost productivity! With 10 employees, this translates to $1,250 per week in performance variance, for 100 employees, the numbers are $12,500 per week or $650,000 per year. Of equal importance, as we will momentarily detail, various intervention strategies can be used to select psychologically well job applicants. Current employees can also be more effectively trained and placed based upon knowledge of their PWB. In our concluding sections, we provide suggestions for proactive business executives interested in developing progressive, employee-centered intervention strategies designed to serve the dual purpose of enhancing both PWB and employee performance.

How to Build a Happy Workforce

Employee-focused, positive psychological-based interventions at work can take three general forms: composition, training, and situational engineering. Composition emphasizes selecting and placing people into appropriate positions, training emphasizes assisting workers so that they "fit" their jobs more closely, and situational engineering emphasizes changing the work environment so that it more closely fits the needs of one's employees. Our "extended" happy/productive worker thesis has implications for each approach.

The Composition (or Selection) Approach to Promoting Happiness

Research has clearly established that PWB is stable over time. In fact, one of our studies has established substantial test-retest correlations of up to five years in duration. These findings give clear support to the notion that people who report being happy (or unhappy) at one point in time are likely to be happy (or unhappy) at another point in time, and provide evidence supportive of the notion of the heritability of happiness.

Interesting research on the possible heritability of happiness (and job satisfaction) has been reported by a number of scholars. While beyond the scope of the present discussion, the possibility of a genetic basis for various employee attitudes and emotions has been highly controversial in organizational research. Nevertheless, and very relevant from a management perspective, research supportive of a possible genetic basis does not necessarily imply that well-being stability is solely due to the personal characteristics of the individual. Employee PWB, and level of job satisfaction for that matter, may well be stable over time because one's life or job circumstances are stable as well. For example, an employee may remain at the same job or at a very similar one for any number of reasons. As a result, the "fact" of employee attitudinal stability should not solely be used to argue against the possibility of successful training and situational engineering-based interventions.

We should point out that selecting the happiest employees does raise the specter of some potentially serious ethical issues. The failure to select prospective employees on the basis of their level of PWB could depress these individuals further, which in turn could make these job candidates even more unemployable in the future. This can engender considerable human and societal costs. As a consequence, careful consideration of these and other related issues is of paramount importance for management personnel, employing organizations, and practicing consultants interested in using various measures of PWB to select happy workers.

Training

Another option is to change employees by helping them learn to be happier. There is good evidence that various types of stress management training can have positive effects on worker happiness. A number of strategies exist where individual employees can proactively self-monitor or manage their personal perceptions to enhance positive, and discourage negative, displays of momentary mood and emotion. For example, constructive self-talk is a conscious effort to replace negative with more positive and reinforcing self-talk. There are a number of other cognitive restructuring techniques designed to be beneficial in temporarily altering an employee's current emotional state or providing more permanent or dispositionally-based changes in their behavior. One such trait is learned optimism. Learned optimism is viewed as a developed trait or style emphasizing positive thought patterns. As the name indicates, employees can be trained to better utilize "learned" optimism techniques, both within and outside the work environment. As one benefit, research has clearly demonstrated that optimistic employees perform more effectively on a wide range of jobs and occupations, especially those involving significant interactions with others.

Metropolitan Life Case

As everyone knows, selling is not easy. It requires great persistence in the face of seemingly consistent rejection. The executives at Metropolitan Life learned this fact all too well. While they rigorously selected less than 1 in 10 sales agent applicants, half would quit in the first year. Equally disheartening, of those who stayed, most produced less and less the longer they remained with the company as sales agents. In any event, by the end of the fourth year, 80% were gone. As it turned out, employee optimism predicted level of sales. Sales agents ranked in the top half on an optimism scale sold 37% more insurance on average in their first 2 years than those agents who scored in the lower half of the scale and were more pessimistic. Even more impressive, agents who scored in the top 10% on optimism sold 88% more than those in the bottom 10%. As executives at Metropolitan Life discovered, the best news was that an optimistic approach is learnable.

Situational Engineering

The third approach to possible interventions involves changing the environment so that it promotes, or at least does not impair, worker PWB. Situational engineering would appear to be a promising technique, in that there is evidence that working conditions strongly affect employee PWB. As with the selection and training approaches, situational engineering provides a variety of options for organizations to create a happier, more satisfied, workforce. In fact, research has documented that something as simple as providing tangible social support can help reduce the negative impact of stressful jobs. More generally, employers can manipulate or reengineer any number of organizational factors (i.e., physical, role, task, and/or interpersonal demands) shown to be related to increased displays of employee emotion at work. For example, work-family conflict seems to diminish life satisfaction and increase negative displays of emotion. Alternatively, family-friendly policies, such as flextime and child-care programs, should increase employee PWB. Finally, we should not neglect the more obvious change strategies. Research has shown that equitable pay tends to promote high levels of PWB. In short, there are a number of available options for designing human resource techniques to enhance PWB and subsequent employee performance.

Concluding Thoughts

Applied research's interest in employee happiness has long centered on the happy/productive worker thesis. However, the results have sometimes proved disappointing. Fortunately, recent work shows great promise. It seems that the generations of managers and business executives who believed that a happy worker is a productive worker are correct when considering employee happiness as PWB. Of noteworthy relevance in the "holy grail" pursuit of providing greater insight into the happy/productive worker thesis is the further development of such positive-based approaches as the broaden-and-build model. The broaden-and-build model provides the necessary framework to explain the possible interactive role of PWB on the job satisfaction/job performance relation. Considered individually, PWB has demonstrated statistically significant relations to employee performance. The psychological well-being/job performance correlation is consistently in the .30–.50 range. Furthermore, results were discussed here that clearly demonstrate that consideration of the interaction effects of PWB on the job satisfaction/job performance relation is significantly more statistically robust.

In addition to PWB, the broaden-and-build model supports the possible adaptive and interactive nature of a number of other positive-based employee emotions. Joy, exhilaration, optimism, and interest all share the potential ability to broaden an employee's momentary thought–action experiences and provide valuable assistance in helping to further build the employee's personal resource arsenal. This means that in addition to studies on happy/productive workers, we may eventually see [and we actively encourage] research on serene/thoughtful workers, caring/helpful workers, joyous/honest workers, and exhilarated/creative workers:

We close by emphasizing an important point. Employee PWB has both theoretical and applied relevance in today's society. Using the Positive Psychology/Positive Organizational Behavior (POB) framework, it seems evident that promoting employee PWB is an intrinsic good for which all should work. If this approach promotes better job performance, which the findings strongly suggest is the case, then so much the better. Regardless, the pursuit of employee PWB remains valuable for its own sake. In closing, roughly 2,500 years ago, Aristotle posed the question of what constitutes the good life. Similar to Aristotle, our response is that the pursuit of happiness (*eudaimonia* to Aristotle), properly defined, is a pivotal first step in any attempt to address this age-old question.

Selected Bibliography

For a further discussion of the happy/productive worker thesis and related topics, see E. Mayo, *The Problems of an Industrial Civilization* (New York: MacMillan, 1933); B. M. Staw, "Organizational Psychology and the Pursuit of the Happy/Productive Worker," *California Management Review* 28 (1986): 40–43; B. M. Staw and J. Ross, "Stability in the Midst of Change: A Dispositional Approach to Job Attitudes," *Journal of Applied Psychology* 70 (1985): 469–480; B. M. Staw, N. E. Bell, and J. A. Clausen, "The Dispositional Approach to Job Attitudes: A Lifetime Longitudinal Test," *Administrative Science Quarterly* 31 (1986): 56–77; R. Cropanzano and T. A. Wright, "When a 'Happy' Worker Is a 'Productive' Worker: A Review and Further Refinement of the Happy-Productive Worker Thesis," *Consulting Psychology Journal: Practice and Research* 53 (2001): 182–199;

T. A. Wright, "The Role of 'Happiness' in Organizational Research: Past, Present, and Future Directions," in P. L. Perrewe and D. C. Ganster, eds., *Research in Occupational Stress and Well-Being*, Vol. 4 (Amsterdam: JAI Press, 2005). For those interested in reading more about the nun study, see D. D. Danner, D. A. Snowden, and W. V. Friesen, "Positive Emotions in Early Life and Longevity Findings from the Nun Study," *Journal of Personality and Social Psychology* 80 (2001): 804–813. For a fascinating look at early work on advertising, see the following work, all by D. B. Lucas and C. E. Benson, "The Relative Value of Positive and Negative Advertising Appeals as Measured by Coupons Returned," *Journal of Applied Psychology* 13 (1929): 274–300; "The Historical Trend of Negative Appeals in Advertising," *Journal of Applied*

Psychology 13 (1929): 346–356; "The Recall Values of Positive and Negative Advertising Appeals," *Journal of Applied Psychology* 14 (1930): 218–238; "Some Sales Results for Positive and Negative Advertisements," *Journal of Applied Psychology* 14 (1930): 363–370.

Highly readable overviews of the broaden-and-build model of positive emotions are contained in B. L. Fredrickson, "What Good Are Positive Emotions?" *Review of General Psychology* 2 (1998): 300–319; B. L. Fredrickson, "The Role of Positive Emotions in Positive Psychology: The Broaden-and-Build Theory of Positive Emotions," *American Psychologist* 56 (2001): 219–226; B. L. Fredrickson, "Positive Emotions and Upward Spirals in Organizations," in K. S. Cameron, J. E. Dutton, and R. E. Quinn, eds., *Positive Organizational Scholarship: Foundations of a New Discipline* (San Francisco: Berrett-Koehler, 2003).

To read more about the positive psychology/positive organizational behavior movements, see F. Luthans, "Positive Organizational Behavior: Developing and Maintaining Psychological Strengths," *Academy of Management Executive* 16 (2002): 57–72; F. Luthans, "The Need for and Meaning of Positive Organizational Behavior," *Journal of Organizational Behavior* 23 (2002): 695–706; T. A. Wright, "Positive Organizational Behavior: An Idea Whose Time Has Truly Come," *Journal of Organizational Behavior* 24 (2003): 437–442.

For a further discussion of the "repair shop" perspective, see C. D. Ryff and B. Singer, "The Contours of Positive Human Health," *Psychological Inquiry* 9 (1998): 1–28; C. L. M. Keyes and J. Haidt, "Introduction: Human Flourishing—The Study of That Which Makes Life Worthwhile," in C. L. M. Keyes and J. Haidt, eds., *Flourishing: Positive Psychology and the Life Well-Lived* (Washington, D.C.: American Psychological Association, 2003).

For a good overview of what psychological well-being is and how it is defined, see E. Diener, E. M. Suh, R. E. Lucas, and H. L. Smith, "Subjective Well-Being: Three Decades of Progress," *Psychological Bulletin* 125 (1999): 276–302.

The following empirical work by Staw and his colleagues is highly supportive of the happy/productive worker thesis: B. M. Staw and S. G. Barsade, "Affect and Managerial Performance: A Test of the Sadder-but-Wiser vs. Happier-and-Smarter Hypotheses," *Administrative Science Quarterly* 38 (1993): 304–331; B. M. Staw, R. I. Sutton, and L. H. Pelled, "Employee Positive Emotion and Favorable Outcomes at the Workplace," *Organization Science* 5 (1994): 71–91; T. A. Wright and B. M. Staw, "Affect and Favorable Work Outcomes: Two Longitudinal Tests of the Happy-Productive Worker Thesis," *Journal of Organizational Behavior* 20 (1999): 1–23.

The present authors have consistently demonstrated that PWB is related to various measures of job performance. For one of the first studies examining the relation between PWB and performance, see T. A. Wright, D. G. Bonett, and D. A. Sweeney, "Mental Health and Work Performance: Results of a Longitudinal Field Study," *Journal of Occupational and Organizational Psychology* 66 (1993): 277–284; T. A. Wright and R. Cropanzano, "Psychological Well-Being and Job Satisfaction as Predictors of Job Performance," *Journal*

of Occupational Health Psychology 5 (2000): 84–94; T. A. Wright, R. Cropanzano, P. J. Denney, P. J., and G. L. Moline, "When a Happy Worker Is a Productive Worker: A Preliminary Examination of Three Models," *Canadian Journal of Behavioral Science* 34 (2002): 146–150.

For a further discussion on halo effects, see T. L. Robbins and A. S. DeNisi, "A Closer Look at Interpersonal Affect as a Distinct Influence on Cognitive Processing in Performance Evaluation," *Journal of Applied Psychology* 79 (1994): 341–353.

For work on the meaning of work, see A. Wrzesniewski, "Finding Positive Meaning in Work," in K. S. Cameron, J. E. Dutton, and R. E. Quinn, eds., *Positive Organizational Scholarship: Foundations of a New Discipline* (San Francisco: Berrett-Koehler, 2003); M. G. Pratt and B. E. Ashforth, "Fostering Meaningfulness in Working and at Work," in K. S. Cameron, J. E. Dutton, and R. E. Quinn, eds., *Positive Organizational Scholarship: Foundations of a New Discipline* (San Francisco: Berrett-Koehler, 2003).

For a fascinating look at the possible physiological basis for human emotions, see B. L. Fredrickson and R. W. Levenson, "Positive Emotions Speed Recovery from the Cardiovascular Sequelae of Negative Emotions," *Cognition and Emotion* 12 (1998): 191–220.

To read further on the possible moderating effect of psychological well-being on the job satisfaction to job performance relation, see T. A. Wright and R. Cropanzano, "The Role of Psychological Well-Being as a Moderator of the Relation Between Job Satisfaction and Job Performance," Paper presented at the 2003 meeting of the *Society for Industrial and Organizational Psychology*, Orlando, Florida.

For a further discussion of work intervention strategies, see D. R. Ilgen, "Teams Imbedded in Organizations: Some Implications," *American Psychologist* 54 (1999): 129–139; R. Cropanzano and T. A. Wright, "A Five-Year Study of Change in the Relationship Between Well-Being and Job Performance," *Consulting Psychology Journal: Practice and Research* 51 (1999): 252–265.

For some entertaining reading on the possible heritability of happiness (and job satisfaction), see R. D. Arvey, T. J. Bouchard, N. L. Segal, and L.M. Abraham, "Job Satisfaction: Environmental and Genetic Components," *Journal of Applied Psychology* 74 (1989): 187–192; T. J. Bouchard, D. T. Lykken, M. McGue, N. Segal, and A. Tellegen, "The Sources of Human Psychological Differences: The Minnesota Study of Twins Reared Apart," *Science* 250 (1990): 223–228. For an alternative interpretation to Arvey et al., see R. Cropanzano and K. James, "Some Methodological Considerations for the Behavioral Genetic Analysis of Work Attitudes," *Journal of Applied Psychology* 75 (1990): 433–439.

To learn more about the benefits of learned optimism, see M.E.P. Seligman, *Authentic Happiness* (New York: Free Press, 2002); M. E. P. Seligman, *Learned Optimism: How to Change Your Mind and Your Life* (New York: Pocket Books, 1998).

For a more comprehensive review of research on organizational reengineering, see J. C. Quick, J. D. Quick, D. L. Nelson, and L. L. Hurrell, *Preventive Stress Management in Organizations* (Washington, D.C.: American Psychological Association, 1997).

BUILDING THE CIVILIZED WORKPLACE*

Robert I. Sutton

Nasty people don't just make others feel miserable; they create economic problems for their companies.

Lars Dalgaard is CEO and cofounder of SuccessFactors, one of the world's fastest-growing software companies—and the fastest with revenues over $30 million. Dalgaard recently listed some milestones that his California-based company passed in its first seven years:

- the use of its software by more than two million employees at over 1,200 companies around the world
- the use of its software by employees speaking 18 languages in 156 countries
- growth three times that of the company's nearest competitor
- enthusiastic recommendations of the product by nearly all customers
- dramatically low employee turnover
- employing no jerks

That's right—no jerks—although the word SuccessFactors really uses (except on its Web site) is a mild obscenity that starts with the letter *A* and sort of rhymes with "castle." All the employees SuccessFactors hires agree in writing to 14 "rules of engagement." Rule 14 starts out, "I will be a good person to work with—not territorial, not be a jerk." One of Dalgaard's founding principles is that "our organization will consist only of people who absolutely love what we do, with a white-hot passion. We will have utmost respect for the individual in a collaborative, egalitarian, and meritocratic environment—no blind copying, no politics, no parochialism, no silos, no games,—just being good!"

Dalgaard is emphatic about applying this rule at SuccessFactors because part of its mission is to help companies focus more on performance and less on politics. Employees aren't expected to be perfect, but when they lose their cool or belittle colleagues, inadvertently or not, they are expected to repent. Dalgaard himself is not above the rule—he explained to me that, given the pressures of running a rapidly growing business, he too occasionally "blows it" at meetings. At times, he has apologized to all 400-plus people in his company, not just to the people at the meeting in question, because "word about my behavior would get out."

As Dalgaard suggests, there is a business case against tolerating nasty and demeaning people. Companies that put up with jerks not only can have more difficulty recruiting and retaining the best and brightest talent but are also prone to higher client churn, damaged reputations, and diminished investor confidence. Innovation and creativity may suffer, and cooperation could be impaired, both within and outside the organization—no small matter in an increasingly networked world.

The problem is more widespread than you might think. Research in the United Kingdom and the United States suggests that jerk-infested workplaces are common: a 2000 study by Loraleigh Keashly and Karen Jagatic[1] found that 27 percent of the workers in a representative sample of 700 Michigan residents experienced mistreatment by someone in the workplace. Some occupations, such as medical ones, are especially bad. A 2003 study[2] of 461 nurses found that in the month before it was conducted, 91 percent

---

1. Personal insults
2. Invading coworker's personal territory
3. Uninvited physical contact
4. Threats and intimidation, verbal and nonverbal
5. Sarcastic jokes and teasing used as insult delivery systems
6. Withering e-mails
7. Status slaps intended to humiliate victims
8. Public shaming or status degradation rituals
9. Rude interruptions
10. Two-faced attacks
11. Dirty looks
12. Treating people as if they were invisible

EXHIBIT 1   **The dirty dozen**

had experienced verbal abuse, defined as mistreatment that left them feeling attacked, devalued, or humiliated. Physicians were the most frequent abusers.

There is good news and bad news about workplace jerks. The bad news is that abuse is widespread and the human and financial toll is high. The good news is that leaders can take steps to build workplaces where demeaning behavior isn't tolerated and nasty people are shown the door.

How Workplace Jerks Do Their Dirty Work

Researchers who write about psychological abuse in the workplace define it as "the sustained display of hostile verbal and nonverbal behavior, excluding physical contact." At least for me, that definition doesn't quite capture the emotional wallop these creeps pack. The workplace jerk definition I use is this: do people feel oppressed, humiliated, de-energized, or belittled after talking to an alleged jerk? In particular, do they feel worse about themselves?

Workplace jerks do their dirty work in all sorts of ways; I've listed 12 common ones—the dirty dozen—to illustrate the range of these subtle and not-so-subtle moves, which can include physical contact (Exhibit 1). Researchers who study workplace abuse and bullying have identified scores of others. I suspect you can add many more that you've seen, personally experienced—or committed.

Lists like these are useful but leave a sterilized view of how workplace jerks act and the damage they inflict. Stories, often painful ones, are necessary to understand how workplace bullies demean and de-energize people. Consider the story of this victim of multiple humiliations:

> "Billy," he said, standing in the doorway so that everyone in the central area could see and hear us clearly. "Billy, this is not adequate, really not at all." As he spoke he crumpled the papers that he held. My work. One by one he crumpled the papers, holding them out as if they were something dirty and dropping them inside my office as everyone watched. Then he said loudly, "Garbage in, garbage out." I started to speak, but he cut me off. "You give me the garbage, now you clean it up." I did. Through the doorway I could see people looking away because they were embarrassed for me. They didn't want to see what was in front of them: a 36-year-old man in a three-piece suit stooping before his boss to pick up crumpled pieces of paper.[3]

The damage done

The human damage done by that kind of encounter is well documented—especially the harm that superiors do to their subordinates. Bennett Tepper studied abusive supervision in a representative study of 712 employees in a midwestern city.[4] He asked them if their bosses had engaged in abusive behavior, including ridicule, put-downs, and the silent treatment—demeaning acts that drive people out of organizations and sap the effectiveness of those who remain. A six-month follow-up found that employees with abusive supervisors quit their jobs at accelerated rates. Those still trapped felt less committed to their employers and experienced less satisfaction from work and life, as well as heightened anxiety, depression, and burnout. Dozens of other studies have uncovered similar findings; the victims report reduced levels of job satisfaction, productivity, concentration, and mental and physical health.

Nasty interactions have a far bigger impact on the mood of people who experience them than positive interactions do. Recent research shows just how much. Theresa Glomb, Charles Hulin, and Andrew Miner did a clever study[5] in which 41 employees of a manufacturing plant in the Midwest carried palm-size computers for two to three weeks. At four random intervals throughout the workday, each employee had to report any recent interaction with a supervisor or a coworker and whether it was positive or negative, as well as their current mood. The researchers found that negative interactions affected the moods of these employees five times more strongly than positive ones.

All these factors suggest an effect on costs. One reader of a short article I wrote on workplace jerks[6] felt that more companies would be convinced if they estimated "the total cost of jerks," or TCJ (Exhibit 2). If you want to develop a rough estimate of your company's TCJ, take a look at my list of possible costs and attach your best monetary estimate to each, as well as to any other factors you regard as relevant. This exercise can help you face up to the damage that jerks do to your organization. When I told a Silicon Valley executive about the TCJ method, he replied that it was more than a concept at his company. Management had calculated the extra costs generated by a star salesperson—the assistants he burned through, the overtime costs, the legal costs, his anger-management training, and so on—and found that the extra cost of this one jerk for one year was $160,000.

Finally, if word leaks out that your organization is led by mean-spirited jerks, the damage to its reputation can drive away potential employees and shake investor confidence. Neal Patterson, the CEO of Cerner, learned this lesson in 2001 when he sent an e-mail intended for just the top 400 people in this health care software company. Patterson complained that few employees were working full 40-hour weeks and that "as managers—you either do not know what your employees are doing; or you do not care." Patterson said that he wanted to see the employee parking lot "substantially full" from 7:30 AM to 6:30 PM weekdays and "half full" on Saturdays. If that didn't happen, he would take harsh measures. "You have two weeks," he warned. "Tick, tock."[7] Patterson's e-mail was leaked on the Internet, provoking harsh criticism from management experts, including my Stanford colleague Jeffrey Pfeffer, who described it as "the corporate equivalent of whips and ropes and chains." Pfeffer went a bit overboard for my taste. But investors weren't pleased either: the company's stock value plummeted by 22 percent in three days. Patterson handled the aftermath well: he sent an apology to his employees and admitted that he wished he had never sent the e-mail. The share price did bounce back. Patterson learned the hard way that when CEOs come across as bullies, they can scare their investors as well as their underlings.

Enforcing the no-jerks rule

Executives who are committed to building a civilized workplace don't just take haphazard action against one jerk at a time; they use a set of integrated work practices to battle the problem.

	Possible costs in calculating your TCJ (total cost of jerks)
Damage to victims and witnesses	• Distraction from tasks—more effort devoted to coping with or avoiding nasty encounters or avoiding blame, less devoted to tasks • Honesty may not be the best policy—reduced psychological safety and climate of fear undermine employees' ability to offer suggestions and learn from failures • Loss of motivation and energy at work • Stress-induced psychological and physical illness • Prolonged bullying turning victims into jerks themselves • Absenteeism and turnover in response to abusive supervisors or peers
Woes of certified jerks	• Hesitation on part of victims and witnesses to cooperate with jerks or tell them bad news • Retaliation from victims and witnesses • Humiliation when "outed" • Job loss • Long-term career damage
Wicked consequences for management	• Time spent appeasing, calming, counseling, or disciplining jerks • Time spent cooling-out victimized employees, as well as customers, contract employees, suppliers, and other key victimized outsiders • Time spent reorganizing departments and teams so that jerks do less damage • Time spent interviewing, recruiting, and training after jerks and their victims depart
Legal and human-resource management costs	• Anger management and other training to reform jerks • Legal costs for inside and outside counsel • Settlement fees and successful litigation by victims • Settlement fees and successful litigation by alleged jerks (e.g., wrongful-termination claims)
When jerks reign: negative effects on organizations	• Reduced creativity and innovation • Reduced discretionary effort • Dysfunctional internal competition • Impaired cooperation from outside organizations and people • "Combat pay"—higher rates charged by outsiders • Impaired ability to attract the best and brightest

EXHIBIT 2 What is your TCJ?

Source: Robert I. Sutton, *The No Asshole Rule: Building a Civilized Workplace and Surviving One That Isn't,* New York: Warner Business Books, 2007

At the workplaces that enforce the no-jerks rule most vehemently and effectively, an employee's performance and treatment of others aren't seen as separate things. Phrases like "talented jerk," "brilliant bastard," or "a bully and a superstar" are oxymorons. Jerks are dealt with immediately: they quickly realize (or are told) that they have blown it, apologize, reflect on their nastiness, ask for forgiveness, and work to change their ways. Repeat offenders aren't ignored or forgiven again and again—they change or depart.

Five intertwined practices are useful for enforcing the no-jerks rule.

Make the rule public by what you say and, especially, do

Plante & Moran, a company on *Fortune*'s "100 Best Places to Work" list for nine years in a row, proclaims its rule openly: "The goal is a 'jerk-free' workforce at this accounting firm," and "the staff is encouraged to live by the Golden Rule." At Barclays Capital, COO Rich Ricci says that "we have a no-jerk rule around here," especially in selecting senior executives. *BusinessWeek* explains what this means for the employees of Barclays Capital: "Hotshots who alienate colleagues are told to change or leave."[8] Talking about the rules is just the first step; the real test happens when someone acts like a jerk. If people don't feel comfortable blowing the whistle on the offender, your company will both be seen as hypocritical and fill up with jerks, so don't adopt the rule unless you mean it. SuccessFactors shows how to back talk with action. Consider this post on the company's public blog site by company employee Max Goldman:

> My own personal experience with [the no-jerks rule] is very simple. Once, my boss was being a jerk, I told him so. Instead of getting mad, he accepted the comment and we moved on. Later, he thanked me for telling him. My boss thanked me for calling him a jerk. Let me repeat that. My boss thanked me for calling him a jerk. Calling the behavior what it was helped everyone work better together and get more done. Can you do that at your company?

Weave the rule into hiring and firing policies

Consider how the Seattle law firm Perkins Coie, which earned a spot on *Fortune*'s "100 Best Places to Work" list in 2007 for the fourth year in a row, applies the rule during job interviews. Partners Bob Giles and Mike Reynvaan were once tempted to hire a rainmaker from another firm but realized that doing so would violate the rule. As they put it, "We looked at each other and said, 'What a jerk.' Only we didn't use that word."[9]

Similarly, Southwest Airlines has always emphasized that people are "hired and fired for attitude." Herb Kelleher, the company's cofounder and former CEO, shows how this works: "One of our pilot applicants was very nasty to one of our receptionists, and we immediately rejected him. You can't treat people that way and be the kind of leader we want."[10] As Ann Rhoades, a former Southwest vice president, told me, "We don't do it to our people; they don't deserve it. People who work for us don't have to take the abuse."

Teach People How to Fight

The no-jerks rule doesn't mean turning your organization into a paradise for conflict-averse wimps. People in the best groups and organizations know how to fight. Intel, the world's largest semiconductor maker, gives all full-time employees training in the "constructive confrontation" that is a hallmark of the company's culture. Leaders and corporate trainers emphasize that bad things happen when the bullies win using personal attacks, disrespect, and intimidation. When that happens, only the loudest and strongest voices get heard; there is no diversity of views; communication is poor, tension high, and productivity low; and people first resign themselves to living with the nastiness—and then resign from the company.

To paraphrase a primary theme in Karl Weick's classic book, *The Social Psychology of Organizing,*[11] this approach means learning to "argue as if you are right and to listen as if you are wrong." That is what Intel tries to teach through lectures, role-playing, and, most essentially, through observing the way managers and leaders fight—and when. The company's motto is "disagree and then commit," because second-guessing, complaining, and arguing after a decision is made sap effort and attention and thus make it unclear whether the decision went wrong because it was a bad idea or because it was a good idea implemented with insufficient energy and commitment.

Apply the rule to customers and clients too

Organizations that are serious about enforcing the no-jerks rule apply it not just to employees but also to customers, clients, students, and everyone else who might be encountered at work. They do so because their people don't deserve the abuse, customers (or taxpayers) don't pay to endure or witness demeaning jerks, and persistent nastiness that is left unchecked can create a culture of contempt infecting everyone it touches.

The late Joe Gold—the founder of Gold's Gym, which now has more than 550 locations in 43 countries—applied a variation of the no-jerks rule to customers. He didn't mince words; "To keep it simple you run your gym like you run your house. Keep it clean and in good running order. No jerks allowed, members pay on time, and if they give you any crap, throw them out." Gold applied the rule to customers from the time he opened his first gym, a block from Muscle Beach, in Venice, California, where early customers included Arnold Schwarzenegger.

Manage the little moments

Putting the right practices and policies in place is useless if they don't set the stage for civilized conversations and interactions. People must treat the person in front of them, right now, in the right way, and they must feel safe to point out when their peers and superiors blow it. The power of efforts to work on "the little moments" can be seen in an organizational change at the US Department of Veterans Affairs. To reduce the bullying of employees, psychological abuse, and aggression at 11 sites with more than 7,000 people, each site appointed an action team of managers and union members that developed a customized intervention process. But there were key similarities among all of the sites: employees learned about the damage that aggression causes, used role-playing exercises to get into the shoes of bullies and victims, and learned to reflect before and after they interacted with other people. Action team members and site leaders also made a public commitment to model civilized behavior themselves. At one site, for example, managers and employees worked to eliminate seemingly small slights such as glaring, interruptions, and treating people as if they were invisible—small things that had escalated into big problems.

The results included less overtime (saving taxpayers' money) and sick leave, fewer complaints from employees, and shorter waiting times for the veterans who were the patients at the 11 sites. A comparison of surveys undertaken before and after these interventions, which started in mid-2001, found a substantial decrease, across the 11 sites, in 32 of 60 kinds of bullying—things like glaring, swearing, the silent treatment, obscene gestures, yelling and shouting, physical threats and assaults, vicious gossip, and sexist and racist remarks.

Being a jerk is contagious

The most important single principle for building a workplace free of jerks, or to avoid acting like one yourself, is to view being a jerk as a kind of contagious disease. Once disdain, anger, and contempt are ignited, they spread like wildfire. Researcher Elaine Hatfield calls this tendency "emotional contagion":[12] if you display contempt, others (even spectators) will respond in much the same way, creating a vicious circle that can turn everyone in the vicinity into a mean-spirited monster just like you. Experiments by Leigh Thompson and Cameron Anderson, as they told the *New York Times,*[13] show that when even compassionate people join a group with a leader who is "high energy, aggressive, mean, the classic bully type," they are "temporarily transformed into carbon copies of the alpha dogs." Being around people who look angry makes you feel angry, too. Hatfield and her colleagues sum up this emotional-contagion research with an Arabic proverb: "A wise man associating with the vicious becomes an idiot."

A swarm of jerks creates a civility vacuum, sucking the warmth and kindness out of everyone who enters and replacing them with coldness and contempt. As we have seen, organizations can screen out and reform these contagious jerks and, if those efforts fail, expel them before the infection spreads. But treating nastiness as a contagious disease also suggests some useful self-management techniques.

Consider some wise advice that I heard from the late Bill Lazier, a successful executive who spent the last 20 years of his career teaching business and entrepreneurship at Stanford. Bill gave this advice to our students: when you get a job offer or an invitation to join a team, take a close look at the people you will work with, successful or not. If your potential colleagues are self-centered, nasty, narrow minded, or unethical, he warned, you have little chance of turning them into better human beings or of transforming the workplace into a healthy one, even in a tiny company. In fact, the odds are that you will turn into a jerk as well.

Notes

1. Loraleigh Keashly and Karen Jagatic, "The nature, extent, and impact of emotional abuse in the workplace: Results of a statewide survey," Academy of Management conference, Toronto, August 8, 2000.

2. Laura Sofield and Susan W. Salmond, "Workplace violence: A focus on verbal abuse and intent to leave the organization," *Orthopaedic Nursing,* July–August 2003, Volume 22, Number 4, pp. 274–83.

3. From an interview with Harvey Hornstein, author of *Brutal Bosses and Their Prey,* New York: Riverhead Press, 1996.

4. Bennett J. Tepper, "Consequences of abusive supervision," *Academy of Management Journal,* June 2000, Volume 43, Number 2, pp. 178–90.

5. Andrew G. Miner, Theresa M. Glomb, and Charles Hulin, "Experience sampling mood and its correlates at work: Diary studies in work psychology," *Journal of Occupational and Organizational Psychology* June 2005, Volume 78, Number 2, pp. 171–93.

6. Robert I. Sutton, "Not worth the trouble," in "Breakthrough ideas for 2004: The HBR list," *Harvard Business Review,* February 2004, Volume 82, Number 2, pp. 19–20.

7. Edward Wong, "A stinging office memo boomerangs; chief executive is criticized after upbraiding workers by e-mail," *New York Times,* April 5, 2001.

8. "Barclays: Anything but stodgy," *BusinessWeek,* April 10, 2006.

9. Shirleen Holt, "Giving the goodies: Many employers see advantages in maintaining workplace perks," *Seattle Times,* March 23, 2003.

10. Allan Cohen, James Watkinson, and Jenny Boone, "Southwest Airlines CEO grounded in real world," SearchCIO.com, March 28, 2005.

11. Karl Weick, *The Social Psychology of Organizing,* New York: McGraw-Hill, 1979.

12. Elaine Hatfield, John T. Cacioppo, and Richard L. Rapson, *Emotional Contagion,* Cambridge, England: Cambridge University Press, 1994.

13. Benedict Carey, "Fear in the workplace: The bullying boss," *New York Times,* June 22, 2004.

Individual and Organizational Motivation

THAT URGE TO ACHIEVE
David C. McClelland

MOTIVATION: A DIAGNOSTIC APPROACH
David A. Nadler
Edward E. Lawler III

INNER WORK LIFE: UNDERSTANDING THE SUBTEXT OF BUSINESS PERFORMANCE
Teresa M. Amabile
Steven J. Kramer

P art of being a good manager is understanding what motivates employees and knowing how to design an organization that inspires people to work at their full potential. There are individual differences in motivation patterns, which means that motivation is yet another type of mental map that helps us better understand ourselves and others at work.

There are many internal human needs that drive motivation. David McClelland, renowned psychologist and founder of McBer and Company, devoted his academic career to studying three primary human needs—achievement, power, and affiliation. McClelland wrote the classic article "That Urge to Achieve" and answered the question that often plagues managers—why some employees in the same work environment are hard workers and others are not.

Internal needs, however, are only one piece of the motivation puzzle. Employees are also influenced by the workplace, particularly by the actions of their managers. They make decisions about how hard to work based on their expectations about the results and rewards of their effort, which is the basis of expectancy theory, developed by Victor Vroom. David Nadler, chairman of Mercer Delta Consulting and vice chairman of March & McLennan Companies, and Edward Lawler, professor and founder of the University of Southern California's Center for Effective Organizations, provide their take on expectancy theory in a classic article entitled "Motivation: A Diagnostic Approach." Failure to understand this theory often results in de-motivated employees (and students). Although managers cannot easily change the internal needs employees bring to work, they can place people in jobs that fit their needs, make sure they are capable of doing a good job, and then reward them appropriately.

Furthermore, it behooves managers to think very carefully about how their actions influence employees personally. One of the most interesting wrinkles in the recent motivation literature concerns the sensemaking that employees do around workplace events. Teresa Amabile, psychologist and Director of Research at the Harvard Business School, and her husband, Steven Kramer, an independent researcher and writer, conducted a study on the "inner work life" of employees. This term refers to the dynamic interplay among personal perceptions, emotions, and motivation. After analyzing 12,000 daily diary entries from workers to understand their private thoughts and feelings, they could trace their impact on employee creativity, productivity, commitment, and collegiality and performance. The researchers also identify which managerial behaviors have the most impact on inner work life.

THAT URGE TO ACHIEVE*

David C. McClelland

Most people in this world, psychologically, can be divided into two broad groups. There is that minority which is challenged by opportunity and willing to work hard to achieve something, and the majority which really does not care all that much.

For nearly 20 years now, psychologists have tried to penetrate the mystery of this curious dichotomy. Is the need to achieve (or the absence of it) an accident, is it hereditary, or is it the result of environment? Is it a single, isolatable human motive, or a combination of motives—the desire to accumulate wealth, power, fame? Most important of all, is there some technique that could give this will to achieve to people, even whole societies, who do not now have it?

While we do not yet have complete answers for any of these questions, years of work have given us partial answers to most of them and insights into all of them. There is a distinct human motive, distinguishable from others. It can be found, in fact tested for, in any group.

Let me give you one example. Several years ago, a careful study was made of 450 workers who had been thrown out of work by a plant shutdown in Erie, Pennsylvania. Most of the unemployed workers stayed home for a while and then checked back with the U.S. Employment Service to see if their old jobs or similar ones were available. But a small minority among them behaved differently: the day they were laid off, they started job-hunting.

They checked both the United States and the Pennsylvania Employment Office; they studied the "Help Wanted" sections of the papers; they checked through their union, their church, and various fraternal organizations; they looked into training courses to learn a new skill; they even left town to look for work, while the majority when questioned said they would not under any circumstances move away from Erie to obtain a job. Obviously the members of that active minority were differently motivated. All the men were more or less in the same situation objectively: they needed work, money, food, shelter, job security. Yet only a minority showed initiative and enterprise in finding what they needed. Why? Psychologists, after years of research, now believe they can answer that question. They have demonstrated that these men possessed in greater degree a specific type of human motivation. For the moment let us refer to this personality characteristic as "Motive A" and review some of the other characteristics of the persons who have more of the motive than other persons.

*Reprinted with author's permission from *Think Magazine*, published by IBM, 1996.

Suppose they are confronted by a work situation in which they can set their own goals as to how difficult a task they will undertake. In the psychological laboratory, such a situation is very simply created by asking them to throw rings over a peg from any distance they may choose. Most persons throw more or less randomly, standing now close, now far away, but those with Motive A seem to calculate carefully where they are most likely to get a sense of mastery. They stand nearly always at moderate distances, not so close as to make the task ridiculously easy, nor so far away as to make it impossible. They set moderately difficult, but potentially achievable goals for themselves, where they objectively have only about a one-in-three chance of succeeding. In other words, they are always setting challenges for themselves, tasks to make them stretch themselves a little.

But they behave like this only if *they* can influence the outcome by performing the work themselves. They prefer not to gamble at all. Say they are given a choice between rolling dice with one-in-three chances of winning and working on a problem with a one-in-three chance of solving in the time allotted, they choose to work on the problem even though rolling the dice is obviously less work and the odds of winning are the same. They prefer to work at a problem rather than leave the outcome to chance or to others.

Obviously they are concerned with personal achievement rather than with the rewards of success per se, since they stand just as much chance of getting those rewards by throwing the dice. This leads to another characteristic the Motive A persons show—namely, a strong preference for work situations in which they get concrete feedback on how well they are doing, as one does, say in playing golf, or in being a salesperson, but as one does not in teaching, or in personnel counseling. Golfers always know their score and can compare how well they are doing with par or with their own performance yesterday or last week. Teachers have no such concrete feedback on how well they are doing in "getting across" to their students.

The *n*Ach Person

But why do certain persons behave like this? At one level the reply is simple: because they habitually spend their time thinking about doing things better. In fact, psychologists typically measure the strength of Motive A by taking samples of a person's spontaneous thoughts (such as making up a story about a picture they have been shown) and counting the frequency with which she mentions doing things better. The count is objective and can even be made these days with the help of a computer program for content analysis. It yields what is referred to technically as an individual's *n*Ach score (for "need for Achievement"). It is not difficult to understand why people who think constantly about "doing better" are more apt to do better at job-hunting, to set moderate achievable goals for themselves, to dislike gambling (because they get no achievement satisfaction from success), and to prefer work situations where they can tell easily whether they are improving or not. But why some people and not others come to think this way is another question. The evidence suggests it is not because they are born that way, but because of special training they get in the home from parents who set moderately high achievement goals but who are warm, encouraging, and non-authoritarian in helping their children reach these goals.

Such detailed knowledge about one motive helps correct a lot of common sense ideas about human motivation. For example, much public policy (and much business policy) is based on the simpleminded notion that people will work harder "if they have to." As a first approximation, the idea isn't totally wrong, but it is only a half-truth. The majority of unemployed workers in Erie "had to" find work as much as those with higher *n*Ach, but they certainly didn't work as hard at it. Or again, it is frequently assumed that any strong motive will lead to doing things better. Wouldn't it be fair to say that most of the Erie workers were just "unmotivated?" But our detailed knowledge of various human motives shows that each one leads a person to behave in *different ways*. The contrast is not between being "motivated" or "unmotivated" but between being motivated toward A or toward B or C, etc.

A simple experiment makes the point nicely: subjects were told that they could choose as a working partner either a close friend or a stranger who was known to be an expert on the problem to be solved. Those with higher *n*Ach (more "need to achieve") chose the experts over their friends, whereas those with more *n*Aff (the "need to affiliate with others") chose friends over experts. The latter were not "unmotivated"; their desire to be with someone they liked was simply a stronger motive than their desire to excel at the task. Other such needs have been studied by psychologists. For instance, the need for Power is often confused with the need for Achievement because both may lead to "outstanding" activities. There is a distinct difference. People with a strong need for Power want to command attention, get recognition, and control others. They are more active in political life and tend to busy themselves primarily with controlling the channels of communication both up to the top and down to the people so that they are more "in charge." Those with high *n*Power are not as concerned with improving their work performance daily as those with high *n*Ach.

It follows, from what we have been able to learn, that not all "great achievers" score high in *n*Ach. Many generals, outstanding politicians, great research scientists do not, for instance, because their work requires other personality characteristics, other motives. A general or a politician must be more concerned with power relationships, a research scientist must be able to go for long periods without the immediate feedback the person with high *n*Ach requires, etc. On the other hand, business executives, particularly if they are in positions of real responsibility or if they are salespeople, tend to score high in *n*Ach. This is true even in a Communist country like Poland: apparently there, as well as in a private enterprise economy, a manager succeeds if he is concerned about improving all the time, setting moderate goals, keeping track of his or the company's performance, etc.

Motivation and Half-Truths

Since careful study has shown that common sense notions about motivation are at best half-truths, it also follows that you cannot trust what people tell you about their motives. After all, they often get their ideas about their own motives from common sense. Thus a general may say he is interested in achievement (because he has obviously achieved), or a businesswoman that she is interested only in making money (because she has made money), or one of the majority of unemployed in Erie that he desperately wants a job (because he knows he needs one); but a careful check of what each one thinks about and how each one spends his or her time may show that each is concerned about quite different things. It requires special measurement techniques to identify the presence of *n*Ach and other such motives. Thus what people say and believe is not very closely related to these "hidden" motives, which seem to affect people's "style of life" more than their political, religious, or social attitudes. Thus *n*Ach produces enterprising women and men among labor leaders or managers, Republicans or Democrats, Catholics or Protestants, capitalists or communists.

Wherever people begin to think often in *n*Ach terms, things begin to move. People with higher *n*Ach get more raises and are promoted more rapidly, because they keep actively seeking ways to do a better job. Companies with many such people grow faster. In one comparison of two firms in Mexico, it was discovered that all but one of the top executives of a fast-growing firm had higher *n*Ach scores than the highest scoring executive in an equally large but slow-growing firm. Countries with many such rapidly growing firms tend to show above-average rates of economic growth. This appears to be the reason why correlations have regularly been found between the *n*Ach content in popular literature (such as popular songs or stories in children's textbooks) and subsequent rates of national economic growth. A nation that is thinking about doing better all the time (as shown in its popular literature) actually does do better economically speaking. Careful quantitative studies have shown this to be true in Ancient Greece, in Spain in the Middle Ages, in England from 1400 to 1800, as well as among contemporary nations, whether capitalist or communist, developed or underdeveloped.

MOTIVATION: A DIAGNOSTIC APPROACH*

David A. Nadler

Edward E. Lawler III

- What makes some people work hard while others do as little as possible?
- How can I, as a manager, influence the performance of people who work for me?
- Why do people turn over, show up late to work, and miss work entirely?

These important questions about employees' behavior can only be answered by managers who have a grasp of what motivates people. Specifically, a good understanding of motivation can serve as a valuable tool for understanding the causes of behavior in organizations, for predicting the effects of any managerial action, and for directing behavior so that organizational and individual goals can be achieved.

Existing Approaches

During the past 20 years, managers have been bombarded with a number of different approaches to motivation. The terms associated with these approaches are well known—*human relations*, *scientific management*, *job enrichment*, *need hierarchy*, *self-actualization*, etc. Each of these approaches has something to offer. On the other hand, each of these different approaches also has its problems in both theory and practice. Running through almost all of the approaches with which managers are familiar are a series of implicit but clearly erroneous assumptions.

Assumption 1: All employees are alike   Different theories present different ways of looking at people, but each of them assumes that all employees are basically similar in their makeup. Employees all want economic gains, or all want a pleasant climate, or all aspire to be self-actualizing, etc.

Assumption 2: All situations are alike   Most theories assume that all managerial situations are alike, and that the managerial course of action for motivation (for example, participation, job enlargement, etc.) is applicable in all situations.

Assumption 3: One best way   Out of the other two assumptions there emerges a basic principle that there is "one best way" to motivate employees.

When these "one best way" approaches are tried in the "correct" situation they will work. However, all of them are bound to fail in some situations. They are therefore not adequate managerial tools.

*Reprinted with permission from *Perspectives on Behavior in Organizations* (New York: McGraw-Hill, 1977): 26–34. By permission of the authors.

A New Approach

During the past 10 years, a great deal of research has been done on a new approach to looking at motivation. This approach, frequently called *expectancy theory*, still needs further testing, refining, and extending. However, enough is known that many behavioral scientists have concluded that it represents the most comprehensive, valid, and useful approach to understanding motivation. Further, it is apparent that it is a very useful tool for understanding motivation in organizations.

The theory is based on a number of specific assumptions about the causes of behavior in organizations.

Assumption 1: Behavior is determined by a combination of forces in the individual and forces in the environment   Neither the individual nor the environment alone determines behavior. Individuals come into organizations with certain "psychological baggage." They have past experiences and a developmental history, which has given them unique sets of needs, ways of looking at the world, and expectations about how organizations will treat them. These all influence how individuals respond to their work environment. The work environment provides structures (such as a pay system or a supervisor), which influence the behavior of people. Different environments tend to produce different behavior in similar people just as dissimilar people tend to behave differently in similar environments.

Assumption 2: People make decisions about their own behavior in organizations   While there are many constraints on the behavior of individuals in organizations, most of the behavior that is observed is the result of individuals' conscious decisions. These decisions usually fall into two categories. First, individuals make decisions about *membership behavior*—coming to work, staying at work, and in other ways being a member of the organization. Second, individuals make decisions about the amount of *effort* they will direct towards performing their jobs. This includes decisions about how hard to work, how much to produce, at what quality, etc.

Assumption 3: Different people have different types of needs, desires, and goals Individuals differ on what kinds of outcomes (or rewards) they desire. These differences are not random; they can be examined systematically by an understanding of the differences in the strength of individuals' needs.

Assumption 4: People make decisions among alternative plans of behavior based on their perceptions (expectancies) of the degree to which a given behavior will lead to desired outcomes   In simple terms, people tend to do those things which they see as leading to outcomes (which can also be called "rewards") they desire and avoid doing those things they see as leading to outcomes that are never desired.

In general, the approach used here views people as having their own needs and mental maps of what the world is like. They use these maps to make decisions about how they will behave, behaving in those ways that their mental maps indicate will lead to outcomes that will satisfy their needs. Therefore, they are inherently neither motivated nor unmotivated; motivation depends on the situation they are in, and how it fits their needs.

The Theory

Based on these general assumptions, expectancy theory states a number of propositions about the process by which people make decisions about their own behavior in organizational settings. While the theory is complex at first view, it is in fact made of a series of fairly straightforward observations about behavior. Three concepts serve as the key building blocks of the theory:

PERFORMANCE-OUTCOME EXPECTANCY Every behavior has associated with it, in an individual's mind, certain outcomes (rewards or punishments). In other words, the individual believes or expects that if he or she behaves in a certain way, he or she will get certain things.

Examples of expectancies can easily be described. An individual may have an expectancy that if he produces 10 units he will receive his normal hourly rate while if he produces 15 units he will receive his hourly pay rate plus a bonus. Similarly an individual may believe that certain levels of performance will lead to approval or disapproval from members of her work group or from her supervisor. Each performance can be seen as leading to a number of different kinds of outcomes and outcomes can differ in their types.

VALENCE Each outcome has a "valence" (value, worth, attractiveness) to a specific individual. Outcomes have different valences for different individuals. This comes about because valences result from individual needs and perceptions, which differ because they in turn reflect other factors in the individual's life.

For example, some individuals may value an opportunity for promotion or advancement because of their needs for achievement or power, while others may not want to be promoted and leave their current work group because of needs for affiliation with others. Similarly, a fringe benefit such as a pension plan may have great valence for an older worker but little valence for a young employee on his or her first job.

EFFORT-PERFORMANCE EXPECTANCY Each behavior also has associated with it in the individual's mind a certain expectancy or probability of success. This expectancy represents the individual's perception of how hard it will be to achieve such behavior and the probability of his or her successful achievement of that behavior.

For example, you may have a strong expectancy that if you put forth the effort, you can produce 10 units an hour, but that you have only a fifty-fifty chance of producing 15 units an hour if you try.

Putting these concepts together, it is possible to make a basic statement about motivation. In general, the motivation to attempt to behave in a certain way is greatest when:

a. The individual believes that the behavior will lead to outcomes (performance outcome expectancy).
b. The individual believes that these outcomes have positive value for him or her (valence).
c. The individual believes that he or she is able to perform at the desired level (effort performance expectancy).

Given a number of alternative levels of behavior (10, 15, and 20 units of production per hour, for example) the individual will choose that level of performance which has the greatest motivational force associated with it, as indicated by the expectancies, outcomes, and valences.

In other words, when faced with choices about behavior, the individual goes through a process of considering questions such as, "Can I perform at that level if I try?" "If I perform at that level, what will happen?" "How do I feel about those things that will happen?" The individual then decides to behave in that way which seems to have the best chance of producing positive, desired outcomes.

A General Model

On the basis of these concepts, it is possible to construct a general model of behavior in organizational settings (see Figure 1). Working from left to right in the model, motivation is seen as the force on the individual to expend effort. Motivation leads to an observed level of effort by the individual. Effort, alone, however, is not enough.

A person's motivation is a function of:

a. Effort-to-performance expectancies
b. Performance-to-outcome expectancies
c. Perceived valence of outcomes

FIGURE 1   The Basic Motivation-Behavior Sequence

Performance results from a combination of the effort that an individual puts forth and the level of ability which he or she has (reflecting skills, training, information, etc.). Effort thus combines with ability to produce a given level of performance. As a result of performance, the individual attains certain outcomes. The model indicates this relationship in a dotted line, reflecting the fact that sometimes people perform but do not get desired outcomes. As this process of performance-reward occurs, time after time, the actual events serve to provide information which influences the individual's perceptions (particularly expectancies) and thus influences motivation in the future.

Outcomes, or rewards, fall into two major categories. First, the individual obtains outcomes from the environment. When an individual performs at a given level he or she can receive positive or negative outcomes from supervisors, co-workers, the organization's rewards systems, or other sources. These environmental rewards are thus one source of outcomes for the individual. A second source of outcomes is the individual. These include outcomes that occur purely from the performance of the task itself (feelings of accomplishment, personal worth, achievement, etc.). In a sense, the individual gives these rewards to himself or herself. The environment cannot give them or take them away directly; it can only make them possible.

Supporting Evidence

Over 50 studies have been done to test the validity of the expectancy-theory approach to predicting employee behavior.[1] Almost without exception, the studies have confirmed the predictions of the theory. As the theory predicts, the best performers in organizations tend to see a strong relationship between performing their jobs well and receiving rewards they value. In addition they have clear performance goals and feel they can perform well. Similarly, studies using the expectancy theory to predict how people choose jobs also show that individuals tend to interview for and actually take those jobs which they feel will provide the rewards they value. One study, for example, was able to correctly predict for 80 percent of the people studied which of several jobs they would take.[2] Finally, the theory correctly predicts that beliefs about the outcomes associated with performance (expectancies) will be better predictors of performance than will feelings of job satisfaction since expectancies are the critical causes of performance and satisfaction is not.

Questions about the Model

Although the results so far have been encouraging, they also indicate some problems with the model. These problems do not critically affect the managerial implications of the model, but they should be noted. The model is based on the assumption that individuals make very rational decisions after a thorough exploration of all the available alternatives and on weighing the possible outcomes of all these alternatives. When we talk to or observe individuals, however, we find that their decision processes are frequently less thorough. People often stop considering alternative behavior plans when they find one that is at least moderately satisfying, even though more rewarding plans remain to be examined.

People are also limited in the amount of information they can handle at one time, and therefore the model may indicate a process that is much more complex than the one that actually takes place. On the other hand, the model does provide enough information and is consistent enough with reality to present some clear implications for managers who are concerned with the question of how to motivate the people who work for them.

Implications for Managers

The first set of implications is directed toward the individual manager who has a group of people working for him or her and is concerned with how to motivate good performance. Since behavior is a result of forces both in the person and in the environment, you as manager need to look at and diagnose both the person and the environment. Specifically, you need to do the following:

Figure out what outcomes each employee values   As a first step, it is important to determine what kinds of outcomes or rewards have valence for your employees. For each employee you need to determine "what turns him or her on." There are various ways of finding this out, including; (a) finding out employees' desires through some structured method of data collection, such as a questionnaire; (b) observing the employees' reactions to different situations or rewards; or (c) the fairly simple act of asking them what kinds of rewards they want, what kind of career goals they have, or "what's in it for them." It is important to stress here that it is very difficult to change what people want, but fairly easy to find out what they want. Thus, the skillful manager emphasizes diagnosis of needs, not changing the individuals themselves.

Determine what kinds of behavior you desire   Managers frequently talk about "good performance" without really defining what good performance is. An important step in motivating is for you yourself to figure out what kinds of performances are required and what are adequate measures or indicators of performance (quantity, quality, etc.). There is also a need to be able to define those performances in fairly specific terms so that observable and measurable behavior can be defined and subordinates can understand what is desired of them (e.g., produce 10 products of a certain quality standard-rather than only produce at a high rate).

Make sure desired levels of performance are reachable   The model states that motivation is determined not only by the performance-to-outcome expectancy, but also by the effort-to-performance expectancy. The implication of this is that the levels of performance that are set as the points at which individuals receive desired outcomes must be reachable or attainable by these individuals. If the employees feel that the level of performance required to get a reward is higher than they can reasonably achieve, then their motivation to perform well will be relatively low.

Link desired outcomes to desired performances   The next step is to directly, clearly, and explicitly link those outcomes desired by employees to the specific performances you desire. If your employee values external rewards, then the emphasis should be on the rewards systems concerned with promotion, pay, and approval. While the linking of these rewards can be initiated through your making statements to your employees, it is extremely important that employees see a clear example of the reward process working in a fairly short period of time if the motivating "expectancies" are to be created in the employees' minds. The linking must be done by some concrete public acts, in addition to statements of intent.

If your employee values internal rewards (e.g., achievement), then you should concentrate on changing the nature of the person's job, for he or she is likely to respond well to such things as increased autonomy, feedback, and challenge, because these things will lead to a situation where good job performance is inherently rewarding. The best way to check on the adequacy of the internal and external reward system is to ask people what their perceptions of the situation are. Remember it is the perceptions of people that determine their motivation, not reality. It doesn't matter for example whether you feel a subordinate's pay is related to his or her motivation. Motivation will be present only if the subordinate sees the relationship. Many managers are misled about the behavior of their subordinates because they rely on their own perceptions of the situation and forget to find out what their subordinates feel. There is only one way to do this: ask. Questionnaires can be used here, as can personal interviews.

Analyze the total situation for conflicting expectancies   Having set up positive expectancies for employees, you then need to look at the entire situation to see if other factors (informal work groups, other managers, the organization's reward systems) have set up conflicting expectancies in the minds of the employees. Motivation will only be high when people see a number of rewards associated with good performance and few negative outcomes. Again, you can often gather this kind of information by asking your subordinates. If there are major conflicts, you need to make adjustments, either in your own performance and reward structure, or in the other sources of rewards or punishments in the environment.

Make sure changes in outcomes are large enough   In examining the motivational system, it is important to make sure that changes in outcomes or rewards are large enough to motivate significant behavior. Trivial rewards will result in trivial amounts of effort and thus trivial improvements in performance. Rewards must be large enough to motivate individuals to put forth the effort required to bring about significant changes in performance.

Check the system for its equity   The model is based on the idea that individuals are different and therefore different rewards will need to be used to motivate different individuals. On the other hand, for a motivational system to work it must be a fair one—one that has equity (not equality). Good performers should see that they get more desired rewards than do poor performers, and others in the system should see that also. Equity should not be confused with a system of equality where all are rewarded equally, with no regard to their performance. A system of equality is guaranteed to produce low motivation.

Implications for Organizations

Expectancy theory has some clear messages for those who run large organizations. It suggests how organizational structures can be designed so that they increase rather than decrease levels of motivation or organization members. While there are many different implications, a few of the major ones are as follows:

Implication 1: The design of pay and reward systems   Organizations usually get what they reward, not what they want. This can be seen in many situations, and pay systems are a good example.[3] Frequently, organizations reward people for membership (through pay tied to seniority, for example) rather than for performance. Little wonder that what the organization gets is behavior oriented toward "safe," secure employment rather than effort directed at performing well. In addition, even where organizations do pay for performance as a motivational device, they frequently negate the motivational value of the system by keeping pay secret, therefore preventing people from observing the pay-to-performance relationship that would serve to create positive, clear, and strong performance-to-reward expectancies. The implication is that organizations should put more effort into rewarding people (through pay, promotion, better job opportunities, etc.) for the performances that are desired, and that to keep these rewards secret is clearly self-defeating. In addition, it underscores the importance of the frequently ignored performance evaluation or appraisal process and the need to evaluate people based on how they perform clearly defined specific behaviors, rather than on how they score on ratings of general traits such as "honesty," "cleanliness," and other, similar terms that frequently appear as part of the performance appraisal form.

Implication 2: The design of tasks, jobs, and roles   One source of desired outcomes is the work itself. The expectancy-theory model supports much of the job enrichment literature, in saying that by designing jobs which enable people to get their needs fulfilled, organizations can bring about higher levels of motivation.[4] The major difference between the traditional approaches to job enlargement or enrichment and the expectancy-theory approach is the recognition by expectancy theory that different people have different needs and, therefore, some people may not want enlarged or enriched jobs. Thus, while the design of tasks that have more autonomy, variety, feedback, meaningfulness, etc., will lead to higher motivation in some, the organization needs to build in the opportunity for individuals to make choices about the kind of work they will do so that not everyone is forced to experience job enrichment.

Implication 3: The importance of group structures   Groups, both formal and informal, are powerful and potent sources of desired outcomes for individuals. Groups can provide or withhold acceptance, approval, affection, skill training, needed information, assistance, etc. They are a powerful force in the total motivational environment of individuals. Several implications emerge from the importance of groups. First, organizations should consider the structuring of at least a portion of rewards around group performance rather than individual performance. This is particularly important where group members have to cooperate with each other to produce a group product or service, and where the individual's contribution is often hard to determine. Second, the organization needs to train managers to be aware of how groups can influence individual behavior and to be sensitive to the kinds of expectancies that informal groups set up and their conflict or consistency with the expectancies that the organization attempts to create.

Implication 4: The supervisor's role   The immediate supervisor has an important role in creating, monitoring, and maintaining the expectancies and reward structures that will lead to good performance. The supervisor's role in the motivation process becomes one of defining clear goals, setting clear reward expectancies, and providing the right rewards for different people (which could include both organizational rewards and personal rewards, such as recognition, approval, or support from the supervisor). Thus, organizations need to provide supervisors with an awareness of the nature of motivation as well as the tools (control over organizational rewards, skill in administering those rewards) to create positive motivation.

Implication 5: Measuring motivation   If things like expectancies, the nature of the job, supervisor-controlled outcomes, satisfaction, etc. are important in understanding how well people are being motivated, then organizations need to monitor employee perceptions along these lines. One relatively cheap and reliable method of doing this is through standardized employee questionnaires. A number of organizations already use such techniques, surveying employees' perceptions and attitudes at regular intervals (ranging from once a month to once every year-and-a-half) using either standardized surveys or surveys developed specifically for the organization. Such information is useful both to the individual manager and to top management in assessing the state of human resources and the effectiveness of the organization's motivational systems.[5]

Implication 6: Individualizing organizations Expectancy theory leads to a final general implication about a possible future direction for the design of organizations. Because different people have different needs and therefore have different valences, effective motivation must come through the recognition that not all employees are alike and that organizations need to be flexible in order to accommodate individual differences. This implies the "building in" of choice for employees in many areas, such as reward systems, fringe benefits, job assignments, etc., where employees previously have had little say. A successful example of the building in of such choice can be seen in the experiments at TRW and the Educational Testing Service with "cafeteria fringe-benefits plans," which allow employees to choose the fringe benefits they want, rather than taking the expensive and often unwanted benefits that the company frequently provides to everyone.[6,7]

Summary

Expectancy theory provides a more complex model of humankind for managers to work with. At the same time, it is a model that holds promise for the more effective motivation of individuals and the more effective design of organizational systems. It implies, however, the need for more exacting and thorough diagnosis by the manager to determine (a) the relevant forces in the individual, and (b) the relevant forces in the environment, both of which combine to motivate different kinds of behavior. Following diagnosis, the model implies a need to act—to develop a system of pay, promotion, job assignments, group structures, supervision, etc.—to bring about effective motivation by providing different outcomes for different individuals.

Performance of individuals is a critical issue in making organizations work effectively. If a manager is to influence work behavior and performance, he or she must have an understanding of motivation and the factors that influence an individual's motivation to come to work, to work hard, and to work well. While simple models offer easy answers, it is the more complex models that seem to offer more promise. Managers can use models (such as expectancy theory) to understand the nature of behavior and build more effective organizations.

Notes

1. For reviews of the expectancy theory research see T. R. Mitchell, "Expectancy Models of Job Satisfaction, Occupational Preference and Effort: A Theoretical, Methodological, and Empirical Appraisal," *Psychological Bulletin 81* (1974): 1053–1077. For a more general discussion of expectancy theory and other approaches to motivation see E. E. Lawler, *Motivation in Work Organizations* (Belmont, CA: Brooks/Cole, 1973).

2. E. E. Lawler, W. J. Kuleck, J. G. Rhode, and J. F. Sorenson, "Job Choice and Postdecision Dissonance," *Organizational Behavior and Human Performance 13* (1975): 133–145.

3. For a detailed discussion of the implications of expectancy theory for pay and reward systems, see E. E. Lawler, *Pay and Organizational Effectiveness: A Psychological View* (New York: McGraw Hill, 1971).

4. A good discussion of job design with an expectancy theory perspective is in J. R. Hackman, G. R. Oldham, R. Janson, and K. Purdy, "A New Strategy for Job Enrichment," *California Management Review* (Summer 1975): 57.

5. The use of questionnaires for understanding and changing organizational behavior is discussed in D. A. Nadler, *Feedback and Organizational Development: Using Data Based Methods* (Reading, MA: Addison-Wesley, 1977).

6. The whole issue of individualizing organizations is examined in E. E. Lawler, "The Individualized Organization: Problems and Promise," *California Management Review 17* (2) (1974): 31–39.

7. For a more detailed statement of the model see E. E. Lawler, "Job Attitudes and Employee Motivation: Theory, Research and Practice," *Personnel Psychology 23* (1970): 223–237.

INNER WORK LIFE*

Understanding the Subtext of Business Performance

Teresa M. Amabile

Steven J. Kramer

If your organization demands knowledge work from its people, then you undoubtedly appreciate the importance of sheer brainpower. You probably recruit high-intellect people and ensure they have access to good information. You probably also respect the power of incentives and use formal compensation systems to channel that intellectual energy down one path or another. But you might be overlooking another crucial driver of a knowledge worker's performance—that person's inner work life. People experience a constant stream of emotions, perceptions, and motivations as they react to and make sense of the events of the workday. As people arrive at their workplaces they don't check their hearts and minds at the door. Unfortunately, because inner work life is seldom openly expressed in modern organizations, it's all too easy for managers to pretend that private thoughts and feelings don't matter.

As psychologists, we became fascinated a decade ago with day-to-day work life. But our research into inner work life goes well beyond intellectual curiosity about the complex operations of emotions, perceptions, and motivations. It addresses the very pragmatic managerial question of how these dynamics affect work performance. To examine this question, we constructed a research project that would give us a window into the inner work lives of a broad population of knowledge workers. Specifically, we recruited 238 professionals from 26 project teams and had them complete daily diary entries, in a standard format, for the duration of their projects. Nearly 12,000 diary entries later, we have discovered the dynamics of inner work life and the significant effect it can have on the performance of your people—and, by implication, your entire organization.

It may stun you, if you are a manager, to learn what power you hold. Your behavior as a manager dramatically shapes your employees' inner work lives. But the key levers in your hands for driving motivation and performance may not be the ones you'd suspect.

More Than Meets the Eye

Think about your own most recent day at the office, and try to recall it in some detail. What would hidden observers have been able to learn had they been watching you go through that day? They might have read e-mails you composed, looked over the numbers you plugged into spreadsheets, reviewed the reports you prepared. They would have noted your interactions, in formal meetings or hallway encounters, with colleagues, subordinates, and superiors and listened in on a presentation you delivered. They would have heard your end of various telephone conversations, perhaps with customers, suppliers, or consultants. Maybe they would have watched you sitting quietly for a while, looking off into space, jotting down a few notes.

But would these observers really understand your inner work life that day? Of course not. In having those conversations and writing those reports, you were not only dealing with the task at hand. As events unfolded, you were also forming and adjusting perceptions about the people you work with, the organization you are part of, the work you do, and even yourself. You were experiencing emotions, maybe mild states of satisfaction or irritation, maybe intense feelings of pride or frustration. And these perceptions and emotions were intertwining to affect your work motivation from moment to moment—with consequences for your performance that day.

This is what we mean by inner work life: the dynamic interplay among personal *perceptions*, ranging from immediate impressions to more fully developed theories about what is happening and what it means; *emotions,* whether sharply defined reactions (such as elation over a particular success or anger over a particular obstacle) or more general feeling states, like good and bad moods; and *motivation*—your grasp of what needs to be done and your drive to do it at any given moment. Inner work life is crucial to a person's experience of the workday but for the most part is imperceptible to others. Indeed, it goes largely unexamined even by the individual experiencing it.

In order to study inner work lives, we needed a level of access beyond that of an observer. Thus, we relied on the classic form of the personal diary. Every day, we sent a standard e-mail to every participant requesting a brief description, for our eyes only, of an event that stood out in his or her mind from that workday. (See the sidebar "How We Studied State of Mind" for more details on the study.) Their remarks tended to make clear what they thought of the event—what it said to them about their work, their team, their organization, or themselves—and how it made them feel. Beyond that, we had participants rate themselves and each of their teammates monthly along various dimensions (creativity, work quality, commitment to the work, and contributions to team cohesiveness). Because whole teams participated in the study, we were able to triangulate responses from colleagues, strengthening our understanding of notable events and their effects. Finally, rather than relying solely on a team's diaries to assess its overall performance, we also included evaluations by knowledgeable people outside the team.

We were immediately rewarded with evidence of the richness and intensity of people's inner work lives and the proof that they were influenced strongly by the events of the day. What also emerged over time was evidence of the interplay among perceptions, emotions, and motivations—an inner work life system. (See the exhibit "Processing Work Events: What Happens Inside.") This discovery fits well with what is already known about the human brain. Recent research in neuroscience has found that emotion and cognition (which includes perception of events) are tightly intertwined. Areas of the brain associated with rational thought and decision making have direct connections to areas associated with feelings. They do not exist in separate psychological compartments, and they interact in complex ways. Like any system, the brain cannot be understood simply by looking at each individual component. Inner work life functions the same way: It is crucial to consider all components and their interactions.

When something happens at work—some workday event—it immediately triggers cognitive, emotional, and motivational processes. People's minds start "sensemaking": They try to figure out why the event happened and what its implications are. These perceptions feed the emotions evoked by the event, and the emotions, in turn, feed the perceptions. Depending on what happens with these

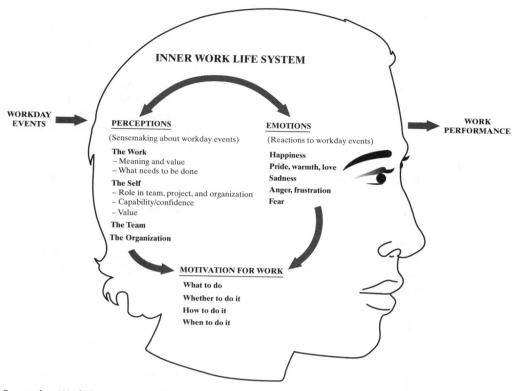

INNER WORK LIFE SYSTEM

Processing Work Events: What Happens Inside
Every worker's performance is affected by the constant interplay of perceptions, emotions, and motivations triggered by workday events, including managerial action—yet inner work life remains mostly invisible to management.

cognitive and emotional processes, motivation can shift, which, in turn, affects how people perform their work. We discerned these processes in the diaries of every team we studied and in most of the people who worked on those teams.

Consider how the dynamics played out with Infomap, a nine-person team of information technologists at DataBrook, a subsidiary of DreamSuite Hotels, that we tracked through various projects across a five-month period. (We have disguised all names and other identifying information about the people and their company.) One urgent project, dubbed the "BigDeal" project, came up suddenly in the fourth month of our study and had enormous financial implications. DreamSuite was being sued for more than $145 million, and its legal department required a great deal of analysis of financial records in order to defend the company. Infomap had eight days to complete the work.

PERCEPTION As the diary entries shown in the exhibit "The Reality Management Never Sees" reveal, the project had significant effects on the inner work lives of the team members. What first becomes clear in studying the diary entries is that people's "events of the day" caused them to form perceptions. Clark's diary entry for May 26, for example, describes the start of the project and the activity surrounding it. Clearly he is engaging in sensemaking, and he comes away with positive perceptions of the "extreme importance" of the work done in his office, the "problem-solving capability" of his team, and the "supportive" nature of management. We see the same kind of reflection by Chester as the project winds up on May 31. His sensemaking produces positive perceptions of the team's co-leader (Ellen), the team itself, other groups in the organization, and top management. These perceptions were triggered by specific events—for example, the extraordinary efforts of Ellen, who rolled up her sleeves and worked alongside the team.

EMOTION We also see the impact of daily events on people's emotions. Helen is inordinately pleased when an upper manager brings refreshments to the team. Marsha reacts to an example of outstanding teamwork with great pleasure. The work atmosphere on May 31 is "happy and light," she notes—even though they were working on Memorial Day, which should have been a holiday for everyone. Chester's upbeat emotions on May 31 are likewise unmistakable.

There is evidence, too, even in the span of these few diary entries, of interplay between perceptions and emotions. When a high-level executive delivers bottled water and pizza to the people working after hours, not only does the event cause happy surprise, it also sends a real signal to the workers. That seemingly trivial event caused people on the BigDeal project to perceive their work and themselves as important and valued, which evoked additional positive emotions. Similar emotions arose when other colleagues and teams offered to pitch in, reinforcing the positive perceptions that team members had formed of those people—and leading, over time, to even more positive emotions.

MOTIVATION High levels of motivation are also on display in the BigDeal project diaries. The entry by Marsha on May 27, for example, reveals that she has just worked 15 hours straight. Yet she describes what she's just endured as "one of the best days I've had in months!!" She notes, in that entry, that "our entire office worked like a real team" and referred to their work as the "big project." Her previous diary entries allowed us to understand how her motivation on May 27 resulted from positive emotions and perceptions. We found, in those entries, that she often felt elated when the team worked closely together, and she perceived herself and her work as more valued when others in the organization signaled its importance. These effects of emotion and perception on motivation make perfect sense. If people are sad or angry about their work, they won't care about doing it well. If they are happy and excited about it, they will leap to the task and put great effort behind it. The same goes for perception. If people perceive the work, and themselves, as having high value, their motivation will be high. Just as important, if they perceive a clear path forward, with little ambiguity about what will constitute progress, motivation levels rise. The BigDeal project had all this going for it. People felt highly valued and certain about what needed to be accomplished. Ultimately, this translated to high performance on the project. Not only did the team get the work done on time, but its high quality made an immediate and measurable contribution to the company's success.

The BigDeal project is all the more striking in comparison with the other projects we tracked for this team. In other periods, we were able to see the same inner work life system operating—but in much less positive ways. Despite the experiences during the BigDeal project, all was not rosy between the team and upper-level management. When, early in our study, an acquisition was announced, employees interpreted the event as a hostile takeover and reacted to it emotionally. Diary entries during that time used terms like "boneheaded" and "bigoted bunch of plantation owners" to describe top management. When layoffs were announced after the acquisition, the entire team perceived the process as unfair. They expressed considerable fear and anger in their diaries and a markedly decreased level of motivation ("People are walking around scared and afraid for their jobs" and "What kills me is, after this, they will turn around and wonder why everyone doesn't just throw themselves in front of a train for the company . . . what dopes"). In fact, during the entire

How We Studied State of Mind

Ten years ago, we set out on a quest to understand what really happens at work. As psychologists, we were fascinated by the unexplored territory of day-to-day life inside organizations and, more specifically, inside the hearts and minds of the professionals working in those organizations. Our aim was to explore daily inner work life—the emotions, perceptions, and motivations that people experience as they react to and make sense of the events of their workdays—and how it affects performance. Our questions were basic: What affects a person's inner work life? Is there anything predictable about how it is shaped by specific events unfolding in the workday and by the organizational context? Does inner work life affect performance? We decided that the best way to get to the heart of these questions was to collect daily diaries from the people themselves.

Over a period of three years, we recruited 238 professionals from 26 project teams in seven companies and three industries to participate in our study. Over 80% of the participants were college educated, and all of the projects required complex, creative work for successful completion. Thus, the term "knowledge workers" fits our participants well. We e-mailed diary forms to the participants every day (Monday through Friday) during the entire course of their projects, asking them each to complete the forms privately at the end of the workday. The average project length was a bit over four months, but some were as long as eight or nine months. About 75% of the forms were returned to us completed and on time, yielding nearly 12,000 individual diary reports.

The diary form had several numerical questions, asking participants to rate their own perceptions of various aspects of the work environment, their mood, and their motivation that day, as well as their own work and the team's work that day. There was also an open-ended question asking people to list the main work tasks they engaged in that day. The most important question was also open-ended; it asked people to briefly report one event that stood out in their minds from the workday.

Although this question simply asked for an event—a concrete description of something specific that happened and who was involved—we found that, very often, people didn't stop there. They told us, sometimes in great detail, about their perceptions of the event and the thoughts that it engendered. They told us about how the event made them feel. And sometimes they told us how it affected their motivation and performance that day. These were the data that led to our primary discoveries of how constant and pervasive inner work life is and how it operates as a complex system. Together with the numerical data we collected on the diary forms and many other sources of data on the participants, the teams, the projects, and the companies, the daily diary narratives served as the basis for our conclusions about inner work life, what affects it, and how, in turn, inner work life affects performance.

time we studied the team—with the exception of the BigDeal project—the team members perceived their company's executive leaders as aloof and oblivious to the team's good work and reacted with varying levels of sadness, anger, and disgust.

Were managers aware of the team's intensely positive perceptions, emotions, and motivations during the BigDeal project? Were they aware of its extremely negative inner work life at other times? Maybe. But when we met with the team, they made it clear that they generally displayed their emotions and described their perceptions only to each other or kept them entirely private. Our research suggests that most managers are not in tune with the inner work lives of their people; nor do they appreciate how pervasive the effects of inner work life can be on performance.

What Gets Done When People Have Good Days?

There is a long-standing debate among management scholars on the question of how work performance is influenced by people's subjective experiences at work. One side says that people perform better when they are happier and internally motivated by love of the work. Others assert that people do their best work under pressure and when externally motivated by deadlines and competition with peers. There is research evidence to support each of these positions.

Having taken a microscope to this question, we believe strongly that performance is linked to inner work life and that the link is a positive one. People perform better when their workday experiences include more positive emotions,

The Reality Management Never Sees

Most managers are unclear about what is going on in their employees' inner work lives and have even less of an idea of what events affect them. Consider these diary entries by the Infomap team at DataBrook, a subsidiary of DreamSuite Hotels. (We have disguised all names and company information. We've also edited the diary entries slightly for clarity and brevity.) This nine-person team of information technologists was tapped to work on an urgent assignment, dubbed "BigDeal," that had enormous financial implications. DreamSuite was being sued for more than $145 million, and its legal department required a great deal of analysis of financial records in order to defend the company. Infomap members worked long hours throughout the eight days they had been given to complete the project, including over a holiday weekend. Yet their spirits were remarkably upbeat. What was causing such a positive outlook despite the burdensome workload and schedule?

DataBrook upper management, which generally paid little attention to Infomap, spent time in the Infomap work

Wednesday

Today's significant team event was one that Tom and I were not involved in. Our office has been asked to produce some ad hoc data... [for the BigDeal project]. Our director, manager, and many users have been in the offfice all day to monitor our progress, while Ellen called Helen in from vacation to help adress the problem. **While I was not involved, I've made this my event for the day because I was able to witness the extreme importance of the financial data that we handle in this office, the problem-solving capability of my team, and the supportive involvement of our immediate management.** It was a very positive experience. **CLARK**

Tuesday

I was called in to work on the BigDeal project. So DreamSuite has to go to court. So Big Deal. What about my vacation?

I'm angry about being called in. But I think I did some really good work under the pressure. And I feel that I really supported the team. **HELEN**

TEAM MEMBER IS CALLED IN FROM VACATION

MAY 25TH	MAY 26TH

PROJECT KICKOFF

Wednesday

More work today on the big DreamSuite lawsuit problem.

The boss's boss came by to offer encouragement. That was nice. He bought us bottled water! Not the cheap stuff I buy, either.

We are getting tired! Nobody's snapped yet, though. I have to admit that I love working under pressure. HELEN

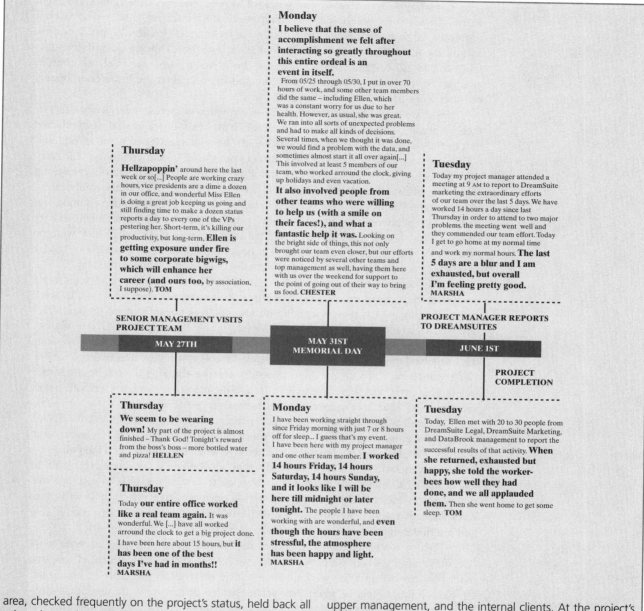

Thursday

Hellzapoppin' around here the last week or so[...] People are working crazy hours, vice presidents are a dime a dozen in our office, and wonderful Miss Ellen is doing a great job keeping us going and still finding time to make a dozen status reports a day to every one of the VPs pestering her. Short-term, it's killing our productivity, but long-term, **Ellen is getting exposure under fire to some corporate bigwigs, which will enhance her career (and ours too,** by association, I suppose). **TOM**

Monday

I believe that the sense of accomplishment we felt after interacting so greatly throughout this entire ordeal is an event in itself.

From 05/25 through 05/30, I put in over 70 hours of work, and some other team members did the same – including Ellen, which was a constant worry for us due to her health. However, as usual, she was great. We ran into all sorts of unexpected problems and had to make all kinds of decisions. Several times, when we thought it was done, we would find a problem with the data, and sometimes almost start it all over again[...] This involved at least 5 members of our team, who worked arround the clock, giving up holidays and even vacation. **It also involved people from other teams who were willing to help us (with a smile on their faces!), and what a fantastic help it was.** Looking on the bright side of things, this not only brought our team even closer, but our efforts were noticed by several other teams and top management as well, having them here with us over the weekend for support to the point of going out of their way to bring us food. **CHESTER**

Tuesday

Today my project manager attended a meeting at 9 AM to report to DreamSuite marketing the extraordinary efforts of our team over the last 5 days. We have worked 14 hours a day since last Thursday in order to attend to two major problems. the meeting went well and they commended our team effort. Today I get to go home at my normal time and work my normal hours. **The last 5 days are a blur and I am exhausted, but overall I'm feeling pretty good.** MARSHA

SENIOR MANAGEMENT VISITS PROJECT TEAM

MAY 27TH

MAY 31ST MEMORIAL DAY

PROJECT MANAGER REPORTS TO DREAMSUITES

JUNE 1ST

PROJECT COMPLETION

Thursday

We seem to be wearing down! My part of the project is almost finished – Thank God! Tonight's reward from the boss's boss – more bottled water and pizza! **HELLEN**

Thursday

Today **our entire office worked like a real team again.** It was wonderful. We [...] have all worked arround the clock to get a big project done. I have been here about 15 hours, but **it has been one of the best days I've had in months!!** MARSHA

Monday

I have been working straight through since Friday morning with just 7 or 8 hours off for sleep... I guess that's my event. I have been here with my project manager and one other team member. **I worked 14 hours Friday, 14 hours Saturday, 14 hours Sunday, and it looks like I will be here till midnight or later tonight.** The people I have been working with are wonderful, and **even though the hours have been stressful, the atmosphere has been happy and light.** MARSHA

Tuesday

Today, Ellen met with 20 to 30 people from DreamSuite Legal, DreamSuite Marketing, and DataBrook management to report the successful results of that activity. **When she returned, exhausted but happy, she told the worker-bees how well they had done, and we all applauded them.** Then she went home to get some sleep. **TOM**

area, checked frequently on the project's status, held back all other demands on the team's time, and provided encouragement and support in a number of small ways. Other groups within the organization cheerfully pitched in as needed. Ellen, the project manager and team co-leader—who was recovering from surgery—not only did a great deal of the actual work but also served as a liaison between the team, upper management, and the internal clients. At the project's completion, although exhausted from the final five-day (and night) sprint, the team members were happy and pleased with the experience.

Clearly, management's engagement and behavior—even seemingly trivial and routine actions—made the difference. The diary excerpts tell the tale in people's own words.

stronger intrinsic motivation (passion for the work), and more favorable perceptions of their work, their team, their leaders, and their organization. Moreover, these effects cannot be explained by people's different personalities or backgrounds—which we did account for in our analyses. Put simply, every moment that they are performing their jobs, employees are "working under the influence" of their inner work lives.

So what do we mean by performance as it relates specifically to knowledge work? In settings where people must work collaboratively to solve vexing problems, high performance depends on four elements: creativity, productivity, commitment, and collegiality. We looked at each of these—using quantitative data from the monthly team ratings and the daily diary forms, as well as content analysis of the diary narratives—and mapped them against the three components of inner work life.

First, we traced the influence of positive emotion on people's creativity—that is, their ability to come up with novel and useful ideas. Many previous studies, conducted as carefully controlled laboratory experiments, have demonstrated a causal relationship between emotion—also termed "affect" or "mood"—and creativity. Our diary study, which used real-world settings and a more naturalistic approach to measuring the effect of emotion on creativity, confirms that this is not merely a laboratory phenomenon. Positive emotion was tied to higher creativity, and negative emotion was tied to lower creativity. Across all 26 teams, people were over 50% more likely to have creative ideas on the days they reported the most positive moods than they were on other days. This finding is based not on people's self-ratings of creativity but on evidence in the diary narrative that they actually did creative thinking that day.

There was even a surprising carry-over effect. The more positive a person's mood on a given day, the more creative thinking he or she did the *next* day—and, to some extent, the day after that—even taking into account the person's mood on those later days. This was clearly the experience of Marsha on the Infomap team. Of her 68 diary entries, 20 contained evidence of creative thinking. Fully 80% of those creative-thinking days followed days on which Marsha's general mood was higher than average for her. Her negative emotions on the days preceding creative-thinking days were the mirror image. Her anger was below average on 75% of the preceding days, her fear was below average on 65%, and her sadness was below average on 60% of them.

Second, we looked at how people's perceptions of their work context affected creativity. Again, our diary study adds more detailed evidence to previous research findings. People in our study were more creative when they interpreted the goings-on in their organizations in a positive light—that is, when they saw their organizations and leaders as collaborative, cooperative, open to new ideas, able to evaluate and develop new ideas fairly, clearly focused on an innovative vision, and willing to reward creative work. They were less creative when they perceived political infighting and internal competition or an aversion to new ideas or to risk taking.

Finally, we analyzed the impact of motivation, the third aspect of inner work life, on creativity. Over the past 30 years, we have garnered a great deal of research evidence supporting what we call the intrinsic motivation principle of creativity: People are more creative when they are motivated primarily by the interest, enjoyment, satisfaction, and challenge of the work itself—not by external pressures or rewards. Most of this evidence comes from laboratory experiments. When intrinsic motivation is lowered, creativity dips as well. Our diary data add to the evidence. Our study participants were more creative in their individual work on the days when they were more highly intrinsically motivated. What's more, the projects distinguished by the greatest levels of creativity overall were the ones in which team members displayed the highest intrinsic motivation in their day-to-day work.

Our findings were quite similar when we shifted our focus from creativity to the other elements of performance: productivity, commitment to the work, and collegiality (specifically, contributions to team cohesiveness). People performed better on all these fronts when they were in a good mood and worse when they were in a bad mood. Productivity, commitment, and collegiality also increased when people held positive perceptions about their work context. At a "local" level, this meant perceiving that they were supported by their team leaders and colleagues, creatively challenged by their tasks, trusted to make decisions with reasonable autonomy, and given sufficient resources and time to complete assignments. More broadly, it meant they perceived the organizational context as collaborative and open, not rife with political game playing or crippling conservatism. Finally, intrinsic motivation levels predicted performance levels across the board. People were more productive, committed, and collegial when they were more motivated—especially by the satisfactions of the work itself.

Clearly, inner work life matters to performance—how creatively people will think, how productive they will be, how much commitment they will show to their work, how collegial they will be. And many of the events that shape inner work life are caused, directly or indirectly, by managers.

What Good Management Does

When we ask people in business to guess which events caused by managers have the greatest influence on inner work life, they often think of interpersonal events—the kinds of person-to-person encounters where, for example, the manager praises a subordinate, works collaboratively with a subordinate as a peer, makes things more fun and relaxing, or provides emotional support. Or the opposite. These sorts of events do, indeed, have a real impact on people's perceptions, emotions, and motivations. Recall what a difference they made to the BigDeal team.

But, interestingly, our research shows that the most important managerial behaviors don't involve giving people daily pats on the back or attempting to inject lighthearted fun into the workplace. Rather, they involve two fundamental things: enabling people to move forward in their work and treating them decently as human beings.

ENABLE PROGRESS When we compared our study participants' best days (when they were most happy, had the most positive perceptions of the workplace, and were most intrinsically motivated) with their worst days, we found that the single most important differentiator was a sense of being able to make progress in their work. Achieving a goal, accomplishing a task, or solving a problem often evoked great pleasure and sometimes elation. Even making good progress toward such goals could elicit the same reactions.

Sometimes the successes were clearly important for the project. For example, when Louise (an Infomap software engineer coding a new version of a major program) solved a problem to bring her within reach of the goal, she wrote, "I figured out why something was not working correctly. I felt relieved and happy because this was a minor milestone for me. I am 90% complete with this version of enhancements." A few weeks later, she accomplished an important step on a different programming assignment: "Yippee! I think I completed part of a project that has been a pain in the butt! I am taking reports over to the user for their viewing pleasure." But even very mundane successes led to positive feelings. For instance, a diary entry by Tom, another Infomap programmer, said, "I smashed that bug that's been frustrating me for almost a calendar week. That may not be an event to you, but I live a very drab life, so I'm all hyped." This is the kind of joy that people feel when they can simply accomplish what they need to.

Not surprisingly, there is a flip side to this effect. Across our entire database, the worst days—the most frustrating, sad, and fearful days—were characterized by setbacks in the work. Again, the magnitude of the event is not important: Even seemingly small setbacks had a substantial impact on inner work life. On April 19, Tom's failure to make measurable progress in his work cast a pall on his day: "No event today, just the continuing frustration of the week—trying to install a fairly simple change in code to an enormously complicated method of installation and production execution. Honest, you don't want to hear the details." On April 12, Louise reported being irritable about an obstacle she couldn't get around. "I changed a program today and got a syntax error . . . I was angry with myself."

It was clear from the diary data that being able to make progress in the work is a very big deal for inner work life. The next question, then, is which managerial behaviors affect employees' ability to do so. Our research points to several: for example, providing direct help (versus hindrance), providing adequate resources and time (versus inadequate resources or unnecessary time pressure), and reacting to successes and failures with a learning orientation (versus a purely evaluative orientation). But one of the most important managerial behaviors turns out to be the setting of clear goals. People make more progress when managers clarify where the work is heading and why it matters. In our diary study, the teams that made greater progress had more events in which the project goals and the team members' individual work goals were clear or were changed carefully and where people knew why their work mattered to the team, the organization, and the organization's customers. By contrast, teams that made less progress reported more events that muddied, confused, or haphazardly changed the goals. Sometimes those teams would be given a goal by management, only to be assigned several other tasks that conflicted with that goal. Often, those teams had a sense of futility about their work, because of uncertainty about how or even whether their efforts would make a difference.

The people on the Infomap team generally made good progress in their work—on the BigDeal project and others—and it was primarily because Ellen, the project manager and one of the team's leaders, relentlessly sought clarity from the team's clients about their needs and expectations. This clarity was sometimes hard to come by, and, in those instances, progress was impeded. Consider the following example, in which a client had requested a software development project with a firm deadline but with little more than a vague sense of what the final computer program was supposed to do. Repeatedly over several days, Ellen contacted the client manager to discuss specifics. Repeatedly, she was brushed off. Marsha, to whom Ellen had assigned the project, wrote in her April 6 diary:

> We had a meeting to discuss the CRR project that I have been working on; the meeting was with just Ellen and Helen. The users have never given us written requirements for the project, and yet they just sent us a note asking if we will make the May 6 deadline. I am just forging ahead and coding like crazy . . . here's hoping they like what they never have asked for. Ellen is trying very hard to get them to commit themselves.

Eventually, Ellen did manage to get specifications from the client team's manager, and, with a Herculean effort, Marsha did succeed in getting the project done well and on time. But all of Marsha's hard work before the specifications were nailed down was relatively directionless and based on supposition, which impeded both real progress and her own sense of accomplishment. By contrast, during the BigDeal project, the managers who needed the work done communicated in detail with Ellen from the outset to clarify the project goals, specify their needs, and explain to everyone involved why the project was so important. Although there were many technical problems to overcome, there was no ambiguity about the goal. The effects on progress were dazzling.

Managerial events facilitating or impeding progress may be so powerful because they have multiple direct and indirect effects on performance. The direct effects are fairly obvious. For example, when goals are not articulated clearly, work proceeds in wrong directions and performance suffers. Less directly, the frustration of spinning one's wheels sours inner work life, leading to lower motivation; people facing seemingly random choices will be less inspired to act on any of them. And there is a further effect. When a manager's actions impede progress, that behavior sends a strong signal. People trying to make sense of why higher-ups would not do more to facilitate progress draw their own conclusions—perhaps that their work is unimportant or that their bosses are either willfully undermining them or hopelessly incompetent.

MANAGE WITH A HUMAN TOUCH   None of this emphasis on the managerial behaviors that influence progress diminishes the importance of the interpersonal managerial events that we mentioned earlier—events in which people are or are not treated decently as human beings. Although such events weren't quite as important in distinguishing the best days from the worst days, they were a close second. We frequently observed interpersonal events working in tandem with progress events. Praise without real work progress, or at least solid efforts toward progress, had little positive impact on people's inner work lives and could even arouse cynicism. On the other hand, good work progress without any recognition—or, worse, with criticism about trivial issues—could engender anger and sadness. Far and away, the best boosts to inner work life were episodes in which people knew they had done good work and managers appropriately recognized that work.

• • •

Peter Drucker once wrote, "So much of what we call management consists of making it difficult for people to do work." The truth of this has struck us as our ongoing analyses reveal more of the negative managerial behaviors that affect inner work life. But we have also been struck by the wealth of managerial opportunities for improving inner work life. Managers' day-to-day (and moment-to-moment) behaviors matter not just because they directly facilitate or impede the work of the organization. They're also important because they affect people's inner work lives, creating ripple effects on organizational performance. When people are blocked from doing good, constructive work day by day, for instance, they form negative impressions of the organization, their coworkers, their managers, their work, and themselves; they feel frustrated and unhappy; and they become de-motivated in their work. Performance suffers in the short run, and in the longer run, too. But when managers facilitate progress, every aspect of people's inner work lives are enhanced, which leads to even greater progress. This positive spiral benefits the individual workers—and the entire organization. Because every employee's inner work life system is constantly operating, its effects are inescapable.

Discovering how inner work life affects organizational performance is clearly valuable. But as researchers we hope we have also made progress on another front. Inner work lives matter deeply to the people living them. Studies of the modern workweek show that knowledge workers today, as compared with workers of past eras, spend more time in the office and more time focused on work issues while outside the office. As the proportion of time that is claimed by work rises, inner work life becomes a bigger component of life itself. People deserve happiness. They deserve dignity and respect. When we act on that realization, it is not only good for business. It affirms our value as human beings.

CHAPTER

7

Ethics and Values

MANAGING TO BE ETHICAL: DEBUNKING FIVE BUSINESS ETHICS MYTHS
Linda Klebe Treviño
Michael E. Brown

THINK MACRO, ACT MICRO: FINANCE CAPITALISM AND ETHICS ACTION METHODS
Richard P. Nielsen

BUSINESS ETHICS: THE ROLE OF CULTURE AND VALUES FOR AN ETHICAL WORKPLACE
Nancy Lockwood

Ethics and values are yet another example of mental maps that help us understand individual differences in the workplace. Ethical conflicts often arise from incompatible ideas and assumptions about right and wrong. Another source of ethical conflict is determined by how different groups define the issue—for instance, where is the boundary that determines which stakeholders' interests have to be considered in addition to one's own interests? Some of the most blatant scandals in recent years grew out of business decisions that failed to take into consideration the best interests of employees, customers, investors, or even one's fellow citizens.

The number and severity of these scandals raised questions about the cause of such serious ethical lapses and what we can do to prevent them in the future. In "Managing to Be Ethical: Debunking Five Business Ethics Myths," Linda Treviño and Michael Brown, well-published business ethicists at Pennsylvania State University, demolish common beliefs about business ethics. Building on theory, research, and examples, they contend that executives have to actively manage ethics and provide ethical leadership in order to create ethical organizations. Their description of Arthur Andersen's transition from an ethical to an unethical firm highlights the crucial role played by leadership and organizational culture.

In addition to managerial actions, there can also be systemic reasons and incentives that drive unethical behavior. Richard Nielsen, management professor at Boston College and member of the Board of Directors of the Society for Business Ethics, looks at systemic corruption in "Think Macro, Act Micro: Finance Capitalism and Ethics Action." He accurately predicted its result—the U.S. economic crisis that hit in 2008. Nielsen updated his article for the ninth edition of the *OB Reader* in light of recent events. He goes beyond identifying a large-scale, macro problem to contribute one of the best practical guides for people confronted with unethical behavior in the workplace and society. Nielsen lists six types of ethics interventions and reform methods and provides numerous examples of their use.

Trust is a key outcome of ethical behavior and the first casualty of unethical behavior. It plays a major role in business, particularly given the relationship between trust and customer retention, employee retention, and innovation. Nancy Lockwood, a researcher at the Society for Human Resource Management, provides practical advice that goes beyond lip service for managers and companies in "Business Ethics: The Role of Culture and Values for an Ethical Workplace." She also describes generational differences with respect to ethics.

MANAGING TO BE ETHICAL: DEBUNKING FIVE BUSINESS ETHICS MYTHS*

Linda Klebe Treviño

Michael E. Brown

The twenty-first century has brought corporate ethics scandals that have harmed millions of employees and investors, and sent shock waves throughout the business world. The scandals have produced "perp walks" and regulatory backlash, and business ethics is once again a hot topic. Academics and managers are asking: What caused the recent rash of corporate wrongdoing, and what can we do, if anything, to prevent similar transgressions in the future? Perhaps because everyone has opinions about ethics and personal reactions to the scandals, a number of pat answers have circulated that perpetuate a mythology of business ethics management. In this article, we identify several of these myths and respond to them based upon knowledge grounded in research and practice.

Myth 1: It's Easy to be Ethical

A 2002 newspaper article was entitled "Corporate ethics is simple: If something stinks, don't do it." The article went on to suggest "the small test," or "If you don't want to tell your mom what you're really doing . . . or read about it in the press, don't do it."[1] The obvious suggestion is that being ethical in business is easy if one wants to be ethical. A further implication is that if it's easy, it doesn't need to be managed. But that suggestion disregards the complexity surrounding ethical decision making, especially in the context of business organizations.

Ethical Decisions are Complex

First, ethical decisions aren't simple. They're complex by definition. As they have for centuries, philosophers argue about the best approaches to making the right ethical decision. Students of business ethics are taught to apply multiple normative frameworks to tough dilemmas where values conflict. These include consequentialist frameworks that consider the benefits and harms to society of a potential decision or action, deontological frameworks that emphasize the application of ethical principles such as justice and rights, and virtue ethics with its emphasis on the integrity of the moral actor, among other approaches.[2] But, in the most challenging ethical dilemma situations, the solutions provided by these approaches conflict with each other, and the decision maker is left with little clear guidance. For example, multinational businesses with manufacturing facilities in developing countries struggle with employment practice issues. Most Americans believe that it is harmful and contrary to their rights to employ children. But children routinely contribute to family income in many cultures. If corporations simply refuse to hire them or fire those who are working, these children may resort to begging or even more dangerous employment such as prostitution. Or they and their families may risk starvation. What if respecting the rights of children in such situations produces the greater harm? Such business decisions are more complex than most media reports suggest, and deciding on the most ethical action is far from simple.

Moral Awareness is Required

Second, the notion that "it's easy to be ethical" assumes that individuals automatically know that they are facing an ethical dilemma and that they should simply choose to do the right thing. But decision makers may not always recognize that they are facing a moral issue. Rarely do decisions come with waving red flags that say, "Hey, I'm an ethical issue. Think about me in moral terms!"[3] Dennis Gioia was recall coordinator at Ford Motor Company in the early 1970s when the company decided not to recall the Pinto despite dangerous fires that were killing the occupants of vehicles involved in low-impact rear-end collisions. In his information-overloaded recall coordinator role, Gioia saw thousands of accident reports, and he followed a cognitive "script" that helped him decide which situations represented strong recall candidates and which did not. The incoming information about the Pinto fires did not penetrate a script designed to surface other issues, and it did not initially raise ethical concerns. He and his colleagues in the recall office didn't recognize the recall issue as an ethical issue. In other examples, students who download their favorite music from the Internet may not think about the ethical implications of "stealing" someone else's copyrighted work. Or a worker asked to sign a document for her boss may not recognize this as a request to "forge" legal documents.

Researchers have begun to study this phenomenon, and they refer to it as moral awareness, ethical recognition, or ethical sensitivity. The idea is that moral judgment processes are not initiated unless the decision maker recognizes the ethical nature of an issue. So, recognition of an issue as an "ethical" issue triggers the moral judgment process, and understanding this initial step is key to understanding ethical decision-making more generally.

T. M. Jones proposed that the moral intensity of an issue influences moral issue recognition,[4] and this relationship has been supported in research. Two dimensions of moral intensity—magnitude of consequences and social consensus—have been found in multiple studies to influence moral awareness.[5] An individual is more likely to identify an issue as an ethical issue to the extent that a particular decision or action is expected to produce harmful consequences and to the extent that relevant others in the social context view the issue as ethically problematic. Further, the use of moral language has been found to influence moral awareness.[6] For example, in the above cases, if the words "stealing" music (rather than downloading) or "forging" documents (rather than signing) were used, the individual would be more likely to think about these issues in ethical terms.

Ethical Decision Making is a Complex, Multi-Stage Process

Moral awareness represents just the first stage in a complex, multiple-stage decision-making process[7] that moves from moral awareness to moral judgment (deciding that a specific action is morally justifiable), to moral motivation (the commitment or intention to take the moral action), and finally to moral character (persistence or follow-through to take the action despite challenges).

The second stage, moral judgment, has been studied within and outside the management literature.[8] Lawrence Kohlberg's well-known theory of cognitive moral development has guided most of the empirical research in this area for the past 30 years.[9] Kohlberg found that people develop from childhood to adulthood through a sequential and hierarchical series of cognitive stages that characterize the way they think about ethical dilemmas. Moral reasoning processes become more complex and sophisticated with development. Higher stages rely upon cognitive operations that are not available to individuals at lower stages, and higher stages are thought to be "morally better" because they are consistent with philosophical theories of justice and rights.

At the lowest levels, termed "preconventional," individuals decide what is right based upon punishment avoidance (at stage 1) and getting a fair deal for oneself in exchange relationships (at stage 2). Next, the conventional level of cognitive moral development includes stages 3 and 4. At stage 3, the individual is concerned with conforming to the expectations of significant others, and at stage 4 the perspective broadens to include society's rules and laws as a key influence in deciding what's right. Finally, at the highest "principled" level, stage 5, individuals' ethical decisions are guided by principles of justice and rights.

Perhaps most important for our purposes is the fact that most adults in industrialized societies are at the "conventional" level of cognitive moral development, and less than 20 percent of adults ever reach the "principled" level, where thinking is more autonomous and principle-based. In practical terms, this means that most adults are looking outside themselves for guidance in ethical dilemma situations, either to significant others in the relevant environment (e.g., peers, leaders) or to society's rules and laws. It also means that most people need to be led when it comes to ethics.

The Organizational Context Creates Additional Pressures and Complexity

Moral judgment focuses on deciding what's right—not necessarily *doing* what is right. Even when people make the right decision, they may find it difficult to follow through and do what is right because of pressures from the work environment. Research has found that principled individuals are more likely to behave in a manner consistent with their moral judgments, and they are more likely to resist pressures to behave unethically.[10] However, most people never reach the principled level. So, the notion that being ethical is simple also ignores the pressures of the organizational context that influence the relationship between moral judgment and action.

Consider the following ethical-dilemma situation. You find yourself in the parking lot, having just dented the car next to you. The ethical decision is relatively simple. It's about you and your behavior. No one else is really involved. You have harmed someone else's property, you're responsible, and you or your insurance company should pay for the repairs. It's pretty clear that you should leave a note identifying yourself and your insurance company. Certainly, there may be negative consequences if you leave that note. Your insurance rates may go up. But doing the right thing in this situation is fairly straightforward.

Contrast that to business-context situations. It is much harder to "just say no" to a boss who demands making the numbers at all costs. Or to go above the boss's head to someone in senior management with suspicions that "managing earnings" has somehow morphed into "cooking the books." Or to walk away from millions of dollars in business because of concerns about crossing an ethical line. Or to tell colleagues that the way they do business seems to have crossed that line. In these situations, the individual is operating within the context of the organization's authority structure and culture—and would likely be concerned about the consequences of disobeying a boss's order, walking away from millions of dollars in business, or blowing the whistle on a peer or superior. What would peers think? How would the leadership react? Would management retaliate? Is one's job at risk?

It may seem curious that people often worry about whether others will think of them as too ethical. But all of us recognize that "snitches" rarely fit in, on the playground or in life, and whistle-blowers are frequently ostracized or worse.[11] The reasons for their ostracism are not fully understood, but they may have to do with humans' social nature and the importance of social group maintenance. Research suggests that people who take principled stands, such as those who are willing to report a peer for unethical behavior, are seen as highly ethical while, at the same time, they are thought to be highly unlikable.[12] Nearly a third of respondents to the 2003 National Business Ethics Survey[13] said "their co-workers condone questionable ethics practices by showing respect for those who achieve success using them." Further, about 40 percent of respondents said that they would not report misconduct they observed because of fear of retaliation from management. Almost a third said they would not report misconduct because they feared retaliation from co-workers.

If you think this applies only to the playground or the factory floor, ask yourself why we haven't seen more CEOs proclaiming how appalled they are at the behavior of some of their peers after recent ethics scandals. Yes, we heard from a few retired CEOs. But very few active senior executives have spoken up. Why not? They're probably uncomfortable passing moral judgment on others or holding themselves up as somehow ethically better than their peers. So, social context is important because people, including senior executives, look to others for approval of their thinking and behavior.

In sum, being ethical is not simple. Ethical decisions are ambiguous, and the ethical decision-making process involves multiple stages that are fraught with complications and contextual pressures. Individuals may not have the cognitive sophistication to make the right decision. And most people will be influenced by peers' and leaders' words and actions, and by concerns about the consequences of their behavior in the work environment.

Myth 2: Unethical Behavior in Business is Simply the Result of "Bad Apples"

A recent headline was "How to Spot Bad Apples in the Corporate Bushel."[14] The bad-apple theory is pervasive in the media and has been around a long time. In the 1980s, during a segment of the *McNeil Lehrer Report* on PBS television, the host was interviewing guests about insider trading scandals. The CEO of a major investment firm and a business school dean agreed that the problems with insider trading resulted from bad apples. They said that educational institutions and businesses could do little except to find and discard those bad apples after the fact. So, the first reaction to ethical problems in organizations is generally to look for a culprit who can be punished and removed. The idea is that if we rid the organization of one or more bad apples, all will be well because the organization will have been cleansed of the perpetrator.

Certainly there are bad actors who will hurt others or feather their own nests at others' expense—and they do need to be identified and removed. But, as suggested above, most people are the product of the context they find themselves in. They tend to "look up and look around," and they do what others around them do or expect them to do.[15] They look outside themselves for guidance when thinking about what is right. What that means is that most unethical behavior in business is supported by the context in which it occurs—either through direct reinforcement of unethical behavior or through benign neglect.

An example of how much people are influenced by those around them was in the newspaper in November 2002. Police in New Britain, Connecticut, confiscated a 50-ft. long pile of stolen items, the result of a scavenger hunt held by the "Canettes,"

New Britain High School's all-girl drill team. According to the *Hartford Courant*, police, parents, and school personnel were astonished that 42 normally law-abiding girls could steal so many items in a single evening. But the girls had a hard time believing that they had done anything wrong. One girl said: "I just thought it was a custom . . . kind of like a camaraderie thing, [and] if the seniors said it was okay and they were in charge, then it was OK!" In another incident in May 2003, suburban Chicago high school girls engaged in an aggressive and brutal "hazing ritual" that landed five girls in the hospital.[16] We might say that these are teenagers and adults are different. But many of these teenagers are about to start jobs, and there are only a few years between these high school students and young people graduating from college. Most adults are more like these teens than most of us think or would prefer to think. The influence of peers is powerful in both cases.

When asked why they engaged in unethical conduct, employees will often say, "I had no choice," or "My boss told me to do it." Stanley Milgram's obedience-to-authority experiments, probably the most famous social psychology experiments ever conducted, support the notion that people obey authority figures even if that means harming another person.[17] Milgram, a Yale psychologist, conducted his obedience-to-authority experiments in the Hartford community on normal adults. These experiments demonstrated that nearly two-thirds of normal adults will harm another human being (give them alleged electric shocks of increasing intensity) if asked to do so by an authority figure as part of what was billed as a learning experiment. Were these people bad apples? We don't think so. Most of them were not at all comfortable doing what they were being asked to do, and they expressed sincere concern for the victim's fate. But in the end most of them continued to harm the learner because the authority figure in a lab coat told them to do so.

How does this apply to work settings? Consider the junior member of an audit team who discovers something problematic when sampling a firm's financials and asks the senior person on the audit team for advice. When the leader suggests putting the problematic example back and picking another one, the young auditor is likely to do just that. The leader may add words such as the following: "You don't understand the big picture" or "Don't worry, this is my responsibility." In this auditing example, the harm being done is much less obvious than in the learning experiment and the junior auditor's responsibility even less clear, so the unethical conduct is probably easier to carry out and more likely to occur.

The bottom line here is that most people, including most adults, are followers when it comes to ethics. When asked or told to do something unethical, most will do so. This means that they must be led toward ethical behavior or be left to flounder. Bad behavior doesn't always result from flawed individuals. Instead, it may result from a system that encourages or supports flawed behavior.

A corollary of the bad-apples argument is that ethics can't be taught or even influenced in adults because adults are autonomous moral agents whose ethics are fully formed by the time they join work organizations, and they can't be changed. This is simply not true. We know from many empirical studies[18] that the large majority of adults are not fully formed when it comes to ethics, and they are not autonomous moral agents. They look outside themselves for guidance in ethical-dilemma situations, and they behave based to a large extent upon what those around them—leaders and peers—expect of them. So, we have to look at the very powerful signals that are being sent about what is expected. We also know that the development of moral reasoning continues into adulthood. Those who are challenged to wrestle with ethical dilemmas in their work will develop more sophisticated ways of thinking about such issues, and their behavior will change as a result.

Myth 3: Ethics Can be Managed Through Formal Ethics Codes and Programs

If people in organizations need ethical guidance and structural support, how can organizations best provide it? Most large organizations now have formal ethics or legal compliance programs. In 1991 the U.S. Sentencing Commission created sentencing guidelines for organizations convicted of federal crimes (see www.ussc.gov for information). The guidelines removed judicial discretion and required convicted organizations to pay restitution and substantial fines depending upon whether the organization turns itself in, cooperates with authorities, and whether it has established a legal compliance program that meets seven requirements for due diligence and effectiveness. These formal programs generally include the following key elements: written standards of conduct that are communicated and disseminated to all employees, ethics training, ethics advice lines and offices, and systems for anonymous reporting of misconduct. The Sarbanes-Oxley law, passed during the summer of 2002, requires corporations to set up an anonymous system for employees to report fraud and other unethical activities. Therefore, companies that did not previously have such reporting systems are busy establishing them.

Research suggests that formal ethics and legal compliance programs can have a positive impact. For example, the Ethics Resource Center's National Business Ethics Survey[19] revealed that in organizations with all four program elements (standards, training, advice lines, and reporting systems) there was a greater likelihood (78 percent) that employees would report observed misconduct to management. The likelihood of reporting declined with fewer program elements. Only half as many people in organizations with no formal program said that they would report misconduct to management.

Yet, creating a formal program, by itself, does not guarantee effective ethics management. Recall that Enron had an ethics code, and the board voted to bypass its conflict-of-interest policy.[20] Not surprisingly, research suggests that actions speak louder than words. Employees must perceive that formal policies go beyond mere window dressing to represent the real ethical culture of the organization. For example, the National Business Ethics Survey reports that when executives and supervisors emphasize ethics, keep promises, and model ethical conduct, misconduct is much lower than when employees perceive that the "ethics walk" is not consistent with the "ethics talk."[21] In another study[22] formal program characteristics were found to be relatively unimportant compared with more informal cultural characteristics such as messages from leadership at both the executive and supervisory levels. In addition, perceived ethics program follow-through was found to be essential. Organizations demonstrate follow-through by working hard to detect rule violators, by following up on ethical concerns raised by employees, and by demonstrating consistency between ethics and compliance policies and actual organizational practices. Further, the perception that ethics is actually talked about in day-to-day organizational activities and incorporated into decision-making was found to be important.

So, for formal systems to influence behavior, they must be part of a larger, coordinated cultural system that supports ethical conduct every day. Ethical culture provides informal systems, along with formal systems, to support ethical conduct.[23] For example, the research cited above found that ethics-related outcomes (e.g., employee awareness of ethical issues, amount of observed misconduct, willingness to report misconduct) were much more positive to the extent that employees perceived that ethical conduct was rewarded and unethical conduct was punished in the organization. Further, a culture that demands unquestioning obedience to authority was found to be particularly harmful while a culture in which employees feel fairly treated was especially helpful.

The Fall of Arthur Andersen

Barbara Toffler's book *Final Accounting: Ambition, Greed, and the Fall of Arthur Andersen*[24] can help us understand this notion of ethical (or unethical) organizational culture. Andersen transformed over a number of years from having a solid ethical culture to having a strong unethical culture. The company's complete demise is a rather dramatic example of the potential results of such a transformation.

In the mid-1990s, Arthur Andersen did not have a formal ethics office, but it did have formal ethical standards and ethics training. Ironically, it also established a consulting group whose practice was aimed at helping other businesses manage their ethics. Barbara Toffler was hired to run that practice in 1995 after spending time on the Harvard Business School faculty and in her own ethics consulting business. After joining Andersen, Toffler learned quickly that the firm's own ethical culture was slipping badly, and she chronicles that slippage in her book.

The book opens with the following statement: "The day Arthur Andersen loses the public's trust is the day we are out of business." Steve Samek, country managing partner, made that statement on a CD-ROM concerning the firm's Independence and Ethical Standards in 1999. It was reminiscent of the old Arthur Andersen. Andersen's traditional management approach had been a top-down, "one firm" concept. Arthur Andersen had built a strong ethical culture over the years where all of the pieces fit together into a seamless whole that supported ethical conduct. No matter where they were in the world, if customers were dealing with Andersen employees, they knew that they could count on the same high-quality work and the same integrity. Employees were trained in the "Andersen Way," and that way included strong ethics. Training at their St. Charles, Illinois, training facility was sacred. It created a cadre of professionals who spoke the same language and shared the same "Android" values.

Founders create culture, and Arthur Andersen was no exception. Toffler says that in the firm's early days, the messages from the top about ethical conduct were strong and clear. Andersen himself said, "My own mother told me, 'Think straight—talk straight.' . . . This challenge will never fail anyone in a time of trial and temptation." "Think straight, talk straight" became a mantra for decades at Arthur Andersen. Partners said with pride that integrity mattered more than fees. And stories about the founder's ethics became part of the firm's lore. At the young age of 28, Andersen faced down a railway executive who demanded that his books be approved—or else. Andersen said, "There's not enough money in the city of Chicago to induce me to change that report." Andersen lost the business, but later the railway company filed for bankruptcy, and Arthur Andersen became known as a firm one could trust. In the 1930s Andersen talked about the special responsibility of accountants to the public and the importance of their independence of judgment and action. Arthur Andersen died in 1947 but was followed by leaders with similar convictions who ran the firm in the 1950s and 1960s, and the ethical culture continued for many years. Pretty much through the 1980s, Andersen was considered a stable and prestigious place to work. People didn't expect to get rich; rather, they wanted "a good career at a firm with a good reputation."

But, the ethical culture eventually began to unravel, and Toffler attributes much of this to the fact that the firm's profits increasingly came from management consulting rather than auditing. The leadership's earlier commitment to ethics came to be drowned out by the firm's increasing laser-like focus on revenues. Auditing and consulting are very different, and the cultural standards that worked so well in auditing didn't fit the needs of the consulting side of the business. But this mismatch was never addressed, and the resulting mixed signals helped precipitate a downward spiral into unethical practices. Serving the client began to be defined as keeping the client happy and getting return business. And tradition became translated into unquestioning obedience to the partner, no matter what one was asked to do. For example, managers and partners were expected to pad their prices. Reasonable estimates for consulting work were simply doubled or more as consultants were told to back into the numbers.

The training also began falling apart when it came to hiring experienced people from outside the firm—something that happened more and more as consulting took over. New employees had always been required to attend a three-day session designed to indoctrinate them into the culture of the firm, but new consultants were told not to forego lucrative client work to attend. So, Toffler never made it to the training, and many other consultants didn't either.

By the time Toffler arrived at Andersen, the firm still had a huge maroon ethics binder, but no one bothered to refer to it. Ethics was never talked about. And, she says, "When I brought up the subject of internal ethics, I was looked at as if I had teleported in from another world." The assumption, left over from the old days in auditing, was that "we're ethical people; we recruit people who are screened for good judgment and values. We don't need to worry about this stuff." But, as we all learned, their failure to worry about ethics led to the demise of the firm.

Could a formal ethics office have helped Arthur Andersen? Probably not, unless that office addressed the shift toward consulting, identified the unique ethical issues faced in the consulting side of the business, developed ethical guidelines for consulting, and so on. It is easy for formal ethics offices and their programs to be marginalized if they don't have the complete support of the organization's leadership and if they are inconsistent with the broader culture. In fact, Andersen still had ethics policies and they still talked about ethics in formal documents. But the business had changed along with the culture that guided employee actions every day, while the approach to ethics management had not kept pace.

Myth 4: Ethical Leadership is Mostly About Leader Integrity

In our discussion of Arthur Andersen, we suggested the importance of leadership. But what is executive ethical leadership? The mythology of ethical leadership focuses attention narrowly on individual character and qualities such as integrity, honesty, and fairness. The *Wall Street Journal* recently ran a story on its website entitled "Plain Talk: CEOs Need to Restore Character in Companies." It said, "The chief problem affecting corporate America right now is not the regulatory environment or snoozing board directors. It's character."[25] But as Arthur Andersen demonstrated, leaders must be more than individuals of high character. They must "lead" others to behave ethically.

Recent research has found that certain individual characteristics are necessary but not sufficient for effective ethical leadership. Such leadership at the executive level is a reputational phenomenon. In most large organizations, employees have few face-to-face interactions with senior executives. So, most of what they know about a leader is gleaned from afar. In order to develop a reputation for ethical leadership, an executive must be perceived as both a "moral person" and a "moral manager."[26]

Being perceived as a "moral person" is related to good character. It depends upon employee perceptions of the leader's traits, behaviors, and decision-making processes. Ethical leaders are thought to be honest and trustworthy. They show concern for people and are open to employee input. Ethical leaders build relationships that are characterized by trust, respect and support for their employees. In terms of decision-making, ethical leaders are seen as fair. They take into account the ethical impact of their decisions, both short term and long term, on multiple stakeholders. They also make decisions based upon ethical values and decision rules, such as the golden rule.

But being perceived as a "moral person" is not enough. Being a "moral person" tells followers what the leader will do. It doesn't tell them what the leader expects *them* to do. Therefore, a reputation for ethical leadership also depends upon being

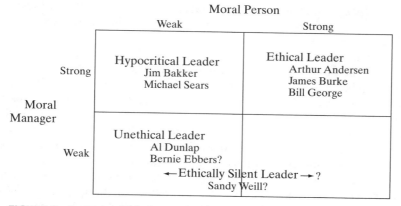

FIGURE 1 **Executive Ethical Leadership Reputation Matrix**

Source: Figure adapted with permission from Treviño, L. K., Hartman, L. P., Brown, M. 2000. "Moral person and moral manager: How executives develop a reputation for ethical leadership" *California Management Review*, 42(4): 128–142.

perceived as a "moral manager," one who leads others on the ethical dimension, lets them know what is expected, and holds them accountable. Moral managers set ethical standards, communicate ethics messages, role model ethical conduct, and use rewards and punishments to guide ethical behavior in the organization.

Combining the "moral person" and "moral manager" dimensions creates a two-by-two matrix (see Figure 1). A leader who is strong on both dimensions is perceived to be an *ethical* leader. We can point to Arthur Andersen as an exemplar of ethical leadership. He was known as a strong ethical person who also clearly led his organization on ethics and values. People knew what they could expect of him, and they knew what he expected of them from an ethics perspective. Another example of ethical leadership is James Burke, CEO of Johnson & Johnson during the early 1980s Tylenol crisis (when Tylenol was laced with cyanide in the Chicago area). Burke handled that crisis masterfully, recalling all Tylenol at a huge financial cost to the firm. But his ethical leadership had begun much earlier when he first took the CEO helm. He focused the organization's attention on the company's long-standing credo and its values. He demanded that senior executives either subscribe to the credo or remove it from the wall. He didn't want to run a hypocritical organization. He also launched the credo survey, an annual survey that asks employees how the company is doing relative to each of the credo values. Bill George, recently retired CEO of Medtronic, is a more current example of an ethical leader. In his book *Authentic Leadership,* George calls for responsible ethical leadership in corporate America while recounting his own struggles to stay true to the company's mission and to himself.[27]

A leader who is neither a moral person nor a moral manager is an *unethical leader.* In our research, Al Dunlap was frequently identified as an unethical leader. Subject of a book entitled *Chainsaw,*[28] Dunlap was known as an expert turnaround manager. But while at Sunbeam, he also became known for "emotional abuse" of employees. As a result of his demands to make the numbers at all costs, employees felt pressure to use questionable accounting and sales techniques, and they did. Dunlap also lied to Wall Street, assuring them that the firm would reach its financial projections. In the end, Dunlap could no longer cover up the sorry state of affairs, and he left a crippled company when the board fired him in 1998. In 2002, he paid a $500,000 fine for financial fraud and agreed never to serve as an officer or director of a public corporation. Unfortunately, there are many candidates for a more current example of unethical leadership: Dennis Kozlowski from Tyco, Bernie Ebbers from WorldCom, and Richard Scrushy from Health South are just a few executive names attached to recent business scandals.

Leaders who communicate a strong ethics/values message (who are moral managers), but who are not perceived to be ethical themselves (they are not moral persons) can be thought of as *hypocritical leaders*. Nothing makes people more cynical than a leader who talks incessantly about integrity, but then engages in unethical conduct himself and encourages others to do so, either explicitly or implicitly. Hypocritical leadership is all about ethical pretense. The problem is that by spotlighting integrity, the leader raises expectations and awareness of ethical issues. At the same time, employees realize that they can't trust the leader.

Jim Bakker, the founder of PTL Ministries, is our favorite example of a hypocritical leader. At its peak, his television ministry had 2000 employees and reached more than 10 million homes. Bakker preached about doing the Lord's work while raising funds for his Heritage USA Christian theme park. The problem was that he sold more memberships than could ever be honored. He tapped millions of dollars donated by his followers to support PTL operating expenses, including huge salaries and bonuses for his family and high ranking PTL officials. PTL filed for bankruptcy in 1987, and Bakker spent eight years in prison.[29]

Michael Sears, recently fired from Boeing for offering a job to an Air Force procurement specialist while she was overseeing negotiations with Boeing, represents a more recent example of a hypocritical leader. Sears had played a significant role at the Boeing Leadership Center which is known for its programs related to ethics. Also, shortly before his firing, Sears released advance copies of his book *Soaring Through Turbulence*, which included a section on maintaining high ethical standards.[30]

We call the final combination *ethically silent leadership*. It applies to executives who are neither strong ethical nor strong unethical leaders. They fall into what employees perceive to be an ethically neutral leadership zone. They may be ethical persons, but they don't provide leadership in the crucial area of ethics, and employees aren't sure where the leaders stand on ethics or if they care. The ethically silent leader is not perceived to be unethical but is seen as focusing intently on the bottom line without setting complementary ethical goals. There is little or no ethics message coming from the top. But silence represents an important message. In the context of all the other messages being sent in a highly competitive business environment, employees are likely to interpret silence to mean that the top executive really doesn't care how business goals are met, only that they are met, so employees act on that message. Business leaders don't like to think that their employees perceive them as ethically silent. But given the current climate of cynicism, unless leaders make an effort to stand out and lead on ethics, they are likely to be viewed that way.

Sandy Weill, CEO of Citigroup, may fit the "ethically silent leader" category. The company has been playing defense with the media, responding to ugly headlines about ethics scandals, especially at its Smith Barney unit, where stock analysts were accused of essentially "selling" their stock recommendations for banking business. Weill's management style is to hire competent people to run Citigroup's units and to let them do their jobs. That may work well for other aspects of the business, but ethics must be managed from the top and center of the organization. According to *Fortune* magazine, Weill has now "gotten religion," if a bit late. Weill has "told his board that he feels his most important job from now on is to be sure that Citigroup operates at the highest level of ethics and with the utmost integrity." New procedures and business standards are being developed at corporate headquarters, and a new CEO was appointed at Smith Barney. However, *Fortune* also cites cynicism about this recent turnabout, noting that Weill is often "tone deaf" on ethical issues.[31]

So, developing a reputation for ethical leadership requires more than strong personal character. Employees must be "led" from the top on ethics just as they must be led on quality, competitiveness, and a host of other expected behaviors. In order to be effective ethical leaders, executives must demonstrate that they are ethical themselves, they must make their expectations of others' ethical conduct explicit, and they must hold all of their followers accountable for ethical conduct every day.

Myth 5: People are Less Ethical Than They Used to be

In the opening to this article, we said that business ethics has once again become a hot topic. The media have bombarded us with information about ethics scandals, feeding the perception that morals are declining in business and in society more generally.

According to a poll released by the PR Newswire in summer 2002, 68 percent of those surveyed believe that senior corporate executives are less honest and trustworthy today than they were a decade ago.[32] But unethical conduct has been with us as long as human beings have been on the earth, and business ethics scandals are as old as business itself. The Talmud, a 1500-year-old text, includes about 2 million words and 613 direct commandments designed to guide Jewish conduct and culture. More than 100 of these concern business and economics. Why? Because "transacting business, more than any other human activity, tests our moral mettle and reveals our character," and because "working, money, and commerce offer . . . the best opportunities to do good deeds such as . . . providing employment and building prosperity for our communities and the world."[33]

So unethical behavior is nothing new. It's difficult to find solid empirical evidence of changes over time. But studies of student cheating have found that the percentage of college students who admit to cheating has not changed much during the last 30 years.[34] Some types of cheating have increased (e.g., test cheating, collaboration on individual assignments). Other types of cheating have declined (e.g., plagiarism, turning in another student's work). Certainly, given new technologies and learning approaches, students have discovered some clever new ways to cheat, and professors have their work cut out for them keeping up with the new methods. But the amount of overall cheating hasn't increased that much. Further, when employees were asked about their own work organizations, the 2003 National Business Ethics Survey found that employee perceptions of ethics are generally quite positive. Interestingly, key indicators have actually improved since the last survey conducted in 2000.[35]

Alan Greenspan said it well on July 16, 2002: "It is not that humans have become any more greedy than in generations past. It is that the avenues to express greed [have] grown so enormously." So, unethical behavior is nothing new, and people are probably not less ethical than they used to be. But the environment has become quite complex and is rapidly changing, providing all sorts of ethical challenges and opportunities to express greed.

If ethical misconduct is an ongoing concern, then organizations must respond with lasting solutions that embed support for ethics into their cultures rather than short-term solutions that can easily be undone or dismissed as fads. The risk is that the current media focus on unethical conduct will result in "faddish" responses that offer overly simplistic solutions and that result inevitably in disillusionment and abandonment. Faddish solutions often result from external pressures to "do something" or at least look like you're doing something. The current focus on scandal certainly includes such pressures.[36] But the recognition that unethical conduct is a continuing organizational problem may help to convince managers that solutions should be designed that will outlast the current intense media focus.

What Executives Can Do: Guidelines for Effective Ethics Management

Building upon what we have learned, we offer guidelines for effective ethics management. The overarching goal should be to create a strong ethical culture supported by strong ethical leadership. Why culture? Because we've seen that being ethical is not simple, and that people in organizations need ethical guidance and support for doing the right thing. Executive leaders must provide that structure and ethical guidance, and they can do that best by harnessing multiple formal and informal cultural systems.[37] People should respond positively to the kind of structure that aims to help them do the right thing. If management says, "We want you to do the right thing, the ethical thing, and we're going to try to create a culture that helps you to do that," employee response should be quite positive so long as employees believe that management is sincere and they observe consistency between words and actions.

First: Understand the Existing Ethical Culture

Leaders are responsible for transmitting culture in their organizations, and the ethical dimension of organizational culture is no exception. According to Schein, the most powerful mechanisms for embedding and reinforcing culture are: (1) what leaders pay attention to, measure, and control; (2) leader reactions to critical incidents and organizational crises; deliberate role modeling, teaching, and coaching by leaders; (3) criteria for allocation of rewards and status; and (4) criteria for recruitment, selection, promotion, retirement, and excommunication.[38]

If leaders wish to create a strong ethical culture, the first step is to understand the current state: What are the key cultural messages being sent about ethics? It's a rare executive who really understands the ethical culture in an organization. And the higher you go in the organization, the rosier the perception of the ethical culture is likely to be.[39] Why? Because information often gets stuck at lower organizational levels, and executives are often insulated from "bad news," especially if employees perceive that the organization "shoots the messenger." Executives need anonymous surveys, focus groups, and reporting lines, and people need to believe that the senior leaders really want to know, if they are to report honestly on the current state of the ethical culture.

In surveys, ask for employee perceptions of supervisory and executive leadership and the messages they send by their communications and behavior. And listen to what employees say. Ask employees whether they perceive that they are treated fairly, and whether the company acts as if it cares about them, its customers, and other stakeholders. Find out what messages the reward system is sending. Do employees believe that ethical "good guys" are rewarded and unethical "bad guys" are punished in the organization? What do employees think is required in order to succeed or to be fired? Follow the kinds of calls coming in to ethics telephone lines. Learn whether employees are asking questions and reporting problems. Use this information to identify needs for training and other interventions. In focus groups, find out who the organizational heroes are. Is it the sales representative who steps on peers in order to get ahead or a manager who is known for the highest integrity? Ask what stories veterans would tell a new hire about ethics in your organization.

Second: Communicate the Importance of Ethical Standards

Employees need clear and consistent messages that ethics is essential to the business model, not just a poster or a website. Most businesses send countless messages about competition and financial performance, and these easily drown out other messages. In order to compete with this constant drumbeat about the short-term bottom line, the messages about ethical conduct must be just as strong or stronger and as frequent. Simply telling people to do the right thing, is not enough. They must be prepared for the types of issues that arise in their particular business and position, and they must know what to do when ethics and the bottom line appear to be in conflict. Executives should tie ethics to the long-term success of the business by providing examples from their own experience or the experiences of other successful employees.

Make sure that messages coming from executive and supervisory leaders are clear and consistent. Train employees to recognize the kinds of ethical issues that are likely to arise in their work. Demand discussion of ethics and values as part of routine business decision making. When making important decisions, ask, "Are we doing the 'right' (i.e., ethical) thing? Who could be hurt by this decision? How could this affect our relationships with stakeholders and our long-term reputation?" Share those deliberations with employees. Finally, be sure to let employees know about exemplary ethical conduct. For example, the famous story about Arthur Andersen losing the railway business because he refused to alter the books was recounted over and over again in the firm and made it absolutely clear that "think straight, talk straight" actually meant something in the firm.

Third: Focus on the Reward System

The reward system may be the single most important way to deliver a message about what behaviors are expected. B.F. Skinner knew what he was talking about. People do what's rewarded, and they avoid doing what's punished.[40] Let's look at the positive side first: Can we really reward ethical behavior? In the short term, we probably cannot. For the most part, ethical behavior is simply expected, and people don't expect or want to be rewarded for doing their jobs the right way.[41] But in the longer term, ethical behavior can be rewarded by promoting and compensating people who are not only good at what they do, but who have also developed a reputation with customers, peers, subordinates, and managers as being of the highest integrity. The best way to hold employees accountable for ethical conduct is to incorporate evaluation of it into 360° performance management systems and to make this evaluation an explicit part of compensation and promotion decisions. The idea is that the bottom line and ethical performance both count; unless individuals have both, they should not advance in the organization.

Also, exemplary behavior can be rewarded. At Lockheed Martin's annual Chairman's meeting, a "Chairman's Award" goes to an employee who exhibited exemplary ethical conduct in the previous year. All senior corporate leaders are expected to expend effort each year to find examples of exemplary ethical conduct in their own business units and make nominations. The award ceremony, attended by all 250 senior executives, is exactly the kind of "ritual" that helps to create an ethical culture. Stories are shared and they become part of the organization's lore, the potential impact growing as the stories accumulate over time.[42]

Perhaps even more important than rewarding ethical conduct is taking care not to reward unethical conduct. That's what began to happen at Arthur Andersen as generating revenue became the only rewarded behavior, and it didn't matter how you did it. For example, consultants were rewarded for making a project last by finding reasons (legitimate or not) to stay on. Toffler says, "Like the famous Roach Motel, consultants were taught to check in, but never check out."[43] So, clients were overcharged, consulting jobs were dragged out, and colleagues were "screwed" along the way because the rewards supported such unethical conduct.

And what about discipline? Unethical conduct should be disciplined swiftly and fairly when it occurs at any level in the organization. The higher the level of the person disciplined, the stronger the message that management takes ethics seriously. That's what is behind the "perp walks" we have observed in the media. The public wants to see that fraudulent conduct among America's executives will not be tolerated. Similarly, inside organizations, employees want to see misconduct disciplined, and disciplined harshly.[44] Overall, employees must perceive that good guys get ahead and bad guys don't—they get punished. But, remember, it's often not enough to punish or remove a bad guy or a bad apple. The system should be checked to see if the existing reward system or other messages contributed to the bad behavior.

Fourth: Promote Ethical Leadership Throughout the Firm

Recall that being a "moral person" who is characterized by integrity and fairness, treats people well, and makes ethical decisions is important. But those elements deal only with the "ethical" part of ethical leadership. To be ethical leaders, executives have to think about the "leadership" part of the term. Providing ethical "leadership" means making ethical values visible—communicating about not just the bottom-line goals (the ends) but also the acceptable and unacceptable means of getting there (the means). Being an ethical leader also means asking very publicly how important decisions will affect multiple stakeholders—shareholders, employees, customers, society—and making transparent the struggles about how to balance competing interests. It means using the reward system to clearly communicate what is expected and what is accepted. That means rewarding ethical conduct and disciplining unethical conduct, even if the rule violator is a senior person or a top producer. Find a way to let employees know that the unethical conduct was taken seriously and the employee disciplined.

Ethical cultures and ethical leaders go hand in hand. Building an ethical culture can't be delegated. The CEO must be the Chief Ethics Officer of his or her organization.[45] Many CEOs may feel that they would rather pass on this challenge—that they don't really know how to do it—or they may prefer to believe that everyone in their organization is already ethical. But ethics is being "managed" in their organizations with or without their attention to it. Benign neglect of the ethical culture simply leads to employees reaching the conclusion, rightly or wrongly, that leaders don't care as much about ethics as they do about other things. Leaders develop a reputation in this arena. Chances are that if the leader hasn't thought much about this reputation or hasn't been very proactive about it, people in the organization will likely label him or her as an ethically neutral leader. That doesn't mean that the leader *is* ethically neutral or doesn't take ethics into account in decision making. It does mean that people aren't sure where the leader stands on the frequent conflicts between ethics and the bottom line. Without explicit guidance, they assume that the bottom-line messages are the most important.

As we've said, senior executives are extremely important. They set the tone at the top and oversee the ethical culture. But from an everyday implementation perspective, front-line supervisors are equally important because of their daily interactions with their direct reports. An ethical culture ultimately depends upon how supervisors treat employees, customers, and other stakeholders, and how they make decisions. Do they treat everyone honestly, fairly and with care? Do supervisors point out when their group is facing a decision with ethical overtones? Do they consider multiple stakeholder interests and the long-term reputation of the organization in decision making? Do they hold themselves and their people accountable for ethical conduct? Or, do they focus only on short-term bottom-line results?

Ethics Isn't Easy

Unethical conduct in business has been with us as long as business transactions have occurred. People are not necessarily more unethical today, but gray areas abound along with many opportunities to cross into unethical territory. Much unethical conduct is the result not just of bad apples but of neglectful leadership and organizational cultures that send mixed messages about what is important and what is expected. It isn't easy to be ethical. Employees must recognize ethical issues in their work, develop the cognitive tools to make the right choices, and then be supported in those choices by the organizational environment. Executives must manage the ethical conduct of their employees as proactively as they manage any important behavior. And the complexity of the management system should match the complexity of the behavior being managed.

The best way to manage ethical conduct is by aligning the multiple formal and informal cultural systems in support of doing the right thing. Cultural messages about the importance of trust and long-term relationships with multiple stakeholders must get at least as much attention as messages about the short-term bottom line, and employees must be held accountable for ethical conduct through performance management and reward systems.

Endnotes

1. St. Anthony, N. "Corporate Ethics Is Simple: If Something Stinks, Don't Do It," *Star Tribune (Minneapolis-Saint Paul) Newspaper of the Twin Cities.* 28 June 2002.
2. For a simple overview of these theories, see Treviño, L. K., & Nelson, K. *Managing Business Ethics: Straight Talk About How to Do It Right, 3rd ed.* New York: Wiley (2003).
3. Gioia, D. "Pinto fires and personal ethics: A script analysis of missed opportunities," *Journal of Business Ethics*, 11 (5,6) (1992): 379–389; Gioia, D. A. 2003. Personal reflections on the Pinto Fires case. In Treviño & Nelson.
4. Jones, T. M. 1991. "Ethical decision making by individuals in organizations: An issue-contingent model," *Academy of Management Review*, 16: 366–395.
5. May, D. R., & Pauli, K. P. 2000. "The role of moral intensity in ethical decision making: A review and investigation of moral recognition, evaluation, and intention." Manuscript presented at the meeting of the National Academy of Management, Toronto, August 2000.
6. Butterfield, K., Treviño, L. K., & Weaver, G. 2000. "Moral awareness in business organizations: Influences of issue-related and social context factors," *Human Relations*, 53(7): 981–1018.
7. Rest, M. 1986, *Moral Development: Advances in Research and Theory.* New Jersey: Praeger.
8. Weber, J. 1990. "Managers' moral reasoning: Assessing their responses to three moral dilemmas," *Human Relations* 43: 687–702; Weber, J., & Wasieleski, 2001. "Investigating influences on managers' moral reasoning: The impact of context, personal, and organizational factors," *Business and Society*, 40(1): 79–111; Treviño, L. K.

1986. "Ethical decision making in organizations: A person-situation interactionist model," *Academy of Management Review*, 11(3): 601–617; Treviño, L. K. 1992. "Moral reasoning and business ethics," *Journal of Business Ethics*, 11: 445–459.
9. Kohlberg, L. 1969. Stage and sequence: "The cognitive-developmental approach to socialization," In *Handbook of socialization theory and research.* D. A. Goslin, ed. Rand McNally, 347–380.
10. Thoma, S. J. 1994. "Moral judgment and moral action." In J. Rest and D. Narvaez (deeds'.). *Moral Development in the Professions: Psychology and Applied Ethics.* Hillsdale, NJ: Erlbaum: 199–211.
11. Miceli, M., & Near, J. 1992. *Blowing the Whistle.* New York: Lexington Books.
12. Treviño, L. K., & Victor, B. 2004. "Peer reporting of unethical behavior: A social context perspective," *Academy of Management Journal*, 353: 38–64.
13. Ethics Resource Center. 2003. *National Business Ethics Survey: How Employees View Ethics in Their Organizations.* Washington, DC.
14. PR Newswire. "How to spot bad apples in the corporate bushel," 13 January 2003. Ithaca, NY.
15. Treviño and Nelson; Jackall, R. 1988. *Moral Mazes: The World of Corporate Managers.* New York: Oxford University Press.
16. Drill team benched after scavenger incident, "Sleepover busted," *Hartford Courant*, 15 November 2002; Paulson. A. "Hazing case highlights girl violence," *Christian Science Monitor*, 9 May 2003.

17. Milgram, S. 1974. *Obedience to Authority: An Experimental View.* New York: Harper and Row.

18. Rest, J. S. (Ed.). 1986. *Moral Development: Advances in Research and Theory.* New York: Praeger. Rest, J. S., et al. 1999. *Postconventional Moral Thinking: A Neo-Kohlbergian Approach.* Mahwah, NJ: Erlbaum.

19. Ethics Resource Center, 2003. op. cit.

20. Schmitt, R. B. "Companies add ethics training: Will it work?," *Wall Street Journal* (Eastern edition), 4 November 2002: B1.

21. Ethics Resource Center, 2003. op. cit.

22. Treviño, L. K. et al. 1999. "Managing ethics and legal compliance: What works and what hurts," *California Management Review*, 41(2): 131–151.

23. Treviño and Nelson.

24. Toffler, B. L., with J. Reingold. 2003. *Final Accounting: Ambition, Greed, and the Fall of Arthur Andersen.* New York: Broadway Books. All of the following material on Toffler's experience at Arthur Andersen is from this source.

25. Kansas, D. "Plain talk: CEOs need to restore character in companies," WSJ.COM. Dow Jones and Company, Inc., 7 July 2002.

26. Treviño, L. K., Hartman, L. P., and Brown, M. 2000. "Moral person and moral manager: How executives develop a reputation for ethical leadership," *California Management Review*, 42(4): 128–142; Treviño, L. K., Brown, M., and Pincus-Hartman, 2003. "A qualitative investigation of perceived executive ethical leadership: Perceptions from inside and outside the executive suite," *Human Relations*, 56(1): 5–37.

27. George, B. 2003. *Authentic Leadership: Rediscovering the Secrets to Creating Lasting Value.* San Francisco: Jossey-Bass.

28. Byrne, J. 1999. *Chainsaw: The Notorious Career of Al Dunlap in the Era of Profit-at-Any-Price.* New York: HarperBusiness.

29. Tidwell, G. 1993. "Accounting for the PTL scandal," *Today's CPA.* July/August: 29–32.

30. Frieswick, K. Boing. *CFO Magazine*, 1 January 2004. www.cfo.com.

31. Treviño and Nelson; Loomis, C. "Whatever it takes," *Fortune*, 25 November 2002: 76.

32. PR Newswire. "Big majority believes tough new laws needed to address corporate fraud; modest majority at least somewhat confident that Bush will support such laws." 27 July 2002.

33. Kahaner, L. 2003. *Values, Prosperity and the Talmud: Business Lessons from the Ancient Rabbis.* New York: Wiley.

34. McCabe, D., and Treviño, L. K. 1996. "What we know about cheating in college," *Change: The Magazine of Higher Learning.* January/ February: 28–33; McCabe, D. L., Treviño, L. K., and Butterfield, K. 2001. "Cheating in academic institutions: A decade of research," *Ethics and Behavior*, 11(3): 219–232.

35. Ethics Resource Center, 2003. op cit.

36. Abrahamson, E. 1991. "Managerial fads and fashions," *Academy of Management Review*, 16: 586–612; Carson, 1999; Gibson, J. W., and Tesone, D. V. 2001. Management fads: Emergence, evolution, and implications for managers. *The Academy of Management Executive*, 15: 122–133.

37. Treviño and Nelson, K.

38. Schein, E. H. 1985. *Organizational Culture and Leadership.* San Francisco, CA: Jossey-Bass.

39. Treviño, L. K., Weaver, G. A., and Brown, M. 2000. "Lovely at the top." Paper presented at the Academy of Management meeting, Toronto, August.

40. Skinner, B. F. 1972. *Beyond Freedom and Dignity.* New York: Bantam Books.

41. Treviño, L. K., and Youngblood, S. A. 1990. "Bad apples in bad barrels: A causal analysis of ethical decision-making behavior," *Journal of Applied Psychology*, 75: 376–385.

42. Treviño and Nelson.

43. Toffler, p. 123.

44. Treviño, L. K. 1992. "The social implications of punishment in organizations: A justice perspective," *Academy of Management Review*, 17: 647–676; Treviño, L. K., and Ball, G. A. 1992. "The social implications of punishing unethical behavior: Observers' cognitive and affective reactions," *Journal of Management*, 18: 751–768.

45. Treviño, Hartman, and Brown.

THINK MACRO, ACT MICRO: FINANCE CAPITALISM AND ETHICS ACTION METHODS*

Richard P. Nielsen

Give us serenity to accept what cannot be changed, courage to change what should be changed, and wisdom to distinguish the one from the other.

—Reinhold Niebuhr

It is a common phenomenon for organizational systems to influence behaviors. For example, performance appraisal and compensation systems can influence safety behaviors. If safety is measured and rewarded, there is often a better chance for an

---

*Written for *The Organizational Behavior Reader.*

organization to maintain high safety levels compared to an organization that only measures and rewards cost reductions. Under the pressures to meet cost reduction numbers, managers can sometimes postpone or even ignore safety issues. The same can be true for even more macro systems such as the political-economic system that an organization operates within. This article considers how a particularly important and relatively new form of capitalist system, finance capitalism, can influence ethical behaviors. With a better understanding of the organizational and political-economic systems and pressures that influence behaviors, we can better select the types of ethics action methods that can increase the ethical and reduce the unethical.

Think Macro: Finance Capitalism and Unethical Behavior

There are at least five types of capitalism: small family-owned business capitalism; large family-owned business capitalism; managerial capitalism; state-owned enterprise capitalism; and, finance capitalism (Schumpeter, 1947; Chandler, 1977; Beaud, 1981; Baskin and Miranti, 1997; Ferguson, 2008; Nielsen, 2008; Appleby, 2010).

Within managerial capitalism, there are at least three important forms: German-bank financed, Japanese network, and U.S.-British stock market-financed managerial capitalism (Chandler, 1977; Nielsen, 2003a; Nielsen, 2005; The Economist, 2004a; Financial Times, 2004).

Within finance capitalism there are at least four important forms: short-run shareholder value capitalism; high leverage, hedge fund capitalism; high leverage, private-equity–leveraged buyout capitalism; and, high leverage banking (Useem, 1996; Bogle, 2005; Nielsen, 2008, 2009; Cohan, 2009; Davis, 2009; Posner, 2009).

In small family-owned capitalism, control is exercised by the family that owns and manages the business. In large family-owned capitalism, the family still owns controlling shares of the company and family members occupy key managerial positions.

In managerial capitalism, family members withdraw from the business and sell most of the family shares. Families sell their ownership shares for family financial diversification reasons and for personal reasons—i.e., often, later generations of family members are not interested in managerial careers. Professional, non-family managers replace family members as the key managers who control the business. In this type of managerial capitalism, when outside investors are dissatisfied with the financial performance of the business, they sell their shares and buy shares of other companies.

In German-bank-financed managerial capitalism, most of a company's stock is owned by large banks who, for the most part, treat their stock holdings as if they were long-term loans. In Japanese-network managerial capitalism, most of a company's stock is owned by the suppliers and customers of the company. In the United States and the United Kingdom stock market managerial capitalism, most of a company's stock is owned directly by individuals and families. This type of capitalism began to disappear in the U.S. as early as the mid-1970s (Drucker, 1980; Useem, 1996).

Today, the dominant form of capitalism and business organization in the United States, the United Kingdom, and spreading around the world is finance capitalism. In finance capitalism, financial institutions control corporations and large sectors of the political-economy. Most individual and family shares are owned indirectly through financial institutions such as mutual funds, pension funds, investment banks, insurance companies, trust funds, and private bankers who control and, when they choose, vote the shares (Useem, 1996; Bogle, 2005; Ferguson, 2008; Davis, 2009).

While there has always been some form of finance capitalism since the beginning of capitalism, the modern forms of finance capitalism began around 1980 and grew to dominance by 2000. It is also spreading rapidly around the world (Useem, 1996; Tagliabue, 1998; Baker and Smith, 1999; The Economist, 2002; Margolis and Walsh, 2003; Ferguson, 2008; Appleby, 2010). However, as a result of the financial crisis and great recession of 2008 that is continuing, many governments around the world, including the United States and the United Kingdom, appear to be trying to increase social and political control of financial institutions (Braithwaite and Guha, 2010; Forsyth, 2010; Morgenson, 2010).

As referred to above there are at least four important forms of modern finance capitalism: short-run shareholder value capitalism; high leverage, hedge fund capitalism; high leverage, private-equity–leveraged buyout capitalism; and, high leverage banking (Useem, 1996; Bogle, 2005; Nielsen, 2008, 2010; Cohan, 2009; Davis, 2009; Posner, 2009.)

What is shareholder value capitalism? Useem (1996, pp. 1, 11) explains, "If the principles of family capitalism dominated industrialization at the turn of the century, and if the concepts of managerial capitalism rose to dominance by mid-century, the new rules of investor [shareholder value] capitalism are coming to prevail by century's end. . . . Managerial capitalism tolerated a host of company objectives besides shareholder value. Investor [shareholder value] capitalism does not. . . . The developing relationships between investors and managers resemble neither markets nor organizations. Rather, they are emerging as enduring networks, a lattice of informal ties that come to guide a continuous two-way exchange of information and exercise of influence. . . . Now, when a large investor is dissatisfied with a company's top management, it often retains much of the holding but (along with other large investors) presses for improved performance. If results are not forthcoming, it lobbies the directors, votes against management, or even seeks new management—as the executives of the Bank of Boston, Kmart, Morrison Knudsen, Philip Morris, and W.R. Grace learned to their dismay." The same can also be said for the firing of the chief executive officers of General Motors and IBM in the 1980s (Nielsen, 2003a).

There is an important theoretical difference between long-term and short-term shareholder value maximization. In long-term shareholder value capitalism, it is theoretically possible to include the reasonable satisfaction of the needs of other stakeholders such as employees, bondholders, local community, etc. However and in practice, many if not most corporate performance appraisal and reward systems are based on yearly and even quarterly performance numbers. Under severe short-term performance pressures, it can be very difficult for managers to pay adequate attention to the needs of multiple stakeholders and even the long-term interests of shareholders (Bogle, 2005; Davis, 2009; Posner, 2009).

The key ethical issues structurally related to the short-term shareholder value form of finance capitalism are: misrepresentation of sales, costs, and profits in order to foster short-term stock prices; delaying funding of maintenance, safety, and other important costs in order to lower costs and increase short-term profitability; sacrificing long-term employment, health care, and pension benefits for short-term earnings; lack of attention to long-term environmental and local community needs for short-term earnings; too high debt borrowing and risk assumption in order to boost short-term profitability and share prices; and, lack of investment for long-term organizational development.

Hedge funds are, for the most part, private companies that borrow as much as 20 to 50 times their capital to trade and/or invest. They trade and invest in a wide variety of areas such as: commodities; stocks; high yield and high risk corporate bonds, mortgage bonds, government bonds; credit default swaps (insurance products on high risk bonds); securitized investment vehicles (packages of high risk debt instruments), etc. The key ethical issues structurally related to high leverage hedge funds are: too high debt risks that can negatively affect financial and economic system liquidity and health; transparency; and, social control.

When interest rates are low, the supply of capital is high, and investment returns are positive, hedge funds can achieve extraordinarily high returns of over 20% per year.

However, when interest rates rise, capital is scarcer, and investment returns fall; instead of extraordinary high returns, there can be extraordinarily large losses that can wipe out the capital of investors and help cause systemic damage to the financial and economic systems as has occurred in the great recession of 2008 that is continuing, as well as the collapse of hedge funds in 1998 that led to large increases in unemployment as well as large losses to investors (Donaldson, 2008; Ferguson, 2008; Posner, 2009). There is also a transparency issue. Since most hedge funds are private, they have far fewer public reporting requirements than publicly traded corporations. Similarly, there is a social control issue. Since the organizations are private, the regulatory requirements are much lower than for publicly traded corporations. However, since hedge funds have the power to borrow and invest and lose huge amounts of capital and can help cause massive recessions, the lack of transparency and social control are important issues.

Private Equity–Leveraged Buyout firms, like hedge funds, are for the most part private companies. Some PE-LBO firms and/or deals lean toward the private equity side and some lean toward the leveraged buyout side. Historically, private equity firms invested for the long term in companies that were often considered too risky for ordinary investors. For example, a private equity company would provide start-up funds for the development of new technologies. The leverage part of the PE-LBO is about large borrowing, as with hedge funds, as much as twenty to fifty times invested capital.

The way a PE-LBO firm typically operates is that it buys a publicly traded corporation with mostly borrowed money, takes it private, greatly increases the debt of the acquired company, pays itself dividends with the borrowed money, invests some of the newly borrowed money in the acquired company, restructures the company within one to four years, and then resells the company.

The private equity dimension of PE-LBOs is less problematical than the leveraged buyout dimension. The high leverage dimension shares with the hedge fund form of finance capitalism the increased and large risks to investors and the financial and economic systems of very high leverage borrowing combined with lack of transparency and social control. In the 2008 great recession, there was more subprime PE-LBO debt than subprime mortgage debt (Acharya, Franks, and Servaes, 2007; Berman, 2008; Nielsen, 2008). These PE-LBO firms, like hedge funds, are for the most part private. There is an additional problem with the high leverage dimension of PE-LBOs. If the PE-LBO firm uses most of the increased debt to pay itself dividends rather than investing the new debt into the company the way it was done in managerial capitalism, the risk position of the acquired company is greatly increased. When a PE-LBO firm loses a large amount of money, it can have very direct negative effects on the companies they take over. Not only do they lose the money of investors, they may have to drastically cut employment costs. Not only do they risk losing the money of investors and cutting employment, they risk destroying the wealth producing and economic development capacity of the organizations they take over. In 2008, more than half the bankruptcies in the United States of over $10 million were of firms that had gone through the PE-LBO process (Berman, 2008).

High leverage banking is very different than traditional banking. Traditional banking was characterized by the "originate and hold" model of banking. That is, banks took deposits and originated loans to businesses and individuals that they held and watched over for the life of the loans. Banks would lend between five and ten times their capital.

The high leverage, "originate and distribute" model of banking is very different. Banks would increase their leverage from 5 to 10 times capital to 20 to 50 times capital. That is, the banks would borrow much more money not only from their own depositors but other financial institutions in order to make loans and/or buy loans that they would then distribute and sell to others. Many of these debt products that the banks originated and distributed were high risk mortgage and high risk corporate debt. Even if the loans were not very safe, as long as the banks could sell the loans to someone else, they were able to receive large commissions and fees from the process. In addition, many of these debt products were contained in "off-balance sheet" accounts that often were not included in regulatory scrutiny. In addition, several of these high leverage banks such as Citigroup, Bank of America, Wells Fargo, Goldman Sachs, Morgan Stanley, Lehman Brothers, and J.P. Morgan Chase also developed their own and/or made loans to and invested in hedge funds and private equity–leveraged buyout firms and deals.

The ethics issues structurally related to high leverage banking are similar to the ethics issues structurally related to hedge funds and private equity–leveraged buyout firms: high risk leverage that can endanger the financial and economic systems; short-term decision making; transparency; and, social control.

Increasing banks' leverage from 10 to 50 times capital greatly increases the risks to the banks, the financial system, and the economic system. Banks are not only very important for the safety of investments in banks, they are important for the safety of customers' deposits as well as normal consumer and business lending. If banks lose their capital through greatly increased risk taking, they may also be losing their depositors' money that the depositors were led to believe were safe. If the banks lose much of their capital, they have to cut back on consumer and business lending which can cause a liquidity crisis with respect to refinancing as well as contribute to an economic recession when it can't lend money for normal consumer purchases and business investments. The economic consequences of a great recession can be enormous (Cohan, 2009; Krugman, 2009; Posner, 2009). For example, the real unemployment rate in the United States in 2009 that includes those people who can't find full-time jobs has increased to about 18% (Forsyth, 2009). Millions of people are forced out of their homes because they cannot meet mortgage payments due to both lost jobs and higher re-financing costs. Government and nonprofit organizations are forced to cut back on educational, health care, infrastructure, and safety programs. Millions of people are unable to retire or are only able to retire with greatly reduced incomes. Government debt increases in order to finance the bailouts of the financial institutions and economic stimulus programs. To stimulate the economy, the same banks who helped cause the crisis are lent money by governments at very low rates that, in turn, greatly increase the trading profits of the banks who caused the problems when they reinvest the low cost borrowed money in higher rate government, corporate, and consumer debt instruments.

In addition to the structural ethics issue of high leverage banking that damages the financial and economic systems, there are the ethics issues of short-term decision making, transparency, and social control. When the banks and the bankers make most of their profits from the fees and commissions of originating and distributing debt products, this encourages short-term decision making. That is, even if it is very risky or even unlikely that a distributed debt product will retain value and/or default a few years after it is distributed, that is not the problem of the bankers. The short-term compensation system of short-term fees, commissions, and bonuses encourages short-term rather than sustainable decision making criteria.

There is also the problem of transparency. When the regulations and regulators allow the banks to include many of these "originate and distribute" activities to be considered off-balance sheet, then they are not subject to the same regulatory reporting and scrutiny requirements. Even though most of the banks are public companies and subject to greater social control than private companies, when the regulations and the regulators decide to de-regulate and/or not consider much of the banks' high leverage, high risk, short-term activities, we have similarly little social control of the banks' activities that can and has caused such enormous damage (Cohan, 2009; Posner, 2009).

Features of finance capitalism are also entangled with features of the U.S. political campaign financing system. For example, congressmen may have conflicts of interests that are sometimes acted upon (Levitt, 2002; Cloud, Fields, Cummings, Markon, and Lucchetti, 2001; Hitt and Haburger, 2002). Individuals and groups of individuals who work for hedge funds, private equity–leveraged buyout firms, banks, mortgage companies, insurance companies, bond rating agencies, corporations, and accounting firms make large contributions to the political campaigns of politicians of both parties. In order to get elected and re-elected, politicians need large amounts of money to run political campaigns. Appointing regulators, for example, to the Federal Reserve, the Treasury Department, and the Securities and Exchange Commission, who are considered friendly and sympathetic to the financial institutions, may result in large campaign contributions. Failure to cooperate puts candidates and their parties at risk of losing large amounts of campaign funds. In the short run and in a long series of short runs, this system is a very profitable win-win setup for many of the key managers, employees, accountants, analysts, regulators, and politicians. The CEOs of the largest and/or most profitable financial institutions received between $50 million to, in some cases of hedge funds and PE-LBO firms, over $1 billion a year in compensation. That is a lot of money that can be shared with politicians. The brokers and loan officers received large commissions from the origination and sale of bonds and loans. The analysts were richly compensated from the sales sides of the business. The accounting firms received larger profits from consulting services than from auditing services. The bond rating agencies received large fees from the financial institutions. The politicians and political parties received large and increased campaign contributions. Meanwhile, individuals and families directly and indirectly lost trillions and suffered greatly through lost jobs, lost health care, reduced pensions, reduced incomes, and lost homes (Cohan, 2009; Krugman, 2009; Posner, 2009). Unfortunately, this system does not benefit everyone and perhaps not even most people and certainly not anywhere near equally.

Act Micro: Ethics Action and Intervention Methods

What can managers and employees do about unethical behaviors that are stimulated by such features of the finance capitalism system and organizational systems that put pressure on people to initiate and/or cooperate with unethical behaviors? There are at least six sets of ethics action and intervention methods that can help us to not just mind our own business and act ethically in our individual work lives, but also to act ethically as citizens of our organizational communities to effectively oppose unethical behaviors and build more ethical communities (Nielsen and Bartunek, 1996; Nielsen, 1996, Treviño and Nelson, 2003). The six types of methods are (1) win-lose forcing methods; (2) win-win methods; (3) dialogic methods; (4) internal due process methods; (5) alternative institution building; and (6) social movement methods. There are many more methods within these six categories. Determining which methods will be more and less appropriate and effective often depends on the different types of individual, organizational, and environmental obstacles that characterize the problem situation (Argyris, 1990; Nielsen, 1996). For example, some top executives of corporations have been unwilling and/or unable to engage in dialog about ethical issues (Brown, 2003). Ethical and effective managers and employees may need to understand and be able to practice a wide variety of ethics action-intervention methods, including such difficult methods as secret whistle-blowing, to realize our duties as professionals and citizens of organizations and communities.

Win-Lose Forcing Methods

Win-lose forcing methods include top-down, compliance and punishment-based ethics codes, secret whistle-blowing, public whistle-blowing, and felony RICO prosecutions. Win-lose forcing methods try to establish ethical behaviors through threats of punishment, embarrassment, and exposure. Win-lose methods concentrate on changing behaviors unlike some other types of methods that try to change both how people think and behave (Nielsen and Bartunek, 1996; Nielsen, 1996; Argyris, 2003).

TOP-DOWN ETHICS CODES For the most part, ethics codes are rules and regulations written by top management and their lawyers to control the behavior of lower-level organizational members. Occasionally, codes are more dialogically and participatively developed by people from many layers and parts of an organization (Nielsen, 1996; Treviño and Nelson, 2003). There are rules that require behaviors and rules that prohibit behaviors. For example, there are rules that require employees to obtain verified information from potential borrowers about incomes, assets, and debts. There are rules that forbid employees from taking kick-backs from vendors. There are rules that require compliance with Generally Accepted Accounting Principles. There are rules that forbid misrepresentation of accounting numbers. There are rules that require that potential conflicts of interest be revealed and rules that prohibit acting upon conflicts of interests.

The top-down, compliance codes include punishments for breaking the rules, such as firings, suspensions, demotions, fines, and even felony prosecutions. Organizations that use punishment-based compliance codes tend to be organizations that have been caught doing extensive unethical and illegal behaviors as well as authoritarian, older, larger, bureaucratic organizations. The older, bureaucratic types of organizations are often characterized by a type of Theory X, win-lose, authoritarian type of management and leadership, where top management acts as if lower-level employees were lazy, irresponsible people who have to be closely supervised and controlled (McGregor, 1960). Examples of these types of organizations with very thick rule books are military organizations, government bureaucracies, and older industries such as mining, banking, insurance, and railroad companies.

Another type of organization that often uses ethics codes are organizations that have been caught doing extensive illegal and unethical behaviors. For example, part of the legal settlement with prosecutors in the high leverage banking, mortgage banking, investment banking, mutual fund, and insurance industry scandals of 2000–2009 is the establishment of compliance-based ethics codes. Similarly, this happened in the 1970s when many military and defense contractors were caught doing extensive corruption. The U.S. government "sentencing guidelines" for judges offered companies lighter sentences and penalties if they established ethics programs with compliance codes and ethics officers to administer the codes (Treviño and Nelson, 2003).

A strength of top-down, punishment-based compliance codes is that they clearly articulate that the unethical behaviors are unethical, are forbidden by the organization, and might be punished. A key limitation of such codes is that they can and have been selectively ignored by the top managers who have the discretion on whether and how to enforce the codes. For example, in the high leverage banking, mortgage banking, investment banking, mutual fund, and insurance industry scandals, almost all of the organizations had ethics codes, compliance officers, and ethics officers that did not appear to play any significant or effective role in preventing the unethical behaviors.

Similarly, the ethics codes and ethics officer programs established as a result of the 1970s' junk bond scandals in the financial services industries and the bid-rigging and bribery/extortion scandals in the defense industries appear to have played very little positive role in either exposing or preventing the financial scandals of 1990–2009.

Another problem with top-down, punishment-based compliance codes is that at least in some industries where there are rapid changes in industry practices, such as in financial services, pharmaceutical, and defense industries, the rules tend to prohibit yesterday's unethical behaviors. The belief can be common in such rapidly changing organizations that use compliance codes that if something is not forbidden by the rules, it is permitted, at least until there is another scandal. For example, the rules that were developed out of the pharmaceutical product testing scandals of the 1960s and the rules against the fraudulent junk bond financial reporting of the 1970s did not cover or help much with the more recent scandals [e.g., the pain medicine and coronary artery stent scandals (Krasner, 2004)], the fraudulent high leverage debt securitizations, earnings predictions, earnings reporting, auditing, investment banking, mutual fund late trading, and New York Stock Exchange specialist companies that systematically engaged in front-running trading of their personal and firm investments ahead of buying and selling for customers (Nielsen, 2003a; Kelly and Craig, 2004; Cohan, 2009; Posner, 2009).

PUBLICLY BLOW THE WHISTLE Given the financial pressures managers and employees are under and the limitations of top-down, punishment-based compliance codes, it is often essential for organizational members to blow the whistle outside the organization when top management selectively ignores its own codes and/or suppresses information about code violations (Sender and Zuckerman, 2003). It may also be necessary to simultaneously blow the whistle to the press and the regulators in order to get the regulators to act and do their jobs when financial institutions might prefer that they ignore whistle-blowers. In the absence of public pressure from the media, regulators often ignore whistle-blowing as they did in the Madoff scandals when Harry Markoplos several times notified the Securities and Exchange Commission of legal and ethical violations (Zuckerman and Gauthier-Villars, 2009).

After unsuccessfully trying to get the attention of top management at Enron, Sherron Watkins, an investment manager, testified before the United States Senate about Enron's deceptive accounting and energy investments (Watkins, 2003). Her testimony was very important in exposing and stopping the unethical and illegal behaviors at Enron and indirectly at the investment banks that supported the Enron frauds. Similarly, Peter Rost, a Vice-President of Marketing for Pfizer, publicly blew the whistle to the media that the big pharmaceutical companies were untruthful when they insisted that importing drugs from abroad is unsafe (Barry and Welch, 2004).

When top management ignores it own codes, internal action-intervention methods are often not politically possible. In such cases, external whistle-blowing that asks for outside help from the government, the courts, and/or the media may be necessary. Unfortunately, there is much evidence that public whistle-blowers suffer very effective retaliation (Alford, 2001; Harding, 2002).

SECRETLY BLOW THE WHISTLE OUTSIDE THE ORGANIZATION Noreen Harrington, a veteran manager with experience as a managing director at Goldman Sacks, Stern Asset management, and Barclays Capital, first tried to discuss the ethics of late trading in mutual funds, but top management would not pay serious attention and continued with the unethical practices. Finally, she secretly blew the whistle to New York State Attorney General. This secret whistle-blowing resulted in exposure of the massive unethical practices in the mutual fund industry as well as several important reforms (Sender and Zuckerman, 2003). Harrington explains why she intervened and acted, "All of a sudden, I thought about this from a different vantage point. I saw one face—my sister's face—and then I saw the faces of everyone whose only asset was a 401(k) (pension). At that point I felt the need to try to make the regulators look into these abuses" (Chatzky, 2004, p. 156). Harrington later decided to reveal her identity to the *Wall Street Journal.* The key advantage of secretly blowing the whistle outside the organization is that the whistle-blower is for the most part protected from retaliation. The disadvantage of the method is that the organization is hurt by public exposure of the unethical behavior.

SECRETLY BLOW THE WHISTLE INSIDE THE ORGANIZATION In 2003, a financial analyst secretly blew the whistle about fraudulent earnings in his division of a large financial services company to the Chairman of the Audit Committee of the Board of Directors (Financial Analyst, 2003). Subsequently, the audit committee reviewed the division's numbers and restated them. The misrepresentation was stopped and corrected. The key advantages of this method are that the unethical behavior is sometimes stopped, the secret whistle-blower is protected, and the organization is given the opportunity to solve the ethics problem before it becomes a public embarrassment to the organization. Disadvantages of the method are that the organization may ignore the warning and/or the organization might seek out and punish the internal whistle-blower.

RICO

If the Racketeer Influenced and Corrupt Organizations Act (Blakey and Roddy, 1996) could be applied in felony prosecutions of top managers, this might have a more important deterrence effect compared, for example, to organizations that pay relatively small fines and admit no guilt. The RICO Act permits judges to find top management guilty for the illegal behaviors of subordinates when there is systematic and pervasive corruption in their organizations. Such systematic and pervasive corruption appears to have been the case for several high leverage, subprime mortgage and corporate debt securitizations and distributions, credit default swaps, investment banking, mutual fund, and insurance industry companies. For example, during the WorldCom and related investment banking scandals, Citigroup former CEO and Chairman, Sanford Weill received total compensation over a five-year period of close to $1 billion, but Citigroup paid a fine of "only" $400 million and did not admit any guilt. To date judges have unfortunately not allowed prosecutors to use the RICO Act in this type of case (Bowe, 2004; DeBaise, 2004; Laufer, 2008). Today, top managers of the financial institutions and rating agencies that helped cause the great recession of 2008 not only are not being prosecuted, they are given preferential lending rates, loan guarantees, and government loans by the Federal Reserve and the Treasury Department and are receiving multimillion dollar bonuses and stock grants and in the case of some hedge funds and private equity–leveraged buyout firms, annual compensation between $100 million and $1 billion a year.

Win-Win Methods

The intention of win-lose methods is to force change through, for example, the threats of punishments for violations of ethics codes and/or exposure through external whistle-blowing to the press or government about perpetrators and top managers who initiate and/or cooperate with unethical and illegal behaviors. Unlike these threat based methods, win-win methods try to offer incentives for ethical behavior and incentives for cessation of unethical behaviors (Nielsen, 2009). Two important types of win-win methods are mutual gain negotiating (Fisher and Ury, 1991) and reciprocal networking (Nielsen, 2003a). As with the win-lose forcing methods, the focus of these methods is behavior change rather than changes in how people think.

WIN-WIN NEGOTIATION Within financial services organizations there have been conflicts of interest that have been acted upon with respect to relationships between the investment banking and financial analysis sides of the business. For example, David Komansky, former CEO of Merrill Lynch, and Denis Kozlowski, former CEO of Tyco, discussed how to manipulate research coverage of Tyco by Merrill hiring an analyst that Tyco favored. According to an e-mail introduced at Koslowski's trial sent to Mr. Komansky by Samuel Chapin, Merrill's Vice-Chairman, "To demonstrate the impact this hire has on our relationship, Denis Kozlowski called me on Phua's (the analyst Tyco wanted Merrill to hire) first day of work to award us the lead management of a $2.1 billion bond offering." Instead of incentives like this for unethical behavior, a possible win-win incentive is to offer financial rewards or points toward promotion for ethical behavior.

Organizations can offer rewards to financial analysts who previously misrepresented their evaluations of stocks in cooperation with misrepresented investment banking deals. For example, the financial analyst who had misrepresented the prospects for a stock in exchange for a bonus from the investment banking unit might instead be offered a bonus for the accuracy of his predictions. However, for something like this to work, the relationship between the investment banking side and the analyst side of financial institutions would have to be separated. This has been done as part of the settlement that Citigroup, Goldman, J.P. Morgan Chase, Credit Swiss First Boston, and Merrill Lynch made with the Securities and Exchange Commission and New York Attorney General. In the aftermath of the 2008 great recession and financial institution scandals, there are various efforts around the world to better align compensation schemes to long-term economic sustainability (Braithwaite and Guha, 2010; Gapper, 2010).

ETHICAL NETWORKING Ethical networking operates as follows. Person A helps Person B. Person A asks Person B to help Person C. Person A asks Person B and Person C to help Person D, and so on. Person A can do this because Person A is an ethical person who wants to help others or for reasons of self-interest. It works both ways. Through this method, Person A builds a network of reciprocal win-win relationships with Person A at the center of the win-win network. If Person A wants to intervene to stop an unethical behavior and/or increase an ethical behavior, Person A has the political allies to exercise organizational influence (Nielsen, 2003a). Ethical networking is different than Mafia-type networking in two key areas. First, the network leader is trying to help people rather than exploit others. Second, the network is inclusive rather than exclusive.

A key strength of win-win methods relative to win-lose methods is that most people prefer to be rewarded for behavior change rather than being threatened into behavior change. A key limitation may be that the ethics change agent may not have anything to offer that is an adequate material incentive for stimulating ethical behavior and/or stopping unethical behavior. For example, in the above Citigroup and Tyco-Merrill Lynch cases and in the current subprime mortgage and subprime corporate debt bubbles, the financial rewards from high-level unethical behaviors are often much greater than the material rewards ethics and corruption reformers can offer very highly compensated managers.

Dialogic Methods

There are at least three sets of dialogic methods. There are the ethics arguments/criteria that can be used to discuss an issue. There are different methods for structuring conversations. There are different organizational structures for participating in organizational decision making.

ETHICS ARGUMENTS/REASONS Examples of ethics arguments/criteria include Aristotle's proportionality criterion where something is less right or wrong than too much or too little, Aristotle's common good criterion, Kant's (1797) "treat people as ends in themselves and not solely as means" criterion, Bentham's (1789) utilitarian cost-benefit criterion, Derrida's (1988) postmodern power bias criterion—i.e., the more powerful often write the rules and the histories to favor the more powerful at expense of the less powerful, etc. There are at least twenty different types or arguments/criteria that could be used in an ethics intervention conversation (Nielsen, 2003a).

For example, with respect to a safety issue, one could reason with Aristotle's proportionality argument that our incidence of accidents relative to the industry is too high. Similarly, one could argue that relative to historical norms of prudence, bank leverage rations of 20 to 50 to 1 are much too high and imprudent. One could reason with Aristotle's common-good criterion that unnecessary worker injuries are not good for our organizational community. Similarly, one could argue that risking a liquidity crisis with too high leverage is not in the interest of the common good. One could reason with Kant's "treat people as ends in themselves and not solely as means" criterion that avoidable accidents for the sake of profitability do not treat people as ends in themselves. Similarly, one could argue that bankers passing on bad debt securitizations to others violates the "do unto others as you would have them do unto you" principle. One could consider with Bentham's cost benefit criteria whether the costs of accidents or financial bubbles were greater than the benefits of improved safety or slower and more prudent economic growth. One could reason with Derrida's postmodern criterion that injuries may be occurring more frequently among the least powerful and most vulnerable customers and employees.

DIALOGIC CONVERSATION STRUCTURES There are at least six different methods of structuring dialogic conversations (Nielsen, 1996). For example, one could use the Socratic method, where the interventionist asks questions without advocating positions. One could use Argyris's (1990, 2003) action-learning method where the interventionist combines inquiry with advocacy and experimentation. One could use Woolman's (Nielsen, 1996) method, where the interventionist inquires about organizational system/tradition forces that may be pressuring organizational members to behave in less ethical ways.

DIALOGIC ORGANIZATIONAL STRUCTURES There are many different types of organizational structures for organizing participative decision making (Heller, Pusic, Strauss, and Wilpert, 1998). For example, there are self-managed work teams. There are joint management–employee committees, there are quality circles, there are employee boards and mixed stakeholder group boards that combine internal and external organizational stakeholders in advisory discussions.

The key advantages of dialogic methods are that they can result in belief conversion toward the ethical as well as behavior change toward the ethical and that dialog can be more friendly and less adversarial. The key problems with dialogic methods are that the people engaging in the unethical activities may already understand that what they are doing is unethical and that they understand that they are choosing what they anticipate will be wealth and power rewards instead of ethics. In addition, powerful people who may be engaged in unethical activities can often choose not to engage in dialog. There is often not much political space in organizations to discuss ethics issues with top management.

Internal Due Process Systems

There are at least four different types of internal due process systems: investigation and punishment, grievance and arbitration, mediation, and employee board systems (Nielsen, 2000). Due process systems are very important because in the emotionality of a scandal and the rush to closure, sometimes top managements find scapegoats rather than fundamental reforms. Typically, lower- and middle-level employees take the blame for either actions or pressures that come from top management.

For example in the Citigroup case referred to above, while several middle- and lower-level managers lost their jobs, the Citigroup CEO and Chairman Sanford Weill was not penalized but handsomely rewarded. There is a great deal of variation in the fairness, costs, and flexibility of due process systems.

INVESTIGATION AND PUNISHMENT SYSTEM In an investigation and punishment system, management does an investigation about an unethical behavior and then announces a decision with punishments if the accused is found guilty by management. This type of system is very fast and relatively inexpensive but offers few protections to the accused. This is the type of system that is very popular in U.S. business but is illegal in the European Union since it offers so little protection to the accused employee.

GRIEVANCE AND ARBITRATION SYSTEM In a grievance and arbitration system, several layers of management and employees discuss the case against the accused. If at progressive levels of management and employee representation, agreement can't be reached, a decision is made by an outside arbitrator. This type of system is common in unionized environments and government organizations. It offers a great deal of protection to the accused but is very time-consuming and expensive.

MEDIATION SYSTEM In a mediation system, typically a human resources manager tries to mediate and work out some type of win-win agreement between the parties to an ethics conflict. This type of system is very informal, inexpensive, and flexible. However, its fairness depends to a great extent on the individual character and skills of the mediator.

EMPLOYEE BOARD SYSTEM In an employee board system, a jury of employees investigates a potential ethics violation and makes recommendations and decisions about the individual case and/or changes in an organization's policies and procedures that may have contributed to the ethics problem. This system is also very flexible and fair but is more expensive and time consuming than a mediator system. This is a relatively rare form of due process system in U.S. business since top managements are often reluctant to cede power to an employee board.

Alternative Institution Building

Sometimes it is not possible or it would take too long for organizational ethics efforts to work. In such a situation, it may be possible to build an alternative institution. For example, in several emerging market countries, the state-owned banking systems are so corrupt that it is not possible to reform them. Bankers are often hired and promoted on the basis of political connections. The administrators of the banks often make intentionally bad loans to friends, relatives, and political allies and collect kickbacks from bank purchases. Bank resources are spent on nonbank activities.

For many years, reformers both within and outside state banking systems in many emerging market countries tried to reform the systems, but it was not possible. Instead, the reformers got together to build alternative private banks. Bankers were hired and promoted on the basis of demonstrated abilities rather than political connections. Lower-level employees were hired on the basis of their achievements rather than their political connections. Customers were invited to apply for loans and other financial services based on their achievements and abilities rather than their political connections. In many emerging markets, the private banks are succeeding. Bankers who did excellent work were hired and promoted based on their achievements rather than their political connections. Excellent employees were recruited and promoted. Many of these banks have been growing at a rate of 15 percent a year for the last twenty years. There is little financial corruption in banking purchases and investments. In some cases, the state banks have begun to imitate some aspects of the ethical private banks.

A key strength of this method is that ethical institutions can be created when older corrupt organizations can't be changed. The U.S. Securities and Exchange Commission may be an example of an institution that can't be changed due to its links to political appointments and campaign contributions and may need to be replaced with an alternative institution (Levitt, 2002).

However, sometimes when the new ethical organization succeeds and gains prominence and market share, the older corrupt institutions decide to try to change in order to survive in the new competitive environment where before they were protected by their relative monopoly position.

Key limitations of this method are that it can take enormous resources to build an alternative institution and there is often very strong opposition to the new institution that is perceived by the old guard as a threat to their institutional position. Unfortunately, sometimes the reverse happens, and the private institutions that were founded to become corruption reform institutions become as corrupt as the public institutions that they were originally trying to reform.

Social Movement Methods

Social movement methods are used when the problem is too big for one individual, group, or even organization to address. Examples of social movements include the U.S. civil rights movement, the Swedish Natural Step environmental movement, the Korean People's Solidarity for Participatory Democracy corruption reform movement, the worldwide auditing and corporate governance reform movement, and the financial institutions reform movement that resulted from the great recession of 2008 (Davis and Thompson, 1994; McAdam, 1982; Nielsen, 2000; Kelly and Craig, 2004; Davis, 2004; Krugman, 2009; Posner, 2009). Typically, social movement methods combine the resources and efforts of many individuals, groups, organizations, and even professional associations.

A common series of processes within a social movement includes the following (Nielsen, 2000). An example from the auditing and corporate governance reform movement is described.

a. Dialog among friends about biases in traditions and systems that also discover political opportunities for reform. Many accounting firm partners, accounting professors, business journalists, and top managers from pension funds, mutual fund companies, and diversified financial services organizations have known about and talked about governance and auditing problems for many years. The investment banking, mutual fund, and insurance industry scandals as well as the worldwide decline of stock markets in the 2000–2002 period that was partially caused by these ethical scandals provided political opportunities for reform.

b. Dialog among friends about personal values among reformers and leaders of established, directly shared interest organizations that result in alliances between reformers and established organization leaders. Some individual leaders were able to mobilize support from their professional accounting associations, media organizations, investment officer associations, pension fund associations, mutual fund associations, etc. to formally back reforms in corporate governance, securities, and auditing legislation.

c. Reframing among the leaders of established organizations and members concerning the meaning of membership in terms of active support for reform of biases in traditions/systems. Some of the leaders of professional associations also asked the members of their associations to individually and collectively support the reforms.

d. Win-win development of specialized reform organizations. For example, the Public Company Accounting Oversight Board was established by the U.S. Congress in 2002 to focus on auditing and governance reforms. The Board has publicly asked practicing accounting auditors to blow the whistle to the Board about illegal and unethical activities of their firms and the clients of their auditing firms (Associated Press, 2004).

e. Selected win-lose actions against opponents to reform. For example, with the information provided by the secret whistle-blowers, the Oversight Board as well as prosecutors can require companies to release e-mails, documents, and other types of information that can then be used to prosecute individual and organizational violators.

f. Trailing, win-win development of support of the reform movement through instrumental alliances with external support groups. For example, after corporate governance successes, reformers ask current supporters for more help and ask potential new allies to support the movement.

A key strength of the social movement method is that it is able to help develop large social changes that would have been impossible for individuals, groups, organizations, and associations acting alone. In addition, very important friendships are developed in the long struggle for positive social change. A key limitation of social movement methods is that they require an enormous amount of time from key leaders who are often not compensated financially very much or at all. This requires an enormous personal commitment of a few key leaders, which typically takes a great deal of time away from family and normal career endeavors. In addition, social movements require an enormous amount of resources from key supporting organizations and individuals. Social movements may also have to be more or less continuous since the particular form of problem that caused the original movement may change. For example, while the reforms in accounting and investment banking as a result of the 2002 investment banking scandals have been worthwhile, they did not appear to help very much with the high leverage debt and securitization bubbles of the 2008 great recession. Reform movements may need to be continuous and able to adapt to new forms. As Schumpeter (1947) observed about the creative destructive movements of new forms of capitalism replacing older forms, the same may be necessary for reform movements. That is, reform movements may also have to continuously reinvent themselves to meet the new ethical challenges of new forms of capitalism such as modern high leverage, finance capitalism.

Conclusion

As illustrated above, there have been and probably still are various types of unethical behaviors that are at least partially caused by features of our organizational and political-economic systems. That is, the types of unethical business behaviors are linked to the types of capitalism, in the recent period, to the "finance capitalism" type. Fortunately, there are many effective ethics action and intervention methods that we can use to resist unethical behaviors and build ethical organizational communities.

Unfortunately, as *The Economist* (2004b, p. 83) observed about the 2002 investment bank and mutual fund scandals and may also be true of the 2008 financial crisis scandals, "Like the investment bank settlement, this week's agreement (mutual fund industry) is less punitive than the seven-figure sum suggests. As with the Wall Street penalties, the mutual-fund fines are easily digestible. . . . As in the investment-bank case, no senior executives of the parent companies have been held liable." As they did then and so far again in the 2008 financial crisis scandals, the government regulators and prosecutors in the investment banking, mutual fund, and insurance industry corruption scandals have allowed the CEOs of the largest financial institutions to keep and increase their massive compensation packages, albeit more in stock than cash bonuses, while having their organizations pay no or relatively small fines and even receive massive bailouts from taxpayers and receive massive preferential low interest loans from the Federal Reserve that are then used to generate very large trading profits without admitting guilt for the massive corruption and unethical behaviors (Solomon, 2004). As John Kay (2010: 9) of the *Financial Times* has observed, "The credit crunch of 2007–2008 was the third phase of a larger and longer financial crisis. The first phase was the emerging market defaults of the 1990s. The second was the new economy boom and bust at the turn of the century. The third was the collapse of markets for structured debt products, which had grown so rapidly in the five years up to 2007. . . . At the end of each phase, regulators and financial institutions declared that lessons had been learnt. While measures were implemented which, if they had been introduced five years earlier, might have prevented the most recent crisis from taking the particular form it did, these responses addressed the particular problem that had just occurred, rather than the underlying generic problems of skewed incentives and dysfunctional institutional structures."

Therefore, while we might prefer to use the dialogic and win-win methods, the win-lose forcing methods of asking for outside help through secret external whistleblowing to the press and to prosecutors as well as aggressive regulation and even application of felony RICO Act (Blakey and Roddy, 1996) prosecutions against CEOs and board chairmen of the largest financial institutions may also be necessary.

It is often not enough to "mind our own business" and act ethically in our individual work lives when there are serious unethical behaviors around us. We have an ethical obligation to act, to ask others inside and outside the organization for help if necessary, and to intervene to help others in resisting unethical and corrupt behaviors and in building ethical organizational communities.

Thinking globally at a micro level about how the larger political-economic systems may be at least in part causing unethical behaviors can help us understand the systematic nature of the problem. Acting locally at a micro level with application of ethics action-intervention methods can help solve the problems. As Aristotle observed, "The student of ethics must apply himself to politics." As the political theorist Edmund Burke advocated, "When bad men [and/or good people pressured by problematical systems] combine, the good must associate; else they will fall one by one, an unpitied sacrifice in a contemptible struggle." And as Reinhold Niebuhr asks, "Grant us serenity to accept what cannot be changed, courage to change what should be changed, and wisdom to distinguish the one from the other." It is the conclusion of this paper that while there is much that cannot be changed with respect to the type of capitalism and political-economy that we may live within during any generation, at least in the short and medium term, there is also much that can be changed; and, with wisdom to know the difference and with practical ethics action and intervention methods, we can help make a positive and ethical difference.

References

Alford, C. Fred. 2001. Whistleblowers: Broken Lives and Organizational Power. Ithaca, N.Y.: Cornell University Press.

Argyris, C.R., Putnam, R., and Smith, D.M. 1985. Action Science. San Francisco: Jossey-Bass.

Argyris, C.R. 1990. Overcoming Organizational Defenses. Boston: Allyn and Bacon.

Argyris, C.R. 2003. "A Life Full of Learning," Organization Studies, 24:7: 1178–1192.

Acharya, V.V., Franks, J. & Servaes, H. 2007. "Private Equity: Boom and Bust?" Journal of Applied Corporate Finance, 19, 4: 44–53.

Appleby, Joyce. 2010. The Relentless Revolution: A History of Capitalism. New York: Norton.

Associated Press. 2004. "Group Encourages Whistleblowing," The Boston Globe, August 24: 8.

Auletta, K. 1986. Greed and Glory on Wall Street: The Fall of the House of Lehman. New York: Random House.

Baker, George and Smith, George. 1999. The New Financial Capitalists. Cambridge: Cambridge University Press.

Barry, Patricia. 2004. "The Insiders," AARP Bulletin, November, p. 10.

Baskin, J.B. & Miranti, P.J. (1997). A History of Corporate Finance. Cambridge: Cambridge University Press.

Bauman, Zygmunt. 1993. Postmodern Ethics. Oxford: Blackwell Publishers.

Beaud, Michael. 1981. A History of Capitalism. N.Y.: Monthly Review Press.

Bentham, J. 1789, 1897. An Introduction to the Principles of Morals and Legislation. Oxford: Oxford University Press.

Berman, D.K. (2008). "Buyout Shops Show Timing Is Everything in Deal Making Arena," The Wall Street Journal, February 26: C1, C5.

Blakey, G.R. and Roddy, K.P. 1996. "Reflections on Reves v. Ernst & Young: Its Meaning and Impact on Substantive, Accessory, Aiding, Abetting and Conspiracy Liability under RICO," American Criminal Law Review, 33, 5: 1345–1702.

Bogle, J.C. 2005. The Battle For The Soul of Capitalism. New Haven: Yale University Press.

Bowe, Christopher. 2004. "Tyco Trial: Judge Drops 'Mafia' Charge," Financial Times, March 6: 9.

Bowe, Christopher and Silverman, Gary. 2004. "Merrill Rewarded After Hiring Analyst Tyco Favored," Financial Times, February 3: 1.

Braithwaite, Tom & Guha, Krishna. 2010. Banks Face Revolutionary Reform. Financial Times, January 22: 2.

Brown, Ken. 2003. "Wall Street Plays Numbers Game with Earnings, Despite Reforms," Wall Street Journal, July, 22: 1, 2.

Chandler, Alfred D. 1977. The Visible Hand: The Managerial Revolution in American Business. Cambridge: Harvard University Press.

Chatzky, Jean. 2004. "Meet the Whistle-Blower," Money, February: 156.

Cloud, David S., Fields, Gary, Cummings, Jeanne, Markon, Jerry, and Lucchetti, Aaron. 2001. "Money and Connections Paved the Way Home for Fugitive Marc Rich," Wall Street Journal, January 29: 1, 6.

Cohan, W.D. 2009. House of Cards. N.Y.: Doubleday.

Craig, Susanne and Brown, Ken. 2004. Wall Street Journal, March 29: C1, C5.

Davis, G.F. and Thompson, T.A. 1994. "A Social Movement Perspective on Corporate Control," Administrative Science Quarterly 39: 141–173.

Davis, Ann. 2004. "Wall Street, Companies It Covers, Agree on Honesty Policy," Wall Street Journal, March 11: C1, C6.

Davis, G.F. 2009. The Rise and Fall of Finance and the End of the Society of Organizations. Academy of Management Perspectives, August: 27–44.

DeBaise, Colleen. 2004. "Tyco Corruption Count Is Dropped," Wall Street Journal, March 8: C4.

Derrida, Jacques. 1988. Limited INC. Evanston, IL.: Northwestern University Press.

Donaldson, Thomas. 2008. "Hedge Fund Ethics," Business Ethics Quarterly, 18, 3: 405–416.

The Economist. 2002. "The End of Tycoons: A New Generation, a New Economy, and a New Capitalism Are Changing the Way in Which Business Is Done in East Asia," April 29: 67–69.

The Economist. 2004a. "Capitalism's New Kings: How Private Equity Is Changing the Business World," November 27: 9–10.

The Economist. 2004b. "America's Mutual-Fund Scandal," March 20: 83.

Ferguson, Niall. 2008. The Ascent of Money: A Financial History of the World. N.Y.: The Penguin Press.

Financial Analyst. 2003. "The Financial Analyst Prefers to Remain Anonymous."

Financial Times. 2004. "Private Equity," November 30: 1–2.

Fisher, Roger and Ury, William. 1991. Getting to Yes. New York: Penguin.

Forsyth, Randall W. 2009. A Tale of Two Credit Markets, Barron's, November 16: 11.

Forsyth, Randall W. 2010. The New Dismal. Barron's, January 25: 7–8.

Gapper, John. 2010. "Goldman's Restraint On Bonuses Is Too Little, Too Late," Financial Times, January 22: 3.

Harding, James. 2002. "Whistle While You Work (and Face the Consequences)," Financial Times, February 10:9.

Hartman, Edwin M. 1996. Organizational Ethics and the Good Life. New York: Oxford University Press.

Heller, F., Pusic, E. Strauss, G. and Wilpert, B. 1998. Organizational Participation: Myth and Reality. Oxford: Oxford University Press.

Hitt, Greg and Hamburger, Tom. 2002. "New Campaign Law Restores PAC's Appeal," Wall Street Journal, July 29: A4.

Kant, Immanuel. 1797, 1994. "The Metaphysical Principles of Virtue," in Ethical Philosophy. Indianapolis/Cambridge: Hackett Publishing: 52.

Kay, John, 2010. "Unfettered finance has been the cause of all our crises," Financial Times, January 6: 9.

Kelly, Kate and Craig, Susanne. 2004. "NYSE Traders Will Pay Fines of $240 million," Wall Street Journal: C1, C3.

Krasner, Jeffery. 2004. "Stents Sold Despite High Failure Rates," The Boston Globe, December 26: 1, A42.

Krugman, Paul. 2009. The Return of Depression Economics. New York: Norton.

Laufer, William S. 2008. Corporate Bodies and Guilty Minds: The Failure of Corporate Criminal Liability. Chicago: The University of Chicago Press.

Levitt, Arthur. 2002. Take on the Street: What Wall Street and Corporate America Don't Want You To Know. New York: Pantheon Books.

Li, Stan X. and Berta, Whitney Blair. 2002. "The Ties That Bind: Strategic Actions and Status Structure in the U.S. Investment Banking Industry." Organization Studies, 23, 3: 339–368.

McAdam, D. 1982. Political Process and the Development of Black Insurgency 1930–1970. Chicago: University of Chicago Press.

McGregor, D. 1960. The Human Side of Enterprise. New York: McGraw-Hill.

Morgenson, Gretchen. 2010. "Resetting the Moral Compass," New York Times, January 24: BU1–3.

Nielsen, Richard P. and Bartunek, Jean M. 1996. "Opening Narrow, Routinized Schemata to Ethical Stakeholder Consciousness and Action," Business and Society, 35, 4: 483–519.

Nielsen, Richard P. 1996. The Politics of Ethics: Methods for Acting, Learning and Sometimes Fighting, With Others in Addressing Ethics Problems in Organizational Life. New York: Oxford University Press, the Ruffin Series in Business Ethics.

Nielsen, Richard P. 2003. "Corruption Networks and Implications for Ethical Corruption Reform," Journal of Business Ethics, 42: 125–149.

Nielsen, Richard P. 2000. "Do Internal Due Process Systems Permit Adequate Political and Moral Space for Ethics Voice, Praxis, and Community?" Journal of Business Ethics, 24, 1: 1–27.

Nielsen, Richard P. 1998. "Can Ethical Character Be Stimulated and Enabled? An Action- Learning Approach to Teaching and Learning Organization Ethics," Business Ethics Quarterly, 8, 3, July: 581–604.

Nielsen, Richard P. 2008. The Private Equity-Leveraged Buyout Form of Finance Capitalism: Ethical and Social Issues and Potential Reforms. Business Ethics Quarterly, 18, 4: 379–404.

Nielsen, Richard P. 2009. Varieties of Win-Win Solutions To Problems With Ethical Dimensions. Journal of Business Ethics, 88: 333–349.

Nielsen, Richard P. 2010. "High Leverage Finance Capitalism, The Economic Crisis, Structurally Related Ethics Issues, and Potential Reforms," Business Ethics Quarterly, 20: 2.

Posner, R.A. 2009. A Failure of Capitalism. Cambridge: Harvard University Press.

Schumpeter, J. A. 1947. Capitalism, Socialism, and Democracy. New York: Harper and Brothers.

Sender, H. and Zuckerman, G. 2003. "Behind the Mutual Fund Probe: Three Informants Opened Up," Wall Street Journal, December 14: 1, 6.

Solomon, Deborah. 2004. "As Corporate Fines Grow, SEC Debates How Much Good They Do," Wall Street Journal, November 12: 1, A6.

Syre, Steven. 2002. "Beyond the Zeroes," Boston Globe, December 22: E2.

Treviño, Linda K. and Nelson, Katherine A. 2003. Managing Business Ethics. New York: John Wiley.

Useem, Michael. 1996. Investor Capitalism. New York: Basic Books.

Watkins, Sherron. 2003. "Former Enron Vice President Sherron Watkins on the Enron Collapse," Academy of Management Executive, 17, 4: 119–125.

Zuckerman, Gregory & Gauthier-Villars, David. 2009. "A Lonely Lament From A Whistle-Blower," Wall Street Journal, February 3: C3.

BUSINESS ETHICS: THE ROLE OF CULTURE AND VALUES FOR AN ETHICAL WORKPLACE*

Nancy Lockwood

Introduction

In the business world today, issues of trust, respect, fairness, equity and transparency are gaining more attention. Business ethics includes organizational values, guidelines and codes, legal compliance, risk management, and individual and group behavior within the workplace. Effective leadership, with open dialogue and thoughtful deliberation, develops the foundation of an ethical workplace, is woven into the fabric of the organizational culture and is mirrored in ethical decision-making. Toward this

*Reprinted with permission of the SHRM Research Quarterly, *The Society for Human Resource Management*, Alexandria, VA (2004): 1–8.

end, all organizational leaders have a key role in establishing corporate values and modeling ethical behavior for their workforce, organization and community.

The importance of ethical leadership has grown exponentially. A 2009 special report from the Business Roundtable Institute of Corporate Ethics and the Arthur W. Page Society focuses on the issue of leadership and trust. *The Dynamics of Public Trust in Business—Emerging Opportunities for Leaders* emphasizes that trust is a critical factor in business. The report points out that "even in the best of times, the dynamism of trust requires continual monitoring and rebalancing as economic and social situations change." Companies can create positive business ethics by generating goodwill, communicating openly and taking advantage of opportunities for leaders to create value based on a foundation of accountability, responsibility and integrity. Ultimately, trust— through good business ethics—"positively impacts business success in a number of critical areas, such as employee performance, customer retention and innovation."[1]

While not inclusive of all aspects of business ethics, this research article focuses on organizational culture and values as integral in the foundation of an ethical workplace. The primary audiences—human resource professionals, people managers and senior management—will find this article useful to thoughtfully consider the state of business ethics in their respective companies, identify related challenges and opportunities, and rethink how better to communicate, restructure and/or reframe policies and practices that influence the organization's ethical stance.

Business Imperative

Organizational culture and ethical leadership are at the core of business ethics. Each shapes and reinforces corporate values, and influences employee attitudes and behaviors. Broadly defined, business ethics includes ethical conduct, legal compliance and, in some cases, corporate social responsibility. Ethics-related outcomes can be seen in nearly every aspect of a company, from employee perceptions of fairness, to employee engagement and retention, and ultimately, as U.S. and global executives note, to reputation and sustainability (see SHRM's 2008 Executive Roundtable Symposium on Sustainability and Human Resource Management).[2]

The establishment of business ethics as policy is not new. A number of business codes were established and in use in the 1920s. In fact, the retailer J. C. Penny Company introduced a company code of conduct in 1913.[3] The focus on business ethics, particularly ethics policies and programs, rapidly grew in the United States in the 1980s and 1990s in response to government and legal pressures. The Defense Industry Initiative (DII), created in the 1980s in response to government regulations, was developed for defense contractors to comply with a high standard of conduct. DII was the first organized attempt at creating standard ethics and compliance programs. In 1999, a survey of a sample of *Fortune* 1000 companies by researchers Weaver, Treviño and Cochran found that only 20% had adopted ethics polices prior to 1976 and 60% since the mid-1980s.[4] A series of high-visibility corporate scandals (such as Enron, Arthur Anderson, WorldCom) resulted in the Sarbanes-Oxley Act (SOX) of 2002, the goal of which is to foster truthful communication between company officers and shareholders in publicly traded companies.

In today's global marketplace, HR, ethics and compliance officers, and organizational leadership must also be cognizant of cultural differences that influence business ethics. In different countries, there are cultural variations around business ethics, such as cultural norms, legislation, communication styles, etc. In Europe, for example, there is a history of socially mandated employee involvement in businesses, where the U.S. style of codes of conduct may not be applicable. Other cultural differences, such as indirect communication styles and the need to save face, require sensitivity for ethics-related communications. U.S. corporate ethics programs tend to reflect American cultural norms, such as individualism. In contrast, collectivist societies use different communication styles to address interpersonal and ethical problems. Whether in domestic or global companies, ultimately, the commitment to business ethics and the foundation is built through organizational culture, with ethical values reflected in the workplace.

Leadership and Organizational Culture

Corporate integrity is reflected in leadership. "Because sound ethical behavior continues to erode within society, it is vital that an organization's leaders model the ethical behavior they require from staff members," notes Norman Howard, Director of Human Resources, W. K. Kellogg Foundation. "Thus, the culture of an organization plays a critical and essential role in defining the importance of ethics both in how it respects employees and how it conducts business."

An ethical culture is developed through communication, rules, leadership, rewards, rituals and stories. The realm of business ethics and organizational culture includes the views of employees and management, individual and organizational values, and constant compliance and principle-driven ethics. Attitudes and behaviors are reinforced over time through codes of conduct, behavioral modeling by senior staff, ethical decision processes and ethics training. Three key questions to ask within an organization are: 1) how does the company culture portray organizational values; 2) do company policies reflect corporate values that form the platform for ethical leadership and corporate governance; and 3) are employees treated fairly and consistently?[5] Leadership determines how effectively this is accomplished. As pointed out in an article titled "The Ethical Commitment: Building Value-Based Cultures," employees want to trust management and know that their needs and well-being are considered. Managers demonstrate trustworthiness when they listen to employees, account for their actions and explain reasons for decisions.[6] Data from the 2009 National Business Ethics Survey, conducted by the Ethics Resource Center, reveal employees' views about whether leadership sets a good example of ethical behavior, with 80% approval for top management and 86% for direct supervisors.[7]

Finally, regular assessments of company ethics by HR and senior management are critical (see Figure 1). This may include policies and programs, the code of conduct, ethics communications, ethics training and employee, opinion surveys. Key questions to consider are: 1) is the company sending the message that it promotes ethical behavior; 2) is it concerned with the welfare of employees or is the goal to

- Do you give your employees an opportunity to express their views before decisions are made?
- Are all employees treated with respect and dignity?
- Does the company promote consistent application of the rules across situations?
- Does the company discourage the influence of personal biases on decisions?
- Are the needs of employees considered?
- Are decisions made based on accurate information?
- Is honest feedback provided about why decisions are made?
- Are the rights of employees respected?
- Are managers consistent in their views about appropriate ethical standards?
- Are opportunities provided to appeal decisions that employees disagree with?

FIGURE 1   Ten Questions to Assess Your Company and Its Procedures About Decision-Making

Source: Adapted from Tyler, T., Dienhard, J., & Thomas, T. (2008, Winter). The ethical commitment to compliance: Building value-based cultures. *California Management Review, 50*(1), 31–51.

protect the company; and 3) is the formal ethics program outsourced for cost savings (on the Internet), thoughtfully focused on the nuances of the organizational culture, and to what degree is senior management involved?[8]

Organizational Ethics Standards and Practices

In some organizations, HR may be responsible for ethics in terms of programs, discipline and communication. In a company without a formal ethics and compliance function, the chief HR professional often serves as the ethics officer, and the HR department promotes ethical conduct and training. The SHRM/ Ethics Resource Center 2008 survey report *The Ethics Landscape in American Business: Sustaining a Strong Ethical Work Environment* documents that the majority (83%) of HR professionals believe that the HR department is a primary resource for ethics-related issues. Many feel that they are not part of the ethics infrastructure, yet are often requested to assist or remedy situations caused by ethical violations. However, the key findings show that HR professionals, in general, are in agreement that nonmanagement employees, supervisors and top management: 1) support them in following their organization's ethics standards; 2) talk about the importance of workplace ethics and doing the right thing in their work; 3) set a good example of ethical behavior; and 4) are held accountable if they are found to be in violation of the organization's ethics standards.[9]

The platform for an ethical workplace is the code of conduct. It describes a value system and ethical principles and outlines specific ethical rules embodied by the organization. Written standards of ethical conduct cover a number of areas, such as compliance and laws, confidential or proprietary information, conflicts of interest, use of company assets, and acceptance of or providing gifts, gratuities and entertainment. The purpose of a code of conduct is to raise ethical expectations; focus on dialogue about ethical issues; encourage ethical decision-making; and prevent misconduct and establish a platform for enforcement.[10] Through the code of conduct, with clear language and specific illustrations of how ethical principles apply to the workplace setting, organizations put employees—including management—on notice that there are consequences of not complying and expectations for certain behavior.[11]

Two broad incentive categories encourage ethical behavior: reward and recognition systems, and performance evaluation systems. Companies may use public acknowledgment of individuals or teams who go "above and beyond the call of duty" as a vehicle to reinforce ethical behavior. For example, an annual ceremony to present the "President's Award for Integrity and Business Ethics" is one way to thank employees for their exemplary work and set examples for others. Performance reviews may include a section on corporate values, such as how the employee demonstrates respect, inspires others, engenders trust and confidence, keeps commitments, etc. Such recognition helps maintain focus on the company's philosophy about business ethics, the real impact on the workplace culture by the employees and the company's standing in the marketplace.

Ethics and Generational Differences

Understanding generational differences—and finding common ground—helps improve communication in the workplace (see Figure 2). The SHRM white paper *Ethics and Generational Differences: Interplay Between Values and Ethical Business Decisions* examined how different generations approach questions of integrity and purpose. The authors point out that "with value systems and motivation at the heart of ethics—and divergent value systems seemingly inherent within the four generational groups—the existence of varied ethical perspectives among co-workers is not a surprise."[12]

- Develop an internal campaign, with ethics as the #1 value for the organization and employees.
- Avoid stereotyping employees according to their generation.
- Clearly identify the priorities of the company and then link them to the priorities and values of employees to support business decisions.
- When possible, learn the values and motivation of employees and then connect them to individual and organizational goals.
- Focus on business results, not on methodology (as long as it is ethical). All groups want to contribute and achieve but may do so differently.
- To make ethical guidelines relevant to everyone, establish ongoing training and support sessions.
- Look for commonality among employees of different generations.
- Embrace diversity of opinion and methodology.
- Err on the side of more communication, such as using different types of media: face-to-face meetings, e-mail blasts, etc.
- Remember to respect the dimensions of differing generations (age, technological savvy, alternative work experiences, innovation, etc.)

FIGURE 2   Key Points for Ethical Business Management of Different Generations

Adapted from: Guss, E., & Miller, M. C. (2008 October). *Ethics and generational differences: Interplay between values and ethical business decisions* [white paper]. Retrieved from www.shrm.org.

A common area of tension among generations focuses on work ethic, and conflict often stems from how it is defined. Traditionalists and Baby Boomers may criticize the two younger generations about their lack of work ethic, since older generations often equate strong work ethic to being part of the organization (and being physically present in the office) for long periods of time. Baby Boomers consider a combination of factors—collaboration, teamwork and meetings—as evidence of work ethic. Generation X and Millennials see work ethic as working hard—often autonomously—with a positive impact on the company while also living a full life outside of their job. Yet, research shows that no matter one's age, people value achievement, balance and responsibility, and want credible, trustworthy leadership (see SHRM's *Research Quarterly* "The Multigenerational Workplace").[13]

The commitment of the Millennial generation (Gen Y) to volunteerism points to idealism and the confidence that one individual can positively affect society. Volunteerism is an opportunity for organizations to showcase ethical and moral behavior through community service (see *Volunteerism—Moving Up on the Strategic Agenda*).[14] A recent study from Deloitte found that nearly two-thirds of respondents aged 18 to 26 prefer to work at firms that offer opportunities to their employees to volunteer their professional skills at nonprofit organizations.[15] "It is the idealism that this generation of young employees brings to the workplace that can also portend the potential vulnerability of their moral compass," says human resource consultant Joy Gaetano, SPHR, president of Gaetano Group and a SHRM Ethics Special Expertise Panel member. "An organization that can establish clear ethical guidelines, set policy standards and provide a culture that nurtures ethical decision-making and values gains respect as an 'employer of choice' where a young employee can focus on optimizing his or her workplace talent rather than feel compromised by workplace conduct."

Ethical Decision-Making

Values drive decision-making. In the sometimes confusing maze of decisions, employees and managers may at times feel conflicted by their personal values and

- What is the biggest ethical dilemma you have experienced in your career?
- How did you respond?
- What was the outcome?
- What did you learn?
- How did you transfer this learning or experience into teachable moments for others?

FIGURE 3 Questions and Lessons for Ethical Decision-Making

Source: Tichy, N. M. (2003). Students meet ethical dilemma in their workplace challenges. In N. M. Tichy & A. R. McGill (Eds.), *The Ethical Challenge: How to Lead with Unyielding Integrity* (pp. 211–230). San Francisco: Jossey-Bass.

the corporate message. In today's busy workplace, managers have to make decisions quickly, are influenced by short-term pressures and therefore may fail to adequately focus on social norms and ethical principles. When confronted with ethical decisions, guidelines about ethical-decision making are valuable tools and can be presented in a corporate ethics program, during a staff meeting or as part of an employee-manager mentorship. These guidelines provide a framework for learning (e.g., where do workers learn what is acceptable in the workplace) as well as opportunities to reinforce corporate values. Such discussions are important in management training—for new managers, managers new to the company and longer-term managers alike—to highlight how value-based decision-making fits within the organization's mission and vision (see Figure 3).

The concept of moral motivation—*why should I do the right thing?*—is the focus of a recent article in the *Journal of Business Ethics.* The authors explored moral motivation through the lens of applicability to corporate ethics programs. The value of this study lies in offering a basis for discussion of how and why decisions are made (i.e., what is the ethical foundation/reasoning). The ethical theories of moral philosophers (Aristotle's ethics of virtue, Kant's categorical imperative and Mill's utilitarianism/greatest happiness principle) identify key ethical leadership skills that are important for today's workplace: 1) practical wisdom—personal integrity and good character, 2) moral reasoning—compliance with corporate ethics, and 3) moral feelings—cost/benefit analysis (for all stakeholders).[16]

Mini-Case Study

John's Decision

John Hart was a division manager at Atlantic Soda, a large bottling conglomerate with more than 30 companies. He was asked to meet with Bill Goodwin (his boss) and Bob Martin (regional division manager for a competitor, Mid-Major Pop). John had joined the firm six months earlier and was known for his track record of hard work and excellent sales results. In Atlantic's culture of rewarding performance and talent, John had already been promoted twice. At the meeting, Goodwin discussed the intense price competition between Atlantic Soda and Major Pop. He suggested that they establish a mutual set of prices. The two principals agreed. However, John would have the responsibility to implement this arrangement in his region.

This true story illustrates an opportunity for an ethical decision. Pressures were exerted by John's manager to sway the decision. John had options to consider: personal/company achievement or his personal and the company's integrity. He made the wrong choice and went to jail for his part in the price fixing, a violation of the Sherman Antitrust Act.[17]

Corporate Ethics Programs

Ethics training is a key part of business ethics. It assists employees and management in clarifying their own ethical paradigms and doing the right thing when confronted with ethical dilemmas. In conjunction with a code of ethics, ethics training serves as an organization's guiding framework. Training can be delivered in many ways, such as web-based training, webcasts and in-person training programs, thus accommodating schedules and different learning preferences and taking advantage of cost-savings opportunities. Legislation makes compliance critical (see *U.S. Sentencing Guidelines for Organizations,* adopted in 1991 and updated in 2004, www.ussc.gov/orgguide.htm). Publicly traded companies subject to the Sarbanes-Oxley Act of 2002 (SOX) must have a code of ethics designed to deter wrongdoing, including a statement promoting financial integrity that clearly applies to senior financial officers (see SHRM article about the Sarbanes-Oxley Act). Additional U.S. federal laws that cover unethical business practices include the Foreign Corrupt Practices Act of 1977 (FCPA), which prohibits corrupt payments to foreign officials for the purpose of obtaining or keeping business; mail and wire fraud statutes, 18 U.S.C. § 1341, 1343; The Travel Act, 18 U.S.C. § 1952, which provides for federal prosecution of violations of state commercial bribery statutes; and Federal Sentencing Guidelines, particularly §8.B2.1, regarding the components of an effective compliance and ethics program.

Based on the Federal Sentencing Guidelines, the Ethics Resource Center (ERC) outlines six elements necessary for a comprehensive ethics and compliance program: 1) written standards for ethical conduct; 2) training on ethics; 3) a mechanism to seek ethics-related advice or information; 4) a process to report misconduct anonymously; 5) disciplinary action of employees who violate the organization's ethics standards or the law; and 6) inclusion of ethical behavior within each employee's regular performance appraisal. The SHRM/ERC 2008 survey report on ethics found that most organizations do not have a comprehensive ethics and compliance program. Only 23% of HR professionals reported that their companies had all six elements, yet other factors were in place: 88% of HR professionals said that their organizations disciplined employees who violated the company standards, 75% had written standards for ethical conduct, 74% had a mechanism to report violations confidentially or anonymously, and 66% had orientation or training on ethics. In contrast, more than 50% of organizations did not have a specific mechanism for employees to seek advice on ethics-related matters, and 57% did not evaluate employees on ethical conduct in their performance reviews. The most common types of misconduct seen by HR professionals were abusive or intimidating behavior toward employees (excluding sexual harassment); e-mail and/or Internet abuse; inaccurate reporting of actual hours worked; employee behavior putting the employee's interests above those of the organization's; and employees taking sick days when they are not sick.[18]

The *2009 National Business Ethics Survey* from ERC found that during the recession, 81% of employees have confidence in their company's executives, only 23% believe that the recession has negatively affected the ethical culture within the company, and 10% believe that in order to stay in business during the recession, their company has lowered its ethical standards. Employees see their leadership—even during these difficult economic times—as trustworthy, with 81% of respondents trusting that company executives are telling the truth about the well-being of the organization. The study also found that with more focus on business ethics, misconduct decreases: specifically, misconduct declined after 2002, when SOX was passed, then increased over the next four years, and then declined again during the recession (see Figure 4).[19]

FIGURE 4   The Increase and Decrease of Misconduct Over Time

Source: Ethics Resource Center. (2009, October). 2009 *National Business Ethics Survey,* www.ethics.org

Ethics and Perceptions of Fairness

Perceptions of fairness are closely tied to business ethics, at the root of which are questions of justice. Also known as "organizational justice," it encompasses fairness of outcomes and allocation of resources, fairness of decision-making processes and fairness of interpersonal treatment from the supervisor. In today's litigious environment, organizations must be transparent, equitable, consistent and fair in their policy development and administration. The following example illustrates how policy applied inconsistently can negatively affect employee morale. Individual values and moral positions of an employee may end up in juxtaposition with the policies and behavior of the employer, through confusion, inconsistency, and poor management communication and practices, bringing forth questions of fairness.

Mini-Case Study

A Lack of Transparency

An employee had worked for nearly 30 years at a well-established, fiscally sound bank in the commercial market. Unexpectedly, she found herself needing to take time off for the care of her sick husband. Saturday morning, her husband was rushed to the hospital to undergo emergency surgery, and on Monday he was placed in intensive care. On that Monday, the employee made a request to her manager to use some of her 10 months of accrued sick leave to care for her husband. FMLA was approved, but she was told that according to the HR department, she must use vacation time rather than sick leave.

After being out for a couple of weeks, with more than two-thirds of her FMLA entitlement remaining, the employee returned to work. Her manager and a senior HR officer ushered her into a meeting to discuss the terms of her return to work. "We're concerned about your ability to come back. We can't have you taking long lunches or leaving early to visit your husband." The employee assured them that this had not been her plan but asked why it would be a problem if an occasional need were to arise. "If we let you do it, we'd have to let everyone do it." Although she had planned to retire in less than six months, at this point, the employee was very upset and her view of the company was negatively affected by this exchange and lack of support. She later learned that sick leave use for family members was discretionary at the determination of the manager. An HR officer also informally counseled her, saying "if your own doctor were to say you are too stressed to work, your sick hours would more than carry you through your planned retirement date, plus you'll get another annual profit-sharing check." This sentiment was echoed to her by several other bank officers.

The poorly communicated and inappropriately administered policies—such as the FMLA leave—coupled with lack of sensitivity by management and subsequently perceived unfairness—largely contributed to the distress of the employee. This example illustrates how lack of transparency of company policies can create confusion and lead to an unethical subculture. In this case, vague policies allowed line and human resource managers to permit or deny leave on a case-by-case basis. While denying sick leave may save the company money in the short term, the cost is also reflected in decreased employee morale, with the likely loss of valuable human capital.

Transparent procedures are important. They allow managers to emphasize the importance of decision-making for all employees to minimize the belief that some receive favorable treatment or differences based on other biases. When focus is placed on respecting employees and their rights, the quality of interpersonal relationships in the workplace improves. When people are treated with dignity and courtesy, commitment to the organization increases along with productivity.[20] Ultimately, the question that HR and organizational leaders should ask is, are our own policies inadvertently shaping our corporate cultures in ways that will undermine the reputation of the company and ultimately cost the company the loss of talent, production, customer service and profits?

Global Perspective

One popular topic for HR professionals in the last few years has been the need to develop a global mindset, but this need has been viewed mostly through the context of individual development. SHRM interviewed Lorelei Carobolante, SCRP, GMS, GPHR, SHRM Global Special Expertise Panel member and CEO/president of G2nd Systems, who has extensive expertise in the area of intercultural communications.

"We often fail to recognize that the establishment of such cultural norms within an organization has many more business ramifications than the often-cited cases of employees assigned to foreign locations and their struggle to become effective contributors," says Carobolante. "As our workforce, anywhere in the world, is becoming more culturally diverse, developing a global mindset is just as important at the local level as it is globally. It applies as equally to a manager in Singapore as to a manager in Toledo, Ohio. For example, we often associate *communication style* with culturally different norms and therefore typically consider it merely an issue of 'etiquette.' Sometimes, we also appreciate its effect on productivity, but we rarely recognize its ethical implications."

"When a manager provides employees with the same desk, the same computer, the same tools, but fails to provide instructions that are equally understood and interpreted by native and non-native English-speaking employees, not only does the manager foster a lack of productivity from employees who cannot understand the subtle implications derived from culturally based expressions, but the manager then does not actively support (and can potentially damage) an employee's ability to excel, be successful and develop his or her professional career," Carobolante continues.

"When a manager is able to communicate in a culturally neutral fashion, employees are not put at a disadvantage in their ability to succeed as a result of poor communication skills by the manager. Even if an employee is uncertain about the meaning of what he or she is told, the employee most likely will not ask for clarification—for fear of being perceived as less intelligent [or having an English proficiency or cultural-difference problem]."

This example clearly illustrates the relationship between business ethics and productivity, and the ethical responsibility for clear communication on the part of the manager, as Carobolante explains. A lack of understanding of these dynamics often leads to:

1. **Poor team performance**, as some employees can establish relationships, while others find it difficult.
2. **Inconsistent productivity** across the organization, as some employees are well attuned with the goals, while others, though equally talented, tend to isolate themselves.
3. **Employee dissatisfaction**, as isolation tends to facilitate a sense of inequality and unfair treatment and leads to decline in employee engagement—a direct connection to productivity.
4. Ultimately, **employee retention problems**, as talented individuals who do not feel appreciated and lose faith in their ability to grow within the organization will leave the company.

As Carobolante concludes, "What is most difficult to recognize is the ethical responsibility associated with today's new globally diverse workplace, which requires managers to communicate effectively across multiple cultures at the same time so that *all* employees will have equal levels of participation, thus being able to contribute their expertise, creativity and commitment to reach the organization's goals."

In Closing

The message sent by leadership through organization culture determines the tone of business ethics in the workplace—how it is defined, perceived, promoted, demonstrated and "lived." Based on a foundation of solid and clear corporate values for ethical behavior, the right decisions can be made, thus fostering trust, fairness, transparency and compliance. With organizations becoming more global and more virtual, leaders must understand people of different backgrounds, cultures, values and perspectives. Ultimately, the ethical workplace is the common link between culture, values and leadership and productivity, organizational reputation and sustainability.

Endnotes

1. Business Roundtable—Institute for Corporate Ethics. (2009). *The dynamics of public trust in business—Emerging opportunities for leaders.* Retrieved July 16, 2009, from www.corporate-ethics.org.
2. Society for Human Resource Management & the Ethics Resource Center (2008, June). *The ethics landscape in American business.* Alexandria, VA: Authors.
3. Weaver, G. R. (1993). Corporate codes of ethics: Purpose, process and content issues. *Business and Society, 32(1),* 44–58.
4. Weaver, G. R., Treviño, L. K., & Cochran, P. (1999). Corporate ethics programs as control systems: Influence of executive commitment and environmental factors. *Academy of Management Journal, 42(1);* 41–57.
5. Ibid.
6. Tyler, T., Dienhart, J., & Thomas, T. (2008, Winter). The ethical commitment to compliance: Building value-based cultures. *California Management Review, 50(2),* 31–51.
7. Ethics Resource Center. (2009, November). *2009 National Business Ethics Survey.* Retrieved from www. ethics.org.
8. Treviño, L. K., & Weaver, G. R. (2003). *Managing ethics in business organizations.* Stanford, CA: Stanford University Press.
9. Society for Human Resource Management & the Ethics Resource Center. (2008, June). *The ethics landscape in American business.* Alexandria, VA: Author.
10. Ethics Resource Center. (2006). *Critical elements of an organizational ethical culture.* Retrieved September 25, 2009, from www.ethics.org/resource/critical-elements-organizational-ethical-culture.

11. Berenbeim, R. E., & Dubinsky, J. E. (2008, January). Working at the intersection of human resources and business ethics: The need for collaboration. *Executive Action series [The Conference Board],* 2–9.

12. Guss, E., & Miller, M. C. (2008, October). *Ethics and generational differences: Interplay between values and ethical business decisions* [white paper]. Retrieved from www.shrm.org.

13. Deal, J. J. (2007). *Retiring the generation gap: How employees young and old can find common ground.* San Francisco: Jossey-Bass and the Center for Creative Leadership.

14. Society for Human Resource Management. (2008, July). *Volunteerism: Moving up on the strategic agenda.* Alexandria, VA: Author.

15. Deloitte. (2008). *2007 volunteer IMPACT survey.* Retrieved September 10, 2009, from www.deloitte.com.

16. De Colle, S., & Werhane, P. H. (2007, Spring). Moral motivation across ethical theories: What can we learn for designing corporate ethics programs? *Journal of Business Ethics, 81,* 751–764.

17. Urbany, J. E., Reynolds, T. J., & Phillips, J. M. (2008, Summer). How to make values count in everyday decisions. *MITSloan Management Review.* Retrieved July 16, 2009, from www.sloanreview.mit.edu.

18. Society for Human Resource Management & the Ethics Resource Center. (2008, June). *The ethics landscape in American business.* Alexandria, VA: Authors.

19. Ethics Resource Center. (2009, November). *2009 National Business Ethics Survey.* Retrieved from www.ethics.org.

20. Tyler, T., Dienhart, J., & Thomas, T. (2008, Winter). The ethical commitment to compliance: Building value-based cultures. *California Management Review, 50*(2), 31–51.

8

Personal Growth and Work Stress

ON THE REALIZATION OF HUMAN POTENTIAL: A PATH WITH A HEART
  Herbert A. Shepard

THE BALANCING ACT—AT WORK AND AT HOME
  Jonathan D. Quick
  Amy B. Henley
  James Campbell Quick

Given the job insecurity engendered by downsizing, restructuring, and mergers and acquisitions, employees are taking on more responsibility for managing their own careers in recent years. The financial crisis and increased unemployment rate have exacerbated the need for people to be proactive about their careers. The burden clearly lies on employees to continuously learn skills that are in demand to maintain their employability. Nevertheless, companies that want to develop and retain a workforce capable of implementing their strategic goals are well aware that training and career development are crucial issues. Both employees and employers, therefore, can profit from educating themselves on career issues and developing career management skills.

Career development begins with self-awareness, which facilitates the all-important fit between the job and the person. Herb Shepard, one of the earliest organizational behavior writers and organization development practitioners, wrote a classic essay entitled," On the Realization of Human Potential: A Path with a Heart." Shepard criticizes the societal institutions that prevent people from seeking their own road to fulfillment, a phenomenon that still occurs. We've included this article to encourage you to consider whether your own path is the right one for you.

Stress is a key consideration in many careers. "The Balancing Act—At Work and At Home" was written by Jonathan Quick, a physician and president and CEO of Management Systems for Health; Amy Henley, professor at Kennesaw State University; and James Campbell Quick, a prolific psychology professor at the University of Texas–Arlington. They take a compelling look at how work demands—including stress—can negatively impact employees' family life and nonwork activities. They argue that effectively balancing the mutual demands of both work and nonwork roles is an essential component of managing today's workforce. After examining the sources of work–family conflict, including work demands, home demands, and self-imposed demands, they conclude with a discussion of effective strategies for balancing work and nonwork roles that can be implemented by both employees and employers.

ON THE REALIZATION OF HUMAN POTENTIAL: A PATH WITH A HEART*

Herbert A. Shepard

A Vision Unfulfilled

The central issue is a life fully worth living. The test is how you feel each day as you anticipate that day's experience. The same test is the best predictor of health and longevity. It is simple.

If it's simple, why doesn't everyone know it? The answer to that question is simple, too. We have been brought up to live by rules that mostly have nothing to do with making our lives worth living; some of them in fact are guaranteed not to. Many of our institutions and traditions introduce cultural distortions into our vision, provide us with beliefs and definitions that don't work, distract us from the task of building lives that are fully worth living, and persuade us that other things are more important.

The human infant is a life-loving bundle of energy with a marvelous array of potentialities, and many vulnerabilities. It is readily molded. If it is given a supportive environment, it will flourish and continue to love its own life and the lives of others. It will grow to express its own gifts and uniqueness, and to find joy in the opportunity for doing so. It will extend these talents to the world and feel gratified from the genuine appreciation of others. In turn, it will appreciate the talents of others and encourage them, too, to realize their own potential and to express their separate uniqueness.

But if a child is starved of a supportive environment, it will spend the rest of its life trying to compensate for that starvation. It becomes hungry for what it has been denied, and compulsively seeks to satisfy perceived deficiencies. In turn, these perceived deficiencies become the basis for measuring and relating to others. As Maslow pointed out, such deficiency motivation does not end with childhood (Maslow, 1962; Maslow and Chang, 1969). Rather, the struggle makes a person continually dependent on and controllable by any source that promises to remove the deficiencies.

Deficiency Motivation in Operation

Frequently we refer to deficiency motivation in terms of needs: needs for approval, recognition, power, control, status; needs to prove one's masculinity, or smartness, or successfulness in other's eyes—and in one's own eyes, which have been programmed to see the world in terms of one's deficiencies. An emphasis on such needs can lead to a denial of individual uniqueness and may make us vulnerable to exploitation. In either case, the outcome for the individual can be devastating, and the rich promise of human potential remains unfulfilled.

---

*Reprinted with permission from M. B. Arthur, L. Bailyn, D. J. Levinson, and H. A. Shepard, *Working with Careers* (New York: Columbia University School of Business, 1984), pp. 25–46.

DENIAL OF UNIQUENESS The way this process takes place can be illustrated by a fable, "The School for Animals":

> *Once upon a time the animals got together and decided to found a school. There would be a core curriculum of six subjects: swimming, crawling, running, jumping, climbing and flying. At first the duck was the best swimmer, but it wore out the webs of its feet in running class, and then couldn't swim as well as before. And at first the dog was the best runner, but it crash landed twice in flying class and injured a leg. The rabbit started out as the best jumper, but it fell in climbing class and hurt its back. At the end of the school year, the class valedictorian was an eel, who could do a little bit of everything, but nothing very well.[1]*

The school for animals, of course, is much like our schools for people. And the notion of a common, unindividualized curriculum has permeated the whole fabric of our society, bringing with it associated judgments about our worth as human beings. It is all too easy for uniqueness to go unrecognized, and to spend a lifetime trying to become an eel.

EXPLOITATION OF UNIQUENESS A second, perhaps subtler way that deficiency motivation can operate is illustrated by the story of the cormorant. Dr. Ralph Siu, when asked what wisdom the ancient oriental philosophers could contribute to modern men in modern organizations on how to preserve their mental health, developed a list of "advices." One of them was as follows:

> *Observe the cormorant in the fishing fleet. You know how cormorants are used for fishing. The technique involves a man in a rowboat with about half a dozen or so cormorants, each with a ring around the neck. As the bird spots a fish, it will dive into the water and unerringly come up with it. Because of the ring, the larger fish are not swallowed but held in the throat. The fisherman picks up the bird and squeezes out the fish through the mouth. The bird then dives for another, and the cycle repeats itself.*
>
> *Observe the cormorant. . . . Why is it that of all the different vertebrates the cormorant has been chosen to slave away day and night for the fisherman? Were the bird not greedy for fish, or not efficient in catching it, or not readily trained, would society have created an industry to exploit the bird? Would the ingenious device of a ring around its neck, and the simple procedure of squeezing the bird's neck to force it to regurgitate the fish have been devised? Of course not. (Siu, 1971)*

The neo-Taoist alerts us to how the cormorant's uniqueness is exploited by the fisherman for his own selfish use. Similarly, human motives can get directed to making others prosper, but not always in a way that benefits the person providing the talent. Human life can too easily parallel that of the captive cormorant.

Institutions and Deficiency Motivation

Let us stay with Dr. Siu's cormorant story a little longer. His advice continues:

> Greed, talent, and capacity for learning, then, are the basis of exploitation. The more you are able to moderate and/or hide them from society, the greater will be your chances of escaping the fate of the cormorant. . . . It is necessary to remember that the institutions of society

are geared to making society prosper, not necessarily to minimize suffering on your part. It is for this reason, among others, that the schools tend to drum into your mind the high desirability of those characteristics that tend to make society prosper—namely, ambition, progress, and success. These in turn are valued in terms of society's objectives. All of them gradually but surely increase your greed and make a cormorant out of you. (Siu, 1971)

The further point here is even more far-reaching: that the institutions and organizations in which we spend our lives collude with one another in causing denials, deflections, or distortions of human potential. In particular, three sets of institutions—parents, schools, and organizations—demand consideration.

PARENTS First, parents, sincerely concerned for their children's ability to survive in the world, unwittingly ignore their individuality and measure their offspring's progress by a simple set of common standards. What parents are not delighted to be able to say that their children are ambitious, talented, and have a great capacity for learning? It is something to boast about, rather than something to hide. Outside confirmation of achievement earns love and recognition, its absence draws disapproval. Any evidence of "A" student behavior is immediately rewarded. Lesser performance calls for added effort so that deficiencies can be corrected. Much of this parental energy is targeted toward helping children qualify for an occupational future that will in no way reflect their true interests and abilities. The expression or suppression of talent is externally defined, and parents stand as the most immediate custodians of society's standards and its dogma.

SCHOOLS In our schools, the ideal is the "Straight A" student. It is this student who is most sought after, either at the next stage of institutional learning, or by employers from the world of work. What "Straight A" means is that the student has learned to do a number of things at a marketable level of performance, regardless of whether the student has any interest in or innate talent for the activity, and regardless of whether it brings pain, joy, or boredom. The reward is in the grade, not the activity. On the one hand, schools collaborate with parents to reinforce this concern over grades as ends in themselves. On the other, as Dr. Siu points out, the school's objectives are to serve the needs of society, not necessarily those of the student. Once more, a person's uniqueness is not valued for its own sake. Schools are selective about the talents they identify, and represent outside interests in the talents that they choose to develop.

ORGANIZATIONS Lastly, in organizations, the continued external denial or manipulation of talent has its direct career consequences. Organizations have implicit ways of teaching about careers, regardless of whether they have explicit career planning and development programs. Reward systems are geared to common deficiencies—needs for status, approval, power—and a career consists of doing the right things to move up the ladder. A vice president of one company counselled his subordinates: "The work day is for doing your job; your overtime is for your promotion."

In many companies the message about careers is very clear: not only is your career more important than the rest of your life, it is more important than your life. In one large corporation, great emphasis was placed on moving young professionals and managers through many company functions as their preparation for general management responsibility. The career plan was well understood: "When you're rotated, don't ask if it's up, down or sideways; the time to worry is when you stop rotating." In such companies, successful careers are based on working hard at any job you are given whether you like it or not, and on conforming to the organization's unwritten rules and to the expectations of your superiors in such matters as office manners, dress, presentation style, language, and prejudices.

Do these paths have "heart"? Do they provide for the expression of human potential and facilitate individual growth? For some, as much through good luck as good management, they do. But perhaps a greater number ultimately lose their way, and get labeled as suffering from "burnout" or "retiring on the job."

In one company that recruits only top graduates, devotes a great deal of managerial time to tracking their performance, and moves each one along at what is judged to be an appropriate pace into jobs that are judged to be suited to his or her talents and potentials, the amount of burnout observed in mid-career management ranks became a matter of concern. As a result, the company offered career planning workshops to mid-career managers, the main objective of which was, according to one executive: " . . . to revitalize them by reminding them that in an ultimate sense each of them is in business for themself!"

For deficiency-motivated people, moving up the hierarchy of management is likely to be such a compelling need that they may desert careers that did have some heart for them. In an informal survey of industrial research scientists conducted by the author some years ago, it was possible to identify the ones for whom their career path had a heart, by their response to the question: "What is your main goal over the next two or three years?" Some responded in such terms as, "Some equipment I've tried to get for three years has finally made it into this year's budget. With it, I can pursue some very promising leads." Others responded in such terms as, "I hope to become a department head." But the second group seemed to have lost its zest. Many of them enjoyed their work and had no real desire to leave it in order to direct the work of others. They were just singing the preferred organizational song.

Don Juan, in teaching Carlos Casteneda about careers, asserted that to have a path of knowledge, a path with a *heart*, made for a joyful journey and was the only conceivable way to live. But he emphasized the importance of thinking carefully about our paths before we set out on them. For by the time people discover that their path "has no heart," the path is ready to kill them. At that point, he cautions, very few people stop to deliberate, and leave that path (Castaneda, 1968).[2] For example, in a life/career planning workshop for the staff of a mid-west military research laboratory, a 29-year-old engineer confessed that he was bored to death with the laboratory work, but his eyes lit up at the prospect of teaching physical education and coaching athletic teams at the high school level. He emerged with a career plan to do just that, and to do it in his favorite part of the country, northern New England. He resolved to do it immediately upon retirement from his civil service job as an engineer, at age 65—a mere 36 years away!

Thus, all these institutions—parents, schools, and organizations—are suspect when they attempt to give career guidance. Suspect if, like the school for animals, they discourage uniqueness and enforce conformity. Suspect if, like the fisherman with his cormorant, they harness talent only to serve their vested interests. Suspect if they address only the development of a career, so that the rest of life becomes an unanticipated consequence of the career choice. Suspect if they stress only the how-to's of a career and not its meaning in your life. And suspect, too, if they describe a career as a way to make a living, and fail to point out that the wrong career choice may be fatal. In sum, suspect because they are not concerned with whether a life is fully worth living.

A Framework for Understanding Human Potential

An outcome of people's experience with society and its institutions is that many adults cannot remember, if they ever knew, what their unique talents and interests were. They cannot remember what areas of learning and doing were fulfilling for them, what paths had heart. These have to be discovered and rediscovered.

For many, the relationship between formal schooling and subsequent occupation needs to be re-examined. In adult life/career planning workshops, the author has found that of the things participants actually enjoy doing, less than 5 percent are things they learned in school as part of formal classroom work. A related outcome is that adults distinguish between work and play. Work is something you have to be "compensated" for, because it robs you of living. Play is something you usually have to pay for, because your play is often someone else's work. Children have to be taught these distinctions carefully, for they make no sense to anyone whose life is fully worth living. As one philosopher put it:

> *A master in the art of living draws no sharp distinction between his work and his play, his labor and his leisure, his mind and his body, his education and his recreation. He scarcely knows which is which. He simply pursues his vision of excellence through whatever he is doing and leaves others to determine whether he is working or playing. To himself he always seems to be doing both.*[3]

But pursuing a vision of excellence is not always simple. What does "vision of excellence" mean? How do you acquire your own? We can be reasonably sure that it has little to do with getting A's, excelling against others in competition, or living up to someone else's standards. It is one's own unique vision. It will not emerge in school, if each person must be comparable to every other person so that grades and rank can be assigned. Such a system defines individuality as differences in degree, not in kind. Consider, too, the word "genius." To most of us it means a person with a high IQ. But differences in IQ are differences of degree, whereas the notion of "unique" makes it impossible to rank and compare.

In the search for your own unique vision, you need a different definition of *genius*, one closer to the dictionary definition as "the unique and identifying spirit of a person or place." By this definition, your genius consists of those of your talents that you love to develop and use. These are the things that you can now or potentially could do with excellence, which are fulfilling in the doing of them; so fulfilling that if you also get paid to do them, it feels not like compensation, but like a gift.

Discovering Genius and Developing Autonomy

Discovering your genius may be easy or difficult. At some level of your being you already know it; you are fortunate if it is in your conscious awareness. If not, there are several routes to discovery, and many sources of pertinent information.

The first source is *play*. Make a list of the things you enjoy doing and find the common themes. Observe what you do when you are not obliged to do anything. What activities are you likely to engage in? What catches your eye when you thumb through a magazine? When you are in an unfamiliar environment, what interests you, what catches your attention? What are the contents of your fantasies and daydreams? What do you wish you were doing? Your sleep-dreams are also important. Record them, for some of them contain important wishes that you may want to turn into plans.

The second source is your own *life history*. Record in some detail the times in your past when you were doing something very well and enjoying it very much. What themes or patterns of strength, skill, and activity pervade most of those times? What were the sources of satisfaction in them?

The third source is *feedback* from others. What do those who know you have to say about your strengths and talents? As they see it, what seems to excite you, give you pleasure, engage you? And if you can find people who knew you when you were a child, can they recall what used to capture your attention and curiosity, what activities you enjoyed, what special promise and talents you displayed?

The fourth source is *psychological instruments*, which provide a variety of ways of helping you to organize and interpret your experience. There are many such instruments that can provide you with clues to your interests, strengths, and sources of satisfaction. Perhaps the most valuable is the Myers-Briggs Type Indicator, which is based on the insights of the psychologist Carl Jung. A recent book, based on these ideas, identifies four basic temperaments, four quite different ways of approaching life (Keirsey and Bats, 1978). One of these is oriented to tradition and stability in the world, and devoted to making systems work and to the maintenance of order. The second type loves action, freedom, excitement, and the mastery of skills. The third type is oriented to the future and to mastery of the unknown. The fourth loves to work in the service of humanity and bring about a better world. One can learn to perform competently in activities that do not fit one's temperament, and to some extent one must, but it always feels like "work." In contrast, if the activities are in accord with one's temperament, it feels more like "play." It follows that your temperament is one of the important components of your genius.

As you take these four routes, you may find the same messages about yourself over and over again—and you may also find a few surprises and contradictions. In general, the truth strategy you employ is the one enunciated in *Alice in Wonderland*: "What I tell you three times is true." You may emerge from the search with some hunches to explore further; you may emerge with certainty about a new direction to take; or you may simply affirm what you already knew—confirming or disconfirming the life and career choices you have already made. This discovery or affirmation of your genius is a first step, but it needs also to be nourished and developed, and you need to learn how to create the conditions that will support you in practicing it. The second step then, is to acquire the resources you need in order to build a world for yourself that supports you in the pursuit and practice of your genius. The process of acquiring these resources can be called the *development of autonomy*—learning the skills needed to build that world.

Consider the Following Case:

Jerome Kirk, a well-known sculptor, discovered his genius through play, though not until his late twenties. Alone on an island off the Maine coast for a week, he amused himself by fashioning sculptures out of driftwood. It was a dazzling experience. But his education had prepared him for work in the field of personnel administration. For the following 20 years he developed his skill as a sculptor, "while earning a living" as a personnel administrator—and he was quite successful in this profession. After 20 years, his sculptures matched his own vision of excellence, he was a recognized artist, and the income from his art was sufficient to enable him to devote all his time to it. It was the realization of a dream. His comment: "I was good in the personnel field, but I never really enjoyed it. It wasn't me. And now I'm utterly convinced that if a person really loves something, and focuses his energy there, there's just no way he can fail to fulfill his 'vision of excellence.' "[4]

The point of this story is not to idealize the creative arts. For others, discovery of genius would take them in a different direction, perhaps toward greater interaction with people rather than away from it. But the story does illustrate the qualities that get released when a person discovers his or her genius. Passion, energy, and focus all came as a natural by-product of Kirk's discovery. These were the qualities needed to develop the autonomy that ultimately allowed Kirk to realize his dream. They were inspired by the knowledge of his genius that he carried within him. The same qualities will be evident in any person who has discovered his or her genius, whether it is in sculpture or in the leadership of organizations (Vaill, 1982).

Living Out Your Potential

You began your life as a bundle of life-loving energy with a marvelous array of potentialities. As you grew up you learned to do many things and not to do other things. Some of these things were good for you, some bad for you, some good for others, some bad for others. Out of the things you learned, you fashioned an identity, a self-image. Thus, your self-image is a cultural product, and the distortion it contains may prevent you from recognizing yourself anymore as a bundle of life-loving energy with a marvelous array of potentialities. Acquiring a renewed identity, an identification with what is truly wonderful about yourself and therefore worth nourishing and loving, is not an easy task. It requires a lot of unlearning and letting go, as well as new learning and risk-taking.

How can you tell when you have achieved this goal? What can you feel from communion with others that confirms your own life as fully worth living? What should living out your potential mean in relationship to the outer world? Three qualities are critical indications that you have achieved a life fully worth living. They can be called tone, resonance, and perspective. Tone refers to feeling good about yourself, resonance to feeling good about your relationships, and perspective to feeling good about the choices in your life. To experience these qualities consistently is to know that you are living life well. Once again, though, our society interferes with and disguises the messages that we receive. Therefore, it is necessary not only to grasp the essence of these qualities, but also to recognize and to separate oneself from the distortions of them that our culture imposes.

TONE Tone refers to your aliveness as an organism. When you think of good muscle tone, you think of a relaxed alertness, a readiness to respond. As used here, the term tone refers to your entire being, your mental and emotional life as well as your muscle and organ life. Hence anxiety is as much the enemy of tone as drugs or being overweight. Lowen expressed this idea as follows:

> *A person experiences the reality of the world only through his body. . . . If the body is relatively unalive, a person's impressions and responses are diminished. The more alive the body is, the more vividly does he perceive reality and the more actively does he respond to it. We have all experienced the fact that when we feel particularly good and alive, we perceive the world more sharply. . . . The aliveness of the body denotes its capacity for feeling. In the absence of feeling, the body goes "dead" insofar as its ability to be impressed by or respond to situations is concerned. . . . It is the body that melts with love, freezes with fear, trembles in anger, and reaches for warmth and contact. Apart from the body these words are poetic images. Experienced in the body, they have a reality that gives meaning to existence (Lowen, 1967).*

But the self-images we forge on our journey through society's institutions often deprive us of our ability to maintain tone. We are no longer in touch with our bodies or with our genuine feelings, and our self-images have been distorted.

One of the most common distortions is to comprise your self-image out of some role or roles you play in society. Great actors and actresses use their capacity for total identification with another human being as a basis for a great performance, but their self-image is not that of a person portrayed. That costume is removed at the end of each performance. Cornelia Otis Skinner declared that the first law of the theater is to love your audience. She meant, of course, that the actor or actress, rather than the character portrayed, must love the audience. You cannot love the audience unless you love yourself, and yourself is not a role. Thus, it is vitally important to recognize your roles as costumes you wear for particular purposes, and not to let them get stuck to you. Your prospects at retirement from your profession or organization will otherwise be for a very short life.

A second common distortion is to make your head (your brain) your self-image, and the rest of you part of your environment. Cutting your body into two segments places enormous stress on it, and your tone will suffer severely. "You don't exist within your body. Your body is a person" (Lowen, 1967). A third distortion is to make your gender your self-image. The sexual-reproductive aspects of people are among their most wonderful potentialities, but to identify with your gender leads you to spend the first years of your life learning some bad habits that you spend the rest of your life trying to liberate yourself from.

Other common distortions include being the public relations representative of your family (often forced on boys and girls), being an underdog, a clown, or a representative of superior values. All such distortions will exact their price by robbing you of tone: by causing you to eat too much or drink too much or worry too much or keep your body in continuous stress, and miss the joy of being alive.

RESONANCE The second quality for living out your genius is your capacity for resonance. This involves an enhanced, stimulated, and yet relaxed vitality that you can experience in interaction with particular others and particular environments. Discovering those others and those environments that are able to provide resonance can be one of the most fulfilling aspects of the journey through a life fully worth living. The word *resonance* is chosen rather than the word *love*, with which it has much in common, because the very meaning of love has become distorted in our society. It has become a commodity in short supply, a marketable item, a weapon used to control others; it is difficult to distinguish love from exploitation or imprisonment.

The term *resonance* is chosen for other reasons as well. It conveys the notion of being "in tune" with other people and environments; it suggests the synergy and expansion of tone when your energy has joined with the energy of others. It also implies harmony. Harmony is a beautiful arrangement of different sounds, in contrast to mere noise, which is an ugly arrangement. Resonance, as used here, implies people's capacity to use their differences in ways that are beautiful rather than ugly.

The world you build that supports you in the pursuit of your genius is not worth living in if it lacks resonance. But once again, your capacity to build and maintain resonant relationships, and to transform dead or noisy relationships into resonant ones, may have been damaged. To regain that capacity first requires that you become aware of the cultural forces that have damaged it, and robbed you of the potential resonance in your life.

Perhaps the greatest distortion to resonance that we face comes from our intensely adversarial society. Almost everything is perceived in competitive, win-lose, success-failure terms. "Winning isn't everything. It's the *only* thing!" We have been encouraged to believe that the world is our enemy. One must be either on the defensive or offensive, or both at once. One must conquer, control, exploit, or be conquered, controlled, exploited. One must fight or run away. As a result one experiences others and is experienced by them either as hostile, aggressive, aloof, or as frightened, shy, withdrawn. Under these circumstances, resonance is hard to come by and short-lived. For many people, win-lose competitiveness does not dominate all aspects of their lives, but is induced by particular kinds of situations—and destroys the potential resonance and synergy of those situations.

For example, many seminars and staff meetings bring in thoughts of winning or losing, succeeding or failing, proving oneself or making points. These displace the potential resonance and synergy that can evolve when a group works creatively together, building on one another's thoughts, stimulating each other's ideas, and mixing work and laughter.

Three further cultural themes that can cripple the capacity for resonance are materialism, sexism, and violence. Materialism is defined as the tendency to measure one's self-worth by the number and kinds of possessions one has, and the tendency to turn experiences into things so that they can be possessions. Collectibles are a way of "life." Sexism is defined as the tendency to turn sexual relationships and partners into materials, and to use sexual labels to sum oneself and others up—gay, macho, or liberated. Morality and fidelity have lost all but their sexual meanings. Lastly, "Violence is as American as apple pie."[5,6] We have more guns than people. Our folk heroes were violent men.

Various combinations of adversarial, materialistic, sexist, and violent themes are commonly destructive of resonance in intimate relationships, such as marriage. Jealousy, possessiveness, and feelings of being exploited can dominate the relationship and the partners become each other's prisoners and jailers. But if they are able to free themselves of these distortions, the relationship can be transformed and resonance restored. If you think of any intimate relationships as consisting of three creatures: yourself, the other person, and the couple, you can see that the phrase "a life fully worth living" applies to each. It follows that you would reserve for the couple only those things that are growthful and fulfilling for it. In pursuing the other aspects of your life, your partner can be a resource to you, and you a resource to your partner. Rather than being each other's jailers, you become the supporters of each other's freedom—and this will enhance your resonance. An application of this principle is not difficult for most parents to grasp: your delight in seeing your child leading a fulfilling life as a result of the support you provided. Cultural distortions make it more difficult to understand that the principle applies equally to intimate relationships among adults.

PERSPECTIVE The third important quality of a worthwhile life is the perspective necessary to guide choices and to inform experience. If you have only one way of looking at the situation you are in, you have no freedom of choice about what to do. And if you have only one framework for understanding your experience, all of your experiences will reinforce that framework. If your outlook is adversarial, you will interpret whatever happens as evidence that the world is hostile, and your choices will be limited to fighting or running away. If you fight, it will confirm your belief that the world is hostile. If you run away, you will know that you were wise to do so. If your perspective is differentiated—if you can see, for example, the potential of a new relationship to be either collaborative or adversarial—you enlarge your range of choices. Thus, if you are aware of "the multiple potential of the moment," you will usually be able to make a choice that will make the next moment better for you and for the others in the situation.

The cultural distortions that lock you into a limited undifferentiated perspective, which lead you to make self-destructive choices, are the same ones that interfere with your tone and self-image, or your capacity for resonance. The messages of adversarialism, materialism, and sexism seek to dictate to you how you should see the world. And your life roles, as defined by other people, are an all too convenient set of prescriptions for your behavior. Take heed of your own feelings, ask what may be causing them, and whether cultural forces are at work. That such distortions are blocking your access to a useful perspective is evidenced whenever you find yourself humorless. The essence of humor is a sudden shift in point of view. To be without humor is to be dying, and laughter is one of the most valuable sources of health and well-being on the journey called a life fully worth living (Cousins, 1979).

Thus tone, resonance, and perspective are the signs that you have discovered your genius and have developed the autonomy to live by it, rather than by society's dictates.

Prospects for Change

The foregoing pages have offered a framework for understanding human potential, parts of which may be familiar, parts of which may be new. In some ways the categories of genius, autonomy, tone, resonance, and perspective are arbitrary, and they should only be used when they fit your purposes. And, clearly, these aspects of life are not separable. The expression of genius needs autonomy. Poor tone, low resonance, and limited perspective almost always have a confirming effect upon one another, and serve to limit autonomy. The essential point is to work in a direction that will begin to free human potential, and to rid it of its cultural fetters.

A Role for Institutions

The view presented here is critical of the way society's institutions impose cultural distortions on people, and prevent them from finding a path with a heart. Does this mean that, for the well-being of all of us, our institutions should refrain from showing any interest in careers? Does it mean that there can be no institution with a vested interest in people having a life that is fully worth living?

I believe the answer to both questions is no. Two concurrent forces are operating to change the culture quite rapidly. One of these is the dawning realization in many American organizations that the theories of management and organization on which our society has operated in the past have failed us, and will not serve us in the future. They have failed because they have regarded human beings as part of a social machine and have treated as irrelevant individual spirit and well-being. Nor have these theories capitalized on individuals' needs and capacities to work harmoniously with each other. This realization of past failure is bringing about a transformation in industrial organizations, and non-industrial organizations will eventually catch up. The second force for change is technological progress, especially the rapid development of electronic communications and computers. The more that routine operations are performed by machines, the more demand there is that the non-routine operations be performed with excellence. This kind of excellence in human performance can only be attained by persons who are fully alive and operating in the area of their genius. Only if the path has a heart will it sustain excellence.

When the aerospace industry was in its infancy, the technical challenge, and hence the need for creativity and teamwork, was immense. One of the most successful companies recognized this fully in its organizational structure and culture.

It invented new organizational forms that were suited to its mission and the capacities of its members to work together creatively. In the process, it created most of the principles and processes that are in use today in what has come to be called organization development. Among other things, it offered its members Life and Career Planning workshops, to help them identify their talents and interests. The approach was somewhat different from the one outlined in this paper, but its intent was the same. The spirit of these workshops was summed up in the way the company introduced them: "What you do with your life and career is your responsibility. But because you are a member of this company, the company shares some of that responsibility with you. Perhaps it's 80 percent yours, 20 percent the company's. This workshop is the company's effort to contribute towards its 20 percent." In a similar spirit, another company offers workshops based on their version of Dalton and Thompson's career-stages model, to help employees identify their position on the path, understand their potential more clearly, and find ways of fulfilling it (Dalton, Thompson, and Price, 1977).

These companies have a vested interest in having their members rediscover their genius. Our hope for changing the order of things is that more and more organizations will follow their example. But we must insist that their interventions be explicitly on their members' behalf. And their processes must seek to liberate people from their cultural surroundings—including organizational cultures—rather than to reaffirm their dependencies. Then their example can be picked up by the schools, who can help others much earlier in their lives. Parents, in turn, will come to appreciate the freedom of spirit that they can encourage in their own children. The path with a heart is also the path to improving our institutions. Let our teaching about careers stand for nothing less.

Notes

1. The version here is that told by Leo Buscaglia (1982). However, an earlier version has been attributed to Casberg (1961), although no published source could be found.
2. Whether these sentiments really reflect Don Juan's thoughts, or only Castaneda's (see Harris, 1979: 322–323), is irrelevant to the present discussion, which emphasizes the content of what is being expressed.
3. Author unknown.
4. Personal communication.
5. Attributed to Vince Lombardi.
6. Attributed to H. Rap Brown.

References

Buscaglia, L., *Love* (New York: Random House, 1982).

Castaneda, C., *The Teaching of Don Juan, A Yaqui Way of Knowledge* (Berkeley: University of California Press, 1968).

Cousins, N., *The Anatomy of an Illness* (New York: Norton, 1979).

Dalton, G. W., Thompson, P. H., and Price, R. L., "The Four Stages of Professional Careers: A New Look at Performance by Professionals," *Organizational Dynamics,* Summer 1977: 19–42.

Harris, M. *Cultural Materialism: The Struggle for a Science of Culture* (New York: Random House, 1979).

Keirsey, D., and Bates, M., *Please Understand Me* (Del Mar, CA: Nemesis Books, 1978).

Lowen, A., *The Betrayal of the Body* (New York: Macmillan, 1967).

Maslow, A. H., *Toward a Psychology of Being* (New York: Van Nostrand, 1962).

Maslow, A. H., and Chang, H., *The Healthy Personality* (New York: Van Nostrand, 1969).

Siu, R., "Work and Serenity," *Journal of Occupational Mental Health,* 1971: 1,5.

Vaill, P. "The Purposing of High Performance Systems," *Organizational Dynamics,* Fall 1982 23–29.

THE BALANCING ACT—AT WORK AND AT HOME*

Jonathan D. Quick

Amy B. Henley

James Campbell Quick

Thomas and Caroline have been married for 30 years. Both are very successful in their careers: she has steadily climbed her way up to a division manager for a Fortune 500 organization, while he has built a strong private medical practice in their community. Along the way, there have been tradeoffs. Work interfered with their personal lives and family goals at times. There have been disagreements about how much work should be brought home, and feelings of neglect when one partner was preoccupied with thoughts of work instead of focusing on the family. He feels that she brings too much work home with her, and she feels that he spends too much time at the office. They both believe that they have too many social obligations and not enough free time. This couple does not agree about a significant decision that was made early in their marriage—whether or not to have children. Caroline says that the decision not to have children was a choice they consciously made to focus on their respective careers and future success. However, Thomas disagrees and states that this path in their lives was not a chosen one. What would cause two individuals, in what appears to be a successful marriage, to have such differing viewpoints regarding a critical decision made in their marital lives?

This vignette illustrates the complexity of the interactions, intersections, and overlaps between the domains of work life and home life with the private domain of the self. We capture these three separate domains, their intersections, and their overlaps in Figure 1. An overlap does not necessarily lead to conflict. Alternatively, it may lead to balance and dynamic interaction. If, for example, work and home life are mutually reinforcing, then there is balance, not conflict. However, if they are not mutually reinforcing, then there is potential conflict. Or, if they are in dysfunctional competition for an individual's time or other resources, then there is active conflict. We plan to explore these issues of conflict and balance throughout the article.

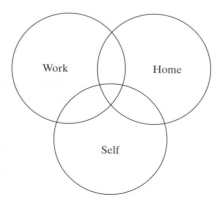

FIGURE 1 The Balancing Act—Work, Home, Self

What's at Stake?

Why should the happy, healthy, productive worker make it a priority to effectively balance the demands from his or her family and work? Quite simply, because so much is at stake when we fail to manage these often-competing demands. Conflict between a person's work responsibilities and family obligations can significantly impact all aspects of the individual's life. There are key consequences that accompany the failure to effectively balance the two domains for the employees themselves, their families and organizations. As a result, not only does the individual suffer from pressures associated with work–family conflict, but the impact extends to spouses, children, bosses, subordinates, etc.

Consider the following example: Robert works an average of 60 hours a week as a sales manager in a rapidly expanding technology firm. He's been married for 11 years and has one daughter, age 8, and a son, age 5. Robert sees that his high performance now at work could pay off in quick advancement up the corporate ladder. As a result, he puts the majority of his energy into his work life and often pushes family requests and obligations to the background. While his wife is understanding at first, over time she begins to put pressure on Robert to spend more time with her and the kids. As a result, Robert becomes tense and feels guilty when he stays late at work to meet with a client or finish a report. His work performance begins to slide, only putting more pressure on Robert. Eventually, Robert becomes so tense and frustrated that his ability to function effectively in either the family or work domain is hindered. His work suffers, and both his organization and his family are affected by the work–family spillover that occurs. Robert becomes trapped in seemingly endless cycle impacting all aspects of his life.

It is obvious that work–family conflict, or the failure to effectively balance work and family demands, has unique consequences for the individual employee or executive involved, his or her family, and the organization. These outcomes affect the employee in all aspects of life and are not isolated to the work domain. As the amount of work–family conflict that an individual is experiencing increases, his or her job satisfaction and life satisfaction fall. These individuals report lower levels of general happiness and subjective well-being than workers who do not experience work–family conflict. Research has also shown that their psychological distress levels increase, and negative health consequences often result. Failure to balance the demands between work and family has been linked with higher levels of depression and increased alcohol use. In regards to their work domain itself, workers tend to become less committed to an organization when they are experiencing work–family conflict. Individuals may see the organization as the cause of distress in their lives, thereby resulting in decreased levels of attachment to that organization. It should be no surprise that workers who are experiencing work–family conflict also report higher intentions to leave their current organizations as well as increased reports of actual turnover.

Effects on the Family and Organization

The effects of work–family conflict are not isolated to merely the individual employee, but extend to the family as well. Family performance often suffers as a result of the competing demands of work and family domains. In turn, work–family conflict has been associated with lower levels of marital satisfaction for both spouses and increased instances of divorce and family strife. The increasing number of dual-career couples also creates a unique dynamic in the balance of work and family, because research has shown that the amount of work–family conflict experienced by one partner directly affects the amount of work–family conflict experienced by the other partner. This spillover of conflict from one spouse to another makes balancing the competing demands of work and family all the more complex, in that now the focus is on managing the demands of two individuals, their respective careers, and their mutual family environment. Reported parental problems have been associated with higher levels of work–family conflict, as have instances of juvenile delinquency and violence. Increased stress levels and tension within the home that often accompany work–family conflict affect the day-to-day functionality of the family unit. This can be observed in seemingly minor details, such as the dad who rarely sees his kids in the morning before they go to school or the mom who consistently breaks her promises to attend key school events, which over time can create feelings of resentment and hurt in the family and affect the overall vitality of the family domain.

Organizations are also victims of the employee's inability to balance work and home demands. Work–family conflict directly affects the job satisfaction, career satisfaction, and performance of the worker, thereby indirectly influencing overall organizational performance. Absenteeism is often higher for individuals experiencing work–family conflict, resulting in increased labor costs for the organization. Because intentions to leave and actual turnover are greater for sufferers of work–family conflict, the organization must incur the costs of replacing these employees in the form of recruitment, selection, and training. Health-care costs for the organization can also rise as workers suffer from the negative health ramifications that often result from the distress associated with work–family conflict.

What Forms Does it Take?

Based upon the extensive ramifications associated with work–family conflict, it is obvious that the failure to balance work and family obligations should be of significant concern for both executives and their organizations. But how does work–family conflict occur? What forms does it take? Jeffrey Greenhaus and Nicholas Beutell have identified three distinct types of work–family conflict that can occur when work stressors, such as role overload, extensive pressure, lack of autonomy, and role ambiguity, limit the ability for workers to effectively manage their work and family lives. While they differ in terms of their nature, all three can result in the negative outcomes discussed above.

Time-based conflict occurs when the time devoted to work makes it difficult to fulfill the obligations and requirements of the family role and can impact the worker in either of two ways. One form of this conflict addresses the simple zero-sum nature of time management. In other words, any time spent by the worker in one domain makes it physically impossible for that worker to spend that same time in the other domain. To understand the effect of this type of work–family conflict, consider the executive who consistently stays late at the office and misses the family evening meal. Over time, this individual is left out of the communication within the family that takes place during this daily activity. As a result, he or she can become increasingly isolated from the family. Time-based conflict can also occur when the employee is physically present in the family domain, but mentally preoccupied with work concerns. So while this individual is trying to meet their family obligations in body, his or her mind is still at work. For example, the parent who attends a child's sporting event or birthday party but spends the majority of the time on a cell phone dealing with problems at the office is not truly committing his or her full self to this time in the family domain.

Strain-based conflict occurs when the pressures of the work role spill over and affect interactions within the family domain. Greenhaus and Beutell define this type of work–family conflict as "strain from participation in one role makes it difficult to fulfill requirements of another." In other words, the employee who has a particularly stressful day at work comes home in a bad mood and takes it out on his family. He may snap at his spouse for no particular reason or be so tired from the workday's events that he doesn't feel like playing baseball when his child asks. While these individuals are not directly preoccupied with office tasks as in time-based conflict, the negative effects of work stressors are manifested within the home environment as workers displace their negative emotions that stem from work experiences and express them within the family.

Behavior-based conflict is the third and final type of work–family conflict. This type of conflict occurs when behaviors that are acceptable, and even rewarded, in the work domain are incompatible with the behaviors that are desired in the home domain. Problems occur then when the employee fails to recognize the need to adjust her behaviors between the two domains. For example, an authoritative boss who must give clear direction to her employees at work in order to get the job done may find that her attempts to behave in the same manner at home with her children are not equally successful and can even result in hurt feelings and resentment. Likewise, the key executive who spends the majority of his day solving problems may encounter resistance when he comes home to a wife who wants him to simply listen attentively to her problems without necessarily instructing her on how to solve them. The key component in this type of work–family conflict involves the need to adjust the behavior between the work and family domains.

Sources of Work–Family Conflict

Work–family conflict is a reality for those who live in families, and even for those executives who do not live in families—yet must catch the crossover effects of colleagues' or employees' conflicts as they spill into the workplace. One of the keys to conflict management is an understanding of the sources of work–family conflict. The core of the conflict comes from three separate, competing, and overlapping sets of demands which, respectively, originate in the home, the workplace, and within one's self. We address the demands of each of these sources of demands separately.

Much that has been written about work–family conflict focuses on conflicting time demands. We offer a different perspective. Rather than framing the conflict in terms of time, we suggest framing it in terms of energy, attention, and engagement. This perspective becomes important in both understanding the conflict and in managing the conflict. For example, if time is seen as the central issue, this then converts the conflict into a form of mathematical problem. If energy is seen as the central issue, then it becomes more of a human issue than a math problem, and each family, as we saw in the opening vignette, can work out their own balancing act for work–family.

Home Demands

Every home needs a wonderful wife, and it does not have to be the woman. As more and more women continue both a professional and a family life, home demands have changed. Now more pressure accrues to the male working spouse or a surrogate chosen by the husband and wife jointly, in the case of traditional family homes. Home demands fall into two broad categories, one physical or material and the other interpersonal. The physical or material demands concern framing and maintaining the home, which are especially substantive in large, elaborate homes. For families with financial resources to hire staff and delegate a range of tasks such as cooking, cleaning, and laundry, this frees both husband and wife to devote more energy to interpersonal aspects of home life. For families without such resources, the challenges are more complicated.

Children within the family add another dimension to the home demands. Because the American culture often assigns primary home responsibility to women, the stereotypic response to their struggle with work–family balance is unfairly written off as of their own making. Prior to becoming chairman and chief executive officer (CEO) of Hewlett-Packard Co., Lew Platt had a direct experience with the conflict in his own life after his first wife Susan died in 1981 and left him to raise two daughters. At the time of his wife's death, Mr. Platt was a general manager at HP with significant professional responsibilities, and no longer a spousal partner who took the primary lead at home and within the family. He quickly grasped the dilemma that many of HP's women managers were faced with on an ongoing basis.

What made Mr. Platt's loss particularly poignant was the critical ages of his daughters: nine and eleven. There are several critical ages in the development of children, and the developmental opportunity comes only once chronologically. Author and Focus on Family founder James Dobson made a conscious decision during the early years of his children's lives to devote more energy to his family and less energy to his career development. While Dr. Dobson's personal and family choice was his, and others may choose differently, it is important to be fully aware of the key developmental and personal issues at stake for one's spouse, children, and other family members as decisions are made. For example, the critically and terminally ill child in a family may call forth the need for extended family or faith community family members to supplement the energy and concern of the parents in the family.

Work Demands

We have described in detail elsewhere (see Annotated Bibliography) the wide array of task, role, physical, and interpersonal demands for people at work. These demands create either stress or challenge for the individual depending upon individual idiosyncrasy and vulnerability. The sources of work stress are independent of a person's home life and other considerations. However, from the standpoint of work–family conflict, the work demands that may be most problematic are role ambiguity and overload, career stage, and family stage. The work role may contribute to work–family conflict when the role expectations are unclear or the volume of work is greater than the time and energy available for that role. Thus, the confusion and volume overload can spill into the home in both unaware and unintended ways, with adverse impact.

Career stage is a second consideration relevant to work–family conflict. In recollecting at age 93 the early stages of his career and its effect on his family life, a distinguished physician and educator observed that he did not have to work as hard as he did at age 33 to be as successful as he was over his entire career. Of course, such retrospective observation is much easier when one has fulfilled a highly successful career. The physician-educator was fortunate that he did not lose his family in the process, and retrospective guilt can be unwarranted. One world renowned cancer researcher experienced some of the same reflective guilt as the physician educator and, upon engaging in a family process of reconciliation, discovered that his wife and children had, in fact, not felt shortchanged throughout their lives with him. Still, a young executive's or professional's striving to achieve in the early career stage may place unwitting pressure on the family.

In addition to the career stage being an important source of work demands creating conflict with the family, one's stage in family life can a source of overlapping conflict. Working parents with small and adolescent children often feel the conflict and tension of the competing role demands from work and home life. While family-friendly work environments may help ease the tension, individual preferences for separation or integration of these two major life domains are important considerations in this regard as well.

Self-Imposed Demands

Individuals often contribute to their own work–family conflicts by way of self-imposed demands. The most problematic self-imposed demands for work–family conflict center around over-achievement drive and workaholism. These self-imposed demands share some overlapping variance with Type A Behavior Pattern, often known as coronary-prone behavior and occasionally the Sisyphus Complex. Preoccupation with work was first suspected as a risk for cardiovascular disease by the Dutch cardiologist Von Dusch, who observed in the 1860s that an excessive involvement with work contributed to heart disease. Workaholism contributes to work–family conflict to the extent that it prevents one from strategic disengagement from work for alternative purposes in life. Table 1 contains a set of 20 self-assessment questions to help assess whether or not you are a workaholic.

Amplifying the Conflict

In addition to the three sources of work–family conflict just discussed, there are a number of factors that can amplify or enflame the conflict beyond its natural origins. These factors may exacerbate work–family conflict, may be symptoms of work–family conflict, or may be immediate consequences of work–family conflict. The five factors are alcohol and other substances, sleep disturbances, business travel, toxic corporate cultures, and the e-mail paradox. These are not intended to be an exhaustive set of factors, and families may discover for themselves specific accelerants that ignite an otherwise routine work–family conflict into a full-blown wildfire. Identifying these factors within the family and then knowing the early warning signs

Table 1   How Do You Know If You Are a Workaholic?

1. Do you get more excited about your work than about family or anything else?
2. Are there times when you can charge through your work and other times when you can't?
3. Do you take work with you to bed? on weekends? on vacation?
4. Is work the activity you like to do best and talk about most?
5. Do you work more than 40 hours a week?
6. Do you turn your hobbies into money-making ventures?
7. Do you take complete responsibility for the outcome of your work efforts?
8. Have your family or friends given up expecting you on time?
9. Do you take on extra work because you are concerned that it won't otherwise get done?
10. Do you underestimate how long a project will take and then rush to complete it?
11. Do you believe that it is okay to work long hours if you love what you are doing?
12. Do you get impatient with people who have other priorities besides work?
13. Are you afraid that if you don't work hard you will lose your job or be a failure?
14. Is the future a constant worry for you even when things are going very well?
15. Do you do things energetically and competitively, including play?
16. Do you get irritated when people ask you to stop doing your work in order to do something else?
17. Have your long hours hurt your family or other relationships?
18. Do you think about your work while driving, falling asleep, or when others are talking?
19. Do you work or read during meals?
20. Do you believe that more money will solve the other problems in your life?

Reprinted with permission from Workaholics Anonymous, World Service Organization (2002).

of their pending activation can go a long way in early detection and prevention of specific conflicts for the family and the workplace.

Alcohol and Other Substances

Alcohol abuse is one of the most potential destructive forces in family life, and for those who have lived with an alcoholic, the personality-changing dynamics of the abuser are clear. For those in the workplace, the abuse of alcohol or other substances may be very difficult to detect. For example, a senior military documents security officer was widely known in Washington, DC, to abstain from alcohol consumption, as was his wife. The couple never drank at any political, military, or diplomatic functions. However, after an investigation was triggered when a Top Secret document went missing, it was discovered that the couple were alcoholics who carefully concealed their abuse in the privacy of their home.

While this is a dramatic Jekyll-and-Hyde case of alcohol abuse, it reveals the insidious effects that alcohol or other substance abuse may have in terms of work–family conflict. The common characteristic of the home in which alcohol is abused is disorder and the experience of a lack of control. For families of abusers, this experience is both deeply disturbing and very disorienting. It may be akin to being in a funny house at the amusement park.

Sleep Disturbances

Stress is a known cause of sleep disturbances and insomnia, one early warning sign of change in an individual's life. However, sleep disturbances in turn may play a causal or inflammatory role in work–family conflict, depending upon the individual's response to the sleep disturbance. Not all sleep disturbances are problematic and, to the extent that they are short-term responses to peak workloads or changing work demands, they may simply be short-term symptoms of the mind–body adjustment to these changing conditions.

However, chronic and long-term sleep disturbances are of concern for the individual, the family, and the organization. For the individual, sleep deprivation can lead to attention deficits that may contribute to health problems and even accidents in the workplace. For the family, one member's sleep disturbance may become "contagious" with other family members. For the organization, sleep disturbances and deprivation may lead to loss of productivity. One senior municipal executive experienced a two-year period of rather severe insomnia for which medical treatment found little effect. This senior executive's emotional reactivity was enhanced, leading to chronic interpersonal conflicts with members of his city council, which in turn had spillover effects into his marriage and home life.

Travel . . . and More Travel

Travel can exacerbate work–family conflicts in at least two ways. The first way is due to the emotional separation caused by the physical distance of the traveling family member. If the family is a secure base of emotional operation for a husband or wife, travel serves to interrupt the periodic emotional reassurance and social support that intimate family relationships provide. The famous folk singers Peter, Paul, and Mary found during one year that they were on the road well over 200 days, significantly cutting into their individual family relationships. Strong family bonds can withstand reasoned periods of separation due to travel, but any fragility within the family bonds is strained by the separation.

The second way in which travel exacerbates work–family conflict is the additional burden which such travel places on the at-home spouse. There are a variety of functional and mundane aspects of home life, such as taking out the garbage, which simply must be managed if the home is to be healthy for the family. Most families divide duties among parents and children, or contract with domestic help for child-care and other important home duties. Who assumes the traveling parent's duties in the absence of that parent?

Toxic Corporate Cultures

Peter Frost has brought our attention to the organizational problem of toxic emotions and pain that is often endemic to work life. William Cohen and his clinical psychologist wife further brought attention to the paranoid organization and other dysfunctional forms of corporate cultures. In some organizations, it does seem that it is necessary to be a little bit paranoid, or a little bit schizophrenic, or somewhat manic to succeed within that specific corporate culture. This in no way suggests neither that these corporate cultures are healthy, nor that they should be emulated by other executives or organizations. The problem from a healthy family standpoint is that unhealthy corporate cultures have unhealthy spillover effects into the family.

The "pressure cooker" corporate culture is particularly problematic for those seeking a healthy work–family balance. Organizations that are pressure cookers simply drive their employees, not allowing time for energy recovery nor strategic disengagement from production. The old joke in Schenectady, New York, was that you could tell a General Electric Company man by his blood pressure. There are peak work periods, however, when long hours may be appropriate. For example, when the Rotary International year comes to an end in June, Russell-Hampton President Bob Lyons joins other employees in manning the phones every day and in working 14-hour days in the office as thousands of Rotary Clubs around the world order the President's Awards recognitions.

The E-Mail Paradox

An emergent factor that may amplify work–family conflict is the ever-present e-mail system, which creates a paradox. E-mail is a double-edged sword that may simplify and streamline, or become a 24-7 cowbell that strangles the family life out of the employee. When an executive or employee allows e-mail to overwhelm his or her attention with expectations of rapid response, then this electronic aide intrudes upon family life in an adverse manner. This is the negative side of e-mail which can exacerbate work–family conflict.

On the positive side, e-mail can be a simplifying tool that allows an executive to send praise and positive reinforcement quickly, simply, and personally. For example, university president Jim Spaniolo has found that e-mail is a wonderful way to communicate positive feedback and to send personal, congratulatory notes to colleagues everywhere who are performing well. Spaniolo is always careful to reserve any difficult or potentially confusing communication to one-on-one, face-to-face contact that ensures the accuracy of such difficult communications. Used appropriately, e-mail can give executives and employees alike the discretionary control in their communication that enables them to accommodate work–family demands and reduce resultant conflicts.

Balancing Strategies: How can We Effectively Balance Work and Family?

It is obvious that work–family conflict has serious ramifications for the individual employee, his or her family, and organization. While a large amount of research has documented the nature of work–family conflict and the negative outcomes often associated with it, less attention has been focused on the ways employees can effectively balance these often incompatible pressures from their work and family domains. However, many options exist for the worker who wishes to alleviate some of this conflict in her life. These management strategies occur at the individual level in terms of managing work responsibilities, family obligations, and self-imposed expectations.

Within the Workplace

First, the employee must take an active role in the management of his work responsibilities. While some characteristics of the work environment may appear to be out of one's personal control, there are many active choices that executives and employees can make to help balance their work and personal lives. As discussed above, individuals experiencing work–family conflict are typically faced with irregular or inflexible work hours, extensive travel, and work overload. The first key to balancing such work demands involves time management: such as setting clear and reasonable goals for work tasks, negotiating travel demands and meeting obligations, and the delegation of assignments when feasible.

To help achieve effective time management, Boris A. Baltes and Heather A. Heydens-Gahir have suggested that a life-management strategy known as selection, optimization, and compensation (SOC) be applied to reduce work–family conflict. When using this strategy, employees first identify and set goals to give them clear direction in how to exert their energy—i.e., selection. In the second phase, optimization, individuals acquire, refine, and use the necessary means to achieve those goals set in the first stage of the process. This stage is often characterized by modeling personal behavior after others whom we find successful, learning new skills relevant to achieving our goals, and actively scheduling time and energy. In the final stage of SOC, individuals use additional resources to compensate for their lack of ability to fully meet those goals that were outlined in the first stage. For example, an executive may have to utilize live-in child-care options to help achieve her goal of providing a supportive environment for her children when work demands force her to be away from home. The key objective of this life-management strategy involves focusing on what the important goals are for a person and then directing resources, such as time, to fulfilling those goals.

Boundary management also represents a key coping strategy for balancing the demands between work and home. According to Ellen Kossek and Raymond Noe, this approach recognizes that individuals must play an active role in managing the "joint enactment" of both work and family roles. Therefore, this option seeks to achieve work–family synthesis while allowing an individual to remain in his or her current position. Such a synthesis is attempted through the concept of boundary management that organizes and separates role demands and expectations based on the boundaries set by the individual. Some individuals choose to set strong boundaries by making the domains mutually exclusive and allowing no interaction between them, while others choose to apply no boundaries at all and allow constant interaction and overlap between family and work life.

Christena Nippert-Eng identified two strategies for managing work–family conflict, based on their position along this continuum of boundary management. Segmentation describes the approach in which clear boundaries are laid between the two domains and overlap is rarely permitted. Individuals utilizing this strategy establish a high level of boundary separation and aim to keep their work and family roles completely distinct. These employees deal with work demands during the established work time and home concerns only during the established home hours. Conflict is reduced because individuals are focused on only one domain at a time, and, therefore, fulfilling only the demands associated with that particular role.

Integration, on the other hand, is utilized when few boundaries exist between domains and no clear distinctions are made regarding the appropriate time for enactment of either role. Individuals using this strategy to reduce work–family conflict will make themselves available to either domain at any time. Therefore, conflict is reduced because the domain with the most pressing need is always addressed, regardless of the time of day or the individual's physical location. For example, individuals applying integration to their domains will accept work calls at home on Saturday, but may also leave work on a Tuesday morning to run an errand with their children.

Finally, the personal management of work responsibilities can be achieved through choices made when structuring and choosing career paths and job assignments. Research shows that as employees receive more autonomy and flexibility in their positions, their level of work–family conflict significantly decreases. Therefore, individuals attempting to balance their work demands should seek avenues in their careers which allow greater flexibility and autonomy. These choices may be made when deciding whether to accept a promotion or position with a new organization or by simply communicating the need for greater control in their current positions. Employees should also actively understand themselves and their personal needs when making job choices and seek a degree of person-organization fit which complements the various priorities in their lives. Such active management of work responsibilities can significantly alleviate the amount of work–family conflict experienced.

Within the Family

While executives and employees must manage their job responsibilities when negotiating between work and family lives, family obligations also play a significant role in the balancing act. Numerous pressures in the family environment—such as the presence of young children, the primary responsibility for caring for children, and the management of care for elder family members—can all stimulate conflict between the work and family domains. However, individuals can take steps to manage their family obligations while simultaneously fulfilling their responsibilities at work.

The design of the family structure itself can intensify the degree of work–family conflict experienced. Work–family conflict increases as families become larger and more complex, such as through dual-career families with increasing levels of obligation. However, research has shown that these factors can be mitigated by support within the family. Employees who report that their spouses provide career support, personal support, and help with the children experience less difficulty in balancing the two domains. Communication within the family plays a key role in fostering this social support. For example, simply letting your spouse know that this is a particularly stressful time at the office and you may have to work late the next few weeks can help everyone in the family adjust to changes in responsibility without feelings of abandonment or resentment.

When managing family obligations, it important to realize that the quantity of time is not always the key factor. Instead, quality of time spent in the family role may be even more important. The majority of the average waking workday is spent either in the work environment, commuting to and from work, or handling other work obligations, leaving little time in the day to accomplish home responsibilities. However, Jim Loehr and Tony Schwartz point out that managing energy, not time, is the key to higher performance and personal renewal. In other words, it may not be the amount of time spent with the family, but the nature of that time. Three hours of energetic, fully engaged, time spent with the family on a weeknight may not equal the amount of time spent at the office that day, but may be more rewarding in terms of the energy and fulfillment achieved. Also, the chosen time spent with the family may be equally important. For example, the average weeknight may not be very significant to the family, but the weeknight that a child has a piano recital or a spouse is receiving an award may be of considerable importance. In other words, while quality time is important, the right time may carry even greater significance.

Self-Management

The final component that must be managed when balancing work and family responsibilities focuses on self-imposed expectations and reactions to role demands. Self-management is a central ingredient in high levels of emotional competence. Key individual difference factors influence the degree of work–family conflict experienced. Neuroticism, Type A tendencies, and negative affectivity have all been found to increase perceptions of work–family conflict. Additionally, predispositions to stress, such as a lack of personality hardiness, and differences in ability to cope with life stressors will further limit an individual's ability to effectively balance work and family demands. It is important that employees recognize the role that their individual personalities play in shaping their reactions to these life stressors. It is interesting to note that as workers age, they report less work–family conflict, thus reflecting the impact of learning experiences on the ability to recognize and manage work–family interactions.

Self-imposed expectations of one's performance in work and/or family roles can be directly related to the level of psychological involvement one feels toward that role. As work becomes more important to us in terms of how we define ourselves, the decisions we make and the direction toward which we expend our energy are affected. This concept is most clearly reflected when considering the classic workaholic mentioned previously. While lack of adequate attention to one's job can result in poor performance and dismissal, an intense obsession and preoccupation with one's job can pose a significant risk for one's health and family. It is difficult for executives—in that commitment, long hours, high performance, and job involvement are all characteristics common to success in today's organizations. However, when taken to the extreme, these behaviors can become destructive for both the individual and her family. Workaholics often suffer from chronic fatigue, obsessive worry, short temper, poor communication, insomnia, and mood fluctuations. In turn, their performance at work may suffer, leading to more pressure and extreme behaviors. All of these negative outcomes inevitably influence the family environment and the attempt to effectively balance the two domains.

The individual must play an active role in self-management in order to balance work and family lives. A key step in this process is the realization of the need to balance both of these aspects of their lives and the examination of self-expectations. It is important for employees to be aware of the demands that they place upon themselves in order to understand how to generate reasonable expectations that allow for a balance between the two domains. This self-knowledge must be gained in order to create the awareness that an individual needs to alter his or her perceptions, behaviors, and lifestyles. The resulting increased awareness will open the door for the individual to seek the support that helps reduce work–family conflict. Employees must be willing to ask for the support they need, whether from their partner or their organization, in order to benefit from this valuable source of strength. Communication of individual needs to all those affected by a poor work–family balance—for example, partners, children, supervisors, plays an important role in this process. The acceptance of support, when offered—is essential for managing these dual obligations.

While the failure to balance work and family lives effectively holds significant ramifications for individuals, their families, and their organizations, it is important for employees to realize that they have options available to help manage the amount of work–family conflict they experience. There are three key components which must all be addressed to achieve this desired balance: managing work responsibilities, managing family obligations, and managing self-imposed expectations. Each of these components represents a distinct aspect of the worker's life over which he must exhibit a degree of control to effectively manage all of the conflicting pressures often found in work and family domains. For the individual, it is important to realize that he plays an active role in determining the degree of work–family conflict he experiences.

A Word to the Wise Executive

Effectively balancing the mutual demands of both work and non-work lives is an essential component of managing today's workforce. While the demands between the alternative domains may create a conflict for some employees, we believe that each of these aspects of an individual's life can coexist successfully. In other words, conflict does not have to occur, and the alternative aspects of an individual's life can be complementary, rather than competitive. The key consideration for employees, executives, and organizations is the active management of each role. Once that is achieved, the probability of engaging fully in all domains increases greatly.

It is obvious that many opportunities exist for conflict between an executive's work and non-work roles, due to time demands and the ever-present strain associated with demanding organizational positions. However, management strategies can enable the executive to find a balance in his or her life in which success in each of the life roles is attainable. We do not believe that success in the work role necessarily constitutes decreased functioning in the non-work role or vice versa. Instead, both roles, as well as self-expectations, can be managed, and even embraced, simultaneously. All of the contributing forces, such as self, family, and organizational demands, can co-exist without creating conflict. The key factor is that individuals are aware of the potential impact of each role on the other roles in their lives. Consequently, the active management of energy, as opposed to time, can enable executives to achieve in all areas. Therefore, the potential solution to work–family conflict is more complex than simply spending the same amount of quantitative hours in each domain. Instead, the understanding of which time, and the quality of that time, becomes much more important. As a result, executives may still spend a greater number of hours outside of the home domain, but the total hours spent enacting the family role may become less influential on life and family satisfaction than the nature of those hours.

Selected Bibliography

Insight into the development and types of work–family conflict can be achieved by reading Jeffrey Greenhaus and Nicholas Beutell's article entitled "Sources of Conflict Between Work and Family Roles," *Academy of Management Review*, 1985: 10, 76–88. A thorough explanation of the effects of work–family conflict, in terms of individual, family, and societal implications, can be found in Donna Wiley's 1987 article "The Relationship Between Work–Nonwork Role Conflict and Job-Related Outcomes: Some Unanticipated Findings," which appeared in the *Journal of Management*, as well as Linda Thomas and Daniel Ganster's article "Impact of Family-Supportive Work Variables on Work–Family Conflict and Strain: A Control Perspective," *Journal of Applied Psychology* 80: 6–15. Further evidence is documented in the article entitled "Compelling Evidence of the Need for Corporate Work/Life Balance Initiatives: Results from a National Survey of Stressful Life Events," by Charles Hobson, Linda Delunas, and Dawn Kesic from the *Journal of Employment Counseling* 38: 38–44. Other information on the issues of work/life balance can be gained from reading Joan Kofodimos's *Balancing Act* (San Francisco: Jossey-Bass, 1993) and the *Harvard Business Review*'s book on *Work and Life Balance* (Cambridge: Harvard Business School Press, 2000) and accessing web-based resources such as www.worklifebalance.com or www.worklifebalancecenter.org.

Additional in-depth readings on stress, the demands that more broadly cause it in addition to work–family conflict, its array of psychological, behavioral, and medical consequences, the various moderating variables in the stress process, and the range of individual and organizational interventions for healthy stress management are available in *Preventive Stress Management in Organizations* by James Campbell Quick,

Jonathan D. Quick, Debra L. Nelson, and Joseph J. Hurrell, Jr. (Washington, DC: American Psychological Association, 1997), the *Handbook of Work Stress*, edited by Julian Barling, Kevin Kelloway, and Michael Frone (Thousand Oaks, CA: Sage Publications, 2005), and the *Handbook of Stress, Medicine, and Health*, Second Edition, edited by Cary L. Cooper (Boca Raton, FL: CRC Press, 2005).

To gain an understanding of the alternatives that individuals can use to simultaneously manage work, family, and self-expectations, interested readers should pick up Jim Loehr and Tony Schwartz's book entitled *The Power of Full Engagement* (New York: Free Press, 2003). These authors stress that managing energy, as opposed to time, is the key ingredient for successfully engaging in all areas of one's life. Additionally, Boris Baltes and Heather Heydens-Gahir have suggested that the life-management strategy of selection, optimization, and compensation (SOC) can be a useful tool for individuals seeking to find a work–family balance in their lives. Their suggestions can be found in the article "Reduction of Work–Family Conflict through the Use of Selection, Optimization, and Compensation Behaviors," which was printed in the *Journal of Applied Psychology*, 2003, 88: 1005–1018.

Finally, two key pieces illustrate the need for individuals to play an active role in managing the joint enactment of both work and family roles. Ellen Kossek and Raymond Noe suggest that boundary management is a key factor for individuals faced with conflicting role demands ("Work–Family Role Synthesis: Individual and Organizational Determinants," *International Journal of Conflict Management* 10: 102–129). They propose that individuals can achieve a work–family synthesis while continuing to meet the obligations of each life role. In a similar vein, Christena Nippert-Eng proposes in her book *Home and Work: Negotiating Boundaries through Everyday Life* (Chicago: University of Chicago Press, 1996) that an effective balance between work and family can be achieved along a continuum of boundary management. She presents two alternative approaches in which individuals either clearly segment their lives into work and family time, or integrate the two domains with each other. Each of these tools can help individuals, organizations, and families understand the role they play in balancing the competing demands in employees' lives.

Creating Effective Work Groups

The chapters in this part of the book are devoted to the key interpersonal skills that both employees and managers need to work successfully with others.

9 Interpersonal Communication

ACTIVE LISTENING
Carl R. Rogers
Richard E. Farson

DEFENSIVE COMMUNICATION
Jack R. Gibb

MINDFUL COMMUNICATION
David C. Thomas
Joyce S. Osland

Communication is the number-one skill recruiters seek in candidates for business jobs. It is the basis for numerous tasks such as giving and following instructions, delegating, settling conflicts, and influencing and leading others. Communication extends beyond the actual stated words to the symbolic meaning of one's actions as a manager.

Communication also extends to understanding the meaning people are trying to convey to us. One of the most important work skills is active listening. Carl Rogers, a noted psychologist, is famous for his groundbreaking work on active listening. Rogers and Richard Farson, a psychologist who founded the Western Behavioral Science Institute, wrote "Active Listening," a classic description of this crucial skill. The article provides a perspective into the manufacturing-based management of the 1950s when it was written and when most people in charge were males and gender-neutral language was not a concern. Despite these historical artifacts, the authors' insights into active listening are timeless.

In another classic communication article, "Defensive Communication," Jack Gibb, an expert on group development, expanded on Rogers's work. Gibb explains why it's important to avoid making other people defensive when you communicate with them and distinguishes between behaviors that result in defensive versus supportive communication climates.

Many factors, such as family and socioeconomic backgrounds, the region where people grew up, gender, education, and culture, influence the way we communicate. Given the demands of global business and multicultural teams, more businesses are paying greater attention to lessons from the field of intercultural communication. Two international management professors, David Thomas, Director of Simon Fraser University's Centre for Global Workforce

Strategy, and Joyce Osland, Director of San Jose State University's Global Leadership Advancement Center, distill some of these lessons in "Mindful Communication." This selection is written as a basic primer for businesspeople who want to decode messages accurately and be more effective in global business interactions. Thomas and Osland describe the basic style differences to look for and provide practical advice for intercultural encounters. Becoming more mindful makes for better communication, whether or not cultural barriers are involved.

ACTIVE LISTENING*

Carl R. Rogers

Richard E. Farson

The Meaning of Active Listening

One basic responsibility of the supervisor or manager is the development, adjustment, and integration of individual employees. He tries to develop employee potential, delegate responsibility, and achieve cooperation. To do so, he must have, among other abilities, the ability to listen intelligently and carefully to those with whom he works.

There are, however, many kinds of listening skills. The lawyer, for example, when questioning a witness, listens for contradictions, irrelevancies, errors, and weaknesses. But this is not the kind of listening skill we are concerned with. The lawyer usually is not listening in order to help the witness adjust, cooperate, or produce. Our emphasis will be on listening skills of the supervisor or manager that will help employees gain a clearer understanding of their situations, take responsibility, and cooperate with each other.

Two Examples

The kind of listening we have in mind is called "active listening." It is called "active" because the listener has a very definite responsibility. He does not passively absorb words which are spoken to him. He actively tries to grasp the facts and the feelings in what he hears, and he tries, by his listening, to help the speaker work out his own problems.

To get a clearer picture of what active listening means, let us consider two different approaches to the same work problem. The example is set in the printing industry, but the behavior of the men could surface in any organization.

EXAMPLE 1

FOREMAN	Hey, Al, I don't get this rush order. We can't handle any 50,000 run today. What do they think we are?
SUPERVISOR	But that's the order. So get it out as soon as you can. We're under terrific pressure this week.
FOREMAN	Don't they know we're behind schedule already because of that press breakdown?
SUPERVISOR	Look, Kelly, I don't decide what goes on upstairs. I just have to see that the work gets out and that's what I'm gonna do.
FOREMAN	The guys aren't gonna like this.
SUPERVISOR	That's something you'll have to work out with them, not me.

*Reprinted with permission of the authors.

EXAMPLE 2

FOREMAN	Hey, Ross, I don't get this rush order. We can't handle any run of 50,000 today. What do they think we are?
SUPERVISOR	They're pushing you pretty hard, aren't they Kelly?
FOREMAN	They sure are and I'm getting sore. We were just about back to schedule after the press breakdown. Now this comes along.
SUPERVISOR	As if you didn't have enough work to do, huh?
FOREMAN	Yeah. I don't know how I'm going to tell the pressman about this.
SUPERVISOR	Hate to face him with a rush order now, is that it?
FOREMAN	I really do. Joe is under a real strain today. Seems like everything we do around here is rush, rush, rush!
SUPERVISOR	I guess you feel it's unfair to load anything more on him today.
FOREMAN	Well, yeah. I know there must be plenty of pressure on everybody to get the work out, but—well, Joe doesn't deserve all the rush orders. But, if that's the way it is—I guess I'd better get the word to him and see how I can rearrange the work flow.

There are obviously many differences between these two examples. The main one, however, is that Ross, the supervisor in the second example, is using the active listening approach. He is listening and responding in a way that makes it clear that he appreciates both the meaning and the feeling behind what Kelly is saying.

Active listening does not necessarily mean long sessions spent listening to grievances, personal or otherwise. It is simply a way of approaching those problems which arise out of the usual day-to-day events of any job.

To be effective, active listening must be firmly grounded in the basic attitudes of the user. We cannot employ it as a technique if our fundamental attitudes are in conflict with its basic concepts. If we try, our behavior will be empty and sterile, and our associates will be quick to recognize such behavior. Until we can demonstrate a spirit which genuinely respects the potential worth of the individual, which considers his rights and trusts his capacity for self-direction, we cannot begin to be effective listeners.

What We Achieve by Listening

Active listening is an important way to bring about changes in people. Despite the popular notion that listening is a passive approach, clinical and research evidence clearly shows that sensitive listening is a most effective agent for individual personality change and group development. Listening brings about changes in people's attitudes toward themselves and others and also brings about changes in their basic values and personal philosophy. People who have been listened to in this new and special way become more emotionally mature, more open to their experiences, less defensive, more democratic, and less authoritarian.

When people are listened to sensitively, they tend to listen to themselves with more care and make clear exactly what they are feeling and thinking. Group members tend to listen more to each other, become less argumentative, more ready to incorporate other points of view. Because listening reduces the threat of having one's ideas criticized, the person is better able to see them for what they are and is more likely to feel that his contributions are worthwhile.

Not the least important result of listening is the change that takes place within the listener himself. Besides the fact that listening provides more information about people than any other activity, it builds deep, positive relationships and tends to alter constructively the attitudes of the listener. Listening is a growth experience.

How to Listen

The goal of active listening is to bring about changes in people. To achieve this end, it relies upon definite techniques—things to do and things to avoid doing. Before discussing these techniques, however, we should first understand why they are effective. To do so, we must understand how the individual personality develops.

The Growth of the Individual

Through all of our lives, from early childhood on, we have learned to think of ourselves in certain, very definite ways. We have built up pictures of ourselves. Sometimes these self-pictures are pretty realistic but at other times they are not. For example, an average, overweight lady may fancy herself a youthful, ravishing siren, or an awkward teenager regard himself as a star athlete.

All of us have experiences which fit the way we need to think about ourselves. These we accept. But it is much harder to accept experiences which don't fit. And sometimes, if it is very important for us to hang on to this self-picture, we don't accept or admit these experiences at all.

These self-pictures are not necessarily attractive. A man, for example, may regard himself as incompetent and worthless. He may feel that he is doing his job poorly in spite of favorable appraisals by the organization. As long as he has these feelings about himself, he must deny any experiences which would seem not to fit this self-picture, in this case any that might indicate to him that he is competent. It is so necessary for him to maintain this self-picture that he is threatened by anything which would tend to change it. Thus, when the organization raises his salary, it may seem to him only additional proof that he is a fraud. He must hold onto this self-picture, because, bad or good, it's the only thing he has by which he can identify himself.

This is why direct attempts to change this individual or change his self-picture are particularly threatening. He is forced to defend himself or to completely deny the experience. This denial of experience and defense of the self-picture tends to bring on rigidity of behavior and create difficulties in personal adjustment.

The active-listening approach, on the other hand, does not present a threat to the individual's self-picture. He does not have to defend it. He is able to explore it, see it for what it is, and make his own decision as to how realistic it is. He is then in a position to change.

If I want to help a man or woman reduce defensiveness and become more adaptive, I must try to remove the threat of myself as a potential changer. As long as the atmosphere is threatening, there can be no effective communication. So I must create a climate which is neither critical, evaluative, nor moralizing. The climate must foster equality and freedom, trust and understanding, acceptance and warmth. In this climate and in this climate only does the individual feel safe enough to incorporate new experiences and new values into his concept of himself. Active listening helps to create this climate.

What to Avoid

When we encounter a person with a problem, our usual response is to try to change his way of looking at things—to get him to see his situation the way we see it, or would like him to see it. We plead, reason, scold, encourage, insult, prod—anything to bring about a change in the desired direction—that is, in the direction we want him to travel. What we seldom realize, however, is that under these circumstances we are usually responding to *our own* needs to see the world in certain ways. It is always difficult for us to tolerate and understand actions which are different from the ways in which *we* believe *we* should act. If, however, we can free ourselves from the need to influence and direct others in our own paths, we enable ourselves to listen with understanding, and thereby employ the most potent available agent of change.

One problem the listener faces is that of responding to demands for decisions, judgments, and evaluations. He is constantly called upon to agree or disagree with someone or something. Yet, as he well knows, the question or challenge frequently is a masked expression of feelings or needs which the speaker is far more anxious to communicate than he is to have the surface questions answered. Because he cannot speak these feelings openly, the speaker must disguise them to himself and to others in an acceptable form. To illustrate, let us examine some typical questions and the type of answers that might best elicit the feeling beneath them.

Employee's Question	Listener's Answer
Just who is responsible for getting this job done?	Do you feel that you don't have enough authority?
Don't you think talent should count more than seniority in promotions?	What do you think are the reasons for your opinion?
What does the boss expect us to do about those broken-down machines?	You're tired of working with worn-out equipment, aren't you?
Don't you think my performance has improved since the last review?	Sounds as if you feel your work has picked up over these last few months.

These responses recognize the questions but leave the way open for the employee to say what is really bothering him. They allow the listener to participate in the problem or situation without shouldering all responsibility for decision-making or actions. This is a process of thinking *with* people instead of *for* or *about* them.

Passing judgment, whether critical or favorable, makes free expression difficult. Similarly, advice and information are almost always seen as efforts to change a person and thus serve as barriers to his self-expression and the development of a creative relationship. Moreover, advice is seldom taken and information hardly ever utilized. The eager young trainee probably will not become patient just because he is advised that, "The road to success is a long, difficult one, and you must be patient." And it is no more helpful for him to learn that "only one out of a hundred trainees reach top management positions."

Interestingly, it is a difficult lesson to learn that *positive evaluations* are sometimes as blocking as negative ones. It is almost as destructive to the freedom of a relationship to tell a person that he is good or capable or right, as to tell him otherwise. To evaluate him positively may make it more difficult for him to tell of the faults that distress him or the ways in which he believes he is not competent.

Encouragement also may be seen as an attempt to motivate the speaker in certain directions or hold him off rather than as support. "I'm sure everything will work out okay" is not a helpful response to the person who is deeply discouraged about a problem.

In other words, most of the techniques and devices common to human relationships are found to be of little use in establishing the type of relationship we are seeking here.

What to Do

Just what does active listening entail, then? Basically, it requires that we get inside the speaker, that we grasp, from his point of view, just what it is he is communicating to us. More than that, we must convey to the speaker that we are seeing things *from his point of view*. To listen actively, then, means that there are several things we must do.

LISTEN FOR TOTAL MEANING Any message a person tries to get across usually has two components: the content of the message and the *feeling* or attitude underlying this content. Both are important, both give the message *meaning*. It is this total *meaning* of the message that we must try to understand. For example, a secretary comes to her boss and says, "I've finished that report." This message has obvious factual content and perhaps calls upon the boss for another work assignment. Suppose, on the other hand, that the secretary says, "Well! I'm finally finished with your damn report!" The factual content is the same, but the total meaning of the message has changed—and changed in an important way for both supervisor and worker. Here sensitive listening can facilitate the work relationship in this office. If the boss were to respond by simply giving his secretary some letters to type, would the secretary feel that she had gotten her total message across? Would she feel free to talk to her boss about the difficulty of her work? Would she feel better about the job, more anxious to do good work on her next assignment?

Now, on the other hand, suppose the supervisor were to respond, "Glad to get that over with, huh?" or "That was a rough one, wasn't it?" or "Guess you don't want another one like that again," or anything that tells the worker that he heard and understands. It doesn't necessarily mean that her next work assignment need be changed or that he must spend an hour listening to the worker complain about the problems she encountered. He may do a number of things differently in the light of the new information he has from the worker—but not necessarily. It's just that extra sensitivity on the part of the supervisor that can transform an average working climate into a good one.

RESPOND TO FEELINGS In some instances the content is far less important than the feeling which underlies it. To catch the full flavor or meaning of the message one must respond particularly to the feeling component. If, for instance, our secretary had said, "I'd like to pile up all those carbons and make a bonfire out of them!", responding to content would be obviously absurd. But to respond to her disgust or anger in trying to work with the report recognizes the meaning of this message. There are various shadings of these components in the meaning of any message. Each time the listener must try to remain sensitive to the total meaning the message has to the speaker. What is she trying to tell me? What does this mean to her? How does she see this situation?

NOTE ALL CUES Not all communication is verbal. The speaker's words alone don't tell us everything he is communicating. And, hence truly sensitive listening requires that we become aware of several kinds of communication besides verbal. The way in which a speaker hesitates in his speech can tell us much about his feelings. So too can the inflection of his voice. He may stress certain points loudly and clearly, and he may mumble others. We should also note such things as the person's facial expressions, body posture, hand movements, eye movements, and breathing. All of these help to convey his total message.

What We Communicate by Listening

The first reaction of most people when they consider listening as a possible method for dealing with human beings is that listening cannot be sufficient in itself. Because it is passive, they feel, listening does not communicate anything to the speaker. Actually, nothing could be farther from the truth.

By consistently listening to a speaker, you are conveying the idea that:

> *I'm interested in you as a person, and I think that what you feel is important. I respect your thoughts, and even if I don't agree with them, I know that they are valid for you. I feel sure that you have a contribution to make. I'm not trying to change you or evaluate you. I just want to understand you. I think you're worth listening to, and I want you to know that I'm the kind of person you can talk to.*

The subtle but most important aspect of this is that it is the *demonstration* of the message that works. Although it is most difficult to convince someone that you respect him by *telling* him so, you are much more likely to get this message across by really *behaving* that way—by actually *having* and *demonstrating* respect for this person. Listening does this most effectively.

Like other behavior, listening behavior is contagious. This has implications for all communications problems, whether between two people, or within a large organization. To insure good communication between associates up and down the line, one must first take the responsibility for setting a pattern of listening. Just as one learns that anger is usually met with anger, argument with argument, and deception with deception, one can learn that listening can be met with listening. Every person who feels responsibility in a situation can set the tone of the interaction, and the important lesson in this is that any behavior exhibited by one person will eventually be responded to with similar behavior in the other person.

It is far more difficult to stimulate constructive behavior in another person but far more valuable. Listening is one of these constructive behaviors, but if one's attitude is to "wait out" the speaker rather than really listen to him, it will fail. The one who consistently listens with understanding, however, is the one who eventually is most likely to be listened to. If you really want to be heard and understood by another, you can develop him as a potential listener, ready for new ideas, provided you can first develop yourself in these ways and sincerely listen with understanding and respect.

Testing for Understanding

Because understanding another person is actually far more difficult than it at first seems, it is important to test constantly your ability to see the world in the way the speaker sees it. You can do this by reflecting in your own words what the speaker seems to mean by his words and actions. His response to this will tell you whether or not he feels understood. A good rule of thumb is to assume that one never really understands until he can communicate this understanding to the other's satisfaction.

Here is an experiment to test your skill in listening. The next time you become involved in a lively or controversial discussion with another person, stop for a moment and suggest that you adopt this ground rule for continued discussion. Before either participant in the discussion can make a point or express an opinion of his own, he must first restate aloud the previous point or position of the other person. This restatement must be in his own words (merely parroting the words of another does not prove that one has understood, but only that he has heard the words). The restatement must be accurate enough to satisfy the speaker before the listener can be allowed to speak for himself.

You might find this procedure useful in a meeting where feelings run high and people express themselves on topics of emotional concern to the group. Before another member of the group expresses his own feelings and thought, he must rephrase the *meaning* expressed by the previous speaker to that person's satisfaction. All the members in the group should be alert to the changes in the emotional climate and the quality of the discussion when this approach is used.

Problems in Active Listening

Active listening is not an easy skill to acquire, it demands practice. Perhaps more important, it may require changes in our own basic attitudes. These changes come slowly and sometimes with considerable difficulty. Let us look at some of the major problems in active listening and what can be done to overcome them.

The Personal Risk

To be effective in active listening, one must have a sincere interest in the speaker. We all live in glass houses as far as our attitudes are concerned. They always show through. And if we are only making a pretense of interest in the speaker, he will quickly pick this up, either consciously or subconsciously. And once he does, he will no longer express himself freely.

Active listening carries a strong element of personal risk. If we manage to accomplish what we are describing here—to sense the feelings of another person, to understand the meaning his experiences have for him, to see the world as he sees it, we risk being changed ourselves. For example, if we permit ourselves to listen our way into the life of a person we do not know or approve of—to get the meaning that life has for him, we risk coming to see the world as he sees it. We are threatened when we give up, even momentarily, what we believe and start thinking in someone else's terms. It takes a great deal of inner security and courage to be able to risk one's self in understanding another.

For the manager, the courage to take another's point of view generally means that he must see *himself* through another's eyes—he must be able to see himself as others see him. To do this may sometimes be unpleasant, but it is far more difficult than *unpleasant*. We are so accustomed to viewing ourselves in certain ways—to seeing and hearing only what we want to see and hear—that it is extremely difficult for a person to free himself from the need to see things his way.

Developing an attitude of sincere interest in the speaker is thus no easy task. It can be developed only by being willing to risk seeing the world from the speaker's point of view. If we have a number of such experiences, however, they will shape an attitude which will allow us to be truly genuine in our interest in the speaker.

Hostile Expressions

The listener will often hear negative, hostile expressions directed at himself. Such expressions are always hard to listen to. No one likes to hear hostile words or be the target of hostility. And it is not easy to get to the point where one is strong enough to permit these attacks without finding it necessary to defend himself or retaliate.

Because we all fear that people will crumble under the attack of genuine negative feelings, we tend to perpetuate an attitude of pseudo-peace. It is as if we cannot tolerate conflict at all for fear of the damage it could do to us, to the situation, to the others involved. But of course the real damage is done by the denial and suppression of negative feelings.

Out-of-Place Expressions

Expressions dealing with behavior that are not usually acceptable in our society also pose problems for the listener. These out-of-place expressions can take the extreme forms that psychotherapists hear—such as homicidal fantasies or expressions of sexual perversity. The listener often blocks out such expressions because of their obvious threatening quality. At less extreme levels, we all find unnatural or inappropriate behavior difficult to handle. Behavior that brings on a problem situation may be anything from telling an "off-color" story in mixed company to seeing a man cry.

In any face-to-face situation, we will find instances of this type which will momentarily, if not permanently, block any communication. In any organization, expressions of weakness or incompetency will generally be regarded as unacceptable and therefore will block good two-way communication. For example, it is difficult to listen to a manager tell of his feelings of failure in being able to "take charge" of a situation in his department because all administrators are supposed to be able to "take charge."

Accepting Positive Feelings

It is both interesting and perplexing to note that negative or hostile feelings or expressions are much easier to deal with in any face-to-face relationship than are positive feelings. This is especially true for the manager because the culture expects him to be independent, bold, clever, and aggressive and manifest no feelings of warmth, gentleness, and intimacy. He therefore comes to regard these feelings as soft and inappropriate. But no matter how they are regarded, they remain a human need. The denial of these feelings in himself and his associates does not get the manager out of a problem of dealing with them. The feelings simply become veiled and confused. If recognized they would work for the total effort; unrecognized, they work against it.

Emotional Danger Signals

The listener's own emotions are sometimes a barrier to active listening. When emotions are at their height, when listening is most necessary, it is most difficult to set aside one's own concerns and be understanding. Our emotions are often our own worst enemies when we try to become listeners. The more involved and invested we are in a particular situation or problem, the less we are likely to be willing or able to listen to the feelings and attitudes of others. That is, the more we find it necessary to respond to our own needs, the less we are able to respond to the needs of another. Let us look at some of the main danger signals that warn us that our emotions may be interfering with our listening.

DEFENSIVENESS The points about which one is most vocal and dogmatic, the points which one is most anxious to impose on others—these are always the points one is trying to talk oneself into believing. So one danger signal becomes apparent when you find yourself stressing a point or trying to convince another. It is at these times that you are likely to be less secure and consequently less able to listen.

RESENTMENT OF OPPOSITION It is always easier to listen to an idea which is similar to one of your own than to an opposing view. Sometimes, in order to clear the air, it is helpful to pause for a moment when you feel your ideas and position being challenged, reflect on the situation, and express your concern to the speaker.

CLASH OF PERSONALITIES Here again, our experience has consistently shown us that the genuine expression of feelings on the part of the listener will be more helpful in developing a sound relationship than the suppression of them. This is so whether the feelings be resentment, hostility, threat, or admiration. A basically honest relationship, whatever the nature of it, is the most productive of all. The other party becomes secure when he learns that the listener can express his feelings honestly and openly to him. We should keep this in mind when we begin to fear a clash of personalities in the listening relationship. Otherwise, fear of our own emotions will choke off full expression of feelings.

Listening to Ourselves

To listen to oneself is a prerequisite to listening to others. And it is often an effective means of dealing with the problems we have outlined above. When we are most aroused, excited, and demanding, we are least able to understand our own feelings and attitudes. Yet, in dealing with the problems of others, it becomes most important to be sure of one's own position, values, and needs.

The ability to recognize and understand the meaning which a particular episode has for you, with all the feelings which it stimulates in you, and the ability to express this meaning when you find it getting in the way of active listening, will clear the air and enable you once again to be free to listen. That is, if some person or situation touches off feelings within you which tend to block your attempts to listen with understanding, begin listening to yourself. It is much more helpful in developing effective relationships to avoid suppressing these feelings. Speak them out as clearly as you can, and try to enlist the other person as a listener to your feelings. A person's listening ability is limited by his ability to listen to himself.

Active Listening and Organization Goals

"How can listening improve productivity?"
"We're in business, and it is a rugged, fast, competitive affair. How are we going to find time to counsel our employees?"
"We have to concern ourselves with organizational problems first."
"We can't afford to spend all day listening when there is work to do."
"What's morale got to do with service to the public?"
"Sometimes we have to sacrifice an individual for the good of the rest of the people in the organization."
Those of us who are trying to advance the listening approach in organizations hear these comments frequently. And because they are so honest and legitimate, they pose a real problem. Unfortunately, the answers are not so clear-cut as the questions.

Individual Importance

One answer is based on an assumption that is central to the listening approach. That assumption is: The kind of behavior which helps the individual will eventually be the best thing that could be done for the work group. Or saying it another way: The things that are best for the individual are best for the organization. This is a conviction of ours, based on our experience in psychology and education. The research evidence from organizations is still coming in. We find that putting the group first, at the expense of the individual, besides being an uncomfortable individual experience, does not unify the group. In fact, it tends to make the group less a group. The members become anxious and suspicious.

We are not at all sure in just what ways the group does benefit from a concern demonstrated for an individual, but we have several strong leads. One is that the group feels more secure when an individual member is being listened to and provided for with concern and sensitivity. And we assume that a secure group will ultimately be a better group. When each individual feels that he need not fear exposing himself to the group, he is likely to contribute more freely and spontaneously. When the leader of a group responds to the individual, puts the individual first, the other members of the group will follow suit, and the group comes to act as a unit in recognizing and responding to the needs of a particular member. This positive, constructive action seems to be a much more satisfying experience for a group than the experience of dispensing with a member.

Listening and Productivity

As to whether or not listening or any other activity designed to better human relations in an organization actually makes the organization more productive—whether morale has a definite relationship to performance is not known for sure. There are some who frankly hold that there is no relationship to be expected between morale and productivity—that productivity often depends upon the social misfit, the eccentric, or the isolate. And there are some who simply choose to work in a climate of cooperation and harmony, in a high-morale group, quite aside from the question of achievement or productivity.

A report from the Survey Research Center at the University of Michigan on research conducted at the Prudential Life Insurance Company lists seven findings related to production and morale. First-line supervisors in high-production work groups were found to differ from those in low-production groups in that they:

1. Are under less close supervision from their own supervisors.
2. Place less direct emphasis upon production as the goal.
3. Encourage employee participation in the making of decisions.
4. Are more employee-centered.
5. Spend more of their time in supervision and less in straight production work.
6. Have a greater feeling of confidence in their supervisory roles.
7. Feel that they know where they stand with the company.

After mentioning that other dimensions of morale, such as identification with the company, intrinsic job satisfaction, and satisfaction with job status, were not found significantly related to productivity, the report goes on to suggest the following psychological interpretation:

> People are more effectively motivated when they are given some degree of freedom in the way in which they do their work than when every action is prescribed in advance. They do better when some degree of decision making about their jobs is possible than when all decisions are made for them. They respond more adequately when they are treated as personalities than as cogs in a machine. In short, if the ego motivation of self-determination, of self-expression, of a sense of personal worth can be tapped, the individual can be more effectively energized. The use of external sanctions, or pressuring for production may work to some degree, but not to the extent that the more internalized motives do. When the individual comes to identify himself with his job and with the work of his group, human resources are much more fully utilized in the production process.

The Survey Research Center has also conducted studies among workers in other industries. In discussing the results of these studies, Robert L. Kahn writes:

> In the studies of clerical workers, railroad workers, and workers in heavy industry, the supervisors with the better production records gave a larger proportion of their time to supervisory functions, especially to the interpersonal aspects of their jobs. The supervisors of the lower-producing

*sections were more likely to spend their time in tasks which the men them-
selves were performing, or in the paper-work aspects of their jobs.*

Maximum Creativeness

There may never be enough research evidence to satisfy everyone on this question.
But speaking from an organizational point of view, in terms of the problem of developing resources for productivity, the maximum creativeness and productive effort of
the human beings in the organization are the richest untapped source of power available. The difference between the maximum productive capacity of people and that
output which the organization is now realizing is immense. We simply suggest that
this maximum capacity might be closer to realization if we sought to release the motivation that already exists within people rather than try to stimulate them externally.

This releasing of the individual is made possible first of all by listening, with
respect and understanding. Listening is a beginning toward making the individual feel
himself worthy of making contributions, and this could result in a very dynamic and
productive organization. Profit making organizations are never too rugged or too busy
to take time to procure the most efficient technological advances or to develop rich
sources of raw materials. But technology and materials are but paltry resources in comparison with the resources that are already within the people in the organization.

G. L. Clements, of Jewel Tea Co., Inc., in talking about the collaborative
approach to management says:

> *We feel that this type of approach recognizes that there is a secret ballot
> going on at all times among the people in any business. They vote for or
> against their supervisors. A favorable vote for the supervisor shows up
> in the cooperation, teamwork, understanding, and production of the
> group. To win this secret ballot, each supervisor must share the problems
> of his group and work for them.*

The decision to spend time listening to employees is a decision each supervisor
or manager has to make for himself. Managers increasingly must deal with people and
their relationships rather than turning out goods and services. The minute we take a
man from work and make him a supervisor he is removed from the basic production of
goods or services and now must begin relating to men and women instead of nuts and
bolts. People are different from things, and our supervisor is called upon for a different
line of skills completely. These new tasks call for a special kind of person. The development of the supervisor as a listener is a first step in becoming this special person.

DEFENSIVE COMMUNICATION*

Jack R. Gibb

One way to understand communication is to view it as a people process rather than as
a language process. If one is to make fundamental improvement in communication, he
must make changes in interpersonal relationships. One possible type of alteration—
and the one with which this paper is concerned—is that of reducing the degree of
defensiveness.

*Reprinted with permission from *The Journal of Communication* 11(3) (1961): 141–148.

Definition and Significance

"Defensive behavior" is behavior which occurs when an individual perceives threat or anticipates threat in the group. The person who behaves defensively, even though he also gives some attention to the common task, devotes an appreciable portion of his energy to defending himself. Besides talking about the topic, he thinks about how he appears to others, how he may be seen more favorably, how he may win, dominate, impress or escape punishment, and/or how he may avoid or mitigate a perceived or anticipated attack.

Such inner feelings and outward acts tend to create similarly defensive postures in others; and, if unchecked, the ensuing circular response becomes increasingly destructive. Defensive behavior, in short, engenders defensive listening, and this in turn produces postural, facial, and verbal cues which raise the defense level of the original communicator.

Defensive arousal prevents the listener from concentrating upon the message. Not only do defensive communicators send off multiple value, motive, and affect cues, but also defensive recipients distort what they receive. As a person becomes more and more defensive, he becomes less and less able to perceive accurately the motives, the values, and the emotions of the sender. The writer's analysis of tape recorded discussions revealed that increases in defensive behavior were correlated positively with losses in efficiency in communication.[1] Specifically, distortions became greater when defensive states existed in the groups.

The converse also is true. The more "supportive" or defense reductive the climate the less the receiver reads into the communication distorted loadings which arise from projections of his own anxieties, motives, and concerns. As defenses are reduced, the receivers become better able to concentrate upon the structure, the content, and the cognitive meanings of the message.

Categories of Defensive and Supportive Communication

In working over an eight-year period with recordings of discussions occurring in varied settings, the writer developed the six pairs of defensive and supportive categories presented in Table 1. Behavior which listeners perceive as possessing any of the characteristics listed in the left-hand column arouses defensiveness, whereas that which they interpret as having any of the qualities designated as supportive reduces defensive feelings. The degree to which these reactions occur depend upon the personal level of defensiveness and upon the general climate in the group at the time.[2]

Table 1 Categories of Behavior Characteristic of Supportive and Defensive Climates in Small Groups

Defensive Climates	Supportive Climates
1. Evaluation	1. Description
2. Control	2. Problem orientation
3. Strategy	3. Spontaneity
4. Neutrality	4. Empathy
5. Superiority	5. Equality
6. Certainty	6. Provisionalism

Evaluation and Description

Speech or other behavior which appears evaluative increases defensiveness. If by expression, manner of speech, tone of voice, or verbal content the sender seems to be evaluating or judging the listener, then the receiver goes on guard. Of course, other factors may inhibit the reaction. If the listener thinks that the speaker regards him as an equal and is being open and spontaneous, for example, the evaluativeness in a message will be neutralized and perhaps not even perceived. This same principle applies equally to the other five categories of potentially defense-producing climates. The six sets are interactive.

Because our attitudes toward other persons are frequently, and often necessarily, evaluative, expressions which the defensive person will regard as nonjudgmental are hard to frame. Even the simplest question usually conveys the answer that the sender wishes or implies the response that would fit into his value system. A mother, for example, immediately following an earth tremor that shook the house, sought for her small son with the question: "Bobby, where are you?" The timid and plaintive "Mommy, I didn't do it" indicated how Bobby's chronic mild defensiveness predisposed him to react with a projection of his own guilt and in the context of his chronic assumption that questions are full of accusation.

Anyone who has attempted to train professionals to use information-seeking speech with neutral affect appreciates how difficult it is to teach a person to say even the simple "Who did that?" without being seen as accusing. Speech is so frequently judgmental that there is a reality base for the defensive interpretations which are so common.

When insecure, group members are particularly likely to place blame, to see others as fitting into categories of good or bad, to make moral judgments of their colleagues, and to question the value, motive, and affect loadings of the speech which they hear. Since value loadings imply a judgment of others, a belief that the standards of the speaker differ from his own causes the listener to become defensive.

Descriptive speech, in contrast to that which is evaluative, tends to arouse a minimum of uneasiness. Speech acts which the listener perceives as genuine requests for information or as material with neutral loadings is descriptive. Specifically, presentations of feelings, events, perceptions, or processes which do not ask or imply that the receiver change behavior or attitude are minimally defense-producing. The difficulty in avoiding overtone is illustrated by the problems of news reporters in writing stories about unions, Communists, [African Americans], and religious activities without tipping off the "party" line of the newspaper. One can often tell from the opening words in a news article which side the newspaper's editorial policy favors.

Control and Problem Orientation

Speech which is used to control the listener evokes resistance. In most of our social intercourse someone is trying to do something to someone else—to change an attitude, to influence behavior, or to restrict the field of activity. The degree to which attempts to control produce defensiveness depends upon the openness of the effort, for a suspicion that hidden motives exist heightens resistance. For this reason attempts of non-directive therapists and progressive educators to refrain from imposing a set of values, a point of view, or a problem solution upon the receivers meet with many barriers. Since the norm is control, non-controllers must earn the perceptions that their efforts have no hidden motives. A bombardment of persuasive "messages" in the fields of politics, education, special causes, advertising, religion, medicine, industrial relations, and guidance has bred cynical and paranoidal responses in listeners.

Implicit in all attempts to alter another person is the assumption by the change agent that the person to be altered is inadequate. That the speaker secretly views the listener as ignorant, unable to make his own decisions, uninformed, immature, unwise, or possessed of wrong or inadequate attitudes is a subconscious perception which gives the latter a valid base for defensive reactions.

Methods of control are many and varied. Legalistic insistence on detail, restrictive regulations and policies, conformity norms, and all laws are among the methods. Gestures, facial expressions, other forms of non-verbal communication, and even such simple acts as holding a door open in a particular manner are means of imposing one's will upon another and hence are potential sources of resistance.

Problem orientation, on the other hand, is the antithesis of persuasion. When the sender communicates a desire to collaborate in defining a mutual problem and in seeking its solution, she tends to create the same problem orientation in the listener, and, of greater importance, she implies that she has no predetermined solution, attitude, or method to impose. Such behavior is permissive in that it allows the receiver to set his own goals, make his own decisions, and evaluate his own progress—or to share with the sender in doing so. The exact methods of attaining permissiveness are not known, but they must involve a constellation of cues, and they certainly go beyond mere verbal assurances that the communicator has no hidden desires to exercise control.

Strategy and Spontaneity

When the sender is perceived as engaged in a stratagem involving ambiguous and multiple motivations, the receiver becomes defensive. No one wishes to be a guinea pig or a role player, and no one likes to be the victim of some hidden motivation. That which is concealed, also, may appear larger than it really is, with the degree of defensiveness of the listener determining the perceived size of the suppressed element. The intense reaction of the reading audience to the material in the *Hidden Persuaders* indicates the prevalence of defensive reactions to multiple motivations behind strategy. Group members who are seen as "taking a role," as feigning emotion, as toying with their colleagues, as withholding information, or as having special sources of data are especially resented. One participant once complained that another was "using a listening technique" on him!

A large part of the adverse reaction to much of the so-called human relations training is a feeling against what are perceived as gimmicks and tricks to fool or to "involve" people, to make a person think he is making his own decision, or to make the listener feel that the sender is genuinely interested in him as a person. Particularly violent reactions occur when it appears that someone is trying to make a stratagem appear spontaneous. One person has reported a boss who incurred resentment by habitually using the gimmick of "spontaneously" looking at his watch and saying, "My gosh, look at the time—I must run to an appointment." The belief was that the boss would create less irritation by honestly asking to be excused.

Similarly, the deliberate assumption of guilelessness and natural simplicity is especially resented. Monitoring the tapes of feedback and evaluation sessions in training groups indicates the surprising extent to which members perceive the strategies of their colleagues. This perceptual clarity may be quite shocking to the strategist, who usually feels that he has cleverly hidden the motivational aura around the "gimmick."

This aversion to deceit may account for one's resistance to politicians who are suspected of behind-the-scenes planning to get his vote; to psychologists whose listening apparently is motivated by more than the manifest or content-level interest in his behavior, or to the sophisticated, smooth, or clever person whose "one-upmanship" is marked with guile. In training groups the role-flexible person frequently is resented because his changes in behavior are perceived as strategic maneuvers.

Conversely, behavior which appears to be spontaneous and free of deception is defense reductive. If the communicator is seen as having a clean id, as having uncomplicated motivations, as being straightforward and honest, and as behaving spontaneously in response to the situation, he is likely to arouse minimal defense.

Neutrality and Empathy

When neutrality in speech appears to the listener to indicate a lack of concern for his welfare, he becomes defensive. Group members usually desire to be perceived as valued persons, as individuals of special worth, and as objects of concern and affection. The clinical, detached, person-is-an-object-of-study attitude on the part of many psychologist-trainers is resented by group members. Speech with low affect that communicates little warmth or caring is in such contrast with the affect-laden speech in social situations that it sometimes communicates rejection.

Communication that conveys empathy for the feelings and respect for the worth of the listener is particularly supportive and defense reductive. Reassurance results when a message indicates that the speaker identifies himself with the listener's problems, shares his feelings, and accepts his emotional reactions at face value. Abortive efforts to deny the legitimacy of the receiver's emotions by assuring the receiver that he need not feel bad, that he should not feel rejected, or that he is overly anxious, though often intended as support giving, may impress the listener as lack of acceptance. The combination of understanding and empathizing with the other person's emotions with no accompanying effort to change him apparently is supportive at a high level.

The importance of gestural behavior cues in communicating empathy should be mentioned. Apparently spontaneous facial and bodily evidences of concern are often interpreted as especially valid evidence of deep-level acceptance.

Superiority and Equality

When a person communicates to another that he feels superior in position, power, wealth, intellectual ability, physical characteristics, or other ways, he arouses defensiveness. Here, as with the other sources of disturbance, whatever arouses feelings of inadequacy causes the listener to center upon the affect loading of the statement rather than upon the cognitive elements. The receiver then reacts by not hearing the message, by forgetting it, by competing with the sender, or by becoming jealous of him.

The person who is perceived as feeling superior communicates that he is not willing to enter into a shared problem-solving relationship, that he probably does not desire feedback, that he does not require help, and/or that he will be likely to try to reduce the power, the status, or the worth of the receiver.

Many ways exist for creating the atmosphere that the sender feels himself equal to the listener. Defenses are reduced when one perceives the sender as being willing to enter into participative planning with mutual trust and respect. Differences in talent, ability, worth, appearance, status, and power often exist, but the low defense communicator seems to attach little importance to these distinctions.

Certainty and Provisionalism

The effects of dogmatism in producing defensiveness are well known. Those who seem to know the answers, to require no additional data, and to regard themselves as teachers rather than as co-workers tend to put others on guard. Moreover, in the writer's experiment, listeners often perceived manifest expressions of certainty as connoting inward feelings of inferiority. They saw the dogmatic individual as needing to be right, as wanting to win an argument rather than solve a problem, and as seeing his ideas as truths to be defended. This kind of behavior often was associated with acts which others regarded as attempts to exercise control. People who were right seemed to have low tolerance for members who were "wrong" (i.e., who did not agree with the sender).

One reduces the defensiveness of the listener when he communicates that he is willing to experiment with his own behavior, attitudes, and ideas. The person who appears to be taking provisional attitudes, to be investigating issues rather than taking sides on them, to be problem solving rather than debating, and to be willing to experiment and explore tends to communicate that the listener may have some control over the shared quest or the investigation of the ideas. If a person is genuinely searching for information and data, he does not resent help or company along the way.

Conclusion

The implications of the above material for the parent, the teacher, the manager, the administrator, or the therapist are fairly obvious. Arousing defensiveness interferes with communication and thus makes it difficult—and sometimes impossible—for anyone to convey ideas clearly and to move effectively toward the solution of therapeutic, educational, or managerial problems.

Endnotes

1. J. R. Gibb, "Defense Level and Influence in Small Groups," *Leadership and Interpersonal Behavior*, eds. L. Petrullo and B. M. Bass (New York: Holt, Rinehart & Winston, 1961): 66–81.

2. J. R. Gibb, "Sociopsychological Processes of Group Instruction," *The Dynamics of Instructional Groups*, ed. N. B. Henry (Fifty-Ninth Yearbook of the National Society for the Study of Education, Part 11, 1960): 115–135.

MINDFUL COMMUNICATION*

David C. Thomas

Joyce S. Osland

Interpersonal skills are competencies that all people have to some degree. They have to do with how people understand the world. We think of them as interpersonal because they are related to how people exert influence over others on a one-to-one basis. In fact, exercising interpersonal influence over others requires a range of multidimensional and complex skills. We are focusing on two of the most critical global competencies, mindful communication and creating and building trust.

Mindful Communication

Communication involves significantly more than speaking the same language. Communication is the act of transmitting messages to another person who interprets

*Adapted and reprinted with permission from *The Blackwell Handbook of Global Management: A Guide to Managing Complexity* (Blackwell Publishing, 2004): 94–108.

Todd works for an American company in Korea. Sometimes he wonders why he ever accepted a position overseas—there seems to be so much that he just doesn't understand. Todd's secretary, Chungmin, speaks English with him because he is not fluent in Korean. Nevertheless, one incident in particular occurred the previous Friday when Chungmin made a mistake and forgot to type a letter. Todd considered this a small error but made sure to mention it when he saw her during lunch in the company cafeteria. Ever since then, Chungmin has been acting rather strange and distant. When she walks out of his office, she closes the door more loudly than usual. She will not even look him in the eye, and she has been acting very moody. She even took a few days' sick leave, which she has not done in many years. Todd has no idea how to understand her behavior. Perhaps she really is ill or feels a bit overworked.

When Chungmin returned to work the following Wednesday, Todd called her into his office. "Is there a problem?" he asked. "Because if there is, we need to talk about it. It's affecting your performance. Is something wrong? Why don't you tell me? It's okay."

At this, Chungmin looked quite distressed. She admitted the problem had something to do with her mistake the previous Friday, and Todd explained that it was no big deal. "Forget it," he said, feeling satisfied with himself for working this out. "In the future, just make sure to tell me if something is wrong." But over the next few weeks, Chungmin took six more sick days and did not speak to Todd once.

Adapted from Cushner, K., & Brislin, R. W. *Cultural Interactions: A Practical Guide*, Thousand Oaks, CA: Sage, 1996.

the message by giving it meaning. In order for such exchange of meaning to occur, the sender and receiver must share common understanding. We call this shared understanding *grounding*. Such grounding is updated constantly over the course of any communication.[1] When individuals have less shared understanding, they lack common information, which explains why the difficulty of communication increases.

The miscommunication in the opening vignette also illustrates the transactional nature of the communication process.[2] Both Todd and Chungmin were sending and receiving messages, adapting their communication based on what they thought the other person was communicating to them, escalating the problem. Both have mistaken assumptions about the extent of grounding they share and expect the other person to communicate according to their own cultural script.[3] As a result, both Todd and Chungmin are communicating in a "mindless" manner. They are simply reacting to the situation in a semiautomatic way based on their own cultural grounding without considering possible cultural differences. For example, what Todd saw as giving constructive feedback, Chungmin perceived as a very rude public reprimand, which she attributed to Todd's thoughtlessness. She responded, mindlessly, by using a Korean script for expressing her displeasure through subtle cues. Because Todd was a novice at intercultural interaction, he failed to perceive this message accurately (he lacked knowledge of Korean culture and grounding) and had difficulty figuring out and making an accurate attribution for Chungmin's behavior. He tried to solve the problem by having an open and frank discussion with Chungmin, another U. S. communication script that was not well received.

Once negative emotions were involved, Chungmin had even less motivation to decode Todd's communication accurately. She responded with more subtle cues to show her discomfort and began to stereotype Todd as an Ugly American. Like an airplane in an ever tightening spin, Todd and Chungmin's failure to correctly diagnose the situation and behave effectively resulted in a negative spiral that only an expert interculturalist could pull out of. The best way to recover from this type of situation is to avoid it in the first place, by learning to engage in mindful communication across cultures.

In this part of the chapter, we first explore what mindful communication is. The two most critical contributors to mindful communication are knowledge of the culture and communication skills, both of which we investigate. We then describe how to build competency in mindful communication and close with a brief summary.

What *Mindful* Communication Is

Mindfulness means attending to one's internal assumptions, cognitions, and emotions, and simultaneously attuning to the other's assumptions, cognitions, and emotions. It also involves learning to see behavior or information presented in the situation as novel or fresh: viewing a situation from several vantage points or perspectives; attending to the context and the person in which we are perceiving the behavior; and creating new categories through which this new behavior may be understood.[4] The antithesis of mindfulness, *mindlessness*, is exemplified in the following vignette.

Mindlessness

Yesterday, my wife called me at work and asked me to pick up some groceries for dinner on my way home. I have a carefully selected route home that I have designed to minimize traffic, and I follow it every day. In order to stop at the grocery store, I would have to make a slight adjustment to the route. Only after I arrived home to be greeted with the question, "Where are the groceries?", did I realize that I had automatically driven my normal route straight home.

The act of driving an automobile is a complex behavior, but most of us do it this semiautomatic way. And in this case, even when we have been cued to break out of our script, we fall back into it. Much of our behavior, including communication behavior, occurs in this scripted, seemingly mindless manner, which is a semi-reflexive response to the situation. As shown in the opening vignette, the adverse results of mindless communication across cultures are all too apparent. Someone who does not share the same cultural grounding easily misunderstands semi-reflexive communication guided by cultural norms. Mindfulness, on the other hand, puts us in a stage of readiness to interact with people who are different from ourselves. As such, it is a mediating step in linking knowledge with skillful practice.

Mindful communication can be judged by the criteria of appropriateness, effectiveness, and satisfaction.[5] Appropriate communication matches the expectations of both sender and receiver and is perceived as proper. Effective communication achieves mutual shared meaning and the goals desired by the communicators. Finally, satisfaction occurs when a communicator's desired identity image is affirmed rather than disconfirmed during the interaction. Competence in intercultural communication involves (1) the heightened mindfulness described above, which builds on (2) the acquisition of in-depth knowledge, and the development of (3) communication skills. We address both knowledge and communication in the following sections.

Knowledge of the Culture

An in-depth knowledge of the culture of the other party in a cross-cultural communication is an important first step in negotiating shared meaning. Understanding cultural values is the foundation for comprehending and decoding the behavior of others and ourselves. Cultural values result in different communication norms that individuals use to guide behavior in certain settings. Knowledge of cultural identities, values, attitudes, and communication practices such as those described previously makes for greater predictability and more accurate attributions. This knowledge allows a better grasp on the internal logic and modal behavior of another culture, which can serve as a first best-guess[6] about behavior in another culture. For instance, individualists tend to express themselves in low-context, direct communication because they value efficiency and are asserting an independent self-identity.

Developing cultural knowledge and sensitivity, a process supported by a global mindset, helps global managers understand the habitual verbal and nonverbal messages and the interaction styles they observe in the multicultural workplace and overseas. Global managers need general knowledge they can extrapolate to incidents to form hypotheses about cultural behavior. Knowledge provides the basic lesson that not all cultures communicate in the same way. Therefore, special attention and caution are required before accurate interpretations can be made. Key elements of knowledge that are important to mindful intercultural communication include knowledge about the communication process itself and about the effects of language, communication style, and nonverbal communication.

The Communication Process

Communication occurs within social systems, and each communicator has a personal context, a field of experience. These backgrounds cause people to encode and decode messages in a unique fashion, which makes it necessary to find a shared field of experience or common grounding. Like all behavior, much communication proceeds in a routine manner without much conscious thought and is consistent with the cultural field in which it is embedded. The communication process can be influenced, however, by "noise," anything that interferes with the intended communication, such as environmental, physiological, and emotional states.

The entire communication process is embedded in culture, which affects how messages are encoded (converted to symbolic form) and sent by some means (a channel) to the receiver, who then interprets (decodes) the message. In this chapter, we define mindful intercultural communication as *a symbolic exchange in which individuals interactively negotiate shared meanings.*[7] The effectiveness of this exchange is critical in a business environment characterized by an ever-increasing number of intercultural interactions. Mastering the intercultural communication process is a fundamental requirement of effective international management.

The basic model of intercultural interaction presented in this section provides a tool for examining the effects of culture on communication. As shown in Figure 1, we can envision intercultural communication as involving three related stages, all affected by culture.

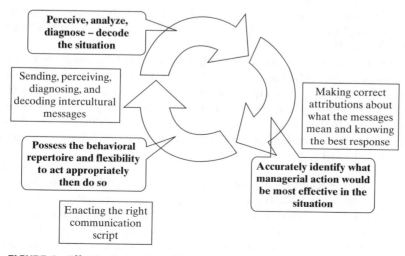

FIGURE 1 **Effective Intercultural Communication**

The first stage concerns how messages are sent, perceived, diagnosed, and decoded. In the second stage, individuals must identify how to respond, which involves making attributions about the meaning of the message they have received. Finally, individuals must choose from their repertoire of possible responses and enact those that they think are most appropriate in the third stage. This requires a degree of behavioral flexibility that often separates novices from experts. Expert intercultural communicators are better at diagnosing and decoding messages and more skilled at choosing and enacting effective scripts. The effectiveness of the communication depends on a lack of distortion, which can occur at any stage of the process. Common sources of distortion, explained in the following section, include language, communication style, non-verbal communication, social categorization and stereotyping, and the willingness to communicate.

Language

An obvious consideration in intercultural communication is the language being used. Three aspects of language influence the ability to create shared meanings. These are language fluency, language accommodation, and second-language use.

LANGUAGE FLUENCY With reference to our basic model on intercultural interaction, fluency in a foreign language affects a global manager's ability to accurately perceive and diagnose the situation and limits the behavioral repertoire with which he or she can respond. However, the relationship between language fluency and effective communication is not so straightforward that we can simply say more fluency is always better. First, compared to a total lack of fluency, a small amount of language skill (knowing a few words) is beneficial to a manager. To reach a higher level of benefit in intercultural interactions, however, individuals need to develop a much more advanced degree of fluency that permits "conversational currency" (being able to make conversation about everyday things such as local sporting events, and so on).[8] Second, the willingness to communicate with others who are culturally different may be more important than fluency itself.[9] Finally, fluency in a foreign language creates certain perceptions among host-country nationals. Fluent foreign managers are perceived as having beliefs more closely aligned with the locals. Furthermore, host-country nationals may also assume that higher degrees of language fluency by a manager are linked to higher competency in other areas, such as knowledge of cultural norms. For example, cultural blunders by a foreign manager are more likely to be forgiven when people are less fluent; fluency sometimes brings higher expectations for culturally appropriate behavior.[10]

People often restrict their communication to those who speak their own language. For example, when large MNCs buy a local company in countries with a different language, they sometimes appoint as their liaison or local manager the host-country national who is most fluent in the language of the MNC. This person is not necessarily the most competent or best able to teach them about the local subsidiary and context; however, the transaction costs of communicating with them are the lowest.[11]

LANGUAGE ACCOMMODATION In our opening vignette, Chungmin accommodated to Todd's inability to speak Korean and spoke English. Language accommodation often relates to the behavioral flexibility stage of our model and identifying the behavior that is most appropriate to the particular situation. Determining who will accommodate can be complex and depends on the motives of the parties in the interaction, the identities of the parties, and the situation itself.[12] Japanese managers, for example, tend to believe that it is not possible for foreigners to be really fluent in the Japanese language and will automatically switch to the foreigner's language. The effort that one party puts into accommodating the other's language is often appreciated and reciprocated. In business situations, the default language is often English, but as we will see in the next section, expecting people to work in a second language may have drawbacks.

SECOND-LANGUAGE USE Most intercultural communication involves at least one of the parties switching to a second language. Often this means switching into English. Using a second or bridge language (second language for both parties) may be the most appropriate behavioral response, but the use of a second language has a number of implications for cross-cultural communication. First, working in a second language can create cognitive strain, requiring more effort on the part of second-language users and putting them at a disadvantage. Over long periods of time, second language use can be exhausting. Second, if the native language speaker is unable to recognize signals that indicate lack of understanding or does not work to create an environment where it is acceptable to check for understanding, the second-language speaker may pretend to understand in order to appear competent or avoid embarrassment. To avoid distortion, both participants must devote more attention to the communication process in order to achieve a negotiated meaning.

Communication Style

Having a language in common does not ensure mutual understanding. Todd and Chungmin spoke the same language, but the differences in their communication styles distorted their communication. Communication style differences are logical extensions of the internalized values and norms of their respective cultures. They are often a barrier to effectively perceiving, analyzing, and decoding intercultural interactions. To avoid misinterpretations and false attributions, managers who work across cultures must learn the culturally based rules that govern the style, conventions, and practices of language use. Some of the most common style differences are high-context versus low-context communication, direct versus indirect communication, succinct versus elaborate communication, and self-enhancement versus self-effacement. We now review each of these style differences.

HIGH- AND LOW-CONTEXT STYLES[13] Cultures vary in terms of the extent to which they use language itself to communicate the message. Low-context communication relies on explicit verbal messages to convey intention or meaning, whereas in high-context communication most of the information is either contained in the physical context or internalized in the person; very little is in the coded or explicit part of the message. In the opening vignette, Todd, in accordance with his low-context style, expected Chungmin to communicate in words. Given her high-context style, she expected him to read the meaning in her nonverbal communication and actions, as the Indonesian mother did below.

High-Context Communication

An Indonesian woman invited the mother of the young man who was courting her daughter to tea. The woman was not pleased with the possibility that her daughter might marry into a family that she viewed as having a lower socioeconomic status. During the visit she never mentioned the relationship of their children, but she served bananas with the tea, an unlikely combination. The message that her son did not belong with the woman's daughter any more than bananas go with tea was subtle and implicit; nonetheless, the young man's mother received the message loud and clear.

Source: Thomas, D., *Essentials of International Management: A Cross-Cultural Perspective*, Thousand Oaks, CA: Sage, 2000.

As shown in this example, high-context communication involves multilayered contexts (historical context, social norms, roles, situational and relational contexts), and the listener is expected to understand the nuances of the implicit messages. In contrast, in the low-context communication style, the onus lies on the sender to transmit a clear, explicit message that listeners can easily decode. High-context style is more likely in collectivist cultures such as Asia and Latin America, whereas low-context style is found in individualist cultures such as Switzerland, Germany, and the United States.

DIRECT VERSUS INDIRECT COMMUNICATION Cultures also vary in the extent to which their language and tone of voice reveal or hide intent. Speakers who use a direct style specify their intentions in a forthright manner, whereas in the indirect style nuances in verbal statements hide the speaker's meaning. People from cultures using indirect styles (typically collectivists, such as Chungmin in the opening vignette) may perceive those with a direct style as blunt or insensitive. Conversely, Westerners (such as Todd), who prefer a direct style, often perceive the indirect style of Eastern cultures as insincere and untrustworthy. This is understandable, because in collectivist cultures being polite and avoiding embarrassment often takes precedence over *truth*, as truth is defined in individualist cultures. For collectivists, the social setting determines the degree of directness or truthfulness that is appropriate.

SUCCINCT VERSUS ELABORATE COMMUNICATION Communication styles also vary in terms of the quantity of talk (or silence) used to communicate. Styles range from succinct (low quantity of talk), to exacting (just the right amount of words), to elaborate (a high quantity of talk).[14] Failure to recognize these differences often results in misattributions that are barriers to negotiated shared meanings. People with a succinct style may discount elaborate speakers as illogical or inefficient and may even stop listening to them. Elaborate speakers may assume that succinct communicators have very little to say or contribute. The periods of silence used in Eastern cultures are often misunderstood by Westerners, who interpret them as a lack of understanding and then try to shorten them with further explanation or with moving on to the next point. In multicultural work groups, members of highly verbal cultures often fill in the silences and do not allow enough room for people with a more succinct style to talk.

Arab cultures have an elaborate style, involving detailed descriptions, repetition, verbal elaboration and exaggeration, and the use of metaphor, similes, and proverbs. In contrast, the exacting style, typical of England, Germany, Finland, and Sweden, emphasizes clarity and precise meanings. These cultures perceive the use of too many words as exaggeration, while the use of too few words is viewed as ambiguity. The succinct styles of China, Japan, Korea, and Thailand are characterized by understatements and meaningful pauses. To some extent, the succinct style of collectivist cultures employs silence as a way of controlling the communication interaction in the same way that individualists use talking.[15]

SELF-ENHANCEMENT VERSUS SELF-EFFACEMENT The self-enhancement verbal style emphasizes the importance of boasting about one's accomplishments and abilities. The self-effacement verbal style, on the other hand, emphasizes the importance of humbling oneself via verbal restraints, hesitations, modest talk, and the use of self-deprecation concerning one's effort or performance.[16] Failures to establish shared meanings occur when people from self-enhancing cultures do not perceive the accomplishments and real worth of people from self-effacing cultures. Furthermore, employees from self-effacing cultures find "selling themselves" to gain promotion in self-enhancing cultures difficult and even repugnant. For example, when counseled to explain why he was the best person for a promotion, a Chinese engineer opted instead to quit one U.S. firm for another that was more cross-culturally sensitive and accustomed to working with Asians. Negative perceptions can also occur when the boastful mode of self-enhancers is not well received in self-effacing cultures. Collectivist Asian cultures are generally self-effacing, while Arab and African-American cultures are self-enhancing.

This style difference also relates to the use of praise—how frequently praise is used, what is praised, and the appropriate response to it. For example, Americans use praise frequently and are prone to praise people who are close to them, such as friends or family; they are also likely to praise physical appearance. Japanese are more likely to praise strangers, and Arabs are more likely to praise skill and work than physical characteristics. Response to praise also varies across cultures. In cultures like China, where modesty is a virtue, praise may cause embarrassment. The Hong Kong Chinese, for example, tend to deflect praise, whereas British people are more likely to politely accept it.[17]

Nonverbal Communication

Nonverbal communication (such as Chungmin slamming the door and avoiding eye contact) conveys important messages and is produced more automatically than words. It includes body movements and gestures, facial expressions and facial gazing, tone of voice, and the emphasis of certain words. According to some researchers, as much as 70 percent of communication between people in the same language group is non-verbal.[18] It is possible that people rely even more heavily on the non-verbal component in cross-cultural communications.

Non-verbal communication helps to regulate intercultural interaction by providing information about our feelings and emotional state, adding meaning to our verbal messages, and governing the timing and sequencing of the interaction. Non-verbal behaviors serve the same functions across cultures. As with language, however, nonverbal systems of communication have a significant amount of variation around the world. Failures in establishing shared meanings occur because the same nonverbal behavior can have very different meanings across cultures, and because the same meaning is conveyed by different nonverbal cues in different cultures. For example, in Samoa people sit down to show respect, whereas in many cultures they stand up; showing the sole of one's shoe in a Moslem society is a sign of great disrespect; and, while in North America repeatedly crooking the index finger with the palm up beckons another person to come closer, this same gesture is obscene in some cultures.

As with all intercultural behavior, individuals often fall into the trap of using their own cultural lenses to interpret and explain non-verbal gestures. The challenge is to interpret nonverbal communication as intended by the senders, not as it would be perceived in our own culture.

Table 1 outlines some of the most common categories of non-verbal behaviors and their influence in intercultural communication.

Communication Skills

Intercultural communication skills are our ability to interact effectively in a given situation; they consist of mindful observation, mindful listening, identity confirmation, and collaborative dialogue.[20] They also include the willingness to communicate.

Mindful observation involves an analytical sequence of observing, describing, interpreting, and suspending evaluation when we encounter new behavior. Mindful observation and reliance on description of cultural behavior that is different from one's own is more effective than are reflexive and often evaluative attributions about this behavior. When a Samoan student visited one of the authors, he immediately seated himself without being invited to do so and averted his eyes. Instead of evaluating this behavior as casual and disrespectful, the mindful response would be to think

Table 1	Categories of Non-verbal Behavior
Tone of voice	Pitch, volume, speed, tension, variation, enunciation, and a number of other voice qualities such as breathiness or creakiness convey different meaning based on cultural norms.
Proxemics[19]	People follow predictable patterns when establishing distance between themselves and others that are consistent with cultural norms. However, what is appropriate in one culture may seem unusual or even offensive in another.
Body position	The way people position their body conveys information in all cultures. People learn which body position is appropriate in a given situation in the same way that they internalize other aspects of culture. The vast array of possible body positions is difficult to categorize in any systematic way.
Gestures	Hand gestures are used both intentionally and unintentionally in communication. Those gestures that are used as a substitute for words are called emblems. Because the hand can be configured in numerous ways and with great precision, the number of possible hand gestures is quite extensive. To further complicate matters, the same hand gesture can have different meanings in different parts of the world.
Facial expression	Underlying emotional states seem to be closely linked to facial expression. The six basic emotions of anger, fear, sadness, disgust, happiness, and surprise are evident in facial expressions around the world from a very early age. However, individuals often deliberately seek to override the link between their emotions and their facial expressions as a result of display rules appropriate to their culture.
Eye contact (gaze)	All cultures utilize eye contact (gaze) in non-verbal communication. Maintaining and avoiding eye contact communicate important messages. Cultural differences in gaze patterns seem to be fixed relatively early in life and persist regardless of subsequent cross-cultural experiences.

"He sat down immediately upon entering the room and is not making eye contact with me. Perhaps this is appropriate behavior in Samoa, even though in my culture it is disrespectful. I need to check this out before making any judgments or reacting to this behavior." Investigation revealed that for Samoans to stare at or occupy a position physically above a person of higher status is exceedingly impolite. Mindful observation involves a reflective inner dialogue grounded in non-judgmental description and interpretation. It also requires self-awareness so people can monitor and control their reactions to the "different" behaviors and interactions.

Mindful listening refers to hearing more than just the words that are said. It also involves checking for accurate perception and paraphrasing the speaker's message into one's own words. Checking for mutual understanding and shared meanings is critical in order to overcome all the possible barriers in an intercultural interaction.

Identity confirmation means addressing people by their preferred titles, labels and identities, and using inclusive rather than exclusive language. This behavior indicates a sensitivity to and respect for the perceptions people have of themselves. For example, in Latin American cultures, people of a certain rank usually expect to be addressed with the formal verb tense (*Usted* rather than *tú*) until they signal otherwise, with the title that reflects their occupation (*Ingeniero* [Engineer] Gonzalez) or educational degree (*Licenciado* [college graduate] Martinez), or with a deferential term of respect (*Don* or *Doña*) before their first name. Ignoring these communication rules disconfirms their sense of identity or the way they see themselves.

Collaborative dialogue means suspending one's assumptions about culturally different people and refraining from imposing one's views on them. Engaging in collaborative dialogue is analogous to what has been called an ethno-relative perspective.[21] In contrast to ethnocentrism (viewing one's own culture as superior), an ethno-relative approach involves greater recognition and acceptance of cultural differences. It assumes that behavior can be understood only within a cultural context rather than judged on a universal standard of right or wrong.

Willingness to communicate is involved in both perceiving and decoding the intercultural situation and identifying appropriate behavioral responses to that situation. This willingness to communicate is influenced both by the way we view other groups and how receptive we are to communication. When people categorize others and themselves as members of particular groups, such as a cultural group, they make assumptions that affect their beliefs, attitudes, and behaviors. They see people less as individuals and more as members of the group to which they belong. They assume group members are relatively more similar with regard to their beliefs and behavior, and the group is believed to be a more important cause of their behavior than individual characteristics.[22]

The in-group out-group boundary that results from social categorization has several implications for the way individuals select, structure, and process social information. First, this categorization invokes a comparison of one's own group with other cultural groups, resulting in intergroup bias. While it can be either positive or negative, inter-group bias most often favors one's own group. People are more likely to respond favorably to information from an in-group member. Novices to international work are often heard making such negative comparisons between host-country nationals and their own culture ("People are more reliable, ethical, trustworthy, and so on, in my country"). Expert interculturalists avoid comparisons and sweeping generalizations and use stereotypes only when they are helpful as a first "best-guess" about how others might act. Second, in-group members sometimes develop their own brand of communication, especially the nonverbal component, which can be very difficult for an out-group member to interpret correctly. Finally, when people categorize others as out-group members, they tend to rely on stereotypes when interacting with them. Stereotyping means assigning identical characteristics to all members of a group, regardless of the actual variation among them.[23] Based on relatively little information, stereotypes are resistant to change even in light of new information and are rarely accurately applied to specific individuals.[24]

Stereotypes affect the senders' ability to communicate their messages because they interfere with their ability to be "heard" and accurately judged. The senders' stereotype about receivers also determines how much and what type of information they will share with them. Stereotypes create expectations of how out-group members will behave. These expectations, in turn, influence the way in which we interpret incoming messages and the predictions we make about out-group member behavior.

Early research on stereotypes indicated that people could nurture intense stereotypes about other national cultures even though they had never met a person from that culture.[25] Such cultural stereotypes are often associated with other groups with which one's culture has had a long (often negative) history. National stereotypes may also be susceptible to what is called social dominance theory,[26] which involves a hierarchy of nationalities based on generally accepted status. High status may be attached to a particular nation because of economic dominance or other desirable characteristics. For example, some cultures give Canadians and Norwegians high status because of their generous foreign aid and peacemaking roles. According to this theory, the extent to which one's national group has high status will influence the attitude of others toward a communicator. Their message is more likely to be attended to by others.

The final factor with regard to the willingness of individuals to communicate is receptiveness. Receptiveness involves both cosmopolitanism and satisficing behavior. Cosmopolitanism refers to the willingness to engage with others who are different.[27]

People with a cosmopolitan mindset are more likely to seek out and communicate with "strangers," even when doing so requires extra effort.

One's willingness to continue making an effort to communicate across cultures can be affected by satisficing. Satisficing in decision making refers to accepting a decision that is "good enough" because the costs of maximizing are too great.[28] In an intercultural context, we find satisficing in two areas, in the plateauing that occurs in both language acquisition and cultural understanding.[29] When these skills are good enough to get by, some people stop learning. There is no motivation to reach a higher level of cultural understanding or fluency unless an event occurs that initiates another round of cultural sensemaking or a return to the dictionary or language teacher.

Developing Competence in Mindful Communication

Communication competence is a strong predictor of job performance, psychological adjustment, overall intercultural effectiveness in living in the host culture, the extent of social interaction with host nationals, and transfer of technology.[30] We suggest the path to communication competence is through mindful communication. Experts in mindful intercultural communication possess these competencies: empathy, respect, interest in the local culture and people, flexibility, tolerance, nonjudgmental attitudes, initiative, open-mindedness, sociability, positive self-image, positive attitudes, and stress tolerance.[31] Kealey contends that effective intercultural communicators are characterized by adaptation skills, cross-cultural skills, and partnership skills,[32] all of which are necessary for global managers.

There is a large body of research indicating that cross-cultural training can be effective in sensitizing individuals to cultural issues, enhancing cultural self-awareness and empathy, decreasing the use of negative stereotypes, developing complex rather than oversimplified thinking about another culture, and facilitating cross-cultural interaction.[33] Such training significantly increases employee productivity, business skills, and commitment to the employer.[34] In today's diverse, virtual workplace, mindful communication has become essential even for people without a passport.

Endnotes

1. For a discussion of the concept of grounding, see Clark, H. H., and Brennan, S. E., "Grounding in Communication" in L. B. Resnick, J. M. Levine, and S. D. Teasley, eds., *Perspectives on `Socially Shared Cognition* (Washington, D. C.: American Psychological Association, 1991).

2. J. T. Wood (1997) provides a good description of the transactional communication process in *Communication in Our Lives* (New York: Wadsworth, 1997).

3. For a description of cultural scripts, see Triandis, H. C., Marin, G., Lisansky, J., and Betancourt, H., *Simpatía* as a Cultural Script of Hispanics, *Journal of Personality and Social Psychology*, 47(6), 1984: 1363–1375.

4. For more on the concept of mindfulness see Thich, N. H., *Peace Is Every Step: The Path of Mindfulness in Everyday Life*, (New York: Bantam Books, 1991) and Langer, E. J.,

The Power of Mindful Learning, (Reading, MA: Addison-Wesley, 1997).

5. For a more complete discussion see Ting-Toomey, S. (1999), *Communicating across Cultures*, New York: The Guilford Press.

6. The idea of using stereotypical behavior as a first best guess is presented in Adler, N. J. (1997), *International Dimensions of Organizational Behavior*, 3rd ed., Cincinnati: South-Western.

7. Many of the ideas about the influence of culture on communication presented in this section are drawn from Stella Ting-Toomey's excellent book, *Communicating across Cultures* (1999).

8. The idea of "conversational currency" was first presented by Brein, D., and David, K. H. (1971), "Intercultural

Communication and the Adjustment of the Sojourner," *Psychological Bulletin*, 76(3): 215–230.

9. Empirical evidence of this idea is presented in Benson, P. G. (1978), "Measuring Cross-Cultural Adjustment: The Problem of Criteria," *International Journal of Intercultural Relations*, 2(1): 21–37.

10. For a more complete discussion of this point see Hui, H. C., and Cheng, I. W. M. (1987), "Effects of Second Language Proficiency of Speakers and Listeners on Person Perception and Behavioural Intention: A Study of Chinese Bilinguals," *International Journal of Psychology*, 22: 421–430.

11. For more information on the relationship between intercultural communication and organizational learning, see Taylor, S., and Osland, J. S. (2002), "The Impact of Intercultural Communication on Global Organizational Learning, in M. Easterby-Smith and M. A. Lyles (eds.), *Handbook of Organizational Learning and Knowledge*, Oxford: Blackwell: 212–232.

12. A more complete discussion of language accommodation can be found in Gallois, C., and Callan, V. (1997), *Communication and Culture: A Guide for Practice*, Chichester: John Wiley.

13. The high- and low-context communication style was first identified by Hall, E. T. (1976), *Beyond Culture*, New York: Doubleday. Also see Ting-Toomey (1999): 272.

14. This style consideration is well documented in Gudykunst, W. B., Ting-Toomey, S., and Chua, E. (1988), *Culture and Interpersonal Communication*, Newbury Park: CA: Sage.

15. For more information about the cultural use of this style see Giles, H., Coupland, N., and Wiemann, J. M. (1992), "Talk Is Cheap. . . . but My word Is My Bond: Beliefs About Talk," in K. Bolton and H. Kwok (eds.), *Sociolinguistics Today: International Perspectives*, London: Routledge: 218–243.

16. For more information on this style difference see Ting-Toomey (1999).

17. Two empirical studies with regard to praise across cultures are Barnlund, D. C., and Araki, S. (1985), "Intercultural Encounters: The management of Compliments by Japanese and Americans," *Journal of Cross-Cultural Psychology*, 16: 9–26; and Loh, T. W. C. (1993), "Responses to Compliments Across Languages and Cultures: A Comparative Study of British and Hong Kong Chinese," research report no. 30, City University of Hong Kong.

18. Based on Noller, P. (1984), *Nonverbal Communication and Marital Interaction*, Oxford: Pergamon.

19. *Proxemics* is the term that has been coined to describe the study the way in which people use personal space in their interactions with others. See Hall, E. T. (1966), *The Hidden Dimension*, Garden City, NY: Doubleday.

20. Ting-Toomey (1999).

21. See Bennett, M. (1993), "Towards ethnorelativism: A Developmental Model of Intercultural Sensitivity," in R. M. Paige (ed.), *Education for the Intercultural Experience*, Yarmouth, ME: Intercultural Press: 21–71.

22. For a more complete discussion of social categorization see Wilder, D. A. (1986), "Social Categorization: Implications for Creation and Reduction of Intergroup Bias," in L. Berkowitz (ed.), *Advances in Experimental Social Psychology*, New York: Academic Press, Vol. 19: 291–355.

23. See E. Aronson (1976), *The Social Animal*, San Francisco: W. H. Freeman, for one of the original descriptions of stereotyping.

24. For more information on stereotypes see Ashmore, R. D., and Del Boca, F. K. (1981), "Conceptual Approaches to Stereotypes and Stereotyping," in D. L. Hamilton (ed.), *Cognitive Processes in Stereotyping and Intergroup Behavior*, Hillsdale, NJ: Erlbaum: 1–35.

25. For example, see Katz, D., and Braly, K. W. (1933), "Verbal Stereotypes and Racial prejudice," *Journal of Abnormal and Social Psychology*, 28: 280–290.

26. See Sidanius, J. (1993), "The Psychology of Group Conflict and the Dynamics of Oppression: A Social Dominance Perspective," in S. Iyenger and W. McGuire (eds.), *Explorations in Political Psychology*, Durham, NC: Duke University Press.

27. See Hannerz, U (1996), "Cosmopolitans and Locals in World Culture," in U. Hannerz, *Transnational Connections: Culture, People, Places*, London: Routledge: 102–111.

28. For more information on satisficing see Simon, H. A. (1955), "A Behavioral Model of Rational Choice," *Quarterly Journal of Economics*, 69: 129–138.

29. For a more complete discussion of satisficing in an intercultural context see Osland, J. S. (1995), *The Adventure of Working Abroad: Hero Tales from the Global Frontier*, San Francisco, CA: Jossey-Bass; and Osland, J., and Bird, A. (2000), "Beyond Sophisticated Stereotyping: Cultural Sensemaking in Context," *Academy of Management Executive*, 14(1), 65–87.

30. These findings are located in Ruben, B. D., and Kealey, D. J. (1979), "Behavioral Assessment of Communication Competency and the Prediction of Cross-Cultural Adaptation," *International Journal of Intercultural Relations*, 3: 15–48; Hammer, M. R. (1989), "Intercultural Communication Competence, in M. K. Asante and W. B. Gudykunst (eds.), *Handbook of International and Intercultural Communication*, Newbury Park, CA: Sage: 247–260; Hawes, F., and Kealey, D. J. (1981), "An Empirical Study of Canadian Technical assistance," *International Journal of Intercultural Relations*, 5(3): 239–258; and Clarke, C., and Hammer, M. R. (1995), "Predictors of Japanese and American Managers' Job success, Personal Adjustment, and Intercultural Interaction Effectiveness," *International Management Review*, 35(2): 153–170.

31. This list is compiled from the work of Kealey, D. J., and Ruben, B. D. (1983), "Cross-Cultural Personnel Selection Criteria, Issues, and Methods," in D. Landis and R. W. Brislin (eds.), *Handbook of Intercultural Training, Vol. 1: Issues in*

Training and Design, New York: Pergamon; Kealey, D. J. (1996), "The challenge of International Personnel Selection," in D. Landis and R. S. Bhagat (eds.), *Handbook of Intercultural Training*, 2nd ed., Thousand Oaks, CA: Sage: 81–105; and Chen, G. M., and Starosta, W. J. (1996), "Intercultural Communication Competence: A Synthesis, *Communication Yearbook*, 19: 353–383.

32. See Kealey (1996).

33. Bhawuk, D. P. S., and Brislin, R. W. (2000), "Cross-Cultural Training: A Review," *Applied Psychology*, 49(1): 162–191; Hammer, M. R., and Martin, J. N. (1996), "The Effects of Cross-cultural Training on American Managers in a Japanese–American Joint Venture," *Journal of Applied Communication Research*, 20(2): 161–182; Black, J. S., and Mendenhall, M. (1990), Cross-Cultural Training Effectiveness: A Review and a Theoretical Framework for Future Research, *Academy of Management Review* 15(1): 113–136.

34. Hammer, M. R. (1995), "Making the Case with the Corporation: Tracking the Effects of an International Management Development Program," Presentation Given at the 21st annual congress of the Society for Intercultural Education, Training, and Research, Phoenix, AZ, May 14–17.

10 Perception and Attribution

STEREOTYPE THREAT AT WORK
Loriann Roberson,
Carol T. Kulik

COMMUNICATING ACROSS CULTURES
Nancy J. Adler

This chapter deals with perception, the process by which we select, organize, and evaluate the stimuli in our environment to make it meaningful for ourselves. As a result, people can look at the same event or behavior and take away very different impressions and conclusions about what they "saw." People also make attributions, assigning causes to the behaviors they observe, in unique ways. Dealing with conflicting perceptions and attributions makes many aspects of organizational life more challenging—in particular, communication, teamwork, performance evaluation, and strategic decisions. One of the most common perception-related problems is stereotyping, which occurs when we attribute behavior or attitudes to people on the basis of the group or category to which they belong.

Loriann Roberson, professor of psychology and education at Columbia University, and Carol Kulik, a human resources professor at the University of South Australia, examine how stereotype threat—the fear of being judged according to a negative stereotype—can adversely affect performance. Reviewing over a dozen years of research, they suggest that stereotype threat may be a pervasive organizational phenomenon that affects a broad array of employees. Roberson and Kulik provide practical guidelines for reducing the negative consequences of stereotype threat when it does occur and for creating environments in which stereotype threat is minimized.

The potential for inaccurate perceptions, mistaken attributions, and stereotyping is very obvious in cross-cultural interactions. Nancy Adler, a well-known international management consultant and McGill University scholar, describes the primary difficulties of "Communicating Across Cultures." She provides numerous examples of cultural errors in perception and a framework for understanding why they occur. Adler contends that stereotypes can be both helpful and harmful and provides advice on using them in a positive way.

STEREOTYPE THREAT AT WORK*

Loriann Roberson

Carol T. Kulik

EXECUTIVE OVERVIEW

Managing diversity in organizations requires creating an environment where all employees can succeed. This paper explains how understanding "stereotype threat"—the fear of being judged according to a negative stereotype—can help managers create positive environments for diverse employees. While stereotype threat has received a great deal of academic research attention, the issue is usually framed in the organizational literature as a problem affecting performance on tests used for admission and selection decisions. Further, articles discussing stereotype threat usually report the results of experimental studies and are targeted to an academic audience. We summarize 12 years of research findings on stereotype threat, address its commonplace occurrence in the workplace, and consider how interventions effective in laboratory settings for reducing stereotype threat might be implemented by managers in organizational contexts. We end the paper with a discussion of how attention to stereotype threat can improve the management of diversity in organizations.

Ongoing demographic trends (increasing percentages of African Americans, Hispanics, and Asians in the American workforce, an aging population, expanding female labor force participation) have made diversity a fact of organizational life. When these trends were first identified in the mid-1980s, they were heralded as an opportunity for organizations to become more creative, to reach previously untapped markets, and in general to achieve and maintain a competitive advantage (Cox, 1994; Robinson & Dechant, 1997; Thomas & Ely, 1996).

However, employee diversity does not *necessarily* boost creativity, market share, or competitive advantage. In fact, research suggests that left unmanaged, employee diversity is more likely to damage morale, increase turnover, and cause significant communication problems and conflict within the organization (Jackson et al., 1991; Jehn, Neale, & Northcraft, 1999; Tsui, Egan, & O'Reilly, 1992; Zenger & Lawrence, 1989). Thus, "managing diversity" has become a sought-after managerial skill, and concerns about effective diversity management have spawned an industry of diversity training programs, diversity videos, and diversity consultants. But despite several decades of effort and millions of dollars invested, the evidence suggests that organizations continue to do a poor job of managing diversity. A recent comprehensive report concluded that organizations rarely are able to leverage diversity and capitalize on its potential benefits (Hansen, 2003; Kochan et al., 2003). What's the problem? Are we missing a key piece of the diversity management puzzle?

Most of the attention in the diversity management literature has been focused on the organizational decision maker—the manager who is prejudiced against certain groups and who allows these prejudices to influence how he or she treats employees. These individual-level prejudices become institutionalized—meaning, they become embodied in organizational policies and practices that systematically disadvantage some employees. In their efforts to reduce discrimination, organizations are increasingly concerned about hiring non-prejudiced managers, redesigning biased selection, appraisal, and promotion procedures, and generally eradicating stereotypes from managerial decision making (Greengard, 2003; Rice, 1996). If we eliminate stereotypes from organizational decision making, the logic goes, we'll create an organization where all employees can flourish and advance.

Unfortunately, even if an organization were successful in hiring only non-prejudiced managers and eliminating stereotypes from its formal decision making, stereotypes would still exist in broader society. As a result, every employee walking through the door of the organization knows the stereotypes that *might* be applied to him or her and wonders whether organizational decision makers and co-workers will endorse those stereotypes. Here, we discuss the effects of these stereotypes, and highlight an important aspect of diversity management that has not received much attention by diversity or management scholars: stereotype threat, the fear of being judged and treated according to a negative stereotype about members of your group (Steele, Spencer, & Aronson, 2002). Research on stereotype threat has shown that societal stereotypes can have a negative effect on employee feelings and behavior, making it difficult for an employee to perform to his or her true potential. Research has also indicated that stereotype threat can result in employees working harder, but not better. When stereotype threat is present, performance declines. Therefore, a non-prejudiced manager who uses objective performance indicators as a basis for decision making risks underestimating the employee's true ability. When an organizational context contains the conditions that create stereotype threat, nontraditional employees experience additional barriers to success despite the good intentions of everyone involved. Therefore, stereotype threat places certain demands on the manager of diverse employees—demands to create conditions that minimize the occurrence of stereotype threat, so that all employees can perform effectively.

Stereotype threat has been discussed almost exclusively as an issue for high stakes testing, particularly in educational arenas. For example, we're all familiar with the opportunities that hang on scores from tests such as the Scholastic Aptitude Test (SAT), the Graduate Record Examination (GRE) and the Graduate Management Achievement Test (GMAT): without the "right" scores, a student won't be able to get into the best college for his or her chosen field. In 1999, PBS aired a documentary concluding that stereotype threat was suppressing the standardized test performance of African American students (Chandler, 1999). These effects on high stakes tests are important, but stereotype threat is not limited to African-American students taking large-scale standardized academic tests. It is also present in the everyday, routine situations that are a part of all jobs. Thus, knowledge of stereotype threat and its corrosive effects on performance is needed to understand the work experience of members of stereotyped groups and to manage diversity more effectively in the organization. In this article, we answer the following questions: What is stereotype threat and what are its effects? How can stereotype threat be reduced?

We begin with a short review of the concept and the research evidence. We then describe the conditions that increase the risk of stereotype threat. Because these conditions regularly occur in the workplace, stereotype threat is also likely to be a common part of many people's work experience. Finally, we present strategies for reducing stereotype threat from the academic research literature, and consider if and how those strategies might be applied in organizations. We also discuss how attention to stereotype threat adds value to current organizational approaches to managing diversity.

Stereotype Threat at Work

Every job involves being judged by other people, whether you are giving a sales presentation to clients, representing your work team at a meeting, or showing your boss your work for some informal feedback. Being evaluated can raise anxieties for anyone. Apprehension in these kinds of situations is a common phenomenon, and in fact, a little anxiety can even boost performance (Cocchiara & Quick, 2004; Reio & Callahan,

2004; Yerkes & Dodson, 1908). But anxieties can be heightened for those employees who are members of a negatively stereotyped group, especially when they are performing a kind of task on which, according to the stereotype, members of their group do poorly. Consider these statements by people who are members of stereotyped groups:

> *From a marketing manager: "You can see in someone's eyes when you are first introduced that you're dead in the water just because you're seen as old." Many older workers refer to "the look" on someone's face as they are introduced. A 57 year old accounts supervisor recounted that on meeting someone face to face for the first time, she was told with a tone of disappointment, "Oh, you have such a young voice on the phone." (Blank & Shipp, 1994)*
>
> *From a White loan officer (concerned about being perceived as racist or sexist): "I'm always worried about how I was heard. How will I be interpreted? Did I say the wrong thing?" (Blank & Shipp, 1994)*
>
> *From a Black manager: "I felt Whites had a lot of negative ideas about Blacks. I felt evaluated when I asked questions. Asking questions became painful for me." (Dickens & Dickens, 1991)*
>
> *From an overweight worker: " . . . I work extra hard because I know the stereotype, and I feel I need to prove myself. I work harder than most of my coworkers who do the same job. Yet my (skinny, size-10) boss continually talks about me behind my back to my coworkers—she says that I'm lazy and that I don't take any initiative, and who knows what else. She sees me for maybe half an hour out of the work week, which is hardly enough time to judge me on my work . . . It doesn't matter that I know the job inside-out, or that my customer-service skills are top-notch. It doesn't matter that I'm on time and do any stupid little task that I'm asked. All that matters is the width of my ass." (Personal blog, 2005)*

The individuals quoted here are members of different identity groups, but they all voice a common concern: the fear of being seen and judged according to a negative stereotype about their group, and the concern that they might do something that would inadvertently confirm the negative stereotype (Steele, 1997; Steele et al., 2002). These individuals are experiencing "stereotype threat."

Stereotype threat describes the psychological experience of a person who, while engaged in a task, is aware of a stereotype about his or her identity group suggesting that he or she will not perform well on that task. For example, a woman taking a math test is familiar with the common stereotype that "girls aren't good at math." Or a Black faculty member preparing his case for promotion is aware that some people believe that Blacks are intellectually inferior. This awareness can have a disruptive effect on performance—ironically resulting in the individual confirming the very stereotype he or she wanted to disconfirm (Kray, Thompson, & Galinsky, 2001). Anyone can experience anxiety while performing a task with important implications (a test to get into graduate school or a presentation to a big client), but stereotype threat places an *additional* burden on members of stereotyped groups. They feel "in the spotlight," where their failure would reflect negatively not only on themselves as individuals, but on the larger group to which they belong. As singer and actress Beyoncé Knowles said in an interview with *Newsweek* in 2003: "It's like you have something to prove, and you don't want to mess it up and be a negative reflection on black women" (quoted in Smith, 2004, p. 198).

In the first (and now classic) study on stereotype threat, Claude Steele and Joshua Aronson (1995) asked Black and White students to take a very difficult test. The test was composed of items from the verbal section of the Graduate Record Examination, and it was deliberately designed to tax students' ability. For some students, this test was described simply as a laboratory problem-solving task. However, for other students, the test was described as a "genuine test of your verbal abilities and limitations." The important difference between these two descriptions was that race stereotypes were irrelevant in the "laboratory task" version—there was no reason for a Black participant to expect race to impact his or her performance, or to think that other people might expect race to have an impact. However, in the scenario where the test was described as a genuine test of abilities and limitations (the stereotype threat condition), the racial stereotype (that Blacks lack intellectual ability) *was* relevant, and the researchers predicted that Black participants would be both aware of the stereotype and want to avoid confirming it.

When Steele and Aronson examined the results, they found that White students' performance was largely unaffected by the test instructions—the White students performed about equally well whether the test had been described as an ability test or as a laboratory problem-solving task. However, the instructions made a big difference in the performance of Black students. They performed less well in the ability test condition than in the problem-solving condition—even though the test was equally difficult in both conditions. In fact, after Steele and Aronson controlled for pre-study differences in ability (measured by the students' SAT scores), they found that Black and White students in the laboratory problem-solving condition performed about the same—but Black students underperformed relative to Whites in the ability test condition (Steele & Aronson, 1995).

This basic experimental design, in which researchers compare the performance of two groups (one group is negatively stereotyped, the other is not) in two task conditions (one condition presents the task as stereotype-relevant, the other does not), has been replicated many times over the last twelve years with consistent results. The negatively stereotyped group underperforms when the stereotype is seen as relevant to the task. This research is summarized in Table 1.

As the table shows, the stereotype threat phenomenon has been documented in a large number of groups, across a wide range of diversity dimensions, and in many different performance domains. In the top (unshaded) part of the Table, the "Who was affected?" column includes the people we generally think of as disadvantaged in the workplace due to negative stereotypes—racial and ethnic minorities, members of lower socio-economic classes, women, older people, gay and bisexual men, and people with disabilities. The academic literature sometimes describes members of these groups as "stigma conscious" (Aronson et al., 1999). That means that members of these groups can be very aware of the social stereotypes other people associate with their group. Since the relevant stereotype is very likely to come to mind, concerns about stereotype confirmation are easily aroused. As a result, very subtle contextual variations (a slight wording difference in the way a test is described, for example) may be enough to make the stereotype salient and disrupt performance.

But research has shown that this phenomenon does not apply only to people in disadvantaged groups. In fact, the bottom (shaded) part of Table 1 shows that even members of high status groups can experience stereotype threat. For example, we don't normally think of White men as being disadvantaged in the workplace. White men generally enjoy more hiring opportunities, higher salaries, and more organizational status than women or members of racial minority groups with comparable education and ability (Hite, 2004; Parks-Yancy, 2006). However, even high status groups have some negative stereotypes associated with them, and one of the stereotypes most strongly associated with the White group is the belief that Whites are racist (Frantz et al., 2004). The research suggests that many Whites are chronically concerned with not appearing racist (and inadvertently confirming the stereotype). Therefore, task situations that are described as dependent on racial attitudes can trigger stereotype threat in Whites (and result in participants looking more prejudiced than they might actually be) (Frantz et al., 2004).

Table 1	Examples of Examples of Stereotype Threat[1]		
Who was Affected?	**How did the Researchers Create Stereotype Threat?**	**What Stereotype was Activated?**	**What Happened?**
Black students	Told the students that they were about to take a very difficult test that was a "genuine test of your verbal abilities and limitations"	"Blacks lack intellectual ability"	The students performed less well on the test
Latino students	Told the students that they were about to take a very difficult mathematical and spatial ability test that would provide a "genuine test of your actual abilities and limitations"	"Latinos lack intellectual ability"	The students performed less well on the test
Low socioeconomic status (SES) students	Asked the students to provide background information including their parents' occupation and education, then told them they were about to take a difficult test that would "assess your intellectual ability for solving verbal problems"	"Low SES students lack intellectual ability"	The students attempted to solve fewer problems and had fewer correct answers on the test
Women	Reminded the women that "previous research has sometimes shown gender differences" in math ability, then asked them to take a test that "had shown gender differences in the past"	"Women have weak math ability"	The women performed more poorly on the math test
Older individuals (60 years and older)	Gave the older people a series of memory tests and presented them with a list of "senile" behaviors ("can't recall birthdate") too quickly for conscious awareness. Then researchers gave the older people the memory tests a second time	"Older people have bad memory"	The older people had a significant decline in memory performance from pretest to posttest
Gay and bisexual men	Asked the men to indicate their sexual orientation on a demographic survey, then videotaped the participants while they engaged in a "free play" activity with children	"Gay men are dangerous to young children"	Judges rated the men as more anxious and less suitable for a job at a daycare center
People with a head injury history	Told participants that a "growing number" of neuropsychological studies find that individuals with head injuries "show cognitive deficits on neuro-psychological tests," then gave participants a series of tests assessing memory and attention	"Persons with a head injury history experience a loss of cognitive performance"	The participants performed worse on tests of general intellect, immediate memory, and delayed memory
Whites	Told participants that a "high proportion of Whites show a preference for White people" before asking them to complete the IAT (implicit attitude test) that would measure their "unconscious racial attitudes toward Blacks and Whites"	"Whites are racist"	The participants had a larger IAT effect (the difference in response time between incompatible and compatible trials), suggesting a preference for White faces
White students	Gave the students a packet of newspaper articles emphasizing a "growing gap in academic performance between Asian and White students" before asking them to take a very challenging math test	"White students have less mathematical ability than Asian students"	The students solved fewer problems on the math test

(continued)

Table 1	*Continued*		
Men	Reminded participants that "it is a well-known fact that men are not as apt as women to deal with affect . . . and to process affective information as effectively" then asked them to indicate whether a series of words were "affective" or not	"Men are less capable than women in dealing with affective (emotional) information"	The men made more errors on the task
White men	Told the men that they would be engaged in a golf task that measured their "natural athletic ability." The men completed a demographic survey that included a question about their racial identity, then took the test	"White men have less athletic prowess than Black men"	The men made more strokes (performed worse) on the golf task

[1] The research summarized in this table include the following articles: Steele, C. M., & Aronson, J. (1995). Stereotype threat and the intellectual test performance of African Americans. *Journal of Personality and Social Psychology, 69,* 797–811; Gonzales, P. M., Blanton, H., & Williams, K. J. (2002). The effects of stereotype threat and double-minority status on the test performance of Latino women. *Personality and Social Psychology Bulletin, 28,* 659–670; Croize, J., & Claire, T. (1998). Extending the concept of stereotype threat to social class: The intellectual underperformance of students from low socioeconomic backgrounds. *Personality and Social Psychology Bulletin, 24,* 588–594; Spencer, S. J., Steele, C. M., & Quinn, D. M. (1999). Stereotype threat and women's math performance. *Journal of Experimental Social Psychology, 35,* 4–28; Bosson, J. K., Haymovitz, E. L, & Pinel, E. C. (2004). When saying and doing diverge: The effects of stereotype threat and self-reported versus non-verbal ability. *Journal of Experimental Social Psychology, 40,* 247–255; Suhr, J. A., & Gunstad, J. (2002). "Diagnosis threat": The effect of negative expectations on cognitive performance in head injury. *Journal of Clinical and Experimental Neuropsychology, 24,* 448–457; Frantz, C. M., Cuddy, A. J. C., Burnett, M., Ray, H., & Hart, A. (2004). A threat in the computer: The race implicit association test as a stereotype threat experience. *Personality and Social Psychology Bulletin, 30,* 1611–1624; Aronson, J., Lustina, M. J., Good, C., Keough, K., Steele, C. M., & Brown, J. (1999). When White men can't do math: Necessary and sufficient factors in stereotype threat. *Journal of Experimental Social Psychology, 35,* 29–46; Leyens, J., Desert, M., Croizet, J., & Darcis, C. (2000). Stereotype threat: Are lower status and history of stigmatization preconditions of stereotype threat? *Personality and Social Psychology Bulletin, 26,* 1189-1199; Stone, J., Lynch, C. I., Sjomeling, M., & Darley, J. M. (1999). Stereotype threat effects on Black and White athletic performance. *Journal of Personality and Social Psychology, 77,* 1213–1227.

Further, members of any group may experience stereotype threat when their identity group is negatively compared with another group. For example, comparative stereotypes suggest that Whites have less mathematical ability than Asians, men are less effective in processing affective (emotional) information than women, and White men have less athletic prowess than Black men. These negative comparisons can induce stereotype threat, and members of the target group demonstrate the short-term performance detriments associated with stereotype threat, as the studies listed in the table have found. One conclusion that can be drawn from looking at the table is that stereotype threat can affect all of us because each of us is a member of at least one group about which stereotypes exist. If you think about the stereotypes that could be applied to your own social group, you might recall situations where you personally experienced stereotype threat. If you think about the stereotypes that could apply to your employees, you can also identify the situations where they might be vulnerable to stereotype threat.

The research referred to in the table has decisively shown that stereotype threat has a negative impact on short term performance. But an unresolved question is *why* does stereotype threat have this negative impact? Researchers have suggested several different answers to this question (the literature calls these answers "mediating" explanations), but there is no consensus on which is the "right" answer. The dominant explanation has to do with anxiety (Aronson, Quinn, & Spencer, 1998), but there is still some disagreement over how anxiety affects performance. One argument suggests that anxiety increases a person's motivation and effort. Stereotype threatened participants are very motivated to perform well, and sometimes they try *too* hard or are too cautious in performing (Cadinu et al., 2003). For example, Steele and Aronson (1995) found that the Black participants in their research spent too much time trying to answer a small number of problems. They worked too hard on getting the right answer, and they disadvantaged themselves by not answering enough questions. Another argument proposes the opposite—that anxiety decreases a person's motivation and effort (Cadinu et al., 2003). The explanation is that stereo-type threatened participants lose confidence that they can perform well, and in a self-fulfilling way this undermines performance. Given that the evidence thus far is still mixed and unclear, we will have to wait for further research to provide a more defin-itive answer to the *why* question. However, research has clearly identified the condi-tions under which stereotype threat is more and less likely to occur. This brings us to the next section of our paper.

Conditions for Stereotype Threat

We've seen that the content of stereotypes about groups includes beliefs about the abilities of group members to perform certain kinds of tasks. Stereotype threat will only occur for those tasks associated with the stereotype. But simply being *asked* to perform a stereotype-relevant task is not enough to create stereotype threat. Research has identified two additional conditions needed for stereotype threat to emerge: task difficulty and personal task investment. In addition, the context can influence the perceived relevance of the stereotype for performance of the task or job. We have diagrammed these conditions, and the stereotype threat process, in Figure 1.

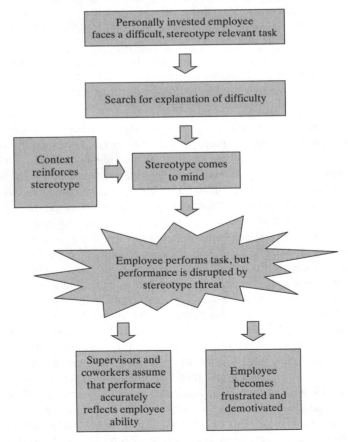

FIGURE 1 The stereotype threat process

Stereotype Relevance of the Task: What Does it Take to Perform Well?

Stereotype threat is situation specific, felt in situations where one can be "judged by, treated and seen in terms of, or self-fulfill a negative stereotype about one's group" (Spencer, Steele, & Quinn, 1999, p. 6). These situations occur when doing well on the task requires an ability on which, according to the stereotype, the person performing the task has a deficit. In the studies we have reviewed, the stereotype relevance of the task has often been created by telling participants that the task is a direct "test" of the stereotyped ability. So, for example, math tests have been used to create a stereotype relevant task for women and verbal or cognitive ability tests used to create stereotype relevant tasks for African Americans and Hispanics. But stereotype relevance isn't limited to standardized tests. Laura Kray and her colleagues surveyed participants to show that negotiation tasks are stereotype relevant for women. The researchers found that people believed that good negotiators were "assertive and concerned with personal gain" *and* that "men are more likely to be assertive than women" (Kray, Galinsky, & Thompson, 2002). Therefore, it logically follows that "men are better negotiators than women."

Research has shown that in our society many people believe successful managers have attributes more similar to those of men and Whites than to those of women, Hispanics, or African Americans (Chung-Herrera & Lankau, 2005; Heilman, Block, Martell, & Simon, 1989; Tomkiewicz, Brenner, & Adeyemi-Beilo, 1998). But beliefs about the traits necessary for jobs can also be organization specific. The potential for stereotype threat exists any time employees' beliefs about the particular traits needed for good job performance are linked to stereotypes about groups.

Task Difficulty: Why is this so Hard?

Stereotype threat is most likely to influence performance on very difficult tasks—those that are at the limits of a person's abilities (Steele et al., 2002). On easier tasks, stereotype threat doesn't have much negative effect. According to psychologist Claude Steele, experiencing frustration with task accomplishment is an important trigger for stereotype threat (Steele et al., 2002). On a simple task there is little frustration—the person is doing well and knows it. But with a difficult task, progress is not so smooth. People who experience frustration with a task try to explain their difficulty to themselves: "Why is this so hard? Is this job just impossible? Am I not working hard enough? Am I having a bad day?" They also think about how others (co-workers, supervisors) will explain their difficulty: "Will they think I'm not working hard enough?" But when the person is a member of a stereotyped group, the stereotype is also likely to come to mind as a potential explanation that others might use: "Will they think the stereotype is true? It's going to look like the stereotype *is* true."

A negative dynamic operates between task difficulty and stereotype threat. When a task is difficult, stereotype threat evokes concern over performance. But this concern also has a greater *impact* on the performance of difficult tasks. Difficult jobs require concentration and focus; all of one's cognitive/mental resources must be directed toward accomplishing the work. If some of those resources are diverted towards worrying about one's skills and how one will be viewed by others, performance decrements occur (Beilock & Carr, 2005; Verbeke & Bagozzi, 2000). Thus, difficult tasks trigger stereotype threat, and also are most affected by it.

In work settings then, difficult, complex, and challenging tasks are where stereotype threat is most likely to occur. This creates a dilemma for managers. Task difficulty is not just a fact in many (especially professional) jobs, it is a desired condition. For years, job design experts have recommended that every job contain some challenging aspects to increase job involvement and avoid boredom and skill atrophy (Greenberg, 1996; Hackman & Oldham, 1980). In fact, giving demanding assignments to new hires is sometimes recommended as a good way to develop employees. Early demanding experiences predict later career success (Habermas & Bluck, 2000). In many organizations, "stretch" assignments (assignments for which an employee is not yet fully qualified, "stretching" the employee's skills and abilities) (McCauley, Eastman, & Ohlott, 1995) are used as developmental tools throughout a person's tenure (Noe, 1999). Stretch assignments are needed for skill development, but managers must be aware of the extra potential for stereotype threat these assignments might involve for stereotyped employees, and counteract this risk. (We discuss how managers might do this later in the paper.)

In addition, tasks that are new and unfamiliar to the person performing them may be more at risk for stereotype threat than routine, familiar ones. New employees in particular are likely to find task accomplishment challenging as they learn their responsibilities. Thus, managers also must be aware of the higher potential for stereotype threat for their new hires.

Personal Task Investment: How Important is this to Who I Am?

Personal task investment refers to how important doing well on the task is to the individual's self esteem and identity. Some employees strongly identify with a particular skill or competency as a part of who they are. We often hear people say, "I'm good with people," or "I'm a techie." For these people, the skill is a part of how they define themselves. For such invested people, doing well in that task domain is important for their self-esteem and for feeling good about themselves. Researchers have argued that people who are personally invested in the task would be most influenced by stereotype threat because they are the ones who really care about their performance (Steele, 1997; Steele et al., 2002). If you want your work performance to say something about you personally, then the prospect of being viewed in terms of a negative stereotype is most disturbing. Studies have consistently confirmed this. Those invested in the task are more negatively affected by stereotype threat than those without such personal task investment.

What does this mean, practically? People tend to be invested in tasks they are good at (Steele, 1997). So the heavy impact of stereotype threat on the personally invested means that "the most capable members of stereotyped groups tend to be the most adversely affected in their performance by stereotype threat" (Kray et al., 2002, p. 388). This carries an important reminder for managers: the employees who care about their work and really want to do well are generally the ones that a manager is least likely to worry about since they are the ones he or she thinks will succeed on their own, and thus don't need coaxing, coaching, or extra attention. Yet, these are the people *most* likely to be affected by stereotype threat, and therefore, most in need of a manager's efforts to address and reduce it. For example, a manager might think that because the talented Hispanic salesperson graduated at the top of his class, he's already proven that stereotypes don't apply to him and isn't bothered by them. Or that the efficient accountant who earned her CPA despite caring for four children no longer worries about not being taken seriously by male managers. But it's exactly these employees, the ones who have made a big investment in their work, who might be most likely to suffer the effects of stereotype threat.

The Context: Is this a Place Where Stereotypes Operate?

We've seen that the most important condition for stereotype threat is stereotype relevance: stereotype threat only occurs when the stereotype seems relevant to performing the task (Steele et al., 2002). In the academic research described earlier, stereotype relevance was created by the way the researchers described the tasks in a laboratory setting. In work settings, the relevance of the stereotype for performance can also be signaled and reinforced by the diversity (or the lack of diversity) of people who are currently performing the job. Rosabeth Moss Kanter used the term "token" to describe individuals who are different from others on a salient demographic dimension—race, sex, or age (Kanter, 1977). Kanter and others have shown that tokens feel very "visible"—that they stand out from the rest of the group. In addition, those in the majority are more likely to view tokens in terms of their distinguishing characteristic: as *the* woman or *the* Asian. Because everyone (the tokens and the tokens' colleagues) is more aware of group memberships under these conditions, associated stereotypes are more likely to come to mind (Niemann & Dovidio, 1998). In addition, the numerical differences reinforce the relevance of the stereotype for performance in the setting. Consider the solitary woman in a team of software engineers. Being the "only one" suggests that the stereotype about women lacking quantitative skills is true, and therefore sex is relevant to job performance. After all, the reasoning goes, if "those people" were good at this kind of job, wouldn't we see more of them performing it? Two studies have provided evidence of the link between token status and stereotype threat. In one, laboratory experimenters found that token women showed lower performance than non-tokens only on a math task (a stereotyped domain) and not on a verbal task (a non stereotyped domain) (Inzlicht & BenZeev, 2003). In the other, field researchers found that Black managers who were tokens in their work group reported higher levels of stereotype threat than non-tokens (Roberson, Deitch, Brief, & Block, 2003).

Thus, group representation can raise the relevance of the stereotype for performance. Work situations involving lone members of a social or demographic group are common. For example, in the field research described above, 18% of the Black managers were tokens in their work group (Roberson et al., 2003). Managers need to be aware of this effect of the environment and find ways to neutralize it.

In summary, these conditions make stereotype threat more likely for members of negatively stereotyped groups:

- The employee is invested in doing well, on:
- A difficult, stereotype relevant task, where:
- The context reinforces the stereotype

When stereotype threat occurs, performance is disrupted. But the effects of stereotype threat go beyond short-term performance decrements. The Black managers who experienced stereotype threat in the field research said that they spent more time monitoring their performance (for example, by comparing themselves to peers) and were more likely to discount performance feedback that they received from the organization (Roberson et al., 2003). So, for example, a Black employee who is regularly exposed to stereotype threat about his intellectual ability might dismiss performance feedback from his White manager that would have helped him to meet organizational performance expectations and get on the promotion "fast track."

But maybe these responses are functional. If your manager holds a negative stereotype about you, maybe you *should* discount feedback from that person (or at least, take it with a large grain of salt). If you can't trust your manager, monitoring the performance of your peers might yield more credible information with which to assess your performance. And if stereotype threat causes people to work harder, couldn't that be a positive benefit? Earlier, we quoted Beyoncé Knowles as feeling like she had "something to prove." Beyonce has clearly been able to channel those feelings in a positive way in order to become a successful performer. Maybe a strong motivation to disprove a negative stereotype about your group can increase persistence and determination to succeed. Research on achievement goals has shown that a desire to prove one's ability can be a powerful form of motivation (Elliott & Harackiewicz, 1996), most effective in improving performance and persistence on simple tasks that are familiar to the performer (Steele-Johnson, Beauregard, Hoover, & Schmidt, 2000; Vandewalle, 2001). If you know *how* to perform a task, this kind of motivation can help you to perform better. But remember the Black students in Steele and Aronson's research—the ones who spent a lot of time answering very few questions? Those students were very motivated, but they were working on very complex, challenging problems and their efforts did not pay off. This kind of motivation often works for you, but it can work against you.

Questions about whether employee responses to stereotype threat can be functional or potentially beneficial indicate that we need to know a lot more about the long-term consequences of repeated exposure to stereotype threat. To answer these questions, research has to study stereotype threat over time in real-world organizational settings. So far, the research suggests that repeated exposure to stereotype threat may have serious, and primarily negative, side effects. Stereotype threat is accompanied by physiological reactions such as an increase in blood pressure, leading researchers to speculate that long-term exposure to stereotype threat conditions might contribute to chronic health problems such as hypertension (Blascovich, Spencer, Quinn, & Steele, 2001). Stereotype threat is also associated with lower job satisfaction (Niemann & Dovidio, 1998; Roberson et al., 2003). Researchers have further suggested that repeated, regular exposure to stereotype threat may lead a person to disengage (or "disidentify") with the performance domain (Steele, 1997). That solo female in your engineering group may begin to think that an alternative career path might be preferable. This leads one to wonder whether long-term exposure to stereotype threat could be one cause of turnover for women and racial/ethnic minorities in professional and managerial jobs. Indeed, some studies have found that members of these groups leave jobs at a higher rate than White men (Horn, Roberson, & Ellis, 2007).

Fortunately, research on the conditions under which stereotype threat is most likely to occur also provides information about reducing the risk of stereotype threat. Recent studies have directly examined ways to reduce or eliminate stereotype threat by changing the conditions that produce the effect—in essence, interrupting the process. These studies are important because they point to some steps that can be taken by managers to lessen the possibility that stereotype threat operates for their employees. We now turn to specific strategies for reducing the likelihood of stereotype threat.

Interrupting the Stereotype Threat Process

Strategies for Reducing Stereotype Threat

We have mentioned that stereotype threat effects are strongest for people who are highly identified with the task domain. Researchers fear that over time, stereotyped people may find one way to reduce stereotype threat themselves—by disidentifying with the affected task domain. In other words, they break the psychological connection between their performance and their self-esteem so that doing well on that kind of task is less important. This is the only solution under the individual's control, but it is also perhaps the worst solution, costly for both the individual who gives up a valued part of the self, and for the organization that loses an engaged and motivated employee. Here we describe some alternatives to this worst case scenario—other strategies for reducing stereotype threat. These strategies, demonstrated to be effective in laboratory studies, all involve changing the conditions for stereotype threat. The strategies, and the points in the process at which they intervene, are shown in Figure 2.

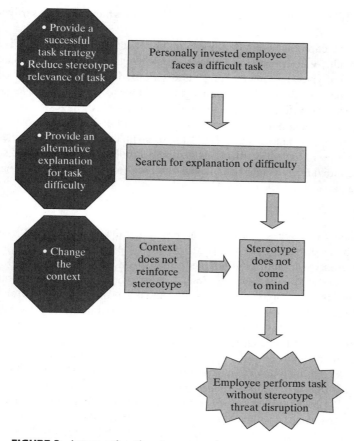

FIGURE 2 Interrupting the stereotype threat process

Provide a Successful Task Strategy

We know that stereotype threat influences people only on very difficult tasks—those at the outer limits of ability and skill. Evidence suggests that stereotype threatened people seek to distance themselves from the stereotype by acting opposite to it (Aronson, 2002). They often put their noses to the grindstone, work harder and longer to prove the stereotype wrong—to show it does not apply to them. In the original study by Steele and Aronson, stereotype threatened Black students worked harder and more diligently at the task, expending more effort than the unthreatened. Unfortunately, working harder and more carefully didn't increase performance. The task they were working on was extremely difficult, right at the outer limit of their abilities. Effort *alone* couldn't boost performance—what the students needed was an effective strategy for solving the problems.

A recent study provided stereotype threatened participants with a strategy to successfully counteract the stereotype. In a negotiation task, women were explicitly told about gender stereotypes suggesting that women are less assertive than men and tend not to act in their own self-interest; these characteristics reduce their effectiveness in negotiations. The women in the study were able to counteract the stereotype by acting particularly assertively when making opening offers to their partners, and this strategy improved their performance in the negotiation. However, the women acted this way only when they were *explicitly* told about gender's effect on negotiation. The women already knew how to act assertively—all they needed to perform successfully was a cue that this context was one in which acting assertively was a good strategy (Kray et al., 2001).

This research suggests that one way to reduce stereotype threat is to teach affected employees behavioral strategies for improving performance and counteracting negative stereotypes. This intervention addresses task difficulty—one of the conditions for stereotype threat. Having good strategies available to cope with challenges makes the task seem less difficult and less frustrating. This research suggests that when using stretch assignments, managers should set goals, and also help employees develop strategies towards attaining them. The "sink or swim" attitude toward stretch assignments common in many organizations can be particularly detrimental for stereotype threatened individuals. If managers discuss and suggest task strategies to employees, stereotype threat should be reduced.

Reduce the Stereotype Relevance of the Task

We also know that stereotype threat happens when the stereotype is relevant to the task; when performance on a task is believed to reflect an ability or trait that differentiates stereotyped and nonstereotyped groups (e.g., women and men; Blacks and Whites). Several studies have eliminated stereotype threat effects by refuting or diminishing the stereotype relevance of the task. In one study, researchers asked men and women to take a difficult math test composed of items from the GRE exam. All participants were told that they were taking the math test as part of an effort to develop new testing procedures for the university. Half of the participants were also informed that this particular test had been shown not to produce gender differences—that men and women performed equally well. The other half were not given any information about gender differences. The researchers predicted that stereotype threat would operate when there was no information given about gender differences, because when labeled simply as a "math test," the gender stereotype that "women can't do math" would be relevant. However, being told explicitly that there were no gender differences would reduce the relevance of the stereotype to the task, and hence reduce stereotype threat. By presenting the test as one with no gender differences, the stereotype would be irrelevant to interpreting performance on the test. These results were confirmed: women underperformed relative to men in the "no information" (stereotype relevant) condition, but performed equally to men in the "no gender difference" (stereotype irrelevant) condition (Spencer et al., 1999).

Another study reduced the stereotype relevance of the task in a slightly different way, by emphasizing characteristics shared by both groups. Male and female college students participated in a negotiation exercise. For half of the participants, researchers made gender stereotypes relevant by saying that the most effective negotiators are "rational and assertive" rather than "emotional and passive" (cueing gender stereotypes). For the other half, researchers eliminated the relevance of the gender stereotype for performance. They told this half of the participants that "rational and assertive" people do better than "emotional and passive" individuals. But then they added, "people who are in competitive academic environments, like you, do exceptionally well in the negotiation. This is true for men and women alike." This description highlighted characteristics important for performance that are shared by both men and women, diminishing the stereotype relevance of the task. This strategy was also successful in decreasing stereotype threat and gender differences in performance (Kray et al., 2001).

These studies show that reducing the stereotype relevance of the task—one of the conditions for stereotype threat—is effective in removing stereotype threat. But is this a realistic strategy in organizations? In the laboratory, it is possible to label an unfamiliar task as one showing group differences or not. It is easy to manipulate participants' beliefs about whether a task reflects group differences when those participants have no prior experience with the task. The situation is different with real world tasks or jobs where employees and co-workers may have strong opinions about the types of people who do well in various jobs or roles. Consider technical or mathematical tasks. Belief in gender differences on such tasks is widespread (Brown & Josephs, 1999), so when faced with a technical or mathematical task, a woman may not believe a manager who says it does not reflect gender differences. It might be more effective for managers instead to use the strategy in the second experiment. For example, rather than try to discredit gender differences, one could make gender differences irrelevant by stressing *common* characteristics of employees that are relevant for performing the task. This could be done by identifying characteristics important for task success that are unlinked to group stereotypes. Perhaps a manager could inform all employees that they were hired precisely because they have the skills needed to do well. For example, "We have such good hiring procedures—the people who we bring in, both men and women, have the skills to perform well."

Provide an Alternative Explanation for Task Difficulty

Task difficulty is a trigger for stereotype threat because people try to explain their difficulty to themselves: on a stereotype relevant task, where the context reinforces the stereotype, they are more likely to think of the stereotype as a potential explanation. The resulting anxiety and distress then disrupts performance. Several studies have shown that by giving an explanation for task difficulty *besides* the stereotype, stereotype threat can be reduced.

In one study, men and women students who came to the laboratory were told they would take a math test being developed by the psychology department for placement purposes. Immediately after this general description, half of the students were asked to begin the test, and were given 20 minutes to complete 20 problems. The other half were told that there would be a practice session before the test, administered on a computer. The experimenter explained that this would help them to "warm up," allowing a better assessment of their true ability level on the actual test. However, when the experimenter turned on the computer, the screen was unreadable (the computer had been rigged). After fiddling with the knobs and controls to no avail, the experimenter then announced that the students would have to take the test without the benefit of warming up, and this extenuating circumstance would be noted on their answer sheets. The researchers designed this study because they reasoned that being denied the "warm up" opportunity would provide a viable alternative to the gender stereotype as an explanation for any experienced task difficulty, reducing stereotype threat effects for women. Results confirmed this: men's performance was not affected by the test conditions. However, the performance of women was greatly affected. Women performed better on the math test when they were denied their "warm up" opportunity (Brown & Josephs, 1999).

In another study, researchers induced stereotype threat for White men by heightening the salience of the stereotype that Whites have less natural athletic ability than Blacks. The researchers then informed half of these participants that the lab space where they would perform athletic tasks had recently been renovated, and that the lab administration wanted "to know if the new changes made research participants feel tense or uneasy." Because of this concern, the participants would be asked to rate the lab space and its effects on their emotions after the experiment (Stone, Lynch, Sjomeling, & Darley, 1999). This information provided participants with another explanation (the renovated lab space) for any anxiety they experienced during the task. White men who received this alternative explanation for poor performance performed better than those who did not.

Again, however effective these manipulations are in the laboratory, their feasibility for the work setting may be limited. Managers certainly shouldn't lie to their employees (as in the first study) to give them an excuse for task difficulty and poor performance. But managers could remind employees about real-life factors that might be constraining their performance (e.g., a difficult client, limited resources, or a tight deadline). Another feasible strategy for providing an alternative explanation comes from a third study. The experimenters induced stereotype threat for women using the usual setup—telling participants that they would be completing a standardized math test for a study of gender differences. One group received just these instructions. With another group, in addition to these instructions, the experimenters described the phenomenon of stereotype threat and said, " . . . if you are feeling anxious while taking this test, this anxiety could be the result of these negative [gender] stereotypes that are widely known in society and have nothing to do with your actual ability to do well" (Johns, Schmader, & Martens, 2005: 176). These instructions had a positive effect on test performance. Women underperformed on the math test relative to men when given only the "math test" description. When stereotype threat was explained and offered as a possible cause of their anxiety, the performance of men and women was similar.

Telling people who might be affected by stereotype threat about the phenomenon has some advantages. Stereotype threat is real, and its effects on performance are well-documented. You might think that explicitly raising the issue of stereotype threat with a potentially affected employee might make matters worse by drawing attention to the stereotype—better to keep quiet and act like it doesn't exist. But instead the opposite appears to be true. Telling employees that you know stereotype threat can happen, and that they should be aware of it, gives them a different attribution for their difficulty and anxiety (it's not the stereotype, it's the stereotype *threat*).

Change the Context

The context is another condition that can affect the likelihood of stereotype threat. We discussed how one aspect of the context—the diversity of people performing the job—can reinforce or diminish the relevance of stereotypes. The research showing that tokens are more likely to experience stereotype threat also suggests a way to reduce stereotype threat: change the context by removing people from token situations.

This strategy may work in the laboratory, but how can managers realistically achieve this goal? In organizations, the composition of work groups is already constrained by employee skills, task interdependence, and other factors. Managers can't shuffle employees around based on their *demographics* to avoid token situations. However, several studies have changed the context using another strategy that does not involve changing the demographic make-up of the work group: presenting a role model who contradicts the stereotype. In one study, participants were administered a difficult math test by either a male or female experimenter. The experimenters gave identical instructions designed to accomplish two goals: 1) induce stereotype threat in the women by presenting the test as diagnostic of ability; and 2) create perceptions of the experimenter's competence in math. Scores on the math test showed that women underperformed relative to men only when the test was administered by a male experimenter. A follow-up study revealed that it was not the physical presence of the female experimenter, but rather her perceived competence that protected the women from stereotype threat. Seeing a woman who was competent in the math domain boosted women's beliefs in their own mathematical abilities and maintained their performance (Marx & Roman, 2002).

Other researchers found similar results when role models were presented in a different way. One study asked participants to read and critique four biographical essays. Half of the participants read essays concerning successful women in a variety of fields such as medicine and law. The other half read essays concerning successful corporations. Then all the participants completed a math test administered by a male experimenter. Results indicated that the role model manipulation reduced stereotype threat: Women scored worse than men on the test when they had read about successful corporations, but women scored at the same level as men when they had read about successful women (McIntyre, Paulson, & Lord, 2003).

These studies suggest that managers may be able to change the context for stereotyped employees by boosting the salience and visibility of role models. Note that in the "essay" study, the physical presence of a role model was not necessary—what was important was that the competence of the role model was salient. This strategy could be feasibly implemented in organizations. Managers can increase access to role models by encouraging employee participation in mentoring programs, professional associations, and employee network groups (Friedman & Holtom, 2002; Friedman, Kane, & Cornfield, 1998). If managers maintain a diverse network of associates themselves, they can be more aware of potential role models for all of their employees, and attempt to connect people.

Implications for Diversity Management

Would a greater focus on reducing stereotype threat add anything new to diversity management? We think it would. Existing diversity management programs tend to have two major objectives (Kellough & Naff, 2004): One goal is to change managers' *attitudes*—to reduce negative attitudes, stereotypes, and prejudice against members of different groups. Much diversity training is geared toward this goal. A second related goal is to change managers' *behaviors*—how they select, appraise, and develop employees (Brief & Barsky, 2000). For example, managers are encouraged, and often required, to specify explicit behavioral and performance standards for promotion or advancement, and to adhere to these in making decisions. These are important objectives. However, these objectives ignore two realities. First, changing attitudes and reducing stereotypes is a long term endeavor. Stereotypes are embedded in the culture, and reinforced outside of the work setting (Brief, 1998). Until society changes, stereotypes about different groups will remain. Even if a particular manager is unprejudiced, others in the workgroup may not be, and employees may still feel stereotype threat. While we need to try to reduce stereotypes, in the foreseeable future we have to deal with existing attitudes, and try to reduce the *impact* of stereotypes on affected employees. Second, while increasing the objectivity of measurement and decisions is necessary, the presence of stereotype threat means that performance *itself* may convey biased information about a person's true ability. So the well-intentioned manager who relies on objective performance data without understanding the impact of stereotype threat will still unfairly underestimate performance. Focusing on stereotype threat takes these realities into account, and highlights two principles that are currently downplayed in most diversity management efforts:

1. **Acknowledge stereotypes and address them directly.** Unfortunately, the goal of eliminating stereotypes from organizational decision making sometimes leads organizational members to deny their existence. People sometimes confuse stereotype awareness with stereotype endorsement (Adler, 2002). Yet research has shown that even unprejudiced people are familiar with the content of common stereotypes and can easily describe what prejudiced people believe about members of certain groups (Devine, 1989). Putting our strategies into action means that a manager has to honestly acknowledge the stereotypes that

exist. The manager who acknowledges the existence and potential impact of stereotypes does not have to endorse or support those stereotypes. Only a manager who acknowledges stereotypes can acknowledge the opportunity for stereotype threat and take corrective action.

The strategies for reducing stereotype threat further imply that managers should talk explicitly about stereotypes with their potentially threatened employees (Kray et al., 2001). Rarely are stereotypes directly named and described—particularly to the affected parties. Although many people (managers and subordinates alike) might see this as a risky step, explicit discussion about stereotypes can be useful in reducing their impact. If supervisors and subordinates trust one another, it can be a good strategy. David Thomas' comparison of successful and plateaued non-White executives demonstrated that successful executives found mentors early in their careers who were able to talk directly about race and the challenges it presented (Thomas, 2001; Thomas & Gabarro, 1999). Such openness about the existence of stereotypes and stereotype threat provides employees with alternative explanations for task difficulty and also may decrease concerns that they will be judged in light of the stereotype. Many managers would shy away from such a frank discussion, but the evidence says that evasion is not always helpful. Honest engagement of the problem and an exploration of action strategies to counteract perceptions can increase trust, reduce stereotype threat, and improve performance. How can managers be encouraged to take these risks? Perhaps diversity training should focus on providing managers with the skills and confidence to talk about stereotypes with their employees.

2. **Shift the focus from the manager to the environment.** Diversity management programs tend to focus on the manager as the target of change. Diversity training programs, for example, are designed to change managerial attitudes and behavior (Bendick, Egan, & Lofhjelm, 2001). In contrast, the strategies for reducing stereotype threat focus on the *environment* as the target of change. In other words, changing the conditions that lead to stereotype threat. Managers need to attend to managing the environment and reducing the cues that signal to employees that stereotypes are operating.

Effective diversity management has always meant creating an environment where all can succeed (Cox, 1994; Thomas, 1991). Knowledge of stereotype threat increases our understanding of what that really means. It is more than being personally nonprejudiced and unbiased. It means actively reducing cues that limit the contributions of *all* employees. Only in this way can the benefits of diversity be realized.

References

Adler, N. J. (2002). *International dimensions of organizational behavior,* Fourth Edition. Cincinnati OH: South-Western Publishing.

Aronson, J. (2002). Stereotype threat: Contending and coping with unnerving expectations. In J. Aronson (Ed.) *Improving academic achievement: Impact of psychological factors on education* (pp. 279–301). San Francisco: Elsevier.

Aronson, J., Lustina, M. J., Good, C., Keough, K., Steele, C. M., & Brown, J. (1999). When White men can't do math:

Necessary and sufficient factors in stereotype threat. *Journal of Experimental Social Psychology, 35,* 29–46.

Aronson, J., Quinn, D. M., & Spencer, S. J. (1998). Stereotype threat and the academic underperformance of minorities and women. In Swim, J. K. & Stangor, C. (Eds.), *Prejudice: The target's perspective* (pp. 83–103). New York: Academic Press.

Beilock, S. L., & Carr, T. H. (2005). When high-powered people fail: Working memory and "choking under pressure" in math. *Psychological Science, 16,* 101—105.

Bendick, M., Egan, M. L., & Lofhjelm, S. M. (2001). Workforce diversity training: From anti-discrimination compliance to organizational development. *Human Resource Planning, 24,* 10–36.

Blank, R., & Shipp, S. (1994). *Voices of diversity: Real people talk about problems and solutions in a workplace where everyone is not alike.* New York: AMACOM.

Blascovich, J., Spencer, S. J., Quinn, D., & Steele, C. (2001). African Americans and high blood pressure: The role of stereotype threat. *Psychological Science, 12,* 225–229.

Brief, A. P. (1998). *Attitudes in and around organizations.* Thousand Oaks, CA: Sage.

Brief, A. P., & Barsky, A. (2000). Establishing a climate for diversity: The inhibition of prejudiced reactions in the workplace. *Research in Personnel and Human Resources Management, 19,* 91–129.

Brown, R. P., & Josephs, R. A. (1999). A burden of proof: Stereotype relevance and gender differences in math performance. *Journal of Personality and Social Psychology, 76,* 246–257.

Cadinu, M., Maass, A., Frigerio, S., Impagliazzo, L., & Latinotti, S. (2003). Stereotype threat: The effect of expectancy on performance. *European Journal of Social Psychology, 33,* 267–285.

Chandler, M. (1999, October 4). *Secrets of the* SAT (FRONT-LINE, #1802). New York and Washington, D.C.: Public Broadcasting Service.

Chung-Herrera, B. G., & Lankau, M. J. (2005). Are we there yet? An assessment of fit between stereotypes of minority managers and the successful-manager proto-type. *Journal of Applied Social Psychology, 35,* 2029–2056.

Cocchiara, F. K., & Quick, J. C. (2004). The negative effects of positive stereotypes: Ethnicity-related stressors and implications on organizational health. *Journal of Organizational Behavior, 25,* 781–785.

Cox, T. H. Jr. (1994). *Cultural diversity in organizations: Theory, research, and practice.* San Francisco, CA: Berrett-Koehler.

Devine, P. G. (1989). Stereotypes and prejudice: Their automatic and controlled components, *Journal of Personality and Social Psychology, 56,* 5–18.

Dickens, F., & Dickens, J. B. (1991). *The Black manager: Making it in the corporate world.* New York: AMACOM.

Elliott, A. J., & Harackiewicz, J. M. (1996). Approach and avoidance achievement goals and intrinsic motivation: A mediational analysis. *Journal of Personality and Social Psychology, 70,* 461–475.

Frantz, C. M., Cuddy, A. J. C., Burnett, M., Ray, H., & Hart, A. (2004). A threat in the computer: The race implicit association test as a stereotype threat experience. *Personality and Social Psychology Bulletin, 30,* 1611–1614.

Friedman, R. A., & Holtom, B. (2002). The effects of network groups on minority employee turnover intentions. *Human Resource Management, 41,* 405–421.

Friedman, R. A., Kane, M., & Cornfield, D. B. (1998). Social support and career optimism: Examining the effectiveness of network groups among Black managers. *Human Relations, 51,* 1155–1177.

Greenberg, J. (1996). *Managing behavior in organizations: Science in service to practice.* Upper Saddle River, NJ: Prentice Hall.

Greengard, S. (2003). Gimme attitude. *Workforce, 82,* 56–60.

Habermas, T., & Bluck, S. (2000). Getting a life: The emergence of the life story in adolescence. *Psychological Bulletin, 12,* 748–769.

Hackman, J. R., & Oldham, G. R. (1980). *Work redesign.* Reading, MA: Addison-Wesley.

Hansen, F. (2003). Diversity's business case doesn't add up. *Workforce, 82,* 28–32.

Heilman, M. E., Block, C. J., Martell, R. F., & Simon, M. C. (1989). Has anything changed? Current characterizations of men, women, and managers. *Journal of Applied Psychology, 74,* 935–942.

Hite, L. M. (2004). Black and White women managers: Access to opportunity. Hitman *Resource Development Quarterly, 15,* 131–146.

Horn, P. W., Roberson, L., & Ellis, A. D. (2007). *Challenging conventional wisdom about who quits: Revelations from corporate America.* Manuscript submitted for publication, Arizona State University.

Inzlicht, M., & Ben Zeev, T. (2003). Do high-achieving female students underperform in private? The implications of threatening environments on intellectual processing. *Journal of Educational Psychology, 95,* 796–805.

Jackson, S. E., Brett, J. F., Sessa, V. I., Cooper, D. M., Julin, J. A., & Peyronnin, K. (1991). Some differences make a difference: Individual dissimilarity and group heterogeneity as correlates of recruitment, promotions, and turn-over. *Journal of Applied Psychology, 76,* 675–689.

Jehn, K, A., Neale, M., & Northcraft, G. (1999). Why differences make a difference: A field study of diversity, conflict, and performance in workgroups. *Administrative Science Quarterly, 44,* 741–763.

Johns, M., Schmader, T., & Martens, A. (2005). Knowing is half the battle: Teaching stereotype threat as a means of improving women's math performance. *Psychological Science, 16,* 175–179.

Kanter, R. (1977). *Men and women of the organization.* New York: Basic Books.

Kellough, J. E., & Naff, K. C. (2004). Responding to a wake up call: An examination of Federal Agency Diversity Management Programs. *Administration & Society, 36,* 62–91.

Kochan, T., Bezrukova, K., Ely, R., Jackson, S., Joshi, A., Jehn, K., Leonare, J., Levine, D., & Thomas, D. (2003). The effects of diversity on business performance: Report of the diversity research network. *Human Resource Management, 42,* 3–21.

Kray, L, J., Galinsky, A. D., & Thompson, L. (2002). Reversing the gender gap in negotiations: An exploration of stereotype regeneration. *Organizational Behavior and Human Decision Processes, 87,* 386–409.

Kray, L. J., Thompson, L., & Galinsky, A. (2001). Battle of the sexes: Gender stereotype confirmation and reactance in negotiations. *Journal of Personality and Social Psychology, 80,* 942–958.

Marx, D. M., & Roman, J. S. (2002). Female role models: Protecting women's math test performance. *Personality and Social Psychology Bulletin, 28,* 1183–1193.

McCauley, C., Eastman, L., & Ohlott, P. (1995). Linking management selection and development through stretch assignments. *Human Resource Management, 34,* 93–115.

McIntyre, R. B., Paulson, R. M., & Lord, C. G. (2003). Alleviating women's mathematics stereotype threat through salience of group achievements. *Journal of Experimental Social Psychology, 39,* 83–90.

Niemann, Y. F., & Dovidio, J. F. (1998). Relationship of solo status, academic rank, and perceived distinctiveness to job satisfaction of racial/ethnic minorities. *Journal of Applied Psychology, 83,* 55–71.

Noe, R. A. (1999). *Employee training and development.* Boston: Irwin McGraw-Hill.

Parks-Yancy, R. (2006). The effects of social group membership and social capital resources on career. *Journal of Black Studies, 36,* 515–545.

Personal blog. (2005, June 3). Available at: http://www.big fatblog.com/archives/001607.php.

Reio, Jr., T. G., & Callahan, J. L. (2004). Affect, curiosity, and socialization-related learning: A path analysis of antecedents to job performance. *Journal of Business and Psychology, 19,* 3–22.

Rice, F. (1996). Denny's changes its spots. *Fortune, 133,* 133–138.

Roberson L., Deitch, E., Brief, A. P., & Block, C. J. (2003). Stereotype threat and feedback seeking in. the workplace. *Journal of Vocational Behavior, 62,* 176–188.

Robinson, G., & Dechant, K. (1997). Building a business case for diversity. *Academy of Management Executive. 11,* 21–31.

Smith, J. L. (2004). Understanding the process of stereotype threat: A review of mediational variables and new performance goal directions. *Educational Psychology Review, 16,* 177–206.

Spencer, S. J., Steele, C. M., & Quinn, D. M. (1999). Stereotype threat and women's math performance. *Journal of Experimental Social Psychology, 35,* 4–28.

Steele, C. M. (1997). A threat in the air: How stereotypes shape intellectual identity and performance. *American Psychologist, 52,* 613–629.

Steele, C. M., & Aronson, J. (1995). Stereotype threat and the intellectual test performance of African Americans. *Journal of Personality and Social Psychology, 85,* 440–452.

Steele, C. M., Spencer, S. J., & Aronson, J. (2002). Contending with group image: The psychology of stereotype and social identity threat. *Advances in Experimental Social Psychology, 34,* 379–440.

Steele-Johnson, D., Beauregard, R. S., Hoover, P. B., & Schmidt, A. M. (2000). Goal orientation and task demand effects on motivation, affect, and performance. *Journal of Applied Psychology, 85,* 724–738.

Stone, J., Lynch, C. L., Sjomeling, M., & Darley, J.M. (1999). Stereotype threat effects on Black and White athletic performance. *Journal of Personality and Social Psychology, 77,* 1213–1.227.

Thomas, D. A. (2001). The truth about mentoring minorities: Race matters. *Harvard Business Review, 79,* 98–107.

Thomas, D. A., & Ely, R. J. (1996). Making differences matter: A new paradigm for managing diversity. *Harvard Business Review, 74,* 79–91.

Thomas, D. A., & Gabarro, J. J. (1999). *Breaking through: The making of minority executives in corporate America.* Boston, MA: Harvard Business School Press.

Thomas, R. R. Jr. (1991). *Beyond race and gender: Unleashing the power of your total work force by managing diversity.* NY: AMACOM.

Tomkiewicz, J., Brenner, O. C., & Adeyemi-Bello, T. (1998). The impact of perceptions and stereotypes on the managerial mobility of African Americans. *Journal of Social Psychology, 138,* 88–92.

Tsui, A. Egan, T., & O'Reilly, C. (1992). Being different: Relational, demography and organizational attachment. *Administrative Science Quarterly, 37,* 549–579.

Verbeke, W., & Bagozzi, R. (2000). Sales call anxiety: Exploring what it means when fear rules a sales encounter. *Journal of Marketing, 64,* 88–102.

Vandewalle, D. (2001). Goal orientation: Why wanting to look successful doesn't always lead to success. *Organizational Dynamics, 30,* 162–171.

Yerkes, R. M., & Dodson, J. D. (1908). The relation of strength of stimulus to rapidity of habit formation. *Journal of Comparative Neurology, 18,* 459–482.

Zenger, T., & Lawrence, B. (1989). Organizational demography: The differential effects of age and tenure distributions on technical communications. *Academy of Management Journal, 32,* 353–376.

COMMUNICATING ACROSS CULTURES*

Nancy J. Adler

All business activity involves communication. Within the global business environment, activities such as leading, motivating, negotiating, decision making, and exchanging information and ideas are all based on the ability of managers and employees from one culture to communicate successfully with colleagues, clients,

---

*Excerpted with permission from *International Dimensions of Organizational Behavior* (South-Western: College Publishing, 2002): 73–102.

and suppliers from other cultures. Communicating effectively challenges managers worldwide even when the work force is culturally homogeneous, but when employees speak a variety of languages and come from an array of cultural backgrounds, effective communication becomes considerably more difficult (6:3–5, 121–128; 16:1).

Cross-Cultural Communication

Communication is the exchange of meaning: It is my attempt to let you know what I mean. Communication includes any behavior that another person perceives and interprets: It is your understanding of what I mean. Communication includes sending both verbal messages (words) and non-verbal messages (tone of voice, facial expression, behavior, and physical setting). It includes consciously sent messages as well as messages that the sender is totally unaware of having sent. Whatever I say and do, I cannot *not* communicate. Communication therefore involves a complex multilayered, dynamic process through which we exchange meaning.

Every communication has a message sender and a message receiver. The sent message is never identical to the received message. Why? Communication is not direct, but rather indirect; it is a symbolic behavior. I cannot communicate my ideas, feelings, or information directly; rather, I must externalize or symbolize them before they can be communicated. *Encoding* describes the producing of a symbol message. *Decoding* describes the receiving of a meaning from a symbol message. Message senders must encode their meaning into a form that the receiver will recognize—that is, into words and behavior. Receivers must then decode the words and behavior—the symbols—back into messages that have meaning for them.

For example, because the Cantonese word for *eight* sounds like *faat*, which means prosperity, a Hong Kong textile manufacturer, Mr. Lau Ting-Pong, paid $85 million in 1988 for car registration number 8. A year later, a European millionaire paid $4.8 million at Hong Kong's Lunar New Year auction for vehicle registration number 7, a decision that mystified the Chinese, since the number 7 has little significance in the Chinese calculation of fortune (12).

The process of translating meanings into words and behaviors—that is, into symbols—and back again into meanings is based on a person's cultural background and differs accordingly for each person. The greater the difference in background between senders and receivers, the greater the difference in meanings attached to particular words and behaviors.

Cross-Cultural Misperception

Do the French and the Chinese see the world in the same way? No. Do Venezuelans and Ghanaians see the world in the same way? Again, no. No two national groups see the world in exactly the same way. Perception is the process by which individuals select, organize, and evaluate stimuli from the external environment to provide meaningful experiences for themselves (1; 7; 8; 10). For example, when Mexican children simultaneously view tachistoscopic pictures of a bullfight and a baseball game, they only remember seeing the bullfight. Looking through the same tachistoscope, American children only remembered seeing the baseball game (2). Similarly, adult card players, when shown cards by researchers, fail to see black hearts and diamonds, or red clubs and spades.

Why didn't the children see both pictures? Why did the adults fail to see the unexpected playing card colors? The answer lies in the nature of perception. Perceptual patterns are neither innate nor absolute. They are selective, learned, culturally determined, consistent, and inaccurate.

- *Perception is* **selective.** At any one time there are too many stimuli in the environment for us to observe. Therefore, we screen out most of what we see, hear, taste, and feel. We screen out the overload and allow only selected information through our perceptual screen to our conscious mind (3).
- *Perceptual patterns are* **learned.** We are not born seeing the world in one particular way. Our experience teaches us to perceive the world in certain ways.
- *Perception is culturally* **determined.** We learn to see the world in a certain way based on our cultural background.
- *Perception tends to remain* **consistent.** Once we see something in a particular way, we continue to see it that way.
- *Perception is* **inaccurate.** We see things that do not exist and do not see things that do exist. Our background, values, interests, and culture act as filters and lead us to distort, block, and even create what we choose to see and to hear. We perceive what we expect to perceive. We perceive things according to what we have been trained to see, according to our cultural map.

For example, read the following sentence and quickly count the number of *F*'s in the sentence:

Finished Files Are the Result of Years of Scientific Study Combined with the Experience of Years.

Most non-native English speakers see all six *F*'s. Many native English speakers only see three *F*'s, they do not see the *F*'s in the word *of* because *of* is not an important word in understanding the sentence's meaning. We selectively see those words that are important according to our cultural conditioning (in this case, our linguistic conditioning). Once we see a phenomenon in a particular way, we usually continue to see it in that way. Once we stop seeing *of*'s, we do not see them again (even when we look for them); we do not see things that do exist. One particularly astute manager at Canadian National Railways makes daily use of perceptual filters to her firm's advantage. She gives reports written in English to bilingual Francophones to proofread and those written in French to bilingual Anglophones. She uses the fact that the English secretaries can "see" more errors—specially small errors—in French and that the French secretaries can "see" more errors in English.

"The distorting impact of perceptual filters causes us to see things that do not exist. In an executive development program, for example, U.S. executives were asked to study the picture shown in Figure 1 and then to describe it to a second colleague who had not seen the picture. The second colleague then attempted to describe the picture to a third colleague who had not seen the picture, and so on. Finally, the fifth colleague described his perception of the picture to the group of executives and compared it with the original picture. Among the numerous distortions, the executives, similar to other groups, consistently described the black and the white man as fighting; the knife as being in the hand of the black man; the white man as wearing a business suit; and the black man as wearing laborer's overalls. Clearly the inaccurate stereotype of blacks (as poorer, working class and more likely to commit crimes) and of whites (as richer, upper class, and less likely to perpetrate violent crime) altered the observers' perceptions, thus totally changing the meaning of the picture. The executives' personal and cultural experiences, and therefore their perceptual filters, allowed them to see things that did not exist and to miss seeing things that did exist."

FIGURE 1   **Perceptual Filters Change the Story**

Cross-Cultural Misinterpretation

Interpretation occurs when an individual gives meaning to observations and their relationships; it is the process of making sense out of perceptions. Interpretation organizes our experience to guide our behavior. Based on our experience, we make assumptions about our perceptions so we will not have to rediscover meanings each time we encounter similar situations. For example, we make assumptions about how doors work, based on our experience of entering and leaving rooms; thus we do not have to relearn how to open a door each time we encounter a new door. Our consistent patterns of interpretation help us to act appropriately and quickly within our day-to-day world.

Categories

Since we are constantly bombarded with more stimuli than we can absorb and more perceptions than we can keep distinct or interpret, we only perceive those images that may be meaningful to us. We group perceived images into familiar categories that help us to simplify our environment, become the basis for our interpretations, and allow us to function in an otherwise overly complex world. Categorization helps me to distinguish what is most important in my environment and to behave accordingly.

Categories of perceived images become ineffective when we place people and things in the wrong groups. Cross-cultural miscategorization occurs when I use my home country categories to make sense out of situations abroad. For example, a Korean businessman entered a client's office in Stockholm and encountered a woman sitting behind the desk. Assuming that she was a secretary, he announced that he wanted to see Mr. Silferbrand. The woman responded by saying that the secretary would be happy to help him. The Korean became confused. In assuming that most women are secretaries rather than managers, he had misinterpreted the situation and acted inappropriately. His categorization made sense because most women in Korean offices are secretaries, but it proved inaccurate and counterproductive here, since this particular Swedish woman was not a secretary.

Stereotypes

Stereotyping involves a form of categorization that organizes our experience and guides our behavior toward ethnic and national groups. Stereotypes never describe individual behavior; rather, they describe the behavioral norm for members of a particular group. Stereotypes, like other forms of categories, can be helpful or harmful depending on how we use them. Effective stereotyping allows people to understand and act appropriately in new situations. A stereotype becomes helpful when it is:

- *Consciously held.* People should be aware that they are describing a group norm rather than the characteristics of a specific individual.
- *Descriptive rather than evaluative.* The stereotype should describe what people from this group will probably be like and not evaluate those people as good or bad.
- *Accurate.* The stereotype should accurately describe the norm for the group to which the person belongs.
- *The first best guess.* about a group prior to having direct information about the specific person or persons involved.
- *Modified.* based on further observation and experience with the actual people and situations.

A subconsciously held stereotype is difficult to modify or discard even after we collect real information about a person, because it is often thought to reflect reality. If a subconscious stereotype also inaccurately evaluates a person or situation, we are likely to maintain an inappropriate, ineffective, and frequently harmful guide to reality. Indrei Ratiu (9), in his work with INSEAD, a leading international business school in France, and the London Business School, found that managers identified as "most internationally effective" by their colleagues altered their stereotypes to fit the actual people involved, whereas managers identified as "least internationally effective" continued to maintain their stereotypes even in the face of contradictory information. Highly effective managers use the stereotype as a first best guess about the group's behavior prior to meeting any individuals from the group. As time goes on, they modify or discard the stereotype entirely; information about each individual supersedes the group stereotype. By contrast, the least internationally effective managers maintain their stereotypes. In drawing conclusions too quickly on the basis of insufficient information—premature closure (7)—their stereotypes become self-fulfilling (11). To be effective, global managers, therefore, become aware of their cultural stereotypes and learn to set them aside when faced with contradictory evidence. They do not *pretend* not to stereotype.

In conclusion, some people stereotype effectively and others do not. Stereotypes become counterproductive when we place people in the wrong group, when we incorrectly describe group norms, when we inappropriately evaluate the group or category, when we confuse the stereotype with the description of a particular individual, and when we fail to modify the stereotype based on our actual observations and experience.

Sources of Misinterpretation

Misinterpretation can be caused by inaccurate perceptions of a person or situation that arise when what actually exists is not seen. It can be caused by an inaccurate interpretation of what is seen; that is, by using my meanings to make sense out of your reality. Culture strongly influences, and in many situations determines, our interpretations. Both the categories and the meanings we attach to them are based on our cultural background. Sources of cross-cultural misinterpretation include subconscious cultural "blinders," a lack of cultural self-awareness, projected similarity, and parochialism.

Subconscious Cultural Blinders

Because most interpretation goes on at a subconscious level, we lack awareness of the assumptions we make and their cultural basis. Our home culture reality never forces us to examine our assumptions or the extent to which they are culturally based, because we share our cultural assumptions with most other citizens from our country. All we know is that things do not work as smoothly or logically when we work outside our own culture as when we work with people more similar to ourselves. For example:

> *Canadians conducting business in Kuwait became surprised when their meeting with a high-ranking official was not held in a closed office and was constantly interrupted. Using the Canadian-based cultural assumptions that important people have large private offices with secretaries to monitor the flow of people into the office, and that important business takes precedence over less important business and is therefore not interrupted, the Canadians interpreted the Kuwaiti's open office and constant interruptions to mean that the official was neither as high ranking nor as interested in conducting the business at hand as they had previously thought. The Canadians' interpretation of the office environment led them to lose interest in working with the Kuwaiti.*

The problem is that the Canadians' interpretation derives from their own North American norms, not from Middle Eastern cultural norms. The Kuwaiti may well have been a high-ranking official who was very interested in doing business. The Canadians will never know.

Lack of Cultural Self-Awareness

Although we may think that a major obstacle in conducting business around the world is in understanding foreigners, the greater difficulty involves becoming aware of our own cultural conditioning. As anthropologist Edward Hall explains, "What is known least well, and is therefore in the poorest position to be studied, is what is closest to oneself" (5:45). We are generally least aware of our own cultural characteristics and are quite surprised when we hear foreigners describe us. For example, many Americans are surprised to discover that foreigners see them as hurried, overly law-abiding, very hard working, extremely explicit, and overly inquisitive (see the box "Cross-Cultural Awareness: Americans As Others See Them"). Asking a foreign national to describe businesspeople from your country is a powerful way to see yourself as others see you.

To the extent that we can begin to see ourselves clearly through the eyes of people from other cultures, we can begin to modify our behavior, emphasizing our most appropriate and effective characteristics and minimizing those least helpful. To the extent that we are culturally self-aware, we can begin to predict the effect our behavior will have on others.

Projected Similarity

Projected similarity refers to the assumption that people are more similar to you than they actually are or that another person's situation is more similar to your own situation than it in fact is. Projecting similarity reflects both a natural and a common process. American professors asked managers from 14 countries to describe the work

---

Cross-Cultural Awareness: Americans as Others See Them

People from other countries often become puzzled and intrigued by the intricacies and enigmas of American culture. Below is a selection of actual observations by people from around the world visiting the United States. As you read them, ask yourself in each case if the observer is accurate and how you would explain the trait in question.

India: "Americans seem to be in a perpetual hurry. Just watch the way they walk down the street. They never allow themselves the leisure to enjoy life; there are too many things to do."

Kenya: "Americans appear to us rather distant. They are not really as close to other people—even fellow Americans—as Americans overseas tend to portray. It's almost as if an American says, 'I won't let you get too close to me.' It's like building a wall."

Turkey: "Once we were out in a rural area in the middle of nowhere and saw an American come to a stop sign. Though he could see in both directions for miles and no traffic was coming, he still stopped!"

Colombia: "The tendency in the United States to think that life is only work hits you in the face. Work seems to be the one type of motivation."

Indonesia: "In the United States, everything has to be talked about and analyzed. Even the littlest thing has to be 'Why, Why, Why?' I get a headache from such persistent questions."

Ethiopia: "Americans are very explicit; [they] want a 'yes' or 'no.' If someone tries to speak figuratively, the American is confused."

Iran: "The first time my [American] professor told me, 'I don't know the answer; I will have to look it up,' I was shocked. I asked myself, 'Why is he teaching me?' In my country a professor would give the wrong answer rather than admit ignorance."[1]

Source: L. R. Kohl, Survival Kit for *Overseas Living: For Americans Planning to Live and Work Abroad*, 4th ed. (London: Nicholas Brealey Publishing in association with Intercultural Press, Yarmouth, Maine, 2001), pp. 47–49. *Based on Kohls* (15: 47–49); adapted by Adler, 2007.

---

and life goals of a colleague in their work team from another country (4). In every case the managers assumed that their foreign colleagues were more like themselves than they actually were. Projected similarity involves assuming, imagining, and actually perceiving similarity when differences exist. Projected similarity particularly handicaps people in cross-cultural situations. As a South African, I assume that my Greek colleague is more South African than he actually is. As an Egyptian, I assume that my Chilean colleague is more similar to me than she actually is. When I act based on this assumed similarity, I often find that I have acted inappropriately and thus ineffectively.

At the base of projected similarity is a subconscious parochialism. I assume that there is only one way to be: my way. I assume that there is only one way to see the world: my way. I therefore view other people in reference to me and to my way of viewing the world. People may fall into an illusion of understanding while being unaware of [their] misunderstandings. "I understand you perfectly but you don't understand me" is an expression typical of such a situation. Or all communicating parties may fall into a collective illusion of mutual understanding. In such a situation, each party may wonder later why other parties do not live up to the "agreement" they had reached.

Most global managers do not see themselves as parochial. They believe that as world travelers they are able to see the foreigner's point of view. This is not always true. While it is important to understand and respect the other culture's point of view, it is not necessary to either accept or adopt it. Understanding and respect do not imply acceptance. However, a rigid adherence to our own belief system expresses a form of parochialism, and parochialism underlies projected similarity.

Cross-Cultural Misevaluation

Even more than perception and interpretation, cultural conditioning strongly affects evaluation. Evaluation involves judging whether someone or something is good or bad. Cross-culturally, we use our own culture as a standard of measurement, judging that which is like our own culture as normal and good and that which is different as abnormal and bad. Our own culture becomes a self-reference criterion: Since no other culture is identical to our own, we tend to judge all other cultures as inferior.

Evaluation rarely helps in trying to understand, communicate with, or do business with people from another culture. The following example highlights the consequences of misevaluation:

> *A Swiss executive waits more than an hour past the appointed time for his Spanish colleague to arrive and to sign a supply contract. In his impatience he concludes that Spaniards must be lazy and totally unconcerned about business. The Swiss executive has misevaluated his colleague by negatively comparing him to his own cultural standards for business punctuality. Implicitly, he has labeled his own culture's behavior as good ("The Swiss arrive on time and that is good") and the other culture's behavior as bad ("The Spanish do not arrive on time and that is bad").*

Communication: Getting their Meaning, not Just their Words

Effective cross-cultural communication is possible; however, global managers cannot approach communication in the same way as do domestic managers. First, effective global managers "know that they don't know." They assume difference until similarity is proven rather than assuming similarity until difference is proven.

Second, in attempting to understand their colleagues from other cultures, effective global managers emphasize description, by observing what is actually said and done, rather than interpreting or evaluating it. Describing a situation is the most accurate way to gather information about it. Interpretation and evaluation, unlike description, are based more on the observer's own culture and background than on the observed situation. My interpretations and evaluations therefore tell me more about myself than about the actual situation. Although managers, as decision makers, must evaluate people (e.g., performance appraisal) and situations (e.g., project assessment) in terms of organizational standards and objectives, effective global managers delay judgment until they have had sufficient time to observe and interpret the situation from the perspective of all cultures involved.

Third, when attempting to understand or interpret an international situation, effective global managers try to see it through the eyes of their international colleagues. This role reversal limits the myopia of viewing situations strictly from one's own perspective.

Fourth, once effective global managers develop an explanation for a situation, they treat the explanation as a guess (as a hypothesis to be tested) and not as a certainty. They systematically check with colleagues both from home and abroad to make certain that their guesses—their initial interpretations—are plausible. This checking process allows them to converge meanings—to delay accepting their interpretations of the situation until they have confirmed them with others.

Understanding: Converging Meanings

There are many ways to increase the chances for accurately understanding businesspeople from other cultures. Each technique is based on presenting the message through multiple channels (for example, stating your position and showing a graph to summarize the same position), paraphrasing to check that colleagues from other cultures have understood your meaning (and not just your words), and converging meanings (always double-checking with the other person to verify that you have communicated what you had intended to communicate).

Endnotes

1. Individual country quotes taken from J. P. Feig and G. Blair, *There Is a Difference*, 2nd ed. (Washington, D.C.: Meridian House International, 1980).

References

Asch, S. "Forming Impressions of Persons," *Journal of Abnormal and Social Psychology 40* (1946), 258–290.

Bagby, J. W. "Dominance in Binocular Rivalry in Mexico and the United States," in I. Al-Issa and W. Dennis, eds., *Cross-Cultural Studies of Behavior* (New York: Holt, Rinehart and Winston, 1970), 49–56. Originally in *Journal of Abnormal and Social Psychology 54* (1957): 331–334.

Berry, J.; Kalin, R.; and Taylor, D. *Multiculturalism and Ethnic Attitudes in Canada* (Ottawa: Minister of Supply and Services, 1977).

Burger, P., and Bass, B. M. *Assessment of Managers: An International Comparison* (New York: Free Press, 1979).

Hall, E. T. *Beyond Culture* (Garden City, NY: AnchorPress/Doubleday, 1976). Also see E. T. Hall's *The Silent Language* (Doubleday, 1959, and Anchor Books, 1973) and *The Hidden Dimension* (Doubleday, 1966, and Anchor Books, 1969).

Kanungo, R. N. *Biculturalism and Management* (Ontario: Butterworth, 1980).

Lau, J. B., and Jelinek, M. "Perception and Management," *Behavior in Organizations: An Experiential Approach* (Homewood, IL: Irwin, 1984), 213–220.

Prekel, T. "Multi-Cultural Communication: A Challenge to Managers," paper delivered at the International Convention of the American Business Communication Association, New York, November 21, 1983.

Ratui, I. "Thinking Internationally: A Comparison of How International Executives Learn," *International Studies of Management and Organization, 13*, no. 1–2 (1983): 139–150. Reprinted by permission of publisher, M. E. Sharpe, Inc., Armonk, N.Y.

Singer, M. "Culture: A Perceptual Approach," L. A. Samovar and R. E. Porter, eds., *Intercultural Communication: A Reader* (Belmont, Calif.: Wadsworth, 1976), 110–119.

Snyder, M. "Self-Fulfilling Stereotypes," *Psychology Today* (July 1982): 60–68.

South China Morning Post, "Mystery Man Gives a Fortune for Lucky '7' " (January 22, 1989): 3; and "Lucky '7' to Go on Sale" (January 4, 1989): 4.

11 Group Dynamics and Work Teams

COLLABORATING WITH VIRTUALITY: LEVERAGING ENABLING CONDITIONS TO IMPROVE TEAM EFFECTIVENESS
Cristina Gibson

LEADING TEAMS WHEN THE TIME IS RIGHT: FINDING THE BEST MOMENTS TO ACT
Ruth Wageman
Colin M. Fisher
J. Richard Hackman

Understanding group dynamics has always been an important skill; the proliferation of teams in the workplace, however, has focused even more attention on this area. The development of technology that allows people to collaborate from almost any location has contributed to the increasing use of virtual teams—teams in which members work in different physical locations and communicate electronically. Our first article, "Collaborating with Virtuality: Leveraging Enabling Conditions to Improve Team Effectiveness," was newly revised and updated for this edition by Cristina Gibson, one of the foremost authorities on virtual teams and a professor at University of California–Irvine. She examines the factors that contribute to the effectiveness of virtual teams. As she notes, virtual teams are first and foremost teams. And, like most teams, they require certain elements to be effective, including design factors, such as team structure, and enabling conditions, such as shared understanding and trust. Gibson goes on to highlight specific strategies for ensuring that virtual teams reach and sustain peak effectiveness.

Creating and sustaining team effectiveness can be challenging, even for the most experienced leaders. "Leading Teams When the Time is Right: Finding the Best Moments to Act" was written by Ruth Wageman, psychologist and Director of Research for the Hay Group, Colin Fisher, Harvard doctoral student, and Richard Hackman, a Harvard psychologist renowned for his work on teams. They argue that leaders must know not only *how* to create the conditions enabling team performance but also *when* to intervene to effectively help the team. The timing of team coaching can dramatically affect team members' receptiveness to recommendations for change. Drawing on a wealth of practical examples, they provide guidance and advice on diagnosing team problems and opportunities, timing interventions appropriately, and implementing remedies to sustain team performance.

COLLABORATING WITH VIRTUALITY: LEVERAGING ENABLING CONDITIONS TO IMPROVE TEAM EFFECTIVENESS*

Cristina Gibson

Imagine a team responsible for prototyping a new wireless device that will enable children and families to transmit pictures to one another. This team includes members of six organizations from four European countries. The team members rarely meet in the same room; instead they communicate via a comprehensive intranet created for the project, an e-mail system, and teleconferences. What challenges might they face in doing their work? What makes this collaboration different than a typical project in a high technology firm? What advantages do they have over traditional teams? What techniques should the team use to increase their effectiveness? These are the issues that are addressed here.

This collaboration is an example of what many scholars and practitioners refer to as a *virtual team*. Yet, the term "virtual" conjures up images of virtual reality video games, or worse yet, mirages that don't really exist! So what is so special about this form of collaboration? "Virtual teams" are first and foremost teams—that is, collections of individuals who are interdependent in their tasks, who share responsibility for outcomes, and who see themselves and are viewed by others as a team (Hackman, 1987). There are four key factors that often make these teams unique: electronic dependence, geographic dispersion, diversity, and dynamic structure (Gibson & Gibbs, 2006).

Electronic Dependence

To be considered to at least some extent "virtual," a team must have some degree of electronic dependence. That is, highly virtual teams rely upon electronically mediated communication to stay in touch and get their work done. They use a variety of technologies including telephone, faxes, teleconferences, e-mail, videoconferences, collaborative design tools, and knowledge management systems. These teams may meet face-to-face from time to time, but they could not do their work and effectively coordinate their activities without technological support. Of course, teams that are co-located also use teleconferencing and e-mail, and just the use of technology does not make a team virtual. It is the degree of reliance on electronic communication that increases virtuality.

Geographic Dispersion

Beyond technological features, perhaps the second most prominent feature of highly virtual teams that sets them apart from co-located teams is that members of virtual teams work from many different locations: They are often spread out over cities, continents, and time zones. Thus, members cannot take for granted that other members share their contextual knowledge or have a common frame of reference (Riopelle et al, 2003). In fact, the more contexts represented on a virtual team, the more information there is to be shared. In particular, members need to share more information about context and in much greater detail than they would if working in the same location (Cramton & Orvis, 2003). Interestingly, recent research indicates that it is the subjective perception of the degree of dispersion (i.e., perceived proximity) rather than actual number of miles or time zones that predicts the effects of being in different locations (Gibson et al., 2010). Colleagues in different countries may feel closer to one another than those in the same city (albeit different offices) if the team works at developing that closeness.

---

*Written for the *Organizational Behavior Reader*.

Cultural Diversity

Virtuality often brings together members that represent highly diverse groups, including different nations, regions, organizations, or professions (Gibson & Cohen, 2003). The co-mingled national, organizational and professional cultures each have their own shared understanding, sensemaking, beliefs, expectations, and behaviors (Gibson & Manuel, 2003). On some virtual teams, members share many cultural characteristics; on others there is a high degree of cultural differences.

Thus, virtual teams are not just technological systems; they are sociotechnological systems: social systems completely intertwined with technology systems (Maznevski & Chuboda, 2000). Since different cultures are often involved, silence and lack of responses via technology can have multiple meanings for virtual team members, including indifference, technical failure, discomfort, or confusion (Cramton & Orvis, 2003). A fascinating and somewhat ironic finding is that when members of virtual teams share many cultural characteristics (e.g., all are Westernized, all share the same function, etc.), subtle cultural differences may go unnoticed but then cause real surprises as the team interacts (Elron & Vigoda, 2003). Cultural differences on virtual teams coincide with differences in the way in which people use language. These differences can be very subtle, yet profound. For example, across cultures, communication varies in the extent to which people use implicit versus explicit language (e.g., the use of qualifiers such as "maybe" "perhaps" or "somewhat"), the extent to which messages are context free or context specific, the degree to which messages contain emotional content or a serious tone, and the degree to which informal versus formal channels of communication are used (Gibson & Gibbs, 2006; Gibson & Manuel, 2003). In highly virtual teams, it is often necessary to create a "hybrid" culture, structure, and set of operating policies that represent a compromise among various alternatives preferred in the team (Riopelle et al., 2003).

Dynamic Structure

Finally, teams that are highly virtual often have a team structure that is dynamic and evolving (Gibson & Gibbs, 2006). In fact, even the participants may be unknown in advance; e.g., they may not be available due to other meetings, or they may choose not to attend based on other priorities. Therefore, a rigid sequence of activities cannot be imposed on the work, tools cannot be structured to assume presence of any given participant (King & Majchrzak, 2003), and work structures must often emerge. Recent evidence indicates that skills in external adjustment (defined as changes made in a team in the manner in which it interacts with external constituents) enable a virtual team to effectively address their dynamic nature (Gibson and Dibble, 2008). Overadjustment is detrimental, as is failing to adjust when necessary so that finding the optimal level of adjustment is key (Gibson and Dibble, 2010). Importantly, in highly virtual teams, initial structure, start-up, and formation activities are potentially more critical than in co-located teams because they provide common ground needed to bridge differences and develop basic operating structure (Riopelle et al., 2003). Further, team collaboration in a virtual environment is unique because it requires both synchronous (members working simultaneously) and asynchronous (members working sequentially or rotating) work.

In summary, teams range in their degree of virtuality, from slightly virtual to extremely virtual. A team that does all its work through e-mail, text exchanges, and teleconferences, never meeting face-to-face, is more virtual than a team that meets face-to-face monthly. A team that spans multiple continents and time zones is more virtual than one whose members are located in the same city. A team that has more cultural diversity is higher in virtuality, and teams that have very dynamic structures have greater virtuality. Increased virtuality adds complexity that must be managed. Yet, as explained below, successfully managing that complexity has enormous benefits.

A Framework for Virtual Collaboration

Many factors work together to determine team effectiveness. What team members and leaders actually do is create the conditions that support effectiveness. They do not work using just one behavior or pulling one lever at a time; they use multiple techniques. As a result, a comprehensive framework must include multiple design and implementation factors that help to create the conditions that support virtual collaboration in teams (Stanko and Gibson, 2008; Kirkman, Gibson and Kim, in press). One well-received framework for team effectiveness in virtual collaborations (see Figure 1) includes *design factors* that managers facilitate, which contribute to the establishment of *enabling conditions*, which in turn increase *effectiveness outcomes* (Cohen & Gibson, 2003). This framework also suggests that electronic dependence, geographic dispersion, diversity, and dynamic structure amplify the effects of the design factors on the enabling conditions (Gibson & Gibbs, 2006; Gibson et al. 2010; Gibson and Dibble, 2010). Each component of the framework is addressed in the sections that follow.

Design Factors

Design factors include features pertaining to the organization and team context, technology use, team member characteristics, and work and team processes (Cohen & Gibson, 2003). Several factors are embedded in each of these categories. For

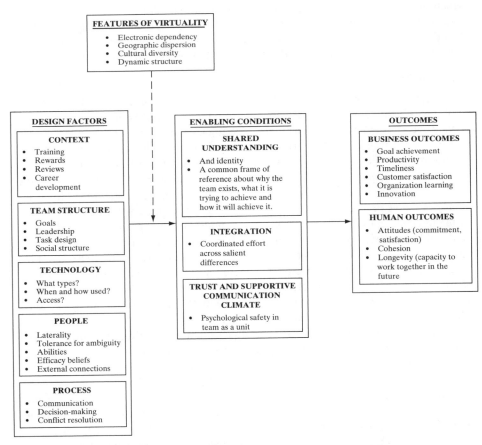

FIGURE 1 Framework for Virtual Collaboration

(Adapted from Gibson and Cohen, 2003)

example, reward systems and decision-making policies are part of the organizational context. How an organization's reward system is structured, how its policies are designed, and how its practices are implemented may make it more likely (or less likely) that its teams will succeed when working virtually. Those who establish, lead, and support virtual teams can influence organizational systems, structures, policies, and practices. These levers, discussed below, can be pulled to promote enabling conditions and effectiveness.

ORGANIZATION AND TEAM STRUCTURE. The systems, structures, and policies that make up the organizational context and team context are important for virtual collaboration. There are often vast differences in job design and staffing patterns across participants and partners. Without common support systems, building competencies and expertise is difficult and this can hamper overall development, knowledge management, and sensemaking (Mohrman et al., 2003). Likewise, virtuality may make *individual level* rewards (a common practice in many organizations) less advisable due to the increased needs for *team-level* cohesion, mutual accountability, and interdependence (Lawler, 2003). Finally, time is a critical resource that organizations must provide for virtual work. Virtual teaming typically lengthens the work day for virtual team members, and time zone dispersion narrows the window for real-time team interaction (Klein & Kleinhanns, 2003). Multitasking is a common strategy during meetings, which can distract members to such an extent that they miss an opportunity to provide valuable input. Likewise, the focus of members is often diluted by their local tasks and priorities (e.g., out of "site" is often out of mind), resulting in missed deadlines of process loss (Klein & Kleinhanns, 2003). Process loss is any aspect of group interaction that inhibits good problem solving. Virtual team members often complain that too much time is spent on merely sharing information in meetings rather than doing truly collaborative tasks such as decision making or problem solving (Klein & Kleinhanns, 2003).

However, in terms of decision-making policies, teams that operate across contexts have a strong potential advantage over co-located teams with respect to their ability to implement decisions, because of the strong ties distributed members can develop locally with clients, customers, and other external constituents (Maznevski & Athanassiou, 2003). In addition, similar to a decentralized organization structure, some forms of electronic media, such as text-based conferencing and discussion groups, have been found to facilitate a more equal and full representation of team member inputs (Tyran et al, 1992). Finally, it is less likely that a vocal and assertive member can dominate a group that relies primarily on text-based electronic media (Tyran et al., 2003), and virtuality often decreases power and hierarchy issues in teams (Elron & Vigoda, 2003). (See Table 1.)

INFORMATION TECHNOLOGY. Tools for electronic communication provide the infrastructure for virtual collaboration. When implemented well, teammates are able to

Table 1 Tips for Addressing Organization and Team Context in Virtual Collaboration

- Share measurement systems and metrics across sites—the more comprehensive, the more useful
- Align incentive systems across subunits and recognize team level efforts
- Create knowledge management systems such as team intranet, archives, index and templates
- Develop sponsors and champions who value virtual teaming
- Provide a human link in the form of a facilitator
- Develop a common training program across sites to strengthen necessary skills

work around the clock without violating the personal time of any one member (Griffith et al., 2003). The technology needs to ensure team members from any location can effectively coordinate their work and should also support team development and work on tasks. Many commercialized products exist to support collaboration in virtual teams. The challenge for practitioners is to figure out which technologies are most appropriate for their teams.

Interestingly, research has demonstrated that use of advanced technologies (e.g., videoconferencing) is relatively uncommon in virtual teams, with most team members preferring to use email as the primary mode of communication (Kirkman et al. 2004; Raven, 2003). This may be because the use of technology is complicated by the composition of most virtual teams; that is, members have different access to, and norms around use of, technologies (Cramton & Orvis, 2003). Across members of teams operating virtually, the quality and capacity of the infrastructure for communication vary, limiting access and feasibility of high-bandwidth technologies such as videoconferencing. In addition, members often have different formats and protocols for storing knowledge (e.g., Lotus Notes databases versus Access or Outlook repositories) (King & Majchrzak, 2003). These variations in availability of advanced technology and resources to support them can cause major communication breakdowns (Klein & Kleinhanns, 2003). Some members may only have access to electronic communication during certain hours, and norms for how often members should check in for messages (e.g., email, voicemail, use of instant messaging) differ from context to context. These features are unique and surprisingly salient in teams that rely heavily on electronic communication. For example, research suggests that creative and reflective processes are often easier in synchronous mode (e.g., through teleconferences or webconferences); in fact, reflection will likely take longer if done asynchronously because responses may not be made with people in the same frame of mind, leading to a loss of "mind-share" between responses (Klein & Kleinhanns, 2003). (See Table 2.)

TEAM MEMBERS. Collaborating virtually often brings together representatives from numerous company locations and permits interaction among parties that might otherwise duplicate effort or even work at cross-purposes (Riopelle et al., 2003). Virtuality potentially increases the number of participants and overall contributions

---

Table 2 Tips for Addressing Technology Issues in Virtual Collaboration

- Simple is often ideal, but must match technology to the task and structure
- Steps to include:
  - Identify options and preferences
  - Match technology to the task and people
  - Ensure access, connectivity and compatibility
  - Train members to use tools and provide ongoing technical support
  - Develop guidelines and templates for use of different media
  - Conduct a limited number of critical face-to-face meetings
- Include explicit norms for team member interaction such as:
  - How often to communicate
  - Expected response time
  - Which media to use
  - Prioritization of issues
  - Confidentiality and legal clarity

Based on Gibson and Cohen (2003).

to meetings, and allows members to maintain access to their home computing environment and desktop tools, which facilitates knowledge capture and search (King & Majchrzak, 2003). By virtue of different locations, members can tap into multiple sources of information and knowledge, and this broad spectrum of knowledge can be leveraged on behalf of the team and the organization. The process of obtaining information is greatly facilitated by building relationships within and outside the team; members hear about what is important from other people they know, they are alerted to knowledge and information that is potentially useful, and they interpret meaning in part based on knowledge of its origins. Good relationships with the right people can help team members acquire knowledge and analysis that competitors cannot obtain (Maznevski & Athanssiou, 2003). Furthermore, if diverse intelligence is leveraged in virtual work, it allows better outcomes than the best individual team member could achieve (Klein & Kleinhanns, 2003).

Recent research indicates that team members' connections with others outside the team (e.g., in other organizations, in government agencies, or personal networks) are particularly critical for adjustment processes (Gibson and Dibble, 2010). Such connections provide legitimacy, as well as access to resources not represented inside the team.

The people who work in highly virtual teams should possess certain capabilities to work effectively with their teammates. First, they need sufficient task-related knowledge and skills. They also need to have the skills to work collaboratively in virtual space. For example, they need lateral skills to work with people quite different from themselves. Team members need to have a tolerance for ambiguity to deal with the unstructured communication that characterizes much of virtual teamwork. It is also critical that team members believe in the ability of the team to accomplish its objectives. Efficacy beliefs have been shown to predict the ability of a team to adjust and perform (Gibson and Dibble, 2010). The personality dimensions and skills that team members possess will influence the establishment of enabling conditions. (See Table 3.)

TEAM AND WORK PROCESSES.   Internal team processes can help or hinder the creation of enabling conditions. In highly virtual teams, there is less opportunity to engage in informal and social interaction, communication is more formal, and there is less time allocated for nontask behavior (Hinds & Weisband, 2003). Further, involvement in

Table 3   Tips for Improving Team Member Skills in Virtual Collaboration

- Build "laterality" by becoming familiar with:
  - Each other's competence and unique personal attributes
  - Personal needs, concerns, interests, priorities and fears of team members
  - Use "round robin sense making" where each member tells what they know about a particular issue
  - Be sensitive to cultural differences in intentions and interpretations
- Establish similarities across members (e.g., education, goals, fate, etc.)
- Create a careful balance between specialization and generalization to take advantage of functional expertise
- Develop, recognize and reward basic communication skills including:
  - Surfacing differences
  - Testing for understanding
  - Active listening
  - Mutual perspective taking

Based on Gibson and Cohen (2003).

the team is often less central than involvement with a member's local environment, so there is less emotional attachment, vested interest, and identification. In turn, this means lower familiarity and intimacy and less self disclosure. English as a second language may exacerbate this and result in less depth and candor in exchanges, which increases psychological distance (Elron & Vigoda, 2003) and fears of misuse, miscommunication, and misinterpretation of knowledge (King & Majchrazk, 2003). As a result, there is often a higher perception of risk, which increases ambiguity and complexity of information exchanged. Even when English is designated as the official language of the collaborative effort and even when sophisticated technologies or translation procedures are used, language presents a key challenge to collective sensemaking processes in virtual teams (Mohrman et al,. 2003).

In addition, communication through text-based media is more laborious and so people tend not to type out details they would communicate verbally (Graetz et al., 1998). As a result, computer-mediated groups have lower communication efficiency than co-located groups (DeSanctis & Monge, 1999). The details, qualifications, social rituals, and cues that reveal meaning are often left out of text messages, and this may hinder interpretation, cohesion, and relationships in teams (Gibson & Zellmer-Bruhn, 2001). In the absence of rich auditory and visual cues such as voice intonation, understanding of complex messages is inhibited, and there is less feedback that information has not been understood (Hinds & Weisband, 2003). Receivers often fail to let a sender know their perception of the message that was sent (Gibson & Manuel, 2003). Adjustment to a shared norm of communication may be resented, particularly if that norm is more inclined toward a given culture (e.g., Israelis resent having to be more indirect due to the preferred style of U.S. participants) (Elron & Vigoda, 2003).

Finally, highly virtual teams may need more time to make sure all voices are adequately heard. Differences in phonics and syntax, unfamiliar accents, and inappropriate use of vocabulary can make it extremely hard or impossible to understand each other (Klein & Kleinhanns, 2003). Specifically, participants who are not physically located at or near headquarters or with the core of the team may be at a disadvantage because they do not have as many opportunities to participate in informal exchanges (Mohrman et al., 2003). All of these phenomena may hinder creativity and satisfaction, which are linked to team effectiveness.

In terms of conflict, relationship conflict (related to interpersonal or emotional issues), which has demonstrated dysfunctional impacts in teams, is more likely to be filtered out of computer-mediated communication (Griffith et al., 2003). Further, in teams that are highly virtual, conflict management is often more explicit and therefore may avoid the common problem of misunderstandings found in less explicit forms of communication. Similarly, highly involved virtual team members are often better able to notice conflict than less involved virtual team members (Griffith et al., 2003).

However, although teams do experience advantages related to conflict due to the virtual nature of their work, the flip side of these benefits may create challenges. For example, members of highly virtual teams often do not have the opportunity to serendipitously engage in sensemaking, and communication is often limited to short time episodes; this is efficient in some ways but may potentially increase opportunities for misunderstandings (Riopelle et al., 2003). Consensus is more difficult to reach in virtual teams, particularly in those teams working on complex, nontechnical issues (Hollingshead & McGrath, 1995). In addition, conflict is likely to be hidden longer in highly virtual teams, and there may be higher levels of process-based conflict (Griffith et al., 2003).

In terms of influence processes, rationality and sanction are used more frequently in highly virtual teams, and these tend to be the most functional forms

Table 4 Tips for Addressing Work Processes Issues in Virtual Collaborations

- Clearly delineate "who knows what" and member roles
- Explicitly address multiple team membership and "mind share"
- Responsibility lies with individuals to:
  - Make needed information available to others
  - Monitor relevant information
  - Tag information so people can quickly determine its relevance
- Meetings are designed to collectively *use* information
  - Follow good meeting management principles and teleconference etiquette
- Discuss conflict-resolution approaches
- Explicitly create cooperative norms
- Develop norms around pacing of differentiation/integration (when to let ideas flow openly and when to reach closure and move on)

Based on Gibson and Cohen (2003).

of influence (Elron & Vigoda, 2003). On the other hand, the less popular and socially acceptable influence tactics, such as pressure, sanction, and legitimating are typically used less frequently because lower familiarity and intimacy serve as gatekeepers to these tactics (Elron & Vigoda, 2003). Political behavior takes on a more careful and covert form in highly virtual teams because communication is more frequently documented. Cultural boundaries and differences restrain people from using extremely aggressive influence and politics (Elron, Shamir, & Ben Ari, 1999), and there are fewer stable political coalitions based on cultural subgroups in virtual teams (Elron & Vigoda, 2003). Members of highly virtual teams are often on "their best behavior" because they consider themselves as "ambassadors" of the groups they represent (Elron & Vigoda, 2003). Yet, ironically, in virtual teams, crisis and conflict are often the impetus that most clearly signals the need for integration and helps to bridge differences represented on the team (Riopelle et al., 2003). (See Table 4.)

Enabling Conditions

Careful management of the design factors helps to establish three enabling conditions in highly virtual team collaborations: 1) shared understanding about the team's goals, tasks, work processes, and member characteristics; 2) integration or coordination across key organizational systems and structures; and 3) mutual trust in the team (Cohen & Gibson, 2003). These are discussed next.

SHARED UNDERSTANDING AND IDENTITY. In most teams, it is important to establish commonalities in beliefs, expectations, and perceptions. Highly virtual teams need to develop this shared understanding about what they are trying to achieve (their goals), how they will achieve them (work and group processes), what they need to do (their tasks), and what each team member brings to the team task (member knowledge, skills, and abilities) (Cohen & Gibson, 2003). When teams involve people from different disciplines, business units, organizations, and cultures, their members will have different ways of perceiving tasks and key issues and of making sense of their situation (Earley & Gibson, 2002). Dougherty (1992) described new product development team members as inhabiting different "thought worlds" because of these differences. By developing shared understandings, virtual teams learn how to bridge the chasm between "thought worlds" (Hinds & Weisband, 2003). Shared

Table 5 Tips for Creating Shared Understanding In Virtual Collaborations

- Launch the team with face-to-face time and opportunities for both formal and informal interactions:
  - Establish clear leadership role(s)
  - Review broad organizational goals (often shared)
  - Review team mission
  - Identify collective work product(s)
  - Agree on objectives, measures, targets (less likely shared)
  - Establish integration mechanisms needed across teams
- Review with management and add processes for assessing the team
- As work continues, schedule time for informal team building ("scheduled informality")

Based on Gibson and Cohen (2003).

identity, defined as a sense of oneness or belonging to a social group, provides a feeling of connectedness or consubstantiality (shared substance) between individuals that can facilitate communication, understanding, and a sense of shared purpose. Recent research indicates that shared identity helps overcome many challenges of perceived lack of proximity (Gibson et al. 2010). (See Table 5.)

INTEGRATION AND ADJUSTMENT. A second key enabling condition captures the process of establishing ways in which the parts of an organization can work together to create value, develop products, or deliver services (Cohen & Gibson, 2003). The parts of the organization (or organizations) represented by team members who work virtually are likely to be highly differentiated in response to global competitive pressures and uncertain business environments. This differentiation across organizational units means that they are likely to have different policies, organizational structures, and systems. These differences can hinder effective collaboration in virtual teams both directly and indirectly. When organizational units have different information technology infrastructures, for example, connectivity can be a serious problem. At the most basic level, virtual team members may not be able to send e-mails to team members from other business units. In a more subtle way, business unit policies, structures, and systems influence employee behaviors. They provide incentives for certain behaviors and disincentives for others. Incentives for cross-unit collaboration may be lacking. Policies, structures, and systems also shape employee perspectives and worldviews on what is and is not important. The greater the degree of differentiation in an organization, the greater the need for integration.

The type of relationships and linkages that are important in a virtual team depends on which task characteristics are dominant. Some virtual tasks relate primarily to integration (e.g., combining knowledge to develop a new product). Others require differentiation (e.g., customizing for different markets), and still others are learning tasks (e.g., benchmarking). Integration tasks require extensive internal networks of relationships. Differentiation tasks require extensive links external to the team, and ties can be weaker. Finally, learning tasks require a balance of the two types of networks (Maznevski & Athanassiou, 2003). Configurations of networks are often combined in virtual teams with varied tasks to achieve the best of all worlds.

In virtual teams, the flow of knowledge and information is related to the development of networks of relationships in the team, particularly the subgroups that often form. Interestingly, if subgroups tend to coincide with the different subtasks of the group (i.e., different types of expertise to apply to different client problems), then knowledge will flow more effectively; if the subgroups don't coincide with subtasks,

Table 6   Tips For Increasing Integration in Virtual Collaborations

- Carefully select members and partners (e.g., organizations) to be involved
- Build relationships by using a counterpart strategy of linking people in similar roles across sites
- Create social and structural integration mechanisms such as:
  - Periodic orientations
  - Informal gatherings
  - Social information exchange
  - "Round-robin" participation
  - "Buddy system" and "mirror image structures" (dyadic accountability)
  - Clarify formal and informal roles

Based on Gibson and Cohen (2003).

then knowledge flows are often compromised (Maznevski & Athanassiou, 2003). Integration works hand in hand with adjustment. Without integrated effort, adjusting to changes that occur in the team or outside the team is difficult (Gibson and Dibble, 2010). (See Table 6.)

TRUST AND SUPPORTIVE COMMUNICATION CLIMATE.   The third enabling condition is *mutual trust and support* in the team. Mutual or collective trust is a shared psychological state that is characterized by an acceptance of vulnerability based on expectations of intentions or behaviors of others within the team (Cummings & Bromiley, 1996; Rousseau, Sitkin, Burt & Camerer, 1998). Teams that have established mutual trust are safe environments for their members. Members are willing to take risks with one another and to let their vulnerabilities show. Given that many factors known to contribute to social control and coordination—such as geographical proximity, similarity in backgrounds, and experience with each other—are often absent in virtual teams, the development of collective trust is critical, yet difficult to establish (Gibson & Manuel, 2003). People tend to trust those whom they perceive as similar to themselves. Further, electronically mediated communication lacks the interpersonal cues that are so important for building trust. Since nonverbal communication can be an important source of information when assessing the trustworthiness of a new teammate, the use of text-based electronic communication (e.g., e-mail), in particular, may impede the development of trust in virtual teams (Gibson & Manuel, 2003).

Further, text-based electronic communication makes it more difficult for team members to formulate impressions of their teammates and make inferences about one another's knowledge (Walther, 1993). Thus, members of highly virtual teams often err on the side of dispositional attributions (i.e., assuming behavior was caused by personality) because they lack situational information and are overloaded, and this may in turn make them less likely to try to modify problematic situations. Finally, geographic distance, different contexts, and reliance on technology lead to less similarities across members and greater possibility of divisive subgroups (Cramton & Orvis, 2003). Interdependence is often higher *within* subgroups (e.g., within a subset of members who are all from the same organization) than across subgroups (Gibson & Vermeulen, 2003). Without opportunities to demonstrate reliability and responsiveness across subgroups, collective trust cannot exist, and a negative cycle of divisive conflict will likely ensue (Gibson & Manuel, 2003). Co-located teammates can often establish credibility with each other by a process that is not explicitly designed, but members of highly virtual teams must create much more explicit routines that will allow this to happen (Maznevski & Athanassiou, 2003). Gibson and Gibbs (2006) found that when team members developed a

Table 7 Tips for Increasing Trust in Virtual Collaborations

- Assess and celebrate openness and psychological safety
- Acknowledge "risky" disclosures
- Celebrate supportive responses
- Continuously evaluate the trust climate and intervene when necessary
- Develop a supportive climate:
  - Active listening
  - Listening for ideas
  - Framing techniques
  - Following-up techniques

Based on Gibson and Cohen (2003).

trusting psychologically safe communication climate in their virtual teams, this enabled them to leverage the dimensions of virtuality (electronics dependence, geographic dispersion, cultural diversity, and dynamic structure) to increase innovation. Without such a climate, these characteristics were a liability. (See Table 7.)

Outcomes

A comprehensive framework for team effectiveness must include both business outcomes and human outcomes. Possible business outcomes are goal achievement, productivity, timeliness, customer satisfaction, organization learning, innovation, and cycle time. Possible human outcomes are team member attitudes, such as commitment and satisfaction, cohesion and longevity, and the capacity to work together in the future.

Conclusion

As demonstrated, operating virtually can amplify the benefits of teamwork. The greater the degree of electronic dependence, geographic dispersion, diversity, and dynamic structure, the higher the potential benefit. Virtuality enables the best talent irrespective of location to be applied to solve business problems, create products, and deliver services. Problems can be framed in ways that allow for innovative solutions when people can apply knowledge from one domain to another. Thus, collaborating virtually has the potential of producing high-quality, innovative business solutions. Plus, face-to-face meetings can be scheduled when needed, but people can do most of the work from their primary, distant work settings. Thus, collaborating virtually offers efficiency benefits as well. The potential to produce high quality, innovative solutions at lower costs offers organizations competitive advantage. The key is to harness this potential.

References

Alderfer, C.P. 1977. Group and Intergroup Relations. In J.R. Hackman and J.L. Suttle (eds.), *Improving the Quality of Work Life*. Palisades, CA: Goodyear.

Cohen, S.G., & Gibson, C.B. (2003). In the beginning: Introduction and framework. In C.B. Gibson & S.G. Cohen (Eds.), *Virtual Teams that Work: Creating Conditions for Virtual Team Effectiveness* (pp. 1–19). San Francisco: Jossey-Bass.

Cramton, D.C., & Orvis, K.L. (2003). Overcoming barriers to information sharing in virtual teams. In C.B. Gibson & S.G. Cohen (Eds.), *Virtual Teams that Work: Creating Conditions for Virtual Team Effectiveness* (pp. 214–230). San Francisco: Jossey-Bass.

Cummings, L.L., & Bromiley, P. "The Organizational Trust Inventory (OTI): Development and Validation." In R.M. Kramer and T.R. Tyler (eds.), *Trust in Organizations: Frontiers of Theory and Research*. Thousand Oaks, CA: Sage, 1996.

DeSanctis, G., & Monge, P. (1999). Introduction to special issue: Communication processes in virtual organizations. *Organization Science*, 19(6): 693–703.

Dougherty, D. (1992). Interpretive barriers to successful product innovation in large firms. *Organization Science*, 13: 77–92

Earley, P.C. and Gibson, C.B. (2002). *Multinational Teams: A New Perspective*. Mahwah, NJ: Lawrence Erlbaum Associates.

Elron, E. & Vigoda, E. (2003). Influence and political processes in virtual teams. In C.B. Gibson & S.G. Cohen (Eds.), *Virtual Teams that Work: Creating Conditions for Virtual Team Effectiveness* (pp. 317–334). San Francisco: Jossey-Bass.

Elron, E., Shamir, B., & Ben-Ari, E. 1999. Why don't they fight each other? Cultural diversity and operational unity in multinational forces. *Armed Forces and Society*, 26: 73–98.

Gibson, C.B., & Gibbs, J. (2006). Unpacking the concept of virtuality. The effects of geographic dispersion, electronic dependence, dynamic structure and national diversity on team innovation. *Administrative Science Quarterly*, 51(3): 451–498

Gibson, C.B., & Cohen, SG. (2010). Investigating the "1" in Virtuality. Work in progress, Working paper, Extending University of California, Irvine.

Gibson, C.B., & Cohen, S.G. (2003). The last word: Conclusions and implications. In C.B. Gibson & S.G. Cohen (Eds.), *Virtual Teams that Work: Creating Conditions for Virtual Team Effectiveness* (pp. 403–421). San Francisco: Jossey-Bass.

Gibson, C.B., & Dibble, R. (2010). Excess may do harm: Examining the diminishing returns of adjustment team-based collaborations. Working paper, University of California, Irvine.

Gibson, C.B., & Dibble, R. (2008). Culture inside and out: Developing the collective capability to externally adjust. In S. Ang & L. Van Dyne (Eds.) *Advances in Cultural Intelligence*, (pp. 221–240). New York: Sharpe.

Gibson, C.B., & Manuel, J.A. (2003). Building trust: Effective multicultural communication processes in virtual teams. In C.B. Gibson & S.G. Cohen (Eds.), *Virtual Teams that Work: Creating Conditions for Virtual Team Effectiveness* (pp. 59–86). San Francisco: Jossey-Bass.

Gibson, C.B., & Vermeulen, F. (2003). A healthy divide: Subgroups as a stimulus for team learning. *Administrative Science Quarterly, 48*, 202–239.

Gibson, C.B., & Zellmer-Bruhn, M. (2001). Metaphor and meaning: An intercultural analysis of the concept of teamwork. *Administrative Science Quarterly*, 46: 274–303.

Graetz, K.A., and others. (1998). Information sharing in face-to-face, teleconferencing, and electronic chat teams. *Small Group Research*, 29(6): 714–743.

Hackman, J.R. (1987). The Design of Work Teams. In J.W. Lorsch (ed.), *Handbook of Organizational Behavior*. Englewood Cliffs, NJ: Prentice-Hall.

Hinds, P.J., & Weisband, S.P. (2003). Knowledge sharing and shared understanding in virtual teams. In C.B. Gibson & S.G. Cohen (Eds.), *Virtual Teams that Work: Creating Conditions for Virtual Team Effectiveness* (pp. 21–36). San Francisco: Jossey-Bass.

Hollingshead, A., & McGrath, J. (1995). Computer-assisted groups: A critical review of the empirical research. In R. Guzzo and E. Salas (Eds.). *Team Effectiveness and Decision Making in Organizations*. San Francisco: Jossey-Bass.

King, N. & Majchrzak, A. (2003). Technology alignment and adaptation for virtual teams involved in unstructured knowledge work. In C.B. Gibson & S.G. Cohen (Eds.), *Virtual Teams that Work: Creating Conditions for Virtual Team Effectiveness* (pp. 265–291). San Francisco: Jossey-Bass.

Kirkman, B. L., Gibson, C. B. and Kim R. (In press) Across borders and technologies: Advancements in virtual teams research. In S.W. Kozlowski (Ed.) Oxford Handbook of Industrial and Organizational Psychology.

Kirkman, B.L., Rosen, B., Tesluk, P.E., & Gibson, C.B. (2004). The impact of team empowerment on virtual team performance: The moderating role of face-to-face interaction. *Academy of Management Journal, 47*, 175–192.

Klein, J.A., & Kleinhanns, A. (2003). Closing the time gap in virtual teams. In C.B. Gibson & S.G. Cohen (Eds.), *Virtual Teams that Work: Creating Conditions for Virtual Team Effectiveness* (pp. 381–400). San Francisco: Jossey-Bass.

Lawler, E.E. III (2003). Pay systems for virtual teams. In C.B. Gibson & S.G. Cohen (Eds.), *Virtual Teams that Work: Creating Conditions for Virtual Team Effectiveness* (pp. 121–144). San Francisco: Jossey-Bass.

Maznevski, M.L., & Athanassiou, N.A. (2003). Designing the knowledge-management infrastructure in virtual teams: Building and using social networks and social capital. In C.B. Gibson & S.G. Cohen (Eds.), *Virtual Teams that Work: Creating Conditions for Virtual Team Effectiveness* (pp. 196–230). San Francisco: Jossey-Bass.

Maznevski, M.L., & Chudoba, K.M. (2000). Bridging space over time: Global virtual-team dynamics and effectiveness. *Organization Science, 11*, 473–492.

Mohrman, S.A., Klein, J.A., & Finegold, D. (2003). Managing the global new product development network: A sense-making perspective. In C.B. Gibson & S.G. Cohen (Eds.), *Virtual Teams that Work: Creating Conditions for Virtual Team Effectiveness* (pp. 37–58). San Francisco: Jossey-Bass.

Riopelle, K., Gluesing, J.C., Alcordo, T.C., Baba, M.L., Britt, D., McKether, W., Monplaisir, L., Ratner, H.H., & Wagner, K.H. (2003). Context, task, and the evolution of technology use in global virtual teams. In C.B. Gibson & S.G. Cohen (Eds.), *Virtual Teams that Work: Creating Conditions for Virtual Team Effectiveness* (pp. 239–264). San Francisco: Jossey-Bass.

Rousseau, D.M., Sitkin, S.B., Burt, R.S., & Camerer, C. (1998). Not so different after all: A cross-disciplinary view of trust. *Academy of Management Review*, 23(3), 393–404.

Stanko, T. & Gibson, C. B. (2009). Virtuality here and now: A review of the concept of virtual work. In R.S. Bhagat & R. M. Steers (Eds.) *Handbook of Culture, Organizations and Work*, (pp. 272–304). Cambridge University Press.

Tyran, K.L., Dennis, A.R., Vogel D.R., & Nunamaker, J.F. (1992). The application of electronic meeting technology to support strategic management. *MIS Quarterly*, 16(3): 313–334.

Tyran, K.L., Tyran, C.K. & Shepherd, M. (2003). Exploring emergent leadership in virtual teams. In C.B. Gibson & S.G. Cohen (Eds.), *Virtual Teams that Work: Creating Conditions for Virtual Team Effectiveness* (pp. 183–195). San Francisco: Jossey-Bass.

Walther, J.B. 1993. Impression development in computer-mediated interaction *Western Journal of Communication*, 57: 381–398.

LEADING TEAMS WHEN THE TIME IS RIGHT: FINDING THE BEST MOMENTS TO ACT*

Ruth Wageman

Colin M. Fisher

J. Richard Hackman

"I am aware that success is more than a good idea. It is timing, too." Anita Roddick.

We have all heard the phrase "timing is everything." While that claim overstates the case, good timing *is* a vital element of high-quality team leadership. Regardless of whether one holds a formal position of authority or is a regular team member who informally provides leadership, the timing of interventions can make all the difference. Timing can be the key to assuring that leadership actions help a team rather than distract or misdirect members, or make no difference at all. This article explores what is involved in providing just the right kinds of leadership at just the right times.

Good timing means taking action to help a team at those special times when the team is ready to receive and use the help that is offered. For example, a project team we observed that was thoughtlessly carving up its work into individual pieces was stopped by the team leader and redirected by a well-timed question: "How are you going to integrate all those separate parts?" Bad timing is either making an intervention at an inappropriate time or failing to act at the moment when help is badly needed. For example, another project team leader poorly timed his efforts to get members to address their uneven levels of participation in the work. Insensitive to timing, this leader stepped in at precisely the moment when members began intensely debating the next step in their work—not a good moment to intervene. Or, just as ineffective, we have seen all too many leaders miss the opportunity to ask, "What didn't work well in that meeting we just had?" Asking that question at the next team event two weeks later, when the meeting is but a distant memory, is too late.

Some of the moments when a team will be open to leadership actions are highly predictable—for example, when members first come together, around the midpoint of their work, and when a significant piece of work has been completed. But there are other times, unpredictable times, when leader interventions also can be helpful. During the course of a day's work, for example, members can fall into intense, unanticipated conflict, or become stuck, or embark on an extended discussion of a trivial or task-irrelevant subject. A well-timed intervention that helps the team deal with developments like these can head off a downward spiral of increasing frustration, and raise the chances that the team will get back onto a more productive path.

The best team leaders exhibit good timing in both of these circumstances—at the predictable times in a team's work life, when members are reliably open to leadership interventions, and at those unpredictable times when developing events require immediate action. We refer to the former as *Type I timing* and to the latter as *Type II timing*. We discuss them each below.

*Reprinted from *Organizational Dynamics*, 38(3), R. Wagerman, C. M. Fisher, and J. R. Hackman, "Leading Teams When the Time Is Right: Finding the Best Moments to Act," pp. 192–203, © 2009, with permission from Elsevier.

Timing Type I: Knowing When a Team Will *Predictably* Be Ready for Leadership Interventions

Having great Type I timing is a matter of getting well prepared for *predictable times* in the life of a team when members are especially open to helpful interventions. It involves knowing what kinds of interventions will help a team at particular points in its lifecycle, and having those interventions already established in one's leadership repertoire. Even well considered and well-executed actions are unlikely to be helpful if the team is not ready for them. In fact, ill-timed interventions may actually do more harm than good, by distracting or diverting a team from other issues that do require members' attention at that time. For example, some years ago, Richard Hackman (in collaboration with Janet Weiss and Ken Brousseau) set out to show that groups offered a strategy-focused coaching intervention when they start their work will perform better than teams that plunge directly into the work—but only when the most obvious way of proceeding is *not* actually the optimum. Although the findings supported that prediction, perhaps the more important lesson from the study was that it turned out to be nearly impossible to get teams to actually *have* a discussion of strategy at the start of their work period. Members needed to focus on getting some actual experience with each other and with the task before they were able to have a useful discussion of how best to go about accomplishing the work.

So when *are* teams most open to intervention? A line of research conducted by Connie Gersick, in which she carefully tracked a number of project teams whose performance periods ranged from just a few days to several months, points the way. Gersick found that every group developed a distinctive approach toward its task as soon as it started work, and stayed with that approach until precisely halfway between its first meeting and its project deadline. Moreover, almost all teams underwent a major transition at that calendar midpoint. In a concentrated burst of changes, they dropped old patterns of behavior, reengaged with outside supervisors, and explored new perspectives on their work. Then, following their transition, teams entered a period of focused task execution that persisted until very near the project deadline, at which time a new set of issues having to do with termination processes arose and captured members' attention.

Gersick's findings provide a refreshing alternative to standard "forming-storming-norming-performing" models of group development, one that recognizes the importance of calendar time in developmental processes. Moreover, her findings suggest that the *readiness* of teams for leader interventions waxes and wanes across the team life cycle. Different issues are naturally on team members' minds at different times, and interventions that address issues that are "alive" for a team at a particular time are especially likely to take root and be helpful. Actions taken when a team is not ready for them—for example, talking about team member relationships at a time when a team is fully occupied with getting an urgent piece of work accomplished—are unhelpful and often disrupt the positive aspects of a team's work processes.

We describe below the particular kinds of interventions that are most helpful when a team is launched, when it reaches its midpoint, and when a significant piece of work has been completed. But some of the most powerful interventions a leader can make to facilitate teamwork are accomplished even *before* team members come together to begin their work. As we will see, how a group and its work are set up makes an enormous difference in how group process and performance unfold. Therefore, there are four predicable times at which team leaders can reliably help their teams both perform their tasks well and learn from their work together: (1) before the group exists, (2) at the initial launch, (3) at the calendar midpoint, and (4) at the end of a performance period.

Before the Group Exists

Whether a team succeeds or fails is often determined before the team ever meets. Initial team design choices powerfully shape team effectiveness on several dimensions: how well the team serves its clients, how much the team itself learns, and the development and well-being of individual members. It is ironic, therefore, that so many team leaders approach the initial meeting of a team without having made the preparations that can help a team get onto a positive trajectory. Excellent pre-work involves knowing what a high-quality team design entails, and then getting as many of those conditions in place as possible before convening the team.

We and our colleagues have conducted a great deal of research on a wide variety of teams to identify the design conditions that reliably foster team effectiveness. The conditions we describe come from studies of senior leadership teams from around the world, of analytic teams in the U.S. intelligence community, of teams of grass-roots organizers, and of a range of consulting, production, service, sales and project teams. These teams come from small businesses, huge multinational conglomerates, and all kinds and sizes of organization in between. Many are from not-for-profit and public sector organizations. The teams work in a variety of industries, come from at least 12 nations, and include organizations you have never heard of as well as many high-profile players.

In brief, the conditions for team effectiveness we have identified are (1) creating a real work team (rather than a set of people who are a team in name only), (2) specifying a compelling direction or purpose for the team, (3) creating an enabling team structure, and (4) providing an organizational context that supports teamwork, and (5) coaching the team as a team. These conditions are described in more detail in the accompanying sidebar.

Collectively, these design features create a high and sturdy platform on which to launch a work team. Shaping the features of the team's design is an essential team leadership activity, because a high-quality team design establishes powerful and persistent positive influences on the key processes that drive performance over time. *Creating* a good team design can be a quite challenging leadership task, however, one that requires both conceptual work and behavioral skill.

THINKING IT THROUGH.   Great pre-work always involves cognitive activity—in particular, careful thought about which design conditions are most critical for the work the team will be doing. For example, thinking through the task demands, and defining the capabilities members must have to perform the work well is largely an analytic task. And that task should be done long before a team is brought together. We have, for example, seen far too many chief executive officers (CEOs) take as a given that their "team" refers to all their direct reports. The best of them, by contrast, first ask: "What do I want of my leadership team? Which of my senior leaders have what it takes to think about the whole enterprise, and to make decisions in collaboration with their peers?" The answers to those questions determine who is invited to the table.

Sidebar: Conditions for Team Effectiveness

1. **Real team.** Real teams (1) have clear *boundaries;* (2) are *interdependent* for some common purpose; and (3) have at least some *stability of* membership, which gives members time and opportunity to learn how to work together well.

2. **Compelling direction.** The specification of the team's overall purposes is (1) *challenging* (which energizes members), (2) *clear* (which orients them to their main purposes) and (3) *consequential* (which engages the full range of their talents).

3. **Enabling structure.** Three structural features are key in fostering competent teamwork. (1) *Task design.* The team task is a whole and meaningful piece of work for which members have autonomy to exercise judgment about work procedures, and that provides members with regular and trustworthy data about how well the team is doing. (2) Team *composition.* The team is as small as possible, has members with ample task and interpersonal skills, and consists of a good *mix* of

(continued)

members. (3) *Core norms of* conduct. The team clearly and explicitly specifies both those member behaviors that are especially valued and those that are unacceptable.

4. **Supportive organizational context.** In addition to the material resources needed for the work, three features of the organizational context are especially consequential: (1) the reward system provides positive consequences for excellent team performance. (2) The educational system makes available technical assistance or training for any aspects of the work for which members are not already knowledgeable, skilled, or experienced. (3) The information system provides the team with whatever data and projections members need to select or invent strategies for carrying out the work that are fully appropriate for the team's task and situation.

When the first four conditions are in place, it becomes useful to provide the fifth:

5. **Available, expert coaching.** The team has available to it someone expert in helping members make good use of their collective resources as they work together.

Similarly, crafting an initial statement of purpose is conceptual work. It involves thinking through one's choice of words and how to provide clarity. It means finding ways to link the statement of team direction to members' values or to the overall purposes of the organization, to make it compelling to team members. This cognitive planning puts a team leader in the best possible position to engage the energy of members, to be sure that the work the leader has in mind really does call for a team of people, and to identify who should be put on the team.

Getting the key design conditions in place is a sequential process. For example, there is very little a team leader can do about choosing the right people and creating constructive norms of conduct in a team before first having thought through what the task is, how to make it a *team* task, and how it will be communicated to the team in a compelling way.

GETTING IT DONE.   Team leaders sometimes find it difficult or impossible to create a good team design, especially in organizations that have been fine-tuned over the years to support work performed by *individual* employees. Creating true team tasks, for example, can be quite a challenge. Sometimes it requires reassembling pieces of work that, for the sake of efficiency, have been partitioned into small, routinized subtasks doled out to individuals. Similarly, state-of-the-art performance appraisal systems that provide good measures of individual contributions are often completely inappropriate for assessing and rewarding work done by teams. Creating a team-favorable design, therefore, often requires skilled negotiations with managerial colleagues to obtain resources and to make organizational changes. And those activities are far better done in advance of the team beginning its work rather than later, when a poor design is already creating difficulties for the team.

A second kind of behavioral pre-work is to rehearse one's intended statement of purpose before actually convening the team. Practicing the team launch offers a leader the opportunity to draw on the advice and reactions of a trusted advisor as a sounding board. For many leaders, hearing an advisor's perspective on how one's words come across, and what is actually being communicated, is the best preparation possible for a high-quality team launch.

Launching the Team

A leader's behavior at the launch of any work team serves a vital function—namely, to breathe life into the team's basic design and thereby help the team start functioning on its own. Good team beginnings are especially critical because the majority of key leadership functions are fulfilled, for better or for worse, by the time a team is only a few *minutes* old. And it is the beginning that offers the best chance to engage members' motivation with the work at hand.

When team members first come together, the most pressing piece of business is to get oriented to one another and to the task. This orientation involves establishing the boundary that distinguishes members from nonmembers, starting to differentiate roles and formulate norms about how members will work together, and engaging with (and, inevitably, redefining) the group task.

Some leaders are fortunate because long-standing organizational processes for launching teams are already in place. At PepsiCo Inc., for example, we found that there were very strong norms about how people should operate both as team leaders and as team members. A carefully scripted "on-boarding" process for teams was in place that showed leaders and members how to bring the core conditions for team effectiveness to life in the first meeting. That process included: (1) identifying and highlighting the core capabilities that each member brought to the team's work; (2) articulating the team purpose and inviting members to respond; (3) creating a sense of shared identity, emphasizing what "we" share and "our accountabilities"; (4) identifying the main resources the team would need and how to get them; and (5) putting the norms and expectations for members on the table for the group to revise and ratify. Collectively, these elements of the launch script animated all the essential conditions for team effectiveness. And they established a positive trajectory for teams that made later coaching interventions immeasurably easier.

When a launch is successful, the leader has helped a group move from being just a list of names to a real, bonded team. The official task that the team was assigned gets examined, assessed, and then redefined to become the slightly different task that the team commits to tackle together. And the team has begun developing and trying out the initially specified team norms, to be gradually revised and made the team's own.

Even so, it does not all happen at once—some cycling back to issues that the leader may have thought were already settled inevitably occurs. In the course of a launch, for example, members typically test the leader's statement of purpose, they may ask clarifying questions that have a confrontational undertone, and they eventually redefine the purpose at least to some degree. That is one reason why it is so important for the leader who commissions the team to achieve clarity in his or her mind during pre-work. It is during pre-work that a leader can get her own mind clear on just what is needed from the team, and about those aspects of the purpose that are negotiable—and those that are not.

Sometimes leaders ask the team members to debate their work strategy at the launch meeting. That is almost always a bad idea. When teams are just starting out, they are not yet ready to address questions about alternative ways of going about the work. In fact, as we have seen, it is nearly impossible to get groups to actually have a productive discussion of performance strategy at launch. The beginning of a work cycle turns out to be an inappropriate time for a coaching intervention that focuses on work strategy. It may not be until the midpoint of the team's work cycle that members become fully ready for interventions intended to help them settle on a strategy that they actually will use in completing their work.

Consulting at the Midpoint

Major changes in how a team works are unlikely to happen until there is some natural break in the work. As Gersick's research demonstrated, the midpoint is an especially pronounced and predictable breakpoint. Halfway through a cycle, a meeting, or a project, teams tend naturally to reorganize and reorient their processes in preparation for the second half. The midpoint, therefore, is a time when a team is likely to be ready (or, in some cases, even eager) for consultative leader interventions, which help members revise and refine their work strategy.

Some of the most deft team coaching we have seen takes place during these predictable "downtimes." Well-conducted midpoint consultations often involve asking a team to reflect on which approaches to the work are effective and which are misdirected, off-base, or simply not working. Even the best teams have a tendency to get caught up in the heat of a difficult decision, or to get mired in inappropriate behavior and digressions. We see patient and dexterous leaders let that process go on for a while. Then, when the team is fully ready to reflect on how things have been going, the leader poses questions such as "How is that working?" "What's not helping?" "What do we wish we had or hadn't done?" "What shall we do differently for the next half?" The discussion that ensues can be the best way to help the team generate a good way of moving forward with the work.

For example, a business unit president of a global mining firm used the last hour of the first day of his two-day management team meeting to conduct a midcourse review. He briefly described some of the behaviors in the team that had improved since the members had begun working together three months before, the norms that he saw them consistently enforcing, and the few things they still did not do well despite trying hard: "Like me jumping on top of Hailey's comment without even understanding her point, when we said we wouldn't do that." He then invited the team members to add their own comments and observations about the team's work processes. It turned out to be an important opportunity for the team to change a few key features of their work process, such as how well they addressed each others' business concerns. And they experienced significantly greater traction in their decision making in the next day's work.

The midpoint, then, is a time when members are most likely to welcome and be helped by interventions that encourage them to assess their work progress, to review how they are applying members' efforts and talents to the work, and to consider how they might want to alter their task performance strategies to better align them with external demands and internal resources. A good midcourse review also can uncover important gaps in team members' knowledge and skill for the work at hand, especially when the problem or client is new to the team, and when anticipating all the necessary capabilities would have been an exercise in clairvoyance. Midpoints are *not* good times for teaching team members new skills, however. If it becomes clear at the midpoint that the work is suffering because of missing capabilities, it may be better to engage the team in locating people outside the group who can provide some help than to take time out for members themselves to hone their knowledge or skills. As will be seen next, learning is best done later, when the group has reached the end of a performance period.

Harvesting Lessons Learned at the End

The final predictable opportunity for helpful team leadership occurs when the work is finished or a significant subtask has been accomplished. At the end of a task cycle, a team has all the information they are likely to get about what members can learn from their team experiences. Members are ready to internalize and use the lessons they learn from their work. Anxieties about getting a piece of work organized and finished on time dissipate once the work is completed, the main reason that learning-focused interventions are best done at the end: People do not learn well when they brim with anxieties. Finally, there usually is *time* for reflection once the task has been finished. The post-performance period, therefore, is an especially crucial time for leaders to undertake learning-focused coaching.

Excellent debriefs not only build the team's reservoir of talent for subsequent work, but also contribute directly to the personal learning of individual team members. Some years ago, Ruth Wageman, then a doctoral student, was conducting research on task interdependence among field service teams at Xerox Corporation. Her academic advisor, Richard Hackman, accompanied her to a meeting with the managers who would be involved in the project. At the end of the meeting, one of the

Xerox managers asked, as was customary at the company, two debriefing questions: "What did we do especially well today? And what needs some improvement?" Various items were called out in response to the first question. There was but a single suggestion for the second item, however: "The professor's interpersonal skills." The professor joined in the laughter. But later he reflected back on his behavior in that meeting—and he found that there were indeed some ways in which he could have behaved more competently and helpfully in team interactions. Those reflections, and the learning they spawned, never would have happened if the Xerox service organization had not routinely and habitually conducted post-meeting debriefings.

Without direct intervention, team members are not likely to conduct a systematic debriefing. If the team has succeeded, they will be more interested in celebrating than in reflecting. If it has failed, they may be driven more to rationalize why the poor outcome was not really their fault than to explore what might be learned from it. Finally, even if members do take the time to reflect on possible explanations for the team's level of performance, leader coaching can be helpful in bringing those explanations into alignment with reality before the team either moves on to another task together or disbands to address other work.

Conclusion

Team leader pre-work sets the stage for team effectiveness. By creating conditions that foster team effectiveness before a team meets, a leader substantially lessens the chances that the team will succumb to intractable process losses. Moreover, pre-work increases the likelihood that members will generate real synergies, or process gains. In addition, getting the first four conditions in place goes a long way toward making the fifth condition—competent coaching—possible. If the team is poorly designed, there is very little a leader can do in real time to redress the difficulties that the team is almost certain to have. But if the basic conditions for effectiveness *are* in place, then real-time leadership actions can help a team get over rough spots and take advantage of opportunities that a poorly designed team would overlook or mishandle.

Once the team is underway, expert team leaders focus on three predictable times when coaching can be especially helpful: beginnings, midpoints, and ends. At the beginning of a team's work, motivational interventions that focus on the level of *effort* the team applies to its work are especially helpful. Such interventions can help minimize free riding (a process loss) and build high-shared commitment to the team and its work (a process gain). For example, articulating a specific, challenging goal and attaching a valuable reward to achieving it are leadership actions that can motivate members to focus intently on the task at hand and to work hard to accomplish it.

At the midpoint of a team's work, consultative interventions that help the team revise and improve its *performance strategies* are especially helpful. Such interventions can help the group avoid over-reliance on habitual routines that may be inappropriate for the team's task (a process loss) and instead invent work strategies that are particularly well-suited for the task and situation (a process gain). For example, a team leader of a problem-solving team can introduce the team to people who have tackled similar problems and invite team members to explore alternative ways of getting the work done.

Finally, at the end of a performance period, educational interventions that help the team make good use of the full complement of members' *knowledge and skill* can be especially helpful. Such interventions can minimize the mis-weighting of members' contributions (that is, when the importance given to individual members' contributions does not match their actual talent for the task, a process loss), and foster peer-to-peer teaching and coaching that can increase the team's capabilities (a process gain).

Clearly, a team that applies ample effort to its work, that uses a performance strategy that is well-aligned with its task and situation, and that appropriately draws on members' knowledge and skills is much more likely to perform well than a team that manages these processes poorly. Leader interventions can be extremely helpful to teams in managing these essential performance processes—but, as we have seen, it is vital that each one be addressed at the specific, predictable time in the team's life when members are ready to receive help and use it.

Timing Type II: Knowing When to Address the *Unpredictable* Nuances of Group Dynamics

> *The [project] team had been preparing its presentation for the client, but they really weren't seeing it through the client's eyes. . . . It was clear from the first slide they showed me when I walked in the room that we had very different expectations for what the clients needed to see. . . . I knew I needed to lead them to a place where they could look at [all the information they had assembled] from the client's perspective. . . . So I had to make a snap decision whether to say right away, "This is not what we're looking for," or whether to wait until after the presentation and act as if we had come to this conclusion.*
>
> TONY, a partner at a global consulting firm,
> on coaching one of his project teams before a meeting with a client.

Tony had a choice to make during his meeting with the team he was supervising. He had quickly diagnosed an unexpected problem, but he also needed to weigh the pros and cons of intervening earlier or later. Intervening immediately, he could see, would save time and get the team onto a good trajectory more quickly, but might undermine the team's sense of autonomy and short-circuit any learning that members could harvest from figuring it out for themselves. On the other hand, while waiting would allow Tony to get a better sense of what was going on and why, the team could end up wasting valuable time before the meeting with the client.

Tony's dilemma typifies the second type of timing that team leaders must master. Our emphasis on predictable times of readiness could be viewed as suggesting that leadership actions are irrelevant or ineffectual during the great majority of a team's life—that is, in the extended periods that lie between its beginning and midpoint, and midpoint and end. It is true that teams are remarkably impervious to major interventions made during times of low readiness. However, by actively watching for emerging opportunities to motivate, consult to, and educate teams, team leaders can make significant contributions to the team and its work.

To exercise great Type II timing, team leaders must diagnose group problems and opportunities as they occur and craft competent interventions on the fly. As will be seen, both diagnosis and intervention require a finely honed sense of timing and considerable coaching skill.

Diagnosis on the Fly

It may seem unnecessary to say, but we have found many team leaders need reminding that: *Diagnosing a team's problems and opportunities requires that one actually observe the team doing its work.* Too many team leaders, when they do not have formal responsibilities that require their presence with the team, choose to work on other matters rather than observe the team in action. Others pitch in to help the team with its work rather than keep an eye on team processes. Still others, although fewer in number, have learned about the importance of coaching interventions at beginnings, midpoints, and ends—and pay close attention to what is going on in the team *only* then, thereby potentially missing important developments that occur between the predictable times.

Occasionally, however, we have observed team leaders who get good data about team processes throughout the team's entire life cycle. Moreover, some organizations have developed policies that explicitly encourage this. At Tony's organization, for example, the firm's partners scheduled three hours per week to check in, observe, and raise questions with each project team that they supervised. This policy created ample opportunity for the partners to identify struggling teams before they caused problems for clients and to develop team members' individual and collective capacities in real time.

Whenever a team leader observes a team at work, he or she should focus on the team's standing on the three performance processes. Team leaders can discern subtle but critical dynamics by scanning the team interactions and asking themselves a short set of diagnostic questions—"How are they doing on effort? Are there signs of mindless routines, or does their strategy seem well-suited? Is there anything going on here that is causing the team to underuse some talent?"

However, dramatic moments in the interaction can often lead team leaders to overfocus on one process and miss opportunities to be genuinely helpful with others. For example, at a management team meeting at the Center for Application of Substance Abuse Technologies (CASAT), several team members complained vocally that work was unfairly distributed among team members. Executive Director Gary Fisher, captured by the intense feelings expressed, focused on the emotional and interpersonal aspects of what he heard in the meeting. In response, he called an all-day meeting in which team members aired their interpersonal issues and decided to redistribute responsibilities more equally. However, the team's performance problems persisted—and were ultimately solved by a small, strategic shift in their work operations. By focusing energy on the surface content of team member complaints, rather than by watching the problem as it was occurring, Gary not only misdiagnosed a simple task strategy issue, but wasted the team's time and resources. To avoid such misdiagnoses, team leaders must balance their attention across the three performance processes and properly diagnose unexpected issues as they emerge.

Merely paying attention to these processes is not enough, however. Team leaders also must competently *interpret* what they see. For instance, we often show our management students a reenacted video of a real-life leadership team. In one tense moment, the team is engaged in a heated discussion as they try to decide how to reduce the organization's overhead costs by 20 percent. Some students see in this discussion a productive debate about work strategy, and they do not see a constructive purpose to intervening in the team's process. Others, however, are concerned that interpersonal conflict between members is undermining the team's effort on the task and argue that the chief executive should intervene. Either interpretation might be appropriate, but each will affect both the timing and type of intervention the leader should choose. Team leaders with good knowledge of the task and of the team and its history are in the best position to make accurate diagnoses of what team dynamics *mean* for the three key performance processes.

One word of caution: A common error we see team leaders make in diagnosing team processes is focusing too much on the quality of members' interpersonal relationships. Relationship dynamics are easy to see, especially when conflicts and disagreements develop, but they can prompt interventions that miss the mark, as Gary Fisher's experience dealing with the negative emotions in his management team illustrated. Although some leaders assume that harmonious interaction is a sign that a team is working well, interventions focused on improving relationships do not actually foster team effectiveness over the long term. In fact, as Robert Kaplan documented years ago (in an article tellingly titled "The conspicuous absence of evidence that process consultation enhances task performance"), relationship-focused interventions impair team effectiveness as often as they help—by distracting members from the work at hand. Team-building exercises that emphasize trust or cohesion are indeed enjoyable and engaging, but they often divert members' attention from task-focused activities that actually have a chance of improving performance outcomes.

It is true that building harmonious interpersonal relations among members can reduce the amount of conflict that exists among members—but conflict about the best ways to do the work, or about the relative worth of different ideas that members propose, actually can foster creativity and, ultimately, team effectiveness. Unless a team leader observes that interpersonal difficulties are diminishing the team's motivation, or members' capacity to develop appropriate strategies, or their ability to leverage one another's talents, interventions that target interpersonal relationships are unlikely to help the team with its work.

Crafting Real-Time Interventions

Once team leaders diagnose the signs a team needs help, they must contend with the key issue of timing on the fly: How *soon* should they intervene? Should they act immediately, as soon as a problem surfaces, or let things play out for a while? The dilemma is that intervening quickly is more likely to correct the problem before it becomes intractable. But early action makes a team dependent on its leader and undermines the team's capacity for self-correction. Intervening later allows the leader to gather more data and offers room for the team to learn from its experience and correct its own mistakes. But delay also increases the chances that a problem will become too large ever to be corrected. Here is how Tony, the consulting firm partner, concerned about his team's upcoming presentation, handled this trade-off:

> I decided to [wait to intervene and] let them walk me through [their presentation], just in case I was missing something. I also felt that, from interacting with the team, the engagement manager had the thinnest skin, and I wanted to steer them in a way which wouldn't make him defensive or question his leadership. So, I had [two other team members] role-play the presenter and the client, while the engagement manager and the other team members watched. I didn't say much while this was happening, but the other members of the team started to ask questions from the client's perspective, and they quickly realized that they didn't really have recommendations that fit. And I did this on purpose so they could learn but not feel bad about themselves and I wouldn't have to lecture them. They could both test out the material for this particular project and, hopefully, learn a technique to help them better prepare for meetings in the future . . . Rather than beating them over the head with [what I thought they should do], I wound up walking them to a place where they could find that out on their own.

In this example, Tony detected a problem in team strategy. But he believed that the additional data he and the team would gain by waiting was valuable enough that he chose not to intervene when he first noticed the problem. He also made the judgment that, because he would not be working with this team regularly, the team *had* to have the ability to self-correct. Had the client meeting been sooner, or had his coaching meeting with the team been of shorter duration, he might reasonably have chosen to intervene more quickly.

Tony's intervention was also appropriately modest. Because the effort, strategy, and use of talent in a team are set on a trajectory by the team's initial design, team leaders swim against strong existing currents when they attempt trajectory-changing interventions in real time. Major changes therefore are best made during those predictable times, discussed earlier, when teams are ready for them. Moreover, as Ruth Wageman documented in her study on self-managing teams, teams that are poorly designed and launched are not helped by real-time process interventions. Well-designed teams, on the other hand, do benefit from modest interventions that aim to achieve small, positive shifts in team effort, strategy, and knowledge and skill.

One way in which team leaders can intervene in the periods between beginnings, midpoints, and ends is by using operant techniques (i.e. positive and negative feedback) to reinforce constructive but infrequently observed team behaviors—for example, praising a team for eliciting participation from quieter members, or pointing out that members' attention to the key issue has slipped. Such interventions can both increase the frequency of desirable behaviors and decrease the frequency of behaviors that are distracting or disruptive.

However, operant interventions only influence the frequency of *existing* behaviors. What actions can a team leader take in the moment to elicit effective behavior that is *not* being exhibited in the team? Leadership research often differentiates between "directive" and "participative" leader styles of intervening. Essentially, directive interventions tell teams what to do and what not to do with a minimum of input from members. They undoubtedly are faster and clearer in the moment. Participative interventions, generally executed by asking questions of the team, invite discussion and the invention of new and alternative ways of behaving. They take time that otherwise could be spent working on the task, but they can clarify team members' understanding of what is needed, and strengthen their commitment to behave differently.

Even though participative interventions often sacrifice short-term efficiency, they also may elicit new behaviors quickly that would not have emerged spontaneously. That is precisely what happened in the example above. Tony set the team up so that members could question each other and identify their own mistakes, and then solve their problems without his direction. This time-consuming intervention helped the team add new ways of preparing for client meetings to its repertoire. Moreover, the new behavior was more valuable to Tony and to the client than the small amount of time that would have been saved had he quickly told the team what he thought was wrong and what they should do about it.

A directive approach, by contrast, may be especially useful when a team is stuck, is headed for a major disaster, or is fixating on inappropriate matters. For example, Yuki Fujiyama, who runs a major business unit for a large financial services organization, found her leadership team consumed by a heated debate about an unpopular cost-allocation process that the chief financial officer (CFO) had recently introduced. Seeing that the team was on an unproductive tangent from which it was unlikely to recover, she stopped the debate cold, asserting that the team would spend no more time second-guessing its CFO and would turn, instead, to their planned discussion of strategic priorities.

Such pointed interventions that let members know that they are significantly off track can sometimes be highly constructive, especially if one also addresses *why* the behavior is problematic and what behaviors might be more appropriate. However, Fujiyama did take the risk that her team would read her actions as political support of a particular team member rather than as a statement about the kind of work that should be the team's focus. It is better for a leader to explicitly state why she expects what she expects from the team than to allow members to draw their own sometimes-sinister conclusions.

Team Re-Launch as an Intervention Strategy

Even competent, well-timed interventions sometimes cannot save a team from an accelerating downward trajectory. Poorly designed teams with unclear purposes, for example, can develop persistent dysfunctions, in which team leaders and members know there are significant problems with effort, strategy, or use of talent. Unfortunately, the dysfunctions persist no matter who intervenes or how. For example, the senior leadership team of a global mining company returned again and again to the same issues without ever coming together to make a decision. Upon reflection, the CEO saw that while his initial choice of team members looked promising, he inadvertently had included in the team too many people from too many different levels and functions of the organization ever to reach common ground. All the clever coaching in the world was not going to bring that team to a point of effectiveness.

In such situations, team leaders who have diagnosed the problem must lie in wait for an opportunity to change the basic design of the team, or create such an opportunity themselves. In the above example, the CEO had all the authority he needed to redefine the team's membership and purpose—all he had to do was to wait for the right moment. In his case, the approach of the new fiscal year created a naturally occurring point of inflection in the organization. He acknowledged that the team as configured was not working and announced that he was disbanding the team and "starting over" at the start of the new fiscal year, with a new configuration of members, a new name, and a new meeting schedule. Armed with the lessons of prior experience, he cut the size down to a handful of top executives, all of whom had previously demonstrated the ability to work collaboratively on the kinds of enterprise issues he wanted the team to tackle. Renaming the team made it palatable to those who were not invited to be part of the new team, especially since he preserved the original team for less frequent information-sharing meetings.

Many leaders find this idea of a team "re-launch," as we term it, a source of considerable relief. It's liberating to realize one does not have to live with continuing frustrations and dysfunctions. "Re-launch" does not offer an excuse for not getting the team design right in the first place, but it does offer real recourse to team leaders who are coping with persistently ineffective teams. It can help them to reconfigure the purpose or composition or norms that are ill-designed, and enable the team to have a fresh start.

When Timing is Beyond your Control

There are times in organizational life when team leaders have no realistic possibility of exhibiting good timing. Two such times are when institutional rhythms overwhelm the predictable pacing of teams' work and when catastrophic events prevent leaders from having any real choice about the timing of their activities.

Institutional Rhythms

The presence of powerful temporal forces that affect an entire organization can make it nearly impossible to properly time team interventions. When an organization begins to move toward a major event like a merger or new product launch, for example, teams invariably are swept along and their natural rhythms are disrupted. In these cases, leaders cannot expect to see the periods of readiness for interventions that come so predictably in normal circumstances, and Type I timing becomes impossible. Only Type II timing is relevant—assessing how teams are doing as events unfold and crafting interventions in real time as needed. Leaders who still try to do their main coaching at the beginnings, midpoints, and ends of team life cycles are almost certain to be both frustrated and unsuccessful. There are times when one simply must go with the larger flow.

An apparent obstacle to well-timed coaching is work that is performed continuously around the clock and throughout the year. How can one exploit the opportunities for intervention at beginnings, midpoints, and ends if there *are* no beginnings, midpoints, or ends? In fact, we find that there almost always are: If they do not exist naturally, then teams or their managers create them. For example, the semiconductor manufacturing teams that David Abramis and Richard Hackman studied at the Signetics Corporation some years ago operated continuously throughout the year: There were no natural breaks in the flow of the work. But managers at the plant arbitrarily partitioned the year into six-week performance periods. Both team dynamics and the tendency of team leaders to coach at those times were highly responsive to the beginnings, midpoints, and ends of those entirely made-up temporal periods.

The creation of quarters to demark financial reporting periods and semesters to organize educational activities in schools have the same character—they are arbitrary, but nonetheless powerful in shaping the rhythm of collective activity. Temporal rhythms are deeply rooted in human experience, and we do not do well when we do not have them. If rhythms fail to occur naturally (for example, through seasonal or biological cycles), we make up some markers and then entrain our activities to them. These made-up markers are surrogates for real beginnings, midpoints, and ends— but they create opportunities for team leadership interventions that are just as real as the real thing.

Catastrophic Events

How can a leader do well-timed coaching when all hands are on deck dealing with an unanticipated crisis or catastrophe? Sometimes there really is not much that can be done: When the hurricane comes, it is the hurricane rather than the team leader that determines what happens when. That said, it also is true that there usually are many more opportunities than one might imagine for well-timed leader interventions even in crisis situations.

Consider, for example, an operating room that is convened in real time when a patient develops an unexpected problem that requires immediate surgery. The team in the operating room—the surgeon, the anesthesiologist, the nurses—will not look much different from a team that is performing a procedure that has been scheduled well in advance. The difference, as a pediatric surgeon at a major Boston hospital told us, is that in an emergency situation there is simply no time to have the team briefing that he likes to conduct prior to beginning a scheduled procedure.

In fact, it's a judgment call. Which is worse for the patient: to take a short delay during which the patient's condition may deteriorate while the surgical team gets its act together, or to run the risk that an unlaunched team may have failures of coordination that pose an even graver threat than that of a brief delay? Our guess is that most surgeons would worry more about the delay than about the possibility of team process problems. We are tempted to come down on the other side. There are relatively few occasions when deferring the start of a procedure for a few minutes will have mortal consequences even in medical emergencies, and relatively more occasions when a procedure that should have proceeded quickly and smoothly did not because of team-related communication miscues and coordination failures.

What if all staff on the surgical service had previously been trained in strategies for conducting a quick launch of a surgical team and had practiced those strategies frequently enough that they became second nature? Would that make it possible for the team to have a reasonable launch even as members were arriving and making preparations for their own roles in the upcoming procedure? And could the same kind of thing be done for mid-procedure check-ins about team strategy and for quick and efficient post-procedure debriefings? We are not aware of any research that bears directly on these questions. But we are confident that there are many more opportunities for well-timed team interventions even in crisis situations than are generally recognized. Just because a crisis appears does not mean that timing becomes irrelevant; indeed, it very well could be that the timing of team-oriented interventions is even more consequential in crisis conditions than it is in normal times.

What it Takes to have a Great Sense of Timing

A great sense of timing requires certain human capacities beyond the basic necessities of team leadership skills. In addition to knowing about the key performance processes that influence team effectiveness and the times when a team is likely to be open to coaching interventions, team leaders also need the ability to sense social systems—that is, to be able to recognize the root causes driving the behavioral patterns they see in teams. Great timing also requires that leaders master their own natural tendencies to analyze endlessly and to recognize when one must act first and analyze later. We explore below what is involved in these two special leadership capabilities.

Ability to Sense Social Systems

Leading teams requires identifying the *systemic* conditions that create obstacles to team performance or, alternatively, that increase the chances of team effectiveness. System-focused action is creating the right design features for a team and then occasionally intervening on the fly, in ways that elicit and reinforce effective collaboration. Consistent with these observations, we find that the team leaders with the best timing are those who are adept both in comprehending the systemic nature of teams and organizations and in taking actions that respect and take full advantage of systemic forces.

Competent team leadership interventions, therefore, require a diagnostic frame of mind, in which a leader asks "What are the critical functions that are *not* being fulfilled in this system right now?" That kind of diagnostic question allows a leader to identify the actions that have the best possible chance of strengthening a team in its particular context at a particular time. For example, one leader of a regional medical products company had superb system-sensing skill. He recognized that it was unclear purposes and trivial tasks that were the most likely root causes of members' disengagement in a series of team meetings. Other observers might have seen the boredom, restlessness, and surreptitious e-mail checking as signs that members were challenging his authority. But his recognition of the underlying issue allowed him to take well-timed action, clarifying purposes and redesigning the team's shared work, when the situation presented an opportunity to do so. This diagnostic frame of mind, coupled with an understanding of the main conditions that elicit and reinforce effective collaboration, illustrates what we mean by the skill of sensing social systems.

IMPULSE TO ACT VS. ANALYZE   Team leaders differ in their propensity to act first (and analyze later) vs. analyze first (and act later). Our observations suggest that these differences sometimes can impede a leader's ability to act at the right moment. Consider, for example, a leader who strongly agrees with the following statement: "It is reckless to act without careful advance planning." Such a leader will wait, observe, and learn before taking action. Leaders who have a strong propensity to analyze are more likely to intervene later rather than sooner in team dynamics and have a better chance of getting the *content* of their interventions right. That is, they put themselves in position to understand what is causing the team to struggle and what actions in their own repertoire are likely to be helpful. Moreover, they run a low risk of undermining the team's ability to self-manage and solve its own problems because the team will have plenty of room to self-correct before its leader intervenes. But such individuals may miss entirely the critical moments in the team when the group is most able to be helped by prompt action.

Now consider the action-prone leader, one who would agree with the statement: "Endless analysis creates more problems than does thoughtless action." Such an individual intervenes quickly, with relatively little observational data about what is going on in the team. Action-oriented leaders are likely to act on problems long before they become intractable or damaging to team performance. But those actions may be taken on the basis of an incomplete or incorrect understanding of the group dynamic. Such leaders also may unintentionally prevent their teams from self-correcting and thereby encourage them to remain dependent on the leader to take care of things.

Among the best team leaders we have observed are those who have learned to shift orientation depending on the situations their teams face. Sometimes these leaders act swiftly; other times they defer action until they have done considerable observation and analysis. The success of this "shifting" strategy of course depends upon the degree to which action—or analysis-prone behaviors actually are under leaders' voluntary control. Sometimes action-prone behavior is driven by a leader's anxiety that the team's trajectory will get out of control and that he will take the blame for the consequences. And analysis-prone behavior can be driven by a leader's lack of confidence in his team leadership repertoire. Developing both capacities—to act swiftly or to wait and analyze more data—may best be done under conditions of relatively low pressure, so that those who hold responsibility for leading teams can learn to choose their approach deliberately when the moment matters.

Conclusion

Effective team leadership ensures that the functions that are most critical to a team in achieving its purposes are identified and fulfilled when the moment is right. Anyone who contributes to that—whether a formal team leader, a regular team member, or even an outside manager or consultant—is exhibiting team leadership. This article has described what it means to have great timing in anyone's team leadership activities. It takes a working knowledge of what teams need and when they need it. It means putting the conditions for team effectiveness in place in the right sequence, then exploiting predictable points of readiness in teams, and, finally, watching for real-time opportunities to help teams on the fly. These different aspects of great timing place a heavy demand on the cognitive, emotional, and behavioral capacities of individuals. Therefore, when a given leadership activity requires knowledge or skill that is beyond one individual's capabilities, the best team leaders do not hesitate to call on others to lend a hand in helping the team move forward. Team leadership is not a solo act. It, too, is a team activity.

12 Problem Solving

PUTTING YOUR COMPANY'S WHOLE BRAIN TO WORK
Dorothy Leonard
Susaan Straus

COLLABORATING FOR SYSTEMIC CHANGE
Peter M. Senge
Benyamin B. Lichtenstein
Katrin Kaeufer
Hilary Bradbury
John S. Carroll

A talent for problem solving has always been a requirement for managers and executives. With the advent of programs designed to increase organizational effectiveness, such as self-managed work teams, employee empowerment, total quality efforts, continuous improvement programs, reengineering, and organizational learning, problem-solving skills are needed by employees at all levels. Without problem-solving expertise, organizations cannot work as effectively and efficiently as they should, and their long-term survival and ability to adapt are threatened. The selections in this chapter reflect both a micro and macro approach to problem solving.

Myopia often keeps individuals, teams, and organizations from accurately seeing and defining problems; it also hinders their ability to come up with creative solutions. Therefore, one of the basic tenets of good problem solving is drawing on diverse perspectives. Dorothy Leonard, business professor and innovation and creativity consultant, and Susaan Straus, management consultant and executive coach, tackle this issue in "Putting Your Company's Whole Brain to Work." Individuals do not approach problem solving in the same way, which can be a source of conflict in today's highly integrated ways of working. Leonard and Straus underscore the importance of understanding, appreciating, and working effectively with people who have different cognitive preferences and communication styles.

Many firms take a systemic approach to problem solving. Peter Senge, founder of the Society for Organizational Learning; Benyamin Lichtenstein, professor of management and entrepreneurship at University of Massachusetts–Boston; Katrin Kaeufer, research director of the Presencing Institute; Hilary Bradbury, director of Sustainable Business Programs at the University of Southern California's Marshall School; and John Carroll, MIT professor, examine how such a systematic approach can be applied to the challenge of creating sustainable enterprises. They argue that effective problem solving requires careful attention to the conceptual, relational, and action-driven aspects inherent in these endeavors. They examine several intriguing examples of collaborative problem solving and draw out useful practical lessons for effectively implementing collaborative problem solving directed at systemic change.

PUTTING YOUR COMPANY'S WHOLE BRAIN TO WORK*

Dorothy Leonard

Susaan Straus

Innovate or fall behind: The competitive imperative for virtually all businesses today is that simple. Achieving it is hard, however, because innovation takes place when different ideas, perceptions, and ways of processing and judging information collide. That, in turn, often requires collaboration among various players who see the world in inherently different ways. As a result, the conflict that should take place constructively among ideas all too often ends up taking place unproductively among people who do not innately understand one another. Disputes become personal, and the creative process breaks down.

Stakes are high enough. That said, we all tend to have one or two preferred habits of thought that influence our decision-making styles and our interactions with others—for good or for ill.

The most widely recognized cognitive distinction is between left-brained and right-brained ways of thinking. This categorization is more powerful metaphorically than it is accurate physiologically; not all the functions commonly associated with the left brain are located on the left side of the cortex and not all so-called right-brained functions are located on the right. Still, the simple description does usefully capture radically different ways of thinking. An analytical, logical, and sequential approach to problem framing and solving (left-brained thinking) clearly differs from an intuitive, values-based, and nonlinear one (right-brained thinking).

Cognitive preferences also reveal themselves in work styles and decision-making activities. Take collaboration as opposed to independence. Some people prefer to work together on solving problems, whereas others prefer to gather, absorb, and process information by themselves. Each type does its best work under different conditions. Or consider thinking as opposed to feeling. Some people evaluate evidence and make decisions through a structured, logical process, whereas others rely on their values and emotions to guide them to the appropriate action.

The list goes on. Abstract thinkers, for instance, assimilate information from a variety of sources, such as books, reports, videos, and conversations. They prefer learning about something rather than experiencing it directly. Experiential people, in contrast, get information from interacting directly with people and things. Some people demand quick decisions no matter the issue, whereas others prefer to generate a lot of options no matter the urgency. One type focuses on details, whereas the other looks for the big picture: the relationships and patterns that the data form.

Not surprisingly, people tend to choose professions that reward their own combination of preferences. Their work experience, in turn, reinforces the original preferences and deepens the associated skills. Therefore, one sees very different problem-solving approaches among accountants, entrepreneurs, social workers, and artists. Proof to an engineer, for example, resides in the numbers. But show a page of numerical data to a playwright, and, more persuaded by his intuition, he may well toss it aside. Of course, assessing people's likely approaches to problem solving only by their discipline can be as misleading as using gender or ethnicity as a guide. Within any profession, there are always people whose thinking styles are at odds with the dominant approach.

The best way for managers to assess the thinking styles of the people they are responsible for is to use an established diagnostic instrument as an assessment tool. A well-tested tool is both more objective and more thorough than the impressions of even the most sensitive and observant of managers. Dozens of diagnostic tools and descriptive analyses of human personality have been developed to identify categories of cognitive approaches to problem solving and communication. All the instruments agree on the following basic points:

- Preferences are neither inherently good nor inherently bad. They are assets or liabilities depending on the situation. For example, politicians or CEOs who prefer to think out loud in public create expectations that they sometimes cannot meet; but the person who requires quiet reflection before acting can be a liability in a crisis.
- Distinguishing preferences emerge early in our lives, and strongly held ones tend to remain relatively stable through the years. Thus, for example, those of us who crave certainty are unlikely ever to have an equal love of ambiguity and paradox.
- We can learn to expand our repertoire of behaviors, to act outside our preferred styles. But that is difficult—like writing with the opposite hand.
- Understanding others' preferences helps people communicate and collaborate.

Managers who use credible personality instruments find that their employees accept the outcomes of the tests and use them to improve their processes and behaviors.

How We Act

All the assessment in the world means nothing unless new understanding brings different actions. Personality instruments will help you understand yourself and will help others understand themselves. The managerial challenge is to use the insights that these instruments offer to create new processes and encourage new behaviors that will help innovation efforts succeed.

UNDERSTAND YOURSELF Start with yourself. When you identify your own style, you gain insight into the ways your preferences unconsciously shape your style of leadership and patterns of communication. You may be surprised to discover that your style can stifle the very creativity you seek from your employees. Consider the experiences of two managers of highly creative organizations. Each was at odds with his direct reports—but for very different reasons.

Jim Shaw, executive vice president of MTV Networks, is a left-brained guy in a right-brained organization. Said Shaw:

I have always characterized the creative, right-brained, visionary-type people here as dreamers. What I've realized is that when a dreamer expressed a vision, my gut reaction was to say, "Well, if you want to do that, what you've got to do is A, then B, then you have to work out C, and because you've got no people and you've got no satellite up-link, you'll have to do D and E." I've learned that saying that to a creative type is like throwing up on the dream. When I say that stuff too soon, the dreamer personalizes it as an attack. I've learned not to put all of the things that need to be done on the table initially. I can't just blurt it all out—it makes me look like a naysayer. What I've learned to do is to leak the information gradually, then the dreamer knows that I am meeting him halfway.

Jerry Hirshberg, president of Nissan Design International, ran into precisely the opposite problem. Hirshberg discovered that some of his employees craved the very kind of structure that he personally abhorred. Before this epiphany, he inundated them with information and expected creativity in return. In short, he tried to manage his employees the way *he* would have wanted to be managed. Hirshberg found, however, that a few individuals reacted to every suggestion with a "Yes but. . . ." Initially, he interpreted such hesitancy as an anti-innovation bias. But he eventually realized that some of his employees preferred to have more time both to digest problems and to construct logical approaches to his intuitively derived ideas. Given a bit of extra time, they would return to the project with solid, helpful, and insightful plans for implementation. Ironically, it was their commitment to the success of the initiative that caused the employees to hesitate: They wanted the best possible result. Hirshberg recognized that their contributions were as critical as his own or those of any of the other "right-brainers" in the company.

Both Shaw and Hirshberg came to realize that their own cognitive preferences unconsciously shaped their leadership styles and communication patterns. In fact, their automatic reactions initially stifled the very creativity they sought from their employees. And note that it was just as important for the predominantly right-brained manager to recognize the contributions of the logicians as it was for the left-brained manager to acknowledge the organic approach of the visionaries. Except in theoretical models, creativity is not the exclusive province of one side or the other.

If you want an innovative organization, you need to hire, work with, and promote people who make you uncomfortable. You need to understand your own preferences so that you can complement your weaknesses and exploit your strengths. The biggest barrier to recognizing the contributions of people who are unlike you is your own ego. Suppose you are stalled on a difficult problem. To whom do you go for help? Usually to someone who is on the same wavelength or to someone whose opinion you respect. These people may give you soothing strokes, but they are unlikely to help spark a new idea. Suppose you were to take the problem instead to someone with whom you often find yourself at odds, someone who rarely validates your ideas or perspectives. It may take courage and tact to get constructive feedback, and the process may not be exactly pleasant. But that feedback will likely improve the quality of your solution. And when your adversary recovers from his amazement at your request, he may even get along with you better because the disagreement was clearly intellectual, not personal.

FORGET THE GOLDEN RULE Don't treat people the way you want to be treated. Tailor communications to the receiver instead of the sender. In a cognitively diverse environment, a message sent is not necessarily a message received. Some people respond well to facts, figures, and statistics. Others prefer anecdotes. Still others digest graphic presentations most easily. Information must be delivered in the preferred "language" of the recipient if it is to be received at all.

For example, say you want to persuade an organization to adopt an open office layout. Arguments appealing to the analytical mind would rely on statistics from well-documented research conducted by objective experts that prove that open architecture enhances the effectiveness of communication. Arguments geared toward the action-oriented type would answer specific questions about implementation: How long will the office conversion take? Exactly what kind of furniture is needed? What are the implications for acoustics? Arguments aimed at people-oriented individuals would focus on such questions as, How does an open office affect relationships? How would this setup affect morale? and Are people happy in this sort of setup? Arguments crafted for people with a future-oriented perspective would include graphics as well as artists' renderings of the proposed environment. In short, regardless of how you personally would prefer to deliver the message, you will be more persuasive and better understood if you formulate messages to appeal to the particular thinking style of your listener.

CREATE "WHOLE-BRAINED" TEAMS Either over time or by initial design, company or group cultures can become dominated by one particular cognitive style. IBM, in the days when it was known as "Big Blue," presented a uniform face to the world; Digital Equipment prided itself on its engineering culture. Such homogeneity makes for efficient functioning—and limited approaches to problems or opportunities. Companies with strong cultures can indeed be very creative, but within predictable boundaries—say, clever marketing or imaginative engineering. When the market demands that such companies innovate in different ways, they have to learn new responses. Doing so requires adopting a variety of approaches to solving a problem—using not just the right brain or the left brain but the *whole* brain.

Consider the all-too-common error made by John, a rising star in a large, diversified instrument company: He forfeited an important career opportunity because he failed to see the need for a whole-brained team. Appointed manager of a new-product development group, John had a charter to bring in radically innovative ideas for products and services for launch in three to six years. "Surprise me," the CEO said.

Given a free hand in hiring, John lured in three of the brightest M.B.A.'s he could find. They immediately went to work conducting industry analyses and sorting through existing product possibilities, applying their recently acquired skills in financial analysis. To complete the team, John turned to the pile of résumés on his desk sent to him by human resources. All the applicants had especially strong quantitative skills, and a couple were engineers. John was pleased. Surely a group of such intelligent, well-trained, rigorous thinkers would be able to come up with some radical innovations for the company. Ignoring advice to hire some right-brained people to stimulate different ideas, he continued to populate his group with left-brained wizards. After 18 months, the team had rejected all the proposed new projects in the pipeline on the basis of well-argued and impressively documented financial and technical risk analysis. But the team's members had not come up with a single new idea. The CEO was neither surprised nor pleased, and the group was disbanded just short of its second anniversary.

In contrast, Bob, a successful entrepreneur embarking on his latest venture, resisted the strong temptation to tolerate only like-minded people. He knew from his prior ventures that his highly analytical style alienated some of his most creative people. Despite his unusual degree of self-awareness, Bob came within a hair's breadth of firing a strong and experienced manager, Wally, his director of human resources. According to Bob, after several months on board, Wally appeared to be "a quart and a half low." Why? Because Bob was inattentive in budget meetings and focused on what he perceived as trivia—day care, flextime, and benefits. Before taking action, however, Bob decided to look at the management team through the lens of thinking styles. He soon realized that Wally was exactly the kind of person he needed to help him grow his small company. Wally contributed a key element that was otherwise missing in the management team: a sensitivity to human needs that helped the company foresee and forestall problems with employees. So Bob learned to meet Wally halfway. Describing his success in learning to work with Wally, he told us, "You would have been proud of me. I started our meetings with five minutes of dogs, kids, and station wagons." Although the concern Wally demonstrated for the workers in the company did not eliminate union issues completely, it did minimize antagonism toward management and made disputes easier to resolve.

The list of whole-brained teams that continue to innovate successfully is long. At Xerox PARC, social scientists work alongside computer scientists. For instance, computer scientist Pavel Curtis, who is creating a virtual world in which people will meet and mingle, is working with an anthropologist who understands how communities form. As a result, Curtis's cyberspace meeting places have more human touches and are more welcoming than they would have been had they been designed only by scientists. Another example is the PARC PAIR (PARC Artist In Residence) program, which links computer scientists with artists so that each may influence the other's perceptions and representations of the world. At Interval Research, a California think tank dedicated to multimedia technologies, Director David Liddle invites leaders from various disciplines to visit for short "sabbaticals." The purpose is to stimulate a cross-fertilization of ideas and approaches to solving problems. The resulting exchanges have helped Interval Research create and spin off several highly innovative start-ups. And Jerry Hirshberg applies the whole-brain principle to hiring practices at Nissan Design by bringing designers into his organization in virtual pairs. That is, when he hires a designer who glories in the freedom of pure color and rhythm, he will next hire a very rational, Bauhaus-trained designer who favors analysis and focuses on function.

Complete homogeneity in an organization's cognitive approach can be very efficient. But as managers at Xerox PARC, Interval Research, and Nissan Design have learned, no matter how brilliant the group of individuals, their contributions to innovative problem solving are enhanced by coming up against totally different perspectives.

LOOK FOR THE UGLY DUCKLING Suppose you don't have the luxury of hiring new people yet and find your organization mired in a swamp of stale thinking patterns. Consider the experience of the CEO of the U.S. subsidiary of a tightly controlled and conservative European chemical company. Even though the company's business strategy had never worked well in the United States, headquarters pushed the CEO to do more of the same. He knew he needed to figure out a fresh approach because the U.S. company was struggling to compete in a rapidly changing marketplace. But his direct reports were as uniformly left-brained as his superiors in Europe and were disinclined to work with him to figure out new solutions.

Rather than give up, the CEO tested thinking preferences further down in the organization. He found the cognitive disparity that he needed in managers one layer below his direct reports—a small but dynamic set of individuals whose countercultural thinking patterns had constrained their advancement. In this company, people with right-brained preferences were seen as helpful but were not considered top management material. They were never promoted above a certain level.

The CEO changed that. He elevated three managers with right-brained proclivities to the roles of senior vice president and division head–lofty positions occupied until then exclusively by left-brained individuals. The new executives were strong supporters of the CEO's intentions to innovate and worked with him to develop new approaches to the business. They understood that their communication strategy with headquarters would be critical to their success. They deliberately packaged their new ideas in a way that appealed to the cognitive framework of their European owner. Instead of lecturing about the need to change and try new ideas as they had in the past, the Americans presented their ideas as ways of solving problems. They supported their positions with well-researched quantitative data and with calculated anticipated cost savings and ROI—and described how similar approaches had succeeded elsewhere. They detailed the specific steps they would follow to succeed. Within two years, the U.S. subsidiary embarked on a major organizational redesign effort that included such radical notions as permitting outside competition for internal services. The quality of internal services soared—as did the number of innovations generated by the company in the United States.

MANAGE THE CREATIVE PROCESS Abrasion is not creative unless managers make it so. Members of whole-brained teams don't naturally understand one another, and they can easily come to dislike one another. Successful managers of richly diverse groups spend time from the outset getting members to acknowledge their differences—often through a joint exploration of the results of a diagnostic analysis—and devise guidelines for working together before attempting to act on the problem at hand. Managers who find it awkward or difficult to lead their groups in identifying cognitive styles or in establishing guidelines can usually enlist the aid of someone who is trained in facilitation.

People often feel a bit foolish creating rules about how they will work together. Surely, the thinking goes, we are all adults and have years of experience in dealing with group dynamics. That, of course, is the problem. Everyone has practiced dysfunctional behavior for years. We learn to value politeness over truth at our mothers' knees. (Who hasn't mastered the art of the white lie by age 16?) We often discount an argument if it has an element of emotion or passion. We opt out if we feel ignored—people with unappreciated thinking styles learn to sit against the wall during meetings (the organizational back-of-the-bus). And we usually don't even notice those behaviors because they are so routine.

But the cost of allowing such behaviors to overtake a group is too high. Bob Meyers, senior vice president of interactive media at NBC, uses a sports analogy to make the point: "On a football team, for example, you have to use all kinds of people. Like the little, skinny guy who can only kick the ball. He may not even look as if he belongs on the team. This guy can't stand up to the refrigerator types that play in other positions. But as long as he does his job, he doesn't need to be big. He can just do what he does best. The catch is that the team needs to recognize what the little skinny guy can do—or they lose the benefit of his talent."

Managing the process of creative abrasion means making sure that everyone is at the front of the bus and talking. Some simple but powerful techniques can be helpful. First, clarify why you are working together by keeping the common goal in front of the group at all times. "If the goal is a real-world one with shared accountability and timetables attached," one manager observed, "then everyone understands the relevance of honoring one another's differences."

Second, make your operating guidelines explicit. Effective guidelines are always simple, clear, and concise. For example, one group set up the following principles about handling disagreements: "Anyone can disagree about anything with anyone, but no one can disagree without stating the reason," and "When someone states an objection, everyone else should listen to it, try to understand it, treat it as legitimate, and counter with their reasons if they don't agree with it." Some principles are as simple as "Discuss taboo subjects," "Verify assumptions," and "Arrive on time with your homework done."

Third, set up an agenda ahead of time that explicitly provides enough time for both divergent discussion to uncover imaginative alternatives and convergent discussion to select an option and plan its implementation. Innovation requires both types of discussion, but people who excel at different types can, as one manager observed, "drive each other nuts." Another manager said, "If you ask people comfortable with ambiguity whether they prefer A or B, they will ask, 'How about C?'" Meanwhile, the people who crave closure will be squirming in their seats at the seemingly pointless discussion. Moreover, if one approach dominates, the unbalanced group process can risk producing an unacceptable or unfeasible new product, service, or change. Clearly allocating time to the two different types of discussion will contain the frustrations of both the decisive types, who are constantly looking at their watches wanting the decision to be made now, and the ambiguous types, who want to be sure that all possible avenues for creativity have been explored. Otherwise, the decisive members generally will pound the others into silence by invoking time pressures and scheduling. They will grab the first viable option rather than the best one. Or if the less decisive dominate, the group may never reach a conclusion. Innovation requires both divergent and convergent thinking, both brainstorming and action plans.

DEPERSONALIZE CONFLICT Diverse cognitive preferences can cause tremendous tensions in any group, yet innovation requires the cross-fertilization of ideas. And because many new products are systems rather than stand-alone pieces, many business projects cannot proceed without the cooperation of people who receive different messages from the same words and make different observations about the same incidents. The single most valuable contribution that understanding different thinking and communication styles brings to the process of innovation is taking the sting out of intellectual disagreements that turn personal.

Consider the experience of the product manager of a radically new product for a medical supplies company. Facing a strict deadline of just 14 months to design and deliver a new surgical instrument, the manager's team needed to pull together fast. Design felt misled by marketing, however, and manufacturing couldn't understand design's delay in choosing between two mechanical hinges. The disagreements turned personal, starting with "you always . . . " and ending with " . . . irresponsible ignorance." Two months into the project, the manager began to wonder whether he should disband the team and start over again. But he knew that his boss, the vice president of marketing, would not agree to extend the deadline. "I was desperate," he recalled. "I decided to make one last attempt at getting them to work together."

The manager decided to experiment with an offsite gathering of his staff, including sessions diagnosing cognitive preferences. When they returned to work, the team members used the new language they had learned to label their differences in opinion and style. "At first, using the terms was kind of a joke," the manager recalled. "They'd say things like, 'Well, of course I want the schedule right now. I'm a J!' Yet you could tell that people were really seeing one another in a different light, and they weren't getting angry." The team made its deadline; perhaps even more important, several members voluntarily joined forces to work on the next iteration of the product. This willingness to work together generated more value for the company than just "warm fuzzies." Critical technical knowledge was preserved in one small, colocated group—knowledge that would have been scattered had project members dispersed to different product lines. Moreover, keeping part of the team together resulted in a rapid development time for the derivative product.

People who do not understand cognitive preferences tend to personalize conflict or avoid it—or both. The realization that another person's approach is not wrongheaded and stubborn, but merely predictably different, diffuses anger. For example, at Viacom, a planning session involving two managers had ground to a halt. One manager simply wouldn't buy into the idea that the other was presenting. Suddenly, the presenter slapped his head and said, "Oooohhh! I get it! You're left-brained! Give me half an hour to switch gears, and I'll be right back. Let me try this one more time." The left-brained manager laughingly agreed—he understood the paradigm—and the meeting resumed with the presenter armed with quantitative data and a much more cohesive and logical presentation. Establishing that kind of effective two-way communication led to a common understanding of the issues at hand and, ultimately, a solution.

Understanding that someone views a problem differently does not mean you will agree. But an important element in understanding thinking styles is recognizing that no one style is inherently better than another. Each style brings a uniquely valuable perspective to the process of innovation, just as each style has some negatives associated with it. Stereotypes of the cold-hearted logician, the absentminded, creative scientist, and the bleeding-heart liberal have some basis in reality. If people even partially internalize the inherent value of different perspectives, they will take disagreements less personally and will be better able to argue and reach a compromise or a consensus with less animosity. They will be open to the possibility that an alien view of the world might actually enhance their own. They will be better equipped to listen for the "a-ha" that occurs at the intersection of different planes of thought.

Caveat Emptor

Personality analysis of the type we describe is no more than a helpful tool, and it has many limitations. The diagnostic instruments measure only one aspect of personality: preferences in thinking styles and communication. They do not measure ability or intelligence, and they do not predict performance. Neither the MBTI® nor the HBDI measure other qualities that are critical to successful innovation such as courage, curiosity, integrity, empathy, or drive.

Preferences tend to be relatively stable, but life experiences can affect them. For example, repeated application of the MBTI® over a period of years has revealed a tendency for people to drift from a thinking style toward a feeling style when they have children. For the most part, however, studies done with both the MBTI® and the HBDI suggest that people retain their dominant preferences throughout a variety of work and social circumstances.

One critical warning label should be attached to any of these diagnostic instruments: only trained individuals should administer them. Not only can results be incorrectly interpreted (for instance, what are intended to be neutral descriptions of preferences might be labeled "right" or "wrong" behavior), but they can also be misused to invade people's privacy or to stereotype them. Of course, it is a human tendency to simplify in order to comprehend complexities; we stereotype people all the time on the basis of their language, dress, and behavior. Because these diagnostics have the weight of considerable psychological research behind them, however, they can be dangerous when misused. Without structured, reliable diagnoses, judgments are likely to be superficial and flawed. And without a substantial investment of time and resources, managers can't expect abrasion to be creative.

One of the paradoxes of modern management is that, in the midst of technical and social change so pervasive and rapid that it seems out of pace with the rhythms of nature, human personality has not altered throughout recorded history. People have always had distinct preferences in their approaches to problem solving. Why then is it only now becoming so necessary for managers to understand those differences? Because today's complex products demand integrating the expertise of individuals who do not innately understand one another. Today's pace of change demands that these individuals quickly develop the ability to work together. If abrasion is not managed into creativity, it will constrict the constructive impulses of individuals and organizations alike. Rightly harnessed, the energy released by the intersection of different thought processes will propel innovation.

COLLABORATING FOR SYSTEMIC CHANGE*

Peter M. Senge

Benyamin B. Lichtenstein

Katrin Kaeufer

Hilary Bradbury

John S. Carroll

For more than a century and a half, industrial growth has been weaving an ever-thickening web of interdependence around the world. Today, consumer choices on one side of the planet affect living conditions for people on the other side. Complex supply chains span the globe; for example, the average pound of food travels between 1,500 and 2,500 miles before it reaches an American consumer.[1] But these developments do not alter biological or social realities that have taken shape over thousands and millions of years. Consequently, businesses operating within this growing web are facing a host of "sustainability" problems: social and ecological imbalances created by this globalization, such as a widening social divide between haves and have-nots, global climate change, exponentially growing chemical and material waste, and loss of habitat and species.

Traditionally, businesses have thought such problems to be the result of economic externalities that require governments' attention. But while governments are a crucial part of lasting change, relying on governmental leadership to effectively deal with sustainability is questionable for many reasons. The first limitation is geography. Even the largest governmental institutions are limited by their borders and can't attack sustainability problems that are global in nature. The second limitation is time. Elected officials are limited by their election cycles and struggle to deal with problems that develop over decades and don't align with their time in office. Moreover, due to increased fragmentation in democratic societies, problems that transcend those of specialized interests tend to fall by the wayside.

For these and many more reasons, businesses are finding themselves compelled to exercise leadership around a host of sustainability issues. In particular, recognizing the limitations of what can be done in isolation, many business leaders have already formed collaborative initiatives like the World Business Council for Sustainable Development, the Coalition for Environmentally Responsible Economies and Societies, and the Global Reporting Initiative. In spite of such initiatives, however, there are challenges we are just beginning to recognize. (See "About the Research," p. 337.)

For example, in 1991, Unilever—the consumer products giant based in London—initiated a worldwide collaborative effort toward creating a global certification regime for sustainable fishing involving fishing companies, distributors, retailers,

*Reprinted with permission from *MIT Sloan Management Review* 48(2) (Winter 2007): 65–71.

local governments, and nongovernmental organizations. Unfortunately, as soon as this Marine Stewardship Council was formed, it was immersed in controversy.[2] Environmental NGOs interpreted aggressive goals to certify major fisheries as a corporate drive to certify "business-as-usual" overfishing.[3] Conversely, NGO efforts to contest certification were criticized by the multinational corporations as stalling progress toward sustainability. One of the first projects of the MSC—to certify the Alaskan pollock fishery (the largest white fish fishery in the world)—became a multiyear legal battle. Similar difficulties have plagued other efforts to establish certification mechanisms in forestry, and organic and nongenetically modified foods.

Two conclusions stand out from efforts like the MSC. First, recognition of the need for such collaboration is growing. Second, it is exceedingly difficult to engage a diverse group of partners in successful collaborative systemic change. Although some relevant research exists,[4] cross-sector collaboration at this scale is largely unexplored. The need is great, but the challenge is equally great.

The Society for Organizational Learning

Beginning in the late 1990s, organizational members of the Society for Organizational Learning began several initiatives focusing on collaborative solutions to a variety of sustainability issues.[5] The group's goals have included the application of systems thinking, working with mental models, and fostering personal and shared vision to face these complex sustainability issues.[6]

Through its work, SoL has learned that successful collaborative efforts embrace three interconnected types of work—*conceptual, relational,* and *action driven*—that together build a healthy "learning ecology" for systemic change. Failing to appreciate the importance of each is likely to frustrate otherwise serious and well-funded attempts at collaboration on complex problems. What follows are examples from particular projects in which this learning ecology provided an important foundation for substantive progress.

Conceptual Work: Framing Complex Issues

Making sense of complex issues like sustainability requires systems-thinking skills that are not widely shared. When effective collaboration is the aim, developing a shared conceptual "systems sense" is even more important.

Illustrative Conceptual Projects: Integrating Sustainability Frameworks

A dozen SoL organization members including Shell, Harley Davidson, HP, Xerox, and Nike formed the SoL Sustainability Consortium in 1999 to gain a better understanding of how learning tools could support their efforts to integrate sustainability concerns into their business practices.[7] One of the first conceptual projects that emerged in the consortium grew from the confusion of members about the many different sustainability frameworks and tools they encountered,[8] including the Natural Step,[9] Natural Capitalism,[10] ISO 14001,[11] Zero Emissions Research Initiative,[12] biomimicry,[13] WBCSD Indicators,[14] ecological footprints,[15] life-cycle analysis,[16] and cradle to cradle.[17] (See "Describing Different Sustainability Frameworks," p. 339.)

This confusion became an issue because the proliferation of frameworks and tools was actually slowing progress toward sustainability rather than assisting it, especially because people were spending their time arguing about which framework was "right." In response the consortium frameworks group emerged—a subgroup of the consortium that included members from BP, Harley-Davidson, Plug Power, Visteon, MIT, and U.S. Natural Step—that came up with two key ideas for integrating and relating different sustainability approaches.[18]

1. THERE ARE THREE DIFFERENT WORLDVIEWS THAT INFORM THE NOTION OF SUSTAINABILITY[19] These are *rationalism,* which recognizes the need for efficient utilization of resources through "meeting the needs of the present without compromising the ability of future generations to meet their own needs";[20] *naturalism,* which recognizes the need to bring industrial systems into harmony with nature[21] by not depleting resources beyond their rates of regeneration; and *humanism,* which recognizes that sustainability depends on an intrinsic human desire to be part of healthy communities that preserve life for ourselves, other species, and future generations.[22]

Each worldview provides a vital counterbalance to the others. For example, popular rationalistic concepts like eco-efficiency can help businesses waste less, but a growing economy can have an increasingly adverse environmental impact, even as it becomes more efficient in using natural resources. By contrast, naturalism addresses the total impact of industrial activity on nature, but unless it evokes a deep human desire to live within those limits, it doesn't necessarily motivate change. Similarly, humanism addresses the deeper motivations for sustainability but does not, by itself, lead to the practical tools and metrics for connecting business operations to sustainability outcomes.[23]

2. DIFFERENT SUSTAINABILITY FRAMEWORKS RELATE TO DIFFERENT LEVELS IN THE MANAGEMENT SYSTEM Many frameworks focus on metrics. This is useful but narrow. Equally important is defining overall outcomes and having guidelines for shaping strategies. Organizational practices that include or go beyond metrics mediate between strategy and outcomes and constitute a critical aspect of any business.

Seeing different sustainability frameworks as working at different management levels clarifies their interdependency and potential complementarity. (See "Integrating Frameworks Across Levels," p. 340.) It also reminds us that management systems must be homegrown. Strategic guidelines and organizational metrics and practices must be tailored to the specific people, culture, market, technology, and history of any enterprise. For example, NIKE Inc., a company that prides itself on innovation for vitality and more healthy personal lifestyles, naturally gravitated to biomimicry—innovation inspired by nature. Today, led by hundreds of independent designers who are part of Nike's larger network, the company is introducing a range of "biomimetic" innovations such as compostable cloth, shoes that are put together with biodegradable adhesives, and an entire line of organic cotton athletic apparel. (Nike even helped to launch the Organic Cotton Exchange to bring more organic cotton onto the world market.) Translating general ideas into specific organizational strategies, practices, and objectives takes imagination, courage, persistence, patience, and passion. In its final report, the consortium subgroup concluded, "The sustainability challenge is fundamentally a learning challenge, a process that requires both 'outer changes' like new metrics and 'inner changes' in taken-for-granted assumptions and ways of operating."[24]

Lessons from the Conceptual Work

The learnings from conceptual work done on particular projects suggest the need for collectively built frameworks that create clarity without denying complexity.

BUILD COMMUNITY THROUGH THINKING TOGETHER AND SHARING When faced with difficult conceptual tasks, it is faster and easier to leave the work to small groups of experts or to outsource it to consultants or academics. But doing so bypasses the collective intelligence embedded in diverse organizations and industries and can result

About the Research

Data for this research were collected and analyzed by a team of four researchers who, over a six-year period, participated in more than a dozen meetings of the SoL Sustainability Consortium as well as being participant observers in all the collaborative projects. Using traditional ethnomethodology, researchers took extensive field notes of each of the consortium meetings and discussed these in post hoc research teleconferences. In addition, 42 semi-structured interviews with participants were conducted, recorded and transcribed over a two-year period. Participants were asked about specific collaborative experiences, as well as their personal and business aspirations for the consortium as a whole. In order to gain a diversity of views, the research team chose individuals representing a range of organizational ranks (senior, mid-level, and junior) and attendance levels (core, frequent, and recent). Data were analyzed and coded for emergent themes, using inductive qualitative methods appropriate for exploratory research.[i] At the same time, individual case studies of collaborative projects were developed and compared in order to identify emergent routines and practices being transferred across projects.[ii] We analyzed all these data for the presence of drivers and interaction patterns within the consortium as a whole, eventually developing a single system map that identified the three domains discussed here.[iii]

The study has been guided by the principles of participatory action research[iv] and community action research,[v] aiming to build a community that builds knowledge in a way that binds together the community. Thus, the researchers actively participated in meetings and projects and, in addition, they periodically presented interpretations from their research engaging participants, facilitators and organizers in regular dialogues on its implications.

i. J.M. Corbin and A.L. Strauss, "The Articulation of Work Through Interaction," Sociological Quarterly 34, no. 1 (March 1993): 71–83; and M.B. Miles and A.M. Huberman, "Qualitative Data Analysis" (Thousand Oaks, California: Sage, 1994).
ii. R.K. Yin, "Case Study Research: Design and Methods" (Beverly Hills, California: Sage Publications, 1984); and K.M. Eisenhardt and L. J. Bourgeois, III, "Building Theories From Case Study Research," Academy of Management Review 14, no. 4 (October 1989): 532–550.
iii. H. Bradbury, D. Good and L. Robson, "What Keeps It Together: Relational Bases for Organizing," in "Creating Collaborative Cultures," ed. S. Shuman (San Francisco: Jossey-Bass/Wiley, in press).
iv. P. Reason and H. Bradbury, "Introduction: Inquiry and Participation in Search of a World Worthy of Human Aspiration," in "Handbook of Action Research: Participative Inquiry and Practice," ed. P. Reason and H. Bradbury (London: Sage Publications, 2001), 1–14; and C.D. Argyris, B. Smith and B. Putnam, "Action Science: Concepts, Methods and Skills For Research and intervention" (San Francisco: Jossey-Bass, 1985).
v. C.O. Scharmer and P. Senge, "Community Action Research," in "Handbook of Action Research: Participative Inquiry and Practice," ed. P. Reason and H. Bradbury (London: Sage Publications, 2001), 238–249.

in output for which there is neither deep understanding nor commitment. In contrast, when conceptual frameworks are developed collaboratively, the process builds community and fosters more extended application and testing. As one member reflected, "Working together to make sense of the different sustainability frameworks showed us that we were not the only company who was confused about sustainability and helped us communicate what sustainability meant in terms of outcomes and strategies in a way that worked in our culture."[25]

ACHIEVE SIMPLICITY WITHOUT REDUCTION[26] Clarity must not come at the expense of oversimplification and trivialization of complex issues. Conceptual working groups can sometimes produce rousing action agendas that include little penetrating insight; similarly, turgid analyses of complex issues can leave people better informed but no more able to take action. Nevertheless, tools like system dynamics[27] and stock-flow diagrams (see "Naturalism and Sustainability," p. 342) can help in digesting the complexity of a problem while communicating key features that guide action. Simple system models highlight key variables and key interrelationships.

Relational Work: Dialogue and Collaborative Inquiry

Success in any collaboration between organizations rests on the quality of relationships that shape cooperation, trust, mutuality, and joint learning.[28] But supporting relationship building is not easy, given the competitive culture and transactional relationships typical in organizational life. Only rarely do groups move beyond "politeness" or win-lose debates into more authentic and reflective interactions characterized by candor, openness, and vulnerability.

From its inception, members of the SoL Sustainability Consortium were committed to skills of reflective conversation and working with mental models as a way to build more productive relationships. As part of bringing new members into the community, a half-day, premeeting workshop introduced basic tools of organizational learning; specific ground rules for effective conversation were made explicit, including such things as confidentiality, radical respect for each other, the imperative to "listen, listen, listen," and inquiry balanced with advocacy. These steps were especially useful in ongoing projects in which people deepened their understanding of one another through genuine dialogue.

Illustrative Relational Projects: Women Leading Sustainability

The first Women Leading Sustainability dialogue was held in 2001 to explore the distinctive nature of women's leadership in sustainability initiatives. Over the years, participants developed a repository of the group's experiences, including stories about leading sustainability initiatives, reflections on personal challenges, and lessons learned through the eyes of their children. In these ways, the group has lived the consortium's dedication to candor and cooperation.

The relational work of WLS has had tangible effects. For example, Simone Amber, founder of a corporate-funded, global Internet-based educational project called SEED, said that the honest dialogue of WLS helped her see how far sustainability efforts go toward helping others, especially those in developing countries. In WLS, participants' motivation for working on sustainability goes beyond business benefits by integrating work, family, and self; and the members have developed a sense of purpose, fueled by a desire for their work to benefit others. These successes are embodied in the group's description of itself: "What matters most about this group is that we assert the importance of taking time for reflection so that our learning evolves through integrating action and reflection." Action and reflection are necessary for good decision making, yet in today's "just do it" culture, time for learning is rarely practiced or valued.

Lessons from the Relational Work

The learnings from relational work done on particular projects suggest that the work must begin with far-reaching and unorchestrated dialogue that in turn sets the tone for systematic initiatives and practices.

DIALOGUE GROUPS EMERGE FROM DEEP QUESTIONS AND LONGINGS Although it is easy to focus on formal strategies and the mechanics of change, we shape our collective futures in "conversations that matter."[29] For example, the Women Leading Sustainability group explored how to connect their "inner" and "outer" lives, how to develop a career path that can provide leadership within the corporation while also being consistent with their core values, and how best to engage stakeholders far beyond their organizations. Such conversations help clarify important issues and provide a "lived experience of how we naturally self-organize to think together, strengthen community, share knowledge and ignite innovation."[30]

Identifying powerful questions cannot be orchestrated or planned. They emerge over time with shifts in strategic context. The key is to recognize and engage them seriously in a spirit of dialogue and joint exploration. For example, John Browne, chief executive officer of BP p.l.c., has arguably done as much to legitimize the importance of climate change in the business world as anyone over the last

Describing Different Sustainability Frameworks

When the Society for Organizational Learning first organized in 1999, one of its first conceptual projects was to find a way to integrate and relate the existing sustainability tools and frameworks.

The Natural Step was founded by the Swedish researcher Karl-Hènrik Robèrt in 1989, who developed the following scientifically based consensus definition of sustainability: In a sustainable society, nature is not subject to systematically increasing (1) concentrations of substances extracted from the earth's crust; (2) concentrations of substances produced by society; and (3) degradation by physical means; and in that society, people are not subject to conditions that systematically undermine their capacity to meet their needs.

Natural capitalism is a strategic framework based on four precepts: (1) radically increase the productivity of resource use; (2) shift to biologically inspired production (for example, biomimicry) with closed loops, no waste, and no toxicity; (3) shift business models away from the making and selling of "things" to providing the service that the "thing" delivers (thereby retaining ownership of products for recycling and remanufacturing); and (4) reinvest in natural and human capital.

ISO 14001 was first published in 1998 and specifies the operational requirements for an environmental management system, providing generalizable objectives and goals with measurable metrics that can guide the environmental activities of organizations in most industries.

Zero Emissions Research Initiative was launched by the United Nations University/Institute of Advanced Studies in 1994 and was renamed Zero Emissions Forum in 1999. ZERI promoted the concept that all industrial inputs can be completely converted into a final product and that waste products can be converted into value-added inputs for another chain of production. In this context, the manufacturing line can be viewed as a series of production cycles and recycling systems.

Biomimicry studies nature's models and imitates or takes inspiration from these designs and processes to create products and human processes. Based on research from multiple disciplines, biomimicry provides a framework for valuing not what we can extract from the natural world but what we can learn from it.

The World Business Council for Sustainable Development brings together 180 international companies in a shared commitment to sustainable development through economic growth, ecological balance, and social progress. The WBCSD has developed a set of eco-efficiency indicators to help measure progress toward economic and environmental sustainability in business.

"Ecological footprints" was first coined in 1992 by the Canadian ecologist William Rees, and is used to manage the use of resources throughout the economy by measuring the total environmental impact of business.

Life-cycle analysis enables a manufacturer to quantify how much energy and raw materials are used and how much solid, liquid, and gaseous waste is generated at each stage of a product's life from creation up to and including the end of its period of use.

Cradle to cradle articulates a set of principles that seek to transform manufacturing design from being purely opportunistic to focusing on the service that products provide. One key principle is the total elimination of waste in manufacturing; all components of manufactured goods would be recycled or reused, thus reversing the "cradle-to-grave" model that governs existing industry.

decade. This started with a day-long meeting of climate scientists and a handful of BP top executives in 1996. "The very fact that we took a whole day on this issue was significant," says former BP chief scientist Bernie Bulkin. "Prior to that, this was a subject that might have gotten 20 minutes on a management team meeting agenda. But, I remember Brown saying that, 'We are grownups. We can think these things through on our own and find out what we really believe. Maybe we come to the same conclusion as the industry association, or maybe we come to a different conclusion.'" This "thinking together" eventually resulted in a historic speech Browne gave at Stanford University, in Stanford, California, in 1997, in which for the first time in public a CEO of a major oil company broke ranks with peers. He declared that it was sufficiently likely that climate change actually was occurring to warrant serious action, and he announced a series of initial commitments that BP would make unilaterally to reduce its emissions and begin investing in alternative technologies.

NURTURING RELATIONAL SPACE CAN BE SYSTEMATIC AND PURPOSEFUL Although the deep questions that drive dialogue cannot be overly planned, there are ways to encourage a relational ecology out of which initiatives will self-organize. For example, many of the founders of Women Leading Sustainability brought specific methods to the group, like personal check-ins and basic principles of dialogue and learning. The provision of free space is a must—and perhaps is the most challenging. Although it sounds simple, free space to simply explore what emerges is virtually nonexistent for today's busy managers.

ONCE IT IS RECOGNIZED AND LEGITIMIZED, DEEPENING RELATIONAL SPACE ALSO INFUSES RESULTS-ORIENTED WORK Effective relational work encourages diverging conversations, asks difficult questions and helps confront dysfunctional practices and attitudes in our organizations and ourselves. Such capacities also benefit action-oriented change initiatives.

Action-Driven Work: Building Collaborative Change Initiatives

Conceptual and relational work are important for effective collaboration, but they are especially important as they come together to enable whole new levels of action. Effectively weaving together all three dimensions requires a new approach that is more personal *and* more systemic than traditional planned change approaches.

Illustrative Action-Oriented Projects: Collaborating for Innovation in Food Systems

Although most consumers in wealthier countries are unaware of problems with global food systems, these are the largest drivers of poverty, social and political instability and local environmental deterioration worldwide. For example, falling prices for coffee have created a "crisis for 25 million coffee producers around the world, [many of whom] now sell their coffee beans for much less than they cost to produce."[31] Long-term trends of falling prices for major agricultural commodities— 40–90 percent declines over the past 50 years for wheat, soy, maize, potatoes, dry beans, and cotton—relentlessly drive down farmer incomes.[31] Whereas wealthy countries like the United States buffer farmers with over $500 billion in annual agricultural subsidies, developing countries do not have that luxury. As a result, the increasing production needed to meet demand and offset falling incomes leads to vast environmental degradation (e.g., over 1.2 billion hectares of topsoil has been lost in the past 50 years—more than the area of China and India combined) as

Different sustainability frameworks relate to different levels in the management system. Companies often develop customized or home-grown versions that combine elements of various frameworks.

Three Management Levels	Associated Sustainability Frameworks
Strategic Guidelines	• The Natural Step • Natural Capitalism • Biomimicry • Cradle to Cradle
Organizational Practices	
• Operating Policies • Metrics	• Zero Emissions Research Initiative • ISO 14001 • Life-Cycle Analysis • Ecological Footprints
Organizational Outcomes	• World Business Council for Sustainable Development

Integrating Frameworks Across Levels

well as increasing worldwide water shortages, since 70 percent of water use is for agriculture. And yet, despite increases in production, 800 million people remain chronically underfed.

The Sustainable Food Lab project was organized around an innovative approach to weaving together conceptual, relational and action space and included about 40 upper-middle and senior leaders.[33] These leaders were committed to a deeply personal action-learning process consisting of three phases: (1) cosensing in order to develop shared understanding of current and emerging realities, (2) coinspiring in order to share new knowledge and commitment, and (3) cocreating in order to design prototypes and pilot a small number of innovations conceived by the lab team. The process began with extended dialogues that brought out the different worldviews within the group, followed by five-day "learning journeys" to Brazil designed to immerse team members in the realities of the food system.[34] Time for reflection and dialogue offered windows into people's different views of reality.

In the midst of a subsequent eight-day retreat for reflection and planning, lab team members undertook two-day wilderness "solos" to catalyze deeper intuitions and commitments. "In many ways, the sustainability challenges stem from losing touch with the larger natural and social world, so these solos seem important," said project coordinator Hal Hamilton. In this case, when the work finally turned to formulating prototyping initiatives, the group discovered new levels of trust, commitment and energy. Eventually, eight different prototyping initiatives and associated teams formed, vetted their aims and wrote initial plans for getting to work. Several of these initiatives have evolved into ongoing action projects in three areas: (1) creating shared standards for sustainable food production so that farmers, buyers and the financial community can influence sound production practices, (2) restructuring specific supply chains to increase opportunities for small and midsize farmers and fishermen, and (3) generating a "demand pull" for more sustainably produced goods and for policies that reward sustainability.

The overall success of this approach to developing action projects was summarized by one of the business participants in the following way: "It amazes me that you can take a group that has been doing individual things and build such a huge amount of trust."

Lessons from the Action-Oriented Work

The learnings from action-oriented work done on particular projects suggest the need to take time to gather input from all stakeholders so that true systemic thinking can give rise to sometimes radically innovative action.

IT CAN TAKE SIGNIFICANT TIME TO BRING TOGETHER THE DIVERSITY OF PLAYERS NEEDED FOR EFFECTIVE COLLABORATIVE ACTION The initial founders of the Sustainable Food Lab—Unilever, Oxfam, the Kellogg Foundation, and the Global Leadership Initiative—spent over two years gathering a sufficiently large and diverse network to undertake the project. While the scale of the challenge is huge, in this case "getting the system in the room"—meaning that the people who are present should represent all aspects and stakeholders of the problem being explored—is a common principle for all system-change processes. This is challenging not only because of the time and effort involved but also because it includes people who will see the world very differently. By defining the project as a cross-sector, multistakeholder initiative, the founders not only signaled that it would take time to engage an appropriately diverse group of participants but also that it would take time to eventually generate action projects for which such diverse participants could truly collaborate.

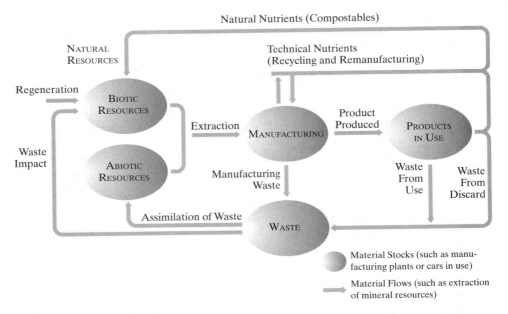

Naturalism and Sustainability

SYSTEMS THINKING IS ESSENTIAL FOR CHANGE, BUT IT ALSO CAN BE MESSY AND UNCOMFORTABLE According to Andre van Heemstra, a management board member at Unilever where the food lab was founded, "The whole awareness of sustainability (in the corporate world) has been growing because systems thinking, in different forms, is enabling us to see more interdependencies than we have seen in the past. It *is* those interdependencies that make you conclude that it is more than stupid—it is reckless to think of commercial sustainability in isolation of either social or environmental sustainability." As a conceptual tool, systems thinking can help to clarify interdependencies and complex change dynamics.[35] But at the same time, seeing systems *together* means allowing for different, sometimes conflicting views.

RADICAL METHODS ARE NEEDED FOR COLLABORATIVE ACTION WORK The basic toolbox from the organizational learning field—which includes systems thinking, building shared vision, and working with mental models and dialogue—is a useful starting point in collaborating for systemic change, but it is just a starting point. New approaches for organizing complex change processes and for large-scale dialogue like the World Cafe[36]—a process for leading collaborative dialogue and knowledge sharing, particularly for larger groups—will also be needed. Traditionally, group and team dynamics approaches have sought to foster deep personal and interpersonal work, but much less is known about opening minds, hearts, and wills across networks that cut across diverse organizational boundaries.

The Collaboration Imperative

Business as usual is reaching an evolutionary dead end. Efficiency improvements are useful but limited and, if extended too far, become counterproductive. It is hard to have healthy businesses, no matter how efficient, in unhealthy social and environmental systems.

Businesses, governments, and NGOs increasingly will confront complex sustainability problems for which isolated efforts are inadequate. Transactional models for improvement (pay for performance, rewards and punishments, benefit-cost relationships, fear as the primary motivator) have never sufficed for dealing with transformational or "adaptive" change, which requires a new mandate for learning across organizations, industries and sectors. We are at the very beginning of recognizing and responding to this historic shift, and we need to learn as quickly as possible.

Distinct but Not Separate Approaches

Although it is convenient for analytic purposes to distinguish the conceptual, relational, and action domains, our experience suggests that they interpenetrate each other in important ways. True systemic change means enacting new ways of thinking, creating new formal structures and, ultimately, transforming relationships. As Hal Hamilton of the food lab says, "The relationships among leaders across normal boundaries might be the most crucial ingredient to major change."

Interweaving conceptual, relational, and action work is especially relevant for the cross-sector collaboration needed for many of the "big issues" confronting society. But there is little precedent for such collaboration—protagonists from different sectors often focus on building political leverage and power rather than creating new knowledge and possibilities together.[37] Only by integrating our thinking, relating, and acting will projects like the food lab become more common and successful.

Leadership and Transactional Networks

While the limits of transactional ways of interacting are apparent, generating change at a scale that matters often requires engaging large communities of diverse participants with different motivations. Efforts like the food lab, by virtue of the deep personal and interpersonal work involved, have many members who share a strong commitment to the success of the enterprise as a whole. But specific projects also must involve a larger number of individuals and organizations in order to be viable. This means including people and organizations that are focused on narrower agendas and do not share the same sense of responsibility for the whole.

The resulting leadership and transactional networks operate on different logics. In effect, leadership networks function like communities, whereas transactional networks operate like markets. Markets are only viable when actors perceive that benefits exceed costs. From a transactional perspective, a collaborative effort is attractive when there is a compelling value proposition, a clear "business case." By contrast, the logic that binds communities revolves around a larger purpose that matters to people. It is not that they are indifferent to benefits and costs, but their primary motivation comes from a commitment to the transcendent aim of sustainable agriculture and its long-term strategic importance for their organizations.

Both types of networks matter for achieving large-scale systemic change. For example, articulating new industry norms that require direct competitors to work together also require enough participants who are genuinely committed to longer-term aims for the industry as a whole. Failing to discern and appreciate these differing motivations can result in stalled initiatives because of an overreliance on transactional players in the early going.

Three Recurring Questions

As we progress along this twofold path of collaborating to achieve practical changes and building learning communities capable of ongoing collaboration, we continue to wrestle with three questions.

1. HOW CAN WE GET BEYOND BENCHMARKING TO BUILDING LEARNING COMMUNITIES? Benchmarking is a well-established form of cross-organizational learning, but a learning community involves much more than site visits or listening to PowerPoint presentations—it involves disclosure and vulnerability. Learning communities are most evident when people are openly discussing real problems and asking for help, and they grow as people offer help simply because they want to. Over time, they nurture common commitment and relationships based on respect and mutuality. Perhaps the biggest question is: Which people and organizations will be willing to move beyond more common transactional relationships to build the leadership networks from which such communities grow?

2. WHAT IS THE RIGHT BALANCE BETWEEN SPECIFYING GOALS AND CREATING SPACE FOR REFLECTION AND INNOVATION? Most collaborative efforts among businesses commence with explicit objectives. But initiatives like the SoL Sustainability Consortium and the Sustainable Food Lab did not; rather, they organized according to a general intention to foster learning communities around broadly articulated sustainability issues. This created a good deal of anxiety but also provided space for exploration. Several short-term projects and dialogue groups materialized but did not achieve the critical mass to continue. On the other hand, no one would have predicted the long-term importance of the Women Leading Sustainability dialogue nor many of the Sustainable Food Lab initiatives aimed at radically shifting social and environmental conditions. These unforeseen developments and larger webs of collaborations would have been unlikely if the issues agenda were predetermined or driven from a central organizing group.

3. WHAT IS THE RIGHT BALANCE BETWEEN PRIVATE INTEREST AND PUBLIC KNOWLEDGE? There is much artistry in building collaborative systemic change initiatives, but at the same time, most of the key members of such networks are from for-profit businesses seeking competitive advantages. Commercial interests and proprietary know-how must be balanced with public interests when tackling systemic issues. SoL believes that balancing private and public interest means focusing on issues that are larger than individual organizations, improving the related systems that can benefit all, and respecting that it takes healthy organizations to address these issues. In this sense, balancing public and private interests resembles the mantra of all great teams and healthy communities: It's up to each of us, and no one can do it alone.

References

1. B. Halweil, "Home Grown: The Case for Local Food in a Global Market," November 2002, www.worldwatch.org/pubs/paper/163.
2. See www.unilever.com/ourvalues/environmentandsociety/sustainability/ fish/default.asp; www.msc.org; and B. May, D. Leadbitter, M. Sutton and M. Weber, "The Marine Stewardship Council (MSC)," in "Eco-labelling in Fisheries; What Is It All About?" ed. B. Phillips, T. Ward and C. Chaffee (Oxford; Blackwell Science, 2003), 14–33.
3. PE. Steinberg, "Fish or Foul: Investigating the Politics of the Marine Stewardship Council" (paper presented at the Conference for Marine Environmental Politics in the 21st

Century, Berkeley, California, April 30-May 2, 1999). globetrotter.berkeley.edu/macarthur/marine/papers/Steinberg-1.html.

4. S. Waddell, "Societal Learning and Change: How Governments, Business and Civil Society Are Creating Solutions to Complex Multi-Stakeholder Problems"(Sheffield, UK; Greenleaf Publishing, 2005).

5. See www.solsustainability.org; S. Schley and J. Laur, "The Sustainability Challenge: Ecological and Economic Development, "The Systems Thinker 7, no. 7 (September 1996): 1–7; and CO. Scharmer and P. Senge, "Community Action Research," in "Handbook of Action Research: Participative Inquiry and Practice," ed. P. Reason and H. Bradbury (London: Sage Publications, 2001), 238–249.

6. P.M. Senge, "The Fifth Discipline; The Art and Practice of the Learning Organization" (New York; Currency Doubleday, 1990/2006); P.M. Senge, A. Kleiner, C. Robers, R. Ross and B. Smith, "The Fifth Discipline Field-book: Strategies and Tools For Building a Learning Organization" (New York: Currency Doubleday, 1994); G. Roth and P.M. Senge, "From Theory to Practice; Research Territory, Processes and Structure at an Organizational Learning Centre," Journal of Organizational Change Management 7, no. 5 (February 1996): 92–106; and www.solonline.org.

7. P.M. Senge and G. Carstedt, "Innovating Our Way to the Next Industrial Revolution," MIT Sloan Management Review 42, no. 2 (winter 2001): 24–38; and J. Ehrenfeld, "Learning and Change in the SoL Consortium" (presentation at the Harley-Davidson Consortium meeting, Milwaukee, Wisconsin, April 9–11,2003), www.solsustainability.org/toolkit.htm.

8. For a more comprehensive list and short analysis of 21 different frameworks, see J. Elkington, "Triple Bottom Line Reporting," 2003, www.ccc.govt.nz/TripleBottomLine.

9. See http://www.naturalstep.org.

10. P. Hawken, A. Lovins and L. Hunter Lovins, "Natural Capitalism: Creating the Next Industrial Revolution" (Boston: Little, Brown, 1999).

11. See http://www.iso14000.com.

12. See http://www.zeri.org.

13. J.M. Benyus, "Biomimicry: Innovation Inspired By Nature"(New York; Morrow, 1997); and www.biomimicry.net.

14. H.A. Verfaillie and R. Bidwell, "Measuring Eco-Efficiency: A Guide to Reporting Company Performance" (Geneva: World Business Council for Sustainable Development, 2000).

15. A. Sturm, M. Wackernagel and K. Müller, "The Winners and Losers in Global Competition: Why Eco-Efficiency Reinforces Competitiveness: A Study of 44 Nations" (Zurich; Verlag Rüegger, 2000); and www.ecological footprint.com.

16. See United Nations Environment Program/Society of Environmental Toxicology and Chemistry cooperation on best available practice in life-cycle assessment, www.setac.org/lca.html.

17. W. McDonough and M. Braungart, "Cradle to Cradle: Remaking the Way We Make Things" (New York; North Point Press, 2002).

18. B.J. Bulkin, J. Ehrenfeld, C. Gray, P. Morris, R. Saillant, T. Savino, T. Reese and P.M. Senge, "Integrating Frameworks For Sustainability," working paper, SoL Sustainability Consortium, Cambridge, Massachusetts, May, 2000 (revised, January 2002), www.solonline.org.

19. These three terms were influenced by the writings of John Ehrenfeld. For example, see J. Ehrenfeld, "Searching for Sustainability: No Quick Fix," Reflections 5, no. 8 (2004): 1–12.

20. World Commission on Sustainable Development; see www.un.org/esa/sustdev/csd/csd.htm.

21. J. Benyus, "Biomimicry" (New York; Morrow, 1997).

22. See www.un.org/Overview/rights.html.

23. A similar project is now underway among consortium members, seeking to clarify the social dimensions of sustainability. See SoL Societal Dimensions Workgroup, "Social Dimensions of Sustainability Frameworks Document" (presentation at SoL Sustainability Consortium, Brewster, Massachusetts, April 26–28, 2005), www.solsustainability.org.

24. The Working Group on Sustainability Frameworks, SoL Sustainability Consortium, *Integrating Frameworks for Sustainability* (Cambridge, Massachusetts, April 2001), www.solsustainability.org/toolkit.htm.

25. Anthony Reese, director of engineering planning, Harley-Davidson Motor Company, 2004.

26. This phrase is a favorite of Karl-Hènrik Robèrt, the Swedish oncologist and pioneer of The Natural Step framework.

27. G.P. Richardson, "Feedback Thought in Social Science and Systems Theory" (Philadelphia: University of Pennsylvania Press, 1991); and Senge et al., "Fifth Discipline Fieldbook," 1994.

28. Y.L. Doz and G. Hamel, "Alliance Advantage: The Art of Creating Value Through Partnering" (Boston: Harvard Business School Press, 1998); and L.C. Abrams, R. Cross, E. Lesser and D.Z. Levin, "Nurturing Interpersonal Trust in Knowledge-Sharing Networks," Academy of Management Executive, 17, no. 4 (2003): 64–77.

29. J. Browne and D. Isaacs, "The World Café: Shaping Our Future Through Conversations That Matter" (San Francisco; Berrett-Koehler, 2005), 5.

30. Ibid.

31. Oxfam International, "Mugged: Poverty in your Coffee Cup" (Oxford, United Kingdom: Oxfam 2002).

32. Food and Agriculture Organization of the United Nations, "The State of Agricultural Commodity Markets," 2004, www.fao.org/docrep/007/y5419e/y5419e00.htm.

33. Business participants included Unilever, General Mills, Rabobank, SYSCO (the world's largest food distributor), Nutreco (the world's largest fish farming company) and Sadia (one of Brazil's few multinational food companies), along with smaller food companies and farm cooperatives. Senior government officials from Europe and South America were involved, along with global NGOs like Oxfam, World Wildlife Fund, Consumers International and The Nature Conservancy and local NGOs from Suriname, Brazil, the United States, the Netherlands, Italy and Germany.

34. Scharmer describes the method-of-learning journey in C.O. Scharmer, "Theory U: Learning From the Future As It Emerges" (Cambridge, Massachusetts: SoL, in press).

35. Sustainability Institute Report, "Commodity Systems Challenges: Moving Sustainability into the Mainstream of Natural Resource Economics," (Hartland, Vermont: Sustainability Institute 2003); and www.sustainer.org/tools_resources/pers.html.

36. Brown and Isaacs, "World Café;" and Senge, "Fifth Discipline," 357–380.

37. As a comparison, see R. Bouwen and T. Taillieu, "Multi-Party Collaboration As Social Learning For Interdependence; Developing Relational Knowing For Sustainable Natural Resource Management," Journal of Community and Applied Social Psychology 14 (2004); 137–153.

13 Managing Creativity

WEIRD IDEAS THAT WORK—BUILDING COMPANIES WHERE INNOVATION IS A WAY OF LIFE
Robert I. Sutton

IMPROVING THE CREATIVITY OF ORGANIZATIONAL WORK GROUPS
Leigh Thompson

M anagers face a dilemma when managing creativity. On the one hand, they need to stimulate new ideas, products, and services. On the other hand, they need to find ways to ensure enough stability so that products and services can be reliably produced. Robert Sutton, a Stanford University professor, examines this dilemma in the article "Weird Ideas That Work— Building Companies Where Innovation Is a Way of Life." His "weird ideas" provide a clear road map for managers who are interested in understanding how to design effective, innovative organizations.

As noted in the chapter on group dynamics, teams can either hinder or facilitate performance. The same is true with creativity. For example, teams often do more poorly than individuals when brainstorming new ideas, but they are better than individuals at developing more creative solutions to certain problems. Leigh Thompson, Northwestern University professor and Executive Director, Kellogg Teams and Groups Center, discusses the barriers that keep teams from being creative. She also provides counterintuitive research findings and practical advice in "Improving the Creativity of Organizational Work Groups."

WEIRD IDEAS THAT WORK—BUILDING COMPANIES WHERE INNOVATION IS A WAY OF LIFE*

Robert I. Sutton

Most managers are quick to *say* that drastically different practices are needed for innovation, as opposed to routine work. You might even react to my weird ideas by saying, "Sure, they're not weird." Yet many managers don't act as if they mean it.

---

*Robert I. Sutton, "Weird Ideas That Work," *Weird Ideas that Work*, Simon and Schuster, 2002, pp. 177–199. Reprinted with permission of the author.

They see practices that spark innovation as strange, even downright wrong. And they act as if practices suited only for routine work are generically good for running all businesses all the time. So they end up stifling innovation instinctively.

This happens to the best managers and companies. Start-ups are as vulnerable as established companies. A typical scenario is that a young company generates some great ideas. Once successful, the company reaches a point where it needs "discipline," or as some venture capitalists say, "It's time for some adult supervision." This means that part of the company—sometimes most of it—is organized for routine work. Tasks like accounting, sales, and human resource management can be done in innovative ways. But when "professional management" is brought into a start-up, routinization takes hold. After all, experimenting with unproven accounting practices can increase the chances a young company will stumble. The trouble starts, however, when the "adult" practices spread to innovative work. Although these managers have the best of intentions, they may unwittingly destroy what made the company vibrant in the first place.

Consider what happened at the Lotus Development Corporation in the mid-1980s. Lotus (which is now part of IBM) was founded in 1982 by Mitchell Kapor and Jonathan Sachs. The company's first product was Kapor and Sachs's Lotus 1-2-3, a business productivity tool. Industry observers give this "killer app" much credit for the success of the IBM personal computer in the mid-1980s. Lotus 1-2-3 sales grew from 53 million in 1982 to 156 million in 1984, which led to an urgent need for experienced professional managers. McKinsey consultant James Manzi was brought in as president in 1984 and became CEO in 1985. Manzi built enormously profitable marketing and sales operations, focusing on building operations modeled after *Fortune* 500 companies. The head of sales was from IBM, as was most of his sales force. Many early employees were resentful of the compensation and other perks granted to the sales force. They saw these salespeople as merely order-takers, because Lotus 1-2-3 was flying off the shelves.

Revenues continued to grow. But Lotus started having trouble developing successful new products. Part of the problem was that techniques suitable only for managing routine work were being used throughout the company. By 1985 or so, around the time the company had grown to over 1,000 employees, many original members felt they no longer fit in at Lotus. Some were simply not competent, but most were creative people who couldn't find a place in the company and found that their skills were no longer valued. Most of the new hires were cut out of the "big company mold," having worked for such firms as Coca-Cola and Procter & Gamble and then going on to get MBA degrees. One disenchanted early hire described them as "boring people who had never created a product or a company spirit."

In 1985, Mitchell Kapor (then chairman of the board) and Freada Klein (then head of organizational development and training) tried an experiment. With Kapor's approval, Klein pulled together the résumés of the first 40 people to join the company. She changed each résumé slightly, usually just disguising the employee's name. Kapor's was changed a bit more because he was known for working as a disk jockey and teaching transcendental meditation. Some of these people had the right technical and managerial skills for the jobs they applied for, but they also had done a lot of "wacko and risky things." They had been community organizers, clinical psychologists, and transcendental meditation teachers (not just Kapor), and several had lived at an ashram.

Not one of the 40 applicants was called back for an interview. Kapor and Klein viewed this as a sign that Lotus was unwittingly screening out innovative people. All signs are that they were correct. The only hit product invented by the company after Lotus 1-2-3, Lotus Notes, was developed 20 miles from headquarters, as Klein put it, "so the team could work unfettered by the narrow Lotus culture." Lotus did need great marketing and sales organizations to cash in on its innovative ideas. The narrowness that came along with these changes, however, was a double-edged sword. It is hard to generate new ideas when practices are used that screen out (and drive out) people with varied ideas and who see things in disparate ways. Kapor and Klein's experiment shows that every company, even a great one like Lotus, needs to be mindful about what it takes to spark innovation. Otherwise, it will be filled with replicants who think alike and act as if the future will be a perfect imitation of the past.[1]

The Best Management Is Sometimes No Management

Leading innovation can require a soft touch, or getting out of the way completely. We have seen how leaders of some of the most innovative companies expect and encourage their so-called subordinates to ignore and defy them. They institute policies like 3M's 15 percent rule or Corning's "Friday Afternoon Experiments" to make sure that employees can follow their hunches, even when their bosses believe those hunches are wrong.[2] Yet some managers still have a hard time bringing themselves to "manage by getting out of the way." After all, everything from Hollywood movies to an MBA education teaches us that management is about overseeing people, giving them orders, goading them on, and inspiring them to perform. As we have also seen, managers can have huge positive effects by creating self-fulfilling prophecies or allocating critical resources to a project. But managers can be oblivious to the harm they cause. Rather than following Pfeffer's advice that, like physicians, managers should "first, do no harm," they take ignorant actions that make things worse. William Coyne, former head of research and development at 3M, tells how a human resource manager once threatened to fire a scientist who was asleep under his bench. Coyne took the HR manager to 3M's "Wall of Patents" to show him that the sleeping scientist had developed some of 3M's most profitable products. Coyne advised, "Next time you see him asleep, get him a pillow."[3] Unfortunately, not all executives are so wise.

Why do so many managers delude themselves into believing they are helping their companies even though they have no effect, or are even hampering innovation?

This delusion, called the self-enhancement bias, helps explain why so many companies hesitate to delegate authority despite strong evidence that it enhances productivity and employee commitment. Yet when managers can bring themselves to get out of the way, good things can happen. Basketball coach Phil Jackson, who won numerous championships with the Chicago Bulls during the Michael Jordan era, and more recently with the Los Angeles Lakers, is a great example. Jackson is renowned for his light touch, for sitting quietly and not calling time-outs during slumps and crucial junctures in the game.[4] Most coaches shout out numerous plays during a game, but "Jackson almost never calls plays; he thinks play-calling makes players feel as if they are on a string (his)."[5] The key to Jackson's success, like David Kelley at IDEO and managers at Corning's lab, is that he has the humility to lead skilled people by giving them what they need to do their jobs and then to leave them alone. When Jackson arrived in Los Angeles, he was ballyhooed as the team's savior, the one person who could lead the underachieving Lakers to a championship. He responded, "I'm no savior . . . . They have to be the savior of themselves."[6] Ironically, he *was* the Laker's savior because he made it clear that winning was up to the players, not him.

Innovation Means Selling, not Just Inventing, New Ideas

Creativity is in the eye of the beholder. As cases from the Beatles' music to Ballard's fuel cell show, no matter how wonderful something new is, it will only be accepted if the right people can be persuaded of its value. Ralph Waldo Emerson was wrong when he said, "If you build a better mousetrap, the world will beat a path to your door." Too many innovations succeed because they are sold better, not because they are objectively superior to those of competitions.

The competition between gas and electric lighting in the 1880s is a good illustration.[7] Researchers Andrew Hargadon and Yellowless Douglas show there was little difference in the illumination provided by gas lamps and the 12-watt light bulbs Thomas Edison sold at the time. Early electric lighting was plagued by blackouts, unreliable lamps and light bulbs, and fires from short circuits and poor wiring. It was more expensive than gas, and "the Welsbach mantle, introduced in 1885 as a response to the incandescent bulb, provided a sixfold increase in the candlepower of gas lamps, changing the flickering of the faint, yellow glow into a clean, white light."[8] Even though electric lighting was not clearly superior, gas lighting was nearly extinct in the United States by 1903. Hargadon and Douglas show how this innovation triumphed largely through Edison's marketing skill and design decisions that, rather than making it as technologically advanced and inexpensive as possible, made electric lighting systems, lamps, and the language used to describe them as similar to gas lighting as possible. Remember, familiarity is comforting.

Selling a completed new product or service is crucial for cashing in on any idea. That is why Bob Metcalfe, who invented the Ethernet and founded 3Com, said, "Most engineers don't understand that selling matters. They think that on the food chain of life, salespeople are below green slime. They don't understand that nothing happens until *something gets sold*."[9] As we have seen, selling starts inside companies long before an innovation is brought to market. Disney employees are invited to pitch ideas for new "attractions" at monthly open forums. At 3M, inventors write proposals for $50,000 "Genesis Grants" to develop prototypes and market tests. The innovation process in every big organization—from Ford, to NASA, to McDonald's, to Virgin Airlines, to Siemens—is punctuated with formal and informal gatherings where innovators try to sell their ideas to peers and bosses. A hallmark of successful innovations in big companies is that they are promoted by persistent and politically skilled champions.[10]

Similarly, all but the wealthiest entrepreneurs must convince investors to support their start-ups. Experienced entrepreneurs and investors Audrey McLean and Mike Lyons teach Stanford students how to do so with an "elevator pitch" exercise. Class that day is conducted *inside* two elevators in a five-story building. Aspiring entrepreneurs are graded on how well they sell their product, market opportunity, and management team to McLean and Lyons during a two-minute elevator ride.

I am writing about innovation, not persuasion. But if an innovator can't sell an idea, or find a representative to do it, then it rarely travels beyond the inventor's mind. This is why so many people practice selling their ideas, study how others do it, seek coaching, and read books such as Robert Cialdini's *Influence*.[11] Innovators especially need to know that judgments of them and their ideas are intertwined, perhaps inseparable. As Arthur Rock, the pioneer venture capitalist who funded Intel and Apple Computer, emphasizes, "I generally pay more attention to the people who prepare a business plan than to the proposal itself." When Rock meets entrepreneurs, he looks for those who "believe so firmly in the idea that everything else pales in comparison," and he claims, "I can usually tell the difference between people who have that fire in their stomachs and those who see their ideas primarily as a way to get rich."[12]

Innovation Requires Both Flexibility and Rigidity

Innovation requires flexibility. Generating different ideas and seeing old things in new ways can only be accomplished by people who can revise their beliefs easily. But recall how much rigidity, how much downright stubbornness, was required for Geoffrey Ballard to develop those fuel cells and for the team at Sun to develop the

Java language. Some rigidity is necessary for developing successful innovations. It helps to define problems narrowly enough so they can be talked about in a constructive way, so people know what to focus attention on and what to ignore, and so ideas can be developed and tested in sufficient depth to see if they are any good.

A useful guideline for striking a healthy balance between rigidity and flexibility is to hold either the solution *or* the problem constant, and to let the other vary. The most common strategy is to find a problem and then to search for and evaluate alternative solutions, to *keep the problem rigid and the possible solutions flexible.* McDonald's has tried thousands of solutions to the problem of getting more people to visit their restaurants. Disney's Imagineers constantly tinker with solutions to the intertwined problems of making the long lines of "guests" in their parks *actually* move quickly and *seem* to move quickly. Gillette's research and development laboratory in Reading, England, will test virtually any material or design if it might lead to a fashionable product that works. The lab's ultimate goal is crystal clear: A closer and more comfortable shave, "The Holy Grail as far as shaving techies are concerned."[13]

The other way to balance rigidity and flexibility is to *hold the solution constant and let the problems vary*, or a "solution-driven search." This is what a two-year-old does with a hammer: hit everything in sight to see what happens. It happens when some new or old technology, product, theory, or service is treated as the possible solution to many as-yet-unknown problems. I mentioned earlier that 3M's Microreplication Technology Center used a three-dimensional surface composed of tiny pyramids to develop a display for laptop computers that used less power than conventional displays. Microreplication was developed in the 1950s to increase the brightness of overhead projectors. 3M managers believed that the microscopic pyramids could be used in many other applications, but did not know exactly how or where. They opened the center to find ways to put Microreplication in as many products as possible. It is now used in dozens of 3M products including recording tape, sandpaper, traffic lights, grinders, and mouse pads.

The Freeplay Group in Cape Town, South Africa, also innovates via a solution-driven search. They invent and sell "self-powered" devices that generate electricity when the user cranks the handle on a 2-inch-wide, 20-foot-long ribbon of carbonized steel flashlight. As the spring unwinds, it produces enough electricity to power a radio (the firm's first product) for 30 minutes. This radio is not just a cool gadget that attracted computer geeks at the Consumer Electronics Show in Las Vegas. It is changing the lives of the world's poorest people, who can now have working radios without using (unattainable) electricity or expensive batteries. Co-CEO Rory Stear says, "We are not just in the radio business. We are in the energy business. We always ask ourselves, what else can we do with this technology?" This solution-driven thinking has led them to develop, or start developing, self-powered products including a flashlight, global-positioning system, land-mine detector, water purifier, and a mechanism for a toy monster truck.[14]

Incite and Uncover Discomfort

As should be obvious by now, discomfort is an inevitable and desirable part of innovation. The weird idea to hire people who make you uncomfortable makes this point directly. Discomfort can also be generated by hiring people you don't need, when employees defy bosses, when people imagine dumb things and try to do them, and when people argue over their precious ideas. Discomfort isn't much fun, but it helps people to avoid and break out of mindless action.

Unfamiliar ideas and things generate negative feelings like irritation, anxiety, and disapproval, as do interruptions of routine action and challenges to taken-for-granted assumptions. If everyone always likes your ideas, it probably means that you are not doing many original things. When Howard Schulz, founder of Starbucks, wanted to partner with former basketball star Magic Johnson to build seven coffee houses in low-income African-American neighborhoods in Los Angeles, other Starbucks executives objected because it was risky. They had built many Starbucks overseas but never in an inner city neighborhood. These executives also reacted with discomfort when, to appeal to African American tastes, Johnson wanted to sell food like sweet potato pie and play music like Miles Davis and Stevie Wonder. Schulz and other Starbucks executives ultimately decided to build these stores and to tailor them to the inner city. This decision to overcome their discomfort proved to be wise: The initial agreement with Johnson was expanded after the first stores posted spectacular sales and profits, and executives' fears that crime would be rampant in and around the stores proved unfounded.[15]

Discomfort plays another role. Many successful ideas were invented because someone got upset about something and then did something about it. Inventor David Levy uses "The Curse Method."[16] Levy says, "Whenever I hear someone curse, it's a sign to invent something."[17] Levy designed the Wedgie lock after he heard a coworker cursing because a thief had stolen his bicycle seat. Levy noticed that the streets near his lab in Cambridge, Massachusetts, were filled with abandoned bikes without seats, suggesting there was a market for a good bicycle seat lock. Being uncomfortable or downright unhappy isn't much fun, but it can be an innovator's inspiration. Says Levy, "When I lie in bed, I try to think of things that suck."[18]

Treat Everything Like a Temporary Condition

The organizing principles for routine work reflect the assumption that everything is a permanent condition; the organizing principles for innovative work reflect the opposite assumption. Both are useful fictions. After all, exploiting existing knowledge is only wise if what worked in the past will keep working. And bringing in varied ideas—seeing things in new ways, and, of course, breaking from the past—only makes sense when, even if old ways still work, they will soon be obsolete. Leaders of innovative companies constantly create alarm and warn that just because things are working well now does not mean that they will work later. Andrew Grove of Intel is famous for being paranoid that a "disruptive" change—a new technology that makes their technology or business model obsolete—will appear. John Chambers of Cisco does pretty much the same thing, as does Jorma Ollila, CEO of the Finnish telephone giant Nokia.

Sustaining innovation requires treating everything from procedures and product lines to teams and organizations as things that might be useful now but will need to be discontinued. It can also mean forming temporary companies, not just temporary projects and teams like AES and Lend Lease. The goal at birth would be a planned and graceful death, with disbanding done once the company had completed a project or intertwined a set of projects. The argument for temporary organizations is that constant disbanding and reforming keeps variance and *vu ja de* high in a company, and makes it difficult for people to engage in mindless action. [*Vu ja de* is what happens when you feel and act as if an experience or object is brand new even if you have had it or seen it hundreds of times.]

This is why some traditional companies, including a team at General Motors Research and Development Center in Warren, Michigan, have examined the film industry to get ideas about sparking innovation. The "Hollywood model" is intriguing because these days a temporary production company is formed to make most films. After the film is completed, any money made by these single-project organizations is distributed, the team is disbanded, and the life-of-project workers go on to their next job. Hollywood was once dominated by large studios like MGM, Warner Brothers, and Paramount, which employed all workers, including directors, writers, and actors. In contrast, contemporary Hollywood producers rely on brokers to supply "packages" of people and to help build the temporary companies that make films. Talent agencies like William Morris and the Creative Artists Agency are among the enduring hubs in a complex network of formal and informal relationships, which explains why, although film production companies are temporary, there is much stability and predictability in the industry.

There are intriguing parallels between Hollywood and new-economy industries. There has been a great rise in contract work—especially by skilled professionals with technical skills—and an associated set of agencies to supply companies with temporary help to meet short-term demands in high-tech industries. Although there is much rhetoric about forming "built-to-last" companies in Silicon Valley, most start-ups in this region are temporary. Those that endure as freestanding firms are rare; far more are acquired by large firms, and demise is even more likely. Regardless of whether employees are classified as temporary or permanent, there is enormous turnover in Silicon Valley. This didn't start in the Internet age: Turnover has averaged over 20 percent per year in high-technology companies since the early 1980s. In both Hollywood and Silicon Valley, people constantly take new roles, work with an ever-changing cast of characters, and new companies are constantly formed with new combinations of existing talent.

Make the Process as Simple as Possible

A hallmark of innovative companies and teams is that they follow the law of parsimony: Make everything as simple as possible (but no simpler). They use work practices that help people focus on what matters and ignore the rest. Needless complexity arises when companies consider every contingency and involve anyone who could possibly improve, support, or be opposed to an idea. These misguided efforts to inject order and control, and to achieve perfection, can tangle aspiring innovators in red tape and condemn them to meeting after meeting with people who barely understand their work (but don't hesitate to give them advice about how to do it). These complex and dysfunctional processes can also require innovators to devote too much time to selling ideas and playing organizational politics, and not enough to developing ideas.

Innovation is easier to sustain in companies that follow the law of parsimony. General Electric's Jack Welch says, "Bureaucracy hates simplicity . . . . Simple messages travel faster, simpler designs reach market faster, and the elimination of clutter allows faster decision making."[19]

Innovation can be simplified by reducing the number of products or services developed and sold. When Steve Jobs returned to Apple in July of 1997, the company was selling so many computer models that, as he put it, "we couldn't even tell our friends which ones to buy." By 1999, Apple had only four computer models: a laptop and desktop for home and educational markets, and a laptop and desktop for business markets. This simplification was crucial to Apple's return to profitability.

Finally, a simple philosophy about what an innovation will be—and will not be—reduces unnecessary distraction and effort. If everyone follows a simple vision, it speeds development, focuses effort, and results in simpler products or services (which will be easier to build or implement). Jeff Hawkins, inventor of the Palm Pilot, also led the development of the hugely successful Palm V, telling the design team, "This product is all about style, it's all about elegance." He said, "I gave examples of products. I said—when the first [StarTac] phone came out, it sold for $1,600, and people were lining up to buy it. Why? Because it was new and it was elegant. So I said—I want to do the StarTac of PDAs." The team pressed Hawkins to add features like more software and a microphone. But he said, "No, no. Palm V is all about elegance and style and I won't entertain anything else." This simple vision, and Hawkins's persistence in putting it into action, made crystal clear to the team where to focus their creative efforts.[20]

Innovation Means Living with Some Nasty Drawbacks

The terms *creativity, innovation*, and *fun* are often used in the same breath. But before you rush ahead to build or join an innovative company, I feel obliged to warn you about the hazards. Working in an innovative place can be annoying and frustrating, or worse. James Adams at Stanford and Barry Staw from the University of California assert that many people *say* they want a creative workplace, but few would be happy if they actually worked in one. Indeed, a few years ago the Intel Corporation removed "Fun" from the list of core values that employees wear on their badges. A cynic might say that Intel has never been a fun place, so at least they are no longer hypocritical about it. After all, Intel is well known for encouraging conflict and internal competition. They even hold classes on how to use "constructive confrontation." Intel might be a bit nastier than absolutely necessary, but to build a company where innovation is a way of life, things need to be done that are unpleasant, or even downright frightening.

The 11 1/2 weird ideas here work, but that doesn't mean you will enjoy hiring people you don't like and who probably won't like you. It doesn't mean you will like being around people who are constantly fighting with you and one another. I don't know about you, but I get aggravated when I ask people who work for me to do something and they defy my request.

Think about the other weird ideas. If you like an orderly workplace, you won't be happy with the chaos that results when your organization is filled with people who have never been taught what they are supposed to do. There are some people who like working in a place where most things fail, are never finished, or reach dead ends. But not most people. When companies are too efficient, it is a warning sign that they are stifling innovation.

Beyond these annoying aspects of innovative places, you should also think hard about the risks that the evolutionary model implies for the average person or company with a new idea. The human tendency to be optimistic means that most of us believe we will be among the small percentage who succeed. But the most likely outcome is that you or your company will be among the many casualties required so that a few can survive and flourish.

I don't want to leave you with the impression that innovative companies are horrible places or that you are destined to lose all your money if you work in one. Many people love the mess and confusion. It is more satisfying to come up with new ideas than to repeat the same actions—and the same thoughts—again and again. It is exciting to work with people who are thrilled about some new idea. Even though many new ideas fail, these setbacks often occur where failure is tolerated, even rewarded. And there are large numbers of people who have become rich working in such places, even if the percentage is small. But you should know the hazards of innovation before devoting your days to it.

Learn to Fail Faster, Not Less Often

If you believe this book, you will cringe when people talk about making innovation more efficient. It usually means they want to use the logic of routine work to manage innovative work. Once companies try to "reduce the number of screw-ups," innovation usually grinds to a halt. The key to more efficient innovation is failing faster, not less often. Consider what Audrey MacLean told me about failure. MacLean was CEO of Adaptive and is now a successful "angel" investor (she calls herself a "mentor capitalist") who has been featured in *Forbes* and *Red Herring* cover stories in recent years. She argues that one unrecognized reason people made so much money investing in Internet firms during the late 1990s was that failure was inexpensive. MacLean notes, "Since it didn't take much time or money to put up a Web site, you could find out pretty quickly if it was going to fly or not. A lot of money was made very quickly when something worked, and not much money was lost on failed experiments."

Barry Staw and Jerry Ross have studied the problem of throwing good money after bad for over 25 years and have developed guidelines for avoiding such situations. The most important one is that people who are responsible for starting some project or company, and who have made public statements saying they are committed to it and it is destined to succeed, should not be involved in deciding its fate. Projects need to be structured so that separate groups make decisions about starting and stopping. This is why most banks use one group to sell loans and a different group to decide whether to pull the plug on troubled loans.

Irrational persistence can also be reduced by eliminating or softening the costs of failure. If people believe that their reputations will be ruined by failure, they may rightly believe that pulling the plug means certain ruin and that—no matter how slim the chances—their only hope is to find some way to succeed. Three of the companies I've talked about here—AES, Hewlett-Packard, and SAS Institute—are well known for such "soft landings." Staw and Ross also advise that "just knowing that one is under the sway of escalation can help." They suggest looking at situations from an outsider's perspective, routinely stopping and asking: "If I took the job for the first time today and found this project going on, would I support it or get rid of it?" This sort of question prompted Intel executives Gordon Moore and Andy Grove to get out of the unprofitable memory-chip business in 1985 and focus on microprocessors, a decision that made Intel billions. An even more aggressive way to avoid escalation situations is to sow the seeds for pulling the plug while a company, project, or product is still a success. Smart executives keep their people vigilant about ways that a current success can turn bad or be eclipsed by competitors.

Open is Good, Closed is Bad

Being open to ideas from other people and places brings in variance and different perspectives, which can help your company avoid getting stuck in the past. And by being open to outsiders, ideas that are old to them, but new to you, can be borrowed or blended with what you already know to invent new management practices, services, and products. The value of openness is perhaps the main lesson from AnnaLee Saxenian's book *Regional Advantage*, which shows why Silicon Valley companies like Hewlett-Packard, Intel, Sun Microsystems, and Cisco have been so innovative, while once-great companies on Boston's Route 128 like DEC, Wang, and Data General declined and died. She shows how Silicon Valley thrives because engineers share ideas so openly, both to get help with technical problems and to show off how much they know.[21] This doesn't happen just inside companies, it happens between engineers from different companies. Not only do engineers routinely violate their intellectual property agreements, several CEOs have admitted to me that being a bit "leaky" in the right conversations is expected and desirable, because everyone understands that it makes innovation happen.

There are, of course, limits to how open a company can and should be about ideas. Concerns about protecting intellectual property are legitimate, and companies that are careful to guard their ideas can make a fortune, at least for a while. Kevin Rivette and David Kline show, for example, that many companies are sitting on unused patents that are worth millions.[22] IBM licensed its unused patents in 1990 and saw its royalties jump from $30 million a year to more than $1 billion in 1999, providing over one-ninth of its annual profits. Intellectual property constraints can also lead to innovation because, if one company owns a solution to some problem, it can spur people in other companies to invent an alternative solution.

Nonetheless, companies that are paranoid about their precious ideas being stolen can kill innovation because, when people from the company get a reputation for listening to other companies' ideas but not talking about their own, the lack of reciprocity may lead others to clam up. Or if people from such companies realize they can't engage in two-way exchanges, they may avoid talking with outsiders who can give them useful advice.

Among the most extreme and impressive illustrations of openness is the development of open source or free software. This includes Linux, currently the only serious challenge to Microsoft Windows. The main benefit of open source development is what is called Linus's Law, that "with more eyes, all bugs are shallow."[23] As the development community grows, each new release grows more resilient and bug free because more people find and fix bugs. The open source community has developed a method of licensing that protects their openness. Open source software is protected by what they call "copylefting" work—not copyrighting it. Open source licenses that follow the copyleft principle add "distribution terms, which are a legal instrument that gives everyone the rights to use, modify, and redistribute the program's code or any program derived from it but only if the distribution terms are unchanged. Thus, the code and the freedoms become legally inseparable."[24]

These restrictions allow the code to stay open. Anyone has access to the source code and is free to modify it, but modifications must be returned to the code base. This causes odd situations in companies and other organizations like universities where a programmer improves some code that their employer wants to copyright and profit from, but the copyleft agreement makes that leverage impossible. An open source Web site points out: "When we explain to the employer that it is illegal to distribute the improved version except as free software, the employer usually decides to release it as free software rather than throw it away."[25] There are philosophical reasons for developing free software, but much of the recent enthusiasm for the open source principle is pragmatic: By being open to diverse people and their ideas, the product keeps getting better and better.

The Attitudes of Innovation

I hope that you use the weird ideas in this book to make your company more innovative. These ideas work. But after a decade of tinkering with them, I've realized that the exact methods used to innovate are less important than building a company where people have the right attitudes toward their work and each other. Psychologists tell us that emotions are the engine that propels human action. Feelings—not cold cognitions—drive people to turn good ideas and intentions into reality. So people who have the right attitudes will not only have an easier time implementing the weird ideas here, their worldview will also drive them to invent and use their own ideas about spurring innovation.

Every innovative company I know of is filled with people who are passionate about solving problems. When I talk to founder and chairman Jeff Hawkins and director of product design engineering Peter Skillman at Handspring about handheld computers, they bounce up and down like my children do when they play with a wonderful new toy. I see the same spirit in Joey Reiman of BrightHouse, the "ideation company" that charges clients like Coca-Cola, Hardee's, and Georgia Pacific $500,000 to $1 million for a single idea. I can see Reiman in my mind's eye, roller skating around a circular stage in Berlin, bellowing to an audience from the advertising firm McCann-Erickson, "We do heartstorming, not brainstorming; creativity is much more about what people feel than what they think." The passion is more subtle in other innovative companies, but you can always find it.

Playfulness and curiosity are related attitudes of innovation. When Kay Zufall started cutting little shapes out of the wallpaper cleaner made at her brother-in-law's factory, she wasn't thinking about trying to develop a new product; she did it because she loves to tinker with ideas and things. Zufall is always trying to make things better and to have some fun along the way. I saw the same spirit in the IDEO engineers who grabbed my new digital camera (one of the first sold) and took it apart on the spot. They couldn't help themselves. They had never seen one before and *had* to see how it was put together. This persistent curiosity leads to odd moments, such as when a waiter asked some IDEO designers why they were taking the napkin holder apart. The answer—"because we wanted to look at how the springs work"— was not treated as credible. But it was true, and it is one of the main reasons IDEO has developed a renowned culture of innovation.

My last attitude of innovation is really a pair of attitudes: the ability to switch emotional gears between cynicism and belief, or between deep doubt and unshakable confidence. These emotions are the tag-team partners of the innovation process. If your company is dominated by only one, you are in trouble. Every innovative company we examined closely here makes use of this blend of emotions, from Disney, to 3M, to Handspring, to Sottsass Associates. People in these places believe that everything is wonderful, that all is possible when generating ideas, but they become cynics—or bring in some cynics—when deciding which to develop and which to stop. Once they pick an idea to develop and implement, belief rises again.

A blend of belief and cynicism can also help you get the most out of this book. As I said at the outset, when you think about my weird ideas, try to suspend disbelief, just for a while. Ask yourself: *What if these ideas are true*? How might I help organize or manage my company differently? How should I act differently to make myself more creative? Play with these ideas in your mind and experiment with them in your company. These weird ideas have firm grounding and have helped other companies develop useful new ideas, but they are not immutable truths. Some cynicism is needed to make the best use of them. Treat them like toys you might buy to mess around with: Try to break them, take apart the pieces to see how they work, try to improve them, and mix them with your other toys. You might develop some of your own counterintuitive ideas along the way. Ultimately, anything that brings in new knowledge, helps people see old things in new ways, or helps a company break from the past will do the trick.

Endnotes

1. This experiment was described to me in a telephone interview I conducted with Freada Klein on October 12, 2000.
2. Fishman, C., "Creative Tension," *Fast Company* (November 2000): 358–88.
3. From a speech that William E. Coyne gave at Motorola University in Schaumburg, IL, July 11, 2000.
4. Shields, D., "The Good Father," *The New York Times Magazine* (April 23, 2000): 58–61.
5. Ibid., 60.
6. Ibid.
7. Hargadon, A., and Y. Douglas, "When Innovations Meet Institutions: Edison and the Design of the Electric Light," working paper, Warrington College of Business Administration, September 2000. University of Florida Gainesville.
8. Ibid., 19.
9. Metcalfe, B., "Invention Is a Flower, Innovation Is a Weed," *MIT Technology Review* (November/December 1999): 56.
10. See, for example, Burgelman, R. A., "A Process Model of Internal Corporate Venturing in the Diversified Firm," *Administrative Science Quarterly* 28 (1983): 223–244.
11. Cialdini, R. B., *Influence: The New Psychology of Modern Persuasion* (New York: Quill, 1984).
12. Rock, A., "Strategy vs. Tactics from a Venture Capitalist," *Harvard Business Review* (November–December 1987).
13. Surowiecki, J., "The Billion-Dollar Blade," *The New Yorker* (June 15, 1998): 43–49.
14. Dahle, C., "The Agenda—Social Justice," *Fast Company* (April 1999): 166–182.

15. Platt, L., "Magic Johnson Builds an Empire," *The New York Times Magazine* (December 10, 2000): 118–121.

16. MacFarquhar, L., "Looking for Trouble," *The New Yorker* (December 6, 1999).

17. Ibid., 80.

18. Ibid., 78.

19. Slater, R., *Jack Welch and the GE Way* (New York: McGraw-Hill, 1999), 135.

20. From an interview Robert Sutton conducted with Jeff Hawkins on August 2, 2000.

21. Saxenian, A., *Regional Advantage: Culture and Competition in Silicon Valley and Route 128* (Cambridge: Harvard University Press, 1996).

22. Rivette, K., and D. Kline, *Rembrandt's in the Attic* (Boston: Harvard Business School Press, 1999).

23. Raymond, E. S., *The Cathedral & the Bazaar, Musings on Linux and Open Source by an Accidental Revolutionary* (O'Reilly: Sebastopol, CA, 1999), 27.

24. www.gnu.org/copyleft/copyleft.html.

25. Ibid.

IMPROVING THE CREATIVITY OF ORGANIZATIONAL WORK GROUPS[*]

Leigh Thompson

Creativity—how to ignite it and how to regenerate it—is a key question that managers and executives pose to management educators and consultants. Several organizational changes and developments make creativity a valuable necessity for the new economy and the organizations that inhabit it. First, flatter organizational structures require companies, divisions, and managers to act in a more entrepreneurial and inventive fashion. The absence of hierarchy and bureaucracy creates fertile opportunity for creative knowledge and action. Second, by nearly all counts, businesses are growing more competitive. Strictly speaking, this means that companies continually need to reinvent themselves. Frank and Cook's book *The Winner-Take-All Society* provides compelling data on how companies are becoming more competitive, resulting in "winners" who gain more and more market share.[1] Third, blurred lines between traditional notions of who's "inside" and who's "outside" the company allow teams to form new relationships with suppliers, complementary businesses, and shadow industries. In *Co-opetition*, Brandenburger and Nalebuff argue that cooperation and competition can co exist in business relationships.[2] Finally, the focus on customer service is more important than ever, and the quest to satisfy and delight the customer or client requires creativity.

Just because the challenges facing a team call for creativity, however, is no guarantee that the team members will be creative. In fact, several factors that seem to foster creativity might actually thwart it.

Creative Realism

Most people think that creative ideas are wild ideas; on the contrary, creativity is the production of novel and useful ideas. Creativity is important for innovation. If creativity pertains to ideas, then innovation pertains to the services and products that result from creative ideas. According to the famous psychologist James Guilford, creative thinking occurs when a problem solver invents a novel solution to a problem.[3] Creative ideas and creative acts are original and valuable. Figure 1 shows a 2×2 grid defining, on the horizontal continuum, creative and conservative ideas.[4] According to the model, teams should strive to achieve creative ideas, which represent highly original and novel ideas, as opposed to conservative, traditional ideas.

FIGURE 1 Four General, Conceptual Domains into Which New Ideas Can Be Classified

Source: Finke, R. A. "Creative realism" in S. M. Smith, T. B. Ward, and R. A. Finke (Eds.), *The Creative Cognition Approach*, Cambridge, MA: MIT Press, 1995, 303–326. Used with permission.

The vertical continuum is the one that is too often overlooked. It distinguishes new ideas that are *realistic* (connected to current ideas and knowledge) from ideas that are *idealistic* (disconnected from current knowledge). If new ideas are not connected to current ideas and knowledge, they are often unimplementable.

The best of all possible worlds is to get ideas in the upper left quadrant. This domain is called *Creative Realism* because these ideas are highly imaginative and highly connected to current structures and ideas. *Conservative Realism* represents ideas that are highly traditional and highly connected to current knowledge and practices. This realm contains little ambiguity and little uncertainty. *Conservative Idealism* is perhaps the worst type of thinking for a company: an extension of a common idea that is unrealistic to begin with. Such ideas exhibit little or no imagination and are not connected to existing knowledge. *Creative Idealism* represents highly original, yet highly unrealistic, ideas.

The key question is how teams can maximize the probability of landing in the upper left (Creative Realism) quadrant. The ideas that flow from this type of thinking are highly original and very useful. An excellent example of Creative Realism was Edison's development of the electric light system.[5] After Edison invented the incandescent light, his next project was to develop an entire system whereby the invention could be made commercially successful. At the time, there were two in-place lighting systems (neither developed by Edison): gas lights and electrical arc lights. Gas lights could be directly controlled for brightness; gas fuel was produced off-site and sent through buried gas mains. Arc lighting was produced by an electrical spark between carbon rods, was very hot, and produced fumes. The generating plant was located at the user's site. Edison's electric lighting system was based on the principles of gas lighting. Edison wrote in his workbooks that he completely imitated the gas system, replacing the gas with electricity. In Edison's electric system, the source of power was remote from the user, and the wires that brought the power were underground. Further, the individual lights were turned on and off by the user. The light bulb in Edison's system was called a burner and was designed to produce the same amount of light as a gas burner.

As we shall see, the efforts that people make to generate ideas in the Creative Realism quadrant sometimes ensure that they won't end up there. As it turns out, the route to creative, useful ideas is often indirect and nonobvious.

Measuring Creativity

In my MBA and executive education courses, I challenge participants to assess their own creativity using a standard creativity measure: Guilford's cardboard-box task.[6] The procedure is very simple: all participants spend ten minutes writing down all of the uses that they can think of for a cardboard box. (The same can be done for a brick, etc.) I am always surprised by the variation in the number, originality, and quality of ideas within the class.

The next step is to instruct participants in how to evaluate creativity, using this very simple task as a model. To do so, I introduce Guilford's three-factor model of creativity: fluency, flexibility, and originality.[7] *Fluency* is simply a measure of *how many* different ideas a person is able to generate. As we will see, Alex Osborn (the father of modern brainstorming) was right: Quantity often does breed quality.[8] The typical range that I get in my MBA and executive classes is 5–40.

Flexibility is a measure of *how many different types* of ideas a person generates. For example, suppose that one person who completes this exercise, Sandy, generates three ideas: using the box as a cage for a hamster, a container for a turtle, and a kennel for a dog. Sandy would receive three points for fluency, because there are three different ideas, but only one point for flexibility, because the ideas are of the same category (i.e., homes for animals). Conversely, Pat suggests using the cardboard box as a god, a telephone (via two boxes and some string), and trading it as currency.[9] Pat would receive a score of three points for fluency (same as Sandy), but score three points for flexibility, because there are three separate categories of ideas—one involving religion, another communication, and the third economics. Clearly, some of Pat's ideas do not meet the requirements for structural connectedness, but as we will see, Pat and her team are in a much better position to set the stage for creative realism than Sandy. Think of flexibility as a kind of mental gymnastics—the ability to entertain different types of ideas, all in a short amount of time. Most people, and in particular most teams, tend to get stuck in one or two types of categories of thought, a kind of cognitive arthritis. The typical range that I get in my MBA and executive classes is 4–17 categories.

Originality is a measure of the uniqueness or originality of the idea. (This is what is meant by creativity on the conservative–creative continuum in Figure 1.) Statistically, original ideas are ideas that are generated by less than 5 percent of a given sample. Thus, in my investigations, if there are 50 executives in a given class, an originality point is given to an idea only if two or fewer people come up with that particular idea. The typical range that I get for originality scores in my MBA and executive classes is 0–14.

There is always a striking correlation among the three measures, such that the people who get the highest scores on originality also get high scores on flexibility and fluency. Thus, there is a strong association between quantity, diversity, and novelty of ideas. According to Guilford, flexibility is the driver. This runs counter to most business notions of creativity, in which diversity of ideas is often not rewarded, quantity is not valued, and *quality* is viewed as the single most important goal. If flexibility is indeed the driver, how do we set the stage for it?

Convergent versus Divergent Thinking

Convergent thinking is thinking that proceeds toward or converges on a single answer. For example, consider a gambling problem: The EV, or expected value, of a 70 percent chance of earning $1,000 is obtained through a simple algorithm, such that $1,000 is multiplied by .7 to obtain $700. In contrast, divergent thinking moves outwards from a problem in many directions and involves thinking without boundaries. Divergent thinking is somewhat like Janusian thinking. Janus was the Roman deity who had two faces looking in opposite directions. In this context, Janusian thinking refers to the ability to cope with conflicting ideas, paradoxes, ambiguity, and doubt. To stimulate Janusian thinking, Tom Verberne suggests asking, "What if the world turned into your worst nightmare or your nicest dream?"[10] Open-ended questions stimulate divergent thinking. After participants answer such questions, have them identify factors that influence the opposing scenarios. This kind of thinking can prevent people from jumping to the most obvious (and often the most expensive) solution. Verberne gives the example of hotel guests complaining to a hotel manager that they have to wait too long for the elevators. The manager refers the problem to an engineer, who suggests installing another elevator. The manager is not convinced to adopt the costly solution, so she asks a psychologist for advice. The psychologist recommends giving people something to do while they wait—for example, putting mirrors and a magazine rack near the elevators. The manager chooses the low-cost option, and the complaints stop. Verberne also suggests role switching, where participants ask what important opportunity or problem faces their organization, take each other's roles within the organization, and ask what's important from the perspective of their new, assumed roles.

Impossibilities can also stimulate divergent thinking. Participants think of ideas that are at present impossible to execute (living on the moon, traveling by satellite, etc.) and then identify conditions that might lead to the idea's fruition.

Many of the factors that make up creative problem solving are related to divergent thinking. Most teams do require some convergent thinking. As we shall see, however, teams tend to focus on convergent thinking at the expense of divergent thinking. Thus, one paradox for teams, when it comes to creativity, is that teams excel at convergent thinking, but individuals excel at divergent thinking. This is paradoxical because intuitively, most people strongly believe that teams are more creative than individuals, when in fact they aren't.

A large body of research in social and organizational psychology reveals that when teams are pitted against individuals, it is teams who excel at tasks requiring convergent thinking. For example, in a classic decision-making game that has a proven best answer, groups of people generate superior decisions with greater frequency than do individuals. Moreover, business and social institutions seem to know this and capitalize on it. Presumably, one reason for having a jury of 12 peers is that the resulting judgment will be more balanced and accurate than if only one person weighs the evidence.

The most difficult task for most teams is divergent thinking, often referred to as "Thinking Outside the Box." As a general observation, the ideas that groups and teams come up with are more clichéd and traditional than the ideas that individuals generate when working on their own. It is as if teams act as a norming device, thereby making group members more likely to conform to one another. In several organizational situations, this is highly desirable, such as when teams want to build cohesion and identity. However, by its very definition, creativity requires diversity of thought and ideas. Marshall Fisher, a cofounder of Century 21 Real Estate, realized that most people, left to their own devices, engage in conformist, convergent thinking. The idea behind his IdeaFisher program is that alternatives need to be freed up. The IdeaFisher program uses keywords and phrases and cross-references them with other like words and phrases to put together diverse and different ideas that normally don't come together in a highly organized fashion.[11] Diversity also means conflict, among other things; and most teams want to avoid conflict at any cost. Conflict avoidance can actually cost a lot.

Brainstorming

Alex Osborn, an advertising executive in the 1950s, wanted to increase the creativity of teams in organizations. He believed that one of the main blocks to organizational creativity was the premature evaluation of ideas. He was convinced that two heads were better than one when it came to generating ideas, but only if people could be trained to *defer judgment* of their own and others' ideas during the idea generation process. Osborn then developed the most widespread business practice used by companies to encourage creative thinking: brainstorming.

In his influential book *Applied Imagination*, Osborn suggested that brainstorming could considerably increase the quality and quantity of ideas produced by group members.[12] Osborn therefore believed that the group product could be greater than the sum of the individual parts if certain conditions were met. Hence, he developed rules to govern the conduct of brainstorming. Contrary to popular corporate lore that brainstorming sessions are wild and crazy free-for-alls where anything goes, Osborn's rules were specific: (1) criticism is ruled out; (2) freewheeling is welcome; (3) quantity is desired; and (4) combination and improvement of ideas are encouraged (see Table 1).

Osborn aptly noted that quantity is a good catalyst for quality: A team is more likely to discover a really good idea if it has a lot of ideas to choose from. But there is even more to brainstorming than mere quantity. Osborn believed that the ideas generated by one person in a team could stimulate ideas in other people in a synergistic fashion.

Many companies still use the original brainstorming rules suggested by Osborn over 40 years ago. Silicon Valley's IDEO design firm lives by these rules. Douglas Dayton of IDEO says that five rules govern every brainstorming session at IDEO: "Have one conversation at a time. Build upon the ideas of others. Defer judgment. Encourage wild ideas (not wild behavior). Stay focused on the subject."[13]

Table 1	Rules for Brainstorming
No Criticism:	Do not criticize ideas. Group members should not evaluate ideas in any way during the generation phase; all ideas should be considered valuable.
Freewheeling Welcome:	Group members should express any idea that comes to mind, no matter how strange, weird, or fanciful. Group members are encouraged not to be constrained nor timid. They should freewheel whenever possible.
Quantity Desired:	Group members should generate as many ideas as possible. Groups should strive for quantity, as the more ideas, the better. A high quantity of ideas increases the probability of finding excellent solutions.
Combining/Improving Ideas Encouraged:	Because all of the ideas belong to the group, members should try to modify and extend the ideas suggested by other members whenever possible.

Source: Adapted from A. F. Osborn. *Applied Imagination* (revised edition). New York: Scribner, 1957.

Osborn claimed to have (but did not provide) research evidence that a team which adopted these rules could generate twice as many ideas as similar numbers of individuals working alone. Thus, the comparison Osborn had in mind was a real group working face-to-face and a control group of sorts, known in the literature as a nominal group.

Does It Work?

This is the question organizational theorists asked about the brainstorming technique. Nearly all laboratory studies have found that group brainstorming leads to the generation of fewer ideas than comparable numbers of solitary brainstormers in both laboratory and organizational settings (i.e., nominal groups).[14] Thus, 40 or so years of research on brainstorming has found that brainstorming is significantly *worse* in terms of fostering creativity than just having the same number of individuals work independently. In fact, virtually all of the empirical investigations of group brainstorming are strongly (not just mildly) negative about its effectiveness compared to solitary brainstorming.

As a typical example, look at the statistics in Table 2, which are actual performance data of brainstorming groups and solitary groups in terms of quantity and quality of ideas. On the basis of these results, which have been replicated several hundred times with a variety of teams brainstorming about all kinds of things, the same pattern emerges again and again. According to Mullen, et al., "It appears particularly difficult to justify brainstorming techniques in terms of any performance outcomes, and the long-lived popularity of brainstorming techniques is unequivocally and substantially misguided."[15]

However, companies who use brainstorming don't like to hear this. Despite the empirical evidence for its ineffectiveness, group brainstorming remains popular in business and industry.[16]

Major Threats to Team Creativity

Four major problems stifle the effectiveness of brainstorming in teams. The basic problem is not teamwork itself, but rather the social-cognitive processes that operate in teamwork and how teams are managed. I refer to these problems as social loafing, conformity, production blocking, and downward norm setting.

Social Loafing

Social loafing is the tendency for people in a group to slack off—that is, not work as hard either mentally or physically in a group as they would alone. Indeed, when

Table 2   Performance Data of Group and Solitary Brainstorming

	Face-to-face brainstorming group	The same number of people working independently (solitary brainstorming)
Quantity: The number of ideas generated	28	74.5
Quality: Percentage of "good ideas" (judged anonymously by independent experts)	8.9%	12.7%

Source: Adapted from Diehl, M., and Stroebe, W. "Productivity Loss in Brainstorming Groups: Toward a Solution of a Riddle" *Journal of Personality and Social Psychology*, 53 (1987): 497–509.

organizational members perceive their own contributions to be unidentifiable and dispensable, they are likely to loaf.[17] If loafing is extreme disinterest in a task, then "flow" is extreme involvement and interest. According to psychologist Mihaly Csikszentmihalyi, people who really enjoy a task often experience a state of "flow." The idea of flow is that an activity is challenging enough to be interesting and rewarding, but not so challenging that the player is threatened or inhibited. Flow is the experience of enjoying an activity so much that it becomes worth doing even though it may have no consequences beyond its own context.[18] Thus, the process is more important than the outcome for people in a flow state.

Conformity

A basic human principle is the desire to be liked and accepted by others, particularly others in one's groups. Several theories of social behavior (e.g., social identity theory) provide compelling evidence that people seek to identify with groups and sometimes will engage in bizarre behaviors to ensure their acceptance by a group.[19] In brainstorming teams this means, for example, that managers may be cautious about their presentation of ideas and suggestions because they fear that others may negatively evaluate the ideas.[20] This, of course, will lead members to respond with "appropriate," traditional, conservative, and highly similar ideas—exactly the kind of behavior that most organizations would like to avoid. For example, word association studies reveal that people make more conventional and clichéd responses when they are in a group than when they are alone. Some companies have liberated teams by using free-association exercises. For example, at Campbell's Soup Company, a group of product developers began brainstorming by randomly selecting the word "handle" from a dictionary. Through free association, someone suggested the word "utensil." This led to "fork." One participant joked about a soup that could be eaten with a fork. The group reasoned (in a convergent fashion) that soup could not be eaten with a fork unless it was thick with vegetables and meat—and Campbell's Chunky Soups, an extraordinarily successful product line, were born.[21]

Conformity can occur when group members are concerned that others in the group will be critical of their suggestions, despite instructions designed to minimize such concerns.[22] Many social conventions in companies suggest that people should stay "on topic" and not present ideas that diverge greatly from those being discussed. This type of conformity is usually not a good idea when it comes to creative thinking.

Production Blocking

A person working alone on a problem can enjoy an uninterrupted flow of thought. In contrast, brainstorming group members cannot speak at the same time; they have to wait for their turns to speak. Consequently, people may forget their ideas or decide during the waiting period not to present them.[23] Their idea production is blocked. Waiting can certainly be frustrating, especially if the meeting is not managed well. Production blocking works both ways too: It is difficult for group members to listen to and process ideas generated by other group members while they are generating their own ideas.

Downward Norm Setting

It is commonly observed that the performance of people working within a group tends to converge over time. For example, at CDW (Computer Discount Warehouse), salespeople working in the same area in the building report monthly sales figures more similar to one another than to those working in other buildings and areas.[24] So far, no problem. However, there is a pervasive tendency for the lowest performers in a group to pull down the average. Indeed, individuals working in brainstorming groups tend to match their performance to that of the least productive member, also known as downward norm setting.[25] It is most likely to occur when there are no strong internal or external incentives for high performance in teams.[26] This low performance level may set the benchmark for the team, in that it is seen as an appropriate or typical level of performance. For example, participants in interactive dyads or groups of four tend to be more similar in their rate of idea generation than noninteracting groups.[27] Unfortunately, the least productive members of the team are often more influential in determining overall team performance than the high performers.

What Goes on During a Typical Brainstorming Session?

What exactly might we expect to observe in a typical company brainstorming session? Video- and tape-recorded interactions reveal an interesting set of events. The four problems noted above combine to cause people in most brainstorming groups to:

- Experience inhibitions, anxiety, and self-presentational concerns
- Reduce their production
- Participate in social rituals, such as telling stories, repeating ideas, and giving positive feedback (a natural pattern of conversation that works well at cocktail parties but kills creativity)
- Set their performance benchmarks too low
- Conform in terms of ideas
- Conform in terms of rate of idea generation

The Faulty-Performance Illusion

Most brainstorming teams have no idea that these behaviors are occurring; most interactive brainstorming teams feel quite confident about their productivity. Thus, though the group's esteem has been soothed via the social rituals, the esteem has a faulty basis. Brainstorming groups, and the companies who use them, are their own worst enemy: They fall prey to the illusion that they function very effectively. They suffer from illusions of invulnerability, collective rationalization, belief in the morality of the group, and stereotyping of outgroups. In fact, the illusion of performance is so self-serving that people often take credit for the ideas generated by others.[28]

Building Team Creativity

Fortunately, teams can take actions to ward off the typical problems that brainstorming produces. The ten strategies outlined below all have a strong scientific research basis, are practical, and are reasonable in cost.

1. Diversify the Team

Team members that have different backgrounds, training, and perspectives are naturally going to offer different categories of thought and ways of looking at a problem compared to homogenous teams. The more heterogeneous a team is, the more likely that the team will excel in all measures of creativity. Indeed, teams in which members are diverse with regard to background and perspective outperform teams with homogeneous members on tasks requiring creative problem solving and innovation.[29] Teams with heterogeneous members generate more arguments, apply a greater number of strategies, detect more novel solutions, and are better at integrating multiple perspectives than teams without conflicting perspectives. For example, IDEO design firm deliberately hires people with diverse backgrounds.

A wonderful working illustration of the diverse-team concept is in place at some microbiology labs. Dunbar undertook a massive and exhaustive study of microbiology laboratories over an extended period of time.[30] He attended all meetings and painstakingly recorded all interactions, both formal and informal, in his search for the conditions that might generate creativity. Over time, some labs distinguished themselves in terms of having more breakthrough discoveries, as evidenced by the number of patents. These successful laboratories did not have larger staff, nor were their scientists better paid or smarter. The key difference involved diversity in training within the lab groups. Lab teams that were more heterogeneous in composition were more likely to engage in divergent thinking, learned from their failures, and freely drew from other domains to address their problems.

2. Analogical Reasoning

Analogical reasoning is the act of applying a concept or idea from a particular domain to another domain. The simplest analogy might be something like this: Green is to go as red is to stop. A much more complex analogy is Kepler's application of concepts from light to develop a theory of orbital motion of planets.[31] Similarly, chemist Friedrich Kekulé discovered the closed hexagonal structure of the benzene ring by imagining a snake biting its own tail. To the extent that teams can recognize when a particular known concept might be useful for solving a new problem, creativity can be enhanced. The problem is that it is not easy to transfer relevant information from one domain to another; people almost always tend to solve problems based on their surface-level similarity to other situations, rather than on their deep, or structural, similarity.

This tendency points to a serious problem with creative teamwork: People usually have the knowledge they need to solve problems, but they fail to access it because it comes from a different context. For example, when people are given the "tumor problem" (concerning how to use a ray to destroy a patient's tumor, the problem being that a ray of sufficient strength will destroy healthy tissue en route to the tumor), an elegant (but not obvious) solution involves using a series of low-intensity rays from different angles that all converge on the tumor spot as their destination.[32] Only about 10 percent of people solve this problem. Gick and Holyoak asked whether performance would improve if the participants were given an analogous problem beforehand involving a general who is trying to capture a fortress but is prevented from making a frontal attack with his entire army. An elegant (and analogous) solution is to divide the army into small groups of ground troops that each approach the fortress from a different road at the same time. Even when the tumor problem was presented immediately after the fortress problem, only 41 percent of people spontaneously transferred the "first divide and then converge" solution. In the research done in our laboratory, we have demonstrated similar lack of transfer with managers and executives.[33] Thus, applying previously learned knowledge to new situations is surprisingly difficult for most managers. This is known as the "inert knowledge" problem.

Many companies are recognizing the box-breaking potential of analogical reasoning as a way of using ideas that people have about other, seemingly unrelated things to solve pressing business problems. Alan Heeks, a Harvard MBA who worked at Procter & Gamble, uses an organic farm as a model for business life. Heeks goes so far as to run workshops at a 132-acre farm where analogies run rampant—participants think about harvesting for their future development, recycling, fertility, and sustainability. Heeks helps participants draw analogies between soil and a company's staff.[34]

The Pennsylvania Chamber of Business in downtown Harrisburg is a broad-based business association representing more than 6,500 companies in Pennsylvania that make use of the private work force. The organization chose the novel *River Horse* by William Least Heat-Moon as an analogy for the changes and transformation their organization is going through.[35] Chamber president Floyd Warner selected the book for his group to read and discuss on a regular basis.

Another use of analogy: When NASA found it necessary to design a satellite that would be tethered to a space station by a thin wire 60 miles long, designers realized that the motion of reeling in the satellite would cause it to act like a pendulum with an ever-widening arc. Stanford scientist Thomas Kane, using the analogy of a yo-yo, determined that a small electric motor on the satellite would allow it to crawl back up the tether to the space station.[36]

As another example, a manufacturer of potato chips faced a frequently encountered problem: Potato chips took up too much shelf space when they were packed loosely, but they crumbled when packed in smaller packages. The manufacturer found a solution by using a direct analogy: Dried leaves are highly similar to potato chips. They crumble very easily and they are bulky. Pressed leaves are flat. Could potato chips be shipped flat? As it turned out, they could not. However, the team realized that leaves are not pressed when they are dry but when they are moist. So, they packed potato chips in stacks, moist enough not to crumble, but dry enough to be nearly flat. The result was Pringles™.[37]

Prem Kamath, head of management resources for Hindustan Lever, described how his firm uses analogies from the movie *Tora! Tora! Tora!* to guard itself against complacency.[38] And Barry Schuler, Marriott International's senior vice president of strategy and planning for information resources, has helped to technically season Marriott's executives by speaking in analogies. Schuler, a former race car driver, sold a new network with the following analogy: "Bill Marriott, Jr. (CEO and chairman of the board) owns several exotic cars. He loves talking about cars. I tell him that the infrastructure—the hardware and system software connecting the network—[is] like the road. Then I ask him, 'Why would you want a thousand roads coming to the same place, when you can have one?' I compare our applications to trucks and cars driving on the road. And Information Resources people are the pit crew."[39] Analogical reasoning involves the application of diverse categories to a company's present problem or challenge. Another example: The D'Arcy advertising firm often holds "kidnappings" in which employees are suddenly whisked away to museums and then asked to think about a certain artist or exhibit as an analogy to their current product or service.[40]

3. Brainwriting

Brainwriting works like this: At various key points in time during a brainstorming session, group members will cease all talking and write down their own ideas silently.[41] Writing ideas instead of speaking them eliminates the problem of production blocking, since group members don't have to wait their turn to generate ideas. It may also reduce conformity, since the written format eliminates the need for public speaking and is typically more anonymous than oral brainstorming. The written ideas can be subsequently shared by the group in a round-robin fashion and summarized on a blackboard or flipchart. For example, investigations of brainstorming groups of four people revealed that brainwriting, followed by a round-robin exchange, eliminated production blocking and social loafing as compared to standard brainwriting.[42] I personally have employed this technique in the executive classroom and have gotten strange reactions: Managers feel uncomfortable sitting in silence; they claim that it breaks their rhythm. But the proof is in the pudding: Brainwriting groups consistently generate more and better ideas than groups who follow their natural instincts. It is worthwhile noting that even if the facilitator does not use brainwriting per se, merely taking breaks can be almost as effective. Even if group members don't write anything down, taking brief breaks can serve a function similar to brainwriting.[43] The more silences and pauses that occur, the more likely it is that a divergent cycle can be created.

4. Nominal Group Technique

The nominal group technique, or NGT, is a variation of the standard brainwriting technique.[44] It begins with a session of brainwriting (independent writing of ideas). These ideas are subsequently shared by the group in a round-robin fashion and summarized on a blackboard. Then the group discusses the ideas for clarification and evaluation. Finally, each person rank-orders the ideas. This technique was compared with an interactive brainstorming process, and the NGT technique overwhelmingly outperformed the standard brainstorming group.[45] Also, nominal groups that perform in the same room generate more ideas than those in separate rooms.[46] One variant of the NGT is the anonymous nominal group technique. Members first write down their ideas on individual sheets of paper or note cards. The meeting facilitator (or a group member) then collects the note cards, shuffles them, and redistributes them randomly to individuals, who read the cards aloud or discuss them in small groups. This variation creates greater acceptance of others' ideas because the ideas are semi-anonymous and prevents individual members from championing only their own ideas.

Another variant of the nominal group technique is the Delphi technique. In this technique, group members do not interact in a face-to-face fashion at any point. This technique is ideally suited for groups whose members are geographically dispersed, making meetings difficult to attend, and for teams whose members experience such great conflict that it is difficult to get through a meeting. This technique requires a leader or facilitator who is trusted by team members. The entire process proceeds through questionnaires followed by feedback, which can be computerized. The leader distributes a topic or question to members and asks for responses from each team member. The leader then aggregates the responses, sends them back out to the team, and solicits feedback. This process is repeated until the issue in question is resolved.

The Delphi technique provides maximum structure, ensures equal input, and avoids production blocking; it is pretty easy to avoid coordination loss when team members never interact directly! The technique is a good alternative for teams who are physically separated but nevertheless need to make decisions. Because members respond independently, conformity pressures and evaluation apprehension are limited. One problem associated with this technique, but not associated with regular or nominal brainstorming, is that it can be quite time-consuming. "Sessions" can last several days, even weeks.

5. Creating an Organizational Memory

Among the biggest drains on group performance are the repetition of ideas and the forgetting of ideas. Groups can create an organizational memory by recording ideas in full view. Group members more often waste time by repeating ideas when ideas are not physically indexed. Recording all ideas improves brainstorming sessions greatly. For example, Buckman Laboratories Inc., a manufacturer of specialty chemicals for aqueous industrial systems based in Memphis, Tennessee, connects all of its associates worldwide with a proprietary knowledge network, K'Netix.[47] Also, Sun Microsystems' Java migration team created a shared-code library, which serves as a central communication hub from which they can check out whole pieces of software codes rather than recreate them every time.[48]

6. Trained Facilitators

A trained facilitator can better follow the rules of brainstorming, help to create an organizational memory, and keep teams on track, in terms of making sure that downward norming does not occur. Indeed, trained facilitators can bring the level of team performance up to that of nominal groups.[49] Furthermore, there can be long-term benefits to this investment: Teams guided by facilitators in several sessions of productive idea generation demonstrate high levels of productivity in subsequent sessions without facilitators.[50] Facilitators can teach teams to share ideas without extensive social interaction or "filler" talk. At IDEO design firm, group leaders are used to facilitate all brainstorming sessions. According to IDEO managers, the key qualification of the facilitators is that they are "good with groups," not that they are experts in the particular product area.

7. High Benchmarks

Brainstorming groups often underperform because they don't have relevant benchmarks. Information about other members' activity levels may increase performance as long as the benchmark is not too high.[51] Providing brainstormers with high performance standards greatly increases the number of ideas generated.[52] Even when members are working independently, announcing to others how many ideas they are generating every five minutes increases the number of ideas generated by the team.[53] Similarly, a facilitator can periodically call the attention of brainstormers to a graph on the computer screen indicating how the team's performance compares with that of other teams. This feedback significantly enhances the number of ideas generated by the group.[54] Simply forewarning teams that they will see a display of all ideas at the end of the session also increases the number of unique ideas generated.[55] It is also helpful for members to record their own ideas after the brainstorm.

8. Membership Change

Groups do not usually remain completely intact; rather, members enter and exit most groups.[56] My colleague, Hoon-Seok Choi, and I have extensively examined small groups that remain perfectly intact (no turnover) versus groups that experience at least one membership change (holding the total number of group members constant). We find dramatic evidence that groups who experience membership change (i.e., an exit of an old member and the entry of a new member) generate more ideas (higher fluency) and more different kinds of ideas (higher flexibility) than do groups who remain intact.

Here is what we think happens: Groups that stay together without any change in membership develop a sort of cognitive arthritis; they get stuck in their same old ruts when it comes to idea generation. In contrast, groups that experience a change in membership are naturally exposed to more ideas due to greater member diversity in task-relevant skills and information. Moreover, when a group experiences a membership change, old members are in a unique position to look at themselves more thoughtfully. That is, the presence of a newcomer can motivate old-timers to revisit their task strategies and develop new and improved methods for performing group tasks.[57] At that point, we think the group is in a better position not only to think about their working style but also to learn from others. Finally, groups that experience membership change are more task-oriented than are groups that keep the same members, due to the transitory nature of interaction among members of groups whose membership changes.[58]

The stepladder technique is a variant of the membership-change technique. In this technique, members are added one by one to a team.[59] Step 1 of the technique involves the creation of a two-person subgroup (the core) that begins preliminary discussion of the group task. After a fixed time interval, another member joins the core group and presents ideas concerning the task. The three-person group then discusses the task in a preliminary manner. The process continues in steps until all members have systematically joined the core group. The complete group then arrives at a final solution. Each group member must have sufficient time to think about the problem before entering into the core group. More important, the entering members must present their preliminary solutions before hearing the core group's preliminary solutions. Self-pacing stepladder groups (which proceed through group activities at a self-determined pace) produce significantly higher quality group decisions than conventional groups.[60] Members with the best individual decisions exert more influence in stepladder groups than in free interaction groups.

9. Electronic Brainstorming

Also known as EBS, electronic brainstorming makes use of computers to interact and exchange ideas. In a typical EBS session, members are seated around a table that contains individual computer stations. A large screen projects all ideas generated by members. Because members don't have to compete for floor time, production blocking is virtually eliminated. And because ideas are anonymously posted, conformity is virtually eliminated.

Mattel Media uses an interesting variation of electronic brainstorming in their team meetings. A self-proclaimed "technographer" records team members' new-product ideas on a laptop, the entries appearing before the group either on a 35-inch color monitor or on the wall. Bernie DeKoven, whose title at Mattel was "Doctor Fun/Staff Design," did not allow anyone to write, in an attempt to minimize production blocking (based on the belief that if you are writing, you are not thinking). Thus, the note-taker recorded everyone's ideas in front of the group. These ideas could be rated, evaluated, and eventually accepted or dumped. Furthermore, everyone left the meeting with a hard copy of the notes in hand, thus providing the organizational memory.

In addition, DeKoven kept a "boneyard"—a file of ideas that were rejected in the meeting. Some of those dismissed notions became valuable later on in the context of other projects. For example, when Andy Rifkin, senior vice president of creative development for Mattel Media, was touring with toy buyers, he got repeated requests for activity-based toys for boys. Picking through the boneyard of a year-old meeting, he found a Hot Wheels CD-ROM concept for designing and decorating cars and printing licenses and tickets. The Hot Wheels Custom Car Designer became a best-selling item in stores.[61]

10. Build a Playground

One of the most popular approaches for stimulating creativity in the short term, as well as instilling long-term passion and motivation, is the creation of the work playground. There is no single recipe for the playground. The basic idea is to break with old ideas about what it means to be at work. In the playground, beige walls turn into tent-shaped fabric sails; "chat-zapping" elevators are replaced with conversation-instigating escalators; and the brainstorming areas (called "chill-out zones" at one office) are painted in funky Technicolor hues.[62] Most importantly, functionality guides the fun playground.

Spaces that are designed to foster creativity involve a lot of fun elements. For example, Southern California's Foote, Cone & Belding advertising agency has reinvented the traditional workspace with 156 surfboards on the walls of its boardroom, removal of all doors from offices, and the use of basketball and Italian bocce ball courts for creative brainstorming.[63] In St. Louis, employees at the D'Arcy Masius Benton & Bowles advertising agency rock climb, visit art museums, and go to the movies on company time, and executives at Aurora Foods encourage employees to write on the walls with markers and experiment with Play-Doh and Slinkies.[64]

Whereas there is little or no research on whether bocce ball courts increase creativity, a powerful body of research suggests that positive affect—whether it comes from reading a funny cartoon or seeing puppies play—increases creativity.[65] The business of space is serious enough that some companies, like Steelcase, have pioneered the workspaces of the future. "Innovation spaces," custom designed by Steelcase, have transformed the way that British Petroleum searches for oil and the way that ultra high-end fashion designer Prada sells clothes to its customers.[66]

Creativity as Part of the Culture

Teams can be much more creative than they often are. Traditional management practices—such as asking for suggestions, only one person speaking at a time, and evaluating options before exhausting them—hurt rather than facilitate creative teamwork. The ten strategies we have reviewed can be applied to a wide range of groups, from intact, long-term, intensive work teams to ad hoc groups and meetings. Table 3 summarizes the strategies and indicates the particular threat to creativity that each addresses.

Creative teamwork is not only good for the bottom line; it can also be an intensely rewarding experience. The paradox is that most of our instincts about creativity are wrong. Tapping into ideas that are creatively realistic requires that companies support teams that do seemingly purposeless and senseless things, such as striving for quantity rather than quality (at least initially), suggesting deliberately impossible-to-realize ideas, and creating havens for individual thinking. Groups and teams can click creatively, but the four threats to creativity—social loafing, conformity, production blocking, and downward norm setting—can kill a naïve attempt at creativity. The ten strategies for enhancing creativity do not carry high price tags; the main challenge will be to make them part of the creative team's culture.

Table 3 How the Key Strategies Deal with the Major Threats to Creative Teamwork

Strategy	Threats to Creativity			
	Social Loafing	Conformity	Production Blocking	Downward Norm Setting
Diversify the team		Diverse teams less likely to have common group norms		
Analogical reasoning		Can lead teams to think about different, nontraditional ideas		
Brainwriting	Especially helpful if the individual group members are accountable	Members are not influenced by others	Everyone can be productive at the same time	Individuals are not aware of others' performance
Nominal group technique	Individuals feel accountable	Members are not influenced by others	Everyone can be productive at the same time	Members less inclined to adjust performance
Creating organizational memory			Group members less likely to repeat ideas	
Trained facilitators	Trained facilitator can keep motivation high	Trained facilitator can use strategies to avoid conformity	Trained facilitator can use strategies to avoid production blocking	
High benchmarks	Clear and high goals reduce loafing			Each member will be reminded of benchmark, which serves as key goal
Membership change	Individuals may be less likely to loaf when newcomers are present	Group norms may be more scrutinized (less conformity)		Teams have exposure to different and potentially higher benchmarks
Electronic brainstorming		Removal of group pressure because of greater (perceived) anonymity	Everyone can be productive at the same time	
Create a playground	If people are motivated and intrigued, they are less likely to loaf	Nonconformist spaces lead to nonconformist behavior		

Endnotes

1. See Frank, R. H., and Cook, P. J. 1996. *The Winner-Take-All Society: Why the Few at the Top Get So Much More Than the Rest of Us* (Reprint edition). New York: Penguin.

2. See Brandenburger, A. M., and Nalebuff, B. J. 1996. *Co-opetition.* New York: Doubleday.

3. See Guilford, J. P. 1950. Creativity. *American Psychologist*, 5: 444–454.

4. See Finke, R. A. 1995. Creative Realism. In S. M. Smith, T. B. Ward, and R. A. Finke (Eds.), *The Creative Cognition Approach*: 303–326. Cambridge, MA: MIT Press.

5. Contrary to popular belief, Edison's idea was not out of the blue. His lighting system was an extension of current lighting systems. For a description of how he developed the ideas, see Basalla. G. 1988. *The Evolution of Technology.* New York: Cambridge University Press. Also Weisberg, R. W. 1997. "Case Studies of Creative Thinking," in S. M. Smith, T. B. Ward, and R. A. Finke (Eds.), *The Creative Cognition Approach*: 53–72. Cambridge, MA: MIT Press.

6. See Guilford, J. P. 1959. *Personality.* New York: McGraw-Hill; also Guilford, J. P., 1967. *The Nature of Human Intelligence.* New York: McGraw-Hill.

7. Ibid.

8. One of the most often overlooked contributions of Osborn's pioneering work on brainstorming is his intuition about the positive relationship between quantity and quality. Osborn correctly noted that demands for "great ideas" will often stifle the creative process. However, it is easy for people to strive for quantity. The probability of having one truly excellent idea can be directly predicted from the number of ideas generated. Moreover, the likelihood of building and integrating ideas can be facilitated with quantity as well.

9. This example was suggested by Professor Terri Kurtzberg, whose dissertation focuses on creativity. She has extensively used the cardboard box task.

10. See Verberne, T. "Creative Fitness," *Training and Development*, 1 August 1997: 68–71.

11. See Camm, M. "Learn How to Clap with One Hand," *Sydney Morning Herald* (Sydney), 24 March 1994: 15.

12. See Osborn, A. F. 1957. *Applied Imagination* (rev. ed.). New York: Scribner.

13. See Gendron, G. "FYI: Growing by Design," *Inc.*, May 1998: 9.

14. Meta-analytic reviews of brainstorming provide compelling data on how individuals outperform groups. A strong example is Mullen, B., Johnson, C., and Salas, E. 1991. "Productivity Loss in Brainstorming Groups: A Meta-Analytic Integration," *Basic and Applied Social Psychology*, 12(1): 3–23. Other papers that address this apparent enigma include Diehl, M., and Stroebe, W. 1987. "Productivity Loss in Brainstorming Groups: Toward a Solution of a Riddle," *Journal of Personality and Social Psychology*, 53(3): 497–509; also Paulus, P. B., and Dzindolet, M. T. 1993. "Social Influence Processes in Group Brainstorming," *Journal of Personality and Social Psychology*, 64(4): 575–586; Jablin, F. M. 1981. "Cultivating Imagination: Factors That Enhance and Inhibit Creativity in Brainstorming Groups," *Human Communication Research*, 7(3): 245–258; Paulus, P. B., Larey, T. S., and Ortega, A. H. 1995. "Performance and Perceptions of Brainstormers in an Organizational Setting," *Basic and Applied Social Psychology*, 17(1–2): 249–265; and Taylor, D. W., Berry, P. C., and Block, C. H. 1958. "Does Group Participation When Using Brainstorming Facilitate or Inhibit Creative Thinking?" *Administrative Science Quarterly*, 3: 23–47.

15. See Mullen, Johnson, & Salas, op. cit., 18.

16. Several scholars who have worked directly with teams in companies report that most companies claim to use brainstorming. However, the question of whether it is used effectively is a matter of debate. For examples of how companies use brainstorming, see Hackman, J. R. 1990. "Work Teams in Organizations: An Oriented Framework," in J. Hackman (Ed.), *Groups That Work and Those That Don't.* San Francisco: Jossey-Bass; also Sutton, R. I., and Hargadon, A. 1996. "Brainstorming Groups in Context: Effectiveness in a Product Design Firm," *Administrative Science Quarterly*, 41(4): 685–718; Swezey, R. W., and Salas, E. (Eds.) 1992. *Teams: Their Training and Performance.* Norwood, NJ: Ablex Publishing Corp.; and Woodman, R. W., Sawyer, J. E., and Griffin, R. W. 1993. "Toward a Theory of Organizational Creativity," *Academy of Management Review*, 18(2): 293–321.

17. A large research literature has examined several factors that might mitigate the powerful social loafing effect. For examples of these methods, see Bouchard. T. J. 1972. "Training, Motivation, and Personality as Determinants of the Effectiveness of Brainstorming Groups and Individuals," *Journal of Applied Psychology*, 56(4): 324–331; also Diehl and Stroebe, op. cit.; Harkins, S. G., and Petty. R. E. 1982. "Effects of Task Difficulty and Task Uniqueness on Social Loafing," *Journal of Personality and Social Psychology*, 43(6): 1214–1229; and Shepperd, J. A. 1993. "Productivity Loss in Performance Groups: A Motivation Analysis," *Psychological Bulletin*, 113(1): 67–81.

18. See Csikszentmihaly, M. 1997. *Finding Flow: The Psychology of Engagement with Everyday Life.* New York: Basicbooks.

19. See Tajfel's work on social identity theory; specifically: Tajfel, H. 1978. *Differentiation Between Social Groups: Studies in the Social Psychology of Intergroup Relations.* New York: Academic Press.

20. See Camacho, L. M., and Paulus, P. B. 1995. "The Role of Social Anxiousness in Group Brainstorming," *Journal of Personality and Social Psychology*, 68(6): 1071–1080.

21. See Higgins, J. 1994. "Creating Creativity," *Training and Development*, 48(11): 11–15.

22. People pay attention to status cues in a group and, as a general principle, lower-status members conform to what they perceive to be the views of high-status members. For examinations of the conformity effect, see Collaros. P. A., and Anderson, L. R. 1969. "Effect of Perceived Expertness Upon Creativity of Members of Brainstorming Groups," *Journal of Applied Psychology*, 53(2, Pt. 1): 159–163; also Diehl and Stroebe, op. cit.; and Harari, O., and Graham, W. K. 1975. "Tasks and Task Consequences as Factors in Individual and Group Brainstorming," *Journal of Social Psychology*, 95(1): 61–65.

23. Production blocking refers to both the difficulty in speaking and processing information simultaneously as well as the difficulty in several people competing for the floor. Diehl and Stroebe, op. cit., offer a direct examination of production blocking; see also Diehl, M., and Stroebe, W. 1991. "Productivity Loss in Idea-Generating Groups: Tracking Down the Blocking Effect," *Journal of Personality and Social Psychology*, 61(3): 392–403; and Stroebe, W., and Diehl, M. 1994. "Why Are Groups Less Effective Than Their members? On Productivity Losses in Idea Generating Groups," *European Review of Social Psychology*, 5: 271–301.

24. This observation was shared by a high-level manager in the company.

25. See Camacho and Paulus, op. cit.; and Paulus and Dzindolet, op. cit.

26. See Shepperd, op. cit.

27. See Camacho and Paulus, op. cit.; Paulus and Dzindolet, op. cit.

28. See Stroebe, W., Diehl, M., and Abakoumkin, G. 1992. "The Illusion of Group Effectivity," *Personality and Social Psychology Bulletin*, 18(5): 643–650.

29. See Jackson, S. E. 1992. "Team Composition in Organizational Settings: Issues in Managing an Increasingly Diverse Workforce," in S. Worchel, W. Wood, & J. A. Simpson (Eds.), *Group Process and Productivity*: 138–173. Newbury Park: Sage.

30. See Dunbar. K. 1997. "How Scientists Think: Online Creativity and Conceptual Change in Science," in T. B. Ward, S. M. Smith, and J. Vaid (Eds.), *Creative Thought: An Investigation of Conceptual Structures and Processes*: 461–493. Washington, D.C.: American Psychological Association.

31. See Gentner, D., Brem, S., Ferguson, R., and Wolff, P. 1997. "Analogy and Creativity in the Works of Johannes Kepler," in T. B. Ward and S. M. Smith (Eds.), *Creative Thought: An Investigation of Conceptual Structures and Processes:* 403–459. Washington, DC: American Psychological Association.

32. This example, first experimentally used by Gick and Holyoak in 1980, points to the vexing problem concerning the general inability of people to transfer knowledge learned in one domain to another.

33. See Thompson, L., Loewenstein, J., and Gentner, D. 2000. "Avoiding Missed Opportunities in Managerial Life: Analogical Training More Powerful Than Individual Case Training," *Organizational Behavior and Human Decision Processes*, 82(1): 60–75. This paper provides data from managers indicating that analogical reasoning is more powerful than the simple case method. Another article by Loewenstein and Thompson provides our view on how managers should be taught; see Loewenstein, J., and Thompson, L. 2000. "The Challenge of Learning," *Negotiation Journal*, October: 399–408.

34. See Cox, A. "Where There's Muck There's Brass: Can a Few Days on the Farm Really Improve Your Performance at Work?" *The Guardian* (London), 2 August 2000.

35. See Jaffe, A. Chamber Gleans Words of Wisdom from Novel's Plot. *The Sunday Patriot News* (Harrisburg, PA), November 2000, D01.

36. See Higgins, op. cit.

37. Ibid.

38. See *The Economic Times*. The Human Touch. 7 November 2000.

39. See Radcliff, D. Marriott: "Want to See the Benefits of IT and Business Alignment?" *Computer World*, 10 April 2000, 58.

40. See Lee, T. "Get Those Creative Juices Flowing," Business Plus section. *St. Louis Post-Dispatch*, 7 January 2002, 8B.

41. Brainwriting has proved to be an effective technique in enhancing the performance of real groups. For direct, empirical examinations, see Geschka, H., Schaude, G. R., and Schlicksupp, H. 1973. "Modern Techniques for Solving Problems," *Chemical Engineering*, August: 91–97; also Paulus, P. B., and Yang, H. 2000. "Idea Generation in Groups: A Basis for Creativity in Organizations," *Organizational Behavior and Human Decision Processes*, 82(1): 76–87.

42. See Paulus and Yang, op. cit.

43. See Horn, E. M. 1993. "The Influence of Modality Order and Break Period on a Brainstorming Task." Honors thesis. University of Texas at Arlington.

44. See Van de Ven, A. H., and Delbecq. A. L. 1974. "The Effectiveness of Nominal, Delphi, and Interacting Group Decision Making Processes," *Academy of Management Journal*, 17(4): 605–621.

45. For a clear demonstration of how NGT is more effective than traditional brainstorming, see Gustafson, D. H., Shukla, R., Delbecq, A., and Walster, W. 1973. "A Comparative Study in Subjective Likelihood Estimates made by Individuals, Interacting Groups, Delphi Groups, and Nominal Groups," *Organizational Behavior and Human Performance*, 9(2): 280–291.

46. See Mullen, Johnson, and Salas, op. cit.

47. See Wah, L. "Making Knowledge Stick," *Management Review*, 1 May 1999, 24–29.

48. Ibid.

49. Trained facilitators are able to address many of the process-loss problems encountered by brainstorming groups. For studies that have empirically examined the effectiveness of trained facilitators, see Offner, A. K.,

Kramer, T. J., and Winter, J. P. 1996. "The Effects of Facilitation, Recording, and Pauses on Group Brainstorming," *Small Group Research*, 27(2): 283–298; also Oxley, N. L., Dzindolet, M. T., and Paulus, P. B. 1996. "The Effects of Facilitators on the Performance of Brainstorming Groups," *Journal of Social Behavior and Personality*, 11(4): 633–646.

50. See Paulus, P. B., Putman, V. L., Coskun, H., Leggett, K. L., and Roland, E. J. 1996. "Training Groups for Effective Brainstorming." Paper presented at the Fourth Annual Advanced Concepts Conference on Work Teams—Team Implementation Issues, Dallas, TX.

51. See Seta, J. J. 1982. "The Impact of Comparison Processes on Co-actors' Task Performance," *Journal of Personality and Social Psychology*, 42(2): 281–291.

52. See Paulus and Dzindolet, op. cit.

53. See Paulus, P. B., Larey, T. S., Putman, V. L., Leggett, K. L., and Roland, E. J. 1996. "Social Influence Processes in Computer Brainstorming," *Basic and Applied Social Psychology*, 18(1): 3–14.

54. See Shepherd, M. M., Briggs, R. O., Reinig, B. A., Yen, J., and Nunamaker, J. F. Jr. 1995–1996. "Invoking Social Comparison to Improve Electronic Brainstorming: Beyond Anonymity," *Journal of Management Information Systems*, 12(3): 155–170.

55. See Roy, M. C., Gauvin, S., and Limayem, M. 1996. "Electronic Group Brainstorming: The Role of Feedback on Productivity," *Small Group Research*, 27(2): 215–247.

56. This is based on research by Hoon-Seok Choi and myself conducted over the past year. A paper that reviews our research can be obtained from either myself or Professor Hoon-Seok Choi, Management & Organizations Department, Kellogg School of Management, Northwestern University, Evanston, IL 60208.

57. See Sutton, R. L., and Louis, M. R. 1987. "How Selecting and Socializing Newcomers Influences Insiders," *Human Resource Management*, 26(3): 347–361.

58. See Ziller, R. C. 1965. "Toward a Theory of Open and Closed Groups," *Psychological Bulletin*, 64(3): 164–182.

59. See Rogelberg, S. G., Barnes-Farrell, J. L., and Lowe, C. A. 1992. "The Stepladder Technique: An Alternative Group Structure Facilitating Effective Group Decision Making," *Journal of Applied Psychology*, 77(5): 730–737.

60. See Rogelberg, S. G., and O'Connor, M. S. 1998. "Extending the Stepladder Technique: An Examination of Self-Paced Stepladder Groups," *Group Dynamics: Theory, Research, and Practice*, 2(2): 82–91.

61. See Grossmann, J. "We've Got to Start Meeting Like This," *Inc.*, 1 April 1998.

62. See Long, S. "This CEO Handles Complaints Himself," *The Straits Times*, 12 April 2002.

63. See *P. R. Newswire*, "Surfboards in the BoardRoom and Bocce Ball Out Back," 25 September 2001.

64. See Lee, op. cit.

65. For an extensive review of the effects of positive affect on creativity, see Isen, A. M., Daubman, K. A., and Nowicki, G. P. 1987. "Positive Affect Facilitates Creative Problem Solving," *Journal of Personality and Social Psychology*, 52(6): 1122–1131.

66. For a look at how the fashion company Prada is rethinking creativity, see Brown, J. "Prada Gets Personal," *BusinessWeek*, 18 March 2002, EB8. For an in-depth treatment of how BP is searching for oil in the depths of the sea, see Verrengia, J. B. "Finding Footprints Under Arctic Ice," *Associated Press*, 8 April 2002, via www.msnbc.com.

CHAPTER

14

Conflict and Negotiation

How Management Teams can have a Good Fight

Kathleen M. Eisenhardt

Jean L. Kahwajy

L. J. Bourgeois III

Managing Face-to-Face International Negotiations

John L. Graham

William Hernández Requejo

Learning to manage conflict, an essential skill for both managers and employees, can be a difficult and sometimes uncomfortable process. The negative results of poorly managed conflict are readily observed in many organizations. When there is too much conflict, we find people consumed by negative feelings who fail to perceive common goals they may share with their adversaries. Valuable time, energy, and resources are devoted to competitive actions and counteractions that simply escalate the hostilities. The absence of conflict, however, is not the answer. A recurring theme in organizational behavior, as evidenced in this book, is the benefit of surfacing and listening to diverse opinions. Fighting for ideas in a constructive manner creates a healthy, moderate level of conflict that is far preferable to either too much or too little conflict.

One characteristic of effective teams is the ability to challenge ideas and disagree constructively. "How Management Teams Can Have a Good Fight" was written by Kathleen Eisenhardt, Stanford professor and Research Director of the Stanford Technology Ventures Program; Jean Kahwajy, consultant; and L. J. Bourgeois III, management professor at Darden Business School. They focus on constructive conflict in teams. Their decade-long research program on the relationships among conflict, politics, and speed in strategic decision making in top-management teams made it possible for them to follow and observe several teams in action. They contrast teams in which conflict produced healthy disagreement with those in which conflict ended up in interpersonal hostility. The outcome is six tactics that teams can use for managing interpersonal conflict.

The second article also includes lessons that can be learned from contrasting effective and ineffective practice. In "Managing Face-to-Face International Negotiations," John Graham, expert on international negotiation and director of the University of California-Irvine Center for Citizen Peacebuilding, and consultant William Hernández Requejo examine how skilled negotiators successfully reach agreements when negotiating in multiple cultural contexts. Illustrated by numerous practical examples, their advice provides useful insights into how successful international managers develop trust, communicate, persuade, and collaborate to reach creative mutual solutions.

HOW MANAGEMENT TEAMS CAN HAVE A GOOD FIGHT*

Kathleen M. Eisenhardt

Jean L. Kahwajy

L. J. Bourgeois III

Top managers are often stymied by the difficulties of managing conflict. They know that conflict over issues is natural and even necessary. Reasonable people, making decisions under conditions of uncertainty, are likely to have honest disagreements over the best path for their company's future. Management teams whose members challenge one another's thinking develop a more complete understanding of the choices, create a richer range of options, and ultimately make the kinds of effective decisions necessary in today's competitive environments.

But, unfortunately, healthy conflict can quickly turn unproductive. A comment meant as a substantive remark can be interpreted as a personal attack. Anxiety and frustration over difficult choices can evolve into anger directed at colleagues. Personalities frequently become intertwined with issues. Because most executives pride themselves on being rational decision makers, they find it difficult even to acknowledge—let alone manage—this emotional, irrational dimension of their behavior.

The challenge—familiar to anyone who has ever been part of a management team—is to keep constructive conflict over issues from degenerating into dysfunctional interpersonal conflict, to encourage managers to argue without destroying their ability to work as a team.

We have been researching the interplay of conflict, politics, and speed in strategic decision making by top-management teams for the past 10 years. In one study, we had the opportunity to observe closely the work of a dozen top-management teams in technology-based companies. All the companies competed in fast-changing, competitive global markets. Thus all the teams had to make high-stakes decisions in the face of considerable uncertainty and under pressure to move quickly. Each team consisted of between five and nine executives; we were allowed to question them individually and also to observe their interactions firsthand as we tracked specific strategic decisions in the making. The study's design gives us a window on conflict as top-management teams actually experience it and highlights the role of emotion in business decision making.

In 4 of the 12 companies, there was little or no substantive disagreement over major issues and therefore little conflict to observe. But the other 8 companies experienced considerable conflict. In 4 of them, the top-management teams handled conflict in a way that avoided interpersonal hostility or discord. We've called those companies Bravo Microsystems, Premier Technologies, Star

---

Electronics, and Triumph Computers. Executives in those companies referred to their colleagues as *smart, team player*, and *best in the business.* They described the way they work as a team as *open, fun*, and *productive.* The executives vigorously debated the issues, but they wasted little time on politicking and posturing. As one put it, "I really don't have time." Another said, "We don't gloss over the issues; we hit them straight on. But we're not political." Still another observed of her company's management team, "We scream a lot, then laugh, and then resolve the issue."

The other four companies in which issues were contested were less successful at avoiding interpersonal conflict. We've called those companies Andromeda Processing, Mega Software, Mercury Microdevices, and Solo Systems. Their top teams were plagued by intense animosity. Executives often failed to cooperate, rarely talking with one another, tending to fragment into cliques, and openly displaying their frustration and anger. When executives described their colleagues to us, they used words such as *manipulative, secretive, burned out*, and *political.*

The teams with minimal interpersonal conflict were able to separate substantive issues from those based on personalities. They managed to disagree over questions of strategic significance and still get along with one another. How did they do that? After analyzing our observations of the teams' behavior, we found that their companies used the same six tactics for managing interpersonal conflict. Team members:

- worked with more, rather than less, information and debated on the basis of facts;
- developed multiple alternatives to enrich the level of debate;
- shared commonly agreed-upon goals;
- injected humor into the decision process;
- maintained a balanced power structure; and
- resolved issues without forcing consensus.

Those tactics were usually more implicit than explicit in the decision-making work of the management teams, and if the tactics were given names, the names varied from one organization to the next. Nonetheless, the consistency with which all four companies employed all six tactics is testimony to their effectiveness. Perhaps most surprising was the fact that the tactics did not delay—and often accelerated— the pace at which the teams were able to make decisions.

Focus on the Facts

Some managers believe that working with too much data will increase interpersonal conflict by expanding the range of issues for debate. We found that more information is better—if the data are objective and up-to-date—because it encourages people to focus on issues, not personalities. At Star Electronics, for example, the members of the top-management team typically examined a wide variety of operating measures on a monthly, weekly, and even daily basis. They claimed to "measure everything." In particular, every week they fixed their attention on indicators such as bookings, backlogs, margins, engineering milestones, cash, scrap, and work-in-process. Every month, they reviewed an even more comprehensive set of measures that gave them extensive knowledge of what was actually happening in the corporation. As one executive noted, "We have very strong controls."

Star's team also relied on facts about the external environment. One senior executive was charged with tracking such moves by competitors as product introductions, price changes, and ad campaigns. A second followed the latest technical developments through his network of contacts in universities and other companies.

"We over-M.B.A. it," said the CEO, characterizing Star's zealous pursuit of data. Armed with the facts, Star's executives had an extraordinary grasp of the details of their business, allowing them to focus debate on critical issues and avoid useless arguments rooted in ignorance.

At Triumph Computer, we found a similar dedication to current facts. The first person the new CEO hired was an individual to track the progress of engineering-development projects, the new-product lifeblood of the company. Such knowledge allowed the top-management team to work from a common base of facts.

In the absence of good data, executives waste time in pointless debate over opinions. Some resort to self-aggrandizement and ill-formed guesses about how the world might be. People—and not issues—become the focus of disagreement. The result is interpersonal conflict. In such companies, top managers are often poorly informed both about internal operations, such as bookings and engineering mile-stones, and about external issues, such as competing products. They collect data narrowly and infrequently. In these companies, the vice presidents of finance, who oversee internal data collection, are usually weak. They were often described by people in the companies we studied as "inexperienced" or "detached." In contrast, the vice president of finance at Premier Technologies, a company with little inter-personal conflict, was described as being central to taking "the constant pulse of how the firm is doing."

Management teams troubled by interpersonal conflict rely more on hunches and guesses than on current data. When they consider facts, they are more likely to examine a past measure, such as profitability, which is both historical and highly refined. These teams favor planning based on extrapolation and intuitive attempts to predict the future, neither of which yields current or factual results. Their con-versations are more subjective. The CEO of one of the four high-conflict teams told us his interest in operating numbers was "minimal," and he described his goals as "subjective." At another such company, senior managers saw the CEO as "visionary" and "a little detached from the day-to-day operations." Compare those executives with the CEO of Bravo Microsystems, who had a reputation for being a "pragmatic numbers guy."

There is a direct link between reliance on facts and low levels of interpersonal conflict. Facts let people move quickly to the central issues surrounding a strategic choice. Decision makers don't become bogged down in arguments over what the facts *might* be. More important, reliance on current data grounds strategic discus-sions in reality. Facts (such as current sales, market share, R&D expenses, competi-tors' behavior, and manufacturing yields) depersonalize the discussion because they are not someone's fantasies, guesses, or self-serving desires. In the absence of facts, individuals' motives are likely to become suspect. Building decisions on facts creates a culture that emphasizes issues instead of personalities.

Multiply the Alternatives

Some managers believe that they can reduce conflict by focusing on only one or two alternatives, thus minimizing the dimensions over which people can disagree. But, in fact, teams with low incidences of interpersonal conflict do just the opposite. They deliberately develop multiple alternatives, often considering four or five options at once. To promote debate, managers will even introduce options they do not support.

For example, Triumph's new CEO was determined to improve the company's lackluster performance. When he arrived, new products were stuck in development, and investors were getting anxious. He launched a fact-gathering exercise and asked senior executives to develop alternatives. In less than two months, they developed four. The first was to sell some of the company's technology. The second was to undertake a major strategic redirection, using the base technology to enter a new market. The third was to redeploy engineering resources and adjust the marketing approach. The final option was to sell the company.

Working together to shape those options enhanced the group's sense of teamwork while promoting a more creative view of Triumph's competitive situation and its technical competencies. As a result, the team ended up combining elements of several options in a way that was more robust than any of the options were individually.

The other teams we observed with low levels of interpersonal conflict also tended to develop multiple options to make major decisions. Star, for example, faced a cash flow crisis caused by explosive growth. Its executives considered, among other choices, arranging for lines of credit from banks, selling additional stock, and forming strategic alliances with several partners. At Bravo, managers explicitly relied on three kinds of alternatives: sincere proposals that the proponent actually backed; support for someone else's proposal, even if only for the sake of argument; and insincere alternatives proposed just to expand the number of options.

There are several reasons why considering multiple alternatives may lower interpersonal conflict. For one, it diffuses conflict: Choices become less black and white, and individuals gain more room to vary the degree of their support over a range of choices. Managers can more easily shift positions without losing face.

Generating options is also a way to bring managers together in a common and inherently stimulating task. It concentrates their energy on solving problems, and it increases the likelihood of obtaining integrative solutions—alternatives that incorporate the views of a greater number of the decision makers. In generating multiple alternatives, managers do not stop at obvious solutions; rather, they continue generating further—usually more original—options. The process in itself is creative and fun, setting a positive tone for substantive, instead of interpersonal, conflict.

By contrast, in teams that vigorously debate just one or two options, conflict often does turn personal. At Solo Systems, for instance, the top-management team considered entering a new business area as a way to boost the company's performance. They debated this alternative versus the status quo but failed to consider other options. Individual executives became increasingly entrenched on one side of the debate or the other. As positions hardened, the conflict became more pointed and personal. The animosity grew so great that a major proponent of change quit the company in disgust while the rest of the team either disengaged or slipped into intense and dysfunctional politicking.

Create Common Goals

A third tactic for minimizing destructive conflict involves framing strategic choices as collaborative, rather than competitive, exercises. Elements of collaboration and competition coexist within any management team: executives share a stake in the company's performance, yet their personal ambitions may make them rivals for power. The successful groups we studied consistently framed their decisions as collaborations in which it was in everyone's interest to achieve the best possible solution for the collective.

They did so by creating a common goal around which the team could rally. Such goals do not imply homogeneous thinking, but they do require everyone to share a vision. As Steve Jobs, who is associated with three high-profile Silicon Valley companies—Apple, NeXT, and Pixar—has advised, "It's okay to spend a lot of time arguing about which route to take to San Francisco when everyone wants to end up there, but a lot of time gets wasted in such arguments if one person wants to go to San Francisco and another secretly wants to go to San Diego."

Teams hobbled by conflict lack common goals. Team members perceive themselves to be in competition with one another and, surprisingly, tend to frame decisions negatively, as reactions to threats. At Andromeda Processing, for instance, the team focused on responding to a particular instance of poor performance, and team members tried to pin the blame on one another. That negative framing contrasts with the positive approach taken by Star Electronics executives, who, sharing a common goal, viewed a cash crisis not as a threat but as an opportunity to "build the biggest war chest" for an impending competitive battle. At a broad level, Star's executives shared the goal of creating "the computer firm of the decade." As one Star executive told us, "We take a corporate, not a functional, viewpoint most of the time."

Likewise, all the management team members we interviewed at Premier Technologies agreed that their common goal—their rallying cry—was to build "the best damn machine on the market." Thus in their debates they could disagree about critical technical alternatives—in-house versus offshore manufacturing options, for example, or alternative distribution channels—without letting the conflict turn personal.

Many studies of group decision making and intergroup conflict demonstrate that common goals build team cohesion by stressing the shared interest of all team members in the outcome of the debate. When team members are working toward a common goal, they are less likely to see themselves as individual winners and losers and are far more likely to perceive the opinions of others correctly and to learn from them. We observed that when executives lacked common goals, they tended to be closed-minded and more likely to misinterpret and blame one another.

Use Humor

Teams that handle conflict well make explicit—and often even contrived—attempts to relieve tension and at the same time promote a collaborative esprit by making their business fun. They emphasize the excitement of fast-paced competition, not the stress of competing in brutally tough and uncertain markets.

All the teams with low interpersonal conflict described ways in which they used humor on the job. Executives at Bravo Microsystems enjoyed playing gags around the office. For example, pink plastic flamingos—souvenirs from a customer—graced Bravo's otherwise impeccably decorated headquarters. Similarly, Triumph Computers' top managers held a monthly "dessert pig-out," followed by group weight watching. Those seemingly trivial activities were part of the CEO's deliberate plan to make work more fun, despite the pressures of the industry. At Star Electronics, making the company "a fun place" was an explicit goal for the top-management team. Laughter was common during management meetings. Practical jokes were popular at Star, where executives—along with other employees—always celebrated Halloween and April Fools' Day.

At each of these companies, executives acknowledged that at least some of the attempts at humor were contrived—even forced. Even so, they helped to release tension and promote collaboration.

Humor was strikingly absent in the teams marked by high interpersonal conflict. Although pairs of individuals were sometimes friends, team members shared no group social activities beyond a standard holiday party or two, and there were no conscious attempts to create humor. Indeed, the climate in which decisions were made was often just the opposite—hostile and stressful.

Humor works as a defense mechanism to protect people from the stressful and threatening situations that commonly arise in the course of making strategic decisions. It helps people distance themselves psychologically by putting those situations into a broader life context, often through the use of irony. Humor—with its ambiguity—can also blunt the threatening edge of negative information. Speakers can say in jest things that might otherwise give offense because the message is simultaneously serious and not serious. The recipient is allowed to save face by receiving the serious message while appearing not to do so. The result is communication of difficult information in a more tactful and less personally threatening way.

Humor can also move decision making into a collaborative rather than competitive frame through its powerful effect on mood. According to a large body of research, people in a positive mood tend to be not only more optimistic but also more forgiving of others and creative in seeking solutions. A positive mood triggers a more accurate perception of others' arguments because people in a good mood tend to relax their defensive barriers and so can listen more effectively.

How Teams Argue but Still Get Along

Tactic	Strategy
Base discussion on current, factual information	Focus on issues, not personalities
Develop multiple alternatives to enrich the debate	
Rally around goals	Frame decisions as collaborations aimed at achieving the best possible solution for the company
Inject humor into the decision-making process	
Maintain balanced power structure	Establish a sense of fairness and equity in the process
Resolve issues without forcing consensus	

Balance the Power Structure

We found that managers who believe that their team's decision-making process is fair are more likely to accept decisions without resentment, even when they do not agree with them. But when they believe the process is unfair, ill will easily grows into interpersonal conflict. A fifth tactic for taming interpersonal conflict, then, is to create a sense of fairness by balancing power within the management team.

Our research suggests that autocratic leaders who manage through highly centralized power structures often generate high levels of interpersonal friction. At the other extreme, weak leaders also engender interpersonal conflict because the power vacuum at the top encourages managers to jockey for position. Interpersonal conflict is lowest in what we call *balanced power structures*, those in which the CEO is more powerful than the other members of the top-management team, but the members do wield substantial power, especially in their own well-defined areas of responsibility. In balanced power structures, all executives participate in strategic decisions.

At Premier Technologies, for example, the CEO—described by others as a "team player"—was definitely the most powerful figure. But each executive was the most powerful decision maker in some clearly defined area. In addition, the entire team participated in all significant decisions. The CEO, one executive observed, "depends on picking good people and letting them operate."

The CEO of Bravo Microsystems, another company with a balanced power structure, summarized his philosophy as "making quick decisions involving as many people as possible." We watched the Bravo team over several months as it grappled with a major strategic redirection. After many group discussions, the final decision was made at a multiday retreat involving the whole team.

In contrast, the leaders of the teams marked by extensive interpersonal conflict were either highly autocratic or weak. The CEO at Mercury Microdevices, for example, was the principal decision maker. There was a substantial gap in power between him and the rest of the team. In the decision we tracked, the CEO dominated the process from start to finish, identifying the problem, defining the analysis, and making the choice. Team members described the CEO as "strong" and "dogmatic." As one of them put it, "When Bruce makes a decision, it's like God!"

At Andromeda, the CEO exercised only modest power, and areas of responsibility were blurred within the top-management team, where power was diffuse and ambiguous. Senior executives had to politick amongst themselves to get anything accomplished, and they reported intense frustration with the confusion that existed at the top.

Most executives expected to control some significant aspect of their business but not the entirety. When they lacked power—because of either an autocrat or a power vacuum—they became frustrated by their inability to make significant decisions. Instead of team members, they became politicians. As one executive explained, "We're all jockeying for our spot in the pecking order." Another described "maneuvering for the CEO's ear."

The situations we observed are consistent with classic social-psychology studies of leadership. For example, in a study from the 1960s, Ralph White and Ronald Lippitt examined the effects of different leadership styles on boys in social clubs. They found that boys with democratic leaders—the situation closest to our balanced power structure—showed spontaneous interest in their activities. The boys were highly satisfied, and within their groups there were many friendly remarks, much praise, and significant collaboration. Under weak leaders, the boys were disorganized, inefficient, and dissatisfied. But the worst case was autocratic rule, under which the boys were hostile and aggressive, occasionally directing physical violence against innocent scapegoats. In imbalanced power situations, we observed adult displays of verbal aggression that colleagues described as violent. One executive talked about being "caught in the cross fire." Another described a colleague as "a gun about to go off." A third spoke about "being beat up" by the CEO.

Seek Consensus with Qualification

Balancing power is one tactic for building a sense of fairness. Finding an appropriate way to resolve conflict over issues is another—and, perhaps, the more crucial. In our research, the teams that managed conflict effectively all used the same approach to resolving substantive conflict. It is a two-step process that some executives call *consensus with qualification*. It works like this: executives talk over an issue and try to reach consensus. If they can, the decision is made. If they can't, the most relevant senior manager makes the decision, guided by input from the rest of the group.

When a competitor launched a new product attacking Premier Technologies in its biggest market, for example, there was sharp disagreement about how to respond. Some executives wanted to shift R&D resources to counter this competitive move, even at the risk of diverting engineering talent from a more innovative product then in design. Others argued that Premier should simply repackage an existing product, adding a few novel features. A third group felt that the threat was not serious enough to warrant a major response.

After a series of meetings over several weeks, the group failed to reach consensus. So the CEO and his marketing vice president made the decision. As the CEO explained, "The functional heads do the talking. I pull the trigger." Premier's executives were comfortable with this arrangement—even those who did not agree with the outcome—because everyone had had a voice in the process.

People usually associate consensus with harmony, but we found the opposite: teams that insisted on resolving substantive conflict by forcing consensus tended to display the most interpersonal conflict. Executives sometimes have the unrealistic view that consensus is always possible, but such a naive insistence on consensus can lead to endless haggling. As the vice president of engineering at Mega Software put it, "Consensus means that everyone has veto power. Our products were too late, and they were too expensive." At Andromeda, the CEO wanted his executives to reach consensus, but persistent differences of opinion remained. The debate dragged on for months, and the frustration mounted until some top managers simply gave up. They just wanted a decision, any decision. One was finally made when several executives who favored one point of view left the company. The price of consensus was a decimated team.

In a team that insists on consensus, deadlines can cause executives to sacrifice fairness and thus weaken the team's support for the final decision. At Andromeda, executives spent months analyzing their industry and developing a shared perspective on important trends for the future, but they could never focus on making the decision. The decision-making process dragged on. Finally, as the deadline of a board meeting drew imminent, the CEO formulated and announced a choice—one that had never even been mentioned in the earlier discussions. Not surprisingly, his team was angry and upset. Had he been less insistent on reaching a consensus, the CEO would not have felt forced by the deadline to act so arbitrarily.

How does consensus with qualification create a sense of fairness? A body of research on procedural justice shows that process fairness, which involves significant participation and influence by all concerned, is enormously important to most people. Individuals are willing to accept outcomes they dislike if they believe that the process by which those results came about was fair. Most people want their opinions to be considered seriously but are willing to accept that those opinions

---

Building a Fighting Team

How can managers encourage the kind of substantive debate over issues that leads to better decision making? We found five approaches that help generate constructive disagreement within a team:

1. *Assemble a heterogeneous team, including diverse ages, genders, functional backgrounds, and industry experience.* If everyone in the executive meetings looks alike and sounds alike, then the chances are excellent that they probably think alike, too.

2. *Meet together as a team regularly and often.* Team members that don't know one another well don't know one another's positions on issues, impairing their ability to argue effectively. Frequent interaction builds the mutual confidence and familiarity team members require to express dissent.

3. *Encourage team members to assume roles beyond their obvious product, geographic, or functional responsibilities.* Devil's advocates, sky-gazing visionaries, and action-oriented executives can work together to ensure that all sides of an issue are considered.

4. *Apply multiple mind-sets to any issue.* Try role-playing, putting yourself in your competitors' shoes or conducting war games. Such techniques create fresh perspectives and engage team members, spurring interest in problem solving.

5. *Actively manage conflict.* Don't let the team acquiesce too soon or too easily. Identify and treat apathy early, and don't confuse a lack of conflict with agreement. Often, what passes for consensus is really disengagement.

cannot always prevail. That is precisely what occurs in consensus with qualification. As one executive at Star said, "I'm happy just to bring up my opinions."

Apart from fairness, there are several other reasons why consensus with qualification is an important deterrent to interpersonal conflict. It assumes that conflict is natural and not a sign of interpersonal dysfunction. It gives managers added influence when the decision affects their part of the organization in particular, thus balancing managers' desires to be heard with the need to make a choice. It is an equitable and egalitarian process of decision making that encourages everyone to bring ideas to the table but clearly delineates how the decision will be made.

Finally, consensus with qualification is fast. Processes that require consensus tend to drag on endlessly, frustrating managers with what they see as time-consuming and useless debate. It's not surprising that the managers end up blaming their frustration on the shortcomings of their colleagues and not on the poor conflict-resolution process.

Linking Conflict, Speed, and Performance

A considerable body of academic research has demonstrated that conflict over issues is not only likely within top-management teams but also valuable. Such conflict provides executives with a more inclusive range of information, a deeper understanding of the issues, and a richer set of possible solutions. That was certainly the case in the companies we studied. The evidence also overwhelmingly indicates that where there is little conflict over issues, there is also likely to be poor decision making. "Groupthink" has been a primary cause of major corporate- and public-policy debacles. And although it may seem counterintuitive, we found that the teams that engaged in healthy conflict over issues not only made better decisions but moved more quickly as well.

Without conflict, groups lose their effectiveness. Managers often become withdrawn and only superficially harmonious. Indeed, we found that the alternative to conflict is usually not agreement but apathy and disengagement. Teams unable to foster substantive conflict ultimately achieve, on average, lower performance. Among the companies that we observed, low-conflict teams tended to forget to consider key issues or were simply unaware of important aspects of their strategic situation. They missed opportunities to question falsely limiting assumptions or to generate significantly different alternatives. Not surprisingly, their actions were often easy for competitors to anticipate.

In fast-paced markets, successful strategic decisions are most likely to be made by teams that promote active and broad conflict over issues without sacrificing speed. The key to doing so is to mitigate interpersonal conflict.

MANAGING FACE-TO-FACE INTERNATIONAL NEGOTIATIONS*

John L. Graham

William Hernández Requejo

The most difficult aspect of an international business negotiation is the actual conduct of the face-to-face meeting. Assuming that the appropriate people have been chosen to represent a firm, and that those representatives are well prepared, and that the process has been designed to maximize knowledge flows, things can still go

*Reprinted from *Organizational Dynamics*, 38(2), John L. Graham and William Hernandez Requejo, "Managing Face-to-Face International Negotiations," pp. 167–177, © 2009, with permission from Elsevier.

wrong at the negotiation table. Obviously, if these other preliminaries haven't been managed properly, then things will go wrong during the meetings.

Non-Task Sounding

Trust and connections can make a big difference in the United States. They're often great to have, but not essential. In all relationship-oriented cultures around the world (e.g., Japan, China, Brazil, or Spain), they are essential. Getting started in the States means: (1) sending a letter explaining your business purpose and dropping a name or two if possible; (2) a follow-up call for an appointment; (3) five minutes of small talk across her desk (this is the non-task sounding); and (4) you're talking business. There are a few more steps to the dance in Asia, Latin America, Southern Europe, India, Africa, and Middle East.

Most business professionals are loath to use their legal system (attorneys and courts) to clean things up if the business goes sour. They depend on strong and trusting relationships between the people on both sides to mitigate conflicts down the road. And, time and money are *invested* in building those relationships *before* getting down to business. Five minutes of non-task sounding in the United States can translate into five days, weeks, or even months of non-task sounding in Shanghai, Lagos, Rio de Janeiro, or Jeddah. There is no other way because in such countries real business cannot be conducted until a good interpersonal relationship has been established.

In the United States people tend to trust until given reason not to. In the relationship-oriented cultures of Asia, Africa, Latin America, and Southern Europe suspicion and distrust characterize all meetings with strangers. In such places it is difficult to earn trust because business will not even begin without it. Instead, trust must be transmitted via personal connections or intermediaries. That is, a trusted business associate of yours must pass you along to one of his trusted business associates and so on. So the key first step in non-task sounding in many countries is finding the personal links to your intended target organization and/or executive.

Role of Intermediaries

Those links can be hometown, family, school, or previous business ties. In some places they can be institutional—as in Japan where your banker can do the introductions. In China or India, the links must be based on personal experience. For example, you call your former classmate and ask him to set up a dinner meeting with his friend. Expensive meals at nice places are key to demonstrating that you understand the value of strategic personal relationships. If things go well and his friend accepts the role of your intermediary, he will set up a meeting with your potential client or business partner whom he knows quite well.

Often, your intermediary will then arrange a lunch or dinner the night before a visit to the client's offices. We have found this to be particularly true when dealing with international financial institutions such as Banco Santander, BBVA, or Deutsche Bank. The intermediary will attend both. Your intermediary will insist that you spend big bucks on the meal. This is important. Your sincerity will be gauged by the size of the check for this ritual sharing of food. For someone who grabs a sandwich at his desk for lunch this will seem inefficient. However, a $500 meal may in fact be a great investment in many places around the world such as Hong Kong or Milan.

The talk at these initial meetings may range widely, even inanely from the American perspective. Even though your intermediary has "blessed" the relationship, your foreign partner will still endeavor to sound you out in the broadest senses—trustworthiness, sincerity, integrity, competence, and so on. S/he will be looking for feelings of interpersonal harmony and connection. There is no rushing this process. Rick Lynch, chief executive officer (CEO) of Heineken in China, notes that while this "empty questioning" may test your own patience, even your endurance, you should take it as a sign of progress—they're interested.

At some point when you have "passed" the total-you test, the client or the intermediary will bring up business. This signals the end to non-task sounding in relationship-cultures. Only the client or intermediary can give this signal. We repeat, only the client or intermediary can give this signal. NOT YOU! And even then, after brief discussion of business, your foreign client may lapse back into more non-task sounding. The management implications are clear. In foreign countries, actually even in the United States, always, ALWAYS, let the client or intermediary bring up business.

Sam Su, President of YUM! Brands in China feels that most Americans can make it through the dinner, but at the client's offices the next day they can't keep from making proposals. This is often incredibly rude from the Chinese perspective. Even when they've been told by their own experienced staff to continue the small talk until the client broaches business, most high-powered Americans can't stand the "delays."

We talked with a group of American executives representing MicroAge International, a computer hardware manufacturing company, trying to develop a business relationship with a Spanish distributor. Their complaint was that every time they went to Madrid the trip was exhausting because the Spaniards insisting on continuous late night eating and drinking. That combined with jet lag made the discussions during the days literally physically demanding. We recommended they invite the Spaniards to Arizona to visit their offices to continue the work. Our clients responded, "We've tried that, but it's still party late into the night there as well, and here we have to contend with our families!"

Other minor considerations: Business cards will be required and small gifts (exchanged before leaving the offices) will be appropriate in many countries such as Japan, China, and Malaysia. For meetings in the United States, setting and formality will be marginally less important for operational level executives, but not much less. Particularly when the foreign firm is the one courted, long periods of non-task sounding, including dinner at a very good restaurant or at your home, are advised.

Role for C-Level Executives

The role of C-level executives in negotiations internationally is often ceremonial. By ceremonial, we do not mean unimportant! Ordinarily they are brought into negotiations only to sign the agreement, after all issues have been settled by lower level executives. On occasion, top executives are included earlier in the talks to communicate commitment and importance. In either case, their main activity is non-task sounding. Only vague statements should be made about the potential for a strong, long-lasting business relationship. Specifics must be left up to managers and staff.

Getting top American executives to understand the importance of non-task sounding and to make these adjustments in their behavior may be difficult. One successful way has been to supply them with a list of appropriate questions to ask during the initial meetings with their high-level counterparts. Soccer's a good topic almost everywhere, but a little knowledge about cricket will go a long way in Sydney. Ask your local representatives or intermediaries what topics are appropriate and do a little studying ahead of time.

The American executives should be prepared with business cards in the local language and should exchange them if the other side offers. However, when presidents of companies meet, business cards often are not required. Of course, American presidents should be well briefed about their foreign counterparts in advance.

Finally, when high-level meetings are held in the United States, we recommend a similar approach. Top-level foreign executives, particularly from East Asian cultures, will not be prepared to bargain and will not be persuaded, even when in the United States. It's simply not their role. When American hosts wish to demonstrate the importance of the visit and the deal, we advise sending a limousine to pick up the foreign party at their hotel. The initial meeting between top executives should not be held across a boardroom table, and certainly not across the American executive's desk. Rather, a more comfortable, living room or a private room in a high-class restaurant type of atmosphere is preferable. Remember, the extra expense is an investment!

Task-Related Exchange of Information

A task-related exchange of information implies a two-way communication process. However, when Americans meet foreigners across the negotiation table, the information flow is very often unidirectional—from the American side to the other. In the paragraphs that follow we will recommend actions for American bargainers that will help them to manage efficiently the give-and-take of information.

Giving Information

The most obvious problem associated with providing information to international clients will be the language. It is true that many more foreign executives can speak and understand English than Americans can use any second language. English is, after all, the international language of business and technology. However, Americans should be careful of misunderstandings arising from the other side's limited knowledge of English. Confusion can result when foreign executives, because of politeness, indicate they understand when in fact they do not. When any doubt exists, Americans should use visual media (PowerPoint and brochures) and provide copious written support materials and an interpreter if the other side hasn't. Even when an international partner does provide an interpreter, there may be critical stages of the negotiations when your own interpreter should be included on your negotiation team. Be sure to talk to and listen to the executive on the other side of the table even when she or he speaks in the local language. The interpreter should not be the sole focus of your attention.

Regarding written materials, imagine for a moment that you are a Vietnamese executive trying to choose between two competitive offerings. One is written in your native language, and the other is written in a foreign language. Which proposal will you "like" better? Which company will you choose as a vendor? Perhaps you can get by with technical or engineering details in English, but the sections of the proposal that will be reviewed and evaluated by upper Vietnamese management, particularly Party officials, must be written in their native language. We've heard more than once that translation of documents is expensive and takes time. In fact, several of our clients have been reluctant to authorize the expenditures for high quality translation. These have usually been executives at small and medium size firms that just have not experienced or noticed the lack of understanding during their presentations to foreign customers and partners. But would you rather have your client spending his time reading your proposal in his second language? And how expensive is losing your next deal?

Once managers are comfortable with the language situation, they can turn their attention to more subtle aspects of giving information to their foreign counterparts. The first of these has to do with the order of presentation. In the United States managers tend to say what they want and explain the reasons behind their requests only if necessary. That's why the task-related exchange of information goes so quickly. This isn't the ritual in many countries. For example, in Japan they are used to long descriptions of background and context before specific proposals are made, because there, the time invested in detailed discussions obviates heavy-handed persuasive tactics and yields seemingly obvious answers to negotiation problems. Given this mode of operation, it is not surprising to hear the American executive's complaint about the thousands of questions the Japanese ask.

Clearly then, communicating your bargaining interests, your company's needs and preferences, will take longer in almost all foreign countries. Language problems and lengthy explanations will require more meetings, involving more of your people (technical experts) and more of theirs. We strongly recommend patience with this process and anticipation of increased time and money spent at this stage. But at some point American bargainers will have to terminate such questioning. While answering "a thousand" questions may be tedious but necessary, answering two thousand questions may not be productive. Instead of answering a repetitious question about delivery again, a variety of responses may work better:

1. "Apparently delivery is key issue for you. Can you remind me again why?"
2. Summarize your previous answer after something like: "I already gave that information to Mr. Park yesterday, but to reiterate . . . "
3. Offer to write down the requested information so that it may be shared with all concerned foreign executives.
4. Generally, a repeated question should be answered the second time in about three minutes. The third time it's asked, the answer should be a one-minute summary. If the same question is asked a fourth time, it's probably a persuasive tactic and not information gathering. The appropriate response is then silence or a change of subject.

Managers should recognize one other thing about foreign questions. The other side often understands, and even expects, that some questions cannot be answered. But they will go ahead and ask them anyway. This is in sharp contrast to the American practice of only asking questions that will be answered. That is, if an American manager asks a question and doesn't get an answer, he often gets upset. This is not necessarily the case with the executives in many other countries such as Israel, for example. Israeli directness often leads to questions uncomfortable for Americans. But, a response of, "I just can't answer that one," will not necessarily bother an inquisitive Israeli executive.

Finally, we recommend that American bargainers guard against the tendency of making concessions during this exchange of information. We have found that often American negotiators, impatient with the process, will actually make concessions during this second stage of negotiations, before they have even determined the foreign negotiator's position, needs, and interests. For example, it is common for Americans to focus on land prices in international real estate transactions, making concessions on that issue before hearing about access, water rights, and other potentially crucial issues. It will take great patience indeed to avoid the natural urge to get to the third stage, persuasion, by making concessions in the hopes that they will reciprocate.

Getting Information

Of course, getting information *before* negotiations begin is hugely important. James Sebenius advocates "mapping the players and the process" in international negotiations. We agree, and your intermediary or local advisors will be essential in this activity. Key information will be issues related to the larger context of your business—government or party involvement and the larger economic plans of local, provincial, and/or even national authorities—things not considered or uncovered during your own environmental scanning. Also, crucial will be knowledge of the key decision makers. In family businesses in Hispanic cultures or Saudi Arabia it's almost always the patriarch; in state owned enterprises in Vietnam or China it's the top Party official.

Hopefully, your foreign clients will be courting your business like the Chinese government did with 7-Eleven Inc. prior to the 2008 Olympic Games. In such a situation they will be the ones making proposals and supplying you with more information than you probably want. But should your firm be initiating the contact or trying to make the sale, expect great difficulties getting feedback to your proposals. If you ask a group of Thai executives what they think of your price quote and proposal, they will invariably say, something like, "Let us take a look or let us study (or do some research on) it." They may even respond in such a manner even if they think it stinks.

Let's review the reasons behind this "strange" behavior. First, executives in many relationship-oriented cultures (e.g., the Philippines or Thailand) want to maintain your face and interpersonal harmony. From his point of view a negative, albeit honest, answer at the negotiation would disrupt the harmony established. American executives are often unable to read the subtle, nonverbal, negative cues that accompany the "Let us study it." Another local executive would read the nonverbal message that "it stinks," but even the most experienced Americans are sometimes unable to process this subtle message.

In the United States, another key source of information regarding your client's reaction to your proposals is his or her facial expression. Most of us process such information unconsciously, but we all do pay attention to this channel. Indeed, many American executives report great frustration because of the Japanese negotiator's "poker face." Indeed, some Japanese managers report increasing their eye contact when dealing with Americans to demonstrate interest, but controlling their facial expressions to hide negative reactions.

Indeed, the most efficient way to get feedback from a foreign client may be through the indispensable intermediary. Having talked about all the difficulties in getting honest feedback from many of your foreign partners, you should also understand that some cultures are on the other end of the scale. For example, both German and Israeli negotiators are famous for their sometimes brutal honesty. If a German executive thinks your proposal stinks, she'll very directly tell you so. An Israeli might take it a step further and tell you it's insulting. Israelis highly value what they call *doogri,* that is, expressing their feelings directly and accurately. Israelis complain they can't get a straight answer from Americans! The problem then for Americans is to not take offense at their pushy use of English and their apparently aggressive manner. It's their cultural mores.

Persuasion

From the American perspective persuasion is the heart of a negotiation. In America, managers have a wide range of persuasive tactics that can be and often are employed to change clients' minds. Among them are promises, recommendations, appeals to industry norms, providing more information, asking questions, and the more aggressive threats and warnings. We have observed Americans using all such persuasive tactics. However, the appropriateness and effectiveness of these approaches varies in other countries. Things are a bit more complicated in many places.

For example, Honeywell Bull had won negotiation rights for an order of 100 ATMs from the Bank of China. Toward the end of the negotiations, the Bank of China buyer asked for deeper price cuts. But to him it wasn't just a matter of thrift. He appealed, "If the price isn't reduced further I will lose face." This is Chinese for "the deal will be off and we'll talk to your competitor." The Honeywell Bull executive responded that he had some room to move in the bid, but the lower price would not allow for training in the U.S. for the Chinese managers. The Chinese side then asked for a break and came back smiling in 10 minutes agreeing to all the terms. Some might conclude that for Chinese executives, seeing New York, Hollywood, and Las Vegas is more important than a face-saving price reduction. However, the clever negotiator will understand that his staff's travel to the States gave much more face to the Chinese executive than any mere price break.

When the persuasion starts in your negotiations in many countries you can expect to hear about your competitors and threats to do business elsewhere. Of course, Americans do the same thing, but with more finesse perhaps. Korean managers at companies such as Samsung Electronics Co. and LG seem to use this tactic with little compunction. Because American negotiators tend to be in a hurry and tend to focus on "one thing at a time," the development of a symmetrical set of alternatives begins only when troubles crop up with the focal business deal. So most Americans feel like they're being "two timed" when the "there's-more-than-one-game-in-town" threat is delivered. Americans get mad when the Koreans are just blandly pointing out what they believe should be obvious to everyone.

Another important factor in relationship-oriented cultures is the context in which specific tactics are used. Aggressive influence tactics such as threats or warnings, which can only be used by negotiators in higher power positions (usually buyers), should be communicated through intermediaries and informally. And even then, only subtle and indirect threats, commands, and so on, are appropriate. Getting mad ruins relationships. Loud voices and angry tones destroy even longstanding interpersonal harmony. So the intermediary or local representative can be doubly important from the American perspective. First, s/he provides a method of more accurately reading foreign clients, and, second, it makes available to American bargainers persuasive tactics that would be completely inappropriate during the formal talks.

To sum up, if an impasse is reached with foreign clients, rather than trying to persuade in the usual American manner, we recommend use of the following eight persuasive tactics, in the following order and in the following circumstances:

1. Ask more questions. We feel that the single most important advice we can give is to use questions as a persuasive tactic. This is true in not only relationship-oriented cultures, but anywhere in the world, including the United States. One prominent negotiations expert suggests that sometimes it's "smart to be a little bit dumb" in business negotiations. Ask the same questions more than once—"I didn't completely understand what you meant. Can you please explain that again?" If your clients or potential business partners have good answers, then it's perhaps best if you compromise on the issue. But often, under close scrutiny, their answers aren't very good. And with such a weak position exposed they will be obligated to concede. Also, questions often put more information on the table providing leads toward more creative solutions. For all these reasons questions can elicit key information and can be powerful persuasive devices.

2. Educate. Condescension will kill this approach, so be careful. But, re-explain your company's situation, needs, and preferences. You might also make oblique reference to the "internationally recognized business practices" about which most managers in fast developing countries (e.g., India and China) are becoming more interested. Some executives supply foreign customers with information about their own competitors, again with the intent of education about the overall marketplace.

3. Silence. If you are still not satisfied with their response, try silence. Let them think about it and give them an opportunity to change their position. However, you should recognize that foreign executives are often much better at the use of this tactic than you. If silence is a tactic you find difficult to use, you should at least be aware that some of your foreign partners will use it frequently and naturally.

4. If tactics 1 through 3 produce no concessions, it will be time to change the subject or call a recess and put to work the intermediary. But rather than going directly

to the more aggressive tactics (warnings and threats) we recommend repeating the first three tactics using that important communication channel—the intermediary or local representative. The questions and explanations may expose new information or objections that couldn't be broached at the negotiation table.

5. Aggressive influence tactics (warnings and threats, particularly those emphasized with expressions of emotions) may be used in negotiations with most East Asians, for example, only at great risk and in special circumstances. First, they should only be used via the intermediary or your local representative, and even then they should be used in the most indirect manner possible. Second, they should be used only when the American company is clearly in the stronger position. Even in these two circumstances, use of such aggressive persuasive tactics will damage the interpersonal harmony, which may in the long run be to your company's disadvantage. If power relations ever shift (and they always do), the other side will be quick to exploit the change in events. However, if the American side exercises restraint and maintains the interpersonal harmony, then if and when power relations shift, often the other side will consider the American company's interests.

   This latter point is difficult for most Americans to believe. But we have witnessed Chinese executives behave in this way several times. For example, a corporate vice president at Honeywell Bull threatened a senior executive at China Post with a lawsuit, demanding final acceptance of a signed contract. The China Post executive responded, "Go ahead. You may win the case. But, you will be finished in the China market." At a subsequent meeting the Honeywell Bull country manager, schooled in the Chinese style of business negotiations and possessing a good relationship with the China Post executive, was able to smooth things over by appealing to the interests of the long term. The customer responded, "This is the right attitude, I will see what I can do to expedite the final acceptance."

6. If tactics 1 through 5 have not produced concessions on their part, we suggest the use of time to enable them to consider new information and to reach a decision satisfying almost everyone involved on their side, from technical experts to government officials. Bargainers in many countries (e.g., Japan, Malaysia, or Thailand) don't make concessions immediately following persuasive appeals without broader consultation. Indeed, the combination of collective decision-making and social hierarchy can make things quite complicated with clients from relationship-cultures. Unfortunately, time is perhaps the most difficult tactic for American bargainers to use. Americans are in a hurry to solve the problem and settle the deal. "Letting things hang" goes against their nature. But it may be necessary. And hopefully, they will run into their time limits before you run into yours. Also, use of this tactic will require the cooperation and understanding of your home office.

   It should be remembered that executives from most other cultures are skilled in the use of time as a persuasive tactic. Often, group decision-making and the long-term approach to business deals seem to enhance the effectiveness of tactical delays for foreign bargaining with Americans. Richard Solomon, President of the U.S. Institute for Peace, explains in his excellent book on the Chinese negotiation style: "Do not expect quick or easy agreement. A Chinese negotiator will have trouble convincing his superiors that he has fully tested the limits of his counterpart's position if he has not protracted the discussions."

7. The next persuasive tactic to use is asking the intermediary to arbitrate your differences. Let them call your clients and meet with them separately as a go-between. We have seen intermediaries often successfully settle otherwise irreconcilable differences.

8. Finally, if all else fails, it may be necessary to bring together the top executives of the two companies in the hope of stimulating more cooperation. A refusal at this stage means the business is finished.

To conclude our discussion of persuasive tactics, we want to emphasize the importance of these recommendations. A mistake at this stage, even a minor one, can have major consequences for your international business relationships. American managers will have to be doubly conscientious to avoid blunders here because often the foreigners' style of persuasion is so different and apparently ambiguous. Remember that the managers from relationship-oriented cultures in particular are looking to establish a long-term business relationship of mutual benefit. Threats and the like don't fit into their understanding of how such a relationship should work. You should also recognize that we are recommending adoption of a Japanese approach to persuasion when bargaining with almost all foreign clients and business partners. We realize our approach takes longer, but in the end you and your company will benefit by such an approach. Finally, smart American negotiators will anticipate the foreigner's use of the persuasive tactics just described.

Concessions and Agreement

The final stage of business negotiations involves concessions, building toward agreement. Negotiation requires compromise, or as the Chinese say, "Finding *the way*." Usually, both sides give up something to get even more. But the approach used for compromise can vary substantially around the world, particularly East to West.

American and European managers often report great difficulties in measuring progress in their negotiations in Asia. After all, in America managers are half done when half the issues are settled. But in Japan or Malaysia nothing seems to get settled. Then, surprise, you're done. Often, Americans make unnecessary concessions right before agreements are announced by the other side. American bargainers in Asia should expect this holistic approach and be prepared to discuss all issues simultaneously and in an apparently haphazard order. Progress in the talks should not be measured by how many issues have been settled. Rather, Americans must try to gauge the quality of the business relationship. Important signals of progress will be:

1. Higher level foreign executives being included in the discussions;
2. Their questions beginning to focus on specific areas of the deal;
3. A softening of their attitudes and position on some of the issues;
4. At the negotiation table, increased talk among themselves in their native tongue, which may often mean they're trying to decide something;
5. Calls for additional meetings, increased bargaining, and use of the intermediary; and
6. They ask about things potential benefits such as overseas training or even future business.

As part of your team's preparations, it will be important to document concession strategies. When they're agreed to and written down before negotiations begin, it's easier for everyone on your side to stick to the "concession schedule." Americans need to follow such schedules with care. Trading concessions with foreign bargainers will not work because they view nothing to be settled until everything is settled. We advise making no concession until all issues and interests have been exposed and fully discussed. Then concessions should be made, on minor issues first, to help establish the relationship.

Finally, concessions should not be decided upon at the negotiation table. Rather, Americans are advised to reconsider each concession away from the social pressure of the formal negotiations. This again is a Japanese practice that Americans will do well emulating. Having strategically limited authority can be an important check on runaway concession making.

Minor Distractions

Before closing our discussion of the process of business negotiations, it is important to mention briefly three foreign behaviors that will seem rude to American bargainers but are nothing more than common habits for executives in many other countries. First, Iranian clients will often break into side conversations—in Farsi. Ordinarily, the purpose of these side conversations is clarification of something the Americans have said, that is, they are getting the translation straightened out among themselves. Second, Chinese executives will often enter or leave negotiations in the middle of your comments. This reflects their busy schedule and a different view of "meeting etiquette." Finally, it can be particularly disturbing to be talking to a group of Saudi or Japanese and discover that one, perhaps even the senior executive, is "listening while doing other things" or "listening with his eyes shut." Usually this shouldn't be taken personally; it simply reflects a different view of appropriate behavior at meetings. Further, busy foreign executives may also be signaling that they are comfortable with how things are going—if they are not comfortable, they will remain quite attentive.

The New Creativity

Getting to "yes" isn't good enough

Perhaps the most famous negotiation parable involves an argument over an orange. The most obvious approach was to simply cut it in half, each person getting a fair share. But, when the negotiators began talking to each other, exchanging information about their interests, a better solution to the problem became obvious. The person wanting the orange for juice for breakfast took that part and the person wanting the rind for making marmalade took that part. Both sides ended up with more. Neither agreement is particularly creative. The parable of the orange becomes a story about creativity when both parties decide to cooperate in planting an orange tree. In a similar way, Boeing Co. buys composite plastic wings for its new 787 Dreamliner, designed and manufactured by Japanese suppliers, and then sells the completed 787s back to Japanese airlines, all with a nice subsidy from the Japanese government. This is what we mean by creativity in negotiations.

At business schools these days we are beginning to learn a lot about creative processes. Courses are being offered and dissertations being proffered with "innovation" the key buzz word at academic conferences and in corporate boardrooms. The more we hear about innovation and creative processes the more we are beginning to appreciate that the Japanese approach to international business negotiations, by nature, uses many of the techniques commonly emphasized in any discussion of creative processes. Indeed, there appears to be a deeply fundamental explanation why the Japanese have been able to build such a successful society, despite their lack of natural resources and relative isolation. While Japanese society does have its own obstacles to creativity—hierarchy and collectivism are two—they have developed a negotiation style that in many ways obviates such disadvantages.

We also must give credit to the luminaries in field who have long advocated creativity in negotiations. Howard Raiffa and his colleagues recommend:

> . . . the teams should think and plan together informally and do some joint brainstorming, which can be thought of as "dialoguing" or "pre-negotiating." The two sides make no tradeoffs, commitments, or arguments about how to divide the pie at this early stage.

Roger Fisher and William Ury title their Chapter 4 in *Getting to Yes,* "Invent[ing] Options for Mutual Gain." David Lax and James Sebenius, in their important new book, *3-D Negotiations,* go past getting to yes, and talk about "creative agreements" and "great agreements." Lawrence Susskind and his associates advocate the use of "parallel informal negotiations" toward building creative negotiation outcomes. Our goal here is to push these ideas to the forefront in thinking about business negotiations. The field generally is still stuck in the past, talking about "making deals" and "solving problems." Even the use of terms like "win-win" exposes the vestiges of the old competitive thinking. Our point is that a business negotiation is not something that can be won or lost, and the competitive metaphor limits creativity. The problem-solving metaphor does as well. Thus, we urge managers to accept only creative outcomes!

One of the smartest people we know working in the area of creative processes is Lynda Lawrence at Idea-Works, a Newport Beach consulting firm (www.ideaworksconsulting.com). Lawrence's expertise combines practice and research—the rich experiences of founding and managing her own advertising agency with a comprehensive study of the topic. She also co-teaches a course in Innovation Processes (Creativity and Diffusion of Innovations) at the Merage School of Business at UC Irvine. She has developed a list of "10 Ways to Generate More Ideas" that we have included here as Exhibit 1. Read down her list and consider how these techniques might be used to stimulate creative thinking in your negotiations.

1. Establish ***common goals*** of what this "collaboration" would create. A more workable deal? Some common long-term goals? A closer partnership?
2. Establish the ***rules of engagement.*** The purpose of the exercise is to resolve differences in creative ways that work better for both parties. All ideas are possibilities, and research shows that combining ideas from different cultures can result in better outcomes than those from a single culture.
3. ***Trust is key,*** and difficult to establish in many cultures. "Certain techniques might speed up that process a little such as being offsite, for example, or establishing physical proximity that unconsciously signals intimacy."
4. ***Add diversity*** (gender, culture, extroverts, different work specialties, experts, outsiders) to the group.
5. ***Use storytelling.*** This both helps establish who you are and what point of view you are bringing to this collaboration.
6. ***Work in small groups.*** Add physical movement. Tell the participants to relax, play, sing, have fun, and silence is Ok.
7. Work holistically and use visuals. If, for example, there are three sticking points where neither side is happy, agree to use on those points by spending a short time—10 minutes—on each point where both sides offer "crazy" suggestions. Use techniques of ***improvisation.*** Neither side should be offended by the ***crazy ideas.*** No one should criticize. Explain that by exploring crazy ideas that better ideas are often generated.
8. ***Sleep on it.*** This enables the unconscious to work on the problems, and gives participants time to collect opinions before meeting again the next day. Other kinds of breaks coffee,etc. (are also helpful.)
9. Doing this process ***over several sessions*** allows both sides to feel that progress is being made, and actually generates better and more polished ideas that both sides can invest in.
10. It is the process of creating something together, rather than the specific proposals, which creates ***bonding*** around a shared task and establishes new ways of working together. Each side feels honored and Americans can feel that something is being accomplished.

EXHIBIT 1   10 Ways to Generate More Ideas
Source: Lynda Lawrence, Chief Idea Officer, Idea Works Consulting (www.ideaworksconsulting.com)

For the Japanese reader, some things on this list will be quite familiar. That is, based on our careful studies of negotiation styles in more than 20 cultures around the world, it is clear that the Japanese approach to business negotiations is, *by nature*, best at incorporating many tools of creativity. For example, it's easy to get Japanese in close physical proximity (#3); they've been living that way for millennia. In Japanese companies there are not typically marketing specialists as different from engineers as different from finance analysts. Each executive may have worked in several functional areas, limiting the "chimney effect" often associated disparagingly with American firms (#4). Physical movement (#6)—picture the start of the day at your typical Japanese factory. The Japanese also seem to work best in small groups (#6). Silence is definitely okay (part of #6). The Japanese invented *karaoke* (#6 and singing). The Japanese have difficulty criticizing others, especially foreigners (#7). The use of visuals and holistic thinking are natural for Japanese (#7). Breaks are also a common procedure for Japanese (#8). Japanese will work better with familiar folks (#9).

Perhaps we're stretching to make a few of these connections, and as we've already implied, some of these techniques will seem foreign to Japanese negotiators. For example, diversity is not a strong suit for Japanese—purposefully adding women and other elements of diversity (#4) to their groups would seem odd. Moreover, the Japanese are working on some of their own creativity disadvantages. For example, in Japanese elementary schools you can find rows and columns of third graders bowing and chanting in unison their school motto that ironically might include " . . . we will be independent thinkers."

Indeed, we notice similar changes in the Chinese school systems (imitating the Japanese) as they try to bridge what they also see as a creativity gap vis-à-vis the U.S. Ann Hulbert in the *New York Times Magazine* recently asked the uncomfortable questions: Can China create schools that foster openness, flexibility, and innovations? And what happens to China if it does? She adds, "Even as Americans seek to emulate China's test-centered and math-focused pedagogy, Chinese educators are trying to promote a Western emphasis on critical thinking at home . . . Throughout China, middle school exams have been abolished and vacation review classes are widely discouraged . . . The Chinese government worries that too many students have become the sort of stressed-out, test-acing drone who lacks the skills necessary in the global marketplace."

However, the key things the Japanese do in international negotiation that Americans can and should learn are the following: (1) The Japanese are the absolute champion information vacuums in global business. They keep their mouths shut and let everyone else do the talking. Thus, they use the diversity of their international colleagues (customers, suppliers, competitors, scientists, etc.) to a greater extent than any other group. We often disparage it as copying and borrowing, but in fact being open to everyone's ideas has always been the key to creativity and human progress. The Japanese, like everyone else around the world, are ethnocentric. But, at the same time they very much respect foreign ideas. (2) The Japanese will only work with cooperative negotiators when they have a choice. Trust and creativity go hand in hand. And, they will work to train other managers to negotiate more creatively for their own good. Witness the highly successful 25-year manufacturing joint venture in Fremont, California, between Toyota Motor Corp. and General Motors Corp. as a prominent example.

We challenge you to employ Lawrence's list in your own negotiations—in planning, execution, and follow-up. For example, playing golf or hitting a tennis ball with your partners can not only build personal relationships and trust, but also the *physical movement* can actually stimulate creative thinking. Or, give clients a couple of days to consider your tough requests—*sleeping on it* can lead to new ideas about commercial relationships. Indeed, the overnight part of #8 is particularly important. Anthropologist and consumer expert Clotaire Rapaille suggests that the transitions between wakefulness and sleep can act as a kind of creative "whack on the side of the head" that allows the mind to work differently, " . . . calming their brainwaves, getting them to that tranquil point just before sleep." Such tactics and tools should permeate your planning and interactions, both at home and abroad.

Application of principles of creativity will be practically and overtly appropriate in at least three points in your negotiations. Above we noted that Howard Raiffa and others suggest that they be used in pre-negotiation meetings. Second, we advocate their use when impasses are reached. For example, in the negotiations regarding the multi-billion-dollar Camisea natural gas project in Peru, the involved firms and environmentalist groups reached what seemed to be an irreconcilable difference: roads and a huge pipeline through the pristine forest would be an ecological disaster. The creative solution? Think of the remote gas field as an offshore platform, run the pipeline underground, and fly in personnel and equipment to the compression stations as needed.

Third, once you've gotten to "yes," a scheduled review of the agreement may actually get your business relationship past "yes" to truly creative outcomes. Perhaps you schedule such a review three months after implementation of the agreement has begun. But, the point is time must be set aside for a *creative* discussion of how can we improve on our business relationship. The emphasis of such a session should always be putting new ideas on the table—the answers to the question "what haven't we thought of?"

Conclusions

Implementing corporate strategies through business negotiations in other countries, particularly the unfamiliar, but fast-growing ones, will remain one of the most daunting and interesting challenges facing American executives during the next few decades. Actually, executives from around the world are fast learning to work with one another—particularly as new, large market countries join the World Trade Organization and begin to harmonize commercial practices. Indeed, herein we advocate what we see as a world standard for business negotiations. Young people are flooding into M.B.A. programs around the world and learning about concepts like corporate image, brand equity, and the ins and outs of intellectual property. The Internet is also making a huge difference, making efficient communication more available. While currently in many countries engineers and political persons usually lead companies, the future bodes well for the new business class. Herein we aspire to inspire a new approach in international commerce—one that defines the old ways of competitive and problem-solving negotiation styles as interesting relics, and advocates a new process of negotiations that elevates creativity as the first goal.

In relationship-oriented cultures, such as Indonesia, Nigeria, and China, there are huge advantages to moving first. Old friendships work their magic only when they are *old*! We recommend investing now in such places, if only in a small venture. This activity will allow executives and organizations to learn "the ropes to skip and the ropes to know." Managers will be able to develop the essential connections and the cross-cultural competence of your own staff toward understanding and growing the business there in these new places. Foreign-language skills and cultural knowledge will continue to be crucial. This means selecting, promoting, and *trusting* the advice of your own immigrant-American staff and advisors.

Other than arrogance, condescension, and ethnocentricity, *time* has always been the American bargainer's biggest handicap in international business. Impatience will be your enemy in almost all foreign countries. But, impatience is your friend when it comes to making the decision about whether to go or not. We counsel studied entry, but there is no better time than now to begin your work.

CHAPTER

15

Managing Diversity

Workplace diversity is another issue that requires careful management and attention in organizations. Among both individuals and teams, we find more emphasis placed on understanding the differences people bring to work and the need to incorporate an appreciation of these differences into the way we manage and work with others. Globalization and labor migration have resulted in more work contact with people from other cultures. The definition of diversity, however, extends beyond cultural background to include differences resulting from thinking styles, working styles, age, functional disciplines, years of service, religious beliefs, sexual orientation, marital status, physical appearance/abilities, education, and gender. The readings in this chapter deal with generational, gender, and cultural diversity.

Harriet Hankin, a consultant, examines generational diversity in "Generations: Boomers and Echos and Nexters—Oh My!." Hankin argues that understanding generations is a useful tool for recognizing factors that motivate individuals and influence their perceptions and priorities. If managers understand the forces and influences that shaped each generation, they can design workplaces in which every individual can do his or her best work.

Robin Ely, a Harvard professor who studies organizational race and gender issues, and Deborah Rhode, director of the Stanford Center on the Legal Profession and expert on legal ethics and gender, focus on the topic of gender diversity. They examine America's ambivalence about women and leadership in "Women and Leadership: Defining the Challenges." After addressing the structural and attitudinal barriers women face and the result of their underrepresentation in positions of power, the authors discuss the developmental challenges for women.

Most diversity training programs teach participants about the characteristics of different groups. There is a danger, however, that such information can be also used to stereotype individuals. In "Beyond sophisticated Stereotyping: Cultural Sensemaking in Context," Joyce Osland and Allan Bird, both experts on global leadership, warn against stereotyping people from different cultures using the bipolar value dimensions frequently taught in cross-cultural training programs and courses. During many years as expatriates in various countries, they became intrigued by the paradoxical aspects of complex cultures and devised a sensemaking model that encourages people to consider the context when decoding cultural behavior. Since this article was published, the sensemaking model has been applied more broadly to any type of cultural behavior, paradoxical or not.

GENERATIONS: BOOMERS AND ECHOS AND NEXTERS—OH MY!*

Harriet Hankin

When I got married more than twenty-five years ago, I was shocked by the number of socks my husband brought with him. He cleared out two or three drawers and filled them with socks. Some of them had never been opened and still had tags on them; others had tremendous holes. Being the new and doting wife, I sorted the socks—matched sizes and colors, tossed the "holey" ones, unwrapped the new ones. Big mistake! Bob loved his socks—ALL of them—and I wasn't to throw out a single one. Over the years, Bob's socks have become a running family joke, but the root of the attachment is quite clear. Raised during the depression, he had to wash out his socks each night and keep wearing them over and over again. This was the first time the differences in generations hit home for me—we are shaped by the experiences we live through. Separated by nearly sixteen years, my husband and I are from two different generations. He was eight years old when America was stunned by the attack on Pearl Harbor, December 7, 1941. It was a day that had a tremendous impact on him and has shaped his values and priorities even today.

I, on the other hand, am a Baby Boomer, a label I've always hated. Still, it meant that I always had enough socks and never kept or attempted to darn a "holey" one. Pearl Harbor was a chapter in my history book. I did, however, grow up with the belief that holding a textbook over my head while I crouched under my desk at school would keep me safe from the Russian threat of a nuclear bomb. The assassinations of John F. Kennedy, Martin Luther King, Jr., and Robert Kennedy were life-shaping historic moments for me.

For my daughter's generation, socks are important only as a fashion statement and they probably never heard of the word "darn" in reference to a sock. At twenty-one, my daughter is part of a new generation that seems to care very deeply about the future of our world. Their historical markers include the explosion of the space shuttle *Columbia* (though they don't remember the 1986 *Challenger* explosion), the war in Iraq, and most significantly, the terrorist attacks on the World Trade Center and Pentagon on September 11, 2001.

So, using my little family as a springboard, I can readily identify the significance and potential of three generations. At the same time, I realize that we are not only a product of our home environment and heredity but also of the historical context of our upbringing.

In the future, successful organizations will find the different generations more relevant than ever. Why? In short, because they are all working and will continue to do so.

For the first time in our history, four generations are active in the workforce at one time. They are, in fact, working together, interacting in the workplace. It's not just old man Jones sitting up in the executive suite and young Billy down in the mailroom, never to cross paths. Billy is probably up in Mr. Jones's office, helping him set up his computer to retrieve specific data he needs every day. As I am finding in so many areas, old paradigms of thinking are just that: old—and outdated. They will not work in the future.

In the past, companies could put generations into three tidy little groups, each with its own area of focus:

- *The Older Generation:* retired or getting ready to retire and concerned with their pensions
- *The Middle Generation:* the bulk of the workforce focused primarily on benefits and compensation
- *The Younger Generation:* the workforce of future, in need of training and education

Think about it. Many companies solved most of their workforce issues within these three silos. Need to shake things up? Save some money? Get rid of the "dead wood" and have an early retirement drive. Want to motivate your workers? Give them "family friendly" benefits and an annual picnic. Want to whip those up-and-comers into shape and attract the best and the brightest at the same time? Put together a management training program, complete with lectures, guest speakers, and job rotations. It was so easy, wasn't it? Now look! People are working who are 20, 40, 60, and even 80. It's all getting so complicated—or is it?

In the future, companies will face many generations active in the workforce simultaneously, thanks mainly to increased longevity and people looking to remain on the job years past what used to be considered retirement age. How will companies need to adjust their human resource functions—from recruiting and training to benefits and compensation—based on the different needs and expectations of the different generations? If they are looking to develop satisfied, productive workforces blending a wide variety of skills and experiences—which, of course, they should be—companies will start answering these questions today.

In this chapter, I will define the generations, delve a little deeper into what makes them tick, and then look at the implications for employers of these generations all working together. According to the book *Generations at Work* by Ron Zemke, Claire Raines, and Bob Filipczak:

> *The three generations that occupy today's workplace and the fourth generation that is entering it are clearly distinguishable by all these criteria—their demographics, their early life experiences, the headlines that defined their times, their heroes, music, and sociology, and their early days in the workplace. Their differences can be a source of creative strength and a source of opportunity, or a source of stifling stress and unrelenting conflict. Understanding generational differences is critical to making them work for the organization and not against it. It is critical to creating harmony, mutual respect, and joint effort where today there is suspicion, mistrust, and isolation.[1]*

Defining the Generations

Here is a thumbnail sketch of each of the major generations of today. I found some differences in birth years attributed to each, so I took the most common or that used by the Census Bureau. All the names, nicknames, birth years, and overlap became confusing. Laying it out this way was helpful to me. Consider it as a vertical timeline.

The Silent Generation

- Born 1922 to 1945.
- Key Influences: The Great Depression and the New Deal; World War II; Holocaust; Hiroshima; radio and movies.
- Other Names: The Veterans; Seniors; The Greatest Generation.

The Baby Boomers

- Born 1946 to 1964.
- Key Influences: Vietnam War; assassinations of JFK, Martin Luther King, Jr., and Robert Kennedy; putting a man on the Moon; Watergate; Cold War and bomb shelters; television; women's liberation, sexual revolution; environmental concerns (Green Party, Exxon *Valdez*).
- Other Names: Boomers; "Me" Generation.

Generation X

- Born 1965 to 1976.
- Key Influences: Demolition of the Berlin Wall; *Challenger* disaster; Clinton sex scandal; the skyrocketing growth of the stock market and the abundant economy in the 1980s and 1990s; 24-hour live, remote news coverage; the dot-com economy; hi-tech start-ups.
- Other Names: Baby Bust; Xers.

Baby Boom Echo

- Born 1977 to 2000.
- Key Influences: Oklahoma City bombing; Rodney King beating; O.J. Simpson trial; Columbine High School massacre; Y2K; Internet; September 11, 2001, terrorist attacks; corporate scandals (Enron); video games; instant messaging.
- Other Names: Generation Y; Nexters; Internet Generation; Millennials (for those born in the 1980s and 1990s).

Millennium Generation

- Born Since 2000.
- Key Influences: Yet to be determined.
- Other Names: I call this generation the Millennials. I feel that twenty years is a large span for one generation and I want to make the point that children who are just coming into the world with the new century will have their own set of influences. These babies will be the ones living the trends we are predicting now. This generation, and the one yet to come, will be the workforce that picks up where the Boomers leave off.

How Generations Enhance Understanding

There are varying views about whether understanding the generations is a useful tool for understanding what motivates an individual. Both sides of the argument make relevant points. On the one hand is the argument that factors other than birth year have a major impact on who one is: upbringing, education, affluence or lack of it, and even geography, just to name a few. I agree. On the other hand, members of a generation do share a history that reflects the news, views, politics, and entertainment that shaped their youth. I think both influences are relevant.

For employers, however, generations are perhaps the most consistent indicator of work needs. While a person can move, get an education, or change financial circumstances, a birth date never changes. It is a useful and dependable benchmark for certain information and is critical for longitudinal studies and trends. Companies and coworkers alike benefit from an understanding of the characteristics of the generations.

People born in the same generation have shared experiences that influence their perceptions and priorities and that shape who they are. They share the historic events, economics, and culture of their time. For example, members of the Silent Generation may remember going to bed hungry, or, similarly to my husband, not having enough socks.

They remember the attack on Pearl Harbor as a cataclysmic event beyond anything they could imagine. They also grew up in a time when holding hands on a date was a really big deal. As a result, they bring a certain set of principles and priorities to work. We call them the Silent Generation because they pretty much would "put up and shut up." They could remember things much worse than anything they were facing in the workplace. They were duty bound and loyal to their employers because people generally worked in one place for life.

Recognizing these key commonalities for a given generation helps guide employers as they seek to attract, retain, and support them as employees. This does not mean buying into and reinforcing stereotypes about the different age groups; it does mean having a basic understanding of the forces and influences that helped shape each generation and being aware of the needs and concerns of each group. As always, each employee is an individual and should be treated as such.

Delving a Little Deeper into the Generations

In order to understand this trend and what it will mean for employers, we have to take a closer look at each of the generations outlined above:

The Silent Generation: Born 1922 to 1945

Let's put the country's most mature generation in perspective. According to Louis Pol, demographer and associate dean of the College of Business Administration at the University of Nebraska at Omaha, the birthrate was fairly stable early in the 20th century. Then, during the Great Depression and World War II, the birthrate declined. At the same time, though, we had massive migrations from Europe to the United States. During these times, people knew greater economic turmoil and hardship than any American generation before or since. They survived through self-discipline, sacrifice, and pure hard work. The New Deal made construction workers out of many who had previously held jobs in other professions. The war led women to join the assembly lines of American factories. After the war, this generation enjoyed, albeit conservatively, a life of steadily increasing affluence and luxury.

The Silent Generation is the most traditional: working fathers, nuclear families, and traditional work ethics. They tend to be highly disciplined, hardworking, and loyal employees who play by the rules. They are the wisdom-keepers of America. They have so much to offer all of the generations—where America came from and what our elders endured to give us all that we take for granted today.

Even if they do not hold managerial positions, many of these senior employees are natural workplace leaders. They know how things are done—and why. They can assist younger workers in finding information they need or in determining who is the right person to go to in a given situation. Much of this type of knowledge is not written down in employee handbooks and job descriptions—it is simply woven into the fabric of a workplace. Still, it is vital in maintaining a thriving team atmosphere.

A natural affinity is developing between this generation and the Baby Boom Echo Generation. The indication for employers is that a mentor relationship between a Senior and an Echo would be a good match. While the Silent Generation has felt undervalued for quite a while, it seems that the tide is turning and that they are becoming open to remaining at work (or coming back to the workplace after they reach retirement age) if given adequate flexibility.

The Baby Boomers: Born 1946 to 1964

At the end of the World War II, we enjoyed an economic boom. It was a time of optimism and industry and growth. Spurred on by returning veterans, the large influx of immigrants, and the general sense of optimism pervading the country, we made babies like crazy. In her article "Generational Divide," Alison Stein Wellner says that America was "in the mood" to make babies after World War II.[2] (If you get the reference to Glenn Miller, give yourself an extra credit point.) During the Baby Boom years, there were more than 75 million births. What's more, each year the birthrate increased over the preceding year until 1964. From 1946 to 1964, there were over 4 million births per year in the United States—that is the definition of the Baby Boom.

The Baby Boom Generation took the steadily increasing affluence that their parents were enjoying after World War II and ran with it. That was their parents' plan—to create the opportunity for their children to have more than they did. Education became a top priority. Many of the Boomers were raised in homes enjoying economic prosperity and a strong nuclear family. Most of their mothers were homemakers; most of their fathers were the family breadwinners.

The Boomers are an interesting group. The sheer size of the group means that society goes where they go. Perhaps the "Silent" Generation just can't be heard above the roar of the Boomers.

The Boomers gave us hippies, communes, and free love. They also gave us the 80-hour workweek. Although generally seen as self-absorbed, Boomers are active in social issues, civil rights, and politics. They are an optimistic, competitive group that focuses deeply on personal accomplishment.

Three in One: Dissecting the Baby Boom

The Baby Boom is often viewed as three generations in one. The leading edge of the Baby Boom, the first six years, came after a much lower birth generation, but in big-growth, high-optimism years. That group was able to study whatever they wanted in college, or even to get good jobs without attending college. They were able to burn their bras, burn the flag, burn their draft cards, burn their brains on drugs, take a couple of years off to find themselves and come back to get a good job.

The next seven years make up the middle of the Baby Boom. These middle Boomers had a very different situation—they could not get good jobs as easily because the older Boomers had clogged the pipeline. They had to have strong, clean transcripts and not take a lot of chances if they wanted to get the same good jobs that the leading edge of the Baby Boom had coasted into.

The tail end, the last five years of the Baby Boom, had a completely different set of circumstances. These late Boomers were at a disadvantage. They had a huge number of Boomers ahead of them in the workforce moving up into middle management. There was no place for the tail end to go. They had to settle for jobs that people previously started right out of high school, except now they needed a college degree to land these jobs. Also prices had greatly escalated for basics, such as housing. The Late Boomers did not have the same sense of entitlement. They had to have an MBA to get that same job that the leading edge of the Boom could have gotten right out of college or maybe even high school. As futurist Edie Weiner puts it, "If you think that the Baby Boom is one generation from beginning to end, then you think Peter, Paul, and Mary, and Metallica are cut from the same cloth, and they clearly aren't, right?"[3]

A recent book by Jonathan Pontell sought to break out the last piece of the Baby Boom into a distinct segment he coined "Generation Jones." He defines this generation as those born from 1954 to 1965. In his view, this generation is too young for the Baby Boom and too old for the Baby Bust/Generation Xers. While some are agreeing with him, others say that his views are just typical of the Baby Boom—self-focused, wanting special recognition.

Boomers and Finances

An interesting debate rages over the amount of money that will be passed down to the Boomers from their Silent Generation parents. One school of thought is that this will determine how long the Boomers will stay working. There are some 50 million Silent Generation Americans, and they are the wealthiest group of seniors in U.S. history. Estimates are that they control as much as two-thirds of the country's financial assets—including 40 percent of the mutual funds, 60 percent of the annuities, and 48 percent of luxury cars. Still, with all this wealth, the amount earmarked for inheritance is dwindling on a couple of fronts. First, the Silent Generation is facing unprecedented health-care costs and other expenses. Second, as they live longer and better, the Silent Generation is less willing to sock it away for their children. In the early 1990s, 56 percent of those over age 65 felt it was important to leave an inheritance. By 2000, that figure had dropped to less than half, 47 percent. This is credited not only to increased life expectancy and rising expenses, but also to a realization that their children are doing even better than they did.

At the same time, Boomers are notoriously poor savers. The Me Generation spends, spends, spends. They buy more products and services than any other generation. They may need that inheritance when it's all said and done.

They have time to start saving, though. Boomers are entering their Golden Age according to sociologists. The positions they hold, the money they make, and the achievements they can attain are just reaching their peak.

How Long Will the Boomers Work?

Boomers will continue to work far beyond what was traditionally considered retirement age. In spite of the fact that many people attribute this to the Boomers' lack of savings, I believe that, in large part, they will continue to work because they want to work. Boomers are so driven to succeed that I cannot imagine that they will settle down and do nothing for the last twenty-five or thirty years of their life. They would get too bored.

Bound by Values

Ken Dychtwald, president of Age Wave, is one of the nation's leading authorities on the Baby Boom. While acknowledging differences among the Boomers, he likens them to a forest of trees sharing the same root system. "Boomers are an extremely diverse generation, an extraordinarily complex yet individualistic collection of men and women," he says. "But under the surface, we're a generation with many, many common values and experiences. We're bound together by deeply rooted values." According to Dychtwald, these values include a belief in meritocracy, a respect for knowledge, and a lack of respect for authority.[4]

I do see them working at something they enjoy, however. After driving themselves to tension headaches and high blood pressure for the first half of their career, the Boomers will seek employment that better aligns with their dreams and aspirations. In addition, the Baby Boom includes the first generation of professional career businesswomen, many of whom will just be hitting their stride in their fifties and beyond. I believe a large number of smart, skillful businesswomen will be rejoining the workforce once their own children have grown. While as many as one in three Boomers say they would stop working if they could afford it, I'm not sure that this will be the reality.

At the same time, the Boomers will move toward better balance between work and home. Many are willing to trade higher pay for more time for themselves and their families. This is a trend we are seeing across the generations, a trend that is gaining support and momentum. Boomers, given their propensity to spend and self-focus, are expected to increase their travel and recreational activities as a means to enhance their work–life balance. They will be less stressed, hopefully, and bring a more balanced, patient perspective to their jobs. In addition, they will gain insight, appreciation, and a broader view as a result of seeing places other than their office and doing things other than their work. After all, this is the group that gave us the term "workaholic," and most "-aholics" need the help of a twelve-step program to get control.

Generation X: Born 1965 to 1976

Douglas Coupland first coined this label in his book *Generation X*. When the book was written in 1992, Generation Xers were "twenty-something." Now many of them are well into their thirties. Generation X is fascinating. On one hand, it is considered a generation raised with even more of a silver spoon and a sense of entitlement and much less political interest than the Baby Boomers. As a result, they are often viewed as slackers with less involvement in, and more pessimistic views about, politics and other issues. On the other hand, some Xers are hard-core traditionalists—optimistic and hardworking. Some are like a second wave of hippies and some are narrow-minded believers in gender roles and stereotypes. Generation X, more than any other generation I studied, is the one that is most elusive because the differences among its members can be so extreme. In many cases, the labels ascribed to them are not only too general, they are outright wrong.

Generation X is also the group most attached to (or blamed for) the dot-com fury and the stock market boom days of the 1980s and 1990s. According to Benjamin Soskis, this is largely a misperception. Fewer than 5 percent of Gen Xers are employed in computer-related industries. Moreover, a 1998 investor study by the Investment Company Institute found that the median stockholding of Xers was $20,000 and the median age for investors was 47, i.e., more Boom than Bust.

▌Bookend Boomers

Sometimes called the Bookend or Sandwich generation, Boomers are surrounded by issues from elder parents on one end and children in their twenties on the other. Young adult offspring continue to put demands on their time and energy, demands that the Boomers themselves never would have thought to make of their own parents. At the same time, more and more Boomers are being put in the position of needing to parent their parents, who are elderly and in declining health. This will be relevant to employers whose Boomer employees face stresses, time demands, and money constraints, all of which require company support and understanding.

Fifty-one million Americans are considered members of Generation X. Just like those generations that came before them, Xers grew up in a different world. The divorce of their parents has often been cited as the event having the single greatest impact upon them. The high rate of divorce and increased number of working mothers led to Xers being the first generation of latch-key kids. As a result, traits of independence, resilience, and adaptability are often among their attributes.

Generation X feels strongly that they do not need someone looking over their shoulders. They also desire immediate and ongoing feedback and are equally comfortable giving feedback to others. Other traits of this group include working well in multicultural settings, desire for some fun in the workplace, and a pragmatic approach for getting things done.

Generation X also saw their parents get laid off and face job insecurity in a way that previous generations never did. They have redefined loyalty. Instead of remaining loyal to their employer, they have a commitment to the work—to the teams with whom they work and to the bosses for whom they work.

Baby Boom Echo: Born 1977 to 2000

By 1977, many Boomers decided to have children, and the birthrate began to climb again. This created a surge in the population and a generation called the Baby Boom Echo. I found many different starting and ending years attributed to the Baby Boom Echo—beginning anywhere from 1976 to 1982 and ending around 1994 to 2001.

The Baby Boom Echo is entering the workforce now and will be coming on in force through the first quarter of the 21st century. Nearly 75 million strong, this generation is coming of age as powerful and positive. Their parents, the Boomers, are seen as the most child-centered caregivers in American history. This brings us to another label—the Soccer Mom. Parents of the Echo are shuttling their children everywhere—soccer, softball, karate, dance, tutors, singing, and piano—and that's just one child! With the taxi service come high expectations of achievement, as the highly competitive Boomer parents see their children as both an extension and a reflection of themselves. It seems that even when it comes to parenting, the Boomers are all about "me." At any rate, the Baby Boom Echo is seen as a largely self-confident group, sometimes even cocky. They like to set goals and go for them. Since they have had to be good at time management since day one, Echos are multitaskers and team players. In fact, they typically prefer to work in groups rather than alone. They also tend to socialize in groups rather than as couples.

High-tech is second nature to them. Many of the Echos have never seen a dial phone and cannot imagine that we saw *The Wizard of Oz* only once a year. In spite of the showers of attention they received, they do expect to work hard. They desire structure and direction in the workplace. Perhaps as a result of years of having coaches and headstrong parents, the Echos are respectful of positions and titles and desire a relationship with their boss. This may not always sit well with Generation X, who are largely hands-off, independent workers. On the other hand, the Echo is the group, as I mentioned before, that is expected to work very well with the Seniors.

One reason for this affinity may be the hardships witnessed by the Baby Boom Echo. In between soccer and softball, this generation saw parents lose their jobs in record numbers due to layoffs and "right-sizing." The Echos saw retirees struggling to get by, and seniors taking jobs at McDonald's to make ends meet. The recession of the late 1990s and into the 2000s brought an abrupt end to the Roaring '80s and '90s, similar to the abrupt end of the Roaring '20s. Another interesting commonality between the World War II generation and the Baby Boom Echo is their faith in the military. A poll for the Harvard Institute of Politics finds that 75 percent of 1,200 undergraduates surveyed report trusting the military "to do the right thing" all or most of the time.[5]

Encouraging the Connection

Hewlett-Packard (HP) is one company that is taking advantage of the natural affinity between the Silent Generation and the Baby Boom Echo. In 1995, the company began a mentoring program pairing HP employees with thousands of middle- and high-school students. Primarily through the use of e-mail communication, the program is credited with having a tremendous positive impact on the students.

Employers are already looking forward to getting the rest of the Baby Boom Echo into the workforce, expecting this large and positive group to change society for the better and increase productivity. Echos are generally found to be more favorable about their work situation and to feel that management has a clearly communicated vision. They are looking for guidance, and 75 percent report that their managers are available when needed.[6] They are also expected to be fiercely loyal to managers whom they trust to teach and nurture them—much as they trusted their coaches.

According to the book *Generations at Work*, by Ron Zemke, Claire Raines, and Bob Filipczak, seven attributes characterize the Baby Boom Echo:

1. Their supervisory style is not fixed. How closely they monitor and manage, for instance, is a product of each individual's track record and personal preferences. Control and autonomy are a continuum, not solitary options.
2. Their leadership style is situationally varied. Some decisions are consensually made; others are made by the manager, but with input and consultation.
3. They depend less on positional than on personal power.
4. They know when and how to make personal policy exceptions, without causing a team riot.
5. They are thoughtful when matching individuals to a team, or matching a team or individual to an assignment.
6. They balance concern for tasks and concern for people. They are neither slave drivers nor country club managers.
7. They understand the elements of trust and work to gain it from their employees. They are perceived as fair, inclusive, good communicators, and competent in their own right.[7]

While some sources anticipate that this will be the next generation of workaholics, I don't agree. According to Mercer Human Resources Consulting, 64 percent of Baby Boom Echo employees reported reaching a balance between home and work. Only about 40 percent of the other generations reported finding such a balance. In addition, other trends, such as spirituality in the workplace, are at play that will continue to reinforce balance as a priority.

At the same time, however, this generation is not afraid of hard work. They will be more efficient, working smarter instead of longer. A 2001 study found that 88 percent of the Echos surveyed had specific goals for the next five years and were confident about reaching them.[8] This type of goal-oriented optimism would not be expected from either Boomers or Xers. Echos reflect their parents' priority around education. Not only are they well educated in the traditional sense, but also most hit the workforce with relevant work experience or internships to their credit. In addition, Echos are expected to continue their education throughout adulthood, consistently seeking out job-related and other types of training.

What Echos Want

While companies are eager for the hardworking Echos to join the workforce, they will find that this generation has strong demands for their employers—demands that they will expect to be met. In their book *Managing Generation Y*, Bruce Tulgan and Carolyn A. Martin cite Echo expectations of the workplace including challenging work that matters, clearly delegated assignments balanced with freedom and flexibility, increased responsibility as a reward for accomplishment, ongoing training/learning opportunities, and mentor relationships. In another book, *Generations*, authors William Strauss and Neil Howe predict that the Baby Boom Echos, who are also expected to become politically active, will require even more dramatic employment adjustments, such as:

- Pay equity among all workers
- Fewer job definitions
- A reestablished middle class
- Downgraded salaries for CEOs and other executives
- Trade barriers
- Government regulation of labor standards
- Revitalized unions[9]

Not only demanding, the Echos may also be needy and harder to please. They are expected to require more direction and supervision than the Boomers or Xers. Companies will need strong team leaders to manage them. Training, orientation, and consistent feedback will also be important to their success. A majority (67 percent) expressed an interest in the opportunity to take time away for training—compared to 52 percent or less for the other generations. Echos also reported being less satisfied at work—significantly less satisfied than the other generations—with both their job and their companies. Less than half of Echos said they feel fairly treated at work, compared to 64 percent of all generations. In addition, while 75 percent of Xers feel that they are being challenged with interesting work, only 64 percent of Echos do. One reason for this may be that they feel they are ready to move to the next rung of the corporate ladder, but haven't yet done so.[10]

Company loyalty and motivation of the Baby Boom Echos is influenced by factors other than pay, especially when compared to the other generations. As mentioned above, Echos are very loyal to their managers, whom they view as caring coaches. When asked about factors that affect their commitment and motivation to work, 82 percent cited flexible working arrangements, a figure much higher than that for the other generations. While the other generations most often cited base pay as the primary work factor, fewer Echos did. Still, more than half of the Echos said they would be willing to leave their current employer for another offering better benefits.

The Millennium Generation: Born Since 2000

As I mentioned in the thumbnail sketches of the generations at the beginning of this chapter, I am breaking out a fifth, new generation that I call the Millennium Generation, or the Millennials, to describe babies being born since the turn of the 21st century.* As interesting as all this generational information is, it is only part of the picture. New babies are being born every day, and historical, political, and even

---

*Many writers use the term *millennials* to refer to people born in the late 1980s and 1990s. Again, the terminology can be confusing. I prefer my usage; it was, after all, in 2000 that we celebrated in "millennium."

entertainment events will influence them in ways that I cannot even dare to imagine. With my futurist hat firmly in place, I see young people entering the workplace who will be comfortable with diversity, who will expect equal pay as an everyday occurrence, and who will be flexible and interested in carving out their own niche both at home and at work. Technology will be so advanced that the time-clock-punching mentality will be a thing of the past. Results will rule. Recognition and reward will follow naturally and without angst or struggle.

One thing is for sure. Millennials will live a long time. By 2020, we may have five generations working side by side. Surveys and studies will continue to pour out of established and prestigious sources as each generation enters each phase of their lives. Companies will have instant access to all of this information. More importantly, though, companies will have a front-row seat for the interactions, associations, and priorities of the four or five generations working side by side. This firsthand information will prove the most valuable in determining how to best manage the generations for maximum employee satisfaction and productivity.

Many Generations: One Workforce

Insight into the differences among the generations is beneficial to employers seeking to create a workplace where people can do their best work. Generalizations aside, every one in every generation is a person. At the end of the day, each individual wants to be recognized as such: an individual, not a number or statistic or label. This is not preaching, this is priority insight #1.

What generation are you in? As I already mentioned, I am considered a Baby Boomer. In researching the generations, I found characteristics I shared with my Boomer brethren, and ones I did not. No big surprise! I bet you would say the same thing. More importantly, though, I found a common thread throughout all of the generations—as individuals, regardless of their age, they share a desire for individual dignity. In the workplace this translates into:

- Respect
- Fair treatment
- Equality
- Balance
- Flexibility
- Appropriate feedback
- Job enhancement and advancement opportunities

Generational Diversity

First off, it's inevitable that the generations will all be present in the workforce at the same time. Smart businesses, however, will proactively seek generational diversity in their employee base for a number of reasons, including:

- *Wisdom and Experience:* A new appreciation for the corporate wisdom, but also the life wisdom, of the older workers is renewing their role as a valuable asset.
- *Fresh Ideas and Fearlessness:* Younger workers bring a value in their "why not" ways that have come as a result of their fresh approach and independence.
- *Individual Wisdom and Skills:* Regardless of their age, each individual brings a unique skill and experience set. Finding just the right blend for a given position requires that we open up opportunities across the generations and reach out for the diverse and wonderful things they each can offer.
- *The Need for More Workers:* Many sources predict worker shortages in the millions in the first half of the 21st century.

- *Reflection of the Marketplace:* All these vital and active generations will be the vital and active marketplace from which your customers will come. An employee base that mirrors the marketplace is largely accepted and expected to be more effective.

Conclusion

What we are seeing today, early in the 21st century, is just the tip of the iceberg. We can find examples of four generations active in the workplace scattered here and there. At this point, they are novel enough even to be newsworthy. By 2050, though, four or even five generations will be working together in full force. It won't just be Seniors working at Burger King or serving as ex-officio board members, and it won't just be young people, still wet behind the ears, needing to learn to fit in and earn their stripes. Many generations of workers—all strong, all valuable, and all side-by-side—will provide unprecedented opportunities for development and profitability. Combining the wisdom and experience of the older worker with the energy and stamina of the young, the workplace of the future stands to gain considerably.

Finding and keeping the best and the brightest from all the generations will be the challenge of the future. Management, compensation, scheduling, and training will all be affected by the multigenerational workforce.

Notes

1. Ron Zemke, Claire Raines, and Bob Filipczak, *Generations at Work: Managing the Clash of Veterans, Boomers, Xers, and Nexters in Your Workplace* (New York: AMACOM, 2000).
2. Alison Stein Wellner, "Generational Divide," *American Demographics*, October 2000: 52–56, 58.
3. Edie Weiner, interview, August 2003.
4. Quoted in Wellner, "Generational Divide", 545.
5. Robin Toner, "Trust in the Military Heightens Among Baby Boomers' Children," *The New York Times*, May 27, 2003: A1.
6. Eric Hazard, "Mercer (HR Consulting): Gen Y Positive About Career but Not Satisfied," www.PlanSponsor.com, July 16, 2003.
7. Zemke, Raines, and Filipczak, *Generations at Work*.
8. Ibid, 144.
9. William Strauss and Neil Howe, *Generations: The History of America's Future, 1584 to 2069* (New York: William Morrow, 1992).
10. Hazard, "Mercer (HR Consulting): Gen Y Positive About Career."

WOMEN AND LEADERSHIP: DEFINING THE CHALLENGES*

Robin J. Ely

Deborah L. Rhode

In 1999, When Carly Fiorina assumed leadership of Hewlett-Packard (HP), she announced: "I hope that we are at the point that everyone has figured out that there is not a glass ceiling" (Markoff, 1999). Seven years later, in a memoir chronicling her highly public ouster from HP, Fiorina recounted endless examples of the sexism she had earlier denied, including routine descriptions of her as a "bimbo" or a "bitch" (Fiorina, 2006). That about-face well captures America's contemporary ambivalence about women and leadership. The increasing prominence of leaders like Carly

Fiorina, Hillary Clinton, Nancy Pelosi, and Condoleezza Rice underscores the changes in gender roles over the last half century. More than 90 percent of surveyed Americans are willing to vote for a qualified female presidential candidate, up from a third in the 1930s. Yet only half think the country is ready to elect one (Mandel, 2007:291–292). In Gallup polls, 61 percent of men and 45 percent of women believe that the sexes have equal job opportunities (Jones, 2005). But a cottage industry of studies makes clear that women's under-representation in leadership positions is at least partly attributable to traditional gender expectations and practices (Eagly and Carli, 2007a; Rhode and Kellerman, 2007).

Initially, the hope was that filling the pipeline would take care of the problem, but it is now clear that time alone is not the answer. For more than two decades, women have been earning about one-third of the MBAs awarded in the United States, yet they constitute only 2 percent of *Fortune* 500 CEOs and 8 percent of top leadership positions (Wilson, 2004). For almost a quarter century, women have made up more than 40 percent of new entrants to the legal profession, but they are still less than one-fifth of law firm partners, federal judges, and *Fortune* 500 general counsels. The gap widens for women of color, who account for only about 4 percent of congressional legislators, and 1 to 2 percent of corporate officers, top earners, law firm partners, and general counsels (Center for American Women in Politics, 2006). Women constitute a majority of American voters, but hold only 16 percent of congressional seats (Center for American Women in Politics, 2006; Center for Women in Government and Civil Society, 2006). In other nations, the patterns are similar. Although gender quotas for public positions have brought women an increasing share of political leadership, they lag far behind in corporate and elite professional settings (Dahlerup, 2007:227; Eagly and Carli, 2007a). In Europe, women account for about a third of managerial positions but only 3 percent of CEOs (European Commission, 2007).

These statistics point up the barriers women face in gaining leadership roles, but as Carly Fiorina's experience suggests, traditional gender expectations and practices also shape people's experiences even after they reach the top. A fundamental challenge to women's leadership arises from the mismatch between the qualities traditionally associated with leaders and those traditionally associated with women (Catalyst, 2007; Eagly and Carli, 2007a). The assertive, authoritative, and dominant behaviors that people link with leadership tend not to be viewed as typical or attractive in women (Catalyst, 2007; Eagly and Carli, 2007b). Reactions to Hillary Clinton's candidacy for the 2008 Democratic presidential nomination are illustrative. She has been roundly criticized for lacking "people skills" (Vedantam, 2007) and opposed by online groups bearing such names as "Life's a B*tch, Don't Vote for One . . . Anti Hillary Clinton '08" and "Hillary Clinton Is a Man and I Won't Vote for Him." Yet when she has publicly expressed caring and compassion, people have questioned both her authenticity and her toughness. "Can Hillary Cry Her Way Back to the White House?" asked *New York Times* Op Ed columnist Maureen Dowd (2008:A21). Clinton is in good company. Reflecting on the "myth of the iron lady," *Washington Post* staff writer Shankar Vedantam notes a pattern in the phrases used to describe many countries' first female leaders: "England's Margaret Thatcher," he notes, "was called 'Attila the Hen.' Golda Meir, Israel's first female prime minister was 'the only man in the Cabinet.' Richard Nixon called Indira Gandhi, India's first female prime minister, 'the old witch.' And Angela Merkel, the current chancellor of Germany, has been dubbed 'the iron frau.' "

Although attitudes toward women as a group are generally positive, even more positive than attitudes toward men (Eagly and Mladinic, 1989), these views do not hold for women who occupy traditionally male roles, especially when they excel in those roles (Eagly, Makhijani, and Klonsky, 1992; Heilman et al., 2004; Rudman and Click, 2001). In experiment after experiment, when women achieve in distinctly male arenas, they are seen as competent but are less well liked than equally successful men (Heilman et al., 2004:416). By the same token, when women performing traditionally male roles are seen as nice, they are liked but not respected (Rudman and Glick, 2001:744). In short, women, unlike men, face trade-offs between competence (i.e., success) and likability in traditionally male roles.

In leadership contexts, these biases play out on several levels: in the ways that organizations structure leadership paths and positions, in the ways that people perceive women leaders, and in the ways that women leaders perceive themselves and what they must do to succeed (Hogue and Lord, 2007). At each level, a woman's qualifications for leadership are called into question. Organizations consistently, if unwittingly, communicate that women are not well-suited for leadership roles. Just as others may view her leadership through a cultural lens distorted by gender bias, so too may a woman have difficulty developing a viable view of herself as a leader. Recent theory suggests that individuals who are unable to firmly ground their self-identity in the leadership role may be missing a critical requirement for leadership development (Lord and Hall, 2005). In that respect, gender bias presents a significant problem not only for women but also for organizations (Hogue and Lord, 2007:370).

Women leaders clearly navigate a different societal and organizational terrain from their male counterparts, a terrain deeply rooted in cultural ambivalence. In this chapter, we explore this landscape, how women leaders might navigate it more effectively, and how organizations might support them and stand to gain in the process. Specifically, we examine how ambivalence about women emerges in organizational structures and practices, as well as in individual attitudes; how the resulting double bind women face shapes their experiences and identities in leadership roles; and how these dynamics in turn may limit their capacity to exercise leadership effectively. Drawing on recent theory about the role of identity in developing leadership expertise, and applying a goal-based approach to the self, we speculate about how women might succeed and how organizations might assist them. Finally, we propose a research agenda to investigate these issues at both the individual and organizational level.

Barriers to Women's Leadership

Some women achieve leadership positions in spite of barriers to their advancement, but these barriers nonetheless shape their developmental and leadership experiences. In this section, we briefly review the research on structural and attitudinal obstacles to women leaders' advancement and speculate about the effects on career patterns.

Structural Barriers

Differential structures of opportunity and power block women's access and advancement to leadership positions (Kanter, 1977; Reskin, 1988; Ridgeway, 1993; Strober, 1984). For example, men's predominance in positions of organizational power, together with differences in the composition of men's and women's social and professional networks, give men greater access to information and support (Burt, 1992; Ibarra, 1992; Podolny and Baron, 1997). Women in traditionally male-dominated settings often have difficulty breaking into the "old boys" loop of advice and professional development opportunities (Catalyst, 2003; Heffernan, 2004; O'Brien, 2006; Ragins, 1998). Isolation and exclusion are particularly likely for women of color (American Bar Association, 2006; Bell and Nkomo, 2001; Catalyst, 2003, 2004a). Surveys of upper-level American managers find that almost half of women of color and close to one-third of white women cite a lack of influential mentors as a major barrier to advancement (Catalyst, 1999, 2004a). In law, 62 percent of women of color and 60 percent of white women, but only 4 percent of white men, felt excluded from formal and informal networking opportunities (American Bar Association, 2006).

The problem of exclusion is compounded by organizational structures and practices that tend to reflect and support men's experiences (Acker, 1990; Bailyn, 2006; Martin, 1996; Rapoport et al., 2002). For example, women are disadvantaged by the convergence of their biological and professional clocks and by the escalating time demands of leadership positions. The increasing pace and competitiveness of organizational life, coupled with technological advances, have created a culture of constant accessibility and blurred the boundaries of home and work. With BlackBerrys, cell phones, e-mails, and faxes, leaders remain tethered to their offices. Although such technologies have made it easier for a woman to work from home, they have also made it harder not to. Excessive hours are a major reason that many highly qualified women step off the leadership track (Stone and Lovejoy, 2004). Some evidence suggests that women of color are particularly likely to face challenges given their greater responsibilities as single parents or caretakers of elderly and extended family members (Catalyst, 2003; Hewlett, Luce, and West, 2005).

Excessive workloads also leave limited time for the informal socializing and mentoring that promote professional development. The small number of women in top positions cannot begin to provide adequate support for every subordinate who needs it, and some female leaders worry about appearances of favoritism if they focus their effort on other women (Rhode and Kellerman, 2007). Junior women who are scrambling to build careers while raising children have similar difficulty finding time for the social activities that help forge professional relationships. After the workday ends, men are picking up tips over golf and drinks; women are picking up "laundry, dinner, and the house" (Wellington and Catalyst, 2001).

Although men have assumed an increasing share of household responsibilities over the last quarter century, women continue to shoulder the major burden. Government data indicate that about one-fifth of men engage in some kind of housework on an average day, while more than half of women do (U.S. Bureau of Labor Statistics, 2006). Women put in about twice as much time on childcare as men (Bianchi, Robinson, and Milkie, 2006). In one representative survey of high-achieving women, four of ten felt that their husbands created more domestic work than they contributed (Hewlett and Vita Leon, 2001). In another study involving well-educated professional women who had left the paid workforce, two-thirds cited their husbands' role as a reason for the decision, including their lack of support in childcare and other domestic tasks, and their expectation that wives should be the ones to cut back on employment (Stone and Lovejoy, 2004). Unlike most male leaders, most aspiring female leaders lack the support of spouses who are full-time homemakers or who are working only part-time (Williams, 2000). Women with families also face more constraints on travel and relocation than similarly situated men. Until the home becomes an equal opportunity employer, women will pay the price in the world outside it.

Employment policies reflect and further reinforce gender differences in family roles and responsibilities. The vast majority of American workplaces fail to offer the same paid parental leave to fathers as to mothers, and few men take any extended period of time away from their jobs for family reasons (Rhode and Williams, 2007). In law, three-quarters of those with part-time schedules are female (National Association of Law Placement, 2007). Similar leave and part-time patterns prevail in other professions, as well as in other nations, except in the small minority of countries that mandate "use it or lose it" paid leave for fathers. Work/family policies that disadvantage men also disadvantage women. The effect is to entrench unequal family responsibilities, which perpetuates unequal workplace opportunities.

Related problems stem from the lack of flexible schedules, meaningful part-time positions, and affordable quality childcare. Although women in top managerial and professional positions often are in workplaces that offer reduced or flex-time arrangements, few of these women take advantage of them. Most believe, with reason, that any limitation in hours or availability would jeopardize their career prospects, and that they would end up working more than their status and compensation justified (Crittendon, 2001; Rhode and Williams, 2007). So, for example, almost all of America's large law firms (98 percent) permit part-time schedules, but only about 5 percent of lawyers use them (National Association of Law Placement, 2007). Supervisors now would rarely greet a pregnancy with the advice that the CEO of Archer Daniels once received: "Get yourself fixed and put it on your expense account" (Birger, 2006). But such attitudes remain embedded in workplace cultures and reward structures.

Taken together, these inadequate workplace policies and unequal family responsibilities help account for gender differences in paid leadership positions. Almost 20 percent of women with graduate or professional degrees have stepped out of the labor force, compared with only 5 percent of similarly credentialed men (Wallis, 2004). In a study by the Center for Work-Life Policy of some three thousand highly educated Americans, nearly four in ten women reported voluntarily leaving the workforce at some point over their careers. The same proportion reported sometimes choosing a job with lesser compensation and fewer responsibilities than they were qualified to assume in order to accommodate family responsibilities. By contrast, only one in ten men left the workforce primarily for family-related reasons (Hewlett and Luce, 2005). Although other surveys find some variation in the number of women who opt out to accommodate domestic obligations, all of these studies find substantial gender differences. Yet the overwhelming majority of these women want to return to work, and most do so, although generally not without significant career costs and difficulties (Hewlett and Luce, 2005; Rhode and Williams, 2007). Similar obstacles arise in other advanced industrial nations (Foroohar, 2006; International Labor Organization, 2004).

Societal and organizational structures that heighten women's willingness to reduce or suspend their workforce participation carry an unwelcome by-product. The effect is to reinforce assumptions about women's lesser career commitment and to make them seem less worthy of mentoring, training, and challenging assignments (Rhode and Williams, 2007). These assumptions are buttressed by other cognitive biases. People are, for example, more likely to notice and recall information that confirms their prior stereotypes than information that contradicts them; the dissonant data are filtered out (Festinger, 1957). For example, if employers assume that a working mother will sometimes give priority to family over job, they will more easily remember the times when she left early than the times when she stayed late. The result is often to reduce women's opportunities for career development, which increases their willingness to step off the leadership track. Women's attrition, in turn, reinforces stereotypes about women's lesser commitment and creates a self-perpetuating cycle of gender inequalities (Deutsch, 2005; Hewlett and Luce, 2005).

In organizations with few if any women in positions of power, gender is particularly salient and negatively affects women lower in the organizational ranks, despite balanced representation at those levels.

In a study of women associates in law firms, gender roles were more stereotypical and more problematic in firms with low proportions of senior women (Ely, 1995). Compared with women in firms with higher proportions of senior women, these women associates were more likely to consider feminine attributes as a hindrance to success, and were less able to develop professional styles that were both personally satisfying and consistent with the firm's requirements for success. Women's representation in upper-level positions also influenced the quality of their relationships with each other. Women associates in firms with few senior women were less likely to experience their shared gender as a positive basis for identification with women, less likely to perceive senior women as role models with legitimate authority, more likely to experience competition in relationships with female peers, and less likely to find support in these relationships (Ely, 1994). These findings suggest that women's relative presence or absence in powerful organizational positions affects the conditions that their junior female colleagues need to succeed.

Attitudinal Barriers

To be sure, the bias that Virginia Schein once labeled as "think manager—think male" has diminished over time (Koch, Luft, and Kruse, 2005; Schein, 2001:675–676). Women are becoming more like men in their career aspirations and achievements and are more willing to see themselves as having characteristics associated with authority (Dennis and Kunkel, 2004; Eagly, 2005:459–174; Koch et al., 2005). So too, recent theories of leadership have stressed the importance of interpersonal qualities commonly attributed to women, such as cooperation, collaboration, and interpersonal sensitivity. An emerging body *of* scholarship suggests that the most effective style of leadership in today's world is "transformational" (Avolio et al., 2004; Luthans and Avolio, 2003; May et al., 2003). Leaders who take this approach emphasize gaining the trust and confidence of followers and empowering them to develop their own potential. Meta-analyses of studies involving thousands of leaders suggest that women are somewhat more transformational than men, especially in providing support for subordinates (Eagly, Johannesen-Schmidt, and van Engen, 2003). Women are also less likely than men to engage in the leadership styles judged least effective: "laissez-faire" hands-off approaches and transactional "passive management by exception" approaches that call for intervention only when situations become extreme (Eagly et al., 2003; Judge and Piccolo, 2004).

Yet despite these trends, the legacy of traditional gender stereotypes remains. Women have long suffered from a double standard and double bind in the exercise of authority. They are thought too aggressive or not aggressive enough, and what appears assertive in a man appears abrasive in a woman (Eagly and Carli, 2007b; Eagly and Karau, 2002; Rudman and Click, 2001; Babcock and Laschever, 2003). In its report *The Double-Bind Dilemma for Women in Leadership: Damned If You Do, Doomed If You Don't,* Catalyst documented the persistence of this double standard among senior American and European business leaders (Catalyst, 2007). As noted above, women who conform to traditional feminine stereotypes are often liked but not respected: they are judged too soft, emotional, and unassertive to make tough calls and project the necessary "presence" in positions of authority (Catalyst, 2007; Eagly and Carli, 2007b). Asian women are particularly likely to be stereotyped as passive, reserved, and lacking in ambition, and Latina women are frequently viewed as overemotional (Catalyst, 2003; Giscombe and Mattis, 2002).

By contrast, women who adopt more masculine traits are often respected but not liked: they are seen as domineering, strident, and cold. "Dragon Lady" and "Bully Broad" are epithets of choice (Babcock and Laschever, 2003; Eagly and Karau, 2002). Self-promoting behavior that appears self-confident or entrepreneurial in men often looks pushy and "unfeminine" in women. African American women are especially vulnerable to such stereotypes, and risk being seen as overly aggressive and confrontational (Catalyst, 2004a). A review of more than a hundred studies found that women are rated lower when they adopt authoritative, masculine styles, particularly when the evaluators are men (Butterfield and Grinnell, 1999; Catalyst, 2007; Cleveland, Stockdale, and Murphy, 2000). In effect, women face a trade-off between competence and likability in circumstances where effective leadership requires both.

Recent research suggests that two coexisting and complementary forms of sexism—one benevolent and the other one hostile—lie at the root of this dilemma.

Benevolent sexism is "a subjectively favorable, chivalrous ideology that offers protection and affection to women who embrace conventional roles" and is used to reward women who conform to traditional gender role expectations. Hostile sexism is "antipathy toward women who are viewed as usurping men's power" and is used to punish women who challenge the status quo (Glick and Fiske, 2001:109). Taken together, these two forms of prejudice reflect ambivalence about women, promoting polarized responses to them. Women who appear feminine are at risk for benevolent sexism, which disqualifies them for leadership. Women who demonstrate the masculine traits associated with leadership may evoke hostile sexism, which leads to ostracism and rejection.

This double bind helps account for why women continue to be rated lower than men on most of the qualities associated with leadership (Catalyst, 2005; Eagly and Carli, 2007b). People more readily credit men with leadership ability and more readily accept men as leaders (Eagly and Carli, 2007b; Rudman and Kilianski, 2007). More Americans prefer a male to a female boss, and women have a stronger preference than men (Carroll, 2006). An analysis of some sixty-one studies in which the leadership behavior of men and women was similar, or their paper credentials were equal, revealed that overall men were rated higher, particularly for male-dominated positions (Eagly, Makhijani, and Klonsky, 1992). Such findings are consistent with other studies on gender bias in performance evaluations and in explanations of success and failure (Foschi, 1996; Valian, 1999). Even in experimental situations where male and female performance is objectively equal, women are held to higher standards and their competence is rated lower (Foschi, 1996). In another meta-analysis of fifty-eight studies, when women did well on traditionally masculine tasks, the common explanation was hard work; when men did well, the assumed reason was generally competence (Swim and Sanna, 1996).

Such biases are compounded by in-group favoritism, especially among groups with high status. Extensive research documents the preferences and presumptions of competence that individuals accord to those who are like them in important respects, including gender. Members of high status in-groups tend to attribute accomplishments of fellow members to intrinsic characteristics, such as intelligence, drive, and commitment. By contrast, the achievements of low status out-group members are often ascribed to luck or special treatment (Crocker, Major, and Steele, 1998; Foschi, 2000). Accordingly, the men who dominate leadership positions tend to support and channel career development opportunities to male subordinates who appear more likely to succeed than their female counterparts. Women's effective performance may not be enough to break the pattern if it is attributed to factors other than ability. In one recent study of 2,800 managers, supervisors who rated female subordinates somewhat higher than men in competence still rated the women lower in long-term leadership potential (Coughlin, 2005).

When women perform consistently and substantially above expectations in male-dominated contexts, however, their effectiveness may carry special positive weight. This effect is particularly true of women of color, who routinely encounter lower expectations of competence (Eagly and Carli, 2007a). When small numbers of women occupy prominent roles, they are subject to special scrutiny and polarized assessments (Kanter, 1977). Superstars attract special notice and receive higher evaluations than their male counterparts, but women who are just below that level tend to get disproportionately lower evaluations (Biernat and Kobrynowicz, 1997; Heilman, 2001; Heilman, Martell, and Simon, 1998). At the same time, the presence of a few highly regarded women at the top creates the illusion that the glass ceiling has been shattered for everyone else. And when superstars fail or opt out, their departures attract particular notice and reinforce stereotypes about women's lesser capabilities and commitment (Kephart and Schumacher, 2005; Stanley, 2004).

These perceptions about performance can, in turn, prevent women from getting assignments that would demonstrate their abilities, thus creating a cycle of self-fulfilling prophecies. In professional contexts, women, particularly women of color, are left off the partnership track, and in corporate sectors, they receive fewer line responsibilities that lead to top executive positions (International Labor Organization, 2004; Wilkins and Gulati, 1996). In a recent study by the American Bar Association (2006), 44 percent of women of color and 39 percent of white women, compared with only 2 percent of white men, reported being passed over for desirable work assignments. The absence of important line experience is the major reason that surveyed CEOs gave for women's under-representation in leadership positions (Wellington, Kropf, and Gerkovich, 2003).

Many women also internalize these stereotypes, which creates a psychological glass ceiling. In general, women see themselves as less deserving than men of rewards for the same performance and as less qualified for key leadership positions (Babcock and Laschever, 2003; Barron, 2003). This lesser sense of entitlement may discourage them from engaging in assertive, self-promoting behaviors and from taking risks that are critical for developing key leadership skills (Hogue and Lord, 2007). As one comprehensive overview of gender in negotiations put it, "Women don't ask" (Babcock and Laschever, 2003). Part of the reason is that women who do ask confront other problems. For example, experimental research on negotiation also suggests that male participants penalize women more than men for their attempts to negotiate greater compensation (Bowles and McGinn, 2008). An unwillingness to seem too "pushy" or "difficult," and an undervaluation of their own worth, often deter women from negotiating effectively for what they want or need. Their reluctance is understandable in settings where men's dislike of assertive women can undermine career advancement. In one Catalyst survey, 96 percent of female executives said that it was critical or fairly important "to develop a style with which male managers are comfortable" (Catalyst, 2004c). In short, the legacy of gender stereotypes subjects aspiring female leaders to higher standards and greater constraints than their male counterparts.

Individual, Organizational, and Societal Consequences

Research findings concerning barriers to women's leadership raise an obvious question. What difference does it make? Are the consequences for individuals, organizations, and society sufficient to justify expending considerable time and resources to address these problems?

To many observers, women's underrepresentation in positions of influence is unproblematic; women's absence reflects women's choices. As one *New York Times Magazine* cover story famously put it: "Why don't women run the world? Maybe it's because they don't want to" (Belkin, 2003). Or at least they don't want to make the personal and family sacrifices that leadership demands. Yet the assumption that individual preferences explain social inequalities ignores all the evidence of bias summarized above, as well as the constraints that drive career patterns. A focus on the choices of women also deflects attention from those of men and the way that their decisions as spouses, employers, and policy makers limit the options available to women. In fact, recent evidence suggests that the sexes have increasingly similar employment aspirations and that women's unequal opportunities to realize their potential ill serves all concerned.

In a comprehensive 2007 assessment, Alice Eagly and Linda Carli reviewed studies on women's career preferences and workplace commitments. In general, they found that gender differences have weakened among men and women in similar occupations, although women still place a higher priority on good hours and working with or helping other people, and young men particularly value leisure time

(Eagly and Carli, 2007a). Although women are still much more willing than men to assume full-time homemaker roles, employees who are similarly well established in managerial careers report similar leadership ambitions (Catalyst, 2004b; Eagly and Carli, 2007a). Among those with comparable jobs and family situations, female employees report greater work effort than men (Bielby and Bielby, 1988).

Moreover, many of the women who step off the leadership track are not entirely happy with the decision. For some, the decision reflects less a desire to become a full-time homemaker than frustration with inadequate professional opportunities or work/family accommodations (Rhode and Williams, 2007). For others, the problems surface only later when women discover the long-term career costs of even relatively short absences (Crittendon, 2001; Hewlett and Luce, 2005). In one study by the Columbia Center for Work-Life Policy, a quarter of those who wanted to return to work were unable to find jobs, and a majority failed to obtain full-time professional employment (Hewlett and Luce, 2005).

The result is to shortchange both individuals and employers. The barriers to women's advancement undermine organizational performance and compromise fundamental principles of equal opportunity and social justice. Some research suggests that having more women in leadership positions has tangible payoffs. In weak corporate governance firms, boards with fewer women performed worse (Adams and Ferreira, 2007). A lack of gender diversity can also limit an organization's opportunities for learning and renewal. Women tend to engage in different social relations and economic activities from men and bring different experiences and perspectives to their workplaces. Organizations that fail to tap this knowledge miss out on a valuable resource for rethinking and improving their performance (Ely and Thomas, 2001; Meyerson and Ely, 2003; for example, see Groysberg, 2008).

A further consideration is demographic. Women are now a majority of college and master's degree graduates and represent an equal share of the talent available for leadership. Reducing the obstacles to women's success also reduces the costs of attrition. It increases employees' morale, commitment, and retention, and decreases the expenses associated with recruiting, training, and mentoring replacements (Rhode and Williams, 2007). Removing barriers also helps to ensure that women are able to develop to their fullest potential. In an increasingly competitive and multicultural environment, organizations cannot afford to squander their human resources.

So too, society as a whole has a stake in ensuring that people are able—and believe they are able—to contribute fully to public and private sector institutions. Our economy depends on effective corporate performance, and our political system depends on public confidence in meritocratic processes. As the United States Supreme Court recognized in a decision sustaining law school affirmative action programs, "In order to cultivate a set of leaders with legitimacy in the eyes of the citizens, it is necessary that the path to leadership be open to talented and qualified individuals of every race and ethnicity" (*Grutter v. Bollinger,* 2003). The same is true of gender. By diversifying leadership opportunities, organizations leverage their talent, create role models, challenge stereotypes, and enlarge aspirations among underrepresented groups. To that end, we need to focus more attention on how to develop women's leadership goals and skills.

Identity, Gender, and the Development of Leadership Skills

How people become leaders and who they are as leaders are fundamentally questions about identity (Lord and Hall, 2005; for a review, see van Knippenberg et al., 2004). To develop the deep cognitive structures associated with leadership expertise, the leadership role must become a central part of one's sense of self (Lord and Hall, 2005:592). In this view, as leaders progress from novice to expert, they shift from an individual-oriented identity focused on self to a collective-oriented identity focused on self-and-others. The novice's central concern is with emulating leadership behaviors in order to project an image of the self as a leader. By contrast, the expert develops an increasing capacity to pursue internally held values and personalized strategies in service of goals that include others. In short, the leader's focus shifts from "doing" to "being," from "how I behave" to "who I am."

Our focus here is on how structural and attitudinal barriers to women's leadership interfere with this crucial developmental process. The result is to make it difficult for talented, enterprising, motivated women to seek and benefit from the sorts of developmental experiences that are more readily available to their similarly credentialed male counterparts. Women, we argue, can become stuck in *doing*.

Drawing from the theories of Robert Lord and colleagues, we provide a brief overview of this perspective on leadership development (see, for example, Hogue and Lord, 2007; Lord and Hall, 2005). We then suggest how gender may play out in this process. Finally, we propose a research agenda to develop and test these ideas, one focused on both individuals and organizations.

Identity and the Development of Leadership Skills: From Doing to Being

With leaders' shift from an individual to collective orientation comes a qualitative change both in their information processing skills and in the types of knowledge these skills enable leaders to use. Individually oriented leaders are concerned with differentiating themselves from others and with learning leadership behaviors that will lead others to accept them as leaders (Lord and Hall, 2005:596). Learning the surface structures of leadership—how to meet the accepted definitions of what leaders should be and do—is the first central skill leaders acquire. Such definitions are based largely on an idealized representation of what leadership involves, from which the novice formulates general heuristics and applies them to all superficially similar situations (Lord and Hall, 2005:598–599). At this stage, relevant skills include displaying the emotions seen as appropriate for leaders. Social interactions serve to validate (or challenge) the individual's self-view as a leader (Lord and Hall, 2005:596). The developmental work of novices involves proactively seeking and experimenting with provisional identities—images they adapt from role models as trials for possible but not yet fully formed "selves" (Ibarra, 1999).

As leaders gain experience, these identities become more firmly established. Different self-concepts emerge in different situations (Lord and Hall, 2005:592). As contexts change, different identities become salient, eliciting different skills, goals, and self-regulatory structures. Increasingly oriented toward a relational rather than individual identity, leaders at this stage begin to consider others in their self-definition as a leader (Andersen and Chen, 2002; Fletcher, 2006). Greater motivation to attempt new leadership activities further enhances these leaders' skill and identity development.

Finally, expert leaders rely on deep structures of knowledge, drawing on principles and values rather than surface features to respond to situational requirements, and adjusting their identities accordingly. This approach necessitates a deliberate shift in focus away from concerns about self to concerns about others, the organization, and even society as a whole. Increased cognitive capacity enables expert leaders to gauge their progress in various tasks and interpersonal activities and to adjust their behavior accordingly (Lord and Hall, 2005:593). A personal understanding of identity and core values is an important source of flexibility in applying leadership skills. By no longer patterning their behavior on others, these leaders can rely on more sophisticated and personalized strategies for managing their emotions and responding to those of others, particularly during times of crisis. Expert leaders also build relevant knowledge and leadership capacities in subordinates, making effective delegation possible (Lord and Hall, 2005:603).

In sum, a leader's identity solidifies with experience as leadership roles and skills become more central to his or her sense of self. Those skills become increasingly contextualized and their application more driven by internally held values, further strengthening the link between one's personal identity and the leadership role. Thus, the leader's identity takes on an increasingly important function in guiding knowledge acquisition, goal formation, and interpretations of social situations.

The Challenge for Women

This perspective on leadership sheds new light on gender-related barriers by placing them in a developmental context. If a central developmental task is to integrate the leadership role into the core self, then this task is fraught at the outset with an inherent contradiction for the woman leader—a contradiction between her female identity and the masculine traits associated with leadership. With little support or direction, a woman leader must convey a credible image—one that strikes just the right blend of masculinity and femininity—to an audience that is deeply ambivalent about her authority. From this viewpoint, the likability-competence trade-off would be most critical in the novice phase of development, when learning to behave in accordance with idealized images of leadership is the key task. With this framing, the double bind is a problem to be addressed as a means to an end, rather than as an end in itself. Accordingly, many of the structural and attitudinal barriers women leaders face may compromise their early developmental experiences and impede their transition to later stages.

Research suggests that in the evolution from follower to leader, men and women both experience a gap between their identity and the image they wish to convey, but that the strategies they use to bridge the gap differ (Ibarra, 1999; Ibarra and Petriglieri, 2007). In a study of identity development among young professionals transitioning to a managerial role, men relied on imitation strategies, which involved experimenting with traits and behaviors selected from a broad array of role models. By contrast, women tended to rely on true-to-self strategies, transferring to the new role behaviors that had worked for them in the past (Ibarra, 1999). Further analysis revealed differences in self-presentation styles as well (Ibarra and Petriglieri, 2007). Men were more "acquisitive," aggressively seeking to signal credibility by displaying behaviors that conformed to their firm's norms, even when they felt insecure, while women engaged in "protective" self-presentation, modestly asserting more neutral, uncertain, or qualified images in an effort to avoid disapproval. With clients, women sought to prove their competence by demonstrating technical mastery over the long term; in contrast, men were intent on making a positive first impression. Women cited their reliance on "substance rather than form" as a more "authentic" strategy than their male counterparts', and thus as a source of pride. Nevertheless, because displaying technical competence drew on already well-honed self-presentation skills, women's strategies failed to close the gap between identity and image in their new role. Men not only built a broader repertoire of possible selves, they also experienced more congruence between their provisional identity and the kind of professional they aspired to become. When the best of their male counterparts have built the foundations of a new identity and are ready to move on, equally high-potential women may still be searching for the raw materials.

These differences partly reflect men's and women's different structural positions in their workplaces and cultural attitudes about gender and leadership. To further leadership skills, novices need to identify role models, proactively experiment with provisional identities, and evaluate experiments against internal standards and external feedback (Ibarra, 1999). Yet women generally have fewer supports than men for learning how to convey the image of a leader, receive less latitude for making mistakes in the learning process (Foschi, 1996), and experience less social acceptance for their leadership attempts (Hogue and Lord, 2007). These challenges may be particularly acute for women of color (Giscombe and Mattis, 2002). In the study of identity development described earlier, women reported having few role models whose styles were feasible or congruent with their self-concepts and worried that either "acting like a man" or "acting like a woman" would diminish their credibility (Ibarra and Petriglieri, 2007:19). These findings are consistent with research showing that in firms with few women in powerful positions—the norm in most professions and industries—junior women had difficulty identifying with senior women, seeing them as credible role models (Ely, 1994), and finding ways of being a woman that were both personally satisfying and professionally valued (Ely, 1995). For many women transitioning into a leadership role, the provisional self may be an "impossible self" (Ibarra and Petriglieri, 2007).

An Agenda for Future Research

The self-help shelves of bookstores are overstocked with strategies to promote women's leadership: "how-to" publications that advise aspiring women to be more like men, less like men, or simply more savvy in managing their career development and family obligations (Eagly and Carli, 2007a; Rhode and Kellerman, 2007). These "leadership lite" publications offer such commonsense homilies as don't sleep with your supervisor, advertise mistakes, show bad manners, or neglect relationships; the best also echo experts' suggestions about the need to demonstrate competence, seek high-visibility challenging assignments, and develop a style that blends assertiveness and warmth (Catalyst, 2006; Eagly and Carli, 2007a).

The jazzed-up, dumbed-down sound bites available in publications like *Play Like a Man, Ten Secrets of Successful Women,* and *Nice Girls Don't Get the Corner Office* may sell books, but they won't level the playing field because they erroneously assume that the essence of leadership lies simply in *what leaders do.* If leadership is also about *who leaders are,* and the contexts in which they lead, then this advice may be shortsighted. We wish to reframe the problem at both the individual and organizational levels. At the individual level, one central problem is developmental: the way gender biases affect capacities for developing leadership identity. At the organizational level, the primary problem is structural: the way unconscious biases and workplace practices constrain women's leadership opportunities and performance. Our research agenda examines the difficulties on both dimensions.

Identity Processes in Women's Leadership Development

Although theory is rich on how leaders develop, we have little direct empirical evidence about how these processes may differ for women and men and less still about how they unfold in organizations. Herminia Ibarra and Jennifer Petriglieri's (2007) qualitative accounts of women and men's identity transitions in the shift from individual-contributor to managerial roles are a promising start, but many questions remain unanswered.

One set of questions concerns whether, in light of cultural attitudes toward women in authority and the small number of effective female role models, women's leadership identity might need to develop differently from men's. Drawing on a "goal approach" to the self (for reviews, see Dweck, Higgins, and Grant-Pillow, 2003; Crocker, Moeller, and Burson, 2010), we explore what the process might look like for women. A growing body of social psychological research suggests that personal goals form the core of self-systems. Peoples' different goals influence their emotional states, attributions, expectancies, and relationships with others.

PERFORMANCE VERSUS LEARNING GOALS A large body of research on goals for the self concerns people's orientation toward performance versus learning (for reviews, see Dweck and Leggett, 1988; Dweck et al., 2003). When people hold *performance* goals, they want to *demonstrate* a valued attribute and validate a self-image that includes this attribute. This is both a private strategy designed for self-reinforcement and a public impression-management strategy designed for others. By contrast, when people hold *learning* goals, they want to *develop* a valued attribute. In theory, a novice leader might focus on either demonstrating or developing attributes associated with leadership and could construct a provisional self with either goal orientation. We suspect, however, that because this process involves image construction, it more readily lends itself to performance goals.

More than two decades of research attest to the differences these goals make. Those seeking to validate a self-image prefer tasks that will make them look smart over tasks that will foster learning, and prefer partners who will reinforce them rather than challenge them to grow. Compared with those holding learning goals, people with performance goals are more likely to greet new tasks with apprehension or anxiety than with excitement, more likely to experience difficulty on a task as failure, and less likely to take actions to remedy their deficiencies. When a task is used as a means to validate the self, a setback decreases enjoyment of the task, dampens intrinsic motivation, and implies inability, which lowers subsequent expectations of success. Performance goals also lead to more superficial processing of information (e.g., rote memorization) aimed at demonstrating competence rather than increasing understanding, and that focus diminishes performance. Ironically enough, on difficult tasks, performance goals undermine performance. Learning goals enhance it. Although efforts to project the image of leadership may encourage both men and women to seek performance goals, we suspect that the particular identity challenges confronting women leaders often heighten their concerns about how others view them and increase their tendency to pursue a performance-oriented *strategy*. Moreover, although performance goals can be self-defeating for anyone, they may be particularly so for women, whose identity task is more difficult than men's. Seeking external validation for an image that reflects the perfect blend of seemingly incompatible attributes—those of a leader and those of a woman—is almost surely a losing proposition. Research might fruitfully explore the impact of performance versus learning goals on novice leaders' identity transitions and whether these goals have a differential effect on women's and men's success.

PREVENTION VERSUS PROMOTION STRATEGIES A second line of research considers the strategic and motivational character of the pursuit of goals. Those who emphasize *prevention* primarily seek to avoid failure. By contrast, those who emphasize *promotion* are primarily driven to approach success. *Prevention* strategies derive from an internalized sense of what one *ought* to do and focus on responsibilities, safety, and security. *Promotion* strategies derive from an internalized sense of what one would ideally *like* to do and focus on aspiration advancement, and accomplishments (for reviews, see Dweek et al., 2003; Higgins, 1997). Those with a protection focus generally use fewer means to pursue their goals compared with those with a promotion focus.

The catch-22 women experience in the workplace—too feminine or not feminine enough—may encourage a prevention-oriented approach to leadership identity. So, for example, in Ibarra and Petrigleiri's (2007) study, women tended to prefer a protective style, seeking to avoid disapproval. Men's more acquisitive approach to identity construction may reflect a promotion focus, which is easier for them than for women to adopt because their gender identity is not inconsistent with the masculine traits associated with leadership. These differences may help to explain why the women in the Ibarra-Petriglieri study produced a narrower repertoire of strategies than men.

Research on women's and men's strategies for developing leadership identities may further illuminate the gender dynamics of leadership. For example, we suspect that women leaders' prevention-focused identity strategies may elicit more negative competence ratings from followers, whereas promotion-focused ones may elicit more negative likability ratings. Whether leaders view situations as threats or opportunities can trigger different motivational structures in followers (Avolio et al., 2004; Lord and Brown, 2004). Research suggests that labeling situations as threats may elicit in followers a more cautious orientation (Lord and Hall, 2005). If women's leadership already raised anxiety (Kram and McCollom-Hampton, 1998; Lerner, 1981), the cautious, prevention-focused strategies may trigger further concern about competence. By contrast, viewing situations as opportunities should foster a more creative orientation in followers (Avolio et al 2004; Lord and Hall, 2005). Yet gender stereotypes may lead followers to experience women's use of promotion-focused strategies as inappropriate or over-claiming. In short, the strategic choices women face during identity transitions to leadership roles may also constitute double bind.

Research has demonstrated that although people differ substantially in the goals that are most immediately accessible to them, clear situational cues can induce different goals, along with their allied affect and strategies (Dweck et al, 2003:249). In other words, goals are malleable and open to intervention. With such intervention in mind Jennifer Crocker and her colleagues have proposed an alternative to performance goals—one that is compatible with learning but more encompassing (see Crocker et al., 2010). This alternative may facilitate women's leadership development by providing a more viable path to the integrated, values-based identity that is characteristic of expert leaders. Although systematic scrutiny of these ideas has only just begun, this framework is consistent with a great deal of psychological theory and research, and has the potential to inform future study of women and leadership.

EGOSYSTEM VERSUS ECOSYSTEM MOTIVATION An understanding of women's career development may also benefit from exploring distinctions between "egosystem" and "ecosystem" motivations. In essence, performance goals are part of individuals' egosystem, which makes self-worth contingent on having desirable qualities and having those qualities recognized by others. When people operate in an egosystem framework, they seek validation of their desired qualities and thus are oriented toward performance goals. The self is primarily experienced as an object to be judged.

By contrast, ecosystem motivation assesses the self as part of a larger whole, a system in which individual actions have consequences for others and repercussions for the system as a whole. Under this approach, people view the relationship between the self and others as positive rather than zero sum—what is good for oneself can also be good for others. They prioritize the needs of others, not out of virtue or self-sacrifice, but rather out of a commitment to collective well-being, through such goals as fostering teamwork, an organizational mission, or broader social ideals. In this framework, the self is not an object but an agent acting in service of common ends. Although ecosystem motivation may encourage self-evaluation, its objective is not simply to assess one's self-worth or standing, but rather to identify strengths and weaknesses in order to accomplish broader goals. Feelings of self-worth may be a by-product of such goals, but positive self-evaluations or feelings of self-worth are not an end in themselves. Because they are not focused on self-image, ecosystem goals facilitate openness to learning. They motivate people to use their ignorance as a signal that they need to draw on the talents and skills of others; failure becomes a clue that assumptions may be faulty, and a mistake becomes a signal to reassess practices. These goals may not quell fears and anxieties about rejection or incompetence in the short term, as do self-validation goals, but they provide a powerful reason to move forward in spite of those fears and anxieties (Ely, Meyerson, and Davidson, 2006). In addition, while egosystem motivation narrows the focus of attention to cues that are relevant to the needs of the self, ecosystem motivation broadens it, encouraging a long-term perspective on personal goals. This perspective enables people to become more mindful, to notice a broader array of social and environmental cues, and to develop a wider repertoire of strategies. Ecosystem goals can push in different directions than a desire to be "nice" or "likeable." Acting on ecosystem motivation sometimes involves making others uncomfortable or unhappy, as in the case of a manager who must lay people off or give unsettling feedback to those whose performance is deficient. As this example suggests, there can be a trade-off between these two types of goals. Being overly concerned with self-image can lead one to overlook what is best for the organization as a whole, and acting on behalf of the organization can sometimes damage one's image.

What is critical about these motivational systems is that they refer to goals or intended consequences, not to specific behaviors. Almost any action can be taken with an egosystem or an ecosystem motivation. For example, one can be generous to enhance one's reputation as a virtuous person or to benefit others without regard for self-enhancement. Withholding support could similarly serve either objective. For example, a person might say "no" to a request in order to appear tough-minded or in order to prod the other person to become more independent.

This framework suggests that ecosystem goals may be a more constructive path to leadership for women. Focusing their attention on collective goals rather than simply on self-image may help women to escape the double bind. An experimental study of the effects of leaders' mindfulness on evaluations of women leaders is consistent with this suggestion (Kawakami, White, and Langer, 2000). Among women leaders with a masculine style, those who sought to make a genuine connection with their audience were rated higher in warmth, genuineness, and leadership skill than those who focused on a script.

Moreover, although much of the theory on ecosystem motivation remains untested, early findings suggest that holding these goals may foster precisely the kinds of behaviors that are essential for leadership expertise (Avolio et al, 2004; Lord and Hall, 2005). Compared with people who chronically seek to validate their self-images, those who chronically seek to be constructive and supportive of others are clearer about their goals, more open to learning from failure, and evidence better self-regulation (Crocker et al., 2010). Over time, holding collectively oriented goals produces upward spirals of giving and receiving support and increases interpersonal trust (Crocker and Canevello, 2008). By replacing self-image goals with more collective concerns, women may be better able to develop the identity orientation characteristic of expert leaders.

The Organizational Context

Women's capacity for leadership, of course, depends not simply on their individual development of goals and identities, but also on the organizational contexts within which opportunities for leadership arise. Organizations can either reinforce or disrupt sex-based roles and practices, and thus are key sites for intervention and reform (Ely and Meyerson, 2000; Ely and Padavic, 2007). They are correspondingly critical sites for research. (For examples, see Ely and Meyerson's [2007] analysis of how organizational conditions disrupted masculinity on offshore oil platforms and Meyerson, Ely, and Wernick's [2007] speculation on how such conditions may affect women's leadership.)

One set of questions involves how organizational structures affect leadership identity. For example, how might organizations alter norms and practices to better support women's identity and role transitions? Can men also benefit from such organizational changes? What organizational conditions encourage a focus on self-image versus collective goals, and are these conditions related to women's rise into leadership positions? How does the organization's demographic structure (e.g., the proportion and placement of women in senior positions) affect junior women's identity transitions when moving into leadership roles? How does this structure influence how women conceptualize and take up authority? These questions call for research that focuses on the interplay between organizational features and individual-level processes. Organizational scholars are uniquely positioned to conduct such studies by examining how organizational features "magnify and blunt" individual cognitive, emotional, and behavioral processes (Staw and Sutton, 1992:26).

A second cluster of research questions involves how to create cultures that value and promote gender diversity and equity in leadership positions. Scholars and practitioners generally agree that the most important factor in ensuring equal access to leadership opportunities is a commitment to that objective, which is reflected in workplace priorities, policies, and reward structures (Rhode and Kellerman, 2007; Ridgeway and Correll, 2000; Powell, 1998; Wellington et al., 2003). Yet we know little about what causes some organizations to develop and sustain this commitment. Why did the heads of Deloitte Touche embrace the business case for diversity when so many other accounting firms with the same problems failed to respond, even after seeing the extraordinary payoffs that Deloitte achieved from gender-related initiatives?

For organizations that fail to treat diversity as a bottom-line issue, what strategies are most effective in promoting change? Under what circumstances does greater transparency produce constructive responses? What kind of pressure is most effective, and how can it be mobilized? For example, some evidence suggests that most female investors would like to see their pension funds support companies with good track records on women's issues, but we know little about how such preferences might translate into organizational leverage (Calvert Group, 2004; Grosser and Moon, 2005). Other research suggests that certain kinds of pressure, such as class action suits brought by women, provoke more resistance and harassment than litigation brought by other groups, such as racial minorities (James and Wooten, 2006). More systematic evaluation of different forms of political and legal pressure should be a priority.

We also need to know more about the effectiveness of particular governmental interventions and internal initiatives. In countries that require companies to report data on women's representation and advancement (Grosser and Moon, 2005), do the requirements result in significant improvements? In this country, what information is available indicates that many employers now invest substantial time and money in diversity programs that have no significant or measurable impact on outcomes. Although some small-scale studies find that diversity training may improve awareness and attitudes, more systematic, large-scale studies find no effects (Kalev, Dobbin, and Kelly, 2006), or evidence of backlash from white male participants (Bendick, Egan, and Lofthejelm, 1998; Krawiec, 2003; Nelson, Acker, and Melvin, 1996). Many ostensible beneficiaries of these programs express doubt about their effectiveness; only a third of woman of color surveyed by Catalyst felt that diversity efforts created a supportive environment for their group (Giscombe and Mattis, 2002). Virtually no evidence documents improvements in the representation of women in upper-level positions as a result of such training (Kalev et al., 2006; Krawiec, 2003).

Mentoring initiatives also merit attention, especially in light of the role they might play in the development of leadership identity. Although virtually all experts agree about the value of mentors, less than a quarter of surveyed female managers have expressed satisfaction with the availability of mentoring at their workplaces (Catalyst, 2004c). Similar unhappiness is common in other professional contexts, such as large law firms (American Bar Association, 2006). Yet inadequate attention has focused on analyzing the underlying causes and assessing institutional responses, such as formal and electronic mentoring systems and women's networks (Headlam-Wells, 2004). We know that relationships that arise from formal assignments are rarely as successful as those that arise naturally (Catalyst, 2004c; Cleveland et al., 2000). But we know too little about what kinds of incentives and oversight might make required or voluntary mentoring work better. We also lack sufficient data about the significance of women's networks that are emerging in workplaces and professional associations. These networks sponsor a range of activities that build career skills, forge policy coalitions, and link managerial and professional employees with colleagues and potential clients and customers (Kalev et al., 2006; Nance-Nest, 2006; Rhode and Kellerman, 2007). Given the significant time and money now invested in these networks, it would be useful to know more about their effectiveness in generating business and advancement opportunities.

Work/family policies similarly require more systematic assessment. In surveys of high-achieving women, between two-thirds and four-fifths identify work/family issues as a major part of the problem and the solution for women's advancement. Most of these women rate scheduling flexibility as more important than compensation (Hewlett and Luce, 2005; Wellington et al., 2003). Organizations have responded with a wide array of initiatives concerning flex time, part time, telecommuting, and leave policies, as well as childcare assistance and reentry support. Programs that are accessible in principle, however, are often inadequate in practice. Many women who opt for flexible or reduced schedules find that their hours are not respected, their compensation is not proportionate to performance, and their second-class status deprives them of desirable assignments and career development opportunities (Rhode and Williams, 2007). New ways to address these concerns are beginning to emerge. A growing number of employers are offering consulting arrangements and career assistance for women who have temporarily left the labor force, and executive education programs are beginning to target women seeking to transition back (McGinn, 2006). Law firms are experimenting with alternative structures that allow different hours and compensation trade-offs, or that eliminate up or out partnership tracks entirely and match attorneys with cases that fit their expertise and scheduling preferences (Belkin, 2008; Jones, 2007). Nonprofit research and policy organizations are developing more innovative scheduling and compensation structures that enable individuals to have a life as well as leadership opportunities.

All of these initiatives deserve more attention from the academic community. Business, professional, and public policy schools should be at the forefront of teaching and research on gender, diversity, and leadership. Society has an enormous stake in ensuring equal access to leadership opportunities and effective development of leadership potential. To make that possible, we need more knowledge about what works in the world. Research institutions have a unique opportunity and corresponding obligation to help fill the gap.

References

Acker, J. "Hierarchies, Jobs, Bodies: A Theory of Gendered Organizations." *Gender and Society* 4 (1990): 139–158.

Adams, R., and D. Ferreira. "Gender Diversity in the Boardroom." Working paper, London School of Economics, 2007.

American Bar Association, Commission on Women in the Profession. *Visible Invisibility: Women of Color in Law Firms.* Chicago: ABA Foundation, 2006.

Andersen, S.N. and S. Chen. "The Relational Self: An Interpersonal Social-Cognitive Theory." *Psychological Review* 109 (2002): 619–645.

Avolio, B.J., W.L. Gardner, F.O. Walumbwa, F. Luthans, and D.R. May. "Unlocking the Mask: A Look at the Process by Which Authentic Leaders Impact Follower Attitudes and Behaviors." *Leadership Quarterly* 15 (2004): 801–823.

Babcock, L., and S. Laschever. *Women Don't Ask: Negotiation and the Gender Divide.* Princeton University Press, 2003.

Bailyn, L. *Breaking the Mold: Redesigning Work for Productive and Satisfying Lives.* Itliaca, NY: Cornell University Press, 2006.

Barron, L. "Ask and You Shall Receive? Gender Differences in Negotiators' Beliefs About Requests for a Higher Salary." *Human Relations* 56 (2003): 635–662.

Belkin, L. "The Opt-Out Revolution." *New York Times Magazine,* October 26, 2003, 42.

___. "Who's Cuddly Now? Law Firms." *The New York Times,* January 24, 2008, 1.

Bell, E., and S. Nkomo. *Our Separate Ways.* Cambridge, MA: Harvard Business School Press, 2001.

Bendick, M., M. Egan, and S. Lofthejelm. *The Documentation and Evaluation of Antidiscrimination Training in the United States.* Washington, D.C.: Bendick and Egan Economic Consultants, 1998.

Bianchi, S., J. Robinson, and M. Milkie. *Changing Rhythms of American Family Life.* New York: Russell Sage Foundation, 2006.

Bielby, D., and W. Bielby. "She Works Hard for the Money: Household Responsibilities and the Allocation of Work Effort." *American Journal of Sociology* 93 (1988): 1031–1059.

Biernat, M., and D. Kobrynowicz. "Gender and Race-Based Standards of Competence: Lower Minimum Standards but Higher Ability Standards for Devalued Groups." *Journal of Personality and Social Psychology* 72 (1997): 544–557.

Birger, J. "The Outsider." *Fortune,* October 16, 2006, 137.

Bowles, H., and K. McGinn. "Untapped Potential in the Study of Negotiation and Gender Inequality in Organizations." *Academy of Management Annals* 2 (2008): 99–132.

Burt, R. *Structural Holes.* Cambridge, MA: Harvard University Press, 1992.

Butterfield, D.A., and J.P. Grinnell. " 'Re-viewing' Gender, Leadership, and Managerial Behavior: Do the Decades of Research Tell Us Anything?" In *Handbook of Gender and Work,* edited by G. Powell, 223–238. Thousand Oaks, CA.: Sage Publications, 1999.

Calvert Group. *The Calvert Women's Principles: A Global Code of Conduct for Corporations.* Bethesda, MD: The Calvert Group, 2004.

Carroll, J. "Americans Prefer Male Boss to Female Boss." Gallup Brain, 2006. http://institution.gallup.com/content/Default.aspx?ci=24346.

Catalyst. *Women of Color in Corporate Management: Opportunities and Barriers.* New York: Catalyst, 1999.

___. *Advancing Asian Women in the Workplace: What Managers Need to Know.* New York: Catalyst, 2003.

___. *Advancing African-American Women in the Workplace: What Managers Need to Know.* New York: Catalyst, 2004a.

___. *The Bottom Line: Connecting Corporate Performance and Gender Diversity.* New York: Catalyst, 2004b.

___. *Women and Men in U.S. Corporate Leadership: Same Workforce, Different Realities.* New York: Catalyst, 2004c.

___. *Women Take Care, Men Take Charge: Stereotyping of Business Leaders Exposed.* New York: Catalyst, 2005.

___. *The Double Bind Dilemma for Women in Leadership: Damned If You Do; Doomed If You Don't.* New York: Catalyst, 2007.

Center for American Women in Politics. *Election Results Show Advances for Women.* New Brunswick, NJ: Eagleton Institute of Politics, Rutgers, State University of New Jersey, 2006.

Center for Women in Government and Civil Society. *Women in State Policy Leadership 1998–2005.* Albany, NY: State University of New York Center for Women in Government and Civil Society, 2006.

Cleveland, J., M. Stockdale, and K. Murphy. *Women and Men in Organizations: Sex and Gender Issues at Work.* Mahwah, NJ: Lawrence Erlbaum Associates, 2000.

Coughlin, L. "The Time Is Now: A Leader's Personal Journey." In *Enlightened Power: How Women Are Transforming the Practice of Leadership,* edited by L. Coughlin, 1–16. Hoboken, NJ: John Wiley & Sons, 2005.

Crittendon, A. *The Price of Motherhood: Why the Most Important Job in the World Is Still the Least Valued.* New York: Metropolitan/Owl, 2001.

Crocker, J., and A. Canevello. "Creating and Undermining Social Support in Communal Relationships: The Role of Compassionate and Self-image Goals." *Journal of Personality and Social Psychology* 95, no. 3 (2008): 555–575.

Crocker, J., B. Major, and C. Steele. "Social Stigma." In *Handbook of Social Psychology,* edited by D.T. Gilbert, S.T. Fiske, and G. Kubdzey, 504—553. Boston: McGraw-Hill, 1998.

Crocker, J., S. Moeller, and A. Burson. "The Costly Pursuit of Self-Esteem: Implications for Self-Regulation." In *Handbook of Personality and Self-Regulation,* edited by R. Hoyle. West Sussex, England: Wiley-Blackwell, 2010.

Dahlerup, D. "Will Gender Balance in Politics Come By Itself?" In *Women and Leadership: The State of Play and Strategies for Change,* edited by B. Kellerman and D. Rhode, 251–270. San Francisco: Jossey Bass, 2007.

Dennis, M.R., and A.D. Kunkel. "Perceptions of Men, Women, and CEOs: The Effects of Gender Identity." *Social Behavior and Personality* 32 (2004): 155–172.

Deutsch, C. "Behind the Exodus of Executive Women: Boredom." *The New York Times,* May 1, 2005.

Dowd, M. "Can Hillary Cry Her Way to the White House?" *The New York Times,* January 9, 2008, A21.

Dweck, C, E. Higgins, and H. Grant-Pillow. "Self-Systems Give Unique Meaning to Self Variables." In *Handbook of Self and Identity,* edited by M.R. Leary, 239–252. New York: Guilford, 2003.

Dweck, C, and E. Leggett. "A Social-Cognitive Approach to Motivation and Personality." *Psychological Review* 95 (1988): 256–273.

Eagly, A. "Achieving Relational Authenticity in Leadership: Does Gender Matter?" *Leadership Quarterly* 16 (2005): 459–474.

Eagly A, and L. Carli. "Overcoming Resistance to Women Leaders." In *Women and Leadership: The State of Play and Strategies for Change,* edited by B. Kellerman and D. Rhode, 127–148. San Francisco: Jossey-Bass, 2007a.

____. *Through the Labyrinth: The Truth About How Women Become Leaders.* Boston: Harvard Business School Press, 2007b.

Eagly, A., M. Johannesen-Schmidt, and M.L. van Engen. "Transformational, Transactional, and Laissez-faire Leadership Styles: A Meta-analysis Comparing Women and Men." *Psychological Bulletin* 95 (2003): 569–591.

Eagly, A., and S. Karau. "Role Congruity Theory of Prejudice Toward Female Leaders." *Psychological Review* 109 (2002): 573–598.

Eagly, A., M.G. Makliijani, and B.G. Klonsky. "Gender and the Evaluation of Leaders: A Meta-analysis." *Psychological Bulletin* 111 (1992): 3–22.

Eagly, A., and A. Mladinic. "Gender Stereotypes and Attitudes Toward Women and Men." *Personality and Social Psychology Bulletin* 15 (1989): 543–548.

Ely, R. "The Effects of Organizational Demographics and Social Identity on Relationships Among Professional Women." *Administrative Science Quarterly* 39 (1994): 203–238.

____. "The Power in Demography: Women's Social Constructions of Gender Identity at Work." *Academy of Management Journal* 38 (1995): 589–634.

Ely, K., and D. Meyerson. "Theories of Gender: A New Approach to Organizational Analysis and Change." In *Research in Organizational Behavior.* Vol. 22, edited by B. Staw and R. Sutton, 105–153. Elsevier, 2000.

____. "Unmasking Manly Men: The Organizational Reconstruction of Men's Identity." Working paper 07–054. Harvard Business School, Boston, 2007.

Ely, R., D. Meyerson, and M. Davidson. "Rethinking Political Correctness." *Harvard Business Review* 84, no. 9 (September 2006).

Ely, R., and I. Padavic. "A Feminist Analysis of Organizational Research on Sex Differences." *Academy of Management Review* 32 (2007): 1121–1143.

Ely, R., arid D. Thomas. "Cultural Diversity at Work: The Moderating Effects of Work Group Perspectives on Diversity." *Administrative Science Quarterly* 46 (2001): 229–273.

European Commission, Database. "Social and Economic Domain Decision-Making in the Top Publicly Quoted Companies." 2007. http://ec.europa.eu/emplopnent_social/women_men_stats/out/ measures_out438-en.htm.

Festinger, L. *Theory of Cognitive Dissonance.* Stanford, CA: Stanford University Press, 1957.

Fiorina, C. *Tough Choices: A Memoir.* New York: Penguin Group, 2006.

Fletcher, J.K. "Leadership, Power and Positive Relationships at Work." In *Exploring Positive Relationships at Work: Building a Theoretical and Research Foundation,* edited by J. Dutton and B.R. Ragins, 347–370. NJ: Lawrence Erlbaum Press, 2006.

Foroohar, R. "Unlikely Boomtowns." Newsweek.com. July 3, 2006.

Foschi, M. "Double Standards in the Evaluation of Men and Women." *Social Psychology Quarterly* 59 (1996): 237–254.

____. "Double Standards for Competence: Theory and Research." *Annual Review of Sociology* 26 (2000): 21–42.

Giscombe, K., and M.G. Mattis. "Leveling the Playing Field for Women of Color in Corporate Management: Is the Business Case Enough?" *Journal of Business Ethics 37* (2002): 103–119.

Glick, P., and S. Fiske. "An Ambivalent Alliance: Hostile and Benevolent Sexism as Complementary Justifications for Gender Inequality." *American Psychologist 56* (2001): 109–118.

Grosser, K., and J. Moon. "Gender Mainstreaming and Corporate Social Responsibility: Reporting Workplace Issues." *Journal of Business Ethics* 62 (2005): 327–340.

Groysberg, B. "How Star Women Build Portable Skills." *Harvard Business Review* 86, no. 2 (February 2008): 74–81.

Grutter v. Bollinger. 539 U.S. 306 (2003).

Headlam-Wells, J. "E-mentoring for Aspiring Women Managers." *Women in Management Review* 19 (2004): 212–218.

Heffernan, M. *The Naked Truth: The Working Woman's Manifesto on Business and What Really Matters.* San Francisco: Jossey-Bass, 2004.

Heilman, M. "Description and Prescription: How Gender Stereotypes Prevent Women's Ascent up the Organizational Ladder." *Journal of Social Issues* 57 (2001): 657–674.

Heilman, M., R. Martell, and M. Simon. "The Vagaries of Sex Bias: Conditions Regulating the Undervaluation, Equivaluation, and Overvaluation of Female Job Applicants." *Organizational Behavior and Human Decision Processes* 41 (1998): 98–110.

Heilman, M., A. Wallen, D. Fuchs, and M. Tamkins. "Penalties for Success: Reactions to Women Who Succeed at Male Gender-Typed Tasks." *Journal of Applied Psychology* 89 (2004): 416–427.

Hewlett, S., and C. Luce. "Off-Ramps and On-Ramps: Keeping Talented Women on the Road to Success." *Harvard Business Review* 83, no. 3 (March 2005): 43–54.

Hewlett, S., C. Luce, and C. West. "Leadership in Your Midst: Tapping the Hidden Strength of Minority Executives." *Harvard Business Review* 83, no. 11 (November 2005): 74–79.

Hewlett, S., and N. Vita Leon. *High Achieving Women.* New York: Center for Work Life Policy, 2001.

Higgins, E.T. "Beyond Pleasure and Pain." *American Psychologist* 52 (1997): 1280–1300.

Hogue, M., and R. Lord. "A Multilevel, Complexity Theory Approach to Understanding Gender Bias in Leadership." *Leadership Quarterly* 18 (2007): 370–390.

Ibarra, H. "Homophily and Differential Returns: Sex Differences in Network Structure and Access in an Advertising Firm." *Administrative Science Quarterly* 37 (1992): 422–447.

___. "Provisional Selves: Experimenting with Image and Identity in Professional Adaptation." *Administrative Science Quarterly* 44 (1999): 764—791.

Ibarra, H., and J. Petriglieri. "Impossible Selves: Image Strategies and Identity Threat in Professional Women's Career Transitions." Working paper, INSEAD, 2007.

International Labor Organization, 2004. "Breaking Through the Glass Ceiling: Women in Management," Geneva Switzerland: International Labor Organization.

James, E., and L. Wooten. "Diversity Crisis: How Firms Manage Discrimination Lawsuits." *Academy of Management Journal* 49 (2006): 1103–1118.

Jones, J. "Gender Differences in Views of Job Opportunity: Fifty-Three Percent of Americans Believe Opportunities Are Equal." Gallup Brain, August 2, 2005. http://brain.gallup.com.

Jones, L. "The Rise of the New Model Firm." *National Law Journal,* May 21, 2007. http:www//.axiom.legal.com.

Judge, T, and R. Piccolo. "Transactional and Transformational Leadership: A Meta-analytic Test of Their Relative Validity." *Journal of Applied Psychology* 89 (2004): 901–910.

Kalev, A., F. Dobbin, and E. Kelly. "Best Practices or Best Guesses: Diversity Management and Remediation of Inequality." *American Sociological Review* 71 (2006): 589–617.

Kanter, R. *Men and Women of the Corporation.* New York: Basics Books, 1977.

Kawakami, C, J. White, and E. Langer. "Mindful and Masculine: Freeing Women Leaders from the Constraints of Gender Roles." *Journal of Social Issues* 56 (2000): 49–63.

Kephart, P., and L. Schumacher. "Has the 'Glass Ceiling' Cracked? An Exploration of Women Entrepreneurship." *Journal of Leadership and Organizational Studies* 12 (2005): 2–15.

Koch, S., R. Luft, and L. Kruse. "Women and Leadership—20 Years Later. A Semantic Connotation Study." *Social Sciences Information* 44 (2005): 3–23.

Kram, K. and M. McCollom-Hampton. "When Women Lead: The Visibility-Vulnerability Spiral." In *The Psychodynamics of Leadership,* edited by E. Klein, F. Gabelnick, and P. Herr, 193–218. Madison, CT: Psychosocial Press, 1998.

Krawiec, K. "Cosmetic Compliance and the Failure of Negotiated Governance." *Washington University Law Quarterly* 81 (2003): 487–544.

Lerner, H. "Early Origins of Envy and Devaluation of Women: Implications for Sex Role Stereotypes." In *Women and Mental Health,* edited by E. Howell and M. Bayes, 26–40. New York: Basic Books, 1981.

Lord, R., and D. Brown. *Leadership Processes and Follower Self-Identity.* Mahwah, NJ:Lawrence Erlbaum, 2004.

Lord, R., and R. Hall. "Identity, Deep Structure and the Development of Leadership Skill."*Leadership Quarterly* 16 (2005): 591–615.

Luthans, E, and B. Avolio. "Authentic Leadership: A Positive Development Approach." In *Positive Organizational Scholarship,* edited by K.S. Cameron, J.E. Dutton, and R.E. Quinn, 241–258. San Francisco, CA: Berrett-Koehler Publishers, 2003.

Mandel, R. "She's the Candidate! A Woman for President." In *Women and Leadership: The State of Play and Strategies for Change,* edited by B. Kellerman and D. Rhode, 283–303. San Francisco: Jossey-Bass, 2007.

Markoff, J. "Hewlett-Packard Picks Rising Star at Lucent as Its Chief Executive." *The New York Times,* July 20, 1999, C1.

May, D.R., A. Chan, T. Hodges, and B.J. Avolio. "Developing the Moral Component of Authentic Leadership." *Organizational Dynamics* 32 (2003): 247–260.

McGinn, D. "Getting Back on Track." Newsweek.com, September 25, 2006.

Meyerson, D., and R. Ely. "Using Difference to Make a Difference." In *Women and Leadership: The State of Play and Strategies for Change,* edited by D. Rhode. Stanford, CA: Stanford University Press, 2003.

Meyerson, D.E., R.J. Ely, and L. Wernick. "Disrupting Gender, Revising Leadership." In *Women and Leadership: The State of Play and Strategies for Change,* edited by D. Rhode and B. Kellerman, 453–473. San Francisco: Jossey-Bass, 2007.

Nance-Nest, S. "Wall Street Women: Forming Their Own Inside Circle." April: 10, 2006. http://www.womensenews.org/.

National Association of Law Placement. "Few Lawyers Work Part Time: Most Who Do So Are Women." Press release, December 5, 2007.

Nelson, T., M. Acker, and M. Melvin. "Irrepressible Stereotypes."*Journal of Experimental Social Psychology 32* (1996): 13–38.

O'Brien, T. "Up the Down Staircase." *The New York Times,* March 19, 2006.

Podolny, J., and J. Baron. "Resources and Relationships: Social Networks and Mobility in the Workplace." *American Sociological Review 62* (1997): 673–693.

Powell, G. *Handbook of Gender and Work.* Thousand Oaks, CA: Sage Publications, 1998.

Ragins, B. "Gender and Mentoring Relationships: A Review and Research Agenda in the Next Decade." In *Handbook of Gender and Work,* edited G. Powell, 347–369. Thousand Oaks, CA: Sage Publications, 1998.

Rapoport, R., L. Bailyn, J. Fletcher, and B.H. Pruitt. *Beyond Work-Family Balance: Advancing Gender Equity and Workplace Performance.* San Francisco: Jossey-Bass, 2002.

Reskin, B. "Bringing the Men Back In: Sex Differentiation and the Devaluation of Women's Work." *Gender and Society 2* (1988): 58–81.

Rhode, D., and B. Kellerman. "Women and Leadership: The State of Play." In *Women and Leadership: The State of Play and Strategies for Change,* edited by B. Kellerman and D. Rhode, 1–64. Hoboken, NJ: John Wiley & Sons, 2007.

Rhode, D., and J. Williams. "Legal Perspectives on Employment Discrimination." In *Sex Discrimination in the Workplace,* edited by F. Crosby, M. Stockdale, and A. Ropp. Santa Cruz, CA: University of California, 2007.

Ridgeway, C. "Gender, Status, and the Social Psychology of Expectations." In *Theory on Gender/Feminism on Theory,* edited by P. England, 175–198. New York: Aldine Press, 1993.

Ridgeway, C, and S. Correll. "Limiting Inequality Through Interaction: The End(s) of Gender." (Essay for special issue on Utopian Visions). *Contemporary Sociology* 29 (2000): 118.

Rudman, L., and P. Glick. "Prescriptive Gender Stereotypes and Backlash Toward Agentic Women."*Journal of Social Issues* 57 (2001): 743–762.

Rudman, L., and S. Kilianski. "Implicit and Explicit Attitudes Toward Female Authority." *Personality and Social Psychology Bulletin* 26 (2007): 1315–1328.

Schein, V "A Global Look at the Psychological Barriers to Women's Progress in Management." *Journal of Social Issues* 57 (2001): 675–688.

Stanley, A. "For Women to Soar Is Rare: To Fail Is Human." *The New York Times,* July 13, 2004.

Staw, B., and R. Sutton. "Macro Organizational Psychology." In *Social Psychology in Organizations: Advances in Theory and Research,* edited by J.K. Murnighan, 350–384. Englewood Cliffs, NJ: Prentice Hall, 1992.

Stone, P., and M. Lovejoy. "Fast-Track Women and the Choice to Stay Home." *Annals of the American Academy of Political and Social Science* 596 (2004): 62–83.

Strober, M. "Toward a General Theory of Occupational Sex Segregation: The Case of Public School Teaching." In *Sex Segregation in the Workplace: Trends, Explanations, Remedies,* edited by B. Reskin, 144–156. Washington, DC: National Academy Press, 1984.

Swim, J.K., and L.J. Sanna. "He's Skilled, She's Lucky: A Meta-analysis of Observers' Attributions for Women's and Men's Successes and Failures." *Personality and Social Psychology Bulletin* 22 (1996): 507–519.

U.S. Bureau of Labor Statistics. "News: American Time-use Survey—2005 Results Announced by BLS." 2006. http://wwwbls.gov/news.release/pdf/atus.pdf.

Valian, V. *Why So Slow? The Advancement of Women.* Cambridge, MA: MIT Press, 1999.

van Knippenberg, D., B. van Knippenberg, D. Cremer, and M. Hogg. "Leadership, Self, and Identity: A Review and Research Agenda." *Leadership Quarterly* 15 (2004): 825–856.

Vedantam, S. "The Myth of the Iron Lady." *Washingtonpost.com.* November 12, 2007, A-03.

Wallis, C. "The Case for Staying Home." *Time,* March 22, 2004, 51.

Wellington, S., and Catalyst. *Be Your Own Mentor.* New York: Random House, 2001.

Wellington, S., S.B. Kropf, and P. Gerkovich. "What's Holding Women Back?" *Harvard Business Review* 81, no. 6 (June 2003): 18–19.

Wilkins, D.B., and M. Gulati. "Why Are There So Few Black Lawyers in Corporate Law Firms? An Institutional Analysis." *California Law Review* 94 (1996) 493–625.

Williams, J. *Unbending Gender: Why Family and Work Conflict and What to Do About It.* New York: Oxford University Press, 2000.

Wilson, M. *Closing the Leadership Gap: Why Women Can and Must Help Run the World.* New York: Feminist Press, City University of New York, 2004.

BEYOND SOPHISTICATED STEREOTYPING: CULTURAL SENSEMAKING IN CONTEXT*

Joyce S. Osland

Allan Bird

If U.S. Americans are so individualistic and believe so deeply in self-reliance, why do they have the highest percentage of charitable giving in the world and readily volunteer their help to community projects and emergencies?

In a 1991 survey, many Costa Rican customers preferred automatic tellers over human tellers because "at least the machines are programmed to say 'Good morning' and 'Thank you.' "[1] Why is it that so many Latin American cultures are noted for warm interpersonal relationships and a cultural script of simpatía (positive social behavior),[2] while simultaneously exhibiting seeming indifference as service workers in both the private and public sectors?

Based on Hofstede's[3] value dimension of Uncertainty Avoidance, the Japanese have a low tolerance for uncertainty while Americans have a high tolerance. Why then do the Japanese intentionally incorporate ambiguous clauses in their business contracts, which are unusually short, while Americans dot every *i*, cross every *t*, and painstakingly spell out every possible contingency?

Many people trained to work in these cultures found such situations to be paradoxical when they first encountered them. These examples often contradict and confound our attempts to neatly categorize cultures. They violate our conceptions of what we think particular cultures are like. Constrained, stereotypical thinking is not the only problem, however. The more exposure and understanding one gains about any culture, the more paradoxical it often becomes. For example, U.S. Americans are individualistic in some situations (e.g., "the most comprehensive of rights and the right most valued is the right to be left alone"[4]) and collectivist in others (e.g., school fundraising events).

Long-term sojourners and serious cultural scholars find it difficult to make useful generalizations since so many exceptions and qualifications to the stereotypes, on both a cultural and individual level, come to mind. These cultural paradoxes are defined as situations that exhibit an apparently contradictory nature.

Surprisingly, there is little mention of cultural paradoxes in the management literature.[5] Our long-term sojourns as expatriates (a combined total of 22 years), as well as our experience in teaching cross-cultural management, preparing expatriates to go overseas, and doing comparative research, has led us to feel increasingly frustrated with the accepted conceptualizations of culture. Thus, our purpose is to focus attention on cultural paradoxes, explain why they have been overlooked and why they exist, and present a framework for making sense of them. Our intent is to initiate a dialogue that will eventually provide teachers, researchers, and people who work across cultures with a more useful way to understand culture.

A look at the comparative literature reveals that cultures are described in somewhat limited terms.[6] There are 22 dimensions commonly used to compare cultures, typically presented in the form of bipolar continua, with midpoints in the first examples, as shown in Table 1. These dimensions were developed to yield greater cultural understanding and allow for cross-cultural comparisons. An unanticipated consequence of using these dimensions, however, is the danger of stereotyping entire cultures.

Sophisticated Stereotyping

In many parts of the world, one hears a generic stereotype for a disliked neighboring ethnic group—"The (fill in the blank) are lazy, dirty thieves, and their women are promiscuous." This is a low-level form of stereotyping, often based on lack of personal contact and an irrational dislike of people who are different from oneself. Professors and trainers work very hard to dispel such stereotypes. Rarely, however, do we stop to consider whether we are supplanting one form of stereotyping for another. For example, when we teach students and managers how to perceive the Israelis using Hofstede's[7] cultural dimensions, they may come to think of Israelis in terms of small power distance, strong uncertainty avoidance, moderate femininity, and moderate individualism. The result is to reduce a complex culture to a shorthand description they may be tempted to apply to all Israelis. We call this *sophisticated stereotyping*, because it is based on theoretical concepts and lacks the negative attributions often associated with its lower-level counterpart. Nevertheless, it is still limiting in the way it constrains individuals' perceptions of behavior in another culture.

Table 1	Common Cultural Dimensions	
Subjugation to Nature	**Harmony**	**Mastery of Nature**
Past	Present	Future
Being	Containing and controlling	Doing
Hierarchical relationships	Group	Individualistic
Private space	Mixed	Public
Evil human nature	Neutral or mixed	Good
Human nature as changeable		Human nature as unchangeable
Monochronic time		Polychronic time
High-context language		Low-context language
Low uncertainty avoidance		High uncertainty avoidance
Low power distance		High power distance
Short-term orientation		Long-term orientation
Individualism		Collectivism
Masculinity		Femininity
Universalism		Particularism
Neutral		Emotional
Diffuse		Specific
Achievement		Ascription
Individualism		Organization
Inner-directed		Outer-directed
Individualism (competition)		Group-organization (collusion)
Analyzing (reductivist)		Synthesizing (larger, integrated wholes)

Sources: Kluckhohn and Strodtbeck (1961); Hall and Hall (1990); Hofstede (1980); Parsons and Shils (1951); Trompenaars and Hampden Turner (1993); Trompenaars (1994). The dimensions are bipolarcontinua, with the first six containing midpoints.

Do we recommend against teaching the cultural dimensions shown in Table 1 so as to avoid sophisticated stereotyping? Not at all. These dimensions are useful tools in explaining cultural behavior. Indeed, cultural stereotypes can be helpful—provided we acknowledge their limitations. They are more beneficial, for example, in making comparisons between cultures than in understanding the wide variations of behavior within a single culture. Adler[8] encourages the use of "helpful stereotypes," which have the following limitations: They are consciously held, descriptive rather than evaluative, accurate in their description of a behavioral norm, the first best guess about a group prior to having direct information about the specific people involved, and modified based on further observations and experience. As teachers, researchers, and managers in cross-cultural contexts, we need to recognize that our original characterizations of other cultures are best guesses that we need to modify as we gain more experience.

For understandable, systemic reasons, business schools tend to teach culture in simple-minded terms, glossing over nuances and ignoring complexities. An examination of the latest crop of organizational behavior and international business textbooks revealed that most authors present only Hofstede's cultural dimensions, occasionally supplemented by Hall's theory of high- and low-context cultures.[9] Although these disciplines are not charged with the responsibility of teaching culture in great depth, these are the principal courses in many curricula where business students are exposed to cross-cultural concepts. Another handicap is that many business professors do not receive a thorough grounding in culture in their own disciplines and doctoral programs. One could further argue that we are joined in this conspiracy to give culture a quick-and-dirty treatment by practitioners and students who are looking for ways to simplify and make sense of the world.

The limitations of sophisticated stereotyping become most evident when we confront cultural paradoxes. This is the moment we realize our understanding is incomplete, misleading, and potentially dangerous. Perhaps because cultural paradoxes reveal the limitations in our thinking, they are often left unmentioned, even though virtually anyone with experience in another culture can usually identify one or two after only a moment's reflection.

Why Don't We Know More About Cultural Paradoxes?

With one exception,[10] the cross-cultural literature contains no mention or explanation of cultural paradoxes. This absence can be explained by:

- homegrown perceptual schemas that result in cultural myopia;
- lack of cultural experience that leads to misinterpretation and failure to comprehend the entire picture;
- cultural learning that plateaus before complete understanding is achieved;
- Western dualism that generates theories with no room for paradox or holistic maps;
- features of cross-cultural research that encourage simplicity over complexity; and
- a between-culture research approach that is less likely to capture cultural paradoxes than a within-culture approach.

Perceptual Schemas

When outsiders look at another culture, they inevitably interpret its institutions and customs using their own lenses and schemas; cultural myopia and lack of experience prevent them from seeing all the nuances of another culture.

In particular, a lack of experience with the new culture creates difficulties for new expatriates trying to make sense of what they encounter. The situation is analogous to putting together a jigsaw puzzle. Though one may have the picture on the puzzle box as a guide, making sense of each individual piece and understanding where and how it fits is exceedingly difficult. As more pieces are put into place, however, it is easier to see the bigger picture and understand how individual pieces mesh. Similarly, as one acquires more and varied experiences in the new culture, one can develop an appreciation for how certain attitudes and behaviors fit the puzzle and create an internal logic of the new culture.

The danger with sophisticated stereotyping is that it may lead individuals to think that the number of shapes that pieces may take is limited and that pieces fit together rather easily. As Barnlund notes: "Rarely do the descriptions of a political structure or religious faith explain precisely when and why certain topics are avoided or why specific gestures carry such radically different meanings according to the context in which they appear."[11]

Expatriates and researchers alike tend to focus first on cultural differences and make initial conclusions that are not always modified in light of subsequent evidence.[12] Proactive learning about another culture often stops once a survival threshold is attained, perhaps because of an instinctive inclination to simplify a complex world. This may lead us to seek black-and-white answers rather than tolerate the continued ambiguity that typifies a more complete understanding of another culture.

One of the best descriptions of the peeling away of layers that characterizes deeper cultural understanding is found in a fictionalized account of expatriate life written by an expatriate manager, Robert Collins.[13] He outlines ascending levels on a Westerner's perception scale of Japanese culture that alternate, in daisy-petal-plucking fashion, between seeing the Japanese as significantly different or not really that different at all:

> *The initial level on a Westerner's perception scale clearly indicates a "difference" of great significance. The Japanese speak a language unlike any other human tongue . . . . They write the language in symbols that reason alone cannot decipher. The airport customs officers all wear neckties, everyone is in a hurry, and there are long lines everywhere.*
>
> *Level Two is represented by the sudden awareness that the Japanese are not different at all. Not at all. They ride in elevators, have a dynamic industrial/ trade/financial system, own great chunks of the United States, and serve cornflakes in the Hotel Okura.*
>
> *Level Three is the "Hey, wait a minute" stage. The Japanese come to all the meetings, smile politely, nod in agreement with everything said, but do the opposite of what's expected. And they do it all together. They really are different.*
>
> *But are they? Level Four understanding recognizes the strong group dynamics, common education and training, and the general sense of loyalty to the family—which in their case is Japan itself. That's not so unusual, things are just organized on a larger scale than any social unit in the West. Nothing is fundamentally different.*
>
> *Level Five can blow one's mind, however. Bank presidents skipping through streets dressed as dragons at festival time; single ladies placing garlands of flowers around huge, and remarkably graphic, stone phallic symbols; Ministry of Finance officials rearranging their bedrooms so as to sleep in a "lucky" direction; it is all somewhat odd. At least, by Western standards. There is something different in the air.*
>
> *And so on. Some Westerners, the old Japan hands, have gotten as far as Levels 37 or 38.[14]*

The point of Collins's description is that it takes time and experience to make sense of another culture. The various levels he describes reflect differing levels of awareness as more and more pieces of the puzzle are put into place. Time and experience are essential because culture is embedded in the context. Without context it makes little sense to talk about culture. Yet just as its lower-order counterpart does, sophisticated stereotyping tends to strip away or ignore context. Thus, cognitive schemas prevent sojourners and researchers from seeing and correctly interpreting paradoxical behavior outside their own cultures.

Theoretical Limitations

Another reason for the inattention to cultural paradoxes stems from the intersection between cognitive schemas and theory. Westerners have a tendency to perceive stimuli in terms of dichotomies and dualisms rather than paradoxes or holistic pictures.[15] The idea of paradox is a fairly recent wrinkle on the intellectual landscape of management theorists[16] and has not yet been incorporated into cultural theories in a managerial context.

Cross-cultural research is generally held to be more difficult than domestic studies. Hofstede's[17] work represented a major step forward and launched a deluge of studies utilizing his dimensions. Hundreds of studies have used one or more of Hofstede's dimensions to explore similarities and differences across cultures regarding numerous aspects of business and management. However, Hofstede himself warned against expecting too much of these dimensions and of using them incorrectly. For example, he defended the individualism-collectivism dimension as a useful construct, but then went on to say: "This does not mean, of course, that a country's Individual Index score tells all there is to be known about the backgrounds and structure of relationship patterns in that country. It is an abstraction that should not be extended beyond its limited area of usefulness."[18]

When we fail to specify under what conditions a culture measures low or high on any of the common cultural dimensions, or to take into consideration the impact of organizational culture, it misleads rather than increases our understanding of comparisons of culture and business practices. Such an approach prevents rather than opens up opportunities for learning and exploration.

A final explanation for the failure to address cultural paradoxes can be traced to the emic/etic distinction commonly used in the cultural literature. An emic perspective looks at a culture from within its boundaries, whereas an etic perspective stands outside and compares two or more cultures. To make between-culture differences more prominent, the etic approach minimizes the inconsistencies within a culture. Most cultural approaches in management adopt a between-culture approach, playing down the within-culture differences that expatriates must understand in order to work successfully in the host country.

Anthropologist Claude Levi-Strauss warned that explanation does not consist of reducing the complex to the simple, but of substituting a more intelligible complexity for one that is less intelligible.[19] In failing to acknowledge cultural paradoxes or the complexity surrounding cultural dimensions, we may settle for simplistic, rather than intelligently complex, explanations.

Sources of Paradox in Cultural Behavior

Behavior that looks paradoxical to an expatriate in the initial stages of cultural awareness may simply reflect the variance in behavioral norms for individuals, organizational cultures, subcultures, as well as generational differences and changing sections of the society. In addition, expatriates may also form microcultures[20] with specific members of the host culture. The cultural synergy of such microcultures may not be reflective of the national culture. These false paradoxes need to be discarded before more substantive paradoxes can be evaluated.

Based on an analysis of all the paradoxes we could find, we have identified six possible explanations for cultural behaviors that appear truly paradoxical. They are:

- the tendency for observers to confuse individual with group values;
- unresolved cultural issues;
- bipolar patterns;
- role differences;
- real versus espoused values; and
- value trumping, a recognition that in specific contexts certain sets of values take precedence over others.

Confusing individual with group values is exemplified by the personality dimension labeled allocentrism versus idiocentrism, which is the psychological, individual-level analog to the individualism–collectivism dimension at the level of culture.[21] Allocentric people, those who pay primary attention to the needs of a group, can be found in individualistic cultures, and idiocentric people, those who pay more attention to their own needs than to the needs of others, in collectivist cultures. What we perceive as cultural paradox may not reflect contradictions in cultural values, but instead may reveal the natural diversity within any culture that reflects individual personality and variation.

Unresolved cultural issues are rooted in the definition of culture as a learned response to problems. Some paradoxes come from problems for which there is no clear, happy solution. Cultures may manifest a split personality with regard to an unresolved problem.[22] As a result, they shuttle back and forth from one extreme to the other on a behavioral continuum. U.S. Americans, for example, have ambivalent views about sex, and, as one journalist recently noted: "Our society is a stew of prurience and prudery."[23] Censorship, fears about sex education, and sexual taboos coexist uncomfortably with increasingly graphic films and TV shows and women's magazines that never go to press without a feature article devoted to sex. This melange is more than a reflection of a diverse society that has both hedonists and fundamentalists with differing views of sex; both groups manifest inconsistent behaviors and attitudes about sex, signaling an enduring cultural inability to resolve this issue.

Bipolar patterns make cultural behavior appear paradoxical because cultural dimensions are often framed, perhaps inaccurately, as dualistic, either–or continua. Cultures frequently exhibit one of these paired dimensions more than the other, but it is probable that both ends of the dimensions are found in cultures—but only in particular contexts. For example, in Latin America, ascribed status, derived from class and family background, is more important than its polar opposite, achieved status, which is based on talent and hard work. When it comes to professional soccer, however, achieved status trumps class and ascription.

Often some groups and roles appear to deviate from cultural stereotypes. For example, in the United States, autocratic behavior is frequently tolerated in CEOs, even though the United States is characterized as an egalitarian culture. Such behavior may also be an example of a high power distance context in a low power distance culture: We accept that CEOs possess an unequal degree of power and that they will behave in a different manner than most U.S. Americans.

There is also a difference between real versus espoused values. All cultures express preferences for ideal behaviors—for what should be valued and how people should act. Nevertheless, people do not always act consistently with ideal behaviors and values. For example, U.S. Americans may simultaneously pay lip service to the importance of equality (an espoused value), while trying to acquire more power or influence for themselves (a real value).

A final possible explanation of cultural paradoxes derives from a holistic, contextual view of culture in which values co-exist as a constellation, but their salience differs depending on the situation. Using the Gestalt concept of figure-ground, at times a particular value becomes dominant (figure), while in other circumstances, this same value recedes into the background (ground).[24] In India, for example, collectivism is figural when individuals are expected to make sacrifices for their families or for the larger society—such as Hindu sons who postpone marriage until their sisters marry, or daughters who stay single to care for their parents. In other circumstances, however, collectivism fades into the background and individualism comes to the fore and is figural when Indians focus more upon self-realization—for example, elderly men who detach themselves from their family to seek salvation.[25] Taking the figure-ground analogy a step further, depending on the context, one cultural value might trump another, lessening the influence another value normally exerts.[26] For example, we find it useful to view culture as a series of card games in which cultural values or dimensions are individual cards. Depending on the game, previous play, and the hand one is dealt, players respond by choosing specific cards that seem most appropriate in a given situation. Sometimes a particular card trumps the others; in another round, it does not. In a given context, specific cultural values come into play and have more importance than other values. To a foreigner who does not understand enough about the cultural context to interpret why or when one value takes precedence over another, such behavior looks paradoxical. Members of the culture learn these nuances more or less automatically. For example, children learn in what context a socially acceptable white lie is more important than always telling the truth. A true understanding of the logic of another culture includes comprehending the interrelationships among values, or how values relate to one another in a given context.

A Model of Cultural Sensemaking

To make sense of cultural paradoxes and convey a holistic understanding of culture, we propose a model of cultural sensemaking. The model shown in Figure 1 helps explain how culture is embedded in context.[27] Cultural sensemaking is a cycle of sequential events:

- *Indexing Context.* The process begins when an individual identifies a context and then engages in indexing behavior, which involves noticing or attending to stimuli that provide cues about the situation. For example, to index the context of a meeting with a subordinate, we consider characteristics such as prior events (recent extensive layoffs), the nature of the boss–subordinate relationship within and without work (golfing partner), the specific topic under discussion (employee morale), and the location of the interaction (boss's office).
- *Making Attributions.* The next step is attribution, a process in which contextual cues are analyzed in order to match the context with appropriate schema. The matching process is moderated or influenced by one's social identity (e.g., ethnic or religious background, gender, social class, organizational affiliation) and one's history (e.g., experiences and chronology). A senior U.S. American manager who fought against the Japanese in World War II will make different attributions about context and employ different schema when he meets with a Japanese manager than will a Japanese-American manager of his generation, or a junior U.S. manager whose personal experience with Japan is limited to automobiles, electronics, and sushi.
- *Selecting Schema.* Schemas are cultural scripts, "a pattern of social interaction that is characteristic of a particular cultural group."[28] They are accepted and appropriate ways of behaving, specifying certain patterns of interaction. From personal or vicarious experience, we learn how to select schema. By

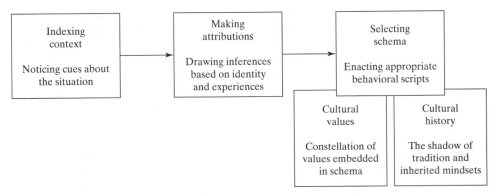

FIGURE 1   Cultural Sensemaking Model

watching and working with bosses, for example, we develop scripts for how to act when we take on that role ourselves. We learn appropriate vocabulary and gestures, which then elicit a fairly predictable response from others.

- *The Influence of Cultural Values.* Schemas reflect an underlying hierarchy of cultural values. For example, people working for U.S. managers who have a relaxed and casual style and who openly share information and provide opportunities to make independent decisions will learn specific scripts for managing in this fashion. The configuration of values embedded in this management style consists of informality, honesty, equality, and individualism. At some point, however, these same managers may withhold information about a sensitive personnel situation because privacy, fairness, and legal concerns would trump honesty and equality in this context. This trumping action explains why the constellation of values related to specific schema is hierarchical.

- *The Influence of Cultural History.* When decoding schema, we may also find vestiges of cultural history and tradition. Mindsets inherited from previous generations explain how history is remembered.[29] For example, perceptions about a colonial era may still have an impact on schemas, particularly those involving interactions with foreigners, even though a country gained its independence centuries ago.

Some Illustrations of Sensemaking

Sensemaking involves placing stimuli into a framework that enables people "to comprehend, understand, explain, attribute, extrapolate, and predict."[30] Let's analyze each of the cultural paradoxes presented in the introduction using the sensemaking model. In the United States, when a charity requests money, when deserving people are in need, or when disaster hits a community (indexing contexts), many U.S. Americans (e.g., religious, allocentric people making attributions) respond by donating their money, goods, or time (selecting schema). The values underlying this schema are humanitarian concern for others, altruism,[31] and collectivism (cultural values). Thus, individualism (a sophisticated stereotype) is moderated by a communal tradition that has its roots in religious and cultural origins (cultural history).

Fukuyama[32] writes that U.S. society has never been as individualistic as its citizens thought, because of the culture's relatively high level of trust and resultant social capital. The United States "has always possessed a rich network of voluntary associations and community structures to which individuals have subordinated their narrow interests."[33] Under normal conditions, one should take responsibility for oneself and not rely on others. However, some circumstances and tasks can overwhelm individual initiative and ingenuity. When that happens, people should help those in need, a lesson forged on the American frontier (cultural history). To further underscore the complexity of culture, in the same contexts noted above, the tax code and prestige associated with philanthropy (cultural history) may be the primary motivations for some citizens (e.g., idiocentric, upwardly ambitious people making attributions) to act charitably (selecting schema), but the value underlying the schema would be individualism.

The Costa Rican example is illustrated in Figure 2. When bank tellers interact with clients (indexing context) many of them (e.g., members of various in-groups, civil servants making attributions) do not greet customers and make eye contact, but concentrate solely on their paperwork (selecting schema). The values that underlie this schema are in-group out-group behavior[34] and power (cultural values). In collectivist cultures such as Costa Rica, members identify strongly with their in-group and treat members with warmth and cooperation. In stark contrast, out-group members are often treated

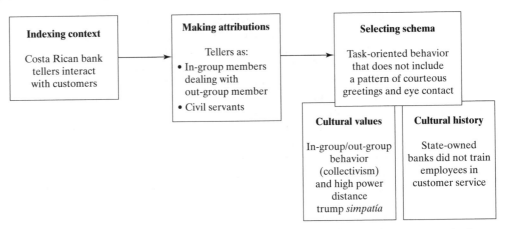

FIGURE 2 Making Sense of Paradoxical Behavior: Seemingly Indifferent Customer Service in a Culture Characterized by Positive, Warm Relations

with hostility, distrust, and a lack of cooperation. Customers are considered as strangers and out-group members who do not warrant the special treatment given to in-group members (family and friends). One of the few exceptions to simpatía and personal dignity in Costa Rica, and Latin America generally, is rudeness sometimes expressed by people in positions of power.[35] In this context, the cultural value of high power distance (the extent to which a society accepts the fact that power in institutions and organizations is distributed unequally)[36] trumps *simpatía*. Whereas simpatía lessens the distance between people, the opposite behavior increases the distance between the powerful and the powerless. Unlike many other contexts in Costa Rica, bank telling does not elicit a cultural script of simpatía, and state-owned banks did not have a history of training employees in friendly customer service (cultural history) at this time.

In the third cultural example, when Japanese business people make contracts (indexing context), they (e.g., business people making attributions) opt for ambiguous contracts (selecting schema). The dominant value underlying this schema is collectivism (cultural value). In this context, collectivism is manifested as a belief that those entering into agreement are joined together and share something in common; thus, they should rely on and trust one another. Collectivism trumps high uncertainty avoidance (sophisticated stereotype) in this context, but uncertainty avoidance is not completely absent. Some of the uncertainty surrounding the contract is dealt with upstream in the process by carefully choosing and getting to know business partners, and by using third parties. An additional consideration is that many Japanese like flexible contracts, because they have a greater recognition of the limits of contracts and the difficulties of foreseeing all contingencies (cultural history). Even though U.S. Americans are typically more tolerant of uncertainty (sophisticated stereotype), they value pragmatism and do not like to take unnecessary risks (cultural values). If a deal falls through, they rely on the legal system for a resolution (cultural history).

Working From a Sensemaking Approach

Sophisticated stereotypes are useful in the initial stages of making sense of complex behaviors within cultures. However, rather than stereotyping cultures somewhere along a continuum, we can advance understanding by thinking in terms of specific contexts that feature particular cultural values that then govern behavior. Geertz maintains that "culture is best seen not as complexes of concrete behavior patterns— customs, usages, traditions, habit clusters—as has by and large been the case up to now, but as a set of control mechanisms—plans, recipes, rules, instructions (what computer engineers call *programs*)—for the governing of behavior."[37]

Understanding the control mechanisms within a culture requires the acquisition of attributional knowledge, the awareness of contextually appropriate behavior.[38] This is in contrast to factual knowledge and conceptual knowledge. Factual knowledge consists of descriptions of behaviors and attitudes. For example, it is a fact that Japanese use small groups extensively in the workplace. Conceptual knowledge consists of a culture's views and values about central concerns. Sophisticated stereotyping operates in the realm of conceptual knowledge. This category of knowledge is an organizing tool, but it is not sufficient for true cultural understanding. Knowing that the Japanese are a communal society (conceptual knowledge) does not explain the non-communal activities that exist in Japanese organizations or when the Japanese will or will not be communal. For example, why are quality control circles used in some work settings and not in others? Factual and conceptual knowledge about Japanese culture cannot answer that question; only attributional knowledge can.

Managers can acquire attributional knowledge from personal experience, vicariously from others' experience, and from cultural mentoring. The personal experience method involves carefully observing how people from another culture act and react, and then formulating and reformulating hypotheses and cultural explanations for the observed behavior. When expatriates test their hypotheses and find them valid, they form schemas about specific events in the host culture.

One can learn vicariously by reading about other cultures, but the best form of vicarious learning is via cultural assimilator exercises.[39] These are critical incidents of cross-cultural encounters, accompanied by alternative explanations for the behavior of people from the foreign culture. After choosing what they perceive as the most likely answer, trainees then read expert opinions relating why each answer is adequate or inadequate. These opinions are validated by cross-cultural experts and include information about the relative importance of cultural dimensions or context-specific customs in the culture in question.

A cultural mentor can be viewed as a hybrid of vicarious and personal acquisition of attributional knowledge—a sort of live cultural assimilator. Cultural mentors are usually long-term expatriates or members of the foreign culture. The latter are often helpful souls who have lived abroad themselves and understand the challenge of mastering another culture or people not totally in step with their own culture.[40] "They interpret the local culture for expatriates and guide them through its shoals, as well as providing them with the necessary encouragement when it feels like the expatriates will never 'break the code' of another culture and fit in comfortably."[41] Reading an explanation from a book or working through a series of cultural assimilators is different from receiving an explanation of an experience the expatriate has personally lived through and now wishes to understand. Cultural mentors can correct inaccurate hypotheses about the local culture. Expatriates who had cultural mentors overseas have been found to fare better than those who did not have such mentors: They were more fluent in the foreign language; they perceived themselves as better adapted to their work and general living conditions abroad; they were more aware of the paradoxes of expatriate life, indicating a higher degree of acculturation and understanding of the other culture; and they received higher performance appraisal ratings from both their superiors and themselves.[42]

In spite of the benefits of mentoring, few multinationals formally assign a cultural mentor to their expatriates. Yet another way of developing an expatriate's attributional knowledge is to provide more training in the host country rather than relying solely on predeparture culture "inoculations."

Admittedly, there are trade-offs to developing attributional knowledge. The acquisition of cultural knowledge takes a good deal of time and energy, which is not available to all managers. Nor is it reasonable to expect employees who work with people from various cultures on a daily basis to master each culture. Nevertheless, organizing the knowledge they do acquire as context-specific schemas can speed up cultural learning and prevent confusion and errors in making sense of cultural paradoxes.

If we accept that cultures are paradoxical, then it follows that learning another culture occurs in a dialectical fashion—thesis, antithesis, and synthesis. Thesis entails a hypothesis involving a sophisticated stereotype; antithesis is the identification of an apparently oppositional cultural paradox. Synthesis involves making sense of contradictory behavior—understanding why certain values are more important in certain contexts. Behavior appears less paradoxical once the foreigner learns to index contexts and match them with the appropriate schemas in the same way that members of the host culture do. Collins's description of the Westerner's Perception Scale in comprehending Japanese culture[43] illustrates one form of dialectical culture learning, an upwardly spiraling cycle of cultural comprehension.

Using the Model

Because this cultural sensemaking model provides a more complex way of understanding culture, it has clear implications for those who teach culture, for those who work across cultures, and for organizations that send expatriates overseas.

Teaching About Cultural Understanding

Sophisticated stereotyping should be the beginning of cultural learning, not the end, as is so often the case when teaching or learning about culture. Recognition of a more complex, holistic, sensemaking model of culture allows us to respond more effectively when students or trainees provide examples of paradoxes that seem to contradict cultural dimensions. The model also requires a somewhat different teaching approach. We have developed a sequential method that has been effective in our teaching:

- *Help students understand the complexity of their own culture.* To acquaint students with the vast challenge of comprehending culture, we begin with a thorough understanding of the internal logic of one's own culture and its socioeconomic, political, and historical roots. We add complexity by pointing out paradoxes as well as identifying regional, ethnic, religious, organizational, and individual variations in behavior. For example, when Thai students describe their culture as friendly, we ask the following series of questions: "Are all Thais friendly? Are Thais always friendly? Under what circumstances would Thais not exhibit friendly behavior? Why?"
- *Give students cultural dimensions and values as well as sophisticated stereotypes as basic tools.* These dimensions, including the values listed in Table 1, can then be used to explain contrasting behavior from two or more different cultures (e.g., what can sample obituaries from the United States and Mexico reveal about cultural values? What is the typical response of businesses in both countries when a member of an employee's family dies?). Students practice recognizing cultural dimensions in cross-cultural dialogues and cases and learn sophisticated stereotypes. This helps them gain conceptual knowledge about different cultures so they can make between-culture distinctions.
- *Develop students' skills in cultural observation and behavioral flexibility.* One of the difficulties expatriates confront in making sense of a new culture is the contradiction between the expected culture, the sophisticated stereotype taught in predeparture training or gleaned from others, and the manifest

culture, the one actually enacted in a situation.[44] To help students become skilled at observing and decoding other cultures, teach them to think more like anthropologists and give them practice in honing observational and interpretive skills. To help students develop the behavioral flexibility needed to adapt to unanticipated situations, role-playing and videos of cross-cultural interactions can be used.

- *Have students do an in-depth study or experience with one culture.* To go beyond sophisticated stereotypes, students learn the internal logic and cultural history of a single culture. They acquire attributional knowledge from cultural mentors and/or cultural immersion, in addition to extensive research.

- *Focus on learning context-appropriate behavior in other cultures and developing cultural hypotheses and explanations for paradoxical behavior.* Once students have mastered the preceding steps, the emphasis changes to learning schemas for different contexts. For example, student teams are instructed to deliberately demonstrate incorrect behavior; they ask others to point out the mistakes and then replay the scene using correct behavior. To model the crucial behavior of asking for help in understanding cultural mysteries,[45] students use cultural mentors to explain situations they choose to learn about (e.g., "How do managers in ___ encourage employees to perform at high levels? Why does that work for them?") The variation in the mentors' answers ("Some managers are successful doing this while others . . . ") and the qualified answers ("This seems to work unless . . . ; it depends on . . . ") helps students develop more complex understandings of the other culture. To highlight the message of moving beyond cultural stereotypes, use language that focuses on forming and testing hypotheses about contextual behavior: "What are your hypotheses about why a French employee behaves this way in this situation? How can you find out if these hypotheses are correct?"

Sensemaking for Individuals Working Across Cultures

After the training program, and once on assignment in a new culture, this cultural sensemaking approach has other practical implications.

- *Approach learning another culture more like a scientist who holds conscious stereotypes and hypotheses in order to test them.* One of the key differences between managers who were identified by their fellow MBA students as the "most internationally effective" and the "least internationally effective" is that the former changed their stereotypes of other nationalities as they interacted with them while the latter did not.[46]

- *Seek out cultural mentors and people who possess attributional knowledge about cultures.* Perhaps one of the basic lessons of cross-cultural interaction is that tolerance and effectiveness result from greater understanding of another culture. Making sense of a culture's internal logic and decoding cultural paradoxes is easiest with the aid of a willing and knowledgeable informant.

- *Analyze disconfirming evidence and instances that defy cultural stereotypes.* Even people with a great deal of experience in another culture can benefit from analyzing cultural paradoxes. For instance, the question "In what circumstances do Latin Americans fail to exhibit *simpatía*?" led to a more complex cultural understanding for one of the authors, who had already spent nine curious years in that region. Once expatriates can function reasonably well in another culture, it is easy for them to reach plateaus in their cultural understanding and mistakenly assume that they comprehend the entire puzzle. This presents a danger when expatriates inadvertently pass on inaccurate information about the local culture, or make faulty, and even expensive, business decisions based on partial understandings.

- *Learn cultural schemas that will help you be effective.* Knowing how to act appropriately in specific cross-cultural settings results in self-confidence and effectiveness. One cannot memorize all the rules in another culture, but understanding the values that underlie most schemas can often prevent us from making serious mistakes.

How Multinational Organizations Can use the Sensemaking Model

The cultural sensemaking model also has practical implications for multinational organizations.

- *Use cognitive complexity as a selection criterion for expatriates and people in international positions.* Avoid black-and-white thinkers in favor of people who exhibit cognitive complexity, which involves the ability to handle ambiguity and multiple viewpoints. This skill is better suited to a thesis–antithesis approach to understanding the paradoxical nature of culture.
- *Provide in-country cultural training for expatriates that goes beyond factual and conceptual knowledge.* Predeparture cultural training is complemented by on-site training, which has the advantage of good timing. In-country culture training takes place when expatriates are highly motivated to find answers to real cultural dilemmas and when they are ready for greater complexity.[47]
- *Gauge the cultural knowledge possessed by expatriates within a country.* The accuracy and depth of one's cultural understanding is not always linked to the time one has spent in another country; it depends on the degree of involvement with the other culture as well as cultural curiosity and desire to learn. Nevertheless, when companies determine the optimum length of overseas assignments, they should consider how much time is generally necessary to function effectively in a particular culture. If a firm's expatriates stay abroad for only two years, it is less likely that a deep understanding of the culture will be shared among them than if they were to stay for longer periods. As long as the longer-term expatriates do not stop at a low-level plateau of cultural learning, mixing short-term (2–3 years) with longer-term expatriates (6–7 years) with permanent expatriates could produce more shared organizational learning about the culture. It is also essential to recognize that expatriates working for the same organization may be at different levels of cultural understanding.
- *Act like learning organizations with regard to cultural knowledge.* Multinationals benefit from formal mechanisms to develop a more complex understanding of the cultures where they do business through such methods as cultural mentors and in-country cultural training. There should also be mechanisms for sharing cultural knowledge. For example, having returned expatriates give formal debriefing sessions in which they report what they learned in their assignment increases the company's collective cultural knowledge and eases the expatriates' transition home by helping them make sense of a highly significant experience.[48]

Endnotes

1. This was one of the findings of a class research project on the acceptance of ATMs by Dr. Osland's graduate students at INCAE's (Central American Institute of Business Administration) Banking Program in 1991.

2. J. C. Triandis, G. Marin, J. Lisansky, and H. Betancourt, "Simpatía as a Cultural Script of Hispanics," *Journal of Personality and Social Psychology 47*, no. 6 (1984): 1363–1375.

3. G. Hofstede, *Culture's Consequences: International Differences in Work-Related Values* (Beverly Hills: Sage, 1980).

4. *Olmstead v. United States*, 277 U.S. 438, 478 (1928) (J. Brandeis, dissenting).

5. The descriptions of cultural metaphors in *Understanding Global Cultures: Metaphorical Journeys Through 17 Countries* (Thousand Oaks, CA: Sage, 1994) by Martin Gannon and his associates contain passing references to paradoxes, but do not address the issue directly.

6. T. Parsons and E. Shils, *Toward a General Theory of Action* (Cambridge: Harvard University Press, 1951); F. Kluckhohn and F. L. Strodtbeck, *Variations in Value Orientations* (Evanston, IL: Row, Peterson, 1961); Hofstede; H. C. Triandis, "Dimensions of Cultural Variations as Parameters of Organizational Theories," *International Studies of Management and Organization 12*, no. 4 (1982): 139–169; S. Ronen and O. Shenkar, "Clustering Countries on Attitudinal Dimensions: A Review and Synthesis," *Academy of Management Review 10* (1985): 435–454; E. T. Hall and M. R. Hall, *Understanding Cultural Differences* (Yarmouth, ME: Intercultural Press, 1990); A. P. Fiske, "The Four Elementary Forms of Sociality: Framework for a Unified Theory of Social Relations," *Psychological Review 99*, no. 4 (1992): 689–723; S. Schwartz, "Universals in the Content and Structure of Values: Theoretical Advances and Empirical Tests in 20 Countries," *Advances in experimental Social Psychology,* ed. M. Zanna (New York, NY: Academic Press, 1992): 1–66. F. Trompenaars and C. Hampden Turner, *The Seven Cultures of Capitalism* (New York: Doubleday, 1993).

7. Hofstede.

8. N. Adler, *International Dimensions of Organizational Behavior,* 3rd ed. (Cincinnati: South-Western, 1997): 75–76.

9. Hall and Hall.

10. Gannon.

11. D. Barnlund, *Public and Private Self in Japan and the United States* (Yarmouth, ME: Intercultural Press, 1975): 6.

12. J. S. Osland, *The Adventure of Working Abroad: Hero Tales from the Global Frontier* (San Francisco: Jossey-Bass, 1995).

13. R. J. Collins, *Max Danger: The Adventures of an Expat in Tokyo* (Rutland, VT: Charles E.Tuttle Co., 1987).

14. Ibid., 14–15.

15. R. C. Tripathi, "Aligning Development to Values in India," *Social Values and Development: Asian Perspectives*, eds. H. S. Sinha and R. Kao (New Delhi: Sage, 1988): 315–333; J. Wilbur, *A Brief History of Everything* (New York: Shambala 1995).

16. R. Quinn and K. S. Cameron, eds., *Paradox and Transformation* (Cambridge, MA: Ballinger, 1988); K. K. Smith and D. N. Berg, *Paradoxes of Group Life* (San Francisco: Jossey-Bass, 1987).

17. Hofstede.

18. G. Hofstede, in U. Kim, H. S. Triandis, C. Kâgitçibasi, S. Choi, and G. Yoon, eds., *Individualism and Collectivism* (Thousand Oaks. CA: Sage, 1994): XI.

19. C. Levi-Strauss, *La Pensée Sauvage* (Paris: Adler's Foreign Books, Inc., 1962).

20. G. Fontaine, *Managing International Assignments: The Strategy for Success* (Upper Saddle River, NJ: Prentice Hall, 1989).

21. H. C. Triandis, R. Bontempo, M. J. Villareal, M. Asai, and N. Lucca, "Individualism and Collectivism: Cross-Cultural Perspectives on Self-Ingroup Relationships," *Journal of Personality and Social Psychology 54* (1998): 323–338.

22. G. Bateson, *Steps to an Ecology of Mind* (London: Paladin Books, 1973).

23. J. Haught, "What Does Sex Have to Do with It?" *Oregonian*, December 29, 1993, D7.

24. Tripathi, Marin, et al.

25. Ibid.

26. A. Bird, J. S. Osland, M. Mendenhall, and S. Schneider, "Adapting and Adjusting to Other Cultures:What We Know but Don't Always Tell," *Journal of Management Inquiry 8* (1999): 152–165.

27. Context is also embedded in culture, so one could argue that the entire model is situated within the broader culture. For simplicity's sake, however, we chose to focus only on the sensemaking that occurs in deciphering cultural paradoxes.

28. Triandis, Marin, et al.

29. G. Fisher, *Mindsets: The Role of Culture and Perception in International Relations* (Yarmouth, ME: Intercultural Press, 1997).

30. W. H. Starbuck and F. J. Milliken,"Executives' Personal Filters:What They Notice and How They Make Sense," *The Executive Effect: Concepts and Methods for Studying Top Managers*, ed. D. Hambrick (Greenwich, CT: JAI Press, 1988): 51.

31. Barnlund.

32. F. Fukuyama, *Trust* (New York: Penguin Books, 1996).

33. Ibid., 29.

34. Triandis, et al.

35. J. S. Osland, S. De Franco, and A. Osland, "Organizational Implications of Latin American Culture: Lessons for the Expatriate Manager," *Journal of Management Inquiry 8*, no. 2 (1999): 219–234.

36. Hofstede, *Culture's Consequences.*

37. C. Geertz, *The Interpretation of Cultures* (New York: HarperCollins Basic Books, 1973): 44.

38. A. Bird, S. Heinbuch, R. Dunbar, and M. McNulty, "A Conceptual Model of the Effects of Area Studies Training Programs and a Preliminary Investigation of the Model's Hypothesized Relationships," *International Journal of Intercultural Relations 17*, no. 4 (1993): 415–436.

39. The original cultural assimilators were developed by Harry Triandis at the University of Illinois. A recent collection is found in *Intercultural Interactions: A Practical Guide* by R. Brislin, K. Cushner, C. Cherrie, and M. Yong (Thousand Oaks, CA: Sage, 1986 and 1996—second edition).

40. Osland, *Working Abroad.*

41. Ibid., 68.

42. Ibid., 74.

43. Collins.

44. J. Schermerhorn Jr. and M. H. Bond, "Cross-Cultural Leadership Dynamics in Collectivism and High Power Distance Settings," *Leadership and Organization Development Journal 18*, no. 4 (1997): 187–193.

45. On occasion we have heard frustrated cross-cultural trainers grumble that some expatriates view seeking out cultural explanations with the same disdain they reserve for stopping to ask for driving directions.

46. I. Ratiu, "Thinking Internationally: A Comparison of How International Students Learn," *International Studies of Management and Organization 13* (1983): 139–150.

47. Bird, Osland, et al.

48. Osland, *Working Abroad.*

Leadership and Management

This section of the book focuses on the knowledge and essential skills required of effective leaders, managers, team leaders, and self-leaders.

CHAPTER

16 Leadership

LEVEL 5 LEADERSHIP
Jim Collins

IN PRAISE OF THE INCOMPLETE LEADER
Deborah Ancona
Thomas W. Malone
Wanda J. Orlikowski
Peter M. Senge

L eadership is one of the most frequently researched topics in organizational behavior, which makes it difficult to choose among the thousands of articles written on this subject. Our conceptions or schemas of what constitutes a good leader vary from culture to culture and can also change over time within the same culture.

Our first choice came from Jim Collins's best-selling book *Good to Great*, which compared pairs of firms in the same industry whose performance was similar and "good" at one point. He and his researchers examined in depth why some firms went on to become "great" and sustained that level of performance, beating the general stock market by an average of seven times over a fifteen-year period. One of the reasons they identified was a type of leadership they call "Level 5 Leadership." Countries have implicit theories of leadership—an ideal profile for leaders—that influence how leaders are selected, groomed, and evaluated by others. Collins's description of effective leaders who achieve greatness adds a new wrinkle to the U.S. CEO leader profile.

Our second choice further questions the typical conception of the flawless leader. "In Praise of the Incomplete Leader" was written by Deborah Ancona, management professor and director of the MIT Leadership Center; Thomas Malone, management professor and director of the MIT Center for Collective Intelligence; Wanda Orlikowski, MIT communication science professor; and Peter Senge, founder of MIT's Society for Organizational Learning. They note that effective leaders recognize their weaknesses as well as their strengths and take steps to compensate for their limitations while building upon their strengths. The authors suggest that effective leadership requires four capabilities: sensemaking, relating, visioning, and inventing. Because it is rare for an individual to excel at all four capabilities, effective leaders devise ways to tap into the knowledge of others. This has the dual benefit of furthering the leader's goals and developing employees' skills, thus creating an environment in which distributed leadership flourishes.

LEVEL 5 LEADERSHIP*

Jim Collins

You can accomplish anything in life, provided that you do not mind who gets the credit.

HARRY S. TRUMAN[1]

In 1971, a seemingly ordinary man named Darwin E. Smith became chief executive of Kimberly-Clark, a stodgy old paper company whose stock had fallen 36 percent behind the general market over the previous twenty years.

Smith, the company's mild-mannered in-house lawyer, wasn't so sure the board had made the right choice—a feeling further reinforced when a director pulled Smith aside and reminded him that he lacked some of the qualifications for the position.[2] But CEO he was, and CEO he remained for 20 years.

What a twenty years it was. In that period, Smith created a stunning transformation, turning Kimberly-Clark into the leading paper-based consumer products company in the world. Under his stewardship, Kimberly-Clark generated cumulative stock returns 4.1 times the general market, handily beating its direct rivals Scott Paper and Procter & Gamble and outperforming such venerable companies as Coca-Cola, Hewlett-Packard, 3M, and General Electric. (See Figure 1.)

It was an impressive performance, one of the best examples in the twentieth century of taking a good company and making it great. Yet few people—even ardent students of management and corporate history—know anything about Darwin Smith. He probably would have liked it that way. A man who carried no airs of self-importance, Smith found his favorite companionship among plumbers and electricians and spent his vacations rumbling around his Wisconsin farm in the cab of a backhoe, digging holes and moving rocks.[3] He never cultivated hero status or executive celebrity status.[4] When a journalist asked him to describe his management style, Smith, dressed unfashionably like a farm boy wearing his first suit bought at J. C. Penney, just stared back from the other side of his nerdy-looking black-rimmed glasses. After a long, uncomfortable silence, he said simply: "Eccentric."[5] The *Wall Street Journal* did not write a splashy feature on Darwin Smith.

But if you were to think of Darwin Smith as somehow meek or soft, you would be terribly mistaken. His awkward shyness and lack of pretense was coupled with a fierce, even stoic, resolve toward life. Smith grew up as a poor Indiana farmtown boy, putting himself through college by working the day shift at International Harvester and attending Indiana University at night. One day, he lost part of a finger on the job. The story goes that he went to class that evening and returned to work the next day. While that might be a bit of an exaggeration, he clearly did not let a

*(c) 2001 Jim Collins. Jim Collins is author of *Good to Great: Why Some Companies Make the Leap and Others Don't*, and co-author of *Built to Last: Successful Habits of Visionary Companies*. A recipient of the Distinguished Teaching Award while a faculty member at the Stanford University Graduate School of Business, Jim now works from his management-research laboratory in Boulder, Colorado. More of Jim Collins' work can be found at www.jimcollins.com.

BEFORE DARWIN SMITH

Kimberly-Clark, Cumulative Value of $1 Invested,
1951 – 1971

DARWIN SMITH TENURE

Kimberly-Clark, Cumulative Value of $1 Invested,
1971 – 1991

FIGURE 1 **Kimberly-Clark before and during Darwin Smith's tenure**

lost finger slow down his progress toward graduation. He kept working full-time, he kept going to class at night, and he earned admission to Harvard Law School.[6] Later in life, two months after becoming CEO, doctors diagnosed Smith with nose and throat cancer, predicting he had less than a year to live. He informed the board but made it clear that he was not dead yet and had no plans to die anytime soon. Smith held fully to his demanding work schedule while commuting weekly from

Wisconsin to Houston for radiation therapy and lived twenty-five more years, most of them as CEO.[7]

Smith brought that same ferocious resolve to rebuilding Kimberly-Clark, especially when he made the most dramatic decision in the company's history: Sell the mills.[8] Shortly after he became CEO, Smith and his team had concluded that the traditional core business—coated paper—was doomed to mediocrity. Its economics were bad and the competition weak.[9] But, they reasoned, if Kimberly-Clark thrust itself into the fire of the *consumer* paper-products industry, world-class competition like Procter & Gamble would force it to achieve greatness or perish.

So, like the general who burned the boats upon landing, leaving only one option (succeed or die), Smith announced the decision to sell the mills, in what one board member called the gutsiest move he'd ever seen a CEO make. Sell even the mill in Kimberly, Wisconsin, and throw all the proceeds into the consumer business, investing in brands like Huggies and Kleenex.[10]

The business media called the move stupid and Wall Street analysts downgraded the stock.[11] Smith never wavered. Twenty-five years later, Kimberly-Clark owned Scott Paper outright and beat Procter & Gamble in six of eight product categories.[12] In retirement, Smith reflected on his exceptional performance, saying simply, "I never stopped trying to become qualified for the job."[13]

Not What We Expected

Darwin Smith stands as a classic example of what we came to call a Level 5 leader—an individual who blends extreme personal humility with intense professional will. We found leaders of this type at the helm of every good-to-great company during the transition era. Like Smith, they were self-effacing individuals who displayed the fierce resolve to do whatever needed to be done to make the company great.

> **Level 5 leaders channel their ego needs away from themselves and into the larger goal of building a great company. It's not that Level 5 leaders have no ego or self-interest. Indeed, they are incredibly ambitious—but their ambition is first and foremost for the institution, not themselves.**

The term *Level 5* refers to the highest level in a hierarchy of executive capabilities that we identified in our research. (See Figure 2.) While you don't need to move in sequence from Level 1 to Level 5—it might be possible to fill in some of the lower levels later—fully developed Level 5 leaders embody all five layers of the pyramid. I am not going to belabor all five levels here, as Levels 1 through 4 are somewhat self-explanatory and are discussed extensively by other authors. This chapter will focus instead on the distinguishing traits of the good-to-great leaders—namely Level 5 traits—in contrast to the comparison leaders in our study [in matched firms that were not able to make the leap from good to great].

But first, please permit a brief digression to set an important context. We were not looking for Level 5 leadership or anything like it. In fact, I gave the research team explicit instructions to *downplay* the role of top executives so that we could avoid the simplistic "credit the leader" or "blame the leader" thinking common today.

To use an analogy, the "Leadership is the answer to everything" perspective is the modern equivalent of the "God is the answer to everything" perspective that held back our scientific understanding of the physical world in the Dark Ages. In the 1500s, people ascribed all events they didn't understand to God. Why did the crops fail? God did it. Why did we have an earthquake? God did it. What holds the planets in place? God. But with the Enlightenment, we began the search for a more scientific

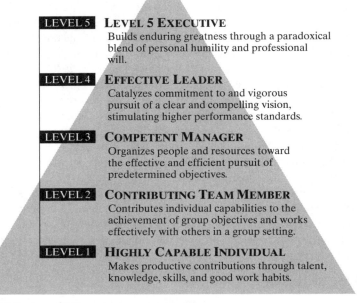

FIGURE 2   Level 5 hierarchy

understanding—physics, chemistry, biology, and so forth. Not that we became atheists, but we gained deeper understanding about how the universe ticks.

Similarly, every time we attribute everything to "Leadership," we're no different from people in the 1500s. We're simply admitting our ignorance. Not that we should become leadership atheists (leadership *does* matter), but every time we throw our hands up in frustration—reverting back to "Well, the answer must be Leadership!"—we prevent ourselves from gaining deeper, more scientific understanding about what makes great companies tick.

So, early in the project, I kept insisting, "Ignore the executives." But the research team kept pushing back, "No! There is something consistently unusual about them. We can't ignore them." And I'd respond, "But the comparison companies also had leaders, even some great leaders. So, what's different?" Back and forth the debate raged.

Finally—as should always be the case—the data won.

The good-to-great executives were all cut from the same cloth. It didn't matter whether the company was consumer or industrial, in crisis or steady state, offered services or products. It didn't matter when the transition took place or how big the company. All the good-to-great companies had Level 5 leadership at the time of transition. Furthermore, the absence of Level 5 leadership showed up as a consistent pattern in the comparison companies. Given that Level 5 leadership cuts against the grain of conventional wisdom, especially the belief that we need larger-than-life saviors with big personalities to transform companies, it is important to note that Level 5 is an empirical finding, not an ideological one.

Humility + Will = Level 5

Level 5 leaders are a study in duality: modest and willful, humble and fearless. To quickly grasp this concept, think of United States President Abraham Lincoln (one of the few Level 5 presidents in United States history), who never let his ego get in the way of his primary ambition for the larger cause of an enduring great nation. Yet those who mistook Mr. Lincoln's personal modesty, shy nature, and awkward manner as signs of weakness found themselves terribly mistaken, to the scale of 250,000 Confederate and 360,000 Union lives, including Lincoln's own.[14]

While it might be a bit of a stretch to compare the good-to-great CEOs to Abraham Lincoln, they did display the same duality. Consider the case of Colman Mockler, CEO of Gillette from 1975 to 1991. During Mockler's tenure, Gillette faced three attacks that threatened to destroy the company's opportunity for greatness. Two attacks came as hostile takeover bids from Revlon, led by Ronald Perelman, a cigar-chomping raider with a reputation for breaking apart companies to pay down junk bonds and finance more hostile raids.[15] The third attack came from Coniston Partners, an investment group that bought 5.9 percent of Gillette stock and initiated a proxy battle to seize control of the board, hoping to sell the company to the highest bidder and pocket a quick gain on their shares.[16] Had Gillette been flipped to Perelman at the price he offered, shareowners would have reaped an instantaneous 44 percent gain on their stock.[17] Looking at a $2.3 billion short-term stock profit across 116 million shares, most executives would have capitulated, pocketing millions from flipping their own stock and cashing in on generous golden parachutes.[18]

Colman Mockler did not capitulate, choosing instead to fight for the future greatness of Gillette, even though he himself would have pocketed a substantial sum on his own shares. A quiet and reserved man, always courteous, Mockler had the reputation of a gracious, almost patrician gentleman. Yet those who mistook Mockler's reserved nature for weakness found themselves beaten in the end. In the proxy fight, senior Gillette executives reached out to thousands of individual investors—person by person, phone call by phone call—and won the battle.

Now, you might be thinking, "But that just sounds like self-serving entrenched management fighting for their interests at the expense of shareholder interests." On the surface, it might look that way, but consider two key facts.

First, Mockler and his team staked the company's future on huge investments in radically new and technologically advanced systems (later known as Sensor and Mach 3). Had the takeover been successful, these projects would almost certainly have been curtailed or eliminated, and none of us would be shaving with Sensor, Sensor for Women, or the Mach 3—leaving hundreds of millions of people to a more painful daily battle with stubble.[19]

Second, at the time of the takeover battle, Sensor promised significant future profits that were not reflected in the stock price because it was in secret development. With Sensor in mind, the board and Mockler believed that the future value of the shares far exceeded the current price, even with the price premium offered by the raiders. To sell out would have made short-term shareflippers happy but would have been utterly irresponsible to long-term shareholders.

In the end, Mockler and the board were proved right, stunningly so. If a shareflipper had accepted the 44 percent price premium offered by Ronald Perelman on October 31, 1986, and then invested the full amount in the general market for ten years, through the end of 1996, he would have come out three times *worse* off than a shareholder who had stayed with Mockler and Gillette.[20] Indeed, the company, its customers, and the shareholders would have been ill served had Mockler capitulated to the raiders, pocketed his millions, and retired to a life of leisure. (See Figure 3.)

Sadly, Mockler was never able to enjoy the full fruits of his effort. On January 25, 1991, the Gillette team received an advance copy of the cover of *Forbes* magazine, which featured an artist's rendition of Mockler standing atop a mountain holding a giant razor above his head in a triumphal pose, while the vanquished languish on the hillsides below. The other executives razzed the publicity-shy Mockler, who

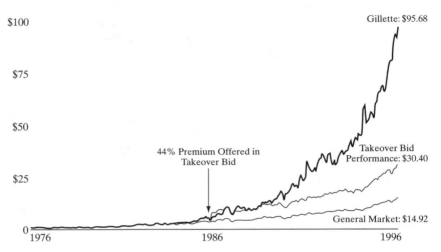

Cumulative Value of $1 Invested, 1976 – 1996
Gillette versus Takeover Bid and Market

This chart shows how an investor would have fared under the following scenarios:
1. $1 invested in Gillette, held from December 31, 1976, through December 31, 1996.
2. $1 invested in Gillette, held from December 31, 1976, *but then sold* to Ronald
   Perelman for a 44.44% premium on October 31, 1986, the proceeds then invested in
   the general stock market.
3. $1 invested in General Market held from December 31, 1976 through December 31, 1996.

FIGURE 3   Colman Mockler's triumph

had likely declined requests to be photographed for the cover in the first place,
amused at seeing him portrayed as a corporate version of Conan the Triumphant.
Walking back to his office, minutes after seeing this public acknowledgment of his
sixteen years of struggle, Mockler crumpled to the floor, struck dead by a massive
heart attack.[21]

I do not know whether Mockler would have chosen to die in harness, but I am
quite confident that he would not have changed his approach as chief executive. His
placid persona hid an inner intensity, a dedication to making anything he touched the
best it could possibly be—not just because of what he would get, but because he simply couldn't imagine doing it any other way. It wouldn't have been an option within
Colman Mockler's value system to take the easy path and turn the company over to
those who would milk it like a cow, destroying its potential to become great, any
more than it would have been an option for Lincoln to sue for peace and lose forever
the chance of an enduring great nation.

Ambition for the Company: Setting Up Successors for Success

When David Maxwell became CEO of Fannie Mae in 1981, the company was losing $1 million every single business day. Over the next nine years, Maxwell trans-
formed Fannie Mae into a high-performance culture that rivaled the best Wall
Street firms, earning $4 million every business day and beating the general stock
market 3.8 to 1. Maxwell retired while still at the top of his game, feeling that the
company would be ill served if he stayed on too long, and turned the company over
to an equally capable successor, Jim Johnson. Shortly thereafter, Maxwell's retirement package, which had grown to be worth $20 million based on Fannie Mae's
spectacular performance, became a point of controversy in Congress (Fannie Mae
operates under a government charter). Maxwell responded by writing a letter to his

successor, in which he expressed concern that the controversy would trigger an adverse reaction in Washington that could jeopardize the future of the company. He then instructed Johnson not to pay him the remaining balance—$5.5 million—and asked that the entire amount be contributed to the Fannie Mae foundation for low-income housing.[22]

David Maxwell, like Darwin Smith and Colman Mockler, exemplified a key trait of Level 5 leaders: ambition first and foremost for the company and concern for *its* success rather than for one's own riches and personal renown. Level 5 leaders want to see the company even more successful in the next generation, comfortable with the idea that most people won't even know that the roots of that success trace back to their efforts. As one Level 5 leader said, "I want to look out from my porch at one of the great companies in the world someday and be able to say, 'I used to work there.' "

In contrast, the comparison leaders, concerned more with their own reputation for personal greatness, often failed to set the company up for success in the next generation. After all, what better testament to your own personal greatness than that the place falls apart after you leave?

In over three quarters of the comparison companies, we found executives who set their successors up for failure or chose weak successors, or both.

Some had the "biggest dog" syndrome—they didn't mind other dogs in the kennel, as long as they remained the biggest one. One comparison CEO was said to have treated successor candidates "the way Henry the VIII treated wives."[23]

Consider the case of Rubbermaid, an unsustained comparison company that grew from obscurity to number one on *Fortune's* annual list of America's Most Admired Companies and then, just as quickly, disintegrated into such sorry shape that it had to be acquired by Newell to save itself. The architect of this remarkable story, a charismatic and brilliant leader named Stanley Gault, became synonymous in the late 1980s with the success of the company. In 312 articles collected on Rubbermaid, Gault comes through as a hard-driving, egocentric executive. In one article, he responds to the accusation of being a tyrant with the statement, "Yes, but I'm a sincere tyrant."[24] In another, drawn directly from his own comments on leading change, the word *I* appears forty-four times ("I could lead the charge"; "I wrote the twelve objectives"; "I presented and explained the objectives"), whereas the word *we* appears just sixteen times.[25] Gault had every reason to be proud of his executive success. Rubbermaid generated forty consecutive quarters of earnings growth under his leadership—an impressive performance, and one that deserves respect.

But—and this is the key point—Gault did not leave behind a company that would be great without *him*. His chosen successor lasted only one year on the job and the next in line faced a management team so shallow that he had to temporarily shoulder four jobs while scrambling to identify a new number two executive.[26] Gault's successors found themselves struggling not only with a management void, but also with strategic voids that would eventually bring the company to its knees.[27]

Of course, you might say, "Yes, Rubbermaid fell apart after Gault, but that just proves his personal greatness as a leader." Exactly! Gault was indeed a tremendous Level 4 leader, perhaps one of the best in the last fifty years. But he was not a Level 5 leader, and that is one key reason why Rubbermaid went from good to great for a brief shining moment and then, just as quickly, went from great to irrelevant.

A Compelling Modesty

In contrast to the very *I*-centric style of the comparison leaders, we were struck by how the good-to-great leaders *didn't* talk about themselves. During interviews with the good-to-great leaders, they'd talk about the company and the contributions of other executives as long as we'd like but would deflect discussion about their own contributions. When pressed to talk about themselves, they'd say things like, "I hope I'm not sounding like a big shot." Or, "If the board hadn't picked such great successors, you probably wouldn't be talking with me today." Or, "Did I have a lot to do with it? Oh, that sounds so self-serving. I don't think I can take much credit. We were blessed with marvelous people." Or, "There are plenty of people in this company who could do my job better than I do."

It wasn't just false modesty. Those who worked with or wrote about the good-to-great leaders continually used words like *quiet, humble, modest, reserved, shy, gracious, mild-mannered, self-effacing, understated, did not believe his own clippings*; and so forth. Board member Jim Hlavacek described Ken Iverson, the CEO who oversaw Nucor's transformation from near bankruptcy to one of the most successful steel companies in the world:

> *Ken is a very modest and humble man. I've never known a person as successful in doing what he's done that's as modest. And, I work for a lot of CEOs of large companies. And that's true in his private life as well. The simplicity of him. I mean little things like he always gets his dogs at the local pound. He has a simple house that's he's lived in for ages. He only has a carport and he complained to me one day about how he had to use his credit card to scrape the frost off his windows and he broke the credit card. "You know, Ken, there's a solution for it; enclose your carport." And he said, "Ah, heck, it isn't that big of a deal. . . . " He's that humble and simple.*[28]

The eleven good-to-great CEOs are some of the most remarkable CEOs of the century, given that only eleven companies from the *Fortune* 500 met the exacting standards for entry into this study. Yet, despite their remarkable results, almost no one ever remarked about them! George Cain, Alan Wurtzel, David Maxwell, Colman Mockler, Darwin Smith, Jim Herring, Lyle Everingham, Joe Cullman, Fred Allen, Cork Walgreen, Carl Reichardt—how many of these extraordinary executives had you heard of?

When we systematically tabulated all 5,979 articles in the study, we found fewer articles surrounding the transition date for the good-to-great companies than for the comparisons, by a factor of two.[29] **Furthermore, we rarely found articles that focused on the good-to-great CEOs.**

The good-to-great leaders never wanted to become larger-than-life heroes. They never aspired to be put on a pedestal or become unreachable icons. They were seemingly ordinary people quietly producing extraordinary results.

Some of the comparison leaders provide a striking contrast. Scott Paper, the comparison company to Kimberly-Clark, hired a CEO named Al Dunlap, a man cut from a very different cloth than Darwin Smith. Dunlap loudly beat on his own chest, telling anyone who would listen (and many who would prefer not to) about what he had accomplished. Quoted in *Business Week* about his nineteen months atop Scott

Paper, he boasted, "The Scott story will go down in the annals of American business history as one of the most successful, quickest turnarounds ever, [making] other turnarounds pale by comparison."[30]

According to *Business Week*, Dunlap personally accrued $100 million for 603 days of work at Scott Paper (that's $165,000 *per day*), largely by slashing the workforce, cutting the R&D budget in half, and putting the company on growth steroids in preparation for sale.[31] After selling off the company and pocketing his quick millions, Dunlap wrote a book about himself, in which he trumpeted his nickname Rambo in Pinstripes. "I love the Rambo movies," he wrote. "Here's a guy who has zero chance of success and always wins. Rambo goes into situations against all odds, expecting to get his brains blown out. But he doesn't. At the end of the day he succeeds, he gets rid of the bad guys. He creates peace out of war. That's what I do, too."[32] Darwin Smith may have enjoyed the mindless Rambo movies as well, but I suspect he never walked out of a theater and said to his wife, "You know, I really relate to this Rambo character; he reminds me of me."

Granted, the Scott Paper story is one of the more dramatic in our study, but it's not an isolated case. In over two thirds of the comparison cases, we noted the presence of a gargantuan personal ego that contributed to the demise or continued mediocrity of the company.[33]

We found this pattern particularly strong in the unsustained comparisons—cases where the company would show a leap in performance under a talented yet egocentric leader, only to decline in later years. Lee Iacocca, for example, saved Chrysler from the brink of catastrophe, performing one of the most celebrated (and deservedly so) turnarounds in American business history. Chrysler rose to a height of 2.9 times the market at a point about halfway through his tenure. Then, however, he diverted his attention to making himself one of the most celebrated CEOs in American business history. *Investor's Business Daily* and the *Wall Street Journal* chronicled how Iacocca appeared regularly on talk shows like the *Today* show and *Larry King Live*, personally starred in over eighty commercials, entertained the idea of running for president of the United States (quoted at one point, "Running Chrysler has been a bigger job than running the country. . . . I could handle the national economy in six months"), and widely promoted his autobiography. The book, *Iacocca*, sold seven million copies and elevated him to rock star status, leading him to be mobbed by thousands of cheering fans upon his arrival in Japan.[34] Iacocca's personal stock soared, but in the second half of his tenure, Chrysler's stock fell 31 percent behind the general market.

Sadly, Iacocca had trouble leaving center stage and letting go of the perks of executive kingship. He postponed his retirement so many times that insiders at Chrysler began to joke that Iacocca stood for "I Am Chairman of Chrysler Corporation Always."[35] And when he did finally retire, he demanded that the board continue to provide a private jet and stock options.[36] Later, he joined forces with noted takeover artist Kirk Kerkorian to launch a hostile takeover bid for Chrysler.[37]

Chrysler experienced a brief return to glory in the five years after Iacocca's retirement, but the company's underlying weaknesses eventually led to a buyout by German carmaker Daimler-Benz.[38] Certainly, the demise of Chrysler as a stand-alone company does not rest entirely on Iacocca's shoulders (the next generation of management made the fateful decision to sell the company to the Germans), but the fact remains: Iacocca's brilliant turnaround in the early 1980s did not prove to be sustained and Chrysler failed to become an enduring great company.

Unwavering Resolve . . . to Do What Must Be Done

It is very important to grasp that Level 5 leadership is not just about humility and modesty. It is equally about ferocious resolve, an almost stoic determination to do whatever needs to be done to make the company great.

Indeed, we debated for a long time on the research team about how to describe the good-to-great leaders. Initially, we penciled in terms like "selfless executive" and "servant leader." But members of the team violently objected to these characterizations.

"Those labels don't ring true," said Anthony Chirikos. "It makes them sound weak or meek, but that's not at all the way I think of Darwin Smith or Colman Mockler. They would do almost anything to make the company great."

Then Eve Li suggested, "Why don't we just call them Level 5 leaders? If we put a label like 'selfless' or 'servant' on them, people will get entirely the wrong idea. We need to get people to engage with the whole concept, to see *both* sides of the coin. If you only get the humility side, you miss the whole idea."

Level 5 leaders are fanatically driven, infected with an incurable need to produce *results*. They will sell the mills or fire their brother, if that's what it takes to make the company great.

When George Cain became CEO of Abbott Laboratories, it sat in the bottom quartile of the pharmaceutical industry, a drowsy enterprise that had lived for years off its cash cow, erythromycin. Cain didn't have an inspiring personality to galvanize the company, but he had something much more powerful: inspired standards. He could not stand mediocrity in any form and was utterly intolerant of anyone who would accept the idea that good is good enough. Cain then set out to destroy one of the key causes of Abbott's mediocrity: nepotism. Systematically rebuilding both the board and the executive team with the best people he could find, Cain made it clear that neither family ties nor length of tenure would have anything to do with whether you held a key position in the company. If you didn't have the capacity to become the best executive in the industry in your span of responsibility, then you would lose your paycheck.[39]

Such rigorous rebuilding might be expected from an outsider brought in to turn the company around, but Cain was an eighteen-year veteran insider *and* a family member, the son of a previous Abbott president. Holiday gatherings were probably tense for a few years in the Cain clan. ("Sorry I had to fire you. Want another slice of turkey?") In the end, though, family members were quite pleased with the performance of their stock, for Cain set in motion a profitable growth machine that, from its transition date in 1974 to 2000, created shareholder returns that beat the market 4.5 to 1, handily outperforming industry superstars Merck and Pfizer.

Upjohn, the direct comparison company to Abbott, also had family leadership during the same era as George Cain. Unlike George Cain, Upjohn's CEO never showed the same resolve to break the mediocrity of nepotism. By the time Abbott had filled all key seats with the best people, regardless of family background, Upjohn still had B level family members holding key positions.[40] Virtually identical companies with identical stock charts up to the point of transition, Upjohn then fell 89 percent behind Abbott over the next twenty-one years before capitulating in a merger to Pharmacia in 1995.

As an interesting aside, Darwin Smith, Colman Mockler, and George Cain came from inside the company. Stanley Gault, Al Dunlap, and Lee Iacocca rode in as saviors from the outside, trumpets blaring. This reflects a more systematic finding from our study. The evidence does not support the idea that you need an outside leader to come in and shake up the place to go from good to great. In fact, going for a high-profile outside change agent is *negatively correlated* with a sustained transformation from good to great.

Ten out of eleven good-to-great CEOs came from inside the company, three of them by family inheritance. The comparison companies turned to outsiders with six times greater frequency—yet they failed to produce sustained great results.[41]

A superb example of insider-driven change comes from Charles R. "Cork" Walgreen 3rd, who transformed dowdy Walgreens into a company that outperformed the stock market by over fifteen times from the end of 1975 to January 1, 2000.[42] After years of dialogue and debate within his executive team about Walgreens' food-service operations, Cork sensed that the team had finally reached a watershed point of clarity and understanding: Walgreens' brightest future lay in convenient drugstores, not food service. Dan Jorndt, who succeeded Walgreen as CEO in 1998, described what happened next:

> *Cork said at one of our planning committee meetings, "Okay, now I am going to draw the line in the sand. We are going to be out of the restaurant business completely in five years." At the time, we had over five hundred restaurants. You could have heard a pin drop. He said, "I want to let everybody know the clock is ticking. . . . " Six months later, we were at our next planning committee meeting and someone mentioned just in passing that we only had five years to be out of the restaurant business. Cork was not a real vociferous fellow. He sort of tapped on the table and said, "Listen, you have four and a half years. I said you had five years six months ago. Now you've got four and a half years." Well, that next day, things really clicked into gear to winding down our restaurant business. He never wavered. He never doubted; he never second-guessed.*[43]

Like Darwin Smith selling the mills at Kimberly-Clark, Cork Walgreen's decision required stoic resolve. Not that food service was the largest part of the business (although it did add substantial profits to the bottom line). The real problem was more emotional. Walgreens had, after all, invented the malted milkshake and food service was a long-standing family tradition dating back to his grandfather. Some food-service outlets were even named after the CEO himself—a restaurant chain named Corky's. But no matter, if Walgreens had to fly in the face of long-standing family tradition in order to focus its resources where it could be the best in the world (convenient drugstores), Cork would do it. Quietly, doggedly, simply.[44]

The quiet, dogged nature of Level 5 leaders showed up not only in big decisions, like selling off the food-service operations or fighting corporate raiders, but also in a personal style of sheer workmanlike diligence. Alan Wurtzel, a second-generation family member who took over his family's small company and turned it into Circuit City, perfectly captured the gestalt of this trait. When asked about differences between himself and his counterpart CEO at Circuit City's comparison company, Wurtzel summed up: "The show horse and the plow horse—he was more of a show horse, whereas I was more of a plow horse."[45]

The Window and the Mirror

Alan Wurtzel's plow horse comment is fascinating in light of two other facts. First, he holds a doctor of jurisprudence degree from Yale—clearly, his plow horse nature had nothing to do with a lack of intelligence. Second, his plow horse approach set the stage for truly *best in show* results. Let me put it this way: If you had to choose between $1 invested in Circuit City or $1 invested in General Electric on the day that the legendary Jack Welch took over GE in 1981 and held to January 1, 2000, you would have been better off with Circuit City—by six times.[46] Not a bad performance, for a plow horse.

You might expect that extraordinary results like these would lead Alan Wurtzel to discuss the brilliant decisions he made. But when we asked him to list the top five factors in his company's transformation, ranked by importance, Wurtzel gave a surprising answer: The number one factor was *luck*. "We were in a great industry, with the wind at our backs."

We pushed back, pointing out that we selected the good-to-great companies based on performance that surpassed their industry's average. Furthermore, the comparison company (Silo) was in the same industry, with the same wind and probably bigger sails! We debated the point for a few minutes, with Wurtzel continuing his preference for attributing much of his success to just being in the right place at the right time. Later, when asked to discuss the factors behind the enduring nature of the transformation, he said, "The first thing that comes to mind is luck. . . . I was lucky to find the right successor."[47]

Luck. What an odd factor to talk about. Yet the good-to-great executives talked a lot about luck in our interviews. In one interview with a Nucor executive, we asked why the company had such a remarkable track record of good decisions; he responded: "I guess we were just lucky."[48] Joseph F. Cullman 3rd, the Level 5 transition CEO of Philip Morris, flat-out refused to take credit for his company's success, attributing his good fortune to having great colleagues, successors, and predecessors.[49] Even the book he wrote—a book he undertook at the urging of his colleagues, which he never intended to distribute widely outside the company—had the unusual title *I'm a Lucky Guy*. The opening paragraph reads: "I was a very lucky guy from the very beginning of my life: marvelous parents, good genes, lucky in love, lucky in business, and lucky when a Yale classmate had my orders changed to report to Washington, D.C., in early 1941, instead of to a ship that was sunk with all hands lost in the North Atlantic, lucky to be in the Navy, and lucky to be alive at eighty-five."[50]

We were at first puzzled by this emphasis on good luck. After all, we found no evidence that the good-to-great companies were blessed with more good luck (or more bad luck, for that matter) than the comparison companies. Then we began to notice a contrasting pattern in the comparison executives: They credited substantial blame to *bad* luck, frequently bemoaning the difficulties of the environment they faced.

Compare Bethlehem Steel to Nucor. Both companies operated in the steel industry and produced hard-to-differentiate products. Both companies faced the competitive challenge of cheap imported steel. Yet executives at the two companies had completely different views of the same environment. Bethlehem Steel's CEO summed up the company's problems in 1983 by blaming imports: "Our first, second, and third problems are imports."[51] Ken Iverson and his crew at Nucor considered the same challenge from imports a *blessing*, a stroke of good fortune ("Aren't we lucky; steel is heavy, and they have to ship it all the way across the ocean, giving us a huge advantage!"). Iverson saw the first, second, and third problems facing the American steel industry not to be imports, but *management*.[52] He even went so far as to speak out publicly against government protection against imports, telling a stunned gathering of fellow steel executives in 1977 that the real problems facing the American steel industry lay in the fact that management had failed to keep pace with innovation.[53]

The emphasis on luck turns out to be part of a pattern that we came to call *the window and the mirror.*

Level 5 leaders look out the window to apportion credit to factors outside themselves when things go well (and if they cannot find a specific person or event to give credit to, they credit good luck). At

the same time, they look in the mirror to apportion responsibility, never blaming bad luck when things go poorly.

The comparison leaders did just the opposite. They'd look out the window for something or someone outside themselves to blame for poor results, but would preen in front of the mirror and credit themselves when things went well. Strangely, the window and the mirror do not reflect objective reality. Everyone outside the window points inside, directly at the Level 5 leader, saying, "He was the key; without his guidance and leadership, we would not have become a great company." And the Level 5 leader points right back out the window and says, "Look at all the great people and good fortune that made this possible; I'm a lucky guy." They're both right, of course. But the Level 5s would never admit that fact.

Cultivating Level 5 Leadership

Not long ago, I shared the Level 5 finding with a gathering of senior executives. A woman who had recently become chief executive of her company raised her hand and said, "I believe what you say about the good-to-great leaders. But I'm disturbed because when I look in the mirror, I know that I'm not Level 5, not yet anyway. Part of the reason I got this job is because of my ego drives. Are you telling me that I can't make this a great company if I'm not Level 5?"

"I don't know for certain that you absolutely must be a Level 5 leader to make your company great," I replied. "I will simply point back to the data: Of 1,435 companies that appeared on the *Fortune* 500 in our initial candidate list, only eleven made the very tough cut into our study. In those eleven, all of them had Level 5 leadership in key positions, including the CEO, at the pivotal time of transition."

She sat there, quiet for moment, and you could tell everyone in the room was mentally urging her to ask *the question.* Finally, she said, "Can you learn to become Level 5?"

Summary: The Two Sides of Level 5 Leadership

Professional Will	Personal Humility
Creates superb results, a clear catalyst in the transition from good to great.	Demonstrates a compelling modesty, shunning public adulation; never boastful.
Demonstrates an unwavering resolve to do whatever must be done to produce the best long-term results, no matter how difficult.	Acts with quiet, calm determination; relies principally on inspired standards, not inspiring charisma, to motivate.
Sets the standard of building an enduring great company; will settle for nothing less.	Channels ambition into the company, not the self; sets up successors for even greater success in the next generation.
Looks in the mirror, not out the window, to apportion responsibility for poor results, never blaming other people, external factors, or bad luck.	Looks out the window, not in the mirror, to apportion credit for the success of the company—to other people, external factors, and good luck.

My hypothesis is that there are two categories of people: Those who do not have the seed of Level 5 and those who do. The first category consists of people who could never in a million years bring themselves to subjugate their egoistic needs to the greater ambition of building something larger and more lasting than themselves. For these people, work will always be first and foremost about what they *get*—fame, fortune, adulation, power, whatever—not what they *build*, create, and contribute.

> **The great irony is that the animus and personal ambition that often drive people to positions of power stand at odds with the humility required for Level 5 leadership. When you combine that irony with the fact that boards of directors frequently operate under the false belief that they need to hire a larger-than-life, egocentric leader to make an organization great, you can quickly see why Level 5 leaders rarely appear at the top of our institutions.**

The second category of people—and I suspect the larger group—consists of those who have the potential to evolve to Level 5; the capability resides within them, perhaps buried or ignored, but there nonetheless. And under the right circumstances—self-reflection, conscious personal development, a mentor, a great teacher, loving parents, a significant life experience, a Level 5 boss, or any number of other factors—they begin to develop.

In looking at the data, we noticed that some of the leaders in our study had significant life experiences that might have sparked or furthered their maturation. Darwin Smith fully blossomed after his experience with cancer. Joe Cullman was profoundly affected by his World War II experiences, particularly the last-minute change of orders that took him off a doomed ship on which he surely would have died.[54] A strong religious belief or conversion might also nurture development of Level 5 traits. Colman Mockler, for example, converted to evangelical Christianity while getting his MBA at Harvard, and later, according to the book *Cutting Edge,* became a prime mover in a group of Boston business executives who met frequently over breakfast to discuss the carryover of religious values to corporate life.[55] Other leaders in our study, however, had no obvious catalytic event; they just led normal lives and somehow ended up atop the Level 5 hierarchy.

I believe—although I cannot prove—that potential Level 5 leaders are highly prevalent in our society. *The problem is not, in my estimation, a dearth of potential Level 5 leaders. They exist all around us, if we just know what to look for.* And what is that? Look for situations where extraordinary results exist but where no individual steps forth to claim excess credit. You will likely find a potential Level 5 leader at work.

For your own development, I would love to be able to give you a list of steps for becoming Level 5, but we have no solid research data that would support a credible list. Our research exposed Level 5 as a key component inside the black box of what it takes to shift a *company* from good to great. Yet inside that black box is yet another black box—namely, the inner development of a *person* to Level 5. We could speculate on what might be inside that inner black box, but it would mostly be just that—speculation. So, in short, Level 5 is a very satisfying idea, a powerful idea, and, to produce the best transitions from good to great, perhaps an essential idea. A "Ten-Step List to Level 5" would trivialize the concept.

My best advice, based on the research, is to begin practicing the other good-to-great disciplines we discovered. We found a symbiotic relationship between Level 5 and the remaining findings. On the one hand, Level 5 traits enable you to implement the other findings; on the other hand, practicing the other findings helps you to become Level 5. Think of it this way: This chapter is about what Level 5s *are*; the rest of the book describes what they *do*. Leading with the other disciplines can help you move in the right direction. There is no guarantee that doing so will turn you into a full-fledged Level 5, but it gives you a tangible place to begin.

Level 5 Leadership

KEY POINTS

- Every good-to-great company had Level 5 leadership during the pivotal transition years.
- "Level 5" refers to a five-level hierarchy of executive capabilities, with Level 5 at the top. Level 5 leaders embody a paradoxical mix of personal humility and professional will. They are ambitious, to be sure, but ambitious first and foremost for the company, not themselves.
- Level 5 leaders set up their successors for even greater success in the next generation, whereas egocentric Level 4 leaders often set up their successors for failure.
- Level 5 leaders display a compelling modesty, are self-effacing and understated. In contrast, two thirds of the comparison companies had leaders with gargantuan personal egos that contributed to the demise or continued mediocrity of the company.
- Level 5 leaders are fanatically driven, infected with an incurable need to produce sustained *results*. They are resolved to do whatever it takes to make the company great, no matter how big or hard the decisions.
- Level 5 leaders display a workmanlike diligence—more plow horse than show horse.
- Level 5 leaders look out the window to attribute success to factors other than themselves. When things go poorly, however, they look in the mirror and blame themselves, taking full responsibility. The comparison CEOs often did just the opposite—they looked in the mirror to take credit for success, but out the window to assign blame for disappointing results.
- One of the most damaging trends in recent history is the tendency (especially by boards of directors) to select dazzling, celebrity leaders and to de-select potential Level 5 leaders.
- I believe that potential Level 5 leaders exist all around us, if we just know what to look for, and that many people have the potential to evolve into Level 5.

UNEXPECTED FINDINGS

- Larger-than-life, celebrity leaders who ride in from the outside are negatively correlated with going from good to great. Ten of 11 good-to-great CEOs came from *inside* the company, whereas the comparison companies tried outside CEOs six times more often.
- Level 5 leaders attribute much of their success to good luck, rather than personal greatness.
- We were not looking for Level 5 leadership in our research, or anything like it, but the data was overwhelming and convincing. It is an empirical, not an ideological, finding.

We cannot say for sure what percentage of people have the seed within, or how many of those can nurture it. Even those of us who discovered Level 5 on the research team do not know for ourselves whether we will succeed in fully evolving to Level 5. And yet, all of us who worked on the finding have been deeply affected and inspired by the idea. Darwin Smith, Colman Mockler, Alan Wurtzel, and all the other Level 5s we learned about have become models for us, something worthy to aspire toward. Whether or not we make it all the way to Level 5, it is worth the effort. For like all basic truths about what is best in human beings, when we catch a glimpse of that truth, we know that our own lives and all that we touch will be the better for the effort.

Endnotes

1. David McCullough, *Truman* (New York: Simon and Schuster, 1992): 564.
2. Robert Spector, based on research and a manuscript by William W. Wicks, *Shared Values: A History of Kimberly-Clark* (Connecticut: Greenwich Publishing Group, 1997): 101.
3. "Darwin Smith May Have Done Too Good a Job," *Business Week*, August 1, 1988, 57; "Rae Takes On the Paper Industry's Tough Lone Wolf," *Globe and Mail*, July 20, 1991; "Former CEO of K-C Dies," *Dallas Morning News*, December 27, 1995, 1D.
4. Research Interview #5-E, page 26.
5. Research Interview #5-E, page 26.
6. "Darwin Smith May Have Done Too Good a Job," *Business Week*, August 1, 1988: 57.
7. "Darwin Smith May Have Done Too Good a Job," *Business Week*, August 1, 1988: 57; "Kimberly-Clark Bets, Wins on Innovation," *Wall Street Journal*, November 22,

1991: A5; "Darwin E. Smith, 69, Executive Who Remade a Paper Company," *New York Times*, December 28, 1995: B9; Robert Spector, based on research and a manuscript by William W. Wicks, *Shared Values: A History of Kimberly-Clark* (Connecticut: Greenwich Publishing Group, 1997): 101.

8. Robert Spector, based on research and a manuscript by William W. Wicks, *Shared Values: A History of Kimberly-Clark* (Connecticut: Greenwich Publishing Group, 1997): 112.

9. *International Directory of Company Histories*, Vol. 3 (Chicago: St. James Press, 1991): 40; "Kimberly-Clark—Aiming for the Consumer," *Financial World*, April 1, 1970: 15.

10. Robert Spector, based on research and a manuscript by William W. Wicks, *Shared Values: A History of Kimberly-Clark* (Connecticut: Greenwich Publishing Group, 1997): 106, 112; "Darwin E. Smith, 69, Executive Who Remade a Paper Company," *New York Times*, December 28, 1995: B9; "Former CEO of K-C Dies," *Dallas Morning News*, December 27, 1995: 1D; Research Interview #5-E, page 6; "Paper Tiger: How Kimberly-Clark Wraps Its Bottom Line in Disposable Huggies," *Wall Street Journal*, July 23, 1987: 1.

11. "The Battle of the Bottoms," *Forbes*, March 24, 1997: 98.

12. "The Battle of the Bottoms," *Forbes*, March 24, 1997: 98.

13. Robert Spector, based on research and a manuscript by William W. Wicks, *Shared Values: A History of Kimberly-Clark* (Connecticut: Greenwich Publishing Group, 1997): 10.

14. Shelby Foote, *The Civil War: A Narrative: Red River to Appomattox* (New York: Random House, 1975): 1040; James M. McPherson, *Battle Cry of Freedom: The Civil War Era* (New York: Ballantine Books, 1989): 854.

15. Gordon McKibben, *Cutting Edge: Gillette's Journey to Global Leadership* (Boston: Harvard Business School Press, 1998): 14.

16. Company "Chronology," Gillette corporate typescript, 1995; Gordon McKibben, *Cutting Edge: Gillette's Journey to Global Leadership* (Boston: Harvard Business School Press, 1998): 198, 199; Rita Ricardo-Campbell, *Resisting Hostile Takeovers: The Case of Gillette* (Connecticut: Praeger Publishers, 1997): 153.

17. Gordon McKibben, *Cutting Edge: Gillette's Journey to Global Leadership* (Boston: Harvard Business School Press, 1998): 159.

18. Rita Ricardo-Campbell, *Resisting Hostile Takeovers: The Case of Gillette* (Connecticut: Praeger Publishers, 1997).

19. Author conversation with Gillette CEO, summer 2000. "We invested almost $1.5 billion in Sensor and Mach 3. We believed that these projects would have been scrapped had the takeover happened."

20. Gordon McKibben, *Cutting Edge: Gillette's Journey to Global Leadership* (Boston: Harvard Business School Press, 1998): 158. Calculations run using CRSP data.

21. Gordon McKibben, *Cutting Edge: Gillette's Journey to Global Leadership* (Boston: Harvard Business School Press, 1998): 254.

22. "Maxwell Relinquishes Rights to $5.5 Million Final Retirement Payment," *PR Newswire*, January 21, 1992; "$5.5 Million Declined by Ex-Official," *Washington Post*, January 22; 1992: F1.

23. "Iacocca's Last Stand," *Fortune*, April 20, 1992: 63.

24. "Sincere Tyranny," *Forbes*, January 28, 1985: 54.

25. "Managing: Leaders of Corporate Change," *Fortune*, December 14, 1992: 104.

26. "Chairman Quits Post," *New York Times*, November 17, 1992, D5; "Rubbermaid's Sad Succession Tale," *New York Times*, July 5, 1987: C1.

27. "Is Rubbermaid Reacting Too Late?" *New York Times*, December 22, 1996: A1.

28. Research Interview #7-D, page 17.

29. Chris Jones and Duane Duffy, "Media Hype Analysis" (unpublished), *Good to Great* research project, summers 1998: 1999.

30. "Did CEO Dunlap Save Scott Paper—or Just Pretty It Up? The Shredder," *Business Week*, January 15, 1996.

31. "Did CEO Dunlap Save Scott Paper—or Just Pretty It Up? The Shredder," *Business Week*, January 15, 1996; "Chain Saw Al to the Rescue?" *Forbes*, August 26, 1996; "After the Fall," *Across the Board*, April 1996: 28–33; "Only the Paranoid Survive," *Worth Online*, October 1996; Albert J. Dunlap with Bob Andelman, *Mean Business: How I Save Bad Companies and Make Good Companies Great* (New York: Fireside, 1997): 20.

32. Albert J. Dunlap with Bob Andelman, *Mean Business: How I Save Bad Companies and Make Good Companies Great* (New York: Fireside, 1997): 132.

33. The cases where a charismatic CEO eventually became a liability for the company were Great Western, Warner-Lambert, Scott Paper, Bethlehem Steel, R. J Reynolds, Addressograph-Multigraph, Eckerd, Bank of America, Burroughs, Chrysler, Rubbermaid, and Teledyne.

34. "President Iacocca," *Wall Street Journal*, July 28, 1982: 1; "Iacocca Hands Over the Keys to Chrysler," *Investor's Business Daily*, January 4, 1993: 1.

35. "Iacocca Hands Over the Keys to Chrysler," *Investor's Business Daily*, January 4, 1993: 1.

36. "How Chrysler Filled Detroit's Biggest Shoes," *Wall Street Journal*, September 7, 1994: B1.

37. "Why Certain Stocks Appear To Be Worth More Than Their Price," *Wall Street Journal*, April 13, 1995, A1; "Chrysler's New Plan: Sell Cars," *Fortune*, June 26, 1995: 19.

38. "Will Success Spoil Chrysler?" *Fortune*, January 10, 1994; "Company of the Year: Chrysler Has the Hot Cars. More Important, It Has a Smart, Disciplined Management Team," *Forbes*, January 13, 1997: 82; "Daimler-Benz Will Acquire Chrysler in $36 Billion Deal That Will Reshape Industry," *New York Times*, May 7, 1998: A6.

39. Research Interview #1-A, page 3; Research Interview #1-G, page 35; "A Drugmaker's Return to Health," *Business Week*, April 26, 1976: 38; Herman Kogan, *The Long White Line: The Story of Abbott Laboratories* (New York: Random House, 1963): 249.

40. The Upjohn Company, *International Directory of Company Histories*, 707; "The Medicine Men of Kalamazoo," *Fortune*, July 1959: 106.

41. Leigh Wilbanks, "CEO Analysis Unit" (unpublished), *Good to Great* research project, summer 1998.

42. University of Chicago Center for Research in Securities Prices data, all dividends reinvested and adjusted for stock splits.

43. Research Interview #10-D, pages 9–10.

44. Herman Kogan and Rick Kogan, *Pharmacist to the Nation* (Deerfield, Ill.: Walgreens Company, 1989), 236; Research Interview #10-F, page 3.

45. Research Interview #2-G, page 10.

46. University of Chicago Center for Research in Securities Prices data, all dividends reinvested and adjusted for stock splits.

47. Research Interview #2-G, page 16.

48. Research Interview #7-H, page 12.

49. Research Interview #8-A, pages 4–5, 9, 10.

50. Joseph F. Cullman 3rd, *I'm a Lucky Guy* (Joseph F. Cullman 3rd, 1998): 1.

51. "Searching for Profits at Bethlehem," *New York Times*, December 25, 1983: C1.

52. "Steel Man Ken Iverson," *Inc.*, April 1, 1986: 40.

53. Jeffrey L. Rodengen, *The Legend of the Nucor Corporation* (Fort Lauderdale, Fla.: Write Stuff Enterprises, 1997): 71.

54. Joseph F. Cullman 3rd, *I'm a Lucky Guy* (Joseph F. Cullman 3rd, 1998).

55. Gordon McKibben, *Cutting Edge: Gillette's Journey to Global Leadership* (Boston: Harvard Business School Press, 1998): 78–79.

IN PRAISE OF THE INCOMPLETE LEADER*

Deborah Ancona

Thomas W. Malone

Wanda J. Orlikowski

Peter M. Senge

We've come to expect a lot of our leaders. Top executives, the thinking goes, should have the intellectual capacity to make sense of unfathomably complex issues, the imaginative powers to paint a vision of the future that generates everyone's enthusiasm, the operational know-how to translate strategy into concrete plans, and the interpersonal skills to foster commitment to undertakings that could cost people's jobs should they fail. Unfortunately, no single person can possibly live up to those standards.

It's time to end the myth of the complete leader: the flawless person at the top who's got it all figured out. In fact, the sooner leaders stop trying to be all things to all people, the better off their organizations will be. In today's world, the executive's job is no longer to command and control but to cultivate and coordinate the actions of others at all levels of the organization. Only when leaders come to see themselves as incomplete—as having both strengths and weaknesses—will they be able to make up for their missing skills by relying on others.

Corporations have been becoming less hierarchical and more collaborative for decades, of course, as globalization and the growing importance of knowledge work have required that responsibility and initiative be distributed more widely. Moreover, it is now possible for large groups of people to coordinate their actions, not just by bringing lots of information to a few centralized places but also by bringing lots of information to lots of places through ever-growing networks within and beyond the firm. The sheer complexity and ambiguity of problems is humbling. More and more decisions are made in the context of global markets and rapidly—sometimes radically—changing financial, social, political, technological, and environmental forces. Stakeholders such as activists, regulators, and employees all have claims on organizations.

*Reprinted by permission of *Harvard Business Review*. From "In Praise of the Incomplete Leader" by Deborah Ancona, Thomas W. Malone, Wanda J. Orlikowski, and Peter M. Senge, February 2007, pp. 92–100. Copyright © 2007 by the Harvard Business School Publishing Corporation; all rights reserved.

No one person could possibly stay on top of everything. But the myth of the complete leader (and the attendant fear of appearing incompetent) makes many executives try to do just that, exhausting themselves and damaging their organizations in the process. The incomplete leader, by contrast, knows when to let go: when to let those who know the local market do the advertising plan or when to let the engineering team run with its idea of what the customer needs. The incomplete leader also knows that leadership exists throughout the organizational hierarchy—wherever expertise, vision, new ideas, and commitment are found.

We've worked with hundreds of people who have struggled under the weight of the myth of the complete leader. Over the past six years, our work at the MIT Leadership Center has included studying leadership in many organizations and teaching the topic to senior executives, middle managers, and MBA students. In our practice-based programs, we have analyzed numerous accounts of organizational change and watched leaders struggle to meld top-down strategic initiatives with vibrant ideas from the rest of the organization.

All this work has led us to develop a model of distributed leadership. This framework, which synthesizes our own research with ideas from other leadership scholars, views leadership as a set of four capabilities: *sensemaking* (understanding the context in which a company and its people operate), *relating* (building relationships within and across organizations), *visioning* (creating a compelling picture of the future), and *inventing* (developing new ways to achieve the vision).

While somewhat simplified, these capabilities span the intellectual and interpersonal, the rational and intuitive, and the conceptual and creative capacities required in today's business environment. Rarely, if ever, will someone be equally skilled in all four domains. Thus, incomplete leaders differ from incompetent leaders in that they understand what they're good at and what they're not and have good judgment about how they can work with others to build on their strengths and offset their limitations.

Sometimes, leaders need to further develop the capabilities they are weakest in. The exhibits throughout this article provide some suggestions for when and how to do that. Other times, however, it's more important for leaders to find and work with others to compensate for their weaknesses. Teams and organizations—not just individuals—can use this framework to diagnose their strengths and weaknesses and find ways to balance their skill sets.

Sensemaking

The term "sensemaking" was coined by organizational psychologist Karl Weick, and it means just what it sounds like: making sense of the world around us. Leaders are constantly trying to understand the contexts they are operating in. How will new technologies reshape the industry? How will changing cultural expectations shift the role of business in society? How does the globalization of labor markets affect recruitment and expansion plans?

Weick likened the process of sensemaking to cartography. What we map depends on where we look, what factors we choose to focus on, and what aspects of the terrain we decide to represent. Since these choices will shape the kind of map we produce, there is no perfect map of a terrain. Therefore, making sense is more than an act of analysis; it's an act of creativity. (See the exhibit "Engage in Sensemaking.")

The key for leaders is to determine what would be a useful map given their particular goals and then to draw one that adequately represents the situation the organization is facing at that moment. Executives who are strong in this capability know how to quickly capture the complexities of their environment and explain them to others in simple terms. This helps ensure that everyone is working from the same map, which makes it far easier to discuss and plan for the journey ahead. Leaders need to have the courage to present a map that highlights features they believe to be critical, even if their map doesn't conform to the dominant perspective.

When John Reed was CEO of Citibank, the company found itself in a real estate crisis. At the time, common wisdom said that Citibank would need to take a $2 billion write-off, but Reed wasn't sure. He wanted a better understanding of the situation, so to map the problem, he met with federal regulators as well as his managers, the board, potential investors, economists, and real estate experts. He kept asking, "What am I missing here?" After those meetings, he had a much stronger grasp of the problem, and he recalibrated the write-off to $5 billion—which turned out to be a far more accurate estimate. Later, three quarters into the bank's eight-quarter program to deal with the crisis, Reed realized that progress had stopped. He began talking to other CEOs known for their change management skills. This informal benchmarking process led him to devise an organizational redesign.

Throughout the crisis, real estate valuations, investors' requirements, board demands, and management team expectations were all changing and constantly needed to be reassessed. Good leaders understand that sensemaking is a continuous process; they let the map emerge from a melding of observations, data, experiences, conversations, and analyses. In healthy organizations, this sort of sensemaking goes on all the time. People have ongoing dialogues about their interpretations of markets and organizational realities.

At IDEO, a product design firm, sensemaking is step one for all design teams. According to founder David Kelley, team members must act as anthropologists studying an alien culture to understand the potential product from all points of view. When brainstorming a new design, IDEO's teams consider multiple perspectives—that is, they build multiple maps to inform their creative process. One IDEO team was charged with creating a new design for an emergency room. To better understand the experience of a key stakeholder—the patient-team members attached a camera to a patient's head and captured his experience in the ER. The result: nearly ten full hours of film of the ceiling. The sensemaking provoked by this perspective led to a redesign of the ceiling that made it more aesthetically pleasing and able to display important information for patients.

Engage in Sensemaking

1. Get data from multiple sources: customers, suppliers, employees, competitors, other departments, and investors.
2. Involve others in your sensemaking. Say what you think you are seeing, and check with people who have different perspectives from yours.
3. Use early observations to shape small experiments in order to test your conclusions. Look for new ways to articulate alternatives and better ways to understand options.
4. Do not simply apply existing frameworks but instead be open to new possibilities. Try not to describe the world in stereotypical ways, such as good guys and bad guys, victims and oppressors, or marketers and engineers.

Relating

Many executives who attempt to foster trust, optimism, and consensus often reap anger, cynicism, and conflict instead. That's because they have difficulty relating to others, especially those who don't make sense of the world the way they do. Traditional images of leadership didn't assign much value to relating. Flawless leaders shouldn't need to seek counsel from anyone outside their tight inner circle, the thinking went, and they were expected to issue edicts rather than connect on an emotional level. Times have changed, of course, and in this era of networks, being able to build trusting relationships is a requirement of effective leadership.

Three key ways to do this are *inquiring, advocating,* and *connecting.* The concepts of inquiring and advocating stem from the work of organizational development specialists Chris Argyris and Don Schon. Inquiring means listening with the intention of genuinely understanding the thoughts and feelings of the speaker. Here, the listener suspends judgment and tries to comprehend how and why the speaker has moved from the data of his or her experiences to particular interpretations and conclusions.

Advocating, as the term implies, means explaining one's own point of view. It is the flip side of inquiring, and it's how leaders make clear to others how they reached their interpretations and conclusions. Good leaders distinguish their observations from their opinions and judgments and explain their reasoning without aggression or defensiveness. People with strong relating skills are typically those who've found a healthy balance between inquiring and advocating: They actively try to understand others' views but are able to stand up for their own. (See the exhibit "Build Relationships.")

We've seen countless relationships undermined because people disproportionately emphasized advocating over inquiring. Even though managers pay lip service to the importance of mutual understanding and shared commitment to a course of action, often their real focus is on winning the argument rather than strengthening the connection. Worse, in many organizations, the imbalance goes so far that having one's point of view prevail is what is understood as leadership.

Effective relating does not mean avoiding interpersonal conflict altogether. Argyris and Schon found that "maintaining a smooth surface" of conviviality and apparent agreement is one of the most common defensive routines that limits team effectiveness. Balancing inquiring and advocating is ultimately about showing respect, challenging opinions, asking tough questions, and taking a stand.

Consider Twynstra Gudde (TG), one of the largest independent consulting companies in the Netherlands. A few years ago, it replaced the role of CEO with a team of four managing directors who share leadership responsibilities. Given this unique structure, it's vital that these directors effectively relate to one another. They've adopted simple rules, such as a requirement that each leader give his opinion on every issue, majority-rules voting, and veto power for each director.

Clearly, for TG's senior team model to work, members must be skilled at engaging in dialogue together. They continually practice both inquiring and advocating, and because each director can veto a decision, each must thoroughly explain his reasoning to convince the others' that his perspective has merit. It's not easy to reach this level of mutual respect and trust, but over time, the team members' willingness to create honest connections with one another has paid off handsomely. Although they don't always reach consensus, they are able to settle on a course of action. Since this new form of leadership was introduced, TG has thrived: The company's profits have doubled, and employee satisfaction levels have improved. What's more, TG's leadership structure has served as a model for cooperation throughout the organization as well as in the firm's relations with its clients.

The third aspect of relating, connecting, involves cultivating a network of confidants who can help a leader accomplish a wide range of goals. Leaders who are strong in this capability have many people they can turn to who can help them think through difficult problems or support them in their initiatives. They understand that the time spent building and maintaining these connections is time spent investing in their leadership skills. Because no one person can possibly have all the answers, or indeed, know all the right questions to ask, it's crucial that leaders be able to tap into a network of people who can fill in the gaps.

Build Relationships

1. Spend time trying to understand others' perspectives, listening with an open mind and without judgment.
2. Encourage others to voice their opinions. What do they care about? How do they interpret what's going on? Why?
3. Before expressing your ideas, try to anticipate how others will react to them and how you might best explain them.
4. When expressing your ideas, don't just give a bottom line; explain your reasoning process.
5. Assess the strengths of your current connections: How well do you relate to others when receiving advice? When giving advice? When thinking through difficult problems? When asking for help?

Visioning

Sensemaking and relating can be called the enabling capabilities of leadership. They help set the conditions that motivate and sustain change. The next two leadership capabilities–what we call "visioning" and inventing–are creative and action oriented: They produce the focus and energy needed to make change happen.

Visioning involves creating compelling images of the future. While sensemaking charts a map of what is, visioning produces a map of what could be and, more important, what a leader wants the future to be. It consists of far more than pinning a vision statement to the wall. Indeed, a shared vision is not a static thing—it's an ongoing process. Like sensemaking, visioning is dynamic and collaborative, a process of articulating what the members of an organization want to create together.

Fundamentally, visioning gives people a sense of meaning in their work. Leaders who are skilled in this capability are able to get people excited about their view of the future while inviting others to help crystallize that image. (See the exhibit "Create a Vision.") If they realize other people aren't joining in or buying into the vision, they don't just turn up the volume; they engage in a dialogue about the reality they hope to produce. They use stories and metaphors to paint a vivid picture of what the vision will accomplish, even if they don't have a comprehensive plan for getting there. They know that if the vision is credible and compelling enough, others will generate ideas to advance it.

In South Africa in the early 1990s, a joke was making the rounds: Given the country's daunting challenges, people had two options, one practical and the other miraculous. The practical option was for everyone to pray for a band of angels to come down from heaven and fix things. The miraculous option was for people to talk with one another until they could find a way forward. In F.W. de Klerk's famous speech in 1990—his first after assuming leadership—he called for a nonracist South Africa and suggested that negotiation was the only way to achieve a peaceful transition. That speech sparked a set of changes that led to Nelson Mandela's release from Robben Island prison and the return to the country of previously banned political leaders.

Create a Vision

1. Practice creating a vision in many arenas, including your work life, your home life, and in community groups. Ask yourself, "What do I want to create?"
2. Develop a vision about something that inspires you. Your enthusiasm will motivate you and others. Listen to what they find exciting and important.
3. Expect that not all people will share your passion. Be prepared to explain why people should care about your vision and what can be achieved through it. If people don't get it, don't just turn up the volume. Try to construct a shared vision.
4. Don't worry if you don't know how to accomplish the vision. If it is compelling and credible, other people will discover all sorts of ways to make it real—ways you never could have imagined on your own.
5. Use images, metaphors, and stories to convey complex situations that will enable others to act.

Few of South Africa's leaders agreed on much of anything regarding the country's future. It seemed like a long shot, at best, that a scenario-planning process convened by a black professor from the University of the Western Cape and facilitated by a white Canadian from Royal Dutch Shell would be able to bring about any sort of change. But they, together with members of the African National Congress (ANC), the radical Pan Africanist Congress (PAC), and the white business community, were charged with forging a new path for South Africa.

When the team members first met, they focused on collective sensemaking. Their discussions then evolved into a yearlong visioning process. In his book, *Solving Tough Problems,* Adam Kahane, the facilitator, says the group started by telling stories of "left-wing revolution, right-wing revolts, and free market Utopias." Eventually, the leadership team drafted a set of scenarios that described the many paths toward disaster and the one toward sustainable development.

They used metaphors and clear imagery to convey the various paths in language that was easy to understand. One negative scenario, for instance, was dubbed "Ostrich": A nonrepresentative white government sticks its head in the sand, trying to avoid a negotiated settlement with the black majority. Another negative scenario was labeled "Icarus": A constitutionally unconstrained black government comes to power with noble intentions and embarks on a huge, unsustainable public-spending spree that crashes the economy. This scenario contradicted the popular belief that the country was rich and could simply redistribute wealth from whites to blacks. The Icarus scenario set the stage for a fundamental (and controversial) shift in economic thinking in the ANC and other left-wing parties—a shift that led the ANC government to "strict and consistent fiscal discipline," according to Kahane.

The group's one positive scenario involved the government adopting a set of sustainable policies that would put the country on a path of inclusive growth to successfully rebuild the economy and establish democracy. This option was called "Flamingo," invoking the image of a flock of beautiful birds all taking flight together.

This process of visioning unearthed an extraordinary collective sense of possibility in South Africa. Instead of talking about what other people should do to advance some agenda, the leaders spoke about what they could do to create a better future for everyone. They didn't have an exact implementation plan at the ready, but by creating a credible vision, they paved the way for others to join in and help make their vision a reality.

Leaders who excel in visioning walk the walk; they work to embody the core values and ideas contained in the vision. Darcy Winslow, Nike's global director for women's footwear, is a good example. A 14-year veteran at Nike, Winslow previously held the position of general manager of sustainable business opportunities at the shoe and apparel giant. Her work in that role reflected her own core values, including her passion for the environment. "We had come to see that our customers' health and our own ability to compete were inseparable from the health of the environment," she says. So she initiated the concept of ecologically intelligent product design. Winslow's team worked at determining the chemical composition and environmental effects of every material and process Nike used. They visited factories in China and collected samples of rubber, leather, nylon, polyester, and foams to determine their chemical makeup. This led Winslow and her team to develop a list of "positive" materials—those that weren't harmful to the environment—that they hoped to use in more Nike products. "Environmental sustainability" was no longer just an abstract term on a vision statement; the team now felt a mandate to realize the vision.

Inventing

Even the most compelling vision will lose its power if it floats, unconnected, above the everyday reality of organizational life. To transform a vision of the future into a

Cultivate Inventiveness

1. Don't assume that the way things have always been done is the best way to do them.
2. When a new task or change effort emerges, encourage creative ways of getting it done.
3. Experiment with different ways of organizing work. Find alternative methods for grouping and linking people.
4. When working to understand your current environment, ask yourself, "What other options are possible?"

present-day reality, leaders need to devise processes that will give it life. This inventing is what moves a business from the abstract world of ideas to the concrete world of implementation. In fact, inventing is similar to execution, but the label "inventing" emphasizes that this process often requires creativity to help people figure out new ways of working together.

To realize a new vision, people usually can't keep doing the same things they've been doing. They need to conceive, design, and put into practice new ways of interacting and organizing. Some of the most famous examples of large-scale organizational innovation come from the automotive industry: Henry Ford's conception of the assembly-line factory and Toyota's famed integrated production system.

More recently, Pierre Omidyar, the founder of eBay, invented through his company a new way of doing large-scale retailing. His vision was of an online community where users would take responsibility for what happened. In a 2001 BusinessWeek Online interview, Omidyar explained, "I had the idea that I wanted to create an efficient market and a level playing field where everyone had equal access to information. I wanted to give the power of the market back to individuals, not just large corporations. That was the driving motivation for creating eBay at the start."

Consequently, eBay outsources most of the functions of traditional retailing—purchasing, order fulfillment, and customer service, for example—to independent sellers worldwide. The company estimates that more than 430,000 people make their primary living from selling wares on eBay. If those individuals were all employees of eBay, it would be the second largest private employer in the United States after Wal-Mart.

The people who work through eBay are essentially independent store owners, and, as such, they have a huge amount of autonomy in how they do their work. They decide what to sell, when to sell it, how to price, and how to advertise. Coupled with this individual freedom is global scale. EBay's infrastructure enables them to sell their goods all over the world. What makes eBay's inventing so radical is that it represents a new relationship between an organization and its parts. Unlike typical outsourcing, eBay doesn't pay its retailers—they pay the company.

Inventing doesn't have to occur on such a grand scale. It happens every time a person creates a way of approaching a task or figures out how to overcome a previously insurmountable obstacle. In their book *Car Launch,* George Roth and Art Kleiner describe a highly successful product development team in the automobile industry that struggled with completing its designs on time. Much of the source of the problem, the team members concluded, came from the stovepipe organizational structure found in the product development division. Even though they were a "colocated" team dedicated to designing a common new car, members were divided by their different technical expertise, experience, jargon, and norms of working.

When the team invented a mechanical prototyping device that complemented its computer-aided design tools, the group members found that it facilitated a whole new way of collaborating. Multiple groups within the team could quickly create physical mock-ups of design ideas to be tested by the various engineers from different specialties in the team. The group called the device "the harmony buck," because it helped people break out of their comfortable engineering specialties and solve interdependent design problems together. Development of a "full body" physical mock-up of the new car allowed engineers to hang around the prototype, providing a central focal point for their interactions. It enabled them to more easily identify and raise cross-functional issues, and it facilitated mutual problem solving and coordination.

In sum, leaders must be able to succeed at inventing, and this requires both attention to detail and creativity. (See the exhibit "Cultivate Inventiveness.")

Balancing the Four Capabilities

Sensemaking, relating, visioning, and inventing are interdependent. Without sensemaking, there's no common view of reality from which to start. Without relating, people work in isolation or, worse, strive toward different aims. Without visioning, there's no shared direction. And without inventing, a vision remains illusory. No one leader, however, will excel at all four capabilities in equal measure.

Typically, leaders are strong in one or two capabilities. Intel chairman Andy Grove is the quintessential sensemaker, for instance, with a gift for recognizing strategic inflection points that can be exploited for competitive advantage. Herb Kelleher, the former CEO of Southwest Airlines, excels at relating. He remarked in the journal *Leader to Leader* that "We are not afraid to talk to our people with emotion. We're not afraid to tell them, 'We love you.' Because we do." With this emotional connection comes equitable compensation and profit sharing.

Apple CEO Steve Jobs is a visionary whose ambitious dreams and persuasiveness have catalyzed remarkable successes for Apple, Next, and Pixar. Meg Whitman,

---

Examining Your Leadership Capabilities

Few people wake up in the morning and say, "I'm a poor sensemaker" or "I just can't relate to others." They tend to experience their own weaknesses more as chronic or inexplicable failures in the organization or in those around them. The following descriptions will help you recognize opportunities to develop your leadership capabilities and identify openings for working with others.

SIGNS OF WEAK SENSEMAKING

1. You feel strongly that you are usually right and others are often wrong.
2. You feel your views describe reality correctly, but others' views do not.
3. You find you are often blindsided by changes in your organization or industry.
4. When things change, you typically feel resentful. (That's not the way it should be!)

SIGNS OF WEAK RELATING

1. You blame others for failed projects.
2. You feel others are constantly letting you down or failing to live up to your expectations.

3. You find that many of your interactions at work are unpleasant, frustrating, or argumentative.
4. You find many of the people you work with untrustworthy.

SIGNS OF WEAK VISIONING

1. You feel your work involves managing an endless series of crises.
2. You feel like you're bouncing from pillar to post with no sense of larger purpose.
3. You often wonder, "Why are we doing this?" or "Does it really matter?"
4. You can't remember the last time you talked to your family or a friend with excitement about your work.

SIGNS OF WEAK INVENTING

1. Your organization's vision seems abstract to you.
2. You have difficulty relating your company's vision to what you are doing today.
3. You notice dysfunctional gaps between your organization's aspirations and the way work is organized.
4. You find that things tend to revert to business as usual.

the CEO of eBay, helped bring Pierre Omidyar's vision of online retailing to life by inventing ways to deal with security, vendor reliability, and product diversification.

Once leaders diagnose their own capabilities, identifying their unique set of strengths and weaknesses, they must search for others who can provide the things they're missing. (See the sidebar "Examining Your Leadership Capabilities.") Leaders who choose only people who mirror themselves are likely to find their organizations tilting in one direction, missing one or more essential capabilities needed to survive in a changing, complex world. That's why it's important to examine the whole organization to make sure it is appropriately balanced as well. It's the leader's responsibility to create an environment that lets people complement one another's strengths and offset one another's weaknesses. In this way, leadership is distributed across multiple people throughout the organization.

. . .

Years ago, one of us attended a three-day meeting on leadership with 15 top managers from different companies. At the close of it, participants were asked to reflect on their experience as leaders. One executive, responsible for more than 50,000 people in his division of a manufacturing corporation, drew two pictures on a flip chart. The image on the left was what he projected to the outside world: It was a large, intimidating face holding up a huge fist. The image on the right represented how he saw himself: a small face with wide eyes, hair standing on end, and an expression of sheer terror.

We believe that most leaders experience that profound dichotomy every day, and it's a heavy burden. How many times have you feigned confidence to superiors or reports when you were really unsure? Have you ever felt comfortable conceding that you were confused by the latest business results or caught off guard by a competitor's move? Would you ever admit to feeling inadequate to cope with the complex issues your firm was facing? Anyone who can identify with these situations knows firsthand what it's like to be trapped in the myth of the complete leader—the person at the top without flaws. It's time to put that myth to rest, not only for the sake of frustrated leaders but also for the health of organizations. Even the most talented leaders require the input and leadership of others, constructively solicited and creatively applied. It's time to celebrate the incomplete—that is, the human—leader.

17 Organizational Culture

Organizational culture greatly influences the way people behave at work. Ever since this discovery was made, scholars and managers alike have been interested in learning how to create, manage, and maintain productive and healthy organizational cultures. Organizational culture can play either a positive or negative role in attracting and retaining employees. When leaders understand the role of organizational culture and manage it effectively, it can serve as the glue that holds organizations together and helps them succeed.

Edgar Schein, management professor emeritus, has contributed much of our current knowledge about organizational culture. The first selection, "Uncovering the Levels of Culture," is a chapter from his book *Organizational Culture and Leadership*, which is considered a classic in its field. Schein defines organizational culture and explains how it works.

Our second article is an updated classic by Larry Greiner, management and organization professor at the University of Southern California. In "Evolution and Revolution as Organizations Grow," Greiner outlines five developmental phases that organizations traverse as they grow. Within each stage, organizations gradually evolve until they reach a crisis that necessitates serious change—a revolution. The resulting solution is eventually outgrown, when the organization has to move on to the next stage. According to Greiner, leaders should understand where their organization is in this developmental scheme, in part because each phase requires a different type of leadership and organizational emphasis. Learning to "grow" the organization can help leaders avoid the pitfalls that derail so many firms.

In "Do the Best Companies Have the Best People?," Stanford University professors Jeffrey Pfeffer and Robert Sutton suggest that talent, while important, may be often overrated in its role in sustaining organizational performance. They argue that the best companies are those that are selective about who they hire, believe that everyone is capable of the best performance, and create and sustain systems that make the best performance possible throughout the organization. They note that organizations can often take poor performers and create environments where they succeed wonderfully. But, managers must be vigilant to ensure that the systems and policies reinforce great performance—a cautionary tale for even the best organizations as recent news reports regarding quality defects in Toyota Motor Company vehicles attest. Pfeffer and Sutton provide useful advice for managers who are interested in nurturing the capabilities of their employees and in developing organizations capable of sustaining superior performance.

UNCOVERING THE LEVELS OF CULTURE*

Edgar H. Schein

The culture of a group can now be defined as

> *A pattern of shared basic assumptions that the group learned as it solved its problems of external adaptation and internal integration, that has worked well enough to be considered valid and, therefore, to be taught to new members as the correct way to perceive, think, and feel in relation to those problems.*

The purpose of this chapter is to show that culture can be analyzed at several different levels, where the term *level* refers to the degree to which the cultural phenomenon is visible to the observer. Some of the confusion of definition of what culture really is results from not differentiating the levels at which it manifests itself. These levels range from the very tangible overt manifestations that one can see and feel to the deeply embedded, unconscious basic assumptions that I am defining as the essence of culture. In between we have various espoused values, norms, and rules of behavior that members of the culture use as a way of depicting the culture to themselves and others.

Many other culture researchers prefer the concept of "basic values" for describing the deepest levels. As I will try to show with later examples, my preference is for "basic assumptions" because these tend to be taken for granted and are treated as nonnegotiable. Values can be and are discussed, and people can agree to disagree about them. Basic assumptions are so taken for granted that someone who does not hold them is viewed as crazy and automatically dismissed. The levels at which culture can be analyzed are shown in Figure 1.

Artifacts

At the surface we have the level of *artifacts*, which includes all the phenomena that one sees, hears, and feels when one encounters a new group with an unfamiliar culture. Artifacts would include the visible products of the group such as the architecture of its physical environment, its language, its technology and products, its artistic creations, and its style as embodied in clothing, manners of address, emotional displays, myths and stories told about the organization, published lists of values, observable rituals and ceremonies, and so on. For purposes of cultural analysis this level also includes the visible behavior of the group and the organizational processes into which such behavior is made routine.

Artifacts	Visible organizational structures and processes (hard to decipher)
Espoused values	Strategies, goals, philosophies (espoused justifications)
Basic underlying assumptions	Unconscious, taken-for-granted beliefs, perceptions, thoughts, and feelings (ultimate source of values and action)

FIGURE 1 **Levels of culture**

The most important point about this level of the culture is that it is easy to observe and very difficult to decipher. The Egyptians and the Maya both built highly visible pyramids, but the meaning of pyramids in each culture was very different—tombs in one and temples as well as tombs in the other. In other words, the observer can describe what she sees and feels but cannot reconstruct from that alone what those things mean in the given group, or whether they even reflect important underlying assumptions.

On the other hand, one school of thought argues that one's own response to physical artifacts such as buildings and office layouts can lead to the identification of major images and root metaphors that reflect the deepest level of the culture (Gagliardi, 1990). This would be especially true if the organization one is deciphering is in the same larger culture as the researcher. The problem is that symbols are ambiguous, and one can only test one's insight into what something might mean if one has also experienced the culture at the level of its values and the level of its basic assumptions.

It is especially dangerous to try to infer the deeper assumptions from artifacts alone because one's interpretations will inevitably be projections of one's own feelings and reactions. For example, when one sees a very informal, loose organization, one may interpret that as inefficient if one's own background is based on the assumption that informality means playing around and not working. Alternatively, if one sees a very formal organization, one may interpret that to be a sign of lack of innovative capacity if one's own experience is based on the assumption that formality means bureaucracy and formalization.

Every facet of a group's life produces artifacts, creating the problem of classification. In reading cultural descriptions, one often notes that different observers choose to report on different sorts of artifacts, leading to noncomparable descriptions. Anthropologists have developed classification systems, but these tend to be so vast and detailed that cultural essence becomes difficult to discern.

If the observer lives in the group long enough, the meanings of artifacts gradually become clear. If, however, one wants to achieve this level of understanding more quickly, one can attempt to analyze the espoused values, norms, and rules that provide the day-to-day operating principles by which the members of the group guide their behavior. This kind of inquiry takes us to the next level of cultural analysis.

Espoused Values

All group learning ultimately reflects someone's original values, someone's sense of what ought to be as distinct from what is. When a group is first created or when it faces a new task, issue, or problem, the first solution proposed to deal with it reflects some individual's own assumptions about what is right or wrong, what will work or not work. Those individuals who prevail, who can influence the group to adopt a certain approach to the problem, will later be identified as "leaders" or founders, but the group as a group does not yet have any shared knowledge because it has not yet taken a common action in response to the new problem. Therefore, whatever is proposed can only have the status of a value from the point of view of the group, no matter how strongly the proponent may believe that he or she is uttering absolute proven truth. Until the group has taken some joint action and its members have together observed the outcome of that action, there is not as yet a shared basis for determining what is factual and real.

For example, in a young business if sales begin to decline, a manager may say, "We must increase advertising" because of her belief that advertising always increases sales. The group, never having experienced this situation before, will hear that assertion as a statement of that manager's values: "She believes that when one is in trouble it is a *good* thing to increase advertising." What the leader initially proposes, therefore, cannot have any status other than a value to be questioned, debated, challenged, and tested.

If the manager convinces the group to act on her belief and if the solution works and if the group has a shared perception of that success, then the perceived value that advertising is "good" gradually starts a process of *cognitive transformation*. First, it will be transformed into a *shared value or belief* and, ultimately, into a *shared assumption* (if action based on it continues to be successful). If this transformation process occurs—and it will occur only if the proposed solution continues to work, thus implying that it is in some larger sense "correct" and must reflect an accurate picture of reality—group members will tend to forget that originally they were not sure and that the proposed course of action was at an earlier time debated and confronted.

Not all values undergo such transformation. First of all, the solution based on a given value may not work reliably. Only values that are susceptible to physical or social validation and that continue to work reliably in solving the group's problems will become transformed into assumptions. Second, value domains dealing with the less controllable elements of the environment or with aesthetic or moral matters may not be testable at all. In such cases consensus through social validation is still possible, but it is not automatic.

By social validation I mean that certain values are confirmed only by the shared social experience of a group. Such values typically involve the group's internal relations, where the test of whether they work or not is how comfortable and anxiety-free members are when they abide by them. Social validation also applies to those broader values that involve relationships to the environment but in a non-testable fashion, such as religion, ethics, and aesthetics.

In these realms the group learns that certain such values, as initially promulgated by prophets, founders, and leaders, work in the sense of reducing uncertainty in critical areas of the group's functioning. And as they continue to work, they gradually become transformed into nondiscussable assumptions supported by articulated sets of beliefs, norms, and operational rules of behavior. The derived beliefs and moral/ethical rules remain conscious and are explicitly articulated because they serve the normative or moral function of guiding members of the group in how to deal with certain key situations and in training new members in how to behave. A set of values that becomes embodied in an ideology or organizational philosophy thus can serve as a guide and as a way of dealing with the uncertainty of intrinsically uncontrollable or difficult events.

Values at this conscious level will predict much of the behavior that can be observed at the artifactual level. But if those values are not based on prior learning, they may also reflect only what Argyris and Schön (1978) have called *espoused values*, which predict well enough what people will say in a variety of situations but which may be out of line with what they will actually *do* in situations where those values should, in fact, be operating. Thus, a company may say that it values people and has high quality standards for its products, but its record in that regard may contradict what it says.

If the espoused values are reasonably congruent with the underlying assumptions, then the articulation of those values into a philosophy of operating can be helpful in bringing the group together, serving as a source of identity and core mission. But in analyzing values one must discriminate carefully between those that are congruent with underlying assumptions and those that are, in effect, either rationalizations or only aspirations for the future. Often such lists of values are not patterned, sometimes they are even mutually contradictory, and often they are inconsistent with observed behavior. Large areas of behavior are often left unexplained, leaving us with a feeling that we understand a piece of the culture but still do not have the culture as such in hand. To get at that deeper level of understanding, to decipher the pattern, and to predict future behavior correctly, we have to understand more fully the category of basic assumptions.

Basic Assumptions

When a solution to a problem works repeatedly, it comes to be taken for granted. What was once a hypothesis, supported only by a hunch or a value, comes gradually to be treated as a reality. We come to believe that nature really works this way. Basic assumptions, in this sense, are different from what some anthropologists call dominant value orientations in that such dominant orientations reflect the preferred solution among several basic alternatives, but all the alternatives are still visible in the culture, and any given member of the culture could, from time to time, behave according to variant as well as dominant orientations (Kluckhohn and Strodtbeck, 1961).

Basic assumptions, in the sense in which I want to define the concept, have become so taken for granted that one finds little variation within a cultural unit. In fact, if a basic assumption is strongly held in a group, members will find behavior based on any other premise inconceivable. For example, a group whose basic assumption is that the individual's rights supersede those of the group members will find it inconceivable that members would commit suicide or in some other way sacrifice themselves to the group even if they had dishonored the group. In a capitalist country, it is inconceivable that one might design a company to operate consistently at a financial loss or that it does not matter whether or not a product works. Basic assumptions, in this sense, are similar to what Argyris has identified as *theories-in-use*, the implicit assumptions that actually guide behavior, that tell group members how to perceive, think about, and feel about things (Argyris, 1976; Argyris and Schön, 1974).

Basic assumptions, like theories-in-use, tend to be those we neither confront nor debate and hence are extremely difficult to change. To learn something new in this realm requires us to resurrect, reexamine, and possibly change some of the more stable portions of our cognitive structure, a process that Argyris and others have called double-loop learning or frame breaking (for example, Argyris, Putnam, and Smith, 1985; Bartunek and Moch, 1987). Such learning is intrinsically difficult because the reexamination of basic assumptions temporarily destabilizes our cognitive and interpersonal world, releasing large quantities of basic anxiety.

Rather than tolerating such anxiety levels we tend to want to perceive the events around us as congruent with our assumptions, even if that means distorting, denying, projecting, or in other ways falsifying to ourselves what may be going on around us. It is in this psychological process that culture has its ultimate power. Culture as a set of basic assumptions defines for us what to pay attention to, what things mean, how to react emotionally to what is going on, and what actions to take in various kinds of situations. Once we have developed an integrated set of such assumptions, which might be called a thought world or mental map, we will be maximally comfortable with others who share the same set of assumptions and very uncomfortable and vulnerable in situations where different assumptions operate either because we will not understand what is going on, or, worse, misperceive and misinterpret the actions of others (Douglas, 1986).

The human mind needs cognitive stability. Therefore, any challenge to or questioning of a basic assumption will release anxiety and defensiveness. In this sense, the shared basic assumptions that make up the culture of a group can be thought of at both the individual and group levels as psychological cognitive *defense mechanisms* that permit the group to continue to function. Recognizing this connection is important when one thinks about changing aspects of a group's culture, for it is no easier to do that than to change an individual's pattern of defense mechanisms. In either case the key is the management of the large amounts of anxiety that accompany any relearning at this level.

To understand how unconscious assumptions can distort data, consider the following example. If we assume, on the basis of past experience or education, that other people will take advantage of us whenever they have an opportunity, we expect to be taken advantage of and then interpret the behavior of others in a way that coincides with those expectations. We observe people sitting in a seemingly idle posture at their desks and interpret their behavior as loafing rather than thinking out an important problem. We perceive absence from work as shirking rather than doing work at home.

If this is not only a personal assumption but one that is shared and thus part of the organization's culture, we will discuss with others what to do about our "lazy" work force and institute tight controls to ensure that people are at their desks and busy. If employees suggest that they do some of their work at home, we will be uncomfortable and probably deny the request because we will assume that at home they would loaf (Bailyn, 1992; Perin, 1991).

In contrast, if we assume that everyone is highly motivated and competent, we will act in accordance with that assumption by encouraging people to work at their own pace and in their own way. If someone is discovered to be unproductive in the organization, we will assume that there is a mismatch between the person and the job assignment, not that the person is lazy or incompetent. If the employee wants to work at home, we will perceive that as evidence of wanting to be productive even if circumstances require him to be at home.

In both cases there is the potential for distortion. The cynical manager will not perceive how highly motivated some of the subordinates really are, and the idealistic manager will not perceive that there are subordinates who are lazy and who are taking advantage of the situation. As McGregor (1960) noted several decades ago, such assumption sets in the human area become the basis of whole management and control systems that perpetuate themselves because if people are treated consistently in terms of certain basic assumptions, they come eventually to behave according to those assumptions in order to make their world stable and predictable.

Unconscious assumptions sometimes lead to ridiculously tragic situations, as illustrated by a common problem experienced by American supervisors in some Asian countries. A manager who comes from an American pragmatic tradition takes it for granted that solving a problem always has the highest priority. When that manager encounters a subordinate who comes from a different cultural tradition, in which good relationships and protecting the superior's "face" are assumed to have top priority, the following scenario can easily result.

The manager proposes a solution to a given problem. The subordinate knows that the solution will not work, but his unconscious assumption requires that he remain silent because to tell the boss that the proposed solution is wrong is a threat to the boss's face. It would not even occur to the subordinate to do anything other than remain silent or even reassure the boss that they should go ahead and take the action if the boss were to inquire what the subordinate thought.

The action is taken, the results are negative, and the boss, somewhat surprised and puzzled, asks the subordinate what he would have done. When the subordinate reports that he would have done something different, the boss quite legitimately asks why the subordinate did not speak up sooner. This question puts the subordinate in an impossible bind because the answer itself is a threat to the boss's face. He cannot possibly explain his behavior without committing the very sin he is trying to avoid in the first place—namely, embarrassing the boss. He might even lie at this point and argue that what the boss did was right and only "bad luck" or uncontrollable circumstances prevented it from succeeding.

From the point of view of the subordinate, the boss's behavior is incomprehensible because it shows lack of self-pride, possibly causing the subordinate to lose respect for that boss. To the boss the subordinate's behavior is equally incomprehensible. The boss cannot develop any sensible explanation of the subordinate's behavior that is not cynically colored by the assumption that the subordinate at some level just does not care about effective performance and therefore must be gotten rid of. It never occurs to the boss that another assumption such as "one never embarrasses a superior" is operating and that to the subordinate that assumption is even more powerful than "one gets the job done."

If assumptions such as these operate only in an individual and represent her idiosyncratic experience, they can be corrected more easily because the person will detect that she is alone in holding a given assumption. The power of culture comes about through the fact that the assumptions are shared and therefore mutually reinforced. In these instances probably only a third party or some cross-cultural education could help to find common ground whereby both parties could bring their implicit assumptions to the surface. And even after they have surfaced, such assumptions would still operate, forcing the boss and the subordinate to invent a whole new communication mechanism that would permit each to remain congruent with her or his culture—for example, agreeing that before any decision is made and before the boss has stuck her neck out, the subordinate will be asked for suggestions and for factual data that will not be face threatening. Note that the solution must keep each cultural assumption intact. One cannot in these instances simply declare one or the other cultural assumption "wrong." One has to find a third assumption to allow them both to retain their integrity.

I have dwelled on this example to illustrate the potency of implicit, unconscious assumptions and to show that such assumptions often deal with fundamental aspects of life—the nature of time and space; human nature and human activities; the nature of truth and how one discovers it; the correct way for the individual and the group to relate to each other; the relative importance of work, family, and self-development; the proper role of men and women; and the nature of the family.

We do not develop new assumptions about each of these areas in every group or organization we join. Each member of a new group will bring her or his own cultural learning from prior groups, but as the new group develops its own shared history, it will develop modified or brand-new assumptions in critical areas of its experience. Those new assumptions make up the culture of that particular group.

Any group's culture can be studied at these three levels—the level of its artifacts, the level of its values, and the level of its basic assumptions. If one does not decipher the pattern of basic assumptions that may be operating, one will not know how to interpret the artifacts correctly or how much credence to give to the articulated values. In other words, the essence of a culture lies in the pattern of basic underlying assumptions, and once one understands those, one can easily understand the other more surface levels and deal appropriately with them.

Summary and Conclusions

Though the essence of a group's culture is its pattern of shared, taken-for-granted basic assumptions, the culture will manifest itself at the levels of observable artifacts and shared espoused values, norms, and rules of behavior. It is important to recognize in analyzing cultures that artifacts are easy to observe but difficult to decipher and that values may only reflect rationalizations or aspirations. To understand a group's culture, one must attempt to get at its shared basic assumptions and one must understand the learning process by which such basic assumptions come to be.

Leadership is originally the source of the beliefs and values that get a group moving in dealing with its internal and external problems. If what a leader proposes works and continues to work, what once was only the leader's assumption gradually comes to be a shared assumption. Once a set of shared basic assumptions is formed by this process, it can function as a cognitive defense mechanism both for the individual members and for the group as a whole. In other words, individuals and groups seek stability and meaning. Once these are achieved, it is easier to distort new data by denial, projection, rationalization, or various other defense mechanisms than to change the basic assumption. As we will see, culture change, in the sense of changing basic assumptions is, therefore, difficult, time consuming, and highly anxiety provoking. This point is especially relevant for the leader who sets out to change the culture of the organization.

The most central issue for leaders, therefore, is how to get at the deeper levels of a culture, how to assess the functionality of the assumptions made at each level, and how to deal with the anxiety that is unleashed when those levels are challenged.

References

Argyris, C. *Integrating the Individual and the Organization* (New York: Wiley, 1976).

Argyris, C. and D. A. Schön, *Theory in Practice: Increasing Professional Effectiveness* (San Francisco: Jossey-Bass, 1974).

Argyris, C. and D. A. Schön, *Organizational Learning* (Reading, MA: Addison-Wesley, 1978).

Argyris, C., R. Putnam, and D. M. Smith, *Action Science* (San Francisco: Jossey-Bass, 1985).

Bailyn, L., "Changing the Conditions of Work: Implications for Career Development," *Career Development in the 1990's: Theory and Practice*, D. H. Montross and C. J. Shinkman (Springfield, IL: Thomas, 1992).

Bartunek, J., and M. K. Moch, "First Order, Second Order, and Third Order Change and Organization Development Interventions: A Cognitive Approach," *Journal of Applied Behavioral Science* 23 (1987): 483–500.

Douglas, M., *How Institutions Think* (Syracuse, NY: Syracuse University Press, 1986).

Gagliardi, P. (ed.), *Symbols and Artifacts: Views of the Corporate Landscape* (New York: de Gruyter, 1990).

Kluckhohn, F. R., and F. L. Strodtbeck, *Variations in Value Orientations* (New York: Harper & Row, 1961).

McGregor, D. M., *The Human Side of Enterprise* (New York: McGraw-Hill, 1960).

Perin, C., "The Moral Fabric of the Office," S. Bacharach, S. R. Barley, and P. S. Tolbert (eds.), *Research in the Sociology of Organizations* (special volume on the professions) (Greenwich, CT: JAI Press, 1991).

EVOLUTION AND REVOLUTION AS ORGANIZATIONS GROW*

Larry E. Greiner

Key executives of a retail store chain hold on to an organizational structure long after it has served its purpose because the structure is the source of their power. The company eventually goes into bankruptcy.

A large bank disciplines a "rebellious" manager who is blamed for current control problems, when the underlying causes are centralized procedures that are holding back expansion into new markets. Many young managers subsequently leave the bank, competition moves in, and profits decline.

The problems at these companies are rooted more in past decisions than in present events or market dynamics. Yet management, in its haste to grow, often overlooks such critical developmental questions as, Where has our organization been? Where is it now? and What do the answers to these questions mean for where it is going? Instead, management fixes its gaze outward on the environment and toward the future, as if more precise market projections will provide the organization with a new identity.

In stressing the force of history on an organization, I have drawn from the legacies of European psychologists who argue that the behavior of individuals is determined primarily by past events and experiences, rather than by what lies ahead. Extending that thesis to problems of organizational development, we can identify a series of developmental phases through which companies tend to pass as they grow. Each phase begins with a period of evolution, with steady growth and stability, and ends with a revolutionary period of substantial organizational turmoil and change—for instance, when centralized practices eventually lead to demands for decentralization. The resolution of each revolutionary period determines whether or not a company will move forward into its next stage of evolutionary growth.

A Model of How Organizations Develop

To date, research on organizational development has been largely empirical, and scholars have not attempted to create a model of the overall process. When we analyze the research, however, five key dimensions emerge: an organization's age and size, its stages of evolution and revolution, and the growth rate of its industry. The Figure 1 "How Companies Grow" shows how these elements interact to shape an organization's development.

AGE OF THE ORGANIZATION The most obvious and essential dimension for any model of development is the life span of an organization (represented on the Figure 1 as the horizontal axis). History shows that the same organizational practices are not maintained throughout a long life span. This demonstrates a most basic point: management problems and principles are rooted in time. The concept of decentralization, for example, can describe corporate practices at one period but can lose its descriptive power at another.

The passage of time also contributes to the institutionalization of managerial attitudes. As these attitudes become rigid and eventually outdated, the behavior of employees becomes not only more predictable but also more difficult to change.

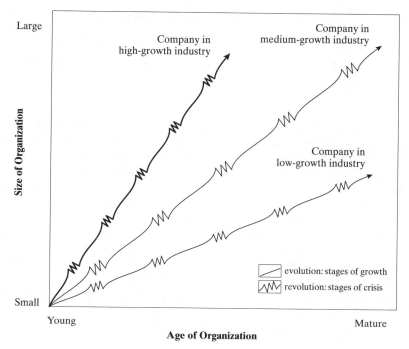

FIGURE 1 How Companies Grow

SIZE OF THE ORGANIZATION This dimension is depicted on the chart as the vertical axis. A company's problems and solutions tend to change markedly as the number of its employees and its sales volume increase. Problems of coordination and communication magnify, new functions emerge, levels in the management hierarchy multiply, and jobs become more interrelated. Thus, time is not the only determinant of structure; in fact, organizations that do not become larger can retain many of the same management issues and practices over long periods.

STAGES OF EVOLUTION As organizations age and grow, another phenomenon emerges: prolonged growth that we can term the *evolutionary period.* Most growing organizations do not expand for two years and then contract for one; rather, those that survive a crisis usually enjoy four to eight years of continuous growth without a major economic setback or severe internal disruption. The term *evolution* seems appropriate for describing these quiet periods because only modest adjustments appear to be necessary for maintaining growth under the same overall pattern of management.

STAGES OF REVOLUTION Smooth evolution is not inevitable or indefinitely sustainable; it cannot be assumed that organizational growth is linear. *Fortune*'s "500" list, for example, has had considerable turnover during the last 50 years. In fact, evidence from numerous case histories reveals periods of substantial turbulence interspersed between smoother periods of evolution.

We can term the turbulent times *periods of revolution* because they typically exhibit a serious upheaval of management practices. Traditional management practices that were appropriate for a smaller size and earlier time no longer work and are brought under scrutiny by frustrated top-level managers and disillusioned lower-level managers. During such periods of crisis, a number of companies fall short. Those that are unable to abandon past practices and effect major organizational changes are likely either to fold or to level off in their growth rates.

The critical task for management in each revolutionary period is to find a new set of organizational practices that will become the basis for managing the next period of evolutionary growth. Interestingly enough, those new practices eventually sow the seeds of their own decay and lead to another period of revolution. Managers therefore experience the irony of seeing a major solution in one period become a major problem in a later period.

GROWTH RATE OF THE INDUSTRY The speed at which an organization experiences phases of evolution and revolution is closely related to the market environment of its industry. For example, a company in a rapidly expanding market will have to add employees quickly; hence, the need for new organizational structures to accommodate large staff increases is accelerated. Whereas evolutionary periods tend to be relatively short in fast-growing industries, much longer evolutionary periods occur in mature or slow-growing industries.

Evolution can also be prolonged, and revolutions delayed, when profits come easily. For instance, companies that make grievous errors in a prosperous industry can still look good on their profit-and-loss statements; thus, they can buy time before a crisis forces changes in management practices. The aerospace industry in its highly profitable infancy is an example. Yet revolutionary periods still occur, as one did in aerospace when profit opportunities began to dry up. By contrast, when the market environment is poor, revolutions seem to be much more severe and difficult to resolve.

Phases of Growth

With the foregoing framework in mind, we can now examine in depth the five specific phases of evolution and revolution. As shown in the Figure 2 "The Five Phases of Growth," each evolutionary period is characterized by the dominant management style used to achieve growth; each revolutionary period is characterized by the dominant management problem that must be solved before growth can continue. The pattern presented in the chart seems to be typical for companies in industries with moderate growth over a long period; companies in faster-growing industries tend to experience all five phases more rapidly, whereas those in slower-growing industries encounter only two or three phases over many years.

It is important to note that each phase is at once a result of the previous phase and a cause for the next phase. For example, the evolutionary management style in Phase 3 is delegation, which grows out of and becomes the solution to demands for greater autonomy in the preceding Phase 2 revolution. The style of delegation used in Phase 3, however, eventually provokes a revolutionary crisis that is characterized by attempts to regain control over the diversity created through increased delegation.

For each phase, managers are limited in what they can do if growth is to occur. For example, a company experiencing an autonomy crisis in Phase 2 cannot return to directive management for a solution; it must adopt a new style—delegation—in order to move forward.

PHASE 1: CREATIVITY In the birth stage of an organization, the emphasis is on creating both a product and a market. The following are the characteristics of the period of creative evolution:

- The founders of the company are usually technically or entrepreneurially oriented, and they generally disdain management activities; their physical and mental energies are absorbed entirely by making and selling a new product.
- Communication among employees is frequent and informal.

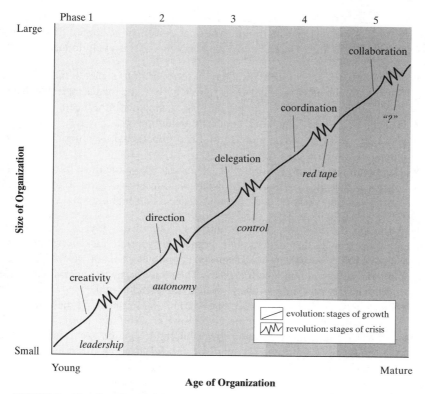

FIGURE 2 The Five Phases of Growth

- Long hours of work are rewarded by modest salaries and the promise of ownership benefits.
- Decisions and motivation are highly sensitive to marketplace feedback; management acts as customers react.

All the foregoing individualistic and creative activities are essential for a company to get off the ground. But as the company grows, those very activities become the problem. Larger production runs require knowledge about the efficiencies of manufacturing. Increased numbers of employees cannot be managed exclusively through informal communication, and new employees are not motivated by an intense dedication to the product or organization. Additional capital must be secured, and new accounting procedures are needed for financial control. The company's founders find themselves burdened with unwanted management responsibilities. They long for the "good old days" and try to act as they did in the past. Conflicts among harried leaders emerge and grow more intense.

At this point, a *crisis of leadership* occurs, which is the onset of the first revolution. Who will lead the company out of confusion and solve the managerial problems confronting it? Obviously, a strong manager is needed—one who has the necessary knowledge and skills to introduce new business techniques. But finding that manager is easier said than done. The founders often resist stepping aside, even though they are probably temperamentally unsuited to the job. So here is the first critical choice in an organization's development: to locate and install a strong business manager who is acceptable to the founders and who can pull the organization together.

PHASE 2: DIRECTION Those companies that survive the first phase by installing a capable business manager usually embark on a period of sustained growth under able, directive leadership. Here are the characteristics of this evolutionary period:

- A functional organizational structure is introduced to separate manufacturing from marketing activities, and job assignments become increasingly specialized.
- Accounting systems for inventory and purchasing are introduced.
- Incentives, budgets, and work standards are adopted.
- Communication becomes more formal and impersonal as a hierarchy of titles and positions grows.
- The new manager and his or her key supervisors assume most of the responsibility for instituting direction; lower-level supervisors are treated more as functional specialists than as autonomous decision-making managers.

Although the new directive techniques channel employees' energy more efficiently into growth, they eventually become inappropriate for controlling a more diverse and complex organization. Lower-level employees find themselves restricted by a cumbersome and centralized hierarchy. They have come to possess more direct knowledge about markets and machinery than do their leaders at the top; consequently, they feel torn between following procedures and taking initiative on their own.

Thus, the second revolution emerges from a *crisis of autonomy*. The solution adopted by most companies is to move toward more delegation. Yet it is difficult for top-level managers who previously were successful at being directive to give up responsibility to lower-level managers. Moreover, the lower-level managers are not accustomed to making decisions for themselves. As a result, numerous companies flounder during this revolutionary period by adhering to centralized methods, while lower-level employees become disenchanted and leave the organization.

PHASE 3: DELEGATION The next era of growth evolves from the successful application of a decentralized organizational structure. It exhibits these characteristics:

- Much greater responsibility is given to the managers of plants and market territories.
- Profit centers and bonuses are used to motivate employees.
- Top-level executives at headquarters limit themselves to managing by exception based on periodic reports from the field.
- Management often concentrates on acquiring outside enterprises that can be lined up with other decentralized units.
- Communication from the top is infrequent and usually occurs by correspondence, telephone, or brief visits to field locations.

The delegation phase allows companies to expand by means of the heightened motivation of managers at lower levels. Managers in decentralized organizations, who have greater authority and incentives, are able to penetrate larger markets, respond faster to customers, and develop new products.

A serious problem eventually emerges, however, as top-level executives sense that they are losing control over a highly diversified field operation. Autonomous field managers prefer to run their own shows without coordinating plans, money, technology, and personnel with the rest of the organization. Freedom breeds a parochial attitude.

Soon, the organization falls into a *crisis of control*. The Phase 3 revolution is under way when top management seeks to regain control over the company as a whole. Some top-management teams attempt a return to centralized management, which usually fails because of the organization's newly vast scope of operations. Those companies that move ahead find a new solution in the use of special coordination techniques.

PHASE 4: COORDINATION The evolutionary period of the coordination phase is characterized by the use of formal systems for achieving greater coordination and by top-level executives taking responsibility for the initiation and administration of these new systems. For example:

- Decentralized units are merged into product groups.
- Formal planning procedures are established and intensively reviewed.
- Numerous staff members are hired and located at headquarters to initiate companywide programs of control and review for line managers.
- Capital expenditures are carefully weighed and parceled out across the organization.
- Each product group is treated as an investment center where return on invested capital is an important criterion used in allocating funds.
- Certain technical functions, such as data processing, are centralized at headquarters, while daily operating decisions remain decentralized.
- Stock options and company wide profit sharing are used to encourage employees to identify with the organization as a whole.

All these new coordination systems prove useful for achieving growth through the more efficient allocation of a company's limited resources. The systems prompt field managers to look beyond the needs of their local units. Although these managers still have a great deal of decision-making responsibility, they learn to justify their actions more carefully to a watchdog audience at headquarters.

A lack of confidence, however, gradually builds between line and staff, and between headquarters and the field. The many systems and programs introduced begin to exceed their usefulness. A *red-tape crisis* is in full swing. Line managers, for example, increasingly resent direction from those who are not familiar with local conditions. And staff people, for their part, complain about uncooperative and uninformed line managers. Together, both groups criticize the bureaucratic system that has evolved. Procedures take precedence over problem solving, and innovation dims. In short, the organization has become too large and complex to be managed through formal programs and rigid systems. The Phase 4 revolution is under way.

PHASE 5: COLLABORATION The last observable phase emphasizes strong interpersonal collaboration in an attempt to overcome the red-tape crisis. Where Phase 4 was managed through formal systems and procedures, Phase 5 emphasizes spontaneity in management action through teams and the skillful confrontation of interpersonal differences. Social control and self-discipline replace formal control. This transition is especially difficult for the experts who created the coordination systems as well as for the line managers who relied on formal methods for answers.

The Phase 5 evolution, then, builds around a more flexible and behavioral approach to management. Here are its characteristics:

- The focus is on solving problems quickly through team action.
- Teams are combined across functions to handle specific tasks.
- Staff experts at headquarters are reduced in number, reassigned, and combined into interdisciplinary teams that consult with, not direct, field units.
- A matrix-type structure is frequently used to assemble the right teams for the appropriate problems.

- Formal control systems are simplified and combined into single multipurpose systems.
- Conferences of key managers are held frequently to focus on major problems.
- Educational programs are used to train managers in behavioral skills for achieving better teamwork and conflict resolution.
- Real-time information systems are integrated into daily decision-making processes.
- Economic rewards are geared more to team performance than to individual achievement.
- Experimenting with new practices is encouraged throughout the organization.

What will be the revolution in response to this stage of evolution? Many large U.S. companies are now in the Phase 5 evolutionary stage, so the answer is critical. Although there is little clear evidence regarding the outcome, I imagine that the revolution arising from the *"?"* crisis will center around the psychological saturation of employees who grow emotionally and physically exhausted from the intensity of teamwork and the heavy pressure for innovative solutions.

My hunch is that the Phase 5 revolution will be solved through new structures and programs that allow employees to periodically rest, reflect, and revitalize themselves. We may even see companies with dual organizational structures: a habit structure for getting the daily work done and a reflective structure for stimulating new perspective and personal enrichment. Employees could move back and forth between the two structures as their energies dissipate and are refueled.

One European organization has implemented just such a structure. Five reflective groups have been established outside the company's usual structure for the purpose of continuously evaluating five task activities basic to the organization. The groups report directly to the managing director, although their findings are made public throughout the organization. Membership in each group includes all levels and functions in the company, and employees are rotated through the groups every six months.

Other concrete examples now in practice include providing sabbaticals for employees, moving managers in and out of hot-spot jobs, establishing a four-day workweek, ensuring job security, building physical facilities for relaxation during the workday, making jobs more interchangeable, creating an extra team on the assembly line so that one team is always off for reeducation, and switching to longer vacations and more flexible work hours.

The Chinese practice of requiring executives to spend time periodically on lower-level jobs may also be worth a nonideological evaluation. For too long, U.S. management has assumed that career progress should be equated with an upward path toward title, salary, and power. Could it be that some vice presidents of marketing might just long for, and even benefit from, temporary duty in field sales?

Implications of History

Let me now summarize some important implications for practicing managers. The main features of this discussion are depicted in the table "Organizational Practices in the Five Phases of Growth," which shows the specific management actions that characterize each growth phase. These actions are also the solutions that ended each preceding revolutionary period.

In one sense, I hope that many readers will react to my model by seeing it as obvious and natural for depicting the growth of an organization. To me, this type of reaction is a useful test of the model's validity.

But at a more reflective level, I imagine some of these reactions come more from hindsight than from foresight. Experienced managers who have been through a developmental sequence can identify that sequence now, but how did they react when in the midst of a stage of evolution or revolution? They can probably recall the limits of their own developmental understanding at that time. Perhaps they resisted desirable changes or were even swept emotionally into a revolution without being able to propose constructive solutions. So let me offer some explicit guidelines for managers of growing organizations to keep in mind.

Know Where you are in the Developmental Sequence   Every organization and its component parts are at different stages of development. The task of top management is to be aware of the stages; otherwise, it may not recognize when the time for change has come, or it may act to impose the wrong solution.

Leaders at the top should be ready to work with the flow of the tide rather than against it; yet they should be cautious because it is tempting to skip phases out of impatience. Each phase produces certain strengths and learning experiences in the organization that will be essential for success in subsequent phases. A child prodigy, for example, may be able to read like a teenager, but he cannot behave like one until he matures through a sequence of experiences.

I also doubt that managers can or should act to avoid revolutions. Rather, these periods of tension provide the pressure, ideas, and awareness that afford a platform for change and the introduction of new practices.

Recognize the Limited Range of Solutions   In each revolutionary stage, it becomes evident that the stage can come to a close only by means of certain specific solutions; moreover, these solutions are different from those that were applied to the problems of the preceding revolution. Too often, it is tempting to choose solutions that were tried before but that actually make it impossible for the new phase of growth to evolve.

Management must be prepared to dismantle current structures before the revolutionary stage becomes too turbulent. Top-level managers, realizing that their own managerial styles are no longer appropriate, may even have to take themselves out of leadership positions. A good Phase 2 manager facing Phase 3 might be wise to find a position at another Phase 2 organization that better fits his or her talents, either outside the company or with one of its newer subsidiaries.

Organizational Practices in the Five Phases of Growth

Category	Phase 1	Phase 2	Phase 3	Phase 4	Phase 5
Management Focus	Make and sell	Efficiency of operations	Expansion of market	Consolidation of organization	Problem solving and innovation
Organizational Structure	Informal	Centralized and functional	Decentralized and geographical	Line staff and product groups	Matrix of teams
Top-Management Style	Individualistic and entrepreneurial	Directive	Delegative	Watchdog	Participative
Control System	Market results	Standards and cost centers	Reports and profit centers	Plans and investment centers	Mutual goal setting
Management Reward Emphasis	Ownership	Salary and merit increases	Individual bonus	Profit sharing and stock options	Team bonus

Finally, evolution is not an automatic affair; it is a contest for survival. To move ahead, companies must consciously introduce planned structures that not only solve a current crisis but also fit the next phase of growth. That requires considerable self-awareness on the part of top management as well as great interpersonal skills in persuading other managers that change is needed.

Realize that Solutions Breed New Problems   Managers often fail to recognize that organizational solutions create problems for the future, such as when a decision to delegate eventually causes a problem of control. Actions in the past determine much of what will happen to a company in the future.

An awareness of this effect should help managers evaluate company problems with a historical understanding instead of pinning the blame on a current development. Better yet, it should place managers in a position to predict problems and thereby to prepare solutions and coping strategies before a revolution gets out of hand.

Top management that is aware of the problems ahead could well decide not to expand the organization. Managers may, for instance, prefer to retain the informal practices of a small company, knowing that this way of life is inherent in the organization's limited size, not in their congenial personalities. If they choose to grow, they may actually grow themselves out of a job and a way of life they enjoy.

And what about very large organizations? Can they find new solutions for continued evolution? Or are they reaching a stage when the government will act to break them up because they are too large?

Clearly, there is still much to learn about processes of development in organizations. The phases outlined here are merely five in number and are still only approximations. Researchers are just beginning to study the specific developmental problems of structure, control, rewards, and management style in different industries and in a variety of cultures.

One should not, however, wait for conclusive evidence before educating managers to think and act from a developmental perspective. The critical dimension of time has been missing for too long from our management theories and practices. The intriguing paradox is that by learning more about history, we may do a better job in the future.

Revolution is Still Inevitable

I wrote the first draft of this article while I was felled by a bad leg during a ski vacation in Switzerland. At the time, the business world was buzzing with numerous faddish techniques. Perhaps it was the size and height of the mountains that made me feel that there were deeper and more powerful forces at work in organizations.

Four basic points still seem valid about the model. First, we continue to observe major phases of development in the life of growing companies, lasting anywhere from 3 to 15 years each. Although scholars debate the precise length and nature of these phases, everyone agrees that each phase contains its own unique structure, systems, and leadership. The growth rate of the industry seems to determine the phases length.

Second, transitions between developmental phases still do not occur naturally or smoothly, regardless of the strength of top management. All organizations appear to experience revolutionary difficulty and upheaval, and many of these organizations falter, plateau, fail, or get acquired rather than grow further. IBM before Lou Gerstner and General Electric before Jack Welch both suffered badly at the end of the fourth phase of coordination, when sophisticated management systems evolved into rigid bureaucracies.

Third, the logic of paradox underlying the model continues to ring true, although it often haunts and confuses the managerial psyche. Managers have difficulty in understanding that an organizational solution introduced

(continued)

by them personally in one phase eventually sows the seeds of revolution.

Fourth, the greatest resistance to change appears at the top because revolution often means that units under each senior executive will be eliminated or transformed. That is why we so often see new chief executives recruited from the outside and why senior managers frequently leave companies. Executives depart not because they are "bad" managers but because they just don't fit with where the company needs to go.

As for the differences that I have observed since the article's original publication, there is obviously much more "death" in the life of organizations today. Few organizations make it through all the phases of growth. If they don't fail, as most do in the initial phase of creativity and entrepreneurship, they often get acquired by companies that are in a later phase.

The phases are not as cleanly marked off as I depicted them. The vestiges of one phase remain as new approaches are introduced. Such overlaps are most notable in the case of the first phase entrepreneur hanging on when professional management is added in the second phase of direction.

There are also miniphases within each evolutionary stage. The delegation phase, for example, does not typically begin with the complete decentralization of the entire organization into multiple product units, as the article implies. Usually one product group is launched, and then others are added over time. Also, as delegation—or *decentralization*, as I now prefer to call this phase—advances, senior managers at the corporate office are not as hands-off as I depicted them. The addition of multiple product or geographic units over time requires a sophisticated level of involvement by senior management to review strategies, evaluate results, and communicate the organization's values—but not to micro-manage the units under them.

I would change some of the things I said about the fifth phase of collaboration. My original description of this phase suggests that the entire organization is turned into a matrix of teams. I now see the matrix as confined largely to senior management, where the heads of geographic areas, product lines, and functional disciplines collaborate as a team in order to ensure that their decisions are coordinated and implemented across global markets. The most significant change in this phase occurs when the previously bureaucratic Phase 4 control-oriented staff and systems are replaced by a smaller number of consulting staff experts who help facilitate, rather than control, decisions.

My speculation that "psychological saturation" is the crisis ending Phase 5 now seems wrong. Instead, I think the crisis is one of realizing that there is no internal solution, such as new products, for stimulating further growth.

Rather, the organization begins to look outside for partners or for opportunities to sell itself to a bigger company.

A sixth phase may be evolving in which growth depends on the design of extra-organizational solutions, such as creating a holding company or a network organization composed of alliances and cross-ownership. GE may have developed a similar model in which a periphery of companies is built around a core "money" company or bank (GE Capital) that attracts capital, earns high returns, and feeds the growth of other units.

I doubt that the advancement of information technology has made much of a difference in the basic aspects of the model. Information technology appears useful as a tool that evolves in different forms to fit each phase. For example, the Phase 2 functional organizational structure requires data that reflect revenue and cost centers, whereas Phase 3 decentralization needs data that measure profit center performance.

I wrote the article mainly about industrial and consumer goods companies, not about knowledge organizations or service businesses, which had yet to come into prominence. After recently studying a number of consulting, law, and investment firms, our research team found that those organizations also experience evolution and revolution as they grow.

In the first, entrepreneurial phase, the professional service firm pursues and tests a variety of market paths. The phase ends with the partners arguing about whether or not to stay together to concentrate on one partner's vision for the future. In the second phase, the firm focuses on one major service and eventually finds itself with a debate among the partners about whether to continue focusing on the current practice or to open another office or add additional services. A third phase of geographic or service expansion typically ends with a struggle over ownership: How much equity are the original partners willing to share with the younger partners who led the expansion and brought in new clients? The fourth phase involves institutionalizing the firm's name, reputation, and its standard way of operating, and ends in a crisis of cultural conformity in the face of which the firm must restore innovation and flexibility.

Finally, as a strong caveat, I always remind myself and others that the "ev and rev" model depicted in this article provides only a simple outline of the broad challenges facing a management concerned with growth. It is not a cookie-cutter solution or panacea. The rate of growth, the effective resolution of revolutions, and the performance of the company within phases still depend on the fundamentals of good management: skillful leadership, a winning strategy, the heightened motivation of employees, and a deep concern for customers.

DO THE BEST ORGANIZATIONS HAVE THE BEST PEOPLE?*

Jeffrey Pfeffer

Robert I. Sutton

Every company devotes enormous effort to choosing and judging its members. Such efforts make sense. There are huge differences between the best and worst performers. And renowned companies do have great people. Consider IDEO, one of the largest and arguably most successful innovation firms in the world. IDEO's products have won more than twice as many *Business Week* Industrial Design Excellence Awards than the next best firm. IDEO's people have designed thousands of products and experiences, everything from the first Apple mouse, to full-size mechanical whales for the Free Willy films, to finding ways for DePaul Health Center's emergency room to make visits less bewildering. IDEO even designed and built a full-sized, working prototype of Dilbert's "dream cubicle" for Scott Adams, the cartoon character's creator.[1]

We spent a lot of time trying to figure out why IDEO is so creative. In the mid-1990s, we did an 18-month study that entailed spending a couple of days a week watching IDEO's designers and talking to them about their work. When we teach managers about IDEO, they often conclude that the firm is creative because it attracts and keeps talented people. David Kelley, the founder and chairman, reinforces this view when after being pressed to reveal IDEO's secrets, he grins and says, "I just hire some smart people and get out of the way." We repeat Kelley's quote to dissuade leaders bent on micro-managing creative work. It is true that IDEO hires smart people and does not monitor them closely. Yet this truth is also fundamentally misleading about the source of IDEO's success and about why other organizations succeed and fail, too.[2] The best evidence indicates that natural talent is overrated, especially for sustaining organizational performance.

Why Smart and Skilled People Fuel Performance

Not everyone agrees that talent and individual attributes are overrated. Psychologist Benjamin Schneider argues that "the people make the place," and that *those who compose* an organization—their abilities and personalities—"come to define how that place looks, feels, and behaves."[3] Schneider says "it only *looks* like organizations determine behavior." He argues that because people are so hard to change, *who* is in an organization is far more important than what happens to them, and that things like training, peer pressure, management action, and rewards have little or no effect.[4] He concludes that organizational culture and performance result mostly from who is hired and sticks around. Jim Collins, in *Good to Great,* echoes this sentiment when he emphasizes the importance of "getting the right people on the bus."[5]

These views are bolstered by research showing that better small groups usually contain better people. Experiments show that in groups doing everything from brainstorming to solving complex problems performance depends on members' individual skill (or lack of it). Psychologist Edwin Locke and his colleagues argue this is just common sense. They point out that in the 1960s, each of the five offensive linemen on the Dallas Cowboys weighed 300 pounds or more, and each was enormously strong and skilled before joining the team, so their teamwork was a trivial factor in their success compared to their individual traits. No matter how motivated, well-trained, or cooperative, a line made up of 200-pound "wimps" would be vastly inferior.[6]

The argument is that human skills, intelligence, physical attributes, and personalities are so enduring and hard to change that what organizations do, including their performance, mostly reflects an additive combination of the kinds of people who join and stay. This view pervades *The War for Talent,* a book by McKinsey consultants Ed Michaels, Helen Handfield-Jones, and Beth Axelrod.[7] They assert that talented people are scarce, better talent makes a huge difference in company performance, and the information revolution means that talent is among the most crucial competitive advantages for any company. They cite their surveys at 120 companies and 27 case studies to show this is the new reality. They advise firms to differentiate and affirm the best people: Aggressively remove "C players"; heap praise, mentoring, rewards, and promotions on "A players"; and offer far more modest kudos, compensation, and the like to the solid "B players," who form the majority of the workforce. This research has some deep flaws—especially, as we mentioned in chapter 2, that the claimed *cause* of performance (managing talent) was measured after its *effect*.[8] But some rigorous studies do imply that great people make great organizations. And there are numerous well-crafted studies that examine why some people are more talented and productive than others.

The Best Are *Much Better Than the Rest*

There are enormous and well-documented differences between the best and worst performers in numerous endeavors. Psychologist Dean Keith Simonton, who has spent his career studying greatness and genius, concludes: "No matter where you look, the same story can be told, with only minor adjustments. Identify the 10 percent who have contributed the most to some endeavor, whether it be songs, poems, paintings, patents, articles, legislation, battles, films, designs, or anything else. Count all the accomplishments that they have to their credit. Now tally the achievements of the remaining 90 percent who struggled in the same area of achievement. The first tally will equal or surpass the second tally. Period."[9] One study showed that a mere 16 composers produced about 50 percent of the classical music that is performed and recorded today, while 235 others produced the remaining half. Another study found that 10 percent of the authors had written about 50 percent of the books in the Library of Congress. Research on computer programmers showed that the most productive programmers were 10 times more productive than the least productive, and five times more productive than average programmers.[10] Such staggering variations suggest a strong argument for bringing aboard and keeping the best people, especially those in the top 10 percent.

Less dramatic but still large differences were uncovered by industrial psychologists Frank Schmidt and John Hunter, who analyzed *all* published studies (spanning 85 years!) "that measured or counted the amount of output for different employees." They found, in comparing superior workers (at the 84th percentile) with average workers (at the 50th percentile), that superior workers in jobs requiring low skill produced 19 percent more than average workers, superior workers in jobs requiring high skill were 32 percent more productive, and for professionals and managers, superior performers produced 48 percent more output than average performers. It is hard to quarrel with their conclusion that such differences can affect an organization's economic health.[11]

Organizations Can *Spot the Best in Advance*

Not only are there huge differences between the best and the worst performers, such differences in who is going to be the best or the worst can be predicted in advance, albeit not with perfect accuracy. Schmidt and Hunter's exhaustive study examined 19 methods that organizations used to select new employees. The best predictor of future job performance was general mental ability, like IQ and related measures of overall smartness. Other strong predictors were work sample tests (candidates do tasks associated with the job, like a typing test), job tryouts (candidates do the whole job for a few hours or days), structured job interviews (every candidate is asked the same questions in the same order), and conscientiousness (reliable and scrupulous people, with a strong sense of purpose and will). The worst predictors were age and graphology (using handwriting analysis to assess personality).[12]

Cognitive ability is not the only kind of intelligence that fuels job performance. Promising research on multiple intelligences, like practical, social, and emotional intelligence, has sparked interest and controversy.[13] The most heated arguments are about whether traditional IQ tests are fair, measure a sufficiently broad range of human abilities, and are strong or weak predictors of performance. We won't drag you through these arguments, many fueled by ideology rather than evidence, but virtually all researchers agree that traditional IQ tests predict job performance, although they disagree on how strongly. And practical intelligence does predict job performance over and above traditional IQ, especially practical problem-solving skills (e.g., focusing on what is important, not what is urgent) and interpersonal skills or social intelligence (e.g., showing respect and listening to others).

Other measures also can predict success in specific jobs. Salespeople face constant rejection and failure in their work, for example, so it seems reasonable that optimists would fare better than pessimists. Psychologists Martin Seligman and Peter Schulman predicted that optimistic salespeople who viewed setbacks as temporary and not their fault would be more successful than those with opposing pessimistic styles. Indeed, their study of 103 newly hired life insurance agents found that optimists sold more insurance and were about twice as likely to still be selling insurance a year later.[14]

In short, there is disagreement about exactly which factors best predict job performance, and no assessment is always accurate. But managers can make evidence-based decisions about who to hire and who to avoid.

Stars (Might) Attract More Stars

Advocates of the talent mind-set emphasize that, if you bring in great people, they will attract and bring in more great people. This argument is especially dear to consultants and executives who recommend that employees be sorted into star "As," ho-hum but acceptable "Bs," and "Cs" who need to shape up or ship out. Bradford Smart contends, based on over 100 consulting engagements, that "in practice, A players hire other A players. B players hire C players. C players hire F players. If you can woo a small critical mass of A players, you can start a favorable chain reaction and build a strong company."[15] Smart's book *Topgrading* emphasizes that the "fact" that "C players don't hire A players" is the biggest single hurdle to building a company filled with A players.[16] *The War for Talent* makes the same point. "We call it the Rule of Crappy People: Bad managers hire very, very bad employees, because they are threatened by anyone who is anywhere near as good as they are."[17]

Despite the vehemence of these claims, we can't find rigorous research on the Rule of Crappy People, or on related assertions that good people hire good people and bad people hire even worse people. The general conclusion that people want to be with others like themselves, and shun different people is, however, supported by research on similarity and attraction effects. In the battle of clashing clichés, study after study shows that birds of a feather flock together, not that opposites attract. Even when people try not to be swayed, they have warmer feelings and offer more positive evaluations of others who look like them, act like them, have the same birthday, or are similar on any dimension they notice. And they downgrade and shun different people.[18]

This similar-to-me effect helps explain why most organizations unwittingly "bring in the clones." Male interviewers prefer hiring males, white interviewers prefer white candidates to blacks and Hispanics, and so on.[19] So future studies may confirm the claims made in *Topgrading* and *The War for Talent* that a "virtuous cycle" starts when you hire A players. For now, the controlled study that comes closest was done with 40 Canadian college students who, based on a personality test, were classified as being in the top or bottom third in conscientiousness. Then they were shown videotapes of two candidates for a job overseeing students in a college dormitory. One candidate acted conscientious, describing himself as diligent, dedicated, and attentive to detail; the other was the opposite, describing himself as spontaneous, laid back, and not very systematic. A similar-to-me effect was observed: conscientious students rated the conscientious candidate as better suited to the job; less conscientiousness students didn't notice much difference between candidates. Conscientiousness was the second strongest predictor of job performance (after IQ) in Schmidt and Hunter's study, and certainly is part of the A player profile. So this research bolsters claims that good people want to hire other good people like themselves, but reveals nothing about the Rule of Crappy People.[20]

Why an Obsession with Individual "Talent" Can Be Hazardous to Organizational Health

Michael Schrage is right: "A collaboration of incompetents, no matter how diligent or well-meaning, cannot be successful."[21] But not being in the top 10 percent isn't the same as being incompetent—90 percent of the people in every organization simply fail to qualify. It is a mathematical fact that only 10 percent of the people are going to be in the top 10 percent. And despite claims in *The War for Talent, Topgrading*, and numerous other books on hiring the best people, the talent mind-set is rooted in a set of assumptions and empirical evidence that are incomplete, misleading, and downright wrong. A moment's consideration will reveal that the war for talent idea rests on three crucial assumptions:

- Individual ability is largely fixed and invariant—there are better and worse people.
- People can be reliably sorted based on their abilities and competence.
- Organizational performance is, in many instances, the simple aggregation of the individual performances; what matters is what individuals do, not the context or system in which they do it.

As we will soon see, each of these assumptions isn't so completely true that one would want to base organizational success on its validity.

Talent Isn't So Easy to Perfectly Identify

What do Steve Young, Kurt Warner, and Jake Delhomme have in common? All eventually became starting National Football League quarterbacks, but only after long stints sitting on the bench or playing in obscure football leagues because they weren't considered good enough for the NFL. All three played in Super Bowls, and Young and Warner won Most Valuable Player awards. Talent management "errors" like these "point out how . . . luck plays a much greater role than anyone would have you believe and sometimes, key players emerge from the most unlikely circumstances."[22] In fact, just about all professional sports teams—a domain where we might expect individual talent to be crucial and readily discerned—have numerous top players who were not deemed as such early in their careers.

Talent is not easy to identify for a number of reasons. First, even the best predictors don't do a very good job of selecting the best people. Take IQ. Intelligence is the most powerful predictor of job performance across studies, but IQ still seldom correlates more than 0.4 with performance. Since the amount of variation explained by a predictor is the correlation squared, intelligence accounts for no more than 16 percent of the variation in performance, leaving some 84 percent *unexplained*. Other alleged predictors have even lower correlations. This doesn't mean that companies should spurn valid indicators of ability when selecting people. But it does mean we all ought to be more circumspect about our ability to discern talent.

Second, performance naturally varies over time. Even the best athletes, the best musicians, and yes, the best professors, have off days. A study of output rates among foundry employees (machine molders, hand molders, and chippers and grinders) found week-to-week consistency in individual employee output that would leave about 50 percent of the variation unexplained. A review of other studies of variation in individual output in industrial settings where output could be precisely measured and both incentives and skills were constant reported that "individual output varied over a fairly large range from week to week."[23] This means that, depending on when you happened to look, A players would appear to be B players, or vice versa. An obvious implication is that you get better measures of performance or ability if you take more than one sample. Unfortunately, this simple insight is routinely ignored: hiring decisions are often based on a single test, work sample, or interview. Similarly, student achievement tests—used to measure whether schools are failing or succeeding—are administered once a year, at most.

Yet another problem with assessing ability or talent is that human judgments are clouded by invariable, potent, and largely inescapable psychological biases. A few years ago, one of us talked to an oil company executive who claimed he could identify top managerial talent at an early age. We asked how he could be so confident in his ability. He responded that the people he identified, who then were tapped for a fast track program, invariably turned out to be successful. This executive never considered that their success could stem mostly from being tapped, not from his ability to spot talent. Consider a more systematic study of managerial bias. Managers provided performance evaluations for two types of employees—subordinates they were involved in hiring versus subordinates they were not involved in hiring. As you might expect, managers gave higher performance evaluations to subordinates they had a voice in hiring, independently of other employee performance measures.[24] This is what happens when people expend effort and make a public commitment to a course of action—they think they have done a good job. If you help choose someone for a position, you will think more highly of that person's abilities compared to someone you didn't help select, in part to justify the decision you have made.

These uncertainties and human frailties mean that for most jobs in most organizations, assessing talent and ability is fraught with error and bias. Most dimensions of work performance are not as objective as how well someone can pitch, hit a ball, or throw a discus. In ambiguous, interdependent, subjective situations, all sorts of biases—including the commitment effect just described, as well as biases from similarity and liking—will intrude and affect how talent is assessed. These biases cloud how talent is judged even when objective performance indicators are present, such as how fast a person can type or how many points a basketball player has scored.[25]

Talent Isn't Fixed—Unless You Believe It Is

Yet another reason why talent is so difficult to assess is that it is a moving target. Despite all the myths, talent is not completely fixed or predetermined at birth or at a young age. Talent depends on a person's motivation and experience. Talent depends on how a person is managed or led. Assessments of talent depend on how it is defined by a given culture in a given era. Talent depends more on effort and having access to the right information and techniques than on natural ability. Talent, in other words, is far more malleable than many people want us to believe.

Consider the cultural and historical factors that shape whether a person is anointed as talented. Today Rembrandt is considered a great painter. Many people today consider Johann Sebastian Bach a great composer, and Mozart as one of the greatest composers. Yet these and many other geniuses were largely unrecognized and unrewarded during their lifetimes. Why? Because what is great art or what is great music depends so much on cultural conventions and reigning definitions of art and music. Judgments about talent depend on interests and tastes. For Bach's contributions to be fully recognized, ideas about music itself had to change so that his music fit the definition of greatness.[26]

Talent or ability also depends on what happens to people and how they are coached, not just their innate skill or motivation. Consider baseball. A study by Lawrence Kahn examined the effect of baseball managers on team and player performance. Kahn measured player ability by the average of their performance over their entire careers, a reliable indicator of player talent. He found that some managers inspired players to perform above their ability, and other managers stymied players, consistently driving players to perform below their ability. Ability or talent did not explain all of a player's performance in a given year. How the player was managed and coached mattered, too.[27]

There is no doubt that inherited abilities limit how well people can do in some pursuits. There aren't any horse racing jockeys who are 7' 3" tall, nor any professional basketball players who are 4'10". But natural talent is overrated. Exceptional performance doesn't happen without exceptional effort, and even allegedly inherited abilities—like IQ and other "smartness" measures—improve markedly and continuously when people work hard, have good coaching, and *believe* they will keep getting better. The nature versus nurture debate persists in academia and society. But natural gifts are useless without lots of practice. People, teams, and organizations that are novices at something almost always do it badly at first; brilliant or at least competent performance is only achieved through raw persistence, coupled with the belief that improvement will happen. What people are able to do as beginners is far less important than whether they try hard and keep learning every day.

Decades of research by University of Florida's Anders Ericsson show that experts and superstars—at least in every endeavor where measurement is possible—act a lot like golf superstar Tiger Woods. By the time Tiger was 6 years old, he was playing golf almost every day and was coached by a skilled pro, Rudy Duran, from ages 4 to 12. Ericsson's research in dozens of domains reveals a similar story—exceptional performance doesn't happen without approximately 10 years of nearly daily, deliberate practice, for about four hours a day, by people who somehow (e.g., coaching, skilled peers or competitors, or books) have access to the best techniques. This 10-year rule holds in every domain he studied—chess, medicine, auditing, programming, bridge, physics, juggling, dance, and music.[28]

Once achieved, exceptional performance can't be maintained without relentless effort either. Dean Keith Simonton shows that in everything from science to the arts the most renowned geniuses—Mozart, da Vinci, Picasso, Einstein, and Darwin—don't have a higher success rate than their ordinary contemporaries. They simply *do more* than others. Everyone has heard of Charles Darwin's *Origin of Species,* but few know of his next book, a narrow and unheralded study of orchids. Simonton also shows that geniuses don't have hot streaks—the periods when they produce the most successes are those when they also produce the most failures.[29]

Practice and effort also counts for surgeons. Faculty in teaching hospitals notice a gifted resident now and then, someone, in surgeon Atul Gawande's words, "who picks up complex manual skills unusually quickly, sees the operative field as a whole, notices trouble before it happens." Yet medical school faculty believe that practice, not natural talent, is required to become a great surgeon, to "be boneheaded enough to stick at practicing this one difficult thing day and night for years on end." Gawande tells us that during his interviews for surgical residencies no one asked him to sew, tested his dexterity, or ever checked if he had steady hands.[30]

What is true for individuals is also true for organizations, groups, and teams. Exceptional performance depends heavily on experience and effort. No matter how gifted (or ordinary) team members are to start out, the more experience they have working together, the better their teams do. Think of the U.S. women's national soccer team, which has won numerous championships including two of the four women's World Cups and two of the three Olympic women's tournaments held to date. The team certainly has had enormously talented players, including Mia Hamm, Brandi Chastain, Julie Foudy, and Joy Fawcett. Yet every team member, including recently retired superstar Mia Hamm, will tell you that the most important factors in their success were the communication, mutual understanding, respect, and ability to work together that developed during the dozen or so years that the stable core group played together. Quantitative research on team effectiveness has demonstrated the power of such joint experience in every setting examined, including string quartets, surgical teams, student groups, top management teams, and airplane cockpit crews.[31] The sole exception is a study of R&D teams. These teams continued getting more and more productive during their first four years or so, but their output then slipped unless they brought in new members and had contact with outsiders—so old teams eventually go stale unless they bring in new ideas.[32]

Experienced teams perform better, because over time members come to trust each other more, communicate more effectively, and learn to blend each other's diverse skills, strengths, and weaknesses. Even a little experience together helps: a disproportionately high percentage of mistakes made during commercial airlines flights happen early in the typically 72-hour stint that a cockpit team spends together. The National Transportation Safety Board's study of incidents (serious mistakes and errors in flights, short of a crash) found that 73 percent happened the first day that crews were together, and fully 44 percent happened on crews' first flights.[33] And teams that have a lot of experience together gain a huge advantage. Professors Kathleen Eisenhardt and Claudia Schoonhoven conducted a study of 98 (of the 102) semiconductor firms founded in the United States between 1978 and 1985. They discovered that when a founding team's members had worked together before (plus had more industry experience and larger teams), firms enjoyed greater financial success in their first two years. This performance advantage became increasingly stronger during the third, fourth, fifth, and sixth years after a company was founded.[34]

These studies all suggest that the "talent mind-set" is dangerous because it treats talent as something fixed. This mind-set causes people to believe that it just isn't worth trying hard because they—or the people they lead—are naturally smart or not, and there is little if anything anyone can do about it. Yet raw cognitive ability—at least performance on tests that measure it—isn't nearly as difficult to enhance as many people think. When people believe they can get smarter, they do. *But*—and this is *very important*—when people believe that cognitive ability is difficult or impossible to change, they don't get smarter.

A series of studies by Columbia University's Carol Dweck shows that when people believe their IQ level is unchangeable, "they become too focused on being smart and looking smart rather than on challenging themselves, stretching and expanding their skills, becoming smarter."[35] Dweck finds that most people believe either that intelligence is fixed *or* that it can be improved through effort and practice. People who see intelligence as fixed believe statements like "if you are really smart at something, you shouldn't have to work hard at it," don't take remedial classes to repair glaring deficiencies, avoid doing things they are not already skilled at because it makes them look dumb, and derive less pleasure from sustained effort and commitment.[36] After all, they believe, if you have to work hard at things, it means you aren't that smart.

Dweck concludes that when people believe they are born with natural and unchangeable smarts, it causes them to learn less over time. They don't bother to keep learning new things and improving old skills, and even when they do try, they don't enjoy it. But people who believe that intelligence is malleable keep getting smarter and more skilled at what they already can do, and are willing to learn new things that they do badly at first.

This research means that your theories of performance and ability become self-fulfilling. If you believe that ability is fixed and communicate this to the people you lead, they will see their performance as an opportunity to judge their competence in terms of where they fall in the distribution of immutable intelligence. If by contrast, you—and they—believe that performance and ability are malleable, they will see tasks as learning opportunities, not tests that determine if they are preordained to be good or bad at something. These findings also mean if you believe that only 10 percent or 20 percent of your people can ever be top performers, and use forced rankings to communicate such expectations in your company, then only those anointed few will probably achieve superior performance.

This research explains why Southwest Airlines tells new employees that they are the "cream, cream, cream of the crop." Southwest is selective about who it hires, but by believing that everyone is capable of the highest performance levels, and having a system that makes it possible, it turns that belief into reality over and over again.

Great Systems Are Often More Important Than Great People

People need to share what they know, coordinate with others, and understand where their jobs fit in because organizations, or networks of organizations, are often complex systems that only can perform well when the pieces mesh together well. People's performance depends on the resources they have to work with, including the help they get from colleagues, and the infrastructure that supports their work. Wide-ranging research on software development, airlines, the air traffic control system, oil refineries, nuclear power plants, aircraft carriers, NASA, and the automobile industry show it is impossible for even the most talented people to do competent, let alone brilliant, work in a flawed system. Yet a well-designed system filled with ordinary—but well-trained—people can consistently achieve stunning performance levels.

NASA's space shuttle program provides a painful illustration. It is a classic case of smart, hardworking, and well-meaning people trapped in a system with such ingrained flaws that even a horrible accident, the *Challenger* shuttle explosion in 1986, didn't change it much. That is the conclusion reached by the Columbia Accident Investigation Board, a blue-ribbon panel charged with determining why the shuttle *Columbia* disintegrated upon reentry on February 1, 2003.[37] One chapter compares the *Columbia* accident with the *Challenger* explosion 17 years earlier. It begins with a comment by board member Sally Ride, the first American woman in space and a member of the Rogers Commission, the earlier task force that examined the *Challenger* accident. Ride concluded that there were remarkable echoes of the *Challenger* accident in the one that befell the *Columbia*.

The report lists one haunting parallel after another. Although nearly all of the personnel involved in the two accidents were different, the system and organizational

culture were largely unchanged. The shuttle program was treated as a routine operation governed by budgets and schedules rather than an experimental operation,
where it was unrealistic to adhere to predictable budgets and schedules—even
though the Rogers Commission had demanded exactly that change. The focus on
budget and schedule meant that *Challenger* and *Columbia* engineering teams were
held to a dangerous decision rule when making "go, no-go" launch decisions.
"Instead of having to prove it was safe to fly, they were asked to prove it was unsafe
to fly." NASA remained a dysfunctional bureaucracy where, rather than deferring to
people with the greatest technical expertise, leaders believed that "an allegiance to
hierarchy, procedure, and following the chain of command" decreased the odds of
failure. People with greater prestige and power routinely ignored and stifled those
with more expertise but less power and overturned their recommendations. In both
tragedies, pressures to cut costs and meet schedules meant that NASA administrators
outsourced so much of the shuttle design, manufacturing, and repair that they didn't
know enough about its components to make informed decisions—they were managing a system they didn't understand.

The Columbia Accident Investigation Board concluded that the organizational
system that caused *Columbia's* failure must finally be fixed or "the scene is set for
another accident." They add that, although people must always take responsibilities
for their actions, "NASA's problems cannot be solved simply by retirements, resig-
nations, or transferring personnel." In other words, the problem is the system, not the
people.

Over 15 years of research in the auto industry also provides compelling evidence for the power of systems over individual talent in a business context. Wharton
Business School's John Paul MacDuffie has combined quantitative studies of every
automobile plant in the world with in-depth case studies to understand why some
plants are more effective than others. MacDuffie has found that lean or flexible production systems, with their emphasis on teams, training, and job rotation, and their
de-emphasis of status differences between employees, build higher quality cars at a
lower cost.[38] Toyota developed and still uses such practices, consistently achieving
lower cost and higher quality than other companies—although some Honda plants
give them a run for the money, and there are signs that General Motors is finally
catching up. Toyota's success stems from its great system, not stunning individual
talent. This starts at the top of the organization. One study showed that Toyota was
the only major automobile company where a change in CEO had no effect on performance.[39] The system is so robust that changing CEOs at Toyota is a lot like changing
lightbulbs; there is little noticeable effect between the old one and the new one.

Or consider the NUMMI (New United Motor Manufacturing) plant in
Fremont, California, a Toyota-General Motors joint venture. When GM closed its
Fremont plant in 1982, it was one of the worst plants in the country, producing cars
with more defects and at a higher cost than nearly any other U.S. plant. Daily absenteeism was nearly 20 percent. Wildcat strikes and drug and alcohol abuse were rampant. Following an agreement between GM and Toyota, the plant was reopened by
Toyota in 1985; 85 percent of the initial workforce was rehired from a pool of
employees who worked at the old, awful plant, and who still belonged to the United
Auto Workers union. Before the plant was reopened, workers were given extensive
training in the Toyota Production System. Over 400 trainers were sent to NUMMI
from Japan and over 600 workers were sent to Japan for training. The year the plant
reopened, the 6,500 Novas it produced were among the lowest cost and highest quality cars made in the United States. Absenteeism was less than 3 percent. Toyota took
a bunch of F players, retrained them, put them into a great system, and magically
they became superstars. A better place made them much better people.[40]

Some will say that automobile manufacturing is not really a setting consistent with the current emphasis on knowledge work, and that NASA and the space shuttle represent a complex, interdependent system in which it would be difficult for a single individual to make a profound difference. So perhaps the best, most compelling, and most interesting study of the relationship between systems and the stars that are imported into them is by Boris Groysberg and his colleagues on the ultimate star system in business: investment analysts. Analysts are treated like stars, hired away at enormous salaries, and many achieve great media notoriety. Because analyst star quality can be measured by their listing in *Institutional Investor* magazine, and because their mobility is traceable, as is their performance, this is a revealing setting to study what happens when stars move. Groysberg found that after a company hires a star, bad things happen all around: "The star's performance plunges, there is a sharp decline in the functioning of the group or team the person works with, and the company's market value falls." In particular, "46% of the research analysts did poorly in the year after they left one company for another . . . their performance plummeted by an average of about 20% and had not climbed back to the old levels even five years later." Groysberg reports that even when stars do maintain or return to their prior status as top performers, they are unlikely to help their new employer over the long haul "because stars don't stay with organizations for long, despite the astronomical salaries firms pay to lure them away from rivals."[41]

Given all the evidence on the importance of systems, something that W. Edwards Deming and the quality movement emphasized for years, why do so many companies still place so much emphasis on getting and keeping great people and so little on building and sustaining great systems? A big part of the answer is that Western countries, like the United States, glorify rugged individualism so much that we make a cognitive error. We forget that history, organizational goals, rewards, and structure are potent causes of what people and organizations do. We give too much credit to individual heroes when organizations do things right and place too much blame on individual scapegoats when things go wrong. This perceptual blindness pervades the talent mind-set, and you see it in story after story in the business press, in corporate histories, and in advice given by gurus and management consultants.

This tendency to overattribute success and failure to individuals can be overcome, but to do so requires focusing on locating and dealing with systemic causes of performance issues. MIT Professors Nelson Repenning and John Sternman contrasted a successful and a failed process improvement effort in a manufacturing firm.[42] In the unsuccessful effort, undertaken to speed product development, managers attributed performance to individual skills and effort, not the system. Heroes and scapegoats were constantly held up as examples, but little learning and change occurred. Managers who missed targets were, in their words, "beat up" by executives. So they pressured workers to try ever harder, resulting in immediate productivity increases, which reinforced the misperception that problems were due to lazy people. But setbacks kept happening. The effort ended in failure despite more monitoring (one project manager was required to give hourly updates to his boss), more precise measures for pinpointing who was to blame, and tougher penalties for poor individual performance. Repenning and Sternman found that this effort failed largely because, rather than improving the system, managers focused on monitoring, motivating, and punishing people.

A different approach was used in the successful effort, which focused on improving cycle time. Managers consciously fought their natural tendency to focus on who deserved credit and blame, and instead worked on strengthening the system. A supervisor explained, "There are two theories. One says 'there is a problem, let's fix it.' The other says 'we've got a problem, someone is screwing up, let's go beat them up.' To make improvement, we could no longer embrace the second theory, we had to use the first.'"[43]

The Right Kind of Talent

This chapter provides numerous lessons about managing talent, but four main guidelines stand out. The content, and especially the spirit, of these guidelines clash with the talent mind-set advocated in many books and by many consultants, but are supported by more and better evidence.

1. Treat Talent as Something Almost Everyone Can Earn, Not That Just a Few People Own

John Wooden was the most successful college basketball coach ever. Over a 12-year period, his teams at the University of California at Los Angeles won the national championship 10 times—no other coach has ever come close to that record. Yet Wooden didn't define success in terms of winning or losing games or championships. To him, it was "knowing you gave your best effort to become the best of what you are capable."[44] This sounds corny, but the best evidence shows that superior performers believe in themselves, try hard, and learn constantly. Wooden believed that some players were more talented than others, and worked to recruit the best, but he believed that all those championships came from effort and teamwork, not just because his people had natural talent. Wooden asserts his definition is also superior to one based on wins and losses because it focuses on things people can control, not things they are powerless over.

The virtues of Wooden's philosophy become crystal clear when it comes to overcoming negative stereotypes. There is strong evidence that many African-Americans are subtly brainwashed to believe that intelligence is fixed and they have inherently lower ability than members of other races. The myth that African-Americans are hardwired to have lower IQs and they can't do anything about it has been perpetuated by everyone from Nobel Prize winner William Shockley to the academic psychologists who wrote the controversial *The Bell Curve*.[45] These stereotypes undermine academic performance even among African-American students who earn the best grades and test scores. Some fascinating research shows, however, that if you can convince people that smarts come from what people do, rather than what they were born with, performance improves markedly. In a study with Stanford undergraduates, randomly selected students were persuaded to believe that intelligence was malleable rather than fixed. Over two months later, they reported being more engaged in and enjoying the academic process more than students in control conditions. Most impressively, students persuaded to believe that smartness was malleable got better grades the next term, especially African-American students.[46]

Managers are not omnipotent. Performance is also driven by advice and support from peers and conscientiousness, and may be marred by personal problems like poor health and family problems. Unfortunately, managers may continue to lavish money, attention, and opportunities on anointed stars, while failing to notice (or admit) that others are performing better and learning faster. Entrenched beliefs can cause them to notice and remember the good things that their favorites do, and ignore and forget the bad. And if they notice their darlings aren't up to snuff, they might be too proud to confess they are wrong. A study of the National Basketball Association (NBA) by Barry Staw and Ha Hoang found, for example, that teams displayed irrational commitment to players they picked early in the college draft.[47] NBA teams pick the most widely heralded players first, followed by players thought to be increasingly less talented. Staw and Hoang's analysis of the 1980–1986 NBA drafts found that players picked earlier were given more playing time, were less likely to be traded to other teams, and had longer careers than lower-paid and less-hyped peers *regardless* of their actual performance. The NBAs head of public relations claimed "coaches play their best players and don't care what the person costs. Wins and losses are all that matters."[48] But Staw and Hoang showed that simply proclaiming and paying a player as a superstar can lead to biased judgments about his actual performance. So if you decide that one of your people is better than the rest, it can cause you to ignore and forget evidence that clashes with your beliefs—and that can be bad for your team or company.

2. The Law of Crappy Systems Trumps the Law of Crappy People

We've emphasized that managers, consultants, gurus, the press, and just about everyone else gives individuals too much credit and blame for organizational performance. This misguided faith in the omnipotence of saviors and villains is due largely to a cognitive error made by most people in Western countries. This fundamental attribution error was uncovered decades ago by psychologist Lee Ross.[49] It means that people place excessive weight on individual personality, preferences, and efforts when trying to explain what people (and groups and organizations) do and why they do it, and underplay the setting, culture, or system. This occurs partly because of how human perception operates. When we look at a situation, like a company, we *see* individuals—individuals acting, making decisions, doing great or awful things. The *context* in which this happens, the industry and general economic environment, the actions of all of those people we don't see, are less obvious and vivid. So it is not surprising that we overattribute actions and consequences to individuals rather than to the constraints under which they operate.

An insidious consequence of this fundamental error is something we have come to call the brain vacuum syndrome. This is where an organization hires one apparently brilliant person after another, and then places them in the same badly designed jobs in the same badly designed system. Each new incumbent seems smart and savvy until they start the job, and in a flash they start acting stupid. We first noticed this syndrome by watching friends who took jobs as deans and associate deans in business schools. These jobs come with much responsibility but little authority and few resources. Demands from students, faculty, staff, university administrators, companies, and alumni are intense, unrealistic, and in conflict. These jobs are hard, perhaps impossible, to do well. But that doesn't stop virtually every major constituency from focusing attention on the incumbent's personality and skills rather than the impossibility of doing the job. To most observers, it seems like every ounce of intelligence, common sense, and skill is sucked out of people the minute they become academic administrators. Much the same thing happened at NASA, where the Columbia Accident Investigation Board was dismayed to see that, although most of the people had been changed, the same system produced the same mistakes seen 17 years earlier—it was a system that made it difficult for smart people to do smart things.

Don't get us wrong. There are people who can't or won't do the jobs they are given. Incompetent people damage organizations and there will always be rotten apples who need to be retrained or moved to different jobs, and if all else fails, fired. But the law (or "rule") of Crappy People is a dangerous half-truth. We propose the "law of Crappy Systems" instead: bad systems do far more damage than bad people, and a bad system can make a genius look like an idiot. Try redesigning systems and jobs before you conclude that a person is "crappy." And if you keep hiring people who seem good, but turn crappy, stop blaming them and fix the system, at least if you want to turn off the brain vacuum.

3. Wisdom: The Most Crucial Talent?

Wisdom, not intelligence, is probably the most important talent for sustaining organizational performance. Organizations need people who think quickly and well when they work alone on problems with known correct answers—that is what IQ tests measure. But having people who know the limits of their knowledge, who ask for help when they need it, and are tenacious about teaching and helping colleagues is probably more important for making constant improvements in an organization, technical system, or body of knowledge. Also, as research on intelligence suggests, such wise actions help people become smarter and smarter.

Our first big clue about the wisdom-performance link came when we studied IDEO. We opened this chapter with founder and chairman David Kelley attributing IDEO's success to "hiring some smart people and getting out of the way." But that is only part of the story. The rest of the story is that Kelley can get out of the way because IDEO has intertwined cultural values, work practices, and rewards—a system—that requires little intervention from senior management. Kelley deserves much credit for designing and tinkering with this system during the 20-plus years that he served as CEO. Gwen Books, who was Kelley's assistant for over a decade, once told us, "David never stops thinking about IDEO, it is like a prototype he is constantly redesigning in his head." The genius of the design is that IDEO was, and still is under current CEO Tim Brown, largely run and policed by peers.

One of the main reasons that IDEO's system works so well is the attitude its people have toward knowledge. We mentioned this attitude of wisdom in chapter 2 as essential for practicing evidence-based management. Recall that wisdom is about "knowing what you know and knowing what you don't know." This attitude enables people to act on their (present) knowledge while doubting what they know, so they can do things *now*, but can keep learning along the way.[50] Wise people realize that all knowledge is flawed, that the only way to keep getting better at anything is to act on what you know now, and to keep updating.

Table 1 displays key elements of how wise (and unwise) people think and act in organizations. These elements stem from theory and research, but an episode at

Table 1 The Attitude of Wisdom: Elements and Antithesis in Organizations	
Wisdom	**Antithesis**
Acting with knowledge (while doubting what you know)	*Acting without knowledge or without doubting your knowledge; also inaction combined with endless analysis or, worse yet, no effort to learn what to do*
• Understanding and acknowledging the limits of your knowledge	• Acting like a know-it-all, not seeming to understand, accept, or acknowledge the limits of your knowledge
• Having humility about your knowledge	• Being arrogant or insecure about your knowledge
• Asking for and accepting help from others	• Not asking for, or refusing, help from others
• Giving help	• Not giving help, even when people clearly need your knowledge and skill
• Being curious—asking questions, listening, constantly striving to learn new things from the events, information, and people around you	• Lacking curiosity about people, things, and ideas; answering questions and talking only to show people how smart you are, without learning anything from them

IDEO provides perhaps the best summary and explanation. Robert Sutton was sitting with two engineers, Larry Schubert and Roby Stancel, who were talking about designing a device for Supercuts, a chain of hair salons that specializes in inexpensive, fast haircuts. They were talking about a device that could be attached to an electric razor to vacuum away cut hair. We were in front of Rickson Sun's workstation. Rickson looked mildly disturbed as he shut his sliding door to muffle the noise of our meeting—a futile gesture because his stylish cubicle had no roof and low walls. Rickson still looked a bit annoyed when he emerged minutes later to tell us that he had once worked on a product with key similarities to the device Larry and Roby were designing—a vacuum system that carried away the fumes from a hot scalpel that cauterized skin during surgery. He also brought out a report describing different kinds of plastic tubing sold by vendors. Larry Schubert commented, "Once Rickson realized he could help us, he had to do it, or he wouldn't be a good IDEO designer."

This simple episode illustrates the attitude of wisdom and why it enables people to keep learning and systems to keep getting better. Larry and Roby are smart people but knew that if they acted like know-it-alls, the design would suffer. They deferred to Rickson's knowledge. They reacted with a kind of confident humility we saw many times at IDEO. When Rickson offered to help, they knew and he knew that to improve the design they had to listen to him, and follow up on his offer to help in the future.

IDEO may sound like a warm and fuzzy organization, but no matter how smart designers are, if they refuse to work cooperatively and act unwise, the consequences are swift and unpleasant. Every now and then, IDEO hires designers who act as if taking time to help others—and asking for help—aren't parts of their job. These selfish designers are the subjects of nasty gossip. They are teased, shunned, and given boring work. Some learn to be wise. Those who don't are treated as if they are invisible; there is no need to fire them, they realize that they better leave.

IDEO is just one organization that fosters and displays an attitude of wisdom. Others include Southwest Airlines, the Toyota Production System, and U.S. Navy aircraft carriers with remarkable safety records. Once you start studying organizations where people keep learning and moving forward, and where systems keep getting better instead of inducing the same errors again and again, you see the attitude of wisdom.

4. Encourage People to Be Noisy and Nosy—It Promotes Wisdom

Here is a trick question. Imagine that you just had a major operation and are given the choice: do you want to stay in a nursing unit that administers the wrong drug or the wrong amount, or forgets to give the right drug, about once every 500 patient days, or would you rather be in a unit that blunders *10* times as often? In the mid-1990s, Harvard Business School's Amy Edmondson was doing what she *thought* was a straightforward study of how leader and coworker relationships influence errors in eight nursing units. Edmondson, and the Harvard physicians funding her research, were flabbergasted when nurse questionnaires showed that the units with *best* leadership and *best* coworker relationships reported making *10 times more errors than the worst!*

Puzzled but determined to understand this finding, Edmondson brought in another researcher to observe these nursing units. Edmondson didn't tell this second researcher about her findings, so he wasn't biased. When Edmondson pieced together what this researcher observed with her findings, she realized that better units reported more errors because people felt psychologically safe to do so. In these units, nurses said "mistakes are natural and normal to document" and "mistakes are serious because of the toxicity of the drugs, so you are never afraid to tell the nurse manager." In the units where errors were rarely reported, nurses said things like "The environment is unforgiving, heads will roll." The physicians who helped sponsor her research changed their view of medical errors 180 degrees. They no longer saw errors as purely objective evidence, but partly as a reflection of whether people are learning from and admitting mistakes or trying to avoid blame and, in the process, possibly covering things up.

Edmondson and her colleagues have since done multiple studies on how hospitals, surgical teams, doctors, and nurses learn from problems and errors, which reveal much about talents and behaviors that promote wisdom. Especially pertinent is a study of nurses that examined 194 patient care failures, everything from problems caused by broken equipment to drug treatment errors. Edmondson and colleague Anita Tucker concluded that those nurses whom doctors and administrators saw as *most talented* unwittingly caused the same mistakes to happen over and over. These "ideal" nurses quietly adjust to inadequate materials without complaint, silently correct others' mistakes without confronting error-makers, create the impression that they never fail, and find ways to quietly do the job without questioning flawed practices. These nurses get sterling evaluations, but their silence and ability to disguise and work around problems undermine organizational learning. Rather than these smart silent types, hospitals would serve patients better if they brought in wise and noisy types instead.

Table 2 lists these talents of wisdom. All of these characteristics help people act on what they know, and keep improving their own skills, peers' skills, and organizational practices and procedures. The crux is, if you want better performance instead of the illusion of it, you and your people must tell everyone about problems you've fixed, point out others' errors so all can learn, admit your own errors, and never stop questioning what is done and how to do it better. These actions can annoy doctors and administrators—or any other authority figure—who prefer quiet and compliant underlings, but if we want organizations that do as much good and as little harm as possible, these talents are essential.[51]

Similar advice came from the Columbia Investigation Board, who emphasized that the risk of future accidents would be reduced if people felt safer to complain, point out mistakes and risks, and ask questions. They concluded:

> *For both accidents there were moments when management's definition of risk might have been reversed were it not for the many missing signals—an absence of trend analysis, imagery data not obtained, concerns not voiced, information overlooked or dropped from meetings . . . [P]eople who are marginal and powerless in*

Table 2	The Talents of Wisdom: People Who Sustain Organizational Learning
Noisy complainers	Repair problems right away and then let every relevant person know that the system failed
Noisy troublemakers	Always point out others' mistakes, but do so to help them and the system learn, not to point fingers
Mindful error-makers	Tell managers and peers about their own mistakes, so that others can avoid making them too. When others spot their errors, they communicate that learning—not making the best impression—is their goal
Disruptive questioners	Won't leave well enough alone. They constantly ask why things are done the way they are done. Is there a better way of doing things?

Source: Based on research by Anita L. Tucker and Amy C. Edmondson.

organizations may have useful information or opinions that they don't express. Even when these people are encouraged to speak, they find it intimidating to contradict a leader's strategy or a group consensus. Extra effort must be made to contribute all relevant information to discussions of risk.[52]

Prestige, Pride, and Performance

A couple years ago, one of us give a speech at a renowned (but declining) high-technology firm that used a forced-ranking system. They called it a stacking system. Managers were required to rank 20 percent of employees as A players, 70 percent as Bs, and 10 percent as Cs. Just as the *War for Talent* advises, they gave the lion's share of rewards to As, modest rewards to Bs, and fired the Cs. But in an anonymous poll, the firm's top 100 or so executives were asked which company practices made it difficult to turn knowledge into action. The stacking system was voted the worst culprit. This is not just one company's experience. A survey of more than 200 human resource professionals from companies employing more than 2,500 people by the Novations Group found that even though more than half of the companies used forced ranking, the respondents reported that forced ranking resulted in lower productivity, inequity and skepticism, negative effects on employee engagement, reduced collaboration, and damage to morale and mistrust in leadership.[53]

Research on the link between talent and organizational performance reveals why these findings aren't surprising. It is not that all employees deserve equal treatment. All human organizations, or for that matter, all mammal groups, have status hierarchies. Some members are valued, respected, and have great influence. Others are held in low esteem, shunned, and made powerless. Those at the top of the heap feel pride; those at the bottom feel shame. It would be impossible, and probably undesirable, for any leader to eliminate status differences. People who help the organization succeed deserve prestige, and those who help it fail deserve to be shunned. Figuring out who deserves a place at the top—and the bottom—of the pecking order, and how to get them where they deserve to be, is part of a manager's job.

But we can't find a shred of evidence that it is better to have just a few alpha dogs at the top and to treat everyone else as inferior. Rather, the best performance comes in organizations where as many people as possible are treated as top dogs. If you want people to keep working together and learning together, it is better to grant prestige to many rather than few, and to avoid big gaps between who gets the most and least rewards and kudos. A related, and equally crucial, lesson is that smart people are typically granted more prestige than they deserve, and wise people are granted less. Smartness is important, but wisdom is more crucial for fueling organizational (and individual) performance over the long haul.

We also can't find any evidence that organizations benefit from routinely firing people in the bottom 10 percent or 20 percent. If an organization selects and trains people right, and places them in an effective system, there is no reason why 10 percent or 20 percent would automatically become incompetent every year. On the other hand, research on maintaining group and organizational culture shows that stigmatizing and removing destructive misfits is crucial to organizational health. There are sound reasons for reserving the bottom rungs for people who never bother to learn new things, don't help others learn, or don't try to improve how the organization works. If reeducating them, or even ignoring and shaming them, doesn't change their ways, it is probably best to expel them. Getting rid of such people signals that their behavior is destructive and unnecessary.

Notes

1. For more information about IDEO, see Thomas Kelley, *The Art of Innovation* (New York: Doubleday, 2001) and http://www.ideo.com/.

2. This research resulted in papers including R. I. Sutton and A. Hargadon, "Brainstorming Groups in Context: Effectiveness in a Product Design Firm," *Administrative Science Quarterly* 41 (1996): 685–718; A. Hargadon and R. I. Sutton, "Building an Innovation Factory," *Harvard Business Review* (May–June 2000): 157–166; A. Hargadon and R. I. Sutton, "Technology Brokering and Innovation in a Product Development Firm," *Administrative Science Quarterly* 42 (1997): 716–749.

3. Benjamin Schneider, "The People Make the Place," *Personnel Psychology* 40 (1987): 437–453.

4. Ibid., 440.

5. Jim Collins, *Good to Great* (New York: HarperCollins, 2001).

6. Edwin A. Locke et al., "The Importance of the Individual in the Age of Groupism," in *Groups at Work,* ed. Marlene E. Tuner (Mahwah, NJ: Erlbaum, 2001), 501–528.

7. Ed Michaels, Helen Handfield-Jones, and Beth Axelrod, *The War for Talent* (Boston: Harvard Business School Press, 2001).

8. For example, in their 1997 sample of 77 companies, the authors report that companies were *first* rated as high or average performers based on return to shareholders during the prior decade, and *then* interviews and surveys were done to measure how these firms were "fighting" the talent wars. A change cannot be caused by something that occurs *after* it happens; yet the authors treated the business practices as "causes" and prior performance as "effect." Even if we assume (as the authors might have) that the 1997 survey and interview data from these companies measured how they had managed talent during the prior 10 years, it is plausible—indeed far more likely—that better financial performance *caused* companies to use the practices that they recommend. Michaels and his colleagues report, for example, that the high-performing companies were more likely than average-performing companies to "pay whatever it takes to prevent losing top performers." Couldn't it be that firms with superior financial performance would simply have more money to lavish on top performers? Perhaps the most questionable claim in the book is made in *The War for Talent*'s last chapter, which tells leaders who follow their advice to "expect a huge impact in a year." We can't find any quantitative evidence in the book (or any other research) that seems to support this claim; rather it seems to be guided by stories about the authors' heroes. Given the limits of case studies we reviewed in chapter 2, and given that so much of the advice in the book is unsupported or clashes with past research, this claim simply isn't warranted.

9. Dean Keith Simonton, *Greatness: Who Makes History and Why* (New York: Guilford Press, 1994), 419–420.

10. This research was published by H. Sackman, W. J. Erikson, and E. E. Grant in 1968. It is described in Frederick P. Brooks Jr.'s *The Mythical Man Month* (Reading, MA: Addison-Wesley, 1995).

11. Frank L. Schmidt and John E. Hunter, "The Validity and Utility of Selection Methods in Personnel Psychology: Practical and Theoretical Implications of 85 Years of Research Findings," *Psychological Bulletin* 124 (1998): 262–274.

12. Ibid.

13. A pair of best sellers by Daniel Goleman and his colleagues—Daniel Goleman, *Emotional Intelligence: Why It Can Matter More Than IQ* (New York: Bantam, 1995); and Daniel Goleman, Richard Boyatzis, and Annie McKee, *Primal Leadership: Realizing the Power of Emotional Intelligence* (Boston: Harvard Business School Press, 2002)—have fueled much recent excitement about the power of emotional intelligence (EI) for predicting employee success. These books draw on past research and original evidence to argue that organization members who are skilled at detecting and managing emotions will have more successful careers and lead more successful organizations than counterparts who are otherwise similar, but who have lower "EQs." We find such claims to be appealing and they do seem consistent with earlier work on practical intelligence. And research may ultimately prove EQ's value for predicting which organization members will succeed and thus who to bring aboard your organization. Unfortunately, however, a spate of recent academic writing and research suggests that there is unclear evidence—and conflicting opinions—about what emotional intelligence is, how to measure it, and if the 19 elements of emotionally intelligent leaders identified by Goleman and his colleagues are original. A balanced summary of the current controversy can be found in a 2005 special issue of the *Journal of Organizational Behavior* that was devoted to emotional intelligence. See Paul E. Spector, "Introduction: Emotional Intelligence," *Journal of Organizational Behavior* 26 (2005): 409–410.

    The upshot is that, even though it seems sensible that people, especially leaders, who are skilled at detecting others' emotions and managing their own feelings will be more successful, the value of bringing in emotional intelligence experts to assess and train your people remains questionable at the moment and the validity of "emotional intelligence" as a coherent concept is debatable.

14. Martin E. P. Seligman and Peter Schulman, "Explanatory Style as a Predictor of Productivity and Quitting Among Life Insurance Sales Agents," *Journal of Personality and Social Psychology* 50 (1986): 832–838.

15. Hank Gilman et al., "The Smart Way to Hire Superstars," *Fortune*, July 10, 2000.

16. Bradford D. Smart, *Topgrading* (New York: Prentice-Hall, 1999), 34.

17. Michaels, Handfield-Jones, and Axelrod, *The War for Talent.*

18. For reviews, see: R. B. Cialdini, *Influence: The Psychology of Persuasion* (New York: Quill, 1993); K. Y. Williams and C. A. O'Reilly, "Demography and Diversity in Organizations: A Review of 40 Years of Research," in *Research in Organizational Behavior*, vol. 20, eds. B. M. Staw and L. L. Cummings (Stamford, CT: JAI Press, 1998): 77–140; J. Pfeffer, "Organizational Demography," in *Research in Organizational Behavior*, vol. 5, ed. L. L. Cummings and B. M. Staw (Greenwich, CT: JAI Press, 1983): 299–357; J. Pfeffer, *New Directions for Organization Theory: Problems and Prospects* (New York: Oxford, 1997).

19. See, for example, R. M. Kanter, *Men and Women of the Corporation* (New York: Basic Books, 1977); R. W. Eder and G. R. Ferris, *The Employment Interview: Theory, Research, and Practice* (Newbury Park, CA: Sage Publications, 1989); Thung-rung Lin, Gregory H. Dobbins, and Jiing-lih Farh, "A Field Study of Race and Age Similarity Effects on Interview Ratings in Conventional and Situational Interviews," *Journal of Applied Psychology* 77 (1992): 363–371.

20. Greg J. Sears and Patricia M. Rowe, "A Personality-Based Similar to Me Effect in the Employment Interview: Conscientiousness, Affect- Versus Competence-Mediated Interpretations, and the Role of Job Relevance," *Canadian Journal of Behavioural Science* 35 (2003): 13–24.

21. Michael Schrage, "The Rules of Collaboration," *Forbes ASAP,* June 5, 1995, 88.

22. Ira Miller, "Dark Horses Become Workhorses," *San Francisco Chronicle,* October 22, 2001.

23. Harold F. Rothe, "Output Rates Among Industrial Employees," *Journal of Applied Psychology* 63 (1978): 40–46.

24. F. D. Schoorman, "Escalation Bias in Performance Appraisals: An Unintended Consequence of Supervisor Participation in Hiring Decisions," *Journal of Applied Psychology* 73 (1988): 58–62.

25. Robert L. Cardy and Gregory H. Dobbins, "Affect and Appraisal Accuracy: Liking as an Integral Dimension in Evaluating Performance," *Journal of Applied Psychology* 71 (1986): 672–678; Barry M. Staw and Ha Hoang, "Sunk Costs in the NBA: Why Draft Order Affects Playing Time and Survival in Professional Basketball," *Administrative Science Quarterly* 40 (1995): 474–494.

26. Edward Rothstein, "Myths About Genius," *New York Times,* January 5, 2002.

27. Lawrence M. Kahn, "Managerial Quality, Team Success, and Individual Player Performance in Major League Baseball," *Industrial and Labor Relations Review* 46 (1993): 531–547.

28. See K. A. Ericsson and A. C. Lehman, "Expert and Exceptional Performance: Evidence of Maximal Adaptation to Task Constraints," *Annual Review of Psychology* 47 (1996): 273–305; K. A. Ericsson, *The Road to Excellence* (New York: Earlbaum, 1996). In addition, Robert Sutton spent many hours talking with K. A. Ericsson during the 2002–2003 academic year, when both served as Fellows at the Center for Advanced Study in the Behavioral Sciences in Palo Alto, California.

29. D. K. Simonton, *Origins of Genius: Darwinian Perspectives on Creativity* (New York: Oxford, 1999).

30. Atul Gawande, *Complications* (New York: Henry Holt, 2002), 19.

31. Richard Hackman, *Leading Teams* (Boston: Harvard Business School Press, 2002).

32. This study by Ralph Katz showed that the productivity of research and development teams continues to improve through the first three or four years that they work together, but teams that have had little change in personnel and little contact with outsiders who have new ideas suffer a drop in creative output. So, at least for creative work, shaking up things by moving members in and out and exposing them to outsiders appears to be wise. But even in this case, there does need to be a balance between stability and shaking things up, as teams did continue to improve for at least the first three years they were together. See R. Katz, "The Effects of Group Longevity on Project Communication and Performance," *Administrative Science Quarterly* 27 (1982): 81–104; R. Katz and T. J. Allen, "Investigating the Not Invented Here Syndrome: A Look at Performance, Tenure, and Communication Patterns of 50 R&D Project Groups," *R&D Management* 12 (1982): 7–19.

33. For a summaries of this and related research, see Earl L. Wiener, Barbara G. Kanki, and Robert L. Helmreich, *Cockpit Resource Management* (San Diego, CA: Academic Press, 1993); Richard Hackman, *Leading Teams* (Boston: Harvard Business School Press, 2002).

34. Kathleen M. Eisenhardt and Claudia Bird Schoonhoven, "Organizational Growth: Linking Founding Team, Strategy, Environment, and Growth Among U.S. Semiconductor Ventures, 1978–1988," *Administrative Science Quarterly* 35 (1990): 504–529.

35. Carol. S. Dweck, "Beliefs that Make Smart People Dumb," in *Why Smart People Can Be So Stupid,* ed. Robert J. Sternberg (New Haven, CT: Yale University Press, 2002), 24–41.

36. Ibid., 31.

37. This and other quotations about the investigations from Harold W. Gehman Jr. et al., *Columbia Accident Investigation Board: Report Volume I* (Washington, DC: Government Printing Office, 2003), http://www.caib.us/.

38. See, for instance, John Paul MacDuffie, "Human Resource Bundles and Manufacturing Performance: Organizational Logic and Flexible Production Systems in the World Auto Industry," *Industrial and Labor Relations Review* 48 (1995): 197–221; Frits K. Pil and John Paul MacDuffie, "The Adoption of High-Involvement Work Practices," *Industrial Relations* 35 (1996): 423–455; John Paul MacDuffie, "The Road to 'Root Cause': Shop Floor Problem Solving at Three Auto Assembly Plants," *Management Science* 43 (1997): 479–502.

39. M. B. Lieberman, L. Lau, and M. Williams, "Firm Level Productivity and Management Influence: A Comparison of U.S. and Japanese Automobile Manufacturers," *Management Science* 36 (1990): 1193–1215.

40. For a summary of the NUMMI experience, see Charles O'Reilly III and Jeffrey Pfeffer, *Hidden Value* (Boston: Harvard Business School Press, 2000).

41. Boris Groysberg, Ashish Nanda, and Nitin Nohria, "The Risky Business of Hiring Stars," *Harvard Business Review* (May 2004): 94.

42. Nelson P. Repenning and John D. Sterman, "Capability Traps and Self-Confirming Attribution Errors in the Dynamics of Process Improvement," *Administrative Science Quarterly* 47 (2002): 265–295.

43. Ibid., 287.

44. Brian D. Brio, *Beyond Success* (New York: Perigee, 1997), 30; John Wooden, *Wooden* (Chicago: Contemporary Books, 1997).

45. Richard J. Hernstein and Charles Murray, *The Bell Curve* (New York: Free Press, 1999).

46. Joshua Aronson, Carrie B. Fried, and Catherine Good, "Reducing the Effects of Stereotype Threat on African American College Students by Shaping Theories of Intelligence," *Journal of Experimental Social Psychology* 22 (2001): 1–13.

47. Staw and Ha, "Sunk Costs in the NBA."

48. Ibid., 487.

49. Lee D. Ross, "The Intuitive Psychologist and His Shortcomings," in *Advances in Experimental Social Psychology,* vol. 10, ed. L. Berkowitz (New York: Random House, 1977), 173–220.

50. See John A. Meacham, "The Loss of Wisdom," in *Wisdom: Its Nature, Origins, and Development,* ed. Robert J. Sternberg (Cambridge, England: Cambridge University Press, 1990), 181–211; and John A. Meacham, "Wisdom and the Context of Knowledge: Knowing What One Doesn't Know One Doesn't Know," in *On the Development of Developmental Psychology,* eds. D. Huhn and J. A. Meacham (Basel, Switzerland: Krager, 1983), 111–134; Robert J. Sternberg, "Implicit Theories of Intelligence, Creativity and Wisdom," *Journal of Personality and Social Psychology* 49 (1985): 607–627.

51. These data and insights are drawn primarily from two articles, Amy C. Edmondson, "Learning from Mistakes Is Easier Said Than Done: Group and Organizational Influences on the Detection and Correction of Human Error," *Journal of Applied Behavioral Science* 32 (1996): 5–28; and Anita L. Tucker and Amy C. Edmondson, "Why Hospitals Don't Learn from Failures: Organizational and Psychological Dynamics that Inhibit System Change," *California Management Review* 45 (2003): 55–72.

52. Gehman et al., Columbia Accident Investigation Board, 203.

53. Novations Group, "Uncovering the Growing Disenchantment with Forced Ranking Performance Management Systems," white paper (Boston, MA: Novations Group, August 2004).

18 Decision Making

D ecision making is more than coming up with a good judgment; managing the process of making the decision is equally important. Most supervisors and managers can point to at least one decision-making debacle in their early career caused by failing to include key players or seek out all the relevant information from the right sources. Managers and leaders also seem to struggle with the question of who should make decisions.

Victor Vroom, management professor and consultant, has devoted many years to answering this question. He and his colleagues developed a contingency theory called the leadership-participation model, which is summarized in the first article, "Leadership and the Decision-Making Process." This updated model assumes that different decision situations require different types of leadership. As with so many contingency theories, the profile of an effective leader or manager is that of someone who is capable of analyzing the context and choosing from various styles the one that is most appropriate.

The rational decision-making process has always been popular among businesspeople, especially in the United States, where rationality is highly valued. Intuitive decision making has traditionally received less respect and attention. There is a growing trend, however, toward acknowledging the contributions of intuitive decision making and acknowledging that rational decision making and intuitive decision making are complementary. In our opinion, the most important contribution to understanding intuitive decision making in recent years is Gary Klein's book, *Sources of Power: How People Make Decisions*. With his colleagues, Klein, chief scientist at Applied Research Associates and an expert on naturalistic decision making, studied and observed decision makers in action in order to discover "How People Really Make

Decisions." This excerpt explains the recognition-primed decision model, which takes most of the mystery out of intuitive decision making and frames it as a form of expert thinking.

In "Tough Calls in a Speed-Driven World," Keith Murnighan, a social psychologist at Northwestern's Kellogg School of Management, and John Mowen, marketing professor at Oklahoma State University, provide a framework to help managers make difficult choices that are timely, confident, and accurate. Their seven-step model is based on extensive research on the differences between excellent and flawed decisions. They explain how and when to use the model effectively and walk us through a case study of a difficult business decision.

LEADERSHIP AND THE DECISION-MAKING PROCESS*

Victor H. Vroom

The Jim Burns Decision

Jim Burns is an emergency response manager in a large company, specializing in ecological control systems. His work runs the gamut from removal and disposal of toxic waste to cleaning up spills of oil and other contaminants. Typically, his firm works on contracts with organizations both public and private, but occasionally Jim is called upon to deal with situations not covered by existing contracts.

This morning Jim received a phone call from the police in a nearby town. They asked for his firm's assistance in dealing with an oil spill that threatened a nearby river. Jim drove to the site with four of his associates, and within an hour the team of five had obtained the following picture of what happened.

While filling an oil tanker, the driver had gone into the cab and had fallen asleep. Before it was noticed, 10,000 gallons of crude oil had escaped and begun making its way five miles downstream and was within four hours of reaching a wildlife sanctuary.

Although the potential for environmental damage is clear, the liability is not. The driver was an employee of a small subcontractor who was uninsured and who would be forced into bankruptcy, if deemed liable. The oil company contacted its insurance company, which denied any responsibility for claims that might be made against it. Representatives of the State Environmental Protection Agency and Department of Fish and Game were contacted, and they offered their moral support, but neither had the half million dollars Jim estimated would be necessary to contain and clean up the spill.

A decision must be made soon about whether to risk the company's money in a matter in which reimbursement, if any, may have to be decided by the courts. The decision is Jim's to make, and he is experienced in making the difficult judgments that are called for. Although conscientious, the members of his team lack this experience and are likely to look to him for direction. Nonetheless, they will have to carry out any action, and Jim has found that their involvement in decisions helps them to work together as a team.

Jim Burns' challenge raises two general issues relevant to solving problems and making decisions in organizations. The first issue involves determining what solution or decision should be adopted. In this case should Jim begin the cleanup or defer any action pending resolution of the liability issues? It is this facet of decision making that is the focus of most business school curricula and of the optimization models developed by management scientists. (To be sure, the nature of this particular problem complicates matters further by the introduction of a potential conflict between organizational goals and broader social concerns.)

The second issue revolves around not *what* should be decided but *how* and with *whom* it should be decided. Should Jim decide himself, or should he involve the team in some way in determining what decision would be made? In this second issue, theories of decision making intersect with theories of leadership style.

Leadership Style

It is the latter perspective that has interested my colleagues and me and has become the focus of a large-scale program of research at Yale. We are interested in what happens between a leader and the leader's associates in decision-making situations. Our interest was inspired by an article by Bob Tannenbaum and Warren Schmidt. Their work distinguished seven different styles, varying in influence by the manager and the size of the area of freedom afforded subordinates.

Being a believer in parsimony, I have collapsed some of their alternatives, resulting in five styles that are labeled Decide, Consult Individually, Consult Group, Facilitate and Delegate. Definitions of each of these styles were given to forty specialists in the field of organization development. The specialists were then asked to locate the styles on a 10-point scale, corresponding to the relative opportunities for influencing the decision that they were likely to provide to group or team members. The definitions of these five processes, adapted from Tannenbaum and Schmidt, and the mean-scale values assigned by the OD professionals, are shown in Exhibit 1.

This language for describing leadership styles can be used in two distinctly different ways. It can be the starting point for the development of a *normative* model

Influence by Leader		Area of Freedom for Group		
0	**3**	**5**	**7**	**10**
	Consult			
Decide	**Individually**	**Consult Group**	**Facilitate**	**Delegate**
You make the decision alone and either announce or "sell" it to the group. You may use your expertise in collecting information that you deem relevant to the problem from the group or others.	You present the problem to the group members individually, get their suggestions, and then make the decision.	You present the problem to the group members in a meeting, get their suggestions, and then make the decision.	You present the problem to the group in a meeting. You act as facilitator, defining the problem to be solved and the boundaries within which the decision must be made. Your objective is to get concurrence on a decision. Above all, you take care to ensure that your ideas are not given any greater weight than those of others simply because of your position.	You permit the group to make the decision within prescribed limits. The group undertakes the identification and diagnosis of the problem, developing alternative procedures for solving it, and deciding on one or more alternative solutions. While you play no direct role in the group's deliberations unless explicitly asked, your role is an important one behind the scenes, providing needed resources and encouragement.

EXHIBIT 1   Vroom's Adaption of Tannenbaum and Schmidt's Taxonomy

that would help managers or leaders to select the style that best fits a given situation. Like our predecessors, we are convinced that each of the styles is appropriate to certain kinds of situations, and that an effective leader is one who explicitly tailors his or her style to demands of the immediate problem at hand.

The taxonomy of leadership styles in Exhibit 1 can also be used to describe what people do. A common vocabulary, independent of its normative uses, may be helpful in communication and setting of expectations between leaders and their colleagues. Furthermore, these concepts can be used by social scientists in developing a descriptive model aimed at understanding how managers actually decide whether and when to share their decision-making power.

Over the last two decades, my colleagues and I at Yale have conducted a program of research designed to provide us with a normative model that can be used by managers in evaluating specific decisions that they face and in selecting the most effective leadership style for each. The result has been the development of an "expert system" that shows substantial promise in helping managers through the myriad of factors that need attention in deciding when and how to involve associates in making decisions. In addition, we have made progress in developing a descriptive model of what managers' decision-making practices actually do. Our studies, which now involve over 100,000 managers, have been aimed at understanding the factors that actually influence what managers do. Specifically, we have looked at such factors as organizational level, cultural influences, and the role of gender in leadership style. This article outlines the normative model first and then examines our progress in understanding its similarities to, and differences from, what managers actually do.

Toward a Normative Model

Decision Quality

Let us first examine what is at stake in the choice of how much and in what way to involve others in solving problems and making decisions. The first, and undoubtedly the most important, is the quality of the decision. Above all we want wise, well reasoned, and analytically sound decisions that are consistent with the goals to be achieved and with potentially available information about the consequences of alternative means of achieving them.

What happens to decision quality as one moves from the autocratic process to more participative processes? Undoubtedly the nature of the decision and its quality will change as we move across the scale. But will decision quality increase or decrease? A conservative answer, and one that we believe to be consistent with the available research evidence, is that the effects of participation on decision quality depend on certain observable features of the decision-making situation. It depends on where the relevant knowledge or expertise resides, that is, in the leader, in the group, or both. It depends on the goals of the potential participants, particularly on the extent to which group or team members support the organizational objectives embedded in the problem. Finally, the amount of synergy exhibited in team-based processes depends on the skills and abilities of team members in working together effectively in solving problems.

Decision Implementation

Although the quality of the decision may be the most important component of its effectiveness, it is not the only component. Many high-quality decisions have been ineffective because they were not effectively implemented. The effectiveness with which a group or team implements a decision can be shown to depend on the extent to which they are committed to its success. Here the evidence is clearer and less equivocal. People do support what they help to build. Under a wide range of conditions, increasing participation leads to greater "buy-in," commitment to decisions, and motivation to implement them effectively. To be sure, there are some situations in which the motivational benefits of greater commitment are nonexistent or irrelevant to implementation. Sometimes the team may not be playing a role in implementation; in other situations, the team may view the leader as the expert or as a person with the legitimate right to make the decision and, as a result, may fully support whatever decision the leader might make.

Costs of Decision Making

Apart from considerations of decision quality and implementation, which determine the effectiveness of the decision, there are considerations of efficiency relevant to the decision process. Use of any decision-making process consumes resources. At the same time it can add to resources, albeit of a different kind. The resources consumed are costs and principally involve the time "used up" in the decision-making process. Increasing the amount of participation will increase the elapsed time to make the decision and, to an even greater degree, increase the number of hours consumed by the process. Both of these meanings of time constitute liabilities of participative leadership styles. Seeking consensus slows down the process and consumes substantially more hours than the directive or even consultative methods of decision making. The first of these costs, increasing the time interval between the occurrence of a problem and obtaining a solution, is most relevant in emergencies where a quick or immediate response is necessary. The second consideration, the hours consumed, is more generally relevant.

Development

Potentially offsetting these costs are developmental benefits of increased participation. Moving from the autocratic to highly participative styles increases the potential value of the group or team to the organization in three ways: (1) It develops the knowledge and competence of individual members by providing them with opportunities to work through problems and decisions typically occurring at higher organizational levels. (2) It increases teamwork and collaboration by providing opportunities to solve problems as part of a team. (3) It increases identification with organizational goals by giving people "a voice" in making significant decisions in *their* organizations. These developmental benefits may be negligible when the decision lacks significance, that is, when the issue being decided is trivial and lacks consequences to the organization. Furthermore, the development benefits may be of negligible value if the group or team members have a nonexistent or tenuous future within the broader organization.

We term a style inefficient when it wastes time without a commensurate return in development. Conversely, it is efficient when it is used judiciously in precisely those situations in which sufficient developmental benefits are realized. It is interesting to note that costs (time) and development, the two components of efficiency, are realized at different points in time. The time costs are immediately realizable. The slowness of response and the number of hours consumed in a group meeting have immediate effects. In contrast, the growth and development of individuals and teams may not pay off for a substantial period of time.

Putting it all Together

So far our inquiry has led us to identify four outcomes of participation, each of which is contingent on one or more situational factors. To be useful to leaders, we must supplement our analysis with a suitable tool for synthesizing the effects that we have postulated. Exhibits 2 and 3 depict decision matrices that constitute such a tool.

In Exhibit 2 we show the Time-Driven Model. It is short-term in its orientation, being concerned with making effective decisions with minimum cost. No value is placed on employee development.

TIME-DRIVEN MODEL

Instruction: The matrix operates like a funnel. You start at the left with a specific decision problem in mind. The column headings denote situational factors which may or may not be present in that problem. You progress by selecting High or Low (H or L) for each relevant situational factor. Proceed down from the funnel, judging only those situational factors for which a judgement is called for, until you reach the recommended process.

Decision Significance	Importance of Commitment	Leader Expertise	Likelihood of Commitment	Group Support	Group Expertise	Team Competence	Recommended Process
H	H	H	H	–	–	–	Decide
			L	H	H	H	Delegate
						L	Consult (Group)
					L	–	Consult (Group)
				L	–	–	Consult (Group)
		L		H	H	H	Facilitate
						L	Consult (Individually)
					L	–	Consult (Individually)
				L	–	–	Consult (Individually)
				H	H	H	Facilitate
						L	Consult (Group)
					L	–	Consult (Group)
				L	–	–	Consult (Group)
	L	H	–	–	–	–	Decide
		L	–	H	H	H	Facilitate
						L	Consult (Individually)
					L	–	Consult (Individually)
				L	–	–	Consult (Individually)
L	H	–	H	–	–	–	Decide
			L	–	–	H	Delegate
						L	Facilitate
	L	–	–	–	–	–	Decide

EXHIBIT 2 **Time-Driven Model**
(Reprinted from A Model of Leadership Style by Victor Vroom) 1999.

DEVELOPMENT-DRIVEN MODEL

PROBLEM STATEMENT	Decision Significance	Importance of Commitment	Leader Expertise	Likelihood of Commitment	Group Support	Group Expertise	Team Competence	
	H	H	-	H	H	H	H	Delegate
							L	Facilitate
						L	-	Consult (Group)
					L	-	-	Consult (Group)
				L	H	H	H	Delegate
							L	Facilitate
						L	-	Facilitate
					L	-	-	Consult (Group)
		L	-	-	H	H	H	Delegate
							L	Facilitate
						L	-	Consult (Group)
					L	-	-	Consult (Group)
	L	H	-	H	-	-	-	Decide
				L	-	-	-	Delegate
		L	-	-	-	-	-	Decide

EXHIBIT 3 **Development-Driven Model**

(Reprinted from A Model of Leadership Style by Victor Vroom) 1999.

In contrast, Exhibit 3 shows the Development-Driven Model. It may be thought of as a long-term model, because it is concerned with making effective decisions with maximum developmental consequences. No value is placed on time.

To use one of these two models, you must have a decision problem in mind that has two properties. First, it must fall within your area of freedom or discretion, that is, it must be up to you to decide. Second, there must be some identifiable group of others who are potential participants in the decision.

One enters the matrix at the left-hand side, at "Problem Statement." Arranged along the top of the matrix are seven situational factors, each of which may be present (H for high) or absent (L for low) in that problem. To obtain the recommended process, you first ascertain whether the decision to be made is a significant one. If so, you select H and answer the second question, concerning the importance of gaining commitment from the group. Continuing this procedure (avoiding the crossing of any horizontal line) will bring you to a recommended process. Sometimes a conclusive determination can be made based on as few as two factors (e.g., L,L); others require three (e.g., L,H,H), four (e.g., H,H,H,H,), or as many as seven factors (e.g., H,H,L,L,H,H,H).

Submitting the same problem to both the Time-Driven and Development-Driven Model can be instructive. Sometimes the two models yield identical recommendations. Where they differ, the Development-Driven Model recommends a higher level of participation. Occasionally, the difference may be greater than one position on the participation scale. For example, in the Jim Burns case with which this article began, the Time-Driven Model recommends Decide (H,H,H,H) and the Development-Driven Model recommends Consultation with the Group (H,H,H,H,L).

DECISION SIGNIFICANCE:	The significance of the decision to the success of the project or organization.
IMPORTANCE OF COMMITMENT:	The importance of team members' commitment to the decision.
LEADER'S EXPERTISE:	Your knowledge or expertise in relation to this problem.
LIKELIHOOD OF COMMITMENT:	The likelihood that the team would commit itself to a decision that you might make on your own.
GROUP SUPPORT FOR OBJECTIVES:	The degree to which the team supports the organization's objectives at stake in this problem.
GROUP EXPERTISE:	Team members' knowledge or expertise in relation to this problem.
TEAM COMPETENCE:	The ability of team members to work together in solving problems.

EXHIBIT 4   **Situational Factors in the Normative Model**

Although the situational factors that identify the columns in Exhibits 2 and 3 are sufficient for the experienced user of these matrices, a less experienced user may wish to refer to explanations of the situational factors in Exhibit 4. To practice using the models, read each of the four cases in Exhibit 5. Underneath each case, we have shown the recommended actions made by the two models, along with the path by which these recommendations are obtained.

Where did the Model Come from?

The model is an outgrowth of 25 years of research on leadership and decision-making processes. We began by collecting cases from managers of successful and unsuccessful decisions and ascertaining which decision process they used on each. If the decisions were unsuccessful, we wanted to find out why, whether it could have been avoided, and if so, how. Our goal was to build a model that would maximize the frequency of successful decisions, while avoiding as many of the unsuccessful ones as possible. Early on, we were joined by social scientists operating in various parts of the world, which helped us to test our concepts. We were somewhat encouraged by the findings (based on six separate studies conducted in three different countries): decisions made in accordance with a decision tree on which we were working at the time were almost twice as likely to be successful as were decisions that were inconsistent with the model.

But these investigations also made it clear that we had a long way to go, so we continued our efforts to extend and refine our early work. Now we have developed a complex set of equations that show great promise in forecasting the consequences of participation on quality, implementation, cost, and development. The decision matrices shown in Exhibits 2 and 3 are derived from the use of these equations and are the simplest way in which the implications of the model can be shown *on paper*.

Setting: Banking;
Your Position: President & Chief Executive
                        Officer

The bank examiners have just left, insisting that many of your commercial real estate loans be written off, thereby depleting already low capital. Along with many other banks in your region, your bank is in serious danger of being closed by the regulators. As the financial problems surfaced, many of the top executives left to pursue other interests, but fortunately, you were able to replace them with three highly competent younger managers. While they had no prior acquaintance with one another, each is a product of fine training program with one of the money center banks in which they rotated through position in each of the banking functions.

Your extensive experience is the industry leads you to the inevitable conclusion that the only hope is a two-pronged approach involving reduction of all but the most critical expenses and the sale of assets to other banks. The task must be accomplished quickly since further deterioration of the quality of the loan portfolio could result in a negative capital position forcing regulators to close the bank.

The strategy is clear to you, but you have many details that will need to be worked out. You believe that you know what information will be needed in order to get the bank on a course for future prosperity. You are fortunate in having three young executives to help you out. While they have had little or no experience in working together you know that each is dedicated to the survival of the bank. Like you, they know what needs to be done and how to do it.

ANALYSIS
   TIME DRIVEN:
   H H H L H H L—CONSULT GROUP
   DEVELOPMENT DRIVEN:
   H H L H H L—FACILITATE

Setting: Repertory Theater;
Your Position: Executive Director

You are the executive director of a repertory theater affiliated with a majority university. You are responsible for both financial and artistic direction of the theater. While you recognize that both of these responsibilities are important, you have focused your efforts where your own talents lie— on insuring the highest level of artistic quality to the theater's productions. Reporting to you is a group of four department heads responsible for production, marketing, development, and administration, along with an assistant dean who is responsible for the actors who are also students in the university. They are a talented set of individuals, and each is deeply committed to the theater and experienced in working together as a team.

Last week you received a comprehensive report from an independent consulting firm commissioned to examine the financial health of the theater. You were shocked by the major conclusion of the report. "*The expenses of operating the theater have been growing much more rapidly than income, and by year's end the theater will be operating in the red. Unless expenses can be reduced, the surplus will be consumed, and within five years the theater might have to be closed.*"

You have distributed the report to your staff and are surprised at the variety of reactions that it has produced. Some dispute the report's conclusions criticizing its assumptions or methods. Others are more shaken, but even they seem divided about what steps ought to be taken and when. None of them or, in fact, anyone connected with the theater would want it to close. It has a long and important tradition both in the university and in its surrounding community.

ANALYSIS
   TIME DRIVEN:
   H H L L H H H—FACILITATE
   DEVELOPMENT DRIVEN:
   H H L H H H—DELEGATE

(continued)

EXHIBIT 5   **Applying the Matrices to the Sample Cases**

Setting: Auto Parts Manufacturer;
Your Position: Country Manager

Your firm has just acquired a small manufacturer of spare auto parts in Southeast Asia. The recent collapse in the economies in this region made values very attractive. Your senior management decided to acquire a foothold in this region. It was less interested in the particular acquired firm, which produces parts for the local market, than it was in using it as a base from which to produce parts at reduced cost for the worldwide market.

When you arrived at your new assignment two weeks ago, you were somewhat surprised by the less than enthusiastic reception that you received from the current management. You attribute the obvious strain in working relations not only to linguistic and cultural differences but also to a deep-seated resentment to their new foreign owners. Your top management team seem to get along very well with one another, but the atmosphere changes when you step into the room.

Nonetheless, you will need their help in navigating your way through this unfamiliar environment. Your immediate need is to develop a plan for land acquisition on which to construct new manufacturing and warehouse facilities. You and your administrative assistant, who accompanied you from your previous assignment, should be able to carry out the plan, but its development would be hazardous without local knowledge.

ANALYSIS
    TIME DRIVEN:
    H L L L—CONSULT INDIVIDUALLY
    DEVELOPMENT DRIVEN:
    H L L—CONSULT GROUP

Setting: Manufacturer of Internal Combustion Engines;
Your Position: Project Manager

Your firm has received a contract from one of the world's largest automobile manufacturers to produce an engine to power their "flagship" sports car. The engine is of Japanese design and is very complex not only by American but by world standards. As project manager, you have been involved in this venture from the outset, and you and your team of engineers have taken pride at the rave reviews the engine has received in the automotive press. Your firm had previously been known as a producer of outboard engines for marine use, and its image is now greatly enhanced as the manufacturer of the power plant of one of the world's fastest sports cars.

Your excitement at being a part of this project was dashed by a report of serious engine problems in cars delivered to customers. Seventeen owners of cars produced in the first month have experienced engine seizures—a circumstance which has caused the manufacturer to suspend sales, to put a halt to current production, and to notify owners of this year's production not to drive the cars! Needless to say, this situation is a disaster and unless solved immediately could expose your firm to extended litigation as well as terminate what had been a mutually beneficial relationship. As the person most informed about the engine, you have spent the last two weeks on the road inspecting several of the seized engines, the plant in which they are installed, and reviewing the practices in your own company's plant in which the engine is manufactured. As a result of this research, you have become convinced that the problem is due to operation of the engine at very high RPM's before it has warmed up to develop sufficient oil pressure. The solution would be to install an electronic control limiting engine RPM's until the engine has reached normal operating temperature.

ANALYSIS
    TIME DRIVEN:
    H H H H—DECIDE
    DEVELOPMENT DRIVEN:
    H H H H L—CONSULT GROUP

EXHIBIT 5   Continued

However, the full power of the model is better revealed in a computer program that allows much more complexity and precision whereas, at the same time, is easier to use. Contained on a CD-ROM, the program has a number of features not possible in a decision matrix. These include: (1) using eleven situational factors, rather than the seven shown in the matrices, (2) permitting five possible responses, corresponding to the degree to which situational factors are present, (3) incorporating the Value of Time and Value of Development as situational factors, rather than portraying them as separate matrices, and (4) guiding managers through the process of analyzing the situations they face with definitions, examples, and other sources of help.

We have found by observing managers' use of the model on problems they are currently facing on their jobs that the model's recommendations can be affected by the way in which the problem is framed. For example, if the problem is seen as a deficiency within the team, efforts to find a solution are less likely to be affected than if the problem is located in the situation. Accordingly, we have provided a help screen for "testing" a manager's framing of the problem, to make sure that it has been defined in a way that is likely to be productive. In addition, we have found in this rapidly changing world that groups defined by a common manager may not be the most effective for solution of organizational problems. Thus, the software provides a help screen called Team Formation, which provides advice on making up a group to solve a particular problem or make a particular decision.

What Determines Managers' Styles?

Toward a Descriptive Model

To study managerial styles (as they are, rather than how our models say they should be), we have developed an innovative measuring device that we term a problem set. It consists of a set of 30 cases, each depicting a manager faced with a decision to make. Exhibit 5 gives examples of some of the shorter cases from a typical set. Cases are based on real situations. Each has been condensed to fit on a single page, providing information on the manager's role, the organizational context, the decision that has to be made, the group of persons that the manager is considering involving, and so on.

The set of cases covers the whole gamut of managerial decisions. Titles include "Saving a Savings Bank," "Trimming Expense Accounts," "Relocating the Head Office," and so forth. However, the cases are not randomly selected. Rather, they vary with respect to the critical factors that the model deems highly relevant to choice of leadership style. Each of the factors contained in the decision matrices shown in Exhibits 2 and 3 is varied across the set of cases, and each is varied independently of each other factor. This latter feature, which statisticians refer to as a multifactorial experimental design, is most important, because it permits determining which of the relevant factors influences each individual manager, in what way, and to what degree. Thus, the problem set becomes a powerful diagnostic tool capable of revealing "the manager's model," that is, the way in which each individual manager responds to decision-making situations.

Although we originally developed the problem set as a research tool, we discovered early on that managers enjoyed and benefited from the experience of thinking through how they would deal with highly different situations, and attempting to make sense out of the different choices they made. To aid in the learning that was resulting from this measuring instrument, we have developed a Java-based computer program that could quickly analyze a manager's choices and produce a five-page individualized report comparing him or her with peers and with the models, both time-driven and development-driven. Furthermore, due to the power of the statistical design underlying the problem set, we are able to show each manager how his or her choices were influenced by each of the situational factors used in the decision matrices. Each manager's individualized analysis also shows how well his or her choices are likely to result in decisions that are (1) of high quality, (2) would be effectively implemented, (3) were economical in use of time, and (4) would have favorable developmental consequences on their team.

Here we will focus not on what *managers have learned* from having a mirror held up to them but rather what *we have learned from managers* about how they go about deciding when and where to share their decision-making power. In a world in which it is common to label managers with terms like autocratic or participative or theory X or Theory Y, it was instructive to see that managers make different choices in different situations. In fact, it makes somewhat more sense to talk about autocratic and participative situations than autocratic or participative managers do. The differences in behavior among managers are about one-third of the size of the differences among situations.

Managers behave situationally. They adapt their behavior to the situations they face. Furthermore, the kinds of situations that evoke autocratic and participative styles are very similar to those in which the normative model would recommend such styles. Each of the seven situational factors shown at the top of Exhibits 2 and 3 affects the average manager in roughly the same way as they affect the behavior of the model. Managers make more participative choices on highly significant decisions, when they need the commitment of the group, when they lack the expertise, when the likelihood of commitment to *their* decision is low, when the group's expertise is high and when the group has a history of working together effectively.

But not all managers behave that way! Some are influenced by only one or two of these factors and seem to ignore the rest. Still others are affected by one of these factors, but in what we believe to be the wrong way. For example, one fifth of the U.S. managers that we have studied (and three quarters of all managers from Poland) are more likely to involve others in insignificant, trivial decisions.

One of the most important functions of the feedback is to draw each individual's attention to those aspects of the situation that they are overlooking. We should make it clear that the model not only responds to the seven situational factors, but also does so configurally. Thus, the effects of one factor depend on the level of certain other factors. For example, where the knowledge resides (in the leader or in the group or both or neither) has more effect on leadership style in highly significant decisions than in those of lesser significance.

Of great interest to us is the fact that managers also behave configurally. There is evidence in our data that managers attend to combinations of factors rather than being influenced by each factor separately. However, these effects are less strong among managers than in the model, suggesting that only a small number of managers behave that way or that, in the typical manager, the configural effects are small in relation to those that are linear.

We said earlier that the situational effects dwarfed the differences among individual managers. Although that statement is true, it does not imply that differences among managers in their typical or overall behavior are insignificant or inconsequential. If one averages the choices of a manager on the 30 cases, one obtains a mean score that reflects, on average, where he or she stands on the scale shown in Exhibit 1. We turn now to consider some of the things that we have found to correlate with differences in where people stand on our 10-point scale of participation.

The first factor is *when* people took the test! Our data have been collected over a 25-year period, and throughout most of that period we have observed an increase in the use of the more participative processes on that scale. Something seems to be producing a move toward higher involvement, more participation, greater empowerment, and more frequent use of teams over time. We do not know precisely what is producing this, but we suspect that it reflects changes in (1) the external environment of organizations (greater rates of change, greater complexity), (2) the flattening of the pyramid (greater spans of control resulting in difficulties in hierarchical control), (3) the growth of information technology, making it easier to get information closer to the occurrence of problems, and (4) the changing nature of the labor force (higher education, higher needs for independence, etc.). Of the demographic factors, the culture in which the organization functions accounts for the greatest variance. High involvement managers are more likely to be found in countries with high per capita GNP, with a strong democratic tradition and with a highly educated work force.

We have also investigated gender differences and have found women managers to be significantly more participative than their male counterparts. Supporting this conclusion, we have found sizeable differences in the reactions to autocratic men and autocratic women managers. In general, being participative is valued by direct reports, but this is truer for women than for men. Participative men and women are equally valued, but autocratic males are strongly preferred to autocratic women.

A third demographic factor that correlates with leadership style as measured by our problem sets is level in the organization. In each organization that we have studied in depth, the higher the level in the organizational ladder, the more participative the manager. To be sure, we have never carried our investigation up to the level of the CEO, where we cannot rely on sample size and the law of large numbers to cancel out chance factors due to personality or to measurement.

We should point out that our findings are restricted to what managers say they would do on a standardized set of cases. Although managers have no incentive to lie (because it will only decrease the accuracy of the computer feedback that they alone will receive), we have no guard against self-deception. As a possible check on such tendencies, we have given the same problem sets to both the managers and to his or her direct reports. The latter are asked to describe how their manager would respond to each case. The result is striking. Virtually all managers are seen by their direct reports as closer to the left side of that scale than they see themselves. We have referred to this difference as the autocratic shift. We do not know whether the biases are in managers' conceptions of themselves, the perceptions of them held by their direct reports, or both.

Conclusion

Historically, the people dimension of management has been viewed as basically intuitive, clinical, and "touchy-feely." The kinds of analytical approaches that are customary in finance, operations, and to a lesser degree, strategy, have not been applied, or even viewed as applicable to issues of behavior. We have violated that norm and have sought to apply analytical methods to the development of better normative and descriptive tools for understanding leadership style. We will be the first to admit that our model is far from perfect. We ignore deliberately what style managers are "good at," what they are accustomed to practicing, and what they are encouraged to use in their "organizational culture." We do this because we believe that what worked in the past is no guarantee of success in the future. We believe that leadership styles deserve a fresh look.

At Yale and in other environments, when I teach the model presented in this paper and provide people with computer feedback on their own leadership style, I stress that both are intended to stimulate reflection and self-examination. They are not tools to be slavishly embraced and used in all decisions. I believe that much of the behavior that is currently driven by habits needs to be converted back into choices. The changing demands of today demand that we reexamine the styles we used in the past and reassess their appropriateness to today's environment.

Selected Bibliography

The original inspiration for this body of work may be found in an article written in the *Harvard Business Review* by Bob Tannenbaum and Warren Schmidt ("How to Choose a Leadership Pattern," *Harvard Business Review,* 1958: 99–101).

My initial work on leadership was done with Philip Yetton (*Leadership and Decision Making,* University of Pittsburgh Press: 1973). Subsequently I collaborated with Arthur G. Jago in writing *The New Leadership* (Prentice Hall: 1988).

How People Really Make Decisions*

Gary Klein

During the past 25 years, the field of decision making has concentrated on showing the limitations of decision makers—that is, that they are not very rational or competent. Books have been written documenting human limitations and suggesting remedies: training methods to help us think clearly, decision support systems to monitor and guide us, and expert systems that enable computers to make the decisions and avoid altogether the fallible humans.

This book was written to balance the others and takes a different perspective. Here I document human strengths and capabilities that typically have been downplayed or even ignored.

In 1985, I did my first study of how firefighters make life-and-death decisions under extreme time pressure. That project led to others—with pilots, nurses, military leaders, nuclear power plant operators, chess masters, and experts in a range of other domains. A growing number of researchers have moved out of the laboratory, to work in the area of naturalistic decision making—that is, the study of how people use their experience to make decisions in field settings. We try to understand how people handle all of the typical confusions and pressures of their environments, such as missing information, time constraints, vague goals, and changing conditions. In doing these studies, my research team and I have slept in fire stations, observed intensive care units, and ridden in M-1 tanks, U.S. Navy AEGIS cruisers, Blackhawk helicopters, and AWACS aircraft. We have learned a lot about doing field research.

Instead of trying to show how people do not measure up to ideal strategies for performing tasks, we have been motivated by curiosity about how people do so well under difficult conditions. We all have areas in which we can use our experience to make rapid and effective decisions, from the mundane level of shopping to the high-stakes level of fire-fighting. Shopping in a supermarket does not seem like an impressive skill until you contrast an experienced American shopper to a recent immigrant from Russia. Moving to the other extreme of high-stakes decisions, an example is a fireground commander working under severe time pressure while in charge of a crew at a multiple-alarm fire at a four-story apartment building. Our research concentrated on this high-stakes world. The fireground commanders seemed to be making effective decisions. See "The Torn Artery" description in Example 1.

Example 1 shows decision making at a very high level. Lieutenant M handled many decision points yet spent little time on any one of them. He drew on his experience to know just what to do. Yet merely saying that he used his experience is not an answer. The challenge is to identify how that experience came into play.

We have found that people draw on a large set of abilities that are sources of power. The conventional sources of power include deductive logical thinking, analysis of probabilities, and statistical methods. Yet the sources of power that are needed in natural settings are usually not analytical at all—the power of intuition, mental simulation, metaphor, and storytelling. The power of intuition enables us to size up a situation quickly. The power of mental simulation lets us imagine how a course of action might be carried out. The power of metaphor lets us draw on our experience by suggesting parallels between the current situation and something else we have come across. The power of storytelling helps us consolidate our experiences to make them available in the future, either to ourselves or to others. These areas have not been well studied by decision researchers.

---

*Excerpted with permission from *Sources of Power: How People Make Decisions* (Cambridge, MA: MIT Press, 1998): 1–35.

EXAMPLE 1
The Torn Artery

My research assistant, Chris Brezovic, and I are sitting in a fire station in Cleveland on a Saturday afternoon in the summer of 1985. We slept only a few hours in the station the night before since we had been up late interviewing the commander during that shift. He was going to stay up all night catching up on his work. We were assigned beds on the second floor. I was told to be ready to get down the stairs and onto the truck no more than 25 seconds after an alarm sounded. (No, we did not slide down the pole, although the station still had one. Too many firefighters had broken ankles that way, so they no longer used the pole.) I even slept with my eyeglasses on, not wanting to waste precious seconds fumbling with them. There was only one call, at around 3:00 in the morning. The horn suddenly began blaring, we all jumped out of bed, ran down the flight of stairs, pulled on our coats and boots, and climbed onto the trucks within the time limit. The fire was pretty small—a blaze in a one-car garage.

Chris and I are feeling a little sleepy that next afternoon when the alarm comes in at 3:21 P.M. for the emergency rescue team. Three minutes later, the truck is driving up to a typical house in a residential neighborhood. It is summer, and young women in bikinis who had been tanning themselves on their lawns are running over to their neighbor's yard.

When we pull to a stop, we see a man laying face down in a pool of blood, his wife crouching over him. As the emergency rescue team goes to work, the woman quickly explains that her husband had been standing on a ladder doing some home repair. He slipped, and his arm went through a pane of glass. He reacted foolishly by pulling his arm out and, in doing so, sliced open an artery. The head of the rescue team, Lieutenant M, later told us that the man had lost two units of blood. If he lost four units, he would be dead. Watching his life leak out of his arm, the man is going into shock.

The first decision facing Lieutenant M is to diagnose the problem. As he ran to the man, even before listening to the wife, he made his diagnosis. He can see from the amount of blood that the man has cut open an artery, and from the dishcloths held against the man's arm he can tell which artery. Next comes the decision of how to treat the wound. In fact, there is nothing to deliberate over. As quickly as possible, Lieutenant M applies firm pressure. Next, he might examine whether there are other injuries, maybe neck injuries, which might prevent him from moving the victim. But he doesn't bother with any more examination. He can see the man is minutes from death, so there is no time to worry about anything else.

Lieutenant M has stopped the bleeding and directs his crew to move the man on a stretcher and to the truck. He assigns the strongest of his crew to the hardest stretcher work, even though the crew member has relatively little experience. Lieutenant M decides that the man's strength is important for quick movement and thinks the crew member has enough training that he will not drop the stretcher as it is maneuvered in through the back of the rescue truck.

On the way to the hospital, the crew puts inflatable pants on the victim. These exert pressure on the man's legs to stabilize his blood pressure. Had the crew put the pants on the man before driving, they would have wasted valuable time. When we reach the hospital I look down at my watch: 3:31 P.M. Only 10 minutes has elapsed since the original alarm.

This book examines some recent findings that have emerged from the field of naturalistic decision making. It also describes how research can be done outside the laboratory setting by studying realistic tasks and experienced people working under typical conditions. Features that help define a naturalistic decision-making setting are time pressure, high stakes, experienced decision makers, inadequate information (information that is missing, ambiguous, or erroneous), ill-defined goals, poorly defined procedures, cue learning, context (e.g., higher-level goals, stress), dynamic conditions, and team coordination (Orasanu and Connolly 1993).

Soelberg's course on decision making at the MIT Sloan School of Management taught students how to perform the classical decision analysis method we can call the rational choice strategy. The decision maker:

1. Identifies the set of options.
2. Identifies the ways of evaluating these options.
3. Weights each evaluation dimension.
4. Does the rating.
5. Picks the option with the highest score.

For his Ph.D. dissertation, Soelberg studied the decision strategies his students used to perform a natural task: selecting their jobs as they finished their degrees. He assumed that they would rely on the rational choice strategy. He was wrong. His students showed little inclination toward systematic thinking. Instead, they would make a gut choice. By interviewing his students, Soelberg found he could identify their favorite job choice and predict their ultimate choice with 87 percent accuracy—up to three weeks before the students themselves announced their choice.

Soelberg had trained his students to use rational methods, yet when it was time for them to make a rational and important choice, they would not do it. Soelberg was also a good observer, and he tried to capture the students' actual decision strategies.

What did the students do during this time? If asked, they would deny that they had made a decision yet. For them, a decision was just what Soelberg had taught: a deliberated choice between two or more options. To feel that they had made such a decision, they had to go through a systematic process of evaluation. They selected one other candidate as a comparison, and then tried to show that their favorite was as good as or better than the comparison candidate on each evaluation dimension. Once they had shown this to their satisfaction (even if it meant fudging a little or finding ways to beef up their favorite), then they would announce as their decision the gut favorite that Soelberg had identified much earlier. They were not actually making a decision; they were constructing a justification.

We hypothesized that the fireground commanders would behave in the same way. We thought this hypothesis—that instead of considering lots of options they would consider only two—was daring. Actually, it was conservative. The commanders did not consider two. In fact, they did not seem to be comparing any options at all. This was disconcerting, and we discovered it at the first background discussion we had with a fireground commander, even before the real interviews. We asked the commander to tell us about some difficult decisions he had made.

"I don't make decisions," he announced to his startled listeners. "I don't remember when I've ever made a decision."

For researchers starting a study of decision making, this was unhappy news. Even worse, he insisted that fireground commanders never make decisions. We pressed him further. Surely there are decisions during a fire—decisions about whether to call a second alarm, where to send his crews, how to contain the fire.

He agreed that there were options, yet it was usually obvious what to do in any given situation. We soon realized that he was defining the making of a decision in the same way as Soelberg's students—generating a set of options and evaluating them to find the best one. We call this strategy of examining two or more options at the same time, usually by comparing the strengths and weaknesses of each, *comparative evaluation*. He insisted that he never did it. There just was no time. The structure would burn down by the time he finished listing all the options, let alone evaluating them.

We sought to explain two puzzles: how the commanders could reliably identify good options and how they could evaluate an option without comparing it to any others.

Our results turned out to be fairly clear. It was not that the commanders were *refusing* to compare options; rather, they did not have to compare options. I had been so fixated on what they were not doing that I had missed the real finding: that the commanders could come up with a good course of action from the start. That was what the stories were telling us. Even when faced with a complex situation, the commanders could see it as familiar and know how to react.

EXAMPLE 2
The Overpass Rescue

A lieutenant is called out to rescue a woman who either fell or jumped off a highway overpass. She is drunk or on drugs and is probably trying to kill herself. Instead of falling to her death, she lands on the metal supports of a highway sign and is dangling there when the rescue team arrives.

The lieutenant recognizes the danger of the situation. The woman is semiconscious and lying bent over one of the metal struts. At any moment, she could fall to her death on the pavement below. If he orders any of his team out to help her, they will be endangered because there is no way to get a good brace against the struts, so he issues an order not to climb out to secure her.

Two of his crew ignore his order and climb out anyway. One holds onto her shoulders and the other to her legs.

A hook-and-ladder truck arrives. The lieutenant doesn't need their help in making the rescue, so tells them to drive down to the highway below and block traffic in case the woman does fall. He does not want to chance that the young woman will fall on a moving car.

Now the question is how to pull the woman to safety. First, the lieutenant considers using a rescue harness, the standard way of raising victims. It snaps onto a person's shoulders and thighs. In imagining its use, he realizes that it requires the person to be in a sitting position or face up. He thinks about how they would shift her to sit up and realizes that she might slide off the support.

Second, he considers attaching the rescue harness from the back. However, he imagines that by lifting the woman, they would create a large pressure on her back, almost bending her double. He does not want to risk hurting her.

Third, the lieutenant considers using a rescue strap—another way to secure victims, but making use of a strap rather than a snap-on harness. However, it creates the same problems as the rescue harness, requiring that she be sitting up or that it be attached from behind. He rejects this too.

Now he comes up with a novel idea: using a ladder belt—a strong belt that firefighters buckle on over their coats when they climb up ladders to rescue people. When they get to the top, they can snap an attachment on the belt to the top rung of the ladder. If they lose their footing during the rescue, they are still attached to the ladder so they won't plunge to their death.

The lieutenant's idea is to get a ladder belt, slide it under the woman, buckle it from behind (it needs only one buckle), tie a rope to the snap, and lift her up to the overpass. He thinks it through again and likes the idea, so he orders one of his crew to fetch the ladder belt and rope, and they tie it onto her.

In the meantime, the hook-and-ladder truck has moved to the highway below the overpass, and the truck's crew members raise the ladder. The firefighter on the platform at the top of the ladder is directly under the woman shouting, "I've got her. I've got her." The lieutenant ignores him and orders his men to lift her up.

At this time, he makes an unwanted discovery: ladder belts are built for sturdy firefighters, to be worn over their coats. This is a slender woman wearing a thin sweater. In addition, she is essentially unconscious. When they lift her up, they realize the problem. As the lieutenant put it, "She slithered through the belt like a slippery strand of spaghetti."

Fortunately, the hook-and-ladder man is right below her. He catches her and makes the rescue. There is a happy ending.

Now the lieutenant and his crew go back to their station to figure our what had gone wrong. They try the rescue harness and find that the lieutenant's instincts were right: neither is usable.

Eventually they discover how they should have made the rescue. They should have used the rope they had tied to the ladder belt. They could have tied it to the woman and lifted her up. With all the technology available to them, they had forgotten that you can use a rope to pull someone up.

The commanders' secret was that their experience let them see a situation, even a nonroutine one, as an example of a prototype, so they knew the typical course of action right away. Their experience let them identify a reasonable reaction as the first one they considered, so they did not bother thinking of others. They were not being perverse. They were being skillful. We now call this strategy *recognition-primed decision making.*

This rescue helped us see several important aspects of decision making. First, the lieutenant's deliberations about options took him only about a minute. That may seem too short, but if you imagine going through it in your mind, a minute is about right.

Second, the decision maker looked at several options yet never compared any two of them. He thought of the options one at a time, evaluated each in turn, rejected it, and turned to the next most typical rescue technique. We can call this strategy a *singular evaluation approach*, to distinguish it from comparative evaluation. Singular evaluation means evaluating each option on its own merits, even if we cycle through several possibilities.

Distinguishing between comparative and singular evaluation strategies is not difficult. When you order from a menu, you probably compare the different items to find the one you want the most. You are performing a comparative evaluation because you are trying to see if one item seems tastier than the others. In contrast, if you are in an unfamiliar neighborhood and you notice your car is low on gasoline, you start searching for service stations and stop at the first reasonable place you find. You do not need the best service station in town.

The difference between singular and comparative evaluation is linked to the research of Herbert Simon, who won a Nobel Prize for economics. Simon (1957) identified a decision strategy he calls *satisficing*: selecting the first option that works. Satisficing is different from optimizing, which means trying to come up with the best strategy. Optimizing is hard, and it takes a long time. Satisficing is more efficient. The singular evaluation strategy is based on satisficing. Simon used the concept of satisficing to describe the decision behavior of businesspeople. The strategy makes even more sense for fireground commanders because of their immense time pressure.

Our model of recognitional decision making was starting to fit together. The experienced fireground commanders could judge a situation as prototypical and know what to do. If their first choice did not work out, they might consider others—not to find the best but to find the first one that works.

But there was still the second puzzle. If they did not compare one course of action to another, how did they evaluate the options? All of the evaluation procedures we knew about required contrast: looking at the degree to which each option satisfies each criterion, weighing the importance of the criteria, tabulating the results, and finding the best option. If the commanders did not compare options, how did they know that a course of action was any good?

The answer lies in the overpass rescue story. To evaluate a single course of action, the lieutenant imagined himself carrying it out. Fireground commanders use the power of mental simulation, running the action through in their minds. If they spot a potential problem, like the rescue harness not working well, they move on to the next option, and the next, until they find one that seems to work. Then they carry it out. As the example shows, this is not a foolproof strategy. The advantage is that it is usually better than anything else they can do.

Before we did this study, we believed that novices impulsively jumped at the first option they could think of, whereas experts carefully deliberated about the merits of different courses of action. Now it seemed that it was the experts who could generate a single course of action, while novices needed to compare different approaches.

In one case we studied commanders who had no experience with the type of incident they faced. This helped us to see better what is required for proficient decision making.

From this episode we learn that there are times for deliberating about options. Usually these are times when experience is inadequate and logical thinking is a substitute for recognizing a situation as typical. Although the commanders in this case study had been firefighters for a long time, they had no experience with a fire this large. Deliberating about options makes a lot of sense for novices, who have to think their way through the decision. It is what I do when I have to buy a house or a car. I have to start from scratch, identifying features I might want, looking at the choices.

EXAMPLE 3
The Christmas Fire

Dotted around the Midwest are oil tank farms: large complexes of storage tanks filled with oil piped in from the Texas and Oklahoma fields and held at these farms before being pumped to specific points in the Midwest. This incident took place at a tank farm. The pipeline field at this farm had 20 tanks, each 45 feet high and 100 feet in diameter and each with a capacity of more than 60,000 barrels of oil.

On Christmas night in the middle of a bitterly cold winter, one of the tanks bursts open. The oil comes pouring out—a bad enough situation—and then ignites. A large oil tank instantly turns into a giant torch and sets fire to another tank. Most of the big power lines of the tanks are down and burning. The telephone lines are also on fire. Burning oil has spilled into a ditch, and fierce winds push the fire along.

The setting is a rural farm community crisscrossed with underground oil pipes. If the flames spread, they can conceivably set the whole town on fire.

The fire departments of the surrounding townships report to the call. These departments are staffed by volunteer firefighters who are used to putting out barn fires and garage fires, and maybe a house fire or two in a year. Now they are looking at a wall of flames 50 to 100 feet high. They have never seen anything like it before in their lives. As one commander described it to us, "Our heads turned to stone."

As they watch, one of the two burning tanks ruptures. A wave of crude oil rides over the highway and engulfs a new tank, number 91, which is filled with oil. A man from the pipeline company tells the fireground commanders that if the fire comes any farther south, it will reach a 20-inch propane gas line. The oil is following gravity northward, "creepin' like a little monster" toward a large chemical plant.

Because of the cold, everyone is bundled up, many wearing face masks. The crews have trouble recognizing if someone is from their own district. It is hard to tell who the commanders are. Worse, there is no source of water in the area. Foam is needed to put out oil fires, but the commanders can locate only a thousand gallons.

In short, they have no resources for fighting the fire and no understanding of what to do. They are afraid the fire will spread to the other tanks. They wonder if they should evacuate the town. They are bewildered.

For two days, they remain uncertain about how to proceed. A commander of one of the fire departments orders a trench to be built to contain the oil. A different commander's idea is to pipe the oil out of tank 91. But no one can tell if the lines are still working, and no one wants to take a chance of leaking oil into a field where the fire might spread. A third commander calls the power company to turn off the electricity to the downed power lines, but the power company does not comply right away. Each department goes off in a different direction.

Eventually the power company turns off power in the early morning of the second day. Crews can approach tank 91.

The plan is to spray foam down onto the fire, if they can get enough foam. It is freezing cold and windy. Where should they position the ladder truck? Should a firefighter, carrying a hose, climb up a ladder to the rim of tank 91? The dikes around the tank make it hard to get close, and the field around the dikes has dangerous ravines. Eventually a ladder truck gets near tank 91, and firefighters spray foam onto the rim of the oil tank. The wind just blows the foam away, and suddenly the origination point fire, in a nearby tank, starts to boil up menacingly. Fearing an eruption, the commander evacuates his men.

Sometime during the second day, one of the chiefs asks a person working at the oil company if all the pipes leading into the complex have been turned off. The reply is that no one knows, since the tangle of pipelines is so confusing. Spurred on by the question, the plant personnel start tracing all the incoming pipelines and find a source of fuel: a large 22-inch pipe that has been pumping new oil directly into one of the burning tanks. During the second day, they get all the pipes turned off.

On the third day, the volunteer fire chiefs finally take organized action: they choose not to try to do anything. They let the fire burn while they devote all their energies to planning. One of the fireground commanders later told us that this was their first effective decision.

Here is how they go about planning. They ask themselves what their options are, and what the advantages and disadvantages are of each. Finally, in the confusion of a runaway oil fire, we find the strongest example of deliberative decision making—by chiefs who are essentially baffled about what is happening: They try rising up a tower to get a man above the rim of a tank to spray foam down onto the fire. Near the rim, he sees cracks with crude oil coming through. The pumps start spraying foam, and the command is given to start the water truck cycle. Because of earlier delays, the water truck freezes up before it can be used. Then the foam pump starts to malfunction, so they give up and call the firefighter down.

Next they try rigging up a nozzle to spray the foam down, but the high winds sweep it away, and the heat cooks it off. They order more foam from a nearby U.S. Air Force base, but the different foams that arrive are incompatible. Finally, they give up, abandon their pride, and call in some consultants. They call in the team of "Boots and Coots," former colleagues of Red Adair, a world-famous fighter of oil well fires.

Boots and Coots arrive, look briefly at the scene, and say that they will need a great deal more foam. "We don't have that much foam," the volunteer fireground commanders argue. "Of course not," Boots and Coots answer. "We've already ordered it. It will be here tomorrow."

From that point on, under the direction of the experts, the fire operations go smoothly. The entire fire is extinguished within the next two days. Although no one is seriously injured, the cost of the fire is estimated at $10 to $15 million.

Defining the Recognition-Primed Decision Model

The recognition-primed decision (RPD) model fuses two processes: the way decision makers size up the situation to recognize which course of action makes sense, and the way they evaluate that course of action by imagining it.

Figure 1 shows the basic strategy, as variation 1. Decision makers recognize the situation as typical and familiar—a typical garage fire, or apartment building fire, or factory fire, or search-and-rescue job—and proceed to take action. They understand what types of *goals* make sense (so the priorities are set), which cues are important (so there is not an overload of information), what to expect next (so they can prepare themselves and notice surprises), and the *typical ways of responding* in a given situation. By recognizing a situation as typical, they also recognize a *course of action* likely to succeed. The recognition of goals, cues, expectancies, and actions is part of what it means to recognize a situation.

Some situations are more complex, as shown by variations 2 and 3 in Figure 1. Variation 2 occurs when the decision maker may have to devote more attention *to diagnosing* the situation, since the information may not clearly match a typical case or may map onto more than one typical case. The decision maker may need to gather more information in order to make a diagnosis. Another complication is that the decision maker may have misinterpreted the situation but does not realize it until some *expectancies* have been violated. At these times, decision makers will respond to the anomaly or ambiguity by checking which interpretation best matches the features of the situation. They may try to build a story to account for some of the inconsistencies.

Variation 3 explains how decision makers evaluate single options by imagining how the course of action will play out. A decision maker who anticipates difficulties may need to *adjust* the course of action, or maybe *reject* it and look for another option.

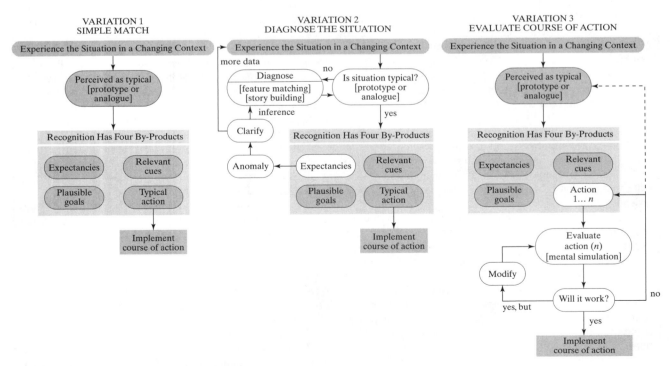

FIGURE 1   Integrated Version of Recognition-Primed Decision Model

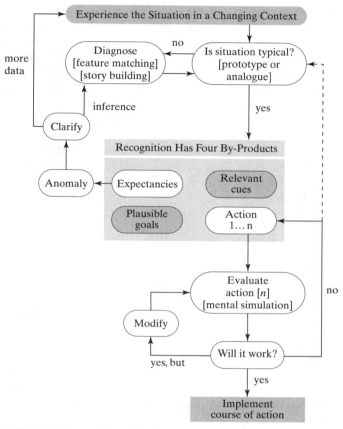

FIGURE 2   **Recognition-Primed Decision Model**

One way to think about these three variations is that variation 1 is basically an "if . . . then" reaction, an antecedent followed by the rule-based response. The expertise is in being able to recognize when the antecedent condition has been met. Variation 2 takes the form "if (???) . . . then," with the decision maker deliberating about the nature of the situation. Variation 3 takes the form if . . . then (???), as the decision maker ponders the outcome of a reaction. Figure 2 shows an integrated version of all three variations.

The Theoretical Importance of the RPD Model

Recognitional decision making can be contrasted with the more classical approaches. Perhaps the most widely known of these models stems from the work of Janis and Mann (1977), who warned that people try to avoid making decisions because of the stress of carrying out the analysis. Janis and Mann offered these prescriptions for making better decisions:

- Thoroughly canvas a wide range of options.
- Survey a full range of objectives.
- Carefully weigh the costs, risk, and benefits of each option.
- Intensively search for new information in evaluating options.
- Assimilate all new information.
- Reexamine the positive and negative consequences of each option.
- Carefully plan to include contingencies if various risks occur.

Janis and Mann probably did not intend this advice for time-pressured situations, but the RPD model predominates even when time is sufficient for comparative evaluations. Yet in one form or another, Janis and Mann's prescriptive advice is held up as an ideal of rationality and finds its way into most courses on cognitive development. The advice is more helpful for beginners than for experienced decision makers. In most applied settings, beginners are not going to be put in a position to make critical decisions.

The prescriptions of Janis and Mann are an example of the rational choice strategy that we had encountered: define the evaluation dimensions, weight each one, rate each option on each dimension, multiply the weightings, total up the scores, and determine the best option—that is, unless you do not have all the data you need, or are not sure how to do the ratings, or disagree with the weights, or run out of time before you have finished.

There are advantages to the rational choice strategy:

- It should result in reliable decisions (that is, the same result each time for the same analysis).
- It is quantitative.
- It helps novices determine what they do not know.
- It is rigorous; it does not leave anything out.
- It is a general strategy, which could apply in all sorts of situations.

The problem is that the assumptions of the rational choice strategy are usually too restrictive. Rarely is there the time or the information needed to make this type of strategy work. Furthermore, if we cannot trust someone to make a big judgment, such as which option is best, why would we trust all of the little judgments that go into the rational choice strategy. Clearly this method is not going to ensure that novices make good choices, and it usually is not helpful for experienced decision makers. It can be useful in working with teams, to calibrate everyone's grasp of the strengths and weaknesses of different options.

The Power of Intuition

Intuition depends on the use of experience to recognize key patterns that indicate the dynamics of the situation. Because patterns can be subtle, people often cannot describe what they noticed, or how they judged a situation as typical or atypical. Therefore, intuition has a strange reputation. Skilled decision makers know that they can depend on their intuition, but at the same time they may feel uncomfortable trusting a source of power that seems so accidental.

Bechara, Damasio, Tranet, and Damasio (1997) found that intuition has a basis in biology. They compared patients who were brain damaged to a group of normal subjects. The brain-damaged subjects lacked intuition, an emotional reaction to anticipated consequences of good and bad decisions. In the normal subjects, this system seemed to be activated long before they were consciously aware that they had made a decision.

For the first formal interview that I did in our first research project with firefighters, I was trying to find some difficult incident where my interviewee, a fireground commander, had to make a tough decision. He could think of only one case, years ago, where he said his extrasensory perception (ESP) had saved the day. I tried to get him to think of a different incident because the one he had in mind was too old, because he was only a lieutenant then, not a commander, and because I do not have much interest in ESP. But he was determined to describe this case, so I finally gave up and let him tell his story.

EXAMPLE 4
The Sixth Sense

It is a simple house fire in a one-story house in a residential neighborhood. The fire is in the back, in the kitchen area. The lieutenant leads his hose crew into the building, to the back, to spray water on the fire, but the fire just roars back at them.

"Odd," he thinks. The water should have more of an impact. They try dousing it again, and get the same results. They retreat a few steps to regroup.

Then the lieutenant starts to feel as if something is not right. He doesn't have any clues; he just doesn't feel right about being in that house, so he orders his men out of the building—a perfectly standard building with nothing out of the ordinary.

As soon as his men leave the building, the floor where they had been standing collapses. Had they still been inside, they would have plunged into the fire below.

"A sixth sense," he assured us, and part of the makeup of every skilled commander. Some close questioning revealed the following facts:

- He had no suspicion that there was a basement in the house.
- He did not suspect that the seat of the fire was in the basement, directly underneath the living room where he and his men were standing when he gave his order to evacuate.
- But he was already wondering why the fire did not react as expected.
- The living room was hotter than he would have expected for a small fire in the kitchen of a single-family home.
- It was very quiet. Fires are noisy, and for a fire with this much heat, he would have expected a great deal of noise.

The whole pattern did not fit right. His expectations were violated, and he realized he did not quite know what was going on. That was why he ordered his men out of the building. With hindsight, the reasons for the mismatch were clear. Because the fire was under him and not in the kitchen, it was not affected by his crew's attack, the rising heat was much greater than he had expected, and the floor acted like a baffle to muffle the noise, resulting in a hot but quiet environment.

This incident helped us understand how commanders make decisions by recognizing when a typical situation is developing. In this case, the events were not typical, and his reaction was to pull back, regroup, and try to get a better sense of what was going on. By showing us what happens when the cues do not fit together, this case clarified how much firefighters rely on a recognition of familiarity and prototypicality. By the end of the interview, the commander could see how he had used the available information to make his judgment. (I think he was proud to realize how his experience had come into play. Even so, he was a little shaken since he had come to depend on his sixth sense to get him through difficult situations, and it was unnerving for him to realize that he might never have had ESP.)

This is one basis for what we call *intuition*: recognizing things without knowing how we do the recognizing. In the simple version of the RPD model, we size the situation up and immediately know how to proceed: which goals to pursue, what to expect, how to respond. We are drawn to certain cues and not others because of our situation awareness. (This must happen all the time. Try to imagine going through a day without making these automatic responses.)

There may be other aspects of intuition than the one I have been describing. I do know that the firefighters' experience enables them to recognize situations quickly.

Many people think of intuition as an inborn trait—something we are born with. I am not aware of any evidence showing that some people are blessed with intuition, and others are not. My claim is that intuition grows out of experience.

We should not be surprised that the commander in this case was not aware of the way he used his experience. Rather than giving him specific facts from memory, the experience affected the way he saw the situation. Another reason that he could not describe his use of experience was that he was reacting to things that were not happening rather than to things that were. A third reason that he was unaware of his use of experience was that he was not drawing on his memory for any specific previous experience. A large set of similar incidents had all blended together.

Described in this way, intuition does not sound very mysterious. In fact, the simple version of the RPD model is a model of intuition.

Intuition is an important source of power for all of us. Nevertheless, we have trouble observing ourselves use experience in this way, and we definitely have trouble explaining the basis of our judgments when someone else asks us to defend them. Therefore, intuition has a bad reputation compared with a judgment that comes from careful analysis of all the relevant factors and shows each inference drawn and traces the conclusion in a clear line to all of the antecedent conditions. In fact, research by Wilson and Schooler (1991) shows that people do worse at some decision tasks when they are asked to perform analyses of the reasons for their preferences or to evaluate all the attributes of the choices.

Intuition is not infallible. Our experience will sometimes mislead us, and we will make mistakes that add to our experience base. Imagine that you are driving around in an unfamiliar city, and you see some landmark, perhaps a gas station, and you say, "Oh, now I know where we are," and (despite the protests of your spouse, who has the map) make a fateful turn and wind up on an unescapable entrance ramp to the highway you had been trying to avoid. As you face the prospect of being sent miles out of your way, you may lamely offer that the gas station you remembered must have been a different one: "I thought I recognized it, but I guess I was wrong."

Practical Implications

- Be sensitive to when you need to compare options and when you do not. For many tasks, we are novices, and the rational choice method helps us when we lack the expertise to recognize situations. Sometimes we may need to use formal methods to look at wide array of alternatives. Other times we may judge that we should rely on our expertise to look in greater depth at a smaller set of alternatives—maybe the first one considered.

- The part of intuition that involves pattern matching and recognition of familiar and typical cases can be trained. The ideas set forth in this chapter imply that we do not make someone an expert through training in formal methods of analysis. Quite the contrary is true, in fact: We run the risk of slowing the development of skills. If the purpose is to train people in time-pressured decision making, we might require that the trainee make rapid responses rather than ponder all the implications. If we can present many situations an hour, several hours a day, for days or weeks, we should be able to improve the trainee's ability to detect familiar patterns. The design of the scenarios is critical, since the goal is to show many common cases to facilitate a recognition of typicality along with different types of rare cases so trainees will be prepared for these as well.

We can summarize the key features of the RPD model in comparison to the standard advice given to decision makers. The RPD model claims that with experienced decision makers:

- The focus is on the way they assess the situation and judge it familiar, not on comparing options.

- Courses of action can be quickly evaluated by imagining how they will be carried out, not by formal analysis and comparison.
- Decision makers usually look for the first workable option they can find, not the best option.
- Since the first option they consider is usually workable, they do not have to generate a large set of options to be sure they get a good one.
- They generate and evaluate options one at a time and do not bother comparing the advantages and disadvantages of alternatives.
- By imagining the option being carried out, they can spot weaknesses and find ways to avoid these, thereby making the option stronger. Conventional models just select the best, without seeing how it can be improved.
- The emphasis is on being poised to act rather than being paralyzed until all the evaluations have been completed.

References

A. Bechara, H. Damasio, D. Tranel, and A. R. Damasio, "Deciding Advantageously Before Knowing the Advantageous Strategy," *Science 275* (1997): 1293–1295.

I. L. Janis and L. Mann, *Decision Making: A Psychological Analysis of Conflict, Choice, and Commitment* (New York: Free Press, 1977).

J. Orasanu and T. Connolly, "The Reinvention of Decision Making," *Decision Making in Action: Models and Methods*, eds. G. Klein, J. Orasanu, R. Calderwood, and C. E. Zsambok (Norwood, NJ: Ablex, 1993): 3–20.

H. A. Simon, *Models of Man: Social and Rational* (New York: Wiley 1957).

P. O. Soelberg, "Unprogrammed Decision Making," *Industrial Management Review 8* (1967): 19–29.

T. D. Wilson and J. W. Schooler, "Thinking Too Much: Introspection Can Reduce the Quality of Preferences and Decisions," *Journal of Personality and Social Psychology 60* (1991): 181–192.

TOUGH CALLS IN A SPEED-DRIVEN WORLD*

J. Keith Murnighan

John Mowen

The value of art is not beauty, but right action.

W. SOMERSET MAUGHAM

Put yourself in the shoes of Jim Bronson. You are 36 years old and have just received the national entrepreneur-of-the-year award. You and your partner have successfully opened 27 Chicago Brew Pubs in the last nine years. It is 1995, and investment bankers are at your door, wanting you to take your company public so that they can make you rich.

In 1986, you left a position as a senior analyst on Wall Street to pursue your dream of successfully developing a restaurant chain. You and your partner, Paul

---

*Adapted and reprinted with permission from *The Art of High Stakes Decision-Making: Tough Calls in a Speed-Driven World* (New York, NY: John Wiley & Sons Inc., 2002): 3–22.

Springfield, make a great team. You favor a conservative approach to growth, whereas Paul, a natural marketer, constantly pushes you to grow faster. Your decisions so far have been phenomenally successful. Your strategy of carefully growing by three pubs a year has really paid off.

Now that you have won this big award, however, the competitive environment in the brewing industry is changing. Investment bankers are interested in other brew pubs, including L. A. Brew Pub, Big Apple, California Brew Pub, Big City Brew Pub, and Simpsons. There is a chance that each company may announce public offerings this year. You realize that within a one-year period, there may be 300 million to 400 million investment dollars flowing into brew pubs.

You now face a classic tough call. Do you continue your strategy of avoiding serious debt and slowly growing your company, or do you go public and exponentially grow your company as the investment bankers propose? You face a soon-to-close window of threat and opportunity. If you continue your present strategy of slow growth, your more highly capitalized competitors could invade your territory and potentially drive you out of business. If you follow the investment bankers' advice and double the number of Chicago Brew Pubs each year for four consecutive years, you could potentially make several million dollars, but it will also place extreme demands on your managerial ability. Either choice could mean great success or dismal failure. You only have a short time to decide. Once your competitors go public, you may not get a second chance.

Jim Bronson and his partner had only a few weeks to make their decision. They worried that if they failed to act, they would fall behind the power curve; that is, their competitors would become so well capitalized that no matter how hard they tried, or how well they made their future decisions, they would be unable to compete effectively. To stay ahead of the curve, they would be unable to compete effectively. To stay ahead of the curve, they would have to make the investment. Yet there was an incredible downside to the high-growth strategy. They faced a tremendously tough call, a true decision dilemma. If you were Jim Bronson, what would you do?

A Crashing Plane

Now change the situation and the time to December 20, 1995. American Airlines flight 965 is running smoothly. You are the pilot. Suddenly, the crash avoidance system barks, "Terrain, terrain . . . pull up, pull up." You pull up the nose of the Boeing 757 to gain lift. At the same time, you shove the throttle forward to increase air speed. The plane climbs, but not sharply enough. It clips some trees and slams into the side of a mountain ridge in Colombia, South America. Amazingly, 4 of the 163 passengers survive.

Like any airplane crash, it was a tremendous tragedy. In many ways, the aftermath made things even worse, when investigations revealed that any of three different choices could have led to no crash at all. First, analysis of the data by investigators suggested that the cause of the crash was pilot error. Apparently, the pilot had punched the wrong coordinates into the airplane's computer, making its readouts inaccurate and confusing. Subsequent choices that depended on these inaccurate readings placed the plane in great danger. Second, the accident occurred during the early stages of landing when the pilot followed standard operating procedures to extend small spoilers (called speed breaks) from the top of the plane's wings to reduce life. When the alarm sounded and a steep climb was necessary, the pilot failed to retract the spoilers. As a result, the plane could not climb steeply enough to clear the mountain. The pilot had fallen behind the power curve, and he did not respond quickly enough when his actions determined the fate of everyone on board his plane.

A third factor also contributed to the tragedy. According to *The Wall Street Journal*, executives at Boeing faced a tough call when they designed the plane, and their choice contributed to the tragedy. Unlike Airbus, Boeing actively decided *not* to build a system into the plane that would automatically retract the spoilers when an emergency climb was necessary. As one retired pilot lamented, "They only needed another two hundred feet to make it, and if that plane had automatically retracting spoilers, they would have made it."

Tough Calls Defined

Tough calls are high-stakes decisions that must be made when information is ambiguous, values conflict, and experts disagree. By their nature, they never offer a clear-cut, obvious choice. Due to the high risk that accompanies such hard choices, they may result in tremendous coups or dreadful blunders. Some people have jobs that require them to make tough calls all the time. Those who are successful and who can handle the pressure become the leaders of their fields. In today's society, they become the chief executive officers (CEOs), the eminent scientists, the pilots, the entrepreneurs, and the national leaders whose decisions impact the lives of thousands, if not millions, of people every year.

Over time, the quality of our decisions determines our future. Each day we make dozens of decisions. Do I wear a seatbelt? Do I have five servings of fruits and vegetables? Do I get an hour of physical activity? We call these habitual decisions "multiplay decisions" because over the course of a few years, we make these routine choices thousands of times. Because their effects accumulate, they can have an enormous impact on our lives. If we choose to develop poor habits, we pay the consequences. Hundreds of books have been written on this type of routine decision making.

We focus on the tough calls that occur less often, but with surprising frequency, in either our personal or our professional lives. Do I sell my company? Do I change my career? Do I report the unethical behavior of my boss? Do I fire an employee? How do I approach the need for increased care for my elderly parents? The answers to these questions have one commonality: The results of these decisions will seriously affect your future as well as the lives of other people.

Our goal is to provide you with a structure and a set of guidelines for making tough calls. Peter Volanakis, the executive vice president of Corning Glass Corporation, argued that managers within an organization should share a common decision-making process for making fast, effective judgments. A sound decision-making process will give you the courage to take responsible high-stakes risks. Volanakis argued that this process will both improve and increase risk taking because managers "have no trouble defending their decision when they know they have taken all the important factors into consideration and used an objective, rational system to evaluate the available information."

We present a process called SCRIPTS for making tough calls. SCRIPTS identifies seven parameters that will ensure that your high-stakes decisions will stand the test of time. The seven parameters are: **s**earch for signals of threats and opportunities, find the **c**auses, evaluate the **r**isks, apply **i**ntuition and emotion, take different **p**erspectives, consider the **t**ime frame, and **s**olve the problem. Just as Somerset Maugham suggested in the quote introducing this chapter, the benefit of following a tested procedure is not in its elegance or beauty. Rather, it is in the positive outcomes that result.

Our high-stakes decisions determine our long-term happiness and success. Indeed, research tells us that we most frequently second-guess the hard choices that we have *not* made. It is not a lack of motivation that prevents success. Rather, it is the fear of making high-stakes decisions. By developing an in-depth understanding of the SCRIPTS process, you will be able to identify high-stakes decisions and how you can make them with the courage that comes from developing the essential ability to make hard choices. You will also learn how to make tough calls with the velocity that our speed-driven world requires.

Illustrating the Four Characteristics of Tough Calls

The Chicago Brew Pub case illustrates the four key characteristics of tough calls. First, the stakes were high—the fate of an organization and the jobs of five hundred employees were at stake. Second, the available information was ambiguous. No one could tell with any certainty, in advance, which course of action would result in the most favorable outcome. Third, basic values were in conflict. On the one hand, Jim Bronson wanted to follow his conservative instincts and build the company slowly and prudently. On the other hand, he knew that a failure to grow the company at this critical time could create difficulties that he might not be able to handle. Fourth, experts disagreed as to the most appropriate choice. The investment bankers urged him to act before the window of opportunity closed. In contrast, traditional bankers counseled him to be extremely wary of the siren song of quick riches.

The fate of American Airlines flight 965 also illustrates the characteristics of tough calls. The pilot faced a crisis situation in which many lives were in his hands. He had to react quickly based on his training, intelligence, and ability to handle stress. The case also identifies two additional aspects of tough calls. First, it illustrates the idea that tough calls can be made by both organizations and individuals. At the individual level, the pilot had to react quickly and skillfully to the crisis. At the organizational level, a team of executives had to decide whether to install a software system that automatically retracted the spoilers.

The flight 965 case also shows that decisions made at one time may impact outcomes many years later. Years prior to the crash, aeronautical engineers and company managers made the decision to leave it to pilots to determine whether to retract the spoilers in an emergency. In the design philosophy of building an airplane, managers must decide whether to maximize a pilot's or a computer's control of the plane and its many systems and safety features. Needless to say, computers can malfunction and cause accidents just like pilots can. The two giant airplane manufacturers, Boeing and Airbus, took alternative routes. Airbus installed software that instructed the computer system to retract the spoilers; Boeing relied on pilots.

The experts at Boeing and the experts at Airbus disagreed in part because of their different organizational value systems. At Boeing, the value system emphasizes allowing pilots to have maximum control of the airplane. At Airbus, the value system focuses to a larger extent on using technology to fly an airplane. Thus experts in each company examined exactly the same data and came to opposite conclusions.

When choices are tough, no absolutely right answer exists. You can consult the most outstanding experts, but they will disagree on what to do. You can use complex computer programs, but they may only add to the confusion when subtle changes of an assumption or estimates of key variables lead to completely different answers.

Even though no one "right" answer exists, you must make the decision and you must bear the consequences.

Types of Tough Calls

We have developed a simple matrix that identifies the types of tough calls that individuals and organizations face. As shown in Figure 1, the two dimensions of the matrix are (1) the time available to make the decision and (2) whether the decision is repeated. The time available to make the decision can range from instantaneous (like the pilot on flight 965) to having months to work out a solution. We must make short-fuse decisions quickly and decisively. Long-fuse decisions give us time to think, bring in experts, and even employ computer simulations.

The second dimension of the matrix represents the frequency with which the same decision is repeated. In our terminology, choices that occur infrequently and are rarely replayed are single-play decisions. At an organizational level, the decision by Boeing not to install automatic retracting spoilers was a single-play decision. Once made, it would be very hard to change. In contrast, banks replay thousands of times the decision concerning the financial criteria to give credit cards to consumers. The decisions that identify these criteria are strategic decisions. Replaying them over and over again illustrates the tactical application of the tough call. On a personal level, getting married, building a home, and undertaking major elective surgery are all examples of single-play decisions (at least for most people). In contrast, having dessert after dinner, selecting the right outfit to wear, and choosing to drive or use mass transit to get to work are all multiplay decisions.

Tough choices are almost always single-play decisions—whether they have a short or long time fuse. American Airlines flight 965 illustrates both types of single-play decisions. The few seconds that the pilot had to respond to the emergency represent the ultimate in crisis decision-making. Thus, **crisis choices** are single-play decisions with a short time fuse, and **strategic decisions** are single-play decisions with a long time fuse. The design decision by Boeing to give pilots maximum control over the plane's functions represents a strategic decision. The decision faced by Jim Bronson represents a strategic decision. The selection of a career represents a strategic decision. Similarly, within organizations, the decision to enter an entirely new market represents a strategic choice. Each of these examples is a single-play decision with an outcome that has the

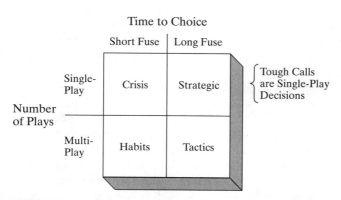

FIGURE 1 **A Matrix of Decision Types**

potential of being a horrible blunder. By their very nature, then, tough choices entail considerable risk.

Multiplay decisions, in contrast, involve the execution of many smaller decisions, often over a long time period. Thus, when multiplay decisions have a short time fuse, we think of them as **habitual**. Habitual choices tend to involve low stakes—if only because we get so used to making them. Some personal examples include choosing whether to wear a seat belt in a car, the mechanics of monthly bill paying, and how we choose which phone calls to return. Examples of habitual decisions in corporations include choices to highlight or ignore small defects in a product and the choice of internal e-mail for ordinary announcements.

Any single execution of a multiplay decision is unlikely to cause major problems. Thus, not wearing a seat belt on one trip to the grocery store is unlikely to cause any problems. When repeated many times over a long time period, however, multiplay decisions can have enormous consequences.

When time is available to make a multiplay decision, what would otherwise become habitual decisions can now be made tactically. **Tactical decisions** result from the development of a plan of action that fits within a broader, strategic decision. When acting rationally, we make our strategic decisions first and then move on to the nitty-gritty of tactics; strategic decisions provide the umbrella under which we make our tactical decisions. When we make strategic decisions, we focus on grand goals and big objectives and expect to achieve them over the long haul. We use tactics to implement our strategies. Like habitual choices, we make many tactical decisions. When we have time, we can make them deliberately.

The Law of Large Numbers and Multiplay Decisions

We have known people who scoff at the importance of habitual and tactical decisions in their personal and professional lives. They are completely correct in suggesting that the outcome of any single tactical habitual decision is unlikely to have much of an impact on their organization. Two facts, however, make multiplay decisions extremely important. First, they occur very frequently; one researcher recently estimated that 95 percent of our decisions are not just habitual but automatic. Second, multiplay decisions playing out over time have an inexorable quality: If you get them right, you will invariably win; but if you get them wrong, you will invariably lose. The law of large numbers explains why.

The law of large numbers is simple. If you do the same thing over and over again, the chances of failure and the chances of success will reveal themselves much more clearly than if you did that thing only once. Stated differently, if you replay a bet many times, your outcome will probably be very close to the bet's underlying expected value. Thus, if the odds are 60–40 for you, placing the bet a thousand times means that you will win very close to six hundred and you will lose very close to four hundred of the bets.

The law of large numbers explains why casinos are so incredibly profitable. The house has a small probability advantage on every single bet, whether made at the craps table, at roulette, or at blackjack. It also has a small probability advantage on every pull of every slot machine. (It's no wonder that they call them one-armed bandits.) Because they have this small advantage over many, many bets, the house's profits almost precisely match its edge in the odds. And the more bets that people make in any one casino, the higher the profits and the more certain they are to occur. This is why casinos treat big winners so well (e.g., offering free rooms and liquor). They know that if they can keep people betting, the law of large numbers will ensure that the house will increase its winnings. The law also explains why polling services can give such good estimates of election outcomes. By randomly sampling voters as they leave voting booths on election day, polling services can project with tremendous accuracy what the outcome of the election will be, long before all of the votes are in. (In fact, getting data from about 2,400 people provides a prediction of the total population's view within about three percentage points.) The law of large numbers is very powerful.

We can see the implications of the law of large numbers for decision-making by considering two different gambles. First, imagine that we have asked you to flip a fair coin. Before you see the result, you must choose heads or tails. If you are right, we will give you $10,000. If you are wrong, you give us $5,000. When we do this with managerial and executive groups, most people choose not to make the bet—even though the expected value is positive and considerable. Indeed, the mathematical calculation gives an expected value of $2,500. Suppose, however, that we change the bet. This time we will toss the coin one hundred times. For each bet that you win, we give you $100; for each bet that you lose, you pay us $50. The expected value of these hundred bets is exactly the same as the expected value of our one big bet—$2,500. When we offer this bet to managers and executives, they all choose to play.

The first bet is a large, single-play decision. The second is a series of smaller, identical multiplay decisions. The law of large numbers operates in the second case but not the first. Over the course of a hundred rounds of the multiplay bet, you will almost certainly win about $2,500. When we do the single-play bet, however, you will either win $10,000 or lose $5,000. The fear of losing $5,000 makes taking the bet too risky for most people, even though the prize for winning is twice as big.

It is critical to remember, however, that the underlying odds of multiplay decisions are what determine their final, cumulative outcome. When you make many choices, you will win in the long run only *if* the overall expected value of your choices is positive. If the expected value is negative, the law of large numbers will lead you to a terrible final outcome.

*SCRIPT*ing Tough Calls

By considering each of seven SCRIPTS parameters, you will improve your odds of successfully navigating your own tough calls in a timely and confident way.

1. Search for signals of threats and opportunities.   **5.** Take different **p**erspectives.
2. Find the **c**auses.   **6.** Consider the **t**ime frame.
3. Evaluate the **r**isks.   **7. S**olve the problem.
4. Apply **i**ntuition and emotion.

Search for Signals of Threats and Opportunities

The first step in making tough calls is to identify signals of threats and opportunities. Unless threats are identified early, they can compound, sometimes rapidly. According to the law of the power curve, the longer we wait to address a problem, the more severe it will become. Master decision makers employ situation analysis to monitor their environment and detect problem signals. To perform effective situation analysis, we must know our goals, have outstanding information systems, and have the expertise necessary to interpret the data and recognize the presence of problem signals.

Signal-detection analysis can help us determine whether to respond to a possible problem. In this approach, the decision maker determines the strength of the signal for action and compares it to a trigger for how much evidence is required before taking action. The trigger for action is based on the relative costs of making the two types of possible errors—a needless blunder or a missed opportunity. As exemplified by the USS *Vincennes* (which shot down an Iran Air passenger plane it mistook for combat aircraft), a needless blunder occurs when an action is taken when it should not have been. As exemplified by the USS *Stark* (which was bombed by an Iraqi combat plane that was not perceived as a threat), a missed opportunity occurs when an action is not taken when it should have been. If a missed opportunity will be more negative than a needless blunder, we should set a hair trigger for action. If a needless blunder will be more negative, we should set a sticky trigger for action.

Decision-makers must be aware of the various biases that impact their detection of signals. In particular, the overconfidence bias may cause a person to set a hair trigger when charting an initial course of action. A hair trigger, however, increases the likelihood of a needless blunder. On the other hand, a previous choice of action allows overconfidence to lead to a sticky trigger. As a result, the decision-maker may have difficulty abandoning a losing course of action.

If we identify a signal of a threat or opportunity, it is critical to determine whether the situation has a short or a long fuse. For short-fuse crises, we truncate the SCRIPTS process and employ guided intuition to solve the problem. For long-fuse problems, we can activate the entire SCRIPTS process. Prior to moving to the second stage of the SCRIPTS process, we summarize the seven principles of signal detection.

The Signal-Detection Principles

1. Employ situation analysis to identify signals of threats and opportunities.
2. Avoid the zone of false hope by identifying problem signals early.
3. Set your trigger so that a mistake will lead to the least-negative outcome.
4. Strive for accuracy in detecting signals by creating outstanding systems for gathering and interpreting data.
5. Recognize that the overconfidence bias can decrease accuracy and influence trigger setting.
6. If you are facing a short-fuse situation, truncate the SCRIPTS process by going directly to guided intuition.
7. Be realistic when making a decision, and be confident when implementing it.

Find the Causes

The causes of a threat or opportunity can range dramatically in complexity. On the one hand, a threat or opportunity may arise from a single factor. Usually, however, when high-stakes decisions are involved, multiple factors converge to create the quandary. As a result, it is critical to take a systems approach to understanding causation.

The use of a systems approach often reveals that the cause of a serious incident is overdetermined; that is, a number of factors have come together to produce the problem. Reality is extremely complex because it is marked by multiple factors coming together to cause threats and opportunities.

ROOT-CAUSE ANALYSIS To this point, we have shown that catastrophes are often overdetermined. We have not, however, described how to find the causes. If you are an engineer or work for a hospital, you will know the answer—root-cause analysis. There are many definitions of root-cause analysis. One of our favorites was developed at Cisco Systems. Managers at this high-tech company define root-cause analysis as the "process of analyzing cause–effect relationships between events in complex systems." We think of root-cause analysis as a structured process for assessing the cause–effect relationships in a system and identifying which component, or components, are responsible for an event. A number of principles apply, including the following:

1. Begin by determining the sequence of events that has led to the incident.
2. Constantly seek answers to the "why" question.
3. Carefully examine human decision making as well as physical systems.
4. Recognize that a single cause can generate many symptoms and may share symptoms with other causes.
5. Understand that there may be more than one root cause.

After the basic problem or problems have been identified, we then seek to find a set of alternative solutions. We recognize that it is important to identify as many solutions as possible. The most frequent error in this phase is to truncate the solution-identification process too early. Other sources of error include the overconfidence bias (overconfidence leads to underestimating threats and failing to collect necessary information), hindsight bias (retrospectively overestimating how well a problem or outcome could have been anticipated), and availability bias (weighting more heavily accessible information in decision making).

Causal Principles

1. Use root-cause analysis to identify the cause or causes of the threat or opportunity.
2. Analyze causes from a systems perspective, and recognize that failures are often overdetermined.
3. Avoid causal illusions by acknowledging that neither you nor mysterious outside forces can influence events governed by chance.
4. Avoid the availability bias by knowing that the cause of an outcome may not be the most available factor that comes to mind.
5. Defensive, ego-driven attributions can lead to a failure to identify causes. Learn more by realizing (a) that the situation is not always the cause of our poor outcomes and (b) that we are not always completely responsible for our good outcomes.
6. Avoid the fundamental attribution error by recognizing that situational factors (e.g., good/bad luck or the difficulty of the task) may be a serious influence in the performance of others.
7. Avoid the hindsight bias; that is, don't exaggerate in hindsight what you could not have anticipated in foresight.

Evaluate the Risks

Six risk factors are important when we evaluate the negative consequences (i.e., the risks) of a missed opportunity or a needless blunder. Each is concerned with anticipating the regret that we would experience following the ultimate outcome. We use the acronym SMILES to identify the six factors:

The Six Risk Dimensions

Social risk: How will others view me? What will it do to my reputation?

Monetary risk: How will the outcome impact my financial and material resources?

Information risk: How much will I learn from the experience?

Life/health risk: Will the outcome threaten my life or health?

Experience risk: How much will I enjoy or hate the experience?

Sink-the-boat risk: Does a false action create the potential for a catastrophic, irretrievable loss?

To assess the consequences of a needless blunder or a missed opportunity, we try to anticipate potential regret for each of the SMILES dimensions.

A critical problem, of course, is determining the actual value of the risks of the different choices available in high-stakes decisions. There is no true "reality" as to what the actual risks and benefits are because they are based on perceptions, not objective reality. The problem is even more difficult because several perceptual and motivational factors often bias our estimates and perceptions. These include the anchoring and insufficient adjustment bias (the tendency to make estimates by starting from an initial point or anchor and then adjusting from that value to generate a prediction), the law of decreasing marginal effect (the positive or negative reaction to each additional unit of something—money, praise, losses, etc.—decreases as the amount increases), entrapment in decisions (not ending a failing project or "throwing good money after bad"), and failing to carry through a course of action (quitting too soon).

One quite effective approach to managing risk involves developing rules of thumb for action. These are easily followed rules that typically result in satisfactory but not always optimal decisions. Heuristics have several advantages: They are quick to implement, they tend to be simple, and they are frequently based on years of experience. One of the most basic is the principle of diversification—or not putting all your eggs in one basket. Another is the use of milestones or objectives that must be met in order for a project to be continued.

Apply Intuition and Emotion

Reason, intuition, and emotion all play an important role in high-stakes decision-making. The tough call is *when* to use reason, *when* to employ intuition, and *when* to allow your emotions to influence your actions. We recommend that when a strategic decision must be made, the decision-maker should use reason and guided intuition. The reasoning process involves moving through the seven SCRIPTS steps prior to taking action. The decision-maker then compares the conclusion derived from the SCRIPTS procedure to the solution that emerges from employing guided intuition.

Whether we are employing the full SCRIPTS procedure or using intuition, emotion can get in the way to bias how we estimate probabilities and how we value outcomes. For example, in crisis situations, the emotions of anger and fear can activate flight or fight responses that are highly dysfunctional. Taking the time to think through the situation and develop options can be critical. Once a decision has been made, however, emotions can add that extra spark to get the decision implemented and to provide the energy to perform the work quickly and efficiently.

Finally, we propose that decision-makers employ a guided-intuition process whether making crisis or strategic decisions. We define guided intuition as the instantaneous use of the SCRIPTS procedure to make experienced-based intuitive decisions. Thoroughly practicing the SCRIPTS procedure on many problems allows the steps to become ingrained and reflexive. When a crisis situation occurs, the decision-maker can then automatically engage this intuitive process, in which causes are sought, risks are identified, alternative perspectives are taken, and time is considered in a matter of seconds or minutes. Thus, the SCRIPTS procedure guides the use of

> ## Principles of Intuition and Emotion
>
> 1. Guided-intuition is best employed by experts when time is short and/or when a rational analysis has resulted in two or more essentially equivalent options.
> 2. Emotions are required to move a decision-maker to action and to implement solutions energetically.
> 3. When time is available, use rational decision analysis to identify alternative courses of action, the probability of success of the options, and the positive and negative outcomes that may occur.
> 4. Emotions exaggerate and bias perceptions of the probability of outcomes and the perceptions of positive and negative values.
> 5. Fear increases the belief that negative outcomes will happen and causes people to view bad outcomes more negatively.
> 6. Optimism increases the belief that good things will happen and increases the perceived value of positive outcomes.

both reason and intuition in high-stakes decision-making. While using intuition or moving through the SCRIPTS procedure, turn down the flames of emotions and avoid letting anger, fear, or greed hijack you. When you identify a solution, however, allow your emotions to provide explosive force to implement the course of action with overwhelming energy and drive.

Take Different Perspectives

The perspective that we employ provides a set of values and salient issues that influence the factors that we consider in our decision-making processes. As a result, it influences our final choice. By explicitly viewing decision problems from divergent perspectives, master decision-makers ensure that they develop a full understanding of the situation. Clear-headed decision-makers know that if they do not plainly evaluate the decision from alternative frames of reference, their decision will almost invariably be misconstrued.

Our perspectives act as lenses that focus our attention on particular decision elements and personal values. In the next section, we discuss eight divergent perspectives that are prevalent in U.S. corporations. We describe how each perspective can have both positive and negative effects on decision making. We then show how the perspectives have influenced decision-makers in a variety of high-stakes contexts. After discussing the critical importance of viewing decisions from an ethical perspective, we conclude the chapter with a discussion of the principle of multiframe superiority.

EIGHT PROFESSIONAL PERSPECTIVES The eight professional perspectives we identify here are engineering/technology, sales/marketing, production, political, legal, accounting/finance, competitive, and ethical. At the risk of overloading on acronyms, note that the eight perspectives can be remembered via the phrase ESP-PLACE.

Engineering/Technology Frame   The first important frame of reference in organizations is the engineering/technology perspective. This frame is at its best when it causes executives to focus on producing innovative, high-quality products in an efficient and timely manner. On the downside, the engineering/technology frame can result in look-alike, cost-ineffective products designed for the engineer rather than the customer. At its worst, the needs and wants of consumers are ignored. This can result in the creation of products that are easy to use for the engineers. For consumers, however, the products may be so complicated as to be nearly incomprehensible and useless.

The Sales/Marketing Frame   The sales/marketing frame represents another lens that many professionals use to view the world. At its best, the sales frame causes managers to take a customer perspective in which they focus on increasing customer satisfaction and developing innovative products that fulfill the needs and wants of consumers. Unfortunately, the sales viewpoint can result in a P. T. Barnum–like focus on hype and gimmicky sales-promotion efforts. At its worst, the sales perspective results in the use of misrepresentation and deceit to foist inferior products onto unsuspecting consumers.

The Production Frame   A production focus represents a third lens that managers use to view the world. At its best, it emphasizes efficiency and productivity. The goal is to optimize output by having long production runs with a similar design and minimal changes to reduce costs. When overdone, however, a production mentality results in a loss of focus on the customer's needs and wants. If the market changes and product innovation fails to keep pace, everyone loses. A production focus can also cause managers to search out and use the latest production technology and then find themselves saddled with dramatic overcapacity. Matching production to the market can be overlooked when a production frame dominates a person's view.

The Political Frame   Another important frame of reference for decision-making is a political focus. On the positive side, a political perspective allows a manager to use a combination of relationships, compromise, power, and persuasion to bring disparate sides together to get things done. When a person views the world with a political lens, the goal also becomes one of staying in power and building alliances with and rewarding those who either contributed to the process or are likely to contribute in the future. On the negative side, a political perspective can lead to decisions that are based on ideology and favoritism rather than on a focus on getting the job done most effectively.

The Legal Frame   A legal frame is another important perspective for managers. At its best, a legal perspective causes executives to carefully consider the relationship of high-stakes decisions to appropriate laws and regulations. Because the U.S. legal system is adversarial in nature, a legal perspective can inculcate a high degree of competitiveness in decision-makers and negotiators. Like the other perspectives, however, an overuse of the legal frame can cause problems. It can lead managers to focus solely on whether a particular action is legal and forget about the effects of the action on consumers and suppliers. As a result, an action can be taken that is legal but that also has extremely negative consequences for public relations. In addition, as we have already seen, the legal frame can result in an extreme competitiveness that alienates potential partners.

The Accounting/Finance Frame   When appropriately used, the accounting/finance perspective keeps costs under control and a company on solid financial footing. When improperly used, it focuses attention on achieving short-term profits and stifles innovation. For example, during the 1990s reengineering craze, U.S. corporations dramatically cut personnel. The short-term result was a dramatic increase in productivity and profitability. Unfortunately, over the longer term, the remaining employees were over-worked. As a result, they could not attend to their customers or to research and development. The net effect was a decrease in consumer satisfaction and new product innovations. These effects were particularly strong in the banking industry; as the headline in the November 2000 issue of the American Banking Association's *Banking Journal* stated, "Put Away the Axe: You Can't Cut Your Way to Profitability Anymore."

The Competitive Frame   Those who employ a competitive perspective think in terms of military campaigns or sports contests. Managers frequently use military and sports terminology in the hallways of giant corporations, start-ups, and small retailers. On the military side, managers will employ phrases that come directly from the jargon of war: an advertising campaign, launching a new product blitz, battling competitors, biting the bullet, identifying the flagship brand, being under the gun. On the sports side, the phrases and metaphors are almost as numerous. We often hear managers describe themselves or others as running a two-minute drill, dropping the ball, running interference, quarterbacking the team, being a team player, punting on an issue, and scoring a touchdown.

Employing a competitive perspective in the language that we use to communicate our ideas influences how we actually perceive the situation. At its best, a competitive perspective emphasizes the values of teamwork, achievement, and winning victories. Each of these values can make a positive contribution to making high-stakes decisions. At its worst, a competitive orientation can result in a cutthroat mentality that emphasizes secrecy and winning at any cost.

The Ethical Frame   The last of our perspectives is an ethical frame of reference. Increasingly, major corporations include a position called the ethics officer. When used appropriately, viewing the world from an ethical perspective will result in long-term benefits. By asking what the "right" thing to do is, managers can avoid talking themselves into taking actions that can lead to short-term profits but long-term disaster. When used improperly, however, the constant questioning of choices that can result from an ethics perspective can slow the decision-making process to a crawl.

Using a multiframe approach is exactly the opposite of our normal tendencies. Most of us recognize that we can't see all aspects of every big decision that we confront and that other sources of information and other perspectives might help us to make better decisions. But as human beings, we love to hear that our opinions are sound, that our inclinations are correct, and that the decisions we are considering are on track. In a word, we yearn for support. Thus, we tend to ask our friends for their opinions when we make big decisions—and our friends tend to be like us. In many instances, they may have exactly the same perspectives that we do. So they are most likely to be convinced by our logic.

We are biased not to ask people who are different from us to evaluate our potential decisions but only to ask people who are similar to us. But different kinds of people are exactly the people whom we should seek out. First, they can help us see things differently and give us some foresight about our potentially disastrous blunders. Second, if they do agree with our decisions, from a totally different perspective, we can be much more confident that we are making the right decision. Thus, the idea of using multiple perspectives means that we must go against our natural tendencies and consciously seek out people with different kinds of insights that can better inform our decision making.

Consider the Time Frame

High-stakes decisions require us to accept trade-offs. It is a rare but wonderful occasion when we can have our cake and eat it, too. We have already discussed one trade-off that managers frequently make—that of freedom versus control. For example, Boeing executives exchanged computerized control of the 757 for giving pilots the freedom to make critical decisions in flight.

The difficulty of present-future trade-offs is compounded by the fact that any single decision can have both good and bad outcomes. These outcomes can occur together or separately, in the present or in the future. This juxtaposition of positive and negative outcomes over time strongly influences both business and personal decisions. Present-future trade-offs can lead to decision myopia, which results from our natural tendency to overweight the present and underweight the future.

Solve the Problem

A THREE-STEP PROCESS FOR SOLVING THE PROBLEM Our approach to solving the problem is to take our philosophy of structured analysis to its logical conclusion. We do this in three steps. The first step is to set our trigger, that is, determine how sticky or how quick it should be. Second, we assess how the evidence that we have been able to accumulate contributes to the probability of success if we act. Finally, we compare our evidence to our trigger setting. If our estimate of the probability of success surpasses the trigger setting, we act; if not, we remain in a status quo position. Through this three-step process, we provide a simple, but powerful, means for making high-stakes decisions. In the sections below, we discuss each step in the solve-the-problem process.

Step 1: Set the Trigger The trigger identifies the amount of evidence that we will require for action. We discussed what it means to set a sticky, a neutral, or a hair trigger, settings based on which type of error is more costly. Thus, we set a sticky trigger when the risk of a needless blunder is substantially higher than the risk of a missed opportunity. An example is the criterion for guilt employed in the criminal justice system in the United States. The instruction that the defendant must be found guilty "beyond a reasonable doubt" means that we have set a sticky trigger because we believe that it is worse to convict an innocent person (a needless blunder) than to let a guilty person go free (a missed opportunity). In contrast, the instructions in civil trials represent a neutral trigger; the jury (the set of decision-makers) is told that a verdict for the plaintiff can be based on a "preponderance of the evidence," which implicitly indicates that the risk of a needless blunder is no greater than the risk of a missed opportunity.

Thus far, we have described the trigger setting in terms of a process of balancing the risk of a missed opportunity versus the risk of a needless blunder. There is a simple way to quantify this balancing process. We recommend the creation of a risk ratio. We produce a risk ratio by dividing the value of the needless blunder by the sum of the values of the missed opportunity and the needless blunder. The risk ratio will range from zero to one because the value of the denominator (the sum of the value of the needless blunder and the value of the missed opportunity) will always be larger than the value of the numerator (the value of the needless blunder). The denominator represents the range of possible outcomes, from the worst to the best. The numerator represents the downside risk if you take the action and are wrong:

$$\text{Risk Ratio} = \frac{\text{the value of a needless blunder}}{\text{the value of a needless blunder} \div \text{the value of a missed opportunity}}$$

Step 2: Assess the Evidence for Acting After setting the trigger, a decision-maker needs to assess the strength of the evidence that the project will succeed. We begin by identifying the milestones that must be achieved for the endeavor to be successful. Then, we multiply the probabilities of each milestone together.

Just as we adjusted the risk ratio when we set the trigger, we must also adjust this probability estimate of success. To do so, we list all of the reasons why action

Principles for Solving the Problem

1. Move through a three-step sequence to calculate a risk ratio, estimate the probability of success if you act, and choose action if your probability-of-success estimate exceeds your risk ratio.
2. When faced with multiple options for action, select the option that has the largest confidence margin.
3. When monetary considerations dominate, use them first in calculating your risk ratio. Then adjust on the basis of the other SMILES risk dimensions.
4. When nonmonetary considerations dominate, start with a risk ratio of .50. Then use the six SMILES dimensions to adjust it.
5. Calculate the likelihood of success by (1) estimating the probability of achieving each milestone necessary for an action to succeed and by multiplying the probabilities together and (2) adjusting your result by considering the effects of intuition, emotions, perspective, and time.

should work and all of the reasons why it may not. This approach borrows ideas that go back at least to Benjamin Franklin when he described how to make complex choices. He suggested beginning the process by taking a sheet of paper and listing the pros and cons of engaging in an action. He next advocated, after contemplation and thought, striking out comparable pros and cons until the process simplified itself and an obvious choice emerged. Our process for solving the problem builds on Franklin's intuitive approach.

Step 3: Compare the Likelihood of Success to the Risk Ratio With the calculations of the risk ratio and the probability of success, we are now in position to make a high-stakes decision. This straightforward step simply entails comparing the two figures. If the likelihood of success is greater than the risk ratio, the evidence points toward action. In contrast, if the likelihood of success is less than the risk ratio, there is a strong indication to not act.

We conclude with a strong suggestion, an admonition, to always identify as many options as possible. One of the most frequent mistakes of high-stakes decision-makers is to focus quickly on a single solution and then act to justify its selection. Once we identify the possible causes of a problem, we should identify as many solutions as possible. By the time we have moved through the SCRIPTS process and have reached the stage of solving the problem, we will quickly eliminate most options.

As master decision-makers, we should strive to employ the three-step process on several alternatives, not just two. In this way, we can be more confident that we haven't eliminated any better solutions.

SCRIPTing the Brew Pub Case

The Chicago Brew Pub case provides examples for each of the seven SCRIPTS parameters. First, Jim Bronson and his partner had to search for signals of threats and opportunities. They recognized that the competitive environment was about to become much more difficult. But Jim also realized that going public would create its own set of problems.

Jim and Chicago Brew Pub did decide to go public. The days just before their initial public offering, however, provided a clear signal of impending difficulties. For 11 days, Jim traveled to 24 states and appeared at 73 meetings. He recognized that this exhausting experience was a harbinger of the difficulties of doubling the number of restaurants for four consecutive years.

The second parameter of tough calls is to find the causes of threats and opportunities. Jim certainly knew what would cause his opportunities to vanish: Only so much money was available to open brew pubs, and unless he acted quickly, the money would dry up. What he failed to ask, however, was why the opportunities appeared in the first place. He knew that the Chicago Brew Pub was the only profitable brew pub chain at the time. Another key question that needed an answer involved whether the market would support a dramatic increase in the number of brew pubs.

Interestingly, Jim told us that neither he nor his partner took any formal steps to evaluate the risks—the third parameter in the SCRIPTS process. One risk factor, however, did impact his decision. He recognized that by going public, they could immediately pay off the $3 million debt that they had taken on to begin a process of franchising restaurants. Thus, on one dimension that was immediately obvious to them, going public would decrease risk.

Next, Jim Bronson and his partner needed to apply intuition and emotion—the fourth SCRIPTS parameter—when they considered their options. When we turn to intuition, it is critical to control the effects of our emotions on our decisions. Emotions such as greed and fear can short-circuit an otherwise effective process employing intuition. Emotions do have a role, however, in high-stakes decision making. They are always present because of the stress that inevitably accompanies the decision process. The key is to employ the energy that emotions create to help implement the decision.

For the fifth parameter of tough calls, take different perspectives, the two partners took different viewpoints. Paul Springfield took a marketing approach and focused on the issue of how to please customers and grow the business. Jim Bronson took a finance perspective that focused on how to hold down costs and make a profit. Their perspectives for making decisions influenced their interpretation of the evidence and the values that they brought to the decision-making process. As in many successful partnerships, the interplay of individuals taking divergent perspectives resulted in a winning strategy for many years.

Professional training provides people with a particular perspective. The best decision-makers recognize the biases that their own frame of reference creates, so they try to increase the number of perspectives that they use to analyze a problem. By viewing a problem through multiple perceptual lenses, they can select the optimum approach (or approaches) for making tough choices.

The sixth SCRIPTS parameter, consider the time frame, also applies here. Of particular importance is the question of how long the window of opportunity will remain open. In the brew pub case, it appeared that the chance to go public would disappear in less than six months. As a result, the partners needed to make a major strategic decision relatively quickly—but not immediately. Time pressure can dramatically affect the quality of our decisions. Master decision-makers can still function extremely well even in such stressful situations. In addition, they recognize that even in our fast-paced world, not all of their decisions need to be made quickly. Indeed, some of the worst disasters result from taking a "ready, fire, aim" approach to making tough choices and acting more quickly than is really necessary.

After considering the first six SCRIPTS parameters, decision makers have the information that they need to take the final step, solve the problem, and make the tough call. We provide a three-step procedure for making the final decision. When time is available, the procedure can be more formal and employ explicit calculations. When time is short, the procedure will need to be less formal and seriously abbreviated. Having more time will allow you to make better decisions, but the SCRIPTS process will still facilitate quick decisions in important ways.

The SCRIPTS process can handle both long- and short-fuse decision situations. By first identifying and understanding the problem, you will immediately know whether your problem is a crisis or a strategic decision. If you are in a crisis, you must truncate lengthier procedures and use your experience, training, and intuition to make the tough call. If your problem is strategic, you can afford to use the more formal three-step procedure. By practicing the three-step procedure on numerous problems, you will begin to equip yourself to make crisis decisions. The rational decision-making procedures that we provide can thus be hard-wired so that your reactions become almost reflexive. In essence, you will begin to develop the kind of experienced intuition that will allow you to cope with crises quickly and effectively.

The Conclusion

You may be wondering what happened to Jim Bronson and his partner and Chicago Brew Pub. After making a small public offering of stock, they paid the investment bankers and retired their debt of $3 million, leaving them with $15 million for expansion. They began opening pubs but quickly realized that it was extremely difficult to find suitable properties in the fast-growing industry. Over the next three years, they opened as many pubs as their experience and sound judgment indicated. By 1998, they had 67 locations.

Early in 1999, however, the industry started collapsing as competitor after competitor entered the market. In Dallas, for example, the number of brew pubs increased from 3 to 40 in two-and-a-half years.

We interviewed Janice Kline, who was the chief financial officer (CFO) for a company that owned 80 restaurant franchises. Beginning in 1996, she carefully watched the explosion of brew pubs because they were competitors of her firm. For her, the growth of the brew pub industry also represented an opportunity. As the competing brew pub companies sought to spend the $400 million in new capital that they had to expand, they needed to purchase existing properties. Janice was more than happy to sell her company's worst properties for inflated prices. Big Apple, for instance, paid handsomely for properties because of their investment bankers' requirement to grow. Janice told us that she simply waited for the inevitable collapse.

It didn't take long. Every analyst employed by the investment bankers failed the tough call as each company that had gone public lost money. In the end, every publicly traded brew pub company either went bankrupt or was purchased at distressed prices by another firm, resulting in almost complete devastation for what was an emerging brew pub industry. In early 1999, there were about eight thousand brew pubs. By 2000, the number had been cut in half. Unfortunately, Chicago Brew Pub was caught in the carnage. In 2000, the company went bankrupt.

The experience of Jim Bronson, Paul Springfield, and Chicago Brew Pub illustrates two additional features of tough calls. First, because hard choices are made under conditions of great risk and uncertainty, even the best decision can have bad consequences. Only through the 20–20 vision of hindsight can we criticize the decision of these two young entrepreneurs to go public.

Second, the need to make decisions on fast time can be illusory. After being approached to take his company public, Jim Bronson recognized that he had to take sufficient time to formulate an effective strategy. Because of the pressure of the investment bankers, however, he perceived that his window of opportunity for making the decision would remain open for only a few weeks. In hindsight, however, had he waited longer, his outcomes would have been much better. Indeed, had he waited a couple of years to take his company public, he may have been able to buy up the other failed brew pubs at a fraction of their true value. Considering the time frame is a critical step in making tough calls. It's all too easy to get caught up with the idea that "I need to make a decision NOW!"

Master decision-makers follow a tested process (such as SCRIPTS) for making decisions, they do much of their own research (or have trusted advisors help them with it), they first gain and then learn from experience, they have fun and experiment, and they implement their decisions with precision. When making tough choices, master decision-makers recognize that even the best decisions can turn out poorly. As a result, they focus on the process rather than the outcome. They recognize that whether the outcome turns out well or badly, they must learn from it and then put it behind them. With a top-notch process, the odds are increased that the outcome of the next tough call will be successful.

19 Power and Influence

THE SCIENCE OF PERSUASION
Robert Cialdini

INFLUENCE WITHOUT AUTHORITY: THE USE OF ALLIANCES, RECIPROCITY, AND EXCHANGE TO ACCOMPLISH WORK
Allan R. Cohen
David L. Bradford

The command-and-control management style, which was more prevalent in the past, went hand in hand with an autocratic approach to using power and influence. In the current work environment, however, people in positions of authority are expected to earn the respect of their subordinates, explain the rationale for their decisions and orders, and focus on commitment rather than control with their employees. Furthermore, many employees work in cross-disciplinary teams—their influence efforts are more often directed horizontally at peers rather than vertically up or down a hierarchy. These changes have resulted in the need for a broader range of skills relating to power and influence. Power is defined as the capacity to influence the behavior of others, whereas influence is the process by which people successfully persuade others to follow their advice, suggestions, or orders.

In the article "The Science of Persuasion," Robert Cialdini, psychology professor at Arizona State University, examines six pervasive influence tactics that we use to persuade one another and discusses how to resist unwanted persuasion. He documents his extensive research on these tactics, providing numerous examples. Cialdini also considers how culture impacts the use and effectiveness of various tactics.

Allan Cohen, Babson College professor and former dean, and David Bradford, Stanford University professor and center director, perceived early on that many employees have to influence people whom they do not supervise. Their classic article, "Influence Without Authority: The Use of Alliances, Reciprocity, and Exchange to Accomplish Work," explains the different "currencies" we can use to influence others and the reciprocal nature of mutual influence.

THE SCIENCE OF PERSUASION*

Robert Cialdini

Social psychology has determined the basic principles that govern getting to "yes"

I'd like to let you in on something of great importance to you personally. Have you ever been tricked into saying yes? Ever felt trapped into buying something you didn't really want or contributing to some suspicious-sounding cause? And have you ever wished you understood why you acted in this way so that you could withstand these clever ploys in the future?

Yes? Then clearly this article is just right for you. It contains valuable information on the most powerful psychological pressures that get you to say yes to requests. And it's chock-full of NEW, IMPROVED research showing exactly how and why these techniques work. So don't delay, just settle in and get the information that, after all, you've already agreed you want.

The scientific study of the process of social influence has been under way for well over half a century, beginning in earnest with the propaganda, public information and persuasion programs of World War II. Since that time, numerous social scientists have investigated the ways in which one individual can influence another's attitudes and actions. For the past 30 years, I have participated in that endeavor, concentrating primarily on the major factors that bring about a specific form of behavior change—compliance with a request. Six basic tendencies of human behavior come into play in generating a positive response: reciprocation, consistency, social validation, liking, authority and scarcity. As these six tendencies help to govern our business dealings, our societal involvements and our personal relationships, knowledge of the rules of persuasion can truly be thought of as empowerment.

Reciprocation

When the Disabled American Veterans organization mails out requests for contributions, the appeal succeeds only about 18 percent of the time. But when the mailing includes a set of free personalized address labels, the success rate almost doubles, to 35 percent. To understand the effect of the unsolicited gift, we must recognize the reach and power of an essential rule of human conduct: the code of reciprocity.

All societies subscribe to a norm that obligates individuals to repay in kind what they have received. Evolutionary selection pressure has probably entrenched the behavior in social animals such as ourselves. The demands of reciprocity begin to explain the boost in donations to the veterans group. Receiving a gift—unsolicited and perhaps even unwanted—convinced significant numbers of potential donors to return the favor.

Charitable organizations are far from alone in taking this approach: food stores offer free samples, exterminators offer free in-home inspections, health clubs offer free workouts. Customers are thus exposed to the product or service, but they are also indebted. Consumers are not the only ones who fall under the sway of reciprocity. Pharmaceutical companies spend millions of dollars every year to support medical researchers and to provide gifts to individual physicians—activities that may subtly influence investigators' findings and physicians' recommendations. A 1998 study in the *New England Journal of Medicine* found that only 37 percent of researchers who published conclusions critical of the safety of calcium channel blockers had previously received drug company support. Among those whose conclusions attested to the drugs' safety, however, the number of those who had received free trips, research funding or employment skyrocketed—to 100 percent.

Reciprocity includes more than gifts and favors; it also applies to concessions that people make to one another. For example, assume that you reject my large request, and I then make a concession to you by retreating to a smaller request. You may very well then reciprocate with a concession of your own: agreement with my lesser request. In the mid-1970s my colleagues and I conducted an experiment that clearly illustrates the dynamics of reciprocal concessions. We stopped a random sample of passersby on public walkways and asked them if they would volunteer to chaperone juvenile detention center inmates on a day trip to the zoo. As expected, very few complied, only 17 percent.

For another random sample of passersby, however, we began with an even larger request: to serve as an unpaid counselor at the center for two hours per week for the next two years. Everyone in this second sampling rejected the extreme appeal. At that point we offered them a concession. "If you can't do that," we asked, "would you chaperone a group of juvenile detention center inmates on a day trip to the zoo?" Our concession powerfully stimulated return concessions. The compliance rate nearly tripled, to 50 percent, compared with the straightforward zoo-trip request.

Consistency

In 1998 Gordon Sinclair, the owner of a well-known Chicago restaurant, was struggling with a problem that afflicts all restaurateurs. Patrons frequently reserve a table but, without notice, fail to appear. Sinclair solved the problem by asking his receptionist to change two words of what she said to callers requesting reservations. The change dropped his no-call, no-show rate from 30 to 10 percent immediately.

The two words were effective because they commissioned the force of another potent human motivation: the desire to be, and to appear, consistent. The receptionist merely modified her request from "Please call if you have to change your plans" to "Will you please call if you have to change your plans?" At that point, she politely paused and waited for a response. The wait was pivotal because it induced customers to fill the pause with a public commitment. And public commitments, even seemingly minor ones, direct future action.

In another example, Joseph Schwarzwald of Bar-Ilan University in Israel and his co-workers nearly doubled monetary contributions for the handicapped in certain neighborhoods. The key factor: Two weeks before asking for contributions, they got residents to sign a petition supporting the handicapped, thus making a public commitment to that same cause.

Social Validation

On a wintry morning in the late 1960s, a man stopped on a busy New York City sidewalk and gazed skyward for 60 seconds, at nothing in particular. He did so as part of an experiment by City University of New York social psychologists Stanley Milgram, Leonard Bickman, and Lawrence Berkowitz that was designed to find out what effect this action would have on passersby. Most simply detoured or brushed by; 4 percent joined the man in looking up. The experiment was then repeated with a slight change. With the modification, large numbers of pedestrians were induced to come to a halt, crowd together, and peer upward.

The single alteration in the experiment incorporated the phenomenon of social validation. One fundamental way that we decide what to do in a situation is to look to what others are doing or have done there. If many individuals have decided in favor of a particular idea, we are more likely to follow, because we perceive the idea to be more correct, more valid.

Milgram, Bickman, and Berkowitz introduced the influence of social validation into their street experiment simply by having five men rather than one look up at nothing. With the larger initial set of upward gazers, the percentage of New Yorkers who followed suit more than quadrupled, to 18 percent. Bigger initial sets of planted up-lookers generated an even greater response: a starter group of 15 led 40 percent of passersby to join in, nearly stopping traffic within one minute.

Taking advantage of social validation, requesters can stimulate our compliance by demonstrating (or merely implying) that others just like us have already complied. For example, a study found that a fund raiser who showed homeowners a list of neighbors who had donated to a local charity significantly increased the frequency of contributions; the longer the list, the greater the effect. Marketers, therefore, go out of their way to inform us when their product is the largest-selling or fastest-growing of its kind, and television commercials regularly depict crowds rushing to stores to acquire the advertised item.

Less obvious, however, are the circumstances under which social validation can backfire to produce the opposite of what a requester intends. An example is the understandable but potentially misguided tendency of health educators to call attention to a problem by depicting it as regrettably frequent. Information campaigns stress that alcohol and drug use is intolerably high, that adolescent suicide rates are alarming, and that polluters are spoiling the environment. Although the claims are both true and well intentioned, the creators of these campaigns have missed something basic about the compliance process. Within the statement "Look at all the people who are doing this undesirable thing" lurks the powerful and undercutting message "Look at all the people who are doing this undesirable thing." Research shows that, as a consequence, many such programs boomerang, generating even more of the undesirable behavior.

For instance, a suicide intervention program administered to New Jersey teenagers informed them of the high number of teenage suicides. Health researcher David Shaffer and his colleagues at Columbia University found that participants became significantly more likely to see suicide as a potential solution to their problems. Of greater effectiveness are campaigns that honestly depict the unwanted activity as damaging despite the fact that relatively few individuals engage in it.

Liking

"Affinity," "rapport," and "affection" all describe a feeling of connection between people. But the simple word "liking" most faithfully captures the concept and has become the standard designation in the social science literature. People prefer to say yes to those they like. Consider the worldwide success of the Tupperware Corporation and its "home party" program. Through the in-home demonstration get-together, the company arranges for its customers to buy from a liked friend, the host, rather than from an unknown salesperson. So favorable has been the effect on proceeds that, according to company literature, a Tupperware party begins somewhere in the world every two seconds. In fact, 75 percent of all Tupperware parties today occur outside the individualistic U.S., in countries where group social bonding is even more important than it is here.

Of course, most commercial transactions take place beyond the homes of friends. Under these much more typical circumstances, those who wish to commission the power of liking employ tactics clustered around certain factors that research has shown to work.

Physical attractiveness can be such a tool. In a 1993 study conducted by Peter H. Reingen of Arizona State University and Jerome B. Kernan, now at George Mason University, good-looking fundraisers for the American Heart Association generated nearly twice as many donations (42 versus 23 percent) as did other requesters. In the 1970s researchers Michael G. Efran and E.W.J. Patterson of the University of Toronto found that voters in Canadian federal elections gave physically attractive candidates several times as many votes as unattractive ones. Yet such voters insisted that their choices would never be influenced by something as superficial as appearance.

Similarity also can expedite the development of rapport. Salespeople often search for, or outright fabricate, a connection between themselves and their customers: "Well, no kidding, you're from Minneapolis? I went to school in Minnesota!" Fund raisers do the same, with good results. In 1994 psychologists R. Kelly Aune of the University of Hawaii at Manoa and Michael D. Basil of the University of Denver reported research in which solicitors canvassed a college campus asking for contributions to a charity. When the phrase "I'm a student, too" was added to the requests, the amount of the donations more than doubled.

Compliments also stimulate liking, and direct salespeople are trained in the use of praise. Indeed, even inaccurate praise may be effective. Research at the University of North Carolina at Chapel Hill found that compliments produced just as much liking for the flatterer when they were untrue as when they were genuine.

Cooperation is another factor that has been shown to enhance positive feelings and behavior. Salespeople, for example, often strive to be perceived by their prospects as cooperating partners. Automobile sales managers frequently cast themselves as "villains" so the salesperson can "do battle" on the customer's behalf. The gambit naturally leads to a desirable form of liking by the customer for the salesperson, which promotes sales.

Authority

Recall the man who used social validation to get large numbers of passersby to stop and stare at the sky. He might achieve the opposite effect and spur stationary strangers into motion by assuming the mantle of authority. In 1955, University of Texas at Austin researchers Monroe Lefkowitz, Robert R. Blake, and Jane S. Mouton discovered that a man could increase by 350 percent the number of pedestrians who would follow him across the street against the light by changing one simple thing. Instead of casual dress, he donned markers of authority: a suit and tie.

Those touting their experience, expertise or scientific credentials may be trying to harness the power of authority: "Babies are our business, our only business," "Four out of five doctors recommend," and so on. There is nothing wrong with such claims when they are real, because we usually want the opinions of true authorities. Their insights help us choose quickly and well.

The problem comes when we are subjected to phony claims. If we fail to think, as is often the case when confronted by authority symbols, we can easily be steered in the wrong direction by ersatz experts—those who merely present the aura of legitimacy. That Texas jaywalker in a suit and tie was no more an authority on crossing the street than the rest of the pedestrians who nonetheless followed him. A highly successful ad campaign in the 1970s featured actor Robert Young proclaiming the health benefits of decaffeinated coffee. Young seems to have been able to dispense this medical opinion effectively because he represented, at the time, the nation's most famous physician. That Marcus Welby, M.D., was only a character on a TV show was less important than the appearance of authority.

Scarcity

While at Florida State University in the 1970s, psychologist Stephen West noted an odd occurrence after surveying students about the campus cafeteria cuisine: ratings of the food rose significantly from the week before, even though there had been no change in the menu, food quality, or preparation. Instead the shift resulted from an announcement that because of a fire, cafeteria meals would not be available for several weeks.

This account highlights the effect of perceived scarcity on human judgment. A great deal of evidence shows that items and opportunities become more desirable to us as they become less available. For this reason, marketers trumpet the unique benefits or the one-of-a-kind character of their offerings. It is also for this reason that they consistently engage in "limited time only" promotions or put us into competition with one another using sales campaigns based on "limited supply."

Less widely recognized is that scarcity affects the value not only of commodities but of information as well. Information that is exclusive is more persuasive. Take as evidence the dissertation data of a former student of mine, Amram Knishinsky, who owned a company that imported beef into the United States and sold it to supermarkets. To examine the effects of scarcity and exclusivity on compliance, he instructed his telephone salespeople to call a randomly selected sample of customers and to make a standard request of them to purchase beef. He also instructed the salespeople to do the same with a second random sample of customers but to add that a shortage of Australian beef was anticipated, which was true, because of certain weather conditions there. The added information that Australian beef was soon to be scarce more than doubled purchases.

Finally, he had his staff call a third sample of customers, to tell them (1) about the impending shortage of Australian beef and (2) that this information came from his company's exclusive sources in the Australian national weather service. These customers increased their orders by more than 600 percent. They were influenced by a scarcity double-whammy: not only was the beef scarce, but the information that the beef was scarce was itself scarce.

Influence across Cultures

Do the six key factors in the social influence process operate similarly across national boundaries? Yes, but with a wrinkle. The citizens of the world are human, after all, and susceptible to the fundamental tendencies that characterize all members of our species. Cultural norms, traditions and experiences can, however, modify the weight that is brought to bear by each factor.

Consider the results of a report published in 2000 by Stanford University's Michael W. Morris, Joel M. Podolny and Sheira Ariel, who studied employees of Citibank, a multinational financial corporation. The researchers selected four societies for examination: the United States, China, Spain and Germany. They surveyed Citibank branches within each country and measured employees' willingness to comply voluntarily with a request from a co-worker for assistance with a task. Although multiple key factors could come into play, the main reason employees felt obligated to comply differed in the four nations. Each of these reasons incorporated a different fundamental principle of social influence.

Employees in the United States took a reciprocation-based approach to the decision to comply. They asked the question, "What has this person done for me recently?" and felt obligated to volunteer if they owed the requester a favor. Chinese employees responded primarily to authority, in the form of loyalties to those of high status within their small group. They asked, "Is this requester connected to someone in my unit, especially someone who is high ranking?" If the answer was yes, they felt required to yield.

Spanish Citibank personnel based the decision to comply mostly on liking/friendship. They were willing to help on the basis of friendship norms that encourage faithfulness to one's friends, regardless of position or status. They asked, "Is this requester connected to my friends?" If the answer was yes, they were especially likely to want to comply.

German employees were most compelled by consistency, offering assistance in order to be consistent with the rules of the organization. They decided whether to comply by asking, "According to official regulations and categories, am I supposed to assist this requester?" If the answer was yes, they felt a strong obligation to grant the request.

In sum, although all human societies seem to play by the same set of influence rules, the weights assigned to the various rules can differ across cultures. Persuasive appeals to audiences in distinct cultures need to take such differences into account.

Knowledge Is Power

I think it noteworthy that many of the data presented in this article have come from studies of the practices of persuasion professionals—the marketers, advertisers, salespeople, fund raisers and their comrades whose financial well-being depends on their ability to get others to say yes. A kind of natural selection operates on these people, as those who use unsuccessful tactics soon go out of business. In contrast, those using procedures that work well will survive, flourish and pass on these successful strategies. Thus, over time, the most effective principles of social influence will appear in the repertoires of long-standing persuasion professions. My own work indicates that those principles embody the six fundamental human tendencies examined in this article: reciprocation, consistency, social validation, liking, authority, and scarcity.

From an evolutionary point of view, each of the behaviors presented would appear to have been selected for in animals, such as ourselves, that must find the best ways to survive while living in social groups. And in the vast majority of cases, these principles counsel us correctly. It usually makes great sense to repay favors, behave consistently, follow the lead of similar others, favor the requests of those we like, heed legitimate authorities and value scarce resources. Consequently, influence agents who use these principles honestly do us a favor. If an advertising agency, for instance, focused an ad campaign on the genuine weight of authoritative, scientific evidence favoring its client's headache product, all the right people would profit— the agency, the manufacturer and the audience. Not so, however, if the agency, finding no particular scientific merit in the pain reliever, "smuggles" the authority principle into the situation through ads featuring actors wearing white lab coats.

Are we then doomed to be helplessly manipulated by these principles? No. By understanding persuasion techniques, we can begin to recognize strategies and thus truly analyze requests and offerings. Our task must be to hold persuasion professionals accountable for the use of the six powerful motivators and to purchase their products and services, support their political proposals or donate to their causes only when they have acted truthfully in the process.

If we make this vital distinction in our dealings with practitioners of the persuasive arts, we will rarely allow ourselves to be tricked into assent. Instead we will give ourselves a much better option: To be informed into saying yes. Moreover, as long as we apply the same distinction to our own attempts to influence others, we can legitimately commission the six principles. In seeking to persuade by pointing to the presence of genuine expertise, growing social validation, pertinent commitments or real opportunities for cooperation, and so on, we serve the interests of both parties and enhance the quality of the social fabric in the bargain.

Surely, someone with your splendid intellect can see the unique benefits of this article. And because you look like a helpful person who would want to share such useful information, let me make a request. Would you buy this [book] for 10 of your friends? Well, if you can't do that, would you show it to just one friend? Wait, don't answer yet. Because I genuinely like you, I'm going to throw in—at absolutely no extra cost—a set of references that you can consult to learn more about this little-known topic.

Now, will you voice your commitment to help? . . . Please recognize that I am pausing politely here. But while I'm waiting, I want you to feel totally assured that many others just like you will certainly consent. And I love that shirt you're wearing.

Persuasive Techniques

FAST FACTS

1. Six basic tendencies of human behavior come into play in generating a positive response to a request: reciprocation, consistency, social validation, liking, authority, and scarcity.
2. The six key factors are at work in various areas around the world as well, but cultural norms and traditions can modify the weight brought to bear by each factor.
3. Knowledge of these tendencies can empower consumers and citizens to make better-informed decisions about, for example, whether to purchase a product or vote for legislation.

Further Reading

G. Richard Shell. *Bargaining for Advantage.* Viking, 1999.

A. J. Pratkanis and E. Aronson. *Age of Propaganda: The Everyday Use and Abuse of Persuasion.* Revised edition. W. H. Freeman and Company, 2001.

Robert B. Cialdini. *Influence: Science and Practice.* Fourth edition. Allyn & Bacon, 2001.

Robert Levine. *The Power of Persuasion: How We're Bought and Sold.* John Wiley & Sons, 2003.

For regularly updated information about the social influence process, visit http://www.influenceatwork.com

---

INFLUENCE WITHOUT AUTHORITY: THE USE OF ALLIANCES, RECIPROCITY, AND EXCHANGE TO ACCOMPLISH WORK*

Allan R. Cohen

David L. Bradford

Bill Heatton is the director of research at a $250 million division of a large west coast company. The division manufactures exotic telecommunications components and has many technical advancements to its credit. During the past several years, however, the division's performance has been spotty at best; multimillion dollar losses have been experienced in some years despite many efforts to make the division

---

*Reprinted from *Organizational Dynamics*, 17(3), Allan R. Cohen and David L. Bradford, "Influence Without Authority: The Use of Alliances, Reciprocity, and Exchange to Accomplish Work," pp. 5–17, © 1989, with permission from Elsevier.

more profitable. Several large contracts have resulted in major financial losses, and in each instance the various parts of the division blamed the others for the problems. Listen to Bill's frustration as he talks about his efforts to influence Ted, a colleague who is marketing director, and Roland, the program manager who reports to Ted.

> *Another program is about to come through. Roland is a nice guy, but he knows nothing and never will. He was responsible for our last big loss, and now he's in charge of this one. I've tried to convince Ted, his boss, to get Roland off the program, but I get nowhere. Although Ted doesn't argue that Roland is capable, he doesn't act to find someone else. Instead, he comes to me with worries about my area.*
>
> *I decided to respond by changing my staffing plan, assigning to Roland's program the people they wanted. I had to override my staff's best judgment about who should be assigned. Yet I'm not getting needed progress reports from Roland, and he's never available for planning. I get little argument from him, but there's no action to correct the problem. That's bad because I'm responding but not getting any response.*
>
> *There's no way to resolve this. If they disagree, that's it. I could go to a tit-for-tat strategy, saying that if they don't do what I want, we'll get even with them next time. But I don't know how to do that without hurting the organization, which would feel worse than getting even!*
>
> *Ted, Roland's boss, is so much better than his predecessor that I hate to ask that he be removed. We could go together to our boss, the general manager, but I'm very reluctant to do that. You've failed in a matrix organization if you have to go to your boss. I have to try hard because I'd look bad if I had to throw it in his lap.*
>
> *Meanwhile, I'm being forceful, but I'm afraid it's in a destructive way. I don't want to wait until the program has failed to be told it was all my fault.*

Bill is clearly angry and frustrated, leading him to behave in ways that he does not feel good about. Like other managers who very much want to influence an uncooperative co-worker whom they cannot control, Bill has begun to think of the intransigent employee as the enemy. Bill's anger is narrowing his sense of what is possible; he fantasizes revenge but is too dedicated to the organization to actually harm it. He is genuinely stuck.

Organizational members who want to make things happen often find themselves in this position. Irrespective of whether they are staff or line employees, professionals or managers, they find it increasingly necessary to influence colleagues and superiors. These critical others control needed resources, possess required information, set priorities on important activities, and have to agree and cooperate if plans are to be implemented. They cannot be ordered around because they are under another area's control and can legitimately say no because they have many other valid priorities. They respond only when they choose to. Despite the clear need and appropriateness of what is being asked for (certainly as seen by the person who is making the request), compliance may not be forthcoming.

All of this places a large burden on organizational members, who are expected not only to take initiatives but also to respond intelligently to requests made of them by others. Judgment is needed to sort out the value of the many requests made of anyone who has valuable resources to contribute. As Robert Kaplan argued in his article "Trade Routes: The Manager's Network of Relationships" (*Organizational Dynamics,* Spring 1984), managers must now develop the organizational equivalent of "trade routes" to get things done. Informal networks of mutual influence are needed. In her book, *The Change Masters* (Simon & Schuster, 1983), Rosabeth Moss Kanter showed that developing and implementing all kinds of innovations require coalitions to be built to shape and support new ways of doing business.

A key current problem, then, is finding ways to develop mutual influence without the formal authority to command. A peer cannot "order" a colleague to change priorities, modify an approach, or implement a grand new idea. A staff member cannot "command" his or her supervisor to back a proposal, fight top management for greater resources, or allow more autonomy. Even Bill Heatton, in dealing with Roland (who was a level below him in the hierarchy but in another department), could not dictate that Roland provide the progress reports that Bill so desperately wanted.

Exchange and the Law of Reciprocity

The way influence is acquired without formal authority is through the "law of reciprocity"—the almost universal belief that people should be paid back for what they do, that one good (or bad) deed deserves another. This belief is held by people in primitive and not-so-primitive societies all around the world, and it serves as the grease that allows the organizational wheel to turn smoothly. Because people expect that their actions will be paid back in one form or another, influence is possible.

In the case of Bill Heatton, his inability to get what he wanted from Roland and Ted stemmed from his failure to understand fully how reciprocity works in organizations. He therefore was unable to set up mutually beneficial exchanges. Bill believed that he had gone out of his way to help the marketing department by changing his staffing patterns, and he expected Roland to reciprocate by providing regular progress reports. When Roland failed to provide the reports, Bill believed that Ted was obligated to remove Roland from the project. When Ted did not respond, Bill became angry and wanted to retaliate. Thus, Bill recognized the appropriateness of exchange in making organizations work. However, he did not understand how exchange operates.

Before exploring in detail how exchange can work in dealing with colleagues and superiors, it is important to recognize that reciprocity is the basic principle behind all organizational transactions. For example, the basic employment contract is an exchange ("an honest day's work for an honest day's pay"). Even work that is above and beyond what is formally required involves exchange. The person who helps out may not necessarily get (or expect) immediate payment for the extra effort requested, but some eventual compensation is expected.

Think of the likely irritation an employee would feel if his or her boss asked him or her to work through several weekends, never so much as said thanks, and then claimed credit for the extra work. The employee might not say anything the first time this happened, expecting or hoping that the boss would make it up somehow. However, if the effort were never acknowledged in any way, the employee, like most people, would feel that something important had been violated.

Exchanges enable people to handle the give-and-take of working together without strong feelings of injustice arising. They are especially important during periods of rapid change because the number of requests that go far beyond the routine tends to escalate. In those situations, exchanges become less predictable, more free-floating, and spontaneous. Nevertheless, people still expect that somehow or other, sooner or later, they will be (roughly) equally compensated for the acts they do above and beyond those that are covered by the formal exchange agreements in their job. Consequently, some kind of "currency" equivalent needs to be worked out, implicitly if not explicitly, to keep the parties in the exchange feeling fairly treated.

Currencies: The Source of Influence

If the basis of organizational influence depends on mutually satisfactory exchanges, then people are influential only insofar as they can offer something that others need. Thus, power comes from the ability to meet others' needs.

A useful way to think of how the process of exchange actually works in organizations is to use the metaphor of "currencies." This metaphor provides a powerful way to conceptualize what is important to the influencer and the person to be influenced. Just as many types of currencies are traded in the world financial market, many types are "traded" in organizational life. Too often people think only of money or promotion and status. Those "currencies," however, usually are available only to a manager in dealing with his or her employees. Peers who want to influence colleagues or employees who want to influence their supervisors often feel helpless. They need to recognize that many types of payments exist, broadening the range of what can be exchanged.

Some major currencies that are commonly valued and traded in organizations are listed in Exhibit 1. Although not exhaustive, the list makes evident that a person does not have to be at the top of an organization or have hands on the formal levers of power to command multiple resources that others may value.

Inspiration-related Currencies	
Vision	Being involved in a task that has larger significance for the unit, organization, customers, or society.
Excellence	Having a chance to do important things really well.
Moral/Ethical Correctness	Doing what is "right" by a higher standard than efficiency.
Task-related Currencies	
Resources	Lending or giving money, budget increases, personnel, space, and so forth.
Assistance	Helping with existing projects or undertaking unwanted tasks.
Cooperation	Giving task support, providing quicker response time, approving a project, or aiding implementation.
Information	Providing organizational as well as technical knowledge.
Position-related Currencies	
Advancement	Giving a task or assignment that can aid in promotion.
Recognition	Acknowledging effort, accomplishment, or abilities.
Visibility	Providing a chance to be known by higher-ups or significant others in the organization.
Reputation	Enhancing the way a person is seen.
Importance/Insiderness	Offering a sense of importance, of "belonging."
Network/Contacts	Providing opportunities for linking with others.
Relationship-related Currencies	
Acceptance/Inclusion	Providing closeness and friendship.
Personal support	Giving personal and emotional backing.
Understanding	Listening to others' concerns and issues.
Personal-related Currencies	
Self-Concept	Affirming one's values, self-esteem, and identity.
Challenge/Learning	Sharing tasks that increase skills and abilities.
Ownership/Involvement	Letting others have ownership and influence.
Gratitude	Expressing appreciation or indebtedness.

EXHIBIT 1   Commonly Traded Organizational Currencies

Part of the usefulness of currencies comes from their flexibility. For example, there are many ways to express gratitude and to give assistance. A manager who most values the currency of appreciation could be paid through verbal thanks, praise, a public statement at a meeting, informal comments to his peers, and/or a note to her boss. However, the same note of thanks seen by one person as a sign of appreciation may be seen by another person as an attempt to brownnose or by a third person as a cheap way to try to repay extensive favors and service. Thus, currencies have value not in some abstract sense but as defined by the receiver.

Although we have stressed the interactive nature of exchange, "payments" do not always have to be made by the other person. They can be self-generated to fit beliefs about being virtuous, benevolent, or committed to the organization's welfare. Someone may respond to another person's request because it reinforces cherished values, a sense of identity, or feelings of self-worth. The exchange is interpersonally stimulated because the one who wants influence has set up conditions that allow this kind of self-payment to occur by asking for cooperation to accomplish organizational goals. However, the person who responds because "it is the right thing to do" and who feels good about being the "kind of person who does not act out of narrow self-interest" is printing currency (virtue) that is self-satisfying.

Of course, the five categories of currencies listed in Exhibit 1 are not mutually exclusive. When the demand from the other person is high, people are likely to pay in several currencies across several categories. They may, for example, stress the organizational value of their request, promise to return the favor at a later time, imply that it will increase the other's prestige in the organization, and express their appreciation.

Establishing Exchange Rates

What does it take to pay back in a currency that the other party in an exchange will perceive as equivalent? In impersonal markets, because everything is translated into a common monetary currency, it generally is easy to say what a fair payment is. Does a ton of steel equal a case of golfclubs? By translating both into dollar equivalents, a satisfactory deal can be worked out.

In interpersonal exchanges, however, the process becomes a bit more complicated. Just how does someone repay another person's willingness to help finish a report? Is a simple thank-you enough? Does it also require the recipient to say something nice about the helper to his or her boss? Whose standard of fairness should be used? What if one person's idea of fair repayment is very different from the other's?

Because of the natural differences in the way two parties can interpret the same activity, establishing exchanges that both parties will perceive as equitable can be problematic. Thus, it is critical to understand what is important to the person to be influenced. Without a clear understanding of what that person experiences and values, it will be extremely difficult for anyone to thread a path through the minefield of creating mutually satisfactory exchanges.

Fortunately, the calibration of equivalent exchanges in the interpersonal and organizational worlds is facilitated by the fact that approximations will do in most cases. Occasionally, organizational members know exactly what they want in return for favors of help, but more often they will settle for very rough equivalents (providing that there is reasonable goodwill).

The Process of Exchange

To make the exchange process effective, the influencer needs to (1) think about the person to be influenced as a potential ally, not an adversary; (2) know the world of the potential ally, including the pressures as well as the person's needs and goals;

(3) be aware of key goals and available resources that may be valued by the potential ally; and (4) understand the exchange transaction itself so that win-win outcomes are achieved. Each of these factors is discussed below.

Potential Ally, Not Adversary

A key to influence is thinking of the other person as a potential ally. Just as many contemporary organizations have discovered the importance of creating strategic alliances with suppliers and customers, employees who want influence within the organization need to create internal allies. Even though each party in an alliance continues to have freedom to pursue its own interests, the goal is to find areas of mutual benefit and develop trusting, sustainable relationships. Similarly, each person whose cooperation is needed inside the organization is a potential ally. Each still has self-interests to pursue, but those self-interests do not preclude searching for and building areas of mutual benefit.

Seeing other organizational members as potential allies decreases the chance that adversarial relationships will develop—an all-too-frequent result (as in the case of Bill Heatton) when the eager influencer does not quickly get the assistance of cooperation needed. Assuming that even a difficult person is a potential ally makes it easier to understand that person's world and thereby discover what that person values and needs.

The Potential Ally's World

We have stressed the importance of knowing the world of the potential ally. Without awareness of what the ally needs (what currencies are valued), attempts to influence that person can only be haphazard. Although this conclusion may seem self-evident, it is remarkable how often people attempt to influence without adequate information about what is important to the potential ally. Instead, they are driven by their own definition of "what should be" and "what is right" when they should be seeing the world from the other person's perspective.

For example, Bill Heatton never thought about the costs to Ted of removing Roland from the project. Did Ted believe he could coach Roland to perform better on this project? Did Ted even agree that Roland had done a poor job on the previous project, or did Ted think Roland had been hampered by other departments' shortcomings? Bill just did not know.

Several factors can keep the influencer from seeing the potential ally clearly. As with Bill Heatton, the frustration of meeting resistance from a potential ally can get in the way of really understanding the other person's world. The desire to influence is so strong that only the need for cooperation is visible to the influencer. As a result of not being understood, the potential ally digs in, making the influencer repeat an inappropriate strategy or back off in frustration.

When a potential ally's behavior is not understandable ("Why won't Roland send the needed progress reports?"), the influencer tends to stereotype that person. If early attempts to influence do not work, the influencer is tempted to write the person off as negative, stubborn, selfish, or "just another bean counter/whiz kid/sales-type" or whatever pejorative label is used in that organizational culture to dismiss those organizational members who are different.

Although some stereotypes may have a grain of truth, they generally conceal more than they reveal. The actuary who understands that judgment, not just numbers, is needed to make decisions disappears as an individual when the stereotype of "impersonal, detached number machine" is the filter through which he or she is seen. Once the stereotype is applied, the frustrated influencer is no longer likely to see what currencies that particular potential ally actually values.

Sometimes, the lack of clear understanding about a potential ally stems from the influencer's failure to appreciate the organizational forces acting on the potential ally. To a great extent, a person's behavior is a result of the situation in which that person works (and not just his or her personality). Potential allies are embedded in an organizational culture that shapes their interests and responses. For example, one of the key determinants of anyone's behavior is likely to be the way the person's performance is measured and rewarded. In many instances, what is mistaken for personal orneriness is merely the result of the person's doing something that will be seen as good performance in his or her function.

The salesperson who is furious because the plant manager resists changing priorities for a rush order may not realize that part of the plant manager's bonus depends on holding unit costs down—a task made easier with long production runs. The plant manager's resistance does not necessarily reflect his or her inability to be flexible or lack of concern about pleasing customers or about the company's overall success.

Other organizational forces that can affect the potential ally's behavior include the daily time demands on that person's position; the amount of contact the person has with customers, suppliers, and other outsiders; the organization's information flow (or lack of it); the style of the potential ally's boss; the belief and assumptions held by that person's co-workers; and so forth. Although some of these factors cannot be changed by the influencer, understanding them can be useful in figuring out how to frame and time requests. It also helps the influencer resist the temptation to stereotype the noncooperator.

Self-Awareness of the Influencer

Unfortunately, people desiring influence are not always aware of precisely what they want. Often their requests contain a cluster of needs (a certain product, arranged in a certain way, delivered at a specified time). They fail to think through which aspects are more important and which can be jettisoned if necessary. Did Bill Heatton want Roland removed, or did he want the project effectively managed? Did he want overt concessions from Ted, or did he want better progress reports?

Further, there is a tendency to confuse and intermingle the desired end goal with the means of accomplishing it, leading to too many battles over the wrong things. In *The Change Masters*, Kanter reported that successful influencers in organizations were those who never lost sight of the ultimate objective but were willing to be flexible about means.

Sometimes influencers underestimate the range of currencies available for use. They may assume, for example, that just because they are low in the organization they have nothing that others want. Employees who want to influence their boss are especially likely not to realize all of the supervisor's needs that they can fulfill. They become so caught up with their feelings of powerlessness that they fail to see the many ways they can generate valuable currencies.

In other instances, influencers fail to be aware of their preferred style of interaction and its fit with the potential ally's preferred style. Everyone has a way of relating to others to get work done. However, like the fish who is unaware of the water, many people are oblivious of their own style of interaction or see it as the only way to be. Yet interaction style can cause problems with potential allies who are different.

For example, does the influencer tend to socialize first and work later? If so, that style of interaction will distress a potential ally who likes to dig right in to solve the problem at hand and only afterward chat about sports, family, or office politics. Does the potential ally want to be approached with answers, not problems? If so, a tendency to start influence attempts with open-ended, exploratory problem solving can lead to rejection despite good intentions.

Nature of the Exchange Transaction

Many of the problems that occur in the actual exchange negotiation have their roots in the failure to deal adequately with the first three factors outlined above. Failure to treat other people as potential allies, to understand a potential ally's world, and to be self-aware are all factors that interfere with successful exchange. In addition, some special problems commonly arise when both parties are in the process of working out a mutually satisfactory exchange agreement.

- *Not knowing how to use reciprocity.* Using reciprocity requires stating needs clearly without "crying wolf," being aware of the needs of an ally without being manipulative, and seeking mutual gain rather than playing "winner takes all." One trap that Bill Heatton fell into was not being able to "close on the exchange." That is, he assumed that if he acted in good faith and did his part, others would automatically reciprocate. Part of his failure was not understanding the other party's world; another part was not being able to negotiate cleanly with Ted about what each of them wanted. It is not even clear that Ted realized Bill was altering his organization as per Ted's requests, that Ted got what he wanted, or that Ted knew Bill intended an exchange of responses.
- *Preferring to be right rather than effective.* This problem is especially endemic to professionals of all kinds. Because of their dedication to the "truth" (as their profession defines it), they stubbornly stick to their one right way when trying to line up potential allies instead of thinking about what will work given the audience and conditions. Organizational members with strong technical backgrounds often chorus the equivalent of "I'll be damned if I'm going to sell out and become a phone salesman, trying to get by on a shoeshine and smile." The failure to accommodate to the potential ally's needs and desires often kills otherwise sound ideas.
- *Overusing what has been successful.* When people find that a certain approach is effective in many situations, they often begin to use it in places where it does not fit. By overusing the approach, they block more appropriate methods. Just as a weight lifter becomes muscle-bound from overdeveloping particular muscles at the expense of others, people who have been reasonably successful at influencing other people can diminish that ability by overusing the same technique.

For example, John Brucker, the human resources director at a medium-size company, often cultivated support for new programs by taking people out to fancy restaurants for an evening of fine food and wine. He genuinely derived pleasure from entertaining, but at the same time he created subtle obligations. One time, a new program he wanted to introduce required the agreement of William Adams, head of engineering. Adams, an old-timer, perceived Brucker's proposal as an unnecessary frill, mainly because he did not perceive the real benefits to the overall organization. Brucker responded to Adams's negative comments as he always did in such cases—by becoming more friendly and insisting that they get together for dinner soon. After several of these invitations, Adams became furious. Insulted by what he considered to be Brucker's attempts to buy him off, he fought even harder to kill the proposal. Not only did the program die, but Brucker lost all possibility of influencing Adams in the future. Adams saw Brucker's attempts at socializing as a sleazy and crude way of trying to soften him up. For his part, Brucker was totally puzzled by Adams's frostiness and assumed that he was against all progress.

He never realized that Adams had a deep sense of integrity and a real commitment to the good of the organization. Thus, Brucker lost his opportunity to sell a program that, ironically, Adams would have found valuable had it been implemented.

As the case above illustrates, a broad repertoire of influence approaches is needed in modern organizations. Johnny-one-notes soon fall flat.

The Role of Relationships

All of the preceding discussion needs to be conditioned by one important variable: the nature of the relationship between both parties. The greater the extent to which the influencer has worked with the potential ally and created trust, the easier the exchange process will be. Each party will know the other's desired currencies and situational pressures, and each will have developed a mutually productive interaction style. With trust, less energy will be spent on figuring out the intentions of the ally, and there will be less suspicion about when and how the payback will occur.

A poor relationship (based on previous interactions, on the reputation each party has in the organization, and/or on stereotypes and animosities between the functions or departments that each party represents) will impede an otherwise easy exchange. Distrust of the goodwill, veracity, or reliability of the influencer can lead to the demand for "no credit; cash up front," which constrains the flexibility of both parties.

The nature of the interaction during the influencer process also affects the nature of the relationship between the influencer and the other party. The way that John Brucker attempted to relate to William Adams not only did not work but also irreparably damaged any future exchanges between them.

Few transactions within organizations are one-time deals. (Who knows when the other person may be needed again or even who may be working for him or her in the future?) Thus, in most exchange situations two outcomes matter: success in achieving task goals and success in improving the relationship so that the next interaction will be even more productive. Too often, people who want to be influential focus only on the task and act as if there is no tomorrow. Although both task accomplishment and an improved relationship cannot always be realized at the same time, on some occasions the latter can be more important than the former. Winning the battle but losing the war is an expensive outcome.

Inconvertible Currencies

We have spelled out ways organizational members operate to gain influence for achieving organizational goals. By effectively using exchange, organizational members can achieve their goals and at the same time help others achieve theirs. Exchange permits organizational members to be assertive without being antagonistic by keeping mutual benefit a central outcome.

In many cases, organizational members fail to acquire desired influence because they do not use all of their potential power. However, they sometimes fail because not all situations are amenable to even the best efforts at influencing. Not everything can be translated into compatible currencies. If there are fundamental differences in what is valued by two parties, it may not be possible to find common ground, as illustrated in the example below.

The founder and chairman of a high-technology company and the president he had hired five years previously were constantly displeased with one another. The president was committed to creating maximum shareholder value, the currency he valued most as a result of his MBA training, his position, and his temperament. Accordingly, he had concluded that the company was in a perfect position to cash in by squeezing expenses to maximize profits and going public. He could see that the company's product line of exotic components was within a few years of saturating its market and would require massive, risky investment to move to sophisticated end-user products.

The president could not influence the chairman to adopt this direction, however, because the chairman valued a totally different currency, the fun of technological challenge. An independently wealthy man, the chairman had no interest in realizing the $10 million or so he would get if the company maximized profits by cutting research and selling out. He wanted a place to test his intuitive, creative research hunches, not a source of income.

Thus, the president's and chairman's currencies were not convertible into one another at an acceptable exchange rate. After they explored various possibilities but failed to find common ground, they mutually agreed that the president should leave—on good terms and only after a more compatible replacement could be found. Although this example acknowledges that influence through alliance, currency conversion, and exchange is not always possible, it is hard to be certain that any situation is hopeless until the person desiring influence has fully applied all of the diagnostic and interpersonal skills we have described.

Influence is enhanced by using the model of strategic alliances to engage in mutually beneficial exchanges with potential allies. Even though it is not always possible to be successful, the chances of achieving success can be greatly increased. In a period of rapid competitive, technological, regulative, and consumer change, individuals and their organizations need all the help they can get.

CHAPTER

20

Empowerment and Coaching

WHY TREATING PEOPLE RIGHT PAYS OFF
Edward E. Lawler III

MANAGEMENT DIALOGUES: TURNING ON THE MARGINAL PERFORMER
John R. Schermerhorn, Jr.
William L. Gardner
Thomas N. Martin

COACHING FOR SUSTAINED DESIRED CHANGE
Melvin L. Smith
Ellen B. Van Oosten
Richard E. Boyatzis

B y this point, you have read several references in different articles about the growing
obsolescence of the command-and-control management style. Managers with this
mentality conceive of their jobs as making decisions, giving orders, and ensuring that
subordinates obey. A more effective approach is high-involvement (high-performance or high-
commitment) management, which focuses on employee commitment and empowerment.
Empowerment is defined as granting employees the autonomy to assume more responsibility
within an organization and strengthening their sense of effectiveness. Managers empower
employees by sharing power, information, and the responsibility to manage their own work as
much as possible.

Renowned management professor, scholar, and consultant Edward Lawler contends in
"Why Treating People Right Pays Off" that achieving competitive advantage requires both hiring
and retaining great people and maintaining great organizational practices. He suggests that treating
people right is about identifying and implementing things that are good for both organizational
performance and individuals, including leaders who create commitment and reward systems that
reinforce core values.

Whereas the first article in this chapter focuses on system-level management practices, the
second article answers the perennial micro-level problem of how to handle and coach poorly performing employees. "Management Dialogues: Turning on the Marginal Performer" was written

by John Schermerhorn, Jr., professor and director of the Center for Southeast Asian Studies at Ohio University, William Gardner, professor and director of the Center for Leadership Studies at Texas Tech University, and Thomas Martin, professor at Southern Illinois University, Carbondale. This reading provides blow-by-blow advice for dealing with performance problems and will prepare you for the inevitable job interview question, "What would you do if you had an employee who wasn't doing an acceptable job?"

Businesses are looking increasingly to external coaches for help with employee performance. A key component of their work is an understanding of the basics of lasting behavioral change. "Coaching for Sustained Desired Change" comes to us from authors at the Organizational Behavior department at Case Western Reserve University: Melvin Smith, professor; Ellen Van Oosten, doctoral student; and Richard Boyatzis, professor and expert on emotional intelligence. They provide a model of individual change and explain its theoretical underpinnings.

WHY TREATING PEOPLE RIGHT PAYS OFF*

Edward E. Lawler III

We are entering a new era in the relationship between organizations and their employees. The world of work is sharply altering most of the century-old understandings between employers and employees. No longer can organizations think of people as either loyal "family members" or as easily replaceable resources when it comes to accomplishing their business objectives.

In this new era, people need to be respected and treated as precious human capital, more essential to an organization's effectiveness than its financial capital. People can now be the primary source of a company's competitive advantage in most businesses. To put it bluntly, how people are treated increasingly determines whether a company will prosper and even survive.

In the past, arguments about the importance of how people are treated have largely fallen on deaf ears in the executive offices and boardrooms of most organizations. Yes, there are many companies that claim that their people are their most important asset, and they even put pictures of them (always smiling) in their annual reports. But most of these companies do not behave like their people are their number one priority. All too often, they treat them as replaceable parts that add little value.

But today, a number of powerful and compelling factors are coalescing into a new reality: to be effective, organizations must excel in organizing and managing their people. In the twenty-first century, treating people right is not an option; it is a necessity.

The Compelling Forces of Change

Every reader of this book knows that the business environment of the twenty-first century is different from what it was twenty or thirty years ago. In fact, the business world today is vastly different from what it was just five years ago. There can be no doubt that the world is changing more rapidly and has become more chaotic, demanding, and competitive than ever before.

But let's get specific about how the world is now different. Let me invite you to take a step back for a moment and consider the business environment throughout most of the second half of the twentieth century.

---

*Adapted and reprinted with permission from *Treat People Right!* (San Francisco, CA: Jossey-Bass, 2003): 3–21.

For organizations, the business environment was relatively stable and predictable and offered numerous opportunities for growth. An organization was assured of at least a degree of success and profitability as long as it produced moderately good products or services and made productive use of its employees. It could gain competitive advantage with relative ease by controlling its sources of raw materials or by obtaining low-cost financial capital and physical assets. Some organizations also gained competitive advantage because they had government-created protection from competition.

For people, too, the old environment was also relatively stable and secure. Most employees who worked for governments or large corporations lived under a "loyalty contract," a tacit agreement with their employers that if they were loyal, they could have a comfortable life with that organization. They had not just a job but a career that included the security of a regular paycheck, benefits, and retirement income. Even for employees not covered under a loyalty contract, the growth and power of the union movement provided many of them with benefits and protections that guaranteed a good quality of life.

Now contrast that with today's business environment.

For most organizations today, the sense of stability and assured success is in question. It is no longer easy to find competitive advantage and, once found, to maintain it for very long. New threats seem to come from everywhere: start-ups, international competitors, legal changes, new technologies. Most organizations must fight tooth and nail to secure their profits and continue their growth. Most also regularly struggle to find qualified people for their leadership and knowledge work jobs. As a result, the past decades have seen the downfall of many venerable companies, as well as the overnight birth and death of many seemingly smart start-ups—witness the many failed dot-coms that originally seemed destined for success.

For most people, the new environment is equally insecure. The promise of a steady job has all but disappeared, with millions of workers downsized, furloughed, laid off, or voluntarily choosing to move from company to company. Many people have found that they simply don't have the skills needed to compete in the marketplace, having lost their personal competitive advantage and their value as human capital. Many of today's workers are finding that although they still have jobs, they are falling behind the business, scientific, and technical needs that organizations have.

These starkly contrasting sketches of the business environment are the result of four major changes:

- The globalization of competition
- The rapid development of scientific and technical knowledge
- The death of the loyalty contract
- The scarcity of skilled employees

Of course, not all of these have affected or will affect every organization in the same way, but most organization have felt or will feel the impact of at least several of them. Most people, too, will feel the impact of several of them at some point during their careers.

Let's explore these forces in greater detail so that you can understand how each affects organizations and people.

Globalization of Competition

The old days of limited competition are over. With the disappearance of communist and totalitarian regimes in many parts of the world, more and more countries are opening up to foreign business and trade. While this increasing globalization has created new markets and growth opportunities for many existing organizations, it has also dramatically elevated the level of competition in nearly all industries.

Many new competitors exist. Over just the past decade, we have seen the emergence of a coalition of Western European countries into a major new economic power, the emergence of India as a global competitor in software and technology, the entrance of the formerly socialist or communist Eastern European bloc countries into the world market, the awakening of the Chinese and Southeast Asian dragons, and the adoption of the North American Free Trade Agreement. Each of these developments has created competitors searching for profits, dominance, and new markets. Many of these newer competitors have distinct advantages in areas ranging from geographical proximity to important markets to high-skilled, relatively low-wage workforces to large storehouses of financial capital with which to buy new plants and equipment as well as to acquire other companies.

While some organizations have found expanded profits in the new global markets, many others have struggled due to increased competition and the complexities involved in operating on the global stage. Globalization has also had a negative impact on millions of people whose jobs have been transferred to foreign countries where the labor is cheaper. They have been forced either to find new jobs, often at lower pay, or to retrain themselves to compete in new industries. If it hasn't already, at some time in the future, globalization is likely to dramatically affect your career, and you will face some important choices about how to manage your career in this new era of global competition.

Greater Scientific and Technical Knowledge

In the past several decades, the bar has been significantly raised with respect to the level of scientific and technological knowledge that organizations need in order to compete. And there is every reason to believe that the growth of new knowledge will continue to accelerate.

The amount of knowledge now required to be competitive has altered the core of what organizations do, the types of products they produce, and how they operate, as well as where they can find competitive advantage. Entire industries, including communications, entertainment, consulting, housing, banking, finance, retailing, and manufacturing, have been forced to rethink their strategies and how they go about their business.

Changes in technology have also caused many of the world's most venerable companies to completely change their direction or invest large amounts of capital to develop new products or to acquire new technologies. And like dinosaurs, a few historic companies (Polaroid and Westinghouse, for example) have been vanquished by faster, smarter competitors who were able to invent or adopt new technologies.

Perhaps the most vivid example of the rapid evolution of technology and its impact on organizations is the Internet. In the blink of an eye, the Internet created a host of new competitors that served customers in new and different ways. While many Internet companies accomplished little other than the expenditure of huge amounts of investment capital, many others truly succeeded in changing the world (think of Amazon.com and eBay), creating the need for competitors to adopt new business models.

Meanwhile, the demand for increased scientific and technical knowledge has put significant pressure on workers everywhere. Increasingly, today's employees in developed countries must have highly sophisticated skills with respect to managing information, developing knowledge, and dealing in abstract concepts. They need to have the ability to think, analyze, and problem-solve. Fewer workers are needed to do the mind-numbing, repetitive manual tasks that formerly dominated the work scene. These are being done by machines or sent to low-wage economies. Needless to say, it has become absolutely clear that people who cannot keep pace with scientific and technological change are quickly losing their value as employees.

Death of the Loyalty Contract

Throughout most of the twentieth century, organizations maintained a tacit agreement with their workers that as long as they were generally productive, their jobs and a reasonable pension plan were guaranteed. This was often referred to as the "loyalty contract."

However, globalized competition, the rise of technology, and the increasing demand for knowledge workers with state-of-the-art skills has made maintaining the loyalty contract unrealistic in the case of most companies. More and more organizations have realized that buying their workers' long-term loyalty is simply not a good investment.

Despite its honorable tradition, today the loyalty contract is in many ways counterproductive. By providing employees with a relatively secure and comfortable lifestyle, it serves to attract and retain only those people who want secure, predictable employment situations. It does not attract or retain those who want to be part of an entrepreneurial organization or who want to be part of a rapidly changing, technologically advanced, or knowledge-intensive organization. A loyalty relationship also does little to encourage individuals to learn new skills, keep up with technology changes, and keep the company financially competitive.

Beginning in the 1980s, more and more companies ended their loyalty contracts. Such revered organizations as General Electric, IBM, and AT&T shattered their contracts by laying off thousands of employees. In retrospect, it is clear that most of these organizations had no choice. At that time, laying off their workers was the best way these firms could adapt to the dramatic changes in their businesses. To have done otherwise would have been fatal for them.

The death of the loyalty contract has had enormous repercussions in today's business environment. One of its major effects has been on the cost, availability, and attitudes of good labor. Most people, especially younger workers, understand and accept that loyalty to their organization is largely a losing proposition. As a result, many of them are no longer willing to be dependent on their employers or amenable to accepting practices and decisions that are not advantageous to them. Without the benefits of the old loyalty contract, today's employees are demanding substitutes such as challenging work, opportunities for learning, and substantive rewards. And when they do not get what they want, today's workers are quick to move on to more attractive employment situations.

The change is significant: Organizations can no longer count on their members' loyalty, so they must continuously compete for talent. They have to focus on attracting and hiring the most talented people and retaining their existing talent. Because of the increased mobility of individuals, organizations need to change the fundamental way they think about their employees. They need to look for approaches to managing them that are advantageous to both themselves and their employees.

Scarcity of Skilled Employees

Two powerful forces are contributing to an increasing shortage of knowledgeable skilled employees: workforce demographics and education.

First, many industrialized countries are facing the burden of an aging population.[1] Increasingly in the United States, Europe, and Japan, a high percentage of the workforce is approaching or has attained the traditional age of retirement. This demographic shift is a result of a combination of relatively low birth rates, especially in countries like Japan, Italy, and Germany, as well as longer life expectancies. Although many potential retirees can remain in the workforce, they have to be sold on the idea of continuing to work. They also may not be able to meet the needs that organizations have for employees with knowledge.

The other force behind the growing scarcity of skilled labor in the United States is an underperforming educational system. It is accepted in the business world that our schools simply do not produce enough well-educated students who are capable of doing the type of complex knowledge work that is increasingly needed in today's world. Fewer and fewer new graduates leave school ready to handle the challenges and intricacies of today's competitive jobs. Particularly lacking are people who can problem-solve and do cutting-edge technical and engineering work.

When it comes to human capital, you must not underestimate the importance of a highly skilled workforce. As tasks become more complicated, the difference between an average performer and a good performer rises dramatically. If you examine a simple, repetitive assembly line job, the difference between the best performer and the worst may only be a few percentage points in productivity. However, the difference between an outstanding knowledge worker and an average one can be 1,000 percent or more.

In the old competitive environment, many jobs did not require highly effective performance for an organization to be successful, so the demand for highly talented people was relatively limited. Many organizations simply did not need to make it a priority to fill jobs with highly talented individuals, other than at the very senior levels of management and in a few key technical areas. In most cases, organizations were satisfied to fill jobs with people who could perform at a "good enough" level because the work was not particularly challenging or difficult and how well it was done did not have a significant impact on the organization's overall performance.

But in the new competitive environment, the situation is radically different. There is now an undeniable need for highly knowledgeable, skilled people, and many corporations are having trouble finding enough of them. With more and more technically difficult and personally demanding jobs, creating an extraordinary workforce is a constant challenge, while the payoff from staffing with top performers can be tremendous.

You may be wondering if the shortage of skilled human capital is just a temporary phenomenon; after all, it did ease after the dot-com bust. I am convinced that the problem is here to stay. While the ups and downs of birth rates and economic cycles will affect the labor market over short time spans, the shortage of highly qualified human capital is likely to remain a reality for decades. The reason is simple: The growth of knowledge and technology continuously creates higher demands for an educated workforce.

The New Competitive Advantage

The four major changes we have just reviewed show every sign of continuing. There is little question that we will experience a further globalization of business and even more competition. The demand for scientific and technical knowledge workers will continue to grow as organizations need to commit more resources to developing and delivering new and more complex products and services. And there is no stopping the increasing need for skilled people to handle more and more complex business management issues, products, and decision making. In light of the increasing demand for talent, people are more and more likely to see themselves as free agents.

In the future, organizations will undoubtedly need to meet new challenges if they are to survive and thrive. To do this, organizations must learn how to attract, retain, motivate, organize, and manage talented individuals. People are the key to helping organizations stay ahead of change and to having a competitive advantage. This calls for a new type of relationship between organizations and people, one that recognizes the true importance of *human capital.*

How should organizations recognize the importance of human capital? History has some important lessons to teach us about what not to do. One thing not to do is to put the human assets on the corporate balance sheet. If human assets truly matter, the argument goes, they should be valued and accounted for. Yet efforts at human asset accounting have failed, largely because they are based on flawed thinking—people are not comparable to the assets already appearing in corporate accounting statements. Assets are owned and can be bought, sold, and manipulated. But people cannot be owned; they make their own decisions, and they have their own unique competencies and capabilities that make managing and organizing them far more complex and challenging than managing buildings, equipment, and other corporate assets. In short, it is a serious mistake to think of people as assets.

However, from an organizational point of view, it is valid to consider people as human *capital* and at least as important as an organization's financial capital. Like financial capital, people need to be treated with care, respect, and commitment if the organization expects them to stay invested. It must also provide them with the returns they need. Just as in managing financial capital, organizations cannot afford to waste their human capital or risk having it go to places where it can get a better return. Like financial capital, human capital needs to be carefully allocated, utilized, and managed.

I recently heard a radio ad that illustrates the erroneous thinking behind the traditional approach to the role of human capital in organizations. The ad was for a company that specializes in outsourcing human resource management for corporations, and the ad ended with the jingle, "We take care of your people so you can take care of your business." This sounds great, but it actually is the opposite of how a company should think about its people. A more appropriate slogan would be something like, "We take care of your people so *they* can take care of your business." As my revision of this slogan indicates, it is the people who must deal with the business in today's world, because they are the business and the best source of competitive advantage.

Talented People and Well-Designed Organizations

Let me clarify one point about treating people right and the importance of human capital. I am not suggesting that having the right people alone will make organizations effective. Treating people right is not just about talented people; it is also about strategies, practices, designs, and policies that make organizations into places where people want to perform well and can work effectively. Extraordinary results can be obtained only by having talented people *and* well-designed organizations with the best management systems.

In fact, opinions differ regarding the importance of talent. Some academics such as Charles O'Reilly and Jeffrey Pfeffer argue that companies can gain competitive advantage and achieve extraordinary results with ordinary people.[2] In their view, if you have the right systems, you don't have to worry about having the best people.

Others have argued that talent is all that counts. For example, Secretary of State Colin Powell, in many of his speeches on leadership, has argued that "organization does not really accomplish anything. Only by attracting the best people will you accomplish great deeds."

My position is that both are wrong. Achieving the competitive advantage needed today requires *both* great people and great organizational practices. It is misleading to claim that organizations can get extraordinary results with ordinary people, just as it is misleading to argue that organizations can get extraordinary results with ordinary management practices. To be effective, organizations need both outstanding people and outstanding management systems, because that is what produces world-class results for both individuals and organizations.

Outstanding individuals and organizational practices tend to reinforce each other and seek each other out because of the momentum they create. Effective organizational practices attract outstanding people, and outstanding people create effective structures and practices. Treating people right is all about identifying and implementing the things organizations can do that are good for organizational performance and individuals.

The Ultimate Goal: A Virtuous Spiral

Treating people right leads to powerful win-win virtuous spirals of success. Virtuous spirals occur when organizations treat people right by implementing the effective practices needed to motivate them and enable them to perform well. Virtuous spirals are actually the ultimate competitive advantage—powerful and hard-to-duplicate sources of positive momentum and higher levels of performance.

A virtuous spiral begins when an organization takes intelligent, strategy-driven, conscious actions to attract, retain, motivate, develop, and effectively organize committed, high-performance individuals. This generates a high-performance organization. It boosts the rewards for employees, which increases their motivation and commitment. The more challenging and rewarding environment that results further reinforces the organization's ability to attract, retain, and develop effective employees, who further positively affect performance. Thus a virtuous spiral forms and expands, carrying the organization and its members to greater heights. Figure 1 captures this in graphic form.

To successfully develop a virtuous spiral, organizations need to emphasize ever-increasing levels of performance, higher rewards for individuals, and increasingly competent employees. As they achieve these goals, a positive performance momentum develops that feeds on itself and provides a powerful competitive advantage.

Virtuous Spiral Organizations

Let me present a few examples of organizations that have achieved impressive results due to their dedication to treating people right. Because I have studied and consulted with these organizations, I can state with considerable confidence that their success is very much due to their ability to create and sustain virtuous spirals.

Microsoft is one of the most impressive examples of a company that has profited from a virtuous spiral relationship with its people for decades. Since the early 1980s, the company has had an environment in which its employees have done well

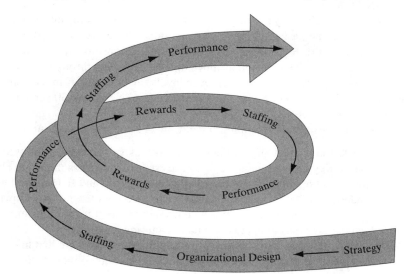

FIGURE 1   Virtuous Spiral

and the company has done well. The employees have had challenging work and of course, one of the most highly rewarding stock plans around. Microsoft has been an enormously attractive place to work, especially for high performers. As a result, it has attracted some of the country's top software engineers and marketing executives.

Because of its relationship with its human capital, Microsoft has been able to generate a powerful dynamic in which success begets success, which begets more success. The company's seemingly unstoppable growth began to slow down only in the late 1990s, when it faced a rapidly changing competitive environment along with government challenges to its growing power. But even in the market downturn of the early years of the new century, Microsoft has continued on a virtuous spiral of increasing growth and success.

Another organization that has clearly enjoyed a virtuous spiral of success for decades is General Electric. Even before Jack Welch became CEO in the early 1980s, GE had already established an environment where highly talented individuals wanted to work because of the opportunities the company offered for career development and financial rewards. Able to attract and retain highly talented individuals, GE has enjoyed decades of enviable growth in profits and as a result has attracted more and more talented individuals. GE is a clear example of a cycle of successful performance leading to successful recruitment and motivation of individuals, which in turn produce even more successful performance.

Southwest Airlines is a third example of an organization that has managed to maintain a virtuous spiral for decades. From its very beginning, Southwest was a human capital–focused organization that sought a high-quality relationship with its employees. Its founder, Herb Kelleher, stressed from day one that the company's competitive advantage is its people. The result has been excellent customer service and an absence of the hostile labor relationship characteristic of every other major airline. Despite being highly unionized, Southwest has never had a strike and is frequently mentioned as one of the best places to work.

Like many other organizations that have created virtuous spirals, there is no one secret to Southwest's success. The company has emphasized the careful selection of employees, building an employee-friendly work environment, giving employees freedom to control their jobs and work environment, profit sharing and stock ownership for all employees, and the opportunity for employees to grow, develop, and advance in the company.

Procter & Gamble is yet another example. Though the company is over one hundred years old, the past forty years of its existence have been marked by many forward-thinking efforts to establish a virtuous spiral relationship with its employees based on employee involvement and the development of leaders throughout the company. P&G was an early adopter of employee involvement practices in its manufacturing plants. It also has a stock ownership plan that has placed over 30 percent of its stock into the hands of its employees.

Other examples of virtuous spiral organizations are worth noting quickly:

- Johnson & Johnson has had a long-term virtuous spiral relationship with its employees. Key to its success are numerous separate business units that allow for a high level of autonomy and a clear mission vision and statement of ethical standards. It, like Procter & Gamble, also has a high level of stock ownership by its employees and has done an outstanding job of instituting employee involvement practices in many of its manufacturing locations.
- Capital One, the financial services firm, is a relatively new firm that has had a virtuous spiral relationship with its employees since its founding. Its human

resource management system focuses on the development of people, and most employees own Capital One stock.

- Harley-Davidson recovered from near extinction in the 1970s by building a strong cooperative relationship with its unions and using employee involvement to improve quality and productivity. It continues to be a market leader both in its business sector and in the way it treats its people.
- Medtronic is a leading manufacturer of medical equipment that has grown rapidly by creating innovative lifesaving products. It goes out of its way to involve all employees in the mission of the company, which is to improve the quality and length of people's lives. As a result, employees profit both financially and intrinsically as a result of working there.
- Applied Materials is the world's leading producer of semiconductor manufacturing equipment. It is frequently listed as one of the best places to work despite the fact that it is in a highly cyclical business. It deals with this by using slowdowns to train and develop people, and it uses stock to be sure that everyone wins when the business is strong.

When Organizations Don't Treat People Right

Organizations that do not attempt to treat people right and to initiate a virtuous spiral are susceptible to the opposite result, the *death spiral.*

Death spirals occur when organizations mistreat their human capital, and as a result, their performance declines, causing repercussions that lead to further declines and in many cases death. When organizations experience declining performance, they are perceived to be in trouble. As a result, they cannot attract the right human capital to fix their situation or the financial assets and the customers they need to reverse their decline. They soon become a place no one wants to be associated with. They become less and less of a competitor and ultimately die. Death spirals can last decades or just a few days.

Perhaps the most recent dramatic example of a death spiral is the complete collapse of Arthur Andersen. In a very short period of time, it went from being one of the world's five premier accounting firms to oblivion. In essence, it lost the reputation of its brand and its attractiveness as an employer. Both customers and employees began leaving the company, and in just a matter of months, its ability to function ended.

The collapse of Arthur Andersen illustrates an important point about death spirals. Organizations like Andersen whose market worth is in its intangible assets, such as its reputation, brand, and human capital, are extremely vulnerable to sudden death spirals. Many knowledge work firms, like consulting firms and publishers, have intangible assets that represent more than 75 percent of their market value; only a small portion of their assets are in their plant, equipment, and financial assets. When such organizations lose their attractiveness as an employer or their reputation as a good place to do business, they can plunge, much like an airplane that has lost its forward momentum. Their performance decreases so quickly that almost overnight they go out of business.

Rapid death spirals rarely happen to old-economy companies in industries like steel, automobiles, and energy because they have more tangible assets. As a result, it usually takes longer for them to fail. They can even defy gravity and exist in a zero-momentum condition if they have significant tangible assets and operate in a forgiving environment. For example, most public utilities have been able to maintain a steady-state existence because of their monopoly power. But when they have been deregulated, they rarely do well: Witness the declines of AT&T, Nortel, and Lucent.

Several major organizations today are in a slow death spiral. General Motors has been for decades and has had great difficulty reversing its downward momentum, losing market share year after year. Two of the great retailers in American history, Montgomery Ward and Sears, have both declined, although at different rates. Montgomery Ward has already gone into bankruptcy, while Sears continues to lose market share. It has new, fierce competitors—namely Wal-Mart, Target, Lowe's, and Home Depot—that continue to take market share away from it in part because they have developed virtuous spirals.

Without exception, organizations that are in death spirals have failed to fully recognize and respond to the compelling forces of change in the world today. None has adequately altered its strategy and management practices to fit the new world or changed its relationship with employees in ways that can reverse the death spirals. These companies are no longer seen as good places to work and have increasing difficulty attracting the kind of human talent that they need in order to be effective.

The world of professional sports provides an excellent juxtaposition between actions that create a virtuous spiral and those that lead to a death spiral. In the 1980s, one of my consulting clients, the NFL, reached an agreement with its players' union that effectively created a virtuous spiral relationship. In essence, it assured labor and management that each would share in any revenue improvements that took place in the business. This resulted in a virtuous spiral relationship that has enriched both the owners and the players. Strikes became a thing of the past, and the game of professional football has grown in popularity and revenue; today it is the most popular spectator sport in the United States.

Just the opposite has happened in professional baseball. Labor and management have never been able to agree on an acceptable revenue-sharing relationship. Instead of creating the kind of virtuous spiral relationship that pro football enjoys, it has created a death spiral. Contract negotiations with the union have been highly acrimonious. There have been eight work stoppages since 1972, one of which led to the cancellation of the World Series. In 2002, after months of hostile negotiations, a contract was reached without a strike, but it did little to forge a cooperative labor-management relationship. TV ratings for the 2002 World Series reached an all-time low, in part because fans were turned off by the threat of a strike. Instead of both sides winning, both management and labor have ended up losing relative to what might have been.

The Seven Principles for Treating People Right and Creating a Virtuous Spiral

By now, I hope that the rationale for treating people right and creating a virtuous spiral is clear. The only question that remains is how to do it. What steps do organizations need to take to treat people right and potentially launch a virtuous spiral?

To be competitive in this new world, an organization must attract and retain highly talented, high-performing individuals. It needs to encourage people to develop the skills and knowledge that the organization needs in order for them to perform effectively. It needs to motivate them to perform their work well and to commit themselves to the success of the organization. Finally, it needs to create an organization design and a leadership capability that lead to effective organizational performance.

Creating a virtuous spiral is something most organizations can do. Through my research and study of many leading organizations, I have identified seven principles that are key to organizations' developing virtuous spirals. These seven principles guide a wide assortment of specific practices that I have seen implemented in exemplary organizations with positive results.

These seven principles are summarized in Exhibit 1.

1. *Attraction and Retention*
   Organizations must create a value proposition that defines the type of workplace they want to be so that they can attract and retain the right people.
2. *Hiring Practices*
   Organizations must hire people who fit with their values, core competencies, and strategic goals.
3. *Training and Development*
   Organizations must continuously train employees to do their jobs and offer them opportunities to grow and develop.
4. *Work Design*
   Organizations must design work so that it is meaningful for people and provides them with feedback, responsibility, and autonomy.
5. *Mission, Strategies, and Goals*
   Organizations must develop and adhere to a specific organizational mission, with strategies, goals, and values that employees can understand, support, and believe in.
6. *Reward Systems*
   Organizations must devise and implement reward systems that reinforce their design, core values, and strategy.
7. *Leadership*
   Organizations must hire and develop leaders who can create commitment, trust, success, and a motivating work environment.

EXHIBIT 1   Seven Principles for Treating People Right and Creating a Virtuous Spiral

Your Own Virtuous Spiral

Let me point out that there are a number of important implications of treating people right that you need to consider if you work with or for an organization.

On the positive side, just as organizations need to view you as human capital, you need to begin seeing yourself as human capital, not an asset. Consider your time, energy, intelligence, and skills. You have the opportunity to invest your knowledge and skills in any organization you want, and you can choose to withdraw it from one organization and invest it elsewhere if better returns are offered. In today's highly competitive world, you are a valuable resource for organizations. If you manage your career right, you will be in demand, and organizations will vie for your services more than they vie for investment dollars. In fact, the more you improve your skills and knowledge and invest in your personal development, the more you can build your own personal virtuous spiral of career success. Figure 2 depicts the type of virtuous spiral that you can create. It shows that increased skills and performance can lead to better jobs and higher rewards.

For you to have the best opportunity to develop a virtuous career spiral, your organization needs to be in a virtuous spiral. Organizations cannot thrive unless their people prosper, but at the same time, people cannot thrive unless their organizations prosper. Although Figures 1 and 2 show separate spirals for organizations and individuals, in practice they are intertwined. They depend on each other and feed off each other.

This suggests that you too need to continuously increase your commitment, dedication, and value to any organization you work for. With the death of the loyalty contract, however, you must also behave and think as a free agent, because no matter where you work, your organization may not be able to keep you employed indefinitely. You need to learn how to negotiate for what you want while getting it because of what you can offer.

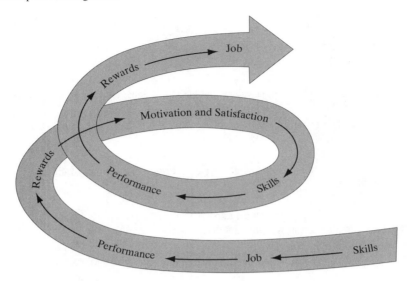

FIGURE 2 Virtuous Career Spiral

Endnotes

1. K. Dychtwald, *Age Power: How the 21st Century Will Be Ruled by the New Old.* New York: Tarcher/Putnam, 1999.

2. C. A. O'Reilly III and J. Pfeffer, *Hidden Value: How Great Companies Achieve Extraordinary Results with Ordinary People.* Boston: Harvard Business School Press, 2000.

MANAGEMENT DIALOGUES: TURNING ON THE MARGINAL PERFORMER*

John R. Schermerhorn, Jr.

William L. Gardner

Thomas N. Martin

Bob is an employee in the R&D laboratory of a large high-technology firm. He was hired by the lab supervisor, Fred, after a thorough recruitment and selection process. Both men were enthusiastic about the appointment. Bob had excellent technical credentials, was glad to be hired by the lab, and really liked Fred. Fred was confident in Bob's abilities and sure that Bob was just the person the lab needed. He passed by Bob's work station during Bob's first day on the job. Here's the way things started off:

FRED   Hi, Bob. First full day on the job, I see?

BOB   Yes, and I'm ready to go to work.

FRED   Good. I just thought I'd stop by first thing to say hi and remind you we're expecting good results. You'll be pretty much on your own here, so it will be your responsibility to stay on top of things.

BOB   Well, that shouldn't be a problem.

FRED   I hope not. But if you hit any snags, don't be afraid to call me.

*Reprinted from *Organizational Dynamics*, 18(4), John R. Schermerhorn, Jr., William L. Gardner, and Thomas N. Martin, "Management Dialogues: Turning on the Marginal Performer," pp. 47–59, © 1990, with permission from Elsevier.

BOB   All right.

FRED   Good enough, Bob. See you later.

Everything seemed in order with this brief but positive exchange between a manager and his new employee. The two men talked easily with each other. Fred quite specifically reminded Bob of his expectations and pledged his support. Bob expressed confidence in his ability to fulfill Fred's expectations, and he acknowledged the offer of support.

But six months later, things had changed dramatically. For example, consider one of Bob's typical workdays. He arrived late for work and looked at the clock, which read 8:55. "Little late this morning," he thought to himself. "Oh well, no big deal. Fred's not around anyway." Later in the day he noted that he had "come up short again" in his work. "But not too bad," he said. "This ought to be enough to keep Fred off my back." Finally, just before quitting time he considered getting a jump on the next day's schedule. But after thinking just a moment, he concluded, "Ah, why sweat it? I'll do it tomorrow."

People like Bob show up in most work sites. Although they initially seem capable and highly motivated, they become marginal performers—workers who do just enough to get by. Many frustrated managers simply consider these people unfortunate employment mistakes that must be tolerated. By contrast, we believe managers can "turn around" many marginal performers and thereby produce large productivity gains for their organization. Such *high-performance management* gets the best from each and every individual contributor.

Let's go back to the opening vignette to determine what went wrong in Fred and Bob's relationship and what could have been done about it. Why did Bob, a capable and motivated person, become a marginal performer? What could Fred have done to turn the situation around so that Bob's high-performance potential would have been realized?

A Comprehensive Approach to Individual Performance

The answers can be found in a management framework based on what we call the *individual performance equation: Performance = Ability × Support × Effort.* Central to the equation is the principle that high levels of work performance result from the combination of a person's job-related abilities, various forms of organizational support, and individual work efforts. The multiplication signs indicate that all three factors must exist for high performance to occur. Take any one or more away, and performance will be compromised. High-performance management starts with the following implications of the individual performance equation.

1. PERFORMANCE BEGINS WITH ABILITY Individual abilities are the skills and other personal characteristics we use in a job. For someone to perform well, he or she must have the skills and abilities required to complete the work. If the person lacks the requisite baseline abilities, it will be very difficult for even extraordinary effort and support to produce high performance.

Because ability is a prerequisite for performance, it is the first factor to consider when searching for explanations of marginal work. Initially, managers must determine whether employees have the skills and aptitudes necessary to succeed. The best way to ensure that they do is to develop selection procedures that properly match individual talents and job demands. In cases where employees lack essential skills, managers should use training and development programs to help them acquire these skills. The manager may also consider replacing or reassigning personnel to achieve a better match of individual abilities with job requirements.

In addition, as Victor Vroom's expectancy theory of motivation points out, individuals must believe in their abilities if they are to exhibit high performance. A person may have the right abilities but may fail to develop the expectation that by using these skills, he or she will achieve the desired performance levels. Thus part of a manager's job is to help build self-confidence among the individual contributors—to help them realize that they have the abilities required to meet high-performance expectations.

2. PERFORMANCE REQUIRES SUPPORT The second but frequently overlooked high-performance factor is support. Even the most hard-working and highly capable individuals will be unable to maximize their performance if they do not have the necessary support.

In searching for the causes of marginal performance, managers need to examine two major dimensions of support. First, they must ask if they have done their part to create a physical work setting that supplies employees with broad opportunities to fully use their abilities. A supportive work environment provides appropriate technologies, tools, facilities, and equipment; offers adequate budgets; includes clearly defined task goals; gives autonomy without the burden of too much red tape and other performance obstacles; and pays a market-competitive base wage or salary. Deficiencies in these areas impose situational constraints that too often frustrate employees' performance efforts.

Second, managers must give proper attention to the social aspects of the work environment. Recent research into job stress, for example, suggests that social support is critical for sustained high performance. Emotional support from a person's supervisor and co-workers, as well as from non-job sources (i.e., spouse, family, and friends), can have long-term positive effects on job performance. Indeed, empathy can help a worker better handle such work stresses as skill underutilization, high workloads, and role ambiguity.

A manager's responsibility thus includes providing every individual contributor with the maximum opportunity to perform at a high level. This advice echoes Robert House's path-goal theory of leadership. Path-goal theory suggests that effective managers use various management styles—directive, supportive, achievement oriented, and participative—as necessary to ensure that employees have clear "paths" as they seek to accomplish their goals. That is, good managers use leadership behaviors that maximize the amount of situational support available to others.

3. PERFORMANCE INVOLVES EFFORT Effort is the final, and perhaps most commonly emphasized, individual performance factor. Here, effort refers to the amount of energy (physical and/or mental) a person applies to perform a task. In other words, it represents someone's willingness to work hard.

Effort is necessary to achieve high-performance results. Capable, well-supported, but uninspired employees are no more likely to succeed than are hard-working persons who lack ability and/or support. Yet unlike the other performance factors, which are subject to direct managerial control, the decision to exert or withhold one's effort rests solely with the individual contributor. To understand why employees sometimes decide *not* to work as hard as possible, it is again useful to consider Vroom's expectancy theory of motivation. According to this perspective, the motivation to work is the product of expectancy, instrumentality, and valence: *Expectancy* is the individual's assessment of the likelihood that his or her work effort will lead to task performance; *instrumentality* is the individual's belief that a given level of performance will lead to certain work outcomes; and *valence* is the value the person attaches to these outcomes. If the level of any one of these factors is low, motivation is likely to suffer. To avoid motivational deficits, managers are advised to make sure individual contributors see clear linkages between how hard they work, their performance results, and their rewards.

Bob, the Marginal Performer

Let's return to the opening vignette and begin to apply the individual performance equation. All three elements of the equation—ability, support, and effort—appear to exist.

Fred set the stage for Bob's high performance by (1) hiring a technically competent person, (2) indicating his intention to provide support, and (3) encouraging Bob to work hard and use his ability to good advantage. Our first clues as to what went wrong are found in a conversation that took place after Bob had been on the job about a month.

Fred happened to pass by Bob's area and noticed Bob was working hard. He thought to himself how fortunate he was to have a dependable go-getter like Bob in his department. Bob noticed Fred approaching and wondered whether Fred would mention his good performance from the past week.

> FRED   Hi, Bob. It sure is good weather, wouldn't you say?
>
> BOB   Yes, it sure is.
>
> FRED   I was just passing through the building on another matter. While I'm here, I thought I'd show you some new schedule changes.
>
> BOB   Oh yes, Darlene (the project manager) told me all about them. Say, how'd we end up last week anyway?
>
> FRED   Pretty good, pretty good. If you have any questions about those schedule changes, just call the project manager. Well, I've got to run. See you later, Bob.

In this interaction Bob obviously wanted Fred's praise. What he got was a lukewarm "Pretty good, pretty good" followed by "I've got to run." Fred passed up a perfect opportunity to recognize directly Bob's accomplishments. From an expectancy theory perspective, this oversight could prove costly. Bob's expectation was probably quite high—he had already shown he could do the job when he wanted to. The valence he attached to possible work outcomes, such as praise, also was probably high. But Bob's instrumentality may have become low because he sensed little or no relationship between performing well and receiving the desired supervisory recognition. The positive reinforcement he both desired and needed was just not there. As a result, his motivation to work hard was reduced.

Things could have gotten better if the motivational dynamics had improved in later interactions between Fred and Bob. Unfortunately, as we'll now see, they didn't. Several weeks later while reading the weekly lab reports, Fred noticed a decline in Bob's performance. This was a serious problem, so Fred decided to chat with Bob right away. Bob had met high performance standards in the past and should still have been able to reach them. When Fred stopped by Bob's work station, they engaged in the following conversation.

> FRED   Hi, Bob, how's it going?
>
> BOB   Pretty good.
>
> FRED   Say, I wanted to check with you about your performance figures for the past couple of weeks. They've been down a little, you know.
>
> BOB   Well, I got stuck on a couple of things that threw me off. But I think I'm back on track now.
>
> FRED   The only reason I'm bringing it up is that you've busted the charts in the past. I know you can do it when you put your mind to it. You're one of our top performers. I figured if you were off on the numbers there must be a reason.
>
> BOB   Well, I'm sure my performance results will be back up this week.
>
> FRED   Okay, good, Bob, Take care now.

Reviewing this interaction, Fred thought it had been right to let Bob know he wasn't happy with his performance. But in this developing scheme, we have an indication that the only time Bob got the desired personal attention from Fred was when he did poorly. As social-learning theorists will tell us, Bob was essentially "learning" through reinforcement to work below his actual performance potential. By giving attention only when Bob turned in marginal, rather than high, performance, Fred was positively reinforcing the wrong behaviors and neglecting critical opportunities to positively reinforce the right ones. As long as this pattern continued, Bob was likely to remain a marginal performer. And, as we will see, a manager's frustrations with this situation can all too easily lead him or her to adopt ever more punitive approaches.

A few weeks later Fred noted that Bob's performance still wasn't back up to standard. While he was not the worst performer in the lab, he surely could have been doing a lot better; Bob's past record was proof positive. Being even more concerned now, Fred went to Bob's work area to discuss things with him.

FRED   Bob, I want to talk to you.

BOB   Hi, Fred, what's on your mind?

FRED   Your lousy performance, that's what! Your output has been down again for the past two weeks. Look, Bob, I know you can hit the numbers, but you're just not putting out. I need someone in here who can get the job done. If it is not you, I'll get someone else. I hope I won't have to do that. Now let's get to it?

BOB   (No response.)

Theorists advise us that Fred's threats reveal a number of shortcomings. For example, behaviors targeted for punishment frequently receive positive reinforcement from another source—like peers and co-workers or even the supervisor's inadvertent actions. For another, managers who use punishment often come to be viewed negatively by the recipients of the punishment. At the very least, then, we can expect that Fred had set the stage for potentially irreparable damage to his working relationship with Bob! It is not clear what Fred really gained as a result of his punitive managerial posture.

One thing is clear from the above episode. Fred was telling Bob that it was *Bob's* responsibility to find out what had gone wrong over the past couple of weeks, then take steps to correct it. Implicitly he was also attributing Bob's marginal performance to one or more things that might be wrong—with Bob! Unfortunately, Fred made a common mistake: He focused only on what the employee might have been doing wrong while overlooking other possible causes for the marginal performance.

Attribution Errors in Performance Management

Take a look at the data in Exhibit 1. It summarizes how managers from the health care and banking industries responded to two questions: (1) "What is the most frequent cause of poor performance by your employees?" and (2) "What is the most frequent cause of poor performance by yourself?" The exhibit shows quite different patterns of responses: When employees' performance deficiencies were at issue, the managers tended to attribute the problem to employees' lack of ability and/or effort; when the manager's own performance deficiencies were at issue, the problem was overwhelmingly viewed as a lack of outside support. But, we must ask, if managers need better support to achieve higher performance, doesn't the same hold true for their employees?

Responses such as these are of no great surprise to those familiar with an area of management research known as attribution theory. When dealing with marginal performers like Bob, the theory predicts that managers like Fred are more likely to

Number of Responses to the Question: Most common cause of poor performance by your employees?	Attribution	Number of Responses to the Question: Most common cause of poor performance by yourself?
22	Lack of Ability	2
15	Lack of Support	66
36	Lack of Effort	6

EXHIBIT 1   Marginal Performance: Attributions Given by Managers and by Employees Themselves

"attribute" any performance problems to some deficiency within the individual—that is, to a lack of ability or lack of effort—rather than to a deficiency in the work situation, like a lack of organizational or managerial support. Given that Bob was considered technically competent when he was hired (thus satisfying the ability factor), Fred probably assumed that Bob's reduced performance resulted from a lack of motivation (a problem with the effort factor).

Managers who view performance problems in such a manner will spend valuable time and money trying to find ways to increase their employees' motivation directly and immediately. When these initial efforts fail, the threatening and punitive approach that Fred used in the last episode is likely to follow.

The fact that employees tend to attribute deficiencies in their performance to external causes, such as inadequate support, rather than to the internal causes their managers favor further complicates such situations. Bob, for example, is more likely to attribute his mediocre performance to a lack of supervisory recognition (an external cause) than to his own laziness (an internal cause)—which Fred seems to assume is the case. When such gaps between attributions exist, employees like Bob typically resent the harsh and punitive responses their managers use. On the other hand, managers get increasingly frustrated because they cannot understand the employee's failure to perform.

If this cycle of mismatched manager-employee attributions is allowed to continue, a worst-case scenario, in the form of what social psychologists call "learned helplessness," may occur. This term refers to the tendency for people who are exposed to repeated punishment or failure to believe they do not possess the skills needed to succeed at their job. As a result they become passive in their work, and they tend to remain so even after situational changes occur that make success once again possible. A feeling that outcomes are beyond one's control, when in fact they are not, is the essence of learned helplessness. People become convinced that they are doomed to fail no matter what they do. As a consequence, employees who experience learned helplessness will usually continue to exhibit passive and maladaptive behavior long after changes (such as increased support or the arrival of a new manager) occur that make success possible.

In Bob's case, learned helplessness resulting from Fred's punitive responses may cause Bob eventually to doubt the very abilities that led to his hiring and early successes. While learned helplessness is a worst-case scenario, it exemplifies the serious complications that can arise if managers fail to address marginal performance in a constructive way. The approach that we recommend for dealing more positively with the marginal performer is outlined below.

Dealing with Bob—A Better Way

Many marginal performers, like Bob, are aware that they are not working up to their potential—and they know why. Given a positive environment for dialogue, they are often willing and able to pinpoint the causes—both personal and situational—of their performance problems. They are also willing to assume their share of the responsibility for correcting them. Toward this end, we suggest the following managerial strategy for "turning around" a marginal performer.

- Bring the performance gap to the marginal performer's attention.
- Ask in a nonthreatening manner for an explanation.
- Describe the implications of the marginal performer's substandard work.
- Restate the original and still-desirable performance objectives.
- Offer the external support necessary for the marginal performer to improve his or her performance.
- Express confidence that the marginal performer will respond as expected.
- Agree on an appropriate time frame for jointly evaluating future performance in terms of the agreed-upon standards.
- Continue the process until it succeeds or the individual admits to an employment mismatch that can be reconciled only by a job change.

To illustrate how these steps can be followed, let's go back in time and pick up our vignette at the point where Fred first noticed that Bob's performance had dropped off. We'll assume he was prepared to adopt this more positive approach to the situation. As Fred's dialogue with Bob develops, we'll occasionally interject some discussion of his actions and Bob's responses. This will help illustrate the steps and potential benefits of the recommended approach.

Fred noticed that Bob's performance had been down for two weeks. After thinking it over, he realized that a capable person like Bob should have been consistently performing at a higher level—but he may have needed some help. Fred decided to walk to Bob's work station and talk to him about the matter at once.

> FRED   Bob? I'd like to talk with you a bit. This last production report shows you came in below standard again the past week.
>
> BOB   Yeah, I guess I was a bit behind.

Immediately, Fred brought the performance gap to Bob's attention. He did this politely, but specifically and face-to-face. Bob readily admitted he had fallen behind.

> FRED   How do you feel about falling behind?
>
> BOB   Well, every time I get rolling I get hit with a schedule change. Sometimes they make sense, sometimes they don't. I'm not always clear about what to do. I didn't want to say much. So I just tried to struggle through on my own.

In the above exchange, Fred gave Bob a chance to express his feelings without putting him on the defensive. His next step was to try to identify the causes for Bob's substandard performance. To do this, Fred asked in a non-threatening manner for an explanation.

> FRED   There certainly have been a lot of schedule changes lately. Which ones are giving you the most problems?
>
> BOB   Mostly the changes with the Series J designs. I'm just not clear on how to handle them.
>
> FRED   Yeah, they can be tricky. Have you asked anyone about them?

BOB   Well, I realize the project manager has a lot on her mind. I just didn't want to bother her with my own problems. And . . .

FRED   And?

BOB   Uh . . . I just didn't want her to think I couldn't do the job.

This back-and-forth talk revealed Bob's belief that his performance suffered from unclear schedule changes, something beyond his control. Fred listened to the content of Bob's message and tried to understand his feelings. He also asked Bob to clarify certain points, such as the types of schedule changes he had the most problems with and the reasons why he didn't ask for help. By remaining open-minded and avoiding common attribution errors, Fred learned a lot about the possible causes of Bob's poor performance. In fact, his active listening revealed that Bob feared he would look incompetent if he brought his problems with the design changes to the project manager's attention. Next, Fred provided Bob with some immediate support to reassure him that he was viewed as a capable and trustworthy worker.

FRED   You shouldn't worry about it, Bob. She thinks highly of you. In fact, she said having you here is really going to make things a lot easier. And your part of the process really counts. The project manager needs your help to meet the deadlines.

BOB   Well, I thought I could work it out, even if it took extra time.

FRED   I'm sure you could, Bob, with your technical skills. But on this project time counts, and there are other people here to help you when needed. It's important that you understand completely what happens when you don't make your numbers because of confusion over the schedule changes. You slow down the next process, and that compounds the schedule changes down the line. Then our standards fall off, and we risk missing the target dates. So you see, your work directly affects the overall performance of the unit.

BOB   Yes, I can see where it would.

After reassuring Bob that he was viewed as a highly capable and dependable worker, Fred made sure Bob understood the implications of his substandard work. Fred explained to Bob what happened when he slowed down on the job and stressed that his performance affected the entire project. This reminded Bob that others depended on his work being done well and on time so they could meet their performance objectives. It highlighted not only the significance of his job in general, but also the significance of high performance in that job. From the perspective of House's path-goal theory, Fred clarified the path Bob needed to follow to achieve the desired goal of high performance. But Fred wasn't finished yet.

FRED   Bob, before going further, let's review the performance objectives we established for you. They are . . . . (Fred and Bob review objectives.)

BOB   Yes, Fred, they're clear to me.

FRED   Well look, Bob, the next schedule change you get hit with, I want you to talk to the project manager or to me before it throws you behind. In the meantime, let's discuss ways of dealing with schedule changes for the Series J designs so that you know how to handle them. Then I'm sure your performance will be back up to the standard level where it belongs. Okay?

BOB   Okay, I'll sure feel better when things are back on track.

During this exchange Fred once again stated Bob's original and still-desired performance objectives. By doing this face-to-face, Fred reinforced the personal dimensions of their relationship, further heightened Bob's commitment to improve, and increased Bob's sense of accountability to Fred. In addition, Fred offered the support necessary for Bob to improve his performance. He urged Bob to ask for help when he ran into problems, something Bob had previously considered an unwelcome intrusion on the project manager. He further suggested that the two of them discuss how to deal with the Series J schedule changes. This was an offer of immediate help for dealing with a perceived job constraint. Finally, Fred expressed confidence that Bob would respond as expected. Bob readily agreed that he would be able to do so.

Following this discussion, Bob probably felt pretty good. Fred then made one more effort to ensure that Bob would get back on and stay on the high-performance track.

> FRED   I feel real good about our conversation, Bob. You're a capable guy, and I know you'll be right back on top soon. Just to make sure things go okay, though, let's talk again after next week's reports are in. What do you think?
>
> BOB   I'll look forward to it. It'll give us a chance to touch base.

Fred established an appropriate time frame and standards for evaluating Bob's future performance. By adding this control, he helped ensure that the promised improvements in productivity would become a reality. Bob was assured that Fred was interested in his ongoing performance and that productivity gains would receive attention. He also saw that a failure to obtain the desired results would require an explanation. By formally scheduling further meetings with Bob, Fred assured himself of opportunities to recognize performance improvements. If such improvements did not occur, the meetings would ensure that Bob's marginal performance would receive further attention before too much time had elapsed. At that point Fred could continue the process with Bob or, if he believed the job was a true mismatch, work with Bob to develop an alternative solution. Thus, the stage seemed set once again for Bob to become the high performer everyone expected him to be.

Broad-Based High-Performance Management

Our continuing example offers managers a starting point for developing personal and situation-specific strategies for dealing with marginal performers. Of course the exact nature of the marginal performance will vary from one person to the next. Our example has dealt with only one type—the capable individual whose work efforts have declined over time. From the individual performance equation, however, we know that marginal performance can arise from a lack of ability, effort, or support, or from some combination of these factors. To deal with the uniqueness of each situation, we suggest asking the diagnostic questions listed in Exhibit 2. The following guidelines also highlight useful actions.

To Maximize Ability

The manager's task is to achieve and maintain an appropriate match between the capabilities of the marginal performer and the job he or she is asked to do. Depending on the nature of the job and the person, one of several options may be selected. In some cases the individual's abilities can be developed through training; in other cases the job may have to be changed so it better fits the individual; and in

Questions to Ask About Ability

Has the individual performed at a higher level in the past?
Is the performance deficiency total, or is it confined to particular tasks?
How well do the individual's capabilities match the job's selection criteria?
Has the individual been properly trained for current task requirements?

Questions to Ask About Support

Have clear and challenging task goals been set?
Are other employees having difficulty with the same tasks?
Is the job properly designed to achieve a "best fit" with the individual's capabilities?
Do any policies and/or procedures inhibit task performance?
Is the manager providing adequate feedback?
Is the individual being fairly compensated?
Is the work environment comfortable?
Is the manager providing sufficient empathy and emotional support?
Are the individual's co-workers providing sufficient emotional support?
Has the manager actually encouraged high performance?

Questions to Ask About Effort

Does the individual lack enthusiasm for work in general? For the assigned tasks in particular?
Are individuals with similar abilities performing at higher levels?
Has the individual been properly recognized for past accomplishments?
Are rewards and incentives provided on a performance-contingent basis?
Is the individual aware of possible rewards and incentives?
Does the individual have an appropriate role model?

EXHIBIT 2 **Questions Managers Can Ask When Dealing with a Marginal Performer**

still others, individuals may have to be replaced with more capable workers. In all cases a job vacancy must be recognized for what it is—perhaps the manager's greatest opportunity to build high-performance potential into a system by hiring a person whose talents and interests match the job's requirements.

Earlier we noted that repeated exposure to failure and punishment can lead to learned helplessness. Because the ability deficits are more imagined than real, however, individuals suffering from learned helplessness will need help in refocusing their concerns toward other performance factors. Take, for example, the case of a newly appointed manager who inherits a team of marginal performers who had received little or no support from their previous supervisor. To restore their feelings of competence, the manager must first help them understand that any past performance problems were not due to a lack of ability. This is the first step of a "turnaround" strategy.

To Maximize Support

The manager's task here is to (1) help marginal performers secure the resources they need to achieve high levels of job performance, and (2) help remove any and all obstacles that inhibit high performance. Success with this factor sometimes requires a dramatic change in the way managers view their responsibilities. Rather than simply being the person who directs and controls the work of others, an effective manager always acts to facilitate their accomplishments. This involves doing much more than telling employees what to do and then following up on them. The truly effective manager creates a supportive work environment by clarifying performance expectations, changing job designs, providing immediate feedback, fostering better interpersonal relations, and eliminating unnecessary rules, procedures, and other job constraints.

Consider again the case of the newly appointed supervisor. Support is an especially critical component of an effort to alleviate learned helplessness. Once marginal performers are convinced through attributional training that they do have the ability required to perform, they must be further persuaded that they will receive the support required to excel. The manager should engage marginal performers in dialogues that identify the types of external support needed to help them apply their abilities to best advantage. Ideally initial task assignments will then be created to produce successful experiences that further bolster employees' new-found self-confidence.

To Maximize Effort

Basic principles of motivation and positive reinforcement should be applied whenever managers deal with marginal performers. First, the marginal performer should be made aware whenever his or her performance falls below standard. He or she should also be told how substandard performance adversely impacts other workers, sub-units, and the organization as a whole. Immediate positive reinforcement should follow performance improvements and all above-standard achievements. Punishment should be avoided. By serving as an enthusiastic role model, a supervisor can further help marginal performers become high achievers.

For the new supervisor dealing with a group of marginal performers, strategies to correct ability and support deficits must be accompanied by assurances that high performance will lead to desired outcomes. The most powerful means of persuasion are successful experiences clearly followed by positive reinforcement—praise, recognition, and other valued rewards. It is also helpful to provide positive role models who obtain desired rewards through skilled utilization and task accomplishment.

Finally, it is important to note that managers' motivational attempts gain leverage from ability and support efforts. The key is what psychologists call the *effectance motive,* a natural motivation that occurs from feelings of self-efficacy. When people feel competent in their work, the argument goes, they can be expected to work harder at it. Competence, in turn, comes from ability and the feeling that one's skills and aptitudes are equal to the tasks at hand. Competence also comes from support and the feeling that one's work environment helps, rather than hinders, task accomplishment.

It is said that the very best motivation is that which comes from within. Thus, managers can gain additional motivational impact by investing in ability and support factors. To the extent that greater perceived ability and support enhance one's sense of competence, internal motivation is a likely consequence. Rather than concentrating only on motivational strategies designed to encourage more work effort externally, managers should make sure they take full advantage of the improved internal motivation that may be derived when ability and support factors are addressed.

A Vast Pool of Resources

Marginal performers present significant challenges to their managers—but they also represent a vast pool of human resources with the potential to offer major productivity gains to their organizations. To capitalize on this potential, managers must be committed to working with marginal performers to identify the causes of their problems and take positive actions to move them toward greater accomplishments. The individual performance equation can provide managers with the insight they need to tap the true potential of the marginal performer. Specifically, it directs a manager's attention toward three major factors that influence individual performance—the often neglected support factor as well as the more commonly recognized ability and effort factors. Guided by this action framework, managers can take advantage of every interaction and every conversation with marginal performers to pursue their turnaround strategies. In the final analysis, the foundations for high-performance management rest with the managers themselves. To achieve the desired results, managers must:

- **Recognize that marginal performers are potential sources of major productivity gains for organizations.** At the very least, they must be considered just as important as any other human resource within the organization.
- **Recognize the need to implement positive turnaround strategies for dealing with marginal performers.** Systematic and well-considered attention, rather than outright neglect and even punishment, is the order of the day—every day of a manager's workweek.
- **Be ready to accept at least partial responsibility for the fact that a subordinate has become a marginal performer.** Many workers learn to be marginal performers from the way they are treated in the workplace—they don't start out to be that way. Bob, for one, sure didn't.

Acknowledgment

The case setting for this article was developed from a vignette presented in Wilson Learning Corporation's instructional video "Dealing with the Marginal Performer" (*Building Leadership Skills,* New York: Wiley, 1986) and examined in William L. Gardner's accompanying instructor's guide. The initial four dialogues reported here are loosely adapted from the video. We are indebted to Wilson Learning Corporation and John Wiley & Sons for allowing us to build upon this case framework.

COACHING FOR SUSTAINED DESIRED CHANGE*

Melvin L. Smith, Ph.D., Ellen B. Van Oosten, and Richard E. Boyatzis, Ph.D.

Although he was Vice President of Information Technology at a mid-sized company, James[†] was confused about his future. He was doing quite well. Or at least it appeared he was. Having grown up in a poor neighborhood in a Midwest city, he did much better than most of his friends—he lived. He went to college and was about to complete an Executive MBA Program. James loved his daughters and had a significant investment account ready to pay for their college. He was divorced, but on amiable terms with his ex-wife and had a girlfriend. He was devout in his faith, contributed his time eagerly to church projects, and was an advocate for Promise Keepers (a movement to encourage fathers to keep their promises to their families and their God). So what was wrong?

When James looked into his future, beyond a few months, it was a blank wall. It did not worry him, consciously. Like heartburn, he ignored his lack of an image for his future and hoped the discomfort would go away. His personal vision essay was devoted entirely to his family and his faith. His coach asked him, "James, you didn't mention anything about work in your essay about your future. Do you have trust funds that you didn't mention?" He laughed, "No, I just thought I'd keep doing what

---
*Excerpted and reprinted from R. Woodman, W. Pasmore, and A. Shami (Eds.), *Research in Organizational Change and Development*, 17, Melvin L. Smith, Ellen B. Van Oosten, and Richard E. Boyatzis, "Coaching for Sustained Desired Change," pp. 145–173, © 2009, with permission from Elsevier.
[†]James is a pseudonym for a real person who prefers not to be identified.

I have been doing." Trying to invoke his passion about the future, his coach probed, "What would you love to do?"

After a long silence, he shrugged his shoulders. It seemed incongruous, a well-dressed, effective executive acting like a teenager who does not know what they want to have as a major in college. His coach pushed, "if you won the Lottery, say $80 million dollars after tax, what would you do?" He told him that maybe he would drive a truck cross-country. This seemed more like an escape fantasy than a dream. A few minutes later, in response to a question as to what would make him feel truly happy that he was fulfilling his purpose in life, he said, "Teaching high school kids, in the inner city, that computers can be their instruments to freedom."

Possibilities then opened up for James. He shared his dream that he could teach workshops on Saturdays or Fridays at local high schools. He talked about setting up IT internships for high school students at local companies. It was as if a dam had opened and ideas flooded his consciousness. He leaned forward and was talking faster than his coach had heard him talk in months. The excitement was contagious, you could feel it. James had an epiphany. His image of his "work" in the future changed him from "been there, done that" to "Wow, I can't wait to get started." James now had a dream—a clear one he could work toward. Two years later, he was actively in pursuit of his dreams. He was running computer workshops and programs for teens in his spare time. He got an offer to coordinate an IT program full time as an administrator/faculty at a local community college; when his firm offered a buy-out package as part of their downsizing, he took it.

In these uncertain and fearful times, many people, like James, around the world are avoiding looking to their future and just trying to get by in the present, or tolerating their situation. It is a dysfunctional response to having a future a person dreams about. Unfortunately, those of us in the helping professions, like teachers, trainers, and coaches, are often adding to this blocking of the future. Managers doing performance reviews and trying to motivate a person to change and improve in the future are often committing the same act of "visionocide." We are contributing to killing off people's dreams and inhibiting their progress toward a more effective future. The source of the misdirected effort and less than desirable consequences lay in misunderstanding how people change.

Much has been written of late regarding the "explosion" of executive coaching as a practice (Feldman & Lankau, 2005). The attention given to executive coaching in the literature over the past few years has increased exponentially (Kampa-Kokesch and Anderson, 2001). There are a number of reasons for the increased popularity and use of executive coaches by mid-to-senior level managers.

The demand for high-caliber managerial talent continues to grow. Companies require managers and leaders who can lead their businesses and respond to the on-going challenges of globalization, deregulation and rapid advances in technology. Another reason for the growth in executive coaching is that executive leadership failures can be costly. Watkins (2003) reports that 58% of new executives hired from outside the company don't succeed in their new position within 18 months. Further, he adds that the average cost of such failures is upwards of one million dollars. We also know that "other high-performance professionals, such as athletes, performers, and public speakers use coaching as a means of improving their performance" and in this sense, they become a benchmark for managers and executives, seeing themselves also as high-performers to study and emulate (Kampa-Kokesch and Anderson, 2001, p. 209). Finally, the recognition that emotional intelligence skills are key to succeeding as a leader and that emotional intelligence abilities can be learned and developed also helps us to understand the demand for executive coaching (Goleman, Boyatzis and McKee, 2002).

Market signals reinforce the growth in the practice of executive coaching in a compelling way. A Google search conducted in December of 2004, using the words "executive coaching" yielded 2,680,000 web site links. A search conducted using the same key words a mere three years later in December of 2007 yielded more than 8,280,000 hits. Additionally, annual spending on coaching for executives in the United States is estimated at roughly $1 billion (Sherman and Freas, 2004). These numbers serve as indicators of the explosion in interest and use of executive coaching services. Further, it has been noted that research (both theoretical and empirical) has lagged behind practice in this growing area of executive coaching (Joo, 2005; Kampa-Kokesch & Anderson, 2001; Kilburg, 1996; Sherman & Freas, 2004). As a result, previous authors have called for additional work that 1) clearly defines coaching, 2) offers theory regarding why and how coaching works, and 3) empirically examines specific outcomes associated with coaching (Feldman & Lankau, 2005; Kilburg, 1996).

In this chapter, we offer a definition of a particular type of coaching, one focused on achieving sustained, desired change in the individual being coached. We call this *coaching with compassion*. We also discuss a theory of intentional change, which we suggest explains why coaching in the manner we will describe indeed leads to sustained, desired change in individuals. The structure of the chapter is as follows. After setting the context for our discussion of coaching, we explain Intentional Change Theory (ICT) and its five stages or "discoveries," as well as discussing the role of mindfulness and less-mindful behavior in that change process. Next, we discuss the coaching relationship, where we focus on the importance of creating a high quality relationship and share the competencies required by those who create that relationship. We provide a guide for coaching for sustained desired change.

Putting Coaching into a Context

While coaching was most frequently associated with sports, historically, its emergence in the field of management and leadership development has grown exponentially over the past decade. Several definitions of executive coaching are found in the literature. It has been described as a conversation following a prescribed and predictable path, leading to superior performance and commitment to sustained improvement and positive relationships (Kolb, Rubin and Osland, 1991). Coaching has also been characterized as a process for skill improvement or behavioral change in team members (Brocato, 2003). A common thread among most definitions of coaching is the description as a facilitative or helping relationship with the purpose of achieving some type of change, learning, and/or new level of individual or organizational performance (Douglas & McCauley, 1999; Hudson, 1999; Kampa-Kokesch and Anderson, 2001; Kilburg, 2000; Quick and Macik-Frey, 2004).

Coaching is one of many forms of helping relationships (Boyatzis, Smith & Blaize, 2006). Within an organizational context, coaching is often discussed in the same vein as mentoring. Because coaching and mentoring share certain common elements, the two are sometimes seen as interchangeable and the literature has not always been clear on the distinctions between the two practices. There are distinctions, however, that should be articulated before we more deeply explore a specific form of coaching to be discussed in this chapter.

Mentoring has been defined as an intense relationship where a senior, more experienced person (the mentor) provides assistance to a junior, less experienced person (the protégé) in order to enhance the latter's professional and personal development (Kram, 1985; Noe, Greenberger, & Wang, 2002; Ragins, 1999). More specifically, Kram (1985) identified two types of assistance that mentors provide to their protégés. The first she describes as career functions, which directly aid the protégé's career advancement. These include exposure, protection, *coaching,* sponsorship, and challenging assignments. Kram describes the second type of assistance as psychosocial functions, which include acceptance and confirmation, friendship, counseling, and role modeling. Given this conceptualization of mentoring, coaching is considered to be one of the many functions or roles of a mentor. However, coaching, as described earlier, may also take place outside of the context of a mentoring relationship.

Other than the fact that coaching may in some cases be considered as a subset of mentoring, how are the two practices distinguished from one another? Tracing each word back to its origin sheds light on a key conceptual distinction. The word "mentor" can be traced back to the Greek word meaning "enduring." The meaning of the word was derived from the trust that Odysseus placed in his friend Mentor to whom he delegated complete responsibility for rearing his son Telemachus during the Trojan War (Hamilton, 1942). Conversely, the root meaning of the verb "to coach," which was first used in the English language in the 1500's, is to convey a valued person from where they are to where they want to be (Whitherspoon & White, 1996). The latter involves a shorter-term duration and a more specific focus, which serves as a useful distinction between mentoring and coaching.

Executive coaches are employed by clients for a variety of reasons. However, consistent with the common thread among the definitions of coaching, most coaching processes focus on a central task of helping a client improve performance or change behavior in a desirable way.

Our focus in this chapter is on the coaching of individuals for *sustained, desired change.* The "change" may be in a person's actions, habits or competencies. It may be in their dreams or aspirations. It may be in the way they feel in certain situations or around certain people. It may be a change in how they look at events at work or in life. It is "desired" in that the person wishes it so or would like it to occur. It is "sustained" in that the changed state endures for a relatively long period of time.

We argue that coaching for sustained, desired change differs from another form of coaching, *coaching for compliance.* This approach refers to directing an individual toward the achievement of some externally defined objectives through a prescribed set of steps. Situations involving coaching for compliance are common, such as with the struggling executive assigned a coach to improve performance metrics or the manager who is "coached" to demonstrate certain company-endorsed competencies within a set period of time. In instances where an individual is coached strictly for compliance to an imposed standard of behavior, the change effort (if successful at all) is typically not sustainable. If the individual being coached doesn't feel the need or have a true desire to change, then long-term behavioral change is unlikely to occur (Boyatzis, 2006). For instance, it has been suggested that mandated coaching and even mentoring programs invoke an instrumental mindset (Higgins & Kram, 2001; Kram, 1985), which in the absence of psychosocial support may lead to ineffective results. Coaching for sustained, desired change, on the other hand, is rooted in a genuine desire to help an individual grow and develop in ways that they choose. It moves beyond a purely instrumental focus tied to externally derived objectives and incorporates the personal vision and values of the individual being coached. It involves helping individuals discover and articulate their ideal future, as well as helping them determine how they might best make a difference with their lives. As we will discuss later in this chapter, Boyatzis, Smith, and Blaize (2006) suggest that this type of coaching, when done with compassion, not only benefits the person being coached, but also generates residual benefits for the person doing the coaching.

Coaching may involve both caring for the person's development *and* serving an organizational (i.e., instrumental) need. In such situations, the instrumental utility of the coaching act does not necessarily preclude the experience of compassion. But, in this situation coaches must be careful to ensure that they are not serving their own desires or goals rather than those of the individual being coached.

Mindfulness and Sustained Desired Change

Sustained, desired changes in an individual's behavior, thoughts, feelings or perceptions are, on the whole, discontinuous. That is, they appear as emergent or catastrophic changes over time and effort. The experience is one of an epiphany or discovery. Self-awareness or mindfulness (of self and context, both social and natural) (Boyatzis & McKee, 2005) is inversely proportionate to the degree of surprise or discovery.

When individuals are more mindful, they will experience the change process as a set of smooth transitions. Coaches can help a person with such necessarily conscious realizations. They may do it by asking questions, being supportive, or offering insight. The more mindful a person is, the easier the role of the coach in provoking these conscious epiphanies.

Krieger (2005) defined mindfulness as

a psychological state in which individuals engage in active information processing while performing their current tasks such that they are actively analyzing, categorizing, and making distinctions in data (p. 127).

In a considerably more expansive definition, Weick and Sutcliffe (2001) described mindfulness as

the combination of ongoing scrutiny of existing expectations, continuous refinement and differentiation of expectations based on newer experiences, willingness and capability to invent new expectations that make sense of unprecedented events, a more nuanced appreciation of context and ways to deal with it, and identification of new dimensions of context that improve foresight and current functioning (p. 42).

These definitions of mindfulness were derived from the work of Langer (1989), who suggested that mindfulness could best be understood as the process of drawing novel distinctions. Langer and Moldoveanu (2000) further offered that this process of drawing novel distinctions can lead to greater sensitivity to one's environment, more openness to new information, the creation of new categories for structuring perception, and enhanced awareness of multiple perspectives in problem solving. Helping an individual achieve a higher state of mindfulness so that they might better leverage each of these consequences of drawing novel distinctions is an important aspect of coaching for sustained desired change.

The converse of mindfulness has been referred to as *mindlessness* and has typically been viewed as a less than ideal state where individuals are on automatic pilot (Langer, 1997), behave like programmed automatons (Langer and Moldoveanu, 2000), or are fixated on a single perspective without awareness of other possibilities (Weick, Sutcliffe, and Obstfeld, 1999). Levinthal and Rerup (2006), however, offer a different perspective, suggesting that *less-mindful behavior* actually has its virtues. They further suggest that mindfulness and less-mindful behavior are not wholly distinct categories, but are instead interrelated processes. And while Levinthal and Rerup argue the possibility of a complementary relationship where both mindful and less-mindful behavior can occur simultaneously, Weick and Sutcliffe (2006) contend that further understanding is needed before we can determine whether it is conceivable that the two processes can truly operate simultaneously or whether they are mutually exclusive and can thus only operate sequentially. Even sequential operation of these processes can be viewed as beneficial, however, if we assume that an individual is capable of moving back and forth fluidly between the two. Drawing on this view, we next discuss how mindfulness and less-mindful behavior each can play a role in the process of an individual making sustained desired change.

A Theory of Intentional Change

Intentional Change Theory (ICT) describes the essential components and processes that encourage sustained, desired change to occur in a person's behaviors, thoughts, feelings and/or perceptions (Boyatzis, 2006). ICT presents a window to view, interpret and understand how individuals and organizations can approach change and as such becomes an important tool in the coaching process. The model includes five phases or discontinuities, called "discoveries" (Boyatzis, 2006; Goleman, Boyatzis and McKee, 2002).

The five phases include: (1) the Ideal Self; (2) the Real Self; (3) creation of a Learning Agenda and Plan; (4) Experimentation and Practice with new behaviors, thoughts or feelings outlined in the Learning Plan, and (5) Trusting Relationships that support a person's development experience. Each discovery is discussed below along with a consideration of associated activities which can be classified as either mindful or less-mindful behavior (see Levinthal and Rerup, 2006). A diagram of the process is presented in Figure 1.

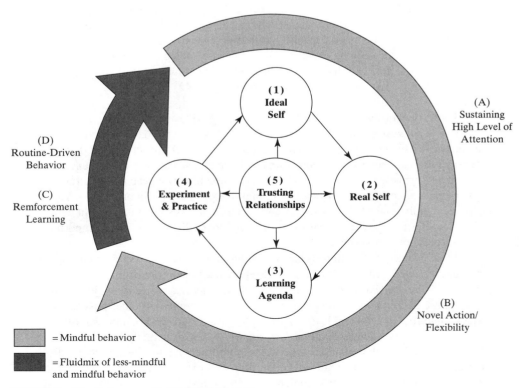

FIGURE 1 **Mindfulness and Intentional Change**

The First Discovery: Catching Your Dreams, Engaging Your Passion

The first discovery and potential starting point for the process of personal development is the discovery of an individual's deepest aspirations for his or her life, called the *Ideal Self.* Three major components comprise the development of this image: (1) an image of a desired future; (2) hope that one can attain it; and (3) inclusion of one's core identity, which serves as a foundation upon which to build the desired image (Boyatzis & Akrivou, 2006).

The last twenty years has revealed literature supporting the power of positive imaging or visioning in sports psychology, meditation and biofeedback research, and other psycho-physiological research (Boyatzis & McKee, 2005). Mindfulness is important at this stage of the intentional change process because without clear and sustained focus on our dreams and desires (Figure 1), we often become anesthetized to them, causing them to lose their power as motivators of goal-directed behavioral change.

In the coaching process, it thus becomes a powerful vehicle for the coach to include a discussion of the individual's ideal self. The reason for this is that when a person reflects upon his or her ideal life and career and creates a personal vision, positive emotions of hope and excitement often follow. The vision then serves as a foundation for the rest of the coaching process and as a source of renewal.

The Second Discovery: How Do Others See Me?

A person's awareness of his/her current self is often elusive. The Real Self, which is addressed by the Second Discovery, is the person that others see and with whom they interact. This discontinuity involves assessing one's strengths and weaknesses and creating a Personal Balance Sheet as an outcome. Maintaining focused attention on who we really are (see again Figure 1) allows us to realize our strengths and weaknesses. For normal reasons, the human psyche protects itself from the automatic "intake" of some information about ourselves. These ego-defense mechanisms protect us. They also conspire to delude us into an image of who we are.

For a person to truly consider changing a part of him or herself, he or she should have a clear sense of what he or she values and wants to keep. These areas in which the Real Self and Ideal Self are consistent or congruent can be considered strengths. Likewise, to consider what you want to preserve about yourself involves admitting aspects of yourself that you wish to change or adjust in some manner. Areas where your Real Self and Ideal Self are inconsistent may be considered gaps (i.e., aspects considered weaknesses or things we wish to change). Self-assessment and 360-degree assessment instruments are examples of resources available and commonly used by coaches to stimulate reflection and encourage mindfulness as a person develops awareness of his/her current capabilities and limitations.

All too often, people explore growth or development by focusing on the "gaps" or deficiencies. Organization-based leadership training programs and managers conducting annual reviews often make the same mistake. There is an assumption that we can "leave well enough alone" and get to the areas that need work. It is no wonder that many programs or procedures intended to help a person develop often result in the individual feeling battered, beleaguered and bruised, not helped, encouraged, motivated, or guided.

The Third Discovery: Mindful Steps toward Change

The next discontinuity in intentional change is development of a learning agenda, which encompasses the individual's personal vision, learning goals and actions in support of those goals. It provides a framework to document a person's desired future as well as the steps he or she chooses to take to create that desired future through the articulation of clear goals. Mindfulness at this stage of the change process (Figure 1) involves remaining open to novel action to be taken in the learning process and exhibiting flexibility in one's preferred learning style and approach to tackling new learning situations.

A learning agenda is unique in that it places the focus more on the development process itself and less on discrete outcomes such as improved performance or greater fulfillment at work. It differs from a traditional *development plan* in that it ideally embodies a *learning orientation* rather than a *performance orientation*. A learning orientation arouses a positive belief in one's capability and the hope of improvement. This encourages people to set personal standards of performance, rather than "normative" standards that mimic what others have done or serve to meet an imposed goal (Beaubien and Payne, 1999). Contrary to a learning orientation, a performance orientation often evokes anxiety and doubts about whether or not change is possible or even desired.

Research supporting the power of this assertion is available through longitudinal studies conducted at the Weatherhead School of Management. Leonard (2008) showed that MBA students who approached development with a learning orientation and set goals desiring to change on certain emotional intelligence competencies, changed significantly on those competencies as compared to other MBAs.

The Fourth Discovery: Metamorphosis

The fourth discovery includes experimentation and practice with desired changes. The essence of this stage is really about implementing the goals and action steps articulated in the prior discovery and taking risks to develop new behavioral "habits." These behaviors become habits by practicing them beyond the point of comfort to the point of mastery. During the experimentation and practice phase, reinforcement learning (Figure 1) occurs as experimental outcomes that meet or exceed aspirations are classified as successes and are reinforced, while outcomes that fall short of expectations are viewed as failures and lead to further experimentation (Levinthal and Rerup, 2006). As successful experiments get reinforced through repeated practice, routine-driven behavior (Figure 1) emerges as the learned behavior is mastered. During this process of metamorphosis, it is still extremely critical to also be mindful. For in this phase of the intentional change process, one must be fully aware of the changes that are occurring in order for them to be integrated into the revised Ideal and Real Selves and in order to keep the positive emotional attractor aroused, thus fueling further change efforts.

There are different approaches to consider when trying to learn new behaviors and there is no one "best" or "right" way. It's best to find the application or situation that is most easily "doable" and where a person has the highest degree of energy to continue to practice. It's often helpful if a person can find ways to leverage learning from current, or on-going experiences happening in his/her professional and/or personal life vs. creating an elaborate, new application. That is, the experimentation and practice can but usually do not need to involve formal learning such as attending training courses or creating a new project assignment. During this part of the process, intentional change looks and feels like a "continuous improvement" process.

The impact of experimentation and practice on development of one's capabilities was empirically proven by Dreyfus (2008). She studied managers of scientists and engineers who were considered superior performers. After observing that the managers used considerably more of certain abilities than their less effective counterparts, she investigated how they developed some of those abilities. One of the distinguishing abilities was Group Management, also called Team Building. She found that many of these middle-aged managers had first experimented with team building skills in high school and college, in sports, clubs, and living groups. Later, when they became "bench scientists and engineers" working on problems in relative isolation, they still used and practiced this ability in activities outside of work. They practiced team building and group management in social and community organizations, such as 4-H Clubs, and professional associations in planning conferences and such.

The Fifth Discovery: Relationships that Enable Us to Learn

Our relationships are an essential part of our environment. The most crucial relationships often exist in groups that have particular importance to us. These relationships and groups give us a sense of identity, guide us as to what is appropriate and "good" behavior, and provide feedback on our behavior. In sociology, they are called reference groups or social identity groups. These relationships create a "context" within which we interpret our progress on desired changes, the utility of new learning, and even contribute significant input to formulation of the Ideal Self (Kram, 1996).

Based on social identity, reference group, and now relational theories, our relationships both mediate and moderate our sense of who we are and who we want to be. We develop or elaborate on our Ideal Self from these contexts. We label and interpret our Real Self from these contexts. We interpret and value strengths (i.e., aspects considered our core that we wish to preserve) from these contexts. We also interpret and value gaps (i.e., aspects considered weaknesses or things we wish to change) from these contexts.

In this sense, our relationships are mediators, moderators, interpreters, sources of feedback, sources of support and permission for the change and learning we seek. They may also be the most important source of protection from relapses or returning to our earlier forms of behavior. The relationship between a coach and a client fits this model in that the coach serves as a significant mirror, holding up a picture of the individual for him or her to see. As an objective third-party, the coach can often make observations and raise provocative questions from a unique seat not accessible to most others.

Research conducted at the Weatherhead School of Management further illustrates the importance of relationships. Wheeler (2008) analyzed the extent to which the MBA graduates worked on their goals in multiple "life spheres" (i.e., work, family, recreational groups, etc.). In a two-year follow-up study of two graduating classes of part-time MBA students, she found those who worked on their goals and plans in multiple sets of relationships improved the most and to a greater degree than those working on goals in only one setting, such as work or within one relationship.

The process of sustained desired change requires behavioral freedom and permission to try something new and see what happens. This "permission" comes from interaction with others in trusting, supportive relationships that facilitate the change process.

SELF-ORGANIZING AND THE PULL OF TWO ATTRACTORS The process of experiencing sustained desired change is an iterative, cyclical process of ongoing development for most people, most of the time. Leveraging complexity theory as a guide, the process of development engages the cycle of in this case, individual change, or the lack of it through two self-organizing properties of the human organism. Two attractors, the Positive Emotional Attractor (PEA) and the Negative Emotional Attractor (NEA), determine whether it is an adaptation to existing conditions or an adaptation to new, emergent conditions.

Intentional Change Theory offers an explanation as to how disequilibrium occurs and suggests forces to drive new self-organizing systems. An attractor becomes the destabilizing force. We call this the Positive Emotional Attractor. It pulls the person toward his/her Ideal Self. In the process of focusing people on future possibilities and filling them with hope, it arouses the Parasympathetic Nervous System (PNS) (Boyatzis, Smith, and Blaize, 2006). Once the PNS is aroused, people have access to more neural circuits and find themselves in a calmer, if not elated state in which the immune system is functioning well and the body is sustained. They are able, in this state, to experience neurogenesis (i.e., the conversion of hippocampal stem cells into new neurons) and the new degrees and extent of learning that becomes possible. It is even suggested that formation of learning goals or learning oriented goals works from this attractor and results in more successful change.

But another attractor is also at play in the system—the Negative Emotional Attractor. In an analogous manner, it arouses the Sympathetic Nervous System (SNS) which helps people to deal with stress and threat and protect themselves. Within the threatened environment and state, the NEA pulls a person toward defensive protection. In this arousal, the body shunts blood to the large muscle groups, closes down non-essential neural circuits, suspends the immune system, and produces Cortisol—important for protection under threat. But Cortisol inhibits or even stops neurogenesis and overexcites older neurons, rendering them useless (Boyatzis, Smith, and Blaize, 2006).

If a person's adaptation is self-organizing, then desired change not already part of this system is only possible when it is intentional. Because of the difficulty in sustaining the effort, it also must be driven by a powerful force. This also helps us to understand why there is both a need for more positivity than negativity in change efforts (Fredrickson and Losada, 2005). A further description of the components of the positive and negative emotional attractors and how they are activated in each of the intentional change theory discoveries is provided in Table 1.

Table 1 Intentional Change and the Positive and Negative Emotional Attractors

Stage of ICT	PEA Components	NEA Components
Ideal Self	Personal vision, efficacy, hope, dreams, values	Ought Self, preoccupation with one element
Real Self	Strengths	Weaknesses
Learning Agenda	Things you are excited about learning or are eager to try	To Do lists, Performance Improvement Plans
Experimentation/ Practice	Trying new things, exploring, getting positive reinforcement and feedback from others about one's new behavior, thoughts, or feelings	Repetitive activities such as skill building seen as somewhat tedious
Trusting Relationships	Trusting support, encouragement for the pursuit of one's dreams	Reminder of progress on one's Learning Plan, constructive or negative feedback on behavior or attempted new behavior

The Coaching Relationship

Relationships with others are an essential part of our environment. Our relationships create a context within which we can interpret our progress on desired changes and consider the utility of new learning. They may also contribute significantly to the formulation of our Ideal Selves (Kram, 1996). In this sense, our relationships are sources of feedback, support, and permission for change and learning. They may also be the most important source of protection from relapses or returning to our earlier forms of behavior (Boyatzis, 2006). The coaching relationship is one of particular importance as individuals attempt to make desired changes in their lives. Further, achieving sustained desired change is facilitated when the coach shows compassion for the person being coached (Boyatzis, Smith and Blaize, 2006).

COACHING WITH COMPASSION Boyatzis, Smith and Blaize (2006) define compassion as having three components: (1) empathy or understanding the feelings of others; (2) caring for the other person; and (3) willingness to act in response to the person's feelings. They suggest that each of the components is a necessary but not sufficient condition of compassion. That is, compassion as they define it requires the presence of all three components. This definition of compassion shares elements with several previously offered definitions (Frost, Dutton, Worline, and Wilson, 2000; Kanov et al., 2004). A key distinguishing factor of the Boyatzis, et al. (2006) conceptualization of compassion, however, is that it incorporates the desire to reach out and help others whether or not their condition is based on suffering and pain. It is closer to compassion as the emotional expression of the virtue of benevolence evident in Confucian philosophy (Van Norden, 1998), specifically the concept of "ren" (Cua, 1998). Alternate reasons to help others may include others' relative distress from not moving toward desired goals or wanting to help them extend and reach for their dreams or new aspirations, both of which support the practice of coaching others for sustained, desired change.

Coaching with compassion thus requires a caring relationship between the coach and the person being coached. A caring relationship in the context of coaching is one where both parties are on the same emotional wavelength (i.e., the coach is attuned to and in touch with the feelings of the person being coached) and both parties have some sense of commitment to the relationship (Goleman, Boyatzis, & McKee, 2002). Goleman, et al. (2002) suggest that a person's emotional intelligence enables them to establish and promote such caring relationships. Quick and Macick-Frey (2004) discuss the importance of deep interpersonal communication in creating such relationships. According to Quick and Macick-Frey, deep interpersonal communication between the coach and the person being coached is the key to building supportive, positive relationships in the work place. They add that it can actually help the person being coached enhance his/her health and approach greater authenticity.

Boyatzis, Smith, and Blaize (2006) also discuss the health benefits of a caring coaching relationship. However, they suggest that not only does the person being coached benefit from such a relationship, but also the person doing the coaching. They argue that coaching, when done with compassion, should ameliorate the negative physiological and psychological effects of power stress. Therefore, coaching with compassion is likely to enhance a coach's overall health, thereby increasing his/her sustainability.

When coaching takes place within an organizational context, where the coach is a leader coaching his or her subordinates, these health benefits and the increased ability to sustain effectiveness over time can contribute significantly to the performance of the organization. We know from experience, however, that not all relationships between leaders and subordinates (or between those who coach others and those who receive that coaching) will necessarily be characterized as caring.

Leader-member exchange (LMX) theory (Graen, Novak, & Sommerkamp, 1982) suggests that leaders actually differentiate among their subordinates and form different types of exchange relationships with each of them, rather than demonstrating a single leadership style across all subordinates. The focus of LMX theory is the dyadic relationship between a leader and a subordinate. High quality relationships have been characterized as consisting of relatively greater degrees of trust, respect, loyalty, liking, intimacy, support, openness, and honesty than is seen in low quality relationships, which have been suggested to be more instrumental in nature and are more likely to be based on very specific (even contractual) obligations (Dansereau, Graen and Haga, 1975; Graen & Scandura, 1987).

While it has been suggested, given that they have limited amounts of time and energy, that leaders are only able to establish high quality relationships with a select number of subordinates (Graen & Scandura, 1987), others contend that leaders should engage in intentional efforts aimed at forming high-quality relationships with all subordinates (Graen & Uhl-Bien, 1995; Uhl-Bien, Graen, & Scandura, 2000). Dutton and Heaphy (2003) further state that, at an even more fundamental level, every interaction represents an opportunity to build high quality connections, which they suggest are characterized by feelings of vitality and aliveness, a heightened sense of positive regard, and felt mutuality (p. 267). Thus, whether the coaching is taking place within or outside of the context of the superior-subordinate relationship, when it is done with compassion as we are suggesting is the case when coaching for sustained desired change, both the coach and the person being coached are likely to benefit in significant ways.

Core Coaching Competencies

We have discussed the benefits of showing compassion in the coaching relationship. However, what are the specific skills necessary to effectively coach individuals for sustained desired change? Brotman, Liberi, & Wasylyshyn (1998) identified twelve competencies that they suggested executive coaches attempting to bring about lasting behavior change must possess—1) approachability, 2) comfort around top management, 3) compassion, 4) creativity, 5) customer focus, 6) integrity and trust, 7) intellectual horsepower, 8) interpersonal savvy, 9) listening, 10) dealing with paradox, 11) political savvy, and 12) self-knowledge. They summarize these competencies as representing someone who is a trusted and approachable person who can establish long-lasting relationships with a variety of others. In much earlier work, Rogers (1961) identified three characteristics that seemed critical for effective "helping" behavior emerging from his work on psychotherapy. Those characteristics were empathy, unconditional positive regard, and genuineness. A variety of other studies have pointed to the importance of empathy in the effectiveness of those in helping relationships, such as coaches (Bohart and Greenberg, 1997; Hall and Bernieri, 2001). Boyatzis (2009) adds that conceptual synthesis of competency studies on various roles within the human resource field suggest that a set of competencies that constitute emotional intelligence as well as several cognitive competencies play an important part (Brotman et. al., 1998; Goleman, 1998; Spencer and Spencer, 1993).

In work outside of the field of executive coaching, but still focused on helping relationships geared toward bringing about sustained desired change, Boyatzis (2005) shares results of a series of studies designed to determine the competencies of alcoholism counselors that predicted the work performance of their clients after they had returned to work. The studies showed that two competencies, empathy and emotional self-awareness, distinguished effective counseling and predicted work performance. Application of these results to executive coaching would confirm that empathy, or sensitivity to the person being coached, is a key characteristic of effective coaches. Coaching for sustained desired change, like counseling, cannot proceed without listening to and understanding the individual being coached, his/her issues, problems, and situation at work and at home. If the individual is viewed as merely a "problem bearing platform," the coach will focus on the problems and tasks rather than the person. In the process, he/she may miss underlying issues or factors contributing to sustaining current behavior and impact. The coach must be sensitive to changes in the individual and his or her process of change to tailor comments and suggestions to that person's needs at that point in time.

A second critical competency revealed in the Boyatzis study was emotional self-awareness. A coach, like a counselor, cannot focus on their clients and understanding their situations if the coach is preoccupied with his own challenges. Similarly, awareness of transference, counter-transference, and projection must be an integral aspect of the functioning of executive coaches. They must be able to separate their own feelings and values from those of the client. This is not to say that the coach's feelings and values are not important. But, the coach has the responsibility to be able to identify and manage his/her feelings and reactions. Whether the coach uses this information as part of understanding the client or as a vehicle for suspending his/her own needs and anxieties, managing oneself is difficult if not impossible without a high degree of self-monitoring, or emotional self-awareness. Boyatzis (2005) thus suggests that to be effective as a counselor, and by extension an executive coach, a person must be sensitive to others. To be sensitive to others, she must also be sensitive to herself. Therefore, consistent with previously discussed views, we suggest that empathy and self-awareness are two critically important competencies for coaching for sustained desired change. Some have argued that psychologists are particularly well equipped for this type of coaching due to their training in psychological dynamics and adult development, as well as the tactics and tools that they utilize to facilitate self-discovery (Brotman, Liberi, and Wasylyshyn, 1998; Feldman and Lankau, 2005; Kilburg, 1996). Others have suggested that being knowledgeable about issues associated with the business context in which executives operate (e.g., leadership, management principles, and organizational politics) is of critical importance (Diedrich and Kilburg, 2001; Feldman and Lankau, 2005; Kampa-Kokesch & Anderson, 2001). Still others have argued that talented executive coaches must be grounded in both psychology and business (Wasylyshyn, 2003). We argue, however, that one's specific background is not as important as the demonstration of the competencies necessary to make a genuine connection with the individual being coached and to facilitate the process of self directed learning and growth. A proposed guide for coaching others for sustained desired change is presented in Figure 2.

As discussed earlier, when coaching someone for sustained desired change, a coach should be a critical catalyst to ensure that the person being coached doesn't get stuck in the pull of one attractor, but instead is able to move somewhat smoothly back and forth. The coach, through observations, support, and timing of interventions, helps a person manage his/her way between the two attractors. When the coach feels the person is too full of the NEA, he creates a positive, supportive climate and emphasizes the PEA. This helps the person restore his balance. The coach can also help in the reverse – if a person believes too many of his reviews or

(Focusing on Compassion and the Positive Emotional Attractor)
Preparation

1. Do I know elements of the person's Ideal Self and Personal Vision?
   a. Do I know his/her dominant values?
   b. Do I know his/her operating philosophy?
   c. Do I know his/her life and/or career stage, or point in his/her life/career cycle? Is he/she approaching or in a mid-life crisis?
   d. Do I know aspects of his/her dreams, fantasies and aspirations for the future?
   e. Do I know what he/she considers his/her passion and calling?
   f. Do I know what he/she considers his/her strengths?
   g. Do I know the level of his/her optimism?
   h. Do I know the level of his/her efficacy?
2. Do I care about him/her?
3. Am I tuned into how he/she is feeling today?

Coaching Discussion

4. Have we discussed his/her dreams about the future?
5. Have we discussed his/her Personal Vision or elements of his/her Ideal Self?
6. Have we discussed who helped him the most to become who he is or get to where he has?
7. Have we discussed personal strengths that can help the individual move closer to or maintain his/her Ideal Self.
8. Have we discussed his/her weaknesses that may inhibit that movement? Which of those are close to a tipping point, suggesting that they can be developed?

Post Coaching Discussion

9. Was the person's awareness of his/her Ideal Self or Personal Vision enhanced as a result of our conversation?
10. Was the person able to make discriminating choices or identify priorities within those things discussed as to which are the most salient?
11. Did we cover a comprehensive array of relevant topics in the person's life and work?

FIGURE 2 Guide to Coaching for Sustained Desired Change

sycophants' praise, the coach can provide a dosage of reality and bring him into the NEA. Managing the balance to keep the person alert, eager, and the momentum for change calls for a great deal of sensitivity and talent on the part of the effective coach in these compassionate relationships.

Concluding Thoughts

A slight, but important modification in the way we coach can yield dramatically improved results. Coaching with compassion, rather than the almost instinctive coaching for compliance or to fix or help another directly, can arouse the sustainable processes that will result in desired change. But it appears to require a deep and holistic approach to coaching others.

Without a great deal of additional empirical research, we are left with fads, theories, and what seem to be good ideas. Our intellectual integrity rests on our willingness to put our methods, practices, and theories to a test. Do they work? In this sense, research should focus on what produces effective coaching, not merely normative or descriptive approaches that some coaches use.

References

Akrivou, K., Boyatzis, R.E., and McLeod, P.L. (2006). The Evolving Group: Towards a Prescriptive Theory of Intentional Group Development, *Journal of Management Development,* 25(7), 689–709.

Beaubien, J.M. & Payne, S.C. (1999). Individual goal orientation as a predictor of job and academic performance: A meta-analytic review and integration. Paper presented at the meeting of the Society for Industrial and Organizational Psychology, Atlanta, GA. April.

Bohart, A.C. & Greenberg, L.S. (1997). *Empathy Reconsidered: New Directions in Psychotherapy.* Washington D.C.: American Psychological Association.

Boyatzis, R.E., (2005). "Core competencies in coaching others to overcome dysfunctional behavior," In V. Druskat, F. Sala & G. Mount (Eds.) *Linking Emotional Intelligence and Performance at Work: Current Research Evidence with Individuals and Groups.* Mahweh, NJ: Erlbaum. 81–95.

Boyatzis, R.E. (2006). Intentional change theory from a complexity perspective. *Journal of Management Development,* 25(7), 607–623.

Boyatzis, R.E. (2009). A behavioral approach to emotional Intelligence. *Journal of Management Development, 28,* 9, 749–770.

Boyatzis, R.E. & Akrivou, K. (2006). The Ideal Self as a Driver of Change. *Journal of Management Development, 25(7),* 624–642.

Boyatzis, R.E. & McKee, A. (2005). *Resonant Leadership: Renewing Yourself and Connecting with Others Through Mindfulness, Hope, and Compassion.* Boston, MA: Harvard Business School Press.

Boyatzis, R.E., Smith, M. & Blaize, N. (2006). Developing Sustainable Leaders through Coaching and Compassion. *Academy of Management Journal on Learning and Education,* 5(1), 8–24.

Brocato, R. (2003). Coaching for improvement: An essential role for team leaders and managers. *The Journal for Quality and Participation,* Spring: 17–23.

Brotman, L.E., Liberi, W.P., & Wasylyshyn, K. M. (1998). Executive coaching: The need for standards of competence. *Consulting Psychology Journal: Practice and Research, 50(1),* 40–46.

Cua, A.S. (1998). Confucian philosophy: Chinese. In E. Carig (Ed.), *Routledge Encyclopedia of Philosophy* (Vol 2, pp. 536–549). London: Routledge.

Dansereau, F., Graen, G., & Haga, W. J. (1975). A vertical dyad linkage approach to leadership within formal organizations: A longitudinal investigation of the role-making process. *Organizational Behavior and Human Performance,* 13, 46–78.

Douglas, C. A., & McCauley, C. D. (1999). Formal developmental relationships: A survey of organizational practices. *Human Resource Development Quarterly, 10(3),* 203–220.

Dreyfus, C. (2008), "Identifying competencies that predict effectiveness of R & D managers," *Journal of Management Development,* Vol. 27 No. 1, pp. 76–91.

Dutton, J.E. & Heaphy, E.D. (2003). The power of high-quality connections. In K.S. Cameron, J.E. Dutton, & R.E. Quinn (Eds.), *Positive Organizational Scholarship: Foundations of a New Discipline* (pp. 264–278). San Francisco: Berrett-Koehler Publishers.

Feldman, D.C., & Lankau, M.J. (2005). Executive coaching: A review and future research agenda. *Journal of Management,* 31, 829–848.

Fredrickson, B.L. and Losada, M. K. (2005). Positive affect and the complex dynamics of human flourishing. *American Psychologist,* 60, 678–86.

Frost, P., Dutton, J., Worline, M, & Wilson, A. (2000). Narratives of compassion in organizations. In S. Fineman (Ed.), *Emotions in organizations* (pp. 25–45). Beverly Hills, CA: Sage Publications.

Goleman, D. (1998). Working with Emotional Intelligence. New York: Bantam.

Goleman, D., Boyatzis, R.E., McKee, A. (2002). *Primal Leadership: Realizing the Power of Emotional Intelligence.* Boston, MA: Harvard Business School Press.

Graen, G., Novak, M., & Sommerkamp, P. (1982). The effects of leader-member exchange and job design on productivity and job satisfaction: Testing a dual attachment model. *Organizational Behavior and Human Performance,* 30, 109–131.

Graen, G.B., & Scandura, T. A. (1987). Toward a psychology of dyadic organizing. *Research in Organizational Behavior,* 9: 175–208.

Graen, G.B., & Uhl-Bien, M. (1995). Relationship-based approach to leadership: Development of leader-member exchange (LMX) theory of leadership over 25 years: Applying a multi-level multi-domain perspective. *Leadership Quarterly,* 6: 219–247.

Hall, J.A. & Bernieri, F.J. (2001). *Interpersonal sensitivity: Theory and measurement.* Mahwah, NJ: Lawrence Erlbaum Associates.

Hamilton, E. (1942). *Mythology: Timeless Tales of Gods and Heroes.* Boston, MA: Little, Brown, & Co.

Higgins M.C. & Kram, K.E. (2001). Reconceptualizing mentoring at work: a developmental network perspective. *Academy of Management Review,* 26: 264–288.

Hudson, F.M. (1999). *The Handbook of Coaching.* San Francisco, CA: Jossey-Bass.

Joo, B.K. (2005). Executive coaching: A conceptual framework from an integrative review of practice and research. *Human Resource Development Review,* 4, 462–488.

Kampa-Kokesch, S. & Anderson, M.Z. (2001). Executive coaching: A comprehensive review of the literature. *Consulting Psychology Journal: Practice and Research,* 53(4), 205–228.

Kanov, J.M., Maitlis, S., Worline, M., Dutton, J., Frost, P., & Lilius, J.M. (2004). Compassion in organizational life. *Journal of Applied Behavioral Science.* 47, 808–827.

Kilburg, R.R. (1996). Toward a conceptual understanding and definition of executive coaching. *Consulting Psychology Journal: Practice and Research, 48(2),* 134–144.

Kilburg, R.R. (2000). *Executive Coaching: Developing Managerial Wisdom in a World of Chaos.* Washington, DC: American Psychological Association.

Kolb, D.A., Rubin, I., & Osland, J. (1991). *The Organizational Behavior Reader.* Englewood Cliffs: Prentice Hall.

Kram, K.E. (1985). *Mentoring at Work. Developmental Relationships in Organizational Life.* Glenview, IL: Scott, Foresman.

Kram, K. E. (1996). A relational approach to careers. In D.T. Hall (Ed.). *The Career is Dead: Long Live the Career* (pp. 132–157). San Francisco, CA: Jossey-Bass.

Krieger, J. (2005). Shared Mindfulness. *Journal of Business Communication, 42,* 135–167.

Langer, E.J. (1989). *Mindfulness.* Cambridge, MA: DeCapo Press.

Langer, E.J. (1997). *The Power of Mindful Learning.* Cambridge, MA: Perseus Publishing.

Langer, E.J., & Moldoveanu, M. (2000). The construct of mindfulness. *Journal of Social Issues, 56,* 1–9.

Leonard, D. (2008), "The impact of learning goals on emotional, social and cognitive competency development," *Journal of Management Development,* Vol. 27 No. 1, pp. 109–128.

Levinthal, D., & Rerup, C. (2006). Crossing an Apparent Chasm: Bridging Mindful and Less-mindful Perspectives on Organizational Learning. *Organization Science, 17,* 503–514.

Noe, R.A., Greenberger, D.B., & Wang, S. (2002). Mentoring: What We Should Know and Where We Might Go. In G.R. Ferris (Ed.), *Research in Personal and Human Resources Management* (Vol. 21, pp. 129–174). Oxford, UK: Elsevier Science.

Quick, J.C. and Macik-Frey, M. (2004). Behind the mask: coaching through deep interpersonal communication (2002 Harry and Miriam Levinson Award Address). *Consulting Psychology Journal, 56,* 67–74.

Ragins, B.R. (1999). Gender and mentoring relationships: Definitions, challenges, and strategies. In G.N. Powell (Ed.), *Handbook of Gender and Work* (pp. 347–370). Thousand Oaks, CA: Sage Publications.

Rogers, C.R. (1961). *On becoming a person: A therapist's view of psychotherapy.* Boston: Houghton Mifflin.

Sherman, S., & Freas, A. (2004). The wild west of executive coaching. *Harvard Business Review, 82(11),* 83–90.

Spencer, L.M. Jr. & Spencer, S. (1993). *Competence at Work: Models for Superior Performance.* New York: John Wiley.

Uhl-Bien, M., Graen, G. B., & Scandura, T. A. (2000). Implications of leader-member exchange (LMX) for strategic human resource management systems: Relationships as social capital for competitive advantage. *Research in Personnel and Human Resource Management, 18,* 137–185.

Van Norden, B.W. (1998). Menius, In E. Craig (Ed.). *Routledge Encyclopedia of Philosophy (Vol. 6, pp.302–304).* London: Routledge.

Wasylyshyn, K.M. (2003). Executive coaching: An outcome study. *Consulting Psychology Journal: Practice and Research, 55(2),* 94–106.

Watkins, Michael. (2003). *The First 90 Days: Critical Success Strategies For New Leaders At All Levels.* Boston, MA: Harvard Business School Press.

Weick, K.E., & Sutcliffe, K.M. (2001). *Managing the Unexpected.* San Francisco, CA: Jossey-Bass.

Weick, K., Sutcliffe, K. & Obstfeld, D. (1999). Organizing for high reliability. *Research in Organizational Behavior, 21,* 81–123.

Wheeler, J. V. (2008), "The impact of social environments on emotional, social, and cognitive competency development," *Journal of Management Development,* Vol. 27 No. l, pp. 129–145.

Witherspoon, R. & White, R.P. (1996). Executive Coaching: A Continuum of Roles. *Consulting Psychology Journal: Practice & Research, 48,* 124–133.

CHAPTER

21

Performance Management

On The Folly of Rewarding A, While Hoping for B
Steven Kerr

Performance Management in Global Teams
Bradley L. Kirkman
Deanne N. Den Hartog

Developing employees to have the skills needed to accomplish an organization's strategic goals, reinforcing good performance, providing feedback, and following up on unacceptable performance are all components of high-involvement management and performance management systems. Leaders and managers, in partnership with human resources, have the overall responsibility for ensuring that their organization's performance management system accomplishes its purpose. The responsibility for evaluating employee performance, however, is more likely to be shared with people throughout the organizational hierarchy. Given the growing use of peer evaluations, reverse evaluations (subordinates evaluating bosses), and multirater evaluations (by subordinates, colleagues, supervisors, and sometimes customers and suppliers), companies that are serious about performance management ensure that a wide range of employees possess the necessary skill to foster improved performance in others.

Leaders and managers should analyze the impact of their organization's performance management system and avoid the design flaws that Steven Kerr describes in an updated version of his classic article "On the Folly of Rewarding A, While Hoping for B." Kerr, a senior advisor at Goldman Sachs and former Chief Learning Officer there and at GE, contends that many systems foster the wrong behavior by using rewards incorrectly. A failure to understand social reinforcement theory invariably results in dysfunctional behavior at work. Kerr notes that a common management folly is hoping for teamwork but rewarding individual behavior.

This problem is addressed in "Performance Management in Global Teams," written by Bradley Kirkman, a professor at Texas A&M who focuses on teams, and Deanne Den Hartog, a Dutch scholar at the Amsterdam Business School who worked on the GLOBE project studying international leadership. They provide guidance on performance management and explain how cultural dilemmas can be avoided.

ON THE FOLLY OF REWARDING A, WHILE HOPING FOR B*

Steven Kerr

Whether dealing with monkeys, rats, or human beings, it is hardly controversial to state that most organisms seek information concerning what activities are rewarded, and then seek to do (or at least pretend to do) those things, often to the virtual exclusion of activities not rewarded. The extent to which this occurs of course will depend on the perceived attractiveness of the rewards offered, but neither operant nor expectancy theorists would quarrel with the essence of this notion.

Nevertheless, numerous examples exist of reward systems that are fouled up in that the types of behavior rewarded are those which the rewarder is trying to discourage, while the behavior desired is not being rewarded at all.

Fouled-Up Systems

In Politics

Official goals are "purposely vague and general and do not indicate . . . the host of decisions that must be made among alternative ways of achieving official goals and the priority of multiple goals . . . "[1] They usually may be relied on to offend absolutely no one, and in this sense can be considered high acceptance, low quality goals. An example might be "All Americans are entitled to health care." Operative goals are higher in quality but lower in acceptance, since they specify where the money will come from, and what alternative goals will be ignored.

The American citizenry supposedly wants its candidates for public office to set forth operative goals, making their proposed programs clear, and specifying sources and uses of funds. However, since operative goals are lower in acceptance, and since aspirants to public office need acceptance (from at least 50.1 percent of the people), most politicians prefer to speak only of official goals, at least until after the election. They of course would agree to speak at the operative level if "punished" for not doing so. The electorate could do this by refusing to support candidates who do not speak at the operative level. Instead, however, the American voter typically punishes (withholds support from) candidates who frankly discuss where the money will come from, rewards politicians who speak only of official goals, but hopes that candidates (despite the reward system) will discuss the issues operatively.

In War

If some oversimplification may be permitted, let it be assumed that the primary goal of the organization (Pentagon, Luftwaffe, or whatever) is to win. Let it be assumed further that the primary goal of most individuals on the front lines is to get home alive. Then there appears to be an important conflict in goals—personally rational behavior by those at the bottom will endanger goal attainment by those at the top.

But not necessarily! It depends on how the reward system is set up. The Vietnam War was indeed a study of disobedience and rebellion, with terms such as *fragging* (killing one's own commanding officer) and *search and evade* becoming part of the military vocabulary. The difference in subordinates' acceptance of authority between World War II and Vietnam is reported to be considerable, and veterans of the Second World War were often quoted as being outraged at the mutinous actions of many American soldiers in Vietnam.

Consider, however, some critical differences in the reward system in use during the two conflicts. What did the GI in World War II want? To go home. And when did he get to go home? When the war was won! If he disobeyed the orders to clean out the trenches and take the hills, the war would not be won and he would not go home. Furthermore, what were his chances of attaining his goal (getting home alive) if he obeyed the orders compared to his chances if he did not? What is being suggested is that the rational soldier in World War II, whether patriotic or not, probably found it expedient to obey.

Consider the reward system in use in Vietnam. What did the soldier at the bottom want? To go home. And when did he get to go home? When his tour of duty was over! This was the case whether or not the war was won. Furthermore, concerning the relative chance of getting home alive by obeying orders compared to the chance if they were disobeyed, it is worth noting that a mutineer in Vietnam was far more likely to be assigned rest and rehabilitation (on the assumption that fatigue was the cause) than he was to suffer any negative consequence.

In his description of the "zone of indifference," Barnard stated that "a person can and will accept a communication as authoritative only when . . . at the time of his decision, he believes it to be compatible with his personal interests as a whole."[2] In light of the reward system used in Vietnam, wouldn't it have been personally irrational for some orders to have been obeyed? Was not the military implementing a system which rewarded disobedience, while hoping that soldiers (despite the reward system) would obey orders?

In Medicine

Theoretically, physicians can make either of two types of error, and intuitively one seems as bad as the other. Doctors can pronounce patients sick when they are actually well (a type 1 error), thus causing them needless anxiety and expense, curtailment of enjoyable foods and activities, and even physical danger by subjecting them to needless medication and surgery. Alternately, a doctor can label a sick person well (a type 2 error), and thus avoid treating what may be a serious, even fatal ailment. It might be natural to conclude that physicians seek to minimize both types of error.

Such a conclusion would be wrong. It has been estimated that numerous Americans have been afflicted with iatrogenic (physician caused) illnesses.[3] This occurs when the doctor is approached by someone complaining of a few stray symptoms. The doctor classifies and organizes these symptoms, gives them a name, and obligingly tells the patient what further symptoms may be expected. This information often acts as a self-fulfilling prophecy, with the result that from that day on the patient for all practical purposes is sick.

Why does this happen? Why are physicians so reluctant to sustain a type 2 error (pronouncing a sick person well) that they will tolerate many type 1 errors? Again, a look at the reward system is needed. The punishments for a type 1 error are real: guilt, embarrassment, and the threat of a malpractice suit. On the other hand, a type 1 error (labeling a well person sick) is a much safer and conservative approach to medicine in today's litigious society. Type 1 errors also are likely to generate increased income and a stream of steady customers who, being well in a limited physiological sense, will not embarrass the doctor by dying abruptly. Fellow physicians and the general public therefore are really rewarding type 1 errors while hoping fervently that doctors will try not to make them.

A current example of rewarding type 1 errors is provided by Broward County, Florida, where an elderly or disabled person facing a competency hearing is evaluated by three court-appointed experts who get paid much more *for the same examination* if the person is ruled to be incompetent. For example, psychiatrists are paid $325 if they judge someone to be incapacitated, but earn only $125 if the person is judged competent. Court-appointed attorneys in Broward also earn more—$325 as opposed to $175—if their clients lose than if they win. Are you surprised to learn that, of 598 incapacity proceedings initiated and completed in the county in 1993, 570 ended with a verdict of incapacitation?[4]

In Universities

Society hopes that professors will not neglect their teaching responsibilities but rewards them almost entirely for research and publications. This is most true at the large and prestigious universities. Clichés such as "good research and good teaching go together" notwithstanding, professors often find that they must choose between teaching and research-oriented activities when allocating their time. Rewards for good teaching are usually limited to outstanding teacher awards, which are given to only a small percentage of good teachers and usually bestow little money and fleeting prestige. Punishments for poor teaching are also rare.

Rewards for research and publications, on the other hand, and punishments for failure to accomplish these, are common. Furthermore, publication-oriented résumés usually will be well-received at other universities, whereas teaching credentials, harder to document and quantify, are much less transferable. Consequently it is rational for university professors to concentrate on research, even to the detriment of teaching and at the expense of their students.

By the same token, it is rational for students to act based upon the goal displacement[5] which has occurred within universities concerning what they are rewarded for. If it is assumed that a primary goal of a university is to transfer knowledge from teacher to student, then grades become identifiable as a means toward that goal, serving as motivational, control, and feedback devices to expedite the knowledge transfer. Instead, however, the grades themselves have become much more important for entrance to graduate school, successful employment, tuition refunds, and parental respect, than the knowledge or lack of knowledge they are supposed to signify.

It therefore should come as no surprise that we find fraternity files for examinations, term paper writing services, and plagiarism. Such activities constitute a personally rational response to a reward system which pays off for grades rather than knowledge. These days, reward systems—specifically, the growing threat of lawsuits—encourage teachers to award students high grades, even if they aren't earned. For example:

> When Andy Hansen brought home a report card with a disappointing C in math, his parents . . . sued his teacher. . . . After a year and six different appeals within the school district, another year's worth of court proceedings, $4,000 in legal fees paid by the Hansens, and another $8,500 by the district . . . the C stands. Now the student's father, auto dealer Mike Hansen, says he plans to take the case to the State Court of Appeals. "We went in and tried to make a deal: They wanted a C, we wanted an A, so why not compromise on a B?" Mike Hansen said. "But they dug in their heels, and here we are."[6]

In Consulting

It is axiomatic that those who care about a firm's well-being should insist that the organization get fair value for its expenditures. Yet it is commonly known that firms seldom bother to evaluate a new TQM, employee empowerment program, or whatever, to see if the company is getting its money's worth. Why? Certainly it is not because people have not pointed out that this situation exists; numerous practitioner-oriented articles are written each year on just this point.

One major reason is that the individuals (in human resources, or organization development) who would normally be responsible for conducting such evaluations are the same ones often charged with introducing the change effort in the first place. Having convinced top management to spend money, say, on outside consultants, they usually are quite animated afterwards in collecting rigorous vignettes and anecdotes about how successful the program was. The last thing many desire is a formal, revealing evaluation. Although members of top management may actually hope for such systematic evaluation, their reward systems continue to reward ignorance in this area. And if the HR department abdicates its responsibility, who is to step into the breach? The consultants themselves? Hardly! They are likely to be too busy collecting anecdotal "evidence" of their own, for use on their next client.

In Sports

Most coaches disdain to discuss individual accomplishments, preferring to speak of teamwork, proper attitude, and one-for-all spirit. Usually, however, rewards are distributed according to individual performance. The college basketball player who passes the ball to teammates instead of shooting will not compile impressive scoring statistics and is less likely to be drafted by the pros. The ballplayer who hits to right field to advance the runners will win neither the batting nor home run titles, and will be offered smaller raises. It therefore is rational for players to think of themselves first, and the team second.

In Government

Consider the cost-plus contract or its next of kin, the allocation of next year's budget as a direct function of this year's expenditures—a clear-cut example of a fouled-up reward system. It probably is conceivable that those who award such budgets and contracts really hope for economy and prudence in spending. It is obvious, however, that adopting the proverb "to those who spend shall more be given" rewards not economy, but spending itself.

In Business

The past reward practices of a group health claims division of a large eastern insurance company provides another rich illustration. Attempting to measure and reward accuracy in paying surgical claims, the firm systematically kept track of the number of returned checks and letters of complaint received from policyholders. However, underpayments were likely to provoke cries of outrage from the insured, while overpayments often were accepted in courteous silence. Since it was often impossible to tell from the physician's statement which of two surgical procedures, with different allowable benefits, was performed, and since writing for clarifications would have interfered with other standards used by the firm concerning percentage of claims paid within two days of receipt, the new hire in more than one claims section was soon acquainted with the informal norm: "When in doubt, pay it out!"

This situation was made even worse by the firm's reward system. The reward system called for annual merit increases to be given to all employees, in one of the following three amounts:

1. If the worker was "outstanding" (a select category, into which no more than two employees per section could be placed): 5 percent
2. If the worker was "above average" (normally all workers not "outstanding" were so rated): 4 percent
3. If the worker committed gross acts of negligence and irresponsibility for which he or she might be discharged in many other companies: 3 percent

Now, since the difference between the five percent theoretically attainable through hard work and the four percent attainable merely by living until the review date is small, many employees were rather indifferent to the possibility of obtaining the extra one percent reward. In addition, since the penalty for error was a loss of only one percent, employees tended to ignore the norm concerning indiscriminant payments.

However, most employees were not indifferent to a rule which stated that, should absences or latenesses total three or more in any six-month period, the entire four or five percent due at the next merit review must be forfeited. In this sense, the firm was *hoping* for performance, while *rewarding* attendance. What it got, of course, was attendance. (If the absence/lateness rule appears to the reader to be stringent, it really wasn't. The company counted "times" rather than "days" absent, and a ten-day absence therefore counted the same as one lasting two days. A worker in danger of accumulating a third absence within six months merely had to remain ill— away from work—during a second absence until the first absence was more than six months old. The limiting factor was that at some point salary ceases, and sickness benefits take over. This was usually sufficient to get the younger workers to return, but for those with 20 or more years' service, the company provided sickness benefits of 90 percent of normal salary, tax-free! Therefore . . .)

Thanks to the U.S. government, even the reporting of wrongdoing has been corrupted by an incredibly incompetent reward system that calls for whistleblowing employees to collect up to 30 percent *of the amount of a fraud* without a stated limit. Thus prospective whistleblowers are encouraged to delay reporting a fraud, even to actively participate in its continuance, in order to run up the total and, thus, their percentage of the take.

I'm quite sure that by now the reader has thought of numerous examples in his or her own experience which qualify as "folly." However, just in case, Table 1 presents some additional examples well worth pondering.

Causes

Extremely diverse instances of systems which reward behavior A although the rewarder apparently hopes for behavior B have been given. These are useful to illustrate the breadth and magnitude of the phenomenon, but the diversity increases the difficulty of determining commonalities and establishing causes. However, the following four general factors may be pertinent to an explanation of why fouled-up reward systems seem to be so prevalent.

Table 1   Common Management Reward Follies

We hope for . . .	But we often reward . . .
• Long-term growth; environmental responsibility	• Quarterly earnings
• Teamwork	• Individual effort
• Setting challenging "stretch" objectives	• Achieving goals; "making the numbers"
• Downsizing; rightsizing; delayering; restructuring	• Adding staff; adding budget; adding Hay points
• Commitment to total quality	• Shipping on schedule, even with defects
• Candor; surfacing bad news early	• Reporting good news, whether it's true or not; agreeing with the boss, whether or not (s)he's right

1. *Fascination with an "Objective" Criterion.* Many managers seek to establish simple, quantifiable standards against which to measure and reward performance. Such efforts may be successful in highly predictable areas within an organization, but are likely to cause goal displacement when applied anywhere else.

2. *Overemphasis on Highly Visible Behaviors.* Difficulties often stem from the fact that some parts of the task are highly visible while other parts are not. For example, publications are easier to demonstrate than teaching, and scoring baskets and hitting home runs are more readily observable than feeding team-mates and advancing base runners. Similarly, the adverse consequences of pro-nouncing a sick person well are more visible than those sustained by labeling a well person sick. Team-building and creativity are other examples of behav-iors which may not be rewarded simply because they are hard to observe.

3. *Hypocrisy.* In some of the instances described, the rewarder may have been getting the desired behavior, notwithstanding claims that the behavior was not desired. For example, in many jurisdictions within the United States, judges' campaigns are funded largely by defense attorneys, while prosecutors are legally barred from making contributions. This doesn't do a whole lot to help judges to be "tough on crime" though, ironically, that's what their campaigns inevitably promise.

4. *Emphasis on Morality or Equity Rather Than Efficiency.* Sometimes consid-eration of other factors prevents the establishment of a system which rewards behavior desired by the rewarder. The felt obligation of many Americans to vote for one candidate or another, for example, may impair their ability to withhold support from politicians who refuse to discuss the issues. Similarly, the concern for spreading the risks and costs of wartime military service may outweigh the advantage to be obtained by committing personnel to combat until the war is over. The 1994 Clinton health plan, the Americans with Disabilities Act, and many other instances of proposed or recent governmental intervention provide outstanding examples of systems that reward inefficiency, presumably in support of some higher objective.

Altering the Reward System

Managers who complain about lack of motivation in their workers might do well to consider the possibility that the reward systems they have installed are paying off for behavior other than what they are seeking. This, in part, is what happened in Vietnam, and this is what regularly frustrates societal efforts to bring about honest politicians and civic-minded managers.

A first step for such managers might be to explore what types of behavior are currently being rewarded. Chances are excellent that these managers will be sur-prised by what they find—that their firms are not rewarding what they assume they are. In fact, such undesirable behavior by organizational members as they have ob-served may be explained largely by the reward systems in use.

This is not to say that all organizational behavior is determined by formal rewards and punishments. Certainly it is true that in the absence of formal reinforce-ment some soldiers will be patriotic, some players will be team oriented, and some employees will care about doing their job well. The point, however, is that in such cases the rewarder is not causing the behavior desired but is only a fortunate by-stander. For an organization to act upon its members, the formal reward system should positively reinforce desired behavior, not constitute an obstacle to be overcome.

Postscript

An irony about this article's being designated a management classic is that numerous people claim to have read and enjoyed it, but I wonder whether there was much in it that they didn't know. I believe that most readers already know, and act on in their non-work lives, the principles that underlie this article. For example, when we tell our daughter (who is about to cut her birthday cake) that her brother will select the first piece, or inform our friends before a meal that separate checks will be brought at the end, or tell the neighbor's boy that he will be paid five dollars for cutting the lawn after we inspect the lawn, we are making use of prospective rewards and punishments to cause other people to care about our own objectives. Organizational life may seem to be more complex, but the principles are the same.

Another irony attached to this "classic" is that it almost didn't see the light of day. It was rejected for presentation at the Eastern Academy of Management and was only published in the *Academy of Management Journal* because Jack Miner, its editor at the time, broke a tie between two reviewers. Nobody denied the relevance of the content, but reviewers were quite disturbed by the tone of the manuscript, and therefore its appropriateness for an academic audience. A compromise was reached whereby I added a bit of the great academic cure-all, data (Table 1 in the original article, condensed and summarized in this update), and a copy editor strangled some of the life from my writing style. In this respect, I would like to acknowledge the extremely competent editorial work performed on this update by John Veiga and his editorial staff. I am grateful to have had the opportunity to revisit the article, and hope the reader has enjoyed it also.

Endnotes

1. C. Perrow, "The Analysis of Goals in Complex Organizations," *Readings on Modern Organizations*, ed. A. Etzioni (Upper Saddle River, NJ: Prentice Hall, 1969). 66.

2. C. I. Barnard, *The Functions of the Executive* (Cambridge, MA: Harvard University Press, 1964). 165.

3. L. H. Garland, "Studies of the Accuracy of Diagnostic Procedures," *American Journal Roentgenological, Radium Therapy Nuclear Medicine 82* (1959): 25–38; and T. J. Scheff, "Decision Rules, Types of Error, and Their Consequences in Medical Diagnosis," *Mathematical Explorations in Behavioral Science*, eds. F. Massarik and P. Ratoosh (Homewood, IL: Irwin, 1965).

4. *Miami Herald*, May 8, 1994. 1a, 10a.

5. Goal displacement results when means become ends in themselves and displace the original goals. See P. M. Blau and W. R. Scott, *Formal Organizations* (San Francisco, CA: Chandler, 1962).

6. "San Francisco Examiner," reported in *Fortune*, February 7, 1994. 161.

PERFORMANCE MANAGEMENT IN GLOBAL TEAMS*

Bradley L. Kirkman

Deanne N. Den Hartog

When organizations globalize, most of the work dedicated to this effort gets done through the collaboration and coordination of many people located in different nations. Often this collaboration takes the form of global work teams. In fact, teams form the basic building blocks of most global organizations. Globalization rarely occurs without teamwork. The "global" aspect of teamwork in organizations adds

*Reprinted with permission from *The Blackwell Handbook of Global Management: A Guide to Managing Complexity* (Oxford, UK: Blackwell, 2004): 250–272.

another layer of complexity to the complicated overall globalization process. Thus, there is a pressing need to understand the role of teamwork in globalization and what factors account for successful global teams.

The purpose of this chapter is to discuss the performance management of teams in an international context. Performance management is problematic in teams of this type because members are likely to bring widely disparate viewpoints about appropriate ways to reward, recognize, evaluate, and train and develop global team members. In this chapter, we first discuss the issue of global team-based rewards and recognition. Second, we highlight the difficult task of evaluating contributors in global teams. Finally, we discuss the importance of training and development in global teams. We also note that many of the issues we discuss in this chapter could be applied to other organizational units in addition to teams, such as work units, departments, divisions, whole organizations, or even one-on-one manager–employee relationships. We focus specifically on teams here due to their wide-spread use in global organizing.

Rewards and Recognition in Global Teams

If the many failures of implementing global teams and other organizational forms world wide could be traced to one single factor, that factor would most likely be inappropriate reward and recognition strategies. Key management decisions related to reward and recognition include:

- Should rewards be based on individual performance, team performance, or both?
- What are the important factors to consider when using team-based pay?
- How can recognition be used in addition to, or instead of, monetary rewards?

Rewarding Global Teams

Managers have many choices for rewarding global teams, but generally the issue comes back to two major strategies: rewarding team members based on individual performance and rewarding team members based on team performance as a whole. Whether organizations are team-based or individual-based, most U.S. managers continue to reward organizational contributions individually. Managers and employees set individual goals and develop individual action plans, and individuals are held accountable for their progress toward their goals. This approach becomes problematic in a team setting because often tasks are accomplished by people working together, interdependently, and individual contributions cannot be identified or, in some cases, are non-existent. Consider the example of a software design team whose members frequently exchange the latest versions of a software program. Software may undergo hundreds or even thousands of iterations; and keeping track of specific, individual contributions neither makes sense in their context nor is feasible. This effect may be exacerbated in many global teams because of their reliance on electronic rather than face-to-face communication, which makes assessing individual contributions even more problematic. As Charles Handy stated when discussing virtual organizations, "How do you manage people whom you do not see?"[1]

Individual-based Rewards

Individual rewards, in most cases, do just what they are designed to do. They elicit behaviors that are consistent with an individual's focus and persistence toward his or her own goals, not those of a team, especially in individualist contexts. For example, the piece-rate pay system, so often used in manufacturing settings worldwide, compensates individuals for the number of units they produce daily. The more an individual produces, the more he or she gets paid. Consider what happens, however, when a team-based work system is implemented in such an environment. Imagine the reaction of a piece-rate-compensated worker being asked to step away from his or her work area for an hour or two to help a new team member learn a task. While helping a new team member, the piece-rate worker produces nothing that will be counted and monetarily rewarded. The new team member who needs the help might as well be reaching into the person's wallet or purse and removing money while being helped! Simply put, individual-based pay motivates individual-based behavior. Unless there is an incentive for teamwork, most human beings won't react positively to simply being told to "act like a team."

Team-based Rewards

At the other end of the spectrum are team-based rewards. Incentives are not based on individual output, but on the output or performance of the team as a whole. Such plans might range from 100 percent team-based pay to as little as 5 to 10 percent, but the intent is the same: to reward team members for performing well as a team. As with individual pay, team members receiving team-based pay will likely be motivated consistent with the manner in which they are paid. Unfortunately, what looks good on paper often does not translate well in the workplace. Some companies that have transitioned to team-based pay systems, such as the apparel maker Levi Strauss in the United States, have fared no better, and in some cases, worse than companies retaining their individual-based pay systems. The underlying reason for much of the failure may be social loafing.[2]

Social loafing is a phenomenon best described by the "tug-of-war" example. Tug-of-war usually involves two groups of individuals pulling in opposite directions on a rope, sometimes across an unpleasant middle ground such as a mud pit or pool of water. One team wins when it successfully pulls the other team into or across the unpleasant middle ground. Studies have shown, however, that as more and more individuals are added to either side of the rope, individual pulling efforts decrease.[3] That is, team members who initially used 100 percent of their pulling strength reduce their efforts to, say, 80 or 90 percent, once new team members are added. Team members simply see no reason to continue exerting maximum effort once their comrades have joined the fray. Social loafing effects have been found in a variety of countries.[4]

The same phenomenon can and does occur in the workplace, and team-based pay can be the culprit. When Levi Strauss abandoned their piece-rate pay system and transitioned to 100 percent team-based pay in the United States, chaos erupted.[5] Slower workers and those who took long lunch breaks or slacked off on the job were verbally assaulted and threatened with physical violence. To maintain order, law-enforcement officers were stationed at one Levi Docker's trouser-producing plant in Powell, Tennessee. Higher-performing team members reacted very negatively to fellow members whom they held responsible for reducing the overall compensation of the team. What's worse, the workers who were most negatively affected by team-based pay were the highest performing under the old piece-rate system. Many saw their take-home pay decrease as rewards were tied to team, not individual, performance. Levi's lost many of these high-performing workers to rival factories before abandoning team-based pay.

Combining Individual and Team-based Rewards

So, if the lesson above is not to use either purely individual-based pay or purely team-based pay in global teams, then the answer must lie somewhere in between. Indeed, most team researchers and compensation specialists argue that a combination of individual- and team-based rewards provides a better solution (even though some research has not supported this claim).[6] Companies can use global team-based pay to encourage teamwork, and individual-based pay to stimulate individual accountability and decrease social loafing. However, such a solution raises another question. What is the best combination of individual- and team-based rewards? Should companies strive for a fifty-fifty balance or lean more heavily in one direction or the other? And, if the latter, how does one decide the direction of emphasis? There is no easy answer here, but part of the answer lies in at least five distinct areas: the nature of the task, the stability of team membership, the national culture of the team members, the national and local labor laws affecting employee compensation, and reward options.

Nature of the Task

By nature of the task, we refer specifically to how *interdependent* the tasks are that the team performs. As defined earlier, task or workflow interdependence is defined as the degree of communication and coordination required between team members to get their jobs done.[7] Low task interdependence might occur in a group of project managers who perform their tasks relatively autonomously in different regions of the world, rarely interacting or exchanging information. High task interdependence would be characteristics of a surgical team or a globally distributed team of software design engineers who constantly exchange information and materials to accomplish tasks. A rule of thumb would be the more interdependent the task, the higher the level of team-based rewards relative to individual-based rewards. This rule of thumb also applies to larger work units as in the case of unit-based pay, such as departments or divisions.

Membership Stability

The stability of team membership is another important factor affecting the proportion of team-based rewards used. If there are frequent composition changes in a global team, it will be difficult to accurately assess the contributions of various members and, in turn, reward based on global team performance. For example, Eastman Chemical (Kodak) abandoned team-based rewards because the company found it impossible to draw indisputable lines around "the team."[8] Managers will likely have to move to a higher level of rewards such as unit-level or organization-level rather than team-based rewards to ensure fair compensation when firm team boundaries cannot be drawn. Perhaps team members themselves can be a part of the design and administration of a rewards and recognition program, especially in countries in which employee participation is commonly used and valued.

National Culture of Team Members

One of the strongest points we can make is that the whole concept of performance management will vary across different countries and cultures. For example, reward and recognition systems are often designed based on Western-oriented notions of goal- and task-oriented conceptualizations of work. These work concepts are unlikely to hold up in Eastern cultures or those cultures in which work is not considered a central life interest.[9] It should come as no surprise that in countries like the United States, Great Britain, and Australia, cultural individualism pervades rewards and recognition programs based on individual performance. The notion of "sharing" rewards or credit for an accomplishment is as foreign a notion in individualistic countries as, say, an "employee of the month" award would be in collectivistic countries like Japan, China, or Malaysia.

Should the managers at Levi Strauss have been surprised at the reaction of their U.S. workers when the company tried to implement team-based rewards?

Perhaps hindsight is a luxury here, but not only were Levi's operating in what many consider to be the most individualistic country in the world,[10] they hired workers who assumed they would be working in a piece-rate system. It doesn't take a lot of imagination to guess what type of worker is attracted and selected into this compensation system: individualistic workers who like to work autonomously and be responsible solely for their outcomes. Simply put, a piece-rate system rewards the fastest individual workers. So, not only did Levi's try to implement team-based pay in a highly individualistic country, they tried to implement it in a facility in which they had hired individualistic workers from the most individualist country in the world.[11]

The impact of individualism–collectivism on team and other unit-based reward strategies can also be seen in more collectivist-oriented countries such as China. In China, harmony is seen as a key element in relationships among workers. Maintaining such harmony ensures smoothly running work processes. A research study on human resource management in China showed that few companies in China implement individual-based rewards, as these types of rewards could lead to so-called "red-eye disease" among workers, an expression commonly used in China to refer to jealousy.[12] Jealousy emanating from individual-based pay could constitute a disruption of harmony and, as such, have a negative impact on working relationships and performance.[13] Such interpersonal dynamics in the workplace may undergo some changes in the coming years owing to China's fast paced economic development and increased openness to Western organizations and management styles. However, paying attention to the different meanings and effects that recognition and reward for performance may have in different cultures is important.

Thus, where global teams are concerned, in addition to looking at tasks, managers need to take into account the heterogeneity level or diversity of individualism–collectivism of the team members. That is, if a global team or work unit comprises primarily members from individualist countries such as those in North America, Western Europe, and Australia (all the members are basically the same on the individualism–collectivism dimension), rewards should be based more on individual performance rather than on team or unit performance.[14] Similarly, if a global team or work unit comprises mostly members from collectivist countries such as those in Asia, Latin America, and Africa (again, the members are basically the same on the individualism–collectivism dimension), managers can use a higher proportion of team- or unit-based rewards compared to individual-based rewards. Reinforcing this strategy, there is evidence that supports the link between one's degree of collectivism and a preference for team-based rewards[15] and between individualism and resistance to team-based work systems in general.[16] One could argue, however, that using a large proportion of team-based rewards might again lead to higher levels of social loafing in collectivistic countries. Research does not support this contention, however. In fact, in an experiment designed to compare social loafing between U.S. and Chinese managers, Americans performed less effectively when working in groups compared to working alone.[17] Chinese managers, on the other hand, never demonstrated a social loafing effect and, in fact, performed better in a group than working alone. These results suggest that the lack of a social loafing effect in collectivistic countries provides additional support for using a high proportion of team- or unit-based rewards.

Perhaps the trickiest reward scenario is for a global team that is characterized by a high level of cultural value heterogeneity on the individualism–collectivism dimension. For example, team members comprising a global team from countries such as those in Asia, Europe, Latin America, and North America would likely bring completely different assumptions and beliefs about the appropriateness of team-based rewards. Team leaders should seek the input of heterogeneous teams before designing and implementing a team-based reward system. It is likely that the parameters of such a system will have to be negotiated among team members with such diverse viewpoints on reward appropriateness. The greater the cultural diversity on a global team, the more likely will be the need for team leaders and members to think through the design and implementation of team- or unit-based reward systems. Taking action quickly on these issues may lead to problems.[18]

Labor Laws

Local labor laws on compensation issues must be considered when deciding between individual-based and higher-level rewards. For example, Genencor International, the second largest biotechnology company in the world and a joint venture between Eastman Chemical and Finland's Cultor, has operations in Argentina, Belgium, Finland, and the United States with headquarters in Rochester, New York. In an attempt to streamline their human resource practices worldwide, managers at Genencor wanted to implement team-based pay at all of their facilities. They were not successful in Finland, however, because of local labor laws and active union involvement at the facilities.[19] Finnish labor unions control and regulate salaries by job levels. Managers found that they were required to conform to national and state labor laws and the industry union-based collective bargaining agreements. While some companies, such as General Electric, have been very successful in dealing with unions, especially in Europe, managers should keep in mind that their ability to manipulate compensation to stimulate teamwork and to establish other performance-related pay plans might be constrained by national labor laws.

Reward Options

A final key point is the role of recognition as it relates to team performance. Employees often value gestures of recognition more than pure financial rewards. For example, when asked what is important in a job, most U.S. workers ranked a "full appreciation of work done" and a "feeling of being in on things" much higher than good wages.[20] Many managers all over the world often overlook recognition as a relatively inexpensive way in which to reinforce desired team-related behaviors. Guidelines for using recognition should be similar to those for designing reward systems for teams. Richard Daft tells the story of an American executive in Japan who offered a holiday trip to the top salesperson, but employees showed no interest. After changing the individual recognition program to group recognition in accordance with the collectivist values of the Japanese employees, the entire group reached the sales target.[21] Thus, recognizing teams or units when the members have, on the whole, collectivist values and recognizing individuals when the members have individualist values are good rules of thumb.

In summary, when designing and implementing global team-based reward systems, managers should be certain to:

- use a combination of individual- and team-based rewards to motivate team-related behavior but avoid social loafing (the balance of this combination will vary by culture);
- use a higher level of team-based relative to individual-based rewards the higher the level of task interdependence in a global team;
- use a higher level of individual-based relative to team-based rewards as the instability of global team membership increases;
- use a higher level of team-based rewards the more collectivistic the global team; use a higher level of individual-based rewards the more individualistic the

global team; and when the heterogeneity level of individualism–collectivism in the team is high, reward systems will be best negotiated among team members with such diverse viewpoints on reward appropriateness;

- pay attention to national and state labor laws and the collective bargaining agreements established with industry unions when designing and implementing reward systems for global teams;
- take into account the importance of recognition to supplement or complement tangible reward systems for global teams, tailoring recognition to the cultural values of each global team member.

Performance Evaluation and Appraisal in Global Teams

As with the reward and recognition of global teams and work units, evaluation of individual global team members and teams as a whole has presented many challenges to those who lead global teams. In most organizations, evaluations are often tied to important rewards such as promotions or highly visible assignments. Thus, there is a clear link between performance evaluation and rewards: in order to be able to design effective performance-related pay systems, one must first be able to measure performance. This holds for both global team and individual-based systems. One of the most frequently observed reasons why performance-related pay systems fail to reach the desired results is that the criteria for performance evaluation are unclear or unfair.[22] Key decisions in global team-based performance appraisal include:

- On what additional knowledge, skills, and abilities (KSAs) should workers be evaluated when they are working in a global team versus individually?
- Who should have input into global team member evaluations (supervisor, peers, customers)?
- How can managers ensure the perceived fairness of the performance evaluation process in multicultural global teams?

Appraisals

Taking the knowledge, skills, and abilities decision first, evaluating global team members on team-relevant KSAs is another way to reinforce and motivate teamwork in organizations in addition to monetary rewards and recognition. There is a link between good reward systems and appraisals; timely and appropriate rewards require an appraisal system that ensures performance is measured adequately. As such, appraisal acts as a basis for the reward.

Effective appraisal systems enable the assessment of task performance and monitor whether people are good team players whose behavior is conducive to the effectiveness of the entire team. Effective appraisal systems should both reward good team players and discourage behaviors that are not conducive to global team effectiveness.[23] Each organization is responsible for conducting job analyses to determine the specific KSAs needed for each global team. Beyond task-specific KSAs are the more general, process-oriented ones, such as conflict resolution, collaborative problem-solving, communication, decision-making, and team member support. In most studies of team effectiveness, these KSAs have been found to be critical to team success.[24] Such processes vary by culture and country.

U.S. researchers have found that conflict about task-related issues (rather than interpersonal-related issues) enhances team performance, especially the quality of team decision-making.[25] Thus, for teams composed predominantly of U.S. and other Western members, managers would be encouraged to stimulate and encourage this type of conflict to increase team performance. There are cultural differences, however, that might make this advice problematic for non-Western global team members. For example, the concept of "face-saving" is related to group harmony and conversational indirectness. In Eastern cultures such as China, Japan, and the Philippines, the loss of face, or public humiliation, can result from receiving negative feedback.[26] Thus, while team members in the United States might openly confront one another in meetings and question the rationale behind decisions in order to enhance decisionmaking, such behaviors in cultures that value face might be cause for extreme shame, ending in retaliation or possibly physical violence such as the Indonesian ship-worker who chased his boss into his quarters with an axe after being publicly berated in front of other crew members.[27]

Evaluation Input

Another key decision in global team-based performance appraisals is who should have input into the evaluation process. Accompanying the increase in the use of 360° feedback, or getting evaluation input from one's boss, peers, and subordinates, in the United States has been the use of peer evaluations in teams.[28] The logic for their use is, who can better assess the performance of team members than the people who work with each other on a daily basis?

Rather than relying solely on just one source of feedback for team member evaluations, many companies integrate multiple sources similar to a 360°-feedback program. Nancy Kurland and Diane Bailey, researchers who study telecommuting, or workers who do their jobs from remote locations and communicate electronically, stated:

> A major challenge for [global team] managers is their inability to physically observe their employees' performance. They question, "How do you measure productivity, build trust, and manage people who are physically out of sight?" If a manager can't see her subordinates in action, then she can't note where the employee is struggling and where he is strong . . . monitoring and measuring [employee] performance remain problematic and a source of concern.[29]

Clearly, assessing the performance of global team members who are geographically dispersed is a challenge. One company on the cutting edge of global virtual team performance evaluation and assessment is Sabre, Inc., the Dallas/Fort Worth, Texas-based reservation company.[30] Sabre provides computer reservation systems for American Airlines, United Airlines, and over 60,000 travel agents in 114 countries. Sabre is also a majority owner of Travelocity.com, the on-line reservation service, and uses global virtual teams in part of its North American Canadian and U.S. operations. Sabre has built comprehensive performance review system, which uses actual customer satisfaction ratings as part of an overall "balanced scorecard"[31] measure, or a measure that includes both financial and non-financial performance indicators, of global team effectiveness. Managers assess individual contributions to team effectiveness by monitoring electronic communications and by systematically collecting data from peers and direct reports using the 360° format. Performance data provide a solid foundation for recognizing and rewarding team and individual performance, developing new training programs to assist virtual teams, and identifying individual team members who could benefit from off-line mentoring and coaching. As one manager at Sabre stated, "Most everyone's work is measured in the results they produce and through statistics, and it can all be pulled out systematically for each individual."[32] For global teams at Sabre, U.S. and Canadian team members can be judged more on what they actually do rather than on what they appear to be doing.

Assessment Across Cultures

Cultural values that would be likely to affect how global team members in different countries give each other feedback are the individualism–collectivism, power distance, and uncertainty avoidance dimensions and the concepts of harmony, assertiveness, and face. Research has shown that collectivists give more generous evaluations to fellow team members than do individualists, and this is especially true if the team member is an in-group rather than an out-group member.[33] In-group members are similar others such as family and close friends while out-group members lie outside these preferred groups. Thus, fair and unbiased peer evaluations may be more difficult to obtain when collectivistic global team members have to rate members of their in-group, especially in face-to-face, rather than virtual teams in which the pressures for conformity may be higher.

Power distance is the second cultural value likely to affect peer evaluations in global teams. Power distance refers to the extent to which power differences and status inequalities in a society are tolerated. In high power-distance countries such as China, Mexico, and the Philippines, subordinates are typically more reluctant to challenge their supervisors than are employees in low power-distance countries such as Finland, Israel, and the United States. In line with this, employees in high power-distance cultures were shown to be more fearful in expressing disagreement with their managers.[34] If global teams are composed of members of different status levels, and lower-status team members are asked to evaluate the performance of higher-status members, evaluations are likely to be positively skewed, especially for face-to-face teams. People in high power-distance cultures are likely to be reluctant to provide negative feedback to superiors, and the acceptability of the idea that subordinates would be allowed to provide such ratings is likely to be less in high power-distance cultures, as this may be perceived to threaten status positions.

Uncertainty avoidance refers to cultures in which members shun ambiguity.[35] People in such cultures want things to be predictable and easy to interpret, and rituals such as elaborate planning and control systems are put into place to ensure this. The concept of lifelong employment in Japan is a good example of how organizations can reduce uncertainty. Looking at performance appraisal, one would expect a much higher degree of formalization in high uncertainty avoidance cultures. The performance appraisal system is likely to be spelled out in more detail, and there are more regulations and procedures in place, ensuring that complaints or grievances are handled through a predesigned structure. For example, German culture ranks high on uncertainty avoidance and research has shown that German employees typically prefer formalized performance evaluations such as clear goals, time frames, and exact measurements.[36]

The emphasis on maintaining harmony found in several Eastern cultures may lead to skewed peer and subordinate ratings in a positive direction, since global team members would be reluctant to jeopardize their relationships with fellow members. Similarly, team members from cultures that are typically highly assertive, aggressive, and dominant in social relationships are more likely to provide negative feedback than those in less assertive cultures.[37] People in highly assertive cultures such as the United States prefer direct feedback and communication and have a "tell it like it is" mentality. For example, at General Electric, all employees are ranked from the top to the bottom of the organization. The bottom 10 percent may be given either an opportunity to improve, or outplacement services. Former CEO Jack Welch argues that such a system is appropriate because softening feedback for under-performing workers is unfair to them and akin to outright lying because it might prevent them from finding opportunities that are more suitable. In contrast, in many Asian cultures the subtleties of conversational indirectness are preferred.[38] We do not want to give the impression that directness is the one best way to provide feedback in order to enhance performance in global teams. The real issue here is maintaining harmony and how that may affect peer and subordinate ratings in global teams. Directness may not be as appropriate in Eastern cultures, but subtle approaches may be just as effective because the elaborate networks that exist in these cultures will ensure that everyone will already know relevant performance feedback.

Similar to the effect it has on open conflict, saving face will likely prevent open discussion of individual global team member performance by fellow members, especially in face-to-face teams. However, this does not mean that peer feedback cannot be used on teams that have members that value saving face. At Motorola in the Philippines, for example, issues regarding team performance are raised in more general form in team meetings.[39] No one is singled out personally, but often this is enough to motivate the under-performing team members to step up their efforts. When performance appraisal data must be collected from global team members, it can be collected anonymously and presented in summary form to mask authorship. Such a strategy has worked very effectively for Motorola's teams in the Philippines and in other countries that value face-saving.

Fairness Across Cultures

The third and final issue for performance evaluation and appraisal in global teams is ensuring perceptions of fairness or justice in the performance appraisal process. In Western management thought, justice in organizations has generally been conceived of as having three dimensions:

- *Distributive justice*—the perceived fairness of the distribution of outcomes. This type of justice emanated from equity theory.[40]
- *Procedural justice*—the perceived fairness of the criteria used to make decisions regarding the distribution of outcomes, including voice, or the opportunity for the employee to have a say in decisions.[41]
- *Interactional justice*—the perceived fairness of how decisions are communicated, including adequate explanations and consideration of employee welfare by managers.[42]

While the perceived fairness of evaluation procedures has received considerable attention in dyadic manager–employee settings,[43] there has been considerably less attention paid to the perceived fairness of *team-based* evaluation settings.[44] One recent study did examine general employee justice concerns during an implementation of self-managing work teams in two U.S. *Fortune* 50 organizations.[45] Many employee concerns centered on issues of the fairness of team-based performance appraisals. Open-ended comments from the study included: "Will peer reviews be fair and objective?"; "Who will fairly judge my contribution to the business?"; and "I hate peer ratings because it is a personality contest and not a question of merit." Clearly, employees in the United States were very concerned about the fairness of team-based performance appraisals. In addition, these employees expressed the desire to have voice in the performance appraisal process. This finding was echoed at the dyadic level by Jerald

Greenberg who found that U.S. employee perceptions of procedural justice in the appraisal decision were based on, among other elements, the ability to rebut or challenge a supervisor's appraisal.[46]

Owing to cultural differences, there are reasons to believe that global team members may have different mental models regarding what constitutes a fair team-based performance appraisal. In other cultural contexts, employees may not conceive of distributive, procedural, and interactional justice in the same manner.[47] For example, while Western conceptualizations of procedural justice include the ability to challenge or rebut decisions, research has shown that in China, procedural justice does not include this component.[48]

The most likely explanation for this difference is the cultural value of power distance.[49] While power distance was originally conceived of as a country- or nation-level phenomenon,[50] like many of the other cultural values, researchers have adopted this dimension to explain variations in individual behavior. For example, Joel Brockner and his colleagues found that when employees did not have a say in managerial decisions, they were less committed to their organizations. However, this effect was much more pronounced in lower power-distance cultures such as the United States and Germany than in high power-distance cultures such as China, Mexico, and Hong Kong.[51] It has also been shown that the relationships between procedural justice and trust in supervisors and between distributive justice and psychological (implied) contract fulfillment were stronger for those lower, rather than higher, in power distance.[52] Simon Lam and his colleagues found similar results with justice–work outcome relationships, with the effects of fairness stronger for those lower, rather than higher, in power distance.[53]

These findings suggest that managers should pay attention to cultural value differences especially power distance, when designing and implementing global team-based performance appraisal systems if team members are to perceive them as fair. This is important because a number of studies have shown that employees who perceive managerial decisions as unjust will react unfavorably.[54] Unfortunately, at times there may be very little managers can do to ensure fairness in employee work assignments in global teams. For example, at ItemField, a New York-based business-to-business software developer, new-hire Israeli team members located in Israel who typically do not work on Friday were told that they had to be on call on Fridays to support the U.S. sales force.[55] Even though Israeli employees were alerted in advance, business demands limited the actions that U.S. managers took to enhance fairness perceptions among their Israeli global team members.

There is also evidence that the performance evaluation process may be fairer (less biased) in globally distributed teams versus face-to-face teams. Differences in such demographic factors as race, gender, and age can lower performance ratings for employees who differ in these aspects from their bosses,[56] and for team members who are different from team leaders.[57] However, when team leaders do not see team members on a daily basis, the opportunities for bias to enter the performance appraisal process may be fewer. In addition, contamination of evaluations by perceptual biases is less likely when team leaders have extensive objective data at their disposal.[58]

When designing and implementing global team-based performance evaluation and appraisal systems, managers should be certain to:

- reward good team players but also discourage behaviors that are not conducive to global team effectiveness;
- in addition to determining task-specific KSAs, include evaluations of global team processes such as conflict resolution, collaborative problem-solving, communication, decision-making, and team member support;

- use multidimensional, balanced performance evaluation systems that include a mixture of objective and subjective ratings such as 360° feedback and altering peer feedback systems based on cultural differences, along with technology-based measures to document global team member achievements such as e-mail and electronic team meeting archives; customer surveys and team member input;
- enhance the fairness of global team peer evaluations by: (1) attempting to broaden team member in-groups by stressing value similarity among members; (2) standardizing the appraisal system by training peer raters and using job-relevant rating scales; (3) enhancing the fairness of peer evaluations by informing employees of when and how ratings will be collected; (4) rewarding team members on their ability and willingness to provide accurate ratings that differentiate between low and high performers; and (5) assessing team members on the individualism-collectivism dimension in order to anticipate potential bias in peer ratings.[59]

Training and Development in Global Teams

One of the most important facets of effective global team implementation is the effective use of team training and development. Working in global teams can be a very foreign concept to many employees, and if managers decide that teams are appropriate, they need guidance in order to effectively shape appropriate global team behaviors. One facet that is often missing from global team training is the inclusion of the whole team in hands-on capability development.[60] Global teams should be treated as a whole unit and training should be applied as the team performs actual job-related tasks.[61] As a result, the value of the training is established in the context of the work that the team does. Key questions to consider with regard to training and development include:

- What are the best methods for training and development in global team-based organizations?
- What should global team members be trained to do?
- How can training be leveraged to increase the amount of global team learning and flexibility?

Best Methods

Regarding methods or techniques for global team training and development, there are at least three general techniques used by training specialists to enhance team member abilities. First, there is the cognitive style, which normally involves traditional classroom instruction in which a trainer covers basic principles of team operation such as forming a team charter, setting ground rules for teams, or managing conflict. Second, there is the behavioral style, or experiential learning, which can involve immersing team members in situations similar to those they are likely to face in their actual jobs. Such simulations might include performing a complex task in a limited amount of time, purposefully engaging in conflict over a valued resource, or role-playing a key event in a team's life cycle. Finally, there is the affective style, which typically involves some level of emotional involvement on the part of team members. This may take the form of heart-to-heart talks between team members such as intimate self-disclosure, or intense personal feedback between global team members guided by experienced facilitators.

With at least three possible methods of training and development, the question still remains: What is the best method to use? The answer is, not surprisingly, all three. Since human beings differ in the manner in which they learn most effectively, that is, some are classroom learners, some have to experience it before they understand, and still others need to be moved emotionally to internalize key learnings, most training and development specialists advocate a combination of these three techniques to enhance the transfer of training for all global team members.

As stated, people differ in the way they learn most effectively. An individual's learning strategy can be seen as a predisposition to use certain types of learning behavior.[62] For example, one can distinguish between *surface* (instruction-oriented) and *deep* (meaning-oriented) learning strategies, the latter fostering managers' career success.[63] The different ways in which people learn reflect different existing modes of thought or cognitive styles. The most widely recognized distinction in this area is between *analytical*, that is, logical, sequential information processing, and *intuitive*, in other words, more integrative and nonlinear thinking styles.[64] There are also cross-cultural differences to be considered in the way people think and prefer to learn; however, the evidence regarding cross-cultural differences in these cognitive styles is somewhat mixed. Whereas some propose a contrast between the "analytic West" and the "intuitive East," many studies find different patterns. In a six-nation study among managers from organizations in both the public and private sectors and management students, the most integrative and nonlinear thinking was seen among managers from the most developed countries (the U.K., Australia, Hong Kong, Singapore), whereas an emphasis on logical and sequential thinking was seen in the developing and Arab countries (Jordan, Nepal).[65] The explanation for the differences may lie in the increasing complexity of management problems in many organizations in highly developed countries. Such high complexity may call for integrative, non-linear thinking.

What about cross-cultural differences in learning preferences? According to Hofstede, people in uncertainty avoidant cultures have been programmed from childhood to feel comfortable in structured environments.[66] Such differences in the need for structure are also reflected in the learning environment. In cultures high on uncertainty avoidance (Germany) one thus often finds structured learning situations with precise objectives, detailed arrangements, and strict timetables. People prefer tasks with a correct answer that they can find and like to be rewarded for accuracy. On the other hand, those from cultures low on uncertainty avoidance (United Kingdom) are more likely to prefer less structure. They prefer open-ended questions, vague objectives and no timetables. They do not believe that there should be a single correct answer and expect to be rewarded for originality.[67] Similar patterns may be expected in a training situation, where people from cultures high on uncertainty avoidance are likely to prefer much more structured processes and assignments compared with people from cultures low on uncertainty avoidance.

Another cultural dimension to consider is power distance. In cultures high on power distance, the role and status of the teacher or trainer are likely to be different from such a role in cultures low on power distance. In cultures high on power distance, the teacher-student relationship is essentially an unequal relationship, in which the more powerful party (teacher) is treated with respect and hardly ever openly receives uninvited criticism from the less powerful party (students). The process is likely to be teacher-centered, with the teacher initiating conversation and deciding on what is to be taught. In contrast, in cultures low on power distance, teachers and students have a more equal relationship. The process is more student-centered: students take more initiative and decide on and pursue what they want to learn. Open communication, questioning teachers, and arguing their opinion is the rule rather than the exception.[68] Again, similar patterns may be expected in a training situation.

Training Content

Beyond the methods and techniques used for training and the learning styles of trainees, the second key issue is the actual content of the training for team members. As discussed in our section on evaluation (performance appraisal), team-relevant knowledge, skills, and abilities (KSAs) must be identified by each organization for each job, so that global team members will know and can be trained for the most job-relevant KSAs. Also relevant are interpersonal processes such as communication, decision-making, and conflict resolution, all critical for global team success. In addition to KSAs and global team processes, development of self-management skills among global team members is important. Since the purpose of many global teams is to be proactive and take on the many responsibilities traditionally reserved for management, starting team members down the path of self-management to increase global team effectiveness is critically important.

The main question then becomes: How much autonomy is appropriate for most global teams? There are several contingency factors that are crucial to consider here. First is the type of global team. Research has shown that autonomy is highly effective for line-level work teams but can have detrimental effects on cross-functional project teams that have a high level of complexity and rich information-processing requirements.[69] In these types of teams strong leadership is needed to help team members manage complexity.

Second, there is the level of task interdependence, defined earlier in this chapter as the degree of coordination and communication needed between members to perform a task. Granting teams high autonomy when tasks are interdependent results in higher levels of team effectiveness; in contrast, for tasks low in interdependence, giving autonomy to a team can actually result in lower team effectiveness.[70]

Third, there are several cultural values that are likely to affect initial acceptance of training on self-management. Global team members from high power-distance countries such as Mexico, China, and the Philippines may have difficulty engaging in self-management-related activities such as setting their own goals or taking initiative without asking for supervisory permission. Also, management in such countries may be less likely to allow the global team members a high level of autonomy. A being orientation refers to the extent to which people in a society focus on non-work activities. People in high being-oriented societies work only as much as they need in order to live and would likely resist taking on the additional responsibilities associated with a high degree of self-management. Determinism refers to the extent to which people in a society believe that their outcomes are determined by forces outside of their control such as luck, fate, or a deity. Because self-management requires that employees set their own goals and take actions to bring them closer to achieving their goals, employees high in determinism would likely resist self-management in teams.[71]

Recent research has supported a link between these cultural values and employee resistance to self-management in teams in different countries.[72] So, does this mean that managers should not try to train employees on self-management in countries that are high in power distance, being orientation, and/or determinism? The answer is not so much whether employees are trained on self-management or not, but *how* such training occurs and gets carried out.[73] For example, employees in high power-distance countries are likely to need more reinforcement that organizational authorities support their taking on more self-management in their global teams. Perhaps having high-level keynote speakers during training sessions would encourage high power-distance employees to internalize the self-management training. Training modules could be designed around more routine tasks that would become self-managing, rather than higher-level tasks such as hiring and firing fellow team members or initiating management-level decisions. Self-management training and development need to be adapted to fit the cultural values of team members in different countries.[74]

Leveraging Global Team Training

A final key issue for training and development involves leveraging global team training and development for maximum team learning and flexibility. In a true team-based organization, learning is required across functions, levels, and even organizations.[75] Such learning requires norms that are very different to those present in traditional organizations. For example, true team learning requires that organizations encourage team members to surface bad news and act on it.[76] However, if the organizational *status quo* maintains the typical reaction of negatively evaluating the messenger of bad news, organizational learning will not take place. Only organizations that encourage experimentation and innovation and set up mechanisms for shared team reflection, or what Amy Edmondson calls a climate of psychological safety,[77] will be likely to be able to successfully capitalize on this learning.[78]

In this respect, differences among people as they deal with errors are of interest. In organizational life, errors are unavoidable. Even with the best checks and procedures there is almost always some margin for error. Focusing too much on error prevention, through bureaucratic procedures and checks, and having a negative approach to errors, by punishment of those responsible, may lead global team members to low levels of risk-taking and exploration.[79] In such circumstances, people may cover up errors or blame others rather than take responsibility for their errors and share their experiences so others can learn from them. In describing his role in the Barings Bank disaster in 1993, for instance, Nick Leeson noted that a major reason he started an unauthorized shadow account was that he was afraid to admit errors.[80] Leeson found a way to hide errors and their negative consequences and make up for them without having to admit to them. Barings had a very punishing culture, quickly firing those that made mistakes or were not successful enough, which apparently reinforced covering up mistakes.[81]

As Peter Senge notes, a learning organization needs to have a positive attitude toward exploration and errors.[82] Thus, an important management issue becomes "the design and nurture of work environments in which it is possible to learn from mistakes and to collectively avoid making the same ones in the future."[83] In order to be able to learn from errors, it is necessary to use active rather than passive approaches.[84] Thus, a strategy that ensures negative consequences of errors such as loss of time, accidents, and faulty products are minimized (a control goal) and at the same time fosters the potential positive side of errors (learning, innovation, resilience—a learning goal), seems optimal.[85] Error orientations are shared within teams and even organizations. The above example of the punishing culture at Barings that resulted in Leeson's trying to cover up errors illustrates the reinforcement outcomes of covering up errors. In a Dutch study, error aversion (feeling strained by and covering up errors) was negatively related to team performance; and a mastery orientation (taking on the challenges of error occurrences) was positively related to organizational performance.[86] A link between dealing with errors and uncertainty avoidance seems likely.[87] Cultures high on uncertainty avoidance are likely to be low on risk-taking and probably have a more negative view of errors. In line with this, these cultures may then be high on error strain and covering up errors and low on learning from them.[88] The concept of saving face is critical for how global team members handle the discussion of errors. If team members are concerned about admitting mistakes to avoid humiliation, this could severely hamper global team learning. On the other hand, if the global team members knew how to decode and design for this dynamic, conceivably they might understand what was going on, take appropriate actions, save face, and promote team learning.

As stated above, to reflect on one's actions and surroundings is crucial to organizational learning. For example, reflection can be important for recognizing how certain present ways of operating can be obsolete, owing to environmental changes.[89] Teams often use "habitual routines" to guide team behavior. Habitual routines exist when groups repeatedly exhibit a functionally similar pattern of behavior in similar situations without explicitly selecting this pattern over alternative ways of behaving.[90] Although having some "ground rules" on what to do in certain circumstances seems helpful to smooth interactions and effective functioning, groups tend to stick to the patterns of interactions that are set early in their life, even when circumstances have changed and these patterns are no longer adequate. Reflexive behavior in teams seems important to counteract the tendency to rely on routines that may be no longer effective.

At the team level, reflexivity is defined as the extent to which group members overtly reflect on and communicate about the group's objectives, strategies (decision-making) and processes (communication), and adapt these to current or anticipated circumstances.[91] Differences between people in reflexivity are also important. As was seen above, teams need to reflect on errors, but also analyze their success, think about whether current group composition is adequate to meet objectives, talk about their use of time and resources, and decide how to deal with changes in the environment.[92] Besides reflecting on such issues, teams also need to engage in action planning to ensure that envisioned changes are acted upon. Reflexivity can thus be seen as an iterative three-stage process of reflection, planning, and taking action. Reflexivity is especially important for the effective functioning of teams involved in complex decision-making. Such teams have high autonomy and work in highly uncertain and unpredictable environments.[93] Research has found reflexivity to be positively related to subjective as well as objective measures of team performance in the United Kingdom as well as in the Netherlands.[94]

A trusting and open team climate and non-authoritarian leadership styles are conducive to reflexivity in teams. However, only few teams actually take the time to reflect on their strategies and actions on a regular basis.[95] Given the fact that in many organizations global teams are increasingly autonomous and need to make increasingly complex decisions, more attention to the creation of work environments that are conducive to reflexivity and learning seems relevant to help improve global team functioning.[96] For example, the United States, Brazilian, and Italian team members on Whirlpool Corporation's North American Appliance Group developed a chlorofluorocarbon-free refrigerator using a global team. To enhance team learning, the team met face to face every four months to discuss the project and the ground rules necessary to stimulate creative, out-of-bounds thinking. A key to the project's success was the informal social gathering that took place, allowing team members to build relationships and develop a climate for freedom of expression.[97] Similarly, Mobil Corporation has its global team members huddle in one location at the launch of a new product so the members can build the relationships necessary for true learning to take place.[98] Beyond anecdotal evidence, to date levels of team reflexivity have not been thoroughly compared across different cultures. However, reflexivity seems most likely to occur in cultures that are relatively low on power distance. In high power-distance cultures, team members are less likely to speak up or disagree with team leaders or other higher-status members. This may hamper reflexivity and global team learning in general.

The planning aspect of reflexivity is likely to be linked to uncertainty avoidance. For example, Rauch and colleagues compared German and Irish small enterprises.[99] Germany and Ireland are similar on all but one of Hofstede's culture dimensions. Where the German culture is high on uncertainty avoidance, Ireland ranks as one of Europe's lowest on uncertainty avoidance. Thus, Germany has a culture in which one would expect business owners to plan more and in greater detail. Customers will expect such planning and doing things "right," and meeting customer expectations in such an environment should be linked to careful and detailed planning. In contrast, in Ireland planning is seen as less necessary. Customers will have less respect for plans, show unplanned behavior themselves, and expect high flexibility. Planning too much will render small business owners inflexible. Thus, Rauch and colleagues expected and found that planning had a positive influence on small business success in Germany and a negative influence on small business success in Ireland. The cultural appropriateness of planning will influence its success.

Training and development systems aimed to maximize global team learning and success need to take cultural values such as those ensuing from power distance and uncertainty avoidance into account. Culture differences will lead to different expectations of the role of the trainer or teacher, differences in the likelihood of people "speaking up" during the learning process, different preferences in structure and planning approaches, and different approaches to errors—all variables that may play a role in designing effective learning environments for global teams. When designing and implementing global team-based training and development systems, managers should be certain to:

- use a combination of training techniques to enhance the transfer of training for all the members of a global team (cognitive, behavioral, and affective styles);
- use structured learning situations with precise objectives, detailed arrangements, and strict timetables for team members high in uncertainty avoidance cultural contexts; and open-ended questions, vague objectives, and few timetables for team members low in certainty avoidance contexts: use teacher-centered training for team members in cultures high in power distance and student-centered training for team members with cultures low in power distance;
- train global team members to be self-managing when appropriate (as with work teams versus project teams, highly interdependent versus highly independent teams that have relatively low levels of power distance, being orientation, and determinism);
- leverage global team training and development for maximum team learning and flexibility (increase global team psychological safety, avoid a focus on error prevention, and increase team reflexivity).

Conclusion

We have discussed global team performance management in the areas of rewards and recognition, performance evaluation and appraisal and training and development. In each of these areas, we have seen how the cultural values of those belonging to global teams had important implications for the design and administration of global team performance management. Clearly, there is not one ideal way to manage global team performance or the performance of other work units, such as departments or divisions. Implementing a best practice without regard for culture would likely result in a high level of employee resistance to such initiatives.[100] To increase the chances for effective global teams and work units, managers should take into account the complexity of the cultural differences represented on the team. Only then will organizations be able to realize the true global team effectiveness.

Notes

1. Handy, C. (1995). "Trust and the Virtual Organization," *Harvard Business Review, 73:* 40–48.
2. Latane, B., Williams. K. D., and Harkins, S. (1979). "Many Hands Make Light the Work: The Causes and Consequences of Social Loafing," *Journal of Personality and Social Psychology, 37,* 822–832.
3. Moede, W. (1927). "Die Richtlinien Der Leistungs-Psychologic," *Industrielle Psychotechnik," 4,* 193–207; Ringelmann, M. (1913). *Aménagement des fumeriers et des purins*, Paris: Librarie agricole de la Maison rustique.
4. Thompson, L. 2000. *Making the Team: A Guide for Managers.* Upper Saddle River, NJ: Prentice Hall.
5. King, R. T., Jr. 1998. "Jeans Therapy: Levi's Factory Workers are Assigned to Teams, and Morale Takes a Hit," *Wall Street Journal*, 232: Al, A6.
6. Wageman, R. 1998. "Interdependence and Group Effectiveness," *Administrative Science Quarterly, 40:* 145–180.
7. Shea, G. P., and Guzzo, R. A. (1987). "Groups as Human Resources," in G. Ferris and K. Rowland (eds.). *Research in Personnel and Human Resources Management*, Greenwich. CT: JAI Press, Vol. 5: 323–356.
8. Lipnack, J., and Stamps; J. (2000). *Virtual Teams: People Working Across Boundaries with Technology*, 2nd edn. New York: Wiley.
9. Trompenaars, F. (1993). *Riding the Waves of Culture: Understanding Diversity in Global Business*. Chicago: Irwin.
10. Hofstede, G. (1980). *Culture's Consequences: International Differences in Work-Related Values*. Beverly Hills, CA: Sage.
11. *Ibid.;* Au, K. Y. (1999). "Intra-Cultural Variation: Evidence and Implications for International Business," *Journal of International Business Studies*, 30: 799–812.
12. Verburg. R. M. (1996). "Developing HRM in Foreign-Chinese Joint Ventures," *European Management Journal*, 14(5), 518–525.
13. Verburg, R. M, Drenth, P. J. D., Koopman, P. L. Van Muijen, J. J., and Wang, Z. M. (1999), "Managing Human Resources Across Cultures: A Comparative Analysis of Practices in Enterpreneurial Organizations in China and the Netherlands," *International Journal of Human Resource Management*, 10(3): 391–410.
14. Kirkman, B. L., Gibson, C. B., and Shapiro, D. L. (2001). "Exporting Teams: Enhancing the Implementation and Effectiveness of Work Teams in Global Affiliates," *Organizational Dynamics,* 30(1), 12–29.
15. Cable, D. M., and Judge, T. A. 1994. "Pay Preferences and Job Search Decisions: A Person-Environment Fit Perspective," *Personnel Psychology*, 47: 317–348. Kirkman, B. L., and Shapiro, D. L. (2000). "Understanding Why Team Members Won't Share: An Examination of Factors Related to Employee Receptivity to Team-Based Rewards," *Small Group Research*, 31: 175–209.
16. Kirkman, B. L., and Shapiro, D. L. (2001a). "The Impact of Employee Cultural Values on Productivity, Cooperation, and Empowerment in Self-Managing Work Teams," *Journal of Cross-Cultural Psychology*, 32(5): 597–617; Kirkman. B. L., and Shapiro, D. L., (2001b), "The Impact of Cultural Values on Job Satisfaction and Organizational Commitment in Self-Managing Work Teams: The Mediating Role of Employee Resistance," *Academy of Management Journal*, 44(3): 557–569.
17. Earley, P. C. (1989). "Social Loafing and Collectivism: A Comparison of the United States and the People's Republic of China," *Administrative Science Quarterly*, 34: 565–581.
18. Maznevski, M. L., and Chudoba, K. M. (2001). "Bridging Space Over Time: Global Virtual Team Dynamics and Effectiveness," *Organization Science*, 11(5): 473–492.
19. Kirkman et al. (2001).
20. Kovach, K. A. (1987). "What Motivates Employees? Workers and Supervisors Give Different Answers," *Business Horizons* 30: 61.
21. Daft, R. L., (1987). *Management.* Chicago: Dryden Press.
22. Richardson. R. (2001). "Performance-Related Pay: Another Management Fad?," *Inaugural Addresses Series in Research in Management*, EIA-2001-01-ORG. Rotterdam: Erasmus Research Institute of Management, Erasmus University.
23. Gibson, C. B., and Kirkman, B. L. (1999). "Our Past, Present, and Future in Teams: The Role of Human Resources Professionals in Managing Team Performance,"

in A. I. Kraut and A. K. Korman (eds.). *Evolving Practices in Human Resources Management: Responses to a Changing World of Work,* San Francisco: Jossey-Bass, 90–117.

24. Campion, M. A., Medsker, G. J., and Higgs, A. C. (1993). "Relations Between Work Group Characteristics and Effectiveness: Implications for Designing Effective Work Groups," *Personnel Psychology*, 46: 823–850; Campion, M. A., Papper, E. M., and Medsker, G. J. (1996). "Relations Between Work Group Characteristics and Effectiveness: A Replication and Extension," *Personnel Psychology*, 49: 429–452; Hyatt, D. E., and Ruddy, T. M. (1997). "An Examination of the Relationship Between Work Group Characteristics and Performance: Once More into the Breech," *Personnel Psychology*, 50: 553–585.

25. Pelled, L. H., Eisenhardt, K. M., and Xin, K. R. (1999). "Exploring the Black Box: An Analysis of Work Group Diversity, Conflict, and Performance," *Administrative Science Quarterly*, 44: 1–28.

26. Earley, P. C. (1997). *Face, Harmony, and Social Structure: An Analysis of Organizational Behavior across Cultures.* New York: Oxford University Press.

27. Daft (1987).

28. Saavedra, R., and Kwun, S. K. (1993). "Peer Evaluation in Self-Managing Work Groups," *Journal of Applied Psychology*, 78: 450–462.

29. Kurland, N. B., and Bailey, D. E., (1999). "Telework: The Advantages and Challenges of Working Here, There, Anywhere, and Anytime," *Organizational Dynamics*, 28(2): 53–67.

30. Kirkman, B. L., Rosen, B., Gibson, C. B., Tesluk, P. E., and McPherson, S. O. (2003), "Five Challenges to Virtual Team Performance: Lessons from Sabre, Inc.," *Academy of Management Executive*, 16(3): 67–79.

31. Kaplan, R. S., and Norton, D. P. (1996). "Using the Balanced Scorecard as a Strategic Management System," *Harvard Business Review*, 74: 75–85.

32. *Ibid.*

33. Gomez, C. B., Kirkman, B. L., and Shapiro, D. L. (2000). "The Impact of Collectivism and Ingroup/Outgroup Membership on the Evaluation Generosity of Team Members," *Academy of Management Journal*, 43(6): 1097–1106.

34. Adsit, D. J., London. M., Crom, S., and Jones, D. (1997). "Cross-Cultural Differences in Upward Ratings in a Multinational Company," *International Journal of Human Resource Management*, 8(4): 385–401.

35. Hofstede (1980); Hofstede, G. (2001). *Culture's Consequences: Comparing Values, Behaviors, Institutions, and Organizations across Nations.* Thousand Oaks, CA: Sage.

36. Lindholm, N. (1999). "National Culture and Performance Management in MNC Subsidiaries," *International Studies of Management and Organization*, 29(4): 45–66.

37. Den Hartog, D. N. (2003). "Assertiveness," in R. J. House, P. J. Hanges, M. Javidan, P. W. Dorfman, V. Gupta. and GLOBE Associates (eds.). *Cultures, Leadership, and Organization: A 62 Nation GLOBE Study.* Thousand Oaks, CA: Sage, vol. 1.

38. *Ibid.*; Holtgraves, T. (1997). "Styles of Language Use: Individual and Cultural Variability in Conversational Indirectness," *Journal of Personality and Social Psychology*, 73: 624–637.

39. Kirkman et al. (2001).

40. Adams, J. S. (1965). "Inequity in Social Exchange," in L. Berkowitz (ed.), *Advances in Experimental Social Psychology.* New York: Academic Press, vol. 2, 267–299.

41. Lind, E. A., and Tyler, T. R. (1988). *The Social Psychology of Procedural Justice.* New York: Plenum.

42. Bies, R. J., and Moag, J. S. (1986). "International Justice: Communication Criteria of Fairness," in R. Lewicki, M. Bazerman, and B. Sheppard (eds.). *Research on Negotiation in Organizations*, Greenwich, CT: JAI Press. vol. 1, 43–55.

43. Cropanzano, R., and Greenberg, J. (1997). "Progress in Organizational Justice: Tunneling Through the Maze," in C. L. Cooper and I. T. Robertson (eds.). *International Review of Industrial and Organizational Psychology*, New York: John Wiley, vol. 2, 317–372; Greenberg, J. (1986). "Determinants of Perceived Fairness of Performance Evaluations," *Journal of Applied Psychology*, 71(2): 310–342; Greenberg, J. (1990). "Organizational Justice: Yesterday, Today, and Tomorrow," *Journal of Management*, 16: 399–432; Korsgaard, M. A. and Roberson, L. (1995). "Procedural Justice in Performance Evaluation: The Role of Instrumental and Non-Instrumental Voice in Performance Appraisal Discussion," *Journal of Management*, 21: 657–669.

44. Colquitt, J. A., Noe, R. A., and Jackson, C. L., 2002. "Justice in Teams: Antecedents and Consequences of Procedural Justice Climate," *Personnel Psychology*, 55(1): 83–109.

45. Kirkman, B. L., Shapiro, D. L., Novelli, L., Jr., and Brett. J. M. 1996. "Employee Concerns Regarding Self-Managing Work Teams: A Multidimensional Justice Perspective," *Social Justice Research,* 9(1): 47–67.

46. Greenberg (1986).

47. Lind, E. A., and Earley, P. C. 1992. "Procedural Justice and Culture," *International Journal of Psychology*, 27(2): 227–242; Greenberg. J. A. (2001). "Studying Organizational Justice Cross-Culturally: Fundamental Challenges," *International Journal of Conflict Management*, 12(4), 365–375.

48. Kirkman, B. L., Lowe, K. B., and Peng, D. (2000). "The Role of Procedural Justice, Perceived Organizational Support, and Individualism-Collectivism in Motivating Organizational Citizenship Behavior of Employees in the People's Republic of China," paper presented at the annual meeting of the Academy of Management, Toronto, Canada, August.

49. Pillai, R., Scandura. T. A., and Williams, E. A. (1999). "Leadership and Organizational Justice: Similarities and Differences Across Cultures," *Journal of International Business Studies*, 30(4): 763–779.

50. Hofstede (1980).

51. Brockner. J., Ackerman. G., Greenberg, J., Gelfand, M. J., Francesco, A. M., Chen, Z. X., Leung, K., Bierbrauer, G., Gomez, C., Kirkman, B. L., and Shapiro, D. L. (2001). "Culture and Procedural Justice: The Moderating Influence of Power Distance on Reactions to Voice," *Journal of Experimental Social Psychology*, 37(4): 300–315.

52. Lee, C., Pillutla, M., and Law, K. S., 2000. "Power-Distance, Gender, and Organizational Justice," *Journal of Management*, 26, 685–704.

53. Lam, S. S. K., Schaubroeck, J., and Aryee. S. (2002). "Relationship Between Organizational Justice and Employee Work Outcomes: A Cross-National Study," *Journal of Organizational Behavior*, 23: 1–18.

54. Cropanzano and Greenberg (1997).

55. Alexander, S. (2000). "Virtual Teams Going Global," *Infoworld*, 22(46), 55–56.

56. See, e.g., Kraiger, K., and Ford, J. K. (1985). "A Meta-Analysis of Rater Race Effects in Performance Ratings," *Journal of Applied Psychology*, 70(1): 56–65. See also Pulakos, E. D., Oppler, S. H., White, L. A., and Borman, W. C., (1989). "Examination of Race and Sex Effects on Performance Ratings," *Journal of Applied Psychology*, 74(5): 70–78.

57. Baugh, S. G., and Graen. G. B. (1997). "Effects of Team Gender and Racial Composition on Perceptions of Team Performance in Cross-Functional Teams," *Group & Organization Management*, 22(3): 366–383. See also Kirkman. B. L., Tesluk. P. E., and Rosen, B. (in press), "The Impact of Demographic Heterogeneity and Team Leader-Team Member Demographic Fit on Team Empowerment and Effectiveness," *Group and Organization Management.*

58. Kirkman et al. (in press).

59. Gomez et al. (2000).

60. Gibson and Kirkman (1999).

61. Mohrman, S. A., Cohen, S. G., and Mohrman, A. M., Jr. (1995), *Designing Team-Based Organizations: New Forms for Knowledge Work.* San Francisco: Jossey-Bass.

62. Biggs, J. B. (1993). "What Do Inventories of Students' Learning Processes Really Measure? A Theoretical Review and Clarification," *British Journal of Educational Psychology*, 63: 3–19.

63. Hoeksema, L. H., Van de Vliert, E., and Williams, A. R. T. (1996). "The Interplay Between Learning Strategy and Organizational Structure in Predicting Career Success," *International Journal of Human Resource Management*, 8: 307–327.

64. Allinson, C. W., and Hayes, J. 2000. "Cross-National Differences in Cognitive Style Implications for Management," *International Journal of Human Resource Management*, 11(1): 161–170.

65. *Ibid.*

66. Hofstede, G. (1991). *Cultures and Organizations: Software of the Mind*, London: McGraw-Hill.

67. *Ibid.*

68. *Ibid.*

69. Cohen, S. G., and Bailey, D. E., (1997). "What Makes Teams Work: Group Effectiveness Research from the Shop Floor to the Executive Suite," *Journal of Management*, 23, 239–290.

70. Langfred, C. W. (2000). "Work-Group Design and Autonomy: A Field Study of the Interaction between Task Interdependence and Group Autonomy," *Small Group Research*, 31: 54–70.

71. Kirkman, B. L., and Shapiro, D. L., (1997). "The Impact of Cultural Values on Employee Resistance to Teams: Toward a Model of Globalized Self-Managing Work Team Effectiveness," *Academy of Management Review*, 22(3): 730–757.

72. Kirkman and Shapiro (2001a, 2001b).

73. Elenkov, D. S. (1998). "Can American Management Concepts Work in Russia? A Cross-Cultural Comparative Study," *California Management Review*, 40: 133–156; Kirkman and Shapiro (2001b); Nicholls, C. E., Lane, H. W., and Brechu, M. B. (1999). "Taking Self-Managed Teams to Mexico," *Academy of Management Executive*, 13: 15–27.

74. Kirkman, B. L., Lowe, K. B., and Gibson. C. B. (2002). "Two Decades of *Culture's Consequences:* A Review of the Empirical Research on Hofstede's Cultural Value Dimensions," working paper. Georgia Institute of Technology.

75. Mohrman et al. (1995).

76. Edmondson, A. (1999). "Psychological Safety and Learning Behavior in Work Teams," *Administrative Science Quarterly*, 44: 350–383; Kasl, E., Marsick, V. J., and Dechant. K. (1997). "Teams as Learners: A Research-Based Model of Team Learning," *Journal of Applied Behavioral Science*, 33(2): 227–246.

77. Edmondson (1999).

78. Gibson and Kirkman (1999); Mohrman et al. (1995).

79. Edmondson (1999).

80. Leeson, N. (1996). *Rogue Trader*, London: Little, Brown.

81. Rawnsley, J. (1995). *Total Risk: Nick Leeson and the Fall of Barings Bank.* New York: Harper; Van Dyck. C. (2000). *Putting Errors to Good Use: Error Management Culture in Organizations.* Amsterdam: KLI Dissertation series. 2000–3.

82. Senge, P. M. (1990). *The Fifth Discipline: The Art and Practice of the Learning Organization*, New York: Currency Doubleday.

83. Edomondson (1999), p. 25.

84. Frese, M. (1995). "Error Managment in Training: Conceptual and Empirical Results," in C. Zucchermaglio, S. Bandura, and S. U. Stucky (eds.), *Organizational Learning and Technological Change,* New York: Springer.

85. Van Dyck (2000).

86. *Ibid.*

87. Hofstede (1991).

88. Rybowiak, V., Garst, H., Frese, M., and Baltinic. B. (1999). "Error Orientation Questionnaire (E.O.Q): Reliability, Validity, and Different Language Equivalence," *Journal of Organizational Behavior.* 20: 527–547.

89. Tjosvold. D. (1991). *Team Organization: An Enduring Competitive Advantage.* New York: John Wiley.

90. Gersick, C. J., and Hackman, J. R. (1990). "Habitual Routines in Task-Performing Groups," *Organizational Behavior and Human Decision Processes*, 17: 65–97.

91. West, M. A., Garrod, S., and Carletta. J. (1997). "Group Decision-Making and Effectiveness. Unexplored Boundaries," in C. L. Cooper and S. E. Jackson, (eds.), *Creating Tomorrow's Organizations: A Handbook for Future Research in Organizational Behavior.* Chichester: John Wiley, 293–316.

92. West, M. A. (1996), "Reflexivity and Work Group Effectiveness: A Conceptual Intergration," in M. A. West (ed.), *Handbook of Work Group Psychology,* Chichester: John Wiley, 555–579.

93. *Ibid.*

94. Carter. S. M., and West, M. A. (1998). "Reflexivity, Effectiveness, and Mental Health in BBC-TV Production Teams," *Small Group Research*, 29: 583–601; Schippers. M. C., Den Hartog, D. N., and Koopman, P. (2001). "Reflexivity in Teams: The Development of a Questionnaire and the Relationship with Trust, Leadership, and Performance of Work Teams," manuscript submitted for publication.

95. West (1996).

96. Maznevski and Chudoba (2001).

97. Geber. B. (1995). "Virtual teams," *Training*, 32(4): 36–40.

98. Solomon. C. M. (1998). "Building Teams Across Borders," *Global Workforce*, November: 12–17.

99. Rauch A., Frese. M., and Sonnentag, S. (2000). "Cultural Differences in Planning/Success Relationships: A Comparison of Small Enterprises in Ireland, West Germany, and East Germany," *Journal of Small Business Management*, 38(4): 28–41.

100. Kirkman and Shapiro (1997).

Managing Effective Organizations

In this section, we're going to make a more obvious transition from micro-level topics in organizational behavior dealing with individuals and groups to macro-level issues that affect the entire organization. In addition to a thorough grounding in the topics we have already covered, organization design and managing change are heavily dependent on systems thinking and analytical skills.

CHAPTER

22 Organization Design

THE ORGANIZATION OF THE FUTURE: STRATEGIC IMPERATIVES AND CORE COMPETENCIES
FOR THE TWENTY-FIRST CENTURY

David A. Nadler

Michael L. Tushman

MAKING MERGERS AND ACQUISITIONS WORK: STRATEGIC AND PSYCHOLOGICAL PREPARATION

Mitchell Lee Marks

Philip H. Mirvis

IF YOU MUST DOWNSIZE, DO IT RIGHT

Wayne F. Cascio

Organizations cannot function at peak capacity if they are not well designed. Managers have various "building blocks" at their disposal (such as strategy, structure, systems, type of staff, competencies, managerial style, and rewards). Most design experts assume that a good, complementary "fit" among these various components is necessary to organizational success—with some exceptions that allow for evolution and adaptation to change.

One element of designing organization structures is to consider the future demands they will face. A classic article on taking stock of where we are and where business needs to go is "The Organization of the Future: Strategic Imperatives and Core Competencies for the Twenty-first Century," by David Nadler, chairman of Mercer Delta Consulting and vice chairman of March & McLennan Companies, and Michael Tushman, Harvard professor and consultant. Based on the changes they see in the environment, Nadler and Tushman list six strategies that are essential for organizations of the future. Then they identify the organizational competencies and architecture needed to carry out these strategies.

The second article, "Making Mergers and Acquisitions Work: Strategic and Psychological Preparation," notes that three out of four mergers and acquisitions fail to achieve their financial and strategic objectives. Mitchell Marks and Philip Mirvis, internationally recognized consultants on mergers and acquisitions, discuss the managerial actions that lead to successful combinations.

Employment downsizing and restructuring continue to be major tactics used in hopes of enhancing organizational competitiveness and performance. As with mergers and acquisitions, downsizing and restructuring efforts frequently fail to produce long-term payoffs. In "If You

Must Downsize, Do It Right," Wayne Cascio, business professor at the University of Colorado–Denver, concludes that downsizing alone does not result in long-term success. In fact, research shows that downsizing firms, taken as a group, never do better than firms that do not downsize. Given these caveats, Cascio outlines key considerations and downsizing strategies to help firms downsize as wisely as possible.

THE ORGANIZATION OF THE FUTURE: STRATEGIC IMPERATIVES AND CORE COMPETENCIES FOR THE 21ST CENTURY*

David A. Nadler

Michael L. Tushman

Poised on the eve of the next century, we are witnessing a profound transformation in the very nature of our business organizations. Historic forces have converged to fundamentally reshape the scope, strategies, and structures of large, multi-business enterprises.

Driven by new competitive demands and fueled by an abundance of capital, companies have massively rearranged their portfolios, adding and discarding businesses to sharpen their strategic focus. Those discreet and dramatic portfolio plays, characterized by the high-profile mergers and acquisitions of the past three years, have provided a constant flow of front page news. But beyond the headlines lies a more subtle story, one with greater long-term significance than the acquisitive appetites of auto makers and telecom giants. Heading into the new century, the most important business development is the pursuit of competitive advantage in an uncertain world through new approaches to organization design.

These new approaches should lead those of us concerned with the theory and practice of organizational design to reconsider those ideas still grounded in the post-War, pre-Internet world that lasted through the 1980s. As this remarkable decade draws to a close, it's appropriate to reflect on the state of organization design and to distill those timeless ideas that will guide us in designing the effective organization of the future.

Our purpose here is first to present our perspectives on the most relevant lessons of organization design. We'll then examine the challenges of the new environment and their implications for tomorrow's organizations. Next, we'll identify six new strategic imperatives that flow from this reshaped environment. We'll conclude by proposing a set of organizational challenges that encompass the most critical design issues for the organization of the future.

A Perspective on Organization Design

What we think of today as "organization design" began to evolve in the aftermath of World War II. Building on the research of the 1920s and 1930s and the experience of the 1940s, the notion of the "organization as machine" gave way to a more subtle perspective on the social and technical aspects of the organization. Much of our contemporary thinking can be traced to the landmark work *Organization and Environment* by Lawrence and Lorsch (1969), which introduced several profound ideas. The first was "contingency theory"—the notion that organizations are most effective when their design characteristics match their environment. The second

*Reprinted from *Organizational Dynamics*, 28(1), David A. Nadler and Michael L. Tushman, "The Organization of the Future: Strategic Imperatives and Core Competencies for the 21st Century," pp. 45–59, © 1999, with permission from Elsevier.

major idea flowed from the first; if two units of the same organization operate in different environments, each should take on different characteristics. That creates a dual demand for both "differentiation" and "integration," or the capacity to link different units within the same organization.

The twin principles of "integration and differentiation" are more relevant than ever, given the complexity of modern organizations. The new challenge is to effectively manage dramatically different businesses that overlap or even compete against one another within a single, strategically focused enterprise. What's more, there will be a growing need for integration patterns—joint ventures, alliances, etc.—that extend beyond traditional corporate boundaries.

We believe there are four core lessons of organization design that will retain their relevance in the coming decade:

1. The environment drives the strategic architecture of the enterprise, either through anticipation of, or reaction to, major changes in the marketplace. Every industry evolves through cycles of incremental change punctuated by turbulent periods of disequilibrium that call for radical or discontinuous change. The organization's capacity to understand its environment and to make the right kinds of strategic changes at the appropriate point in the cycle will determine its competitive strength.

2. Strategy drives organizational architecture, a term that describes the variety of ways in which the enterprise structures, coordinates, and manages the work of its people in pursuit of strategic objectives. Over the years, we have described this concept as the congruence model of organizational behavior (Figure 1). This model views the organization as an open system that transforms input from the external environment into output of various types. The organization, consisting of the formal and informal arrangements, the people, and the core work, is driven by an articulated strategy. The more closely each component of the organization is aligned with the others—and with the strategy—the more effective the overall performance. Consequently, effective organizations design patterns of formal and informal structures and processes best suited to their strategic objectives.

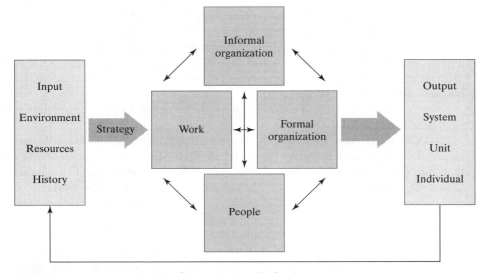

FIGURE 1 **Congruence Model of Organizational Behavior**

3. The relationship between strategy and organization design is reciprocal. How an enterprise is organized will influence its focus and time horizons, either encouraging or restricting its people's ability to develop creative strategies.

4. The basic dilemma of organizational design remains unchanged. This raises several questions: How do we design and manage both differentiation and integration? How do we group people, processes, and operating units in ways appropriate to their unique competitive environments and strategic requirements, while maintaining their link to the larger organization? How do we encourage both divergence and cohesion? The key to effective design requires an appreciation of the underlying duality of this challenge.

Assuming these are the relevant lessons that should continue to guide us, our task in the remainder of this paper is to address three key issues:

1. What are the key characteristics of the changing business environment? What are the critical changes that will drive new thinking in strategic and organizational architecture?

2. What are the strategic imperatives that flow from the environmental changes we've identified?

3. What organizational challenges will be created by the new strategic imperatives? How will effective organizations translate strategic imperatives into new organizational architectures and new leadership priorities?

To answer these questions, we begin by considering the historic trends that have already begun to reshape the competitive environment.

The New Business Environment

In many ways, today's business environment has changed qualitatively since the late 1980s. The end of the Cold War radically altered the very nature of global politics and economics. In just a few short years, the triumph of capitalism has spawned a variety of trends with profound consequences: the opening of markets, true global competition, widespread industry deregulation, and an abundance of accessible capital. We have experienced both the benefits and perils of a truly global economy, with both Wall Street and Main Street feeling the pangs of economic dislocation half a world away.

At the same time, we have fully entered the information age. Startling breakthroughs in information technology have irreversibly altered the ability to conduct business unconstrained by the traditional limitations of time or space. Today, it's almost impossible to imagine a world devoid of intranets, e-mail, and laptops. With stunning speed, the Internet is profoundly changing the way we work, shop, do business, and communicate.

In less than 10 years, the changes wrought by new information technology have been phenomenal.

As a consequence, we have truly entered the post-industrial economy. We are rapidly shifting from an economy based on manufacturing and commodities to one that places the greatest value on information, services, support, and distribution. That shift, in turn, places an unprecedented premium on "knowledge workers," a new class of affluent, educated, and mobile people who view themselves as free agents in a seller's market.

Beyond the realm of information technology, the accelerated pace of technological change in virtually every industry has created entirely new businesses, wiped out others, and produced a pervasive demand for continuous innovation. New product, process, and distribution technologies provide powerful levers for creating competitive value. More companies are learning the importance of destructive technologies—innovations that hold the potential to make a product line, or even an entire business segment, virtually obsolete.

Another major trend has been the fragmentation of consumer and business markets. There's a growing appreciation that superficially similar groups of customers may have very different preferences in terms of what they want to buy and how they want to buy it. Now, new technology makes it easier, faster, and cheaper to identify and serve targeted micromarkets in ways that were physically impossible or prohibitively expensive in the past. Moreover, the trend feeds on itself, a business's ability to serve sub-markets fuels customers' appetites for more and more specialized offerings.

Implications of Environmental Change

We all know that change has become an inherent part of business. What's more significant is the rapidly accelerating velocity of change. More specifically, the lifespan of product, process, and distribution technologies has contracted with breathtaking speed.

The critical issue is time. The rapidly increasing velocity of change warps organizational time and space, bending the very shape of the enterprise. It's not just simply a matter of doing the same things, only faster; it's more like the difference between checkers and three-dimensional chess. The massive demands imposed by time compression will force organizations to:

- Compete and innovate simultaneously in multiple venues and in overlapping time frames; and
- Find creative ways to design and implement new organizational architectures in half the time required by current processes without sacrificing the benefits traditionally associated with deliberate planning and appropriate participation.

Together, these changes in the business environment challenge our fundamental assumptions of organizational design. Historically, the purpose of organizational structures was to institutionalize stability; in the organization of the future, the goal of design will be to institutionalize change. In that sense, we stand in the midst of a profound shift in the design and purpose of organizational design.

The New Strategic Imperatives

We believe that the changing environment we've just described creates six strategic imperatives for the organization of the future. It will be required to: increase strategic clock speed; focus portfolios, with various business models; abbreviate strategic life cycles; create "go-to-market" flexibility; enhance competitive innovation; and manage intra-enterprise cannibalism. We will describe each in turn.

1. INCREASE STRATEGIC CLOCK SPEED From a strategic standpoint, speed is quickly becoming a critical success factor. In a strategic context, speed involves an organizational capacity to understand, anticipate, and respond appropriately to those external changes that fundamentally alter the rules of engagement and the sources of value in a given industry or business segment. Examples abound: the deregulation of telecommunications and other utilities, the emergence of new technologies such as wireless communication, the development of e-commerce, and the rise of "category killer" outlets in consumer segments such as home improvement (Home Depot) and toys (Toys "R" Us). Virtually every industry has seen vast changes in the way it designs, produces, or reaches the market with its offerings.

Timing is everything. During periods of radical, discontinuous change, the first movers enjoy significant advantages. Those who perceive the early signs of discontinuity in the environment and then rapidly fashion an appropriate new strategy are infinitely more successful than those who miss the warning signs or delay their response. Those who move slowly find they must react to competitors; those who wait too long find themselves struggling for survival.

2. FOCUS PORTFOLIOS, WITH VARIOUS BUSINESS MODELS Over the past 40 years, there's been significant change in the underlying strategies that defined our large and complex business enterprises. Through the mid-1960s, the classical form or organizational architecture consisted of companies with a single dominant business design that was largely duplicated down through the pyramid of divisions and operating companies. These shared designs allowed for tight linkages and a sense of consistency.

The mid-1960s saw the rise of the conglomerate. Driven by a thirst for growth, a fundamental belief that "bigger is better," and a desire to offset the cyclical downturns in specific industries, companies diversified their portfolios in unprecedented ways. Within each corporation, there might be dozens of companies with wholly unrelated strategies and entirely different business designs. The holding company model involved only the most minimal linkages across the enterprise, with each business operating essentially as an independent agent in pursuit of financial goals dictated from above.

Now we're witnessing the emergence of the new "strategic enterprise." The changing marketplace no longer rewards unfocused growth and gross market share. Instead, companies are reshaping their portfolios in the pursuit of strategic focus, concentrating on those businesses where they can create sustainable value by applying their core competencies to provide competitive advantage. They are spinning off or selling businesses that either dilute focus, in terms of resources and managerial energy, or whose potential value cannot be leveraged within the larger enterprise. In effect, companies are breaking up and reassembling the traditional value chain.

This sharpened focus is leading companies to seek new ways to compete within a given competitive space, operating simultaneously in mature, emerging, and future segments of the same markets. Consequently, we're going to see more and more variations in business design within a single enterprise. In this context, we use the term *business design* as defined by Slywotzky and Morrison as encompassing four dimensions: which customers to pursue, how to capture value (i.e., profit), how to maintain a unique value proposition, and what scope of activities to pursue.

For example, consider the case of Lucent Technologies, a spinoff created by AT&T in 1995 from four of its businesses and much of Bell Labs. As part of AT&T, those businesses were locked in a strategic dilemma created by deregulation: In order to realize their full value, they would have to do business with AT&T's widening array of direct competitors. That created major conflicts for everyone concerned. Once Lucent became independent from AT&T, its value as a manufacturer and supplier of telecommunications equipment and systems skyrocketed; its profits more than quadrupled between 1995 and 1998, and its stock price rose from $13.50 a share in 1996 to nearly $120, adjusted for splits.

But it wasn't long before Lucent realized that it, too, would have to reshape its business design. Just a few years after the spinoff, Lucent exited the consumer business, where it lacked the front-end linkages—sales, distribution, customer base—to sufficiently leverage its back-end technology and production strengths. Instead, Lucent chose to focus exclusively on business communications. In early 1999, it acquired Ascend Communications Inc., a move that represented a $20 billion bet on data networking—a business involving substantially different technology than Lucent's traditional circuit switching. Now, the challenge for Lucent is figuring out how to manage these two different—and, in some ways, directly competing—business designs.

3. ABBREVIATED STRATEGIC LIFE CYCLES Each industry progresses through a fairly predictable life cycle. There may be huge differences in the duration of that cycle depending upon the industry segment, but the pattern of cycles is consistent. Understanding those cycles is essential for leaders. Different stages in the cycle of industry evolution—the well-known "S-curve"—demand different strategies at various points along the curve.

But waves of change in industry leadership suggest that firms must engage in both incremental and discontinuous technical change, as well as architectural innovation—taking the same product and taking it to different markets. Thus in photolithography for disk drives, leading firms were unable to take known technologies and move to new customers. Dynamic capabilities seem to be rooted in shaping streams of different types of innovation in a given product class.

The consequences of the sweeping and rapid changes in the environment discussed earlier have had the effect of substantially shortening those evolutionary cycles for every industry. In the past, companies large and small, including AT&T, General Motors, and even IBM, could get along for a decade, and sometimes longer, without any fundamental changes in strategy. Those days are gone. Rather than thinking in terms of decades, the pace of change in the environment will require the organization of the future to significantly change its underlying strategy on a regular basis of between 18 months and 5 years, depending upon the industry. Indeed, it's not uncommon to hear executives, as they talk about strategic cycles, talk in terms of "Web years," signifying a compressed timeframe of 3 months rather than 12.

4. CREATE "GO-TO-MARKET" FLEXIBILITY The fragmentation of markets, one of the significant changes in the environment, has enormous strategic implications for organizations. In order to reach each market segment in the most effective way, companies have begun focusing more intensely than ever before on the rising demand for "go-to-market" variability. Various market segments offer widely divergent demands for the same core product or service in terms of pricing options, sales and service support, speed of delivery, customization, and so forth. Today, no organization can succeed with a "one size fits all" approach to the marketplace.

The most highly publicized changes, of course, have involved the Internet and the emergence of so-called "e-commerce"; by some accounts, sales of goods over the Internet rose from being barely measurable in 1996 to more than $4 billion during the 1998 Christmas season. Waves of change in distribution channels are coming faster all the time. It was only a few years ago that independent booksellers were wilting under the pressure of the book superstores, such as Barnes & Noble and Borders. Then, practically overnight, Amazon.com reshaped the industry, putting the leading competitors on the defensive and forcing them to follow the upstart onto the Web, despite their enormous investments in brick-and-mortar outlets.

Implicit in the notion of "go-to-market" variability is the potential it creates for conflicting internal priorities. Consider the auto industry. By some estimates, we are quickly approaching the point when more than half of all new car buyers in the United States start out by searching the Internet for information, comparing models, options, prices, and financing alternatives before they ever set foot in a showroom. What many shoppers are looking for is a vehicle's factory invoice price, the essential number that equips them to bargain knowledgeably with the local dealer. That's not good news for the dealer; but at this point, the auto companies have no choice but to cater to the demands of sophisticated customers for more and better information. At the same time, reeling from assaults by Car-Max and other high-volume used-car chains, the auto companies have to think seriously about starting their own used-car outlets—an historic shift in distribution that would put a further squeeze on profits of their own franchised dealerships.

5. ENHANCE COMPETITIVE INNOVATION It has practically become an article of faith that innovation provides a critical source of competitive advantage. But the accepted definition of *innovation* is too narrow; we would argue that the scope of innovation must be expanded to include the full range of an organization's capabilities.

Innovation traditionally focused on products and processes. More recently, distribution has attracted attention as an area where significant innovation can lead to dramatic gains. But the combination of product, process, and distribution still fails to capture the full potential for organizational innovation.

We believe the successful organization of the future will also develop exceptional skills to innovate in two other areas: strategy development and organization design. If the most critical characteristic of the new business environment is the accelerating pace of change, then the ability to quickly and creatively develop and implement new strategies and the organization designs required to make them work will become a major source of competitive differentiation.

6. MANAGE INTRA-ENTERPRISE CANNIBALISM What we call *purposeful cannibalism*— the need to develop and support new strategies, product lines, and distribution channels that might eventually dry up existing revenue streams—is not a new idea. Visionary business leaders have done it for years. But two elements of intra-enterprise cannibalism are new.

The first change is that cannibalism has been rare. Business historians praise Tom Watson Jr. for his foresight in developing the IBM 360, which held the potential to wipe out many of the company's best-selling product lines. His willingness to put a major revenue stream at risk was remarkable in large part because it was so uncommon. In the successful organization of the future, the idea of cannibalism will become routine, an accepted part of each company's strategy.

The other change relates, once again, to speed. In the future, it won't suffice to make one big bet each decade. The pace of innovation and the abbreviated strategic cycles will force companies to place multiple bets on an ongoing basis, acknowledging that a new product may be well on its way to obsolescence by the time it reaches the market.

Lucent Technologies' $20 billion acquisition of Ascend, which we mentioned earlier, involved more than a strategy of multiple bets on alternative technologies. There's a good chance that the newly acquired data networking strategy based on packet switching may actually displace the circuit switching technology that now provides the bulk of Lucent's profits. And before long, it's entirely possible that Lucent will have to invest in alternative packet switching strategies as new technologies come along and require new business designs.

Organizational Challenges

The six strategic imperatives described above create a compelling need for some new and unconventional organizational architectures. As we said earlier, organizational architecture throughout much of this century was generally viewed as a way to institutionalize and manage stability. But today, the challenge is to design organizational architectures that are flexible and adaptive, that enable the organization to perform effectively in the face of uncertainty—not just day-to-day, but in the broader context of profound discontinuous change.

In our view, the new strategic imperatives create a corresponding set of challenges for the organization of the future; to succeed, organizations will be forced to become proficient in eight core competencies (Figure 2).

1. INCREASE ORGANIZATIONAL CLOCK SPEED The strategic imperative of timely anticipation and speedy response to change will require the design of organizations with the capacity to do everything faster. The ability to configure the organization in ways that ensure a constant and acute awareness of impending changes in the marketplace will become an essential capability that will separate the leaders from the laggards.

Beyond that, organizations will have to find creative ways to achieve unprecedented speed in all their operating and support processes. They'll want to significantly reduce their time to market and time to volume. They'll want to accelerate decision-making up and down the line. They'll need to substantially cut the time it takes to design and implement strategic and organizational changes. Enlightened leaders already understand that speed doesn't mean operating the same way as in the past, only faster; they know that radical improvements in speed involve doing things differently. In order to increase strategic clock speed, organizations will face three challenges.

First, senior leaders will need a much deeper understanding of the quickening cycle times in their industries. They will have to alter their assumptions about large-scale change, both in terms of the frequency and speed of major change initiatives. Once upon a time, CEOs were expected to be the stewards of stability. Through the 1980s, a CEO might expect to lead one or, in extreme cases, two episodes of radical change. Today, and in the coming decades, leaders of complex organizations should enter their jobs with the expectation that they might well be required to reinvent their organizations three, four, or even more times over the course of their tenure. That will require a fundamentally different attitude about the role of the CEO as an agent of change.

Second, successful enterprises will need to develop sensitive organizational antennae—the roles, structures, and processes that will significantly enhance their ability to detect the early warning signs of value migration. In particular, they will have to keep close watch on minor players and industry outliers, the frequent sources of major innovation. They are the ones to monitor most carefully; they are the ones

FIGURE 2 Strategic Imperatives and Organizational Challenges

most likely to employ new technologies and distribution patterns to nullify the dominant conventional business designs.

Finally, companies will need to redesign their organizational architectures in ways that encourage the "capacity to act" in response to indications of environmental change. In too many organizations, managers lack clear accountabilities, support from above, adequate resources, and sufficient information; faced with major opportunities or challenges, they freeze in their tracks. The growing demand for speed in every facet of the business will require organizations to fashion the formal structures, processes, and roles as well as the informal operating environment necessary to encourage managers throughout the enterprise to act swiftly and independently.

2. DESIGN STRUCTURAL DIVERGENCE The changing environment is requiring enterprises to employ a variety of business designs as they develop multiple ways to achieve value within a defined competitive space. The organizational challenge will be to master the art of designed divergence—the ability to create, support, and link, where necessary, a wide variety of related businesses that use dramatically different architectures to pursue varying and sometimes conflicting strategies.

In recent years, we have argued the case for ambidextrous management—the ability to maintain superior performance in established businesses while managing innovation in targeted areas. The organization of the future will have to be more than just ambidextrous; in a sense, it will have to become polydextrous. Rather than operating, in essence, in both the present and the future, polydextrous leadership will also require an ability to coordinate businesses that are both complementary and competitive in the current marketplace (Figure 3). That will require a fundamental

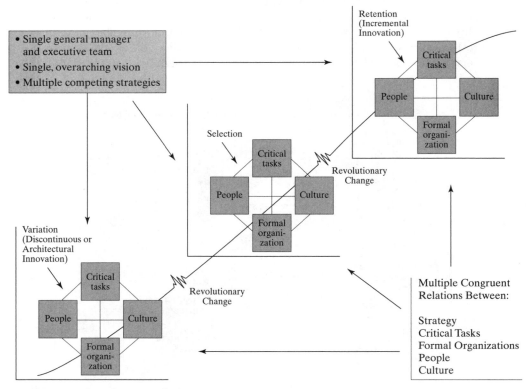

FIGURE 3 **Designed Structural Divergence**

rethinking of the form and purpose of organizational architecture. The framework we have developed over the past 20 years, the Congruence Model, is generally synonymous with consistency. It implies that effective organizations maintain a consistent architecture with minor variations, throughout the enterprise. We now believe that the organization of the future will seek congruence at the enterprise level, providing an effective framework that successfully melds a broad array of different architectures at the business unit level and beyond. Rather than seeking blanket consistency, leaders will come to perceive internal architectural divergence as a powerful source of evolutionary strength.

The most critical issue will be to figure out the appropriate linkages across a broad range of very different businesses. The challenge involves an inherent balancing act: minimizing linkages in order to maximize the focus of independent business units while, at the same time, capitalizing on potential sources of leverage to create value from the joint ownership and management of multiple businesses. In other words, leaders will have to learn when it's best to encourage autonomy and differentiation, and how to create value through the selective use of linking structures and integrative processes.

In reality, the choices are somewhat limited. Businesses can be linked on the back end, through common technology architectures. They can be linked in the middle through infrastructure—manufacturing processes, supply chains, etc. And they can be linked on the front end, through shared customer relationships, distribution channels, sales and service operations, and so on (Figure 4). The more points of linkage, the more diffused the focus. So the issue is to start with a clean slate, to weigh the marginal costs and benefits of each potential linkage, and to arrive at the correct scope and intensity of linkage at each point in the value chain. Corning Inc., for example, has come to the conclusion that its various businesses—photonic devices for telecommunications, stepper lenses for photolithography (for creating chips), ceramic substrates for catalytic converters—offer no leverage on the front end, minimal leverage in the middle, and considerable leverage on the back end, where common technologies provide innovations with applications across its businesses.

3. PROMOTE ORGANIZATIONAL MODULARITY The growing prevalence of abbreviated strategic life cycles will require ever-faster development and implementation of appropriate organizational designs. That requirement clearly calls for both product and process innovation in the domain of organizational design. The implications may be far-reaching, indeed.

In recent decades, we have rejected the notion of "off-the-rack" organization designs. We have steadfastly argued in favor of "custom designs." Our thinking was based on two fundamental beliefs; first, that each design should be suited to the

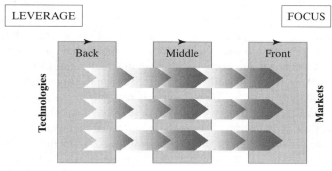

FIGURE 4 Linkage Points

unique demands of the organization—its environment, its strategy, its people, and its culture; and second, that the very process of designing the appropriate structures, processes, systems, and roles held inherent long-term value for the organization and the individuals who took part in the process.

As valuable as it has been, it may well be time to rethink that approach. The transforming requirements of speed might well dictate situations in which there is simply not enough time to engage in a conventional organization design process. We may be approaching a time when theorists and practitioners ought to develop a set of design principles that will allow organizations to quickly select an appropriate architecture for a given strategy.

Many organizations will no longer be able to afford the luxury of spending six or nine months creating and implementing a new design; few companies will be able to wait that long to address the imminent changes in their environment. So the notion of starting each design process with a blank slate will soon become obsolete. The challenge will be to devise a streamlined process, employing modular design, that still retains some of the important benefits—the learning, insight, team-building and ownership—that we attempt to create through the customized design approach.

4. STRUCTURE HYBRID DISTRIBUTION CHANNELS The strategic imperative for go-to-market variability will require organizations to develop different kinds of structures that will enable them to simultaneously manage different channels of distribution in order to serve highly fragmented markets. Xerox Corp.'s early 1999 restructuring—its third in less than a decade—illustrates the kind of new, creative designs that will be required by the organization of the future.

For years, Xerox basically sold a range of generic products through a sales force that called on companies, built relationships, and helped customers to learn about the features and benefits of those products. But changes in the environment battered the business design that had served Xerox so well. Early in the 1990s, Xerox reorganized into business units that focused on selling particular products to corresponding segments of the office market. But after just a few years, that design, and its later refinements, failed to keep pace with the continued fragmentation of the market. The digital office, the proliferation of small businesses and home offices, the demand for new ways to purchase and service equipment, the unique document requirements of specific industries—they all served to fragment the market for office equipment and solutions.

In many cases, companies were no longer satisfied with just "the box," a free-standing copier sitting in a side office. As the digital office became a reality, more customers demanded a networked, multi-function machine to help them solve production, distribution, and archiving problems; others wanted the software and systems design to make the whole set-up work seamlessly. And in extreme cases, they wanted Xerox not only to supply the system, but to design and operate it as well. At the other end of the spectrum was the so-called SOHO market (Small Office/Home Office), whose customers were primarily interested in products that were inexpensive, high quality, easily installed and operated, and quickly ordered, often by phone or over the Internet. And in the middle was still a substantial conventional market, businesses that were happy to keep dealing with the traditional sales force.

Early in 1999, Xerox reconfigured the front end of the organization to focus on customer segments (Figure 5). These segments recognized the geographic distinctions markets in varying stages of economic development and the specific needs of customers in various industries. Facing these customer segments were an array of targeted operations and business groups. General Markets Operations, for example, was aimed at the lower end of the market, and consequently required the structures, processes, culture, and clock speed needed to meet the demands of the small

FIGURE 5   Xerox Organizational Design

customer. On the other hand, Industry and Solutions Operations focused on solutions rather than products, and was further segmented by industry on the principle that systems solutions in financial services and pharmaceuticals, for example, must be unique and custom-tailored.

The Xerox organization design leverages the back end of the value chain, the common technologies. It involves an uncommonly complex design on the front end, however, one that recognizes that Xerox must provide immense variety in the ways it goes to market if it is to compete successfully in a marketplace characterized by the fragmentation of sub-markets.

5. DESIGN METRICAL RESEARCH AND DEVELOPMENT   The strategic imperative of competitive innovation will require the organization of the future to design the structures and processes that guide research and development in some new and creative ways.

Today, different companies design their R&D processes in different configurations, but in the end, there tends to be a single innovation model patterned around the basic business model. That model is entirely inconsistent with the notion of design divergence. Within the same enterprise, businesses and operations with very different strategies will require dramatically different innovation streams, or processes for turning ideas into marketable products. Organizations that insist on applying a single innovation process symmetrically across the enterprise will inevitably run into trouble.

The problem is that competing simultaneously in both the present and the future requires a range of R&D processes, structures, priorities, and behavior. In a mature business, the emphasis in innovation is on the right solution—the absolutely right solution. The marketplace will accept nothing less. Particularly if you're among the market leaders, you can follow a highly structured process with strictly enforced priorities, deadlines and resource allocations.

The picture is entirely different in emerging markets. There, the priorities are speed and flexibility. If you can be first to market, a roughly right solution is better than none; in the extra time it might take to find the absolutely perfect solution, the market could well pass you by. And in those early stages of product life cycle, the customer calls the shots; R&D operations need the flexibility to respond swiftly to unexpected opportunities and challenges.

Consequently, companies whose strategy requires a range of business designs cannot employ symmetrical innovation processes and hope to succeed. There will still be value in a core R&D function; allocating all R&D to the business units eliminates an important potential source of leverage. But the processes by which R&D operates in relation to each business unit—goal setting, funding mechanisms, conflict resolution, etc.—need to be customized and asymmetrical.

6. CONSTRUCT CONFLICT MANAGEMENT PROCESSES In the past, as we've mentioned, an important role of organization design was to preserve consistency, stability, and perhaps even a degree of harmony within the organization. But as we look to the future, organizations that use design to impose an artificial sense of stability in the face of sweeping environmental change will become their own worst enemy.

Instead, effective leaders will actually use organization design to import the conflict and competition of the marketplace into the very structure of their companies. But as the proliferation of internally competitive strategies becomes commonplace, what are the implications for organizations and their leaders?

In short, conflict management will become an essential organizational capability. Today, an extremely short list of companies—Intel usually tops the list—have established reputations for their ability to creatively manage internal conflict. What is a rare talent today will become a standard requirement before long. The successful organization of the future will need to develop the processes, cultures, and behaviors capable of accommodating and resolving conflict in ways that benefit the customer and strengthen the value proposition.

So far, we've been describing organizational challenges that directly correspond with the new strategic imperatives. There are two additional organizational challenges that apply to the full range of strategic imperatives: the changing nature of organizational coherence, and the magnified role of executive teams. Both address the issue of how to manage the organization of the future as it changes to address the growing demands of speed, variable business design, abbreviated strategic cycles, greater go-to-market variability, competitive innovation, and intra-enterprise cannibalism.

7. ORGANIZATIONAL COHERENCE In recent years, we've witnessed a growing recognition that values, culture, and shared goals are replacing formal structures as the glue that holds organizations together. That trend will rapidly accelerate as the result of the strategic and organizational changes we've discussed here.

As business units and operating companies become increasingly autonomous, to the point of becoming outright competitors with one another, the very nature of organizational coherence will undergo a radical transformation. Job titles, formal structures, and bureaucratic procedures will have less and less importance to people whose primary loyalty will be to their own business group and, even more narrowly, to their own professional discipline. Organizational coherence at the enterprise level will become increasingly difficult to maintain, and will rest almost entirely on a common goal and a small number of shared values—not the formal rhetorical flourishes that are the organization's espoused values, but those few values that truly embody the way people think of themselves and their enterprise.

In that context, the notions of "brand" and identity will assume growing importance within the enterprise. The dominant cultural norms—the HP Way, the feistiness of Sun Microsystems, the insistence on winning at Lucent Technologies, Intel's creative conflict, or Microsoft's self-image as the best and the brightest—these will be the understood, though not always explicit, values that will hold divergent enterprises together. The so-called "soft stuff" will, over time, become the essential stuff.

8. EXECUTIVE TEAMS Where will the leadership come from to generate this intangible coherence while managing the tangible hardware of the enterprise? The answer will be in the executive team.

Consider the degree of complexity we're envisioning for the organization of the future. In a sense, what we're talking about is the capacity to manage paradoxes. Large organizations will have to be managed as if they were small; they'll have to be both global and local; they'll need to promote both internal conflict and overall coherence. It's virtually impossible to imagine how a single person, in the form of the CEO, could possess the staggering combination of leadership skills, managerial talent, and technical knowledge required to meet these assorted strategic and organizational challenges. It's absurd to expect that of one person.

Instead, it will fall more and more to the executive team to become the key mechanism for managing the organization of the future. That does not diminish the role of the CEO; to the contrary, the effective CEO will have to become a deft leader of the executive team, a major job in itself. It will require the combined efforts of the CEO and the executive team, working together, to truly understand and anticipate the changes in the environment. It will be up to them to make the critical strategic decision. It will require their combined efforts to understand the timing and guide the implementation of the constant refinement and tuning the complex organization will demand— redesigning the structure to add focus here or to provide more leverage there.

These sophisticated tasks will require the combined intellect of senior people who share a commitment to the common good of the enterprise. Indeed, the enormity of the challenge suggests that senior leadership will need to be expanded for certain types of work, drawing upon the skills, knowledge, and insights of people who haven't traditionally been viewed as members of the senior-level inner circle. One of the challenges for top leaders will be to determine when, how, and in what situations to make the top team more inclusive rather than less.

What is clear is that the organization of the future, in order to succeed, will become less dependent on the independent actions of disaggregated individuals. To succeed, organizations will have to develop a competency in the design and leadership of executive teams, a collective skill that will be just as important as the ability to design innovative strategies and organizational architectures.

MAKING MERGERS AND ACQUISITIONS WORK: STRATEGIC AND PSYCHOLOGICAL PREPARATION*

Mitchell Lee Marks

Philip H. Mirvis

Fewer than one quarter of mergers and acquisitions achieve their financial objectives, as measured in ways including share value, return on investment, and postcombination profitability. Many factors account for this dismal track record: buying the wrong company, paying the wrong price, making the deal at the wrong time. Another factor, however, seems to be at the core of many failed combinations—the process through which the deal is conceived and executed.[1]

Corporate combinations—the merger of separate entities into a new firm or the acquisition of one firm by another—have become a regular component of the managerial repertoire. Many motives prompt executives to acquire or merge with another organization. Perhaps a combination can help a company pursue a strategy that would otherwise be too costly, risky, or technologically advanced to achieve independently. Other deals are opportunistic, as when a troubled competitor seeks a savior or when a bidding war ensues after a firm is put into play. Still other acquisitions or mergers can be defensive moves to protect market share in a declining or consolidating industry.

The overarching reason for combining with another organization is that the union will provide for the attainment of strategic goals more quickly and inexpensively than if the company acted on its own.[2] In this era of intense and turbulent change, involving rapid technological advances and ever increasing globalization, combinations also enable organizations to gain flexibility, leverage competencies, share resources, and create opportunities that otherwise would be inconceivable.

Despite their frequency, corporate combinations have proven difficult events for organizational researchers to assess. The nature of doing a deal runs counter to the requirements of sound research. For both legal and competitive reasons, merger negotiations are shrouded in secrecy. This hinders data collection, but also means that researchers cannot anticipate and identify research sites before the combination occurs. Even after the announcement of a deal, more questions than answers remain. Executives are harried and employees anxious; no one has the time or the inclination to cooperate with a research program. And combinations pose some substantial methodological dilemmas. For example, when does a merger begin—as it is conceived, when it is announced, or when it receives legal approval? Similarly, there is no discrete ending to a merger.

As a result, most research investigations of the process through which combinations have been managed tend to be retrospective. A typical research design asks senior executives to assess the relative influence of various factors on the outcomes of their past combination activities. With 20/20 hindsight, executives acknowledge the human, organizational, and cultural aspects of the combination-management process. However, the lessons learned from past combinations are not being applied in a systematic manner to the management of current combinations.

Combination Phases

For more than 20 years, we have been involved in an action research program investigating and addressing human, cultural, and organizational aspects of corporate combinations.[3] During this time, we have participated as researchers or consultants in over 70 mergers and acquisitions. These combinations have involved large, medium, and small companies, have been friendly and unfriendly, and have spanned a broad range of industry sectors—including financial services, telecom, high tech, health care, pharmaceuticals, manufacturing, professional services, consumer products, entertainment, and government.

Early in our research program, we collaborated with Management Analysis Center of Cambridge, MA, in a study of combinations in banking and finance.[4] This research showed that significant differences could be identified between typical and successful cases by separating the distinct phases organizations go through in the transition from independent to integrated entities:

- precombination phase, as the deal is conceived and negotiated by executives and then legally approved by shareholders and regulators;

- combination phase, as integration planning ensues and implementation decisions are made;
- postcombination phase, as the combined entity and its people regroup from initial implementation and the new organization settles in.

To be sure, these are not clear-cut phases. Integration planning increasingly occurs in the precombination phase, before the deal receives legal approval. Pfizer and Warner-Lambert launched integration planning teams before their deal closed in June 2000, and AOL's President Robert Pittman moved into an office at Time-Warner's New York City headquarters even as federal regulators were reviewing that corporate marriage. Still, some distinct emphases emerged during the earliest months as a deal was being conceived and negotiated that distinguished the combinations that did and did not meet their strategic and financial objectives.

In the precombination phase, a financial tunnel vision predominated in the typical disappointing cases. Buyers concentrated on the numbers: what the target was worth; what price premium, if any, to pay; what the tax implications were; and how to structure the transaction. The decision to do a deal was typically framed in terms of the combined balance sheet of the companies, projected cash flows, and hoped-for return on investment.

Two interrelated human factors added to this financial bias. First, members of the buy team in most instances came from financial positions or backgrounds. They brought a financial mindset to their study of a partner and their judgments about synergies were mostly informed by financial models and ratios. They often did not know very much about, say, manufacturing or marketing; nor did they bring an experienced eye to assessments of a partner's capabilities in these regards. There was also a tendency for hard criteria to drive out soft matters in these cases. If the numbers looked good, any doubts about organizational or cultural differences tended to be scoffed at and dismissed.

In the successful cases, by contrast, buyers brought a strategic mindset to the deal. They positioned financial analyses in a context of an overarching aim and intent. Successful buyers also had a clear definition of specific synergies they sought in a combination and concentrated on testing them well before momentum built and any negotiations commenced. Here, too, human factors played a part. Members of the buy team in successful cases came from technical and operational, as well as financial, positions. And during the scouting phase, they dug deep into the operations and markets of a candidate when gauging its fit. Sensible buyers considered carefully the risks and problems that might turn a strategically sound deal sour. This does not mean that the financial analyses were neglected or that they were any less important to success. To the contrary, what put combinations on the road toward success was both an in-depth financial understanding of a proposed combination, and a serious examination of what it would take to produce desired financial results.

Putting a Combination on the Path Toward Success

Steering a combination toward the successful path begins in the precombination phase. Many observers liken organizational combinations to organ transplants. The surgery must be well thought out and planned, and the surgical team and patient prepped, prior to the operation, to allow for rapid execution and minimize the likelihood of rejection. We urge clients to be proactive in the precombination phase: planning and preparation are integral to success when companies join forces.

Preparation in a combination covers strategic and psychological matters. The strategic challenges concern key analyses that clarify and bring into focus the sources of synergy in a combination. This involves reality testing potential synergies in light of the two sides' structures and cultures and establishing the desired relationship between the two companies. The psychological challenges cover the actions required to understand the mindsets that people bring with them and develop over the course of a combination. This means raising people's awareness of and capacities to respond to the normal and to-be-expected stresses and strains of living through a combination.

Purpose, Partner, Parameters, and People

The journey toward a successful combination begins well before dealings commence. As strategic intent and selection criteria are set, as a deal is being conceived, and as potential partners are screened, assessed, and negotiated with, executives, staff specialists, and advisors need to continuously address at least four different aspects of their potential combination: purpose, partner, parameters, and people.

Purpose: Putting Strategy to Work

The strategic synergies in a combination should lead to a set of decisions in the precombination phase on the intentions, rationale, and criteria for the deal. They guide eventual action for excavating sources of productive combination.

Strategic Intent

Strategy setting begins with scrutiny of an organization's own competitive and market status, its strengths and weaknesses, its top management's aspirations and goals. The results define a direction for increased growth, profitability, or market penetration in existing businesses, for diversification into new areas, or simply for cash investment—which may or may not involve combination activity.

In successful acquisition programs, the CEO, relevant corporate and division management, and various advisors translate these objectives into specific strategic and investment criteria. Most buying companies have standard metrics for evaluating a candidate that include its earnings, discounted cash flow, and annual return on investment. They also have objectives about the impact of a combination on profitability, the combined organization's earnings per share, and future funding requirements.

Here the typical and successful combination roads part ways. In so many cases, financial fit receives a disproportionate amount of attention and priority in the search for a partner. In successful cases, financial criteria are respected and adhered to, but are balanced by careful consideration of each of the synergies sought in a combination and what it will take to realize them. Knowledge gained from this careful look at synergies not only sharpens the parties' assessment of their potential acquisitions, it also enables leadership to put forward a clear and convincing rationale for the combination that goes beyond the numbers. Most combinations involve expense-reduction. Executives who seek to create value have to be able to demonstrate to staff on both sides that there is more to the deal than cost-cutting—and that involves a crisp statement of how synergies will be realized and what that means for the people involved. Two recent oil industry mergers illustrate how early intentions influence subsequent integration. BP selected Amoco and ARCO as integration partners because both provided good fits with BP's retail operations and oil reserves. Exxon Mobil was a copy-cat merger. Rather than highlight strategic intent, these firms were motivated by a need to catch up with the scale of the new market leader and relied purely on financial analyses. With no strategic intent guiding integration, the result was a political free-for-all in which integration decisions were based on empire building and turf protection rather than strategy.

If the true motives underlying a combination have less to do with strategy and more to do with non-rational forces—for example, the desire to run the largest company in an industry or the fear of being swallowed up by competitors—then a successful combination is unlikely because there are no true benefits to reap by joining forces. Yet combinations based on such motives are not infrequent. A blue-ribbon panel of financial experts concluded 20 years ago that CEO ego was the primary force driving mergers and acquisitions in the United States.[5] More recently, a Columbia University business school study found that the bigger the ego of the acquiring company's CEO, the higher the premium the company is likely to pay for a target.[6]

Clear Criteria

When they have a voice in and can agree on the merits of a strategy, top executives, corporate planners, and line managers operate from a common interest and perspective. To enforce this consensus, corporate leaders assert strategic criteria and make sure the acquisition team searches for candidates that fit them.

A firm first needs to know what it is looking for in an acquisition candidate or merger partner. Having a full and open review of these criteria allows for debate and consensus building between staff and line executives. If conflicts or confusion about these criteria are not fully addressed up front, they will persist down the road. Applying these criteria religiously greatly increases the likelihood of selecting a partner that will bring true productive value to the combination, rather than one that will just be an acquisition for the sake of doing a deal. Understanding precisely what synergies are sought sets the stage for subsequently mining opportunities through the combination planning and implementation phases. The more unified both sides are—within and between themselves—about what is being sought, the more focused they can be in realizing their objectives.

Two sets of criteria help here. One is a generic set of criteria that guide a firm's overall combination program and strategy. These are characteristics of organizations that must be present in any combination partner. At Emerson Electronic, a few factors guide search and selection of all alliance partners, such as not going into business with firms in turnaround situations and not straying beyond its core competency in manufacturing.[7]

The second set of criteria guide the assessment and selection of a specific partner. In its effort to acquire other healthcare providers, a southern California hospital established criteria for what it was looking for in this particular search. These included "maintain/enhance quality of care—bring a continually improving level of quality care to the community served by the hospital" and "geographic distribution—enhance the geographic reach of the hospital across Los Angeles county and throughout southern California." Some selection criteria were at odds with one another, such as finding a partner that is both the "low-cost provider" and "adds prestige." The hospital's executive team prioritized the relative importance of each criterion prior to the selection process. When it came time to evaluate choices, the team then assessed the multiple candidates and weighted the high priority criteria accordingly.

Partner: Search and Selection

Successful acquirers know what they are looking for and conduct a thorough due diligence to ensure that they get what they want. Their screening of candidates covers the obvious strategic and financial criteria, but extends also to include assessments of the human and cultural elements that can undermine an otherwise sound deal. How deep is the management talent in the target? What labor relations issues lurk around the corner? How does the company go about doing its business? Is their culture a good enough fit with ours?

Thorough Screening

The value-creating acquisition of Benham Capital Management Group by Twentieth Century Advisors began with a screening process that integrated human and cultural issues with strategic and operational criteria. Both firms meshed along operational lines in offering only no-load mutual funds and treating small shareholders well; but one senior executive told us that an exchange of corporate values statements during due diligence was among the data indicating that cultural compatibility existed as well; "Their 'Guiding Principles' and our 'Statement of Beliefs' were very similar. Both companies stated honesty as a fundamental belief and you don't too often see that both stated and acted out in the financial-services industry."

A thorough assessment of combination candidates also covers less tangible matters. First, it reveals the motives of the sellers in an acquisition or partners in a merger. Why does leadership of the target want to sell? Are they responding to a business opportunity or are they driven by more personal motives, like wanting to cash out their investment? Does senior leadership want to stay on board after the sale? Do the buyers want the seller's leadership to stay? If so, will there be good chemistry between the leaders of the two sides?

Second, thorough screening gets below the top leadership and considers the mindsets of the two management teams. How do the target's people feel about working with or for the buyer's people? Are they looking for a company with deep pockets to fund them to glory, or are they likely to fight hard to fend off any threats to their autonomy after the deal closes? Does the buyer's management team buy into this deal or do factions exist? Where does the target's team stand? Are the technical and professional staff—who are outside the inner circle, but are needed to make the combination work—involved in the process? Are they apt to depart after a combination is announced? Even if answers to these questions are not deal killers, they indicate what has to be done to win people over during courtship phase.

A thorough precombination screening comes only from speaking directly with a good cross-section of the management team from the potential partner. Automated Data Processing CEO Art Weinbach is clear on the value of face-to-face due diligence with an array of managers from potential partners: "The greater surprises have come to us in the people and the people relationships. We have to spend more time on the people side of the equation in the due-diligence period. That is not as simple as looking at organizational charts; it requires speaking and listening to people both for the formal business issues as well as the less formal how does it really work issues. You learn a lot by listening."[8]

Diligent Due Diligence

In most combination programs, true diligence needs to be put back into due diligence. Typically, the financial people who dominate due-diligence teams get a sense of the partner they want and build a case for combination going forward. It is important to get people on the team who will probe deeply and thoroughly enough to work backward and identify faulty assumptions and what might hinder eventual success.

Take information technology as an example. Proper due diligence ascertains first the extent to which the candidate's system has the capacity to meet its own current and future business needs, and then considers the compatibility between the two sides' systems right now and following anticipated growth. If the capacity and compatibility are not there, then the cost for getting there—and the impact of that cost on the financials of the deal—needs to be determined through a realistic (as opposed to an overly optimistic) evaluation.

Broadening the membership of the team also enhances organizational due diligence. Membership can be expanded to include staff professionals from areas like human resources and information technology, and operating managers who will be working with new partners if the combination is carried out. A functional specialist provides a breadth of analysis that simply cannot be conducted by a corporate generalist. Operations managers have a particularly important role on due-diligence teams. They can find many reasons why a deal that looks good on paper would crash on takeoff. In addition to reviewing operational issues, they can also assess the chemistry between themselves and their counterparts. If it is not there early on, it is not likely to be developed later. Differing viewpoints and preferences for how to conduct business are not in and of themselves reasons to negate a deal, but incongruent values, genuine distrust, and outright animosity should be noted as red flags.

Some organizations we have worked with place up to 20 people on their due-diligence teams. This may be bulky in terms of scheduling logistics and organizing findings, but it pays off when a potential showstopper gets unearthed. One organization convenes two diligence teams to assess candidates and overcome the deal fever that frequently afflicts due diligence. Knowing that a poor partner can exact a huge financial toll and be a tremendous burden on management time and energy, this company goes forward only with combinations that pass muster with both teams.

Due diligence is also a time to size up the breadth and depth of managerial talent in the potential partner. A study of large combinations found that 65 percent of successful acquirers reported managerial talent to be the single most important instrument for creating value in a deal.[9] Smart buyers not only evaluate current executives but also look closely at managers not yet in leadership positions.

Parameters: Defining the Combination

There is a tendency for buyer and seller to get mired in the details of their transaction and lose sight of the big picture. Studies of the acquisition process have found that a fragmentation of financial, strategic, organizational, and cultural analyses leaves the executives involved with different, and often competing, perspectives on how to put their organizations together.[10] In addition, each company has its own way of doing business, its own preferences and power structure, and a history of past decisions, forsaken options, and financial and physical investments. What appears to yield strong financial and strategic synergy between, say, two manufacturing groups may not be realizable because of incompatible structures and systems or sharp differences in cultures.

Defining the End State

Partners in successful combinations share a commonality of purpose and recognize and accept the terms of their relationship. People are able to focus their energy on a common goal and let go of any wishful thinking that may run counter to the realities of the combination. Yet in so many cases, corporate marriage contracts, like those between individuals, tend to be implicit rather than explicit, and are open to interpretation and misunderstanding. Carefully defining the end state of a deal can bring the pleasantries and promises of the precombination courtship to a quick halt. Failing to do so can lead to an even more unpleasant divorce.

While the work of achieving the desired end state will involve many people, the initial step is the responsibility of senior executives involved in doing the deal. In the best cases, the senior executive from the buying side puts his or her cards on the table regarding expectations and assumptions for the combining organizations. The senior executive needs to think through and come to the precombination discussions with a clear sense of which aspects of this desired end state are open to negotiation and which are not during precombination discussions and subsequent planning.

With this in mind, executives who hope to combine their companies are well advised to consider and share their hopes, expectations, and biases for how the postcombination organization will be structured. These intentions are largely determined by the degree of integration anticipated for the combined organization. We use a grid of different types of postcombination change to help executives think through their options and clarify their intentions. (See Figure 1.)

Preservation

This end state where the acquired company faces a modest degree of integration and retains its ways of doing business is typically found in diversified firms that promote cultural pluralism among business units. To succeed, corporate management has to protect the boundary of the subsidiary, limiting intrusions by its corporate staff and minimizing conformance to its rules and systems. Strategic synergies generated in a preservative combination come from the cross-pollination of people and work on joint programs.

Absorption

When the acquired company is absorbed by a parent and assimilated into its culture, the lead companies generally bring in new management and conform the target to corporate reporting relationships and regimens. Acquisitions in the airline industry, such as American's absorption of Air California, Delta's of Western, and USAir's of PSA, are classic examples.

Reverse Takeover

In the mirror image of the absorption combination, the acquired company dictates the terms of the combination and effects cultural change in the lead company. When this unusual type of combination occurs, it typically involves the absorption by an acquired business unit or division of a parallel unit in an acquirer. For example, Marriott Corporation acquired Saga and folded its own contract food-services business into it.

FIGURE 1   Defining the Integration End State

Best of Both

Studies find the achieving of synergy between companies through their partial to full integration to be more successful than others—and most fraught with risk. It can also be the bloodiest. Financial and operational synergies are achieved by consolidation. This means crunching functions together and often leads to reductions in force. The optimal result is full cultural integration—the blending of both companies' policies and practices. The merger of equals between Chemical Bank and Manufacturers Hanover and the combination of Canada's Molson Breweries with Carling O'Keefe are examples.

Transformation

When both companies undergo fundamental change following their combination, synergies come not simply from reorganizing the businesses, but from reinventing the company. This is the trickiest of all the combination types and requires a significant investment and inventive management. Transformation poses a sharp break from the past. Existing practices and routines must be abandoned and new ones discovered and developed. In the integration of Pfizer Animal Health and SmithKline Beecham's animal pharmaceutical business in Europe, President Pedro Lichtinger took two orthodox operations and transformed them into a new organization geared toward the emerging realities of the European Community. In doing so, he broke down traditional country-specific structures and cultures and forged a pan-European strategy, structure, team, and identity as the precombination parties merged.

A senior executive will frequently enter a combination with ideas for differing functions to end up at various points on the grid. In Pfizer's acquisition of Warner-Lambert, financial reporting systems clearly were mandated by the buyer. A reverse acquisition occurred in the consumer-products area, however, where Warner-Lambert's business was much larger. John Niblack, head of Pfizer's R&D function, used the merger to transform that organization. An executive has a picture of where he or she wants combination to end, and makes those intentions clear to all parties. Certainly this end state may change as the partners learn more about each other, and about opportunities and challenges that arise during the combination-planning and implementation phases, but both sides enter into the combination with a shared sense of the desired end state.

Cards on the Table

One of the worst moves any buyer can make is to talk merger and act acquisition. Sometimes buyers think they are doing the right thing by softening their messages and welcoming target personnel as partners. Other times, they are being outright manipulative by wooing the other side with pledges of a merger of equals when their true intention is to dominate. When postcombination parameters do not mesh with precombination promises, the result can only be disenchantment and distrust.

Whatever the intentions of the lead organization, false expectations abound in the target. Sometimes, people innocently misinterpret what they hear because of the inconsistent use of language across partners. Other times, being in a state of psychological denial interferes with partners' truly hearing what is being stated. Still other times, a partner knows quite well what is being said, but presumes that its own political skills will reign and change the situation as the organizations come together.

Announcing the desired end state provides an early opportunity to clear the air of any misperceptions or fantasies about how the two sides will coexist in the combined organization. Beyond checking misperceptions, a well articulated desired end state communicates to the work force that their leadership has a solid sense of where it wants to take the combination. This breeds employee confidence that leadership is managing the combination well. It also gives people something tangible to talk about, rather than turn to the worst-case scenarios, rumors, and naysaying that predominate in most combinations. Finally, a clear and understood desired end state guides combination planning and implementation. With the parameters established, integration planning teams and busy executives can study options and make recommendations within a realistic context rather than worry about having plans shot down by a senior executive because they did not fit preconceived expectations.

People: Managing the Dealings

Combination partners typically enter a deal with distinct mindsets. In an acquisition, the buyer and seller usually have very different psychological perspectives on the deal. Often they bring a one-up versus one-down outlook into their dealings, particularly when the acquiree is strapped for cash and has had a downturn in business performance. In cases where the roles of lead and target are not so well delineated, psychological factors can also influence the relationship. Members of one side may see themselves—or be seen by the other side—as more worldly, technically sophisticated, financially strong, or savvy in the marketplace. Yet the very premise for the merger—that the partners will gain access to or leverage each other's technology, patents, customers, or some other capability that they do not already possess—calls for a true meeting of the minds. The AOL-Netscape integration, for example, was slowed by Netscape's self-perceptions of technical superiority; the people who believed they had invented the Internet were dismayed at combining with a firm they considered the McDonald's of the Internet.

Psychological mindsets certainly influence early dealings and can dominate the critical months of transition planning and implementation. (See Table 1.) And they often carry over into the combined organization. Awareness of these mindsets—both one's own and one's partner's—helps both sides prepare for a successful combination.

Mindset of the Buyer

To the victors go the spoils. Bidding wars and hostile takeovers are certainly exhilarating for the winners. And even for executives involved in a friendly deal, there are few moments in a career that equal the intensity and satisfaction of buying another company.

Acquiring another organization, or assuming the role of lead party in a merger, translates into a strong air of superiority. This attitude frequently carries over into assumptions that the buying company's business acumen—and policies, procedures, people, and systems—are superior to those of the purchased firm. Being the dominant party contributes to condescending attitudes about the other side: On more than one occasion, we heard executives from buying companies crow: "They are still

Table 1 Precombination Mindsets of Buyers and Sellers		
Party	**Mindset**	**What to Expect**
Buyer	Air of superiority	Headiness
	Drive to consolidate gains	Urgency
	Urge to dominate the action	Power moves
Seller	State of shock	Anxiety and anger
	Defensive retreat	Resistance
	Sense of fatalism	Hostility and defeatism

battling the problems we solved five years ago. Wait until we show them how to do things." Thus AOLers themselves felt superior to their counterparts from Netscape.

As the combination begins, lead companies are impelled to move fast and consolidate their gains. A sense of urgency prevails in the lead organization as it wants to put its plans into motion fast. There is always something uncertain about precisely what has been bought—who they are, what they do, whether they really know how to run their business. Corporate staffers pounce on the target to get their hands on things in a hurry.

This fuels managers' momentum in the lead company to dominate the action. They have studied the situation longer and have more detailed plans and priorities. Top management may have promised to go slow and honor traditions during the pre-combination negotiations, but vice presidents, corporate staffers, and managers get the taste of power and have their own designs. Moreover, they are rewarded for meeting budgets and producing results, not for how fairly or smoothly they manage the combination. As a result, lead managers often unilaterally dominate the action and impose their own integration plans. Prior promises mean nothing.

Mindset of the Seller

Why is being acquired so debilitating to an organization? In a hostile deal or one imposed by the board, there is from the start a sense of violation: Executives we have interviewed have likened it to a rape and described their buyer as an attacker or barbarian. Even in friendly deals, acquired managers often describe themselves as being seduced by promises that changes will be minimal, and as being taken advantage of once they are forced to accommodate to the new owner's demands.

A state of shock permeates a company following an acquisition announcement. Executives wander the halls after a combination is announced, unprepared to assume new duties and responsibilities. Executive recruiter John Handy found that 90 percent of nearly one thousand senior and middle executives he studied were psychologically unprepared for the changes in status and organizational structure they would encounter following their company's acquisition.[11] Seeing and sensing the anxiety in their superiors, other employees grow anxious about the combination, how it will be managed, and their personal fate in it.

One way executives cope with their shock is by a defensive retreat. This allows acquired executives to regroup and reformulate a battle plan for countering the enemy. At one acquired manufacturing firm, this led to a strategy of noncompliance and various tactics to resist the overtures of the lead company. Even in mergers of equals, perceived fears of losing status or ways of doing things lead executives to dig in and protect their turf.

Acquirees often feel powerless to defend their interests or control their fate. Even when the deal is friendly or when a company is rescued from a hostile deal by a sympathetic third party, the consequences are frequently out of the acquirees' control. Sellers sometimes respond with passive or aggressive hostility; other times, they withdraw with a sense of defeatism.

Many managers use Elisabeth Kübler-Ross's stages of reactions to death and loss to illustrate their personal reactions to being acquired.[12] Initially, there is denial and disbelief. Upon learning they are up for sale, executives go into a state of shock, denying the reality and their own vulnerability. The workforce can both under- and overreact, predicting that nothing will happen or that everything will change. People in the target company then experience anger. They will be angry at their leadership for selling out and then for cashing in. Later they will be angry with the buyer. While expressions of anger allow people to vent their emotions, many become stuck at this stage and are never able to move on to accommodate to the new situation.

For those who can psychologically move forward, next comes bargaining. People's natural tendency is to look out for themselves. Some will leave what they consider to be a sinking ship. Others will try to make themselves indispensable. Some will cozy up to new management and pitch their importance and value to the organization. Others will guard data or customer relationships as leverage for survival.

Only after time will people accept the reality of the new situation and be ready to work with counterparts in a genuine and committed way. For some, this may be a matter of weeks or months. Others take years. Some individuals never reach the stage of acceptance.

Psychological Preparation

An executive we worked with suggested that preparing for a combination was like "preparing to be hit by a Mack truck." Maybe so, but at least it helps to know that others have gotten up off the pavement and gone on with their lives. Psychological preparation for a combination means raising awareness of the normal and to-be-expected mindsets of combination partners. Preparation alerts executives on both sides to the mindsets of the buyer and the seller, and holds up the mindset of partnership as the standard to achieve.

In many combinations in which we have been involved, employees from both sides have participated in sensitization seminars to foster dialogue about their respective mindsets. Individuals hear about combination mindsets, express their hopes and concerns going forward, and learn tactics for coping with their mindset and that of their counterparts.

Another way to raise awareness of combination mindsets is by educating people through readings, presentations, or discussions of the human realities of a combination. Many organizations distribute books and articles describing the mindsets of buyer and seller, sponsor workshops in which outside experts describe the dynamics of combining, and engage executives in discussing expectations or experiences in going through combinations. In organizations with experience in combinations, veterans of previous mergers and acquisitions can share their first-hand experiences with novices. Central to Cisco's fine reputation as a successful acquirer is its use of a buddy system to link veteran acquirees with newly acquired executives.

Combination Preparation Workshops

A more dynamic approach to raise awareness of these mindsets is through an experiential activity that helps people develop a true feeling of what it is like to acquire or be acquired. This proved to be a powerful intervention when two CEOs of high-technology companies shook hands on what they jointly termed "a merger of equals." Little did they know that they held quite different interpretations of that phrase. The target company CEO assumed this meant that both sides would have equal say in combination decisions. The lead company CEO, however, intended it to mean that his side would have the final say, but would engage its counterparts to determine how to best implement those decisions. Both CEOs prepared their terms according to their personal interpretations and ultimately destroyed the goodwill between them.

The target CEO convened his board and asked it to negate the deal. The target company was in a weak financial condition, however, and the board could not justify that course of action. The deal remained, but so did the bad blood between the two sides.

One of us engaged executives from both sides in a two-day meeting that combined educational with experiential activities. The morning of the first day began with a discussion of human, cultural, and organizational issues in combinations, including the mindsets of buyers and sellers. After a lunch break, the two teams went to work on a business simulation. Acquired executives played the Green Widget

Company and lead company executives the Red Widget Company. Being competitive business people, they threw themselves into the simulation and established strategies and tactics for maximizing their returns. Just five minutes before the close of the first day's session, however, the facilitator announced that the Green company intended to acquire the Red company, reversing their roles in the actual deal. Nothing further was said about the details of the acquisition, though more information was promised for the next morning. Day one adjourned and all were invited to cocktails and dinner.

In the lounge, it was as if the simulation were still on. Red Company executives huddled in one corner, wondering out loud what their fate might be at the hands of their new owners and plotting ways to resist any changes in control. Green Company executives, at the other end of the bar, began planning how they would establish authority in their new acquisition.

The next morning, the two groups identified their negotiating teams and readied their combination strategies. The Red team was determined to protect its independence despite the change in ownership. The Green team aimed toward consolidating operations quickly. Neither team was coached to develop these mindsets; they developed naturally based on their roles. It was then announced that the two sides would participate in a series of negotiating sessions, with time allotted for the teams to report back to their colleagues. After three rounds of negotiations, no progress had been made, target executives were obstinate in their resistance and lead executives grew increasingly disenchanted with the lack of progress in negotiations and planning. In a fit of frustration at the next negotiating session, the Green team head fired the executive who headed the Red team. The facilitators then called an end to the simulation and the two sides were brought together to discuss what they had experienced.

Green Company executives began by asserting how uncooperative and unrealistic their acquired counterparts had been. Red Company executives, in turn, complained that the Greens never intended to listen to any input from their side, were disrespectful to them and their way of doing things, and were not willing to negotiate alternative courses for approaching the combination. Red executives acknowledged that what they saw the Green team doing in the simulation reflected their own tendencies in the real acquisition: They were eager to move ahead with consolidation and assumed things would go their way. More than this, however, the Reds gained a deep understanding of what it is like to have one's organization suddenly taken away in a combination. They became more sympathetic and empathetic toward the plight of their real-life acquired counterparts. The Greens, for their part, came to see how easy it was to slip into the mindset of the buyer and dominate the action. The awareness of self and others raised in the experiential activity led to the creation of formal ground rules for combination planning.

As the combination became legal and integration planning hit full stride, no one expected a complete turnaround in people's behaviors. Yet both sides saw enough movement from their counterparts and give-and-take in their relationships to build confidence in their ability to move forward together.

Commitment from Top Leadership

Another way to rein in the controlling behaviors of the lead company is to have the proper outlook modeled and managed at the top. In the merger of paper producers Abitibi-Price and Stone-Consolidated, we got senior team executives to meet early in the precombination phase, well before the deal became legal. Working with internal human resources professionals, one of us designed an offsite meeting agenda that included frank discussion about the role of the group in leading the combination and the ground rules that would guide its leadership. One ground rule directed executives to reach out to the other side as they proceeded to make staffing and integration decisions. Only if they practiced partnership and overcame the tendency to favor people and practices familiar from their side, the executives acknowledged, could middle-level managers be expected to do the same.

Middle managers who must make the deal work also manifest the mindsets of buyer and seller. Some headiness on the part of lead company managers down the line is inevitable. It is imperative, then, that senior executives set the proper tone, articulate the principles of integration, and bring those principles to life in their own actions. Senior executives must also be prepared to act accordingly when the principles are not followed. A top executive from the lead company in an entertainment merger one of us worked on recalled: "Despite all of the urgings for partnership from our CEO, a sense of 'when in doubt, go with our way' prevailed among middle-level managers from our company. It is very difficult to get people to put aside their way of doing things." In this case, lead company executives listened and responded to complaints from acquired counterparts and spent time coaching their own middle managers. Realistically, acts of domination were not overturned, but the acquired team recognized that a genuine effort was made to counter excessive domination.

Precombination Planning

Some firms are beginning to complement preparation for a specific deal with a more generic approach to precombination planning, particularly in industries, like telecom and healthcare, where combinations have become recurring events. Their aim is to have their act together when a combination opportunity arises.

As these organizations survey their competitive environments and deliberate strategic responses, they see that combinations are increasingly important for getting them where they want to go. Knowing that acquisitions and mergers are essential to meeting their strategic objectives—and in some cases necessary for their basic survival—executives take the opportunity to prepare to meet the organizational challenges in combining entities. A small but growing number of companies have either learned from their own failed combinations or taken seriously the feeble track record of other organizations and recognized the need to beef up their readiness for combining successfully.

Kaiser Permanente, the large health-maintenance organization, determined through its strategic-planning process that multiple acquisitions and strategic alliances would be essential for its long-term growth and survival in the volatile healthcare industry. Kaiser's leadership recognized that it did not have the internal competence to identify and implement combination opportunities. Advice from external consultants, coupled with the urging of an executive with considerable combination experience who had just joined Kaiser's senior team, led to the formation of an internal Acquisitions and Alliances SWAT Team. Middle-level managers from a broad array of functions and geographical units were asked to contribute their perspectives in the full combination process, from target selection to integration. Team members received a crash course in everything from valuation to culture clash. Nearly fifty managers graduated into roles to complement staff professionals and external advisors in targeting and integrating acquisition targets and alliance partners.

At Weyerhauser, the forestry and paper-products giant, consolidation among other industry players and the recognition that new ventures were likely to be pursued through acquisitions and alliances prompted senior executives to enhance their awareness of combination pitfalls and success factors and their readiness to manage a combination. Finance, strategy, and human resources executives joined with operations executives who had managed previous acquisitions in the company for an earnest assessment of their acquisition performance. The open discussion of what had and had not worked in previous combinations, both inside and outside the company, led to a more thorough and rigorous regard for the full set of organizational challenges in a combination.

At both Kaiser and Weyerhauser, organizational preparation began well in advance of combination activity. Even when organizations have not been this foresightful, there is still time to act after the initial combination announcement. In some large acquisitions, several months can pass awaiting legal approval. Most organizations waste this time. Others use it. At Pfizer, even before the Warner-Lambert acquisition received legal approval, merger-management training programs raised awareness of combination mindsets and alerted executives to the realities of the integration process. Internal facilitators participated in a day-long integration-team launch meeting that described pitfalls common to other firms' integration-team efforts and guided team members building effective teamwork in their planning groups.

A particularly in-depth precombination planning session was coordinated by internal organization development professional Ronny Versteenskitse of Seagram Spirits and Wine Group (SSWG). Soon after acquiring Seagram, French entertainment conglomerate Vivendi announced its intention to retain the target's film and music holdings, but divest its liquor and wine businesses. Employees in SSWG were in limbo as their unit was put on the auction block. Rather than wait and see what the buyer would do, Versteenskitse convened a four-day meeting of senior human-resources professionals. The meeting featured discussions of the status of major HR initiatives in the company in *light of the eventual change in ownership,* the fate of employees who would not be retained after the sale, success factors in mergers and acquisitions, and the human and cultural realities of joining forces. On the closing day, executives from BP and Amoco and Chemical Bank and Chase discussed their successful integrations. The meeting concluded with a discussion of strategies for actively dealing with the buyer by sharing the output produced at the meeting and reaching out to form a collaborative relationship with counterparts in the lead organization. There was no assurance that the buyer would be receptive to this outreach, but HR professionals left the conference feeling confident that they were doing the best job possible to prepare themselves, their organization, and their new colleagues for the rigors of integrating previously separate organizations.

Preparing to Move Forward

Actions taken—and not taken—in the precombination phase as a deal is being conceived and negotiated set a direction whereby a merger or acquisition heads down a successful path or veers off toward failure. In this phase, leadership sets its growth objectives and business strategy, and determines what kind of firm it wants to partner with, how, and why. It conducts a search, selects a partner, and negotiates a deal. To enhance the likelihood of a successful combination, leadership uses this period to prepare to join forces strategically and psychologically.

Successful combinations begin with self-scrutiny and analyses that yield a conclusion that a company can realize strategic goals more realistically, rapidly, and/or cost-efficiently through a combination than by acting on its own. This creates the basic rationale for scouting the marketplace with the intention of merging or acquiring. Fleshed out further, it also informs search criteria and is applied in screening candidates. As a partner is identified, strategy comes to life in preparing a business case for how the two parties will create value and in thoroughly analyzing potential costs and risks in putting the two together.

Companies have to organize themselves to buy and sell. On both sides, this means putting together a team that includes not only corporate staff and the CEO but also the executives who ultimately have to lead the combination. In addition to its obvious part in determining strategic and financial fit, thorough screening explores a partner's motivation for doing a deal, its culture, and the makeup of its people. Diligent due diligence, in turn, digs deep to understand if the values of the potential partner are compatible; if the bench strength exists to manage the combination while running the core business; if all parties are on the same wavelength on synergies and what it takes to combine; and if there is enough trust and chemistry to propel the combined organization into becoming more than the sum of its parts. Such diligence counters momentum and the rush to close, giving the parties a chance to get better acquainted and—when warranted—to back out gracefully.

Good strategies do not necessarily produce good combinations. Psychological preparation educates people about the mindsets of winners and losers and readies them to meet and work with their counterparts. Seminars and simulations help employees contend with the concerns that arise early on and increase once integration starts.

In the period between the announcement of a sale and its legal close, executives can begin to identify the optimal points of integration between firms, define a desired cultural end state, and prepare for the grueling work of forming transition teams. They also need to think through how to allocate executive time and talent to the combination process. Meanwhile, preparations can be made to ramp up communications, conduct training, and develop and implement retention and layoff policies.

Strategic and psychological challenges afflict all combinations, even the friendliest and most soundly conceived ones. The more these issues are raised and worked through during the precombination period, the more prepared people will be to take on the challenges of integration and contribute to mining the strategic synergies in a combination. Precombination planning readies people to move forward in their personal and organizational transitions, and establishes the dynamics that endure as the combining teams come together to manage the transition to a unified postcombination organization.

Endnotes

1. For studies of postcombination financial results, see Wright, M., Hoskisson, R. E. and Businetz. L. W. 2001. Firm rebirth: Buyouts as facilitators of strategic growth and entrepreneurship. *The Academy of Management Executive*, 15(1): 111–125; Davidson. K. M. 1991: Why acquisitions may not be the best route to innovation. *Journal of Business Strategy*, 12(3): 50–52; Elsass. P. M. and Veiga, J. F. 1994. Acculturation in acquired organizations: A force-field perspective. *Human Relations*, 47(4): 431–453; Hitt, M. A., Hoskisson. R. E., Ireland, R. D., and Harrison, J. S. 1991. Effects of acquisitions on R&D inputs and outputs. *Academy of management Journal*, 34(4): 693–706; and Lubatkin, M. H. 1983. Mergers and the performance of the acquiring firm. *Academy of Management Review*, 8(2): 218–225.

2. The strategic role of combinations is discussed in Haspeslagh. P. and Jemison, D. B. 1991. *Managing Acquisitions: Creating Value Through Corporate Renewal.* New York: The Free Press.

3. Marks, M. L. and Mirvis, P. H. 1998. *Joining forces: Making One Plus One Equal Three in Mergers, Acquisitions, and Alliances.* San Francisco: Jossey-Bass.

4. Management Analysis Center. 1985. A study of the performance of mergers and acquisitions in the financial services sector. Cambridge, MA.

5. Boucher, W. L. 1980. The process of conglomerate merger. Washington, DC: Bureau of Competition, Federal Trade Commission.

6. Sirower, M. L. 1997. *The Synergy Trap.* New York The Free Press.

7. Conference Board. 1994. *Change Management: Strategic Alliances.* New York.

8. McCreight and Company. 1996. *Ensuring Success with Mergers and Acquisitions.* Wilton, CT.

9. Anslinger, P. L. and Copeland, T. E. 1996. Growth through acquisitions: A fresh look. *Harvard Business Review*, January-February.

10. Jemison, D. B. and Sitkin, S. B. 1986. Acquisitions: The process can be a problem. *Harvard Business Review,* March-April.

11. Handy, J. 1969. How to face being taken over. *Harvard Business Review*, November-December.

12. Kubler-Ross, E. 1969. *On Death and Dying.* New York: Simon and Schuster.

IF YOU MUST DOWNSIZE, DO IT RIGHT*

Wayne F. Cascio

HR matters enormously in good times.
It defines you in the bad.
—JACK and SUZY WELCH, *BusinessWeek* (March 11, 2009, p. 104)

Employment downsizing has become a fact of working life as companies struggle to cut costs and to adapt to changing market demands. Indeed, given the speed and depth of the economic crisis that began in 2007, many companies experienced precipitous drops in sales and revenue. Those drops hit single-line businesses especially hard, because the drops could not be offset by stable revenues or even increases in other lines of business. That led many such businesses to consider downsizing their workforces. Consider this simple, fundamental truth expressed by a small-business owner in recent testimony before Congress: "My ability to maintain employment levels and hire workers depends on whether revenue exceeds costs."[1] Suppose it does not? With credit markets frozen, many organizations had little choice but to downsize their workforces in an effort to save the jobs of those remaining. In this case, downsizing was a reaction to an *emergency situation.*

Downsizing can also be part of a broader *workforce strategy* designed to align closely with the overall strategy of the business. Layoffs become just one tool in a portfolio of alternatives to improve firm performance. Management may view this as an opportunity to enhance the organization's medium- and long-term agility through well-planned and targeted coaching, change and career-management interventions.[2]

Cisco Systems, a company that has changed its workforce strategy in recent years, laid off 20 percent of its workforce in 2001 due to tough times. In 2008, the firm implemented employment downsizing only as a last resort, after deploying several other alternatives. The new, measured approach was more consistent with Cisco's long-term talent-management strategy of building internal talent rather than buying it in the external labor market.[3] In other cases, businesses adopt new strategies that require them to pursue different products or services and new types of customers. The new strategies may motivate firms to lay off employees with obsolete skill sets and to hire new employees with the skills to implement the revised business strategy. In such cases, downsizing makes sense.

Does Downsizing Pay Off?

If we consider the extent of employment downsizing in the United States alone, it is a very common practice, since 8.6 million jobs have been lost since the Great

---

*Reprinted with permission from Society for Human Resource Management.

Recession began in 2007.[4] But does this practice achieve the desired results? Studies have tracked the performance of downsizing firms versus non-downsizing firms for as long as nine years after a downsizing event. The findings: *As a group, the downsizers never outperform the non-downsizers.* Companies that simply reduce headcounts, without making other changes, rarely achieve the long-term success they desire.[5]

In contrast, stable employers do everything they can to retain their employees. Consider what happened in the depths of the economic recession in 2008. While more than three million Americans lost their jobs that year, 81 percent of the top 100 companies in *Fortune's* 2009 list of "Best Employers to Work For" had no layoffs in 2008.

Missed Opportunities

In addition to a smaller payroll, a downsized organization often means:

- Lost business as a result of fewer salespeople.
- Lack of new products since there are fewer R&D staff members.
- Reduced productivity when high performers leave as morale decreases.

Such missed opportunities—resulting from downsizing—can have a huge negative impact on the fortunes of an organization. Beyond missed opportunities, large layoffs tend to result in a substantial decline in employee morale and commitment and a significant increase in stress.[6] And for the bottom line, research indicates that companies with very deep layoffs *underperform* the market by as much as eight percent over the ensuing three years.[7]

Direct and Indirect Costs

The direct costs of layoffs can be significant. Laying off highly paid technology workers in the United States, Europe and Japan results in direct costs of about $100,000 per worker. In 2008, for example, IBM spent $700 million in employee restructuring actions.[8] Surprisingly, however, the indirect costs—often longer-term—of employment downsizing may be even larger than the direct costs. Consider the opportunity costs of lost sales, for example. This hidden cost occurs when experienced sales and marketing representatives with strong client relationships are let go or leave out of concern that they will lose their jobs. In domestic or multinational businesses, where relationships with customers and suppliers have to be nurtured over long periods of time in order to inspire enough trust to transact business, the opportunity costs of lost sales may be considerable.

The shock of changing from a non-downsizing organization to a downsizer is a major reason why rates of voluntary turnover increase among remaining workers. An organization that lays off 10 percent of its workforce can expect to see a 15.5 percent rate of voluntary turnover among surviving employees, compared with a 10.4 percent turnover rate among companies with no layoffs.[9] Since the fully loaded costs of turnover (separation, replacement and training) can be 1.5 to 2.5 times the annual salary paid for the job, those additional costs can be huge.[10]

Layoffs at high-involvement workplaces—those with management strategies that give employees the skills, information, and motivation to be competitive—can be markedly more detrimental than layoffs at an average company.[11] All in all, the significant indirect costs associated with employment downsizing may wipe out the direct savings in labor costs. In light of the serious short- and long-term consequences that typically accompany employment downsizing, it behooves senior executives to consider carefully the strategic impact of such a strategy. The next section presents ten such questions.

Ten Tough Questions To Consider Before Downsizing Employees

If employment downsizing still makes sense after answering these ten questions, then by all means implement it. If not, consider other alternatives.

- Why does employment downsizing make sense for the organization? What are the short-term and long-term rationales? Will the company be able to serve its customers better, to innovate, or to penetrate new markets after downsizing its employees?
- What is the business case for employment downsizing? Are there sound business reasons for closing an operation or worksite, for example, lack of customer demand, excess capacity, or obsolete equipment?
- What is the problem that the organization is trying to solve? Is it short-term cash flow, overstaffing, or lines of business that no longer fit the company's business strategy?
- If the problem is short-term cash flow, are there alternative ways to cut costs? Such alternatives might include options such as cutting temporary staff, eliminating overtime, voluntary retirement offers, reducing work hours, freezing salaries and new hiring, temporary layoffs (furloughs), or reducing travel and entertainment expenses, among others. As part of a broader effort to reduce costs at Commercial Vehicle Group, Inc., for example, the CEO asked four employees to devise a plan to save an additional $50,000. The group identified $600,000 in potential savings, including office supplies and cell phones. "They went after everything," said the CEO.[12]
- Do prospective layoffs include hard-to-find skill sets? When the economy turns around, as it will, will your organization be faced with the problem of trying to re-recruit people with the very same skill sets that you laid off?
- How will the downsizing affect high performers who are difficult to replace? Employee morale is the first casualty in a downsizing. Beyond that, high performers are always in demand, regardless of economic conditions. What will you do to retain them?
- What are the short-term payoffs from a downsizing strategy? You may see increased cash flow from savings in fixed costs (of labor), but don't expect to see a spike in your company's stock price. Investors want to see a long-term strategy, not just a short-term knee-jerk reaction.
- What long-term threats to the organization's strategic success might be associated with employment downsizing? Such threats may take the form of loss of mission-critical skills, loss of institutional memory, inability to meet increases in demand as the economy recovers, and a sustained drop in innovation, as survivors become narrow-minded, risk averse, and self-absorbed.
- What long-term costs might the organization incur by implementing employment downsizing? American firms can expect to see increases in their unemployment tax rates, and almost all firms can expect to see increased rates of voluntary turnover in the year following the downsizing. They may also experience the opportunity costs of lost sales, and brand-equity costs—damage to the company's brand as an employer of choice.
- Do the long-term benefits associated with employment downsizing outweigh its short-term costs? In some cases, the answer may be yes, if an organization disposes of unproductive assets that another firm can use more productively—such as IBM's former PC and printer businesses—now operating successfully as Lenovo and Lexmark.

As one observer noted, "Anyone can lay off personnel, cut budgets, and change an organization chart. It takes true genius and creativity to grow a business."[13] Assuming, however, that an organization decides that downsizing its employees is in its short- and long-term best interests, how should it proceed? What does the research tell us about the best ways for managers to execute this strategy? The next sections address those issues.

Downsizing Strategies

Generally speaking, an organization that decides to eliminate redundant employees does so by using four broad strategies: attrition, voluntary termination (including employee buy-outs and early-retirement offers), compulsory termination, and across-the-board cuts.[14]

Attrition, in which firms do not replace people who leave, is the simplest method. With this approach, employees have the opportunity to exercise free choice in deciding whether to stay or leave, and thus the potential for conflict and feelings of powerlessness is minimized. At the same time, however, attrition may pose serious problems for management, because it is unplanned and uncontrollable.

Voluntary termination, which includes buy-out and early-retirement offers, is a second approach to downsizing a workforce. The main advantage of a buy-out is that it gives employees a choice, which tends to reduce some of the stigma associated with the loss of a job. At the same time, there are three important downsides to buy-outs. One, they are expensive. Employees with long service find them attractive. Two, the best workers may leave. There is demand for their skills, and low-performers may stay because they are less marketable. Three, both high- and low-performing workers may leave out of fear. Many worry that they could be dismissed later without any financial cushion. To illustrate this approach, consider the buy-out plans recently offered by Ford Motor Company and General Motors.[15]

At Ford, offers ranged from $35,000 for workers with 30 or more years of service, who could keep their full retiree benefits, to a flat payment of $100,000 to younger workers who agreed to leave the automaker and to give up retiree health care and Ford pensions. For workers who chose to go to college or vocational school for four years, Ford provided tuition, half their usual pay, and full medical coverage. Workers who chose this plan could keep any accumulated pension but had to leave behind any retiree health benefits. Almost half of Ford's hourly production workers (38,000 workers) took one of the offers.

At GM, 35,000 workers accepted checks ranging from $35,000 to $140,000 to retire early. Another 12,600 employees at GM's former parts unit, Delphi, did the same, helping the automaker slash $5 billion in costs. Unfortunately, that was not enough to save the company. As economic conditions deteriorated during the Great Recession, General Motors was forced into bankruptcy in June 2009. A move that once seemed unthinkable became inevitable after years of losses and market-share declines, capped by a dramatic plunge in sales. More than 2,000 dealerships were closed, as GM shed its Pontiac, Saturn, Hummer, and Saab brands. In addition, more than 20,000 U.S. workers lost their jobs, and investors in $27 billion worth of GM bonds, including mutual funds and thousands of individual investors, ended up with new stock in a reorganized GM worth a fraction of their original investment. Owners of current GM shares had their investments essentially wiped out.[16]

Early-retirement incentives (ERI), in which a company offers more generous retirement benefits in return for an employee's promise to leave at a certain time in the future, are often part of a larger buy-out scheme. Sometimes, early-retirement offers are staggered to prevent a mass exodus. Retention bonuses with different quit dates may be used to ensure an orderly exit.

From an organizational viewpoint, managers assume that early retirement opens up promotional opportunities for younger workers, but one research study found that it is difficult to predict accurately how many older workers will take an

ERI. Typically, about one-third of those offered ERIs accept them, but there is a great deal of variation.[17] Beyond that, high performers may leave if an organization offers open-ended, non-targeted ERIs, and incentives may not work. For example, lump-sum bonuses, such as one-week's extra pay for each year of service, are relatively ineffective in persuading older workers to retire early. On the positive side, poor performers are more likely to take ERIs because they lack confidence about future pay increases.

Compulsory termination, in which departing employees are given no choice, is a third downsizing strategy. Plant closures and the wholesale elimination of departments or business units are examples of this approach. Although it is, of course, unappealing to employees, the managers who make the decisions do have the opportunity to design, and implement criteria based on the needs of the business.[18] Eliminating jobs or entire business units also makes it less likely that employees will prevail in lawsuits alleging discrimination.

A final downsizing strategy, **across-the-board cuts** in every department, is perhaps the least effective downsizing option. Such cuts emphasize standardized treatment of employees, but ignore the strategic importance of different departments to a firm's overall success *and* ignore different performance levels of employees. Suppose one department is comprised of superstars, and another is comprised of slackers. Why should the same percentage of superstars and slackers be laid off? *The Economist* magazine described this problem as "Snip, Snip, Oops!"[19]

Selecting Employees for Downsizing

Once the decision to implement layoffs has been made, a variety of decision criteria are available to determine who goes and who stays. Generally speaking, in the United States employers are free to use whatever criteria they wish in terminating employees, as long as the criteria do not discriminate based on membership in a protected class, are not arbitrary or capricious, and are based on legitimate business reasons. Here are five important guidelines:

1. Identify departments and functions that are strategically critical, along with critical employee skill sets going forward.
2. Identify criteria that reflect legitimate business needs.
3. Use a "funnel" approach to selection; that is, evaluate employees by critical skill sets first, followed by job performance, disciplinary actions, and seniority (to break ties).
4. Document the criteria and processes used.
5. Conduct analyses to ensure that there is not a disproportionate effect of layoffs on members of protected classes, and have all analyses and documentation reviewed by an attorney.

As noted above, begin by identifying specific departments or functions based on their strategic importance. In doing this, companies try to retain *pivotal talent*— those employees with skill sets needed to execute business strategies in the coming years.[20] A firm may move in stages, first selecting specific departments or functions, and then turning to a multiple-hurdle or *funnel approach*. In this approach, managers identify critical skill sets and then take explicit steps to retain employees with those skills, letting them know how important they are to the organization's future success.

Job performance becomes the *most important factor* when there are more people with critical skill sets than there are available positions in the downsized organization. Generally speaking, employers tend to retain people who have performed well in the past and who have not had disciplinary problems. Unfortunately, in some organizations, the lack of reliable and valid measurements of performance forces reliance on other criteria.

Once the available pool of employees is limited to those with critical skills, high performance, and few, if any, disciplinary problems, and the firm still has more workers than required—what is the next step? At this point, many employers use **seniority or tenure** with the organization as the criterion for decision-making.

Ultimately, reducing the workforce can be an opportunity to address performance problems that have festered over the years and to terminate employees whose performance has been weak. However, in all downsizing scenarios, sound professional practice requires that firms conduct adverse-impact analyses before implementing such a strategy. Document the criteria and processes used in downsizing, and have results and materials reviewed by an attorney who specializes in employment law.

Note that even when some adverse impact is expected from downsizing, this option is still viable if the criteria used are job-related and reflect legitimate business needs. Having identified who will go and who will stay, the next step is to manage the downsizing process in a dignified, respectful manner. Our next section addresses that important issue.

Managing the Downsizing Process

Despite a variety of styles and strategies used to let employees go, there is a core set of sound professional practices. Here is one such set.[21]

BE TRANSPARENT ABOUT THE CURRENT CONDITIONS THAT THE ORGANIZATION FACES, AND THE POTENTIAL IMPACT ON THE WORKFORCE. Employees want to hear the truth, and they want to hear it from the CEO. In small businesses, employees often sense when a company is in trouble; pretending things are fine will only hurt a leader's credibility. Provide regular updates at least every 4–6 weeks that include reports on year-over-year revenue, net income, current business strategy, and future prospects. Invite employees to ask questions and raise concerns. Allow them to identify redundant jobs, wasted activities, and bloated cost structures that will improve efficiency and cut costs. People who know what is going on can be part of the solution. Beyond that, if people know that their employers tried to use other options to preserve jobs, and use downsizing as a last resort, that will help to ease the pain. At Reflexite, a company that makes reflective safety products and films, the CEO regularly communicated the effects of the downturn, and employees had been involved in discussions about the business. After exhausting all other options, the firm cut 75 positions in one division. The employees' general reaction? "Losing our jobs is painful, but at least we know you did all you could."[22]

TREAT LAID-OFF EMPLOYEES WITH RESPECT AND SENSITIVITY. Give soon-to-be-terminated employees plenty of advance notice, and, if appropriate, tell them that the organization will write a strong letter of reference on their behalf. Be sure that immediate supervisors—not HR professionals—deliver the news of the layoff to affected employees and that they do so in private. The immediate supervisor must be able to make the business case about the need for layoffs, and the criteria for dismissals. Some companies have an HR representative present along with the immediate supervisor during that process. Allow employees to vent, and always treat them respectfully. The role of HR in this situation is to listen and to empathize, not to argue. Finally, create a severance plan that provides tangible economic benefits, and that reflects management's compassion and understanding of the impact of the termination. Although the trend is for companies to offer less in severance payments, fully 93 percent of them require employees to sign releases of liability in order to receive severance pay.[23] Outplacement assistance that can assist employees in job-hunting and networking can be particularly valuable, but ensure that severance arrangements are consistent across units and divisions.[24]

This is precisely what eBay did when it reduced 10 percent of its global work-force in 2008, almost 1,000 people. U. S. employees were allowed to stay on for up to four weeks to take care of personal needs, to say good-bye to their colleagues, and decide when they would leave. This element of personal control is critical. It provides laid-off employees at least some sense that they are still in command of events that affect them. In addition, all U.S. employees received at least five months of severance pay, plus four months of paid health-care benefits, plus 1–3 months of outplacement services. According to Beth Axelrod, eBay's senior vice-president of HR, "How you treat the leavers has a strong impact on how the stayers feel about the company."

ENSURE THAT PROCEDURES USED TO MAKE DECISIONS ARE SEEN AS JUST AND FAIR. Research has demonstrated time and again that the procedures used to select, notify, and support employees are critically important. This is known as "procedural justice." When laid-off employees perceive downsizing procedures to be fair, they tend to file fewer claims of wrongful termination, and voluntary turnover among surviving employees is much less frequent. So also are incidents of theft, violence, and sabotage. Indeed, procedurally fair treatment has been demonstrated to result in reduced stress and increased performance, job satisfaction, commitment to an organization, and trust.[25] Conversely, when employees feel that they have not been treated fairly, they may retaliate in the form of theft, sabotage, and even violence. One way to promote perceptions of fairness, as we saw in the eBay example earlier, is to give employees a sense of personal control by offering options that might include choice in the forms of severance, actual departure date, and outplacement assistance. The lesson is clear: sound HR practices, as reflected in procedural justice throughout the process, and practices that facilitate commitment and fit with the organization, can reduce the negative effects of downsizing considerably.[26]

ON THE DAY OF DISCHARGE, GIVE EMPLOYEES OPTIONS ON HOW THEY WANT THEIR EXIT HANDLED. That includes when and how to collect their personal things, say their good-byes, and depart with as much grace and dignity as possible. Don't allow an unwarranted fear of sabotage to govern the exit process. Here are some sensible security measures to consider: Protect computer systems by taking away access codes from terminated employees, and have terminated employees turn in their building-access cards to thwart them from returning to the premises. Don't allow long-time, loyal employees to be marched out of the building by security personnel, carrying boxes of their personal belongings and passing by surviving co-workers.

GIVE SURVIVORS A REASON TO STAY, AND NEW HIRES A REASON TO JOIN. Both groups will experience transitions. Explain how the decision to cut staff is necessary for the organization's long-term health. Give survivors hope by describing future business plans, targets, and details. Describe a future full of promise, one that will allow the company to seize business opportunities—with everyone's determination and buy-in. Encourage everyone to participate in inventing the future. Explain that you will be investing in those who remain, building skills by retraining everyone in the new ways of operating.

CAREFULLY EXAMINE THE IMPACT OF EMPLOYMENT DOWNSIZING ON ALL HR SYSTEMS. Recognize that downsizing is just one tool in a portfolio of strategies to improve firm performance. That portfolio includes workforce planning, staffing, compensation, performance management, training, job safety, and employee relations. How should each area change in light of the new strategy or environment facing the organization? Let the 3 C's—care of customers, constant innovation, and committed people—guide that examination. Japanese electronics giant, Matsushita Electric Industrial Co. did just that. It shaved billions of dollars from its cost base by cutting its domestic workforce by 19 percent from 2001–2005, and by closing 30 factories. At the same time it boosted spending on research and development, and renewed its focus on creating innovative products (Panasonic cameras, DVD recorders, and flat-screen televisions). Two years later, its stock was up 33 percent.

Consequences of Downsizing on Those Who Remain

Clearly there are ripple effects of employment downsizing for a variety of stakeholders, from survivors who remain, to those laid off, to the larger communities affected. For purposes of this article, we focus particularly on the consequences of downsizing for survivors and their organizations. Examinations of the broader effects of employment downsizing on other stakeholders are available elsewhere.[27]

Those who remain often feel guilty and depressed.[28] Many studies have found that morale, loyalty, and trust in management decline after a downsizing. So also does organizational commitment, job satisfaction, and job involvement. At the same time, stress levels, intentions to quit, and actual levels of voluntary turnover all increase, due - at least in part - to the loss of a sense of personal control over important events in one's life. This constellation of symptoms is known as "survivor syndrome."[29]

Two groups of survivors that are often overlooked are the managers who do the firing, and the HR professionals who are often present at layoff meetings. The process is highly stressful and exhausting for them, and many require counseling subsequently.[30] Here is how David Pottruck, former co-CEO of Charles Schwab & Co., Inc., described his experience after the firm's first layoff.

> Facing up to our first layoff was probably the worst feeling that I ever had in business. I went through a period of incredible sadness and sense of failure. I couldn't imagine the way we had let down these people and these families who had to depart. We made every effort to undertake that process with as much dignity and generosity for employees as we could. We wanted to make sure that those who were still here respected the way the company dealt with those who left. Because if there were other layoffs. . . We don't want to see any destruction of employees' loyalty to the company.[31]

For both laid-off employees and survivors, keep in mind that there is something known as the psychological contract that guides the relationship between workers and employers. Employees infer a set of expectations from their employer's actions, including the expectation of fair treatment. Downsizing is often interpreted by workers as a breach of the psychological contract, and surviving employees may respond by withholding effort and involvement, or through absences or quitting. For example, high-performing employees often take jobs elsewhere in order to avoid the uncertainties and ambiguities in a downsizing environment.[32]

KEEPING WORKERS ENGAGED AND INVOLVED. A recent study[33] examined how layoffs moderate the relationship between high-involvement work practices and productivity, and how continued investments in high-involvement work practices through the period of layoffs maintain workforce productivity. High-involvement work practices are those that create firm-specific employee capabilities that are difficult for other firms to imitate or transfer. They cover a wide range of systems and routines, from team-based production and semi-autonomous work groups, to gainsharing and flexible work design, to information sharing and opportunities for training and development.

Using a large sample of Canadian firms that responded to a Workplace and Employee Survey conducted by Statistics Canada over a 4-year period, the researchers found a negative relationship between high-involvement work practices and productivity in workplaces with higher layoff rates. Workplaces that continued to invest in high-involvement work practices, however, were able to avoid productivity losses, as compared to workplaces that discontinued such investments.

At the most basic level, survivors want answers to three important questions.

1. Were departing employees treated fairly, with dignity and respect? As we have seen, how an organization treats the leavers sends important signals to those who remain.
2. Why should I stay? This is a "me-question" that survivors want answered. What will be the impact on my career and professional development? Is there a future here worth working towards?
3. Is there a new business strategy? Will the organization ultimately be better off as a result of the downsizing?

Conclusion

Employment downsizing is not a cost-cutting cure-all, nor does it guarantee that short-term savings will exceed long-term costs. At the same time, cash flow is the lifeblood of organizations, and to preserve it, some level of employment downsizing may be necessary. If that is the case, use the research-based findings outlined here to downsize employees humanely and with dignity, and be proactive in dealing with the predictable reactions of survivors. Do the layoffs early rather than later in a recession, in order to avoid dismissing workers just before demand picks up again. Late-recession layoffs can be especially costly in terms of severance and other payments to departing employees, coupled with rehiring costs later. Above all, avoid doing downsizing just because it seems trendy, or because all of your competitors seem to be doing it. Above all, be very conscious of its consequences.

References

1. Mitternight, M., quoted in Wells, S. J. (2009, July). Unemployment insurance: How much more will it cost? *HR Magazine*, p. 37.
2. I would like to thank Gerald Purgay of Right Management for this helpful insight. See, for example, Right Management. (2009). *Restructuring for growth.* Philadelphia, PA: Right Management.
3. Zatzick, C. D., Marks, M. L., & Iverson, R. D. (2009, Fall). Which way should you downsize in a crisis? *Sloan Management Review, 51*(1), 78–86.
4. Zuckerman, M. (2010, Jan. 22). The great recession continues. *The Wall Street Journal,* p. A19.
5. Cascio, W. F., & Young, C. E. (2003). Financial consequences of employment-change decisions in major U.S. corporations: 1982–2000. In K. P. De Meuse & M. L. Marks (Eds.), *Resizing the organization: Managing layoffs, divestitures, and closings* (pp. 131–156). San Francisco: Jossey-Bass. De Meuse, K. P., Bergmann, T. J., Vanderheiden, P. A., & Roraff, C. E. (2004). New evidence regarding organizational downsizing and a firm's financial performance: A long-term analysis. *Journal of Managerial Issues, 16,* 155–177.
6. De Meuse, K. P., Marks, M. L., & Dai, G. (In press). Organizational downsizing, mergers and acquisitions, and

strategic alliances: Using theory and research to enhance practice. In S. Zedeck (Ed.), *Handbook of industrial and organizational psychology.* Washington, DC: APA Books.

7. Cascio, W. F., & Wynn, P. (2004). Managing a downsizing process. *Human Resource Management Journal, 43(4),* 425–436. Lavelle, L. (2002, Feb. 11). Swing that ax with care. *BusinessWeek,* p. 78.

8. Bulkeley, W. M. (2009, Jan. 22). IBM employees report job cuts. *The Wall Street Journal,* p. B7.

9. Trevor, C. O., & Nyberg, A. J. (2008). Keeping your head-count when all about you are losing theirs: Downsizing, voluntary turnover rates, and the moderating role of HR practices. *Academy of Management Journal, 51,* 259–276.

10. Cascio, W. F., & Boudreau, J. W. (2008). *Investing in people.* Upper Saddle River, NJ: Pearson.

11. Zatzick, C. D., & Iverson, R. D. (2006). High-involvement management and workforce reduction: Competitive advantage or disadvantage? *Academy of Management Journal, 49,* 999–1015.

12. Tuna, C. (2009, Feb. 23). Searching for more tools to trim costs. *The Wall Street Journal,* p. B4.

13. Franks, G. F. (2007, Nov. 14). Executives vs. managers. *The Wall Street Journal,* p. A15.

14. Cascio, W. F. (2010), Downsizing and redundancy. In A. Wilkinson, T. Redman, S. Snell & N. Bacon (Eds.), *The Sage Handbook of Human Resource Management,* pp. 334–346. Thousand Oaks, CA: Sage.

15. McCracken. J. (2006, Sept, 15). Ford aims to cut union workforce through buyouts. The Wall Street Journal, pp. A1, A10. GM: A rush to the exits. (2006, July 10). *BusinessWeek,* p. 24.

16. Isidore, C. (2009, June 2). GM bankruptcy: End of an era. Downloaded from http://money.cnn.com/2009/06/01/news/companies/gm bankruptcy/index.htm on January 24, 2010.

17. Feldman, D. C. (2007). Late-career and retirement issues. In H. Gunz & M. Peiperl (Eds.), *Handbook of career studies*, pp. 153–168. Thousand Oaks, CA: Sage.

18. Redman, T., & Wilkinson, A. (2009), Downsizing. In T. Redman & A. Wilkinson, (Eds.), *Contemporary human resources management* (pp. 381–404). London: Harlow, Pearson.

19. Snip, snip, oops! (2001, Oct. 13). *The Economist,* pp. 59, 60.

20. Cascio, W. F., & Boudreau, J. W. (2008). *Investing in people.* Upper Saddle River, NJ: Pearson. Maingault, A. (2009, July). We are planning to layoff and furlough some workers . . . What rules should we follow? *HR Magazine,* p. 16.

21. Cascio, W. F. (2009, Feb. 3). Sackings do not always deliver profit. *The Age* (Melbourne, Australia). Available at http://aap.newscentre.com.au/ahri/090203. Cascio, 2002, op. cit. Cascio, W. F. (2003, Feb.). Cutbacks threaten innovation. *HRMonthly* (Australia), pp. 14–19. Clark, B. (2003, Jan. 10–16). How to maintain employee morale in a period of layoffs. *Denver Business Journal,* p. A30. De Meuse, K. P., Marks, M. L., & Dai, G. (In press). Organizational downsizing, mergers and acquisitions, and

strategic alliances: Using theory and research to enhance practice. In S. Zedeck (Ed.), *Handbook of industrial and organizational psychology.* Washington, D. C.: APA Books. Fox, A. (2009, June). Pulling the plug on Circuit City. *HR Magazine,* pp. 59–64. How to fire people: U r sakd. (2003, June 7). *The Economist,* p. 54. Janove, J. (2009, May 29). Downsize with dignity. Available at www.shrm.org/Legal issues. Livingston, B. (2009, March). Managing in difficult times: 10 things to do to keep people engaged. Available at www.creelmanresearch.com. Making the tech slump pay off. (2002, June 24). *BusinessWeek,* pp. 84–90. My company is laying off employees . . . What is the best course of action? (2009, June 8). Available at www.shrm.org/TemplatesTools/hrqa. Roth, D. (2002, Feb. 4). How to cut pay, lay off 8,000 people, and still have workers who love you. *Fortune,* pp. 62–68. Rowley, I., & Tashiro, H. (2005, March 21). Lessons from Matsushita's playbook. *BusinessWeek,* p. 32. Tozzi, J. (2009, April 15). The right way to handle layoffs. *BusinessWeek*, Available at www.busineweek.com/print/smallbiz. Welch, J., & Welch, S. (2009, March 30). Layoffs: HR's moment of truth. *BusinessWeek,* p. 104. Welch, J., & Welch, S. (2009, May 11). Inventing the future now. *BusinessWeek,* p. 76.

22. Holland, K. (2008, Aug. 24). After a downsizing, how to motivate? *The New York Times.* Retrieved from www.nytimes.com on August 26, 2008.

23. Pressman, A. (2009, Aug. 10). Less for the laid off. *BusinessWeek,* p. 61.

24. See, for example, Dvorak, P., & Lublin, J. S. (2009, Aug. 20). Outplacement firms straggle to do job. *The Wall Street Journal,* pp. A1, A10. Institute for Corporate Productivity. (2009). Outplacement pulse survey. Retrieved from www.i4cp.com/contact. Lublin, J. S. (2009, July 7). More jobless execs foot their outplacement bill. *The Wall Street Journal,* pp. Dl, D6. Right Management. (2007). *The next evolution of outplacement.* Retrieved from www.right.com. Saslow, E. (2009, Aug. 9). *The art of letting employees go.* Retrieved August 15, 2009, from www.washingtonpost.com.

25. Colquitt, J.A., Conlon, D.E., Wesson, M.J., Porter, C.O.L.H. & Ng, K.Y. (2001). Justice at the millennium: A meta-analytic review of 25 years of organizational justice research. *Journal of Applied Psychology,* 86, 425–445. Elovainio, M., Kivimaki, M. & Helkama, K. (2001). Organizational justice evaluations, job control, and occupational strain. *Journal of Applied Psychology, 86,* 418–424. Greenberg, J. (1997) *The quest for justice on the job.* Thousand Oaks, CA: Sage. Kanovsky, M. (2000). Understanding procedural justice and its impact on business organizations. *Journal of Management, 26,* 489–511. Klein, H. J., Becker, T. E., & Meyer, J. P. (Eds.). (2009). *Commitment in organizations.* NY: Routledge.

26. Brockner, J. (2006). Why it's so hard to be fair. *Harvard Business Review, 84(3),* 122–129. Brockner, J., & Wiesenfeld, B. M. (1996). An integrative framework for explaining reactions to decisions: Interactive effects of

outcomes and procedures. *Psychological Bulletin, 120,* 189–208. De Meuse, K. P., Bergmann, T. J., & Vanderheiden, P. A. (1997). Corporate downsizing: Separating myth from fact. *Journal of Management Inquiry, 6,* 168–176. Mishra, A. K., & Spreitzer, G. M. (1998). Explaining how survivors respond to downsizing: The roles of trust, empowerment, justice, and work redesign. *Academy of Management Journal, 23,* 567–588. Trevor, C. O., & Nyberg, A. J. (2008). Keeping your head-count when all about you are losing theirs: Downsizing, voluntary turnover rates, and the moderating role of HR practices. *Academy of Management Journal, 51,* 259–276.

27. See, for example, Granatstein, S., & Young, N. (Producers). (2009, Jan. 25). The winter of our hardship. *60 Minutes* (CBS). Available at www.cbsnews.com/video/watch/ ?id=4752321n&tag=related; photovideo. Leana, C. R., & Feldman, D. C. (1992). *Coping with job loss: How individuals, organizations, and communities respond to lay-offs.* NY: Macmillan/Lexington Books. Uchitelle, L. (2006). *The disposable American: Layoffs and their consequences.* NY: Vintage Books. Zaslow, J. (2006, April 1–2). Down and out in Bloomfield Hills, Michigan. *The Wall Street Journal,* pp. Al, A8.

28. Cullen, L. T. (2002, Nov. 18). Where did everyone go? *Time,* pp. 64–66. Kimes, M. (2009, March 2). Does your team have PLSD (Post-Layoff Survivor Disorder)? *Fortune,* p. 24. Kiviat, B. (2009, Feb. 1). After layoffs there's survivor's guilt. *Time.* Available at www.time. com. Steen, M. (2002 Oct. 31) Worker morale has suffered with economy. *The Mercury News, available at* www.bayarea.com.

29. Allen, T. D., Freeman, D. M., Russell, J. E. A., Reizenstein, R. C, & Rentz, J. O. (2001). Survivor reactions to organizational downsizing: Does time ease the pain? *Journal of Occupational & Organizational Psychology, 74,* 145–164. Brockner, J., Grover, S. & Blonder, M.D. (1988). Predictors of survivors' job involvement following layoffs: A field study. *Journal of Applied Psychology, 73,* 436–442. Brockner, J., Grover, S., Reed, T., De Witt, R., & O'Malley, M. (1987). Survivors' reactions to layoffs: We get by with a little help for our friends. *Administrative Science Quarterly, 32,* 526–541.

Cascio, W.F. (1993). Downsizing: What do we know? What have we learned? *Academy of Management Executive, 7,* 95–103. Devine, K., Reay, T., Stainton, L., & Collins-Nakai, R. (2003). Downsizing outcomes: Better a victim than a survivor? *Human Resource Management, 42* (2), 109–124. Knudsen, H. K., Johnson, J. A., Martin, J. K., & Roman, P. M. (2003). Downsizing survival: The experience of work and organizational commitment. *Sociological Inquiry, 73,* 265–283. Luthans, B. C. and Sommer, S. M. (1999). The impact of downsizing on workplace attitudes. *Group and Organization Management, 24,* 46–70. O'Neil, H. M., & Lenn, D. J. (1995). Voices of survivors: Words that downsizing CEOs should hear. *Academy of Management Executive, 9*(4), 23–34. Wiesenfeld, B.M., Brockner, J., & Thibault, V. (2000). Procedural fairness, managers' self-esteem, and managerial behaviors following a layoff. *Organizational Behavior and Human Decision Processes, 83,* 1–32.

30. McConnon, A. (2007, Oct. 22). I dodged the ax. Now I'm in agony. *BusinessWeek,* p. 94. See also McGregor, J. (2009, July 27). Human resources: they're human too. *BusinessWeek,* p. 19.

31. Pottruck, D. (2002, Nov. 18). Laying people off. *Fortune,* p. 44. See also Morris, B. (2003, Dec. 8). When bad things happen to good companies. *Fortune,* pp. 78–88.

32. Dabos, G., & Rousseau, D. M. (2004). Mutuality and reciprocity in the psychological contracts of employee and employer, *Journal of Applied Psychology, 89,* 52–72. Iverson, R.D, & Pullman, J. A. (2000). Determinants of voluntary turnover and layoffs in an environment of repeated downsizing following a merger: An event-history analysis. *Journal of Management, 26,* 977–1003. Rosenblatt, Z., & Sheaffer, Z. (2001). Brain drain in declining organizations: Toward a research agenda. *Journal of Organizational Behavior, 22,* 409–424. Rousseau, D.M. (In press). The individual-organization relationship: The psychological contract. In S. Zedeck (ed.), *Handbook of Industrial/ Organizational Psychology.* Washington, D. C.: APA Books. Rousseau, D. M., & Schalk, R. (2000). *Psychological contracts in employment: Cross-national perspectives.* Newbury Park: Sage.

33. Zatzick & Iverson, 2006, op. cit.

THE HEART OF CHANGE
John P. Kotter
Dan S. Cohen

TRANSFORMING GIANTS
Rosabeth Moss Kanter

RULES OF THUMB FOR CHANGE AGENTS
Herbert A. Shepard

A turbulent business environment and a global economy demand swift adaptation, which has made it necessary to master our final topic, managing change. Change management is an art as well as a skill. Making a difference at work often boils down to helping your organization or department change, regardless of your position in the hierarchy. To successfully apply the knowledge and skills acquired in your study of organizational behavior requires a good understanding of how the change process works. Change efforts generally fail due to implementation problems rather than the lack of good ideas for change. The art of organizational change involves many of the competencies mentioned throughout the *Reader:* the ability to perceive different mental maps and question their validity, the ability to understand why people and groups behave as they do and appreciate the differences among them, the ability to analyze what's really going on in organizations (including the political and informal aspects), and a thorough understanding of what distinguishes effective and ineffective leaders, employees, teams, managers, and organizations. Furthermore, successful change agents, like successful managers, have a great deal of self-awareness.

The importance of emotional intelligence has spread to the change field. John Kotter, Harvard professor and change expert, and consultant Dan Cohen, in "The Heart of Change," contend that unsuccessful changes often result from relying solely on data analysis and rational persuasion. In contrast, they suggest that successful change efforts rely on an orchestrated, choreographed sequence of steps that tangibly demonstrates the need for change, makes people emotionally feel committed to the change, and then removes barriers to change and reinforces behavior consistent with the change.

Common wisdom held that large organizations find it more difficult than smaller firms to change quickly. In "Transforming Giants," Rosabeth Moss Kanter, Harvard scholar and consultant, and her research team argue that this is not necessarily the case. They conducted interviews on twelve large global firms throughout the world to figure out what makes them agile. In addition to making a profit, these firms were focused on coming up with innovations to make the world a better place. Kanter attributes this to their "guidance systems"—common platforms, standardized processes, and shared values and standards.

At the micro level, change agents need to develop the skill set that leads to in successful change management. One of the first writers to capture the art of organizational change was Herb Shepard. He was an early practitioner of organizational development (OD), a specialized area of organizational behavior focused on planned change. Shepard's "Rules of Thumb for Change Agents" is a classic that contains a great deal of wisdom for both OD consultants and anyone who wants to make changes in his or her organization.

THE HEART OF CHANGE*

John P. Kotter

Dan S. Cohen

The single most important message in this book is very simple. People change what they do less because they are given *analysis* that shifts their *thinking* than because they are *shown* a truth that influences their *feelings*. This is especially so in large-scale organizational change, where you are dealing with new technologies, mergers and acquisitions, restructurings, new strategies, cultural transformation, globalization, and e-business—whether in an entire organization, an office, a department, or a work group. In an age of turbulence, when you handle this reality well, you win. Handle it poorly, and it can drive you crazy, cost a great deal of money, and cause a lot of pain.

The lessons here come from two sets of interviews, the first completed seven years ago, the second within the last two years. About 400 people from 130 organizations answered our questions. We found, in brief, that

- Highly successful organizations know how to overcome antibodies that reject anything new. They know how to grab opportunities and avoid hazards. They see that *bigger leaps* are increasingly associated with winning big. They see that continuous gradual improvement, by itself, is no longer enough.
- Successful large-scale change is a complex affair that happens in *eight stages*. The flow is this: Push urgency up, put together a guiding team, create the vision and strategies, effectively communicate the vision and strategies, remove barriers to action, accomplish short-term wins, keep pushing for wave after wave of change until the work is done, and, finally, create a new culture to make new behavior stick.

- The central challenge in all eight stages is *changing people's behavior*. The central challenge is not strategy, not systems, not culture. These elements and many others can be very important, but the core problem without question is behavior—what people do, and the need for significant shifts in what people do.
- Changing behavior is less a matter of giving people analysis to influence their thoughts than helping them to see a truth to influence their feelings. Both thinking and feeling are essential, and both are found in successful organizations, but the heart of change is in the emotions. The flow of see-feel-change is more powerful than that of analysis-think-change. These distinctions between seeing and analyzing, between feeling and thinking, are critical because, for the most part, we use the latter much more frequently, competently, and comfortably than the former.

When we are frustrated, we sometimes try to convince ourselves there is a decreasing need for large-scale change. But powerful and unceasing forces are driving the turbulence. When frustrated, we sometimes think that problems are inevitable and out of our control. Yet some people handle large-scale change remarkably well. We can all learn from these people. CEOs can learn. First-line supervisors can learn. Nearly anyone caught up in a big change can learn.

The Eight Stages of Successful Large-Scale Change

To understand why some organizations are leaping into the future more successfully than others, you need first to see the flow of effective large-scale change efforts. In almost all cases, there is a flow, a set of eight steps that few people handle well.

The process of change involves subtle points regarding overlapping stages, guiding teams at multiple levels in the organization, handling multiple cycles of change, and more. Because the world is complex, some cases do not rigidly follow the eight-step flow. But the eight steps, summarized in Table 1, are the basic pattern associated with significant useful change—all possible *despite* an inherent organizational inclination not to leap successfully into a better future.

The stories that accompany some of the steps show what can be done to enable this process and appeal to the heart to overcome the obstacles to change.

Step One: Increase Urgency

Whether at the top of a large private enterprise or in small groups at the bottom of a nonprofit, those who are most successful at significant change begin their work by creating a sense of *urgency* among relevant people. In smaller organizations, the "relevant" are more likely to number 100 than 5, in larger organizations 1,000 rather than 50. The less successful change leaders aim at 5 or 50 or 0, allowing what is common nearly everywhere—too much complacency, fear, or anger, all three of which can undermine change. A sense of urgency, sometimes developed by very creative means, gets people off the couch, out of a bunker, and ready to move.

First, people are shocked, then the gut-level sense of complacency shrinks and urgency grows. It's not just a matter of the data saying that changes are necessary in the purchasing process so people alter their behavior. Instead, it's subtler and deeper. It's a loud sound that catches attention in a day filled with thousands of words and dozens of events. It's an image, hard to shake, that evokes a feeling that we must *do* something.

Table 1 The Eight Steps for Successful Large-Scale Change

Step	Action	New Behavior	What Works	What Does Not Work
1	Increase urgency	People start telling each other, "Let's go, we need to change things!"	• Showing others the need for change with a compelling object that they can actually, see, touch, and feel • Showing people valid and dramatic evidence from outside the organization that demonstrates that change is required • Looking constantly for cheap and easy ways to reduce complacency • Never underestimating how much complacency, fear, and anger exists, even in good organizations	• Focusing exclusively on building a "rational" business case, getting top management approval, and racing ahead while mostly ignoring all the feelings that are blocking change • Ignoring a lack of urgency and jumping immediately to creating a vision and strategy • Believing that without a crisis or burning platform you can go nowhere • Thinking that you can do little if you're not the head person
2	Build the guiding team	A group powerful enough to guide a big change is formed and they start to work together well.	• Showing enthusiasm and commitment (or helping someone do so) to help draw the right people into the group • Modeling the trust and teamwork needed in the group (or helping someone to do that) • Structuring meeting formats for the guiding team so as to minimize frustration and increase trust • Putting your energy into step 1 (raising urgency) if you cannot take on the step 2 challenge and if the right people will not	• Guiding change with weak task forces, single individuals, complex governance structures, or fragmented top teams • Not confronting the situation when momentum and entrenched power centers undermine the creation of the right group • Trying to leave out or work around the head of the unit to be changed because he or she is "hopeless"
3	Get the vision right	The guiding team develops the right vision and strategy for the change effort.	• Trying to see, literally, possible futures • Visions that are so clear that they can be articulated in one minute or written up on one page • Visions that are moving—such as a commitment to serving people • Strategies that are bold enough to make bold visions a reality • Paying careful attention to the strategic question of how quickly to introduce change	• Assuming that linear or logical plans and budgets alone adequately guide behavior when you're trying to leap into the future • Overly analytic, financially based vision exercises • Visions of slashing costs, which can be emotionally depressing and anxiety creating • Giving people fifty-four logical reasons why they need to create strategies that are bolder than they have ever created before

(Continued)

Table 1 *Continued*

Step	Action	New Behavior	What Works	What Does Not Work
4	Communicate for buy-in	People begin to buy into the change, and this shows in their behavior.	• Keeping communication simple and heartfelt, not complex and technocratic • Doing your homework before communicating, especially to understand what people are *feeling* • Speaking to anxieties, confusion, anger, and distrust • Ridding communication channels of junk so that important messages can go through • Using new technologies to help people see the vision (intranet, satellites, etc.)	• Undercommunicating, which happens all the time • Speaking as though you are only transferring information • Accidentally fostering cynicism by not walking the talk
5	Empower action	More people feel able to act, and do act, on the vision.	• Finding individuals with change experience who can bolster people's self-confidence with we-won-you-can-too anecdotes • Recognition and reward systems that inspire, promote optimism, and build self-confidence • Feedback that can help people make better vision-related decisions • "Retooling" disempowering managers by giving them new jobs that clearly show the need for change	• Ignoring bosses who seriously disempower their subordinates • Solving the boss problem by taking away their power (making them mad and scared) and giving it to their subordinates • Trying to remove all the barriers at once • Giving in to your own pessimism and fears
6	Create short-term wins	Momentum builds as people try to fulfill the vision, while fewer and fewer resist change.	• Early wins that come fast • Wins that are as visible as possible to as many people as possible • Wins that penetrate emotional defenses by being unambiguous • Wins that are meaningful to others—the more deeply meaningful the better • Early wins that speak to the powerful players whose support you need and do not yet have • Wins that can be achieved cheaply and easily, even if they seem small compared with the grand vision	• Launching fifty projects all at once • Providing the first win too slowly • Stretching the truth

(Continued)

Table 1 Continued

7	Don't let up	People make wave after wave of changes until the vision is fulfilled.	<ul><li>Aggressively ridding yourself of work that wears you down—tasks that were relevant in the past but not now, tasks that can be delegated</li><li>Looking constantly for ways to keep the urgency up</li><li>Using new situations opportunistically to launch the next wave of change</li><li>As always—show 'em, show 'em, show 'em</li></ul>	<ul><li>Developing a rigid four-year plan (be more opportunistic)</li><li>Convincing yourself that you're done when you aren't</li><li>Convincing yourself that you can get the job done without confronting some of the more embedded bureaucratic and political behaviors</li><li>Working so hard you physically and emotionally collapse (or sacrifice your off-the-job life)</li></ul>
8	Make change stick	New and winning behavior continues despite the pull of tradition, turnover of change leaders, etc.	<ul><li>Not stopping at step 7—it isn't over until the changes have roots</li><li>Using new employee orientation to compellingly show recruits what the organization really cares about</li><li>Using the promotions process to place people who act according to the new norms into influential and visible positions</li><li>Telling vivid stories over and over about the new organization, what it does, and why it succeeds</li><li>Making absolutely sure you have the continuity of behavior and results that help a new culture grow</li></ul>	<ul><li>Relying on a boss or compensation scheme, or anything but culture, to hold a big change in place</li><li>Trying to change culture as the first step in the transformation process</li></ul>

Increase Urgency—Gloves on the Boardroom Table

FROM JON STEGNER

We had a problem with our whole purchasing process. I was convinced that a great deal of money was being wasted and would continue to be wasted into the future, and that we didn't even know how much money was being thrown away. I thought we had an opportunity to drive down purchasing costs not by 2 percent but by something in the order of $1 billion over the next five years. A change this big meant a big shift in the process. This would not be possible, however, unless many people, especially in top management, saw the opportunity, which for the most part they did not. So nothing was happening.

To get a sense of the magnitude of the problem, I asked one of our summer students to do a small study of how much we pay for the different kinds of gloves used in our factories and how many different gloves we buy. I chose one item to keep it simple, something all the plants use and something we can all easily relate to.

When the student completed the project, she reported that our factories were purchasing 424 different kinds of gloves! *Four hundred and twenty four*. Every factory had their own supplier and their own negotiated price. The same glove could cost $5 at one factory and $17 at another. Five dollars or even $17 may not seem like much money, but we buy a *lot* of gloves, and this was just one example of our purchasing problem. When I examined what she had found, even I couldn't believe how bad it was.

The student was able to collect a sample of every one of the 424 gloves. She tagged each one with the price on it and the factory it was used in. Then she sorted the bags by division in the firm and type of glove.

We gathered them all up and put them in our boardroom one day. Then we invited all the division presidents to come visit the room. What they saw was a large, expensive table, normally clean or with a few papers, now stacked high with gloves. Each of our executives stared at this display for a minute. Then each said something like, "We buy all these different kinds of gloves?" Well, as a matter of fact, yes we do. "Really?" Yes, really. Then they walked around the table. Most, I think, were looking for the gloves that their factories were using. They could see the prices. They looked at two gloves that seemed exactly alike, yet one was marked $3.22 and the other $10.55.

It's a rare event when these people don't have anything to say. But that day, they just stood with their mouths gaping.

This demonstration quickly gained notoriety. The gloves became part of a traveling road show. They went to every division. They went to dozens of plants. Many, many people had the opportunity to look at the stacks of gloves. The road show reinforced at every level of the organization a sense of "this is how bad it is."

Through more research, again done quickly and inexpensively by one of our students, we discovered what some of our competitors were doing. The "competitive benchmarking" was added to the road show. As a result, we were given a mandate for change. People would say "We must act now," which of course we did, and saved a great deal of money that could be used in much more sensible ways.

Even today, people still talk about the glove story.

Step Two: Build the Guiding Team

With urgency turned up, the more successful change agents pull together a *guiding team* with the credibility, skills, connections, reputations, and formal authority required to provide change leadership. This group learns to operate as do all good teams, with trust and emotional commitment. The less successful rely on a single person or no one, weak task forces and committees, or complex governance structures, all without the stature and skills and power to do the job. The landscape is littered with task forces ill equipped to produce needed change.

A feeling of urgency helps greatly in putting together the right group to guide change and in creating essential teamwork within the group. When there is urgency, more people want to help provide leadership, even if there are personal risks. But additional effort is necessary to get the right people in place with the trust, emotional commitment, and teamwork to do the job. That's the step 2 challenge.

For example, the army officer doesn't pull together his new change team with a rational argument. Instead, he shocks them by taking a risk for the greater good with his comments in a meeting. He then helps them begin to tell emotion-packed stories around a campfire. More positive feelings and trust grow making them act as an effective team.

Step Three: Get the Vision Right

In the best cases, the guiding team creates sensible, clear, simple, uplifting *visions* and sets of strategies. In the less successful cases, there are only detailed plans and budgets that, although necessary, are insufficient, or a vision that is not very sensible in light of what is happening in the world and in the enterprise, or a vision that is created by others and largely ignored by the guiding team. In unsuccessful cases, strategies are often too slow and cautious for a faster-moving world.

In successful large-scale change, a well-functioning guiding team answers the questions required to produce a clear sense of direction. What change is needed? What is our vision of the new organization? What should not be altered? What is the best way to make the vision a reality? What change strategies are unacceptably dangerous? Good answers to these questions position an organization to leap into a better future.

Far too often, guiding teams either set no clear direction or embrace visions that are not sensible. The consequences can be catastrophic for organizations and painful for employees—just ask anyone who has suffered through a useless fad forced on them from above.

Get the Vision Right—The Plane Will Not Move!

FROM DEBBIE COLLARD

A C-17 is a huge aircraft. Its tail rises four stories. Watching it being built is an incredible thing.

Aircraft are typically assembled in a series of locations within one manufacturing facility, locations we call "positions." You start work in one place, then when a set of tasks are completed, you move the plane to a second, and then another until you're done. In the case of the C-17, the main fuselage might be assembled in position A, the tail attached over in position B, the wings attached in position C, the cockpit electronics installed in position D, and so on. For this you have to have a hangar that's large enough for two or three 747-sized aircraft to be in production, along with the equipment. This is a huge amount of square footage. Fifteen hundred of our employees would be in this giant hangar. They would be dealing with many, many thousands of parts. It's an incredible production process that requires complex scheduling and coordination.

The speed with which an airplane moves through the different positions is driven by the schedule. If work is not complete at one position when the schedule says it should move, or if needed parts don't arrive in time, the plane moves anyway and the unfinished work is done at the end. As you can imagine, taking apart a plane at the end of the line, adding parts, and then reassembling leads to quality problems and delays. But this was the way the whole industry did things. No one questioned it. I suppose it was like third-grade children going to school from 8:00 to 3:00 and sitting in rooms with teachers. Of course you do it that way.

As soon as Koz arrived, he made it clear that the priorities for the C-17 program were to excel in terms of quality, schedule, and cost, in that order. He really raised the bar, setting a clear vision of the significantly improved performance we needed. I bet he talked to everyone about this and got much head-nodding. "Sure, boss." And I bet most people wanted that vision and did try a little harder. But many accepted the existing basic production system as the only way to do things, and with that they accepted certain problems as inevitable. The mindset was, "Yeah, it would be nice if we were never out of needed parts, but that's impossible in this industry." So while people made small adjustments, the overall production strategy did not come close to achieving Koz's raised-bar vision.

Then one day he stood up in a management meeting and made an announcement. "We are not going to move an airplane until it is complete in position. Quality is number one, so that's what we are going to focus on. Until the plane is done and done right, no movement. Period."

Everyone thought he was off his rocker. You didn't do things this way. I think some of his direct reports, in particular, thought he was crazy. They were convinced that we would never be able to deliver on time if we did it this way. Never. Wouldn't happen, anybody knows that. Something would always bring everything to a halt. You'd have employees twiddling their thumbs at great expense to the company. You might as well expect cars to be made by secretaries on the fifty-ninth floor of the Sears building in Chicago.

We had all heard the quality speech before, but here was a guy telling us that nothing goes anywhere unless it's properly done. Koz showed complete conviction that this radical idea was right. And if his words didn't win us over, all

(continued)

(continued)

day long we had to look at a plane that was not moving until it was complete in a position. All day long, there it was, not moving. Nope. Sitting there.

After Koz made his proclamation, things began to change faster. The fact that out-of-position work would not be tolerated meant that suddenly having parts arrive on time was critical. Our procurement guys got motivated like I'd never seen before. They started coming up with all kinds of new change strategies for their operation. And—incredible since this couldn't be done—they started succeeding in getting our suppliers to operate in new ways. So we began getting the right parts at the right time! Overall, people just didn't want to be the reason that a plane was held in position for longer than it was supposed to. They didn't want to be embarrassed, they didn't want to hurt the company, they didn't want to hurt their careers, and they didn't want to let Koz down. So they started breaking through walls. As evidence began to accumulate that

this nutty idea might actually be working, more people got with the program. More started finding ways to punch through walls. When they couldn't do it by themselves, they would come to Koz with specific ideas, sometimes very clever ideas, for what was needed and for how problems could be solved. Koz would then work with them to remove the obstacles. So if it helped for Koz to talk to the president of a parts company, he'd do it.

Holding the planes in place eliminated all sorts of bad habits. No longer could we say, "Of course some percentage of parts won't arrive on time. That's just life." No, that's not life. That's life as we knew it.

To make a long story short, we transformed the place, and, as a result, quality has gone up and all of our aircraft have not only been on time, they've been early!

To this day people still tell this story, from the shop floor to the executive offices. "He said the plane would not move. Period."

Step Four: Communicate for Buy-In

Communication of the vision and strategies comes next—simple heartfelt messages sent through many unclogged channels. The goal is to induce understanding, develop a gut-level commitment, and liberate more energy from a critical mass of people. Here, deeds are often more important than words. Symbols speak loudly. Repetition is key. In the less successful cases, there is too little effective communication, or people hear words but don't accept them. Remarkably, smart people undercommunicate or poorly communicate all the time without recognizing their error.

In successful change efforts, the vision and strategies are not locked in a room with the guiding team. The direction of change is widely communicated, and communicated for both understanding and gut-level buy-in. The goal: to get as many people as possible acting to make the vision a reality.

When we communicate about a large-scale change, common responses are: "I don't see why we need to change that much," "They don't know what they're doing," "We'll never be able to pull this off," "Are these guys serious or is this a part of some more complicated game I don't understand?" "Are they just trying to line their pockets at my expense?" and "Good heavens, what will happen to me?" In successful change efforts, a guiding team doesn't argue with this reality, declaring it unfair or illogical. They simply find ways to deal with it. The key is one basic insight: Good communication is not just data transfer. You need to show people something that addresses their anxieties, that accepts their anger, that is credible in a very gut-level sense, and that evokes faith in the vision. Great leaders do this well almost effortlessly. The rest of us usually need to do homework before we open our mouths.

MATCHING WORDS AND DEEDS People in change-successful enterprises do a much better job than most in eliminating the destructive gap between words and deeds. Deeds speak volumes. When you say one thing and then do another, cynical feelings can grow exponentially. Conversely, walking the talk can be most powerful. You say that the whole culture is going to change to be more participatory, and then for the first time ever you change the annual management meeting so that participants have real conversations, not endless talking heads with short, trivial Q&A periods. You speak of a vision of innovation, and then turn the people who come up with good new ideas into heroes. You talk globalization and immediately appoint two foreigners to senior management. You emphasize cost cutting and start with eliminating the extravagance surrounding the executive staff.

Step Five: Empower Action

In the best situations, you find a heavy dose of *empowerment.* Key obstacles that stop people from acting on the vision are removed. Change leaders focus on bosses who disempower, on inadequate information and information systems, and on self-confidence barriers in people's minds. The issue here is removing obstacles, not "giving power." You can't hand out power in a bag. In less successful situations, people are often left to fend for themselves despite impediments all around. So frustration grows, and change is undermined.

In highly successful change efforts, when people begin to understand and act on a change vision, you remove barriers in their paths. You take away the tattered sails and give them better ones. You take a wind in their faces and create a wind at their backs. You take away a pessimistic skipper and give the crew an optimistic boss.

The word "empowerment" comes with so much baggage, you might be tempted to abandon it. We won't. As we use the term, empowerment is not about giving people new authority and new responsibilities. It is all about removing barriers.

REMOVING THE "BOSS" BARRIER Often the single biggest obstacle is a boss—an immediate manager or someone higher in the hierarchy, a first-line supervisor or an executive vice president. Subordinates see the vision and want to help, but are effectively shut down. The supervisor's words, actions, or even subtle vibrations say "This change is stupid." The underlings, not being fools, either give up or spend an inordinate amount of time trying to maneuver around the barrier.

The "boss barrier" is typically handled in one of three ways. We ignore the issue, we send the obstacle to a short training course, or (rarely) we try to fire, demote, or transfer the person. None of these are great solutions, the first for obvious reasons, the second because it usually has little effect, and the third because, if not handled well, fear will escalate and become a disempowering force itself.

In cases of highly successful change, people begin by confronting the issue. In order to be fair, they explain the situation to the individual creating the problem. When explaining fails, as it often does, they try more creative solutions.

Empower Action—Retooling the Boss

FROM TIM WALLACE

There was one superintendent in our company, Joe, who was considered so "old school" that people had warned me he would never change his ways. He had been with the company for over twenty years and he was very proud of our products. Whenever a customer would want a change in the product or how we made it, this man would get bent out of shape. He felt we were giving people a great product and that they were too picky. When someone would suggest something, he would respond in one of two ways: We tried it and it didn't work, or

we thought about it and decided not to try it. It seemed to me he was basically a good man, a talented man, and a man with a lot of valuable experience who was stuck in an old paradigm. He just couldn't see anything from the customer's point of view.

Once, it became so tense that one of our best customers said that we needed to replace Joe. I didn't like the idea of terminating an employee who probably thought he was protecting the company. So I thought about it and then said to the customer, "Let's do something different which might help both of us."

(continued)

(continued)

We asked them if Joe could go to work for their company for six months at our expense. He would work at a different place and have a different boss. To help make this happen, we agreed to keep paying his salary. We further said that after six months we would bring him back into our company as a customer representative, inspecting our products specifically for that customer. This would be a different job than he had before, but an important job. The idea was to convert the guy from being an obstacle for others into someone who would actively help us.

Joe's boss thought the plan wouldn't work—may have even thought it was nuts—but he agreed to go along with it. Joe was at first also very reluctant to accept the idea. "I have my own job to do and I don't want to do something else." I told him we really needed his expertise so that he could tell us what was going on when our tankers arrived at the customer's facility. But he was a real hard rock. He didn't want any part of this plan. So we had his boss tell him that he couldn't have his existing job anymore, that he could take our offer or leave.

Off he went into a different world. His new job was to be a quality inspector at the customer's plant. I don't know how difficult it was on him at first, but he had to change to survive. He had to learn a new job, a new company, and how to look at our products from that customer's point of view. If he didn't, he failed.

Well, he didn't want to fail, so he tried to do the new job. And when he started really looking, he found that an old product of ours, which he thought was very good, didn't meet the customer's needs. He found that they bought this product because they didn't have an alternative and switching would be costly. He found that another product, which he also thought was very high quality, was not seen by the customer that way because of how they needed to use it. And he found that our delivery on another product created additional problems.

So then he came back to us saying "This is no good. You don't understand that by doing this, you are hurting the customer. We've got to change or we risk losing their business."

Joe ended up being the best inspector the customer had ever had. They loved him. When he came back to us he was a new man. The "old school" barrier, the change resistor, became one of our best managers.

I suppose there are many people that you can't do much with, or people that you can't afford the expense of doing much with. But I think you need to be very careful when you hear people saying that so-and-so is hopeless. It might be true, or it might not.

Step Six: Create Short-Term Wins

With empowered people working on the vision, in cases of great success those people are helped to produce *short-term wins*. The wins are critical. They provide credibility, resources, and momentum to the overall effort. In other cases, the wins come more slowly, less visibly, speak less to what people value, and have more ambiguity as to whether they really are successes. Without a well-managed process, careful selection of initial projects, and fast enough successes, the cynics and skeptics can sink any effort.

In successful change efforts, empowered people create short-term wins— victories that nourish faith in the change effort, emotionally reward the hard workers, keep the critics at bay, and build momentum. Without sufficient wins that are visible, timely, unambiguous, and meaningful to others, change efforts inevitably run into serious problems.

In the following Bulletin Board story, four priorities instead of 150 mean focus. Focus means more is achieved quickly. Quick achievements provide so much: a feeling of accomplishment, a sense of optimism. With this, behavior changes. Those who have worked so hard to create the wins are reenergized. Those who have been pessimistically or skeptically sitting on the sidelines begin to help. Cynics make less disruptive noise. So momentum grows.

Bulletin boards are misused all the time. Put them off to the side where people do not congregate. Clutter the boards with fifty pieces of paper. Put up propaganda ("We're all committed to the vision!"). Make vague statements ("We're making progress"). Not in this story.

Step Seven: Don't Let Up

After the first set of short-term wins, a change effort will have direction and momentum. In successful situations, people build on this momentum and make a

Create Short-Term Wins—The List on the Bulletin Boards

FROM ROSS KAO

We have learned that when an organization has a great many things to do to correct its course, those leading the change are tempted to put 150 balls in the air all at one time. There is so much to do, you certainly can find 150 balls to put into play. Everyone can come up with a long list of things. But with so much going on at once, you run the danger of getting nothing finished very fast. This creates problems. It leads to frustration. People wonder where you're leading them— and whether or not you're taking the right approach.

To avoid that, we created something called "the Big Four." We knew what our priorities were. We could have listed the top twenty, but we didn't. Instead, we went public with just four goals. In essence, we said to the entire organization. "These are the top four things that we're working on. And until we get one substantially completed, we're not adding number five."

We literally published: "Here are the top four." At every work site we located large bulletin boards that everyone frequented and posted these top four items. In a factory, the board was in the canteen. It quickly became a device for saying, "Look! We're going to go do something. We're going to get it done. And guess what? Everybody look! It's done. And look, we just added another one to the list. And oh, by the way, this one is going to be done in another two weeks." The next thing you know, people are saying, "You know what? Things are happening. Things *are* getting done."

I remember I was out in the factory and I happened to be standing beside the Big Four list. This guy from the line came by and looked at the list with me. After about half a minute he turns to me and he says, "We're really knocking 'em down." People knew it. They felt the energy.

Now, granted, there were some people running around the organization saying, "You mean what I've been doing isn't important?" "No," we'd say, "that isn't what we mean. We're just telling you that that's not what we're working on right now. You need to know that what we're going to do is get something done with lightning speed. We're going to get it completed, and we're going to make sure we've got enough energy and collective participation to get this thing implemented before we move on to the next item."

For an organization that had been treading water, creating and communicating our quick wins really helped us begin to gather momentum.

---

vision a reality by keeping urgency up and a feeling of false pride down; by eliminating unnecessary, exhausting, and demoralizing work; and by not declaring victory prematurely.

In the best cases, change leaders *don't let up*. Momentum builds after the first wins. Early changes are consolidated. People shrewdly choose what to tackle next, then create wave after wave of change until the vision is a reality. In less successful cases, people try to do too much at once. They unwittingly quit too soon. They let momentum slip to the point where they find themselves hopelessly bogged down.

Step Eight: Make Change Stick

Tradition is a powerful force. Leaps into the future can slide back into the past. We keep a change in place by helping to create a new, supportive, and sufficiently strong organizational culture. A supportive culture provides roots for the new ways of operating. It keeps the revolutionary technology, the globalized organization, the innovative strategy, or the more efficient processes working to make you a winner.

In the best cases, change leaders throughout organizations *make change stick* by nurturing a new culture. A new culture—group norms of behavior and shared values—develops through consistency of successful action over a sufficient period of time. Here, appropriate promotions, skillful new employee orientation, and events that engage the emotions can make a big difference. In other cases, changes float fragile on the surface. A great deal of work can be blown away by the winds of tradition in a remarkably short period of time.

In one organization, staff write a good speech about the values the firm has created and needs to strengthen and retain if their transformation is to be firmly entrenched. But the real power comes when they present a real customer to employees. He tells an inspirational story showing the consequences of living those values.

SEE, FEEL, CHANGE Significantly changing the behavior of a single person can be exceptionally difficult work. Changing 101 or 10,001 people can be a Herculean task. Yet organizations that are leaping into the future succeed at doing just that. Look carefully at how they act and you'll find another pattern. They succeed, regardless of the stage in the overall process, because their most central activity does not center on formal data gathering, analysis, report writing, and presentations—the sorts of actions typically aimed at changing thinking in order to change behavior. Instead, they compellingly *show* people what the problems are and how to resolve the problems. They provoke responses that reduce feelings that slow and stifle needed change, and they enhance feelings that motivate useful action. The emotional reaction then provides the energy that propels people to push along the change process, no matter how great the difficulties.

A core pattern is associated with successful change.

1. SEE. People find a problem in some stage of the change process—too many of their colleagues are behaving complacently, no one is developing a sensible strategy, too many are letting up before the strategy has been achieved. They then create dramatic, eye-catching, compelling situations that help others visualize the problem or a solution to the problem.
2. FEEL. The visualizations awaken feelings that facilitate useful change or ease feelings that are getting in the way. Urgency, optimism, or faith may go up. Anger, complacency, cynicism, or fear may go down.
3. CHANGE. The new feelings change or reinforce new behavior, sometimes very different behavior. People act much less complacently. They try much harder to make a good vision a reality. They don't stop before the work is done, even if the road seems long.

Successful see-feel-change tactics tend to be clever, not clumsy, and never cynically manipulative. They often have an afterglow, where the story of the event is told again and again or where there is a remaining visible sign of the event that influences additional people over time. When done well over all eight stages of a change process, the results can be breathtaking. Mature (old-fashioned, clunky, or heavy) organizations take a leap into the future. Laggards start to become leaders. Leaders jump farther ahead.

The point is not that careful data gathering, analysis, and presentation are unimportant. They are important. Sometimes it is behavior changed by analysis that sends people into a see-feel-change process. Sometimes change launched through feelings creates a radically better approach to analysis. Often small changes are a necessary part of a larger change effort, and the small changes are driven by analysis. Occasionally, careful analysis is required to get show-me-the-numbers finance people or engineers in the mood to see.

But analysis has at least three major limitations. First, in a remarkable number of cases, you don't need it to find the big truths. You may not need to do much work to find that the old strategy isn't working and that a new one isn't being embraced. You don't need a fifty-page report to see there is insufficient new product development and that a number of factors make it impossible for the engineers to do what is necessary. You don't need reams of financial data to learn that you cannot stay out of e-business and that the first step is simply to take

Table 2	Achieving a Change of Behavior within Each of the Eight Steps
Almost Always the Core Method Is: **SEE-FEEL-CHANGE**	**Rarely the Core Method Is:** **ANALYSIS-THINK-CHANGE**
1. *HELP PEOPLE SEE.* Compelling, eye-catching, dramatic situations are created to help others visualize problems, solutions, or progress in solving complacency, strategy, empowerment, or other key problems within the eight steps. *As a result*	1. *GIVE PEOPLE ANALYSIS.* Information is gathered and analyzed, reports are written, and presentations are made about problems, solutions, or progress in solving urgency, teamwork, communication, momentum slippage, or other key problems within the eight steps. *As a result*
2. *SEEING SOMETHING NEW HITS THE EMOTIONS.* The visualizations provide useful ideas that hit people at a deeper level than surface thinking. They evoke a visceral response that reduces emotions that block change and enhances those that support it.	2. *DATA AND ANALYSIS INFLUENCE HOW WE THINK.* The information and analysis change people's thinking. Ideas inconsistent with the needed change are dropped or modified.
3. *EMOTIONALLY CHARGED IDEAS CHANGE BEHAVIOR OR REINFORCE CHANGED BEHAVIOR.*	3. *NEW THOUGHTS CHANGE BEHAVIOR OR REINFORCE CHANGED BEHAVIOR.*

the first step. It isn't necessary for a team of psychologists to study Fred and his team to find out they are failing and must be replaced. Yes, there are many exceptions—deciding on which $100 million IT system to buy, for example—but the general point is valid.

Second, analytical tools have their limitations in a turbulent world. These tools work best when parameters are known, assumptions are minimal, and the future is not fuzzy.

Third, good analysis rarely motivates people in a big way. It changes thought, but how often does it send people running out the door to act in significantly new ways? And motivation is not a thinking word; it's a feeling word.

We fail at change efforts not because we are stupid, overcontrolled, and unemotional beings, although it can seem that way at times. We fail because we haven't sufficiently experienced highly successful change. Without that experience, we are too often left pessimistic, fearful, or without enough faith to act. So we not only behave in less effective ways, we don't even try.

Consider the implications of this pattern in an age of accelerating change, at a time when we are making a mind-boggling transition from an industrial to an information/knowledge economy. Consider the implications in light of how managers, management educators, and others today deal with large-scale change.

Of course there are many difficulties here, but being uninformed and pessimistic does not help. We need more leaps into the future. And although we are becoming better at this, there is no reason that we cannot learn to become much better still.

In light of the stakes, we must become better still.

TRANSFORMING GIANTS*

Rosabeth Moss Kanter

What enables a big business to be agile?

Not too long ago, most people would have called that question a contradiction in terms. The common perception was that profit-seeking behemoths were dysfunctional. They were written off as lumbering, inflexible, reactive, and inherently bureaucratic—as systems so closed they had lost the ability to see the problems in the world around them, let alone be part of the solutions. Yet talk to the leaders of some of the world's biggest companies today, and you hear a different story. They're claiming new abilities to shift organizational gears on a global basis and produce meaningful innovations quickly.

To discover the truth behind these claims, I assembled a research team and ventured deep inside a dozen such giants. After two years of visiting their operations—a process that comprised more than 350 interviews on five continents—I am convinced that the transformation these leaders describe is real. Companies such as IBM, Procter & Gamble, Omron, CEMEX, Cisco, and Banco Real are moving as rapidly and creatively as much smaller enterprises, even while taking on social and environmental challenges of a scale only large entities could attempt—and they are bringing small and midsize businesses with them on the journey.

The key, I've concluded, is that a decisive shift is occurring in what might be called the guidance systems of these global giants. Employees once acted mainly according to rules and decisions handed down to them, but they now draw heavily on their shared understanding of mission and on a set of tools available everywhere at once. They more readily think about the meaning of what they do in terms of the wider world and include external partners in the extended family. Authority is still exercised and activities are still coordinated—but thanks to common platforms, standardized processes, and, above all, widely shared values and standards, coherence now arises more spontaneously. This shift is often heralded, and in most of these companies it has been a long time coming. But now it is happening with dramatic effects.

In this article I will set forth the pillars of this new model of big business—what IBM CEO Sam Palmisano calls the "globally integrated enterprise." I will outline the benefits that accrue to the companies that have those pillars in place, which go beyond innovation to include a whole host of mutually reinforcing effects. I will identify the various mechanisms that have helped these giants establish and maintain high standards world-wide—and can help other companies do the same. Replicating the conditions that are emerging at the most progressive megacorporations will not be easy. But if others follow their lead, soon this new paradigm of capitalism could be viewed as not only a competitive necessity but also a benefit to society. When giants transform themselves from impersonal machines into human communities, they gain the ability to transform the world around them in very positive ways.

I recognize that it has become very fashionable in corporate circles to talk about values, and often there is little behind that talk. However, for the vanguard companies we studied, values truly are a primary consideration. They help the companies find business opportunities and motivate both employees and partners.

At IBM, even before the full rollout of grid computing to commercial customers, the company gave away the technology to scientists searching for cures for HIV-AIDS, heart disease, and cancer. Grid computing enables the aggregation of

---

individual PCs' power through a network, providing the information processing necessary for big, ambitious research. As soon as IBM had perfected the technology, it created a nonprofit partnership, World Community Grid (WCG), through which any organization or individual can donate unused computing power to research projects and see what is being done with the donation in real time. Through WCG, IBM gains an inspiring showcase for its new technology, helps business partners connect with the company in a positive way, and gives individuals anywhere in the world the chance to contribute to something big. In Sao Paulo, Brazil, as I talked with an executive of IBM Latin America, he proudly pointed to the action on the ThinkPad behind his office desk, which was at that moment processing data for a WCG cancer research project.

Shared Values, Principles, and Platforms

To compete effectively, large corporations must respond quickly and creatively to opportunities wherever they arise, and yet have those dispersed activities add up to a unified purpose and accomplishment. The companies that meet this challenge rely in part on clear standards and disciplines, including, at the most basic level, standardized processes.

Consider the "CEMEX Way." Around 2000, the Mexico-headquartered global cement company CEMEX launched this companywide program to identify and disseminate best practices and standardize business processes globally using IT platforms. The point was to foster sameness in areas where sameness would make life easier. In every one of the company's plants, for example, pipes carrying natural gas were painted one color, and pipes containing air were painted another color. This made it simple for transferring employees or visiting managers not to waste time upon their arrival figuring out the setup. The same logic followed for other plant configuration systems, financial recording systems, requisition systems, and so forth.

Standardization does not mean that no enhancements can be made. People at CEMEX are encouraged to recommend improvements. If a change is piloted in one plant setting and proves effective, the new practice is immediately rolled out worldwide. Even when a change is not mandated, a novel approach can be disseminated thanks to web-based information sharing. An oft-cited example is how a successful initiative in the United States to substitute alternative fuels for petroleum coke was quickly adopted elsewhere.

Standardized management practices and technologies in companies are the equivalent of infrastructure in cities: They allow people to stop wasting energy on basic activities and instead focus on higher-order concerns. But providing a platform on which creative people can build is only half the battle. What's also required is a shared set of values to guide their choices and actions.

Values turn out to be the key ingredient in the most vibrant and successful of today's multinationals. I refer not to the printing of wallet cards but to the serious nurturing of values in hearts and minds. Once people agree on what they respect and aspire to, they can make decisions independently and not work at cross-purposes. When they team up on a project, they communicate and collaborate efficiently, even despite great differences in backgrounds and cultural traditions, because they have a strong sense of business purpose and company identity.

At Procter & Gamble, the values and standards captured in the company's statement of purpose, values, and principles (known as the PVP) enable managers in diverse locations to respond quickly and effectively to business opportunities or crises. P&G's purpose, the PVP says, is to "improve the lives of the world's consumers" with high-quality products that represent good value. The list of company values underscores the importance of leadership, ownership, integrity, passion for winning, and trust. The statement has eight principles describing how the company chooses to compete. In talking with P&G managers around the world about their operations, my research team and I heard the PVP invoked repeatedly. A developing-country manager said, "We all want the same thing: what will delight the customer and improve her or his life. To do that, we must treat our people as valued assets."

Likewise, at IBM, three simple sentences about customers, world-improving innovation, respect, and responsibility were repeated everywhere we visited and in meetings I had as a senior adviser to the company. Those values were credited with clarifying decisions and cutting through internal politics. Some of this potency may come from the participatory process by which the three sentences were crafted—a three-day chat session on the Web in 2003 called the Values Jam, in which all the employees could contribute thoughts. (See "Leading Change When Business Is Good," HBR December 2004.)

A strong backbone of shared values has always been a strength of some companies. IBM's twenty-first-century values are a reinvention of values laid down almost a hundred years ago; Omron, a global electronics company headquartered in Japan, identified its core principles in the 1950s. But in the age of globalization, values and principles take on even greater importance, and the vanguard companies we studied have recently redoubled their efforts to bring them front and center.

Shortly after CEMEX's first series of acquisitions outside its home region, in the mid-1990s, the company's leaders articulated core values of collaboration, integrity, and leadership and added a set of standards for behavior that employees were required to sign. The company soon learned to appreciate the challenge of upholding those values in parts of the world with very different ethical standards and social norms. In 1999, for example, CEMEX bought a state-owned enterprise in Egypt and found that obtaining and renewing access to rock quarries there—a necessity for cement companies—traditionally involved offering gifts to the people in charge. That was in clear violation of CEMEX's standards, and local employees initially doubted that the company would succeed without compromising them. Indeed, it took a year and a half rather than the usual month, but eventually CEMEX obtained the approval. Today, the story is often retold in situations where there appears to be a conflict between the company's standards and business objectives.

Getting Close at a Distance

The payoff for companies that have embedded values and principles in their guidance systems comes in many forms. The first benefit is integration, which permits collaboration among diverse people. This has clearly occurred in a series of national cultural projects IBM has taken on in recent years, building on its work to digitize the treasures of the State Hermitage Museum in Saint Petersburg, Russia.

The company's Cairo Technology Development Center prides itself on having world-class engineers (all Egyptian, many of them women). It competes for business globally and wins its share: A recent project for Sony in Hollywood, for example, was handled from Cairo. Aware of their colleagues' work for the Hermitage Museum, and knowing that preserving Egypt's cultural heritage was a government priority, leaders at IBM Egypt proposed a project called Eternal Egypt. It would involve partnering with the Egyptian government's Center for Documentation of Cultural and Natural Heritage and the Ministry of Communications and Information Technology to digitize not only the contents of a museum but also ancient structures such as the pyramids, so that they could be viewed in detail, virtually.

Technological innovation was required. In particular, the project demanded new high-resolution scanning technology for three-dimensional objects, which called for an exchange of ideas with IBM engineers in the United States. For website design, the Cairo team got help from an IBM team in Chicago and experts at IBM's research labs in Haifa, Israel (despite political hostilities and religious differences between the countries). Eternal Egypt was launched to wide acclaim, particularly because of the importance of heritage-based tourism to Egypt's economic development. It also led to a commercial contract to digitize the contents of the Library of Alexandria. And most recently, it became a model for IBM China's Forbidden City project, which will go Eternal Egypt one better by including a virtual tour.

The Eternal Egypt model is an important example, because it demonstrates the true global integration of a company. Innovations do not simply emanate from the home country and radiate outward. They emanate from many places. Know-how is transferred to and from emerging and developed countries through a web of global connections.

Sometimes companies achieve collaboration by bringing people from diverse backgrounds together physically. CEMEX is especially adept at getting people to the problem and gaining speed in the process—for example, seconding large numbers of experienced people to newly acquired operations to work on postmerger integration teams for periods of a few months to a few years. This encourages every manager to train replacements, even if the replacement will be temporary. It ensures deep bench strength, as there are always people well schooled in the CEMEX Way ready to mentor others.

Empowerment in the Field

Common values and standards also allow people at the front lines to make consistent decisions, even under pressure and in the company's most culturally and geographically disparate locations. Among the leading-edge companies we examined, this was the most striking similarity, and sometimes the most difficult thing for outside observers to understand. A strong, broadly internalized guidance system obviates the need for controls that stress obedience and instead promotes autonomy.

Expressing values and standards in universal terms is not meant to inhibit differences. In fact, it helps people see how to meet particular customers' and communities' needs by adding localization to globalization. At P&G Brazil, leaders called this "tropicalizing." As a marketing executive told us: "The values and principles don't change, but we respect the local trade, the local consumer, the local organization."

That sentiment was echoed by the general manager of P&G's Near East unit, which has dual headquarters in Cairo and Beirut. "Whenever we're in a tough situation, we start looking at the principles of the company," he said, "because you will find in them the answer to the problem you're having." He faced just such a crisis when Lebanon was bombed in 2006. On the first day of the war, Near East executives conferred. "My team needed to make a decision: What do we need to do with the people in Beirut?" the manager told us. Together they drew from the PVP to agree on a principle of "people safety" first, followed by agility and determination to drive the business.

It may sound uncontroversial in retrospect and from afar, but consider that attending to people safety for employees and their families meant increasing the number of office locations in Lebanon from one to three (to reduce travel distance to work and incidentally conserve gas, which was scarce during the crisis). It also meant moving people who lived in the areas most affected to hotels. P&G offered all employees working in Lebanon (including Lebanese employees) evacuation to Egypt and housing there for their families and up to three extended family members. About half of the workforce moved. These decisions were made and action was taken before any official permission was requested from headquarters. As a result, P&G evacuated employee families faster than some countries moved diplomatic personnel. Although the evacuation cost a great deal, the decisions were supported by regional bosses in Switzerland and global headquarters in Cincinnati.

Innovating In Markets

Procter & Gamble is also responsive to the diverse needs of customers around the world. But if many top management teams would object to the kind of rogue action taken by P&G's Near East unit, just imagine how they would react to local ideas that present some risk to the brand. This was the situation at P&G in the early 2000s, when it was struggling to grow its business in Brazil.

The company's Brazilian marketing group knew its consumers well; in fact, it had gained a deep understanding of local women by using the kinds of market research tools and processes P&G uses globally. Based on that knowledge, it claimed that the company's Always feminine hygiene product could not succeed at its current price point. A better offering, these marketers insisted, would be a stripped-down version, still employing the essential technology that made the product perform well, but without certain features that added cost beyond their value to lower-income consumers. Naturally, many skeptics at headquarters worried that selling "Always Básico" would dilute the brand's equity. But the experiment was allowed to go forward.

■ One Company's Return on Values

Imagine a developing country where workers like their beer and like it cheap—to the extent that alcohol use has become a serious public health problem. Now imagine you are the country manager there for a multinational corporation that profits by selling alcoholic beverages. Your goal is to gain more market share. Is this anywhere for values to hold sway?

Here's how the story played out in Kenya. UK-headquartered Diageo, the world's leading producer of premium alcoholic beverages, had entered the market with a large investment in East African Breweries but couldn't match the low price of its competition. That was because the competition was home brew, subject to no standards or inspections and sold out of garages. Illicit beer was downright dangerous in a country where water supplies are often contaminated— it was known to cause blindness as well as the intense hangovers and related illnesses that routinely lowered productivity in Kenya's labor-intensive industries. But it was popular because, with no government taxes added to its price, it offered the most sips for the shilling.

Diageo had the benefit of local talent with global thinking who could recognize the opportunity in the situation and seize it. (Over the years, the company encouraged members of the internationally educated African diaspora to return to Africa at expatriate pay rates.) Using Diageo's global resources, including a web-based innovation tool, the local team attacked the problem. Importantly, it put the focus on the best outcome for society and was therefore able to open lines of communication with the national government. The company proposed producing a low-cost beer and making it widely available, giving the buyers of illicit

beer an alternative they would consider reasonable. The safer product would succeed, however, only if the government agreed to reduce the surtax on it, so the price would be truly comparable. The government, of course, had no interest in corporate charity, but it became clear that if more people bought legal beer, taxes would be collected on a greater proportion of the alcohol being consumed. A tax cut, therefore, was likely to yield higher tax revenue overall.

To make the new beer, now called Senator, widely available, Diageo needed to develop a new distribution channel: responsibly managed licensed pubs. The team talked to community leaders throughout Kenya to identify influential solid citizens, such as shopkeepers and sports club owners, who could set these pubs up. Diageo provided equipment and trained them in business operations, eventually establishing 3,000 new outlets.

The launch of Senator Beer saw success on many fronts. Beyond the high market share it immediately claimed, Diageo received a prestigious award for contributing to reduced rates of blindness and increases in workplace productivity. Meanwhile, thousands of new small businesses flourished, and government policies started to change. The work was gratifying to Diageo managers both locally and internationally.

At the time of Diageo's formation in 1997 (by the merger of Guinness and Grand Metropolitan), its leaders had articulated the company's values and operating principles to emphasize both high global standards and local community responsibility. With that kind of guidance system in place, local decision makers—even in a "sin industry"—can have a transformative positive social impact.

Having It Both Ways

When do you know a paradigm is shifting? When long-standing contradictions begin to resolve. In the giants my research team and I studied, I was struck by the number of areas in which they achieved a balance between seemingly opposing goals.

- They both globalize and localize, deriving benefits from the intersections.
- They both standardize and innovate, endeavoring to prevent consistency from becoming stifling conformity.
- They foster a common universal culture but also respect for individual differences, seeking inclusion and diversity.

- They maintain control by letting go of it, trusting people educated in the shared values to do the right thing.
- They have a strong identity but also a strong reliance on partners, whom they collaborate with but do not control.
- They produce both business value and societal value.
- They bring together the "soft" areas (people, culture, and community responsibility) and the "hard" areas (technology and product innovation).
- They do not abandon values in a crisis; in fact, as leaders put them to the test, crises serve to strengthen commitment to values.

The manager who led the project in Brazil described for us the local energy that went into it. A small team of office staff, plant managers, R&D experts, and external advertising agency talent collaborated to bring Always Básico to market as rapidly as possible. Within the plant, a creative team found a way to adjust an existing line and reduce the cost of manufacturing. The manager told us about the day, a mere six months after her team began its work, that everyone stood holding hands and watching the first units come off the line.

Always Básico succeeded beyond the team's projections, and headquarters took note. It wasn't long before Pampers Básico was launched in Brazil. More broadly, the initiative became a model for products for low-income consumers around the world. Knowledge moved horizontally to other product lines and also vertically to other markets. As each similar effort improved on previous ones, the Brazilians took pride in having innovated on behalf of the world.

The story teaches two lessons. First, people versed in universal standards are often most innovative when they apply those standards to local situations. And second, it is critical that the standards be open-ended and aspirational, not constraining or restrictive. We saw the same kind of balance struck by CEMEX, which has managed to innovate continuously despite dealing in a product most people would consider the purest form of commodity. We heard how an idea for making concrete more resistant to salt water—a significant benefit in harbor and marine applications—originated in Egypt and made its way to the Philippines. Other recent innovations include antibacterial concrete for hospitals and farms, and road surfaces made of recycled tires in countries experiencing rapid growth in road construction.

People are even more inclined to be creative when their company's values stress innovation that helps the world. Banco Real, the Brazilian arm of a European bank, discovered this when it put social and environmental responsibility at the core of its search for differentiation. The result was a spate of new financial products, including consumer loans for green projects (such as converting autos or houses), micro-finance for poor communities, and the first carbon credit trading in the region. Banco Real also chose suppliers with higher environmental and social standards and even helped them improve their practices. By 2007, it was enjoying the fruits of its values; it had more than doubled its profitability, grown in size to become the third-largest bank in Brazil, and been rated number one or number two in various surveys. CEO Fabio Barbosa had been elected president of the Brazilian Banking Federation, from which position he could spread Banco Real's model.

A Stronger Basis for Partnering

Companies that have established strong guidance systems find themselves more effective in selecting and working with external partners—increasingly a necessity for competitive success. A more outward- and forward-looking definition of purpose encourages exploration of partnership opportunities that extend well beyond the formal boundaries of the company. It causes people in the company to think about end-to-end responsibilities to the whole ecosystem, from suppliers' suppliers to customers' customers and beyond—to society itself. And it creates coherence across the entire network. "We have partnerships all over the place," P&G chief executive A.G. Lafley said, referring to a sweep from contract manufacturing to advertising and design. "What holds them together is one purpose, one set of values, one set of principles."

Omron's principles, for instance, form the basis for choosing partners and gaining trust. The knowledge that partners would share Omron's values and standards helped the Japanese company's R&D transform what one manager called a "not-invented-here, ivory tower" research approach into collaborative information sharing with partners. Omron leaders consider the company's principles a competitive advantage in securing preferred customers, even when its prices are higher, and winning preferred acquisitions, even when its bids are lower. Recent acquisitions, including some in the United States, rested on discussions of the importance Omron places on people and society. The integration process, leaders said, was "like the joining of two families." Indeed, the target companies largely performed the integration themselves, posting the Omron principles and wearing the Omron uniform at the first postintegration meetings. In most of Omron's offices, daily morning meetings start with the company's motto, "At work for a better life, a better world for all," recited by employees or broadcast by a manager.

The giants we studied gain allies in innovation, influence standards, and improve lives in the countries in which they operate through their partners as well as their direct activities. They work with established companies but also grow their own networks. Consider two different value chains anchored by CEMEX. The first is Patrimonio Hoy, which the company created in Mexico in 1998 to organize low-income consumers into self-financing cells and give them access to low-cost building materials, technical expertise, and services. Within six years, hundreds of thousands of families had been served, and this profitable business model was in operation in Mexico, Colombia, Venezuela, Nicaragua, and Costa Rica. The second is Construrama, a distribution program CEMEX started in 2001 to offer small hardware stores training, support, brand recognition, and easy access to products. CEMEX owns the Construrama brand and handles promotion but doesn't charge distributors, operate stores, or have decision-making authority, although service standards must be met. By 2005, this network in Mexico and Venezuela was the equivalent of the largest retail chain in Latin America, and it was expanding to other developing countries.

Construrama was created in response to competition from The Home Depot and Lowe's, both of which were then entering Latin America. CEMEX wanted its own distribution outlets and found common ground with the small and medium-sized enterprises that were threatened by the large international chains. In building the network, CEMEX hewed to the values and standards it had articulated, favoring partners of integrity who were trusted in their communities, and rejecting candidates whose business tactics didn't meet CEMEX's ethical standards (even if they boasted high growth or high margins). Partners are expected to share the company's values, including participation in community-building philanthropic endeavors—for example, contributing people and materials to expand an orphanage or improve a school.

As companies tackle pieces of the public agenda, the partnerships they forge go beyond the commercial world—and commitment to shared values and standards becomes even more important. A good example is IBM's Reinventing Education (RE) work in the United States. In these initiatives, IBM targeted problems that K-12 school districts identified as their most significant. Researchers from the company's renowned Watson lab created prototypes of tools and tested them quickly, and then assembled the right set of commercial and noncommercial partners to help spread the use of the tools. Some RE solutions, like KidSmart workstations for preschool children, are also spreading worldwide through partnerships with government ministries and nonprofit organizations.

As projects like this become more commonplace, the ability to exercise diplomacy is becoming a job requirement for professionals far down in the organization. We were particularly struck by this at IBM India, where people could rattle off the priorities of government officials and explain how the company's activities are in sync. Lorenzo Zambrano, CEO of CEMEX, related a comment made by one of his country managers: "I was trained as an engineer, and now I have to be a politician." Zambrano's response? "Well, yes—welcome to top management!" The activity involved is not simply a trickled down version of lobbying. Managers bring knowledge to government officials about how rules such as product-testing protocols operate in other countries. (Of course, they have to do this gently and with the sensitivity of guests in a host country—even if they are nationals rather than expats.) They can also apply their diplomacy skills to broader matters. The chairman of IBM Greater China, a Chinese national who had worked his whole life in Asia, visited the White House to encourage U.S.-Chinese cooperation on the environment.

Fire in the Belly

If values and standards served no other purpose in a company, they would still serve as motivational tools. They offer people a basis for engagement with their work, a sense of membership, and an anchor of stability in the midst of constant change.

IBM's Palmisano told me that culture is perhaps the hardest area to influence but fundamental to long-term success. "Management is temporary; returns are cyclical. But if we use these values as connective tissue, that has longevity. If people can get emotionally connected and have pride in the entity's success, they will do what is important to IBM." CEMEX's Zambrano echoed this: "We know that high standards have to be applied everywhere. At first, we thought of our reputation conceptually, as something that we needed to keep improving. Now we know it affects our ability to attract the right people. After all, businesses are networks of people working toward the same end. And everyone has to be proud of what they're doing."

Values arouse aspirations to increase the company's positive impact on the world, and that is worth more to many people than increases in compensation, as a manager in India pointed out to me. This, he believed, was why his rapidly growing unit could attract the best talent without offering the highest pay scales. Centrality of values provides a rationale for longer-term investments where the immediate business case is mixed or unclear, and it permits compassionate decisions that show that people in the company really care, thus taking the edge off the natural cynicism that large companies evoke. In the aftermath of the Lebanon bombing, a P&G manager reflected on the impact of the decision to help employees evacuate. "This was a defining moment for the people," he said, "because they saw that a company that is always saying that people are very important, are the most important asset, was really acting on it. That is where you really believe in the principles and values of the company."

How the Fabric Is Woven

The global giants we studied are operating according to a model that differs from what most people might expect of a multinational corporation. It is not ironfisted hierarchy or some clever engineering of structure that provides coherence to their organizations; it is the effect of commonly held values translating into operations through clear standards and processes—values and standards that are embraced by individuals because they allow autonomy, flexibility, and self-expression. Not only does this approach enable a company to unify geographically and culturally diverse people and guide their daily decision making. It also inspires much higher levels of creativity, leading to more breakthrough innovations.

What about the companies still operating under the old paradigm? Is it possible for them, to make the shift? Conversations we had with company leaders suggest the challenges involved. Some companies find it hard to transmit values and standards to portions of the workforce lacking education or international experience, such as unskilled workers in developing countries. Sometimes specific deep-rooted local realities present stumbling blocks; we heard zcomplaints about the history of corruption in Russia, for example, and a generally poor work ethic in Latvia. Companies committed to upholding global standards often find that their demands go beyond local standards and can seem excessive to local managers. Any one of these issues can rear its head in the aftermath of an acquisition, and the desired alignment of standards and values will not come about overnight.

The key to success with the new model may seem counterintuitive to leaders facing such challenges. More than anything else, we heard in our interviews about a loosening of organizational structures in favor of fluid boundaries and flexible deployment of people. Managers and professionals generally appeared less concerned with where they worked and to whom they reported than with what projects they were able to join or initiate. Rather than focusing on the function or discipline that was their organizational base, they focused on the problem to be solved—and figuring out how to assemble the expertise relevant to it. Think of how IBM's cultural heritage projects, like Eternal Egypt and Forbidden City, draw on people across geographies and roles—some colocating, some working virtually, some committing to long-term assignments, some serving as short-term sources of expertise.

Many of these companies have a tradition of making mobility a part of career development, which ensures a degree of international mixing as well as the carrying of expertise from one place to another. This is one of the ways that P&G, for example, transmits its PVP and cultural norms. But using career structures to do this is relatively slow. On the rise, instead, is the practice of asking managers to wear multiple hats for multiple projects—taking on regional or global assignments from anywhere, while not changing their home address. The P&G Brazil marketing manager who worked on Always Básico next headed a global team looking at low-income consumers. IBM's corporate citizenship manager for Latin America previously headed Reinventing Education efforts worldwide out of her base in Rio de Janeiro, watching over work in Ireland, then South Africa and Vietnam. In fact, at IBM these days, about a third of professionals don't have a regular office to which they report; they work from whatever workstations—at customer sites, homes, or IBM offices—they are currently plugged into.

Working with extended networks of partners across inter- and extra-company boundaries requires large numbers of people to serve as connectors among activities—not as bosses but as brokers, network builders, and facilitators. For example, a director-level IBM executive working at IBM China's development labs is focused mainly on making sure that the most promising ideas pass from one stage of development to the next; he and his team serve primarily as technology-savvy bridges between two steps in the process handled by other teams. The IBM leader who envisioned and championed the World Community Grid spends a great deal of time listening to the priorities of executives in the business units and staying in touch with the research laboratories to understand their latest breakthroughs. He is particularly adept at finding ways that needs and opportunities can be connected, from any part of the value chain.

One last element that seems central to the success of the global giants we studied is that they have explicitly added mutual respect and inclusion to the values they live by. Diversity programs are no longer primarily a response to legal requirements; they are valued because they help people form relationships more quickly and overcome tensions between groups. At Cisco, global diversity is the centerpiece of CEO John Chambers's leadership development agenda.

I was struck by how far one company, Shinhan Financial Group, was willing to take this attitude in its acquisition of a major competitor. Well before any formal integration was permitted by the terms of the deal, the company was forging relationships of respect, achieving "emotional integration" through executive retreats, and asking joint working groups to create common practices voluntarily. Similarly, the values of respect and inclusion embedded in P&G's PVP were said by leaders to have helped make the Gillette integration smooth. A well-designed diversity program also encourages people to recognize their similarities—that they are guided by values sufficiently universal to allow for communication and collaboration despite great differences in their ethnic backgrounds or their local or professional cultures.

A Giant Change

Over the course of a career studying the organizations of huge corporations, I have learned how they typically direct activity in and maintain control over their far-flung operations. What I have seen in recent years is a model different from what has prevailed in the past. In the most influential corporations today, a foundation of values and standards provides a well-understood, widely communicated guidance system that ensures effective operations while enabling people to make decisions appropriate to local situations. This, rather than any traditional control system, is what enables IBM or CEMEX to operate as one enterprise in projects that span many countries and to share a culture that makes people inside and external partners connect as an extended family.

A first-order effect is that the new model helps large companies avoid the traps of bureaucracy that in the past made them seem like dinosaurs. More deeply, it yields a way of doing business that is more localized and humane. When large groups of people are subject to management by values, aspirations, and open boundaries instead of management by traditional controls, their energies and passions are engaged. Social contributions are no longer an afterthought—a luxury enjoyed only by those who are already profitable—but a starting point that helps companies find profitable growth. The interplay of corporate standards and local conditions puts companies in a position to influence the ecosystem around them (especially in emerging markets) and to generate innovation. If these vanguard companies lead others to adopt their way of working, then we will see a new, and I think more promising, kind of capitalism. And if it flourishes, not only will that be good for business, it will also be good for the world.

RULES OF THUMB FOR CHANGE AGENTS*

Herbert A. Shepard

The following aphorisms are not so much bits of advice (although they are stated that way) as things to think about when you are being a change agent, a consultant, an organization or community development practitioner—or when you are just being yourself trying to bring about something that involves other people.

Rule I: Stay Alive

This rule counsels against self-sacrifice on behalf of a cause that you do not wish to be your last.

Two exceptionally talented doctoral students came to the conclusion that the routines they had to go through to get their degrees were absurd, and decided they would be untrue to themselves to conform to an absurd system. That sort of reasoning is almost always self-destructive. Besides, their noble gesture in quitting would be unlikely to have any impact whatever on the system they were taking a stand against.

This is not to say that one should never take a stand or a survival risk. But such risks should be taken as part of a purposeful strategy of change and appropriately timed and targeted. When they are taken under such circumstances, one is very much alive.

But Rule I is much more than a survival rule. The rule means that you should let your whole being be involved in the undertaking. Since most of us have never been in touch with our whole beings, it means a lot of putting together of parts that have been divided, of using internal communications channels that have been closed or were never opened.

Staying alive means loving yourself. Self-disparagement leads to the suppression of potentials, to a win-lose formulation of the world, and to wasting life in defensive maneuvering.

Staying alive means staying in touch with your purpose. It means using your skills, your emotions, your labels and positions, rather than being used by them. It means not being trapped in other people's games. It means turning yourself on and off, rather than being dependent on the situation. It means choosing with a view to the consequences as well as the impulse. It means going with the flow even while swimming against it. It means living in several worlds without being swallowed up in any. It means seeing dilemmas as opportunities for creativity. It means greeting absurdity with laughter while trying to unscramble it. It means capturing the moment in the light of the future. It means seeing the environment through the eyes of your purpose.

Rule II: Start Where the System Is

This is such ancient wisdom that one might expect its meaning had been fully explored and apprehended. Yet in practice the rule—and the system—are often violated.

The rule implies that one should begin by diagnosing the system. But systems do not necessarily *like* being diagnosed. Even the term *diagnosis* may be offensive. And the system may be even less ready for someone who calls himself or herself a

*Reprinted by permission of the author from the *OD Practitioner*, December 1984. Organization Development Network, Portland, Oregon.

"change agent!" It is easy for the practitioner to forget that the use of jargon which prevents laypeople from understanding the professional mysteries is a hostile act.

Starting where the system is can be called the Empathy Rule. To communicate effectively, to obtain a basis for building sound strategy, the change agent needs to understand how clients see themselves and their situation, and needs to understand the culture of the system. Establishing the required rapport does not mean that the change agent who wants to work in a traditional industrial setting should refrain from growing a beard. It does mean that, if he has a beard, the beard is likely to determine where the client is when they first meet, and the client's curiosity needs to be dealt with. Similarly, the rule does not mean that a female change agent in a male organization should try to act like one of the boys, or that a young change agent should try to act like a senior executive. One thing it does mean is that sometimes where the client is, is wondering where the change agent is.

Rarely is the client in any one place at any one time. That is, she or he may be ready to pursue any of several paths. The task is to walk together on the most promising path.

Even unwitting or accidental violations of the Empathy Rule can destroy the situation. I lost a client through two violations in one morning. The client group spent a consulting day at my home. They arrived early in the morning, before I had my empathy on. The senior member, seeing a picture of my son in the living room said, "What do you do with boys with long hair?" I replied thoughtlessly, "I think he's handsome that way." The small chasm thus created between my client and me was widened and deepened later that morning when one of the family tortoises walked through the butter dish.

Sometimes starting where the client is, which sounds both ethically and technically virtuous, can lead to some ethically puzzling situations. Robert Frost* described a situation in which a consultant was so empathetic with a king who was unfit to rule that the king discovered his own unfitness and had himself shot, whereupon the consultant became king.

Empathy permits the development of a mutual attachment between client and consultant. The resulting relationship may be one in which their creativities are joined, a mutual growth relationship. But it can also become one in which the client becomes dependent and is manipulated by the consultant. The ethical issues are not associated with starting where the system is, but with how one moves with it.

Rule III: Never Work Uphill This is a comprehensive rule, and a number of other rules are corollaries or examples of it. It is an appeal for an organic rather than a mechanistic approach to change, for a collaborative approach to change, for building strength and building on strength. It has a number of implications that bear on the choices the change agent makes about how to use him/herself, and it says something about life.

Corollary 1: Don't Build Hills as You Go

This corollary cautions against working in a way that builds resistance to movement in the direction you have chosen as desirable. For example, a program which has a favorable effect on one portion of a population may have the opposite effect on other portions of the population. Perhaps the commonest error of this kind has been in the employment of T-group training in organizations: turning on the participants and turning off the people who didn't attend, in one easy lesson.

---

*Robert Frost, "How Hard It Is to Keep from Being King When It's in You and in the Situation." *In the Clearing* (New York: Holt, Rinehart and Winston, 1962) 74–84.

Corollary 2: Work in the Most Promising Arena

The physician–patient relationship is often regarded as analogous to the consultant-client relationship. The results for system change of this analogy can be unfortunate. For example, the organization development consultant is likely to be greeted with delight by executives who see in his specialty the solution to a hopeless situation in an outlying plant. Some organization development consultants have disappeared for years because of the irresistibility of such challenges. Others have wiled away their time trying to counteract the Peter Principle by shoring up incompetent managers.

Corollary 3: Build Resources

Don't do anything alone that could be accomplished more easily or more certainly by a team. Don Quixote is not the only change agent whose effectiveness was handicapped by ignoring this rule. The change agent's task is a heroic one, but the need to be a hero does not facilitate team building. As a result, many change agents lose effectiveness by becoming spread too thin. Effectiveness can be enhanced by investing in the development of partners.

Corollary 4: Don't Overorganize

The democratic ideology and theories of participative management that many change agents possess can sometimes interfere with common sense. A year or two ago I offered a course to be taught by graduate students. The course was oversubscribed. It seemed that a data-based process for deciding whom to admit would be desirable, and that participation of the graduate students in the decision would also be desirable. So I sought data from the candidates about themselves, and xeroxed their responses for the graduate students. Then the graduate students and I held a series of meetings. Then the candidates were informed of the decision. In this way we wasted a great deal of time and everyone felt a little worse than if we had used an arbitrary decision rule.

Corollary 5: Don't Argue if You Can't Win

Win-lose strategies are to be avoided because they deepen conflict instead of resolving it. But the change agent should build her or his support constituency as large and deep and strong as possible so that she or he can continue to risk.

Corollary 6: Play God a Little

If the change agent doesn't make the critical value decisions, someone else will be happy to do so. Will a given situation contribute to your fulfillment? Are you creating a better world for yourself and others? Or are you keeping a system in operation that should be allowed to die? For example, the public education system is a mess. Does that mean that the change agent is morally obligated to try to improve it, destroy it, or develop a substitute for it? No, not even if he or she knows how. But the change agent does need a value perspective for making choices like that.

Rule IV: Innovation Requires a Good Idea, Initiative, and a Few Friends

Little can be accomplished alone, and the effects of social and cultural forces on individual perception are so distorting that the change agent needs a partner, if only to maintain perspective and purpose.

The quality of the partner is as important as the quality of the idea. Like the change agent, partners must be relatively autonomous people. Persons who are authority-oriented—who need to rebel or need to submit—are not reliable partners: The rebels take the wrong risks and the good soldiers don't take any. And rarely do they command the respect and trust from others that is needed if an innovation is to be supported.

The partners need not be numerous. For example, the engineering staff of a chemical company designed a new process plant using edge-of-the-art technology. The design departed radically from the experience of top management, and they were about to reject it. The engineering chief suggested that the design be reviewed by a distinguished engineering professor. The principal designers were in fact former students of the professor. For this reason he accepted the assignment, charged the company a large fee for reviewing the design (which he did not trouble to examine) and told the management that it was brilliantly conceived and executed. By this means the engineers not only implemented their innovations, but also grew in the esteem of their management.

A change agent experienced in the Washington environment reports that he knows of only one case of successful interdepartmental collaboration in mutually designing funding and managing a joint project. It was accomplished through the collaboration of himself and three similarly-minded young men, one from each of four agencies. They were friends and met weekly for lunch. They conceived the project and planned strategies for implementing it. Each person undertook to interest and influence the relevant key people in his own agency. The four served one another as consultants and helped in influencing opinion and bringing the decision-makers together.

An alternative statement of Rule IV is as follows: Find the people who are ready and able to work, introduce them to one another, and work with them. Perhaps because many change agents have been trained in the helping professions, perhaps because we have all been trained to think bureaucratically, concepts like organization position, representatives or need are likely to guide the change agent's selection of those he or she works with.

A more powerful beginning can sometimes be made by finding those persons in the system whose values are congruent with those of the change agent, who possess vitality and imagination, who are willing to work overtime, and who are eager to learn. Such people are usually glad to have someone like the change agent join in getting something important accomplished, and a careful search is likely to turn up quite a few. In fact, there may be enough of them to accomplish general system change, if they can team up in appropriate ways.

In building such teamwork the change agent's abilities will be fully challenged, as he joins them in establishing conditions for trust and creativity; dealing with their anxieties about being seen as subversive; enhancing their leadership, consulting, problem-solving, diagnosing and innovating skills; and developing appropriate group norms and policies.

Rule V: Load Experiments for Success

This sounds like counsel to avoid risk taking. But the decision to experiment always entails risk. After that decision has been made, take all precautions.

The rule also sounds scientifically immoral. But whether an experiment produces the expected results depends upon the experimenter's depth of insight into the conditions and processes involved. Of course, what is experimental is what is new to the system: it may or may not be new to the change agent.

Build an umbrella over the experiment. A chemical process plant which was to be shut down because of the inefficiency of its operations undertook a union management cooperation project to improve efficiency, which involved a modified form of profit-sharing. Such plans were contrary to company policy, but the regional vice president was interested in the experiment, and successfully concealed it from his associates. The experiment was successful; the plant became profitable. But in this case, the umbrella turned out not to be big enough. The plant was shut down anyway.

Use the Hawthorne effect. Even poorly conceived experiments are often made to succeed when the participants feel ownership. And conversely, one of the obstacles to the spread of useful innovations is that the groups to which they are offered do not feel ownership of them.

For example, if the change agent hopes to use experience-based learning as part of his/her strategy, the first persons to be invited should be those who consistently turn all their experiences into constructive learning. Similarly, in introducing team development processes into a system, begin with the best functioning team.

Maintain voluntarism. This is not easy to do in systems where invitations are understood to be commands, but nothing vital can be built on such motives as duty, obedience, security-seeking, or responsiveness to social pressure.

Rule VI: Light Many Fires

Not only does a large monolithic development or change program have high visibility and other qualities of a good target, it also tends to prevent subsystems from feeling ownership of, and consequent commitment to the program.

The meaning of this rule is more orderly than the random prescription—light many fires—suggests. Any part of a system is the way it is partly because of the way the rest of the system is. To work towards change in one subsystem is to become one more determinant of its performance. Not only is the change agent working uphill, but as soon as he turns his back, other forces in the system will press the subsystem back towards its previous performance mode.

If many interdependent subsystems are catalyzed, and the change agent brings them together to facilitate one another's efforts, the entire system can begin to move.

Understanding patterns of interdependency among subsystems can lead to a strategy of fire-setting. For example, in public school systems, it requires collaboration among politicians, administrators, teachers, parents, and students to bring about significant innovation, and active opposition on the part of only one of these groups to prevent it. In parochial school systems, on the other hand, collaboration between the administration and the church can provide a powerful impetus for change in the other groups.

Rule VII: Keep an Optimistic Bias

Our society grinds along with much polarization and cruelty, and even the helping professions compose their world of grim problems to be "worked through." The change agent is usually flooded with the destructive aspects of the situations he enters. People in most systems are impressed by one another's weaknesses, and stereotype each other with such incompetencies as they can discover.

This rule does not advise ignoring destructive forces. But its positive prescription is that the change agent be especially alert to the constructive forces which are often masked and suppressed in a problem-oriented, envious culture.

People have as great an innate capacity for joy as for resentment, but resentment causes them to overlook opportunities for joy. In a workshop for married couples, a husband and wife were discussing their sexual problem and how hard they were working to solve it. They were not making much progress, since they didn't realize that sex is not a problem, but an opportunity.

Individuals and groups locked in destructive kinds of conflict focus on their differences. The change agent's job is to help them discover and build on their commonalities, so that they will have a foundation of respect and trust which will permit them to use their differences as a source of creativity. The unhappy partners focus on past hurts, and continue to destroy the present and future with them. The change agent's job is to help them change the present so that they will have a new past on which to create a better future.

Rule VIII: Capture the Moment

A good sense of relevance and timing is often treated as though it were a "gift" or "intuition" rather than something that can be learned, something spontaneous rather than something planned. The opposite is nearer the truth. One is more likely to "capture the moment" when everything one has learned is readily available.

Some years ago my wife and I were having a very destructive fight. Our nine-year-old daughter decided to intervene. She put her arms around her mother and asked: "What does Daddy do that bugs you?" She was an attentive audience for the next few minutes while my wife told her, ending in tears. She then put her arms around me: "What does Mommy do that bugs you?" and listened attentively to my response, which also ended in tears. She then went to the record player and put on a favorite love song ("If Ever I Should Leave You"), and left us alone to make up.

The elements of my daughter's intervention had all been learned. They were available to her, and she combined them in a way that could make the moment better.

Perhaps it's our training in linear cause-and-effect thinking and the neglect of our capacities for imagery that makes us so often unable to see the multiple potential of the moment. Entering the situation "blank" is not the answer. One needs to have as many frameworks for seeing and strategies for acting available as possible. But it's not enough to involve only one's head in the situation; one's heart has to get involved too. Cornelia Otis Skinner once said that the first law of the stage is to love your audience. You can love your audience only if you love yourself. If you have relatively full access to your organized experience, to yourself and to the situation, you will capture the moment more often.